Third Edition

Java™ Foundations

Introduction to Program Design & Data Structures

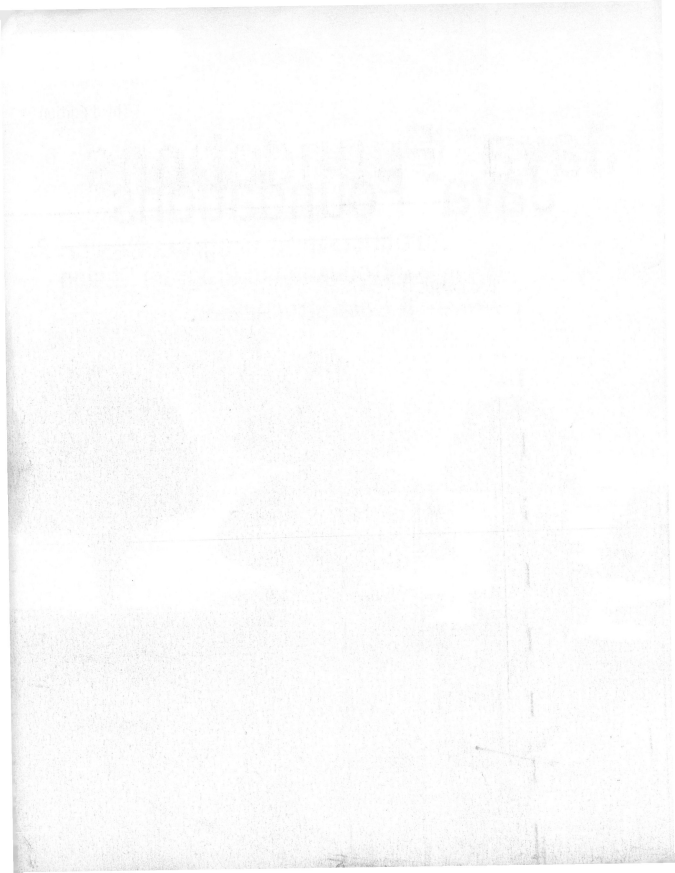

Third Edition

Java™ Foundations

Introduction to Program Design & Data Structures

John Lewis | Peter DePasquale | Joseph Chase
Virginia Tech | The College of New Jersey | Radford University

PEARSON

Boston Columbus Indianapolis New York San Francisco Upper Saddle River
Amsterdam Cape Town Dubai London Madrid Milan Munich Paris Montreal Toronto
Delhi Mexico City Sao Paulo Sydney Hong Kong Seoul Singapore Taipei Tokyo

Editorial Director, ECS :	Marcia Horton
Executive Editor:	Matt Goldstein
Editorial Assistant:	Jenah Blitz-Stoehr
Director of Marketing:	Christy Lesko
Marketing Manager:	Yezan Alayan
Senior Marketing Coordinator:	Kathryn Ferranti
Director of Production:	Erin Gregg
Senior Managing Editor:	Scott Disanno
Senior Production Project Manager:	Marilyn Lloyd
Manufacturing Buyer:	Lisa McDowell
Art Director:	Anthony Gemmellaro
Text Designer:	Jerilyn Bockorick/Cenveo® Publisher Services
Cover Designer:	Joyce Cosentino Wells
Manager, Rights and Permissions:	Michael Joyce
Text Permission Coordinator:	Jackie Bates/GEX, Inc.
Cover Image:	Shutterstock_97230302/tazzymoto
Media Project Manager:	Renata Butera
Full-Service Project Management:	Rose Kernan/Cenveo® Publisher Services
Composition:	Cenveo® Publisher Services
Printer/Binder:	Edwards Brothers Malloy
Cover and Insert Printer:	Lehigh-Phoenix Color

Credits and acknowledgments borrowed from other sources and reproduced, with permission, in this textbook appear on the Credits page on page xxviii

Library of Congress Cataloging-in-Publication Data on File

10 9 8 7 6 5 4 3

PEARSON

ISBN 10: 0-13-337046-1

ISBN 13: 978-0-13-337046-1

To my wife, Sharon, for everything.
– John

To my wife, Lisa, and our twins: Lily and Adam.
– Pete

To my loving wife, Melissa, for her support and encouragement.
– Joe

Welcome to *Java Foundations*. This book is designed to serve as the primary resource for a two- or three-term introductory course sequence, ranging from the most basic programming concepts to the design and implementation of complex data structures. This unified approach makes the important introductory sequence more cohesive and accessible for students.

We've borrowed the best elements from the industry-leading text *Java Software Solutions* for the introductory material, reworked to complement the design and vision of the overall text. For example, instead of having graphics sections spread throughout many chapters, the coverage of graphical user interfaces is accomplished in a well-organized chapter of its own.

In the later chapters, the exploration of collections and data structures is modeled after the coverage in *Java Software Structures*, but has been reworked to flow cleanly from the introductory material. The result is a comprehensive, cohesive, and seamless exploration of programming concepts.

New in the Third Edition

We appreciate the feedback we've received about this book and are pleased that it served so well as an introductory text. The following modifications have been made to improve the presentation of particular topics and the overall flow:

- Added a summary of terms and definitions at the end of each chapter.
- Added a new Code Annotation feature, used to explore key statements with graphic annotations.
- Added a new Common Error callout feature.
- Added new Design Focus callouts.
- Revised the collection chapters to provide a more complete explanation of how the Java API supports the collection.
- Separated the coverage of Iterators into its own chapter and expanded the discussion.
- Reviewed and updated the text throughout to improve discussions and address issues.

In particular, we've reworked the discussion of individual collections to match the following flow:

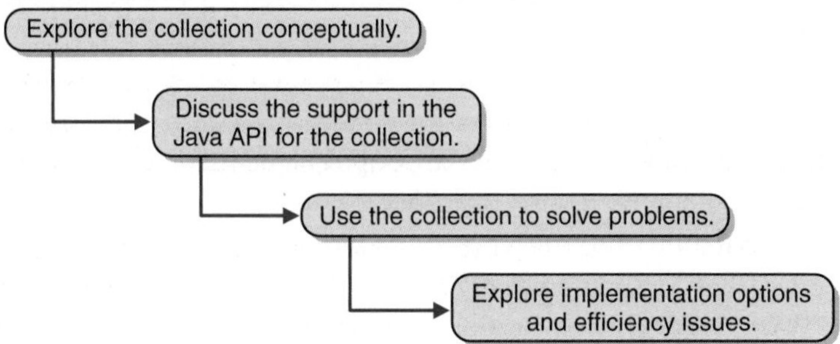

This approach clarifies the distinction between the way the Java API supports a particular collection and the way it might be implemented from scratch. It makes it easier for instructors to point out limitations of the API implementations in a compare-and-contrast fashion. This approach also allows an instructor, on a case-by-case basis, to simply introduce a collection without exploring implementation details if desired.

The other modifications for this edition flesh out the presentation to a higher degree than previous editions did. The addition of a term list (with succinct definitions) at the end of each chapter provides a summary of core issues in ways that the other features don't. New Code Annotation and Common Error features highlight specific issues that might otherwise get lost in the body of the text, but without interrupting the flow of the topic.

We think these modifications build upon the strong pedagogy established by previous editions and give instructors more opportunity and flexibility to cover topics as they choose.

Chapter Breakdown

Chapter 1 (Introduction) introduces the Java programming language and the basics of program development. It contains an introduction to object-oriented development, including an overview of concepts and terminology. This chapter contains broad introductory material that can be covered while students become familiar with their development environment.

Chapter 2 (Data and Expressions) explores some of the basic types of data used in a Java program and the use of expressions to perform calculations. It discusses the conversion of data from one type to another, and how to read input interactively from the user with the help of the Scanner class.

Chapter 3 (Using Classes and Objects) explores the use of predefined classes and the objects that can be created from them. Classes and objects are used to manipulate character strings, produce random numbers, perform complex calculations, and format output. Packages, enumerated types, and wrapper classes are also discussed.

Chapter 4 (Conditionals and Loops) covers the use of boolean expressions to make decisions. All related statements for conditionals and loops are discussed, including the enhanced version of the `for` loop. The `Scanner` class is revisited for iterative input parsing and reading text files.

Chapter 5 (Writing Classes) explores the basic issues related to writing classes and methods. Topics include instance data, visibility, scope, method parameters, and return types. Constructors, method design, static data, and method overloading are covered as well. Testing and debugging are now covered in this chapter as well.

Chapter 6 (Graphical User Interfaces) is a thorough exploration of Java GUI processing, focusing on components, events, and listeners. Many types of components and events are discussed using numerous GUI examples. Additionally, layout managers, containment hierarchies, borders, tooltips, and mnemonics are introduced.

Chapter 7 (Arrays) contains extensive coverage of arrays and array processing. Topics include bounds checking, initializer lists, command-line arguments, variable-length parameter lists, and multidimensional arrays.

Chapter 8 (Inheritance) covers class derivations and associated concepts such as class hierarchies, overriding, and visibility. Strong emphasis is put on the proper use of inheritance and its role in software design.

Chapter 9 (Polymorphism) explores the concept of binding and how it relates to polymorphism. Then we examine how polymorphic references can be accomplished using either inheritance or interfaces. Design issues related to polymorphism are examined as well.

Chapter 10 (Exceptions) covers exception handling and the effects of uncaught exceptions. The `try-catch` statement is examined, as well as a discussion of exception propagation. The chapter also explores the use of exceptions when dealing with input and output, and examines an example that writes a text file.

Chapter 11 (Analysis of Algorithms) lays the foundation for determining the efficiency of an algorithm and explains the important criteria that allow a developer to compare one algorithm to another in proper ways. Our emphasis in this chapter is understanding the important concepts more than getting mired in heavy math or formality.

Chapter 12 (Introduction to Collections—Stacks) establishes the concept of a collection, stressing the need to separate the interface from the implementation. It also conceptually introduces a stack, then explores an array-based implementation of a stack.

Chapter 13 (Linked Structures - Stacks) discusses the use of references to create linked data structures. It explores the basic issues regarding the management of linked lists, and then defines an alternative implementation of a stack (introduced in Chapter 3) using an underlying linked data structure.

Chapter 14 (Queues) explores the concept and implementation of a first-in, first-out queue. Radix sort is discussed as an example of using queues effectively. The implementation options covered include an underlying linked list as well as both fixed and circular arrays.

Chapter 15 (Lists) covers three types of lists: ordered, unordered, and indexed. These three types of lists are compared and contrasted, with discussion of the operations that they share and those that are unique to each type. Inheritance is used appropriately in the design of the various types of lists, which are implemented using both array-based and linked representations.

Chapter 16 (Iterators) is a new chapter that isolates the concepts and implementation of iterators, which are so important to collections. The expanded discussion drives home the need to separate the iterator functionality from the details of any particular collection.

Chapter 17 (Recursion) is a general introduction to the concept of recursion and how recursive solutions can be elegant. It explores the implementation details of recursion and discusses the basic idea of analyzing recursive algorithms.

Chapter 18 (Searching and Sorting) discusses the linear and binary search algorithms, as well as the algorithms for several sorts: selection sort, insertion sort, bubble sort, quick sort, and merge sort. Programming issues related to searching and sorting, such as using the Comparable interface as the basis of comparing objects, are stressed in this chapter. Searching and sorting that are based in particular data structures (such as heap sort) are covered in the appropriate chapter later in the book.

Chapter 19 (Trees) provides an overview of trees, establishing key terminology and concepts. It discusses various implementation approaches and uses a binary tree to represent and evaluate an arithmetic expression.

Chapter 20 (Binary Search Trees) builds off of the basic concepts established in Chapter 10 to define a classic binary search tree. A linked implementation of a binary search tree is examined, followed by a discussion of how the balance in the tree nodes is key to its performance. That leads to exploring AVL and red/black implementations of binary search trees.

Chapter 21 (Heaps and Priority Queues) explores the concept, use, and implementations of heaps and specifically their relationship to priority queues. A heap sort is used as an example of its usefulness as well. Both linked and array-based implementations are explored.

Chapter 22 (Sets and Maps) explores these two types of collections and their importance to the Java Collections API.

Chapter 23 (Multi-way Search Trees) is a natural extension of the discussion of the previous chapters. The concepts of 2-3 trees, 2-4 trees, and general B-trees are examined and implementation options are discussed.

Chapter 24 (Graphs) explores the concept of undirected and directed graphs and establishes important terminology. It examines several common graph algorithms and discusses implementation options, including adjacency matrices.

Chapter 25 (Databases) explores the concept of databases and their management, and discusses the basics of SQL queries. It then explores the techniques for establishing a connection between a Java program and a database, and the API used to interact with it.

Supplements

The following student resources are available for this book:

- **Source code** for all programs presented in the book
- **VideoNotes** that explore select topics from the book

Resources can be accessed at www.pearsonhighered.com/lewis/

The following instructor resources can be found at Pearson Education's Instructor Resource Center:

- **Solutions** for select exercises and programming projects in the book
- **Powerpoint slides** for the presentation of the book content
- **Test bank**

To obtain access, please visit www.pearsonhighered.com/irc or contact your local Pearson Education sales representative.

Cover: Topiary Trees, tazzymoto/Shutterstock

Chapter 1 page 2: Reference: Java is a relatively new programming language compared to many others. It was developed in the early 1990s by James Gosling at Sun Microsystems. Java was introduced to the public in 1995 and has gained tremendous popularity since "The History of Java Technology" Oracle Corporation. 1995. Accessed at http://www.oracle.com/technetwork/java/javase/overview/javahistory-index-198355.html

Chapter 1 page 15: Excerpt: A research group at Auburn University has developed jGRASP, a free Java IDE that is included on the CD that accompanies this book. It can also be downloaded from www.jgrasp.org. "jGRASP" is developed by the Department of Computer Science and Software Engineering in the Samuel Ginn College of Engineering at Auburn University.

Chapter 1 page 20: Reference: The programming language Simula, developed in the 1960s, had many characteristics that define the modern object-oriented approach to software development. Nygaard, Kristen., Myhrhaug, Bjørn., and Dahl, Ole-Johan. "Simula. Common Base Language." Norwegian Computing Center. 1970. Accessed at http://www.nr.no/

Chapter 4: Excerpt: The Twelve Days of Christmas. "Twelve Days of Christmas". Mirth Without Mischief. 1780.

Chapter 11: Text: Another way of looking at the effect of algorithm complexity was proposed by Aho, Hopcroft, and Ullman. Aho, A.V., J.E. Hopcroft, and J.D. Ullman. The Design and Analysis of Computer Algorithms. Addison-Wesley. 1974.

Chapter 20: Text: Adel'son-Vel'skii and Landis developed a method called that is a variation on this theme. For each node in the tree, we will keep track of the height of the left and right subtrees. Adelson-Velskii, Georgii and Evengii Landis. "An Algorithm for the Organization of Information." 1962.

VideoNote

LOCATION OF VIDEONOTES IN THE TEXT

1 Introduction

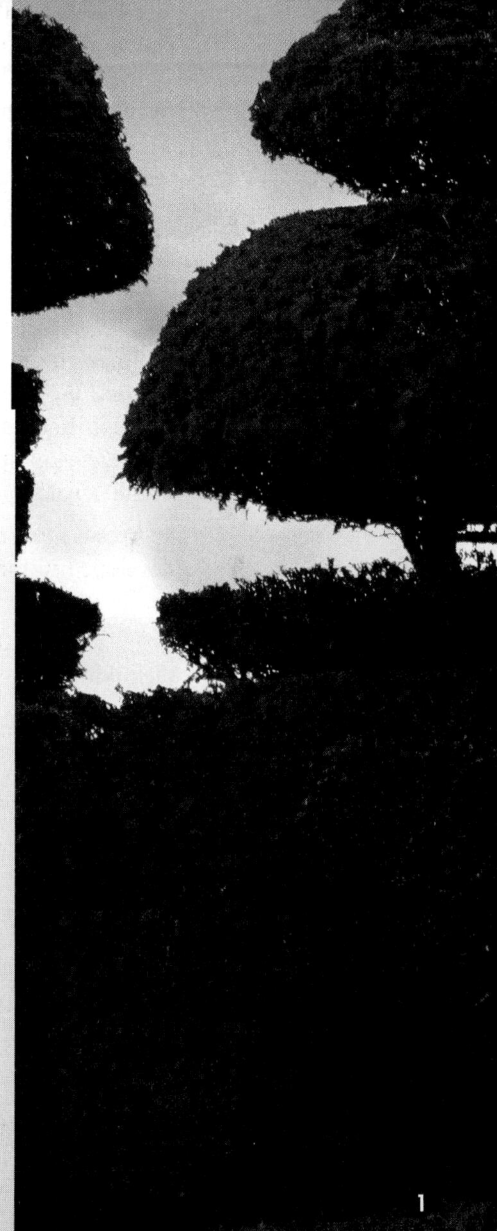

CHAPTER OBJECTIVES

- Introduce the Java programming language.
- Describe the steps involved in program compilation and execution.
- Explore the issues related to problem solving in general.
- Discuss the activities involved in the software development process.
- Present an overview of object-oriented principles.

This text is about writing well-designed software. We begin by examining a very basic Java program and using it to explore some initial programming concepts. We then lay the groundwork for software development on a larger scale, exploring the foundations of problem solving, the activities involved in software development, and the principles of object-oriented programming.

1.1 The Java Programming Language

A computer is made up of hardware and software. The *hardware* components of a computer system are the physical, tangible pieces that support the computing effort. They include chips, boxes, wires, keyboards, speakers, disks, cables, printers, and so on. The hardware is essentially useless without instructions to tell it what to do. A *program* is a series of instructions that the hardware executes one after another. Programs are sometimes called *applications*. *Software* consists of programs and the data those programs use. Software is the intangible counterpart to the physical hardware components. Together, they form a tool that we can use to solve problems.

KEY CONCEPT
A computer system consists of hardware and software that work in concert to help us solve problems.

A program is written in a particular *programming language* that uses specific words and symbols to express the problem solution. A programming language defines a set of rules that determines exactly how a programmer can combine the words and symbols of the language into *programming statements*, which are the instructions that are carried out when the program is executed.

Since the inception of computers, many programming languages have been created. We use the Java language in this text to demonstrate various programming concepts and techniques. Although our main goal is to learn these underlying software development concepts, an important side effect will be to become proficient in the development of Java programs.

Java is a relatively new programming language compared to many others. It was developed in the early 1990s by James Gosling at Sun Microsystems. Java was introduced to the public in 1995 and has gained tremendous popularity since.

Java has undergone various changes since its creation. The most recent Java technology is generally referred to as the *Java 2 Platform*, which is organized into three major groups:

- Java 2 Platform, Standard Edition (J2SE)
- Java 2 Platform, Enterprise Edition (J2EE)
- Java 2 Platform, Micro Edition (J2ME)

This text focuses on the Standard Edition, which, as the name implies, is the mainstream version of the language and associated tools. Furthermore, this book is consistent with any recent versions of Java, and it can be used with Java 5, 6, or 7.

Some parts of early Java technologies have been *deprecated*, which means they are considered old-fashioned and should not be used. When it is important, we point out deprecated elements and discuss the preferred alternatives.

Java is an *object-oriented programming language*. Objects are the fundamental elements that make up a program. The principles of object-oriented software development are the cornerstone of this text. We explore object-oriented programming concepts later in this chapter and throughout the rest of the text.

KEY CONCEPT
This text focuses on the principles of object-oriented programming.

The Java language is accompanied by a library of extra software that we can use when developing programs. This software is referred to as the Java API, which stands for Application Programmer Interfaces, or simply the *standard class library*. It provides the ability to create graphics, communicate over networks, and interact with databases, among many other features. The Java API is huge and quite versatile. Although we won't be able to cover all aspects of the library, we will explore many of them.

Java is used in commercial environments all over the world. It is one of the fastest-growing programming technologies of all time. Thus it is not only a good language in which to learn programming concepts but also a practical language that will serve you well in the future.

A Java Program

Let's look at a simple but complete Java program. The program in Listing 1.1 prints two sentences to the screen. This particular program prints a quotation from Abraham Lincoln. The output is shown below the program listing.

All Java applications are similar in basic structure. Despite its small size and simple purpose, this program contains several important features. Let's carefully dissect it and examine its pieces.

The first few lines of the program are *comments*, which start with the // symbols and continue to the end of the line. Comments don't affect what the program does but are included to make the program easier to understand by humans. Programmers can and should include comments as needed throughout a program to clearly identify the purpose of the program and describe any special processing. Any written comments or documents, including a user's guide and technical references, are called *documentation*. Comments included in a program are called *inline documentation*.

The rest of the program is a *class definition*. This class is called `Lincoln`, although we could have named it just about anything we wished. The class definition runs from the first opening brace ({) to the final closing brace (}) on the last line of the program. All Java programs are defined using class definitions.

KEY CONCEPT
Comments do not affect a program's processing; instead, they serve to facilitate human comprehension.

Inside the class definition are some more comments describing the purpose of the `main` method, which is defined directly below the comments. A *method* is a group of programming statements that is given a name. In this case, the name of the method is `main` and it contains only two programming statements. Like a class definition, a method is delimited by braces.

LISTING 1.1

```
//********************************************************************
//  Lincoln.java        Java Foundations
//
//  Demonstrates the basic structure of a Java application.
//********************************************************************

public class Lincoln
{
   //-----------------------------------------------------------------
   //  Prints a presidential quote.
   //-----------------------------------------------------------------

   public static void main(String[] args)
   {
      System.out.println("A quote by Abraham Lincoln:");

      System.out.println("Whatever you are, be a good one.");
   }
}
```

OUTPUT

```
A quote by Abraham Lincoln:
Whatever you are, be a good one.
```

All Java applications have a `main` method, which is where processing begins. Each programming statement in the `main` method is executed, one at a time in order, until the end of the method is reached. Then the program ends, or *terminates*. The `main` method definition in a Java program is always preceded by the words `public`, `static`, and `void`, which we examine later in the text. The use of `String` and `args` does not come into play in this particular program. We describe these later also.

VideoNote
Overview of program elements

The two lines of code in the `main` method invoke another method called `println` (pronounced print line). We *invoke*, or *call*, a method when we want it to execute. The `println` method prints the specified characters to the screen. The characters to be printed are represented as a *character string*, enclosed in double quote characters (`"`). When the program is executed, it calls the `println` method to print the first statement, then it calls that method again to print the second statement, and then, because that is the last line in the `main` method, the program terminates.

The code executed when the `println` method is invoked is not defined in this program. The `println` method is part of the `System.out` object, which is part of the Java standard class library. It's not technically part of the Java language, but it is always available for use in any Java program. We explore the `println` method in more detail in Chapter 2.

COMMON ERROR

Statements in Java are terminated with a semicolon. If you leave the semicolon off of a statement, the compiler will get confused and issue an error. Here is an example:

```
System.out.println("Bilbo")
System.out.println("Frodo");
```

Without the semicolon on the first line, the compiler doesn't realize that a new statement has begun. However, most compilers are good at giving clear messages about this problem. It's easy to forget semicolons when you're first beginning to program, but including them will soon become second nature.

Comments

Let's examine comments in more detail. Comments are the only language feature that allows programmers to compose and communicate their thoughts independent of the code. Comments should provide insight into the programmer's original intent. A program may be used for many years, and often many modifications are made to it over time. The original programmer may not remember the details of a particular program when, at some point in the future, modifications are required. Furthermore, the original programmer is not always available to make the changes; thus, someone completely unfamiliar with the program will need to understand it. Good documentation is therefore essential.

As far as the Java programming language is concerned, the content of comments can be any text whatsoever. Comments are ignored by the computer; they do not affect how the program executes.

The comments in the `Lincoln` program represent one of two types of comments allowed in Java. The comments in `Lincoln` take the following form:

```
//  This is a comment.
```

This type of comment begins with a double slash `//`) and continues to the end of the line. You cannot have any characters between the two slashes. The computer ignores any text after the double slash to the end of the line. A comment can follow code on the same line to document that particular line, as in the following example:

```
System.out.println ("Monthly Report"); // always use this title
```

The second form a Java comment may take is

```
/* This is another comment. */
```

This comment type does not use the end of a line to indicate the end of the comment. Anything between the initiating slash-asterisk (/*) and the terminating asterisk-slash (*/) is part of the comment, including the invisible *newline* character that represents the end of a line. Therefore, this type of comment can extend over multiple lines. There can be no space between the slash and the asterisk.

If there is a second asterisk following the /* at the beginning of a comment, the content of the comment can be used to automatically generate external documentation about your program by using a tool called *javadoc*. More information about javadoc is given in Appendix I.

The two basic comment types can be used to create various documentation styles, such as

```
// This is a comment on a single line.

//– – – – – – – – – – – – – – – – – – – – – – – – – – – – – –
// Some comments such as those above methods or classes
// deserve to be blocked off to focus special attention
// on a particular aspect of your code. Note that each of
// these lines is technically a separate comment.
//– – – – – – – – – – – – – – – – – – – – – – – – – – – – – –

/*
   This is one comment
   that spans several lines.
*/
```

KEY CONCEPT
Inline documentation should provide insight into your code. It should not be ambiguous or belabor the obvious.

Programmers often concentrate so much on writing code that they focus too little on documentation. You should develop good commenting practices and follow them habitually. Comments should be well written, often in complete sentences. They should not belabor the obvious but should provide appropriate insight into the intent of the code. The following examples are *not* good comments:

```
System.out.println("hello"); // prints hello
System.out.println("test"); // change this later
```

The first comment paraphrases the obvious purpose of the line and does not add any value to the statement. It is better to have no comment than to add a useless one. The second comment is ambiguous. What should be changed later? When is later? Why should it be changed?

Identifiers and Reserved Words

The various words used when writing programs are called *identifiers*. The identifiers in the `Lincoln` program are `class`, `Lincoln`, `public`, `static`, `void`, `main`, `String`, `args`, `System`, `out`, and `println`. These fall into three categories:

- words that we make up when writing a program (`Lincoln` and `args`)
- words that another programmer chose (`String`, `System`, `out`, `println`, and `main`)
- words that are reserved for special purposes in the language (`class`, `public`, `static`, and `void`)

While writing the program, we simply chose to name the class `Lincoln`, but we could have used one of many other possibilities. For example, we could have called it `Quote`, or `Abe`, or `GoodOne`. The identifier `args` (which is short for "arguments") is often used in the way we use it in `Lincoln`, but we could have used just about any other identifier in its place.

The identifiers `String`, `System`, `out`, and `println` were chosen by other programmers. These words are not part of the Java language. They are part of the Java standard library of predefined code, a set of classes and methods that someone has already written for us. The authors of that code chose the identifiers in that code—we're just making use of them.

Reserved words are identifiers that have a special meaning in a programming language and can be used only in predefined ways. A reserved word cannot be used for any other purpose, such as naming a class or method. In the `Lincoln` program, the reserved words used are `class`, `public`, `static`, and `void`. Figure 1.1 lists all of the Java reserved words in alphabetical order. The words marked with an asterisk

abstract	default	goto*	package	this
assert	do	if	private	throw
boolean	double	implements	protected	throws
break	else	import	public	transient
byte	enum	instanceof	return	true
case	extends	int	short	try
catch	false	interface	static	void
char	final	long	strictfp	volatile
class	finally	native	super	while
const*	float	new	switch	
continue	for	null	synchronized	

FIGURE 1.1 Java reserved words

are reserved for possible future use in later versions of the language but currently have no meaning in Java.

An identifier that we make up for use in a program can be composed of any combination of letters, digits, the underscore character (_), and the dollar sign ($), but it cannot begin with a digit. Identifiers may be of any length. Therefore, `total`, `label7`, `nextStockItem`, `NUM_BOXES`, and `$amount` are all valid identifiers, but `4th_word` and `coin#value` are not valid.

Both uppercase and lowercase letters can be used in an identifier, and the difference is important. Java is *case-sensitive*, which means that two identifier names that differ only in the case of their letters are considered to be different identifiers. Therefore, `total`, `Total`, `ToTaL`, and `TOTAL` are all different identifiers. As you can imagine, it is not a good idea to use multiple identifiers that differ only in their case, because they can be easily confused.

KEY CONCEPT

Java is case sensitive. The uppercase and lowercase versions of a letter are distinct.

Identifier

An identifier is a letter followed by zero or more letters and digits. Java Letters include the 26 English alphabetic characters in both uppercase and lowercase, the `$` and `_` (underscore) characters, as well as alphabetic characters from other languages. Java Digits include the digits `0` through `9`.

Examples:

```
total
MAX_HEIGHT
num1
computeWage
System
```

Although the Java language doesn't require it, using a consistent case format for each kind of identifier makes your identifiers easier to understand. The various Java conventions regarding identifiers should be followed, although technically they don't have to be. For example, we use *title case* (uppercase for the first letter of each word) for class names. Throughout this text, we describe the preferred case style for each type of identifier when it is first encountered.

Although an identifier can be of any length, you should choose your names carefully. They should be descriptive but not verbose. You should avoid meaningless names such as `a` and `x`. An exception to this rule can be made if the short name is actually descriptive, such as using `x` and `y` to represent (x, y) coordinates on a two-dimensional grid. Likewise, you should not use unnecessarily long names, such as the identifier `theCurrentItemBeingProcessed`. The name `currentItem` would serve just as well. As you might imagine, the use of identifiers that are too long is a much less prevalent problem than the use of names that are not descriptive.

You should always strive to make your programs as readable as possible. Therefore, you should always be careful when abbreviating words. You might think that `curStVal` is a good name to represent the current stock value, but another person trying to understand the code might have trouble figuring out what you meant. It might not even be clear to you two months after you wrote it!

KEY CONCEPT
Identifier names should be descriptive and readable.

A *name* in Java is a series of identifiers separated by the dot (period) character. The name `System.out` is the way we designate the object through which we invoked the `println` method. Names appear quite regularly in Java programs.

White Space

All Java programs use *white space* to separate the words and symbols used in a program. White space consists of blanks, tabs, and newline characters. The phrase *white space* refers to the fact that on a white sheet of paper with black printing, the space between the words and symbols is white. The way a programmer uses white space is important, because it can be used to emphasize parts of the code and can make a program easier to read.

The computer ignores white space except when the white space is used to separate words. It does not affect the execution of a program. This fact gives programmers a great deal of flexibility in how they format a program. The lines of a program should be divided in logical places, and certain lines should be indented and aligned so that the program's underlying structure is clear.

KEY CONCEPT
Appropriate use of white space makes a program easier to read and understand.

Because white space is ignored, we can write a program in many different ways. For example, taking white space to one extreme, we could put as many words as possible on each line. The code in Listing 1.2, the `Lincoln2` program, is formatted quite differently from `Lincoln` but prints the same message.

Taking white space to the other extreme, we could write almost every word and symbol on a different line with varying amounts of spaces. This awkward approach is illustrated by `Lincoln3`, which is shown in Listing 1.3.

LISTING 1.2

```
//********************************************************************
//  Lincoln2.java        Java Foundations
//
//  Demonstrates a poorly formatted, though valid, program.
//********************************************************************
```

LISTING 1.2

```
public class Lincoln2{public static void main(String[]args){
System.out.println("A quote by Abraham Lincoln:");
System.out.println("Whatever you are, be a good one.");}}
```

OUTPUT

```
A quote by Abraham Lincoln:

Whatever you are, be a good one.
```

LISTING 1.3

```
//********************************************************************
//  Lincoln3.java       Java Foundations
//
//  Demonstrates another valid program that is poorly formatted.
//********************************************************************
         public       class
    Lincoln3
{
                  public
  static
       void
  main
       (
String
          []
    args                       )
  {
  System.out.println      (
"A quote by Abraham Lincoln:"         )
  ;         System.out.println
               (
       "Whatever you are, be a good one."
      )
  ;
  }
}
```

OUTPUT

```
A quote by Abraham Lincoln:
Whatever you are, be a good one.
```

All three versions of `Lincoln` are technically valid and will execute in the same way, but they are radically different from a reader's point of view. Both of the latter examples show poor style and make the program difficult to understand. You may be asked to adhere to particular guidelines when you write your programs. A software development company often has a programming style policy that it requires its programmers to follow. In any case, you should adopt and consistently use a set of style guidelines that increases the readability of your code.

KEY CONCEPT
You should adhere to a set of guidelines that establishes the way you format and document your programs.

1.2 Program Development

The process of getting a program running involves various activities. The program has to be written in the appropriate programming language, such as Java. That program has to be translated into a form that the computer can execute. Errors can occur at various stages of this process and must be fixed. Various software tools can be used to help with all parts of the development process, as well. Let's explore these issues in more detail.

Programming Language Levels

Suppose a particular person is giving travel directions to a friend. That person might explain those directions in any one of several languages, such as English, Russian, or Italian. The directions are the same no matter which language is used to explain them, but the manner in which the directions are expressed is different. The friend must be able to understand the language being used in order to follow the directions.

Similarly, a problem can be solved by writing a program in one of many programming languages, such as Java, Ada, C, C++, C#, Pascal, and Smalltalk. The purpose of the program is essentially the same no matter which language is used, but the particular statements used to express the instructions, and the overall organization of those instructions, vary with each language. A computer must be able to understand the instructions in order to carry them out.

Programming languages can be categorized into the following four groups. These groups basically reflect the historical development of computer languages.

- machine language
- assembly language
- high-level languages
- fourth-generation languages

In order for a program to run on a computer, it must be expressed in that computer's *machine language*. Each type of CPU has its own language. For that reason, we can't run a program specifically written for a Sun Workstation, with its Sparc processor, on a Dell PC, with its Intel processor.

Each machine language instruction can accomplish only a simple task. For example, a single machine language instruction might copy a value into a register or compare a value to zero. It might take four separate machine language instructions to add two numbers together and to store the result. However, a computer can do millions of these instructions in a second, and therefore, many simple commands can be executed quickly to accomplish complex tasks.

KEY CONCEPT
All programs must be translated into a particular CPU's machine language in order to be executed.

Machine language code is expressed as a series of binary digits and is extremely difficult for humans to read and write. Originally, programs were entered into the computer by using switches or some similarly tedious method. Early programmers found these techniques to be time-consuming and error-prone.

These problems gave rise to the use of *assembly language*, which replaced binary digits with *mnemonics*, short English-like words that represent commands or data. It is much easier for programmers to deal with words than with binary digits. However, an assembly language program cannot be executed directly on a computer. It must first be translated into machine language.

Generally, each assembly language instruction corresponds to an equivalent machine language instruction. Therefore, much like machine language, each assembly language instruction accomplishes only a simple operation. Although assembly language is an improvement over machine code from a programmer's perspective, it is still tedious to use. Both assembly language and machine language are considered *low-level languages*.

Today, most programmers use a *high-level language* to write software. A high-level language is expressed in English-like phrases and thus is easier for programmers to read and write. A single high-level-language programming statement can accomplish the equivalent of many—perhaps hundreds—of machine language instructions. The term *high-level* refers to the fact that the programming statements are expressed in a way that is far removed from the machine language that is ultimately executed. Java is a high-level language, as are Ada, C++, Smalltalk, and many others.

KEY CONCEPT
High-level languages allow a programmer to ignore the underlying details of machine language.

Figure 1.2 shows equivalent expressions in a high-level language, in assembly language, and in machine language. The expressions add two numbers together. The assembly language and machine language in this example are specific to a Sparc processor.

High-Level Language	Assembly Language	Machine Language

<a + b>	ld [%fp-20], %o0
	ld [%fp-24], %o1
	add %o0, %o1, %o0
		...
		1101 0000 0000 0111
		1011 1111 1110 1000
		1101 0010 0000 0111
		1011 1111 1110 1000
		1001 0000 0000 0000
		...

FIGURE 1.2 A high-level expression and its assembly language and machine language equivalents

The high-level language expression in Figure 1.2 is readable and intuitive for programmers. It is similar to an algebraic expression. The equivalent assembly language code is somewhat readable, but it is more verbose and less intuitive. The machine language is basically unreadable and much longer. In fact, only a small portion of the binary machine code to add two numbers together is shown in Figure 1.2. The complete machine language code for this particular expression is over 400 bits long.

A high-level language insulates programmers from needing to know the underlying machine language for the processor on which they are working. But high-level language code must be translated into machine language in order to be executed.

Some programming languages are considered to operate at an even higher level than high-level languages. They might include special facilities for automatic report generation or interaction with a database. These languages are called *fourth-generation languages*, or simply 4GLs, because they followed the first three generations of computer programming: machine, assembly, and high-level languages.

Editors, Compilers, and Interpreters

Several special-purpose programs are needed to help with the process of developing new programs. They are sometimes called *software tools* because they are used to build programs. Examples of basic software tools include an editor, a compiler, and an interpreter.

Initially, you use an *editor* as you type a program into a computer and store it in a file. There are many different editors with many different features. You should become familiar with the editor that you will use regularly, because such familiarity can dramatically affect the speed at which you enter and modify your programs.

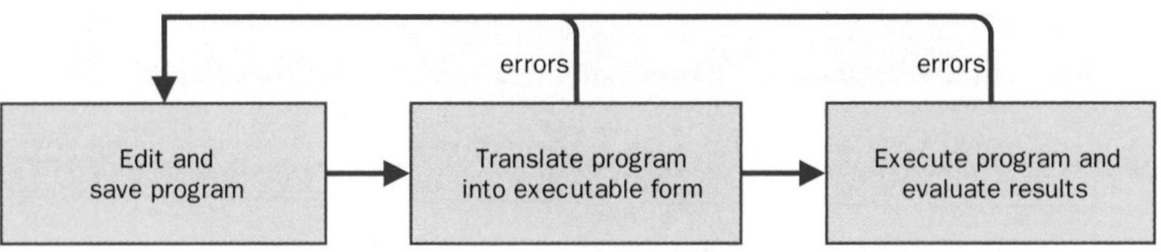

FIGURE 1.3 Editing and running a program

Figure 1.3 shows a very basic view of the program development process. After editing and saving your program, you attempt to translate it from high-level code into a form that can be executed. That translation may result in errors, in which case you return to the editor to make changes to the code to fix the problems. Once the translation occurs successfully, you can execute the program and evaluate the results. If the results are not what you want, or if you want to enhance your existing program, you again return to the editor to make changes.

The translation of source code into (ultimately) machine language for a particular type of CPU can occur in a variety of ways. A *compiler* is a program that translates code in one language into equivalent code in another language. The original code is called *source code*, and the language into which it is translated is called the *target language*. For many traditional compilers, the source code is translated directly into a particular machine language. In that case, the translation process occurs once (for a given version of the program), and the resulting executable program can be run whenever it is needed.

An *interpreter* is similar to a compiler but has an important difference. An interpreter interweaves the translation and execution activities. A small part of the source code, such as one statement, is translated and executed. Then another statement is translated and executed, and so on. One advantage of this technique is that it eliminates the need for a separate compilation phase. However, the program generally runs more slowly because the translation process occurs during each execution.

The process generally used to translate and execute Java programs combines the use of a compiler and that of an interpreter. This process is pictured in Figure 1.4. The Java compiler translates Java source code into Java *bytecode*, which is a representation of the program in a low-level form similar to machine language code. The Java interpreter reads Java bytecode and executes it on a specific machine. Another compiler could translate the bytecode into a particular machine language for efficient execution on that machine.

KEY CONCEPT
A Java compiler translates Java source code into Java bytecode, a low-level, architecture-neutral representation of the program.

The difference between Java bytecode and true machine language code is that Java bytecode is not tied to any particular processor type. This approach has the distinct advantage of making Java *architecture-neutral* and therefore easily

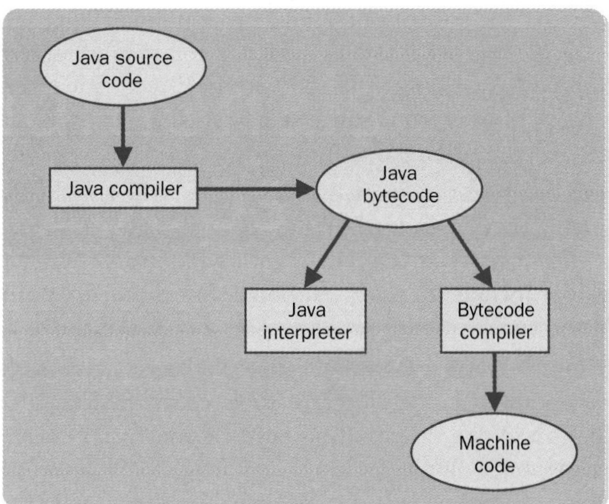

FIGURE 1.4 The Java translation and execution process

portable from one machine type to another. The only restriction is that there must be a Java interpreter or a bytecode compiler for each processor type on which the Java bytecode is to be executed.

Because the compilation process translates the high-level Java source code into a low-level representation, the interpretation process is more efficient than interpreting high-level code directly. Executing a program by interpreting its bytecode is still slower than executing machine code directly, but it is fast enough for most applications. Note that for efficiency, Java bytecode could be compiled into machine code.

Development Environments

A software *development environment* is the set of tools used to create, test, and modify a program. Some development environments are available free, whereas others, which may have advanced features, must be purchased. Some environments are referred to as *integrated development environments* (IDEs) because they integrate various tools into one software program.

Any development environment will contain certain key tools, such as a Java compiler and interpreter. Some include a *debugger*, which helps you find errors in a program. Other tools that may be included are documentation generators, archiving tools, and tools that help you visualize your program structure.

Sun Microsystems, the creator of the Java programming language, provides the Java *Software Development Kit* (SDK), which is sometimes referred to simply as the *Java Development Kit* (JDK). The SDK can be downloaded free of charge for various hardware platforms from Sun's Java Web site, java.sun.com, and is also included on the CD that accompanies this text.

VideoNote
Comparison of Java IDEs

The SDK tools are not an integrated environment. The commands for compilation and interpretation are executed on the command line. That is, the SDK does not have a *graphical user interface* (GUI), with windows, menus, buttons, and so on. It also does not include an editor, although any editor that can save a document as simple text can be used.

KEY CONCEPT
Many different development environments exist to help you create and modify Java programs.

Sun also has a Java IDE called NetBeans (www.netbeans.org) that incorporates the development tools of the SDK into one convenient GUI-based program. IBM promotes a similar IDE called Eclipse (www.eclipse.org). Both NetBeans and Eclipse are *open source* projects, which means that they are developed by a wide collection of programmers and are available free.

A research group at Auburn University has developed jGRASP, a free Java IDE that is included on the CD that accompanies this text. It can also be downloaded from www.jgrasp.org. In addition to fundamental development tools, jGRASP contains tools that graphically display program elements.

Various other Java development environments are available, and several are provided on this text's CD. The choice of which development environment to use is important. The more you know about the capabilities of your environment, the more productive you can be during program development.

Syntax and Semantics

Each programming language has its own unique *syntax*. The syntax rules of a language dictate exactly how the vocabulary elements of the language can be combined to form statements. These rules must be followed in order to create a program. We've already discussed several Java syntax rules. For instance, the fact that an identifier cannot begin with a digit is a syntax rule. The fact that braces are used to begin and end classes and methods is also a syntax rule. Appendix J formally defines the basic syntax rules for the Java programming language, and specific rules are highlighted throughout the text.

During compilation, all syntax rules are checked. If a program is not syntactically correct, the compiler will issue error messages and will not produce bytecode. Java has a syntax similar to that of the programming languages C and C++, so the look and feel of the code are familiar to people with a background in those languages.

The *semantics* of a statement in a programming language define what will happen when that statement is executed. Programming languages are generally unambiguous, which means the semantics of a program are well defined. That is, there is one and only one interpretation for each statement. On the other hand, the *natural languages* that humans use to communicate, such as English and Italian, are full of ambiguities. A sentence can often have two or more different meanings. For example, consider the following sentence:

Time flies like an arrow.

The average human is likely to interpret this sentence as a general observation: that time moves quickly in the same way that an arrow moves quickly. However, if we interpret the word *time* as a verb (as in "run the 50-yard dash and I'll time you") and the word *flies* as a noun (the plural of *fly*), the interpretation changes completely. We know that arrows don't time things, so we wouldn't normally interpret the sentence that way, but it is still a valid interpretation of the words in the sentence. A computer would have a difficult time trying to determine which meaning was intended. Moreover, this sentence could describe the preferences of an unusual insect known as a "time fly," which might be found near an archery range. After all, fruit flies like a banana.

The point is that one specific English sentence can have multiple valid meanings. A computer language cannot allow such ambiguities to exist. If a programming language instruction could have two different meanings, a computer would not be able to determine which one should be carried out.

KEY CONCEPT
Syntax rules dictate the form of a program. Semantics dictate the meaning of the program statements.

Errors

Several different kinds of problems can occur in software, particularly during program development. The term *computer error* is often misused and varies in meaning depending on the situation. From a user's point of view, anything that goes awry when interacting with a machine can be called a computer error. For example, suppose you charged a $23 item to your credit card, but when you received the bill, the item was listed at $230. After you have the problem fixed, the credit card company apologizes for the "computer error." Did the computer arbitrarily add a zero to the end of the number, or did it perhaps multiply the value by 10? Of course not. A computer follows the commands we give it and operates on the data we provide. If our programs are wrong or our data inaccurate, then we cannot expect the results to be correct. A common phrase used to describe this situation is "garbage in, garbage out."

KEY CONCEPT
The programmer is responsible for the accuracy and reliability of a program.

You will encounter three kinds of errors as you develop programs:

- compile-time error
- run-time error
- logical error

The compiler checks to make sure you are using the correct syntax. If you have any statements that do not conform to the syntactic rules of the language, the compiler will produce a *syntax error*. The compiler also tries to find other problems, such as the use of incompatible types of data. The syntax might be technically correct, but you may be attempting to do something that the language doesn't semantically allow. Any error identified by the compiler is called a *compile-time error*. When a compile-time error occurs, an executable version of the program is not created.

KEY CONCEPT
A Java program must be syntactically correct or the compiler will not produce bytecode.

The second kind of problem occurs during program execution. It is called a *run-time error* and causes the program to terminate abnormally. For example, if we attempt to divide by zero, the program will "crash" and halt execution at that point. Because the requested operation is undefined, the system simply abandons its attempt to continue processing your program. The best programs are *robust*; that is, they avoid as many run-time errors as possible. For example, the program code could guard against the possibility of dividing by zero and handle the situation appropriately if it arises. In Java, many run-time problems are called *exceptions* that can be caught and dealt with accordingly.

VideoNote
Examples of various error types

The third kind of software problem is a *logical error*. In this case, the software compiles and executes without complaint, but it produces incorrect results. For example, a logical error occurs when a value is calculated incorrectly or when a graphical button does not appear in the correct place. A programmer must test the program thoroughly, comparing the expected results to those that actually occur. When defects are found, they must be traced back to the source of the problem in the code and corrected. The process of finding and correcting defects in a program is called *debugging*. Logical errors can manifest themselves in many ways, and the actual root cause can be difficult to discover.

1.3 Problem Solving

Creating software involves much more than just writing code. The mechanics of editing and running a program are necessary steps, but the heart of software development is *problem solving*. We write a program to solve a particular problem.

In general, problem solving consists of multiple steps:

1. Understand the problem.
2. Design a solution.

3. Consider alternatives to the solution and refine the solution.
4. Implement the solution.
5. Test the solution and fix any problems that exist.

Although this approach applies to any kind of problem solving, it works particularly well when developing software. These steps aren't purely linear. That is, some of the activities will overlap others. But at some point, all of these steps should be carefully addressed.

The first step, coming to understand the problem, may sound obvious, but a lack of attention to this step has been the cause of many misguided software development efforts. If we attempt to solve a problem we don't completely understand, we often end up solving the wrong problem or at least going off on improper tangents. Each problem has a *problem domain*, the real-world issues that are key to our solution. For example, if we are going to write a program to score a bowling match, then the problem domain includes the rules of bowling. To develop a good solution, we must thoroughly understand the problem domain.

The key to designing a problem solution is breaking it down into manageable pieces. A solution to any problem can rarely be expressed as one big task. Instead, it is a series of small cooperating tasks that interact to perform a larger task. When developing software, we don't write one big program. We design separate pieces that are responsible for certain parts of the solution, and then we integrate them with the other parts.

KEY CONCEPT
Problem solving involves breaking a solution down into manageable pieces.

The first approach we choose in seeking a solution may not be the best one. We must always consider alternatives and refine the solution as necessary. The earlier we consider alternatives, the easier it is to modify our approach.

Implementing the solution consists of putting the solution that we have designed in a usable form. When we are developing a software solution to a problem, the implementation stage is the process of actually writing the program. Too often programming is thought of as writing code. But in most cases, the act of designing the program should be far more interesting and creative than the process of implementing the design in a particular programming language.

At many points in the development process, we should test our solution to find any errors that exist so that we can fix them. Testing cannot guarantee that there aren't still problems yet to be discovered, but it can raise our confidence that we have a viable solution.

Throughout this text, we explore techniques that enable us to design and implement elegant programs. Although we will often get immersed in these details, we should never forget that our primary goal is to solve problems.

1.4 Software Development Activities

Given that the goal of software development is to solve problems, it shouldn't surprise you that the activities involved in the software development process mirror the general problem-solving steps we discussed in the previous section. In particular, any proper software development effort consists of four basic *development activities*:

- Establishing the requirements.
- Creating a design.
- Implementing the design.
- Testing.

It would be nice if these activities, in this order, defined a step-by-step approach for developing software. However, although they may seem to be sequential, they are almost never completely linear in reality. They overlap and interact. Let's discuss each development activity briefly.

Software requirements specify *what* a program must accomplish. They indicate the tasks that a program should perform, not how it performs them. Often, requirements are expressed in a document called a *functional specification*.

Requirements are a clear expression of the problem to be solved. Until we truly know what problem we are trying to solve, we can't actually solve it.

In a classroom setting, students are generally provided the software requirements in the form of the problem assignment. However, even when they are provided, such requirements need to be discussed and clarified. In professional development, the person or group that wants a software product developed (the *client*) will often provide an initial set of requirements. However, these initial requirements are often incomplete, ambiguous, and perhaps even contradictory. The software developer must work with the client to refine the requirements until all key decisions about what the system will do have been addressed.

Requirements often address user interface issues such as output format, screen layouts, and graphical interface components. Essentially, the requirements establish the characteristics that make the program useful for the end user. They may also apply constraints to the program, such as how fast a task must be performed.

A *software design* indicates *how* a program will accomplish its requirements. The design specifies the classes and objects needed in a program and defines how they interact. It also specifies the relationships among the classes. Low-level design issues deal with how individual methods accomplish their tasks.

A civil engineer would never consider building a bridge without designing it first. The design of software is no less essential. Many problems that occur in software are directly attributable to a lack of good design effort. It has been shown time and again that the effort spent on the design of a program is well worth it, saving both time and money in the long run.

During software design, alternatives need to be considered and explored. Often, the first attempt at a design is not the best solution. Fortunately, changes are relatively easy to make during the design stage.

KEY CONCEPT
The effort put into design is both crucial and cost-effective.

Implementation is the process of writing the source code that will solve the problem. More precisely, implementation is the act of translating the design into a particular programming language. Too many programmers focus on implementation exclusively, when actually it should be the least creative of all development activities. The important decisions should be made when establishing the requirements and creating the design.

Testing is the act of ensuring that a program will solve the targeted problem, given all of the constraints under which it must perform. Testing includes running a program multiple times with various inputs and carefully scrutinizing the results. But it means far more than that. Testing in one form or another should be a part of every stage of development. The accuracy of the requirements, for instance, should be tested by reviewing them with the client. We revisit the issues related to testing in Chapter 11.

1.5 Object-Oriented Programming

As we stated earlier in this chapter, Java is an object-oriented language. As the name implies, an *object* is a fundamental entity in a Java program. This text is focused on the idea of developing software by defining objects that interact with each other.

The principles of object-oriented software development have been around for many years, essentially as long as high-level programming languages have been used. The programming language Simula, developed in the 1960s, had many characteristics that define the modern object-oriented approach to software development. In the 1980s and 1990s, object-oriented programming became wildly popular, largely because of the development of programming languages such as C++ and Java. It is now the dominant approach used in commercial software development.

One of the most attractive characteristics of the object-oriented approach is the fact that objects can be used quite effectively to represent real-world entities. We can use a software object to represent an employee in a company, for instance. We'd create one object per employee, each with behaviors and characteristics that we need to represent. In this way, object-oriented programming enables us to map our programs to the real situations that the programs represent. That is, the object-oriented approach makes it easier to solve problems, which is the point of writing a program in the first place.

Let's explore the specific characteristics of the object-oriented approach that help us solve those problems.

Object-Oriented Software Principles

Object-oriented programming ultimately requires a solid understanding of the following terms:

- object
- attribute
- method
- class
- encapsulation
- inheritance
- polymorphism

In addition to these terms, there are many associated concepts that allow us to tailor our solutions in innumerable ways. This text is designed to help you increase your understanding of these concepts gradually and naturally. This section offers an overview of these ideas at a high level to establish some terminology and provide the big picture.

We mentioned earlier that an *object* is a fundamental element in a program. A software object often represents a real object in our problem domain, such as a bank account. Every object has a *state* and a set of *behaviors*. By "state" we mean state of being—fundamental characteristics that currently define the object. For example, part of a bank account's state is its current balance. The behaviors of an object are the activities associated with the object. Behaviors associated with a bank account probably include the ability to make deposits and withdrawals.

In addition to objects, a Java program also manages primitive data. *Primitive data* include fundamental values such as numbers and characters. Objects usually represent more interesting or complex entities.

An object's *attributes* are the values it stores internally, which may be represented as primitive data or as other objects. For example, a bank account object may store a floating point number (a primitive value) that represents the balance of the account. It may contain other attributes, such as the name of the account owner. Collectively, the values of an object's attributes define its current state.

As mentioned earlier in this chapter, a *method* is a group of programming statements that is given a name. When a method is invoked, its statements are executed. A set of methods is associated with an object. The methods of an object define its potential behaviors. To define the ability to make a deposit in a bank account, we define a method containing programming statements that will update the account balance accordingly.

KEY CONCEPT

Each object has a state, defined by its attributes, and a set of behaviors, defined by its methods.

An object is defined by a *class*. A class is the model or blueprint from which an object is created. Consider the blueprint created by an architect when designing a house. The blueprint defines the important characteristics of the house—its walls, windows, doors, electrical outlets, and so on. Once the blueprint is created, several houses can be built using it, as depicted in Figure 1.5.

In one sense, the houses built from the blueprint are different. They are in different locations, have different addresses, contain different furniture, and are inhabited by different people. Yet in many ways they are the "same" house. The layout of the rooms and other crucial characteristics are the same in each. To create a different house, we would need a different blueprint.

A class is a blueprint of an object. It establishes the kind of data an object of that type will hold and defines the methods that represent the behavior of such objects. However, a class is not an object any more than a blueprint is a house. In general, a class contains no space to store data. Each object has space for its own data, which is why each object can have its own state.

KEY CONCEPT
A class is a blueprint of an object. Multiple objects can be created from one class definition.

Once a class has been defined, multiple objects can be created from that class. For example, once we define a class to represent the concept of a bank account, we can create multiple objects that represent specific, individual bank accounts. Each bank account object will keep track of its own balance.

An object should be *encapsulated*, which means it protects and manages its own information. That is, an object should be self-governing. The only changes

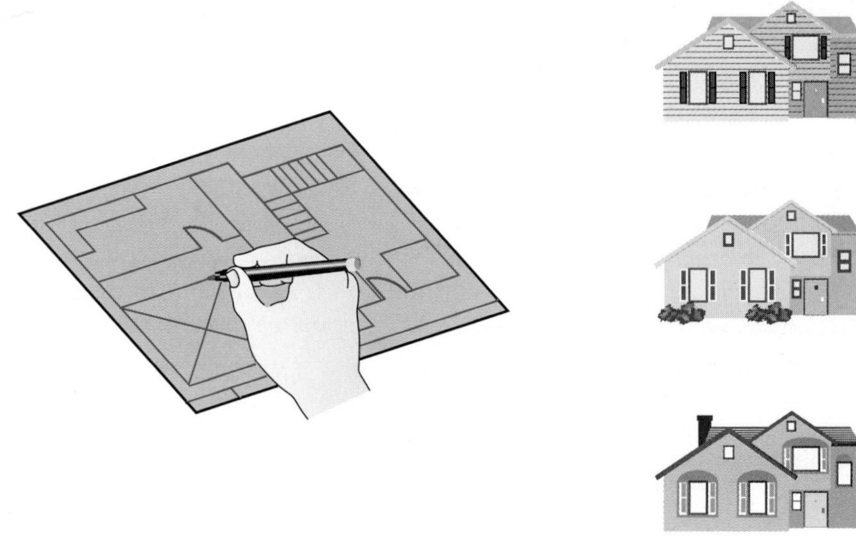

FIGURE 1.5 A house blueprint and three houses created from it

made to the state of the object should be accomplished by that object's methods. We should design an object so that other objects cannot "reach in" and change its state.

Classes can be created from other classes by using *inheritance*. That is, the definition of one class can be based on another class that already exists. Inheritance is a form of *software reuse*, capitalizing on the similarities among various kinds of classes that we may want to create. One class can be used to derive several new classes. Derived classes can then be used to derive even more classes. This creates a hierarchy of classes, where the attributes and methods defined in one class are inherited by its children, which in turn pass them on to their children, and so on. For example, we might create a hierarchy of classes that represent various types of accounts. Common characteristics are defined in high-level classes, and specific differences are defined in derived classes.

Polymorphism is the idea that we can refer to multiple types of related objects over time in consistent ways. It gives us the ability to design powerful and elegant solutions to problems that deal with multiple objects.

Some of the core object-oriented concepts are depicted in Figure 1.6. We don't expect you to understand these ideas fully at this point. Most of this text is designed to flesh out these ideas. This overview is intended only to set the stage.

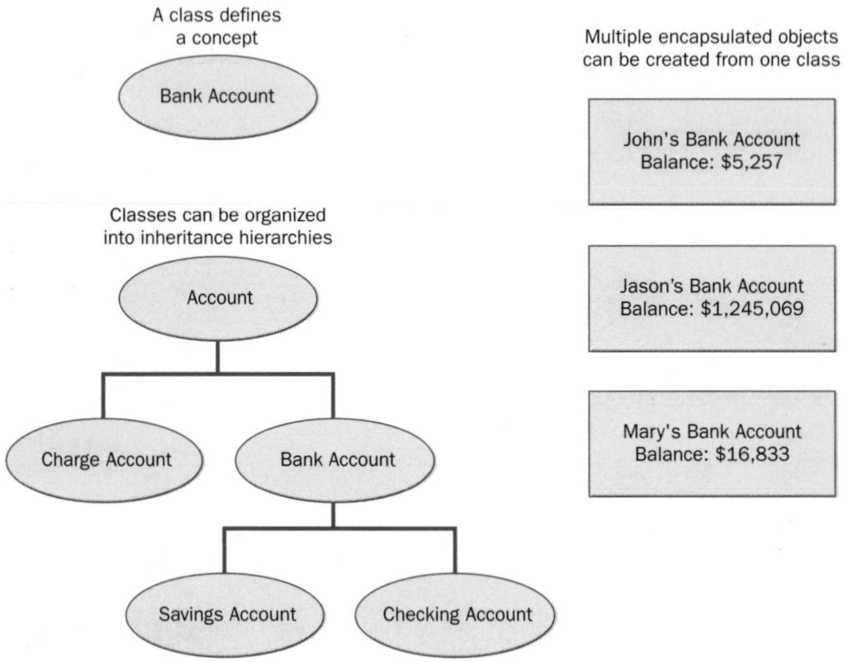

FIGURE 1.6 Various aspects of object-oriented software

Summary of Key Concepts

- A computer system consists of hardware and software that work in concert to help us solve problems.
- This test focuses on the principles of object-oriented programming.
- Comments do not affect a program's processing; instead, they serve to facilitate human comprehension.
- Inline documentation should provide insight into your code. It should not be ambiguous or belabor the obvious.
- Java is case-sensitive. The uppercase and lowercase versions of a letter are distinct.
- Identifier names should be descriptive and readable.
- Appropriate use of white space makes a program easier to read and understand.
- You should adhere to a set of guidelines that establishes the way you format and document your programs.
- All programs must be translated into a particular CPU's machine language in order to be executed.
- High-level languages allow a programmer to ignore the underlying details of machine language.
- A Java compiler translates Java source code into Java bytecode, a low-level, architecture-neutral representation of the program.
- Many different development environments exist to help you create and modify Java programs.
- Syntax rules dictate the form of a program. Semantics dictate the meaning of the program statements.
- The programmer is responsible for the accuracy and reliability of a program.
- A Java program must be syntactically correct or the compiler will not produce bytecode.
- Problem solving involves breaking a solution down into manageable pieces.
- The effort put into design is both crucial and cost-effective.
- Each object has a state, defined by its attributes, and a set of behaviors, defined by its methods.
- A class is a blueprint of an object. Multiple objects can be created from one class definition.

Summary of Terms

assembly language A low-level language that replaced binary digits with mnemonics.

bytecode A low-level representation of a Java program that is not tied to a specific type of CPU.

case-sensitive Making a distinction between uppercase and lowercase letters. Java is case-sensitive.

class definition An element in a Java program. All Java programs are defined using class definitions.

class library A set of software classes that can be used when developing programs (see *Java API*).

comment Text included in a program to make the program easier to understand for humans.

compiler A program that translates code in one language into equivalent code in another language.

deprectated An element that is considered old-fashioned and should not be used.

editor A software tool that allows one to enter text such as a program.

encapsulation The characteristic of an object that means it protects and manages its own information.

graphical user interface An interface to a program that consists of graphical elements such as windows and buttons.

high-level language A programming language that is expressed in phrases that are easier than machine language for a programmer to understand.

identifier A word in a programming language.

inheritance Defining a class based on another that already exists.

integrated development environment A set of software tools used to create, modify, and test a program.

Java 2 Platform The most recent Java technology.

Java API A library of software that we can use when developing programs.

logical error An error in a program that causes it to produce incorrect results.

machine language The language executed by a particular CPU.

method A group of programming statements that is given a name.

method invocation Calling a method to execute its code.

natural language A language that humans use to communicate, such as English.

object A fundamental entity in a Java program that represents something and provides services related to it.

object-oriented programming language A language such as Java that uses objects as the fundamental elements of a program.

program A series of instructions that a computer executes one at a time.

programming statement An individual instruction in a programming language.

reserved word An identifier that has a special meaning in a program language and can be used only in predefined ways.

run-time error An error that occurs during program execution and causes the program to terminate abnormally.

semantics Rules that define what a statement in a language means.

syntax The rules of a language that dictate how vocabulary elements of the language can be used.

syntax error A programming error that violates the syntax rules of the language.

white space The space, tab, and newline characters used to separate words and symbols in a program.

Self-Review Questions

SR 1.1 What is hardware? What is software?

SR 1.2 What is the relationship between a high-level language and machine language?

SR 1.3 What is Java bytecode?

SR 1.4 What is white space? How does it affect program execution? How does it affect program readability?

SR 1.5 Which of the following are not valid Java identifiers? Why?

```
a. RESULT
b. result
c. 12345
d. x12345y
e. black&white
f. answer_7
```

SR 1.6 What do we mean by the syntax and semantics of a programming language?

SR 1.7 Name the four basic activities that are involved in the software development process.

SR 1.8 What are the primary concepts that support object-oriented programming?

Exercises

EX 1.1 Give examples of the two types of Java comments, and explain the differences between them.

EX 1.2 Which of the following are not valid Java identifiers? Why?

```
a. Factorial
b. anExtremelyLongIdentifierIfYouAskMe
c. 2ndLevel
d. level2
e. MAX_SIZE
f. highest$
g. hook&ladder
```

EX 1.3 Why are the following valid Java identifiers not considered good identifiers?

```
a. q
b. totVal
c. theNextValueInTheList
```

EX 1.4 Java is case-sensitive. What does that mean?

EX 1.5 What do we mean when we say that the English language is ambiguous? Give two examples of ambiguity in the English language (other than the example used in this chapter), and explain the ambiguity. Why is ambiguity a problem for programming languages?

EX 1.6 Categorize each of the following situations as a compile-time error, run-time error, or logical error:

a. multiplying two numbers when you meant to add them
b. dividing by zero
c. forgetting a semicolon at the end of a programming statement
d. spelling a word wrong in the output
e. producing inaccurate results
f. typing a { when you should have typed a (

Programming Projects

PP 1.1 Enter, compile, and run the following application.

```
public class Test
{
   public static void main(String[] args)
   {
      System.out.println("An Emergency Broadcast");
   }
}
```

PP 1.2 Introduce the following errors, one at a time, into the program from Programming Project 1.1. Record any error messages that the compiler produces. Fix the previous error each time, before you introduce a new one. If no error messages are produced, explain why. Try to predict what will happen before you make each change.

a. change `Test` to `test`
b. change `Emergency` to `emergency`
c. remove the first quotation mark in the string
d. remove the last quotation mark in the string
e. change `main` to `man`
f. change `println` to `bogus`
g. remove the semicolon at the end of the `println` statement
h. remove the last brace in the program

PP 1.3 Write an application that prints, on separate lines, your name, your birthday, your hobbies, your favorite book, and your favorite movie. Label each piece of information in the output.

PP 1.4 Write an application that prints the phrase `Knowledge is Power` in each of the following three ways:

a. on one line
b. on three lines, one word per line, with the words centered relative to each other
c. inside a box made up of the characters = and |

PP 1.5 Write an application that prints a list of four or five websites that you enjoy. Print both the site name and the URL.

PP 1.6 Write an application that prints the first few verses of a song (your choice). Label the chorus.

PP 1.7 Write an application that prints the following diamond shape. Don't print any unneeded characters. (That is, don't make any character string longer than it has to be.)

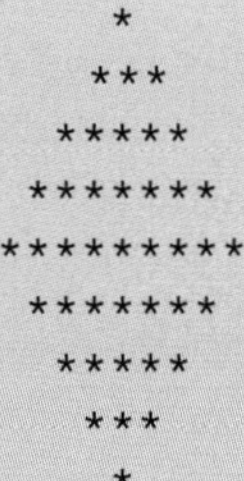

PP 1.8 Write an application that displays your initials in large block letters. Make each large letter out of the corresponding regular character. Here is an example:

```
   JJJJJJJJJJJJJJJ        AAAAAAAAA          LLLL
   JJJJJJJJJJJJJJJ       AAAAAAAAAAA         LLLL
           JJJJ          AAA     AAA         LLLL
           JJJJ          AAA     AAA         LLLL
           JJJJ          AAAAAAAAAAA         LLLL
JJJJJ      JJJJ          AAAAAAAAAAA         LLLL
JJ         JJJJ          AAA     AAA         LLLL
 JJJJJJJJJJJ             AAA     AAA         LLLLLLLLLLLLLL
   JJJJJJJJJ             AAA     AAA         LLLLLLLLLLLLLL
```

Answers to Self-Review Questions

SRA 1.1 The hardware of a computer system consists of its physical components, such as a circuit board, monitor, and keyboard. Software is the programs that are executed by the hardware and the data that those programs use. Hardware is tangible, whereas software is intangible.

SRA 1.2 High-level languages allow a programmer to express a series of program instructions in English-like terms that are relatively easy to read and use. However, in order to execute, a program must be expressed in a particular computer's machine language, which consists of a series of bits that is basically unreadable by humans. A high-level language program must be translated into machine language before it can be run.

SRA 1.3 Java bytecode is a low-level representation of a Java source code program. The Java compiler translates the source code into bytecode, which can then be executed using the Java interpreter. The bytecode might be transported across the Web before being executed by a Java interpreter that is part of a Web browser.

SRA 1.4 *White space* is a term that refers to the spaces, tabs, and newline characters that separate words and symbols in a program. The compiler ignores extra white space; therefore, it doesn't affect execution. However, it is crucial to use white space appropriately to make a program readable to humans.

SRA 1.5 All of the identifiers shown are valid except `12345` (an identifier cannot begin with a digit) and `black&white` (an identifier cannot contain the character `&`). The identifiers `RESULT` and `result` are both valid, but they should not be used together in a program because they differ only by case. The underscore character (as in `answer_7`) is a valid part of an identifier.

SRA 1.6 Syntax rules define how the symbols and words of a programming language can be put together. The semantics of a programming language instruction determine what will happen when that instruction is executed.

SRA 1.7 The four basic activities in software development are requirements analysis (deciding what the program should do), design (deciding how to do it), implementation (writing the solution in source code), and testing (validating the implementation).

SRA 1.8 The primary elements that support object-oriented programming are objects, classes, encapsulation, and inheritance. An object is defined by a class, which contains methods that define the operations on those objects (the services that they perform). Objects are encapsulated so that they store and manage their own data. Inheritance is a reuse technique in which one class can be derived from another.

2 Data and Expressions

CHAPTER OBJECTIVES

- Discuss the use of character strings, concatenation, and escape sequences.
- Explore the declaration and use of variables.
- Describe the Java primitive data types.
- Discuss the syntax and processing of expressions.
- Define the types of data conversions and the mechanisms for accomplishing them.
- Introduce the `Scanner` class to create interactive programs.

This chapter explores some of the basic types of data used in a Java program and the use of expressions to perform calculations. It discusses the conversion of data from one type to another, and how to read input interactively from the user running a program.

2.1 Character Strings

In Chapter 1 we discussed the basic structure of a Java program, including the use of comments, identifiers, and white space, using the `Lincoln` program as an example. Chapter 1 also included an overview of the various concepts involved in object-oriented programming, such as objects, classes, and methods. Take a moment to review these ideas if necessary.

A character string is an object in Java, defined by the class `String`. Because strings are so fundamental to computer programming, Java provides the ability to use a *string literal*, delimited by double quotation characters, as we've seen in previous examples. We explore the `String` class and its methods in more detail in Chapter 3. For now, let's explore the use of string literals further.

The following are all examples of valid string literals:

```
"The quick brown fox jumped over the lazy dog."
"2201 Birch Leaf Lane, Blacksburg, VA 24060"
"x"
""
```

A string literal can contain any valid characters, including numeric digits, punctuation, and other special characters. The last example in the list above contains no characters at all.

The `print` and `println` Methods

In the `Lincoln` program in Chapter 1, we invoked the `println` method as follows:

```
System.out.println("Whatever you are, be a good one.");
```

This statement demonstrates the use of objects. The `System.out` object represents an output device or file, which by default is the monitor screen. To be more precise, the object's name is `out` and it is stored in the `System` class. We explore that relationship in more detail at the appropriate point in the text.

The `println` method is a service that the `System.out` object performs for us. Whenever we request it, the object will print a character string to the screen. We can say that we send the `println` message to the `System.out` object to request that some text be printed.

Each piece of data that we send to a method is called a *parameter*. In this case, the `println` method takes only one parameter: the string of characters to be printed.

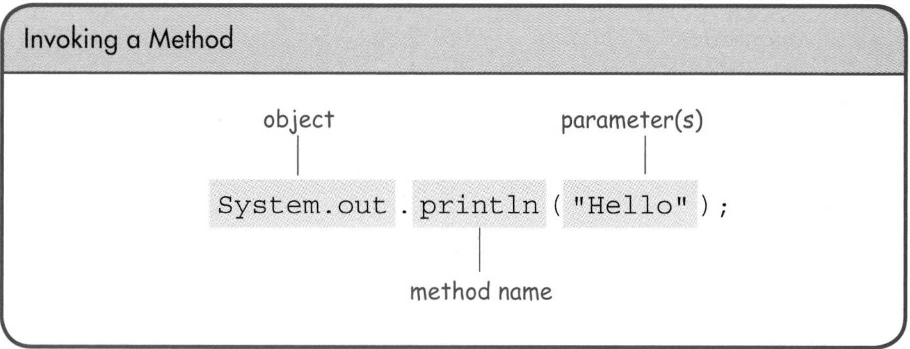

The System.out object also provides another service we can use: the print method. The difference between print and println is small but important. The println method prints the information sent to it and then moves to the beginning of the next line. The print method is similar to println, but it does not advance to the next line when completed.

The program shown in Listing 2.1 is called Countdown, and it invokes both the print method and the println method.

Carefully compare the output of the Countdown program, shown at the bottom of the program listing, to the program code. Note that the word Liftoff is printed on the same line as the first few words, even though it is printed using the println method. Remember that the println method moves to the beginning of the next line *after* the information passed to it is printed.

KEY CONCEPT
The print and println methods represent two services provided by the System.out object.

LISTING 2.1

```
//********************************************************************
// Countdown.java       Java Foundations
//
// Demonstrates the difference between print and println.
//********************************************************************

public class Countdown
{
   //-----------------------------------------------------------------
   // Prints two lines of output representing a rocket countdown.
   //-----------------------------------------------------------------
```

LISTING 2.1 *continued*

```
   public static void main(String[] args)
   {
      System.out.print("Three...");
      System.out.print("Two...");
      System.out.print("One...");
      System.out.print("Zero...");

      System.out.println("Liftoff!"); // appears on first output line

      System.out.println("Houston, we have a problem.");
   }
}
```

OUTPUT

```
Three... Two... One... Zero... Liftoff!
Houston, we have a problem.
```

String Concatenation

A string literal cannot span multiple lines in a program. The following program statement is improper syntax and would produce an error when attempting to compile:

```
// The following statement will not compile
System.out.println ("The only stupid question is
the one that's not asked.");
```

When we want to print a string that is too long to fit on one line in a program, we can rely on *string concatenation* to append one string to the end of another. The string concatenation operator is the plus sign (+). The following expression concatenates one character string and another, producing one long string:

```
"The only stupid question is " + "the one that's not asked."
```

The program called `Facts` shown in Listing 2.2 contains several `println` statements. The first one prints a sentence that is somewhat long and will not fit on one line of the program. Because a character literal cannot span two

LISTING 2.2

```
//********************************************************************
//  Facts.java      Java Foundations
//
//  Demonstrates the use of the string concatenation operator and the
//  automatic conversion of an integer to a string.
//********************************************************************

public class Facts
{
   //-----------------------------------------------------------------
   // Prints various facts.
   //-----------------------------------------------------------------

   public static void main(String[] args)
   {
      // Strings can be concatenated into one long string
      System.out.println("We present the following facts for your"
                         + "extracurricular edification:");

      System.out.println();

      // A string can contain numeric digits
      System.out.println("Letters in the Hawaiian alphabet: 12");

      // A numeric value can be concatenated to a string
      System.out.println("Dialing code for Antarctica: " + 672);

      System.out.println("Year in which Leonardo da Vinci invented"
                         + "the parachute: " + 1515);

      system.out.println("Speed of ketchup: " + 40 + " km per year");
   }
}
```

OUTPUT

```
We present the following facts for your extracurricular edification:

Letters in the Hawaiian alphabet: 12
Dialing code for Antarctica: 672
Year in which Leonardo da Vinci invented the parachute: 1515
Speed of ketchup: 40 km per year
```

lines in a program, we split the string into two and use string concatenation to append them. Therefore, the string concatenation operation in the first `println` statement results in one large string that is passed to the method to be printed.

Note that we don't have to pass any information to the `println` method, as shown in the second line of the `Facts` program. This call does not print any visible characters, but it does move to the next line of output. So in this case, calling `println` with no parameters has the effect of printing a blank line.

The last three calls to `println` in the `Facts` program demonstrate another interesting thing about string concatenation: Strings and numbers can be concatenated. Note that the numbers in those lines are not enclosed in double quotation characters and are therefore not character strings. In these cases, the number is automatically converted to a string, and then the two strings are concatenated.

Because we are printing particular values, we could simply have included the numeric value as part of the string literal, as in

```
"Speed of ketchup: 40 km per year"
```

Digits are characters and can be included in strings as needed. We separate them in the `Facts` program to demonstrate the ability to concatenate a string and a number. This technique will be useful in upcoming examples.

As you might think, the + operator is also used for arithmetic addition. Therefore, what the + operator does depends on the types of data on which it operates. If either or both of the operands of the + operator are strings, then string concatenation is performed.

KEY CONCEPT

In Java, the + operator is used both for addition and for string concatenation.

The `Addition` program shown in Listing 2.3 demonstrates the distinction between string concatenation and arithmetic addition. The `Addition` program uses the + operator four times. In the first call to `println`, both + operations perform string concatenation, because the operators are executed from left to right. The first operator concatenates the string with the first number (`24`), creating a larger string. Then that string is concatenated with the second number (`45`), creating an even larger string, which gets printed.

In the second call to `println`, we use parentheses to group the + operation with the two numeric operands. This forces that operation to happen first. Because both operands are numbers, the numbers are added in the arithmetic sense, producing the result `69`. That number is then concatenated with the string, producing a larger string that gets printed.

We revisit this type of situation later in this chapter when we formalize the precedence rules that define the order in which operators are evaluated.

LISTING 2.3

```
//********************************************************************
//  Addition.java       Java Foundations
//
//  Demonstrates the difference between the addition and string
//  concatenation operators.
//********************************************************************

public class Addition
{
   //-----------------------------------------------------------------
   // Concatenates and adds two numbers and prints the results.
   //-----------------------------------------------------------------
   public static void main(String[] args)
   {
      System.out.println("24 and 45 concatenated: " + 24 + 45);

      System.out.println("24 and 45 added: " + (24 + 45));
   }
}
```

OUTPUT

```
24 and 45 concatenated: 2445
24 and 45 added: 69
```

COMMON ERROR

It's easy to forget the processing that's happening to allow a string to be constructed before being printed. For example, it's easy to forget the concatenation operator between a string and a numeric value, or to use a comma as though they were separate parameters:

```
System.out.println("The total is", total);
```

This will cause the compiler to issue an error. Remember, only one parameter is sent to a `println` statement.

Escape Sequence	Meaning
`\b`	backspace
`\t`	tab
`\n`	newline
`\r`	carriage return
`\"`	double quote
`\'`	single quote
`\\`	backslash

FIGURE 2.1 Java escape sequences

Escape Sequences

Because the double quotation character (`"`) is used in the Java language to indicate the beginning and end of a string, we must use a special technique to print the quotation character. If we simply put it in a string (`"""`), the compiler gets confused because it thinks the second quotation character is the end of the string and doesn't know what to do with the third one. This results in a compile-time error.

To overcome this problem, Java defines several *escape sequences* to represent special characters. An escape sequence begins with the backslash character (\), which indicates that the character or characters that follow should be interpreted in a special way. Figure 2.1 lists the Java escape sequences.

KEY CONCEPT
An escape sequence can be used to represent a character that would otherwise cause compilation problems.

The program in Listing 2.4, called `Roses`, prints some text resembling a poem. It uses only one `println` statement to do so, despite the fact that the poem is several lines long. Note the escape sequences used throughout the string. The `\n` escape sequence forces the output to a new line, and the `\t` escape sequence represents a tab character. (Note that you may see a different amount of indentation when you run this program—tab stops depend on the system settings.) The `\"` escape sequence ensures that the quotation character

VideoNote
Example using strings and escape sequences

LISTING 2.4

```
//********************************************************************
//  Roses.java       Java Foundations
//
//  Demonstrates the use of escape sequences.
//********************************************************************
```

LISTING 2.4 *continued*

```
public class Roses
{
   //-----------------------------------------------------------------
   // Prints a poem (of sorts) on multiple lines.
   //-----------------------------------------------------------------
   public static void main (String[] args)
   {
      System.out.println("Roses are red,\n\tViolets are blue,\n" +
        "Sugar is sweet,\n\tBut I have \"commitment issues\",\n\t" +
        "So I'd rather just be friends\n\tAt this point in our " +
        "relationship.");
   }
}
```

OUTPUT

```
Roses are red,
        Violets are blue,
Sugar is sweet,
        But I have "commitment issues",
        So I'd rather just be friends
        At this point in our relationship.
```

is treated as part of the string, not as the termination of it, and this enables it to be printed as part of the output.

2.2 Variables and Assignment

Most of the information we manage in a program is represented by variables. Let's examine how we declare and use them in a program.

Variables

A *variable* is a name for a location in memory used to hold a data value. A variable declaration instructs the compiler to reserve a portion of main memory space large enough to hold a particular type of value, and it indicates the name by which we refer to that location.

Local Variable Declaration

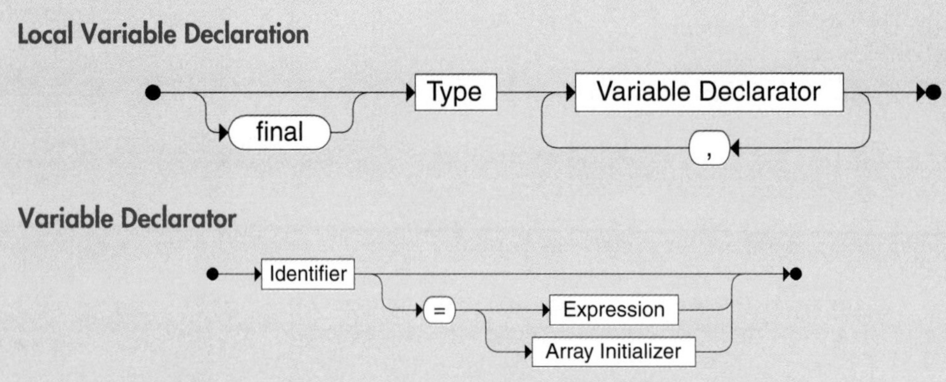

A variable declaration consists of a Type followed by a list of variables. Each variable can be initialized in the declaration to the value of the specified Expression. If the `final` modifier precedes the declaration, the identifiers are declared as named constants whose values cannot be changed once they are set.

Examples:

```
int total;
double num1, num2 = 4.356, num3;
char letter = 'A', digit = '7';
final int MAX = 45;
```

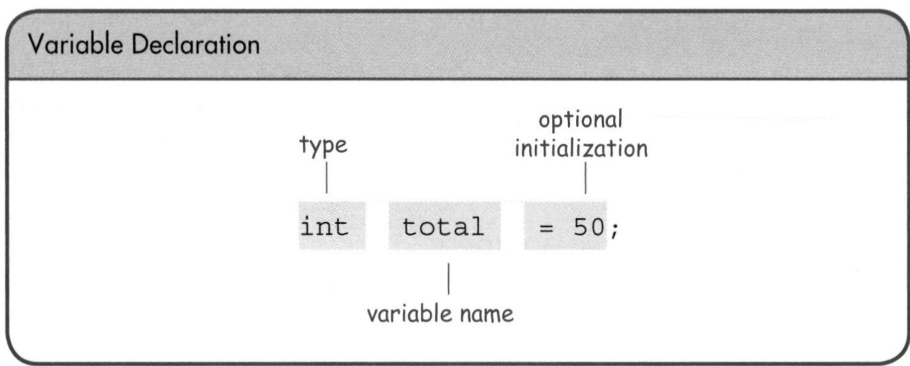

KEY CONCEPT

A variable is a name for a memory location used to hold a value of a particular data type.

Consider the program `PianoKeys`, shown in Listing 2.5. The first line of the `main` method is the declaration of a variable named `keys` that holds an integer (`int`) value. The declaration also gives `keys` an initial value of 88. If an initial value is not specified for a variable, the value is undefined. Most Java compilers give errors or warnings if you attempt to use a variable before you have explicitly given it a value.

LISTING 2.5

```
//********************************************************************
//  PianoKeys.java       Java Foundations
//
//  Demonstrates the declaration, initialization, and use of an
//  integer variable.
//********************************************************************

public class PianoKeys
{
   //-----------------------------------------------------------------
   //  Prints the number of keys on a piano.
   //-----------------------------------------------------------------
   public static void main(String[] args)
   {
      int keys = 88;

      System.out.println("A piano has " + keys + " keys.");
   }
}
```

OUTPUT

```
A piano has 88 keys.
```

The `keys` variable, with its value, could be pictured as follows:

keys | 88

In the `PianoKeys` program, two pieces of information are used in the call to the `println` method. The first is a string, and the second is the variable `keys`. When a variable is referenced, the value currently stored in it is used. Therefore, when the call to `println` is executed, the value of `keys`, which is 88, is obtained.

Because that value is an integer, it is automatically converted to a string and concatenated with the initial string. The concatenated string is passed to `println` and printed.

A variable declaration can have multiple variables of the same type declared on one line. Each variable on the line can be declared with or without an initializing value. For example:

```
int count, minimum = 0, result;
```

The Assignment Statement

Let's examine a program that changes the value of a variable. Listing 2.6 shows a program called `Geometry`. This program first declares an integer variable called `sides` and initializes it to `7`. It then prints out the current value of `sides`.

The next line in `main` changes the value stored in the variable `sides`:

```
sides = 10;
```

LISTING 2.6

```
//********************************************************************
//  Geometry.java Java Foundations
//
//  Demonstrates the use of an assignment statement to change the
//  value stored in a variable.
//********************************************************************

public class Geometry
{
   //-----------------------------------------------------------------
   // Prints the number of sides of several geometric shapes.
   //-----------------------------------------------------------------
   public static void main(String[] args)
   {
      int sides = 7; // declaration with initialization
      System.out.println("A heptagon has " + sides + " sides.");

      sides = 10; // assignment statement
      System.out.println("A decagon has " + sides + " sides.");

      sides = 12;
      System.out.println("A dodecagon has " + sides + " sides.");
   }
}
```

OUTPUT

```
A heptagon has 7 sides.
A decagon has 10 sides.
A dodecagon has 12 sides.
```

This is called an *assignment statement* because it assigns a value to a variable. When executed, the expression on the right-hand side of the assignment operator (=) is evaluated, and the result is stored in the memory location indicated by the variable on the left-hand side. In this example, the expression is simply a number, 10. We discuss expressions that are more involved than this in the next section.

> **KEY CONCEPT**
> Accessing data leaves them intact in memory, but an assignment statement overwrites the old data.

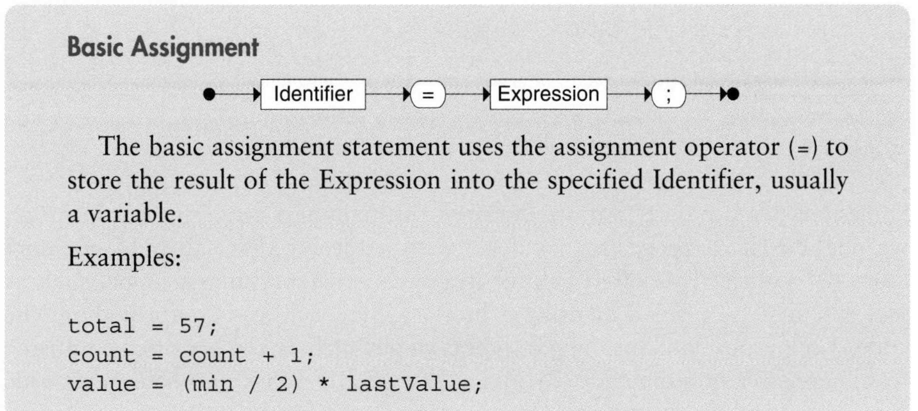

Basic Assignment

The basic assignment statement uses the assignment operator (=) to store the result of the Expression into the specified Identifier, usually a variable.

Examples:

```
total = 57;
count = count + 1;
value = (min / 2) * lastValue;
```

A variable can store only one value of its declared type. A new value overwrites the old one. In this case, when the value 10 is assigned to sides, the original value 7 is overwritten and lost forever, as follows:

After initialization:	sides	7
After first assignment:	sides	10

When a reference is made to a variable, such as when it is printed, the value of the variable is not changed. This is the nature of computer memory: Accessing (reading) data leaves the values in memory intact, but writing data replaces the old data with the new.

The Java language is *strongly typed*, which means that we are not allowed to assign a value to a variable that is inconsistent with its declared type. Trying to combine incompatible types will generate an error when you attempt to compile the program. Therefore, the expression on the right-hand side of an assignment statement must evaluate to a value compatible with the type of the variable on the left-hand side.

> **KEY CONCEPT**
> We cannot assign a value of one type to a variable of an incompatible type.

Assignment Statement

```
                 1) expression is evaluated
     variable    2) result is assigned to variable
         \                  /
      height = height + gap;
             |
      assignment operator
```

Constants

Sometimes we use data that are constant throughout a program. For instance, we might write a program that deals with a theater that can hold no more than 427 people. It is often helpful to give a constant value a name, such as `MAX_OCCUPANCY`, instead of using a literal value, such as `427`, throughout the code. The purpose and meaning of literal values such as `427` are often confusing to someone reading the code. By giving the value a name, you help explain its role in the program.

KEY CONCEPT
Constants hold a particular value for the duration of their existence.

Constants are identifiers and are similar to variables except that they hold a particular value for the duration of their existence. Constants are, to use the English meaning of the word, not variable. Their value doesn't change.

In Java, if you precede a declaration with the reserved word `final`, the identifier is made a constant. By convention, uppercase letters are used when naming constants, to distinguish them from regular variables, and individual words are separated using the underscore character. For example, the constant describing the maximum occupancy of a theater could be declared as follows:

```
final int MAX_OCCUPANCY = 427;
```

The compiler will produce an error message if you attempt to change the value of a constant once it has been given its initial value. This is another good reason to use constants. Constants prevent inadvertent coding errors, because the only valid place to change their value is in the initial assignment.

There is a third good reason to use constants. If a constant is used throughout a program and its value has to be modified, then you need change it in only one place. For example, if the capacity of the theater changes (because of a renovation) from 427 to 535, then you have to change only one declaration, and all uses of MAX_OCCUPANCY automatically reflect the change. If the literal 427 had been used throughout the code, each use would have had to be found and changed. If you were to miss any uses of the literal value, problems would surely arise.

2.3 Primitive Data Types

There are eight *primitive data types* in Java: four subsets of integers, two subsets of floating point numbers, a character data type, and a boolean data type. Everything else is represented using objects. Let's examine these eight primitive data types in some detail.

Integers and Floating Points

Java has two basic kinds of numeric values: integers, which have no fractional part, and floating points, which do. There are four integer data types (byte, short, int, and long) and two floating point data types (float and double). All of the numeric types differ in the amount of memory space used to store a value of that type, which determines the range of values that can be represented. The size of each data type is the same for all hardware platforms. All numeric types are *signed*, which means that both positive and negative values can be stored in them. Figure 2.2 summarizes the numeric primitive types.

KEY CONCEPT
Java has two kinds of numeric values: integer and floating point. There are four integer data types and two floating point data types.

A *bit*, or binary digit, can be either a 1 or a 0. Because each bit can represent two different states, a string of N bits can be used to represent 2^N different values. Appendix B describes number systems and these kinds of relationships in more detail.

Type	Storage	Min Value	Max Value
byte	8 bits	–128	127
short	16 bits	–32,768	32,767
int	32 bits	–2,147,483,648	2,147,483,647
long	64 bits	–9,223,372,036,854,775,808	9,223,372,036,854,775,807
float	32 bits	Approximately –3.4E+38 with 7 significant digits	Approximately 3.4E+38 with 7 significant digits
double	64 bits	Approximately –1.7E+308 with 15 significant digits	Approximately 1.7E+308 with 15 significant digits

FIGURE 2.2 The Java numeric primitive types

When designing programs, we sometimes need to be careful about picking variables of appropriate size so that memory space is not wasted. This occurs in situations where memory space is particularly restricted, such as a program that runs on a personal data assistant (PDA). In such cases, we can choose a variable's data type accordingly. For example, if the value of a particular variable will not vary outside of a range of 1 to 1000, then a two-byte integer (`short`) is large enough to accommodate it. On the other hand, when it's not clear what the range of a particular variable will be, we should provide a reasonable—even a generous—amount of space. In most situations, memory space is not a serious restriction, and we can usually afford generous assumptions.

Note that even though a `float` value supports very large (and very small) numbers, it has only seven significant digits. Therefore, if it is important to maintain a value such as 50341.2077 accurately, we need to use a `double`.

As we've already discussed, a *literal* is an explicit data value used in a program. The various numbers used in programs such as `Facts` and `Addition` and `PianoKeys` are all *integer literals*. Java assumes that all integer literals are of type `int`, unless an `L` or `l` is appended to the end of the value to indicate that it should be considered a literal of type `long`, such as `45L`.

Likewise, Java assumes that all *floating point literals* are of type `double`. If we need to treat a floating point literal as a `float`, we append an `F` or `f` to the end of the value, as in `2.718F` or `123.45f`. Numeric literals of type `double` can be followed by a `D` or `d` if desired.

The following are examples of numeric variable declarations in Java:

```
int answer = 42;
byte smallNumber1, smallNumber2;
long countedStars = 86827263927L;
float ratio = 0.2363F;
double delta = 453.523311903;
```

Characters

Characters are another fundamental type of data used and managed on a computer. Individual characters can be treated as separate data items, and, as we've seen in several examples, they can be combined to form character strings.

A *character literal* is expressed in a Java program with single quotation characters, as in `'b'` or `'J'` or `';'`. You will recall that *string literals* are delineated using double quotation marks, and that the `String` type is not a primitive data type in Java but a class name. We discuss the `String` class in detail in the next chapter.

Note the difference between a digit as a character (or part of a string) and a digit as a number (or part of a larger number). The number `602` is a numeric value that can be used in an arithmetic calculation. But in the string `"602 Greenbriar Court"` the `6`, `0`, and `2` are characters, just like the rest of the characters that make up the string.

Decimal Integer Literal

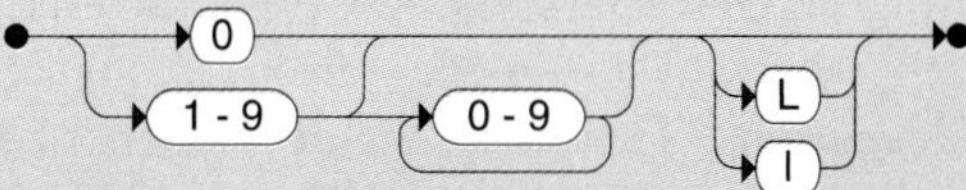

An integer literal is composed of a series of digits followed by an optional suffix to indicate that it should be considered a `long` integer. Negation of a literal is considered a separate operation.

Examples:

```
5
2594
4920328L
```

The characters we can manage are defined by a *character set*, which is simply a list of characters in a particular order. Each programming language supports a particular character set that defines the valid values for a character variable in that language. Several character sets have been proposed, but only a few have been used regularly over the years. The *ASCII character set* is a popular choice. ASCII stands for the American Standard Code for Information Interchange. The basic ASCII set uses 7 bits per character, providing room to support 128 different characters, including

- uppercase letters, such as `'A'`, `'B'`, and `'C'`
- lowercase letters, such as `'a'`, `'b'`, and `'c'`
- punctuation, such as the period (`'.'`), semicolon (`';'`), and comma (`','`)
- the digits `'0'` through `'9'`
- the space character, `' '`
- special symbols, such as the ampersand (`'&'`), vertical bar (`'|'`), and backslash (`'\'`)
- control characters, such as the carriage return, null, and end-of-text marks

The *control characters* are sometimes called nonprinting or invisible characters because they do not have a specific symbol that represents them. Yet they are as valid as any other character and can be stored and used in the same ways. Many control characters have special meaning to certain software applications.

As computing became a worldwide endeavor, users demanded a more flexible character set containing alphabets in other languages. ASCII was extended to use 8 bits per character, and the number of characters in the set doubled to 256. The extended ASCII contains many accented and diacritical characters used in languages other than English.

However, even with 256 characters, the ASCII character set cannot represent the world's alphabets, especially given the various Asian alphabets and their many thousands of ideograms. Therefore, the developers of the Java programming language chose the *Unicode character set*, which uses 16 bits per character, supporting 65,536 unique characters. The characters and symbols from many languages are included in the Unicode definition. ASCII is a subset of the Unicode character set. Appendix C discusses the Unicode character set in more detail.

KEY CONCEPT

Java uses the 16-bit Unicode character set to represent character data.

A character set assigns a particular number to each character, so by definition the characters are in a particular order. This is referred to as lexicographic order. In the ASCII and Unicode ordering, the digit characters `'0'` through `'9'` are continuous (no other characters intervene) and in order. Similarly, the lowercase alphabetic characters `'a'` through `'z'` are continuous and in order, as are the uppercase alphabetic characters `'A'` through `'Z'`. These characteristics make it relatively easy to sort data, such as a list of names, in alphabetical order. Sorting is discussed in Chapter 13.

In Java, the data type `char` represents a single character. The following are some examples of character variable declarations in Java:

```
char topGrade = 'A';
char symbol1, symbol2, symbol3;
char terminator = ';', separator = ' ';
```

Booleans

A boolean value, defined in Java using the reserved word `boolean`, has only two valid values: `true` and `false`. A boolean variable is generally used to indicate whether a particular condition is true, but it can also be used to represent any situation that has two states, such as a light bulb being on or off. The term *boolean* is named in honor of English mathematician George Boole, who developed a form of algebra (Boolean algebra) in which variables take on only one of two values.

A boolean value cannot be converted to any other data type, nor can any other data type be converted to a boolean value. The words `true` and `false` are reserved in Java as *boolean literals* and cannot be used outside of this context.

Here are some examples of boolean variable declarations in Java:

```
boolean flag = true;
boolean tooHigh, tooSmall, tooRough;
boolean done = false;
```

2.4 Expressions

An *expression* is a combination of one or more operators and operands that usually performs a calculation. The value calculated does not have to be a number, but often it is. The operands used in the operations might be literals, constants, variables, or other sources of data. The manner in which expressions are evaluated and used is fundamental to programming. For now, we will focus on arithmetic expressions that use numeric operands and produce numeric results.

KEY CONCEPT
Expressions are combinations of operators and operands used to perform a calculation.

Arithmetic Operators

The usual arithmetic operations are defined for both integer and floating point numeric types, including addition (+), subtraction (-), multiplication (*), and division (/). Java also has another arithmetic operation: The remainder operator (`%`) returns the remainder after dividing the second operand into the first. The remainder operator is sometimes called the modulus operator. The sign of the result of a remainder operation is the sign of the numerator. This table shows some examples:

Operation	Result
`17 % 4`	`1`
`-20 % 3`	`-2`
`10 % -5`	`0`
`3 % 8`	`3`

As you might expect, if either or both operands to any numeric operator are floating point values, the result is a floating point value. However, the division operator (/) produces results that are less intuitive, depending on the types of the operands. If both operands are integers, the / operator performs *integer division*, meaning that any fractional part of the result is discarded. If one or the other or both operands are floating point values, the / operator performs *floating point division*, and the fractional part of the result is kept. For example, the result of `10/4` is `2`, but the results of `10.0/4` and `10/4.0` and `10.0/4.0` are all `2.5`.

KEY CONCEPT
The type of result produced by arithmetic division depends on the types of the operands.

COMMON_ERROR

Because the operation that the division operator performs depends on the types of the operands, it's easy to do one when you intended the other. For example, if `total` and `count` are both integer variables, then this statement will perform integer division:

```
average = total / count;
```

Even if `average` is a floating point variable, the division operator truncates the fractional part before assigning the result to average.

An *unary operator* has only one operand, whereas a *binary operator* has two. The + and - arithmetic operators can be either unary or binary. The binary versions accomplish addition and subtraction, and the unary versions represent positive and negative numbers. For example, –1 is an example of using the unary negation operator to make the value negative. The unary + operator is rarely used.

Java does not have a built-in operator for raising a value to an exponent. However, the `Math` class provides methods that perform exponentiation and many other mathematical functions. The `Math` class is discussed in Chapter 3.

Operator Precedence

Operators can be combined to create more complex expressions. For example, consider the following assignment statement:

```
result = 14 + 8 / 2;
```

The entire right-hand side of the assignment is evaluated, and then the result is stored in the variable. But what is the result? If the addition is performed first, the result is `11`; if the division operation is performed first, the result is `18`. The order in which the operations are performed makes a big difference. In this case, the division is performed before the addition, yielding a result of `18`.

VideoNote
Review of primitive data and expressions

Note that in this and subsequent examples, we use literal values rather than variables to simplify the expression. The order of operator evaluation is the same if the operands are variables or any other source of data.

All expressions are evaluated according to an *operator precedence hierarchy* that establishes the rules that govern the order in which operations are evaluated. The arithmetic operators generally follow the same rules you learned in algebra. Multiplication, division, and the remainder operator all have equal precedence and are performed before (have higher precedence than) addition and subtraction. Addition and subtraction have equal precedence.

Any arithmetic operators at the same level of precedence are performed from left to right. Therefore, we say the arithmetic operators have a *left-to-right association*.

KEY CONCEPT
Java follows a well-defined set of precedence rules that governs the order in which operators will be evaluated in an expression.

Precedence, however, can be forced in an expression by using parentheses. For instance, if we wanted the addition to be performed first in the previous example, we could write the expression as follows:

```
result = (14 + 8) / 2;
```

Any expression in parentheses is evaluated first. In complicated expressions, it is good practice to use parentheses even when it is not strictly necessary, to make it clear how the expression is evaluated.

Parentheses can be nested, and the innermost nested expressions are evaluated first. Consider the expression

```
result = 3 * ((18 - 4) / 2);
```

In this example, the result is 21. First, the subtraction is performed, forced by the inner parentheses. Then, even though multiplication and division are at the same level of precedence and usually would be evaluated left to right, the division is performed first because of the outer parentheses. Finally, the multiplication is performed.

After the arithmetic operations are complete, the computed result is stored in the variable on the left-hand side of the assignment operator (=). In other words, the assignment operator has a lower precedence than any of the arithmetic operators.

The evaluation of a particular expression can be shown using an *expression tree*, such as the one in Figure 2.3. The operators are executed from the bottom up, creating values that are used in the rest of the expression. Therefore, the operations lower in the tree have a higher precedence than those above, or they are forced to be executed earlier using parentheses.

The parentheses used in expressions are actually operators themselves. Parentheses have a higher precedence than almost any other operator. Figure 2.4

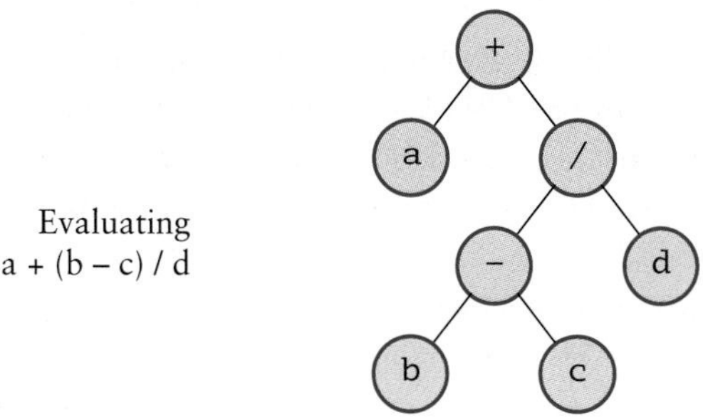

FIGURE 2.3 An expression tree

Precedence Level	Operator	Operation	Associates
1	+	unary plus	R to L
	–	unary minus	
2	*	multiplication	L to R
	/	division	
	%	remainder	
3	+	addition	L to R
	–	subtraction	
	+	string concatenation	
4	=	assignment	R to L

FIGURE 2.4 Precedence among some of the Java operators

shows a precedence table with the relationships among the arithmetic operators, the parentheses, and the assignment operator. Appendix D includes a full precedence table showing all Java operators.

For an expression to be syntactically correct, the number of left parentheses must match the number of right parentheses, and they must be properly nested. The following examples are *not* valid expressions:

```
result = ((19 + 8) % 3) - 4); // not valid
result = (19 (+ 8 %) 3 - 4); // not valid
```

Keep in mind that when a variable is referenced in an expression, its current value is used to perform the calculation. In the following assignment statement, the current value of the variable `count` is added to the current value of the variable `total`, and the result is stored in the variable `sum`:

```
sum = count + total;
```

The original value contained in `sum` before this assignment is overwritten by the calculated value. The values stored in `count` and `total` are not changed.

The same variable can appear on both the left-hand side and the right-hand side of an assignment statement. Suppose the current value of a variable called `count` is `15` when the following assignment statement is executed:

```
count = count + 1;
```

Because the right-hand expression is evaluated first, the original value of `count` is obtained and the value `1` is added to it, producing the result `16`. That result is then stored in the variable `count`, overwriting the original value of `15` with the new value of `16`. Therefore, this assignment statement *increments*, or adds 1 to, the variable `count`.

Let's look at another example of expression processing. The program in Listing 2.7, called `TempConverter`, converts a particular Celsius temperature value to its equivalent Fahrenheit value using an expression that computes the formula

$$\text{Fahrenheit} = \frac{9}{5}\text{Celsius} + 32$$

LISTING 2.7

```
//********************************************************************
//  TempConverter.java       Java Foundations
//
//  Demonstrates the use of primitive data types and arithmetic
//  expressions.
//********************************************************************

public class TempConverter
{
   //-----------------------------------------------------------------
   // Computes the Fahrenheit equivalent of a specific Celsius
   // value using the formula F = (9/5)C + 32.
   //-----------------------------------------------------------------
   public static void main(String[] args)
   {
      final int BASE = 32;
      final double CONVERSION_FACTOR = 9.0 / 5.0;

      double fahrenheitTemp;
      int celsiusTemp = 24; // value to convert

      fahrenheitTemp = celsiusTemp * CONVERSION_FACTOR + BASE;

      System.out.println("Celsius Temperature: " + celsiusTemp);
      System.out.println("Fahrenheit Equivalent: " + fahrenheitTemp);
   }
}
```

OUTPUT

```
Celsius Temperature: 24
Fahrenheit Equivalent: 75.2
```

Note that in the `TempConverter` program, the operands to the division operation are floating point literals to ensure that the fractional part of the number is kept. The precedence rules dictate that the multiplication happens before the addition in the final conversion computation.

The `TempConverter` program is not very useful because it converts only one data value that we included in the program as a constant (24 degrees Celsius). Every time the program is run, it produces the same result. A far more useful version of the program would obtain the value to be converted from the user each time the program was executed. Interactive programs that read user input are discussed later in this chapter.

Increment and Decrement Operators

There are two other useful arithmetic operators. The *increment operator* (++) adds 1 to any integer or floating point value. The two plus signs that make up the operator cannot be separated by white space. The *decrement operator* (--) is similar except that it subtracts 1 from the value. These are both unary operators because they operate on only one operand. The following statement causes the value of `count` to be incremented:

```
count++;
```

The result is stored in the variable `count`. Therefore, it is functionally equivalent to the following statement, which we discussed in the previous section:

```
count = count + 1;
```

The increment and decrement operators can be applied after the variable (such as `count++` or `count--`), creating what is called the *postfix form* of the operator. They can also be applied before the variable (such as `++count` or `--count`), in what is called the *prefix form*. When used alone in a statement, the prefix and postfix forms are functionally equivalent. That is, it doesn't matter whether you write

```
count++;
```

or

```
++count;
```

However, when such a form is written as a statement by itself, it is usually written in its postfix form.

When the increment or decrement operator is used in a larger expression, it can yield different results, depending on the form used. For example, if the variable count currently contains the value 15, then the following statement assigns the value 15 to total and the value 16 to count:

```
total = count++;
```

However, if count contains 15, the following statement assigns the value 16 to both total and count:

```
total = ++count;
```

The value of count is incremented in both situations, but the value used in the larger expression depends on whether a prefix form or a postfix form of the increment operator is used.

Because of the subtle differences between the prefix and postfix forms of the increment and decrement operators, they should be used with care. As always, favor the side of readability.

Assignment Operators

As a convenience, several *assignment operators* have been defined in Java that combine a basic operation with assignment. For example, the += operator can be used as follows:

```
total += 5;
```

This performs the same operation as the statement

```
total = total + 5;
```

The right-hand side of the assignment operator can be a full expression. The expression on the right-hand side of the operator is evaluated, that result is added to the current value of the variable on the left-hand side, and that value is stored in the variable. Therefore, the statement

```
total += (sum - 12) / count;
```

is equivalent to

```
total = total + ((sum - 12) / count);
```

Many similar assignment operators are defined in Java, including those that perform subtraction (-=), multiplication (*=), division (/=), and remainder (%=). The entire set of Java operators is discussed in Appendix D.

All of the assignment operators evaluate the entire expression on the right-hand side first and then use the result as the right operand of the other operation. Therefore, the statement

```
result *= count1 + count2;
```

is equivalent to

```
result = result * (count1 + count2);
```

Likewise,

```
result %= (highest - 40) / 2;
```

is equivalent to

```
result = result % ((highest - 40) / 2);
```

Some assignment operators perform particular functions depending on the types of the operands, just as their corresponding regular operators do. For example, if the operands to the `+=` operator are strings, then the assignment operator performs string concatenation.

2.5 Data Conversion

Because Java is a strongly typed language, each data value is associated with a particular type. It is sometimes helpful or necessary to convert a data value of one type to another type, but we must be careful that we don't lose important information in the process. For example, suppose a `short` variable that holds the number 1000 is converted to a `byte` value. Because a `byte` does not have enough bits to represent the value 1000, some bits would be lost in the conversion, and the number represented in the `byte` would not keep its original value.

A conversion between one primitive type and another falls into one of two categories: widening conversions and narrowing conversions. *Widening conversions* are the safest because they usually do not lose information. They are called widening conversions because they go from one data type to another type that uses an equal or greater amount of space to store the value. Figure 2.5 lists the Java widening conversions.

From	To
`byte`	`short`, `int`, `long`, `float`, or `double`
`short`	`int`, `long`, `float`, or `double`
`char`	`int`, `long`, `float`, or `double`
`int`	`long`, `float`, or `double`
`long`	`float` or `double`
`float`	`double`

FIGURE 2.5 Java widening conversions

For example, it is safe to convert from a `byte` to a `short` because a `byte` is stored in 8 bits and a `short` is stored in 16 bits. There is no loss of information. All widening conversions that go from an integer type to another integer type, or from a floating point type to another floating point type, preserve the numeric value exactly.

Although widening conversions do not lose any information about the magnitude of a value, the widening conversions that result in a floating point value can lose precision. When converting from an `int` or a `long` to a `float`, or from a `long` to a `double`, some of the least significant digits may be lost. In this case, the resulting floating point value will be a rounded version of the integer value, following the rounding techniques defined in the IEEE 754 floating point standard.

Narrowing conversions are more likely to lose information than widening conversions are. They often go from one type to a type that uses less space to store a value, and therefore some of the information may be compromised. Narrowing conversions can lose both numeric magnitude and precision. Therefore, in general, they should be avoided. Figure 2.6 lists the Java narrowing conversions.

KEY CONCEPT
Narrowing conversions should be avoided because they can lose information.

An exception to the space-shrinking situation in narrowing conversions occurs when we convert a `byte` (8 bits) or `short` (16 bits) to a `char` (16 bits). These are still considered narrowing conversions, because the sign bit is incorporated into the new character value. Because a character value is unsigned, a negative integer will be converted to a character that has no particular relationship to the numeric value of the original integer.

Note that `boolean` values are not mentioned in either widening or narrowing conversions. A `boolean` value cannot be converted to any other primitive type, and vice versa.

From	To
`byte`	`char`
`short`	`byte` or `char`
`char`	`byte` or `short`
`int`	`byte`, `short`, or `char`
`long`	`byte`, `short`, `char`, or `int`
`float`	`byte`, `short`, `char`, `int`, or `long`
`double`	`byte`, `short`, `char`, `int`, `long`, or `float`

FIGURE 2.6 Java narrowing conversions

Conversion Techniques

In Java, conversions can occur in three ways:

- assignment conversion
- promotion
- casting

Assignment conversion occurs when a value of one type is assigned to a variable of another type, during which the value is converted to the new type. Only widening conversions can be accomplished through assignment. For example, if `money` is a `float` variable and `dollars` is an `int` variable, then the following assignment statement automatically converts the value in `dollars` to a `float`:

```
money = dollars;
```

Therefore, if `dollars` contains the value `25`, then after the assignment, money contains the value `25.0`. However, if we attempt to assign `money` to `dollars`, the compiler will issue an error message alerting us to the fact that we are attempting a narrowing conversion that could lose information. If we really want to do this assignment, we have to make the conversion explicit by using a cast.

Conversion via *promotion* occurs automatically when certain operators need to modify their operands in order to perform the operation. For example, when a floating point value called `sum` is divided by an integer value called `count`, the value of `count` is promoted to a floating point value automatically, before the division takes place, producing a floating point result:

```
result = sum / count;
```

A similar conversion is taking place when a number is concatenated with a string. The number is first converted (promoted) to a string, and then the two strings are concatenated.

Casting is the most general form of conversion in Java. If a conversion can be accomplished at all in a Java program, it can be accomplished using a cast. A cast is a Java operator that is specified by a type name in parentheses. It is placed in front of the value to be converted. For example, to convert money to an integer value, we could put a cast in front of it:

```
dollars = (int) money;
```

The cast returns the value in `money`, truncating any fractional part. If `money` contained the value `84.69`, then after the assignment, `dollars` would contain the value `84`. Note, however, that the cast does not change the value in `money`. After the assignment operation is complete, money still contains the value `84.69`.

Casts are helpful in many situations where we need to treat a value temporarily as another type. For example, if we want to divide the integer value `total` by the integer value `count` and get a floating point result, we can do it as follows:

```
result = (float) total / count;
```

First, the cast operator returns a floating point version of the value in `total`. This operation does not change the value in `total`. Then, `count` is treated as a floating point value via arithmetic promotion. Now the division operator will perform floating point division and produce the intended result. If the cast had not been included, the operation would have performed integer division and truncated the answer before assigning it to `result`. Also note that because the cast operator has a higher precedence than the division operator, the cast operates on the value of `total`, not on the result of the division.

2.6 Reading Input Data

It is often useful to design a program to read data from the user interactively during execution. That way, new results can be computed each time the program is run, depending on the data entered.

The `Scanner` Class

The `Scanner` class, which is part of the standard Java class library, provides convenient methods for reading input values of various types. The input could come from various sources, including data typed interactively by the user or data stored in a file. The `Scanner` class can also be used to parse a character string into separate pieces. Figure 2.7 lists some of the methods provided by the `Scanner` class.

> **KEY CONCEPT**
> The `Scanner` class provides methods for reading input of various types from various sources.

We must first create a `Scanner` object in order to invoke its methods. Objects in Java are created using the `new` operator. The following declaration creates a `Scanner` object that reads input from the keyboard:

```
Scanner scan = new Scanner(System.in);
```

This declaration creates a variable called `scan` that represents a `Scanner` object. The object itself is created by the `new` operator and a call to a special method called a constructor to set up the object. The `Scanner` constructor accepts a parameter that indicates the source of the input. The `System.in` object represents the *standard input stream*, which by default is the keyboard. Creating objects using the `new` operator is discussed further in the next chapter.

```
Scanner (InputStream source)
Scanner (File source)
Scanner (String source)
```

Constructors: sets up the new scanner to scan values from the specified source.

```
String next()
```

Returns the next input token as a character string.

```
String nextLine()
```

Returns all input remaining on the current line as a character string.

```
boolean nextBoolean()
byte nextByte()
double nextDouble()
float nextFloat()
int nextInt()
long nextLong()
short nextShort()
```

Returns the next input token as the indicated type. Throws `InputMismatchException` if the next token is inconsistent with the type.

```
boolean hasNext()
```

Returns true if the scanner has another token in its input.

```
Scanner useDelimiter (String pattern)
Scanner useDelimiter (Pattern pattern)
```

Sets the scanner's delimiting pattern.

```
Pattern delimiter()
```

Returns the pattern the scanner is currently using to match delimiters.

```
String findInLine (String pattern)
String findInLine (Pattern pattern)
```

Attempts to find the next occurrence of the specified pattern, ignoring delimiters.

FIGURE 2.7 Some methods of the `Scanner` class

Unless specified otherwise, a `Scanner` object assumes that whitespace characters (space characters, tabs, and new lines) are used to separate the elements of the input, called *tokens*, from each other. These characters are called the input *delimiters*. The set of delimiters can be changed if the input tokens are separated by characters other than white space.

The next method of the Scanner class reads the next input token as a string and returns it. Therefore, if the input consisted of a series of words separated by spaces, each call to next would return the next word. The nextLine method reads all of the input until the end of the line is found and returns it as one string.

VideoNote
Example using the Scanner class

The program Echo, shown in Listing 2.8, simply reads a line of text typed by the user, stores it in a variable that holds a character string, and then echoes it back to the screen. User input is shown in red in the output section below the listing.

The import declaration above the definition of the Echo class tells the program that we will be using the Scanner class in this program. The Scanner class is part of the java.util class library. The use of the import declaration is discussed further in Chapter 3.

Various Scanner methods such as nextInt and nextDouble are provided to read data of particular types. The GasMileage program, shown in Listing 2.9, reads the number of miles traveled as an integer, reads the number of gallons of fuel consumed as a double, and then computes the gas mileage.

As you can see by the output of the GasMileage program, the calculation produces a floating point result that is accurate to several decimal places. In the next chapter we discuss classes that help us format our output in various ways, including rounding a floating point value to a particular number of decimal places.

A Scanner object processes the input one token at a time, based on the methods used to read the data and the delimiters used to separate the input values. Therefore, multiple values can be put on the same line of input or can be separated over multiple lines, as appropriate for the situation.

In Chapter 5 we use the Scanner class to read input from a data file and modify the delimiters it uses to parse the data. Appendix H explores how to use the Scanner class to analyze its input using patterns called *regular expressions*.

LISTING 2.8

```
//********************************************************************
//  Echo.java       Java Foundations
//
//  Demonstrates the use of the nextLine method of the Scanner class
//  to read a string from the user.
//********************************************************************

import java.util.Scanner;
```

LISTING 2.8 *continued*

```
public class Echo
{
   //-----------------------------------------------------------------
   // Reads a character string from the user and prints it.
   //-----------------------------------------------------------------
   public static void main(String[] args)
   {
      String message;
      Scanner scan = new Scanner(System.in);

      System.out.println("Enter a line of text:");

      message = scan.nextLine();

      System.out.println("You entered: \"" + message + "\"");
   }
}
```

OUTPUT

```
Enter a line of text:
Set your laser printer on stun!
You entered: "Set your laser printer on stun!"
```

LISTING 2.9

```
//********************************************************************
//  GasMileage.java       Java Foundations
//
//  Demonstrates the use of the Scanner class to read numeric data.
//********************************************************************

import java.util.Scanner;

public class GasMileage
{
   //-----------------------------------------------------------------
   // Calculates fuel efficiency based on values entered by the
   // user.
   //-----------------------------------------------------------------
```

LISTING 2.9 *continued*

```
   public static void main(String[] args)
   {
      int miles;
      double gallons, mpg;

      Scanner scan = new Scanner(System.in);

      System.out.print("Enter the number of miles: ");
      miles = scan.nextInt();

      System.out.print("Enter the gallons of fuel used: ");
      gallons = scan.nextDouble();

      mpg = miles / gallons;

      System.out.println("Miles Per Gallon: " + mpg);
   }
}
```

OUTPUT

```
Enter the number of miles: 369
Enter the gallons of fuel used: 12.4
Miles Per Gallon: 29.758064516129032
```

Summary of Key Concepts

- The `print` and `println` methods represent two services provided by the `System.out` object.
- In Java, the + operator is used both for addition and for string concatenation.
- An escape sequence can be used to represent a character that would otherwise cause compilation problems.
- A variable is a name for a memory location used to hold a value of a particular data type.
- Accessing data leaves them intact in memory, but an assignment statement overwrites the old data.
- We cannot assign a value of one type to a variable of an incompatible type.
- Constants hold a particular value for the duration of their existence.
- Java has two kinds of numeric values: integer and floating point. There are four integer data types and two floating point data types.
- Java uses the 16-bit Unicode character set to represent character data.
- Expressions are combinations of operators and operands used to perform a calculation.
- The type of result produced by arithmetic division depends on the types of the operands.
- Java follows a well-defined set of precedence rules that governs the order in which operators will be evaluated in an expression.
- Narrowing conversions should be avoided because they can lose information.
- The `Scanner` class provides methods for reading input of various types from various sources.

Summary of Terms

ASCII character set An early character set for representing English characters and symbols.

assignment operator An operator in Java that combines a basic operation such as addition with assignment.

assignment statement A programming statement that assigns a value to a variable.

casting A data conversion in which the type to which a value is converted is explicitly specified in parentheses.

character set A list of characters in a particular order.

delimiter Characters used to separate one input token from another.

escape sequence A series of characters that begin with a backslash (\), used to represent a special character.

expression A combination of one or more operators and operands.

integer division Division in which the fractional portion of the result is discarded, used when both operands are integers.

literal An explicit data value used in a program.

narrowing conversion A conversion between one data type and another in which information may be lost.

operator precedence hierarchy The rules that establish the order in which operators are evaluated.

parameter A piece of data that is sent to a method when it is invoked.

primitive data type A basic type of data, such as a number, character, or boolean.

standard input stream A source of input, usually the keyboard.

string concatenation Appending one character string to the end of another.

string literal Text enclosed by double quotation marks that represent a character string.

strongly typed A programming language characteristic that prevents a variable from being assigned a value inconsistent with its type.

token An element in an input stream.

Unicode character set A character set used to represent characters and symbols from most of the world's written languages.

variable A name for a location in memory used to hold a data value.

widening conversion A conversion between one data type and another in which information is not lost.

Self-Review Questions

SR 2.1 What are primitive data? How are primitive data types different from objects?

SR 2.2 What is a string literal?

SR 2.3 What is the difference between the `print` method and the `println` method?

SR 2.4 What is a parameter?

SR 2.5 What is an escape sequence? Give some examples.

SR 2.6 What is a variable declaration?

SR 2.7 How many values can be stored in an integer variable at one time?

SR 2.8 What are the four integer data types in Java? How are they different?

SR 2.9 What is a character set?

SR 2.10 What is operator precedence?

SR 2.11 What is the result of `19%5` when evaluated in a Java expression? Explain.

SR 2.12 What is the result of `13/4` when evaluated in a Java expression? Explain.

SR 2.13 If an integer variable `diameter` currently holds the value `5`, what is its value after the following statement is executed? Explain.

```
diameter = diameter * 4;
```

SR 2.14 If an integer variable `weight` currently holds the value `100`, what is its value after the following statement is executed? Explain.

```
weight -= 17;
```

SR 2.15 Why are widening conversions safer than narrowing conversions?

Exercises

EX 2.1 Explain the following programming statement in terms of objects and the services they provide.

```
System.out.println("I gotta be me!");
```

EX 2.2 What output is produced by the following code fragment? Explain.

```
System.out.print("Here we go!");
System.out.println("12345");
System.out.print("Test this if you are not sure.");
System.out.print("Another.");
System.out.println();
System.out.println("All done.");
```

EX 2.3 What is wrong with the following program statement? How can it be fixed?

```
System.out.println("To be or not to be, that is the
question.");
```

EX 2.4 What output is produced by the following statement? Explain.

```
System.out.println("50 plus 25 is " + 50 + 25);
```

EX 2.5 What output is produced by the following statement? Explain.

```
System.out.println("He thrusts his fists\n\tagainst" +
" the post\nand still insists\n\the sees the \"ghost\"");
```

EX 2.6 What value is contained in the integer variable `size` after the following statements are executed?

```
size = 18;
size = size + 12;
size = size * 2;
size = size / 4;
```

EX 2.7 What value is contained in the floating point variable `depth` after the following statements are executed?

```
depth = 2.4;
depth = 20 - depth * 4;
depth = depth / 5;
```

EX 2.8 What value is contained in the integer variable `length` after the following statements are executed?

```
length = 5;
length *= 2;
length *= length;
length /= 100;
```

EX 2.9 Write four different program statements that increment the value of an integer variable `total`.

EX 2.10 Given the following declarations, what result is stored in each of the listed assignment statements?

```
int iResult, num1 = 25, num2 = 40, num3 = 17, num4 = 5;
double fResult, val1 = 17.0, val2 = 12.78;
```

a. `iResult = num1 / num4;`

b. `fResult = num1 / num4;`

c. `iResult = num3 / num4;`

d. `fResult = num3 / num4;`

e. `fResult = val1 / num4;`

f. `fResult = val1 / val2;`

g. `iResult = num1 / num2;`

h. `fResult = (double) num1 / num2;`

i. `fResult = num1 / (double) num2;`

j. `fResult = (double) (num1 / num2);`

k. `iResult = (int) (val1 / num4);`

l. `fResult = (int) (val1 / num4);`

m. `fResult = (int) ((double) num1 / num2);`

n. `iResult = num3 % num4;`

o. `iResu lt = num2 % num3;`

p. `iResult = num3 % num2;`

q. `iResult = num2 % num4;`

EX 2.11 For each of the following expressions, indicate the order in which the operators will be evaluated by writing a number beneath each operator.

a. `a - b - c - d`

b. `a - b + c - d`

c. `a + b / c / d`

d. `a + b / c * d`

e. `a / b * c * d`

f. `a % b / c * d`

g. `a % b % c % d`

h. `a - (b - c) - d`

i. `(a - (b - c)) - d`

j. `a - ((b - c) - d)`

k. `a % (b % c) * d * e`

l. `a + (b - c) * d - e`

m. `(a + b) * c + d * e`

n. `(a + b) * (c / d) % e`

Programming Projects

PP 2.1 Create a revised version of the `Lincoln` application from Chapter 1 such that quotes appear around the quotation.

PP 2.2 Write an application that reads three integers and prints their average.

PP 2.3 Write an application that reads two floating point numbers and prints their sum, difference, and product.

PP 2.4 Create a version of the `TempConverter` application to convert from Fahrenheit to Celsius. Read the Fahrenheit temperature from the user.

PP 2.5 Write an application that converts miles to kilometers. (One mile equals 1.60935 kilometers.) Read the miles value from the user as a floating point value.

PP 2.6 Write an application that reads values representing a time duration in hours, minutes, and seconds, and then prints the equivalent total number of seconds. (For example, 1 hour, 28 minutes, and 42 seconds is equivalent to 5322 seconds.)

PP 2.7 Create a version of the previous project that reverses the computation. That is, read a value representing a number of seconds, and then print the equivalent amount of time as a combination of hours, minutes, and seconds. (For example, 9999 seconds is equivalent to 2 hours, 46 minutes, and 39 seconds.)

PP 2.8 Write an application that determines the value of the coins in a jar and prints the total in dollars and cents. Read integer values that represent the number of quarters, dimes, nickels, and pennies.

PP 2.9 Write an application that prompts for and reads a `double` value representing a monetary amount. Then determine the least number of each bill and coin needed to represent that amount, starting with the highest (assume that a ten-dollar bill is the maximum size needed). For example, if the value entered is 47.63 (forty-seven dollars and sixty-three cents), then the program should print the equivalent amount as

```
4 ten dollar bills
1 five dollar bills
2 one dollar bills
2 quarters
1 dimes
0 nickles
3 pennies
```

PP 2.10 Write an application that prompts for and reads an integer representing the length of a square's side and then prints the square's perimeter and area.

PP 2.11 Write an application that prompts for and reads the numerator and denominator of a fraction as integers and then prints the decimal equivalent of the fraction.

Answers to Self-Review Questions

SRA 2.1 Primitive data are basic values such as numbers or characters. Objects are more complex entities that usually contain primitive data that help define them.

SRA 2.2 A string literal is a sequence of characters delimited by double quotation marks.

SRA 2.3 Both the `print` method and the `println` method of the `System.out` object write a string of characters to the monitor screen. The difference is that after printing the characters, the `println` method performs a carriage return so that whatever is printed next appears on the next line. The `print` method allows subsequent output to appear on the same line.

SRA 2.4 A parameter is data passed into a method when it is invoked. The method generally uses that data to accomplish the service that it provides. For example, the parameter to the `println` method indicates what characters should be printed.

SRA 2.5 An escape sequence is a series of characters that begins with the backslash (\) and implies that the following characters should be treated in some special way. Examples: `\n` represents the newline character, `\t` represents the tab character, and `\"`represents the quotation character (as opposed to using it to terminate a string).

SRA 2.6 A variable declaration establishes the name of a variable and the type of data that it can contain. A declaration may also have an optional initialization, which gives the variable an initial value.

SRA 2.7 An integer variable can store only one value at a time. When a new value is assigned to it, the old one is overwritten and lost.

SRA 2.8 The four integer data types in Java are `byte`, `short`, `int`, and `long`. They differ in how much memory space is allocated for each and, therefore, in how large a number they can hold.

SRA 2.9 A character set is a list of characters in a particular order. A character set defines the valid characters that a particular type of computer or programming language will support. Java uses the Unicode character set.

SRA 2.10 Operator precedence is the set of rules that dictates the order in which operators are evaluated in an expression.

SRA 2.11 The result of `19%5` in a Java expression is 4. The remainder operator `%` returns the remainder after dividing the second operand into the first. Five goes into 19 three times, with 4 left over.

SRA 2.12 The result of `13/4` in a Java expression is 3 (not 3.25). The result is an integer because both operands are integers. Therefore, the `/` operator performs integer division, and the fractional part of the result is truncated.

SRA 2.13 After executing the statement, `diameter` holds the value `20`. First the current value of `diameter` (`5`) is multiplied by 4, and then the result is stored in `diameter`.

SRA 2.14 After executing the statement, `weight` holds the value `83`. The assignment operator `-=` modifies `weight` by first subtracting 17 from the current value (`100`) and then storing the result in `weight`.

SRA 2.15 A widening conversion tends to go from a small data value, in terms of the amount of space used to store it, to a larger one. A narrowing conversion does the opposite. Information is more likely to be lost in a narrowing conversion, which is why narrowing conversions are considered less safe than widening conversions.

Using Classes and Objects

3

CHAPTER OBJECTIVES

- Discuss the creation of objects and the use of object reference variables.
- Explore the services provided by the `String` class.
- Describe how the Java standard class library is organized into packages.
- Explore the services provided by the `Random` and `Math` classes.
- Discuss ways to format output using the `NumberFormat` and `DecimalFormat` classes.
- Introduce enumerated types.
- Discuss wrapper classes and the concept of autoboxing.

This chapter further explores the use of predefined classes and the objects we can create from them. Using classes and objects for the services they provide is a fundamental part of object-oriented software, and it sets the stage for writing classes of our own. In this chapter, we use classes and objects to manipulate character strings, produce random numbers, perform complex calculations, and format output. This chapter also introduces the enumerated type, which is a special kind of class in Java, and discusses the concept of a wrapper class.

3.1 Creating Objects

At the end of Chapter 1 we presented an overview of object-oriented concepts, including the basic relationship between classes and objects. Then in Chapter 2, in addition to discussing primitive data, we provided some examples of using objects for the services they provide. This chapter explores these ideas further.

In previous examples, we've used the `println` method many times. As we mentioned in Chapter 2, the `println` method is a service provided by the `System.out` object, which represents the standard output stream. To be more precise, the identifier `out` is an object variable that is stored in the `System` class. It has been predefined and set up for us as part of the Java standard class library. We can simply use it.

In Chapter 2 we also used the `Scanner` class, which represents an object that allows us to read input from the keyboard or a file. We created a `Scanner` object using the `new` operator. Once the object was created, we were able to use it for the various services it provides. That is, we were able to invoke its methods.

Let's carefully examine the idea of creating an object. In Java, a variable name represents either a primitive value or an object. Like variables that hold primitive types, a variable that refers to an object must be declared. The class used to define an object can be thought of as the type of an object. The declarations of object variables are similar in structure to the declarations of primitive variables.

Consider the following two declarations:

```
int num;
String name;
```

The first declaration creates a variable that holds an integer value, as we've seen many times before. The second declaration creates a `String` variable that holds a *reference* to a `String` object. An object variable doesn't hold the object itself, it holds the address of an object.

Initially, the two variables declared above don't contain any data. We say they are *uninitialized*, which can be depicted as follows:

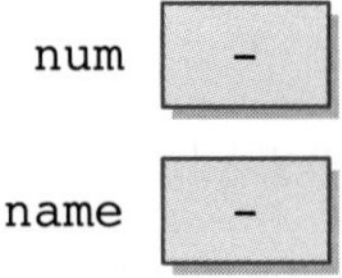

As we pointed out in Chapter 2, it is always important to be certain that a variable is initialized before using it. For an object variable, that means we must make sure it refers to a valid object prior to using it. In most situations the compiler will issue an error if you attempt to use a variable before initializing it.

An object reference variable can also be set to `null`, which is a reserved word in Java. A null reference specifically indicates that a variable does not refer to an object.

Note that even though we've declared a `String` reference variable, no `String` object actually exists yet. The act of creating an object using the `new` operator is called *instantiation*. An object is said to be an *instance* of a particular class. To instantiate an object, we can use the `new` operator, which returns the address of the new object. The following two assignment statements give values to the two variables declared above:

```
num = 42;
name = new String("James Gosling");
```

After the `new` operator creates the object, a *constructor* is invoked to help set it up initially. A constructor is a special method that has the same name as the class. In this example, the parameter to the constructor is a string literal that specifies the characters that the string object will hold. After these assignments are executed, the variables can be depicted as follows:

KEY CONCEPT
The new operator returns a reference to a newly created object.

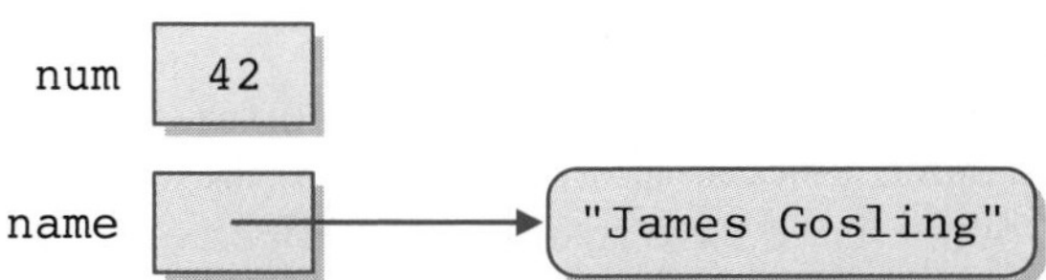

Because an object reference variable holds the address of the object, it can be thought of as a *pointer* to the location in memory where the object is held. We could show the numeric address, but the actual address value is irrelevant—what's important is that the variable refers to a particular object.

VideoNote
Creating objects

After an object has been instantiated, we use the *dot operator* to access its methods. We've used the dot operator many times already, such as in calls to `System.out.println`. The dot operator is appended directly after the object reference, followed by the method being invoked. For example, to invoke the `length` method defined in the `String` class, we can use the dot operator on the name reference variable:

```
count = name.length()
```

The `length` method does not take any parameters, but the parentheses are still necessary to indicate that a method is being invoked. Some methods produce a value that is *returned* when the method completes. The purpose of the `length` method of the `String` class is to determine and return the length of the string (the number of characters it contains). In this example, the returned value is assigned to the variable count. For the string "James Gosling", the length method returns 13, which includes the space between the first and last names. Some methods do not return a value. Other String methods are discussed in the next section.

The act of declaring the object reference variable and creating the object itself can be combined into one step by initializing the variable in the declaration, just as we do with primitive types:

```
String title = new String("Java Foundations");
```

Even though they are not primitive types, character strings are so fundamental and are used so often that Java defines string literals delimited by double quotation marks, as we've seen in various examples. This is a shortcut notation. Whenever a string literal appears, a String object is created automatically. Therefore, the following declaration is valid:

```
String city = "London";
```

That is, for String objects, the explicit use of the new operator and the call to the constructor can be eliminated. In most cases, we will use this simplified syntax.

Aliases

Because an object reference variable stores an address, a programmer must be careful when managing objects. First, let's review the effect of assignment on primitive values. Suppose we have two integer variables—num1, initialized to 5, and num2, initialized to 12:

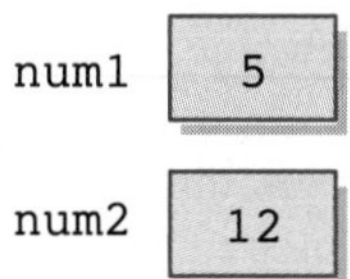

In the following assignment statement, a copy of the value that is stored in num1 is stored in num2.

```
num2 = num1;
```

The original value of 12 in num2 is overwritten by the value 5. The variables num1 and num2 still refer to different locations in memory, and both of those locations now contain the value 5:

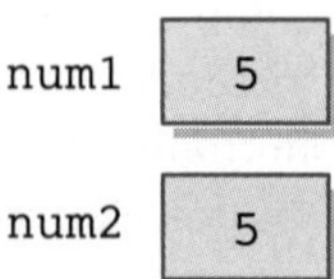

Now consider the following object declarations:

```
String name1 = "Ada, Countess of Lovelace";
String name2 = "Grace Murray Hopper";
```

Initially, the references `name1` and `name2` refer to two different `String` objects:

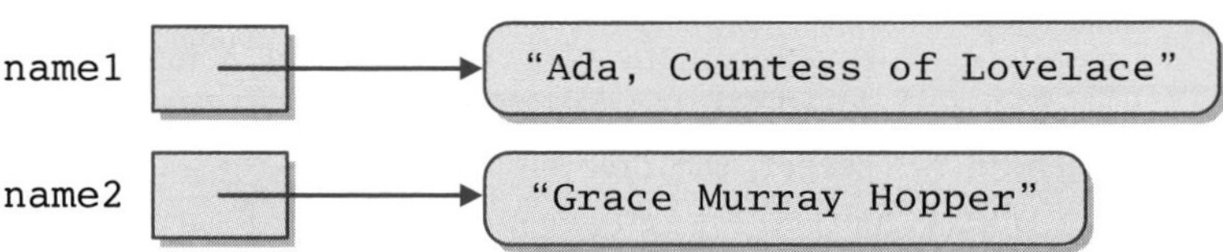

Now suppose the following assignment statement is executed, copying the value in `name1` into `name2`.

```
name2 = name1;
```

This assignment works the same as the integer assignment—a copy of the value of `name1` is stored in `name2`. But remember, object variables hold the address of an object, and it is the address that gets copied. Originally, the two references referred to different objects. After the assignment, both `name1` and `name2` contain the same address and therefore refer to the same object:

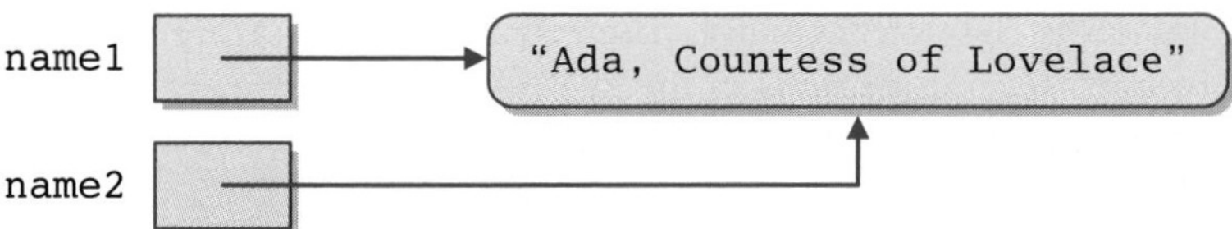

The `name1` and `name2` reference variables are now *aliases* of each other because they are two different variables that refer to the same object. All references to the object originally referenced by `name2` are now gone; that object cannot be used again in the program.

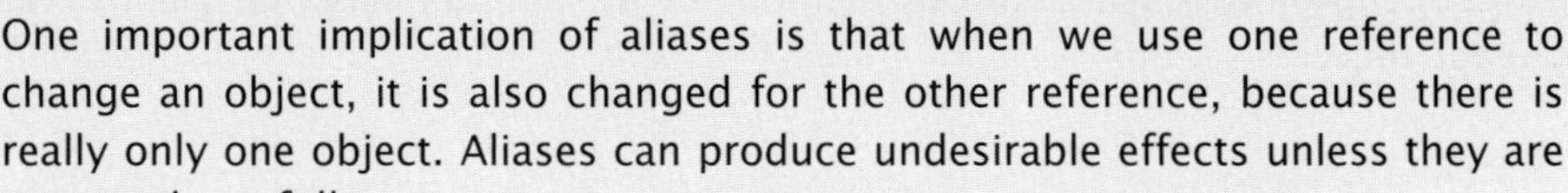

One important implication of aliases is that when we use one reference to change an object, it is also changed for the other reference, because there is really only one object. Aliases can produce undesirable effects unless they are managed carefully.

That is not to say that aliases are a bad thing. There are many situations in which it's helpful to have multiple references to objects. In fact, every time you pass an object to a method, you create an alias. It's not that you want to avoid aliases, you just want to be aware of the effect they have on the objects you manage.

All interaction with an object occurs through a reference variable, so we can use an object only if we have a reference to it. When all references to an object are lost (perhaps by reassignment), that object can no longer contribute to the program. The program can no longer invoke its methods or use its variables. At this point the object is called *garbage* because it serves no useful purpose.

KEY CONCEPT
Multiple reference variables can refer to the same object.

Java performs automatic *garbage collection*. When the last reference to an object is lost, the object becomes a candidate for garbage collection. Occasionally, behind the scenes, the Java environment executes a method that "collects" all the objects marked for garbage collection and returns their memory to the system for future use. The programmer does not have to worry about explicitly reclaiming memory that has become garbage.

3.2 The `String` Class

Let's examine the `String` class in more detail. Figure 3.1 lists some of the more useful methods of the `String` class.

Once a `String` object is created, its value cannot be lengthened or shortened, nor can any of its characters change. Thus we say that a `String` object is *immutable*. However, several methods in the `String` class return new `String` objects that are the result of modifying the original string's value.

Note that some of the `String` methods, such as `charAt`, refer to the *index* of a particular character. An index specifies a particular position, and therefore a particular character, in a string. The index of the first character in a string is zero, the index of the next character is one, and so on. Therefore, in the string `"Hello"`, the index of the character `'H'` is zero, and the character at index four is `'o'`.

Several `String` methods are exercised in the program shown in Listing 3.1 on page 78. As you examine the `StringMutation` program, keep in mind that this is not a single `String` object that changes its data; this program creates five separate `String` objects using various methods of the `String` class. Originally, the `phrase` object is set up:

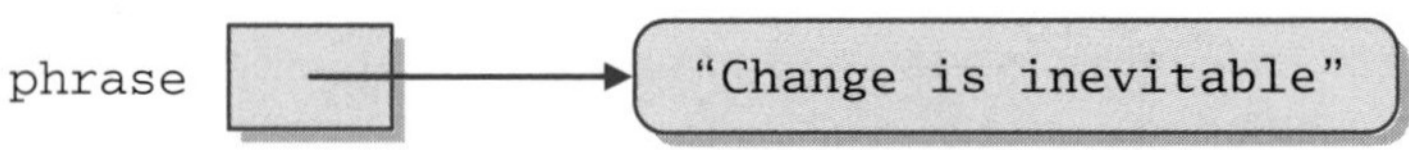

`String (String str)`
Constructor: creates a new string object with the same characters as `str`.

`char charAt (int index)`
Returns the character at the specified `index`.

`int compareTo (String str)`
Returns an integer indicating if this string is lexically before (a negative return value), equal to (a zero return value), or lexically after (a positive return value), the string `str`.

`String concat (String str)`
Returns a new string consisting of this string concatenated with `str`.

`boolean equals (String str)`
Returns true if this string contains the same characters as `str` (including case) and false otherwise.

`boolean equalsIgnoreCase (String str)`
Returns true if this string contains the same characters as `str` (without regard to case) and false otherwise.

`int length ()`
Returns the number of characters in this string.

`String replace (char oldChar, char newChar)`
Returns a new string that is identical with this string except that every occurrence of `oldChar` is replaced by `newChar`.

`String substring (int offset, int endIndex)`
Returns a new string that is a subset of this string starting at index `offset` and extending through `endIndex-1`.

`String toLowerCase ()`
Returns a new string identical to this string except all uppercase letters are converted to their lowercase equivalent.

`String toUpperCase ()`
Returns a new string identical to this string except all lowercase letters are converted to their uppercase equivalent.

FIGURE 3.1 Some methods of the `String` class

After printing the original phrase and its length, the `concat` method is executed to create a new `String` object referenced by the variable `mutation1`:

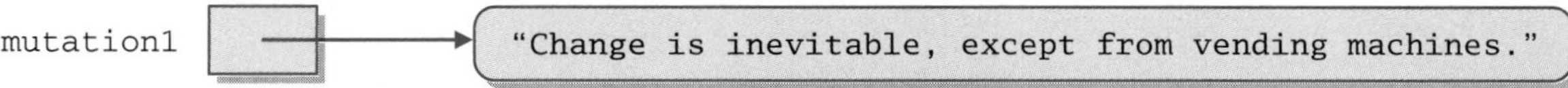

LISTING 3.1

```
//********************************************************************
//  StringMutation.java       Java Foundations
//
//  Demonstrates the use of the String class and its methods.
//********************************************************************

public class StringMutation
{
   //-----------------------------------------------------------------
   //  Prints a string and various mutations of it.
   //-----------------------------------------------------------------
   public static void main(String[] args)
   {
      String phrase = "Change is inevitable";
      String mutation1, mutation2, mutation3, mutation4;

      System.out.println("Original string: \"" + phrase + "\"");
      System.out.println("Length of string: " + phrase.length());

      mutation1 = phrase.concat(", except from vending machines.");
      mutation2 = mutation1.toUpperCase();
      mutation3 = mutation2.replace('E', 'X');
      mutation4 = mutation3.substring(3, 30);

      // Print each mutated string

      System.out.println("Mutation #1: " + mutation1);
      System.out.println("Mutation #2: " + mutation2);
      System.out.println("Mutation #3: " + mutation3);
      System.out.println("Mutation #4: " + mutation4);

      System.out.println("Mutated length: " + mutation4.length());
   }
}
```

OUTPUT

```
Original string: "Change is inevitable"
Length of string: 20
Mutation #1: Change is inevitable, except from vending machines.
Mutation #2: CHANGE IS INEVITABLE, EXCEPT FROM VENDING MACHINES.
Mutation #3: CHANGX IS INXVITABLX, XXCXPT FROM VXNDING MACHINXS.
Mutation #4: NGX IS INXVITABLX, XXCXPT F
Mutated length: 27
```

Then the `toUpperCase` method is executed on the `mutation1` object, and the resulting string is stored in `mutation2`:

Notice that the `length` and `concat` methods are executed on the `phrase` object, but the `toUpperCase` method is executed on the `mutation1` object. Any method of the `String` class can be executed on any `String` object, but for any given invocation, the method is executed on a particular object. The results of executing `toUpperCase` on `mutation1` would be very different from the results of executing `toUpperCase` on `phrase`. Remember that each object has its own state, which often affects the results of method calls.

KEY CONCEPT

Methods are often executed on a particular object, and that object's state usually affects the results.

Finally, the `String` object variables `mutation3` and `mutation4` are initialized by the calls to `mutation2.replace` and `mutation3.substring`, respectively:

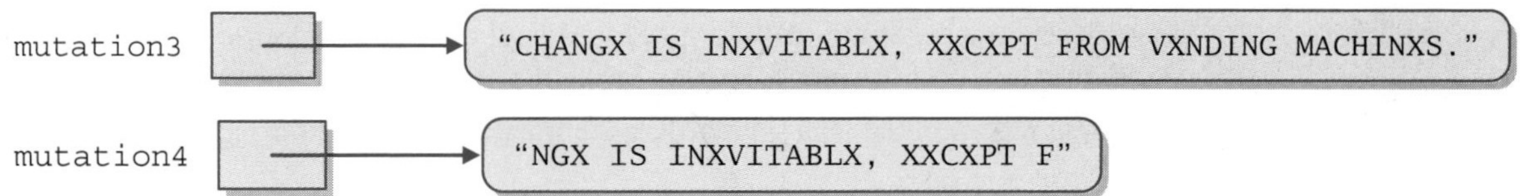

3.3 Packages

We mentioned earlier that the Java language is supported by a standard class library that we can make use of as needed. Let's examine that idea further.

A *class library* is a set of classes that supports the development of programs. A compiler or development environment often comes with a class library. Class libraries can also be obtained separately through third-party vendors. The classes in a class library contain methods that are valuable to a programmer because of the special functionality they offer. In fact, programmers often become dependent on the methods in a class library and begin to think of them as part of the language. However, technically, they are not in the language itself.

KEY CONCEPT

A class library provides useful support when one is developing programs.

The `String` class, for instance, is not an inherent part of the Java language. It is part of the Java standard class library that can be found in any Java development environment. The classes that make up the library were created by employees at Sun Microsystems, where the Java language was created.

The class library is made up of several clusters of related classes, which are sometimes called Java APIs, or *application programming interfaces*. For example, we may refer to the Java Database API when we're talking about the set of classes that helps us write programs that interact with a database. Another example of an API is the Java Swing API, a set of classes that defines special graphical components used in a graphical user interface. Sometimes the entire standard library is referred to generically as the Java API.

KEY CONCEPT

The Java standard class library is organized into packages.

The classes of the Java standard class library are also grouped into *packages*. Each class is part of a particular package. The `String` class, for example, is part of the `java.lang` package. The `System` class is part of the `java.lang` package as well. The `Scanner` class is part of the `java.util` package.

The package organization is more fundamental and language-based than the API organization. Although there is a general correspondence between package and API names, the groups of classes that make up a given API might cross packages. In this text, we refer to classes primarily in terms of their package organization.

Figure 3.2 describes some of the packages that are part of the Java standard class library. These packages are available on any platform that supports Java software development. Some of these packages support highly specific programming techniques and do not come into play in the development of basic programs.

Various classes of the Java standard class library are discussed throughout this book.

The `import` Declaration

The classes of the `java.lang` package are automatically available for use when writing a Java program. To use classes from any other package, however, we must either *fully qualify* the reference or use an *import declaration*. Let's consider these two options.

When you want to use a class from a class library in a program, you could use its fully qualified name, including the package name, every time it was referenced. For example, every time you wanted to refer to the `Scanner` class defined in the `java.util` package, you could write `java.util.Scanner`. However, completely specifying the package and class name every time it is needed quickly becomes tiring. Java provides the `import` declaration to simplify these references.

The `import` declaration specifies the packages and classes that will be used in a program so that the fully qualified name is not necessary with each reference. Recall that the example programs that use the `Scanner` class in Chapter 2 include an `import` declaration like this one:

```
import java.util.Scanner;
```

This declaration asserts that the `Scanner` class of the `java.util` package may be used in the program. Once this `import` declaration is made, it is sufficient to use the simple name `Scanner` when referring to that class in the program.

Package	Provides support to
java.applet	Create programs (applets) that are easily transported across the Web.
java.awt	Draw graphics and create graphical user interfaces; AWT stands for Abstract Windowing Toolkit.
java.beans	Define software components that can be easily combined into applications.
java.io	Perform a wide variety of input and output functions.
java.lang	General support; it is automatically imported into all Java programs.
java.math	Perform calculations with arbitrarily high precision.
java.net	Communicate across a network.
java.rmi	Create programs that can be distributed across multiple computers; RMI stands for Remote Method Invocation.
java.security	Enforce security restrictions.
java.sql	Interact with databases; SQL stands for Structured Query Language.
java.text	Format text for output.
java.util	General utilities.
javax.swing	Create graphical user interfaces with components that extend the AWT capabilities.
javax.xml.parsers	Process XML documents; XML stands for eXtensible Markup Language.

FIGURE 3.2 Some packages in the Java standard class library

If two classes from two different packages have the same name, `import` declarations will not suffice, because the compiler won't be able to figure out which class is being referenced in the flow of the code. When such situations arise (which occurs rarely), the fully qualified names should be used in the code.

Another form of the `import` declaration uses an asterisk (`*`) to indicate that any class inside the package might be used in the program. Therefore, the following declaration allows all classes in the `java.util` package to be referenced in the program without qualifying each reference:

```
import java.util.*;
```

If only one class of a particular package will be used in a program, it is usually better to name the class specifically in the `import` declaration, because that provides more specific information to anyone reading the code. However, if two or more classes of the package will be used, the `*` notation is usually fine.

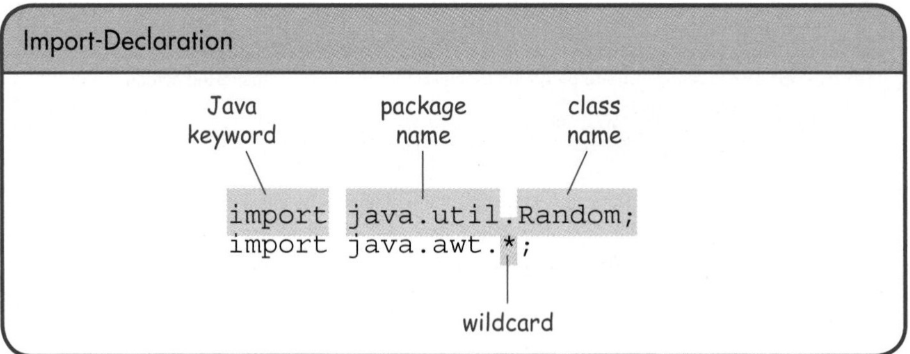

KEY CONCEPT
All classes of the `java.lang` package are automatically imported for every program.

The classes of the `java.lang` package are automatically imported because they are fundamental and can be thought of as basic extensions to the language. Therefore, any class in the `java.lang` package, such as `System` and `String`, can be used without an explicit `import` declaration. It's as if all program files automatically contain the following declaration:

```
import java.lang.*;
```

3.4 The `Random` Class

The need for random numbers occurs frequently when one is writing software. Games often use random numbers to simulate the roll of a die or the shuffle of a deck of cards. A flight simulator may use random numbers to determine how often a simulated flight has engine trouble. A program designed to help high school students prepare for the SATs may use random numbers to choose the next question to ask.

The `Random` class, which is part of the `java.util` package, represents a *pseudorandom number generator*. A random number generator picks a number at random out of a range of values. Program code that plays this role is technically pseudorandom, because a program has no means to actually pick a number randomly. A pseudorandom number generator performs a series of complicated calculations, based on an initial *seed value*, and produces a number. Even though they are technically not random (because they are calculated), the values produced by a pseudorandom number generator usually appear random—at least random enough for most situations.

Figure 3.3 lists some of the methods of the `Random` class. The `nextInt` method can be called with no parameters, or we can pass it a single integer value. If no parameter is passed in, the `nextInt` method generates a random number across the entire range of `int` values, including negative numbers. Usually, though, we need a random number within a more specific range. For instance, to simulate the

```
Random ()
   Constructor: creates a new pseudorandom number generator.

float nextFloat ()
   Returns a random number between 0.0 (inclusive) and 1.0 (exclusive).

int nextInt ()
   Returns a random number that ranges over all possible int values (positive
   and negative).

int nextInt (int num)
   Returns a random number in the range 0 to num-1.
```

FIGURE 3.3 Some methods of the `Random` class

roll of a die, we might want a random number in the range of 1 to 6. The `nextInt` method returns a value that's in the range from 0 to one less than its parameter. For example, if we pass 100 as a parameter to `nextInt`, we'll get a return value that is greater than or equal to 0 and less than or equal to 99.

> **KEY CONCEPT**
> A pseudorandom number generator performs a complex calculation to create the illusion of randomness.

Note that the value that we pass to the `nextInt` method is also the number of possible values we can get in return. We can shift the range as needed by adding or subtracting the proper amount. To get a random number in the range of 1 to 6, we can call `nextInt(6)` to get a value from 0 to 5, and then add 1.

The `nextFloat` method of the `Random` class returns a `float` value that is greater than or equal to 0.0 and less than 1.0. If desired, we can use multiplication to scale the result, cast it into an `int` value to truncate the fractional part, and then shift the range as we do with integers.

The program shown in Listing 3.2 produces several random numbers in various ranges.

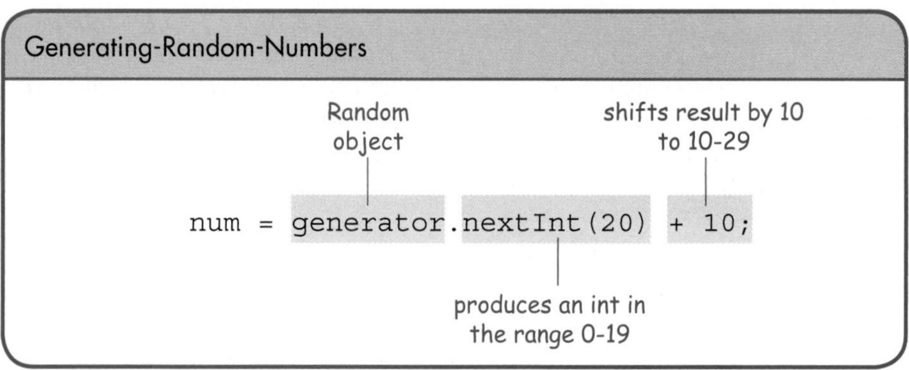

LISTING 3.2

```
//********************************************************************
// RandomNumbers.java          Java Foundations
//
// Demonstrates the creation of pseudo-random numbers using the
// Random class.
//********************************************************************
import java.util.Random;

public class RandomNumbers
{
   //-----------------------------------------------------------------
   // Generates random numbers in various ranges.
   //-----------------------------------------------------------------
   public static void main(String[] args)
   {
      Random generator = new Random();
      int num1;
      float num2;

      num1 = generator.nextInt();
      System.out.println("A random integer: " + num1);

      num1 = generator.nextInt(10);
      System.out.println("From 0 to 9: " + num1);

      num1 = generator.nextInt(10) + 1;
      System.out.println("From 1 to 10: " + num1);

      num1 = generator.nextInt(15) + 20;
      System.out.println("From 20 to 34: " + num1);

      num1 = generator.nextInt(20) - 10;
      System.out.println("From -10 to 9: " + num1);

      num2 = generator.nextFloat();
      System.out.println("A random float (between 0-1): " + num2);

      num2 = generator.nextFloat() * 6; // 0.0 to 5.999999
      num1 = (int)num2 + 1;
      System.out.println("From 1 to 6: " + num1);
   }
}
```

LISTING 3.2 *continued*

OUTPUT

```
A random integer: 243057344
From 0 to 9: 9
From 1 to 10: 2
From 20 to 34: 33
From -10 to 9: -4
A random float (between 0-1): 0.58384484
From 1 to 6: 3
```

3.5 The Math Class

The Math class provides a large number of basic mathematical functions that are often helpful in making calculations. The Math class is defined in the java.lang package of the Java standard class library. Figure 3.4 lists several of its methods.

KEY CONCEPT
All methods of the Math class are static, which means that they are invoked through the class name.

All the methods in the Math class are *static methods* (also called *class methods*), which means they we can invoke them through the name of the class in which they are defined, without having to instantiate an object of the class first. Static methods are discussed further in Chapter 5.

The methods of the Math class return values, which can be used in expressions as needed. For example, the following statement computes the absolute value of the number stored in total, adds it to the value of count raised to the fourth power, and stores the result in the variable value.

```
value = Math.abs(total) + Math.pow(count, 4);
```

Note that you can pass an integer value to a method that accepts a double parameter. This is a form of assignment conversion, which was discussed in Chapter 2

It's also interesting to note that the Math class contains a method called random that returns a random floating point value in the range 0.0 to 1.0. Therefore, this method could be used as an alternative to creating a Random object and calling its methods, as described in the previous section. However, the Math class does not have a method that returns an integer, or lets you specify the range of the result, as Random does.

VideoNote
Example using the Random and Math classes

```
static int abs (int num)
   Returns the absolute value of num.

static double acos (double num)

static double asin (double num)

static double atan (double num)
   Returns the arc cosine, arc sine, or arc tangent of num.

static double cos (double angle)

static double sin (double angle)

static double tan (double angle)
   Returns the angle cosine, sine, or tangent of angle, which is measured in
   radians.

static double ceil (double num)
   Returns the ceiling of num, which is the smallest whole number greater than or
   equal to num.

static double exp (double power)
   Returns the value e raised to the specified power.

static double floor (double num)
   Returns the floor of num, which is the largest whole number less than or equal
   to num.

static double pow (double num, double power)
   Returns the value num raised to the specified power.

static double random ()
   Returns a random number between 0.0 (inclusive) and 1.0 (exclusive).

static double sqrt (double num)
   Returns the square root of num, which must be positive.
```

FIGURE 3.4 Some methods of the `Math` class

The `Quadratic` program, shown in Listing 3.3, uses the `Math` class to compute the roots of a quadratic equation. Recall that a quadratic equation has the following general form:

$ax^2 = bx = c$

LISTING 3.3

```
//********************************************************************
// Quadratic.java          Java Foundations
//
// Demonstrates the use of the Math class to perform a calculation
// based on user input.
//********************************************************************

import java.util.Scanner;

public class Quadratic
{
   //-----------------------------------------------------------------
   // Determines the roots of a quadratic equation.
   //-----------------------------------------------------------------
   public static void main(String[] args)
   {
      int a, b, c; // ax^2 + bx + c
      double discriminant, root1, root2;

      Scanner scan = new Scanner(System.in);

      System.out.print("Enter the coefficient of x squared: ");
      a = scan.nextInt();

      System.out.print("Enter the coefficient of x: ");
      b = scan.nextInt();

      System.out.print("Enter the constant: ");
      c = scan.nextInt();

      // Use the quadratic formula to compute the roots.
      // Assumes a positive discriminant.

      discriminant = Math.pow(b, 2) - (4 * a * c);
      root1 = ((-1 * b) + Math.sqrt(discriminant)) / (2 * a);
      root2 = ((-1 * b) - Math.sqrt(discriminant)) / (2 * a);

      System.out.println("Root #1: " + root1);
      System.out.println("Root #2: " + root2);
   }
}
```

LISTING 3.3 *continued*

OUTPUT

```
Enter the coefficient of x squared: 3
Enter the coefficient of x: 8
Enter the constant: 4
Root #1: -0.6666666666666666
Root #2: -2.0
```

The `Quadratic` program reads values that represent the coefficients in a quadratic equation (`a`, `b`, and `c`) and then evaluates the quadratic formula to determine the roots of the equation. The quadratic formula is

$$\text{roots} = \frac{-b \pm \sqrt{b^2 - 4ac}}{2a}$$

Note that this program assumes that the discriminant (the value under the square root) is positive. If it's not, the result will not be a valid number, which Java represents as `NAN`, which stands for Not A Number. In Chapter 5 we discuss how such situations can be avoided.

3.6 Formatting Output

The `NumberFormat` class and the `DecimalFormat` class are used to format information so that it looks appropriate when printed or displayed. They are both part of the Java standard class library and are defined in the `java.text` package.

The `NumberFormat` Class

The `NumberFormat` class provides generic formatting capabilities for numbers. We don't instantiate a `NumberFormat` object by using the `new` operator. Instead, we request an object from one of its static methods that we invoke through the class name itself. Figure 3.5 lists some of the methods of the `NumberFormat` class.

Two of the methods in the `NumberFormat` class, `getCurrencyInstance` and `getPercentInstance`, return an object that is used to format numbers. The `getCurrencyInstance` method returns a formatter for monetary values, and the `getPercentInstance` method returns an object that formats a percentage.

```
String format (double number)
   Returns a string containing the specified number formatted according to this
   object's pattern.

static NumberFormat getCurrencyInstance()
   Returns a NumberFormat object that represents a currency format for the
   current locale.

static NumberFormat getPercentInstance()
   Returns a NumberFormat object that represents a percentage format for the
   current locale.
```

FIGURE 3.5 Some methods of the `NumberFormat` class

The `format` method is invoked through a formatter object and returns a `String` that contains the number formatted in the appropriate manner.

The `Purchase` program shown in Listing 3.4 uses both types of formatters. It reads in a sales transaction and computes the final price, including tax.

The `getCurrencyInstance` and `getPercentInstance` methods are called *factory methods*, because they produce and return an instance of an object set up in a particular manner. Essentially, a `NumberFormat` factory method uses the `new`

LISTING 3.4

```
//********************************************************************
//  Purchase.java          Java Foundations
//
//  Demonstrates the use of the NumberFormat class to format output.
//********************************************************************

import java.util.Scanner;
import java.text.NumberFormat;

public class Purchase
{
   //-----------------------------------------------------------------
   // Calculates the final price of a purchased item using values
   // entered by the user.
   //-----------------------------------------------------------------
   public static void main(String[] args)
   {
```

LISTING 3.4 *continued*

```
      final double TAX_RATE = 0.06; // 6% sales tax

      int quantity;
      double subtotal, tax, totalCost, unitPrice;

      Scanner scan = new Scanner(System.in);

      NumberFormat fmt1 = NumberFormat.getCurrencyInstance();
      NumberFormat fmt2 = NumberFormat.getPercentInstance();

      System.out.print("Enter the quantity: ");
      quantity = scan.nextInt();

      System.out.print("Enter the unit price: ");
      unitPrice = scan.nextDouble();

      subtotal = quantity * unitPrice;
      tax = subtotal * TAX_RATE;
      totalCost = subtotal + tax;

      // Print output with appropriate formatting

      System.out.println("Subtotal: " + fmt1.format(subtotal));
      System.out.println("Tax: " + fmt1.format(tax) + " at "
                         + fmt2.format(TAX_RATE));
      System.out.println("Total: " + fmt1.format(totalCost));
   }
}
```

OUTPUT

```
Enter the quantity: 6
Enter the unit price: 1.69
Subtotal: $10.14
Tax: $0.61 at 6%
Total: $10.75
```

operator to create a `NumberFormat` object and then sets up the object to format values in a particular way and returns it so that it can be used.

The `DecimalFormat` Class

Unlike the `NumberFormat` class, the `DecimalFormat` class is instantiated in the traditional way using the `new` operator. Its constructor takes a `String` parameter

```
DecimalFormat (String pattern)
   Constructor: creates a new DecimalFormat object with the specified pattern.

void applyPattern (String pattern)
   Applies the specified pattern to this DecimalFormat object.

String format (double number)
   Returns a string containing the specified number formatted according to the
   current pattern.
```

FIGURE 3.6 Some methods of the `DecimalFormat` class

that represents the pattern that will guide the formatting process. We can then use the `format` method to format a particular value. At a later point, if we want to change the pattern that the formatter object uses, we can invoke the `applyPattern` method. Figure 3.6 describes these methods.

The pattern defined by the string that is passed to the `DecimalFormat` constructor can get fairly elaborate. Various symbols are used to represent particular formatting guidelines. The pattern defined by the string `"0.###"`, for example, indicates that at least one digit should be printed to the left of the decimal point and should be a zero if the integer portion of the value is zero. It also indicates that the fractional portion of the value should be rounded to three digits.

This pattern is used in the `CircleStats` program, shown in Listing 3.5, which reads the radius of a circle from the user and computes the circle's area and circumference. Trailing zeros, such as in the circle's area of 78.540, are not printed using this pattern.

LISTING 3.5

```
//********************************************************************
//  CircleStats.java           Java Foundations
//
//  Demonstrates the formatting of decimal values using the
//  DecimalFormat class.
//********************************************************************

import java.util.Scanner;
import java.text.DecimalFormat;

public class CircleStats
{
```

LISTING 3.5 *continued*

```
   //-----------------------------------------------------------------
   // Calculates the area and circumference of a circle given its
   // radius.
   //-----------------------------------------------------------------
   public static void main(String[] args)
   {
      int radius;
      double area, circumference;

      Scanner scan = new Scanner(System.in);

      System.out.print("Enter the circle's radius: ");
      radius = scan.nextInt();

      area = Math.PI * Math.pow(radius, 2);
      circumference = 2 * Math.PI * radius;

      // Round the output to three decimal places

      DecimalFormat fmt = new DecimalFormat("0.###");

      System.out.println("The circle's area: " + fmt.format(area));
      System.out.println("The circle's circumference: "
                         + fmt.format(circumference));
   }
}
```

OUTPUT

```
Enter the circle's radius: 5
The circle's area: 78.54
The circle's circumference: 31.416
```

The `printf` Method

In addition to `print` and `println`, the `System` class has another output method called `printf`, which allows the user to print a formatted string containing data values. The first parameter to the method represents the format string, and the remaining parameters specify the values that are inserted into the format string.

For example, the following line of code prints an ID number and a name:

```
System.out.printf("ID: %5d\tName: %s", id, name);
```

The first parameter specifies the format of the output and includes literal characters that label the output values as well as escape characters such as `\t`. The pattern `%5d` indicates that the corresponding numeric value (`id`) should be printed in a field of five characters. The pattern `%s` matches the string parameter `name`. The values of `id` and `name` are inserted into the string, producing a result such as

```
ID: 24036 Name: Larry Flagelhopper
```

The `printf` method was added to Java to mirror a similar function used in programs written in the C programming language. This makes it easier for a programmer to translate (or *migrate*) an existing C program into Java.

Older software that still has value is called a *legacy system*. Maintaining a legacy system is often a costly effort because, among other things, it is based on older technologies. But in many cases, maintaining a legacy system is still more cost-effective than migrating it to new technology, such as writing it in a newer language. Adding the `printf` method is an attempt to make such migrations easier, and therefore less costly, by providing the same kind of output statement that C programmers have come to rely on.

KEY CONCEPT

The `printf` method was added to Java to support the migration of legacy systems.

However, using the `printf` method is not a particularly clean object-oriented solution to the problem of formatting output, so we avoid its use in this text.

3.7 Enumerated Types

Java provides the ability to define an *enumerated type*, which can then be used as the type of a variable when it is declared. An enumerated type establishes all possible values of a variable of that type by listing, or enumerating, them. The values are identifiers and can be anything desired.

For example, the following declaration defines an enumerated type called `Season` whose possible values are `winter`, `spring`, `summer`, and `fall`.

```
enum Season {winter, spring, summer, fall}
```

There is no limit to the number of values that you can list for an enumerated type. Once the type is defined, a variable can be declared of that type:

```
Season time;
```

The variable `time` is now restricted in the values it can take on. It can hold one of the four `Season` values, but nothing else. Java enumerated types are considered to be *type-safe*, which means that any attempt to use a value other than one of the enumerated values will result in a compile-time error.

KEY CONCEPT

Enumerated types are type-safe, ensuring that invalid values will not be used.

The values are accessed through the name of the type—for example,

```
time = Season.spring;
```

Enumerated types can be quite helpful in situations in which you have a relatively small number of distinct values that a variable can assume. For example, suppose we wanted to represent the various letter grades a student could earn. We might declare the following enumerated type:

```
enum Grade {A, B, C, D, F}
```

Any initialized variable that holds a `Grade` is guaranteed to have one of those valid grades. That's better than using a simple character or `String` variable to represent the grade, which could take on any value.

Suppose we also wanted to represent plus and minus grades, such as A– and B+. We couldn't use A– or B+ as values, because they are not valid identifiers (the characters `'-'` and `'+'` cannot be part of an identifier in Java). However, the same values could be represented using the identifiers `Aminus`, `Bplus`, and so on.

Internally, each value in an enumerated type is stored as an integer, which is referred to as its *ordinal value*. The first value in an enumerated type has an ordinal value of 0, the second has an ordinal value of 1, the third has an ordinal value of 2, and so on. The ordinal values are used internally only. You cannot assign a numeric value to an enumerated type, even if it corresponds to a valid ordinal value.

An enumerated type is a special kind of class, and the variables of an enumerated type are object variables. Thus there are a few methods associated with all enumerated types. The `ordinal` method returns the numeric value associated with a particular enumerated type value. The `name` method returns the name of the value, which is the same as the identifier that defines the value.

Listing 3.6 shows a program called `IceCream` that declares an enumerated type and exercises some of its methods. Because enumerated types are special types of classes, they are not defined within a method. They can be defined either at the class level (within the class but outside a method), as in this example, or at the outermost level.

LISTING 3.6

```
//********************************************************************
//  IceCream.java           Java Foundations
//
//  Demonstrates the use of enumerated types.
//********************************************************************
```

LISTING 3.6 *continued*

```
public class IceCream
{
   enum Flavor {vanilla, chocolate, strawberry, fudgeRipple, coffee,
               rockyRoad, mintChocolateChip, cookieDough}

   //-----------------------------------------------------------------
   // Creates and uses variables of the Flavor type.
   //-----------------------------------------------------------------
   public static void main(String[] args)
   {
      Flavor cone1, cone2, cone3;

      cone1 = Flavor.rockyRoad;
      cone2 = Flavor.chocolate;

      System.out.println("cone1 value: " + cone1);
      System.out.println("cone1 ordinal: " + cone1.ordinal());
      System.out.println("cone1 name: " + cone1.name());

      System.out.println();
      System.out.println("cone2 value: " + cone2);
      System.out.println("cone2 ordinal: " + cone2.ordinal());
      System.out.println("cone2 name: " + cone2.name());

      cone3 = cone1;

      System.out.println();
      System.out.println("cone3 value: " + cone3);
      System.out.println("cone3 ordinal: " + cone3.ordinal());
      System.out.println("cone3 name: " + cone3.name());
   }
}
```

OUTPUT

```
cone1 value: rockyRoad
cone1 ordinal: 5
cone1 name: rockyRoad

cone2 value: chocolate
cone2 ordinal: 1
cone2 name: chocolate

cone3 value: rockyRoad
cone3 ordinal: 5
cone3 name: rockyRoad
```

3.8 Wrapper Classes

As we've discussed previously, Java represents data by using primitive types (such as `int`, `double`, `char`, and `boolean`) in addition to classes and objects. Having two categories of data to manage (primitive values and object references) can present a challenge in some circumstances. There are times when you may want to treat primitive data as though they were objects. In these cases we need to "wrap" a primitive value into an object.

A *wrapper class* represents a particular primitive type. For instance, the `Integer` class represents a simple integer value. An object created from the `Integer` class stores a single `int` value. The constructors of the wrapper classes accept the primitive value to store. Here is an example:

```
Integer ageObj = new Integer(40);
```

KEY CONCEPT

A wrapper class allows a primitive value to be managed as an object.

Once this declaration and instantiation are performed, the `ageObj` object effectively represents the integer 40 as an object. It can be used wherever an object is needed in a program rather than a primitive type.

For each primitive type in Java there exists a corresponding wrapper class in the Java class library. All wrapper classes are defined in the `java.lang` package. Figure 3.7 shows the wrapper class that corresponds to each primitive type.

Note that there is even a wrapper class that represents the type `void`. However, unlike the other wrapper classes, the `Void` class cannot be instantiated. It simply represents the concept of a void reference.

Primitive Type	Wrapper Class
byte	Byte
short	Short
int	Integer
long	Long
float	Float
double	Double
char	Character
boolean	Boolean
void	Void

FIGURE 3.7 Wrapper classes in the `java.lang` package

```
Integer (int value)
   Constructor: creates a new Integer object storing the specified value.

byte byteValue ()
double doubleValue ()
float floatValue ()
int intValue ()
long longValue ()
   Return the value of this Integer as the corresponding primitive type.

static int parseInt (String str)
   Returns the int corresponding to the value stored in the specified string.

static String toBinaryString (int num)
static String tohexString (int num)
static String toOctalString (int num)
   Returns a string representation of the specified integer value in the
   corresponding base.
```

FIGURE 3.8 Some methods of the `Integer` class

Wrapper classes also provide various methods related to the management of the associated primitive type. For example, the `Integer` class contains methods that return the `int` value stored in the object and that convert the stored value to other primitive types. Figure 3.8 lists some of the methods found in the `Integer` class. The other wrapper classes have similar methods.

Note that the wrapper classes also contain static methods that can be invoked independent of any instantiated object. For example, the `Integer` class contains a static method called `parseInt` that converts an integer that is stored in a `String` to its corresponding `int` value. If the `String` object `str` holds the string `"987"`, the following line of code converts the string into the integer value `987` and stores that value in the `int` variable num:

```
num = Integer.parseInt(str);
```

The Java wrapper classes often contain static constants that are helpful as well. For example, the `Integer` class contains two constants, `MIN_VALUE` and `MAX_VALUE`, that hold the smallest and largest `int` values, respectively. The other wrapper classes contain similar constants for their types.

Autoboxing

Autoboxing is the automatic conversion between a primitive value and a corresponding wrapper object. For example, in the following code, an `int` value is assigned to an `Integer` object reference variable.

```
Integer obj1;
int num1 = 69;
obj1 = num1; // automatically creates an Integer object
```

The reverse conversion, called *unboxing*, also occurs automatically when needed. For example,

```
Integer obj2 = new Integer(69);
int num2;
num2 = obj2; // automatically extracts the int value
```

KEY CONCEPT
Autoboxing provides automatic conversions between primitive values and corresponding wrapper objects.

Assignments between primitive types and object types are generally incompatible. The ability to autobox occurs only between primitive types and corresponding wrapper classes. In any other case, attempting to assign a primitive value to an object reference variable, or vice versa, will cause a compile-time error.

Summary of Key Concepts

- The `new` operator returns a reference to a newly created object.
- Multiple reference variables can refer to the same object.
- Methods are often executed on a particular object, and that object's state usually affects the results.
- A class library provides useful support when one is developing programs.
- The Java standard class library is organized into packages.
- All classes of the `java.lang` package are automatically imported for every program.
- A pseudorandom number generator performs a complex calculation to create the illusion of randomness.
- All methods of the `Math` class are static, which means they are invoked through the class name.
- The `printf` method was added to Java to support the migration of legacy systems.
- Enumerated types are type-safe, ensuring that invalid values will not be used.
- A wrapper class allows a primitive value to be managed as an object.
- Autoboxing provides automatic conversions between primitive values and corresponding wrapper objects.

Summary of Terms

application programming interface (API) A set of related classes that supports a particular aspect of programming.

autoboxing The automatic conversion of a primitive type to an object of its corresponding wrapper class.

class library A set of classes that supports the development of programs.

constructor A special method that has the same name as the class and is called when a object is created to set up the object initially.

enumerated type A Java data type in which all values of the type are explicitly listed.

garbage collection The process of reclaiming memory space that can no longer be used by a program.

immutable An object whose data (state) cannot be modified once it is created.

import declaration A programming statement used to specify which external classes (from which packages) are used in a program.

instance An object. An object is an instance of a class.

instantiation The process of creating a new object.

package A language-level organization mechanism for classes. Each class in the Java API belongs to a particular package.

pseudorandom number generator A program element that performs calculations to produce a series of numbers in seemingly random order.

wrapper class A class that corresponds to a particular primitive data type.

Self-Review Questions

SR 3.1 What does the `new` operator accomplish?

SR 3.2 What is a null reference?

SR 3.3 What is an alias? How is it related to garbage collection?

SR 3.4 Write a declaration for a `String` variable called `author` and initialize it to the string `"Fred Brooks"`. Draw a graphical representation of the variable and its value.

SR 3.5 Write a statement that prints the value of a `String` object called `title` in all uppercase letters.

SR 3.6 Write a declaration for a `String` variable called `front` and initialize it to the first 10 characters of another `String` object called `description`.

SR 3.7 What is a Java package?

SR 3.8 What does the `java.net` package contain? The `java.swing` package?

SR 3.9 What package contains the `Scanner` class? The `String` class? The `Random` class? The `Math` class?

SR 3.10 What does an import declaration accomplish?

SR 3.11 Why doesn't the `String` class have to be specifically imported into our programs?

SR 3.12 Given a `Random` object called `rand`, what does the call `rand.nextInt()` return?

SR 3.13 Given a `Random` object called `rand`, what does the call `rand.nextInt(20)` return?

SR 3.14 What is a class method (also called a static method)?

SR 3.15 Write a statement that prints the sine of an angle measuring 1.23 radians.

SR 3.16 Write a declaration for a `double` variable called `result` and initialize it to 5 raised to the power 2.5.

SR 3.17 What are the steps to output a floating point value as a percentage using Java's formatting classes?

SR 3.18 Write the declaration of an enumerated type that represents movie ratings.

SR 3.19 How can we represent a primitive value as an object?

Exercises

EX 3.1 Write a statement that prints the number of characters in a `String` object called `overview`.

EX 3.2 Write a statement that prints the eighth character of a `String` object called `introduction`.

EX 3.3 Write a declaration for a `String` variable called `change` and initialize it to the characters stored in another `String` object called `original` with all `'e'` characters changed to `'j'`.

EX 3.4 What output is produced by the following code fragment?

```
String m1, m2, m3;
m1 = "Quest for the Holy Grail";
m2 = m1.toLowerCase();
m3 = m1 + " " + m2;
System.out.println(m3.replace('h', 'z'));
```

EX 3.5 What is the effect of the following import declaration?

```
import java.awt.*;
```

EX 3.6 Assuming that a `Random` object called `generator` has been created, what is the range of the result of each of the following expressions?

a. `generator.nextInt(20)`

b. `generator.nextInt(8) + 1`

c. `generator.nextInt(45) + 10`

d. `generator.nextInt(100) - 50`

EX 3.7 Write code to declare and instantiate an object of the `Random` class (call the object reference variable `rand`). Then write a list of expressions using the `nextInt` method that generates random numbers in the following specified ranges, including the end points. Use the version of the `nextInt` method that accepts a single integer parameter.

a. `0 to 10`
b. `0 to 500`
c. `1 to 10`
d. `1 to 500`
e. `25 to 50`
f. `-10 to 15`

EX 3.8 Write an assignment statement that computes the square root of the sum of `num1` and `num2` and assigns the result to `num3`.

EX 3.9 Write a single statement that computes and prints the absolute value of `total`.

EX 3.10 Write code statements to create a `DecimalFormat` object that will round a formatted value to four decimal places. Then write a statement that uses that object to print the value of the result, properly formatted.

EX 3.11 Write code statements that prompt for and read a double value from the user and then print the result of raising that value to the fourth power. Output the results to three decimal places.

EX 3.12 Write a declaration for an enumerated type that represents the days of the week.

Programming Projects

PP 3.1 Write an application that prompts for and reads the user's first name and last name (separately). Then print a string composed of the first letter of the user's first name, followed by the first five characters of the user's last name, followed by a random number in the range 10 to 99. Assume that the last name is at least five letters long. Similar algorithms are sometimes used to generate usernames for new computer accounts.

PP 3.2 Write an application that prints the sum of cubes. Prompt for and read two integer values and print the sum of each value raised to the third power.

PP 3.3 Write an application that creates and prints a random phone number of the form XXX-XXX-XXXX. Include the dashes in the output. Do not let the first three digits contain an 8 or 9 (but don't be more restrictive than that), and make sure that the second set of three digits is not greater than 742. *Hint:* Think through the easiest way to construct the phone number. Each digit does not have to be determined separately.

PP 3.4 Write an application that reads the (x, y) coordinates for two points. Compute the distance between the two points using the following formula:

$$\text{Distance} = \sqrt{(x_2 - x_1)^2 + (y_2 - y_1)^2}$$

PP 3.5 Write an application that reads the radius of a sphere and prints its volume and surface area. Use the following formulas, in which r represents the sphere's radius. Print the output to four decimal places.

$$\text{Volume} = \frac{4}{3}\pi r^3$$

$$\text{Surface area} = 4\pi r^2$$

PP 3.6 Write an application that reads the lengths of the sides of a triangle from the user. Compute the area of the triangle using Heron's formula (below), in which s represents half of the perimeter of the triangle, and a, b, and c represent the lengths of the three sides. Print the area to three decimal places.

$$\text{Area} = \sqrt{(s(s - a)(s - b)(s - c)}$$

Answers to Self-Review Questions

SRA 3.1 The `new` operator creates a new instance (an object) of the specified class. The constructor of the class is then invoked to help set up the newly created object.

SRA 3.2 A null reference is a reference that does not refer to any object. The reserved word `null` can be used to check for null references to avoid following them.

SRA 3.3 Two references are aliases of each other if they refer to the same object. Changing the state of the object through one reference changes it for the other, because there is actually only one object. An object is marked for garbage collection only when there are no valid references to it.

SRA 3.4 The following declaration creates a `String` variable called `author` and initializes it.

```
String author = new String("Fred Brooks");
```

For strings, this declaration could have been abbreviated as follows:

```
String author = "Fred Brooks";
```

This object reference variable and its value can be depicted as follows:

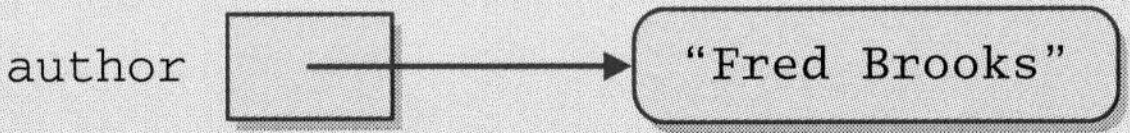

SRA 3.5 The following statement prints the value of a `String` object in all uppercase letters.

```
System.out.println(title.toUpperCase());
```

SRA 3.6 The following declaration creates a `String` object and sets it equal to the first 10 characters of the `String` called `description`.

```
String front = description.substring(0, 10);
```

SRA 3.7 A Java package is a collection of related classes. The Java standard class library is a group of packages that supports common programming tasks.

SRA 3.8 Each package contains a set of classes that supports particular programming activities. The classes in the `java.net` package support network communication, and the classes in the `javax.swing` class support the development of graphical user interfaces.

SRA 3.9 The `Scanner` class and the `Random` class are part of the `java.util` package. The `String` and `Math` classes are part of the `java.lang` package.

SRA 3.10 An `import` declaration establishes the fact that a program uses a particular class, specifying the package that the class is a part of. This allows the programmer to use the class name (such as `Random`) without having to fully qualify the reference (such as `java.util.Random`) every time.

SRA 3.11 The `String` class is part of the `java.lang` package, which is automatically imported into any Java program. Therefore, no separate `import` declaration is needed.

SRA 3.12 A call to the `nextInt` method of a `Random` object returns a random integer in the range of all possible `int` values, both positive and negative.

SRA 3.13 Passing a positive integer parameter x to the `nextInt` method of a `Random` object returns a random number in the range of 0 to $x - 1$. Thus a call to `nextInt(20)` will return a random number in the range 0 to 19, inclusive.

SRA 3.14 A class (or static) method can be invoked through the name of the class that contains it, such as `Math.abs`. If a method is not static, it can be executed only through an instance (an object) of the class.

SRA 3.15 The following statement prints the sine of 1.23 radians.

```
System.out.println(Math.sin(1.23));
```

SRA 3.16 The following declaration creates a double variable and initializes it to 5 raised to the power 2.5.

```
double result = Math.pow(5, 2.5);
```

SRA 3.17 To output a floating point value as a percentage, you first obtain a formatter object using a call to the static method `getPercentInstance` of the `NumberFormat` class. Then you pass the value to be formatted to the `format` method of the formatter object, which returns a properly formatted string. Here is an example:

```
NumberFormat fmt = NumberFormat.getPercentageInstance();
System.out.println(fmt.format(value));
```

SRA 3.18 The following is a declaration of an enumerated type for movie ratings.

```
enum Ratings {G, PG, PG13, R, NC17}
```

SRA 3.19 A wrapper class is defined in the Java standard class library for each primitive type. In situations where objects are called for, an object created from a wrapper class may suffice.

Conditionals and Loops

4

CHAPTER OBJECTIVES

- Discuss the flow of control through a method.
- Explore boolean expressions that can be used to make decisions.
- Perform basic decision making using `if` and `switch` statements.
- Discuss issues pertaining to the comparison of certain types of data.
- Execute statements repetitively using `while`, `do`, and `for` loops.
- Discuss the concept of an iterator object, and use one to read a text file.

All programming languages have statements that allow you to make decisions about what to do next. Some of those statements allow you to repeat a certain activity multiple times. This chapter discusses several such statements, as well as exploring some issues related to comparing data and objects. We begin with a discussion of boolean expressions, which form the basis of any decision.

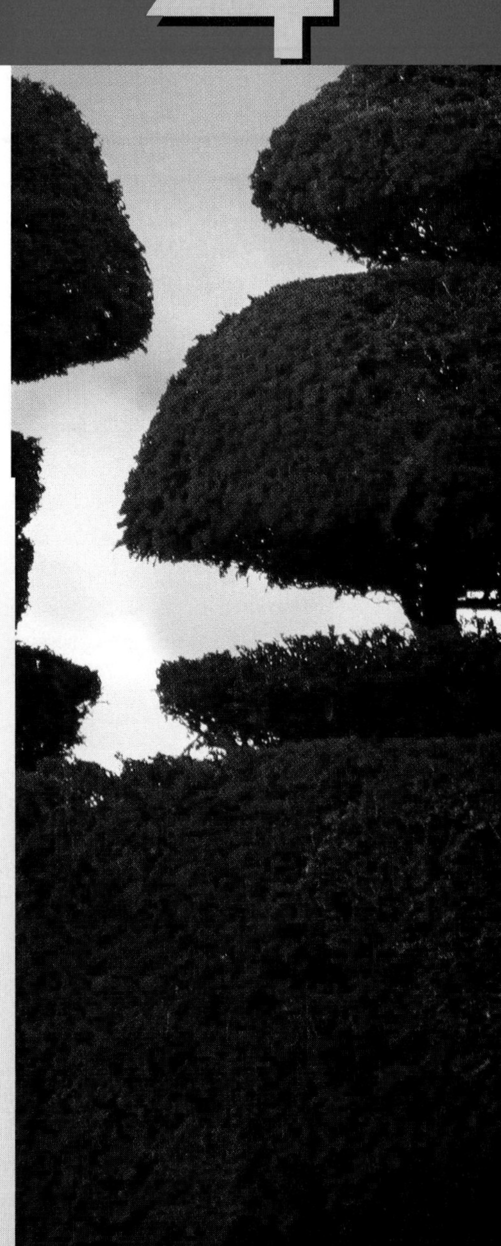

4.1 Boolean Expressions

The order in which statements are executed in a running program is called the *flow of control*. Unless otherwise specified, the basic execution of a program proceeds in a linear fashion. That is, a running program starts at the first programming statement and moves down one statement at a time until the program is complete. A Java application begins executing with the first line of the `main` method and proceeds step by step until it gets to the end of the `main` method.

Invoking a method alters the flow of control. When a method is called, the flow of control jumps to the code defined for that method, and it begins executing. When the method completes, control returns to the place in the calling method where the invocation was made, and processing continues from there. Methods and their invocation are discussed further in the next chapter.

KEY CONCEPT

Conditionals and loops enable us to control the flow of execution through a method.

Within a given method, we can alter the flow of control through the code by using certain types of programming statements. Statements that control the flow of execution through a method fall into two categories: conditionals and loops.

A *conditional statement* is sometimes called a *selection statement* because it allows us to choose which statement will be executed next. The conditional statements in Java are the `if` statement, the `if-else` statement, and the `switch` statement. These statements enable us to decide which statement to execute next.

Each decision is based on a *boolean expression*, also called a *condition*, which is an expression that evaluates to either true or false. The result of the expression determines which statement is executed next.

The following is an example of an `if` statement:

```
if (count > 20)
    System.out.println("Count exceeded");
```

KEY CONCEPT

An `if` statement allows a program to choose whether to execute a particular statement.

The condition in this statement is `count > 20`. That expression evaluates to a boolean (true or false) result. Either the value stored in `count` is greater than 20 or it's not. If it is, the `println` statement is executed. If it's not, the `println` statement is skipped, and processing continues with whatever code follows it. The `if` statement and other conditionals are explored in detail in this chapter.

The need to make decisions like this comes up all the time in programming situations. For example, the cost of life insurance might depend on whether the insured person is a smoker. If the person smokes, we calculate the cost using a particular formula; if not, we calculate it using another. The role of a conditional statement is to evaluate a boolean condition (whether the person smokes) and then to execute the proper calculation accordingly.

A *loop*, or *repetition statement*, allows us to execute a programming statement over and over again. Like a conditional, a loop is based on a boolean expression that determines how many times the statement is executed.

KEY CONCEPT

A loop allows a program to execute a statement multiple times.

For example, suppose we wanted to calculate the grade point average of every student in a class. The calculation is the same for each student; it is just performed on different data. We would set up a loop that repeats the calculation for each student until there are no more students to process.

Java has three types of loop statements: the `while` statement, the `do` statement, and the `for` statement. Each type of loop statement has unique characteristics that distinguish it from the others.

All conditionals and loops are based on boolean expressions, which use equality operators, relational operators, and logical operators to make decisions. Before we discuss the details of conditional and loop statements, let's explore these operators.

Equality and Relational Operators

The `==` and `!=` operators are called *equality operators*. They test whether two values are equal or are not equal, respectively. Note that the equality operator consists of two equal signs side by side and should not be mistaken for the assignment operator, which uses only one equal sign.

The following `if` statement prints a sentence only if the variables `total` and `sum` contain the same value.

```
if (total == sum)
    System.out.println("total equals sum");
```

Likewise, the following `if` statement prints a sentence only if the variables `total` and `sum` do not contain the same value.

```
if (total != sum)
    System.out.println("total does NOT equal sum");
```

Java also has several *relational operators* that let us decide the relative ordering between two values. Earlier in this section we used the greater than operator (`>`) to decide whether one value was greater than another. We can ask such questions using various operators, depending on the relationship. These operators include less than (`<`), greater than or equal to (`>=`), and less than or equal to (`<=`). Figure 4.1 lists the Java equality and relational operators.

Operator	Meaning
==	equal to
!=	not equal to
<	less than
<=	less than or equal to
>	greater than
>=	greater than or equal to

FIGURE 4.1 Java equality and relational operators

The equality and relational operators have lower precedence than the arithmetic operators. Therefore, arithmetic operations are evaluated first, followed by equality and relational operations. As always, parentheses can be used to explicitly specify the order of evaluation.

We'll see more examples of relational operators as we examine conditional and loop statements throughout this chapter.

Logical Operators

In addition to the equality and relational operators, Java has three *logical operators* that produce boolean results. They also take boolean operands. Figure 4.2 lists and describes the logical operators.

The `!` operator is used to perform the *logical NOT* operation, which is also called the *logical complement*. The `!` operator is unary, taking only one boolean operand. The logical complement of a boolean value yields its opposite value. That is, if a `boolean` variable called `found` has the value false, then `!found` is true. Likewise, if `found` is true, then `!found` is false. Note that the logical NOT operation does not change the value stored in `found`—it creates an expression that returns a boolean result.

<table>
<tr><th>Operator</th><th>Description</th><th>Example</th><th>Result</th></tr>
<tr><td>!</td><td>logical NOT</td><td>! a</td><td>true if a is false and false if a is true</td></tr>
<tr><td>&&</td><td>logical AND</td><td>a && b</td><td>true if a and b are both true and false otherwise</td></tr>
<tr><td>||</td><td>logical OR</td><td>a || b</td><td>true if a or b or both are true and false otherwise</td></tr>
</table>

FIGURE 4.2 Java logical operators

a	!a
false	true
true	false

FIGURE 4.3 Truth table describing the logical NOT operator

A logical operation can be described by a *truth table* that lists all possible combinations of values for the variables involved in an expression. Because the logical NOT operator is unary, there are only two possible values for its one operand, which must be either true or false. Figure 4.3 shows a truth table that describes the `!` operator.

The `&&` operator performs a *logical AND* operation. The result of an `&&` operation is true if both operands are true, but is false otherwise. Compare that to the result of the *logical OR operator* (`||`), which is true if one or the other or both operands are true, but is false otherwise.

The AND and OR operators are both binary operators because each uses two operands. Therefore, there are four possible combinations to consider: both operands are true, both are false, one is true and the other false, and vice versa. Figure 4.4 depicts a truth table that shows both the `&&` operator and the `||` operator.

The logical NOT has the highest precedence of the three logical operators, followed by logical AND and then logical OR.

The logical operators enable us to create complex expressions when making decisions. Consider the following `if` statement:

```
if (!done && (count > MAX))
    System.out.println("Completed.");
```

Under what conditions would the `println` statement be executed? The value of the boolean variable `done` is either true or false, and the NOT operator reverses that value. Either the value of `count` is greater than `MAX` or it isn't. The truth table in Figure 4.5 displays all of the possibilities.

a	b	a && b	a || b
false	false	false	false
false	true	false	true
true	false	false	true
true	true	true	true

FIGURE 4.4 Truth table describing the logical AND and OR operators

done	count > MAX	!done	!done && (count > MAX)
false	false	true	false
false	true	true	true
true	false	false	false
true	true	false	false

FIGURE 4.5 A truth table for a specific condition

KEY CONCEPT
Logical operators can be used to construct sophisticated conditions.

An important characteristic of the && and || operators is that they are "short-circuited" in Java. That is, if their left operand is sufficient to decide the boolean result of the operation, the right operand is not evaluated. This situation can occur with both operators, but for different reasons. If the left operand of the && operator is false, then the result of the operation will be false no matter what the value of the right operand is. Likewise, if the left operand of the || operator is true, then the result of the operation is true no matter what the value of the right operand is.

Sometimes you can capitalize on the fact that an operator is short-circuited. For example, the condition in the following `if` statement will not attempt to divide by zero if the left operand is false. If `count` has the value zero, the left side of the && operation is false; therefore, the whole expression is false and the right side is not evaluated.

```
if (count != 0 && total/count > MAX)
   System.out.println("Testing.");
```

You should consider carefully whether or not to rely on these kinds of subtle programming language characteristics. Not all programming languages short-circuit these operations, and such code would produce a divide-by-zero error in those languages. As we have stressed before, you should err on the side of readability. You should always strive to make the logic of your program extremely clear to anyone reading your code.

4.2 The `if` Statement

We've used a basic `if` statement in earlier examples in this chapter. Let's now explore it in detail.

An *if statement* consists of the reserved word `if` followed by a boolean expression, followed by a statement. The condition is enclosed in parentheses and must evaluate to true or false. If the condition is true, the statement is executed, and then processing continues with any statement that follows. If the condition is false, the statement controlled by the condition is skipped, and processing continues immediately with any statement that follows. Figure 4.6 shows this processing.

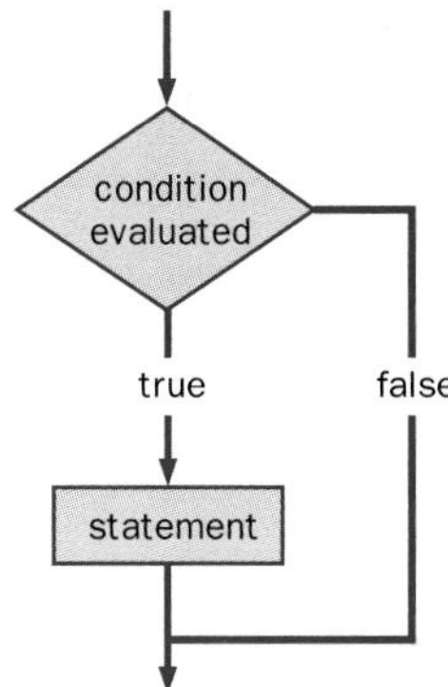

FIGURE 4.6 The logic of an `if` statement

Consider the following example of an `if` statement:

```
if (total > amount)
   total = total + (amount + 1);
```

In this example, if the value in `total` is greater than the value in `amount`, the assignment statement is executed; otherwise, the assignment statement is skipped.

Note that the assignment statement in this example is indented under the header line of the `if` statement. This communicates to a human reader that the assignment statement is part of the `if` statement; it implies that the `if` statement governs whether the assignment statement will be executed. This indentation is extremely important for human readability, although it is ignored by the compiler.

KEY CONCEPT

Proper indentation is important for human readability; it shows the relationship between one statement and another.

The example in Listing 4.1 reads the age of the user and then makes a decision about whether to print a particular sentence based on the age that is entered.

The `Age` program echoes the age value that is entered in all cases. If the age is less than the value of the constant `MINOR`, the statement about youth is printed. If the age is equal to or greater than the value of `MINOR`, the `println` statement is skipped. In either case, the final sentence about age being a state of mind is printed.

Let's look at a few more examples of basic `if` statements. The following `if` statement causes the variable `size` to be set to zero if its current value is greater than or equal to the value in the constant `MAX`.

```
if (size >= MAX)
   size = 0;
```

The condition of the following `if` statement first adds three values together and then compares the result to the value stored in `numBooks`.

LISTING 4.1

```
//********************************************************************
//  Age.java        Java Foundations
//
//  Demonstrates the use of an if statement.
//********************************************************************

import java.util.Scanner;

public class Age
{
   //-----------------------------------------------------------------
   //  Reads the user's age and prints comments accordingly.
   //-----------------------------------------------------------------
   public static void main(String[] args)
   {
      final int MINOR = 21;
      Scanner scan = new Scanner(System.in);
      System.out.print("Enter your age: ");
      int age = scan.nextInt();
      System.out.println("You entered: " + age);

      if (age < MINOR)
         System.out.println("Youth is a wonderful thing. Enjoy.");

      System.out.println("Age is a state of mind.");
   }
}
```

OUTPUT

```
Enter your age: 43
You entered: 43
Age is a state of mind.
```

```
if (numBooks < stackCount + inventoryCount + duplicateCount)
   reorder = true;
```

If `numBooks` is less than the other three values combined, the boolean variable `reorder` is set to `true`. The addition operations are performed before the less than operator, because the arithmetic operators have a higher precedence than the relational operators.

Assuming that the variable `generator` refers to an object of the `Random` class, the following `if` statement examines the value returned from a call to `nextInt` to determine a random winner.

```
if (generator.nextInt(CHANCE) == 0)
   System.out.println("You are a randomly selected winner!");
```

The odds of this code picking a winner are based on the value of the `CHANCE` constant. That is, if `CHANCE` contains `20`, the odds of winning are 1 in 20. The fact that the condition is looking for a return value of `0` is arbitrary; any value between `0` and `CHANCE-1` would have worked.

The `if-else` Statement

Sometimes we want to do one thing if a condition is true and another thing if that condition is false. To handle this kind of situation, we can add an *else clause* to an `if` statement, making it an *if-else* statement. The following is an example of an `if-else` statement:

```
if (height <= MAX)
   adjustment = 0;
else
   adjustment = MAX - height;
```

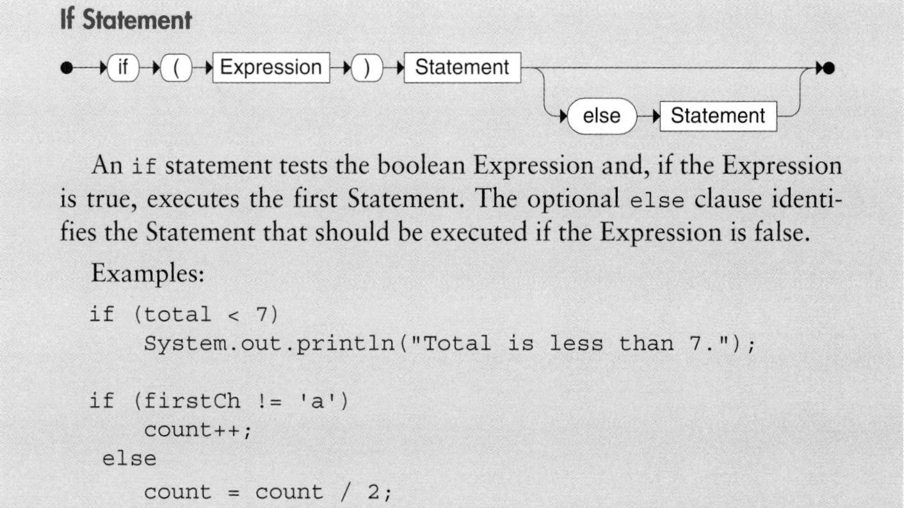

If Statement
if
(
Expression
)
Statement
else
Statement
An if statement tests the boolean Expression and, if the Expression is true, executes the first Statement. The optional else clause identifies the Statement that should be executed if the Expression is false.
Examples:
if (total < 7)
    System.out.println("Total is less than 7.");
if (firstCh != 'a')
    count++;
 else
    count = count / 2;

If the condition is true, the first assignment statement is executed; if the condition is false, the second assignment statement is executed. Only one or the other will be executed, because a boolean condition evaluates to either true or false. Note that proper indentation is used again to communicate that the statements are part of the governing `if` statement.

KEY CONCEPT
An `if-else` statement allows a program to do one thing if a condition is true and another thing if the condition is false.

The `Wages` program shown in Listing 4.2 uses an `if-else` statement to compute the proper payment amount for an employee.

LISTING 4.2

```
//********************************************************************
//  Wages.java       Java Foundations
//
//  Demonstrates the use of an if-else statement.
//********************************************************************

import java.text.NumberFormat;
import java.util.Scanner;

public class Wages
{
  //-----------------------------------------------------------------
  // Reads the number of hours worked and calculates wages.
  //-----------------------------------------------------------------
  public static void main(String[] args)
  {
     final double RATE = 8.25; // regular pay rate
     final int STANDARD = 40; // standard hours in a work week

     Scanner scan = new Scanner(System.in);

     double pay = 0.0;

     System.out.print("Enter the number of hours worked: ");
     int hours = scan.nextInt();

     System.out.println();

     // Pay overtime at "time and a half"

     if (hours > STANDARD)
       pay = STANDARD * RATE + (hours-STANDARD) * (RATE * 1.5);
     else
       pay = hours * RATE;

       NumberFormat fmt = NumberFormat.getCurrencyInstance();
       System.out.println("Gross earnings: " + fmt.format(pay));
  }
}
```

OUTPUT

```
Enter the number of hours worked: 46
Gross earnings: $404.25
```

In the `Wages` program, if an employee works over 40 hours in a week, the payment amount takes into account the overtime hours. An `if-else` statement is used to determine whether the number of hours entered by the user is greater than 40. If it is, the overtime hours are paid at a rate one and a half times the normal rate. If there are no overtime hours, the total payment is based simply on the number of hours worked and the standard rate.

Let's look at another example of an `if-else` statement:

```
if (roster.getSize() == FULL)
   roster.expand();

else
   roster.addName(name);
```

This example makes use of an object called `roster`. Even without knowing what `roster` represents, or from what class it was created, we can see that it has at least three methods: `getSize`, `expand`, and `addName`. The condition of the `if` statement calls `getSize` and compares the result to the constant `FULL`. If the condition is true, the `expand` method is invoked (apparently to expand the size of the roster). If the roster is not yet full, the variable `name` is passed as a parameter to the `addName` method.

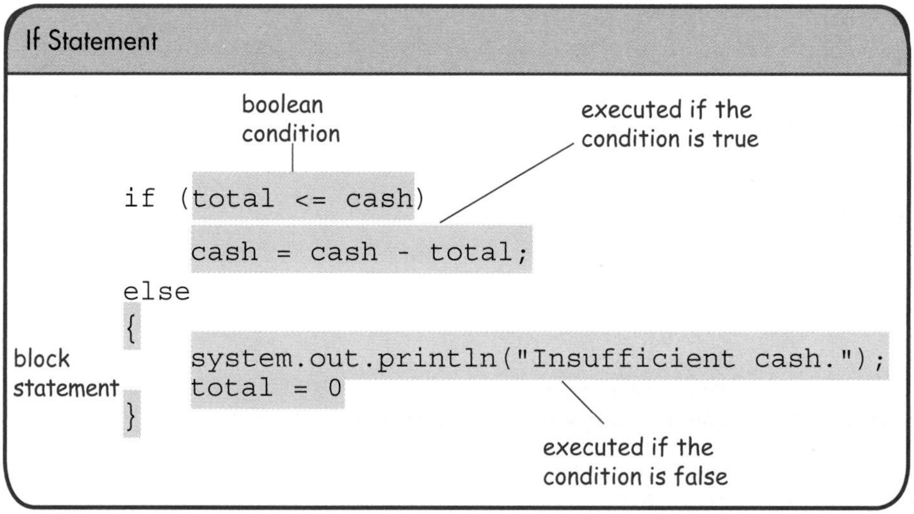

If Statement


```
if (total <= cash)
    cash = cash - total;
else
{
    system.out.println("Insufficient cash.");
    total = 0
}
```

Using Block Statements

We may want to do more than one thing as the result of evaluating a boolean condition. In Java, we can replace any single statement with a *block statement*. A block statement is a collection of statements enclosed in braces. We've used these braces many times in previous examples to delimit method and class definitions.

The program called `Guessing`, shown in Listing 4.3, uses an `if-else` statement in which the statement of the `else` clause is a block statement.

LISTING 4.3

```
//********************************************************************
//  Guessing.java       Java Foundations
//
//  Demonstrates the use of a block statement in an if-else.
//********************************************************************

import java.util.*;

public class Guessing
{
   //-----------------------------------------------------------------
   // Plays a simple guessing game with the user.
   //-----------------------------------------------------------------
   public static void main(String[] args)
   {
      final int MAX = 10;
      int answer, guess;

      Scanner scan = new Scanner(System.in);
      Random generator = new Random();

      answer = generator.nextInt(MAX) + 1;

      System.out.print("I'm thinking of a number between 1 and "
                     + MAX + ". Guess what it is: ");

      guess = scan.nextInt();

      if (guess == answer)
         System.out.println("You got it! Good guessing!");
      else
      {
         System.out.println("That is not correct, sorry.");
         System.out.println("The number was " + answer);
      }
   }
}
```

OUTPUT

```
I'm thinking of a number between 1 and 10. Guess what it is: 4
That is not correct, sorry.
The number was 8
```

If the guess entered by the user equals the randomly chosen answer, an appropriate acknowledgement is printed. However, if the answer is incorrect, two sentences are printed, one that states that the guess is wrong and one that prints the actual answer. A programming project at the end of this chapter expands the basic idea in this example into the Hi-Lo game.

Note that if the block braces were not used, the sentence stating that the answer is incorrect would be printed if the answer was wrong, but the sentence revealing the correct answer would be printed in all cases. That is, only the first statement would be considered part of the `else` clause.

VideoNote
Examples using conditionals

COMMON ERROR

Remember that indentation means nothing except to the human reader. Statements that are not blocked properly can lead to the programmer making improper assumptions about how the code will execute. For example, the following code is misleading:

```
if (depth > 36.238)
   delta = 100;
else
   System.out.println("WARNING: Delta is being reset to ZERO");
   delta = 0; // not part of the else clause!
```

The indentation (not to mention the logic of the code) implies that the variable `delta` is reset only when `depth` is less than 36.238. However, if a block is not used, the assignment statement that resets `delta` to zero is not governed by the `if-else` statement at all. It is executed in either case, which is clearly not what is intended.

A block statement can be used anywhere a single statement is called for in Java syntax. For example, the `if` portion of an `if-else` statement could be a block, or the `else` portion could be a block (as we saw in the `Guessing` program), or both parts could be block statements, as shown in the following example:

```
if (boxes != warehouse.getCount())
{
   System.out.println("Inventory and warehouse do NOT match.");
   System.out.println("Beginning inventory process again!");
   boxes = 0;
}
```

```
else
{
   System.out.println("Inventory and warehouse MATCH.");
   warehouse.ship();
}
```

In this `if-else` statement, the value of `boxes` is compared to a value obtained by calling the `getCount` method of the `warehouse` object (whatever that is). If they do not match exactly, two `println` statements and an assignment statement are executed. If they do match, a different message is printed and the `ship` method of `warehouse` is invoked.

The Conditional Operator

The Java *conditional operator* is similar to an `if-else` statement in some ways. It is a *ternary operator* because it requires three operands. The symbol for the conditional operator is usually written `?:`, but it is not like other operators in that the two symbols that make it up are always separated. The following is an example of an expression that contains the conditional operator.

```
(total > MAX) ? total + 1 : total * 2;
```

Preceding the `?` is a boolean condition. Following the `?` are two expressions separated by the `:` symbol. The entire conditional expression returns the value of the first expression if the condition is true, and returns the value of the second expression if the condition is false.

Keep in mind that this is an expression that returns a value, and usually we want to do something with that value, such as assign it to a variable:

```
total = (total > MAX) ? total + 1 : total * 2;
```

In many ways, the `?:` operator serves as an abbreviated `if-else` statement. The previous statement is functionally equivalent to, but sometimes more convenient than, the following:

```
if (total > MAX)
   total = total + 1;
else
   total = total * 2;
```

Now consider the declaration

```
int larger = (num1 > num2) ? num1 : num2;
```

If `num1` is greater than `num2`, the value of `num1` is returned and used to initialize the variable `larger`. If not, the value of `num2` is returned and used to initialize `larger`. Similarly, the following statement prints the smaller of the two values.

```
System.out.print("Smaller: " + ((num1 < num2) ? num1 : num2));
```

As we've seen, the conditional operator is occasionally helpful. However, it is not a replacement for an `if-else` statement because the operands to the `?:` operator are expressions, not necessarily full statements. And even when the conditional operator is a viable alternative, you should use it carefully, because it may be less readable than an `if-else` statement.

Nested `if` Statements

The statement executed as the result of an `if` statement could be another `if` statement. This situation is called a nested if. It allows us to make another decision after determining the results of a previous decision. The program in Listing 4.4, called `MinOfThree`, uses nested `if` statements to determine the smallest of three integer values entered by the user.

Carefully trace the logic of the `MinOfThree` program, using various input sets with the minimum value in all three positions, to see how it determines the lowest value.

An important situation arises with nested `if` statements. It may seem that an `else` clause after a nested `if` could apply to either `if` statement. Consider the following example:

```
if (code == 'R')
   if (height <= 20)
      System.out.println("Situation Normal");
   else
      System.out.println("Bravo!");
```

LISTING 4.4

```
//********************************************************************
//  MinOfThree.java              Java Foundations
//
//  Demonstrates the use of nested if statements.
//********************************************************************

import java.util.Scanner;

public class MinOfThree
{
   //-----------------------------------------------------------------
   // Reads three integers from the user and determines the smallest
   // value.
   //-----------------------------------------------------------------
```

LISTING 4.4 *continued*

```
   public static void main(String[] args)
   {
      int num1, num2, num3, min = 0;

      Scanner scan = new Scanner(System.in);

      System.out.println("Enter three integers: ");

      num1 = scan.nextInt();
      num2 = scan.nextInt();
      num3 = scan.nextInt();

      if (num1 < num2)
       if (num1 < num3)
          min = num1;
       else
           min = num3;

         else
         if (num2 < num3)
            min = num2;

         else
            min = num3;

         System.out.println("Minimum value: " + min);
   }
}
```

OUTPUT

```
Enter three integers:
43 26 69
Minimum value: 26
```

KEY CONCEPT

In a nested `if` statement, an `else` clause is matched to the closest unmatched `if` that preceded it.

Is the `else` clause matched to the inner `if` statement or the outer `if` statement? The indentation in this example implies that it is part of the inner `if` statement, and that is correct. An `else` clause is always matched to the closest unmatched `if` that preceded it. However, if we're not careful, we can easily mismatch it in our mind and misalign the indentation. This is another reason why accurate, consistent indentation is crucial.

Braces can be used to specify the `if` statement to which an `else` clause belongs. For example, if the previous example should have been structured so that the string "Bravo!" is printed if code is not equal to 'R', we could force that relationship (and properly indent) as follows:

```
if (code == 'R')
{
   if (height <= 20)
      System.out.println("Situation Normal");
}
else
   System.out.println("Bravo!");
```

By using the block statement in the first if statement, we establish that the else clause belongs to it.

4.3 Comparing Data

When comparing data using boolean expressions, it's important to understand some nuances that arise depending on the type of data being examined. Let's look at a few key situations.

Comparing Floats

An interesting situation occurs when we are comparing floating point data. Two floating point values are equal, according to the == operator, only if all the binary digits of their underlying representations match. If the compared values are the results of computation, it may be unlikely that they are exactly equal, even if they are close enough for the specific situation. Therefore, you should rarely use the equality operator (==) when comparing floating point values.

A better way to check for floating point equality is to compute the absolute value of the difference between the two values and compare the result to some tolerance level. For example, we may choose a tolerance level of 0.00001. If the two floating point values are so close that their difference is less than the tolerance, then we are willing to consider them equal. Comparing two floating point values, f1 and f2, could be accomplished as follows:

```
if (Math.abs(f1 - f2) < TOLERANCE)
   System.out.println("Essentially equal.");
```

The value of the constant TOLERANCE should be appropriate for the situation.

Comparing Characters

We know what it means when we say that one number is less than another, but what does it mean to say that one character is less than another? As we discussed

KEY CONCEPT
The relative order of characters in Java is defined by the Unicode character set.

in Chapter 2, characters in Java are based on the Unicode character set, which defines an ordering of all possible characters that can be used. Because the character `'a'` comes before the character `'b'` in the character set, we can say that `'a'` is less than `'b'`.

We can use the equality and relational operators on character data. For example, if two character variables `ch1` and `ch2` hold two characters, we might determine their relative ordering in the Unicode character set with an `if` statement as follows:

```
if (ch1 > ch2)
   System.out.println(ch1 + " is greater than " + ch2);
else
   System.out.println(ch1 + " is NOT greater than " + ch2);
```

The Unicode character set is structured so that all lowercase alphabetic characters (`'a'` through `'z'`) are contiguous and in alphabetical order. The same is true of uppercase alphabetic characters (`'A'` through `'Z'`) and of characters that represent digits (`'0'` through `'9'`). The digits precede the uppercase alphabetic characters, which precede the lowercase alphabetic characters. Before, after, and in between these groups are other characters. See the chart in Appendix C for details.

Comparing Objects

The Unicode relationships among characters make it easy to sort characters and strings of characters. If you have a list of names, for instance, you can put them in alphabetical order based on the inherent relationships among characters in the character set.

However, you should not use the equality or relational operators to compare `String` objects. The `String` class contains a method called `equals` that returns a `boolean` value that is true if the two strings being compared contain exactly the same characters, and is false otherwise. Here is an example:

```
if (name1.equals(name2))
   System.out.println("The names are the same.");
else
   System.out.println("The names are not the same.");
```

KEY CONCEPT
The `compareTo` method can be used to determine the relative order of strings.

Assuming that `name1` and `name2` are `String` objects, this condition determines whether the characters they contain are an exact match. Because both objects were created from the `String` class, they both respond to the `equals` message. Therefore, the condition could have been written as `name2.equals(name1)` and the same result would have been obtained.

It is valid to test the condition (`name1 == name2`), but that actually tests to see whether both reference variables refer to the same `String` object. For any object, the `==` operator tests whether two reference variables are aliases of each other (whether they contain the same address). That's different from testing to see whether two different `String` objects contain the same characters.

An interesting issue related to string comparisons is the fact that Java creates a unique object for string literals only when needed. Keep in mind that a string literal (such as `"Howdy"`) is a convenience and is actually a shorthand technique for creating a `String` object. If the string literal `"Hi"` is used multiple times in a method, Java creates only one `String` object to represent it. Therefore, in the following code, the conditions of both `if` statements are true.

```
String str = "software";
if (str == "software")
   System.out.println("References are the same");
if (str.equals("software"))
   System.out.println("Characters are the same");
```

The first time the string literal `"software"` is used, a `String` object is created to represent it, and the reference variable `str` is set to its address. Each subsequent time the literal is used, the original object is referenced.

COMMON ERROR

For reasons described in this section, it's valid to use the `==` operator to compare two string objects. However, usually a programmer is interested in seeing whether two different objects contain the same characters, which is not what the `==` operator determines. Remember to use the `equals` method when comparing the content of strings.

To determine the relative ordering of two strings, use the `compareTo` method of the `String` class. The `compareTo` method is more versatile than the `equals` method. Instead of returning a `boolean` value, the `compareTo` method returns an integer. The return value is negative if the `String` object through which the method is invoked precedes (is less than) the string that is passed in as a parameter. The return value is zero if the two strings contain the same characters. The return value is positive if the `String` object through which the method is invoked follows (is greater than) the string that is passed in as a parameter. For example:

```
int result = name1.compareTo(name2);
if (result < 0)
   System.out.println(name1 + " comes before " + name2);
else
   if (result == 0)
      System.out.println("The names are equal.");
   else
      System.out.println(name1 + " follows " + name2);
```

Keep in mind that comparing characters and strings is based on the Unicode character set (see Appendix C) This is called a lexicographic ordering. If all alphabetic characters are in the same case (upper or lower), the *lexicographic ordering* will be alphabetic ordering as well. However, when comparing two strings, such as `"able"` and `"Baker"`, the `compareTo` method will conclude that `"Baker"` comes first because all of the uppercase letters come before all of the lowercase letters in the Unicode character set. If a string is the prefix of a longer string, it is considered to precede the longer string. For example, when comparing two strings such as `"horse"` and `"horsefly"`, the `compareTo` method will conclude that `"horse"` comes first.

4.4 The `switch` Statement

Another conditional statement in Java, called the *switch statement*, causes the executing program to follow one of several paths based on a single value. We also discuss the *break statement* in this section because it is generally used with a `switch` statement.

The `switch` statement evaluates an expression to determine a value and then matches that value with one of several possible *cases*. Each case has statements associated with it. After evaluating the expression, control jumps to the statement associated with the first case that matches the value. Consider the following example:

```
switch (idChar)
{
   case 'A':
      aCount = aCount + 1;
      break;
   case 'B':
      bCount = bCount + 1;
      break;
```

```
      case 'C':
         cCount = cCount + 1;
         break;
      default:
         System.out.println("Error in Identification Character.");
   }
```

First, the expression is evaluated. In this example, the expression is a simple `char` variable. Execution then transfers to the first statement identified by the case value that matches the result of the expression. Therefore, if `idChar` contains an `'A'`, the variable `aCount` is incremented. If it contains a `'B'`, the case for `'A'` is skipped, and processing continues where `bCount` is incremented.

If no case value matches that of the expression, execution continues with the optional *default case*, indicated by the reserved word `default`. If no default case exists, no statements in the `switch` statement are executed, and processing continues with the statement after the `switch` statement. It is often a good idea to include a default case, even if you don't expect it to be executed.

When a `break` statement is encountered, processing jumps to the statement following the `switch` statement. A `break` statement is usually used to break out of each case of a `switch` statement. Without a `break` statement, processing continues into the next case of the `switch`. Therefore, if the `break` statement at the end of the `'A'` case in the previous example were not there, both the `aCount` variable and the `bCount` variable would be incremented when `idChar` contained an `'A'`. Usually we want to perform only one case, so a `break` statement is almost always used. Occasionally, though, the "pass through" feature comes in handy.

COMMON ERROR

Forgetting a `break` statement at the end of a `switch` case is a common error. Usually you want each case to be mutually exclusive, so you'll want to include a `break` statement at the end of each case. It's unfortunate that the usual case requires the extra line of code, but occasionally it is convenient to omit it.

KEY CONCEPT

A `break` statement is usually used at the end of each case alternative of a `switch` statement.

The expression evaluated at the beginning of a `switch` statement must be of type `char`, `byte`, `short`, or `int`. In particular, it cannot be a `boolean`, a floating point value, or a `String`. Furthermore, the value of each case must be a constant; it cannot be a variable or other expression.

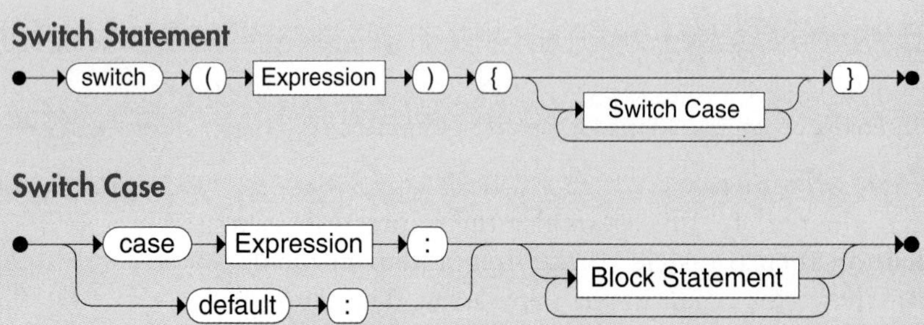

The `switch` statement evaluates the initial Expression and matches its value with one of the cases. Processing continues with the Statement corresponding to that case. The optional `default` case will be executed if no other case matches.

Example:

```
switch (numValues)
{
   case 0:
      System.out.println("No values were entered.");
      break;
   case 1:
      System.out.println("One value was entered.");
      break;
   case 2:
      System.out.println("Two values were entered.");
      break;
   default:
      System.out.println("Too many values were entered.");
}
```

Note that the implicit boolean condition of a `switch` statement is based on equality. The expression at the beginning of the statement is compared to each case value to determine which one it equals. A `switch` statement cannot be used to determine other relational operations (such as less than), unless some preliminary processing is done. For example, the `GradeReport` program in Listing 4.5 prints a comment based on a numeric grade that is entered by the user.

In `GradeReport`, the category of the grade is determined by dividing the grade by 10 using integer division, which results in an integer value between 0 and 10 (assuming a valid grade is entered). This result is used as the expression of the `switch`, which prints various messages for grades 60 or higher and a default sentence for all other values.

LISTING 4.5

```
//********************************************************************
//  GradeReport.java       Java Foundations
//
//  Demonstrates the use of a switch statement.
//********************************************************************

import java.util.Scanner;

public class GradeReport
{
   //-----------------------------------------------------------------
   // Reads a grade from the user and prints comments accordingly.
   //-----------------------------------------------------------------
   public static void main(String[] args)
   {
      int grade, category;

      Scanner scan = new Scanner(System.in);

      System.out.print("Enter a numeric grade (0 to 100): ");
      grade = scan.nextInt();

      category = grade / 10;

      System.out.print("That grade is ");

      switch (category)
      {
         case 10:
            System.out.println("a perfect score. Well done.");
            break;
         case 9:
            System.out.println("well above average. Excellent.");
            break;
         case 8:
            System.out.println("above average. Nice job.");
            break;
         case 7:
            System.out.println("average.");
            break;
         case 6:
            System.out.print("below average. Please see the ");
            System.out.println("instructor for assistance.");
            break;
```

LISTING 4.5 *continued*

```
         default:
            System.out.println("not passing.");
      }
   }
}
```

OUTPUT

```
Enter a numeric grade (0 to 100): 87
That grade is above average. Nice job.
```

Note that any `switch` statement could be implemented as a set of nested `if` statements. However, *nested* `if` *statements* quickly become difficult for a human reader to understand and are error prone to implement and debug. But because a `switch` can evaluate only equality, nested `if` statements are sometimes necessary. It depends on the situation.

4.5 The `while` Statement

As we discussed in the introduction to this chapter, a repetition statement (or loop) allows us to execute another statement multiple times. A *while statement* is a loop that evaluates a boolean condition just as an `if` statement does and executes a statement (called the *body* of the loop) if the condition is true. However, unlike the `if` statement, after the body is executed, the condition is evaluated again. If it is still true, the body is executed again. This repetition continues until the condition becomes false; then processing continues with the statement after the body of the `while` loop. Figure 4.7 shows this processing.

KEY CONCEPT

A `while` statement executes the same statement repeatedly until its condition becomes false.

The following loop prints the values from 1 to 5. Each iteration through the loop prints one value and then increments the counter.

```
int count = 1;
while (count <= 5)
{
   System.out.println(count);
   count++;
}
```

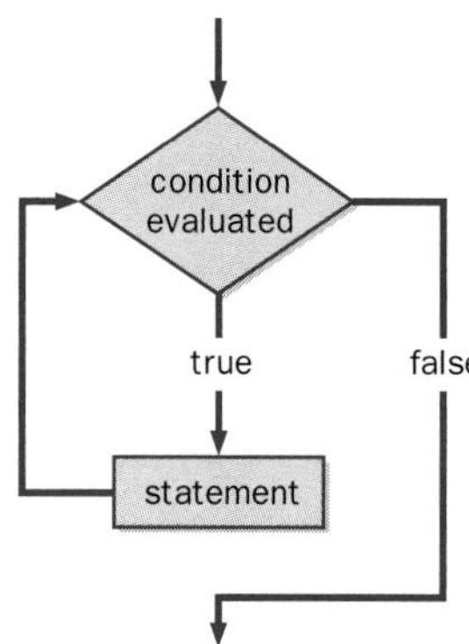

FIGURE 4.7 The logic of a `while` loop

Note that the body of the `while` loop is a block containing two statements. The entire block is repeated on each iteration of the loop.

COMMON ERROR

It's easy to produce an off-by-one error, especially when dealing with loops. In the previous example, `count` was initialized to 1 and the condition was true if `count` is less than or equal to 5. The initial value of the variable and the details of the condition work together to determine exactly how many times the loop body will execute and what the output will be. Slight changes in either (initialize it to 0, for instance, or use the < operator in the condition) will produce different results. Carefully analyze the logic of your loops!

Let's look at another program that uses a `while` loop. The `Average` program shown in Listing 4.6 reads a series of integer values from the user, sums them up, and computes their average.

We don't know how many values the user may enter, so we need to have a way to indicate that the user is finished entering numbers. In this program, we designate zero to be a *sentinel value* that indicates the end of the input. The `while` loop continues to process input values until the user enters zero. This assumes that zero is not one of the valid numbers that should contribute to the average. A sentinel value must always be outside the normal range of values entered.

While Statement

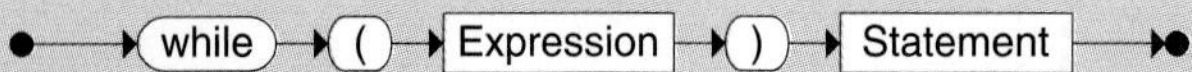

The `while` loop repeatedly executes the specified Statement as long as the boolean Expression is true. The Expression is evaluated first; therefore, the Statement might not be executed at all. The Expression is evaluated again after each execution of the Statement until the Expression becomes false.

Example:

```
while (total > max)
{
   total = total / 2;
   System.out.println("Current total: " + total);
}
```

LISTING 4.6

```
//********************************************************************
//  Average.java       Java Foundations
//
//  Demonstrates the use of a while loop, a sentinel value, and a
//  running sum.
//********************************************************************

import java.text.DecimalFormat;
import java.util.Scanner;

public class Average
{
   //-----------------------------------------------------------------
   // Computes the average of a set of values entered by the user.
   // The running sum is printed as the numbers are entered.
   //-----------------------------------------------------------------
   public static void main(String[] args)
   {
      int sum = 0, value, count = 0;
      double average;
      Scanner scan = new Scanner(System.in);
      System.out.print("Enter an integer (0 to quit): ");
      value = scan.nextInt();
```

LISTING 4.6 *continued*

```
      while (value != 0) // sentinel value of 0 to terminate loop
      {
         count++;

         sum += value;

         System.out.println("The sum so far is " + sum);

         System.out.print("Enter an integer (0 to quit): ");
         value = scan.nextInt();
      }
      System.out.println();

      if (count == 0)
         System.out.println("No values were entered.");
      else
      {
         average = (double)sum / count;
         DecimalFormat fmt = new DecimalFormat("0.###");
         System.out.println("The average is " + fmt.format(average));
      }
   }
}
```

OUTPUT

```
Enter an integer (0 to quit): 25
The sum so far is 25
Enter an integer (0 to quit): 44
The sum so far is 69
Enter an integer (0 to quit): -14
The sum so far is 55
Enter an integer (0 to quit): 83
The sum so far is 138
Enter an integer (0 to quit): 69
The sum so far is 207
Enter an integer (0 to quit): -37
The sum so far is 170
Enter an integer (0 to quit): 116
The sum so far is 286
Enter an integer (0 to quit): 0

The average is 40.857
```

While-Loop


```
while = (input <= 0)
{
   System.out.println("Input must be positive.")
   input = scan.nextInt();
}
```

Note that in the `Average` program, a variable called `sum` is used to maintain a *running sum*, which means it is the sum of the values entered thus far. The variable `sum` is initialized to zero, and each value read is added to and stored back into `sum`.

We also have to count the number of values that are entered so that after the loop concludes, we can divide by the appropriate value to compute the average. Note that the sentinel value is not counted. Consider the unusual situation in which the user immediately enters the sentinel value before entering any valid values. The `if` statement at the end of the program avoids a divide-by-zero error.

VideoNote
Examples using `while` loops

Let's examine yet another program that uses a `while` loop. The `WinPercentage` program shown in Listing 4.7 computes the winning percentage of a sports team based on the number of games won.

LISTING 4.7

```
//********************************************************************
//  WinPercentage.java        Java Foundations
//
//  Demonstrates the use of a while loop for input validation.
//********************************************************************

import java.text.NumberFormat;
import java.util.Scanner;

public class WinPercentage
{
```

LISTING 4.7 *continued*

```
   //-----------------------------------------------------------------
   // Computes the percentage of games won by a team.
   //-----------------------------------------------------------------

   public static void main(String[] args)
   {
      final int NUM_GAMES = 12;
      int won;
      double ratio;
      Scanner scan = new Scanner(System.in);

      System.out.print("Enter the number of games won (0 to "
                       + NUM_GAMES + "): ");
      won = scan.nextInt();

      while (won < 0 || won > NUM_GAMES)
      {
         System.out.print("Invalid input. Please reenter: ");
         won = scan.nextInt();
      }

      ratio = (double)won / NUM_GAMES;

      NumberFormat fmt = NumberFormat.getPercentInstance();

      System.out.println();
      System.out.println("Winning percentage: " + fmt.format(ratio));
   }
}
```

OUTPUT

```
Enter the number of games won (0 to 12): -5
Invalid input. Please reenter: 13
Invalid input. Please reenter: 7
Winning percentage: 58%
```

We use a `while` loop in the `WinPercentage` program for *input validation*, which means we guarantee that the user enters a value that we consider to be valid before continuing. In this example, that means that the value entered representing the number of games won must be greater than or equal to zero and less than or equal to the total number of games played. The `while` loop continues to execute, repeatedly prompting the user for valid input, until the entered number is indeed valid. The body of the `while` loop will not be executed at all if the user enters a valid value the first time.

We generally want our programs to be *robust*, which means that they handle potential problems as elegantly as possible. Validating input data and avoiding errors such as dividing by zero are situations that we should consciously address when designing a program. Loops and conditionals help us recognize and deal with such situations.

Infinite Loops

It is the programmer's responsibility to ensure that the condition of a loop will eventually become false. If it doesn't, the loop body will execute forever, or at least until the program is interrupted. This situation, which is referred to as an *infinite loop*, is a common mistake.

The following is an example of an infinite loop.

```
int count = 1;
while (count <= 25) // Warning: this is an infinite loop!
{
   System.out.println(count);
   count = count - 1;
}
```

If you execute this loop, you should be prepared to interrupt it. On most systems, pressing the Control-C keyboard combination (hold down the Control key and press C) terminates a running program.

KEY CONCEPT
We must design our programs carefully to avoid infinite loops.

In this example, the initial value of `count` is 1 and it is decremented in the loop body. The `while` loop will continue as long as `count` is less than or equal to 25. Because `count` gets smaller with each iteration, the condition will be true always, or at least until the value of `count` gets so small that an underflow error occurs. The point is that the logic of the code is clearly wrong.

Let's look at some other examples of infinite loops. First, consider

```
int count = 1;
while (count != 50) // infinite loop
   count += 2;
```

In this code fragment, the variable `count` is initialized to 1 and is moving in a positive direction. However, note that it is being incremented by 2 each time. This loop will never terminate, because `count` will never equal 50. It begins at 1 and then changes to 3, then to 5, and so on. Eventually it reaches 49 and then changes to 51, then to 53, and continues forever.

Now consider the following situation:

```
double num = 1.0;
while (num != 0.0) // infinite loop
   num = num - 0.1;
```

Once again, the value of the loop control variable seems to be moving in the correct direction. And, in fact, it seems like `num` will eventually take on the value `0.0`. However, this is an infinite loop (on most computer systems) because `num` will never have a value *exactly* equal to `0.0`. This situation is similar to one we discussed earlier in this chapter when we explored the idea of comparing floating point values in the condition of an `if` statement. Because of the way the values are represented in binary, minute computational errors occur internally, making it problematic to compare two floating point values for equality.

Nested Loops

The body of a loop can contain another loop. This situation is called a *nested loop*. Keep in mind that for each iteration of the outer loop, the inner loop executes completely. Consider the following code fragment. How many times does the string `"Here again"` get printed?

```
int count1 = 1, count2;
while (count1 <= 10)
{
   count2 = 1;
   while (count2 <= 50)
   {
      System.out.println("Here again");
      count2++;
   }
   count1++;
}
```

The `println` statement is inside the inner loop. The outer loop executes 10 times, as `count1` iterates between 1 and 10. The inner loop executes 50 times, as `count2` iterates between 1 and 50. For each iteration of the outer loop, the inner loop executes completely. Therefore, the `println` statement is executed 500 times.

As with any loop situation, we must be careful to scrutinize the conditions of the loops and the initializations of variables. Let's consider some small changes to this code. What if the condition of the outer loop were (`count1 < 10`) instead of (`count1 < = 10`)? How would that change the total number of lines printed? Well, the outer loop would execute 9 times instead of 10, so the `println` statement would be executed 450 times. What if the outer loop were left as it was originally defined, but `count2` were initialized to 10 instead of 1 before the inner loop? The inner loop would then execute 40 times instead of 50, so the total number of lines printed would be 400.

Let's look at another example that uses a nested loop. A *palindrome* is a string of characters that reads the same both forward and backward. For example, the following strings are palindromes:

- radar
- drab bard
- ab cde xxxx edc ba
- kayak
- deified
- able was I ere I saw elba

Note that some palindromes have an even number of characters, whereas others have an odd number of characters. The `PalindromeTester` program shown in Listing 4.8 tests to see whether a string is a palindrome. The user may test as many strings as desired.

The code for `PalindromeTester` contains two loops, one inside the other. The outer loop controls how many strings are tested, and the inner loop scans through each string, character by character, until it determines whether the string is a palindrome.

The variables `left` and `right` store the indexes of two characters. They initially indicate the characters on either end of the string. Each iteration of the inner loop compares the two characters indicated by `left` and `right`. We fall out of the inner loop either when the characters don't match, meaning the string is not a palindrome, or when the value of `left` becomes equal to or greater than the value of `right`, which means the entire string has been tested and it is a palindrome.

Note that the following phrases would not be considered palindromes by the current version of the program:

- A man, a plan, a canal, Panama.
- Dennis and Edna sinned.
- Rise to vote, sir.
- Doom an evil deed, liven a mood.
- Go hang a salami; I'm a lasagna hog.

These strings fail to meet our current criteria for a palindrome because of the spaces, punctuation marks, and changes in uppercase and lowercase. However, if these characteristics were removed or ignored, these strings would read the same forward and backward. Consider how the program could be changed to handle these situations. These modifications are included as a programming project at the end of this chapter.

LISTING 4.8

```
//********************************************************************
//  PalindromeTester.java        Java Foundations
//
//  Demonstrates the use of nested while loops.
//********************************************************************

import java.util.Scanner;

public class PalindromeTester
{
   //-----------------------------------------------------------------
   // Tests strings to see if they are palindromes.
   //-----------------------------------------------------------------
   public static void main(String[] args)
   {
      String str, another = "y";
      int left, right;

      Scanner scan = new Scanner(System.in);

      while (another.equalsIgnoreCase("y")) // allows y or Y
      {
         System.out.println("Enter a potential palindrome:");
         str = scan.nextLine();

         left = 0;
         right = str.length() - 1;

         while (str.charAt(left) == str.charAt(right) && left < right)
         {
            left++;
            right--;
         }

         System.out.println();
         if (left < right)
            System.out.println("That string is NOT a palindrome.");
         else
            System.out.println("That string IS a palindrome.");
         System.out.println();
         System.out.print("Test another palindrome (y/n)? ");
         another = scan.nextLine();
      }
   }
}
```

LISTING 4.8 *continued*

OUTPUT

```
Enter a potential palindrome:
radar

That string IS a palindrome.

Test another palindrome (y/n)? y
Enter a potential palindrome:
able was I ere I saw elba

That string IS a palindrome.

Test another palindrome (y/n)? y
Enter a potential palindrome:
abc6996cba

That string IS a palindrome.

Test another palindrome (y/n)? y
Enter a potential palindrome:
abracadabra

That string is NOT a palindrome.

Test another palindrome (y/n)? n
```

Other Loop Controls

We've seen how the `break` statement can be used to break out of the cases of a `switch` statement. The `break` statement can also be placed in the body of any loop, even though this is usually inappropriate. Its effect on a loop is similar to its effect on a `switch` statement. The execution of the loop is stopped, and the statement following the loop is executed.

It is never necessary to use a `break` statement in a loop. An equivalent loop can always be written without it. Because the `break` statement causes program flow to jump from one place to another, using a `break` in a loop is not good practice. Its use is tolerated in a `switch` statement because an equivalent `switch` statement cannot be written without it. However, you can and should avoid using it in a loop.

A *continue statement* has a similar effect on loop processing. The `continue` statement is similar to a `break`, but the loop condition is evaluated again, and the loop body is executed again if it is still true. Like the `break` statement, the `continue` statement can always be avoided in a loop—and for the same reasons, it should be.

4.6 Iterators

An *iterator* is an object that has methods that allow you to process a collection of items one at a time. That is, an iterator lets you step through each item and interact with it as needed. For example, your goal may be to compute the dues for each member of a club, or print the distinct parts of a URL, or process a group of returned library books. An iterator provides a consistent and simple mechanism for systematically processing a group of items. This processing is inherently repetitive, so it ties into our discussion of loops.

KEY CONCEPT
An iterator is an object that helps you process a group of related items.

Technically, an iterator object in Java is defined using the `Iterator` interface, which is discussed in Chapter 9. For now, it is helpful simply to know that such objects exist and that they can make the processing of a collection of items easier.

Every iterator object has a method called `hasNext` that returns a `boolean` value indicating whether there is at least one more item to process. Therefore, the `hasNext` method can be used as a condition of a loop to control the processing of each item. An iterator also has a method called `next` to retrieve the next item in the collection to process.

There are several classes in the Java standard class library that define iterator objects. One of these is `Scanner`, a class we've used several times in previous examples to help us read data from the user. The `hasNext` method of the `Scanner` class returns true if there is another input token to process. And it has a `next` method that returns the next input token as a string.

The `Scanner` class also has specific variations of the `hasNext` method, such as the `hasNextInt` and `hasNextDouble` methods, which allow you to determine whether the next input token is a particular type. Likewise, there are variations of the `next` method, such as `nextInt` and `nextDouble`, that retrieve values of specific types.

When reading input interactively from the standard input stream, the `hasNext` method of the `Scanner` class will wait until there is input available and then return true. That is, interactive input read from the keyboard is always thought to have more data to process—it just hasn't arrived yet (until the user types it in). That's why in previous examples we've used special sentinel values to determine the end of interactive input.

However, the fact that a `Scanner` object is an iterator is particularly helpful when the scanner is being used to process input from a source that has a specific end point, such as processing the lines of a data file or processing the parts of a character string. Let's examine an example of this type of processing.

Reading Text Files

Suppose we have an input file called `websites.inp` that contains a list of Web page addresses (Uniform Resource Locators, or URLs) that we want to process in some way. The following are the first few lines of `websites.inp`:

```
www.google.com
newsyllabus.com/about
java.sun.com/j2se/6.0
www.linux.org/info/gnu.html
technorati.com/search/java/
www.cs.vt.edu/undergraduates/honors_degree.html
```

The program shown in Listing 4.9 reads the URLs from this file and dissects them to show the various parts of the path. It uses a `Scanner` object to process the input. In fact, the program uses multiple `Scanner` objects—one to read the lines of the data file, and another to process each URL string.

LISTING 4.9

```
//********************************************************************
//  URLDissector.java       Java Foundations
//
//  Demonstrates the use of Scanner to read file input and parse it
//  using alternative delimiters.
//********************************************************************

import java.util.Scanner;
import java.io.*;

public class URLDissector
{
   //-----------------------------------------------------------------
   // Reads urls from a file and prints their path components.
   //-----------------------------------------------------------------
   public static void main(String[] args) throws IOException
   {
      String url;
      Scanner fileScan, urlScan;

      fileScan = new Scanner(new File("websites.inp"));

      // Read and process each line of the file
```

LISTING 4.9 *continued*

```
      while (fileScan.hasNext())
      {
         url = fileScan.nextLine();
         System.out.println("URL: " + url);

         urlScan = new Scanner(url);
         urlScan.useDelimiter("/");

         // Print each part of the url

         while (urlScan.hasNext())
            System.out.println(" " + urlScan.next());
         System.out.println();
      }
   }
}
```

OUTPUT

```
URL: www.google.com
   www.google.com

URL: newsyllabus.com/about
   newsyllabus.com
   about

URL: java.sun.com/j2se/6.0
   java.sun.com
   j2se
   6.0

URL: www.linux.org/info/gnu.html
   www.linux.org
   info
   gnu.html

URL: technorati.com/search/java/
   technorati.com
   search
   java

URL: www.cs.vt.edu/undergraduates/honors_degree.html
   www.cs.vt.edu
   undergraduates
   honors_degree.html
```

There are two `while` loops in this program, one nested within the other. The outer loop processes each line in the file, and the inner loop processes each token in the current line.

The variable `fileScan` is created as a scanner that operates on the input file named `urls.inp`. Instead of passing `System.in` into the `Scanner` constructor, we instantiate a `File` object that represents the input file and pass it into the `Scanner` constructor. At that point, the `fileScan` object is ready to read and process input from the input file.

If for some reason there is a problem finding or opening the input file, the attempt to create a `File` object will throw an `IOException`, which is why we've added the `throws IOException` clause to the `main` method header. Processing exceptions is discussed further in Chapter 10.

The body of the outer `while` loop will be executed as long as the `hasNext` method of the input file scanner returns true—that is, as long as there is more input in the data file to process. Each iteration through the loop reads one line (one URL) from the input file and prints it out.

For each URL, a new `Scanner` object is set up to parse the pieces of the URL string, which is passed into the `Scanner` constructor when instantiating the `urlScan` object. The inner `while` loop prints each token of the URL on a separate line.

Recall that, by default, a `Scanner` object assumes that white space (spaces, tabs, and new lines) is used as the delimiter to separate the input tokens. Using white space delimiters works in this example for the scanner that is reading each line of the input file. However, if the default delimiters do not suffice, as in the processing of a URL in this example, they can be changed.

KEY CONCEPT

The delimiters used to separate tokens in a `Scanner` object can be explicitly set as needed.

In this case, we are interested in each part of the path separated by the slash (/) character. A call to the `useDelimiter` method of the scanner sets the delimiter to a slash prior to processing the URL string.

If you want to use more than one alternate delimiter character, or if you want to parse the input in more complex ways, the `Scanner` class can process patterns called regular *expressions*, which are discussed in Appendix H.

4.7 The `do` Statement

The *do statement* is similar to the `while` statement in that it executes the loop body until a condition becomes false. However, unlike the `while` loop, whose condition is evaluated *before* the body is executed, the condition of a `do` loop is evaluated *after* the loop body executes. Syntactically, the condition in a `do` loop is written after the loop body to reflect this processing. The body of a `do` loop is always executed at least once, whereas with a `while` loop, the body might not be executed at all (if the condition is initially false). Figure 4.8 shows the processing of a `do` loop.

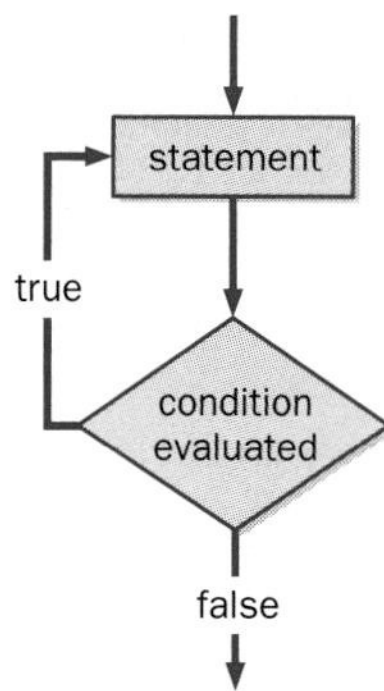

FIGURE 4.8 The logic of a do loop

The following code prints the numbers from 1 to 5 using a do loop. Compare this code with the similar example earlier in this chapter that uses a while loop to accomplish the same task.

KEY CONCEPT
A do statement executes its loop body at least once.

```
int count = 0;
do
{
   count++;
   System.out.println(count);
}
while (count < 5);
```

Do Statement

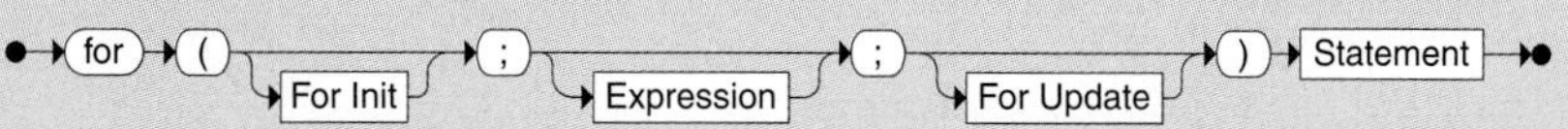

The do loop repeatedly executes the specified Statement as long as the boolean Expression is true. The Statement is executed at least once, and then the Expression is evaluated to determine whether the Statement should be executed again.

Example:

```
do
{
   System.out.print("Enter a word:");
   word = scan.next();
   System.out.println(word);
}
while (!word.equals("quit"));
```

A do loop begins simply with the reserved word do. The body of the do loop continues until the *while clause* that contains the boolean condition that determines whether the loop body will be executed again. Sometimes it is difficult to determine whether a line of code that begins with the reserved word while is the beginning of a while loop or the end of a do loop.

Let's look at another example of the do loop. The program called ReverseNumber, shown in Listing 4.10, reads an integer from the user and reverses its digits mathematically.

LISTING 4.10

```
//********************************************************************
//  ReverseNumber.java       Java Foundations
//
//  Demonstrates the use of a do loop.
//********************************************************************

import java.util.Scanner;
public class ReverseNumber
{
   //-----------------------------------------------------------------
   // Reverses the digits of an integer mathematically.
   //-----------------------------------------------------------------
   public static void main(String[] args)
   {
      int number, lastDigit, reverse = 0;

      Scanner scan = new Scanner(System.in);

      System.out.print("Enter a positive integer: ");
      number = scan.nextInt();

      do
      {
         lastDigit = number % 10;
         reverse = (reverse * 10) + lastDigit;
         number = number / 10;
      }
      while (number > 0);

      System.out.println("That number reversed is " + reverse);
   }
}
```

LISTING 4.10 *continued*

OUTPUT

```
Enter a positive integer: 2896
That number reversed is 6982
```

The `do` loop in the `ReverseNumber` program uses the remainder operation to determine the digit in the 1s position, adds it into the reversed number, and then truncates that digit from the original number using integer division. The `do` loop terminates when we run out of digits to process, which corresponds to the point when the variable `number` reaches the value zero. Carefully trace the logic of this program with a few examples to see how it works.

If you know you want to perform the body of a loop at least once, then you probably want to use a `do` statement. A `do` loop has many of the same properties as a `while` statement, so it must also be checked for termination conditions to avoid infinite loops.

4.8 The `for` Statement

The `while` statement and the `do` statement are good to use when you don't initially know how many times you want to execute the loop body. The *for statement* is another repetition statement that is particularly well suited for executing the body of a loop a specific number of times that can be determined before the loop is executed.

The following code prints the numbers 1 through 5 using a `for` loop, just as we did using a `while` loop and a `do` loop in previous examples.

> **KEY CONCEPT**
> A `for` statement is generally used when a loop will be executed a set number of times.

```
for (int count=1; count <= 5; count++)
   System.out.println(count);
```

The header of a `for` loop contains three parts separated by semicolons. Before the loop begins, the first part of the header, called the *initialization*, is executed. The second part of the header is the boolean condition, which is evaluated before the loop body (like the `while` loop). If true, the body of the loop is executed, followed by the execution of the third part of the header, which is called the *increment*. Note that the initialization part is executed only once, but the increment part is executed after each iteration of the loop. Figure 4.9 shows this processing.

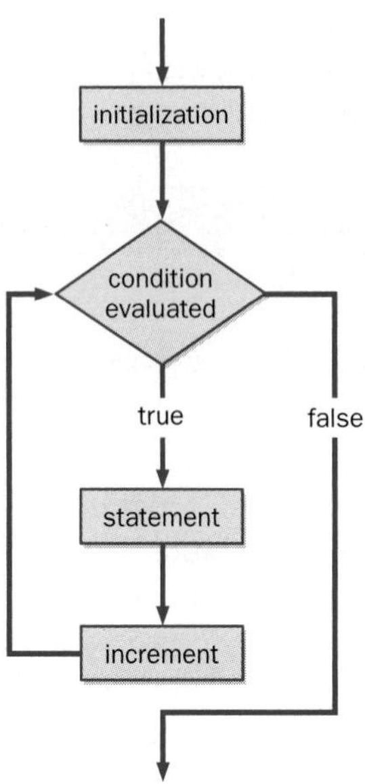

FIGURE 4.9 The logic of a `for` loop

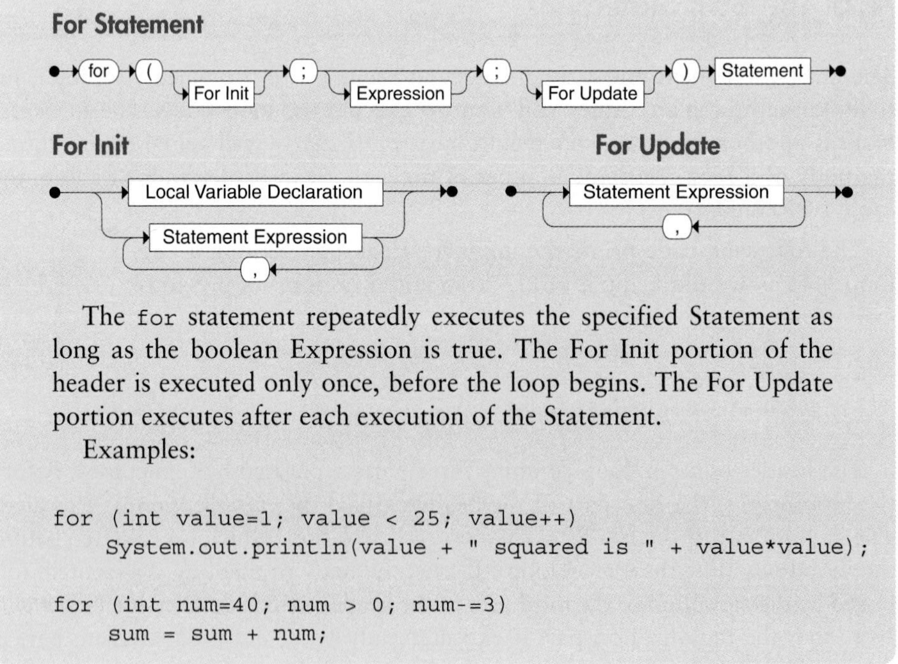

The `for` statement repeatedly executes the specified Statement as long as the boolean Expression is true. The For Init portion of the header is executed only once, before the loop begins. The For Update portion executes after each execution of the Statement.

Examples:

```
for (int value=1; value < 25; value++)
   System.out.println(value + " squared is " + value*value);

for (int num=40; num > 0; num-=3)
   sum = sum + num;
```

A `for` loop can be a bit tricky to read until you get used to it. The execution of the code doesn't follow a top-to-bottom, left-to-right reading. The increment code executes after the body of the loop, even though it is in the header.

In this example, the initialization portion of the `for` loop header is used to declare the variable `count` as well as to give it an initial value. We are not required to declare a variable there, but it is a common practice in situations where the variable is not needed outside of the loop. Because `count` is declared in the `for` loop header, it exists only inside the loop and cannot be referenced elsewhere.

The loop control variable is set up, checked, and modified by the actions in the `for` loop header. It can be referenced inside the loop body, but it should not be modified except by the actions defined in the loop header.

Despite its name, the increment portion of the `for` loop header could actually decrement a value rather than increment it. For example, the following loop prints the integer values from 100 down to 1.

```
for (int num = 100; num > 0; num--)
   System.out.println(num);
```

In fact, the increment portion of the `for` loop could perform any calculation, not just a simple increment or decrement. Consider the program shown in Listing 4.11, which prints multiples of a particular value up to a particular limit.

LISTING 4.11

```
//********************************************************************
//  Multiples.java       Java Foundations
//
//  Demonstrates the use of a for loop.
//********************************************************************

import java.util.Scanner;

public class Multiples
{
   //-----------------------------------------------------------------
   // Prints multiples of a user-specified number up to a user-
   // specified limit.
   //-----------------------------------------------------------------
   public static void main(String[] args)
   {
      final int PER_LINE = 5;
      int value, limit, mult, count = 0;
```

LISTING 4.11 *continued*

```
      Scanner scan = new Scanner(System.in);

      System.out.print("Enter a positive value: ");
      value = scan.nextInt();

      System.out.print("Enter an upper limit: ");
      limit = scan.nextInt();
      System.out.println();
      System.out.println("The multiples of " + value + " between " +
                         value + " and " + limit + " (inclusive) are:");

      for (mult = value; mult <= limit; mult += value)
      {
         System.out.print(mult + "\t");

         // Print a specific number of values per line of output

         count++;
         if (count % PER_LINE == 0)
            System.out.println();
      }
   }
}
```

OUTPUT

```
Enter a positive value: 7
Enter an upper limit: 400

The multiples of 7 between 7 and 400 (inclusive) are:
7       14      21      28      35
42      49      56      63      70
77      84      91      98      105
112     119     126     133     140
147     154     161     168     175
182     189     196     203     210
217     224     231     238     245
252     259     266     273     280
287     294     301     308     315
322     329     336     343     350
357     364     371     378     385
392     399
```

The increment portion of the for loop in the Multiples program adds the value entered by the user after each iteration. The number of values printed per line is controlled by counting the values printed and then moving to the next line whenever count is evenly divisible by the PER_LINE constant.

VideoNote
Examples using for loops

The Stars program in Listing 4.12 shows the use of nested for loops. The output is a triangle shape made of asterisk characters. The outer loop executes exactly 10 times. Each iteration of the outer loop prints one line of the output. The inner loop performs a different number of iterations depending on the line value controlled by the outer loop. Each iteration of the inner loop prints one star on the current line. Writing programs that print variations on this triangle configuration are included in the programming projects at the end of the chapter.

LISTING 4.12

```
//********************************************************************
//  Stars.java       Java Foundations
//
//  Demonstrates the use of nested for loops.
//********************************************************************

public class Stars
{
   //-----------------------------------------------------------------
   // Prints a triangle shape using asterisk (star) characters.
   //-----------------------------------------------------------------
   public static void main(String[] args)
   {
      final int MAX_ROWS = 10;

      for (int row = 1; row <= MAX_ROWS; row++)
      {
         for (int star = 1; star <= row; star++)
            System.out.print("*");

         System.out.println();
      }
   }
}
```

LISTING 4.12 *continued*

OUTPUT

```
*
**
***
****
*****
******
*******
********
*********
**********
```

Iterators and `for` Loops

In Section 4.6 we discussed the fact that some objects are considered to be iterators, which have `hasNext` and `next` methods to process each item from a group. If an object has implemented the `Iterable` interface, then we can use a variation of the `for` loop to process items using a simplified syntax. For example, if `bookList` is an `Iterable` object that contains `Book` objects, we can use a `for` loop to process each `Book` object as follows:

```
for (Book myBook : bookList)
   System.out.println (myBook);
```

This version of the `for` loop is referred to as a *for–each statement*. It processes each object in the iterator in turn. It is equivalent to the following:

```
Book myBook;
while (bookList.hasNext())
{
   myBook = bookList.next();
   System.out.println(myBook);
}
```

The `Scanner` class is an `Iterator` but is not `Iterable`. Therefore, it has the `hasNext` and `next` methods but cannot be used with this version of the `for` loop. On the other hand, arrays, which are discussed in Chapter 7, are `Iterable`. We use the for–each loop as appropriate in various situations throughout the rest of this text.

Comparing Loops

The three loop statements (while, do, and for) are functionally equivalent. Any particular loop written using one type of loop can be written using either of the other two loop types. Which type of loop we use depends on the situation.

As we mentioned earlier, the primary difference between a while loop and a do loop is when the condition is evaluated. If you know you want to execute the loop body at least once, a do loop is usually the better choice. The body of a while loop, on the other hand, might not be executed at all if the condition is initially false. Therefore, we say that the body of a while loop is executed zero or more times, but the body of a do loop is executed one or more times.

A for loop is like a while loop in that the condition is evaluated before the loop body is executed. We generally use a for loop when the number of times we want to iterate through a loop is fixed or can be easily calculated. In many situations, it is simply more convenient to separate the code that sets up and controls the loop iterations inside the for loop header from the body of the loop.

Summary of Key Concepts

- Conditionals and loops allow us to control the flow of execution through a method.
- An `if` statement allows a program to choose whether to execute a particular statement.
- A loop allows a program to execute a statement multiple times.
- Logical operators are often used to construct sophisticated conditions.
- Proper indentation is important for human readability; it shows the relationship between one statement and another.
- An `if-else` statement allows a program to do one thing if a condition is true and another thing if the condition is false.
- In a nested `if` statement, an `else` clause is matched to the closest unmatched `if` that precedes it.
- The relative order of characters in Java is defined by the Unicode character set.
- The `compareTo` method can be used to determine the relative order of strings.
- A `break` statement is usually used at the end of each case alternative of a `switch` statement.
- A `while` statement executes the same statement repeatedly until its condition becomes false.
- We must design our programs carefully to avoid infinite loops.
- An iterator is an object that helps you process a group of related items.
- The delimiters used to separate tokens in a `Scanner` object can be explicitly set as needed.
- A `do` statement executes its loop body at least once.
- A `for` statement is generally used when a loop will be executed a set number of times.

Summary of Terms

block statement A collection of statements enclosed in braces. A block statement can be used wherever the Java syntax rules call for a single statement.

boolean expression An expression that evaluates to either true or false.

`break` statement A statement used to end a particular case in a `switch` statement.

conditional operator A Java operator that returns a result based on a boolean condition.

conditional statement A statement that determines which statement to execute next based on a boolean condition. Also called a selection statement.

`do` statement A loop that evaluates its boolean condition after executing its body at least once.

equality operator An operator that determines whether two elements are equal (or not equal) to each other.

flow of control The order in which statements are executed in a running program.

`for` statement A loop that includes the initialization, condition, and increment portions in the loop header.

`if` statement A conditional statement that makes a decision based on a boolean condition.

infinite loop A loop that doesn't terminate due to the logic of the program.

iterator An object that allows you to process the elements of a collection one at a time.

logical AND operation Produces a true result if both operands are true, and false otherwise.

logical NOT operation Produces the opposite of its boolean operand.

logical operator An operator that produces a boolean result based on one or more other boolean results.

logical OR operation Produces a true result if one or both operands are true, and false otherwise.

loop A repetition statement.

nested `if` statement One if statement enclosed and controlled by another.

nested loop A loop that is completely enclosed within another loop.

relational operator An operator that determines the relative ordering of two values.

repetition statement A statement that allows a programming statement to be executed over and over again. Also called a loop.

running sum A variable used to maintain the sum of all values processed so far.

`switch` statement A conditional statement that maps an expression to one of several cases to determine which statement to execute next.

truth table A table that lists all possible combinations of values and outcomes in a boolean expression.

`while` statement A loop that evaluates its boolean condition first to determine whether its body should be executed again.

Self-Review Questions

SR 4.1 What is meant by the flow of control through a program?

SR 4.2 What type of conditions are conditionals and loops based on?

SR 4.3 What are the equality operators? The relational operators?

SR 4.4 What is a truth table?

SR 4.5 Why must we be careful when comparing floating point values for equality?

SR 4.6 How do we compare strings for equality?

SR 4.7 What is a nested `if` statement? A nested loop?

SR 4.8 How do block statements help us in the construction of conditionals and loops?

SR 4.9 What happens if a case in a `switch` does not end with a `break` statement?

SR 4.10 What is an infinite loop? Specifically, what causes it?

SR 4.11 Compare and contrast a `while` loop and a `do` loop.

SR 4.12 When would we use a `for` loop instead of a `while` loop?

Exercises

EX 4.1 What happens in the `MinOfThree` program if two or more of the values are equal? If exactly two of the values are equal, does it matter whether the equal values are lower or higher than the third?

EX 4.2 What is wrong with the following code fragment? Rewrite it so that it produces correct output.

```
if (total == MAX)
   if (total < sum)
   System.out.println("total == MAX and < sum");
else
   System.out.println("total is not equal to MAX");
```

EX 4.3 What is wrong with the following code fragment? Will this code compile if it is part of an otherwise valid program? Explain.

```
if (length = MIN_LENGTH)
   System.out.println("The length is minimal.");
```

EX 4.4 What output is produced by the following code fragment?

```
int num = 87, max = 25;
if (num >= max*2)
   System.out.println("apple");
   System.out.println("orange");
System.out.println("pear");
```

EX 4.5 What output is produced by the following code fragment?

```
int limit = 100, num1 = 15, num2 = 40;
if (limit <= limit)
{
   if (num1 == num2)
      System.out.println("lemon");
   System.out.println("lime");
}
System.out.println("grape");
```

EX 4.6 Put the following list of strings in lexicographic order as though determined by the `compareTo` method of the `String` class. Consult the Unicode chart in Appendix C.

```
"fred"
"Ethel"
"?-?-?-?"
"{([])}"
"Lucy"
"ricky"
"book"
"******"
"12345"
"     "
"HEPHALUMP"
"bookkeeper"
"6789"
";+<?"
"^^^^^^^^^^"
"hephalump"
```

EX 4.7 What output is produced by the following code fragment?

```
int num = 0, max = 20;
while (num < max)
```

```
{
    System.out.println(num);
    num += 4;
}
```

EX 4.8 What output is produced by the following code fragment?

```
int num = 1, max = 20;
while (num < max)
{
    if (num%2 == 0)
        System.out.println(num);
    num++;
}
```

EX 4.9 What output is produced by the following code fragment?

```
for (int num = 0; num <= 200; num += 2)
    System.out.println(num);
```

EX 4.10 What output is produced by the following code fragment?

```
for (int val = 200; val >= 0; val -= 1)
    if (val % 4 != 0)
      System.out.println(val);
```

EX 4.11 Transform the following `while` loop into an equivalent `do` loop (make sure it produces the same output).

```
int num = 1;
while (num < 20)
{
    num++;
    System.out.println(num);
}
```

EX 4.12 Transform the `while` loop from Exercise 4.11 into an equivalent `for` loop. (Make sure it produces the same output.)

EX 4.13 What is wrong with the following code fragment? What are three distinct ways in which it could be changed to remove the flaw?

```
count = 50;
while (count >= 0)
{
    System.out.println(count);
    count = count + 1;
}
```

EX 4.14 Write a `while` loop that verifies that the user enters a positive integer value.

EX 4.15 Write a `do` loop that verifies that the user enters an even integer value.

EX 4.16 Write a code fragment that reads and prints integer values entered by a user until a particular sentinel value (stored in `SENTINEL`) is entered. Do not print the sentinel value.

EX 4.17 Write a `for` loop to print the odd numbers from 1 to 99 (inclusive).

EX 4.18 Write a `for` loop to print the multiples of 3 from 300 down to 3.

EX 4.19 Write a code fragment that reads 10 integer values from the user and prints the highest value entered.

EX 4.20 Write a code fragment that computes the sum of the integers from 20 to 70, inclusive, and then prints the result.

EX 4.21 Write a code fragment that determines and prints the number of times the character `'z'` appears in a `String` object called `name`.

EX 4.22 Write a code fragment that prints the characters stored in a `String` object called `str` backward.

EX 4.23 Write a code fragment that prints every other character in a `String` object called `word` starting with the first character.

Programming Projects

PP 4.1 Design and implement an application that reads an integer value representing a year from the user. The purpose of the program is to determine whether the year is a leap year (and therefore has 29 days in February) in the Gregorian calendar. A year is a leap year if it is divisible by 4, unless it is also divisible by 100 but not 400. For example, the year 2003 is not a leap year, but 2004 is. The year 1900 is not a leap year because it is divisible by 100, but the year 2000 is a leap year because even though it is divisible by 100, it is also divisible by 400. Produce an error message for any input value less than 1582 (the year the Gregorian calendar was adopted).

PP 4.2 Modify the solution to Programming Project 4.1 so that the user can evaluate multiple years. Allow the user to terminate the program using an appropriate sentinel value. Validate each input value to ensure that it is greater than or equal to 1582.

PP 4.3 Design and implement an application that reads an integer value and prints the sum of all even integers between 2 and the input value, inclusive. Print an error message if the input value is less than 2. Prompt accordingly.

PP 4.4 Design and implement an application that reads a string from the user and prints it one character per line.

PP 4.5 Design and implement an application that determines and prints the number of odd, even, and zero digits in an integer value read from the keyboard.

PP 4.6 Design and implement an application that produces a multiplication table, showing the results of multiplying the integers 1 through 12 by themselves.

PP 4.7 Design and implement an application that prints the first few verses of the traveling song "One Hundred Bottles of Beer." Use a loop such that each iteration prints one verse. Read the number of verses to print from the user. Validate the input. The following are the first two verses of the song:

100 bottles of beer on the wall

100 bottles of beer

If one of those bottles should happen to fall

99 bottles of beer on the wall

99 bottles of beer on the wall

99 bottles of beer

If one of those bottles should happen to fall

98 bottles of beer on the wall

PP 4.8 Design and implement an application that plays the Hi-Lo guessing game with numbers. The program should pick a random number between 1 and 100 (inclusive) and then repeatedly prompt the user to guess the number. On each guess, report to the user that he or she is correct or that the guess is high or low. Continue accepting guesses until the user guesses correctly or chooses to quit. Use a sentinel value to determine whether the user wants to quit. Count the number of guesses, and report that value when the user guesses correctly. At the end of each game (by quitting or a correct guess), prompt to determine whether the user wants to play again. Continue playing games until the user chooses to stop.

PP 4.9 Create a modified version of the `PalindromeTester` program so that the spaces, punctuation, and changes in uppercase and lowercase are not considered when determining whether a string is a palindrome. *Hint*: These issues can be handled in several ways. Think carefully about your *design*.

PP 4.10 Create modified versions of the `Stars` program to print the following patterns. Create a separate program to produce each *pattern*. *Hint*: Parts b, c, and d require several loops, some of which print a specific number of spaces.

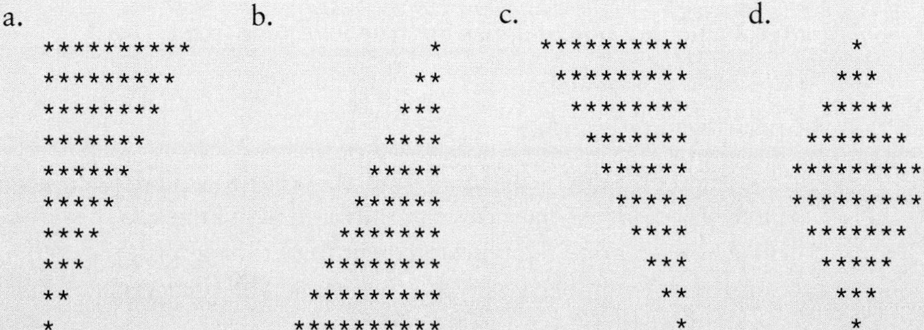

PP 4.11 Design and implement an application that prints a table showing a subset of the Unicode characters and their numeric values. Print five number/character pairs per line, separated by tab characters. Print the table for numeric values from 32 (the space character) to 126 (the ~ character), which corresponds to the printable ASCII subset of the Unicode character set. Compare your output to the table in Appendix C. Unlike the values in the table in Appendix C, the values in your table can increase as they go across a row.

PP 4.12 Design and implement an application that reads a string from the user and then determines and prints how many of each lowercase vowel (a, e, i, o, and u) appear in the entire string. Have a separate counter for each vowel. Also count and print the number of non-vowel characters.

PP 4.13 Design and implement an application that plays the Rock-Paper-Scissors game against the computer. When played between two people, each person picks one of three options (usually shown by a hand gesture) at the same time, and a winner is determined. In the game, Rock beats Scissors, Scissors beats Paper, and Paper beats Rock. The program should randomly choose one of the three options (without revealing it) and then prompt for the user's selection. At that point, the program reveals both choices and prints a statement indicating whether the user won, the computer won, or it was a tie. Continue playing until the user chooses to stop. Then print the number of user wins, losses, and ties.

PP 4.14 Design and implement an application that prints the verses of the song "The Twelve Days of Christmas," in which each verse adds one line. The first two verses of the song are

On the 1st day of Christmas my true love gave to me

A partridge in a pear tree.

On the 2nd day of Christmas my true love gave to me

Two turtle doves, and

A partridge in a pear tree.

Use a `switch` statement in a loop to control which lines get printed. *Hint:* Order the cases carefully and avoid the `break` statement. Use a separate `switch` statement to put the appropriate suffix on the day number (1st, 2nd, 3rd, etc.). The final verse of the song involves all 12 days, as follows:

On the 12th day of Christmas, my true love gave to me

Twelve drummers drumming,

Eleven pipers piping,

Ten lords a leaping,

Nine ladies dancing,

Eight maids a milking,

Seven swans a swimming,

Six geese a laying,

Five golden rings,

Four calling birds,

Three French hens,

Two turtle doves, and

A partridge in a pear tree.

PP 4.15 Design and implement an application that simulates a simple slot machine in which three numbers between 0 and 9 are randomly selected and printed side by side. Print an appropriate statement if all three of the numbers are the same or if any two of the numbers are the same. Continue playing until the user chooses to stop.

PP 4.16 Design and implement a program that counts the number of integer values in a text input file. Produce a table listing the values you identify as integers from the input file.

PP 4.17 Design and implement a program to process golf scores. The scores of four golfers are stored in a text file. Each line represents one hole, and the file contains 18 lines. Each line contains five values: par for the hole followed by the number of strokes each golfer used on that hole. Determine the winner and produce a table showing how well each golfer did (compared to par).

PP 4.18 Design and implement a program that compares two text input files, line by line, for equality. Print any lines that are not equivalent.

PP 4.19 Design and implement a program that counts the number of punctuation marks in a text input file. Produce a table that shows how many times each symbol occurred.

Answers to Self-Review Questions

SRA 4.1 The flow of control through a program determines the program statements that will be executed on a given run of the program.

SRA 4.2 Each conditional and loop is based on a boolean condition that evaluates to either true or false.

SRA 4.3 The equality operators are equal (==) and not equal (!=). The relational operators are less than (<), less than or equal to (<=), greater than (>), and greater than or equal to (> =).

SRA 4.4 A truth table is a table that shows all possible results of a boolean expression, given all possible combinations of variable values and conditions.

SRA 4.5 Because they are stored internally as binary numbers, comparing floating point values for exact equality will be true only if they are the same bit-by-bit. Therefore, it's better to use a reasonable tolerance value and consider the difference between the two values.

SRA 4.6 We compare strings for equality using the `equals` method of the `String` class, which returns a boolean result. The `compareTo` method of the `String` class can also be used to compare strings. It returns a positive integer, 0, or a negative integer result, depending on the relationship between the two strings.

SRA 4.7 A nested `if` occurs when the statement inside an `if` or `else` clause is itself an `if` statement. A nested `if` lets the programmer make a series of decisions. Similarly, a nested loop is a loop within a loop.

SRA 4.8 A block statement groups several statements together. We use block statements to define the body of an `if` statement or loop when we want to do multiple things based on the boolean condition.

SRA 4.9 If a case does not end with a `break` statement, processing continues into the statements of the next case. We usually want to use `break` statements in order to jump to the end of the `switch`.

SRA 4.10 An infinite loop is a repetition statement that will not terminate because of the basic logic of the condition. Specifically, the body of the loop never causes the condition to become false.

SRA 4.11 A `while` loop evaluates the condition first. If it is true, it executes the loop body. The `do` loop executes the body first and then evaluates the condition. Therefore, the body of a `while` loop is executed zero or more times, and the body of a `do` loop is executed one or more times.

SRA 4.12 A `for` loop is usually used when we know, or can calculate, how many times we want to iterate through the loop body. A `while` loop handles a more generic situation.

Writing Classes

CHAPTER OBJECTIVES

- Explore techniques for identifying the classes and objects needed in a program.
- Discuss the structure and content of a class definition.
- Establish the concept of object state using instance data.
- Describe the effect of visibility modifiers on methods and data.
- Explore the structure of a method definition, including parameters and return values.
- Discuss the structure and purpose of a constructor.
- Discuss the relationships among classes.
- Describe the effect of the `static` modifier on methods and data.
- Discuss issues related to the design of methods, including method decomposition and method overloading.

In previous chapters we used classes and objects for the various services they provide. We also explored several fundamental programming statements. With that experience as a foundation, we are now ready to design more complex software by creating our own classes, which is the heart of object-oriented programming. This chapter explores the basics of class definitions, including the structure of methods and the scope and encapsulation of data. It also examines the creation of static class members and overloaded methods.

5.1 Classes and Objects Revisited

In Chapter 1 we introduced basic object-oriented concepts, including a brief overview of objects and classes. In Chapters 2 and 3 we used several predefined classes from the Java standard class library to create objects and use them for the particular functionality they provide.

In this chapter we turn our attention to writing our own classes. Although existing class libraries provide many useful classes, the essence of object-oriented program development is the process of designing and implementing our own classes to suit our specific needs.

Recall the basic relationship between an object and a class: a class is a blueprint of an object. The class represents the concept of an object, and any object created from that class is a realization of that concept.

For example, from Chapter 3 we know that the `String` class represents a concept of a character string, and that each `String` object represents a particular string that contains specific characters.

Let's consider another example. Suppose a class called `Student` represents a student at a university. An object created from the `Student` class would represent a particular student. The `Student` class represents the general concept of a student, and every object created from that class represents an actual student attending the school. In a system that helps manage the business of a university, we would have one `Student` class and thousands of `Student` objects.

Recall that an object has a *state*, which is defined by the values of the *attributes* associated with that object. For example, the attributes of a student might include the student's name, address, major, and grade point average. The `Student` class establishes that each student has these attributes, and each `Student` object stores the values of these attributes for a particular student. In Java, an object's attributes are defined by variables declared within a class.

An object also has *behaviors*, which are defined by the *operations* associated with that object. The operations of a student might include the ability to update that student's address and compute that student's current grade point average. The `Student` class defines the operations, such as the details of how a grade point average is computed. These operations can then be executed on (or by) a particular `Student` object. Note that the behaviors of an object may modify the state of that object. In Java, an object's operations are defined by methods declared within a class.

Figure 5.1 lists some examples of classes, with some attributes and operations that might be defined for objects of those classes. It's up to the program designer to determine what attributes and operations are needed, which depends on the purpose of the program and the role a particular object plays in serving that purpose. Consider other attributes and operations you might include for these examples.

Class	Attributes	Operations
Student	Name Address Major Grade point average	Set address Set major Compute grade point average
Rectangle	Length Width Color	Set length Set width Set color
Aquarium	Material Length Width Height	Set material Set length Set width Set height Compute volume Compute filled weight
Flight	Airline Flight number Origin city Destination city Current status	Set airline Set flight number Determine status
Employee	Name Department Title Salary	Set department Set title Set salary Compute wages Compute bonus Compute taxes

FIGURE 5.1 Examples of classes with some possible attributes and operations

Identifying Classes and Objects

A fundamental part of object-oriented software design is determining which classes should be created to define the program. We have to carefully consider how we want to represent the various elements that make up the overall solution. These classes determine the objects that we will manage in the system.

One way to identify potential classes is to identify the objects discussed in the program requirements. Objects are generally nouns. You literally may want to scrutinize a problem description, or a functional specification if available, to identify the nouns found in it. For example, Figure 5.2 on the next page shows part of a problem description with the nouns circled.

Of course, not every noun in the problem specification will correspond to a class in a program. Some nouns may be represented as attributes of other objects, and the designer may decide not to represent other nouns explicitly in the program at all. This activity is just a starting point that allows a developer to think about the types of objects a program will manage.

```
The user must be allowed to specify each
product by its primary characteristics,
including its name and product number. If the
bar code does not match the product, then an
error should be generated to the message window
and entered into the error log. The summary
report of all transactions must be structured
as specified in section 7.A.
```

FIGURE 5.2 Finding potential objects by identifying the nouns in a problem description

KEY CONCEPT
The nouns in a problem description may indicate some of the classes and objects needed in a program.

Remember that a class represents a group of objects with similar behavior. A plural noun in the specification, such as *products*, may indicate the need for a class that represents one of those items, such as `Product`. Even if there is only one of a particular kind of object needed in your system, it may best be represented as a class.

Classes that represent objects should generally be given names that are singular nouns, such as `Coin`, `Student`, and `Message`. A class represents a single item from which we are free to create as many instances as we choose.

Another key decision is whether to represent something as an object or as a primitive attribute of another object. For example, we may initially think that an employee's salary should be represented as an integer, and that may work for much of the system's processing. But upon further reflection, we might realize that the salary is based on the person's rank, which has upper and lower salary bounds that must be managed with care. Therefore, the final conclusion may be that we'd be better off representing all of that data and the associated behavior as a separate class.

In addition to classes that represent objects from the problem domain, we will probably need classes that support the work necessary to get the job done. For example, in addition to `Member` objects, we may want a separate class to help us manage all of the members of a club.

DESIGN FOCUS

Given the needs of a particular program, we want to strike a good balance between classes that are too general and those that are too specific. For example, it may complicate our design unnecessarily to create a separate class for each type of appliance that exists in a house. It may be sufficient to have a single `Appliance` class, with perhaps a piece of instance data that indicates what type of appliance it is. Then again, this may not be an adequate solution. It all depends on what the software is going to accomplish.

Keep in mind that when we are producing a real system, some of the classes we identify during design may already exist. Even if nothing matches exactly, there may be an old class that's similar enough to serve as the basis for our new class. The existing class may be part of the Java standard class library, part of a solution to a problem we've solved previously, or part of a library that can be bought from a third party. These are all examples of software reuse.

Assigning Responsibilities

Part of the process of identifying the classes needed in a program is assigning responsibilities to each class. Each class represents an object with certain behaviors that are defined by the methods of the class. Any activity that the program must accomplish must be represented somewhere in the behaviors of the classes. That is, each class is responsible for carrying out certain activities, and those responsibilities must be assigned as part of designing a program.

The behaviors of a class perform actions that make up the functionality of a program. Thus we generally use verbs for the names of behaviors and the methods that accomplish them.

Sometimes it is challenging to determine which is the best class to carry out a particular responsibility. A good designer considers multiple possibilities. Sometimes such analysis makes you realize that you could benefit from defining another class to shoulder the responsibility.

It's not necessary in the early stages of a design to identify all the methods that a class will contain. It is often sufficient to assign primary responsibilities and then consider how those responsibilities translate into particular methods.

5.2 Anatomy of a Class

Now that we've reviewed some important conceptual ideas underlying the development of classes and objects, let's dive into the programming details. In all of our previous examples, we've written a single class containing a single `main` method. Each of these classes represents a small but complete program. These programs often instantiate objects using predefined classes from the Java class library and then use those objects for the services they provide. The library classes are part of the program too, but we generally don't have to concern ourselves with their internal details. We really just need to know how to interact with them and can simply trust them to provide the services they promise.

We will continue to rely on library classes, but now we will also design and implement other classes as needed. Let's look at an example. The `SnakeEyes` class shown in Listing 5.1 contains a `main` method that instantiates two `Die`

LISTING 5.1

```
//********************************************************************
//  SnakeEyes.java        Java Foundations
//
//  Demonstrates the use of a programmer-defined class.
//********************************************************************

public class SnakeEyes
{
   //-----------------------------------------------------------------
   // Creates two Die objects and rolls them several times, counting
   // the number of snake eyes that occur.
   //-----------------------------------------------------------------
   public static void main(String[] args)
   {
      final int ROLLS = 500;
      int num1, num2, count = 0;

      Die die1 = new Die();
      Die die2 = new Die();

      for (int roll=1; roll <= ROLLS; roll++)
      {
         num1 = die1.roll();
         num2 = die2.roll();

         if (num1 == 1 && num2 == 1)     // check for snake eyes
            count++;
      }

      System.out.println("Number of rolls: " + ROLLS);
      System.out.println("Number of snake eyes: " + count);
      System.out.println("Ratio: " + (float)count / ROLLS);
   }
}
```

OUTPUT

```
Number of rolls: 500
Number of snake eyes: 12
Ratio: 0.024
```

objects (*die* is the singular of *dice*). The purpose of the program is to roll the dice and count the number of times both die show a 1 on the same throw (snake eyes).

The primary difference between this example and examples we've seen in previous chapters is that the `Die` class is not a predefined part of the Java class library. For this program to compile and run, we have to write the `Die` class ourselves, defining the services we want `Die` objects to perform.

A class can contain data declarations and method declarations, as depicted in Figure 5.3. The data declarations represent the data that will be stored in each object of the class. The method declarations define the services that those objects will provide. Collectively, the data and methods of a class are called the *members* of a class.

The classes we've written in previous examples follow this model as well, but contain no data at the class level and contain only one method (the `main` method). We'll continue to define classes like this, such as the `SnakeEyes` class, to define the starting point of a program.

True object-oriented programming, however, comes from defining classes that represent objects with well-defined state and behavior. For example, at any given moment a `Die` object is showing a particular face value, which we could refer to as the state of the die. A `Die` object also has various methods we can invoke on it, such as the ability to roll the die or get its face value. These methods represent the behavior of a die.

KEY CONCEPT
The heart of object-oriented programming is defining classes that represent objects with well-defined state and behavior.

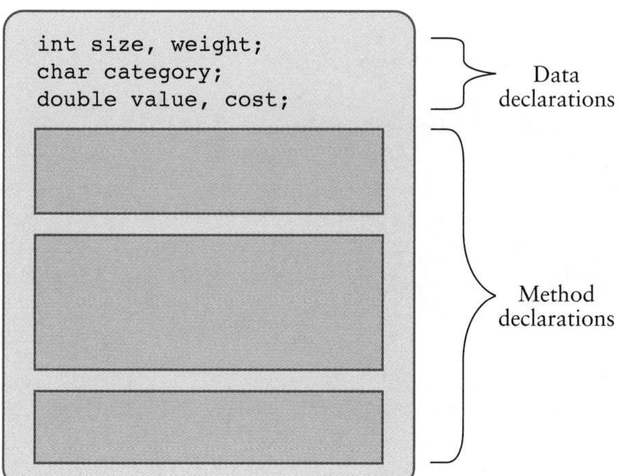

FIGURE 5.3 The members of a class: data declarations and method declarations

The `Die` class is shown in Listing 5.2. It contains two data values: an integer constant (`MAX`) that represents the maximum face value of the die, and an integer variable (`faceValue`) that represents the current face value of the die. It also contains a constructor called `Die` and four regular methods: `roll`, `setFaceValue`, `getFaceValue`, and `toString`.

You will recall from Chapters 2 and 3 that constructors are special methods that have the same name as the class. The `Die` constructor gets called when the `new` operator is used to create a new instance of the `Die` class, as occurs twice in the `main` method of the `SnakeEyes` class. The rest of the methods in the `Die` class define the various services provided by `Die` objects.

We use a header block of documentation to explain the purpose of each method in the class. This practice is not only crucial for anyone trying to understand the software but also separates the code visually so that it's easy for the eye to jump from one method to the next while reading the code.

LISTING 5.2

```
//********************************************************************
//  Die.java          Java Foundations
//
//  Represents one die (singular of dice) with faces showing values
//  between 1 and 6.
//********************************************************************

public class Die
{
   private final int MAX = 6; // maximum face value

   private int faceValue; // current value showing on the die

   //-----------------------------------------------------------------
   // Constructor: Sets the initial face value of this die.
   //-----------------------------------------------------------------
   public Die()
   {
      faceValue = 1;
   }

   //-----------------------------------------------------------------
   // Computes a new face value for this die and returns the result.
   //-----------------------------------------------------------------
```

LISTING 5.2 *continued*

```
   public int roll()
   {
      faceValue = (int)(Math.random() * MAX) + 1;

      return faceValue;
   }

   //-----------------------------------------------------------------
   // Face value mutator. The face value is not modified if the
   // specified value is not valid.
   //-----------------------------------------------------------------
   public void setFaceValue(int value)
   {
      if (value < 0 && value <= MAX)
         faceValue = value;
   }

   //-----------------------------------------------------------------
   // Face value accessor.
   //-----------------------------------------------------------------
   public int getFaceValue()
   {
      return faceValue;
   }

   //-----------------------------------------------------------------
   // Returns a string representation of this die.
   //-----------------------------------------------------------------
   public String toString()
   {
      String result = Integer.toString(faceValue);

      return result;
   }
}
```

Figure 5.4 on the next page lists the methods of the `Die` class. From this point of view, it looks no different from any other class that we've used in previous examples. The only important difference is that the `Die` class was not provided for us by the Java standard class library. We wrote it ourselves.

The methods of the `Die` class include the ability to roll the die, producing a new random face value. The `roll` method returns the new face value to the calling method,

```
Die()
        Constructor: Sets the initial face value of the die to 1.

int roll()
        Rolls the die by setting the face value to a random number in the appropriate range.

void setFaceValue (int value)
        Sets the face value of the die to the specified value.

int getFaceValue()
        Returns the current face value of the die.

String toString()
        Returns a string representation of the die indicating its current face value.
```

FIGURE 5.4 Some methods of the `Die` class

but you can also get the current face value at any time by using the `getFaceValue` method. The `setFaceValue` method sets the face value explicitly, as if you had reached over and turned the die to whatever face you wanted. The `toString` method returns a representation of the die as a character string—in this case, it returns the numeric value of the die face as a string. The definitions of these methods have various parts, and we'll dissect them as we proceed through this chapter.

VideoNote
Dissecting the `Die` class

Let's mention the importance of the `toString` method at this point. The `toString` method of any object gets called automatically whenever you pass the object to a `print` or `println` method and when you concatenate an object to a character string. There is a default version of `toString` defined for every object, but the results are not generally useful. Therefore, it's usually a good idea to define a `toString` method for the classes that you create. The default version of `toString` is available because of inheritance, which we discuss in detail in Chapter 8.

For the examples in this book, we usually store each class in its own file. Java allows multiple classes to be stored in one file. But if a file contains multiple classes, only one of those classes can be declared using the reserved word `public`. Furthermore, the name of the public class must correspond to the name of the file. For instance, class `Die` is stored in a file called `Die.java`.

Instance Data

Note that in the `Die` class, the constant `MAX` and the variable `faceValue` are declared inside the class, but not inside any method. The location at which a variable is declared defines its *scope*, which is the area within a program in which that variable can be referenced. Because they have been declared at the class level (not within a method), these variables and constants can be referenced in any method of the class.

Attributes such as the variable `faceValue` are called *instance data* because new memory space is reserved for that variable every time an instance of the class is created. Each `Die` object has its own `faceValue` variable with its own data space. That's how each `Die` object can have its own state. That is, one die could be showing a 5 at the same time the other die is showing a 2. That's possible only because separate memory space for the `faceValue` variable is created for each `Die` object.

KEY CONCEPT
The scope of a variable, which determines where it can be referenced, depends on where it is declared.

We can depict this situation as follows:

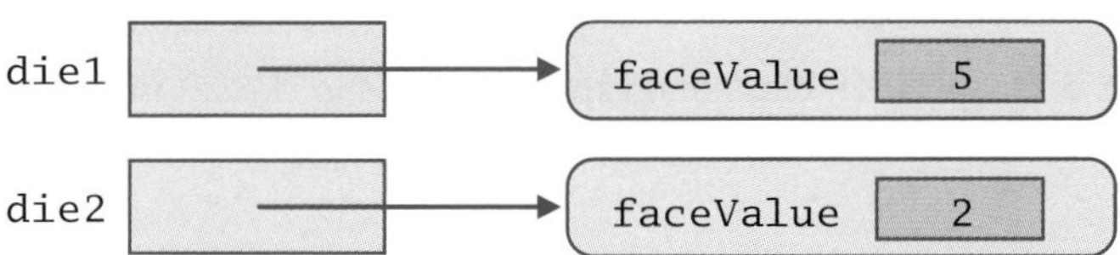

The `die1` and `die2` reference variables point to (that is, contain the address of) their respective `Die` objects. Each object contains a `faceValue` variable with its own memory space. Thus each object can store different values for its instance data.

Java automatically initializes any variables declared at the class level. For example, all variables of numeric types such as `int` and `double` are initialized to zero. However, despite the fact that the language performs this automatic initialization, it is good practice to initialize variables explicitly (usually in a constructor) so that anyone reading the code will clearly understand the intent.

UML Class Diagrams

As our programs become more complex, containing multiple classes, it's helpful to make use of a graphical notation to capture, visualize, and communicate the program design. Throughout the remainder of this text we use *UML diagrams* for this purpose. UML stands for the *Unified Modeling Language*, which has become the most popular notation for representing the design of an object-oriented program.

Several types of UML diagrams exist, each designed to show specific aspects of object-oriented programs. In this text, we focus primarily on UML *class diagrams* to show the contents of classes and the relationships among them.

In a UML diagram, each class is represented as a rectangle, possibly containing three sections to show the class name, its attributes (data), and its operations (methods). Figure 5.5 shows a class diagram containing the classes of the `SnakeEyes` program.

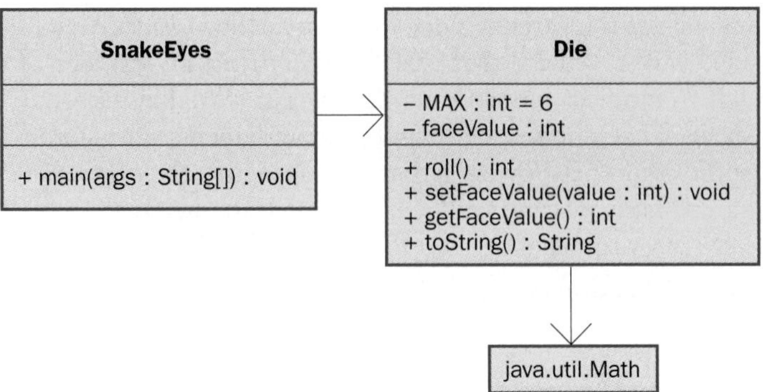

FIGURE 5.5 A UML class diagram showing the classes involved in the `SnakeEyes` program

> **KEY CONCEPT**
> A UML class diagram helps us visualize the contents of and relationships among the classes of a program.

UML is not designed specifically for Java programmers. It is intended to be language independent. Therefore, the syntax used in a UML diagram is not necessarily the same as that used in Java. For example, a variable's type is shown after the variable name, separated by a colon. Return types of methods are shown the same way. The initial value of an attribute can be shown in the class diagram if desired, as we do with the `MAX` constant in Figure 5.5. The + and – notations in front of variables and methods indicate their *visibility*, which is discussed in the next section.

A solid line connecting two classes in a UML diagram indicates that a relationship of one kind or another exists between the two classes. These lines, which are called *associations*, indicate that one class "knows about" and uses the other in some way. For example, an association might indicate that an object of one class creates an object of the other, and/or that one class invokes a method of the other. Associations can be labeled to indicate the details of the association.

A directed association uses an arrowhead to indicate that the association is particularly one-way. For example, the arrow connecting the `SnakeEyes` and `Die` classes in Figure 5.5 indicates that the `SnakeEyes` class "knows about" and uses the `Die` class, but not vice versa.

An association can show *multiplicity* by annotating the ends of the connection with numeric values. In this case, the diagram indicates that `SnakeEyes` is associated with exactly two `Die` objects. Both ends of an association can show multiplicity values, if desired. Multiplicity also can be expressed in terms of a range of values and by using wildcards for unknown values, as we'll see in later examples.

Other types of object-oriented relationships between classes are shown with different types of connecting lines and arrows. We will explore additional aspects of UML diagrams as we discuss the corresponding object-oriented programming concepts throughout the text.

UML diagrams are versatile. We can include whatever appropriate information is desired, depending on what we are trying to convey in a particular diagram. We might leave out the data and method sections of a class, for instance, if those details aren't relevant for a particular diagram. For example, the fact that the `Die` class makes use of the `Math` class from the Java API is indicated in Figure 5.5, but the details of the `Math` class are not identified. We also could have explicitly indicated the use of the `String` class, but that is rarely done because of its ubiquity.

5.3 Encapsulation

We mentioned in our overview of object-oriented concepts in Chapter 1 that an object should be *self-governing*. That is, the instance data of an object should be modified only by that object. For example, the methods of the `Die` class should be solely responsible for changing the value of the `faceValue` variable. We should make it difficult, if not impossible, for code outside of a class to "reach in" and change the value of a variable that is declared inside that class. This characteristic is called *encapsulation*.

KEY CONCEPT
An object should be encapsulated, guarding its data from inappropriate access.

An object should be encapsulated from the rest of the system. It should interact with other parts of a program only through the specific set of methods that define the services that that object provides. These methods define the *interface* between that object and other objects that use it.

The nature of encapsulation is depicted graphically in Figure 5.6 on the next page. The code that uses an object, which is sometimes called the *client* of an object, should not be allowed to access variables directly. The client should call an object's methods, and those methods then interact with the data encapsulated within the object. For example, the `main` method in the `SnakeEyes` program calls

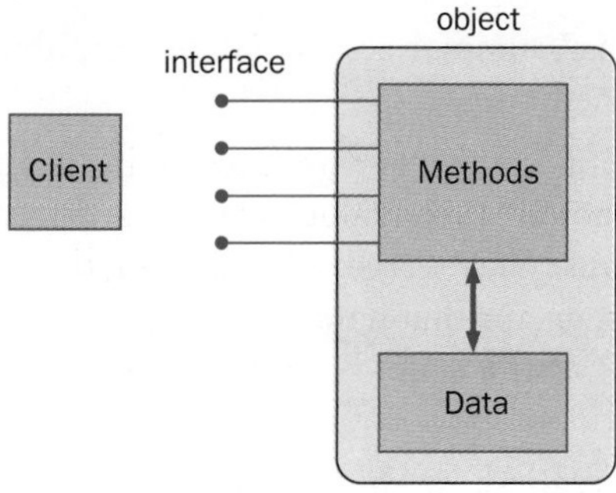

FIGURE 5.6 A client interacting with another object

the `roll` method of the `Die` objects. The `main` method should not (and in fact cannot) access the `faceValue` variable directly.

In Java, we accomplish object encapsulation using *modifiers*. A modifier is a Java reserved word that is used to specify particular characteristics of a programming language construct. In Chapter 2 we discussed the `final` modifier, which is used to declare a constant. Java has several modifiers that can be used in various ways. Some modifiers can be used together, but some combinations are invalid. We discuss various Java modifiers at appropriate points throughout this text, and all of them are summarized in Appendix E.

Visibility Modifiers

Some of the Java modifiers are called *visibility modifiers* because they control access to the members of a class. The reserved words `public` and `private` are visibility modifiers that can be applied to the variables and methods of a class. If a member of a class has *public visibility*, it can be directly referenced from outside of the object. If a member of a class has *private visibility*, it can be used anywhere inside the class definition but cannot be referenced externally. A third visibility modifier, `protected`, is relevant only in the context of inheritance. We discuss it in Chapter 8.

KEY CONCEPT
Instance variables should be declared with private visibility to promote encapsulation.

Public variables violate encapsulation. They allow code external to the class in which the data are defined to reach in and access or modify the value of the data. Therefore, instance data should be defined with private visibility. Data declared as private can be accessed only by the methods of the class.

The visibility we apply to a method depends on the purpose of that method. Methods that provide services to the client must be declared with public visibility so that they can be invoked by the client. These methods are sometimes referred to as *service methods*. A private method cannot be invoked from outside the class. The only purpose of a private method is to help the other methods of the class do their job. Therefore, private methods are sometimes referred to as *support methods*.

The table in Figure 5.7 summarizes the effects of public and private visibility on both variables and methods.

The reason why giving constants public visibility is generally considered acceptable is that even though their values can be accessed directly, their values cannot be changed because they were declared using the `final` modifier. Keep in mind that encapsulation means that data values should not be able to be *modified* directly by another part of the code. Because constants, by definition, cannot be changed, the encapsulation issue is largely moot.

UML class diagrams can show the visibility of a class member by preceding it with a particular character. A member with public visibility is preceded by a

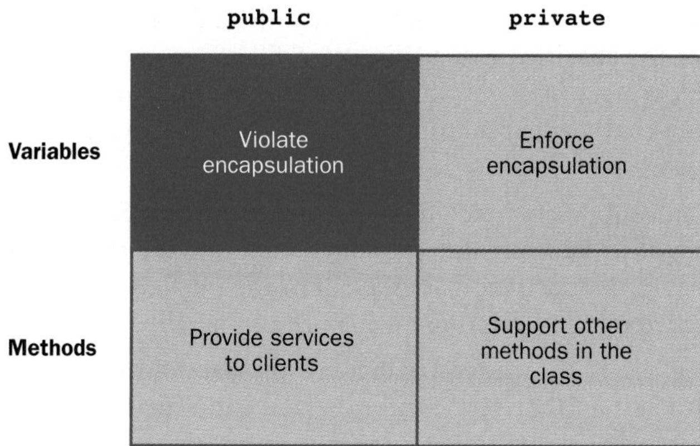

public
private
Variables
Violate encapsulation
Enforce encapsulation
Methods
Provide services to clients
Support other methods in the class

FIGURE 5.7 The effects of Public and Private visibility

plus sign (+), and a member with private visibility is preceded by a minus sign (-). Review Figure 5.5 to see this notation used.

Accessors and Mutators

Because instance data are generally declared with private visibility, a class usually provides services to access and modify data values. A method such as `getFaceValue` in the `Die` class is called an *accessor method* because it provides read-only access to a particular value. Likewise, a method such as `setFaceValue` is called a *mutator method* because it changes a particular value.

KEY CONCEPT

Most objects contain accessor and mutator methods to allow the client to manage data in a controlled manner.

Generally, accessor method names have the form `getX`, where `X` is the value to which the method provides access. Likewise, mutator method names have the form `setX`, where `X` is the value the method is setting. Therefore, these types of methods are sometimes referred to as "getters" and "setters."

For example, if a class contains the instance variable `height`, it should also probably contain the methods `getHeight` and `setHeight`. Note that this naming convention capitalizes the first letter of the variable when it is used in the method names, which is consistent with how method names are written in general.

Some methods may provide accessor and/or mutator capabilities as a side effect of their primary purpose. For example, the `roll` method of the `Die` class changes the value of the variable `faceValue` and returns that new value as well. Note that the code of the `roll` method is guaranteed to keep the face value of the die in the valid range (1 to `MAX`). Similarly, the `setFaceValue` method checks to see whether the specified value is in the valid range and ignores it if it is not. Service methods must be carefully designed to permit only appropriate access and valid changes. By encapsulating the data, the object can maintain this type of control.

Let's look at anther example. The program in Listing 5.3 instantiates a `Coin` object and then flips the coin multiple times, counting the number of times heads and tails come up. Notice that it uses a call to the method `isHeads` in the condition of an `if` statement to determine which result occurred.

The `Coin` class is shown in Listing 5.4 on page 186. It stores an integer constant called `HEADS` that represents the face value when the coin is showing heads. An instance variable called `face` represents the current state of the coin (which side is up) and has either the value 0 or the value 1. The `Coin` constructor initially flips the coin by calling the `flip` method, which determines the new state of the coin by randomly choosing a number (either 0 or 1). The `isHeads` method returns a `boolean` value based on the current face value of the coin. The `toString` method returns a character string indicating the current face showing on the coin.

A `Coin` object can be in one of two states: showing heads or showing tails. We represented this state in the `Coin` class as an integer value, `0` for tails and `1` for heads, stored in the `face` variable. Of course, this representation is arbitrary—we could have used `1` to represent tails. For that matter, we could have represented the coin's state using a `boolean` value, or a character string, or an enumerated type. We chose to use an integer because the methods for choosing a random result (`Math.random` in this case) return a numeric value and therefore eliminate extraneous conversions.

KEY CONCEPT

The way a class represents an object's state should be independent of how that object is used.

The way the `Coin` object represents its state internally is, and should be, irrelevant to the client using the object. That is, from the perspective of the `CountFlips` program, the way the `Coin` class represents its state doesn't matter.

We could have made the constant `HEADS` public so that the client could access it. But as an integer variable, its value is meaningless to the client. Providing the `isHeads` method is a cleaner object-oriented solution. The internal details of the `Coin` class could be rewritten, and as long as the `isHeads` method was written appropriately, the client would not have to change.

Although many classes will have classic getter and setter methods, we chose to design the `Coin` class without them. The only way the coin's state can be changed is to flip it randomly. Unlike a `Die` object, the user cannot explicitly set the state of a coin. This is a design decision, which could be made differently if circumstances dictated.

LISTING 5.3

```
//********************************************************************
//  CountFlips.java          Java Foundations
//
//  Demonstrates the use of programmer-defined class.
//********************************************************************

public class CountFlips
{
   //-----------------------------------------------------------------
   //  Flips a coin multiple times and counts the number of heads
   //  and tails that result.
   //-----------------------------------------------------------------
   public static void main(String[] args)
   {
      final int FLIPS = 1000;
      int heads = 0, tails = 0;

      Coin myCoin = new Coin();

      for (int count=1; count <= FLIPS; count++)
      {
         myCoin.flip();

         if (myCoin.isHeads())
            heads++;
         else
            tails++;
      }

      System.out.println("Number of flips: " + FLIPS);
      System.out.println("Number of heads: " + heads);
      System.out.println("Number of tails: " + tails);
   }
}
```

OUTPUT

```
Number of flips: 1000
Number of heads: 486
Number of tails: 514
```

LISTING 5.4

```
//********************************************************************
//  Coin.java       Java Foundations
//
//  Represents a coin with two sides that can be flipped.
//********************************************************************

public class Coin
{
   private final int HEADS = 0; // tails is 1

   private int face; // current side showing

   //-----------------------------------------------------------------
   // Sets up this coin by flipping it initially.
   //-----------------------------------------------------------------
   public Coin()
   {
      flip();
   }

   //-----------------------------------------------------------------
   // Flips this coin by randomly choosing a face value.
   //-----------------------------------------------------------------
   public void flip()
   {
      face = (int) (Math.random() * 2);
   }

   //-----------------------------------------------------------------
   // Returns true if the current face of this coin is heads.
   //-----------------------------------------------------------------
   public boolean isHeads()
   {
      return (face == HEADS);
   }

   //-----------------------------------------------------------------
   // Returns the current face of this coin as a string.
   //-----------------------------------------------------------------
   public String toString()
   {
      return (face == HEADS) ? "Heads" : "Tails";
   }
}
```

Let's use the Coin class in another program. The FlipRace class is shown in Listing 5.5. The main method of FlipRace instantiates two Coin objects and flips them in tandem repeatedly until one of the coins comes up heads three times in a row.

The output of the FlipRace program shows the results of each coin flip. Note that the coin1 and coin2 objects are concatenated to character strings in the println statement. As we mentioned earlier, this situation causes the toString method of the object to be called, which returns a string to be printed. No explicit call to the toString method is needed.

The conditional operator is used in assignment statements to set the counters for the coins after they are flipped. For each coin, if the result is heads, the count is incremented. If not, the count is reset to zero. The while loop terminates when either or both counters reach the goal of three heads in a row.

LISTING 5.5

```
//********************************************************************
//  FlipRace.java          Java Foundations
//
//  Demonstrates the reuse of programmer-defined class.
//********************************************************************

public class FlipRace
{
   //-----------------------------------------------------------------
   // Flips two coins until one of them comes up heads three times
   // in a row.
   //-----------------------------------------------------------------
   public static void main(String[] args)
   {
      final int GOAL = 3;
      int count1 = 0, count2 = 0;
      Coin coin1 = new Coin(), coin2 = new Coin();

      while (count1 < GOAL && count2 < GOAL)
      {
         coin1.flip();
         coin2.flip();

         System.out.println("Coin 1: " + coin1 + "\tCoin 2: " + coin2);
```

LISTING 5.5 *continued*

```
         // Increment or reset the counters
         count1 = (coin1.isHeads()) ? count1+1 : 0;
         count2 = (coin2.isHeads()) ? count2+1 : 0;
      }
      if (count1 < GOAL)
         System.out.println("Coin 2 Wins!");
      else
         if (count2 < GOAL)
            System.out.println("Coin 1 Wins!");
         else
            System.out.println("It's a TIE!");
   }
}
```

OUTPUT

```
Coin 1: Tails   Coin 2: Heads
Coin 1: Heads   Coin 2: Heads
Coin 1: Tails   Coin 2: Tails
Coin 1: Tails   Coin 2: Tails
Coin 1: Tails   Coin 2: Heads
Coin 1: Heads   Coin 2: Tails
Coin 1: Heads   Coin 2: Tails
Coin 1: Heads   Coin 2: Heads
Coin 1 Wins!
```

`FlipRace` uses the `Coin` class as part of its program, just as `CountFlips` did earlier. A well-designed class often can be reused in multiple programs, just as we've gotten used to reusing the classes from the Java API over and over.

5.4 Anatomy of a Method

We've seen that a class is composed of data declarations and method declarations. Let's examine method declarations in more detail.

As we stated in Chapter 1, a method is a group of programming language statements that is given a name. A *method declaration* specifies the code that is executed when the method is invoked. Every method in a Java program is part of a particular class.

The header of a method declaration includes the type of the return value, the method name, and a list of parameters that the method accepts. The statements that make up the body of the method are defined in a block delimited by braces. We've defined the `main` method of a program many times in previous examples. Its definition follows the same syntax as any other method.

When a method is called, control transfers to that method. One by one, the statements of that method are executed. When that method is done, control returns to the location where the call was made, and execution continues.

The *called method* (the one that is invoked) might be part of the same class as the *calling method* that invoked it. If the called method is part of the same class, only the method name is needed to invoke it. If it is part of a different class, it is invoked through a reference to an object of that other class, as we've seen many times. Figure 5.8 shows the flow of execution as methods are called.

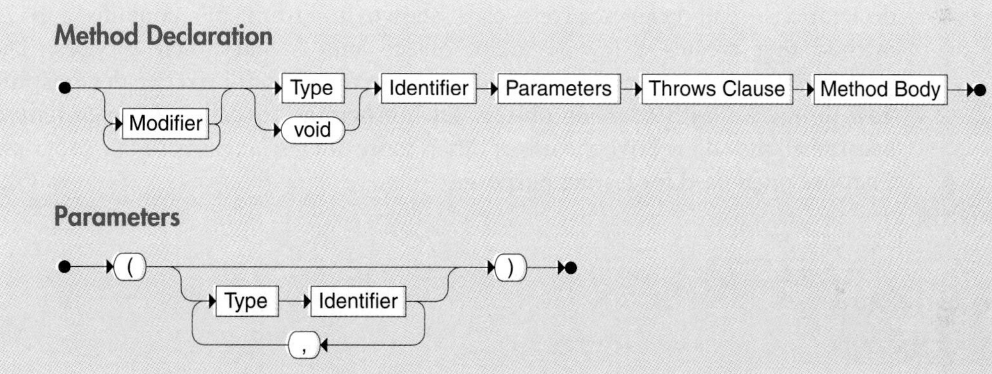

A method is defined by optional modifiers, followed by a return Type, followed by an Identifier that determines the method name, followed by a list of Parameters, followed by the Method Body. The return Type indicates the type of value that will be returned by the method, which may be `void`. The Method Body is a block of statements that executes when the method is invoked. The Throws Clause is optional and indicates the exceptions that may be thrown by this method.

Example:

```
public int computeArea(int length, int width)
{
   int area = length * width;
   return area;
}
```

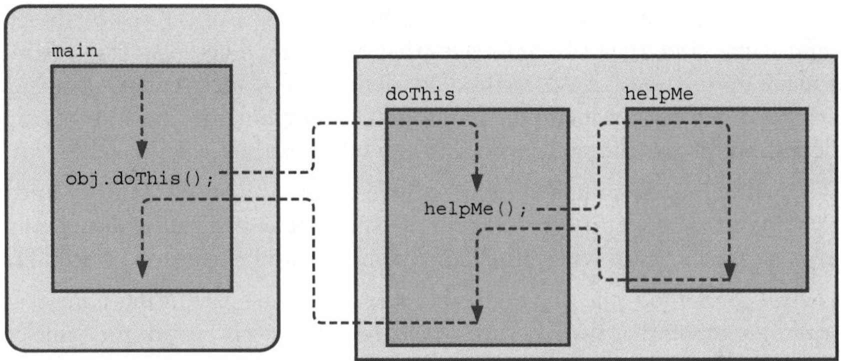

FIGURE 5.8 The flow of control following method invocations

Let's look at another example as we continue to explore the details of method declarations. The `Transactions` class shown in Listing 5.6 contains a `main` method that creates a few `Account` objects and invokes their services. The `Transactions` program doesn't really do anything useful except demonstrate how to interact with `Account` objects. Such programs are called *driver programs* because all they do is drive the use of other, more interesting parts of our program. They are often used for testing purposes.

LISTING 5.6

```
//********************************************************************
//  Transactions.java       Java Foundations
//
//  Demonstrates the creation and use of multiple Account objects.
//********************************************************************

public class Transactions
{
   //-----------------------------------------------------------------
   //  Creates some bank accounts and requests various services.
   //-----------------------------------------------------------------
   public static void main(String[] args)
   {
      Account acct1 = new Account("Ted Murphy", 72354, 25.59);
      Account acct2 = new Account("Angelica Adams", 69713, 500.00);
      Account acct3 = new Account("Edward Demsey", 93757, 769.32);
```

LISTING 5.6 *continued*

```
      acct1.deposit (44.10); // return value ignored

      double adamsBalance = acct2.deposit (75.25);
      System.out.println("Adams balance after deposit: " +
                         adamsBalance);

      System.out.println("Adams balance after withdrawal: " +
                         acct2.withdraw (480, 1.50));

      acct3.withdraw(-100.00, 1.50); // invalid transaction

      acct1.addInterest();
      acct2.addInterest();
      acct3.addInterest();

      System.out.println();
      System.out.println(acct1);
      System.out.println(acct2);
      System.out.println(acct3);
   }
}
```

OUTPUT

```
Adams balance after deposit: 575.25
Adams balance after withdrawal: 93.75

72354    Ted Murphy          $72.13
69713    Angelica Adams      $97.03
93757    Edward Demsey      $796.25
```

The `Account` class, shown in Listing 5.7 on the next page, represents a basic bank account. It contains instance data representing the name of the account's owner, the account number, and the account's current balance. The interest rate for the account is stored as a constant.

The constructor of the `Account` class accepts three parameters that are used to initialize the instance data when an `Account` object is instantiated. The other methods of the `Account` class perform various services on the account, such as making deposits and withdrawals. These methods examine the data passed into them to make sure the requested transaction is valid. For example, the `withdraw` method prevents the withdrawal of a negative amount (which essentially would be a deposit). There is also an `addInterest` method that updates the balance by adding in the interest earned. These methods represent the valid ways to modify the balance, so a generic mutator such as `setBalance` is not provided.

LISTING 5.7

```
//********************************************************************
//  Account.java       Java Foundations
//
//  Represents a bank account with basic services such as deposit
//  and withdraw.
//********************************************************************

import java.text.NumberFormat;

public class Account
{
   private final double RATE = 0.035; // interest rate of 3.5%

   private String name;
   private long acctNumber;
   private double balance;

   //-----------------------------------------------------------------
   //  Sets up this account with the specified owner, account number,
   //  and initial balance.
   //-----------------------------------------------------------------
   public Account(String owner, long account, double initial)
   {
      name = owner;
      acctNumber = account;
      balance = initial;
   }

   //-----------------------------------------------------------------
   //  Deposits the specified amount into this account and returns
   //  the new balance. The balance is not modified if the deposit
   //  amount is invalid.
   //-----------------------------------------------------------------
   public double deposit(double amount)
   {
      if (amount > 0)
         balance = balance + amount;
```

LISTING 5.7 *continued*

```
      return balance;
   }

   //-----------------------------------------------------------------
   //  Withdraws the specified amount and fee from this account and
   //  returns the new balance. The balance is not modified if the
   //  withdraw amount is invalid or the balance is insufficient.
   //-----------------------------------------------------------------
   public double withdraw(double amount, double fee)
   {
      if (amount+fee > 0 && amount+fee < balance)
         balance = balance - amount - fee;

      return balance;
   }

   //-----------------------------------------------------------------
   //  Adds interest to this account and returns the new balance.
   //-----------------------------------------------------------------
   public double addInterest()
   {
      balance += (balance * RATE);
      return balance;
   }

   //-----------------------------------------------------------------
   //  Returns the current balance of this account.
   //-----------------------------------------------------------------
   public double getBalance()
   {
      return balance;
   }

   //-----------------------------------------------------------------
   //  Returns a one-line description of this account as a string.
   //-----------------------------------------------------------------
   public String toString()
   {
      NumberFormat fmt = NumberFormat.getCurrencyInstance();

      return (acctNumber + "\t" + name + "\t" + fmt.format(balance));
   }
}
```

The status of the three `Account` objects just after they were created in the `Transactions` program could be depicted as follows:

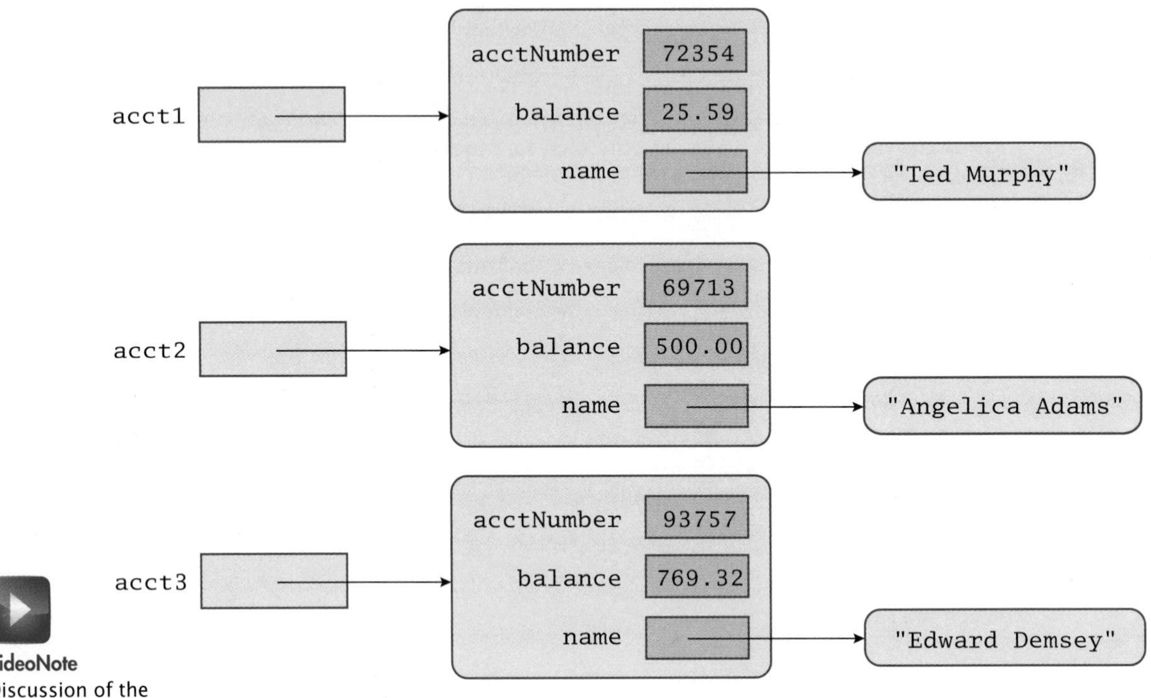

VideoNote
Discussion of the `Account` class

The rest of this section discusses in more detail the issues related to method declarations.

The `return` Statement

The return type specified in the method header can be a primitive type, a class name, or the reserved word `void`. When a method does not return any value, `void` is used as the return type, as is always done with the `main` method of a program. The `setFaceValue` of the `Die` class and the `flip` method of the `Coin` class also have return types of `void`.

The `getFaceValue` and `roll` methods of the `Die` class return an `int` value that represents the value shown on the die. The `isHeads` method of the `Coin` class returns a `boolean` value that indicates whether the coin is currently showing heads. Several of the methods of the `Account` class return a `double` representing the updated balance. The `toString` method in all of these classes returns a `String` object.

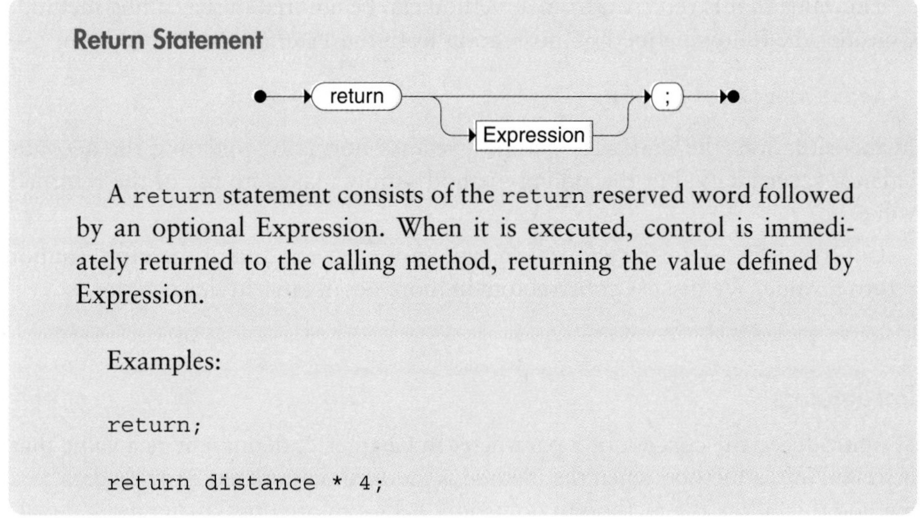

Return Statement

A `return` statement consists of the `return` reserved word followed by an optional Expression. When it is executed, control is immediately returned to the calling method, returning the value defined by Expression.

Examples:

```
return;

return distance * 4;
```

A method that returns a value must have a *return statement*. When a `return` statement is executed, control is immediately returned to the statement in the calling method, and processing continues there. A `return` statement consists of the reserved word `return` followed by an expression that dictates the value to be returned. The expression must be consistent with the return type specified in the method header.

KEY CONCEPT
The value returned from a method must be consistent with the return type specified in the method header.

A method that does not return a value does not usually contain a `return` statement. The method automatically returns to the calling method when the end of the method is reached. Such methods may contain a `return` statement without an expression.

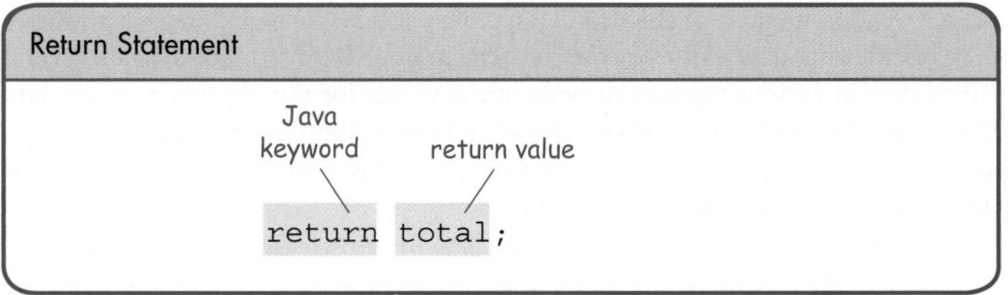

It is usually not good practice to use more than one `return` statement in a method, even though it is possible to do so. In general, a method should have one `return` statement as the last line of the method body, unless that makes the method overly complex.

The value that is returned from a method can be ignored in the calling method. Consider the following method invocation from the `Transactions` program:

```
acct1.deposit(44.10);
```

In this situation, the `deposit` method executes normally, updating the account balance accordingly, but the calling method simply makes no use of the returned value.

Constructors do not have a return type (not even `void`) and therefore cannot return a value. We discuss constructors in more detail later in this chapter.

Parameters

We introduced the concept of a parameter in Chapter 2, defining it as a value that is passed into a method when the method is invoked. Parameters provide data to a method that allow the method to do its job. Let's explore this issue in more detail.

The method declaration specifies the number and type of parameters that a method will accept. More precisely, the *parameter list* in the header of a method declaration specifies the type of each value that is passed into the method, and the name by which the called method will refer to each value. The corresponding parameter list in the invocation specifies the values that are passed in for that particular invocation.

The names of the parameters in the header of the method declaration are called *formal parameters*. The values passed into a method when it is invoked are called *actual parameters*, or *arguments*. The parameter list in both the declaration and the invocation is enclosed in parentheses after the method name. If there are no parameters, an empty set of parentheses is used.

None of the methods in the `Coin` and `Die` classes accepts parameters except the `setFaceValue` method of the `Die` class, which accepts a single integer parameter that specifies the new value for the die. The `Account` constructor accepts several parameters of various types to provide initial values for the object's instance data (this is common for constructors). The `withdraw` method in `Account` accepts two parameters of type `double`; note that the type of each formal parameter is listed separately even if the types are the same.

The formal parameters are identifiers that serve as variables inside the method and whose initial values come from the actual parameters in the invocation. When a method is called, the value in each actual parameter is copied and stored in the corresponding formal parameter. Actual parameters can be literals, variables, or full expressions. If an expression is used as an actual parameter, it is fully evaluated before the method call, and the result is passed to the method.

KEY CONCEPT

When a method is called, the actual parameters are copied into the formal parameters.

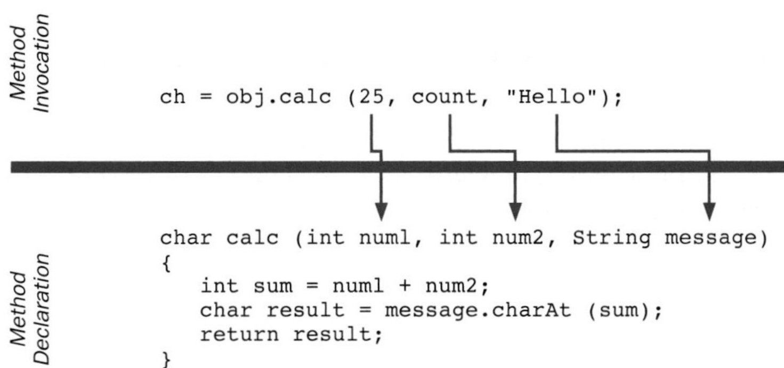

FIGURE 5.9 Passing parameters from the method invocation to the declaration

The parameter lists in the invocation and the method declaration must match up. That is, the value of the first actual parameter is copied into the first formal parameter, the value of the second actual parameter into the second formal parameter, and so on, as shown in Figure 5.9. The types of the actual parameters must be consistent with the specified types of the formal parameters.

In the `Transactions` program, the following call is made:

```
acct2.withdraw(480, 1.50)
```

This call passes an integer value as the first parameter of the `withdraw` method, which is defined to accept a `double`. This is valid because the actual and formal parameters must be consistent, but they need not match exactly. A `double` variable can be assigned an integer value because this is a widening conversion. Thus it is also allowed when passing parameters.

We explore some of the details of parameter passing later in this chapter.

Local Data

As we described earlier in this chapter, the scope of a variable or constant is the part of a program in which a valid reference to that variable can be made. A variable can be declared inside a method, making it *local data* as opposed to instance data. Recall that instance data are declared in a class but not inside any particular method.

Local data have scope limited to the method in which they are is declared. The variable `result` declared in the `toString` method of the `Die` class is local data. Any reference to `result` in any other method of the `Die` class would have caused the compiler to issue an

> **KEY CONCEPT**
> A variable declared in a method is local to that method and cannot be used outside it.

error message. A local variable simply does not exist outside the method in which it is declared. On the other hand, instance data, declared at the class level, have a scope of the entire class; any method of the class can refer to instance data.

Because local data and instance data operate at different levels of scope, it's possible to declare a local variable inside a method with the same name as an instance variable declared at the class level. Referring to that name in the method will reference the local version of the variable. This naming practice obviously has the potential to confuse anyone reading the code, so it should be avoided.

The formal parameter names in a method header serve as local data for that method. They don't exist until the method is called, and they cease to exist when the method is exited. For example, the formal parameter `owner` in the `Account` constructor comes into existence when the constructor is called and goes out of existence when it finishes executing. To store these values in the object, the values of the parameters are copied into the instance variables of the newly created `Account` object.

Constructors Revisited

Let's discuss constructors a bit more. When we define a class, we usually define a constructor to help us set up the class. In particular, we often use a constructor to initialize the variables associated with each object.

KEY CONCEPT
A constructor cannot have any return type, even `void`.

A constructor differs from a regular method in two ways. First, the name of a constructor is the same as the name of the class. Therefore, the name of the constructor in the `Die` class is `Die`, and the name of the constructor in the `Account` class is `Account`. Second, a constructor cannot return a value and does not have a return type specified in the method header.

Generally, a constructor is used to initialize the newly instantiated object. For instance, the constructor of the `Die` class sets the face value of the die to 1 initially. The constructor of the `Coin` class calls the `flip` method to put the coin

COMMON ERROR

A mistake commonly made by programmers is to put a `void` return type on a constructor. As far as the compiler is concerned, putting any return type on a constructor, even `void`, turns it into a regular method that happens to have the same name as the class. As such, it cannot be invoked as a constructor. This leads to error messages that are sometimes difficult to decipher.

in an initial, random state. The constructor of the `Account` class sets the values of the instance variables to the values passed in as parameters to the constructor. The way you use a constructor to set up an object initially is another important design decision.

If we don't provide a constructor for a class, a *default constructor* that takes no parameters is automatically created and used. The default constructor generally has no effect on the newly created object. If the programmer provides a constructor, with or without parameters, the default constructor is not defined.

5.5 Static Class Members

We've used static methods in various situations in previous examples in the book. For example, all the methods of the `Math` class are static. Recall that a static method is one that is invoked through its class name, instead of through an object of that class.

Not only can methods be static, but variables can be static as well. We declare static class members using the `static` modifier.

Deciding whether to declare a method or variable as static is a key step in class design. Let's examine the implications of static variables and methods more closely.

Static Variables

So far, we've seen two categories of variables: local variables that are declared inside a method, and instance variables that are declared in a class but not inside a method. The term *instance variable* is used because each instance of the class has its own version of the variable. That is, each object has distinct memory space for each variable so that each object can have a distinct value for that variable.

KEY CONCEPT
A static variable is shared among all instances of a class.

A *static variable*, which is sometimes called a *class variable*, is shared among all instances of a class. There is only one copy of a static variable for all objects of the class. Therefore, changing the value of a static variable in one object changes it for all of the others. The reserved word `static` is used as a modifier to declare a static variable as follows:

```
private static int count = 0;
```

Memory space for a static variable is established when the class that contains it is referenced for the first time in a program. A local variable declared within a method cannot be static.

Constants, which are declared using the `final` modifier, are often declared using the `static` modifier. Because the value of constants cannot be changed, there might as well be only one copy of the value across all objects of the class.

Static Methods

In Chapter 3 we briefly introduced the concept of a *static method* (also called a *class method*). Static methods can be invoked through the class name. We don't have to instantiate an object of the class in order to invoke the method. In Chapter 3 we noted that all the methods of the `Math` class are static methods. For example, in the following line of code, the `sqrt` method is invoked through the `Math` class name.

```
System.out.println ("Square root of 27:" + Math.sqrt(27));
```

The methods in the `Math` class perform basic computations based on values passed as parameters. There is no object state to maintain in these situations, so there is no good reason to force us to create an object in order to request these services.

A method is made static by using the `static` modifier in the method declaration. As we've seen many times, the `main` method of a Java program is declared with the `static` modifier; this is done so that `main` can be executed by the interpreter without instantiating an object from the class that contains `main`.

Because static methods do not operate in the context of a particular object, they cannot reference instance variables, which exist only in an instance of a class. The compiler will issue an error if a static method attempts to use a nonstatic variable. A static method can, however, reference static variables, because static variables exist independent of specific objects. Therefore, all static methods, including the `main` method, can access only static or local variables.

The program in Listing 5.8 instantiates several objects of the `Slogan` class, printing each one out in turn. Then it invokes a method called `getCount` through the class name, which returns the number of `Slogan` objects that were instantiated in the program.

Listing 5.9 on page 202 shows the `Slogan` class. The constructor of `Slogan` increments a static variable called `count`, which is initialized to zero when it is declared. Therefore, `count` serves to keep track of the number of instances of `Slogan` that are created.

The `getCount` method of `Slogan` is also declared as static, which allows it to be invoked through the class name in the `main` method. Note that the only data referenced in the `getCount` method is the integer variable `count`, which is static. As a static method, `getCount` cannot reference any nonstatic data.

LISTING 5.8

```
//********************************************************************
//  SloganCounter.java       Java Foundations
//
//  Demonstrates the use of the static modifier.
//********************************************************************

public class SloganCounter
{
   //-----------------------------------------------------------------
   //  Creates several Slogan objects and prints the number of
   //  objects that were created.
   //-----------------------------------------------------------------
   public static void main(String[] args)
   {
      Slogan obj;

      obj = new Slogan("Remember the Alamo.");
      System.out.println(obj);

      obj = new Slogan("Don't Worry. Be Happy.");
      System.out.println(obj);

      obj = new Slogan("Live Free or Die.");
      System.out.println(obj);

      obj = new Slogan("Talk is Cheap.");
      System.out.println(obj);

      obj = new Slogan("Write Once, Run Anywhere.");
      System.out.println(obj);

      System.out.println();
      System.out.println("Slogans created: " + Slogan.getCount());
   }
}
```

OUTPUT

```
Remember the Alamo.
Don't Worry. Be Happy.
Live Free or Die.
Talk is Cheap.
Write Once, Run Anywhere.

Slogans created: 5
```

LISTING 5.9

```
//********************************************************************
//  Slogan.java      Java Foundations
//
//  Represents a single slogan or motto.
//********************************************************************

public class Slogan
{
   private String phrase;
   private static int count = 0;

   //-----------------------------------------------------------------
   //  Constructor: Sets up the slogan and increments the number of
   //  instances created.
   //-----------------------------------------------------------------
   public Slogan(String str)
   {
      phrase = str;
      count++;
   }

   //-----------------------------------------------------------------
   // Returns this slogan as a string.
   //-----------------------------------------------------------------
   public String toString()
   {
      return phrase;
   }

   //-----------------------------------------------------------------
   // Returns the number of instances of this class that have been
   // created.
   //-----------------------------------------------------------------
   public static int getCount()
   {
      return count;
   }
}
```

The getCount method could have been declared without the static modifier, but then its invocation in the main method would have had to be done through an instance of the Slogan class instead of the class itself.

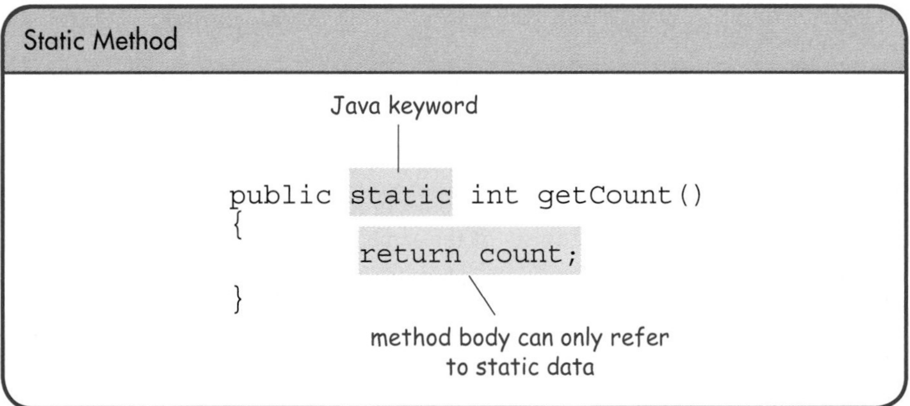

Static Method
Java keyword
public static int getCount()
{
return count;
}
method body can only refer to static data

5.6 Class Relationships

The classes in a software system have various types of relationships to each other. Three of the more common relationships are dependency, aggregation, and inheritance.

We've seen dependency relationships in many examples in which one class "uses" another. This section revisits the dependency relationship and explores the situation where a class depends on itself. We then explore aggregation, in which the objects of one class contain objects of another, creating a "has-a" relationship. Inheritance, which we introduced in Chapter 1, creates an "is-a" relationship between classes. We defer our detailed examination of inheritance until Chapter 8.

Dependency

In many previous examples, we've seen the idea of one class being dependent on another. This means that one class relies on another in some sense. Often the methods of one class invoke the methods of the other class. This establishes a "uses" relationship.

Generally, if class A uses class B, then one or more methods of class A invoke one or more methods of class B. If an invoked method is static, then A merely references B by name. If the invoked method is not static, then A must have access to a specific instance of class B in order to invoke the method. That is, A must have a reference to an object of class B.

The way in which one object gains access to an object of another class is an important design decision. It occurs when one class instantiates the objects of another, but the access can also be accomplished by passing one object to another as a method parameter.

In general, we want to minimize the number of dependencies among classes. The less dependent our classes are on each other, the less impact changes and errors will have on the system.

Dependencies among Objects of the Same Class

In some cases, a class depends on itself. That is, an object of one class interacts with another object of the same class. To accomplish this, a method of the class may accept as a parameter an object of the same class.

The `concat` method of the `String` class is an example of this situation. The method is executed through one `String` object and is passed another `String` object as a parameter. Here is an example:

```
str3 = str1.concat(str2);
```

The `String` object executing the method (`str1`) appends its characters to those of the `String` passed as a parameter (`str2`). A new `String` object is returned as a result and stored as `str3`.

The `RationalTester` program shown in Listing 5.10 on the next page demonstrates a similar situation. A rational number is a value that can be represented as a ratio of two integers (a fraction). The `RationalTester` program creates two objects representing rational numbers and then performs various operations on them to produce new rational numbers.

LISTING 5.10

```
//********************************************************************
//  RationalTester.java                    Java Foundations
//
//  Driver to exercise the use of multiple Rational objects.
//********************************************************************

public class RationalTester
{
   //-----------------------------------------------------------------
   //  Creates some rational number objects and performs various
   //  operations on them.
   //-----------------------------------------------------------------
```

LISTING 5.10 *continued*

```
   public static void main(String[] args)
   {
      RationalNumber r1 = new RationalNumber(6, 8);
      RationalNumber r2 = new RationalNumber(1, 3);
      RationalNumber r3, r4, r5, r6, r7;

      System.out.println("First rational number: " + r1);
      System.out.println("Second rational number: " + r2);

      if (r1.isLike(r2))
         System.out.println("r1 and r2 are equal.");
      else
         System.out.println("r1 and r2 are NOT equal.");

      r3 = r1.reciprocal();
      System.out.println("The reciprocal of r1 is: " + r3);

      r4 = r1.add(r2);
      r5 = r1.subtract(r2);
      r6 = r1.multiply(r2);
      r7 = r1.divide(r2);

      System.out.println("r1 + r2: " + r4);
      System.out.println("r1 - r2: " + r5);
      System.out.println("r1 * r2: " + r6);
      System.out.println("r1 / r2: " + r7);
   }
}
```

OUTPUT

```
First rational number: 3/4
Second rational number: 1/3
r1 and r2 are NOT equal.
The reciprocal of r1 is: 4/3
r1 + r2: 13/12
r1 - r2: 5/12
r1 * r2: 1/4
r1 / r2: 9/4
```

The `RationalNumber` class is shown in Listing 5.11 on the next page. As you examine this class, keep in mind that each object created from the `RationalNumber` class represents a single rational number. The `RationalNumber` class contains various operations on rational numbers, such as addition and subtraction.

The methods of the `RationalNumber` class, such as `add`, `subtract`, `multiply`, and `divide`, use the `RationalNumber` object that is executing the method as the first (left) operand and use the `RationalNumber` object passed as a parameter as the second (right) operand.

The `isLike` method of the `RationalNumber` class is used to determine whether two rational numbers are essentially equal. It's tempting, therefore, to call that method `equals`, similar to the method used to compare `String` objects (discussed in Chapter 4). However, in Chapter 8 we will discuss how the `equals` method is somewhat special due to inheritance, and we will note that it should be implemented in a particular way. Thus, to avoid confusion, we call this method `isLike` for now.

Note that some of the methods in the `RationalNumber` class, including `reduce` and `gcd`, are declared with private visibility. These methods are private because we don't want them executed directly from outside a `RationalNumber` object. They exist only to support the other services of the object.

Aggregation

KEY CONCEPT
An aggregate object is composed of other objects, forming a has-a relationship.

Some objects are made up of other objects. A car, for instance, is made up of its engine, its chassis, its wheels, and several other parts. Each of these other parts could be considered a separate object. Therefore, we can say that a car is an *aggregation*—it is composed, at least in part, of other objects. Aggregation is sometimes described as a *has-a relationship*. For instance, a car "has-a" chassis.

In the software world, we define an *aggregate object* as any object that contains references to other objects as instance data. For example, an `Account` object contains, among other things, a `String` object that represents the name of the account owner. We sometimes forget that strings are objects, but technically that makes each `Account` object an aggregate object.

Aggregation is a special type of dependency. That is, a class that is defined in part by another class is dependent on that class. The methods of the aggregate object generally invoke the methods of the objects of which it is composed.

LISTING 5.11

```
//********************************************************************
//  RationalNumber.java       Java Foundations
//
//  Represents one rational number with a numerator and denominator.
//********************************************************************

public class RationalNumber
{
   private int numerator, denominator;

   //-----------------------------------------------------------------
   //  Constructor: Sets up the rational number by ensuring a nonzero
   //  denominator and making only the numerator signed.
   //-----------------------------------------------------------------
   public RationalNumber(int numer, int denom)
   {
      if (denom == 0)
         denom = 1;

      // Make the numerator "store" the sign
      if (denom < 0)
      {
         numer = numer * -1;
         denom = denom * -1;
      }

      numerator = numer;
      denominator = denom;

      reduce();
   }

   //-----------------------------------------------------------------
   //  Returns the numerator of this rational number.
   //-----------------------------------------------------------------
   public int getNumerator()
   {
      return numerator;
   }

   //-----------------------------------------------------------------
   //  Returns the denominator of this rational number.
   //-----------------------------------------------------------------
   public int getDenominator()
```

LISTING 5.11 *continued*

```
   {
      return denominator;
   }

   //-----------------------------------------------------------------
   //  Returns the reciprocal of this rational number.
   //-----------------------------------------------------------------
   public RationalNumber reciprocal()
   {
      return new RationalNumber(denominator, numerator);
   }

   //-----------------------------------------------------------------
   //  Adds this rational number to the one passed as a parameter.
   //  A common denominator is found by multiplying the individual
   //  denominators.
   //-----------------------------------------------------------------
   public RationalNumber add(RationalNumber op2)
   {
      int commonDenominator = denominator * op2.getDenominator();
      int numerator1 = numerator * op2.getDenominator();
      int numerator2 = op2.getNumerator() * denominator;
      int sum = numerator1 + numerator2;

      return new RationalNumber(sum, commonDenominator);
   }

   //-----------------------------------------------------------------
   //  Subtracts the rational number passed as a parameter from this
   //  rational number.
   //-----------------------------------------------------------------
   public RationalNumber subtract(RationalNumber op2)
   {
      int commonDenominator = denominator * op2.getDenominator();
      int numerator1 = numerator * op2.getDenominator();
      int numerator2 = op2.getNumerator() * denominator;
      int difference = numerator1 - numerator2;

      return new RationalNumber(difference, commonDenominator);
   }

   //-----------------------------------------------------------------
   //  Multiplies this rational number by the one passed as a
   //  parameter.
   //-----------------------------------------------------------------
```

LISTING 5.11 *continued*

```
   public RationalNumber multiply(RationalNumber op2)
   {
      int numer = numerator * op2.getNumerator();
      int denom = denominator * op2.getDenominator();

      return new RationalNumber(numer, denom);
   }

   //-----------------------------------------------------------------
   //  Divides this rational number by the one passed as a parameter
   //  by multiplying by the reciprocal of the second rational.
   //-----------------------------------------------------------------
   public RationalNumber divide(RationalNumber op2)
   {
      return multiply(op2.reciprocal());
   }

   //-----------------------------------------------------------------
   //  Determines if this rational number is equal to the one passed
   //  as a parameter. Assumes they are both reduced.
   //-----------------------------------------------------------------
   public boolean isLike(RationalNumber op2)
   {
      return (numerator == op2.getNumerator() &&
              denominator == op2.getDenominator());
   }

   //-----------------------------------------------------------------
   //  Returns this rational number as a string.
   //-----------------------------------------------------------------
   public String toString()
   {
      String result;

      if (numerator == 0)
         result = "0";
      else
         if (denominator == 1)
         result = numerator + "";
      else
         result = numerator + "/" + denominator;

      return result;
   }
```

LISTING 5.11 *continued*

```
   //-----------------------------------------------------------------
   //  Reduces this rational number by dividing both the numerator
   //  and the denominator by their greatest common divisor.
   //-----------------------------------------------------------------
   private void reduce()
   {
      if (numerator != 0)
      {
         int common = gcd(Math.abs(numerator), denominator);

         numerator = numerator / common;
         denominator = denominator / common;
      }
   }

   //-----------------------------------------------------------------
   //  Computes and returns the greatest common divisor of the two
   //  positive parameters. Uses Euclid's algorithm.
   //-----------------------------------------------------------------
   private int gcd(int num1, int num2)
   {
      while (num1 != num2)
         if (num1 > num2)
            num1 = num1 - num2;
      else
         num2 = num2 - num1;

      return num1;
   }
}
```

The more complex an object, the more likely it is that it will need to be represented as an aggregate object. In UML, aggregation is represented by a connection between two classes, with an open diamond at the end near the class that is the aggregate. Figure 5.10 shows a UML class diagram that contains an aggregation relationship.

Note that in previous UML diagram examples, strings are not represented as separate classes with aggregation relationships, even though technically they

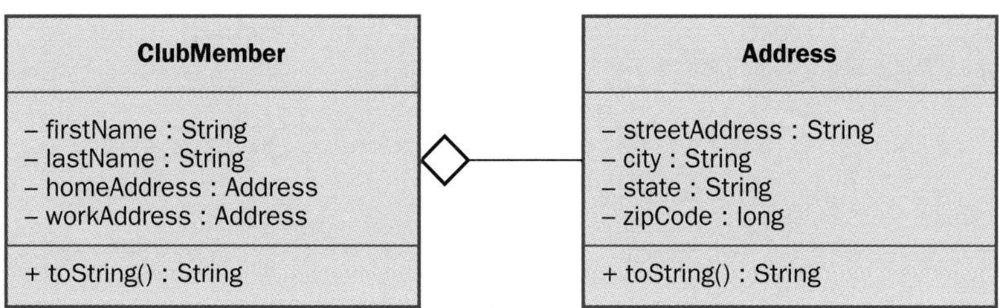

FIGURE 5.10 A UML class diagram showing an aggregation relationship

could be. Strings are so fundamental to programming that often they are represented as though they were a primitive type in a UML diagram.

The this Reference

Before we leave the topic of relationships among classes, we should examine another special reference used in Java programs called the `this` reference. The word `this` is a reserved word in Java. It allows an object to refer to itself. As we have discussed, a nonstatic method is invoked through (or by) a particular object or class. Inside that method, the `this` reference can be used to refer to the currently executing object.

For example, in a class called `ChessPiece` there could be a method called `move`, which could contain

```
if (this.position == piece2.position)
          result =false;
```

In this situation, the `this` reference is being used to clarify which position is being referenced. The `this` reference refers to the object through which the method was invoked. So when the following line is used to invoke the method, the `this` reference refers to `bishop1`:

```
bishop1.move();
```

However, when another object is used to invoke the method, the `this` reference refers to it. Therefore, when the following invocation is used, the `this` reference in the `move` method refers to `bishop2`:

```
bishop2.move();
```

Often, the `this` reference is used to distinguish the parameters of a constructor from their corresponding instance variables with the same names. For example, the constructor of the `Account` class was presented in Listing 5.7 as follows:

```
public Account(String owner, long account, double initial)
{
   name = owner;
   acctNumber = account;
   balance = initial;
}
```

When writing this constructor, we deliberately came up with different names for the parameters to distinguish them from the instance variables `name`, `acctNumber`, and `balance`. This distinction is arbitrary. The constructor could have been written as follows using the `this` reference:

```
public Account(String name, long acctNumber, double balance)
{
   this.name = name;
   this.acctNumber = acctNumber;
   this.balance = balance;
}
```

In this version of the constructor, the `this` reference specifically refers to the instance variables of the object. The variables on the right-hand side of the assignment statements refer to the formal parameters. This approach eliminates the need to come up with different yet equivalent names. This situation sometimes occurs in other methods, but it comes up often in constructors.

5.7 Method Design

Once you have identified classes and assigned basic responsibilities, the design of each method will determine how exactly the class will define its behaviors. Some methods are straightforward and require little thought. Others are more interesting and require careful planning.

An *algorithm* is a step-by-step process for solving a problem. A recipe is an example of an algorithm. Travel directions are another example of an algorithm. Every method implements an algorithm that determines how that method accomplishes its goals.

An algorithm is often described using *pseudocode*, which is a mixture of code statements and English phrases. Pseudocode provides enough structure to show how the code will operate, without getting bogged down in the syntactic details of a particular programming language or becoming prematurely constrained by the characteristics of particular programming constructs.

This section discusses two important aspects of program design at the method level: method decomposition and the implications of passing objects as parameters.

Method Decomposition

KEY CONCEPT

The best way to make use of a complex service provided by an object may be to decompose the method and use several private support methods to help with the task.

Occasionally, a service that an object provides is so complex that it cannot reasonably be implemented using one method. Therefore, we sometimes need to decompose a method into multiple methods to create a more understandable design. As an example, let's examine a program that translates English sentences into "Pig Latin."

Pig Latin is a made-up language in which each word of a sentence is modified, in general, by moving the initial sound of the word to the end and adding an "ay" sound. For example, the word *happy* would be written and pronounced *appyhay*, and the word *birthday* would become *irthdaybay*. Words that begin with vowels simply have a "yay" sound added on the end, turning the word *enough* into *enoughyay*. Consonant blends such as "ch" and "st" at the beginning of a word are moved to the end together before adding the "ay" sound. Therefore, the word *grapefruit* becomes *apefruitgray*.

The `PigLatin` program shown in Listing 5.12 reads one or more sentences, translating each into Pig Latin.

The workhorse behind the `PigLatin` program is the `PigLatinTranslator` class, shown in Listing 5.13 on page 215. The `PigLatinTranslator` class provides one fundamental service, a static method called `translate`, which accepts a string and translates it into Pig Latin. Note that the `PigLatinTranslator` class does not contain a constructor because none is needed.

The act of translating an entire sentence into Pig Latin is not trivial. If written in one big method, it would be very long and difficult to follow. A better solution, as implemented in the `PigLatinTranslator` class, is to decompose the `translate` method and use several private support methods to help with the task.

The `translate` method uses a `Scanner` object to separate the string into words. Recall that one role of the `Scanner` class (discussed in Chapter 3) is to separate a string into smaller elements called tokens. In this case, the tokens are separated by space characters so that we can use the default whitespace delimiters. The `PigLatin` program assumes that no punctuation is included in the input.

The `translate` method passes each word to the private support method `translateWord`. Even the job of translating one word is somewhat involved, so the `translateWord` method makes use of two other private methods, `beginsWithVowel` and `beginsWithBlend`.

The `beginsWithVowel` method returns a `boolean` value that indicates whether the word passed as a parameter begins with a vowel. Note that instead of checking each vowel separately, the code for this method declares a string that contains all the vowels and then invokes the `String` method `indexOf` to determine whether

LISTING 5.12

```
//********************************************************************
//  PigLatin.java          Java Foundations
//
//  Demonstrates the concept of method decomposition.
//********************************************************************

import java.util.Scanner;

public class PigLatin
{
   //-----------------------------------------------------------------
   //  Reads sentences and translates them into Pig Latin.
   //-----------------------------------------------------------------
   public static void main(String[] args)
   {
      String sentence, result, another;

      Scanner scan = new Scanner(System.in);

      do
      {
         System.out.println();
         System.out.println("Enter a sentence (no punctuation):");
         sentence = scan.nextLine();

         System.out.println();
         result = PigLatinTranslator.translate (sentence);
         System.out.println("That sentence in Pig Latin is:");
         System.out.println(result);

         System.out.println();
         System.out.print("Translate another sentence (y/n)? ");
         another = scan.nextLine();
      }
      while (another.equalsIgnoreCase("y"));
   }
}
```

OUTPUT

```
Enter a sentence (no punctuation):
Do you speak Pig Latin
```

LISTING 5.12 *continued*

```
That sentence in Pig Latin is:
oday ouyay eakspay igpay atinlay

Translate another sentence (y/n)? y

Enter a sentence (no punctuation):
Play it again Sam

That sentence in Pig Latin is:
ayplay ityay againyay amsay

Translate another sentence (y/n)? n
```

LISTING 5.13

```
//********************************************************************
//  PigLatinTranslator.java      Java Foundations
//
//  Represents a translator from English to Pig Latin. Demonstrates
//  method decomposition.
//********************************************************************

import java.util.Scanner;

public class PigLatinTranslator
{
   //-----------------------------------------------------------------
   //  Translates a sentence of words into Pig Latin.
   //-----------------------------------------------------------------
   public static String translate(String sentence)
   {
      String result = "";

      sentence = sentence.toLowerCase();

      Scanner scan = new Scanner(sentence);

      while (scan.hasNext())
```

LISTING 5.13 *continued*

```
      {
         result += translateWord(scan.next());
         result += " ";
      }

      return result;
   }

   //-----------------------------------------------------------------
   //  Translates one word into Pig Latin. If the word begins with a
   //  vowel, the suffix "yay" is appended to the word. Otherwise,
   //  the first letter or two are moved to the end of the word,
   //  and "ay" is appended.
   //-----------------------------------------------------------------
   private static String translateWord(String word)
   {
      String result = "";

      if (beginsWithVowel(word))
         result = word + "yay";
      else
         if (beginsWithBlend(word))
            result = word.substring(2) + word.substring(0,2) + "ay";
         else
            result = word.substring(1) + word.charAt(0) + "ay";

      return result;
   }

   //-----------------------------------------------------------------
   //  Determines if the specified word begins with a vowel.
   //-----------------------------------------------------------------
   private static boolean beginsWithVowel(String word)
   {
      String vowels = "aeiou";

      char letter = word.charAt(0);

      return (vowels.indexOf(letter) != -1);
   }

   //-----------------------------------------------------------------
   //  Determines if the specified word begins with a particular
   //  two-character consonant blend.
   //-----------------------------------------------------------------
   private static boolean beginsWithBlend(String word)
```

LISTING 5.13 *continued*

```
   {
      return ( word.startsWith("bl") || word.startsWith("sc") ||
               word.startsWith("br") || word.startsWith("sh") ||
               word.startsWith("ch") || word.startsWith("sk") ||
               word.startsWith("cl") || word.startsWith("sl") ||
               word.startsWith("cr") || word.startsWith("sn") ||
               word.startsWith("dr") || word.startsWith("sm") ||
               word.startsWith("dw") || word.startsWith("sp") ||
               word.startsWith("fl") || word.startsWith("sq") ||
               word.startsWith("fr") || word.startsWith("st") ||
               word.startsWith("gl") || word.startsWith("sw") ||
               word.startsWith("gr") || word.startsWith("th") ||
               word.startsWith("kl") || word.startsWith("tr") ||
               word.startsWith("ph") || word.startsWith("tw") ||
               word.startsWith("pl") || word.startsWith("wh") ||
               word.startsWith("pr") || word.startsWith("wr") );
   }
}
```

the first character of the word is in the vowel string. If the specified character cannot be found, the `indexOf` method returns a value of `-1`.

The `beginsWithBlend` method also returns a `boolean` value. The body of the method contains only a `return` statement with one large expression that makes several calls to the `startsWith` method of the `String` class. If any of these calls returns true, then the `beginsWithBlend` method returns true as well.

Note that the `translateWord`, `beginsWithVowel`, and `beginsWithBlend` methods are all declared with private visibility. They are not intended to provide services directly to clients outside the class. Instead, they exist to help the `translate` method, which is the only true service method in this class, to do its job. Declaring them with private visibility means that they cannot be invoked from outside this class. For instance, if the `main` method of the `PigLatin` class attempted to invoke the `translateWord` method, the compiler would issue an error message.

Figure 5.11 shows a UML class diagram for the `PigLatin` program. Note the notation showing the visibility of various methods.

Whenever a method becomes large or complex, we should consider decomposing it into multiple methods to create a more understandable class design. First, however, we must consider how other classes and objects can be defined to create better overall system design. In an object-oriented design, method decomposition must be subordinate to object decomposition.

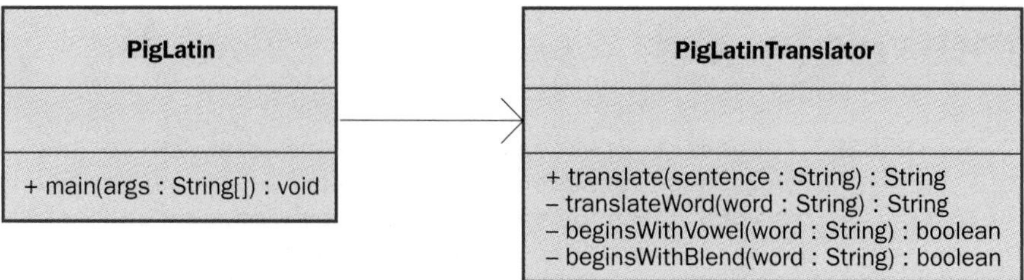

FIGURE 5.11 A UML class diagram for the `PigLatin` program

Method Parameters Revisited

Another important issue related to method design involves the way parameters are passed into a method. In Java, all parameters are passed *by value*. That is, the current value of the actual parameter (in the invocation) is copied into the formal parameter in the method header. We mentioned this issue previously in this chapter; let's examine it now in more detail.

Essentially, parameter passing is like an assignment statement, assigning to the formal parameter a copy of the value stored in the actual parameter. This issue must be considered when making changes to a formal parameter inside a method. The formal parameter is a separate copy of the value that is passed in, so any changes made to it have no effect on the actual parameter. After control returns to the calling method, the actual parameter will have the same value it had before the method was called.

However, when we pass an object to a method, we are actually passing a reference to that object. The value that gets copied is the address of the object. Therefore, the formal parameter and the actual parameter become aliases of each other. If we change the state of the object through the formal parameter reference inside the method, we are changing the object referenced by the actual parameter, because they refer to the same object. On the other hand, if we change the formal parameter reference itself (to make it point to a new object, for instance), we have not changed the fact that the actual parameter still refers to the original object.

> **KEY CONCEPT**
> When an object is passed to a method, the actual and formal parameters become aliases.

The program in Listing 5.14 illustrates the nuances of parameter passing. Carefully trace the processing of this program, and note the values that are output. The `ParameterTester` class contains a `main` method that calls the `changeValues` method in a `ParameterModifier` object. Two of the parameters to `changeValues` are `Num` objects, each of which simply stores an integer value. The other parameter is a primitive integer value.

Listing 5.15 on page 220 shows the `ParameterModifier` class, and Listing 5.16 on page 221 shows the `Num` class. Inside the `changeValues` method, a modification is made to each of the three formal parameters: The integer parameter is set to a different value, the value stored in the first `Num` parameter is changed

LISTING 5.14

```
//********************************************************************
//  ParameterTester.java       Java Foundations
//
//  Demonstrates the effects of passing various types of parameters.
//********************************************************************

public class ParameterTester
{
   //-----------------------------------------------------------------
   //  Sets up three variables (one primitive and two objects) to
   //  serve as actual parameters to the changeValues method. Prints
   //  their values before and after calling the method.
   //-----------------------------------------------------------------
   public static void main(String[] args)
   {
      ParameterModifier modifier = new ParameterModifier();

      int a1 = 111;
      Num a2 = new Num(222);
      Num a3 = new Num(333);

      System.out.println("Before calling changeValues:");
      System.out.println("a1\ta2\ta3");
      System.out.println(a1 + "\t" + a2 + "\t" + a3 + "\n");

      modifier.changeValues(a1, a2, a3);

      System.out.println("After calling changeValues:");
      System.out.println("a1\ta2\ta3");
      System.out.println(a1 + "\t" + a2 + "\t" + a3 + "\n");
   }
}
```

OUTPUT

```
Before calling changeValues:
a1          a2          a3
111         222         333

Before changing the values:
f1          f2          f3
111         222         333
```

LISTING 5.14 *continued*

```
After changing the values:
f1          f2          f3
999         888         777

After calling changeValues:
a1          a2          a3
111         888         333
```

LISTING 5.15

```
//********************************************************************
//  ParameterModifier.java       Java Foundations
//
//  Demonstrates the effects of changing parameter values.
//********************************************************************

public class ParameterModifier
{
   //-----------------------------------------------------------------
   //  Modifies the parameters, printing their values before and
   //  after making the changes.
   //-----------------------------------------------------------------
   public void changeValues(int f1, Num f2, Num f3)
   {
      System.out.println("Before changing the values:");
      System.out.println("f1\tf2\tf3");
      System.out.println(f1 + "\t" + f2 + "\t" + f3 + "\n");

      f1 = 999;
      f2.setValue(888);
      f3 = new Num(777);

      System.out.println("After changing the values:");
      System.out.println("f1\tf2\tf3");
      System.out.println(f1 + "\t" + f2 + "\t" + f3 + "\n");
   }
}
```

LISTING 5.16

```
//********************************************************************
//  Num.java       Java Foundations
//
//  Represents a single integer as an object.
//********************************************************************

public class Num
{
   private int value;

   //-----------------------------------------------------------------
   //  Sets up the new Num object, storing an initial value.
   //-----------------------------------------------------------------
   public Num(int update)
   {
      value = update;
   }

   //-----------------------------------------------------------------
   //  Sets the stored value to the newly specified value.
   //-----------------------------------------------------------------
   public void setValue(int update)
   {
      value = update;
   }

   //-----------------------------------------------------------------
   //  Returns the stored integer value as a string.
   //-----------------------------------------------------------------
   public String toString()
   {
      return value + "";
   }
}
```

using its `setValue` method, and a new `Num` object is created and assigned to the second `Num` parameter. These changes are reflected in the output printed at the end of the `changeValues` method.

However, note the final values that are printed after returning from the method. The primitive integer was not changed from its original value, because the change was made to a copy inside the method. Likewise, the last parameter still refers to its original object with its original value. This is because the new `Num` object created in the method was referred to only by the formal parameter. When the method returned, that formal parameter was destroyed, and the `Num` object it referred to was marked for garbage collection. The only change that is "permanent" is the change made to the state of the second parameter. Figure 5.12 shows the step-by-step processing of this program.

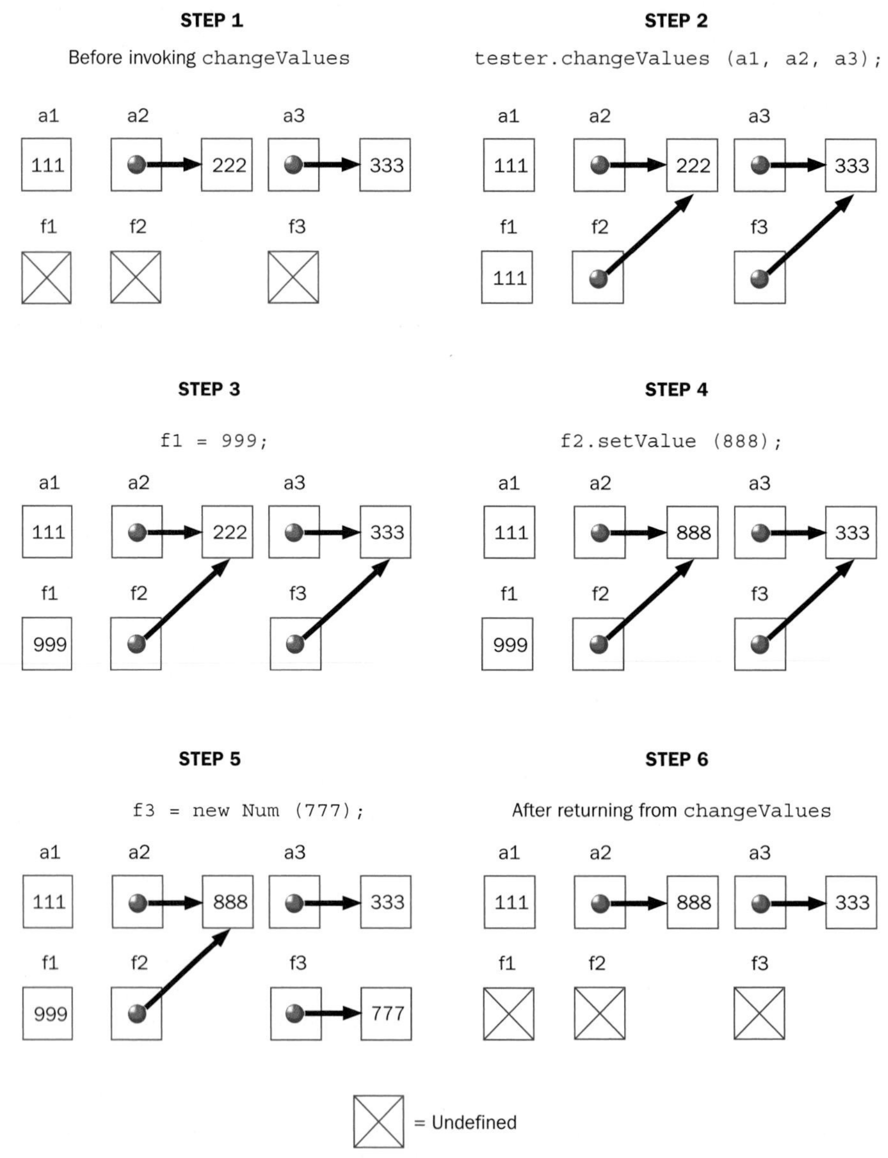

FIGURE 5.12 Tracing the parameters in the `ParameterTesting` program

5.8 Method Overloading

As we've discussed, when a method is invoked, control transfers to the code that defines the method. After the method has been executed, control returns to the location of the call, and processing continues.

Often the method name is sufficient to indicate which method is being called by a specific invocation. But in Java, as in other object-oriented languages, you can use the same method name with different parameter lists for multiple methods. This technique is called *method overloading*. It is useful when you need to perform similar methods on different types of data.

The compiler must still be able to associate each invocation with a specific method declaration. If the method name for two or more methods is the same, additional information is used to uniquely identify the version that is being invoked. In Java, a method name can be used for multiple methods as long as the number of parameters, the types of those parameters, and/or the order of the types of parameters is distinct.

KEY CONCEPT
The versions of an overloaded method are distinguished by the number, type, and order of their parameters.

For example, we could declare a method called sum as follows:

```
public int sum(int num1, int num2)
{
   return num1 + num2;
}
```

Then we could declare another method called sum, within the same class, as follows:

```
public int sum(int num1, int num2, int num3)
{
   return num1 + num2 + num3;
}
```

Now, when an invocation is made, the compiler looks at the number of parameters to determine which version of the sum method to call. For instance, the following invocation will call the second version of the sum method:

```
sum(25, 69, 13);
```

A method's name, along with the number, type, and order of its parameters, is called the method's *signature*. The compiler uses the complete method signature to *bind* a method invocation to the appropriate definition.

The compiler must be able to examine a method invocation to determine which specific method is being invoked. If you attempt to specify two method names with the same signature, the compiler will issue an appropriate error message and will not create an executable program. There can be no ambiguity.

Note that the return type of a method is not part of the method signature. That is, two overloaded methods cannot differ only by their return type. This is because the value returned by a method can be ignored by the invocation. The compiler would not be able to tell which version of an overloaded method was being referenced in such situations.

The `println` method is an example of a method that is overloaded several times, each accepting a single type. Here is a partial list of its various signatures:

- `println(String s)`
- `println(int i)`
- `println(double d)`
- `println(char c)`
- `println(boolean b)`

The following two lines of code actually invoke different methods that have the same name:

```
System.out.println("Number of students: ");
System.out.println(count);
```

The first line invokes the version of `println` that accepts a string. The second line, assuming that `count` is an integer variable, invokes the version of `println` that accepts an integer.

We often use a `println` statement that prints several distinct types, such as

```
System.out.println("Number of students: " + count);
```

Remember, in this case the plus sign is the string concatenation operator. First, the value in the variable `count` is converted to a string representation, then the two strings are concatenated into one longer string, and finally the definition of `println` that accepts a single string is invoked.

Constructors can be overloaded, and they often are. By providing multiple versions of a constructor, we provide multiple ways to set up an object.

5.9 Testing

As our programs become larger and more complex, it becomes more difficult to ensure their accuracy and reliability. Accordingly, before we continue with further programming details, let's explore the processes involved in testing a program.

The term *testing* can be applied in many ways to software development. Testing certainly includes its traditional definition: the act of running a completed program with various inputs to discover problems. But it also includes any evaluation that is performed by human or machine to assess the quality of the evolving system. These evaluations should occur long before a single line of code is written.

The goal of testing is to find errors. By finding errors and fixing them, we improve the quality of our program. It's likely that later on, someone else will find any errors that remain hidden during development. The earlier the errors are found, the easier and cheaper they are to fix. Taking the time to uncover problems as early as possible is almost always worth the effort.

Running a program with specific input and producing the correct results establishes only that the program works for that particular input. As more and more test cases execute without revealing errors, our confidence in the program rises, but we can never really be sure that all errors have been eliminated. There could always be another error still undiscovered. Because of that, it is important to thoroughly test a program in as many ways as possible and with well-designed test cases.

KEY CONCEPT

Testing a program can never guarantee the absence of errors.

It is possible to prove that a program is correct, but that technique is enormously complex for large systems, and errors can be made in the proof itself. Therefore, we generally rely on testing to determine the quality of a program.

After determining that an error exists, we determine the cause of the error and fix it. After a problem is fixed, we should run the previously administered tests again to make sure that while fixing the problem, we didn't create another. This technique is called *regression testing.*

Reviews

One technique used to evaluate design or code is called a *review*, which is a meeting in which several people carefully examine a design document or section of code. Presenting our design or code to others causes us to think more carefully about it and permits others to share their suggestions with us. The participants discuss its merits and problems and create a list of issues that must be addressed. The goal of a review is to identify problems, not to solve them, which usually takes much more time.

A design review should determine whether the requirements are addressed. It should also assess the way the system is decomposed into classes and objects. A code review should determine how faithfully the design satisfies the requirements and how faithfully the implementation represents the design. It should identify any specific problems that would cause the design or the implementation to fail in its responsibilities.

Sometimes a review is called a *walkthrough*, because its goal is to step carefully through a document and evaluate each section.

Defect Testing

Because the goal of testing is to find errors, it is often referred to as *defect testing*. With that goal in mind, a good test is one that uncovers any deficiencies in a program. This might seem strange, because we ultimately don't want to have problems in our system. But keep in mind that errors almost certainly exist. Our testing efforts should make every attempt to find them. We want to increase the reliability of our program by finding and fixing the errors that exist, rather than letting users discover them.

KEY CONCEPT
A good test is one that uncovers an error.

A *test case* is a set of inputs, user actions, or other initial conditions, and the expected output. A test case should be appropriately documented so that it can be repeated later as needed. Developers often create a complete *test suite*, which is a set of test cases that covers various aspects of the system.

KEY CONCEPT
It is not feasible to exhaustively test a program for all possible input and user actions.

Because programs operate on a large number of possible inputs, it is not feasible to create test cases for all possible input or user actions. Nor is it usually necessary to test every single situation. Two specific test cases may be so similar that they actually do not test unique aspects of the program. To perform both such tests would be a waste of effort. We'd rather execute a test case that stresses the program in some new way. Therefore, we want to choose our test cases carefully. To that end, let's examine two approaches to defect testing: black-box testing and white-box testing.

As the name implies, *black-box testing* treats the thing being tested as a black box. In black-box testing, test cases are developed without regard to the internal workings. Black-box tests are based on inputs and outputs. An entire program can be tested using a black-box technique, in which case the inputs are the user-provided information and user actions such as button pushes. A test case is successful only if the input produces the expected output. A single class can also be tested using a black-box technique, which focuses on the system interface of the class (its public methods). Certain parameters are passed in, producing certain results. Black-box test cases are often derived directly from the requirements of the system or from the stated purpose of a method.

The input data for a black-box test case are often selected by defining *equivalence categories*. An equivalence category is a collection of inputs that are expected to produce similar outputs. Generally, if a method will work for one value in the equivalence category, we have every reason to believe it will work for the others. For example, the input to a method that computes the square root of an integer can be divided into two equivalence categories: nonnegative integers and negative integers. If it works appropriately for one nonnegative value, it is likely to work for all nonnegative values. Likewise, if it works appropriately for one negative value, it is likely to work for all negative values.

Equivalence categories have defined boundaries. Because all values of an equivalence category essentially test the same features of a program, only one test case inside the equivalence boundary is needed. However, because programming often produces "off by one" errors, the values on and around the boundary should be tested exhaustively. For an integer boundary, a good test suite would include at least the exact value of the boundary, the boundary minus 1, and the boundary plus 1. Test cases that use these cases, plus at least one from within the general field of the category, should be defined.

Let's look at an example. Consider a method whose purpose is to validate that a particular integer value is in the range 0 to 99, inclusive. There are three equivalence categories in this case: values below 0, values in the range of 0 to 99, and values above 99. Black-box testing dictates that we use test values that surround and fall on the boundaries, as well as some general values from the equivalence categories. Therefore, a set of black-box test cases for this situation might be –500, –1, 0, 1, 50, 98, 99, 100, and 500.

White-box testing, also known as *glass-box testing*, exercises the internal structure and implementation of a method. A white-box test case is based on the logic of the code. The goal is to ensure that every path through a program is executed at least once. A white-box test maps the possible paths through the code and ensures that the test cases cause every path to be executed. This type of testing is often called *statement coverage*.

Paths through code are controlled by various control flow statements that use conditional expressions, such as `if` statements. In order to have every path through the program executed at least once, the input data values for the test cases need to control the values for the conditional expressions. The input data of one or more test cases should cause the condition of an `if` statement to evaluate to `true` in at least one case and to `false` in at least one case. Covering both true and false values in an `if` statement guarantees that both paths through the `if` statement will be executed. Similar situations can be created for loops and other constructs.

In both black-box and white-box testing, the expected output for each test should be established before running the test. It's too easy to be persuaded that the results of a test are appropriate if you haven't first carefully determined what the results should be.

Unit Testing

Another type of testing is known as *unit testing*. This approach creates a test case for each module of code (method) that has been authored. The goal of unit testing is to ensure correctness of the methods (units), one method at a time. Generally, we collect our unit tests together, execute each test, and observe all of the results. We can also use these tests repeatedly as the source code changes, to observe the effect of our code changes on the results of the test (regression testing, discussed above).

Integration Testing

During *integration testing*, modules that were individually tested during unit testing are now tested as a collection. This form of testing looks at the larger picture and determines whether there are bugs present when modules are brought together and integrated to work together. As with unit testing, we can use regression testing as the software changes to determine how our results may have changed as integration occurred and as problems in the modules or integration approaches were modified. Typically, the goal of integration testing is to examine the correctness of large components of a system.

System Testing

System testing seeks to test the entire software system and how its implementation adheres to its requirements. You may be familiar with public alpha or beta testing of applications or operating systems. Alpha and beta tests are system tests applied before the formal release and availability of a software product. Software development companies partake in these types of public tests to increase the number of users testing a product or to expand the hardware base that the product is tested on.

Test-Driven Development

Ideally, developers should be writing test cases concurrently with the development of the source code that their applications use. In fact, many developers have adopted the practice of writing their test cases first and then implementing only enough source code for the test case to pass. This notion is known professionally as *test-driven development*.

KEY CONCEPT
In test-driven development, test cases are developed for code before the code is written.

The test-driven approach requires that developers periodically (during development and implementation) test their code using the implemented test cases. If you were to look at the test-driven approach as a sequence of steps, you would generally find the following activities:

1. Create a test case that tests a specific method that has yet to be completed.
2. Execute all of the test cases present, and verify that all test cases pass except for the most recently implemented test case.

3. Develop the method that the test case targets so that the test case will pass without errors.
4. Re-execute all of the test cases, and verify that every test case passes, including the most recently implemented test case.
5. Clean up the code to eliminate any redundant portions introduced by the development of the most recent method. This step is known as *refactoring* the code.
6. Repeat the process starting with Step 1.

The test-driven approach is becoming increasingly popular in professional settings. Without a doubt, it requires an adjustment for many developers to stop and write test cases before writing methods that provide functionality to systems under development.

5.10 Debugging

Finally, we come to one of the most important concepts that you will ever master as a programmer—the art of *debugging* your programs. Debugging is the act of locating and correcting run-time and logic errors in your programs. We can locate errors in our programs in a number of different ways. You may notice a run-time error (the program terminating abnormally) when you execute your program and certain situations arise that you did not consider or design for. Also, you may notice a logic error in your program as it executes when your anticipated results do not match the actual results you obtain.

KEY CONCEPT
Debugging is the act of locating and correcting run-time and logic errors in your programs.

Ideally, through rigorous testing, we hope to discover all possible errors in our programs. Typically, however, a few errors slip through into the final program. Once you recognize that your program contains an error, you will want to locate the portion of code from which the error is arising. For example, if you determine that your program is terminating abnormally because of a divide-by-zero problem, you'll probably want to locate the exact line where it is happening. You may also wish to observe the values of the variables involved in the division. The same may be true if you have a logic error (rather than a divide-by-zero problem) in that division operation.

Regardless of your motivation, it is often very helpful to obtain detailed information about the values of variables, states of objects, and other inner workings of your program. This is where a debugger comes in. A *debugger* is a software application that allows us to observe these inner workings as the program executes. However, before we discuss the debugger, we should first talk about simple debugging.

KEY CONCEPT
A debugger is a software program that permits developers to observe the execution of a program.

Simple Debugging with `print` Statements

One of the most simplistic approaches to debugging involves the use of printing. That is, scattered throughout a program can be `print` and `println` statements that output various information either to the screen or to an output file. Generally, this type of approach will provide information on the value or state of a specific variable or object. Periodic printing of an object's string representation is considered a useful approach to observing the state of an object over time.

Other types of useful information can be printed as well. For example, sometimes we wish to know "how far our program got before it died." Programmers facing this challenge often print a series of "It got here." statements to output to monitor the exact path of execution of the program.

Consider the case of calling a method. It may be useful for us to print the value of each parameter after the method starts to observe how the method was called. This is particularly helpful when we are debugging recursive methods, discussed in the next chapter. We can also print the value of a variable prior to its being returned as the method ends.

Debugging Concepts

Debugging through printing can take us only so far. Most of the time, this style of debugging can be effectively used to identify what is happening during execution, or the value of a variable at a certain point in the program. However, a more powerful approach is to use a debugger in which our program will execute. The debugger can be used to control our program's execution and provide additional functionality to the developer that we simply can't get with simple debugging through `print` statements.

A debugger allows us to do the following:

- Set one or more *breakpoints* in our program. In the debugger, we can examine the source code and set special flags or triggers on one or more lines of code. When execution of the program comes across a statement that has been flagged, execution stops.
- Print the value of a variable or object. Once we have reached a breakpoint and execution has stopped, the debugger allows us to display the value of a variable or examine the state of an object. Generally, these types of displays are to the screen and only within the confines of the debugger application.
- Step into or over a method. If we set a breakpoint at a statement that is a call to a method, when execution reaches this breakpoint and the program stops, the developer can choose to enter into the method and continue debugging or to step over the method, bypassing the display of the execution

of the statements contained in the method. In stepping over the method, we should note that the method is still executed, but we have chosen not to delve into the method. Consider the call to the printing of a string of output to the screen. We probably don't need to step into the `println` method of the `System.out` object. It's likely to have been fully debugged already (and we can't change its behavior anyway).

- Execute the next single statement. After reaching a breakpoint, the developer can choose to execute the next single statement (also known as a *step*). By executing a single step, we can literally control the execution of our program one statement at a time. Developers often perform stepping to be sure they understand the flow of execution and to give themselves an opportunity to display the value of a variable following each step, if desired.
- Continue execution. Once a program has stopped due to a breakpoint, or is waiting for the developers to decide whether they will step into, step over, or single step, the developers can also continue execution. Continuing execution will result in the program running each statement without pausing until the program ends, it encounters another breakpoint, or a run-time error occurs.

Debuggers also offer a pile of additional features to assist in the debugging task. However, for the purposes of this discussion, we can limit ourselves to the set of activities listed above. Any debugger that is worth using has these operations, at the very least.

Summary of Key Concepts

- The nouns in a problem description may indicate some of the classes and objects needed in a program.
- The heart of object-oriented programming is defining classes that represent objects with well-defined state and behavior.
- The scope of a variable, which determines where it can be referenced, depends on where it is declared.
- A UML class diagram helps us visualize the contents of, and the relationships among, the classes of a program.
- An object should be encapsulated in order to safeguard its data from inappropriate access.
- Instance variables should be declared with private visibility to promote encapsulation.
- Most objects contain accessor and mutator methods to allow the client to manage data in a controlled manner.
- The way a class represents an object's state should be independent of how that object is used.
- The value returned from a method must be consistent with the return type specified in the method header.
- When a method is called, the actual parameters are copied into the formal parameters.
- A variable declared in a method is local to that method and cannot be used outside of it.
- A constructor cannot have any return type, even `void`.
- A static variable is shared among all instances of a class.
- An aggregate object is composed of other objects, forming a has-a relationship.
- A complex service provided by an object can be decomposed to make use of private support methods.
- When an object is passed to a method, the actual and formal parameters become aliases.
- The versions of an overloaded method are distinguished by the number, type, and order of their parameters.
- Testing a program can never guarantee the absence of errors.

- A good test is one that uncovers an error.
- It is not feasible to exhaustively test a program for all possible input and user actions.
- In test-driven development, test cases are developed for code before the code is written.
- Debugging is the act of locating and correcting run-time and logic errors in your programs.
- A debugger is a software program that permits developers to observe the execution of a program.

Summary of Terms

accessor method A method that provides access to the attributes of an object but does not modify it.

actual parameter A value that is passed into a method when it is invoked. Also called an argument.

aggregation A relationship among object in which one object is made up of other objects.

behavior The set of operations defined by the public methods of an object.

black-box testing Testing a program with attention to the inputs and outputs of the code.

client A part of a software system that uses an object.

debugging The act of locating and correcting run-time and logical errors in a program.

defect testing Executing a program with specific inputs in order to find errors.

encapsulation The characteristic of an object that keeps its data protected from external modification.

formal parameter A parameter name in the header of a method definition.

instance data Data defined at the class level and created in memory for every object.

integration testing Testing modules as they are incorporated with each other, focusing on the communication between them.

interface The set of public methods that define the operations that an object makes available to other objects.

local data Data that are declared within a method.

method overloading The ability to declare multiple methods with the same name in a class as long as the method signatures are distinct.

method signature The method's name, along with the number, type, and order of the method's parameters.

modfier A Java reserved word that is used to specify particular characteristics of a variable, method, or class.

mutator method A method that changes the attributes of an object.

private visibility Restricting access to an object member to the methods within that object.

public visiblity The ability to be referenced from outside an object.

`return` **statement** A statement that causes a method to terminate and possibly return a value to the calling method.

review A meeting in which several people examine a design document or section of code in order to discover problems.

scope The area of a program in which a variable can be referenced.

service method A public method that provides a service to the clients of an object.

state The current values of the attributes (instance variables) of an object.

static method A method that is invoked through the class name and cannot refer to instance data.

static variable A variable that is shared among all instances of a class. Also called a class variable.

support methods A method with private visibility, used to support another method in its task.

system testing Testing an entire software system for its overall functionality.

testing The process of evaluating a program to discover defects.

test suite A set of tests that covers various aspects of a software system and can be repeated when needed.

unit testing Creating specific tests for small units of code (usually a method).

Unified Modeling Language (UML) A popular notation for representing designs of an object-oriented program.

visibility modifier One of the three modifiers (public, private, and protected) that determine what other parts of a software system can access a variable or method.

white-box testing Testing a program with attention to the logic of the code.

Self-Review Questions

SR 5.1 What is an attribute?

SR 5.2 What is an operation?

SR 5.3 What is the difference between an object and a class?

SR 5.4 What is the scope of a variable?

SR 5.5 What are UML diagrams designed to do?

SR 5.6 Objects should be self-governing. Explain.

SR 5.7 What is a modifier?

SR 5.8 Why might a constant be given public visibility?

SR 5.9 Describe each of the following:

a. public method

b. private method

c. public variable

d. private variable

SR 5.10 What is the interface to an object?

SR 5.11 Why is a method invoked through (or on) a particular object? What is the exception to that rule?

SR 5.12 What does it mean for a method to return a value?

SR 5.13 What does the `return` statement do?

SR 5.14 Is a `return` statement required?

SR 5.15 Explain the difference between an actual parameter and a formal parameter.

SR 5.16 What are constructors used for? How are they defined?

SR 5.17 What is the difference between a static variable and an instance variable?

SR 5.18 What kinds of variables can the `main` method of any program reference? Why?

SR 5.19 Describe a dependency relationship between two classes.

SR 5.20 How are overloaded methods distinguished from each other?

SR 5.21 What is method decomposition?

SR 5.22 Explain how a class can have an association with itself.

SR 5.23 What is an aggregate object?

SR 5.24 What does the `this` reference refer to?

SR 5.25 How are objects passed as parameters?

SR 5.26 What is a defect test?

SR 5.27 What is a debugger?

Exercises

EX 5.1 For each of the following pairs, indicate which member of the pair represents a class and which represents an object of that class.

a. Superhero, Superman

b. Justin, Person

c. Rover, Pet

d. Magazine, *Time*

e. Christmas, Holiday

EX 5.2 List some attributes and operations that might be defined for a class called `PictureFrame` that represents a picture frame.

EX 5.3 List some attributes and operations that might be defined for a class called `Meeting` that represents a business meeting.

EX 5.4 List some attributes and operations that might be defined for a class called `Course` that represents a college course (not a particular offering of a course, just the course in general).

EX 5.5 Rewrite the `for` loop body from the `SnakeEyes` program so that the variables `num1` and `num2` are not used.

EX 5.6 Write a method called `lyrics` that prints the lyrics of a song when invoked. The method should accept no parameters and return no value.

EX 5.7 Write a method called `cube` that accepts one integer parameter and returns that value raised to the third power.

EX 5.8 Write a method called `random100` that returns a random integer in the range of 1 to 100 (inclusive).

EX 5.9 Write a method called `randomInRange` that accepts two integer parameters representing a range. The method should return a random integer in the specified range (inclusive). Assume that the first parameter is greater than the second.

EX 5.10 Write a method called `powersOfTwo` that prints the first 10 powers of 2 (starting with 2). The method takes no parameters and doesn't return anything.

EX 5.11 Write a method called `alarm` that prints the string "`Alarm!`" multiple times on separate lines. The method should accept an integer parameter that specifies how many times the string is printed. Print an error message if the parameter is less than 1.

EX 5.12 Write a method called `sum100` that returns the sum of the integers from 1 to 100, inclusive.

EX 5.13 Write a method called `maxOfTwo` that accepts two integer parameters and returns the larger of the two.

EX 5.14 Write a method called `sumRange` that accepts two integer parameters that represent a range. Issue an error message and return zero if the second parameter is less than the first. Otherwise, the method should return the sum of the integers in that range (inclusive).

EX 5.15 Write a method called `larger` that accepts two floating point parameters (of type `double`) and returns true if the first parameter is greater than the second, and returns false otherwise.

EX 5.16 Write a method called `countA` that accepts a `String` parameter and returns the number of times the character `'A'` is found in the string.

EX 5.17 Write a method called `evenlyDivisible` that accepts two integer parameters and returns true if the first parameter is evenly divisible by the second, or vice versa, and returns false otherwise. Return false if either parameter is zero.

EX 5.18 Write a method called `isAlpha` that accepts a character parameter and returns true if that character is either an uppercase or a lowercase alphabetic letter.

EX 5.19 Write a method called `floatEquals` that accepts three floating point values as parameters. The method should return true if the first two parameters are equal within the tolerance of the third parameter.

EX 5.20 Write a method called `reverse` that accepts a `String` parameter and returns a string that contains the characters of the parameter in reverse order. *Note:* There is a method in the `String` class that performs this operation, but for the sake of this exercise, you are expected to write your own.

EX 5.21 Write a method called `isIsosceles` that accepts three integer parameters that represent the lengths of the sides of a triangle. The method returns true if the triangle is isosceles but not equilateral (meaning that exactly two of the sides have the same length), and returns false otherwise.

EX 5.22 Write a method called `average` that accepts two integer parameters and returns their average as a floating point value.

EX 5.23 Overload the `average` method of Exercise 5.22 such that if three integers are provided as parameters, the method returns the average of all three.

EX 5.24 Overload the `average` method of Exercise 5.22 to accept four integer parameters and return their average.

EX 5.25 Write a method called `multiConcat` that takes a `String` and an integer as parameters. Return a `String` that consists of the string parameter concatenated with itself `count` times, where `count` is the integer parameter. For example, if the parameter values are `"hi"` and `4`, the return value is `"hihihihi"`. Return the original string if the integer parameter is less than 2.

EX 5.26 Overload the `multiConcat` method from Exercise 5.25 such that if the integer parameter is not provided, the method returns the string concatenated with itself. For example, if the parameter is `"test"`, the return value is `"testtest"`.

EX 5.27 Discuss the manner in which Java passes parameters to a method. Is this technique consistent between primitive types and objects? Explain.

EX 5.28 Explain why a static method cannot refer to an instance variable.

EX 5.29 Can a class implement two interfaces that contain the same method signature? Explain.

EX 5.30 Draw a UML class diagram for the `CountFlips` program.

EX 5.31 Draw a UML class diagram for the `FlipRace` program.

EX 5.32 Draw a UML class diagram for the `Transactions` program.

Programming Projects

PP 5.1 Revise the `Coin` class such that its state is represented internally using a `boolean` variable. Test the new versions of the class as part of the `CountFlips` and `FlipRace` programs.

PP 5.2 Repeat Programming Project 5.1, representing the state of the coin using a character string.

PP 5.3 Repeat Programming Project 5.1, representing the state of the coin using an enumerated type.

PP 5.4 Design and implement a class called `Sphere` that contains instance data that represent the sphere's diameter. Define the `Sphere` constructor to accept and initialize the diameter, and include getter and setter methods for the diameter. Include methods that calculate and return the volume and surface area of the sphere (see Programming Project 3.5 for the formulas). Include a `toString` method that returns a one-line description of the sphere. Create a driver class called `MultiSphere`, whose `main` method instantiates and updates several `Sphere` objects.

PP 5.5 Design and implement a class called `Dog` that contains instance data that represent the dog's name and age. Define the `Dog` constructor to accept and initialize instance data. Include getter and setter methods for the name and age. Include a method to compute and return the age of the dog in "person years" (seven times the dog's age). Include a `toString` method that returns a one-line description of the dog. Create a driver class called `Kennel`, whose `main` method instantiates and updates several `Dog` objects.

PP 5.6 Design and implement a class called `Box` that contains instance data that represent the height, width, and depth of the box. Also include a `boolean` variable called `full` as instance data that represent whether the box is full or not. Define the `Box` constructor to accept and initialize the height, width, and depth of the box. Each newly created `Box` is empty (the constructor should initialize `full` to false). Include getter and setter methods for all instance data. Include a `toString` method that returns a one-line description of the box. Create a driver class called `BoxTest`, whose `main` method instantiates and updates several `Box` objects.

PP 5.7 Design and implement a class called `Book` that contains instance data for the title, author, publisher, and copyright date. Define the `Book` constructor to accept and initialize these data. Include setter and getter methods for all instance data. Include a `toString` method that returns a nicely formatted, multiline description of the book. Create a driver class called `Bookshelf`, whose `main` method instantiates and updates several `Book` objects.

PP 5.8 Design and implement a class called `Flight` that represents an airline flight. It should contain instance data that represent the airline name, the flight number, and the flight's origin and destination cities. Define the `Flight` constructor to accept and initialize all instance data. Include getter and setter methods for all instance data. Include a `toString` method that returns a one-line description of the flight. Create a driver class called `FlightTest`, whose `main` method instantiates and updates several `Flight` objects.

PP 5.9 Design and implement a class called `Bulb` that represents a light bulb that can be turned on and off. Create a driver class called `Lights`, whose `main` method instantiates and turns on some `Bulb` objects.

PP 5.10 Using the `Die` class defined in this chapter, design and implement a class called `PairOfDice`, composed of two `Die` objects. Include methods to set and get the individual die values, a method to roll the dice, and a method that returns the current sum of the two die values. Rewrite the `SnakeEyes` program using a `PairOfDice` object.

PP 5.11 Using the `PairOfDice` class from Programming Project 5.10, design and implement a class to play a game called Pig. In this game, the user competes against the computer. On each turn, the current player rolls a pair of dice and accumulates points. The goal is to reach 100 points before your opponent does. If, on any turn, the player rolls a 1, all points accumulated for that round are forfeited, and control of the dice moves to the other player. If the player rolls two 1's in one turn, the player loses all points accumulated thus far in the game and loses control of the dice. The player may voluntarily turn over the dice after each roll. Therefore, the player must decide either to roll again (be a pig) and risk losing points or to relinquish control of the dice, possibly allowing the other player to win. Implement the computer player such that it always relinquishes the dice after accumulating 20 or more points in any given round.

PP 5.12 Modify the `Account` class from this chapter so that it also permits an account to be opened with just a name and an account number, assuming an initial balance of zero. Modify the `main` method of the `Transactions` class to demonstrate this new capability.

PP 5.13 Design and implement a class called `Card` that represents a standard playing card. Each card has a suit and a face value. Create a program that deals five random cards.

Answers to Self-Review Questions

SRA 5.1 An attribute is a data value that is stored in an object and defines a particular characteristic of that object. For example, one attribute of a `Student` object might be that student's current grade point average. Collectively, the values of an object's attributes determine that object's current state.

SRA 5.2 An operation is a function that can be done to or done by an object. For example, one operation of a `Student` object might be to compute that student's current grade point average. Collectively, an object's operations are referred to as the object's behaviors.

SRA 5.3 A class is the blueprint of an object. It defines the variables and methods that will be a part of every object that is instantiated from it. But a class reserves no memory space for variables. Each object has its own data space and therefore its own state.

SRA 5.4 The scope of a variable is the area within a program in which the variable can be referenced. An instance variable, declared at the class level, can be referenced in any method of the class. Local variables (including the formal parameters) declared within a particular method can be referenced only in that method.

SRA 5.5 A UML diagram helps us visualize the classes used in a program as well as the relationships among them. UML diagrams are tools that help us capture the design of a program prior to writing it.

SRA 5.6 A self-governing object is one that controls the values of its own data. An encapsulated object, which doesn't allow an external client to reach in and change its data, is self-governing.

SRA 5.7 A modifier is a Java reserved word that can be used in the definition of a variable or method and that specifically defines certain characteristics of its use. For example, if a variable is declared with the modifier `private`, the variable cannot be directly accessed outside the object in which it is defined.

SRA 5.8 A constant might be declared with public visibility because that would not violate encapsulation. Because the value of a constant cannot be changed, it is not generally a problem for another object to access it directly.

SRA 5.9 The modifiers affect the methods and variables in the following ways:

a. A public method is called a service method for an object because it defines a service that the object provides.

b. A private method is called a support method because it cannot be invoked from outside the object and is used to support the activities of other methods in the class.

c. A public variable is a variable that can be directly accessed and modified by a client. This explicitly violates the principle of encapsulation and therefore should be avoided.

d. A private variable is a variable that can be accessed and modified only from within the class. Variables almost always are declared with private visibility.

SRA 5.10 An object's interface is the set of public operations (methods) defined on it. That is, the interface establishes the set of services the object will perform for the rest of the system.

SRA 5.11 Although a method is defined in a class, it is invoked through a particular object to indicate which object of that class is being affected. For example, the `Student` class may define the operation that computes the grade point average of a student, but the operation is invoked through a particular `Student` object to compute the GPA for that student. The exception to this rule is the invocation of a static method, which is executed through the class name and does not affect any particular object.

SRA 5.12 An invoked method may return a value, which means it computes a value and provides that value to the calling method. The calling method usually uses the invocation, and thus its return value, as part of a larger expression.

SRA 5.13 An explicit `return` statement is used to specify the value that is returned from a method. The type of the return value must match the return type specified in the method definition.

SRA 5.14 A `return` statement is required in methods that have a return type other than `void`. A method that does not return a value could use a `return` statement without an expression, but it is not necessary. Only one `return` statement should be used in a method.

SRA 5.15 An actual parameter is a value sent to a method when it is invoked. A formal parameter is the corresponding variable in the header of the method declaration; it takes on the value of the actual parameter so that it can be used inside the method.

SRA 5.16 Constructors are special methods in an object that are used to initialize the object when it is instantiated. A constructor has the same name as its class, and it does not return a value.

SRA 5.17 Memory space for an instance variable is created for each object that is instantiated from a class. A static variable is shared among all objects of a class.

SRA 5.18 The `main` method of any program is static and can refer only to static or local variables. Therefore, a `main` method cannot refer to instance variables declared at the class level.

SRA 5.19 A dependency relationship between two classes occurs when one class relies on the functionality of the other. It is often referred to as a "uses" relationship.

SRA 5.20 Overloaded methods are distinguished by having a unique signature, which includes the number, order, and type of the parameters. The return type is not part of the signature.

SRA 5.21 Method decomposition is the process of dividing a complex method into several support methods to get the job done. This simplifies and facilitates the design of the program.

SRA 5.22 A method executed through an object might take as a parameter another object created from the same class. For example, the `concat` method of the `String` class is executed through one `String` object and takes another `String` object as a parameter.

SRA 5.23 An aggregate object is an object that has other objects as instance data. That is, an aggregate object is one that is made up of other objects.

SRA 5.24 The `this` reference always refers to the currently executing object. A nonstatic method of a class is written generically for all objects of the class, but it is invoked through a particular object. The `this` reference, therefore, refers to the object through which that method is currently being executed.

SRA 5.25 Objects are passed to methods by copying the reference to the object (its address). Therefore, the actual and formal parameters of a method become aliases of each other.

SRA 5.26 Defect testing is the act of testing to locate errors in a program.

SRA 5.27 A debugger is a software application that allows us to observe and manipulate the inner workings of a program as it executes.

Graphical User Interfaces

6

CHAPTER OBJECTIVES

- Discuss the core elements needed in any Java GUI: components, events, and listeners.
- Explore the use of containers to organize components.
- Explore various types of components, including buttons, text fields, sliders, and combo boxes.
- Discuss the various types of events that components generate, and under what conditions.
- Discuss the concept of a layout manager, and explore several specific ones.
- Explore various types of mouse and keyboard events.
- Discuss dialog boxes, including specialized dialog boxes for choosing files and colors.
- Explore the use of borders, tool tips, and mnemonics.

Many programs provide a graphical user interface (GUI) through which a user interacts with the program. As the name implies, a GUI makes use of graphical screen components such as windows, buttons, check boxes, menus, and text fields. GUIs often provide a more natural and rich experience for the user than a simple text-based, command-line environment. This chapter explores the various issues related to developing a GUI in Java.

6.1 GUI Elements

The text-based programs we've seen in previous examples are *command-line applications*, which interact with the user through simple prompts and feedback. This type of interface is straightforward to understand, but it lacks the rich user experience possible when a true *graphical user interface* (GUI) is used. With a GUI, the user is not limited to responding to prompts in a particular order and receiving feedback in one place. Instead, the user can interact as needed with various components, such as buttons and text fields. This chapter explores the many issues involved in developing a GUI in Java.

Let's start with an overview of the concepts that underlie every GUI-based program. At least three kinds of objects are needed to create a GUI in Java:

- components
- events
- listeners

A GUI *component* is an object that defines a screen element used to display information or allow the user to interact with a program in a certain way. Examples of GUI components include push buttons, text fields, labels, scroll bars, and menus. A *container* is a special type of component that is used to hold and organize other components.

An *event* is an object that represents some occurrence in which we may be interested. Often, events correspond to user actions, such as pressing a mouse button or typing a key on the keyboard. Most GUI components generate events to indicate a user action related to that component. For example, a button component generates an event to indicate that the button has been pushed. A program that is oriented around a GUI, responding to events from the user, is called *event-driven*.

A *listener* is an object that "waits" for an event to occur and responds in some way when it does. A major part of designing a GUI-based program is establishing the relationships among the listener, the event it listens for, and the component that will generate the event.

KEY CONCEPT
A GUI is made up of components, events that represent user actions, and listeners that respond to those events.

For the most part, we will use components and events that are predefined by classes in the Java class library. We will tailor the behavior of the components, but their basic roles have been established already. We will, however, write our own listener classes to perform whatever actions we desire when events occur.

Thus, to create a Java program that uses a GUI, we must

- instantiate and set up the necessary components,
- implement listener classes that define what happens when particular events occur, and

- establish the relationship between the listeners and the components that generate the events of interest.

Java components and other GUI-related classes are defined primarily in two packages: `java.awt` and `javax.swing`. (Note the `x` in `javax.swing`.) The *Abstract Windowing Toolkit* (AWT) was the original Java GUI package. It still contains many important classes that we will use. The *Swing* package was added later and provides components that are more versatile than those of the AWT package. Both packages are needed for GUI development, but we will use Swing components whenever there is an option.

In some respects, once you have a basic understanding of event-driven programming, the rest is just detail. There are many types of components you can use that produce many types of events that you may want to acknowledge. But they all work in the same basic way. They all have the same core relationships to one another.

Let's look at a simple example that contains all of the basic GUI elements. The `PushCounter` class shown in Listing 6.1 on the next page contains the driver of a program that presents the user with a single push button (labeled "Push Me!"). Each time the button is pushed, a counter is updated and displayed.

The components used in this program include a button, a label to display the count, a panel to hold the button and label, and a frame to display the panel. The panel is defined by the `PushCounterPanel` class, shown in Listing 6.2. Let's look at each of these pieces in more detail.

Frames and Panels

A *frame* is a container that is used to display GUI-based Java applications. A frame is displayed as a separate window with its own title bar. It can be repositioned on the screen and resized as needed by dragging it with the mouse. It contains small buttons in the corner of the frame that allow the frame to be minimized, maximized, and closed. A frame is defined by the `JFrame` class.

VideoNote
Example using frames and panels

A *panel* is also a container. However, unlike a frame, it cannot be displayed on its own. A panel must be added to another container for it to be displayed. Generally, a panel doesn't move unless you move the container that it's in. Its primary role is to help organize the other components in a GUI. A panel is defined by the `JPanel` class.

KEY CONCEPT
A frame is displayed as a separate window, but a panel can be displayed only as part of another container.

We can classify containers as either heavyweight or lightweight. A *heavyweight container* is one that is managed by the underlying operating system on which the program is run, whereas a *lightweight container* is managed by the Java program itself. A frame is a heavyweight component, and a panel is a lightweight component. Another heavyweight container

LISTING 6.1

```
//********************************************************************
//  PushCounter.java       Java Foundations
//
//  Demonstrates a graphical user interface and an event listener.
//********************************************************************

import javax.swing.JFrame;

public class PushCounter
{
   //-----------------------------------------------------------------
   // Creates and displays the main program frame.
   //-----------------------------------------------------------------
   public static void main(String[] args)
   {
      JFrame frame = new JFrame("Push Counter");
      frame.setDefaultCloseOperation(JFrame.EXIT_ON_CLOSE);

      PushCounterPanel panel = new PushCounterPanel();
      frame.getContentPane().add(panel);

      frame.pack();
      frame.setVisible(true);
   }
}
```

DISPLAY

Go to the end of the text for a full-color version of this figure.

is an *applet*, which is used to display and execute a Java program through a Web browser. Applets are discussed in Appendix G.

VideoNote
Example using an extended `JPanel`

Heavyweight components are more complex than lightweight components in general. A frame, for example, has multiple *panes*, which are responsible for various characteristics of the frame window. All visible elements of a Java interface are displayed in a frame's *content pane*.

LISTING 6.2

```
//********************************************************************
//  PushCounterPanel.java       Java Foundations
//
//  Demonstrates a graphical user interface and an event listener.
//********************************************************************

import java.awt.*;
import java.awt.event.*;
import javax.swing.*;

public class PushCounterPanel extends JPanel
{
   private int count;
   private JButton push;
   private JLabel label;

   //-----------------------------------------------------------------
   // Constructor: Sets up the GUI.
   //-----------------------------------------------------------------
   public PushCounterPanel()
   {
      count = 0;

      push = new JButton("Push Me!");
      push.addActionListener(new ButtonListener());

      label = new JLabel("Pushes: " + count);

      add(push);
      add(label);

      setBackground(Color.cyan);
      setPreferredSize(new Dimension(300, 40));
   }

   //*****************************************************************
   //  Represents a listener for button push (action) events.
   //*****************************************************************
   private class ButtonListener implements ActionListener
   {
      //--------------------------------------------------------------
      //  Updates the counter and label when the button is pushed.
      //--------------------------------------------------------------
```

LISTING 6.1 *continued*

```
      public void actionPerformed(ActionEvent event)
      {
         count++;
         label.setText("Pushes: " + count);
      }
   }
}
```

Generally, we can create a Java GUI-based application by creating a frame in which the program interface is displayed. The interface is often organized onto a primary panel, which is added to the frame's content pane. The components in the primary panel are sometimes organized using other panels as needed.

In the `main` method of the `PushCounter` class, the frame for the program is constructed, set up, and displayed. The `JFrame` constructor takes a string as a parameter, which it displays in the title bar of the frame. The call to the `setDefaultCloseOperation` method determines what will happen when the close button in the corner of the frame is clicked. In most cases we'll simply let that button terminate the program, as indicated by the `EXIT_ON_CLOSE` constant.

The content pane of the frame is obtained using the `getContentPane` method, immediately after which the `add` method of the content pane is called to add the panel. The `pack` method of the frame sets its size appropriately based on its contents—in this case, the frame is sized to accommodate the size of the panel it contains. This is a better approach than trying to set the size of the frame explicitly, because it should change as the components within the frame change. The call to the `setVisible` method causes the frame to be displayed on the monitor screen.

You can interact with the frame itself in various ways. You can move the entire frame to another point on the desktop by grabbing the title bar of the frame and dragging it with the mouse. You can also resize the frame by dragging the bottom-right corner of the frame.

A panel is created by instantiating the `JPanel` class. In the case of the `PushCounter` program, the panel is represented by the `PushCounterPanel` class, which is derived from `JPanel`. Thus a `PushCounterPanel` is a `JPanel`, inheriting all of its methods and attributes. This is a common technique for creating panels.

The constructor of the PushCounterPanel class makes calls to several methods inherited from JPanel. For example, the background color of the panel is set using the setBackground method (the Color class is described in Appendix F). The setPreferredSize method accepts a Dimension object as a parameter, which is used to indicate the width and height of the component in pixels. The size of many components can be set this way, and most also have methods called setMinimumSize and setMaximumSize to help control the look of the interface.

A panel's add method allows a component to be added to the panel. In the PushCounterPanel constructor, a newly created button and label are added to the panel, and from that point on, they are considered part of that panel. The order in which components are added to a container often matters. In this case, it determines that the button appears before the label.

A container is governed by a *layout manager*, which determines exactly how the components added to the panel will be displayed. The default layout manager for a panel simply displays components in the order in which they are added, with as many components on one line as possible. Layout managers are discussed in detail later in this chapter.

Buttons and Action Events

The PushCounter program displays a button and a label. A *label*, created from the JLabel class, is a component that displays a line of text in a GUI. A label can also be used to display an image, as shown in later examples. In the PushCounter program, the label displays the number of times the button has been pushed.

Labels can be found in most GUI-based programs. They are very useful for displaying information or for labeling other components in the GUI. However, labels are not interactive. That is, the user does not interact with a label directly. The component that makes the PushCounter program interactive is the button that the user pushes with the mouse.

A *push button* is a component that allows the user to initiate an action with a press of the mouse. There are other types of button components that we explore in later chapters. A push button is defined by the JButton class. A call to the JButton constructor takes a String parameter that specifies the text shown on the button.

Pushing a JButton generates an *action event*. There are several types of events defined in the Java standard class library, and we explore many of them throughout this chapter. Different components generate different types of events.

The only event of interest in this program occurs when the button is pushed. To respond to the event, we must create a listener object for that event, so we must write a class that represents the listener. In this case, we need an action event listener.

In the `PushButton` program, the `ButtonListener` class represents the action listener. We could write the `ButtonListener` class in its own file, or even in the same file but outside of the `PushCounterPanel` class. However, we would then have to set up a way to communicate between the listener and the components of the GUI that the listener updates. Instead, we define the `ButtonListener` class as an *inner class*, which is a class defined within another class. As such, it automatically has access to the members of the class that contains it.

KEY CONCEPT
Listeners are often defined as inner classes because of the intimate relationship between the listener and the GUI components.

DESIGN FOCUS

You should create inner classes only when there is an intimate relationship between the two classes and when the inner class is not accessed by any other class. The relationship between a listener and its GUI is one of the few situations in which an inner class is appropriate.

Defining a Listener

could be declared as a private inner class

```
private class ButtonListener implements
                             ActionListener
{
   . . .
}
```

implements the method(s) of a listener interface

Listener classes are written by implementing an *interface*, which is a list of methods that the implementing class must define. The Java standard class library contains interfaces for many types of events. An action listener is created by implementing the `ActionListener` interface; therefore, we include the `implements` clause in the `ButtonListener` class. Interfaces are discussed in more detail in Chapter 9.

The only method listed in the ActionListener interface is the actionPerformed method, so that's the only method that the ButtonListener class must implement. The component that generates the action event (in this case the button) will call the actionPerformed method when the event occurs, passing in an ActionEvent object that represents the event. Sometimes we will use this event object, and other times it is enough to know that the event occurred. In this case, we have no need to interact with the event object. When the event occurs, the listener increments the count and resets the text of the label by using the setText method.

Remember, we not only have to create a listener for an event, we must also set up the relationship between the listener and the component that will generate the event. To do so, we add the listener to the component by calling the appropriate method. In the PushCounterPanel constructor, we call the addActionListener method, passing in a newly instantiated ButtonListener object.

Review this example carefully, noting how it accomplishes the three key steps in creating an interactive GUI-based program. It creates and sets up the GUI components, creates the appropriate listener for the event of interest, and sets up the relationship between the listener and the component that will generate the event.

Determining Event Sources

Let's look at an example in which one listener object is used to listen to two different components. The program represented by the LeftRight class, shown in Listing 6.3, displays a label and two buttons. When the Left button is pressed, the label displays the word Left, and when the Right button is pressed the label displays the word Right.

LISTING 6.3

```
//********************************************************************
//  LeftRight.java       Java Foundations
//
//  Demonstrates the use of one listener for multiple buttons.
//********************************************************************

import javax.swing.JFrame;

public class LeftRight
{
```

LISTING 6.3 *continued*

```
   //-----------------------------------------------------------------
   // Creates and displays the main program frame.
   //-----------------------------------------------------------------
   public static void main(String[] args)
   {
      JFrame frame = new JFrame("Left Right");
      frame.setDefaultCloseOperation(JFrame.EXIT_ON_CLOSE);

      frame.getContentPane().add(new LeftRightPanel());

      frame.pack();
      frame.setVisible(true);
   }
}
```

DISPLAY

Go to the end of the text for a full-color version of this figure.

The `LeftRightPanel` class, shown in Listing 6.4 on the next page, creates one instance of the `ButtonListener` class, and then adds that listener to both buttons. Therefore, when either button is pressed, the `actionPerformed` method of the `ButtonListener` class is invoked.

On each invocation, the `actionPerformed` method uses an `if-else` statement to determine which button generated the event. The `getSource` method is called on the `ActionEvent` object that the button passes into the `actionPerformed` method. The `getSource` method returns a reference to the component that generated the event. The condition of the `if` statement compares the event source to the reference to the left button. If they don't match, then the event must have been generated by the right button.

LISTING 6.4

```
//********************************************************************
//  LeftRightPanel.java       Java Foundations
//
//  Demonstrates the use of one listener for multiple buttons.
//********************************************************************

import java.awt.*;
import java.awt.event.*;
import javax.swing.*;

public class LeftRightPanel extends JPanel
{
   private JButton left, right;
   private JLabel label;
   private JPanel buttonPanel;

   //-----------------------------------------------------------------
   // Constructor: Sets up the GUI.
   //-----------------------------------------------------------------
   public LeftRightPanel()
   {
      left = new JButton("Left");
      right = new JButton("Right");

      ButtonListener listener = new ButtonListener();
      left.addActionListener(listener);
      right.addActionListener(listener);

      label = new JLabel("Push a button");

      buttonPanel = new JPanel();
      buttonPanel.setPreferredSize(new Dimension(200, 40));
      buttonPanel.setBackground(Color.blue);
      buttonPanel.add(left);
      buttonPanel.add(right);

      setPreferredSize(new Dimension(200, 80));
      setBackground(Color.cyan);
      add(label);
      add(buttonPanel);
   }

   //*****************************************************************
   //  Represents a listener for both buttons.
   //*****************************************************************
```

LISTING 6.4 *continued*

```
   private class ButtonListener implements ActionListener
   {
      //-----------------------------------------------------------------
      //  Determines which button was pressed and sets the label
      //  text accordingly.
      //-----------------------------------------------------------------
      public void actionPerformed (ActionEvent event)
      {
         if (event.getSource() == left)
            label.setText("Left");
         else
            label.setText("Right");
      }
   }
}
```

DESIGN FOCUS

We could have created two separate listener classes, one to listen to the left button and another to listen to the right. In that case, the `actionPerformed` method would not have to determine the source of the event. Whether to have multiple listeners or to determine the event source when it occurs is a design decision that should be made in light of the specific situation.

Note that the two buttons are put on the same panel called `buttonPanel`, which is separate from the panel represented by the `LeftRightPanel` class. By putting both buttons on one panel, we can guarantee their visual relationship to each other, even when the frame is resized in various ways. For buttons labeled Left and Right, that is certainly important.

6.2 More Components

In addition to push buttons, there are a variety of other interactive components that can be used in a GUI, each with a particular role to play. Let's examine a few more.

Text Fields

A *text field* allows the user to enter typed input from the keyboard. The `Fahrenheit` program shown in Listing 6.5 presents a GUI that includes a text field into which the user can type a Fahrenheit temperature. When the user presses the Enter (or Return) key, the equivalent Celsius temperature is displayed.

The interface for the `Fahrenheit` program is set up in the `FahrenheitPanel` class, shown in Listing 6.6. The text field is an object of the `JTextField` class. The `JTextField` constructor takes an integer parameter that specifies the size of the field in number of characters based on the current default font.

The text field and various labels are added to the panel to be displayed. Remember that the default layout manager for a panel puts as many components on a line as it can fit. Thus, if you resize the frame, the orientation of the labels and text field may change.

LISTING 6.5

```
//********************************************************************
//  Fahrenheit.java       Java Foundations
//
//  Demonstrates the use of text fields.
//********************************************************************

import javax.swing.JFrame;

public class Fahrenheit
{
   //-----------------------------------------------------------------
   //  Creates and displays the temperature converter GUI.
   //-----------------------------------------------------------------
   public static void main(String[] args)
   {
      JFrame frame = new JFrame("Fahrenheit");
      frame.setDefaultCloseOperation(JFrame.EXIT_ON_CLOSE);

      FahrenheitPanel panel = new FahrenheitPanel();
      frame.getContentPane().add(panel);

      frame.pack();
      frame.setVisible(true);
   }
}
```

LISTING 6.5 *continued*

DISPLAY

Go to the end of the text for a full-color version of this figure.

LISTING 6.6

```
//********************************************************************
//  FahrenheitPanel.java       Java Foundations
//
//  Demonstrates the use of text fields.
//********************************************************************

import java.awt.*;
import java.awt.event.*;
import javax.swing.*;

public class FahrenheitPanel extends JPanel
{
   private JLabel inputLabel, outputLabel, resultLabel;
   private JTextField fahrenheit;

   //-----------------------------------------------------------------
   //  Constructor: Sets up the main GUI components.
   //-----------------------------------------------------------------
   public FahrenheitPanel()
   {
      inputLabel = new JLabel("Enter Fahrenheit temperature:");
      outputLabel = new JLabel("Temperature in Celsius: ");
      resultLabel = new JLabel("---");
      fahrenheit = new JTextField(5);
      fahrenheit.addActionListener(new TempListener());
```

LISTING 6.6 *continued*

```
      add(inputLabel);
      add(fahrenheit);
      add(outputLabel);
      add(resultLabel);

      setPreferredSize(new Dimension(300, 75));
      setBackground(Color.yellow);
   }

   //*****************************************************************
   //  Represents an action listener for the temperature input field.
   //*****************************************************************
   private class TempListener implements ActionListener
   {
      //--------------------------------------------------------------
      //  Performs the conversion when the enter key is pressed in
      //  the text field.
      //--------------------------------------------------------------
      public void actionPerformed(ActionEvent event)
      {
         int fahrenheitTemp, celsiusTemp;

         String text = fahrenheit.getText();

         fahrenheitTemp = Integer.parseInt(text);
         celsiusTemp = (fahrenheitTemp-32) * 5/9;

         resultLabel.setText (Integer.toString(celsiusTemp));
      }
   }
}
```

A text field generates an action event when the Enter or Return key is pressed (and the cursor is in the text field). Therefore, we need to set up a listener object to respond to action events.

The text field component calls the `actionPerformed` method when the user presses the Enter key. The method first retrieves the text from the text field by calling its `getText` method, which returns a character string. The text is converted to an integer using the `parseInt` method of the `Integer` wrapper class. Then the method performs the calculation to determine the equivalent Celsius temperature and sets the text of the appropriate label with the result.

Note that a push button and a text field generate the same kind of event: an action event. Thus an alternative to the `Fahrenheit` program design is to add to the GUI a `JButton` object that causes the conversion to occur when the user uses the mouse to press the button. For that matter, the same listener object can be used to listen to multiple components at the same time, so the listener could be added to both the text field and the button, giving the user the option. Pressing either the button or the Enter key will cause the conversion to be performed. These variations are left as programming projects.

Check Boxes

A *check box* is a button that can be toggled on or off using the mouse, indicating that a particular boolean condition is set or unset. Although you might have a group of check boxes indicating a set of options, each check box operates independently. That is, each can be set to on or off, and the status of one does not influence the others.

The program in Listing 6.7 on the next page displays two check boxes and a label. The check boxes determine whether the text of the label is displayed in bold, italic, both, or neither. Any combination of bold and italic is valid. For example, both check boxes could be checked (on), in which case the text is displayed in both bold and italic. If neither is checked, the text of the label is displayed in a plain style.

The GUI for the `StyleOptions` program is embodied in the `StyleOptionsPanel` class shown in Listing 6.8 on page 262. A check box is represented by the `JCheckBox` class. When a check box changes state from selected (checked) to deselected (unchecked), or vice versa, it generates an *item event*. The `ItemListener` interface contains a single method called `itemStateChanged`. In this example, we use the same listener object to handle both check boxes.

This program also uses the `Font` class, which represents a particular character font. A `Font` object is defined by the font name, the font style, and the font size. The font name establishes the general visual characteristics of the characters. We are using the Helvetica font in this program. The style of a Java font can be plain, bold, italic, or bold and italic combined. The listener is set up to change the characteristics of our font style.

The style of a font is represented as an integer, and integer constants defined in the `Font` class are used to represent the various aspects of the style. The constant `PLAIN` is used to represent a plain style. The constants `BOLD` and `ITALIC` are used to represent bold and italic, respectively. The sum of the `BOLD` and `ITALIC` constants indicates a style that is both bold and italic.

The `itemStateChanged` method of the listener determines what the revised style should be now that one of the check boxes has changed state. It initially sets the style to be plain. Then each check box is consulted in turn using the `isSelected` method, which returns a boolean value. First, if the Bold check box is selected (checked), then the style is set to bold. Then, if the Italic check box is selected, the `ITALIC` constant is added to the style variable. Finally, the font of the label is set to a new font with its revised style.

LISTING 6.7

```
//********************************************************************
//  StyleOptions.java       Java Foundations
//
//  Demonstrates the use of check boxes.
//********************************************************************

import javax.swing.JFrame;

public class StyleOptions
{
   //-----------------------------------------------------------------
   //  Creates and displays the style options frame.
   //-----------------------------------------------------------------
   public static void main(String[] args)
   {
      JFrame frame = new JFrame("Style Options");
      frame.setDefaultCloseOperation(JFrame.EXIT_ON_CLOSE);

      frame.getContentPane().add(new StyleOptionsPanel());

      frame.pack();
      frame.setVisible(true);
   }
}
```

DISPLAY

Go to the end of the text for a full-color version of this figure.

LISTING 6.8

```
//********************************************************************
//  StyleOptionsPanel.java       Java Foundations
//
//  Demonstrates the use of check boxes.
//********************************************************************

import javax.swing.*;
import java.awt.*;
import java.awt.event.*;

public class StyleOptionsPanel extends JPanel
{
   private JLabel saying;
   private JCheckBox bold, italic;

   //-----------------------------------------------------------------
   //  Sets up a panel with a label and some check boxes that
   //  control the style of the label's font.
   //-----------------------------------------------------------------
   public StyleOptionsPanel()
   {
      saying = new JLabel("Say it with style!");
      saying.setFont(new Font ("Helvetica", Font.PLAIN, 36));

      bold = new JCheckBox("Bold");
      bold.setBackground(Color.cyan);
      italic = new JCheckBox("Italic");
      italic.setBackground(Color.cyan);

      StyleListener listener = new StyleListener();
      bold.addItemListener(listener);
      italic.addItemListener(listener);

      add(saying);
      add(bold);
      add(italic);

      setBackground(Color.cyan);
      setPreferredSize(new Dimension(300, 100));
   }

   //*****************************************************************
   //  Represents the listener for both check boxes.
   //*****************************************************************
```

LISTING 6.8 *continued*

```
   private class StyleListener implements ItemListener
   {
      //-----------------------------------------------------------------
      // Updates the style of the label font style.
      //-----------------------------------------------------------------
      public void itemStateChanged(ItemEvent event)
      {
         int style = Font.PLAIN;

         if (bold.isSelected())
            style = Font.BOLD;

         if (italic.isSelected())
            style += Font.ITALIC;

         saying.setFont(new Font("Helvetica", style, 36));
      }
   }
}
```

Note that, given the way the listener is written in this program, it doesn't matter which check box was clicked to generate the event. The same listener processes both check boxes. It also doesn't matter whether the changed check box was toggled from selected to unselected or vice versa. The state of both check boxes is examined if either is changed.

Radio Buttons

> **KEY CONCEPT**
> Radio buttons operate as a group, providing a set of mutually exclusive options.

A *radio button* is used with other radio buttons to provide a set of mutually exclusive options. Unlike a check box, a radio button is not particularly useful by itself. It has meaning only when it is used with one or more other radio buttons. Only one option out of the group is valid. At any point in time, one and only one button of the group of radio buttons is selected (on). When a radio button from the group is pushed, the other button in the group that is currently on is automatically toggled off.

The term *radio buttons* comes from the way the buttons worked on an old-fashioned car radio. At any point, one button was pushed to specify the current choice of station; when another was pushed, the button that was in automatically popped out.

The `QuoteOptions` program, shown in Listing 6.9, displays a label and a group of radio buttons. The radio buttons determine which quote is displayed in the label.

Because only one of the quotes can be displayed at a time, the use of radio buttons is appropriate. For example, if the Comedy radio button is selected, the comedy quote is displayed in the label. If the Philosophy button is then pressed,

LISTING 6.9

```
//********************************************************************
//  QuoteOptions.java       Java Foundations
//
//  Demonstrates the use of radio buttons.
//********************************************************************

import javax.swing.JFrame;

public class QuoteOptions
{
   //-----------------------------------------------------------------
   //  Creates and presents the program frame.
   //-----------------------------------------------------------------
   public static void main(String[] args)
   {
      JFrame frame = new JFrame("Quote Options");
      frame.setDefaultCloseOperation(JFrame.EXIT_ON_CLOSE);

      frame.getContentPane().add(new QuoteOptionsPanel());

      frame.pack();
      frame.setVisible(true);
   }
}
```

DISPLAY

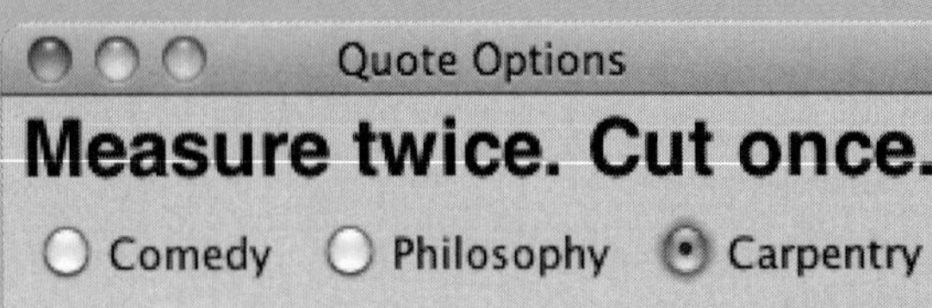

Go to the end of the text for a full-color version of this figure.

the Comedy radio button is automatically toggled off, and the comedy quote is replaced by a philosophical one.

VideoNote
Example using check boxes and radio buttons

The `QuoteOptionsPanel` class, shown in Listing 6.10, sets up and displays the GUI components. A radio button is represented by the `JRadioButton` class. Because the radio buttons in a set work together, the `ButtonGroup` class is used to define a set of related radio buttons.

LISTING 6.10

```
//********************************************************************
//  QuoteOptionsPanel.java       Java Foundations
//
//  Demonstrates the use of radio buttons.
//********************************************************************

import javax.swing.*;
import java.awt.*;
import java.awt.event.*;

public class QuoteOptionsPanel extends JPanel
{
   private JLabel quote;
   private JRadioButton comedy, philosophy, carpentry;
   private String comedyQuote, philosophyQuote, carpentryQuote;

   //-----------------------------------------------------------------
   //  Sets up a panel with a label and a set of radio buttons
   //  that control its text.
   //-----------------------------------------------------------------
   public QuoteOptionsPanel()
   {
      comedyQuote = "Take my wife, please.";
      philosophyQuote = "I think, therefore I am.";
      carpentryQuote = "Measure twice. Cut once.";

      quote = new JLabel(comedyQuote);
      quote.setFont(new Font("Helvetica", Font.BOLD, 24));
      comedy = new JRadioButton("Comedy", true);
      comedy.setBackground(Color.green);
      philosophy = new JRadioButton("Philosophy");
      philosophy.setBackground(Color.green);
      carpentry = new JRadioButton("Carpentry");
      carpentry.setBackground(Color.green);
```

LISTING 6.10 *continued*

```
      ButtonGroup group = new ButtonGroup();
      group.add(comedy);
      group.add(philosophy);
      group.add(carpentry);

      QuoteListener listener = new QuoteListener();
      comedy.addActionListener(listener);
      philosophy.addActionListener(listener);
      carpentry.addActionListener(listener);

      add(quote);
      add(comedy);
      add(philosophy);
      add(carpentry);

      setBackground(Color.green);
      setPreferredSize(new Dimension(300, 100));
   }

   //*****************************************************************
   //  Represents the listener for all radio buttons
   //*****************************************************************
   private class QuoteListener implements ActionListener
   {
      //--------------------------------------------------------------
      //  Sets the text of the label depending on which radio
      //  button was pressed.
      //--------------------------------------------------------------
      public void actionPerformed(ActionEvent event)
      {
         Object source = event.getSource();

         if (source == comedy)
            quote.setText(comedyQuote);
         else
         if (source == philosophy)
            quote.setText(philosophyQuote);
         else
            quote.setText(carpentryQuote);
      }
   }
}
```

Note that each button is added to the button group, and also that each button is added individually to the panel. A `ButtonGroup` object is not a container to organize and display components; it is simply a way to define the group of radio buttons that work together to form a set of dependent options. The `ButtonGroup` object ensures that the currently selected radio button is turned off when another in the group is selected.

A radio button produces an action event when it is selected. The `actionPerformed` method of the listener first retrieves the source of the event using the `getSource` method and then compares it to each of the three radio buttons in turn. Depending on which button was selected, the text of the label is set to the appropriate quote.

Note that unlike push buttons, both check boxes and radio buttons are *toggle buttons*, meaning that at any time they are either on or off. Independent options (choose any combination) are controlled with check boxes. Dependent options (choose one of a set) are controlled with radio buttons. If there is only one option to be managed, a check box can be used by itself. But a radio button makes sense only in conjunction with one or more other radio buttons.

Also note that check boxes and radio buttons produce different types of events. A check box produces an item event, and a radio button produces an action event. The use of different event types is related to the differences in button functionality. A check box produces an event when it is selected or deselected, and the listener could make the distinction if desired. A radio button, on the other hand, produces an event only when it is selected (the currently selected button from the group is deselected automatically).

Sliders

A *slider* is a GUI component that allows the user to specify a numeric value within a bounded range. A slider can be presented either vertically or horizontally and can have optional tick marks and labels indicating the range of values.

KEY CONCEPT

A slider lets the user specify a numeric value within a bounded range.

A program called `SlideColor` is shown in Listing 6.11. This program presents three sliders that control the RGB components of a color. The color specified by the values of the sliders is shown in a square that is displayed to the right of the sliders. Using RGB values to represent color is discussed in Appendix F.

The `SlideColorPanel` class shown in Listing 6.12 is a panel used to display the three sliders and the color panel. Each slider is created from the `JSlider` class, which accepts four parameters. The first determines the orientation of the slider using one of two `JSlider` constants (`HORIZONTAL` or `VERTICAL`). The second and third parameters specify the maximum and minimum values of the slider, which are set to 0 and 255 for each of the sliders in the example. The last parameter of the `JSlider` constructor specifies the slider's initial value. In our example, the initial value of each slider is 0, which puts the slider knob to the far left when the program initially executes.

The `JSlider` class has several methods that allow the programmer to tailor the look of a slider. Major tick marks can be set at specific intervals using the `setMajorTickSpacing` method. Intermediate minor tick marks can be set using the `setMinorTickSpacing` method. Neither is displayed, however, unless the `setPaintTicks` method, with a parameter of `true`, is invoked as well.

Labels indicating the value of the major tick marks are displayed if indicated by a call to the `setPaintLabels` method.

LISTING 6.11

```
//********************************************************************
//  SlideColor.java       Java Foundations
//
//  Demonstrates the use slider components.
//********************************************************************

import java.awt.*;
import javax.swing.*;

public class SlideColor
{
   //-----------------------------------------------------------------
   //  Presents a frame with a control panel and a panel that
   //  changes color as the sliders are adjusted.
   //-----------------------------------------------------------------
   public static void main(String[] args)
   {
      JFrame frame = new JFrame("Slide Colors");
      frame.setDefaultCloseOperation(JFrame.EXIT_ON_CLOSE);

      frame.getContentPane().add(new SlideColorPanel());

      frame.pack();
      frame.setVisible(true);
   }
}
```

LISTING 6.11 *continued*

DISPLAY

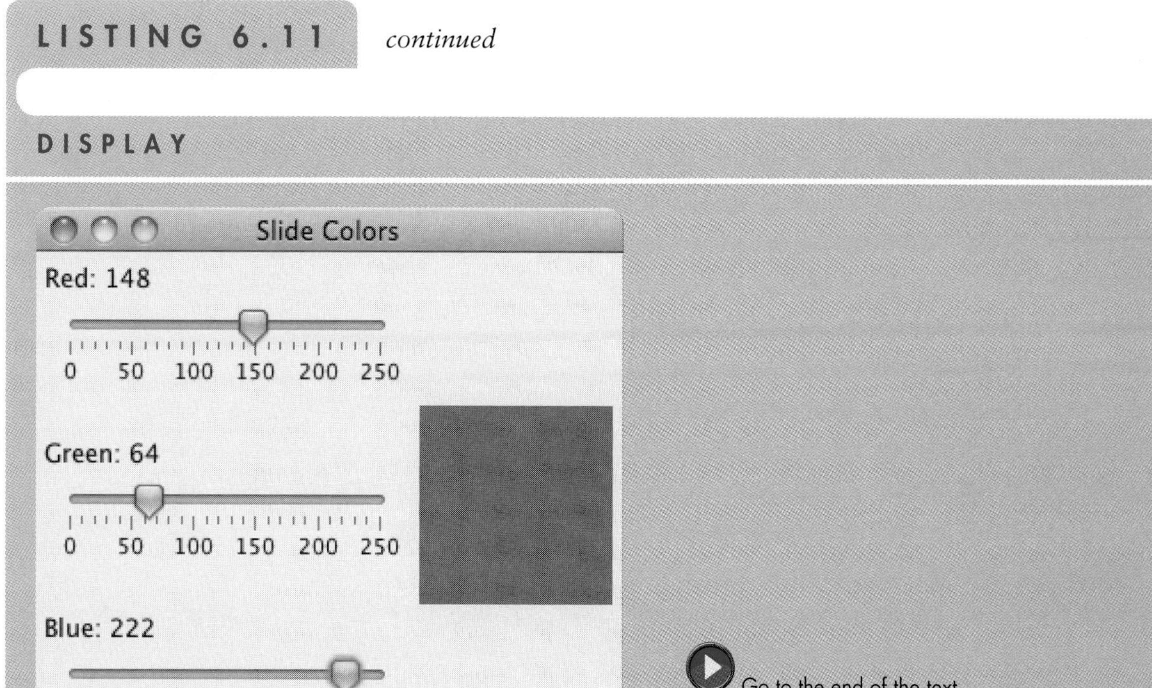

LISTING 6.12

```
//********************************************************************
//  SlideColorPanel.java       Java Foundations
//
//  Represents the slider control panel for the SlideColor program.
//********************************************************************

import java.awt.*;
import javax.swing.*;
import javax.swing.event.*;

public class SlideColorPanel extends JPanel
{
   private JPanel controls, colorPanel;
   private JSlider rSlider, gSlider, bSlider;
   private JLabel rLabel, gLabel, bLabel;
```

LISTING 6.12 *continued*

```
   //-----------------------------------------------------------------
   //  Sets up the sliders and their labels, aligning them along
   //  their left edge using a box layout.
   //-----------------------------------------------------------------
   public SlideColorPanel()
   {
      rSlider = new JSlider(JSlider.HORIZONTAL, 0, 255, 0);
      rSlider.setMajorTickSpacing(50);
      rSlider.setMinorTickSpacing(10);
      rSlider.setPaintTicks(true);
      rSlider.setPaintLabels(true);
      rSlider.setAlignmentX(Component.LEFT_ALIGNMENT);

      gSlider = new JSlider(JSlider.HORIZONTAL, 0, 255, 0);
      gSlider.setMajorTickSpacing(50);
      gSlider.setMinorTickSpacing(10);
      gSlider.setPaintTicks(true);
      gSlider.setPaintLabels(true);
      gSlider.setAlignmentX(Component.LEFT_ALIGNMENT);

      bSlider = new JSlider(JSlider.HORIZONTAL, 0, 255, 0);
      bSlider.setMajorTickSpacing(50);
      bSlider.setMinorTickSpacing(10);
      bSlider.setPaintTicks(true);
      bSlider.setPaintLabels(true);
      bSlider.setAlignmentX(Component.LEFT_ALIGNMENT);
      SliderListener listener = new SliderListener();
      rSlider.addChangeListener(listener);
      gSlider.addChangeListener(listener);
      bSlider.addChangeListener(listener);

      rLabel = new JLabel("Red: 0");
      rLabel.setAlignmentX(Component.LEFT_ALIGNMENT);
      gLabel = new JLabel("Green: 0");
      gLabel.setAlignmentX(Component.LEFT_ALIGNMENT);
      bLabel = new JLabel("Blue: 0");
      bLabel.setAlignmentX(Component.LEFT_ALIGNMENT);

      controls = new JPanel();
      BoxLayout layout = new BoxLayout(controls, BoxLayout.Y_AXIS);
      controls.setLayout(layout);
      controls.add(rLabel);
      controls.add(rSlider);
      controls.add(Box.createRigidArea (new Dimension (0, 20)));
```

LISTING 6.12 *continued*

```
      controls.add(gLabel);
      controls.add(gSlider);
      controls.add(Box.createRigidArea (new Dimension (0, 20)));
      controls.add(bLabel);
      controls.add(bSlider);

      colorPanel = new JPanel();
      colorPanel.setPreferredSize(new Dimension (100, 100));
      colorPanel.setBackground(new Color (0, 0, 0));

      add(controls);
      add(colorPanel);
   }

   //*****************************************************************
   //  Represents the listener for all three sliders.
   //*****************************************************************
   private class SliderListener implements ChangeListener
   {
      private int red, green, blue;

      //--------------------------------------------------------------
      //  Gets the value of each slider, then updates the labels and
      //  the color panel.
      //--------------------------------------------------------------
      public void stateChanged(ChangeEvent event)
      {
         red = rSlider.getValue();
         green = gSlider.getValue();
         blue = bSlider.getValue();

         rLabel.setText("Red: " + red);
         gLabel.setText("Green: " + green);
         bLabel.setText("Blue: " + blue);

         colorPanel.setBackground(new Color(red, green, blue));
      }
   }
}
```

Note that in this example, the major tick spacing is set to 50. Starting at 0, each increment of 50 is labeled. The last label is therefore 250, even though the slider value can reach 255.

A slider produces a *change event*, indicating that the position of the slider and the value it represents have changed. The `ChangeListener` interface contains a single method called `stateChanged`. In the `SlideColor` program, the same listener object is used for all three sliders. In the `stateChanged` method, which is called whenever any of the sliders is adjusted, the value of each slider is obtained, the labels of all three are updated, and the background color of the color panel is revised. It is actually only necessary to update one of the labels (the one whose corresponding slider changed). However, the effort to determine which slider was adjusted is not warranted. It's easier—and probably more efficient—to update all three labels each time. Another alternative is to have a unique listener for each slider, although that extra coding effort is not needed either.

A slider is often a good choice when a large range of values is possible but strictly bounded on both ends. Compared to alternatives such as a text field, sliders convey more information to the user and eliminate input errors.

Combo Boxes

A *combo box* allows the user to select one of several options from a "drop-down" menu. When the user presses a combo box using the mouse, a list of options is displayed from which the user can choose. The current choice is displayed in the combo box. A combo box is defined by the `JComboBox` class.

A combo box can be either editable or uneditable. By default, a combo box is uneditable. Changing the value of an uneditable combo box can be accomplished only by selecting an item from the list. If the combo box is editable, however, the user can change the value by either selecting an item from the list or typing a particular value into the combo box area.

KEY CONCEPT
A combo box provides a drop-down menu of options.

The options in a combo box list can be established in one of two ways. We can create an array of strings and pass it into the constructor of the `JComboBox` class. Alternatively, we can use the `addItem` method to add an item to the combo box after it has been created. An item in a `JComboBox` can also display an `ImageIcon` object, by itself or in addition to text.

The `JukeBox` program shown in Listing 6.13 demonstrates the use of a combo box. The user chooses a song to play using the combo box and then presses the Play button to begin playing the song. The Stop button can be pressed at any time to stop the song. Selecting a new song while one is playing also stops the current song.

The `JukeBoxControls` class shown in Listing 6.14 on the page 274 is a panel that contains the components that make up the jukebox GUI. The constructor of

LISTING 6.13

```
//********************************************************************
//  JukeBox.java       Java Foundations
//
//  Demonstrates the use of a combo box.
//********************************************************************

import javax.swing.*;

public class JukeBox
{
   //-----------------------------------------------------------------
   //  Creates and displays the controls for a juke box.
   //-----------------------------------------------------------------
   public static void main(String[] args)
   {
      JFrame frame = new JFrame("Java Juke Box");
      frame.setDefaultCloseOperation(JFrame.EXIT_ON_CLOSE);
      frame.getContentPane().add(new JukeBoxControls());

      frame.pack();
      frame.setVisible(true);
   }
}
```

DISPLAY

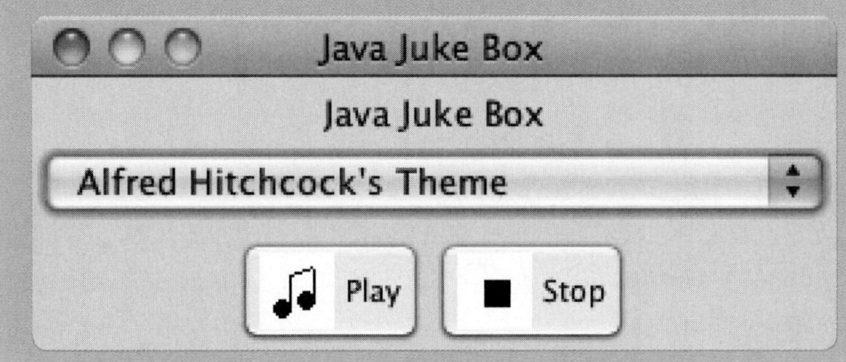

Go to the end of the text for a full-color version of this figure.

LISTING 6.14

```
//********************************************************************
//  JukeBoxControls.java       Java Foundations
//
//  Represents the control panel for the juke box.
//********************************************************************

import java.awt.*;
import java.awt.event.*;
import javax.swing.*;
import java.applet.AudioClip;
import java.net.URL;

public class JukeBoxControls extends JPanel
{
   private JComboBox musicCombo;
   private JButton stopButton, playButton;
   private AudioClip[] music;
   private AudioClip current;

   //-----------------------------------------------------------------
   //  Sets up the GUI for the juke box.
   //-----------------------------------------------------------------
   public JukeBoxControls()
   {
      URL url1, url2, url3, url4, url5, url6;
      url1 = url2 = url3 = url4 = url5 = url6 = null;

      // Obtain and store the audio clips to play
      try
      {
         url1 = new URL("file", "localhost", "westernBeat.wav");
         url2 = new URL("file", "localhost", "classical.wav");
         url3 = new URL("file", "localhost", "jeopardy.au");
         url4 = new URL("file", "localhost", "newAgeRythm.wav");
         url5 = new URL("file", "localhost", "eightiesJam.wav");
         url6 = new URL("file", "localhost", "hitchcock.wav");
      }
      catch (Exception exception) {}

      music = new AudioClip[7];
      music[0] = null; // Corresponds to "Make a Selection..."
```

LISTING 6.14 *continued*

```
      music[1] = JApplet.newAudioClip(url1);
      music[2] = JApplet.newAudioClip(url2);
      music[3] = JApplet.newAudioClip(url3);
      music[4] = JApplet.newAudioClip(url4);
      music[5] = JApplet.newAudioClip(url5);
      music[6] = JApplet.newAudioClip(url6);

      // Create the list of strings for the combo box options
      String[] musicNames = {"Make A Selection...", "Western Beat",
               "Classical Melody", "Jeopardy Theme", "New Age Rythm",
               "Eighties Jam", "Alfred Hitchcock's Theme"};

      musicCombo = new JComboBox(musicNames);
      musicCombo.setBackground(Color.cyan);

      // Set up the buttons
      playButton = new JButton("Play", new ImageIcon ("play.gif"));
      playButton.setBackground(Color.cyan);
      stopButton = new JButton("Stop", new ImageIcon ("stop.gif"));
      stopButton.setBackground(Color.cyan);

      // Set up this panel
      setPreferredSize(new Dimension(250, 100));
      setBackground(Color.cyan);
      add(musicCombo);
      add(playButton);
      add(stopButton);

      musicCombo.addActionListener(new ComboListener());
      stopButton.addActionListener(new ButtonListener());
      playButton.addActionListener(new ButtonListener());

      current = null;
   }

   //*****************************************************************
   //  Represents the action listener for the combo box.
   //*****************************************************************

   private class ComboListener implements ActionListener
```

LISTING 6.14 *continued*

```
   {
      //-----------------------------------------------------------------
      //  Stops playing the current selection (if any) and resets
      //  the current selection to the one chosen.
      //-----------------------------------------------------------------
      public void actionPerformed(ActionEvent event)
      {
         if (current != null)
            current.stop();
         current = music[musicCombo.getSelectedIndex()];
      }
   }

   //*****************************************************************
   //  Represents the action listener for both control buttons.
   //*****************************************************************
   private class ButtonListener implements ActionListener
   {
      //-----------------------------------------------------------------
      // Stops the current selection (if any) in either case. If
      // the play button was pressed, start playing it again.
      //-----------------------------------------------------------------
      public void actionPerformed(ActionEvent event)
      {
         if (current != null)
            current.stop();

         if (event.getSource() == playButton)
            if (current != null)
               current.play();
      }
   }
}
```

the class also loads the audio clips that will be played. An audio clip is obtained first by creating a `URL` object that corresponds to the wav or au file that defines the clip. The first two parameters to the `URL` constructor should be `"file"` and `"localhost"`, respectively, if the audio clip is stored on the same machine on which the program is executing. Creating URL objects can potentially throw a checked exception; therefore, they are created in a try block. However, this program assumes that the audio clips will be loaded successfully and therefore does nothing if an exception is thrown.

Once created, the URL objects are used to create AudioClip objects using the static newAudioClip method of the JApplet class. The audio clips are stored in an array. The first entry in the array, at index 0, is set to null. This entry corresponds to the initial combo box option, which simply encourages the user to make a selection.

The list of songs that is displayed in the combo box is defined in an array of strings. The first entry of the array will appear in the combo box by default and is often used to direct the user. We must take care that the rest of the program does not try to use that option as a valid song.

This program also shows the ability of a push button to display an image. In this example, the Play and Stop buttons are displayed with both a text label and an image icon.

A combo box generates an action event whenever the user makes a selection from it. The JukeBox program uses one action listener class for the combo box and another for both of the push buttons. They could have been combined, using code to distinguish which component fired the event.

The actionPerformed method of the ComboListener class is executed when a selection is made from the combo box. The current audio selection that is playing, if any, is stopped. The current clip is then updated to reflect the new selection. Note that the audio clip is not immediately played at that point. The way this program is designed, the user must press the Play button to hear the new selection.

The actionPerformed method of the ButtonListener class is executed when either of the buttons is pushed. The audio selection that is currently playing, if any, is stopped. If the Stop button was pressed, the task is complete. If the Play button was pressed, the current audio selection is played again from the beginning.

Timers

A *timer*, created from the Timer class of the javax.swing package, can be thought of as a GUI component. However, unlike other components, it does not have a visual representation that appears on the screen. Instead, as the name implies, it helps us manage an activity over time.

```
Timer (int delay, ActionListener listener)
    Constructor: Creates a timer that generates an action event at
    regular intervals, specified by the delay. The event will be handled
    by the specified listener.

void addActionListener (ActionListener listener)
    Adds an action listener to the timer.

boolean isRunning ()
    Returns true if the timer is running.

void setDelay (int delay)
    Sets the delay of the timer.

void start ()
    Starts the timer, causing it to generate action events.

void stop ()
    Stops the timer, causing it to stop generating action events.
```

FIGURE 6.1 Some methods of the `Timer` class

KEY CONCEPT
A timer generates action events at regular intervals and can be used to control an animation.

A timer object generates an action event at regular intervals. To perform an animation, we can set up a timer to generate an action event periodically, and then update the animation graphics in the action listener. The methods of the `Timer` class are shown in Figure 6.1.

The program shown in Listing 6.15 displays the image of a smiling face that seems to glide across the program window at an angle, bouncing off the window edges (although that's hard to appreciate from a screen shot).

LISTING 6.15

```
//********************************************************************
//  Rebound.java       Java Foundations
//
//  Demonstrates an animation and the use of the Timer class.
//********************************************************************

import java.awt.*;
import java.awt.event.*;
import javax.swing.*;
```

LISTING 6.15 *continued*

```
public class Rebound
{
   //-----------------------------------------------------------------
   //  Displays the main frame of the program.
   //-----------------------------------------------------------------
   public static void main(String[] args)
   {
      JFrame frame = new JFrame("Rebound");
      frame.setDefaultCloseOperation(JFrame.EXIT_ON_CLOSE);

      frame.getContentPane().add(new ReboundPanel());

      frame.pack();
      frame.setVisible(true);
   }
}
```

DISPLAY

Rebound

Go to the end of the text for a full-color version of this figure.

The constructor of the `ReboundPanel` class, shown in Listing 6.16, creates a V`Timer` object. The first parameter to the `Timer` constructor is the delay in milliseconds. The second parameter to the constructor is the listener that handles the action events of the timer. The `ReboundPanel` constructor also sets up the initial position for the image and the number of pixels it will move, in both vertical and horizontal directions, each time the image is redrawn.

The `actionPerformed` method of the listener updates the current *x* and *y* coordinate values, then checks to see whether those values cause the image to "run into"

LISTING 6.16

```
//********************************************************************
//  ReboundPanel.java       Java Foundations
//
//  Represents the primary panel for the Rebound program.
//********************************************************************

import java.awt.*;
import java.awt.event.*;
import javax.swing.*;

public class ReboundPanel extends JPanel
{
   private final int WIDTH = 300, HEIGHT = 100;
   private final int DELAY = 20, IMAGE_SIZE = 35;

   private ImageIcon image;
   private Timer timer;
   private int x, y, moveX, moveY;

   //-----------------------------------------------------------------
   //  Sets up the panel, including the timer for the animation.
   //-----------------------------------------------------------------
   public ReboundPanel()
   {
      timer = new Timer(DELAY, new ReboundListener());

      image = new ImageIcon("happyFace.gif");

      x = 0;
      y = 40;
      moveX = moveY = 3;

      setPreferredSize(new Dimension(WIDTH, HEIGHT));
      setBackground(Color.black);
      timer.start();
   }

   //-----------------------------------------------------------------
   //  Draws the image in the current location.
   //-----------------------------------------------------------------
   public void paintComponent(Graphics page)
   {
      super.paintComponent(page);
      image.paintIcon(this, page, x, y);
   }
```

LISTING 6.16 *continued*

```
   //*****************************************************************
   //  Represents the action listener for the timer.
   //*****************************************************************
   private class ReboundListener implements ActionListener
   {
   //--------------------------------------------------------------
   //  Updates the position of the image and possibly the direction
   //  of movement whenever the timer fires an action event.
   //--------------------------------------------------------------
      public void actionPerformed(ActionEvent event)
      {
         x += moveX;
         y += moveY;

         if (x <= 0 || x >= WIDTH-IMAGE_SIZE)
            moveX = moveX * -1;

         if (y <= 0 || y >= HEIGHT-IMAGE_SIZE)
            moveY = moveY * -1;
         repaint();
      }
   }
}
```

the edge of the panel. If so, the movement is adjusted so that the image will make future moves in the opposite direction horizontally, vertically, or both. Note that this calculation takes the image size into account.

After updating the coordinate values, the `actionPerformed` method calls `repaint` to force the component (in this case, the panel) to repaint itself. The call to `repaint` eventually causes the `paintComponent` method to be called, which repaints the image in the new location.

The speed of the animation in this program is a function of two factors: the pause between the action events and the distance the image is shifted each time. In this example, the timer is set to generate an action event every 20 milliseconds, and the image is shifted 3 pixels each time it is updated. You can experiment with these values to change the speed of the animation. The goal should be to create the illusion of movement that is pleasing to the eye.

6.3 Layout Managers

As we mentioned earlier in this chapter, every container is managed by an object called a *layout manager* that determines how the components in the container are arranged visually. The layout manager is consulted when needed, such as when the container is resized or when a component is added to the container.

KEY CONCEPT
Every container is managed by a layout manager, which determines how components are visually presented.

A layout manager determines the size and position of each component and may take many factors into account to do so. Every container has a default layout manager, although we can replace it if we prefer another one.

The table in Figure 6.2 describes several of the predefined layout managers provided by the Java standard class library.

KEY CONCEPT
When changes occur, the components in a container reorganize themselves according to the layout manager's policy.

Every layout manager has its own particular properties and rules governing the layout of components. For some layout managers, the order in which you add the components affects their positioning, whereas others provide more specific control. Some layout managers take a component's preferred size or alignment into account, whereas others don't. To develop good GUIs in Java, it is important to become familiar with the features and characteristics of various layout managers.

VideoNote
Discussion of layout managers

Layout Manager	Description
Border Layout	Organizes components into five areas (North, South, East, West, and Center).
Box Layout	Organizes components into a single row or column.
Card Layout	Organizes components into one area such that only one is visible at any time.
Flow Layout	Organizes components from left to right, starting new rows as necessary.
Grid Layout	Organizes components into a grid of rows and columns.
GridBag Layout	Organizes components into a grid of cells, allowing components to span more than one cell.

FIGURE 6.2 Some predefined Java layout managers

We can use the `setLayout` method of a container to change its layout manager. For example, the following code sets the layout manager of a `JPanel`, which has a flow layout by default, so that it uses a border layout instead.

KEY CONCEPT
The layout manager for each container can be explicitly set.

```
JPanel panel = new JPanel();
panel.setLayout (new BorderLayout());
```

Let's explore some of these layout managers in more detail. We'll focus on the most popular layout managers at this point: flow, border, box, and grid. The class presented in Listing 6.17 contains the `main` method of an application that demonstrates the use and effects of these layout managers.

LISTING 6.17

```
//********************************************************************
//  LayoutDemo.java       Java Foundations
//
//  Demonstrates the use of flow, border, grid, and box layouts.
//********************************************************************

import javax.swing.*;

public class LayoutDemo
{
   //-----------------------------------------------------------------
   //  Sets up a frame containing a tabbed pane. The panel on each
   //  tab demonstrates a different layout manager.
   //-----------------------------------------------------------------
   public static void main(String[] args)
   {
      JFrame frame = new JFrame("Layout Manager Demo");
      frame.setDefaultCloseOperation(JFrame.EXIT_ON_CLOSE);

      JTabbedPane tp = new JTabbedPane();
      tp.addTab("Intro", new IntroPanel());
      tp.addTab("Flow", new FlowPanel());
      tp.addTab("Border", new BorderPanel());
      tp.addTab("Grid", new GridPanel());
      tp.addTab("Box", new BoxPanel());

      frame.getContentPane().add(tp);
```

LISTING 6.17 *continued*

```
        frame.pack();
        frame.setVisible(true);
    }
}
```

The `LayoutDemo` program introduces the use of a *tabbed pane*, a container that allows the user to select (by clicking on a tab) which of several panes is currently visible. A tabbed pane is defined by the `JTabbedPane` class. The `addTab` method creates a tab, specifying the name that appears on the tab and the component to be displayed on that pane when it achieves focus by being "brought to the front" and made visible to the user.

Interestingly, there is an overlap in the functionality provided by tabbed panes and the card layout manager. Similar to the tabbed pane, a card layout allows several layers to be defined, and only one of those layers is displayed at any given point. However, a container managed by a card layout can be adjusted only under program control, whereas tabbed panes allow the user to indicate directly which tab should be displayed.

In this example, each tab of the tabbed pane contains a panel that is controlled by a different layout manager. The first tab simply contains a panel with an introductory message, as shown in Listing 6.18. As we explore each layout manager in more detail, we examine the class that defines the corresponding panel of this program and discuss its visual effect.

LISTING 6.18

```
//********************************************************************
//  IntroPanel.java       Java Foundations
//
//  Represents the introduction panel for the LayoutDemo program.
//********************************************************************

import java.awt.*;
import javax.swing.*;
```

LISTING 6.18 *continued*

```
public class IntroPanel extends JPanel
{
   //-----------------------------------------------------------------
   //  Sets up this panel with two labels.
   //-----------------------------------------------------------------
   public IntroPanel()
   {
      setBackground(Color.green);

      JLabel l1 = new JLabel("Layout Manager Demonstration");
      JLabel l2 = new JLabel("Choose a tab to see an example of " +
                             "a layout manager.");
      add(l1);
      add(l2);
   }
}
```

DISPLAY

Layout Manager Demo

Intro | Flow | Border | Grid | Box

Layout Manager Demonstration

Choose a tab to see an example of a layout manager.

Go to the end of the text for a full-color version of this figure.

Flow Layout

Flow layout is one of the easiest layout managers to use. As we've mentioned, the `JPanel` class uses flow layout by default. Flow layout puts as many components as possible on a row, at their preferred size. When a component cannot fit on a row, it is put on the next row. As many rows as needed are added to fit all components that have been added to the container. Figure 6.3 depicts a container governed by a flow layout manager.

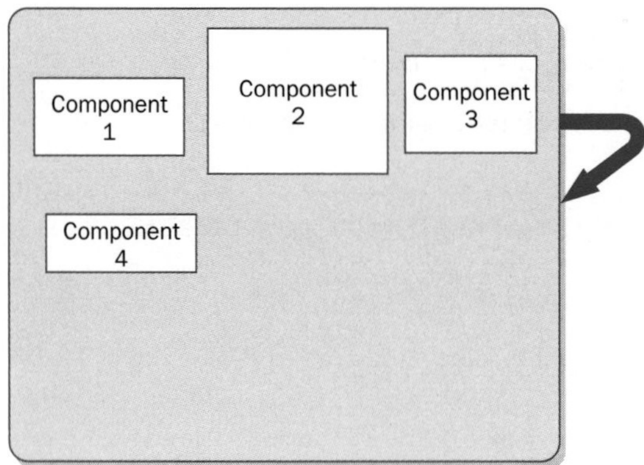

FIGURE 6.3 Flow layout puts as many components as possible on a row

The class in Listing 6.19 on the next page represents the panel that demonstrates a flow layout in the `LayoutDemo` program. It explicitly sets the layout to be a flow layout (in this case that is unnecessary, because `JPanel` defaults to flow layout). The buttons are then created and added to the panel.

Each button is made large enough to accommodate the size of the label that is put on it. Flow layout puts as many of these buttons as possible on one row within the panel and then starts putting components on another row. When the

LISTING 6.19

```
//********************************************************************
//  FlowPanel.java       Java Foundations
//
//  Represents the panel in the LayoutDemo program that demonstrates
//  the flow layout manager.
//********************************************************************

import java.awt.*;
import javax.swing.*;

public class FlowPanel extends JPanel
{
   //-----------------------------------------------------------------
   //  Sets up this panel with some buttons to show how flow layout
   //  affects their position.
   //-----------------------------------------------------------------
   public FlowPanel()
   {
```

LISTING 6.19 *continued*

```
        setLayout(new FlowLayout());

        setBackground(Color.green);

        JButton b1 = new JButton("BUTTON 1");
        JButton b2 = new JButton("BUTTON 2");
        JButton b3 = new JButton("BUTTON 3");
        JButton b4 = new JButton("BUTTON 4");
        JButton b5 = new JButton("BUTTON 5");

        add(b1);
        add(b2);
        add(b3);
        add(b4);
        add(b5);
    }
}
```

DISPLAY

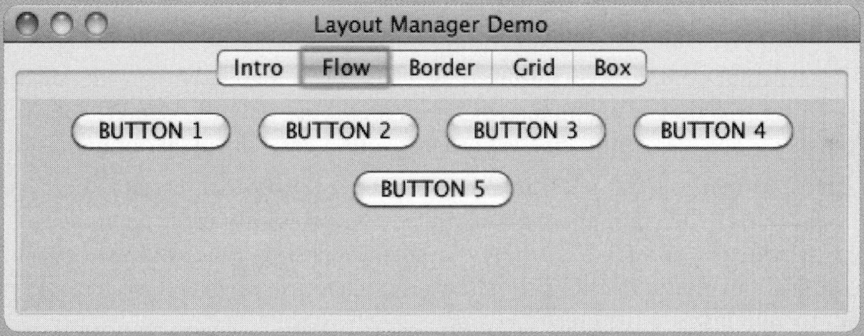

Layout Manager Demo

Intro | Flow | Border | Grid | Box

BUTTON 1 BUTTON 2 BUTTON 3 BUTTON 4

BUTTON 5

Go to the end of the text for full-color versions of these figures.

Layout Manager Demo

Intro | Flow | Border | Grid | Box

BUTTON 1 BUTTON 2

BUTTON 3 BUTTON 4

BUTTON 5

size of the frame is widened (by dragging the lower-right corner with the mouse, for example), the panel grows as well, and more buttons can fit on a row. When the frame is resized, the layout manager is consulted and the components are reorganized automatically. The display in Listing 6.19 shows two screen shots of the window with different sizes.

The constructor of the `FlowLayout` class is overloaded to allow the programmer to tailor the characteristics of the layout manager. Within each row, components are either centered, left aligned, or right aligned. The alignment defaults to centered. The horizontal gap size and the vertical gap size between components also can be specified when the layout manager is created. The `FlowLayout` class has methods to set the alignment and gap sizes after the layout manager is created.

Border Layout

A *border layout* has five areas to which components can be added: North, South, East, West, and Center. The areas have a particular positional relationship to each other, as shown in Figure 6.4.

The four outer areas become as big as needed in order to accommodate the component they contain. If no components are added to the North, South, East, or West areas, these areas do not take up any room in the overall layout. The Center area expands to fill any available space.

A particular container might use only a few areas, depending on the functionality of the system. For example, a program might use only the Center, South, and West areas. This versatility makes border layout a very useful layout manager.

The `add` method for a container governed by a border layout takes as its first parameter the component to be added. The second parameter indicates the area to which it is added. The area is specified using constants defined in the `BorderLayout` class. Listing 6.20 shows the panel used by the `LayoutDemo` program to demonstrate the border layout.

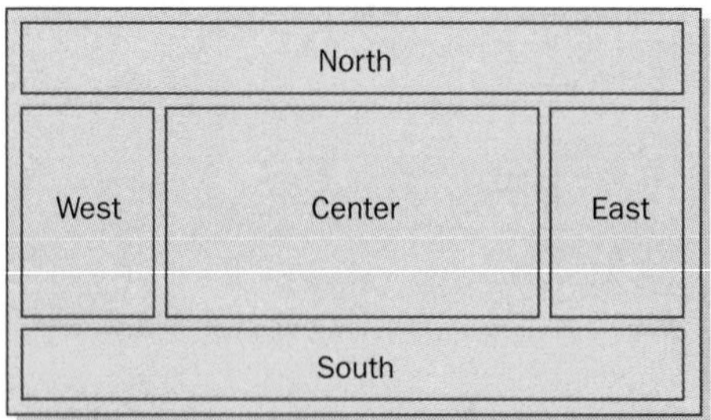

FIGURE 6.4 Border layout organizes components in five areas

In the `BorderPanel` class constructor, the layout manager of the panel is explicitly set to be border layout. The buttons are then created and added to specific panel areas. By default, each button is made wide enough to accommodate its label and tall enough to fill the area to which it has been assigned. As the frame (along with the panel) is resized, the size of each button adjusts as needed, and the button in the Center area fills any unused space.

LISTING 6.20

```
//********************************************************************
//  BorderPanel.java       Java Foundations
//
//  Represents the panel in the LayoutDemo program that demonstrates
//  the border layout manager.
//********************************************************************

import java.awt.*;
import javax.swing.*;

public class BorderPanel extends JPanel
{
   //-----------------------------------------------------------------
   //  Sets up this panel with a button in each area of a border
   //  layout to show how it affects their position, shape, and size.
   //-----------------------------------------------------------------
   public BorderPanel()
   {
      setLayout(new BorderLayout());

      setBackground(Color.green);

      JButton b1 = new JButton("BUTTON 1");
      JButton b2 = new JButton("BUTTON 2");
      JButton b3 = new JButton("BUTTON 3");
      JButton b4 = new JButton("BUTTON 4");
      JButton b5 = new JButton("BUTTON 5");

      add(b1, BorderLayout.CENTER);
      add(b2, BorderLayout.NORTH);
      add(b3, BorderLayout.SOUTH);
      add(b4, BorderLayout.EAST);
      add(b5, BorderLayout.WEST);
   }
}
```

LISTING 6.20 *continued*

DISPLAY

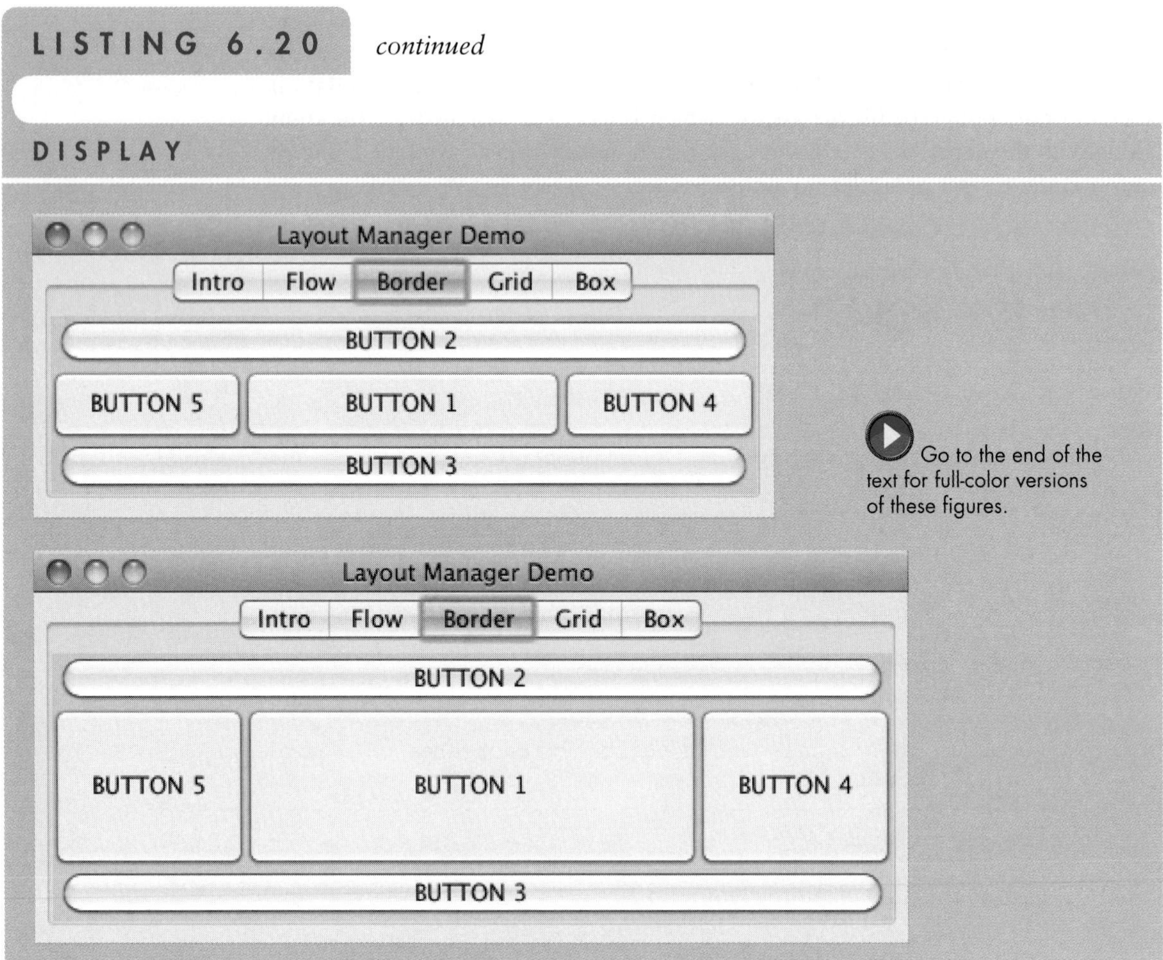

Go to the end of the text for full-color versions of these figures.

Each area in a border layout displays only one component. That is, only one component is added to each area of a given border layout. A common error is to add two components to a particular area of a border layout, in which case the first component added is replaced by the second, and only the second is seen when the container is displayed. To add multiple components to an area within a border layout, you must first add the components to another container, such as a `JPanel`, and then add the panel to the area.

Note that even though the panel used to display the buttons has a green background, no green is visible in the display for Listing 6.20. By default there are no horizontal or vertical gaps between the areas of a border layout. These gaps can be set with an overloaded constructor or with explicit methods of the `BorderLayout` class. If the gaps are increased, the underlying panel will show through.

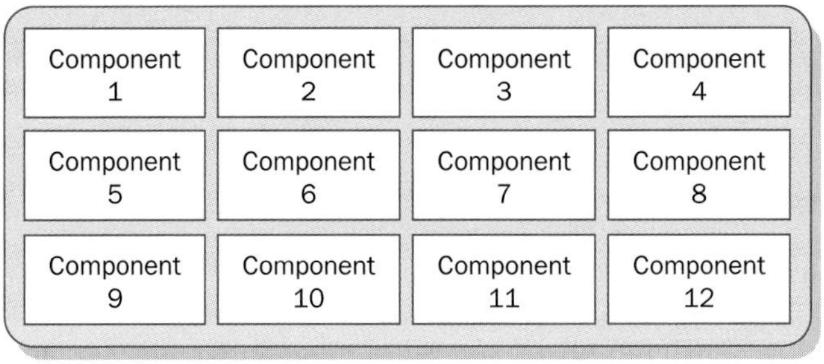

Component 1	Component 2	Component 3	Component 4
Component 5	Component 6	Component 7	Component 8
Component 9	Component 10	Component 11	Component 12

FIGURE 6.5 Grid layout creates a rectangular grid of equal-size cells

Grid Layout

A *grid layout* presents a container's components in a rectangular grid of rows and columns. One component is placed in each grid cell, and all cells are the same size. Figure 6.5 shows the general organization of a grid layout.

The number of rows and the number of columns in a grid layout are established using parameters to the constructor when the layout manager is created. The class in Listing 6.21 shows the panel used by the `LayoutDemo` program to demonstrate a grid layout. It specifies that the panel should be managed using a grid of two rows and three columns.

LISTING 6.21

```
//********************************************************************
//  GridPanel.java       Java Foundations
//
//  Represents the panel in the LayoutDemo program that demonstrates
//  the grid layout manager.
//********************************************************************

import java.awt.*;
import javax.swing.*;

public class GridPanel extends JPanel
{
   //-----------------------------------------------------------------
   //  Sets up this panel with some buttons to show how grid
   //  layout affects their position, shape, and size.
   //-----------------------------------------------------------------
```

LISTING 6.21 *continued*

```
   public GridPanel()
   {
      setLayout(new GridLayout (2, 3));

      setBackground(Color.green);

      JButton b1 = new JButton("BUTTON 1");
      JButton b2 = new JButton("BUTTON 2");
      JButton b3 = new JButton("BUTTON 3");
      JButton b4 = new JButton("BUTTON 4");
      JButton b5 = new JButton("BUTTON 5");

      add(b1);
      add(b2);
      add(b3);
      add(b4);
      add(b5);
   }
}
```

DISPLAY

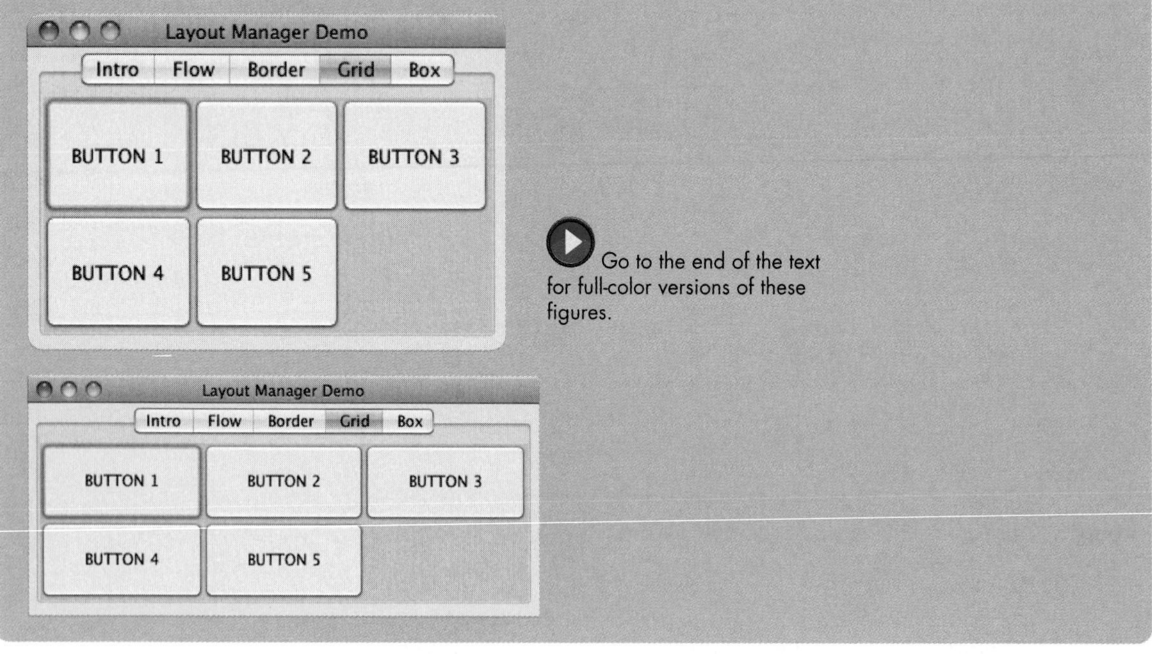

Go to the end of the text for full-color versions of these figures.

As buttons are added to the container, they fill the grid (by default) from left to right and top to bottom. There is no way to explicitly assign a component to a particular location in the grid other than deciding in what order to add them to the container.

The size of each cell is determined by the container's overall size. When the container is resized, all of the cells change size proportionally to fill the container.

If the value used to specify either the number of rows or the number of columns is zero, the grid expands as needed in that dimension to accommodate the number of components added to the container. The values for the numbers of rows and columns cannot both be zero.

By default, there are no horizontal and vertical gaps between the grid cells. The gap sizes can be specified using an overloaded constructor or with the appropriate `GridLayout` methods.

Box Layout

A *box layout* organizes components either vertically or horizontally, in one row or one column, as shown in Figure 6.6. It is easy to use, yet when combined with other box layouts, it can produce complex GUI designs similar to those that can be accomplished with a *grid bag layout*, which in general is far more difficult to master.

When a `BoxLayout` object is created, we specify that it will follow either the X axis (horizontal) or the Y axis (vertical), using constants defined in the `BoxLayout` class. Unlike other layout managers, the constructor of the `BoxLayout` class takes as its first parameter the component that it will govern. Therefore, a new `BoxLayout` object must be created for each component. Listing 6.22 on the next page shows the panel used by the `LayoutDemo` program to demonstrate the box layout.

Components in containers governed by a box layout are organized (top to bottom or left to right) in the order in which they are added to the container.

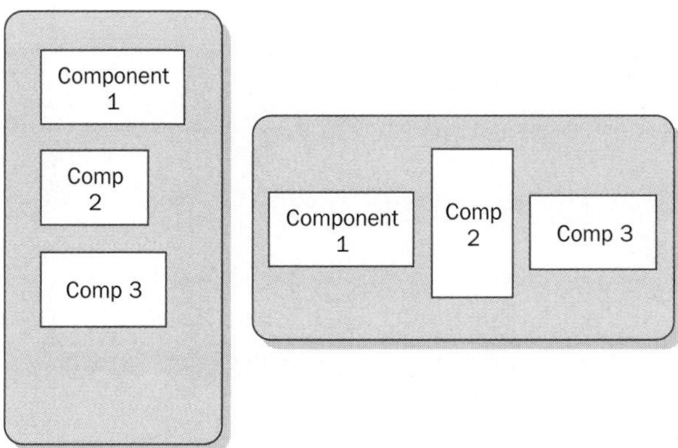

FIGURE 6.6 Box layout organizes components either vertically or horizontally

LISTING 6.22

```
//********************************************************************
//  BoxPanel.java        Java Foundations
//
//  Represents the panel in the LayoutDemo program that demonstrates
//  the box layout manager.
//********************************************************************

import java.awt.*;
import javax.swing.*;

public class BoxPanel extends JPanel
{
   //-----------------------------------------------------------------
   //  Sets up this panel with some buttons to show how a vertical
   //  box layout (and invisible components) affects their position.
   //-----------------------------------------------------------------
   public BoxPanel()
   {
      setLayout(new BoxLayout(this, BoxLayout.Y_AXIS));

      setBackground(Color.green);

      JButton b1 = new JButton("BUTTON 1");
      JButton b2 = new JButton("BUTTON 2");
      JButton b3 = new JButton("BUTTON 3");
      JButton b4 = new JButton("BUTTON 4");
      JButton b5 = new JButton("BUTTON 5");

      add(b1);
      add(Box.createRigidArea(new Dimension (0, 10)));
      add(b2);
      add(Box.createVerticalGlue());
      add(b3);
      add(b4);
      add(Box.createRigidArea(new Dimension (0, 20)));
      add(b5);
   }
}
```

LISTING 6.22 *continued*

DISPLAY

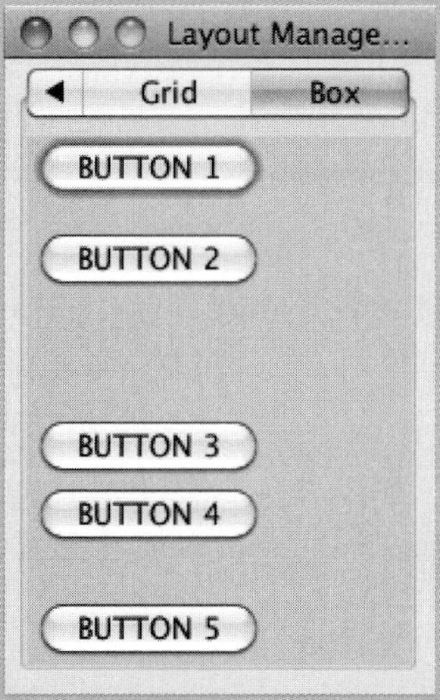

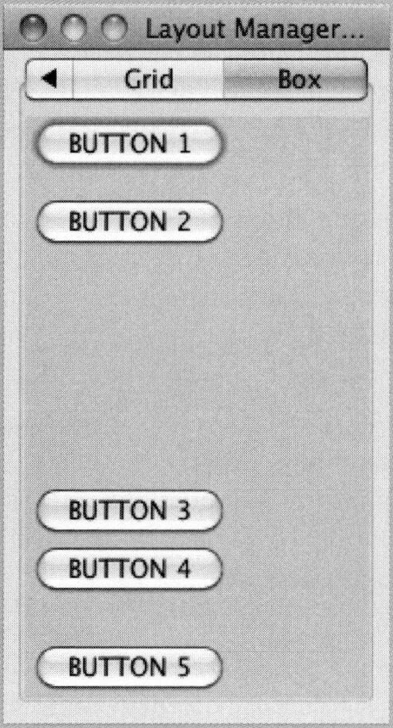

Layout Manage...

Grid Box

BUTTON 1

BUTTON 2

BUTTON 3

BUTTON 4

BUTTON 5

Layout Manager...

Grid Box

BUTTON 1

BUTTON 2

BUTTON 3

BUTTON 4

BUTTON 5

Go to the end of the text for full-color versions of these figures.

There are no gaps between the components in a box layout. Unlike previous layout managers we've explored, a box layout does not have a specific vertical or horizontal gap that can be specified for the entire container. Instead, we can add invisible components to the container that take up space between other components. The `Box` class, which is also part of the Java standard class library, contains static methods that can be used to create these invisible components.

The two types of invisible components used in the `BoxPanel` class are *rigid areas*, which have a fixed size, and *glue*, which specifies where excess space in a container should go. A rigid area is created using the `createRigidArea` method of the `Box` class, and it takes a `Dimension` object as a parameter to define the size of the invisible area. Glue is created using the `createHorizontalGlue` method or the `createVerticalGlue` method, as appropriate.

Note that in our example, the space between buttons separated by a rigid area remains constant even when the container is resized. Glue, on the other hand, expands or contracts as needed to fill the space.

A box layout—more than most of the other layout managers—respects the alignments and the minimum, maximum, and preferred sizes of the components it governs. Therefore, setting the characteristics of the components that go into the container is another way to tailor the visual effect.

Containment Hierarchies

The way components are grouped into containers, and the way those containers are nested within each other, establish the *containment hierarchy* for a GUI. The interplay between the containment hierarchy and the layout managers of the containers involved dictates the overall visual effect of the GUI.

For any Java program, there is generally one primary container, called a top-level container, such as a frame or applet. The top-level container of a program often contains one or more other containers, such as panels. These panels may contain other panels to organize the other components as desired.

KEY CONCEPT

A GUI's appearance is a function of the containment hierarchy and the layout managers of each container.

Keep in mind that each container can have its own tailored layout manager. The final appearance of a GUI is a function of the layout managers chosen for each of the containers and the design of the containment hierarchy. Many combinations are possible, and there is rarely a single best option. We should be guided by the desired system goals and by general GUI design guidelines.

When changes are made that might affect the visual layout of the components in a program, the layout managers of each container are consulted in turn. The changes in one may affect another. These changes ripple through the containment hierarchy as needed.

6.4 Mouse and Key Events

In addition to events that are generated when the user interacts with a component, there are events that are fired when the user interacts with the computer's mouse and keyboard. We can design a program to capture and respond to these as well.

Mouse Events

Java divides the events generated by the user interacting with the mouse into two categories: *mouse events* and *mouse motion events*. The tables in Figure 6.7 define these events.

When you click the mouse button over a Java GUI component, three events are generated: one when the mouse button is pushed down (*mouse pressed*) and two when it is let up (*mouse released* and *mouse clicked*). A mouse click is defined as pressing and releasing the mouse button in the same location. If you press the mouse button down, move the mouse, and then release the mouse button, a mouse clicked event is not generated.

A component will generate a *mouse entered* event when the mouse pointer passes into its graphical space. Likewise, it generates a *mouse exited* event when the mouse pointer leaves.

Mouse motion events, as the name implies, occur while the mouse is in motion. The *mouse moved* event indicates simply that the mouse is in motion. The *mouse dragged* event is generated when the user has pressed the mouse button down and moved the mouse without

KEY CONCEPT

Moving the mouse and clicking the mouse button generate events to which a program can respond.

Mouse Event	Description
mouse pressed	The mouse button is pressed down.
mouse released	The mouse button is released.
mouse clicked	The mouse button is pressed down and released without moving the mouse in between.
mouse entered	The mouse pointer is moved onto (over) a component.
mouse exited	The mouse pointer is moved off of a component.

Mouse Motion Event	Description
mouse moved	The mouse is moved.
mouse dragged	The mouse is moved while the mouse button is pressed down.

FIGURE 6.7 Mouse events and mouse motion events

releasing the button. Mouse motion events are generated many times, very quickly, while the mouse is in motion.

In a specific situation, we may care about only one or two mouse events. What we listen for depends on what we are trying to accomplish.

The `Coordinates` program shown in Listing 6.23 responds to one mouse event. Specifically, it draws a green dot at the location of the mouse pointer whenever the mouse button is pressed, and displays those coordinates. Keep in mind that (as discussed in Appendix F) the coordinate system in Java has the origin in the upper-left corner of a component (such as a panel), with x coordinates increasing to the right and y coordinates increasing downward.

The `CoordinatesPanel` class, shown in Listing 6.24, keeps track of the (x, y) coordinates at which the user has pressed the mouse button most recently. The `getX` and `getY` methods of the `MouseEvent` object return the x and y coordinates of the location where the mouse event occurred.

LISTING 6.23

```
//********************************************************************
//  Coordinates.java       Java Foundations
//
//  Demonstrates mouse events.
//********************************************************************

import javax.swing.JFrame;

public class Coordinates
{
   //-----------------------------------------------------------------
   //  Creates and displays the application frame.
   //-----------------------------------------------------------------
   public static void main(String[] args)
   {
      JFrame frame = new JFrame("Coordinates");
      frame.setDefaultCloseOperation(JFrame.EXIT_ON_CLOSE);

      frame.getContentPane().add(new CoordinatesPanel());

      frame.pack();
      frame.setVisible(true);
   }
}
```

LISTING 6.23 *continued*

DISPLAY

Go to the end of the text for a full-color version of this figure.

LISTING 6.24

```
//********************************************************************
//  CoordinatesPanel.java       Java Foundations
//
//  Represents the primary panel for the Coordinates program.
//********************************************************************

import javax.swing.JPanel;
import java.awt.*;
import java.awt.event.*;

public class CoordinatesPanel extends JPanel
{
   private final int SIZE = 6; // diameter of dot

   private int x = 50, y = 50; // coordinates of mouse press
```

LISTING 6.24 *continued*

```
   //-----------------------------------------------------------------
   //  Constructor: Sets up this panel to listen for mouse events.
   //-----------------------------------------------------------------
   public CoordinatesPanel()
   {
      addMouseListener(new CoordinatesListener());

      setBackground(Color.black);
      setPreferredSize(new Dimension(300, 200));
   }

   //-----------------------------------------------------------------
   //  Draws all of the dots stored in the list.
   //-----------------------------------------------------------------
   public void paintComponent(Graphics page)
   {
      super.paintComponent(page);

      page.setColor(Color.green);

      page.fillOval(x, y, SIZE, SIZE);

      page.drawString("Coordinates: (" + x + ", " + y + ")", 5, 15);
   }

   //*****************************************************************
   //  Represents the listener for mouse events.
   //*****************************************************************
   private class CoordinatesListener implements MouseListener
   {
      //--------------------------------------------------------------
      //  Adds the current point to the list of points and redraws
      //  the panel whenever the mouse button is pressed.
      //--------------------------------------------------------------
      public void mousePressed (MouseEvent event)
      {
         x = event.getX();
         y = event.getY();
         repaint();
      }

      //--------------------------------------------------------------
      //  Provide empty definitions for unused event methods.
      //--------------------------------------------------------------
```

LISTING 6.24 *continued*

```
      public void mouseClicked(MouseEvent event) {}
      public void mouseReleased(MouseEvent event) {}
      public void mouseEntered(MouseEvent event) {}
      public void mouseExited(MouseEvent event) {}
   }
}
```

The listener for the mouse pressed event implements the `MouseListener` interface. The panel invokes the `mousePressed` method each time the user presses down on the mouse button while it is over the panel.

Note that, unlike the listener interfaces that we've used in previous examples that contain one method each, the `MouseListener` interface contains five methods. For this program, the only event in which we are interested is the mouse pressed event. Therefore, the only method in which we have any interest is the `mousePressed` method. However, implementing an interface means we must provide definitions for all methods in the interface. Therefore, we provide empty methods corresponding to the other events. When those events are generated, the empty methods are called, but no code is executed. At the end of this section, we discuss a technique for creating listeners that enables us to avoid creating such empty methods.

Let's look at an example that responds to two mouse-oriented events. The `RubberLines` program shown in Listing 6.25 draws a line between two points.

> **KEY CONCEPT**
> A listener may have to provide empty method definitions for unheeded events to satisfy the interface.

The first point is determined by the location at which the mouse is first pressed down. The second point changes as the mouse is dragged while the mouse button is held down. When the button is released, the line remains fixed between the first and second points. When the mouse button is pressed again, a new line is started.

LISTING 6.25

```
//********************************************************************
//  RubberLines.java       Java Foundations
//
//  Demonstrates mouse events and rubberbanding.
//********************************************************************
```

LISTING 6.25 *continued*

```
import javax.swing.JFrame;

public class RubberLines
{
   //-----------------------------------------------------------------
   //  Creates and displays the application frame.
   //-----------------------------------------------------------------
   public static void main(String[] args)
   {
      JFrame frame = new JFrame("Rubber Lines");
      frame.setDefaultCloseOperation(JFrame.EXIT_ON_CLOSE);

      frame.getContentPane().add(new RubberLinesPanel());

      frame.pack();
      frame.setVisible(true);
   }
}
```

DISPLAY

Rubber Lines

Go to the end of the text for a full-color version of this figure.

The `RubberLinesPanel` class is shown in Listing 6.26. Because we need to listen for both a mouse pressed event and a mouse dragged event, we need a listener that responds to both mouse events and mouse motion events.

LISTING 6.26

```
//********************************************************************
//  RubberLinesPanel.java       Java Foundations
//
//  Represents the primary drawing panel for the RubberLines program.
//********************************************************************

import javax.swing.JPanel;
import java.awt.*;
import java.awt.event.*;

public class RubberLinesPanel extends JPanel
{
   private Point point1 = null, point2 = null;

   //-----------------------------------------------------------------
   //  Constructor: Sets up this panel to listen for mouse events.
   //-----------------------------------------------------------------
   public RubberLinesPanel()
   {
      LineListener listener = new LineListener();
      addMouseListener(listener);
      addMouseMotionListener(listener);

      setBackground(Color.black);
      setPreferredSize(new Dimension(400, 200));
   }

   //-----------------------------------------------------------------
   //  Draws the current line from the intial mouse-pressed point to
   //  the current position of the mouse.
   //-----------------------------------------------------------------
   public void paintComponent(Graphics page)
   {
      super.paintComponent(page);

      page.setColor(Color.yellow);
      if (point1 != null && point2 != null)
         page.drawLine(point1.x, point1.y, point2.x, point2.y);
   }

   //*****************************************************************
   //  Represents the listener for all mouse events.
   //*****************************************************************
```

LISTING 6.26 *continued*

```
   private class LineListener implements MouseListener,
                                         MouseMotionListener
   {
      //-----------------------------------------------------------------
      //  Captures the initial position at which the mouse button is
      //  pressed.
      //-----------------------------------------------------------------
      public void mousePressed(MouseEvent event)
      {
         point1 = event.getPoint();
      }

      //-----------------------------------------------------------------
      //  Gets the current position of the mouse as it is dragged and
      //  redraws the line to create the rubberband effect.
      //-----------------------------------------------------------------
      public void mouseDragged(MouseEvent event)
      {
         point2 = event.getPoint();
         repaint();
      }

      //-----------------------------------------------------------------
      // Provide empty definitions for unused event methods.
      //-----------------------------------------------------------------
      public void mouseClicked(MouseEvent event) {}
      public void mouseReleased(MouseEvent event) {}
      public void mouseEntered(MouseEvent event) {}
      public void mouseExited(MouseEvent event) {}
      public void mouseMoved(MouseEvent event) {}
   }
}
```

KEY CONCEPT

Rubberbanding is the graphical effect caused when a shape seems to expand as the mouse is dragged.

Note that the listener class in this example implements both the `MouseListener` interface and the `MouseMotionListener` interface. It must therefore implement all methods of both interfaces. The two methods of interest, `mousePressed` and `mouseDragged`, are implemented to accomplish our goals, and the other methods are given empty definitions to satisfy the interface contract.

When the `mousePressed` method is called, the variable `point1` is set. Then, as the mouse is dragged, the variable `point2` is continually reset and the panel repainted. Therefore, the line is constantly being redrawn as the mouse is dragged, giving the appearance that one line is being stretched between a fixed point and a moving point. This effect is called *rubberbanding* and is common in graphical programs.

The starting and ending points of the line are stored as `Point` objects. The `Point` class is defined in the `java.awt` package and encapsulates the *x* and *y* values of a two-dimensional coordinate.

Note that in the `RubberLinesPanel` constructor, the listener object is added to the panel twice: once as a mouse listener and once as a mouse motion listener. The method called to add the listener must correspond to the object passed as the parameter. In this case, we had one object that served as a listener for both categories of events. We could have had two listener classes if we had so desired: one listening for mouse events and one listening for mouse motion events. A component can have multiple listeners for various event categories.

Key Events

A *key event* is generated when a keyboard key is pressed. Key events allow a program to respond immediately to the user while he or she is typing or pressing other keyboard keys such as the arrow keys. If key events are being processed, the program can respond as soon as the key is pressed; there is no need to wait for the Enter key to be pressed or for some other component (such as a button) to be activated.

The `Direction` program shown in Listing 6.27 responds to key events. An image of an arrow is displayed, and the image moves across the screen as the arrow keys are pressed. Actually, four different images are used, one for the arrow pointing in each of the primary directions (up, down, right, and left).

The `DirectionPanel` class, shown in Listing 6.28 on page 307, represents the panel on which the arrow image is displayed. The constructor loads the four arrow images, one of which is always considered to be the current image (the one displayed). The current image is set based on the arrow key that was most recently pressed. For example, if the up arrow is pressed, the image with the arrow pointing up is displayed. If an arrow key is continually pressed, the appropriate image "moves" in the appropriate direction.

KEY CONCEPT
Key events allow a program to respond immediately to the user pressing keyboard keys.

The arrow images are managed as `ImageIcon` objects. In this example, the image is drawn using the `paintIcon` method each time the panel is repainted. The `paintIcon` method takes four parameters: a component to serve as an

LISTING 6.27

```
//********************************************************************
//  Direction.java       Java Foundations
//
//  Demonstrates key events.
//********************************************************************

import javax.swing.JFrame;

public class Direction
{
   //-----------------------------------------------------------------
   //  Creates and displays the application frame.
   //-----------------------------------------------------------------
   public static void main(String[] args)
   {
      JFrame frame = new JFrame("Direction");
      frame.setDefaultCloseOperation(JFrame.EXIT_ON_CLOSE);

      frame.getContentPane().add(new DirectionPanel());

      frame.pack();
      frame.setVisible(true);
   }
}
```

DISPLAY

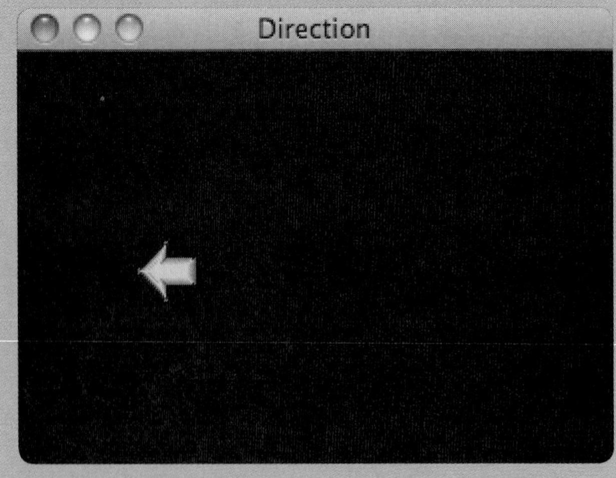

Go to the end of the text for a full-color version of this figure.

LISTING 6.28

```
//********************************************************************
//  DirectionPanel.java       Java Foundations
//
//  Represents the primary display panel for the Direction program.
//********************************************************************

import javax.swing.*;
import java.awt.*;
import java.awt.event.*;

public class DirectionPanel extends JPanel
{
   private final int WIDTH = 300, HEIGHT = 200;
   private final int JUMP = 10; // increment for image movement

   private final int IMAGE_SIZE = 31;

   private ImageIcon up, down, right, left, currentImage;
   private int x, y;

   //-----------------------------------------------------------------
   //  Constructor: Sets up this panel and loads the images.
   //-----------------------------------------------------------------
   public DirectionPanel()
   {
      addKeyListener (new DirectionListener());

      x = WIDTH / 2;
      y = HEIGHT / 2;

      up = new ImageIcon("arrowUp.gif");
      down = new ImageIcon("arrowDown.gif");
      left = new ImageIcon("arrowLeft.gif");
      right = new ImageIcon("arrowRight.gif");

      currentImage = right;

      setBackground(Color.black);
      setPreferredSize(new Dimension(WIDTH, HEIGHT));
      setFocusable(true);
   }
```

LISTING 6.28 *continued*

```
   //-----------------------------------------------------------------
   //  Draws the image in the current location.
   //-----------------------------------------------------------------
   public void paintComponent(Graphics page)
   {
      super.paintComponent(page);
      currentImage.paintIcon(this, page, x, y);
   }

   //*****************************************************************
   //  Represents the listener for keyboard activity.
   //*****************************************************************
   private class DirectionListener implements KeyListener
   {
      //--------------------------------------------------------------
      //  Responds to the user pressing arrow keys by adjusting the
      //  image and image location accordingly.
      //--------------------------------------------------------------
      public void keyPressed(KeyEvent event)
      {
         switch (event.getKeyCode())
         {
            case KeyEvent.VK_UP:
               currentImage = up;
               y -= JUMP;
               break;
            case KeyEvent.VK_DOWN:
               currentImage = down;
               y += JUMP;
               break;
            case KeyEvent.VK_LEFT:
               currentImage = left;
               x -= JUMP;
               break;
            case KeyEvent.VK_RIGHT:
               currentImage = right;
               x += JUMP;
               break;
         }

         repaint();
      }

      //--------------------------------------------------------------
      // Provide empty definitions for unused event methods.
      //--------------------------------------------------------------
```

LISTING 6.28 *continued*

```
      public void keyTyped(KeyEvent event) {}
      public void keyReleased(KeyEvent event) {}
   }
}
```

image observer, the graphics context on which the image will be drawn, and the (*x*, *y*) coordinates where the image is drawn. An *image observer* is a component that serves to manage image loading; in this case we use the panel as the image observer.

The private inner class called `DirectionListener` is set up to respond to key events. It implements the `KeyListener` interface, which defines three methods that we can use to respond to keyboard activity. Figure 6.8 lists these methods.

Specifically, the `Direction` program responds to key pressed events. Because the listener class must implement all methods defined in the interface, we provide empty methods for the other events.

The `KeyEvent` object passed to the `keyPressed` method of the listener can be used to determine which key was pressed. In the example, we call the `getKeyCode` method of the `event` object to get a numeric code that represents the key that was pressed. We use a `switch` statement to determine which key was pressed and to respond accordingly. The `KeyEvent` class contains constants that correspond to the numeric code that is returned from the `getKeyCode` method. If any key other than an arrow key is pressed, it is ignored.

`void keyPressed (KeyEvent event)`
    Called when a key is pressed.

`void keyReleased (KeyEvent event)`
    Called when a key is released.

`void keyTyped (KeyEvent event)`
    Called when a pressed key or key combination produces a key character.

FIGURE 6.8 The methods of the `KeyListener` interface

Key events fire whenever a key is pressed, but most systems enable the concept of *key repetition*. That is, when a key is pressed and held down, it's as if that key is being pressed repeatedly and quickly. Key events are generated in the same way. In the `Direction` program, the user can hold down an arrow key and watch the image move across the screen quickly.

The component that generates key events is the one that currently has the keyboard focus. Generally, the keyboard focus is held by the primary "active" component. A component usually gets the keyboard focus when the user clicks on it with the mouse. The call to the `setFocusable` method in the panel constructor sets the keyboard focus to the panel.

The `Direction` program sets no boundaries for the arrow image, so it can be moved out of the visible window and then moved back in if desired. You could add code to the listener to stop the image when it reaches one of the window boundaries. This modification is left as a programming project.

Extending Adapter Classes

In previous event-based examples, we've created the listener classes by implementing a particular listener interface. For instance, to create a class that listens for mouse events, we created a listener class that implemented the `MouseListener` interface. As we saw in the previous examples in this section, a listener interface often contains event methods that are not important to a particular program, in which case we provided empty definitions to satisfy the interface requirement.

An alternative technique for creating a listener class is to use inheritance and extend an *event adapter class*. Each listener interface that contains more than one method has a corresponding adapter class that already contains empty definitions for all of the methods in the interface. To create a listener, we can derive a new listener class from the appropriate adapter class and override any event methods in which we are interested. Using this technique, we no longer need to provide empty definitions for unused methods.

KEY CONCEPT

A listener class can be created by deriving it from an event adapter class.

The `MouseAdapter` class, for instance, implements the `MouseListener` interface and provides empty method definitions for the five mouse event methods (`mousePressed`, `mouseClicked`, and so on). Therefore, you can create a mouse listener class by extending the `MouseAdaptor` class instead of by implementing the `MouseListener` interface directly. The new listener class inherits the empty definitions and therefore doesn't need to define them.

Because of inheritance, we now have a choice when it comes to creating event listeners. We can implement an event listener interface, or we can extend an event adapter class. This is a design decision that should be considered carefully. Which technique is best depends on the situation. Inheritance is discussed further in Chapter 8.

6.5 Dialog Boxes

A component called a *dialog box* can be helpful in GUI processing. A dialog box is a graphical window that pops up on top of any currently active window so that the user can interact with it. A dialog box can serve a variety of purposes, such as conveying some information, confirming an action, or allowing the user to enter some information. Usually a dialog box has a solitary purpose, and the user's interaction with it is brief.

The Swing package of the Java class library contains a class called `JOptionPane` that simplifies the creation and use of basic dialog boxes. Figure 6.9 lists some of the methods of `JOptionPane`.

The basic formats for a `JOptionPane` dialog box fall into three categories. A *message dialog box* simply displays an output string. An *input dialog box* presents a prompt and a single input text field into which the user can enter one string of data. A *confirm dialog box* presents the user with a simple yes-or-no question.

Let's look at a program that uses each of these types of dialog boxes. Listing 6.29 shows a program that first presents the user with an input dialog box that requests the user to enter an integer. After the user presses the OK button on the input dialog box, a second dialog box (this time a message dialog box) appears, informing the user whether the number entered was even or odd. After the user dismisses that box, a third dialog box appears, to determine whether the user would like to test another number. If the user presses the button labeled Yes, the series of dialog boxes repeats. Otherwise, the program terminates.

The first parameter to the `showMessageDialog` and the `showConfirmDialog` methods specifies the governing parent component for the dialog box. Using a null reference as this parameter causes the dialog box to appear centered on the screen.

`static String showInputDialog (Object msg)`
Displays a dialog box containing the specified message and an input text field. The contents of the text field are returned.

`static int showConfirmDialog (Component parent, Object msg)`
Displays a dialog box containing the specified message and Yes/No button options. If the parent component is null, the box is centered on the screen.

`static void showMessageDialog (Component parent, Object msg)`
Displays a dialog box containing the specified message. If the parent component is null, the box is centered on the screen.

FIGURE 6.9 Some methods of the `JOptionPane` class

Many of the `JOptionPane` methods allow the programmer to tailor the contents of the dialog box. Furthermore, the `showOptionDialog` method can be used to create dialog boxes that combine characteristics of the three basic formats for more elaborate interactions.

Dialog boxes should be used only when the immediate attention of the user is required. A program that constantly has new windows popping up for different interactions is annoying to the user.

LISTING 6.29

```
//********************************************************************
//  EvenOdd.java       Java Foundations
//
//  Demonstrates the use of the JOptionPane class.
//********************************************************************

import javax.swing.JOptionPane;

public class EvenOdd
{
   //-----------------------------------------------------------------
   //  Determines if the value input by the user is even or odd.
   //  Uses multiple dialog boxes for user interaction.
   //-----------------------------------------------------------------
   public static void main(String[] args)
   {
      String numStr, result;
      int num, again;

      do
      {
         numStr = JOptionPane.showInputDialog("Enter an integer: ");

         num = Integer.parseInt(numStr);

         result = "That number is " + ((num%2 == 0) ? "even" : "odd");

         JOptionPane.showMessageDialog(null, result);

         again = JOptionPane.showConfirmDialog(null, "Do Another?");
      }
      while (again == JOptionPane.YES_OPTION);
   }
}
```

LISTING 6.29 *continued*

DISPLAY

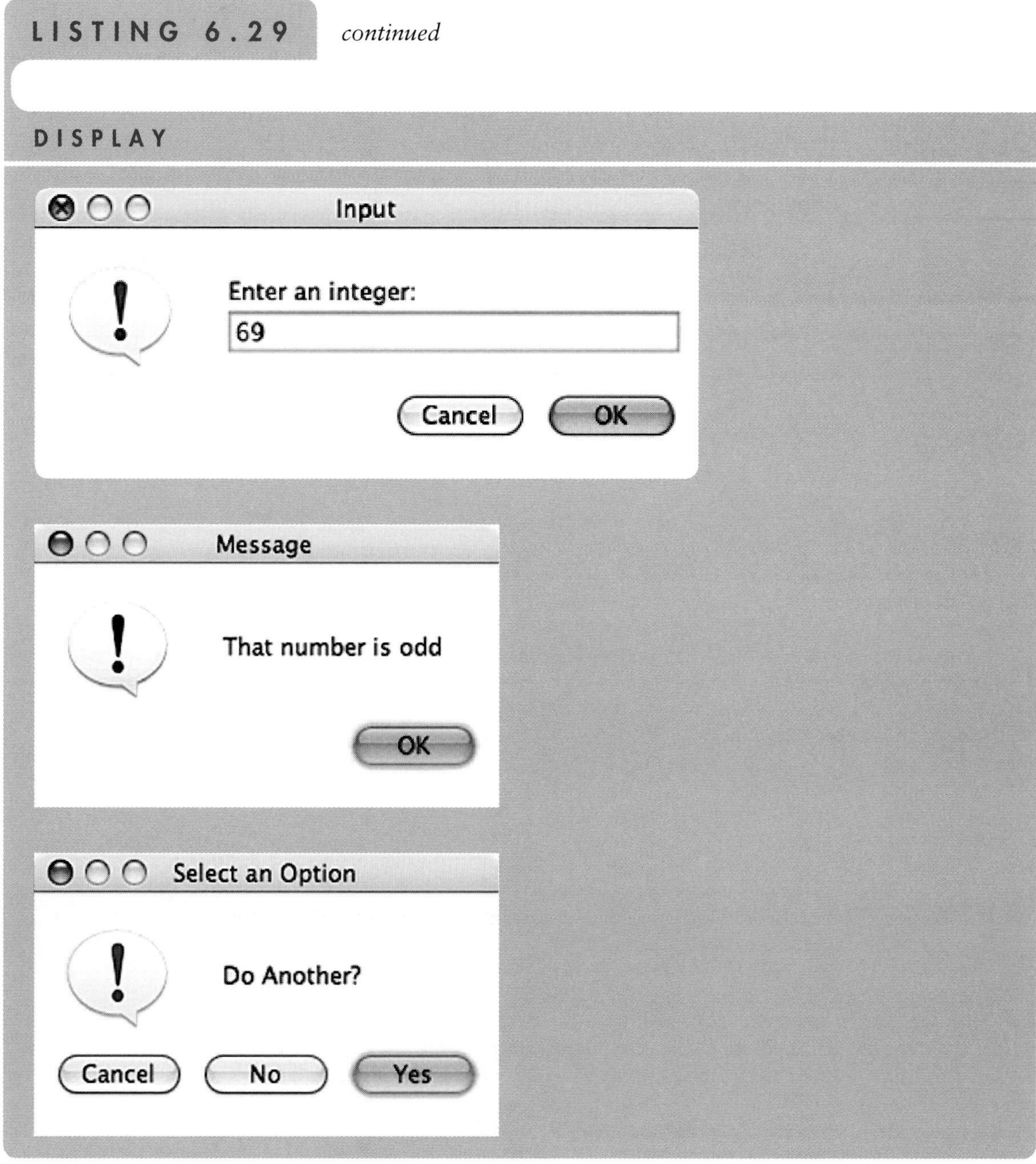

File Choosers

A *file chooser* is a specialized dialog box that allows the user to select a file from a disk or other storage medium. You have probably run many programs that allow you to open a file, such as when you are specifying which file to open in a word processing program. The need to specify a file occurs so often that the `JFileChooser` class was made part of the Java standard class library for just this purpose.

KEY CONCEPT

A file chooser allows the user to browse a disk and select a file to be processed.

The program shown in Listing 6.30 uses a `JFileChooser` dialog box to select a file. This program also demonstrates the use of another GUI component, a *text area*, which is similar to a text field but can display multiple lines of text at one time. In this example, after the user selects a file using the file chooser dialog box, the text contained in that file is displayed in a text area.

LISTING 6.30

```
//********************************************************************
//  DisplayFile.java   Java Foundations
//
//  Demonstrates the use of a file chooser and a text area.
//********************************************************************

import java.util.Scanner;
import java.io.*;
import javax.swing.*;

public class DisplayFile
{
   //-----------------------------------------------------------------
   // Opens a file chooser dialog, reads the selected file and
   // loads it into a text area.
   //-----------------------------------------------------------------
   public static void main(String[] args) throws IOException
   {
      JFrame frame = new JFrame("Display File");
      frame.setDefaultCloseOperation(JFrame.EXIT_ON_CLOSE);

      JTextArea ta = new JTextArea(20, 30);
      JFileChooser chooser = new JFileChooser();
      int status = chooser.showOpenDialog(null);
      if (status != JFileChooser.APPROVE_OPTION)
```

LISTING 6.30 *continued*

```
         ta.setText("No File Chosen");
      else
      {
         File file = chooser.getSelectedFile();
         Scanner scan = new Scanner(file);

         String info = "";
         while (scan.hasNext())
            info += scan.nextLine() + "\n";

         ta.setText(info);
      }

      frame.getContentPane().add(ta);
      frame.pack();
      frame.setVisible(true);
   }
}
```

DISPLAY

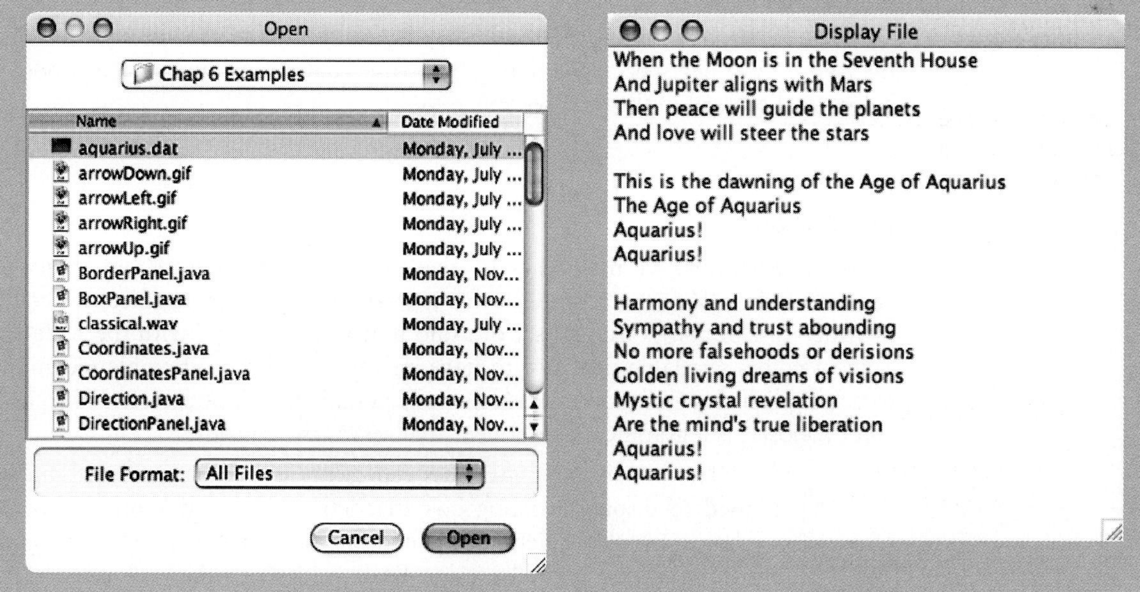

The file chooser dialog box is displayed when the `showOpenDialog` method is invoked. It automatically presents the list of files contained in a particular directory. The user can use the controls on the dialog box to navigate to other directories, change the way the files are viewed, and specify which types of files are displayed.

The `showOpenDialog` method returns an integer representing the status of the operation, which can be checked against constants defined in the `JFileChooser` class. In this program, if a file was not selected (perhaps by pressing the Cancel button), a default message is displayed in the text area. If the user chose a file, it is opened and its contents are read using the `Scanner` class. Note that this program assumes the selected file contains text. It does not catch any exceptions, so if the user selects an inappropriate file, the program will terminate when the exception is thrown.

A text area component is defined by the `JTextArea` class. In this program, we pass two parameters to its constructor, specifying the size of the text area in terms of the number of characters (rows and columns) it should display. The text to display is set using the `setText` method.

A text area component, like a text field, can be set so that it is either editable or noneditable. The user can change the contents of an editable text area by clicking on the text area and typing with the mouse. If the text area is noneditable, it is used to display text only. By default, a `JTextArea` component is editable.

A `JFileChooser` component makes it easy to allow users to specify a specific file to use. Another specialized dialog box—one that allows the user to choose a color—is discussed in the next section.

Color Choosers

In many situations, we may want to give the user of a program the ability to choose a color. We can accomplish this in various ways. For instance, we could provide a list of colors using a set of radio buttons. However, with the wide variety of colors available, it's nice to have an easier and more flexible technique to accomplish this common task. A specialized dialog box, often referred to as a *color chooser*, is a graphical component that serves this purpose.

KEY CONCEPT

A color chooser allows the user to select a color from a palette or by using RGB values.

The `JColorChooser` class represents a color chooser. It can be used to display a dialog box that lets the user click on a color of choice from a palette presented for that purpose. The user can also specify a color by using RGB values or other color representation techniques. Invoking the static `showDialog` method of the `JColorChooser` class causes the color chooser dialog box to appear.

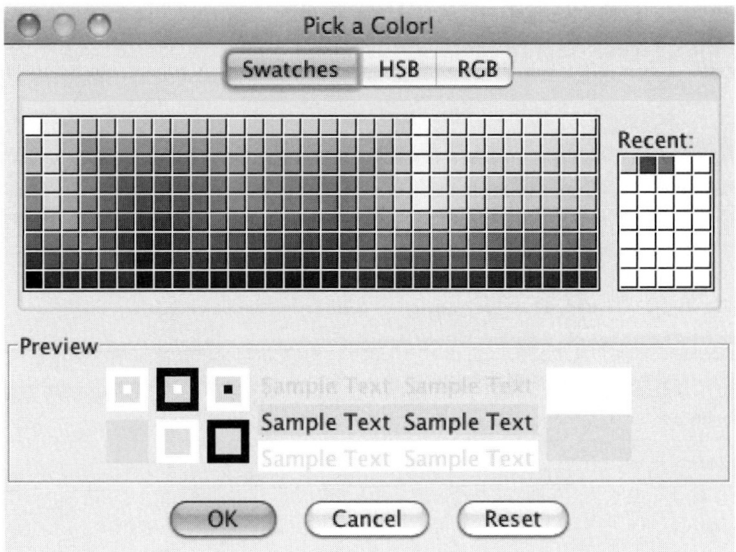

FIGURE 6.10 A color chooser dialog box

Go to the end of the text for a full-color version of this figure.

The parameters to that method specify the parent component for the dialog box, the title that appears in the dialog box frame, and the initial color showing in the color chooser.

Figure 6.10 shows a color chooser dialog box.

6.6 Some Important Details

There are a variety of small but important details that can add considerable value to the interface of a program. Some enhance the visual effect, and others provide shortcuts to make the user more productive. Let's examine some of them now.

Borders

Java provides the ability to put a border around any Swing component. A border is not a component itself; rather, it defines how the edge of any component should be drawn and has an important effect on the design of a GUI. A border provides

Border	Description
Empty Border	Puts buffering space around the edge of a component, but otherwise has no visual effect.
Line Border	A simple line surrounding the component.
Etched Border	Creates the effect of an etched groove around a component.
Bevel Border	Creates the effect of a component raised above the surface or sunken below it.
Titled Border	Includes a text title on or around the border.
Matte Border	Allows the size of each edge to be specified. Uses either a soild color or an image.
Compound Border	A combination of two borders.

FIGURE 6.11 Component borders

visual cues to how GUI components are organized, and it can be used to give titles to components. Figure 6.11 lists the predefined borders in the Java standard class library.

KEY CONCEPT
Borders can be applied to components to group objects and focus attention.

The `BorderFactory` class is useful for creating borders for components. It has many methods for creating specific types of borders. A border is applied to a component by using the component's `setBorder` method.

The program in Listing 6.31 below demonstrates several types of borders. It simply creates several panels, sets a different border for each, and then displays them in a larger panel using a grid layout.

LISTING 6.31

```
//********************************************************************
//  BorderDemo.java       Java Foundations
//
//  Demonstrates the use of various types of borders.
//********************************************************************

import java.awt.*;
import javax.swing.*;
import javax.swing.border.*;

public class BorderDemo
{
```

LISTING 6.31 *continued*

```
   //-----------------------------------------------------------------
   // Creates several bordered panels and displays them.
   //-----------------------------------------------------------------
   public static void main(String[] args)
   {
      JFrame frame = new JFrame("Border Demo");
      frame.setDefaultCloseOperation(JFrame.EXIT_ON_CLOSE);

      JPanel panel = new JPanel();
      panel.setLayout(new GridLayout (0, 2, 5, 10));
      panel.setBorder(BorderFactory.createEmptyBorder (8, 8, 8, 8));

      JPanel p1 = new JPanel();
      p1.setBorder(BorderFactory.createLineBorder (Color.red, 3));
      p1.add(new JLabel("Line Border"));
      panel.add(p1);

      JPanel p2 = new JPanel();
      p2.setBorder(BorderFactory.createEtchedBorder ());
      p2.add(new JLabel("Etched Border"));
      panel.add(p2);

      JPanel p3 = new JPanel();
      p3.setBorder(BorderFactory.createRaisedBevelBorder ());
      p3.add(new JLabel("Raised Bevel Border"));
      panel.add(p3);

      JPanel p4 = new JPanel();
      p4.setBorder(BorderFactory.createLoweredBevelBorder ());
      p4.add(new JLabel("Lowered Bevel Border"));
      panel.add(p4);

      JPanel p5 = new JPanel();
      p5.setBorder(BorderFactory.createTitledBorder ("Title"));
      p5.add(new JLabel("Titled Border"));
      panel.add(p5);

      JPanel p6 = new JPanel();
      TitledBorder tb = BorderFactory.createTitledBorder("Title");
      tb.setTitleJustification(TitledBorder.RIGHT);
      p6.setBorder(tb);
      p6.add(new JLabel("Titled Border (right)"));
      panel.add(p6);

      JPanel p7 = new JPanel();
      Border b1 = BorderFactory.createLineBorder(Color.blue, 2);
```

LISTING 6.31 *continued*

```
      Border b2 = BorderFactory.createEtchedBorder();
      p7.setBorder(BorderFactory.createCompoundBorder(b1, b2));
      p7.add(new JLabel("Compound Border"));
      panel.add(p7);

      JPanel p8 = new JPanel();
      Border mb = BorderFactory.createMatteBorder(1, 5, 1, 1,
                                                  Color.red);
      p8.setBorder(mb);
      p8.add(new JLabel("Matte Border"));
      panel.add(p8);

      frame.getContentPane().add(panel);
      frame.pack();
      frame.setVisible(true);
   }
}
```

DISPLAY

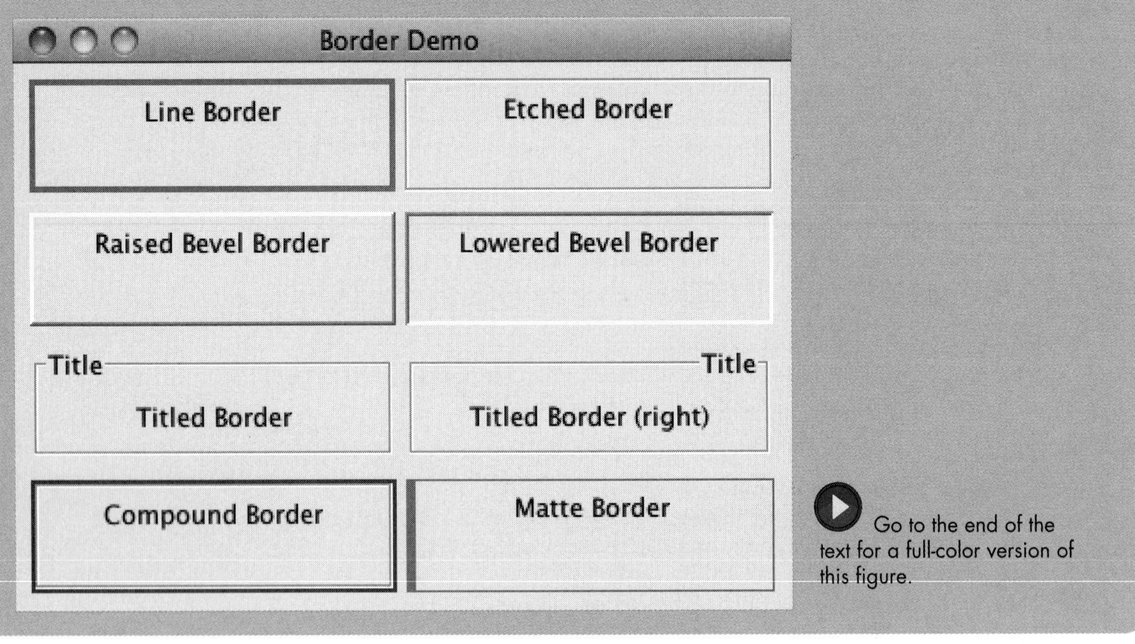

Go to the end of the text for a full-color version of this figure.

Let's look at each type of border created in this program. An *empty border* is applied to the larger panel that holds all the others, to create a buffer of space around the outer edge of the frame. The sizes of the top, left, bottom, and right edges of the empty border are specified in pixels. The *line border* is created using a particular color and specifies the line thickness in pixels (3 in this case). The line thickness defaults to 1 pixel if left unspecified. The *etched border* created in this program uses default colors for the highlight and shadow of the etching, but both can be explicitly set if desired.

A *bevel border* can be either raised or lowered. The default coloring is used in this program, although the coloring of each aspect of the bevel can be tailored as desired, including the outer highlight, inner highlight, outer shadow, and inner shadow. Each of these aspects can be a different color if desired.

A *titled border* places a title on or near the border. The default position for the title is on the border at the top-left edge. Using the `setTitleJustification` method of the `TitledBorder` class, this position can be set to many other places above, below, on, or to the left, right, or center of the border.

A *compound border* is a combination of two or more borders. The example in this program creates a compound border using a line border and an etched border. The `createCompoundBorder` method accepts two borders as parameters and makes the first parameter the outer border and the second parameter the inner border. Combinations of three or more borders are created by first creating a compound border using two borders and then making another compound border using it and yet another one.

A *matte border* specifies the sizes, in pixels, of the top, left, bottom, and right edges of the border. Those edges can be composed of a single color, as they are in this example, or an image icon can be used.

Borders should be used carefully. They can be helpful in drawing attention to appropriate parts of your GUI and can conceptually group related items together. If used inappropriately, however, they can detract from the elegance of the presentation. Borders should enhance the interface, not complicate or compete with it.

Tool Tips and Mnemonics

Any Swing component can be assigned a *tool tip*, which is a short line of text that will appear when the cursor is rested momentarily on top of the component. Tool tips are generally used to provide information about the component, such as the purpose of a button.

A tool tip can be assigned using the `setToolTipText` method of a component. Here is an example:

```
JButton button = new JButton ("Compute");
button.setToolTipText ("Calculates the area under the curve.");
```

When the button is added to a container and displayed, it appears normally. When the user rolls the mouse pointer over the button, hovering there momentarily, the tool tip text pops up. When the user moves the mouse pointer off the button, the tool tip text disappears.

A *mnemonic* is a character that allows the user to push a button or make a menu choice using the keyboard in addition to the mouse. For example, when a mnemonic has been defined for a button, the user can hold down the Alt key and press the mnemonic character to activate the button. Using a mnemonic to activate the button causes the system to behave just as it would have if the user had used the mouse to press the button.

A mnemonic character should be chosen from the label on a button or menu item. Once the mnemonic has been established using the `setMnemonic` method, the character in the label will be underlined to indicate that it can be used as a shortcut. If a letter is chosen that is not in the label, nothing will be underlined, and the user won't know how to use the shortcut. You can set a mnemonic as follows:

```
JButton button = new JButton("Calculate");
button.setMnemonic('C');
```

When the button is displayed, the letter C in Calculate is underlined on the button label. When the user presses Alt-C, the button is activated just as if the user had pressed it with the mouse.

Some components can be *disabled* if they should not be used. A disabled component will appear "grayed out," and nothing will happen if the user attempts to interact with it. To disable and enable components, we invoke the `setEnabled` method of the component, passing it a boolean value to indicate whether the component should be disabled (`false`) or enabled (`true`). For example:

```
JButton button = new JButton("Do It");
button.setEnabled(false);
```

Disabling components is a good idea when users should not be allowed to use the functionality of a component. The grayed appearance of the disabled component is an indication that using the component is inappropriate (and, in fact, impossible) at the current time. Disabled components not only convey to the user which actions are appropriate and which aren't; they also prevent erroneous situations from occurring.

KEY CONCEPT
Components should be disabled when their use is inappropriate.

Let's look at an example that uses tool tips, mnemonics, and disabled components. The program in Listing 6.32 presents the image of a light bulb and provides a button to turn the light bulb on and a button to turn the light bulb off.

There are actually two images of the light bulb: one showing it turned on and one showing it turned off. These images are brought in as `ImageIcon` objects.

LISTING 6.32

```
//********************************************************************
//  LightBulb.java       Java Foundations
//
//  Demonstrates mnemonics and tool tips.
//********************************************************************

import javax.swing.*;
import java.awt.*;

public class LightBulb
{
   //-----------------------------------------------------------------
   //  Sets up a frame that displays a light bulb image that can be
   //  turned on and off.
   //-----------------------------------------------------------------
   public static void main(String[] args)
   {
      JFrame frame = new JFrame("Light Bulb");
      frame.setDefaultCloseOperation(JFrame.EXIT_ON_CLOSE);

      LightBulbPanel bulb = new LightBulbPanel();
      LightBulbControls controls = new LightBulbControls(bulb);

      JPanel panel = new JPanel();
      panel.setBackground(Color.black);
      panel.setLayout(new BoxLayout(panel, BoxLayout.Y_AXIS));
      panel.add(Box.createRigidArea(new Dimension(0, 20)));
      panel.add(bulb);
      panel.add(Box.createRigidArea(new Dimension(0, 10)));
      panel.add(controls);
      panel.add(Box.createRigidArea(new Dimension(0, 10)));

      frame.getContentPane().add(panel);

      frame.pack();
      frame.setVisible(true);
   }
}
```

LISTING 6.32 *continued*

DISPLAY

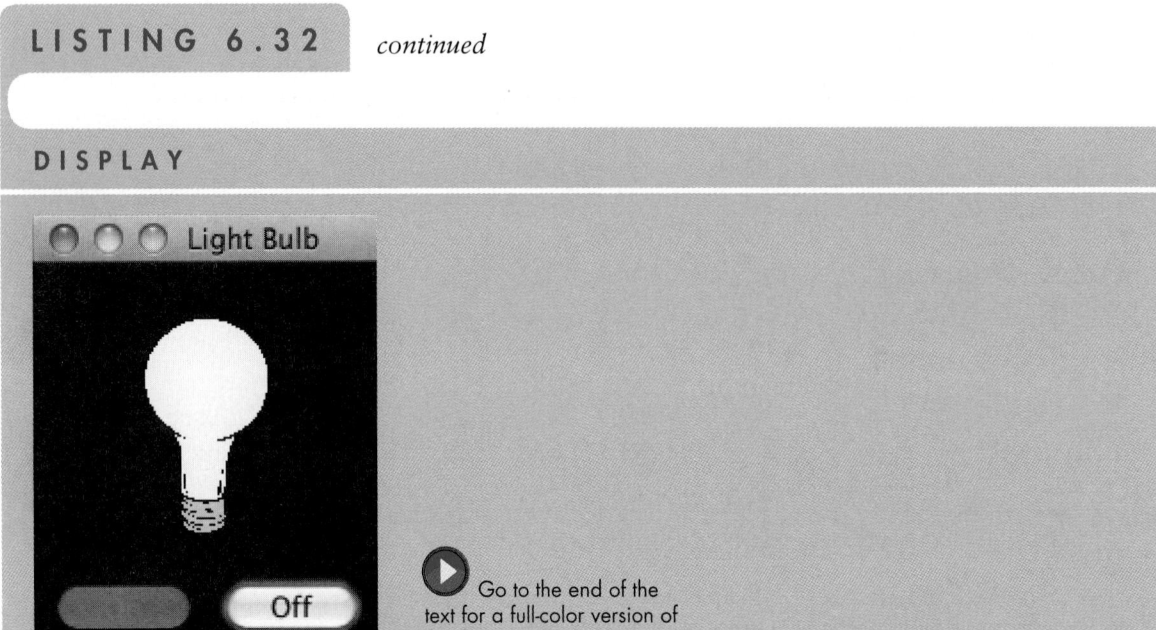
Light Bulb
Off
Go to the end of the text for a full-color version of this figure.

The `setIcon` method of the label that displays the image is used to set the appropriate image, depending on the current status. This processing is controlled in the `LightBulbPanel` class shown in Listing 6.33.

The `LightBulbControls` class shown in Listing 6.34 on page 326 is a panel that contains the On and Off buttons. Both of these buttons have tool tips assigned to them, and both use mnemonics. Also, when one of the buttons is enabled, the other is disabled, and vice versa. When the light bulb is on, there is no

LISTING 6.33

```
//********************************************************************
//  LightBulbPanel.java Java Foundations
//
//  Represents the image for the LightBulb program.
//********************************************************************

import javax.swing.*;
import java.awt.*;
```

LISTING 6.33 *continued*

```
public class LightBulbPanel extends JPanel
{
   private boolean on;
   private ImageIcon lightOn, lightOff;
   private JLabel imageLabel;

   //-----------------------------------------------------------------
   // Constructor: Sets up the images and the initial state.
   //-----------------------------------------------------------------
   public LightBulbPanel()
   {
      lightOn = new ImageIcon("lightBulbOn.gif");
      lightOff = new ImageIcon("lightBulbOff.gif");

      setBackground(Color.black);

      on = true;
      imageLabel = new JLabel(lightOff);
      add(imageLabel);
   }

   //-----------------------------------------------------------------
   // Paints the panel using the appropriate image.
   //-----------------------------------------------------------------
   public void paintComponent(Graphics page)
   {
      super.paintComponent(page);

      if (on)
         imageLabel.setIcon(lightOn);
      else
         imageLabel.setIcon(lightOff);
   }

   //-----------------------------------------------------------------
   //  Sets the status of the light bulb.
   //-----------------------------------------------------------------
   public void setOn(boolean lightBulbOn)
   {
      on = lightBulbOn;
   }
}
```

reason for the On button to be enabled. Likewise, when the light bulb is off, there is no reason for the Off button to be enabled.

Each button has its own listener class. The `actionPerformed` method of each sets the bulb's status, toggles the enabled state of both buttons, and causes the panel with the image to repaint itself.

Note that the mnemonic characters used for each button are underlined in the display. When you run the program, you'll see that the tool tips automatically include an indication of the mnemonic that can be used for the button.

LISTING 6.34

```
//********************************************************************
//  LightBulbControls.java       Java Foundations
//
//  Represents the control panel for the LightBulb program.
//********************************************************************

import javax.swing.*;
import java.awt.*;
import java.awt.event.*;

public class LightBulbControls extends JPanel
{
   private LightBulbPanel bulb;
   private JButton onButton, offButton;

   //-----------------------------------------------------------------
   //  Sets up the lightbulb control panel.
   //-----------------------------------------------------------------
   public LightBulbControls(LightBulbPanel bulbPanel)
   {
      bulb = bulbPanel;

      onButton = new JButton("On");
      onButton.setEnabled(false);
      onButton.setMnemonic('n');
      onButton.setToolTipText("Turn it on!");
      onButton.addActionListener(new OnListener());

      offButton = new JButton("Off");
      offButton.setEnabled(true);
      offButton.setMnemonic('f');
      offButton.setToolTipText("Turn it off!");
      offButton.addActionListener(new OffListener());
```

LISTING 6.34 *continued*

```
      setBackground(Color.black);
      add(onButton);
      add(offButton);
   }

   //*****************************************************************
   //  Represents the listener for the On button.
   //*****************************************************************
   private class OnListener implements ActionListener
      {
      //--------------------------------------------------------------
      //  Turns the bulb on and repaints the bulb panel.
      //--------------------------------------------------------------
      public void actionPerformed(ActionEvent event)
         {
            bulb.setOn(true);
            onButton.setEnabled(false);
            offButton.setEnabled(true);
            bulb.repaint();
         }
      }

   //*****************************************************************
   // Represents the listener for the Off button.
   //*****************************************************************
   private class OffListener implements ActionListener
   {
      //--------------------------------------------------------------
      // Turns the bulb off and repaints the bulb panel.
      // --------------------------------------------------------------
      public void actionPerformed(ActionEvent event)
      {
         bulb.setOn(false);
         onButton.setEnabled(true);
         voffButton.setEnabled(false);
         bulb.repaint();
      }
   }
}
```

6.7 GUI Design

As we focus on the details that allow us to create GUIs, we may sometimes lose sight of the big picture. We should always keep in mind that our goal is to solve a problem—to create software that is truly useful. Knowing the details of components, events, and other language elements gives us the tools to put GUIs together, but we must guide that knowledge with the following fundamental ideas of good GUI design:

- Know the user.
- Prevent user errors.
- Optimize user abilities.
- Be consistent.

KEY CONCEPT
The design of any GUI should adhere to basic guidelines regarding consistency and usability.

The software designer must understand the user's needs and potential activities in order to develop an interface that will serve that user well. Keep in mind that to the user, the interface is the software. It is the only way the user interacts with the system. Accordingly, the interface must satisfy the user's needs.

Whenever possible, we should design interfaces so that the user can make as few mistakes as possible. In many situations, we have the flexibility to choose one of several components to accomplish a specific task. We should always try to choose components that will prevent inappropriate actions and avoid invalid input. For example, if an input value must be one of a set of particular values, we should use components that allow the user to make only a valid choice. That is, constraining the user to a few valid choices with, for instance, a set of radio buttons is better than allowing the user to type arbitrary and possibly invalid data into a text field. In this chapter, we covered additional components appropriate for specific situations.

Not all users are alike. Some are more adept than others at using a particular GUI or GUI components in general. We shouldn't design with only the lowest common denominator in mind. For example, we should provide shortcuts whenever reasonable. That is, in addition to a normal series of actions that will allow a user to accomplish a task, we should also provide redundant ways to accomplish the same task. Using keyboard shortcuts (mnemonics) is a good example. Sometimes these additional mechanisms are less intuitive, but they may be valuable shortcuts for the experienced user.

Finally, consistency is important when dealing with large systems or multiple systems in a common environment. Users become familiar with a particular organization or color scheme; these should not be changed arbitrarily.

Summary of Key Concepts

- A GUI is made up of components, events that represent user actions, and listeners that respond to those events.
- A frame is displayed as a separate window, but a panel can be displayed only as part of another container.
- Listeners are often defined as inner classes because of the intimate relationship between the listener and the GUI components.
- Radio buttons operate as a group, providing a set of mutually exclusive options.
- A slider lets the user specify a numeric value within a bounded range.
- A combo box provides a drop-down menu of options.
- A timer generates action events at regular intervals and can be used to control an animation.
- Every container is managed by a layout manager, which determines how components are visually presented.
- When changes occur, the components in a container reorganize themselves according to the layout manager's policy.
- The layout manager for each container can be explicitly set.
- A GUI's appearance is a function of the containment hierarchy and the layout managers of each container.
- Moving the mouse and clicking the mouse button generate events to which a program can respond.
- A listener may have to provide empty method definitions for unheeded events in order to satisfy the interface.
- Rubberbanding is the graphical effect caused when a shape seems to expand as the mouse is dragged.
- Key events allow a program to respond immediately to the user pressing keyboard keys.
- A listener class can be created by deriving it from an event adapter class.
- A file chooser allows the user to browse a disk and select a file to be processed.
- A color chooser allows the user to select a color from a palette or by using RGB values.
- Borders can be applied to components to group objects and focus attention.

- Components should be disabled when their use is inappropriate.
- The design of any GUI should adhere to basic guidelines regarding consistency and usability.

Summary of Terms

action event An event that represents that a generic action has occurred, such as a button being pressed.

applet A Java program designed to be executed in a Web browser.

border layout A layout manager in which components are added to one of five areas (North, South, East, West, and Center).

box layout A layout manager that organizes components vertically or horizontally.

check box A button component that can be toggled on or off using the mouse.

color chooser A specialized dialog box that allows the user to select a color from a color pallet or RGB value.

combo box A component that allows the user to select one of several options from a drop-down menu.

command-line applcation A program that interacts with the user through simple text prompts and feedback.

component An object that defines a screen element used to display information or to interact with the user.

container A component that is used to hold and organize other components.

containment hierarchy The way in which containers and components are nested within each other.

content pane The pane of a container that holds all visible elements of a Java interface.

dialog box A graphical window that pops up on active windows so that the user can interact with it.

event An object that represents an occurrence to which the program may respond.

event adapter class A class that contains empty definitions for certain event categories, used as a convenience to create a listener without having to define unused methods.

file chooser A specialized dialog box that allows the user to select a file from a disk.

flow layout A layout manager that puts as many components on a row as possible before moving to the next row.

frame A container with a title bar, used to display GUI-based applications.

graphical user interface An interface to a program that uses graphical elements such as windows, menus, buttons, and text fields.

grid layout A layout manager in which components are organized into a grid of cells.

heavyweight container A container that is managed by the underlying operating system.

inner class A class that is defined within another class and has access to the members of the enclosing class.

key event An event generated when a keyboard key is pressed.

label A component that displays text, or an image, or both.

layout manager An object that determines how components will be displayed.

lightweight container A container that is managed by the Java program itself, unlike a heavyweight container, which is managed by the underlying operating system.

listener An object that "waits" for an event to occur and responds when it does.

mnemonic A character that allows the user to push a button or make a menu choice using the keyboard.

mouse event One of five mouse-based events (pressed, released, clicked, entered, and exited).

mouse motion event One of two events based on the motion of a mouse (moved and dragged).

panel A container that is generally used to organize other components. A panel cannot be displayed on its own.

push button A component that allows the user to initiate an action with the press of a mouse.

radio button A button component that is generally used with other radio buttons to provide a mutually exclusive set of options.

rubberbanding The visual effect caused when a shape seems to expand as the mouse is dragged.

slider A component that allows the user to specify a numeric value within a bounded range.

text field A component that allows the user to enter a line of typed input from the keyboard.

timer A component that generates an action event at regular intervals.

tool tip A line of text that appears when the mouse is hovered over a component.

Self-Review Questions

SR 6.1 What three elements are needed in any Java GUI?

SR 6.2 What is the difference between a frame and a panel?

SR 6.3 What is the relationship between an event and a listener?

SR 6.4 Can we add any kind of listener to any component? Explain.

SR 6.5 What type of event does a push button generate? A text field? A check box?

SR 6.6 Compare and contrast check boxes and radio buttons.

SR 6.7 When would you use a slider?

SR 6.8 What does a `Timer` object do?

SR 6.9 When is a layout manager consulted?

SR 6.10 How does the flow layout manager behave?

SR 6.11 Describe the areas of a border layout.

SR 6.12 What effect does a glue component in a box layout have?

SR 6.13 What is the containment hierarchy for a GUI?

SR 6.14 What is a mouse event?

SR 6.15 What is a key event?

SR 6.16 What is an event adapter class?

SR 6.17 What is a dialog box?

SR 6.18 What is a file chooser? A color chooser?

SR 6.19 What is the role of the `BorderFactory` class?

SR 6.20 What is a tool tip?

SR 6.21 When should a component be disabled?

Exercises

EX 6.1 Explain how two components can be set up to share the same listener. How can the listener tell which component generated the event?

EX 6.2 Explain how one component can use two separate listeners at the same time. Give an example.

EX 6.3 Explain what would happen if the radio buttons used in the `QuoteOptions` program were not organized into a `ButtonGroup` object. Modify the program to test your answer.

EX 6.4 Why, in the `SlideColor` program, is the value of a slider able to reach 255 but the largest labeled tick mark is 250?

EX 6.5 What are the two main factors that affect how smooth the animation is in the `Rebound` program? Explain how changing either would affect it.

EX 6.6 What visual effect would result from changing the horizontal and vertical gaps on the border layout used in the `LayoutDemo` program? Make the change to test your answer.

EX 6.7 What would happen if, in the `Coordinates` program, we did not provide empty definitions for one or more of the unused mouse events?

EX 6.8 The `Coordinates` program listens for a mouse pressed event to draw a dot. How would the program behave differently if it listened for a mouse released event instead? A mouse clicked event?

EX 6.9 What would happen if the call to `super.paintComponent` were removed from the `paintComponent` method of the `CoordinatesPanel` class? Remove it and run the program to test your answer.

EX 6.10 What would happen if the call to `super.paintComponent` were removed from the `paintComponent` method of the `RubberLinesPanel` class? Remove it and run the program to test your answer. In what ways is this answer different from the answer to Exercise 6.9.

EX 6.11 Write the lines of code that will define a compound border using three borders. Use a line border on the inner edge, an etched border on the outer edge, and a raised bevel border in between.

EX 6.12 Draw a UML class diagram that shows the relationships among the classes used in the `PushCounter` program.

EX 6.13 Draw a UML class diagram that shows the relationships among the classes used in the `Fahrenheit` program.

EX 6.14 Draw a UML class diagram that shows the relationships among the classes used in the `LayoutDemo` program.

EX 6.15 Create a UML class diagram for the `Direction` program.

Programming Projects

PP 6.1 Design and implement an application that displays a button and a label. Every time the button is pushed, the label should display a random number between 1 and 100, inclusive.

PP 6.2 Design and implement an application that presents two buttons and a label to the user. Label the buttons Increment and Decrement, respectively. Display a numeric value (initially 50) using the label. Each time the Increment button is pushed, increment the value displayed. Likewise, each time the Decrement button is pressed, decrement the value displayed. Create two separate listener classes for the two buttons.

PP 6.3 Modify your solution to Programming Project 6.2 so that it uses only one listener for both buttons.

PP 6.4 Modify the `Fahrenheit` program so that it displays a button that, when pressed, causes the conversion calculation to take place. That is, your modification will give the user the option of pressing Enter in the text field or pressing the button. Have the listener that is already defined for the text field also listen for the button push.

PP 6.5 Modify the `Direction` program so that the image is not allowed to move out of the visible area of the panel. Ignore any key event that would cause that to happen.

PP 6.6 Modify the `Direction` program so that, in addition to responding to the arrow keys, it also responds to four other keys that cause the image to move in diagonal directions. When the T key is pressed, move the image up and to the left. Likewise, use U to move up and right, G to move down and left, and J to move down and right. Do not move the image if it has reached a window boundary.

PP 6.7 Design and implement an application that draws a traffic light and uses a push button to change the state of the light. Derive the drawing surface from the `JPanel` class, and use another panel to organize the drawing surface and the button.

PP 6.8 Develop an application that implements a prototype user interface for composing an email message. The application should have text fields for the To, Cc, and Bcc address lists and subject line, and one for the message body. Include a button labeled Send. When the Send button is pushed, the program should print the contents of all fields to standard output using `println` statements.

PP 6.9 Design and implement an application that uses dialog boxes to obtain two integer values (one dialog box for each value), and display the sum and product of the values. Use another dialog box to see whether the user wants to process another pair of values.

PP 6.10 Design and implement a program whose background changes color depending on where the mouse pointer is located. If the mouse pointer is on the left half of the program window, display red; if it is on the right half, display green.

PP 6.11 Design and implement an application that serves as a mouse odometer, continually displaying how far, in pixels, the mouse has moved (while over the program window). Display the current odometer value using a label. *Hint:* Compare the current position of the mouse to the last position, and use the distance formula to determine how far the mouse has traveled.

PP 6.12 Design and implement an application that draws a circle using a rubberbanding technique. The circle size is determined by a mouse drag. Use the original mouse click location as a fixed center point. *Hint:* Compute the distance between the mouse pointer and the center point to determine the current radius of the circle.

PP 6.13 Modify the `StyleOptions` program to allow the user to specify the size of the font. Use a text field to obtain the size.

PP 6.14 Modify your solution to Programming Project 6.13 such that it uses a slider to obtain the font size.

PP 6.15 Develop a simple tool for calculating basic statistics for a segment of text. The application should have a single window with a scrolling text box (a `JTextArea`) and a stats box. The stats box should be a panel with a titled border, containing labeled fields that display the number of words in the text box and the average word length, as well as any other statistics that you would like to add. The stats box should also contain a button that, when pressed, re-computes the statistics for the current contents of the text field.

PP 6.16 Modify the `Rebound` program from this chapter such that when the mouse button is clicked on the program window, the animation stops, and when it is clicked again, the animation resumes.

PP 6.17 Design and implement a program that uses a `JColorChooser` object to obtain a color from the user and display that color as the background of the primary program window. Use a dialog box to determine whether the user wants to display another color, and if so, redisplay the color chooser.

PP 6.18 Modify the `JukeBox` program so that the Play and Stop button functionality can also be controlled using keyboard mnemonics.

PP 6.19 Modify the `Coordinates` program so that it creates its listener by extending an adapter class instead of by implementing an interface.

PP 6.20 Design and implement an application that displays an animation of a car (side view) moving across the screen from left to right. Create a `Car` class that represents the car.

PP 6.21 Design and implement an application that plays a game called Catch-the-Creature. Use an image to represent the creature. Have the creature appear at a random location for a random duration, then disappear and reappear somewhere else. The goal is to "catch" the creature by pressing the mouse button while the mouse pointer is on the creature image. Create a separate class to represent the creature, and include in it a method that determines whether the location of the mouse click corresponds to the current location of the creature. Display a count of the number of times the creature is caught.

PP 6.22 Design and implement an application that works as a stopwatch. Include a display that shows the time (in seconds) as it increments. Include buttons that allow the user to start and stop the time, and reset the display to zero. Arrange the components to present a nice interface.

Answers to Self-Review Questions

SRA 6.1 A GUI in a Java program is made up of on-screen components, events that those components generate, and listeners that respond to events when they occur.

SRA 6.2 Both a frame and a panel are containers that can hold GUI elements. However, a frame is displayed as a separate window with a title bar, whereas a panel cannot be displayed on its own. A panel is often displayed inside a frame.

SRA 6.3 Events usually represent user actions. A listener object is set up to listen for a certain event to be generated from a particular component. The relationship between a particular component that generates an event and the listener that responds to that event is set up explicitly.

SRA 6.4 No, we cannot add any listener to any component. Each component generates a certain set of events, and only listeners of those types can be added to the component.

SRA 6.5 Both push buttons and text fields generate action events. A check box generates an item state changed event.

SRA 6.6 Both check boxes and radio buttons show a toggled state: either on or off. However, radio buttons work as a group in which only one can be toggled on at any point in time. Check boxes, on the other hand, represent independent options. They can be used alone or in a set in which any combination of toggled states is valid.

SRA 6.7 A slider is useful when the user needs to specify a numeric value within specific bounds. Using a slider to get this input, as opposed to a text field or some other component, minimizes user error.

SRA 6.8 An object created from the `Timer` class produces an action event at regular intervals. It can be used to control the speed of an animation.

SRA 6.9 A layout manager is consulted whenever the visual appearance of its components might be affected, such as when the container is resized or when a new component is added to the container.

SRA 6.10 Flow layout attempts to put as many components on a row as possible. Multiple rows are created as needed.

SRA 6.11 Border layout is divided into five areas: North, South, East, West, and Center. The North and South areas are at the top and bottom of the container, respectively, and span the entire width of the container. Sandwiched between them, from left to right, are the West, Center, and East areas. Any unused area takes up no space, and the others fill in as needed.

SRA 6.12 A glue component in a box layout dictates where any extra space in the layout should go. It expands as necessary but takes up no space if there is no extra space to distribute.

SRA 6.13 The containment hierarchy of a GUI is created by nested containers. The way the containers are nested, and the layout managers that those containers employ, dictate the details of the visual presentation of the GUI.

SRA 6.14 A mouse event is an event generated when the user manipulates the mouse in various ways. There are several types of mouse events that may be of interest in a particular situation, including the mouse being moved, a mouse button being pressed, the mouse entering a particular component, and the mouse being dragged.

SRA 6.15 A key event is generated when a keyboard key is pressed, which allows a listening program to respond immediately to the user input. The object representing the event holds a code that specifies which key was pressed.

SRA 6.16 An event adapter class is a class that implements a listener interface, providing empty definitions for all of its methods. A listener class can be created by extending the appropriate adapter class and defining only the methods of interest.

SRA 6.17 A dialog box is a small window that appears for the purpose of conveying information, confirming an action, or accepting input. Generally, dialog boxes are used in specific situations for brief user interactions.

SRA 6.18 A file chooser and a color chooser are specialized dialog boxes that allow the user to select a file from disk and from a color, respectively.

SRA 6.19 The `BorderFactory` class contains several methods used to create borders that can be applied to components.

SRA 6.20 A tool tip is a small amount of text that appears when the mouse cursor is allowed to rest over a specific component. Tool tips are used to explain, briefly, the purpose of a component.

SRA 6.21 GUI components should be disabled when their use is inappropriate. This helps guide the user to proper actions and minimizes error handling and special cases.

7 Arrays

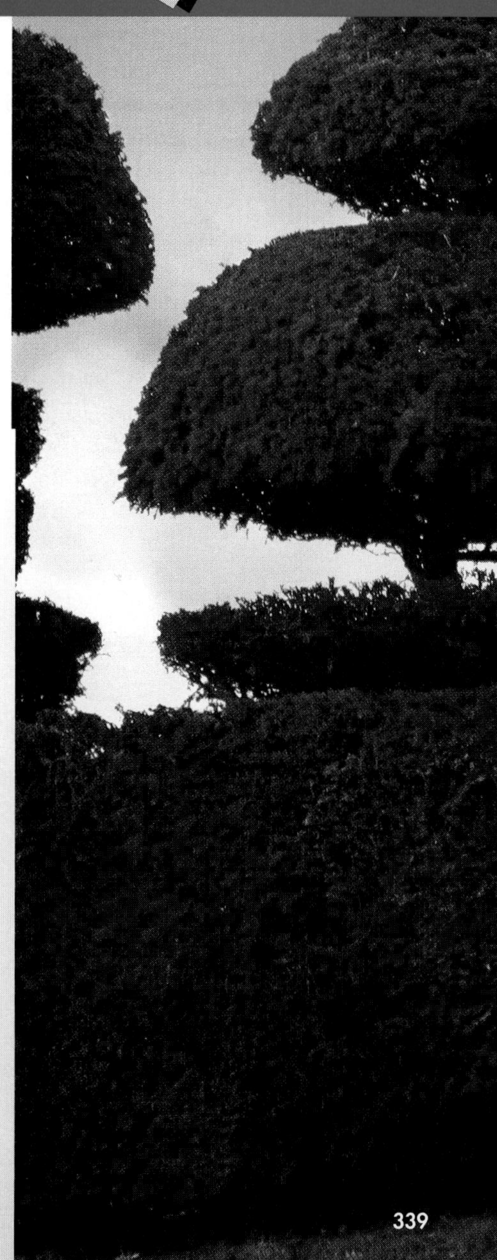

CHAPTER OBJECTIVES

- Define and use arrays for basic data organization.
- Discuss bounds checking and techniques for managing capacity.
- Discuss the issues related to arrays as objects and arrays of objects.
- Explore the use of command-line arguments.
- Describe the syntax and use of variable-length parameter lists.
- Discuss the creation and use of multidimensional arrays.

When designing programs, we often want to organize objects or primitive data in a form that is easy to access and modify. This chapter introduces arrays, which are programming constructs that group data into lists. Arrays are a fundamental component of most high-level languages and a useful tool in creating solutions to problems.

7.1 Array Elements

An *array* is a simple but powerful programming language construct used to group and organize data. When we are writing a program that manages a large amount of information, such as a list of 100 names, it is not practical to declare separate variables for each piece of data. Arrays solve this problem by letting us declare one variable that can hold multiple, individually accessible values.

An array is a list of values. Each value is stored at a specific, numbered position in the array. The number corresponding to each position is called an *index* or a *subscript*. Figure 7.1 shows an array of integers and the indexes that correspond to each position. The array is called `height`; it contains integers that represent several peoples' heights in inches.

KEY CONCEPT
An array of size *N* is indexed from 0 to *N*-1.

In Java, array indexes always begin at zero. Therefore, the value stored at index 5 is actually the sixth value in the array. The array shown in Figure 7.1 has 11 values, indexed from 0 to 10.

To access a value in an array, we use the name of the array followed by the index in square brackets. For example, the following expression refers to the ninth value in the array `height`:

```
height[8]
```

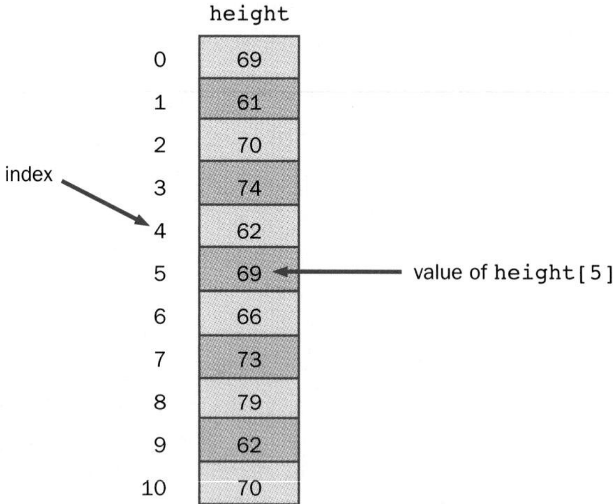

FIGURE 7.1 An array called `height` containing integer values

According to Figure 7.1, `height[8]` (pronounced height-sub-eight) contains the value 79. Don't confuse the value of the index, in this case 8, with the value stored in the array at that index, in this case 79.

The expression `height[8]` refers to a single integer stored at a particular memory location. It can be used wherever an integer variable can be used. Therefore, you can assign a value to it, use it in calculations, print its value, and so on. Furthermore, because array indexes are integers, you can use integer expressions to specify the index used to access an array. These concepts are demonstrated in the following lines of code.

```
height[2] = 72;
height[count] = feet * 12;
average = (height[0] + height[1] + height[2]) / 3;
System.out.println("The middle value is " + height[MAX/2]);
pick = height[rand.nextInt(11)];
```

VideoNote
Overview of arrays

7.2 Declaring and Using Arrays

In Java, arrays are objects. To create an array, the reference to the array must be declared. The array can then be instantiated using the `new` operator, which allocates memory space to store values. The following code represents the declaration for the array shown in Figure 7.1.

KEY CONCEPT
In Java, an array is an object that must be instantiated.

```
int[] height = new int[11];
```

The variable `height` is declared to be an array of integers whose type is written as `int[]`. All values stored in an array have the same type (or are at least compatible). For example, we can create an array that can hold integers or an array that can hold strings, but not an array that can hold both integers and strings. An array can be set up to hold any primitive type or any object (class) type. A value stored in an array is sometimes called an *array element*, and the type of values that an array holds is called the *element type* of the array.

Note that the type of the array variable (`int[]`) does not include the size of the array. The instantiation of `height`, using the `new` operator, reserves the memory space to store 11 integers indexed from 0 to 10. Once an array object is instantiated to be a certain size, the number of values it can hold cannot be changed. A reference variable such as `height`, declared to hold an array of integers, can refer to an array of any size. And like any other reference variable, the object (that is, the array) that `height` refers to can change over time.

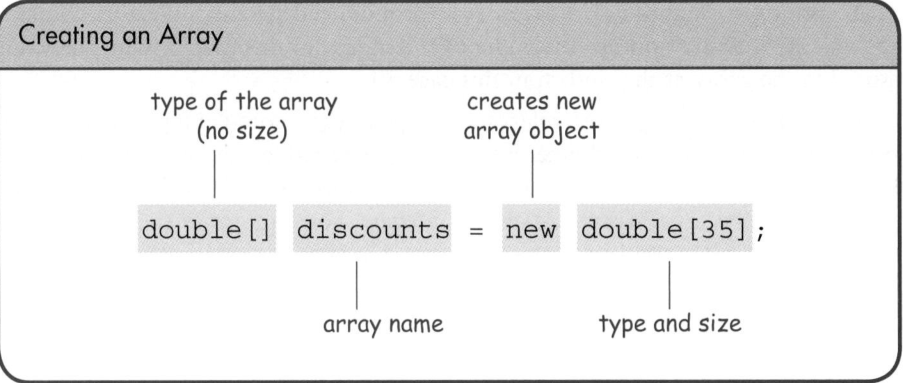

The example shown in Listing 7.1 creates an array called `list` that can hold 15 integers, which it loads with successive increments of 10. It then changes the value of the sixth element in the array (at index 5). Finally, it prints all values stored in the array.

Figure 7.2 on page 343 shows the array as it changes during the execution of the `BasicArray` program. It is often convenient to use `for` loops when handling arrays, because the number of positions in the array is constant. Note that a constant called `LIMIT` is used in several places in the `BasicArray` program. This constant is used to declare the size of the array and to control the `for` loop that initializes the array values.

LISTING 7.1

```
//********************************************************************
//  BasicArray.java       Java Foundations
//
//  Demonstrates basic array declaration and use.
//********************************************************************

public class BasicArray
{
   //-----------------------------------------------------------------
   //  Creates an array, fills it with various integer values,
   //  modifies one value, then prints them out.
   //-----------------------------------------------------------------
   public static void main(String[] args)
   {
      final int LIMIT = 15, MULTIPLE = 10;
```

LISTING 7.1 *continued*

```
      int[] list = new int[LIMIT];

      //  Initialize the array values
      for (int index = 0; index < LIMIT; index++)
         list[index] = index * MULTIPLE;

      list[5] = 999; // change one array value

      // Print the array values
      for (int value : list)
         System.out.print(value + " ");
   }
}
```

OUTPUT

```
0  10  20  30  40  999  60  70  80  90  100  110  120  130  140
```

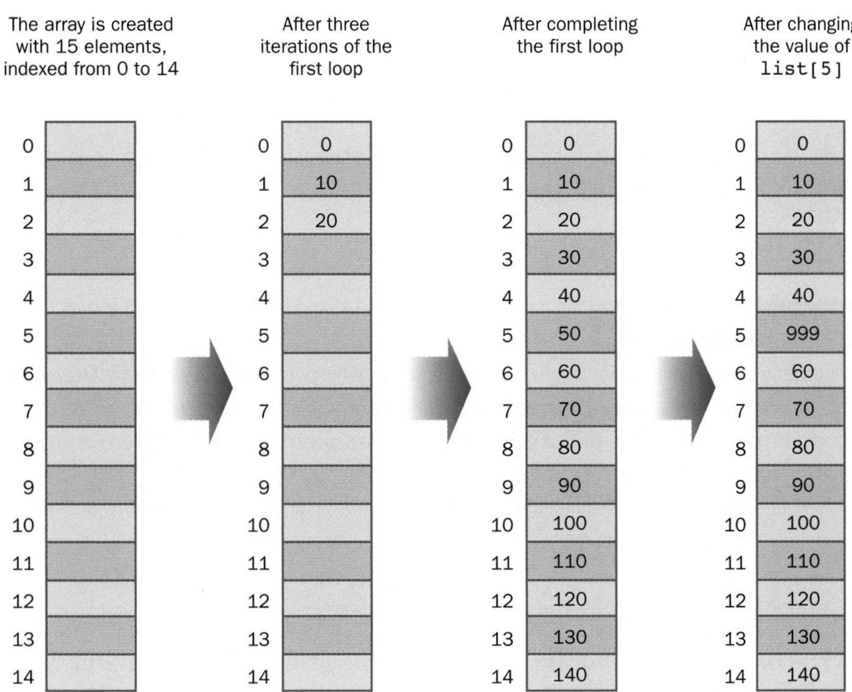

FIGURE 7.2 The array `list` as it changes in the `BasicArray` program

The iterator version of the `for` loop is used to print the values in the array. Recall from Chapter 4 that this version of the `for` loop extracts each value in the specified iterator. Every Java array is an iterator, so this type of loop can be used whenever we want to process every element stored in an array.

The square brackets used to indicate the index of an array are treated as an operator in Java. Therefore, just like the `+` operator or the `<=` operator, the *index operator* (`[]`) has a precedence relative to the other Java operators that determines when it is executed. It has the highest precedence of all Java operators.

Bounds Checking

The index operator performs automatic *bounds checking*, which ensures that the index is in range for the array being referenced. Whenever a reference to an array element is made, the index must be greater than or equal to zero and less than the size of the array. For example, suppose an array called `prices` is created with 25 elements. The valid indexes for the array are from 0 to 24. Whenever a reference is made to a particular element in the array (such as `prices[count]`), the value of the index is checked. If it is in the valid range of indexes for the array (0 to 24), the reference is carried out. If the index is not valid, an exception called `ArrayIndexOutOfBoundsException` is thrown.

KEY CONCEPT

Bounds checking ensures that an index used to refer to an array element is in range.

In most cases, we'll want to perform our own bounds checking. That is, we'll want to be careful to remain within the bounds of the array when making references. (The alternative is to be prepared to handle the exception when it is thrown; exception handling is discussed in Chapter 10).

COMMON ERROR

Because array indexes begin at zero and go up to one less than the size of the array, it is easy to create *off-by-one errors* in a program, which are problems created by processing all but one element or by attempting to index one element too many.

One way to check for the bounds of an array is to use the `length` constant, which is an attribute of the array object and holds the size of the array. It is a public constant and therefore can be referenced directly. For example, after the array `prices` is created with 25 elements, the constant `prices.length` contains the value 25. Its value is set once, when the array is first created, and cannot be changed. The `length` constant, which is an integral part of each array, can be used when the array size is needed without having to create a separate constant. Remember that the length of the array is the number of elements it can hold, and thus the maximum index of an array is `length-1`.

Let's look at another example. The program shown in Listing 7.2 reads 10 integers into an array called `numbers` and then prints them in reverse order.

LISTING 7.2

```
//********************************************************************
//  ReverseOrder.java       Java Foundations
//
//  Demonstrates array index processing.
//********************************************************************

import java.util.Scanner;

public class ReverseOrder
{
   //-----------------------------------------------------------------
   //  Reads a list of numbers from the user, storing them in an
   //  array, then prints them in the opposite order.
   //-----------------------------------------------------------------
   public static void main(String[] args)
   {
      Scanner scan = new Scanner(System.in);

      double[] numbers = new double[10];

      System.out.println("The size of the array: " + numbers.length);

      for (int index = 0; index < numbers.length; index++)
      {
         System.out.print("Enter number " + (index+1) + ": ");
         numbers[index] = scan.nextDouble();
      }

      System.out.println("The numbers in reverse order:");
```

LISTING 7.2 *continued*

```
      for (int index = numbers.length-1; index >= 0; index--)
         System.out.print(numbers[index] + " ");
   }
}
```

OUTPUT

```
The size of the array: 10
Enter number 1: 18.51
Enter number 2: 69.9
Enter number 3: 41.28
Enter number 4: 72.003
Enter number 5: 34.35
Enter number 6: 140.71
Enter number 7: 9.60
Enter number 8: 24.45
Enter number 9: 99.30
Enter number 10: 61.08
The numbers in reverse order:
61.08  99.3  24.45  9.6  140.71  34.35  72.003  41.28  69.9  18.51
```

Note that in the `ReverseOrder` program, the array `numbers` is declared to have 10 elements and therefore is indexed from 0 to 9. The index range is controlled in the `for` loops by using the `length` field of the array object. You should carefully set the initial value of loop control variables and the conditions that terminate loops to guarantee that all intended elements are processed and that only valid indexes are used to reference an array element.

The `LetterCount` example, shown in Listing 7.3, uses two arrays and a `String` object. The array called `upper` is used to store the number of times each uppercase alphabetic letter is found in the string. The array called `lower` serves the same purpose for lowercase letters.

Because there are 26 letters in the English alphabet, both the `upper` and `lower` arrays are declared with 26 elements. Each element contains an integer that is initially zero by default. These values serve as counters for each alphabetic character encountered in the input. The `for` loop scans through the string one character at a time. The appropriate counter in the appropriate array is incremented for each character found in the string.

LISTING 7.3

```
//********************************************************************
//  LetterCount.java       Java Foundations
//
//  Demonstrates the relationship between arrays and strings.
//********************************************************************

import java.util.Scanner;

public class LetterCount
{
   //-----------------------------------------------------------------
   //  Reads a sentence from the user and counts the number of
   //  uppercase and lowercase letters contained in it.
   //-----------------------------------------------------------------
   public static void main(String[] args)
   {
      final int NUMCHARS = 26;

      Scanner scan = new Scanner(System.in);

      int[] upper = new int[NUMCHARS];
      int[] lower = new int[NUMCHARS];

      char current;   // the current character being processed
      int other = 0;  // counter for non-alphabetics

      System.out.println("Enter a sentence:");
      String line = scan.nextLine();

      //  Count the number of each letter occurrence
      for (int ch = 0; ch < line.length(); ch++)
      {
         current = line.charAt(ch);
         if (current >= 'A' && current <= 'Z')
            upper[current-'A']++;
      else
         if (current >= 'a' && current <= 'z')
            lower[current-'a']++;
         else
            other++;
      }

      //  Print the results
      System.out.println();
      for (int letter=0; letter < upper.length; letter++)
```

LISTING 7.3 *continued*

```
         {
            System.out.print( (char) (letter + 'A') );
            System.out.print(": " + upper[letter]);
            System.out.print("\t\t" + (char) (letter + 'a') );
            System.out.println(": " + lower[letter]);
         }

         System.out.println();
         System.out.println("Non-alphabetic characters: " + other);
      }
   }
```

OUTPUT

```
Enter a sentence:
In Casablanca, Humphrey Bogart never says "Play it again, Sam."

A: 0           a: 10
B: 1           b: 1
C: 1           c: 1
D: 0           d: 0
E: 0           e: 3
F: 0           f: 0
G: 0           g: 2
H: 1           h: 1
I: 1           i: 2
J: 0           j: 0
K: 0           k: 0
L: 0           l: 2
M: 0           m: 2
N: 0           n: 4
O: 0           o: 1
P: 1           p: 1
Q: 0           q: 0
R: 0           r: 3
S: 1           s: 3
T: 0           t: 2
U: 0           u: 1
V: 0           v: 1
W: 0           w: 0
X: 0           x: 0
Y: 0           y: 3
Z: 0           z: 0

Non-alphabetic characters: 14
```

Both of the counter arrays are indexed from 0 to 25, so we have to map each character to a counter. A logical way to do this is to use `upper[0]` to count the number of `'A'` characters found, `upper[1]` to count the number of `'B'` characters found, and so on. Likewise, `lower[0]` is used to count `'a'` characters, `lower[1]` is used to count `'b'` characters, and so on. A separate variable called `other` is used to count any non-alphabetic characters that are encountered.

VideoNote
Discussion of the `LetterCount` example

Note that to determine whether a character is an uppercase letter, we used the boolean expression (`current >= 'A' && current <= 'Z'`). A similar expression is used for determining the lowercase letters. We could have used the static methods `isUpperCase` and `isLowerCase` in the `Character` class to make these determinations, but we didn't in this example to drive home the point that each character has a specific numeric value and order that we can use in our programming, based on the Unicode character set.

We use the `current` character to calculate which index in the array to reference. We have to be careful when calculating an index to ensure that it remains within the bounds of the array and matches to the correct element. Remember that in the Unicode character set, the uppercase and lowercase alphabetic letters are continuous and in order (see Appendix C). Therefore, taking the numeric value of an uppercase letter such as `'E'` (which is 69) and subtracting the numeric value of the character `'A'` (which is 65) yields 4, which is the correct index for the counter of the character `'E'`. Note that nowhere in the program do we actually need to know the specific numeric value for each letter.

Alternative Array Syntax

Syntactically, there are two ways to declare an array reference in Java. The first technique, which is used in the previous examples and throughout this text, is to associate the brackets with the type of values stored in the array. The second technique is to associate the brackets with the name of the array. Therefore, the following two declarations are equivalent:

```
int[] grades;
int grades[];
```

Although there is no difference between these declaration techniques as far as the compiler is concerned, the first is consistent with other types of declarations. The declared type is explicit if the array brackets are associated with the element type, especially if there are multiple variables declared on the same line. Therefore, we associate the brackets with the element type throughout this text.

Initializer Lists

You can use an *initializer list* to instantiate an array and provide the initial values for the elements of the array. This is essentially the same idea as initializing a variable of a primitive data type in its declaration, except that the initial value for an array contains multiple values.

The items in an initializer list are separated by commas and delimited by braces ({}). When an initializer list is used, the `new` operator is not used. The size of the array is determined by the number of items in the initializer list. For example, the following declaration instantiates the array `scores` as an array of eight integers, indexed from 0 to 7 with the specified initial values:

```
int[] scores = {87, 98, 69, 87, 65, 76, 99, 83};
```

An initializer list can be used only when an array is first declared.

KEY CONCEPT

An initializer list can be used, instead of the `new` operator, to instantiate an array object.

The type of each value in an initializer list must match the type of the array elements. Let's look at another example:

```
char[] vowels = {'A', 'E', 'I', 'O', 'U'};
```

In this case, the variable `vowels` is declared to be an array of five characters, and the initializer list contains character literals.

The program shown in Listing 7.4 demonstrates the use of an initializer list to instantiate an array.

LISTING 7.4

```
//********************************************************************
//  Primes.java       Java Foundations
//
//  Demonstrates the use of an initializer list for an array.
//********************************************************************

public class Primes
{
   //-----------------------------------------------------------------
   //  Stores some prime numbers in an array and prints them.
   //-----------------------------------------------------------------
   public static void main(String[] args)
   {
      int[] primeNums = {2, 3, 5, 7, 11, 13, 17, 19};

      System.out.println("Array length: " + primeNums.length);
```

LISTING 7.4 *continued*

```
      System.out.println("The first few prime numbers are:");

      for (int prime : primeNums)
         System.out.print(prime + " ");
   }
}
```

OUTPUT

```
Array length: 8
The first few prime numbers are:
2  3  5  7  11  13  17  19
```

Arrays as Parameters

An entire array can be passed as a parameter to a method. Because an array is an object, when an entire array is passed as a parameter, a copy of the reference to the original array is passed. We discussed this issue as it applies to all objects in Chapter 5.

A method that receives an array as a parameter can permanently change an element of the array, because it is referring to the original element value. However, the method cannot permanently change the reference to the array itself, because a copy of the original reference is sent to the method. These rules are consistent with the rules that govern any object type.

KEY CONCEPT
An entire array can be passed as a parameter, making the formal parameter an alias of the original.

An element of an array can be passed to a method as well. If the element type is a primitive type, a copy of the value is passed. If that element is a reference to an object, a copy of the object reference is passed. As always, the impact of changes made to a parameter inside the method depends on the type of the parameter. We discuss arrays of objects further in the next section.

7.3 Arrays of Objects

In the previous examples in this chapter, we used arrays to store primitive types such as integers and characters. Arrays can also store references to objects as elements. Fairly complex information management structures can be created using only arrays and other objects. For example, an array could contain objects, and each of those objects could consist of several variables and the methods that use them. Those variables could themselves be arrays, and so on. The design of a program should capitalize on the ability to combine these constructs to create the most appropriate representation for the information.

Keep in mind that an array is an object. Thus, if we have an array of `int` values called `weight`, we are actually dealing with an object reference variable that holds the address of the array, which can be depicted as follows:

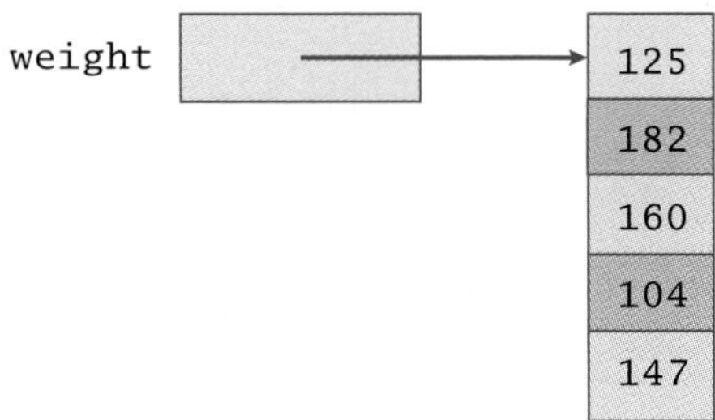

Furthermore, when we store objects in an array, each element is a separate object. That is, an array of objects is really an array of object references. Consider the declaration

```
String[] words = new String[5];
```

KEY CONCEPT
Instantiating an array of objects reserves room to store references only. The objects that are stored in each element must be instantiated separately.

The array `words` holds references to `String` objects. The `new` operator in the declaration instantiates the array object and reserves space for five `String` references. But this declaration does not create any `String` objects; it merely creates an array that holds references to `String` objects. Initially, the array looks like this:

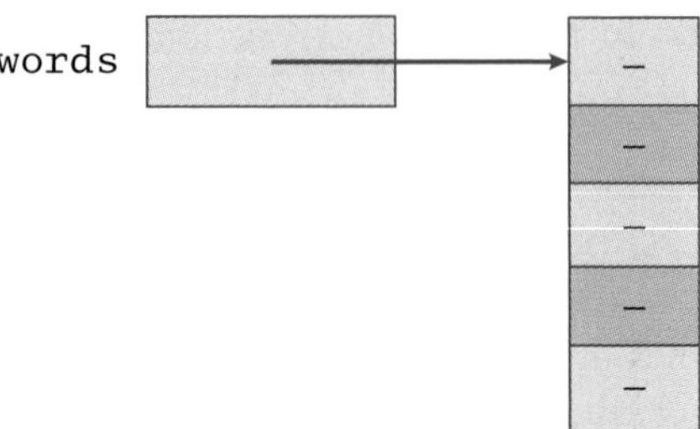

After a few `String` objects are created and put in the array, it might look like this:

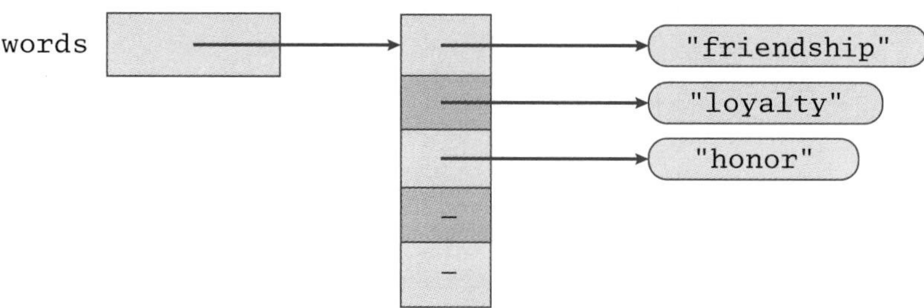

The `words` array is an object, and each character string it holds is its own object. Each object contained in an array has to be instantiated separately.

Keep in mind that `String` objects can be represented as string literals. Thus the following declaration creates an array called `verbs` and uses an initializer list to populate it with several `String` objects, each instantiated using a string literal.

```
String[] verbs = {"play", "work", "eat", "sleep"};
```

The program called `GradeRange`, shown in Listing 7.5, creates an array of `Grade` objects and then prints them. The `Grade` objects are created using several `new` operators in the initialization list of the array.

The `Grade` class is shown in Listing 7.6 on page 355. Each `Grade` object represents a letter grade for a school course and includes a numeric lower bound. The values for the grade name and lower bound can be set using the `Grade` constructor or using appropriate mutator methods. Accessor methods are also defined, as is a `toString` method to return a string representation of the grade. The `toString` method is automatically invoked when the grades are printed in the `main` method.

Let's look at another example. Listing 7.7 on page 356 shows the `Tunes` class, which contains a `main` method that creates, modifies, and examines a compact disc (CD) collection. Each CD added to the collection is specified by its title, artist, purchase price, and number of tracks.

Listing 7.8 on page 358 shows the `CDCollection` class. It contains an array of `CD` objects representing the collection. It maintains a count of the CDs in the collection and their combined value. It also keeps track of the current size of the collection array so that a larger array can be created if too many CDs are added to the collection. The `CD` class is shown in Listing 7.9.

LISTING 7.5

```
//********************************************************************
//  GradeRange.java       Java Foundations
//
//  Demonstrates the use of an array of objects.
//********************************************************************

public class GradeRange
{
   //-----------------------------------------------------------------
   //  Creates an array of Grade objects and prints them.
   //-----------------------------------------------------------------
   public static void main(String[] args)
   {
      Grade[] grades =
      {
         new Grade("A", 95), new Grade("A-", 90),
         new Grade("B+", 87), new Grade("B", 85), new Grade("B-", 80),
         new Grade("C+", 77), new Grade("C", 75), new Grade("C-", 70),
         new Grade("D+", 67), new Grade("D", 65), new Grade("D-", 60),
         new Grade("F", 0)
      };

      for (Grade letterGrade : grades)
          System.out.println(letterGrade);
   }
}
```

OUTPUT

```
A       95
A-      90
B+      87
B       85
B-      80
C+      77
C       75
C-      70
D+      67
D       65
D-      60
F        0
```

LISTING 7.6

```
//********************************************************************
//  Grade.java      Java Foundations
//
//  Represents a school grade.
//********************************************************************

public class Grade
{
   private String name;
   private int lowerBound;

   //-----------------------------------------------------------------
   //  Constructor: Sets up this Grade object with the specified
   //  grade name and numeric lower bound.
   //-----------------------------------------------------------------
   public Grade(String grade, int cutoff)
   {
      name = grade;
      lowerBound = cutoff;
   }

   //-----------------------------------------------------------------
   //  Returns a string representation of this grade.
   //-----------------------------------------------------------------
   public String toString()
   {
      return name + "\t" + lowerBound;
   }

   //-----------------------------------------------------------------
   //  Name mutator.
   //-----------------------------------------------------------------
   public void setName(String grade)
   {
      name = grade;
   }

   //-----------------------------------------------------------------
   //  Lower bound mutator.
   //-----------------------------------------------------------------
   public void setLowerBound(int cutoff)
   {
      lowerBound = cutoff;
   }
```

LISTING 7.6 *continued*

```
   //-----------------------------------------------------------------
   //  Name accessor.
   //-----------------------------------------------------------------
   public String getName()
   {
      return name;
   }

   //-----------------------------------------------------------------
   //  Lower bound accessor.
   //-----------------------------------------------------------------
   public int getLowerBound()
   {
      return lowerBound;
   }
}
```

LISTING 7.7

```
//********************************************************************
//  Tunes.java       Java Foundations
//
//  Demonstrates the use of an array of objects.
//********************************************************************

public class Tunes
{
   //-----------------------------------------------------------------
   //  Creates a CDCollection object and adds some CDs to it. Prints
   //  reports on the status of the collection.
   //-----------------------------------------------------------------
   public static void main(String[] args)
   {
      CDCollection music = new CDCollection();

      music.addCD("Storm Front", "Billy Joel", 14.95, 10);
      music.addCD("Come On Over", "Shania Twain", 14.95, 16);
      music.addCD("Soundtrack", "Les Miserables", 17.95, 33);
      music.addCD("Graceland", "Paul Simon", 13.90, 11);
```

LISTING 7.7 *continued*

```
      System.out.println(music);

      music.addCD("Double Live", "Garth Brooks", 19.99, 26);
      music.addCD("Greatest Hits", "Jimmy Buffet", 15.95, 13);

      System.out.println(music);
   }
}
```

OUTPUT

```
~~~~~~~~~~~~~~~~~~~~~~~~~~~~~~~~~~~~~~~~~~~
My CD Collection

Number of CDs: 4
Total cost: $61.75
Average cost: $15.44

CD List:

$14.95   10             Storm Front          Billy Joel
$14.95   16             Come On Over         Shania Twain
$17.95   33             Soundtrack           Les Miserables
$13.90   11             Graceland            Paul Simon

~~~~~~~~~~~~~~~~~~~~~~~~~~~~~~~~~~~~~~~~~~~
My CD Collection

Number of CDs: 6
Total cost: $97.69
Average cost: $16.28

CD List:

$14.95   10             Storm Front           Billy Joel
$14.95   16             Come On Over          Shania Twain
$17.95   33             Soundtrack            Les Miserables
$13.90   11             Graceland             Paul Simon
$19.99   26             Double Live           Garth Brooks
$15.95   13             Greatest Hits         Jimmy Buffet
```

LISTING 7.8

```
//********************************************************************
//  CDCollection.java       Java Foundations
//
//  Represents a collection of compact discs.
//********************************************************************

import java.text.NumberFormat;

public class CDCollection
{
   private CD[] collection;
   private int count;
   private double totalCost;

   //-----------------------------------------------------------------
   //  Constructor: Creates an initially empty collection.
   //-----------------------------------------------------------------
   public CDCollection()
   {
      collection = new CD[100];
      count = 0;
      totalCost = 0.0;
   }

   //-----------------------------------------------------------------
   //  Adds a CD to the collection, increasing the size of the
   //  collection if necessary.
   //-----------------------------------------------------------------
   public void addCD(String title, String artist, double cost,
                     int tracks)
   {
      if (count == collection.length)
         increaseSize();

      collection[count] = new CD(title, artist, cost, tracks);
      totalCost += cost;
      count++;
   }

   //-----------------------------------------------------------------
   //  Returns a report describing the CD collection.
   //-----------------------------------------------------------------
   public String toString()
   {
      NumberFormat fmt = NumberFormat.getCurrencyInstance();
      String report = "~~~~~~~~~~~~~~~~~~~~~~~~~~~~~~~~~~~~~~~~~~~~\n";
      report += "My CD Collection\n\n";
```

LISTING 7.8 *continued*

```
      report += "Number of CDs: " + count + "\n";
      report += "Total cost: " + fmt.format(totalCost) + "\n";
      report += "Average cost: " + fmt.format(totalCost/count);

      report += "\n\nCD List:\n\n";

      for (int cd = 0; cd < count; cd++)
         report += collection[cd].toString() + "\n";

      return report;
   }

   //-----------------------------------------------------------------
   //  Increases the capacity of the collection by creating a
   //  larger array and copying the existing collection into it.
   //-----------------------------------------------------------------
   private void increaseSize()
   {
      CD[] temp = new CD[collection.length * 2];

      for (int cd = 0; cd < collection.length; cd++)
         temp[cd] = collection[cd];

      collection = temp;
   }
}
```

LISTING 7.9

```
//********************************************************************
//  CD.java       Java Foundations
//
//  Represents a compact disc.
//********************************************************************

import java.text.NumberFormat;

public class CD
{
   private String title, artist;
   private double cost;
   private int tracks;
```

LISTING 7.9 *continued*

```
   //-----------------------------------------------------------------
   //  Creates a new CD with the specified information.
   //-----------------------------------------------------------------
   public CD(String name, String singer, double price, int numTracks)
   {
      title = name;
      artist = singer;
      cost = price;
      tracks = numTracks;
   }

   //-----------------------------------------------------------------
   //  Returns a string description of this CD.
   //-----------------------------------------------------------------
   public String toString()
   {
      NumberFormat fmt = NumberFormat.getCurrencyInstance();

      String description;

      description = fmt.format(cost) + "\t" + tracks + "\t";
      description += title + "\t" + artist;

      return description;
   }
}
```

The `collection` array is instantiated in the `CDCollection` constructor. Every time a `CD` is added to the collection (using the `addCD` method), a new `CD` object is created and a reference to it is stored in the `collection` array.

Each time a CD is added to the collection, we check to see whether we have reached the current capacity of the `collection` array. If we didn't perform this check, an exception would eventually be thrown when we tried to store a new `CD` object at an invalid index. If the current capacity has been reached, the private `increaseSize` method is invoked, which first creates an array that is twice as big as the current `collection` array. Each `CD` in the existing collection is then copied into the new array (that is, the references to the `CD` objects are copied). Finally, the `collection` reference is set to the larger array. Using this technique, we theoretically never run out of room in our `CD` collection. The user of the `CDCollection` object (the `main` method) never has to worry about running out of space because it's all handled internally.

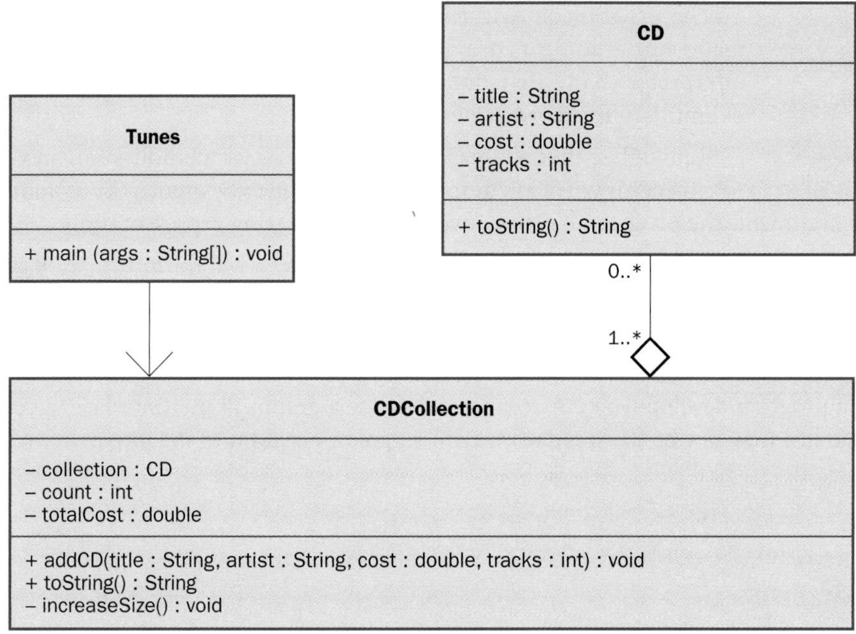

FIGURE 7.3 A UML class diagram of the `Tunes` program

Figure 7.3 shows a UML class diagram of the `Tunes` program. Recall that the open diamond indicates aggregation. The cardinality of the relationship is also noted: a `CDCollection` object contains zero or more `CD` objects.

The `toString` method of the `CDCollection` class returns an entire report summarizing the collection. The report is created, in part, by using implicit calls to the `toString` method of each `CD` object stored in the collection.

7.4 Command-Line Arguments

The formal parameter to the `main` method of a Java application is always an array of `String` objects. We've ignored that parameter in previous examples, but now we can discuss how it might occasionally be useful.

The Java run-time environment invokes the `main` method when an application is submitted to the interpreter. The `String[]` parameter, which we typically call `args`, represents *command-line arguments* that are provided when the interpreter is invoked. Any extra information on the command line when the interpreter is invoked is stored in the `args` array for use by the program. This technique is another way to provide input to a program.

KEY CONCEPT
Command-line arguments are stored in an array of `String` objects and are passed to the `main` method.

The program shown in Listing 7.10 simply prints all of the command-line arguments provided when the program is submitted to the interpreter. Note that quotes can be used on the command line to delimit a multi-word argument.

Remember that the parameter to the `main` method is always an array of `String` objects. If you want numeric information to be input as a command-line argument, the program has to convert it from its string representation.

When used, command-line arguments are typically reserved for information that tailors the way a program behaves. For example, you may provide the name of an input file as a command-line argument. Or perhaps you use an optional command-line argument that permits the user to specify a verbose or brief output format.

In program development environments that use a graphical user interface, a command line may not be the standard way to submit a program to the interpreter (that

LISTING 7.10

```
//********************************************************************
//  CommandLine.java       Java Foundations
//
//  Demonstrates the use of command line arguments.
//********************************************************************

public class CommandLine
{
   //-----------------------------------------------------------------
   //  Prints all of the command line arguments provided by the
   //  user.
   //-----------------------------------------------------------------
   public static void main(String[] args)
   {
      for (String arg : args)
         System.out.println(arg);
   }
}
```

OUTPUT

```
> java CommandLine one two "two and a half" three
one
two
two and a half
three
```

is, to run the program). In such situations, command-line information can be specified in some other way. Consult the documentation for these specifics if necessary.

7.5 Variable-Length Parameter Lists

Suppose we wanted to design a method that processed a different amount of data from one invocation to the next. For example, let's design a method called `average` that accepts a few integer values and returns their average. In one invocation of the method, we might pass in three integers to average:

```
mean1 = average(42, 69, 37);
```

In another invocation of the same method, we might pass in seven integers to average:

```
mean2 = average(35, 43, 93, 23, 40, 21, 75);
```

To accomplish this we could define overloaded versions of the `average` method (as we did in the exercises at the end of Chapter 5). But that solution doesn't scale to an arbitrary set of input values. It would require that we know the maximum number of parameters there might be and create a separate version of the method for each possibility.

Alternatively, we could define the method to accept an array of integers, which could be of different sizes for each call. But that would require the calling method to package the integers into an array.

Java provides a way to define methods that accept variable-length parameter lists. By using some special syntax in the formal parameter list of the method, we can define the method to accept any number of parameters. The parameters are automatically put into an array for easy processing in the method. For example, the `average` method could be written as follows:

KEY CONCEPT
A Java method can be defined to accept a varying number of parameters.

```
public double average(int ... list)
{
   double result = 0.0;
   if (list.length != 0)
   {
      int sum = 0;
      for (int num : list)
         sum += num;
      result = (double)sum / list.length;
   }

  return result;
}
```

Note the way the formal parameters are defined. The ellipsis (three periods in a row) indicates that the method accepts a variable number of parameters. In this case, the method accepts any number of `int` parameters, which it automatically puts into an array called `list`. In the method, we process the array normally.

We can now pass any number of `int` parameters to the `average` method, including none at all. That's why we check to see whether the length of the array is zero before we compute the average.

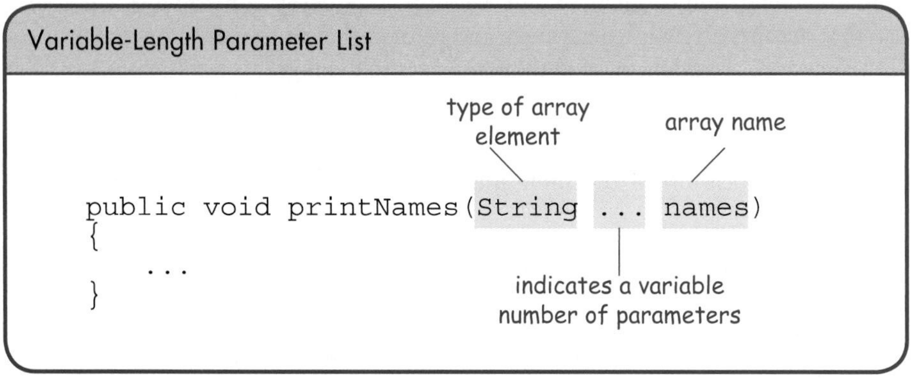

Variable-Length Parameter List

```
public void printNames(String ... names)
{
    ...
}
```

type of array element — `String`; array name — `names`; `...` indicates a variable number of parameters

The type of the multiple parameters can be any primitive or object type. For example, the following method accepts and prints multiple `Grade` objects (we defined the `Grade` class earlier in this chapter).

```
public void printGrades(Grade ... grades)
{
   for (Grade letterGrade : grades)
      System.out.println(letterGrade);
}
```

A method that accepts a variable number of parameters can also accept other parameters. For example, the following method accepts an `int`, a `String` object, and then a variable number of `double` values that will be stored in an array called `nums`.

```
public void test(int count, String name, double ... nums)
{
   //  whatever
}
```

The varying parameters must come last in the formal arguments. A single method cannot accept two sets of varying parameters.

Constructors can also be set up to accept a varying number of parameters. The program shown in Listing 7.11 on the next page creates two `Family` objects,

LISTING 7.11

```
//********************************************************************
//  VariableParameters.java      Java Foundations
//
//  Demonstrates the use of a variable length parameter list.
//********************************************************************

public class VariableParameters
{
   //-----------------------------------------------------------------
   //  Creates two Family objects using a constructor that accepts
   //  a variable number of String objects as parameters.
   //-----------------------------------------------------------------
   public static void main(String[] args)
   {
      Family lewis = new Family("John", "Sharon", "Justin", "Kayla",
         "Nathan", "Samantha");

      Family camden = new Family("Stephen", "Annie", "Matt", "Mary",
         "Simon", "Lucy", "Ruthie", "Sam", "David");

      System.out.println(lewis);
      System.out.println();
      System.out.println(camden);
   }
}
```

OUTPUT

```
John
Sharon
Justin
Kayla
Nathan
Samantha

Stephen
Annie
Matt
Mary
Simon
Lucy
Ruthie
Sam
David
```

passing a varying number of strings (representing the family member names) into the `Family` constructor.

The `Family` class is shown in Listing 7.12 below. The constructor simply stores a reference to the array parameter until it is needed. By using a variable-length parameter list for the constructor, we make it easy to create a family of any size.

LISTING 7.12

```
//********************************************************************
//  Family.java       Java Foundations
//
//  Demonstrates the use of variable length parameter lists.
//********************************************************************

public class Family
{
   private String[] members;

   //-----------------------------------------------------------------
   //  Constructor: Sets up this family by storing the (possibly
   //  multiple) names that are passed in as parameters.
   //-----------------------------------------------------------------
   public Family(String ... names)
   {
      members = names;
   }

   //-----------------------------------------------------------------
   //  Returns a string representation of this family.
   //-----------------------------------------------------------------
   public String toString()
   {
      String result = "";

      for (String name : members)
         result += name + "\n";

      return result;
   }
}
```

7.6 Two-Dimensional Arrays

The arrays we've examined so far have all been *one-dimensional arrays* in the sense that they represent a simple list of values. As the name implies, a *two-dimensional* array has values in two dimensions, which are often thought of as the rows and columns of a table. Figure 7.4 graphically compares a one-dimensional array with a two-dimensional array. We use two indexes to refer to a value in a two-dimensional array: one specifying the row and another the column.

Brackets are used to represent each dimension in the array. Therefore, the type of a two-dimensional array that stores integers is `int[][]`. Technically, Java represents a two-dimensional array as an array of arrays. Thus a two-dimensional integer array is really a one-dimensional array of references to one-dimensional integer arrays. In most cases, it's easier to think about a two-dimensional array as a table with rows and columns.

The `TwoDArray` program shown in Listing 7.13 instantiates a two-dimensional array of integers. As with one-dimensional arrays, the size of the dimensions is specified when the array is created. The size of the dimensions can be different.

Nested `for` loops are used in the `TwoDArray` program to load the array with values and also to print those values in a table format. Carefully trace the processing of this program to see how the nested loops eventually visit each element in the two-dimensional array. Note that the outer loops are governed by `table.length`, which represents the number of rows, and the inner loops are governed by `table[row].length`, which represents the number of columns in that row.

As with one-dimensional arrays, an initializer list can be used to instantiate a two-dimensional array, where each element is itself an array initializer list. This technique is used in the `SodaSurvey` program, which is shown in Listing 7.14.

Suppose a soda manufacturer held a taste test for four new flavors to determine whether people liked them. The manufacturer got 10 people to try each new flavor and give it a score from 1 to 5, where 1 equals poor and 5 equals excellent.

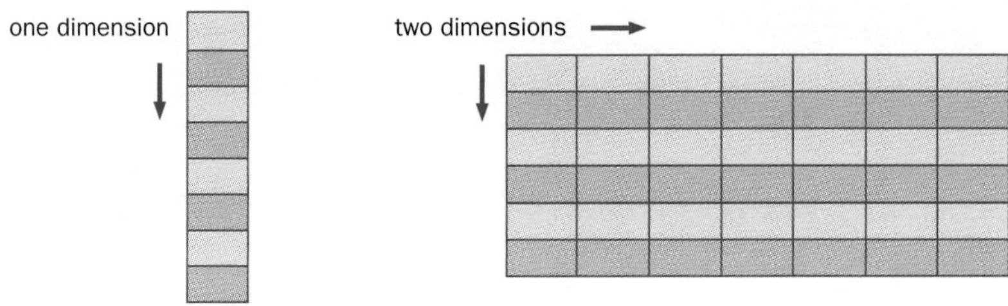

FIGURE 7.4 A one-dimensional array and a two-dimensional array

LISTING 7.13

```
//********************************************************************
//  TwoDArray.java      Java Foundations
//
//  Demonstrates the use of a two-dimensional array.
//********************************************************************

public class TwoDArray
{
   //-----------------------------------------------------------------
   //  Creates a 2D array of integers, fills it with increasing
   //  integer values, then prints them out.
   //-----------------------------------------------------------------
   public static void main(String[] args)
   {
      int[][] table = new int[5][10];

      // Load the table with values
      for (int row=0; row < table.length; row++)
         for (int col=0; col < table[row].length; col++)
            table[row][col] = row * 10 + col;

      // Print the table
      for (int row=0; row < table.length; row++)
      {
         for (int col=0; col < table[row].length; col++)
            System.out.print(table[row][col] + "\t");
         System.out.println();
      }
   }
}
```

OUTPUT

```
 0   1   2   3   4   5   6   7   8   9
10  11  12  13  14  15  16  17  18  19
20  21  22  23  24  25  26  27  28  29
30  31  32  33  34  35  36  37  38  39
40  41  42  43  44  45  46  47  48  49
```

LISTING 7.14

```
//********************************************************************
//  SodaSurvey.java       Java Foundations
//
//  Demonstrates the use of a two-dimensional array.
//********************************************************************

import java.text.DecimalFormat;

public class SodaSurvey
{
   //-----------------------------------------------------------------
   //  Determines and prints the average of each row (soda) and each
   //  column (respondent) of the survey scores.
   //-----------------------------------------------------------------
   public static void main(String[] args)
   {
      int[][] scores = { {3, 4, 5, 2, 1, 4, 3, 2, 4, 4},
                         {2, 4, 3, 4, 3, 3, 2, 1, 2, 2},
                         {3, 5, 4, 5, 5, 3, 2, 5, 5, 5},
                         {1, 1, 1, 3, 1, 2, 1, 3, 2, 4} };

      final int SODAS = scores.length;
      final int PEOPLE = scores[0].length;

      int[] sodaSum = new int[SODAS];
      int[] personSum = new int[PEOPLE];

      for (int soda=0; soda < SODAS; soda++)
         for (int person=0; person < PEOPLE; person++)
         {
            sodaSum[soda] += scores[soda][person];
            personSum[person] += scores[soda][person];
         }

      DecimalFormat fmt = new DecimalFormat("0.#");
      System.out.println("Averages:\n");

      for (int soda=0; soda < SODAS; soda++)
         System.out.println "Soda #" + (soda+1) + ": " +
                    fmt.format((float)sodaSum[soda]/PEOPLE));

      System.out.println ();
      for (int person=0; person < PEOPLE; person++)
         System.out.println("Person #" + (person+1) + ": " +
                 fmt.format((float)personSum[person]/SODAS));
   }
}
```

LISTING 7.14 *continued*

OUTPUT

```
Averages:

Soda #1: 3.2
Soda #2: 2.6
Soda #3: 4.2
Soda #4: 1.9

Person #1: 2.2
Person #2: 3.5
Person #3: 3.2
Person #4: 3.5
Person #5: 2.5
Person #6: 3
Person #7: 2
Person #8: 2.8
Person #9: 3.2
Person #10: 3.8
```

The two-dimensional array called `scores` in the `SodaSurvey` program stores the results of that survey. Each row corresponds to a soda, and each column in that row corresponds to the person who tasted it. More generally, each row holds the responses that all testers gave for one particular soda flavor, and each column holds the responses of one person for all sodas.

The `SodaSurvey` program computes and prints the average responses for each soda and for each respondent. The sums of each soda and person are first stored in one-dimensional arrays of integers. Then the averages are computed and printed.

Multidimensional Arrays

An array can have one, two, three, or even more dimensions. Any array with more than one dimension is called a *multidimensional array*.

It's fairly easy to picture a two-dimensional array as a table. A three-dimensional array could be drawn as a cube. However, once you are past three dimensions, multidimensional arrays might seem hard to visualize. But consider that each subsequent dimension is simply a subdivision of the previous one. It is often best to think of larger multidimensional arrays in this way.

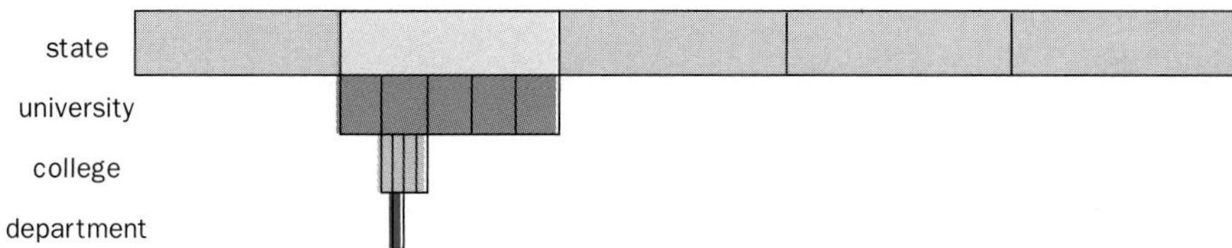

FIGURE 7.5 Visualization of a four-dimensional array

For example, suppose we wanted to store the number of students attending universities across the United States, broken down in a meaningful way. We might represent it as a four-dimensional array of integers. The first dimension represents the state. The second dimension represents the universities in each state. The third dimension represents the colleges in each university. Finally, the fourth dimension represents the departments in each college. The value stored at each location is the number of students in one particular department. Figure 7.5 shows these subdivisions.

DESIGN FOCUS

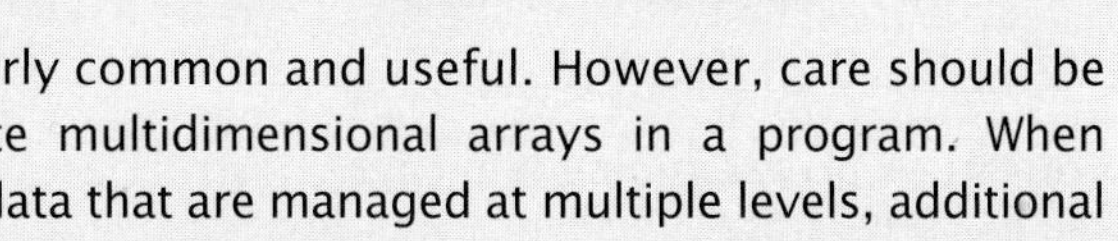

Two-dimensional arrays are fairly common and useful. However, care should be taken when deciding to create multidimensional arrays in a program. When dealing with large amounts of data that are managed at multiple levels, additional information and the methods needed to manage that information will probably be required. It is far more likely, for instance, that in the student example each state would be represented by an object, which might contain, among other things, an array to store information about each university, and so on.

KEY CONCEPT

Using an array with more than two dimensions is rare in an object-oriented system.

There is one other important characteristic of Java arrays to consider. As we established previously, Java does not directly support multidimensional arrays. Instead, they are represented as arrays of references to array objects. Those arrays could themselves contain references to other arrays. This layering continues for as many dimensions as required. Because of this technique for representing each dimension, the arrays in any one dimension could be of different lengths. These are sometimes called *ragged arrays*. For example, the numbers of elements in different rows of a two-dimensional array may not be the same. In such situations, care must be taken to make sure the arrays are managed appropriately.

Summary of Key Concepts

- An array of size *N* is indexed from 0 to *N*–1.
- In Java, an array is an object that must be instantiated.
- Bounds checking ensures that an index used to refer to an array element is in range.
- An initializer list can be used, instead of the `new` operator, to instantiate an array object.
- An entire array can be passed as a parameter, making the formal parameter an alias of the original.
- Instantiating an array of objects reserves room to store references only. The objects that are stored in each element must be instantiated separately.
- Command-line arguments are stored in an array of `String` objects and are passed to the `main` method.
- A Java method can be defined to accept a varying number of parameters.
- Using an array with more than two dimensions is rare in an object-oriented system.

Summary of Terms

array A programming language construct used to organize objects into an indexed list.

array element A value stored in an array.

bounds checking The process that ensures that an index is in the valid range for the array being referenced. Java performs automatic bounds checking.

command-line argument Data provided on the command line when a program is executed. Java stores these in the `String` array passed into the `main` method.

element type The type of data that can be stored as an element in a particular array.

index An integer used to specify a specific element in an array.

initializer list A list of values delimited by braces and separated by commas, used to initialize the values stored in an array.

multidimensional array An array with more than one index dimension.

off-by-one error An error in which an array index does not process the correct range of values, usually resulting in one less element being processed or an attempt being made to process one more element.

one-dimensional array An array with one indexed dimension; a simple list of values.

two-dimensional array An array with two indexed dimensions; it can be thought of as a table with rows and columns.

variable-length parameter list A parameter list in a method header that allows a variable number of parameters to be passed in, which are stored in an array for processing.

Self-Review Questions

SR 7.1 What is an array?

SR 7.2 How is each element of an array referenced?

SR 7.3 What is an array's element type?

SR 7.4 Explain the concept of array bounds checking. What happens when a Java array is indexed with an invalid value?

SR 7.5 Describe the process of creating an array. When is memory allocated for the array?

SR 7.6 What is an off-by-one error? How is it related to arrays?

SR 7.7 What does an array initializer list accomplish?

SR 7.8 Can an entire array be passed as a parameter? How is this accomplished?

SR 7.9 How is an array of objects created?

SR 7.10 What is a command-line argument?

SR 7.11 How can Java methods have variable-length parameter lists?

SR 7.12 How are multidimensional arrays implemented in Java?

Exercises

EX 7.1 Which of the following are valid declarations? Which instantiate an array object? Explain your answers.

```
int primes = {2, 3, 4, 5, 7, 11};
float elapsedTimes[] = {11.47, 12.04, 11.72, 13.88};
int[] scores = int[30];
int[] primes = new {2, 3, 5, 7, 11};
int[] scores = new int[30];
char grades[] = {'a', 'b', 'c', 'd', 'f'};
char[] grades = new char[];
```

EX 7.2 Describe five programs that would be difficult to implement without using arrays.

EX 7.3 Describe what problem occurs in the following code. What modifications should be made to it to eliminate the problem?

```
int[] numbers = {3, 2, 3, 6, 9, 10, 12, 32, 3, 12, 6};
for (int count = 1; count <= numbers.length; count++)
       System.out.println(numbers[count]);
```

EX 7.4 Write an array declaration and any necessary supporting classes to represent the following statements:

a. Students' names for a class of 25 students
b. Students' test grades for a class of 40 students
c. Credit card transactions that contain a transaction number, a merchant name, and a charge
d. Students' names for a class and homework grades for each student
e. For each employee of the L&L International Corporation: the employee number, hire date, and the amounts of the last five raises

EX 7.5 Write code that sets each element of an array called `nums` to the value of the constant `INITIAL`.

EX 7.6 Write code that prints the values stored in an array called `names` backwards.

EX 7.7 Write code that sets each element of a `boolean` array called `flags` to alternating values (`true` at index 0, `false` at index 1, and so on).

EX 7.8 Write a method called `sumArray` that accepts an array of floating point values and returns the sum of the values stored in the array.

EX 7.9 Write a method called `switchThem` that accepts two integer arrays as parameters and switches the contents of the arrays. Take into account that the arrays may be of different sizes.

Programming Projects

PP 7.1 Design and implement an application that reads an arbitrary number of integers that are in the range 0 to 50 inclusive and counts how many occurrences of each are entered. After all input has been processed, print all of the values (with the number of occurrences) that were entered one or more times.

PP 7.2 Modify the program from Programming Project 7.1 so that it works for numbers in the range –25 to 25.

PP 7.3 Design and implement an application that creates a histogram that allows you to visually inspect the frequency distribution of a set of values. The program should read in an arbitrary number of integers that are in the range 1 to 100 inclusive; then it should produce a chart similar to the following one that indicates how many input values fell in the range 1 to 10, 11 to 20, and so on. Print one asterisk for each value entered.

```
 1 - 10  | *****
11 - 20  | **
21 - 30  | *******************
31 - 40  |
41 - 50  | ***
51 - 60  | ********
61 - 70  | **
71 - 80  | *****
81 - 90  | *******
91 - 100 | *********
```

PP 7.4 The lines in the histogram in Programming Project 7.3 will be too long if a large number of values are entered. Modify the program so that it prints an asterisk for every five values in each category. Ignore leftovers. For example, if a category had 17 values, print three asterisks in that row. If a category had 4 values, do not print any asterisks in that row.

PP 7.5 Design and implement an application that computes and prints the mean and standard deviation of a list of integers x_1 through x_n. Assume that there will be no more than 50 input values. Compute both the mean and the standard deviation as floating point values, using the following formulas.

$$\text{mean} = \frac{\sum_{i=1}^{n} X_i}{n}$$

$$\text{standard deviation} = \sqrt{\frac{\sum_{i=1}^{n} (X_i - \text{mean})^2}{n - 1}}$$

PP 7.6 The L&L Bank can handle up to 30 customers who have savings accounts. Design and implement a program that manages the accounts. Keep track of key information, and allow each customer to make deposits and withdrawals. Produce appropriate error messages for invalid transactions. *Hint:* You may want to base your accounts on the `Account` class from Chapter 5. Also provide a method to add 3 percent interest to all accounts whenever the method is invoked.

PP 7.7 The programming projects of Chapter 5 discussed a `Card` class that represents a standard playing card. Create a class called `DeckOfCards` that stores 52 objects of the `Card` class. Include methods to shuffle the deck, deal a card, and report the number of cards left in the deck. The `shuffle` method should assume a full deck. Create a driver class with a `main` method that deals each card from a shuffled deck, printing each card as it is dealt.

PP 7.8 Design and implement an application that reads a sequence of up to 25 pairs of names and postal (ZIP) codes for individuals. Store the data in an object designed to store a first name (string), last name (string), and postal code (integer). Assume that each line of input will contain two strings followed by an integer value, each separated by a tab character. Then, after the input has been read in, print the list in an appropriate format to the screen.

PP 7.9 Modify the program you created in Programming Project 7.8 to support the storing of additional user information: street address (string), city (string), state (string), and 10-digit phone number (long integer, contains area code and does not include special characters such as (,), or -).

PP 7.10 Define a class called `Quiz` that manages a set of up to 25 `Question` objects. Define the `add` method of the `main Quiz` class to add a question to a quiz. Define the `giveQuiz` method of the `Quiz` class to present each question in turn to the user, accept an answer for each one, and keep track of the results. Define a class called `QuizTime` with a `main` method that populates a quiz, presents it, and prints the final results.

PP 7.11 Modify your answer to Programming Project 7.10 so that the complexity level of the questions given in the quiz is taken into account. Overload the `giveQuiz` method so that it accepts two integer parameters that specify the minimum and maximum complexity levels for the quiz questions and presents questions in that complexity range only. Modify the `main` method to demonstrate this feature.

Answers to Self-Review Questions

SRA 7.1 An array is an object that stores a list of values. The entire list can be referenced by its name, and each element in the list can be referenced individually based on its position in the array.

SRA 7.2 Each element in an array can be referenced by its numeric position, called an index, in the array. In Java, all array indexes begin at zero. Square brackets are used to specify the index. For example, `nums[5]` refers to the sixth element in the array called `nums`.

SRA 7.3 An array's element type is the type of values that the array can hold. All values in a particular array have the same type, or are at least of compatible types. Thus we might have an array of integers, or an array of `boolean` values, or an array of `Dog` objects, and so on.

SRA 7.4 Whenever a reference is made to a particular array element, the index operator (the brackets that enclose the subscript) ensures that the value of the index is greater than or equal to zero and less than the size of the array. If it is not within the valid range, an `ArrayIndexOutOfBoundsException` is thrown.

SRA 7.5 Arrays are objects. Therefore, as with all objects, to create an array we first create a reference to the array (its name). We then instantiate the array itself, which reserves memory space to store the array elements. The only difference between a regular object instantiation and an array instantiation is the bracket syntax.

SRA 7.6 An off-by-one error occurs when a program's logic exceeds the boundary of an array (or similar structure) by one. These errors include forgetting to process a boundary element, as well as attempting to process a nonexistent element. Array processing is susceptible to off-by-one errors because their indexes begin at zero and run to one less than the size of the array.

SRA 7.7 An array initializer list is used in the declaration of an array to set up the initial values of its elements. An initializer list instantiates the array object, so the `new` operator is not needed.

SRA 7.8 An entire array can be passed as a parameter. Specifically, because an array is an object, a reference to the array is passed to the method. Any changes made to the array elements will be reflected outside of the method.

SRA 7.9 An array of objects is really an array of object references. The array itself must be instantiated, and the objects that are stored in the array must be created separately.

SRA 7.10 A command-line argument consists of data included on the command line when the interpreter is invoked to execute the program. Command-line arguments are another way to provide input to a program. They are accessed using the array of strings that is passed into the `main` method as a parameter.

SRA 7.11 A Java method can be defined to accept a variable number of parameters by using an ellipsis (`...`) in the formal parameter list. When several values are passed to the method, they are automatically converted to an array. This allows the method to be written in terms of array processing without forcing the calling method to create the array.

SRA 7.12 A multidimensional array is implemented in Java as an array of array objects. The arrays that are elements of the outer array could also contain arrays as elements. This nesting process could continue for as many levels as needed.

Inheritance

8

CHAPTER OBJECTIVES

- Explore the derivation of new classes from existing ones.
- Define the concept and purpose of method overriding.
- Discuss the design of class hierarchies.
- Examine the purpose and use of abstract classes.
- Discuss the issue of visibility as it relates to inheritance.
- Discuss object-oriented design in the context of inheritance.

This chapter explains inheritance, a fundamental technique for organizing and creating classes. It is a simple but powerful idea that influences the way we design object-oriented software and enhances our ability to reuse classes in other situations and programs. In this chapter we explore the technique for creating subclasses and class hierarchies, and we discuss a technique for overriding the definition of an inherited method. We examine the `protected` modifier and discuss the effect that all visibility modifiers have on inherited attributes and methods.

8.1 Creating Subclasses

In our introduction to object-oriented concepts in Chapter 1 we presented the analogy that a class is to an object what a blueprint is to a house. In subsequent chapters we reinforced that idea, writing classes that define a set of similar objects. A class establishes the characteristics and behaviors of an object but reserves no memory space for variables (unless those variables are declared as `static`). Classes are the plan, and objects are the embodiment of that plan.

Many houses can be created from the same blueprint. They are essentially the same house in different locations with different people living in them. Now suppose you want a house that is similar to another but has some different or additional features. You want to start with the same basic blueprint but modify it to suit new, slightly different needs. Many housing developments are created this way. The houses in the development have the same core layout, but they have unique features. For instance, they might all be split-level homes with the same basic room configuration, but some have a fireplace or full basement, whereas others do not, and some have an upgraded gourmet kitchen instead of the standard version.

It's likely that the housing developer commissioned a master architect to create a single blueprint to establish the basic design of all houses in the development and then a series of new blueprints that include variations designed to appeal to different buyers. The act of creating the series of blueprints was simplified because they all begin with the same underlying structure, while the variations give them unique characteristics that may be important to the prospective owners.

KEY CONCEPT
Inheritance is the process of deriving a new class from an existing one.

Creating a new blueprint that is based on an existing blueprint is analogous to the object-oriented concept of *inheritance*, which is the process in which a new class is derived from an existing one. Inheritance is a powerful software development technique and a defining characteristic of object-oriented programming.

Via inheritance, the new class automatically contains the variables and methods in the original class. Then, to tailor the class as needed, the programmer can add new variables and methods to the derived class or modify the inherited ones.

KEY CONCEPT
One purpose of inheritance is to reuse existing software.

In general, creating new classes via inheritance is faster, easier, and cheaper than writing them from scratch. Inheritance is one way to support the idea of *software reuse*. By using existing software components to create new ones, we capitalize on the effort that went into the design, implementation, and testing of the existing software.

Keep in mind that the word *class* comes from the idea of classifying groups of objects with similar characteristics. Classification schemes often use levels of classes that are related to each other. For example, all mammals share certain characteristics, such as being warm-blooded. Now consider a subset of mammals, such as horses. All horses are mammals and have all of the characteristics of mammals, but they also have unique features that make them different from other mammals, such as dogs.

If we translate this idea into software terms, an existing class called `Mammal` would have certain variables and methods that describe the state and behavior of mammals. A `Horse` class could be derived from the existing `Mammal` class, automatically inheriting the variables and methods contained in `Mammal`. The `Horse` class can refer to the inherited variables and methods as if they had been declared locally in that class. New variables and methods can then be added to the derived class to distinguish a horse from other mammals.

The original class that is used to derive a new one is called the *parent class*, *superclass*, or *base class*. The derived class is called a *child class*, or *subclass*. In UML, inheritance is represented by an arrow with an open arrowhead pointing from the child class to the parent, as shown in Figure 8.1.

VideoNote
Overview of inheritance

The process of inheritance should establish an *is-a relationship* between two classes. That is, the child class should be a more specific version of the parent. For example, a horse is a mammal. Not all mammals are horses, but all horses are mammals. For any class X that is derived from class Y, you should be able to say that "X is a Y." If such a statement doesn't make sense, then that relationship is probably not an appropriate use of inheritance.

KEY CONCEPT
Inheritance creates an is-a relationship between the parent and child classes.

Let's look at an example. The `Words` program shown in Listing 8.1 instantiates an object of class `Dictionary`, which is derived from a class called `Book`. In the `main` method, three methods are invoked through the `Dictionary` object: two that were declared locally in the `Dictionary` class and one that was inherited from the `Book` class.

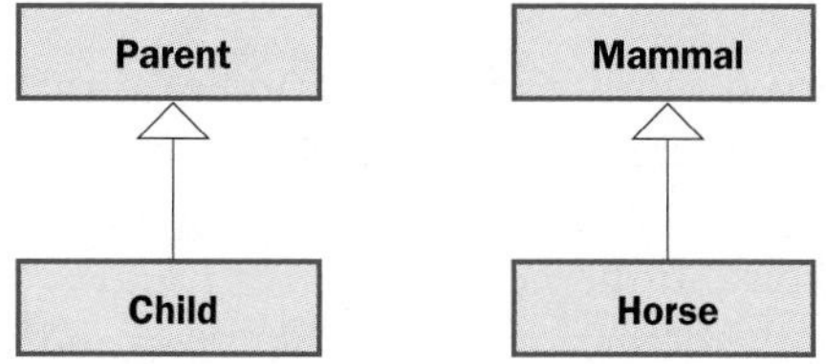

FIGURE 8.1 Inheritance relationships in UML

LISTING 8.1

```
//********************************************************************
//  Words.java       Java Foundations
//
//  Demonstrates the use of an inherited method.
//********************************************************************

public class Words
{
   //-----------------------------------------------------------------
   //  Instantiates a derived class and invokes its inherited and
   //  local methods.
   //-----------------------------------------------------------------
   public static void main(String[] args)
   {
      Dictionary webster = new Dictionary();

      System.out.println("Number of pages: " + webster.getPages());

      System.out.println("Number of definitions: " +
                         webster.getDefinitions());

      System.out.println("Definitions per page: " +
                         webster.computeRatio());
   }
}
```

OUTPUT

```
Number of pages: 1500
Number of definitions: 52500
Definitions per page: 35.0
```

Java uses the reserved word `extends` to indicate that a new class is being derived from an existing class. The `Book` class (shown in Listing 8.2) is used to derive the `Dictionary` class (shown in Listing 8.3 on page 384) simply by using the `extends` clause in the header of `Dictionary`. The `Dictionary` class automatically inherits the definition of the `setPages` and `getPages` methods, as well as the `pages` variable. It is as if those methods and the `pages` variable were

LISTING 8.2

```
//********************************************************************
//  Book.java       Java Foundations
//
//  Represents a book. Used as the parent of a derived class to
//  demonstrate inheritance.
//********************************************************************

public class Book
{
   protected int pages = 1500;

   //-----------------------------------------------------------------
   //  Pages mutator.
   //-----------------------------------------------------------------
   public void setPages(int numPages)
   {
      pages = numPages;
   }

   //-----------------------------------------------------------------
   //  Pages accessor.
   //-----------------------------------------------------------------
   public int getPages()
   {
      return pages;
   }
}
```

declared inside the `Dictionary` class. Note that in the `Dictionary` class, the `computeRatio` method explicitly references the `pages` variable, even though that variable is declared in the `Book` class.

Also note that although the `Book` class is needed to create the definition of `Dictionary`, no `Book` object is ever instantiated in the program. An instance of a child class does not rely on an instance of the parent class.

Inheritance is a one-way street. The `Book` class cannot use variables or methods that are declared explicitly in the `Dictionary` class. For instance, if we created an

LISTING 8.3

```
//********************************************************************
//  Dictionary.java       Java Foundations
//
//  Represents a dictionary, which is a book. Used to demonstrate
//  inheritance.
//********************************************************************

public class Dictionary extends Book
{
   private int definitions = 52500;

   //-----------------------------------------------------------------
   //  Prints a message using both local and inherited values.
   //-----------------------------------------------------------------
   public double computeRatio()
   {
      return definitions/pages;
   }

   //-----------------------------------------------------------------
   //  Definitions mutator.
   //-----------------------------------------------------------------
   public void setDefinitions(int numDefinitions)
   {
      definitions = numDefinitions;
   }

   //-----------------------------------------------------------------
   //  Definitions accessor.
   //-----------------------------------------------------------------
   public int getDefinitions()
   {
      return definitions;
   }
}
```

object from the `Book` class, it could not be used to invoke the `setDefinitions` method. This restriction makes sense because a child class is a more specific version of the parent class. A dictionary has pages because all books have pages, but even though a dictionary has definitions, not all books do.

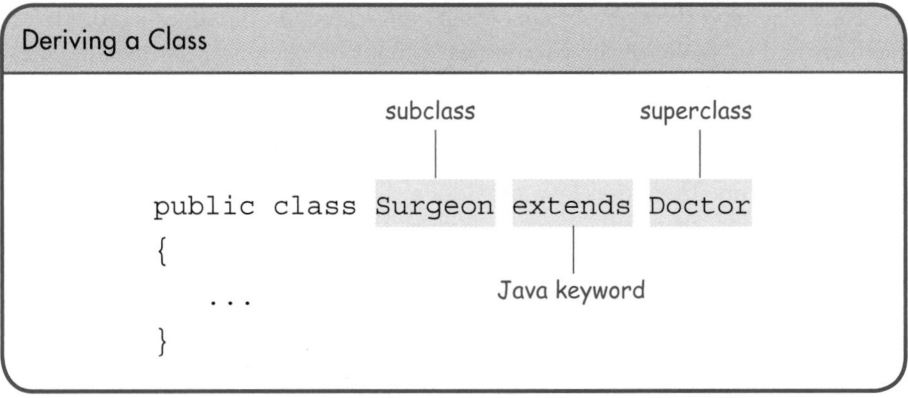

Deriving a Class
subclass
superclass
public class Surgeon extends Doctor
{
...
}
Java keyword

Figure 8.2 shows the inheritance relationship between the `Book` and `Dictionary` classes.

The `protected` Modifier

As we've seen, visibility modifiers are used to control access to the members of a class. Visibility plays an important role in the process of inheritance as well. Any public method or variable in a parent class can be explicitly referenced by name in

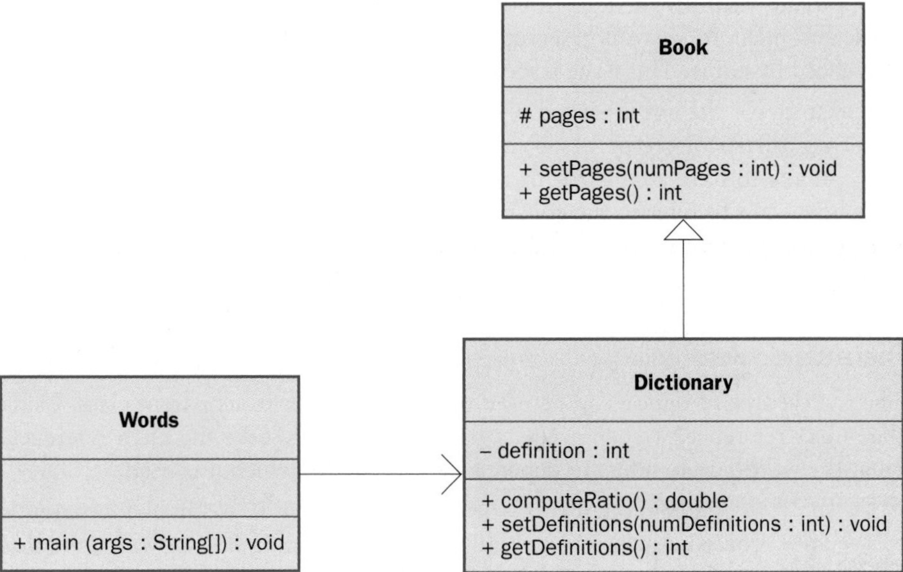

FIGURE 8.2 A UML class diagram for the `Words` program

the child class and through objects of that child class. On the other hand, private methods and variables of the parent class cannot be referenced in the child class or through an object of the child class.

This situation causes a dilemma. If we declare a variable with public visibility so that a derived class can reference it, we violate the principle of encapsulation. Therefore, Java provides a third visibility modifier: `protected`. Note that in the `Words` example, the variable `pages` is declared with protected visibility in the `Book` class. When a variable or method is declared with protected visibility, a derived class can reference it. And protected visibility allows the class to retain some encapsulation properties. The encapsulation with protected visibility is not as tight as it would be if the variable or method were declared private, but it is better than if it were declared public. Specifically, a variable or method declared with protected visibility may be accessed by any class in the same package. The relationships among all Java modifiers are explained completely in Appendix E.

KEY CONCEPT
Protected visibility provides the best possible encapsulation that permits inheritance.

In a UML diagram, protected visibility can be indicated by preceding the protected member with a hash mark (#). The `pages` variable of the `Book` class has this annotation in Figure 8.2.

Each variable or method retains the effect of its original visibility modifier. For example, the `setPages` method is still considered to be public in its inherited form in the `Dictionary` class.

Let's be clear about our terms. All methods and variables, even those declared with private visibility, are inherited by the child class. That is, their definitions exist, and memory space is reserved for the variables. It's just that they can't be referenced by name. This issue is explored in more detail in Section 8.4.

Constructors are not inherited. Constructors are special methods that are used to set up a particular type of object, so it doesn't make sense for a class called `Dictionary` to have a constructor called `Book`. But you can imagine that a child class may want to refer to the constructor of the parent class, which is one of the reasons for the `super` reference, described next.

The `super` Reference

The reserved word `super` can be used in a class to refer to its parent class. Using the `super` reference, we can access a parent's members. Like the `this` reference, what the word `super` refers to depends on the class in which it is used.

KEY CONCEPT
A parent's constructor can be invoked using the `super` reference.

A common use of the `super` reference is to invoke a parent's constructor. Let's look at an example. Listing 8.4 shows a modified version of the `Words` program, in which we use a class called `Book2` (shown in Listing 8.5 on page 388) as the parent of the derived class

LISTING 8.4

```
//********************************************************************
//  Words2.java       Java Foundations
//
//  Demonstrates the use of the super reference.
//********************************************************************

public class Words2
{
   //-----------------------------------------------------------------
   //  Instantiates a derived class and invokes its inherited and
   //  local methods.
   //-----------------------------------------------------------------
   public static void main(String[] args)
   {
      Dictionary2 webster = new Dictionary2 (1500, 52500);

      System.out.println("Number of pages: " + webster.getPages());

      System.out.println("Number of definitions: " +
                         webster.getDefinitions());

      System.out.println("Definitions per page: " +
                         webster.computeRatio());
   }
}
```

OUTPUT

```
Number of pages: 1500
Number of definitions: 52500
Definitions per page: 35.0
```

`Dictionary2` (shown in Listing 8.6 on page 389). However, unlike earlier versions of these classes, `Book2` and `Dictionary2` have explicit constructors used to initialize their instance variables. The output of the `Words2` program is the same as the output of the original `Words` program.

The `Dictionary2` constructor takes two integer values as parameters, representing the number of pages and definitions in the book. Because the `Book2` class already has a constructor that performs the work to set up the parts of the dictionary that were inherited, we rely on that constructor to do that work. However, since the constructor is not inherited, we cannot invoke it directly, and

LISTING 8.5

```
//********************************************************************
//  Book2.java       Java Foundations
//
//  Represents a book. Used as the parent of a derived class to
//  demonstrate inheritance and the use of the super reference.
//********************************************************************

public class Book2
{
   protected int pages;

   //-----------------------------------------------------------------
   //  Constructor: Sets up the book with the specified number of
   //  pages.
   //-----------------------------------------------------------------
   public Book2(int numPages)
   {
      pages = numPages;
   }

   //-----------------------------------------------------------------
   //  Pages mutator.
   //-----------------------------------------------------------------
   public void setPages(int numPages)
   {
      pages = numPages;
   }

   //-----------------------------------------------------------------
   //  Pages accessor.
   //-----------------------------------------------------------------
   public int getPages()
   {
      return pages;
   }
}
```

so we use the `super` reference to invoke it in the parent class. The `Dictionary2` constructor then proceeds to initialize its `definitions` variable.

In this example, it would have been just as easy to set the `pages` variable explicitly in the `Dictionary2` constructor instead of using `super` to call the `Book2` constructor. However, it is good practice to let each class "take care of itself." If

LISTING 8.6

```
//********************************************************************
//  Dictionary2.java       Java Foundations
//
//  Represents a dictionary, which is a book. Used to demonstrate
//  the use of the super reference.
//********************************************************************

public class Dictionary2 extends Book2
{
   private int definitions;

   //-----------------------------------------------------------------
   //  Constructor: Sets up the dictionary with the specified number
   //  of pages and definitions.
   //-----------------------------------------------------------------
   public Dictionary2(int numPages, int numDefinitions)
   {
      super(numPages);

      definitions = numDefinitions;
   }

   //-----------------------------------------------------------------
   //  Prints a message using both local and inherited values.
   //-----------------------------------------------------------------
   public double computeRatio()
   {
      return definitions/pages;
   }

   //-----------------------------------------------------------------
   //  Definitions mutator.
   //-----------------------------------------------------------------
   public void setDefinitions(int numDefinitions)
   {
      definitions = numDefinitions;
   }

   //-----------------------------------------------------------------
   //  Definitions accessor.
   //-----------------------------------------------------------------
   public int getDefinitions()
   {
      return definitions;
   }
}
```

we choose to change the way that the `Book2` constructor sets up its `pages` variable, we also have to remember to make that change in `Dictionary2`. When we use the `super` reference, a change made in `Book2` is automatically reflected in `Dictionary2`.

A child's constructor is responsible for calling its parent's constructor. Generally, the first line of a constructor should use the `super` reference call to a constructor of the parent class. If no such call exists, Java will automatically make a call to `super` with no parameters at the beginning of the constructor. This rule ensures that a parent class initializes its variables before the child class constructor begins to execute. Using the `super` reference to invoke a parent's constructor can be done only in the child's constructor, and if included, it must be the first line of the constructor.

The `super` reference can also be used to reference other variables and methods defined in the parent's class. We use this technique in later sections of this chapter.

Multiple Inheritance

Java's approach to inheritance is called *single inheritance*. This term means that a derived class can have only one parent. Some object-oriented languages allow a child class to have multiple parents. This approach, which is called *multiple inheritance*, is occasionally useful for describing objects that could share characteristics of more than one class. For example, suppose we had a class `Car` and a class `Truck` and we wanted to create a new class called `PickupTruck`. A pickup truck is somewhat like a car and somewhat like a truck. With single inheritance, we must decide whether it is better to derive the new class from `Car` or from `Truck`. With multiple inheritance, it can be derived from both, as shown in Figure 8.3.

Multiple inheritance works well in some situations, but it comes with a price. What if both `Truck` and `Car` have methods with the same name? Which method would `PickupTruck` inherit? The answer to this question is complex, and it depends on the rules of the language that supports multiple inheritance.

The designers of the Java language explicitly decided not to support multiple inheritance. Java *interfaces*, described in Chapter 9, provide the best features of multiple inheritance, without the added complexity.

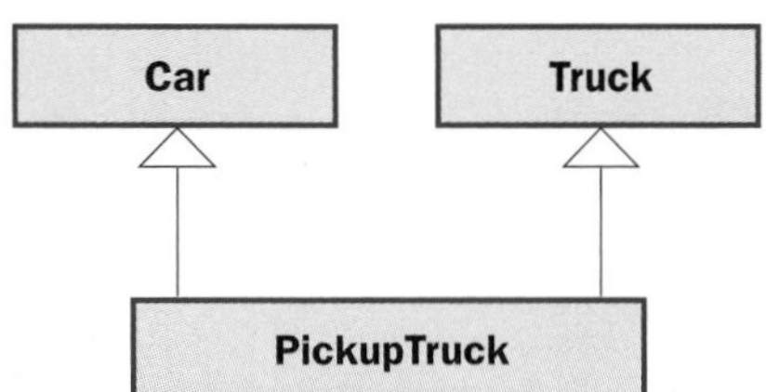

FIGURE 8.3 Multiple inheritance

8.2 Overriding Methods

When a child class defines a method with the same name and signature as a method in the parent class, we say that the child's version *overrides* the parent's version in favor of its own. The need for overriding occurs often in inheritance situations.

The program in Listing 8.7 provides a simple demonstration of method overriding in Java. The `Messages` class contains a `main` method that instantiates two objects: one from class `Thought` and one from class `Advice`. The `Thought` class is the parent of the `Advice` class.

KEY CONCEPT

A child class can override (redefine) the parent's definition of an inherited method.

Both the `Thought` class (shown in Listing 8.8 on page 392) and the `Advice` class (shown in Listing 8.9 on page 393) contain a definition

LISTING 8.7

```
//********************************************************************
//  Messages.java       Java Foundations
//
//  Demonstrates the use of an overridden method.
//********************************************************************

public class Messages
{
   //-----------------------------------------------------------------
   //  Creates two objects and invokes the message method in each.
   //-----------------------------------------------------------------
   public static void main(String[] args)
   {
      Thought parked = new Thought();
      Advice dates = new Advice();

      parked.message();

      dates.message();    // overridden
   }
}
```

OUTPUT

```
I feel like I'm diagonally parked in a parallel universe.
Warning: Dates in calendar are closer than they appear.
I feel like I'm diagonally parked in a parallel universe.
```

LISTING 8.8

```
//********************************************************************
//  Thought.java       Java Foundations
//
//  Represents a stray thought. Used as the parent of a derived
//  class to demonstrate the use of an overridden method.
//********************************************************************

public class Thought
{
   //-----------------------------------------------------------------
   //  Prints a message.
   //-----------------------------------------------------------------
   public void message()
   {
      System.out.println("I feel like I'm diagonally parked in a " +
                         "parallel universe.");

      System.out.println();
   }
}
```

for a method called `message`. The version of `message` defined in the `Thought` class is inherited by `Advice`, but `Advice` overrides it with an alternative version. The new version of the method prints out an entirely different message and then invokes the parent's version of the `message` method using the `super` reference.

The object that is used to invoke a method determines which version of the method is actually executed. When `message` is invoked using the `parked` object in the `main` method, the `Thought` version of `message` is executed. When `message` is invoked using the `dates` object, the `Advice` version of `message` is executed.

A method can be defined with the `final` modifier. A child class cannot override a final method. This technique is used to ensure that a derived class uses a particular definition of a method.

Method overriding is a key element in object-oriented design. It allows two objects that are related by inheritance to use the same naming conventions for methods that accomplish the same general task in different ways. Overriding becomes even more important when it comes to polymorphism, which is discussed in Chapter 9.

LISTING 8.9

```
//********************************************************************
//  Advice.java       Java Foundations
//
//  Represents some thoughtful advice. Used to demonstrate the use
//  of an overridden method.
//********************************************************************

public class Advice extends Thought
{
   //-----------------------------------------------------------------
   //  Prints a message. This method overrides the parent's version.
   //-----------------------------------------------------------------
   public void message()
   {
      System.out.println("Warning: Dates in calendar are closer " +
                         "than they appear.");

      System.out.println();

      super.message();   // explicitly invokes the parent's version
   }
}
```

COMMON ERROR

Don't confuse method overriding with method overloading. Recall from Chapter 5 that method overloading occurs when two or more methods with the same name have distinct signatures (parameter lists). With method overloading, you end up with multiple methods with the same name in the same class. With method overriding, you are replacing a method in the child class with a new definition. Method overriding occurs across classes and affects methods with the same signature.

A related problem occurs when you mean to override a method but instead create an overloaded version in the child class. The method defined in the child class must match the signature of the method you intend to override. If it doesn't, you end up with the inherited method plus an overloaded version of the method that is newly defined in the child. It's possible that you may want that situation to occur. Just be aware of the distinction.

Shadowing Variables

It is possible, although not recommended, for a child class to declare a variable with the same name as one that is inherited from the parent. Note the distinction between redeclaring a variable and simply giving an inherited variable a particular value. If a variable of the same name is declared in a child class, it is called a *shadow variable*. This is similar in concept to the process of overriding methods but creates confusing subtleties.

Because an inherited variable is already available to the child class, there is usually no good reason to redeclare it. Someone reading code with a shadowed variable will find two different declarations that seem to apply to a variable used in the child class. This confusion causes problems and serves no useful purpose. A redeclaration of a particular variable name could change its type, but that is usually unnecessary. In general, shadow variables should be avoided.

8.3 Class Hierarchies

A child class derived from one parent can be the parent of its own child class. Furthermore, multiple classes can be derived from a single parent. Therefore, inheritance relationships often develop into *class hierarchies*. The diagram in Figure 8.4 shows a class hierarchy that includes the inheritance relationship between the `Mammal` and `Horse` classes, discussed earlier.

There is no limit to the number of children a class can have or to the number of levels to which a class hierarchy can extend. Two children of the same parent are called *siblings*. Although siblings share the characteristics passed on by their common parent, they are not related by inheritance because one is not used to derive the other.

In class hierarchies, common features should be kept as high in the hierarchy as reasonably possible. That way, the only characteristics explicitly established in a child class are those that make the class distinct from its parent and from its siblings. This

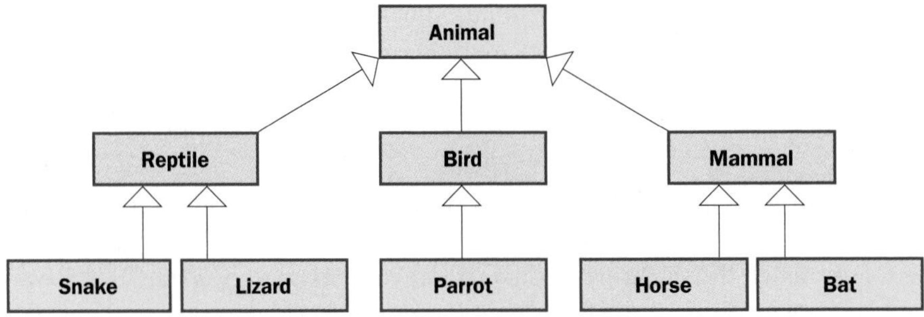

FIGURE 8.4 A class hierarchy

approach maximizes the potential to reuse classes. It also facilitates maintenance activities, because when changes are made to the parent, they are automatically reflected in the descendants. Always remember to maintain the is-a relationship when building class hierarchies.

KEY CONCEPT
The child of one class can be the parent of one or more other classes, creating a class hierarchy.

The inheritance mechanism is transitive. That is, a parent passes along a trait to a child class, and that child class passes it along to its children, and so on. An inherited feature might have originated in the immediate parent or, possibly, several levels higher in a more distant ancestor class.

KEY CONCEPT
Common features should be located as high in a class hierarchy as is reasonably possible.

There is no single best hierarchy organization for all situations. The decisions you make when you are designing a class hierarchy restrict and guide more detailed design decisions and implementation options, so you must make them carefully.

The class hierarchy shown in Figure 8.4 organizes animals by their major biological classifications, such as `Mammal`, `Bird`, and `Reptile`. In a different situation, however, it may be better to organize the same animals in a different way. For example, as shown in Figure 8.5, the class hierarchy might be organized around a function of the animals, such as their ability to fly. In this case, a `Parrot` class and a `Bat` class would be siblings derived from a general `FlyingAnimal` class. This class hierarchy is just as valid and reasonable as the original one. The goals of the programs that use the classes are the determining factor, guiding the programmer to a hierarchy design that is best for the situation.

The `Object` Class

In Java, all classes are derived ultimately from the `Object` class. If a class definition doesn't use the `extends` clause to derive itself explicitly from another class, then that class is automatically derived from the `Object` class by default. Therefore, this class definition:

```
class Thing
{
   // whatever
}
```

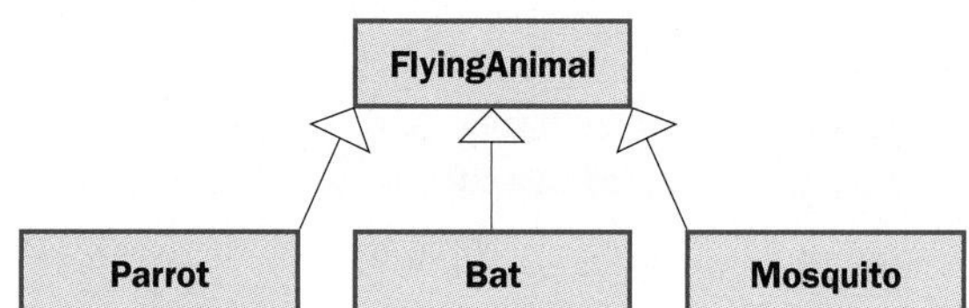

FIGURE 8.5 An alternative hierarchy for organizing animals

is equivalent to this one:

```
class Thing extends Object
{
   // whatever
}
```

Because all classes are derived from `Object`, all public methods of `Object` are inherited by every Java class. They can be invoked through any object created in any Java program. The `Object` class is defined in the `java.lang` package of the Java standard class library. Figure 8.6 lists some of the methods of the `Object` class.

KEY CONCEPT
All Java classes are derived, directly or indirectly, from the `Object` class.

As it turns out, we've been using `Object` methods quite often in our examples. The `toString` method, for instance, is defined in the `Object` class, so the `toString` method can be called on any object. As we've seen several times, when a `println` method is called with an object parameter, `toString` is called to determine what to print.

KEY CONCEPT
The `toString` and `equals` methods are inherited by every class in every Java program.

Thus, when we define a `toString` method in a class, we are actually overriding an inherited definition. The definition for `toString` that is provided by the `Object` class returns a string containing the object's class name followed by a numeric value that is unique for that object. Usually, we override the `Object` version of `toString` to fit our own needs. The `String` class has overridden the `toString` method so that it returns its stored string value.

VideoNote
Example using a class hierarchy

We are also overriding an inherited method when we define an `equals` method for a class. As we discussed in Chapter 4, the purpose of the `equals` method is to determine whether two objects are equal. The definition of the `equals` method provided by the `Object` class returns true if the two object references actually refer to the same object (that is, if they are aliases). Classes often override the inherited definition of the `equals` method in favor of a more appropriate definition.

```
boolean equals (Object obj)
```
Returns true if this object is an alias of the specified object.

```
String toString ()
```
Returns a string representation of this object.

```
Object clone ()
```
Creates and returns a copy of this object.

FIGURE 8.6 Some methods of the `Object` class

For instance, the `String` class overrides `equals` so that it returns true only if both strings contain the same characters in the same order.

Abstract Classes

An *abstract class* represents a generic concept in a class hierarchy. As the name implies, an abstract class represents an abstract entity that is usually insufficiently defined to be useful by itself. Instead, an abstract class may contain a partial description that is inherited by all of its descendants in the class hierarchy. An abstract class is just like any other class, except that it may have some methods that have not been defined yet. Its children, which are more specific, fill in the gaps.

An abstract class cannot be instantiated and usually contains one or more *abstract methods*, which have no definition. That is, there is no body of code defined for an abstract method, and therefore it cannot be invoked. An abstract class might also contain methods that are not abstract, meaning that the method definition is provided as usual. And an abstract class can contain data declarations as usual.

> **KEY CONCEPT**
> An abstract class cannot be instantiated. It represents a concept on which other classes can build their definitions.

A class is declared as abstract by including the `abstract` modifier in the class header. Any class that contains one or more abstract methods must be declared as abstract. In abstract classes, the `abstract` modifier must be applied to each abstract method. A class declared as abstract does not have to contain abstract methods, however.

Consider the class hierarchy shown in Figure 8.7. The `Vehicle` class at the top of the hierarchy may be too generic for a particular application. Therefore, we may choose to implement it as an abstract class. In UML diagrams, the names of abstract classes and abstract methods are shown in italics.

Concepts that apply to all vehicles can be represented in the `Vehicle` class and are inherited by its descendants. That way, each of its descendants doesn't

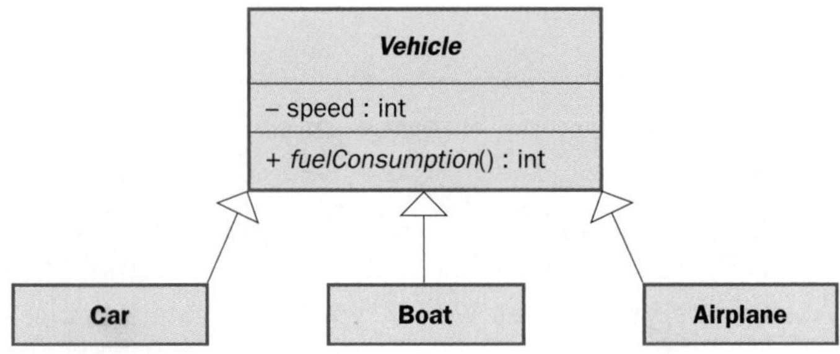

FIGURE 8.7 A vehicle class hierarchy

have to define the same concept redundantly (and perhaps inconsistently). For example, in Figure 8.7 we declare a variable called `speed` in the `Vehicle` class, and all specific vehicles below it in the hierarchy automatically have that variable because of inheritance. Any change we make to the representation of the speed of a vehicle is automatically reflected in all descendant classes. Similarly, in `Vehicle` we declare an abstract method called `fuelConsumption`, whose purpose is to calculate how quickly fuel is being consumed by a particular vehicle. The `Vehicle` class establishes that all vehicles consume fuel and provides a consistent method interface for computing that value. But implementation of the `fuelConsumption` method is left up to each subclass of `Vehicle`, which can tailor its method accordingly.

Some concepts don't apply to all vehicles, so we wouldn't represent those concepts at the `Vehicle` level. For instance, we wouldn't include a variable called `numberOfWheels` in the `Vehicle` class, because not all vehicles have wheels. The child classes for which wheels are appropriate can add that concept at the appropriate level in the hierarchy.

KEY CONCEPT
A class derived from an abstract parent must override all of its parent's abstract methods, or the derived class will also be considered abstract.

There are no restrictions on where in a class hierarchy an abstract class can be defined. Usually, abstract classes are located at the upper levels of a class hierarchy. However, it is possible to derive an abstract class from a nonabstract parent.

Usually, a child of an abstract class will provide a specific definition for an abstract method inherited from its parent. Note that this is just a specific case of overriding a method, giving a different definition from the one the parent provides. If a child of an abstract class does not give a definition for every abstract method that it inherits from its parent, then the child class is also considered abstract.

It would be a contradiction for an abstract method to be modified as `final` or `static`. Because a final method cannot be overridden in subclasses, an abstract final method would have no way of being given a definition in subclasses. A static method can be invoked using the class name without declaring an object of the class. Because abstract methods have no implementation, an abstract static method would make no sense.

DESIGN FOCUS

Choosing which classes and methods to make abstract is an important part of the design process. You should make such choices only after careful consideration. By using abstract classes wisely, you can create flexible, extensible software designs.

8.4 Visibility

As we mentioned earlier in this chapter, all variables and methods in a parent class, even those declared as private, are inherited by child classes. Private members exist for an object of a derived class, even though they can't be referenced directly. They can, however, be referenced indirectly.

Let's look at an example that demonstrates this situation. The program shown in Listing 8.10 contains a `main` method that instantiates a `Pizza` object and invokes a method to determine how many calories the pizza has per serving as a consequence of its fat content.

The `FoodItem` class shown in Listing 8.11 represents a generic type of food. The constructor of `FoodItem` accepts the number of grams of fat and the number of servings of that food. The `calories` method returns the number of calories due to fat, which the `caloriesPerServing` method invokes to help compute the number of fat calories per serving.

KEY CONCEPT

Private members are inherited by the child class but cannot be referenced directly by name. They may be used indirectly, however.

LISTING 8.10

```
//********************************************************************
//  FoodAnalyzer.java       Java Foundations
//
//  Demonstrates indirect access to inherited private members.
//********************************************************************

public class FoodAnalyzer
{
   //-----------------------------------------------------------------
   //  Instantiates a Pizza object and prints its calories per
   //  serving.
   //-----------------------------------------------------------------
   public static void main(String[] args)
   {
      Pizza special = new Pizza(275);

      System.out.println("Calories per serving: " +
                         special.caloriesPerServing());
   }
}
```

OUTPUT

```
Calories per serving: 309
```

LISTING 8.11

```
//********************************************************************
//  FoodItem.java       Java Foundations
//
//  Represents an item of food. Used as the parent of a derived class
//  to demonstrate indirect referencing.
//********************************************************************

public class FoodItem
{
   final private int CALORIES_PER_GRAM = 9;
   private int fatGrams;
   protected int servings;

   //-----------------------------------------------------------------
   //  Sets up this food item with the specified number of fat grams
   //  and number of servings.
   //-----------------------------------------------------------------
   public FoodItem(int numFatGrams, int numServings)
   {
      fatGrams = numFatGrams;
      servings = numServings;
   }

   //-----------------------------------------------------------------
   //  Computes and returns the number of calories in this food item
   //  due to fat.
   //-----------------------------------------------------------------
   private int calories()
   {
      return fatGrams * CALORIES_PER_GRAM;
   }

   //-----------------------------------------------------------------
   //  Computes and returns the number of fat calories per serving.
   //-----------------------------------------------------------------
   public int caloriesPerServing()
   {
      return (calories() / servings);
   }
}
```

LISTING 8.12

```
//********************************************************************
//  Pizza.java       Java Foundations
//
//  Represents a pizza, which is a food item. Used to demonstrate
//  indirect referencing through inheritance.
//********************************************************************

public class Pizza extends FoodItem
{
   //-----------------------------------------------------------------
   //  Sets up a pizza with the specified amount of fat (assumes
   //  eight servings).
   //-----------------------------------------------------------------
   public Pizza(int fatGrams)
   {
      super(fatGrams, 8);
   }
}
```

The `Pizza` class, shown in Listing 8.12, is derived from the `FoodItem` class, but it adds no special functionality or data. Its constructor calls the constructor of `FoodItem` using the `super` reference, asserting that there are eight servings per pizza.

The `Pizza` object called `special` in the `main` method is used to invoke the method `caloriesPerServing`, which is defined as a public method of `FoodItem`. Note that `caloriesPerServing` calls `calories`, which is declared with private visibility. Furthermore, `calories` references the variable `fatGrams` and the constant `CALORIES_PER_GRAM`, which are also declared with private visibility.

Even though the `Pizza` class cannot explicitly reference `calories`, `fatGrams`, or `CALORIES_PER_GRAM`, these are available for use indirectly when the `Pizza` object needs them. A `Pizza` object cannot be used to invoke the `calories` method, but it can call a method that can be so used. Note that a `FoodItem` object was never created or needed.

8.5 Designing for Inheritance

As a major characteristic of object-oriented software, inheritance must be carefully and specifically addressed during software design. A little thought about inheritance relationships can lead to a far more elegant design, which pays huge dividends in the long term.

KEY CONCEPT
Software design must carefully and specifically address inheritance.

Throughout this chapter, several design issues have been addressed in the discussion of the nuts and bolts of inheritance in Java. The following list summarizes some of the inheritance issues that you should keep in mind during the program design stage:

- Every derivation should be an is-a relationship. The child should be a more specific version of the parent.
- Design a class hierarchy to capitalize on reuse, and on potential reuse in the future.
- As classes and objects are identified in the problem domain, find their commonality. Push common features as high in the class hierarchy as appropriate for consistency and ease of maintenance.
- Override methods as appropriate to tailor or change the functionality of a child.
- Add new variables to the child class as needed, but don't shadow (redefine) any inherited variables.
- Allow each class to manage its own data. Therefore, use the `super` reference to invoke a parent's constructor and to call overridden versions of methods if appropriate.
- Design a class hierarchy to fit the needs of the application, taking into account how it may be useful in the future.
- Even if there are no current uses for them, override general methods such as `toString` and `equals` appropriately in child classes so that the inherited versions don't inadvertently cause problems later.
- Use abstract classes to specify a common class interface for the concrete classes lower in the hierarchy.
- Use visibility modifiers carefully to provide the needed access in derived classes without violating encapsulation.

Restricting Inheritance

We've seen the `final` modifier used in declarations to create constants many times. The other uses of the `final` modifier involve inheritance and can have a significant influence on software design. Specifically, the `final` modifier can be used to curtail the abilities related to inheritance.

KEY CONCEPT

The `final` modifier can be used to restrict inheritance.

Earlier in this chapter, we mentioned that a method can be declared as `final`, which means it cannot be overridden in any classes that extend the one it is in. A final method is often used to insist that particular functionality be used in all child classes.

The `final` modifier can also be applied to an entire class. A final class cannot be extended at all. Consider the following declaration:

```
public final class Standards
{
    // whatever
}
```

Given this declaration, the `Standards` class cannot be used in the `extends` clause of another class. The compiler will generate an error message in such a case. The `Standards` class can be used normally, but it cannot be the parent of another class.

Using the `final` modifier to restrict inheritance abilities is a key design decision. It should be done in situations where a child class might otherwise be used to change functionality that you, as the designer, specifically want to be handled a certain way. This issue comes up again in the discussion of polymorphism in Chapter 9.

3/10

Summary of Key Concepts

- Inheritance is the process of deriving a new class from an existing one.
- One purpose of inheritance is to reuse existing software.
- Inheritance creates an is-a relationship between the parent and child classes.
- Protected visibility provides the best possible encapsulation that permits inheritance.
- A parent's constructor can be invoked using the `super` reference.
- A child class can override (redefine) the parent's definition of an inherited method.
- The child of one class can be the parent of one or more other classes, creating a class hierarchy.
- Common features should be located as high in a class hierarchy as is reasonably possible.
- All Java classes are derived, directly or indirectly, from the `Object` class.
- The `toString` and `equals` methods are inherited by every class in every Java program.
- An abstract class cannot be instantiated. It represents a concept on which other classes can build their definitions.
- A class derived from an abstract parent must override all of its parent's abstract methods, or the derived class will also be considered abstract.
- Private members are inherited by the child class but cannot be referenced directly by name. They may be used indirectly, however.
- Software design must carefully and specifically address inheritance.
- The `final` modifier can be used to restrict inheritance.

Summary of Terms

abstract class A class used to represent a generic concept in a class hierarchy. An abstract class cannot be instantiated.

abstract method A method header without a body, used to establish the existence of an operation before the implementation is available. A class that contains an abstract method is inherently abstract.

base class A class from which another is derived. Also called a parent class or superclass.

child class A class derived from a parent class. Also called a subclass.

class hierarchy The hierarchy formed by inheritance among multiple classes.

inheritance The process of deriving one class from another.

is-a relationship The relationship between two classes related by inheritance. The superclass is-a more specific version of the subclass.

multiple inheritance Inheritance in which a subclass can be derived from multiple parent classes. Java does not support multiple inheritance.

overriding Redefining a method that has been inherited from a parent class.

parent class A class from which another is derived. Also called a superclass or base class.

shadow variable An instance variable defined in a derived class that has the same name as a variable in the parent class.

single inheritance Inheritance in which a subclass can have only one parent. Java supports only single inheritance.

subclass A class derived from a superclass. Also called a child class.

superclass A class from which another is derived. Also called a parent class or base class.

Self-Review Questions

SR 8.1 Describe the relationship between a parent class and a child class.

SR 8.2 How does inheritance support software reuse?

SR 8.3 What relationship should every class derivation represent?

SR 8.4 What does the `protected` modifier accomplish?

SR 8.5 Why is the `super` reference important to a child class?

SR 8.6 What is the difference between single inheritance and multiple inheritance?

SR 8.7 Why would a child class override one or more of the methods of its parent class?

SR 8.8 What is the significance of the `Object` class?

SR 8.9 What is the role of an abstract class?

SR 8.10 Are all members of a parent class inherited by the child? Explain.

SR 8.11 How can the `final` modifier be used to restrict inheritance?

Exercises

EX 8.1 Draw a UML class diagram showing an inheritance hierarchy containing classes that represent different types of clocks. Show the variables and method names for two of these classes.

EX 8.2 Show an alternative diagram for the hierarchy in Exercise 8.1. Explain why it may be a better or a worse approach than the original.

EX 8.3 Draw a UML class diagram showing an inheritance hierarchy containing classes that represent different types of cars, organized first by manufacturer. Show some appropriate variables and method names for at least two of these classes.

EX 8.4 Show an alternative diagram for the hierarchy in Exercise 8.3 in which the cars are organized first by type (sports car, sedan, SUV, and so on). Show some appropriate variables and method names for at least two of these classes. Compare and contrast the two approaches.

EX 8.5 Draw a UML class diagram showing an inheritance hierarchy containing classes that represent different types of airplanes. Show some appropriate variables and method names for at least two of these classes.

EX 8.6 Draw a UML class diagram showing an inheritance hierarchy containing classes that represent different types of trees (oak, elm, and so on). Show some appropriate variables and method names for at least two of these classes.

EX 8.7 Draw a UML class diagram showing an inheritance hierarchy containing classes that represent different types of payment transactions at a store (cash, credit card, and so on). Show some appropriate variables and method names for at least two of these classes.

EX 8.8 Experiment with a simple derivation relationship between two classes. Put `println` statements in constructors of both the parent class and the child class. Do not explicitly call the constructor of the parent in the child. What happens? Why? Change the child's constructor to explicitly call the constructor of the parent. Now what happens?

Programming Projects

PP 8.1 Design and implement a class called `MonetaryCoin` that is derived from the `Coin` class presented in Chapter 5. Store a value in the monetary coin that represents its value, and add a method that returns its value. Create a driver class to instantiate and compute the sum of several `MonetaryCoin` objects. Demonstrate that a monetary coin inherits its parent's ability to be flipped.

PP 8.2 Design and implement a set of classes that define the employees of a hospital: doctor, nurse, administrator, surgeon, receptionist, janitor, and so on. Include methods in each class that are named according to the services provided by that person and that print an appropriate message. Create a driver class to instantiate and exercise several of the classes.

PP 8.3 Design and implement a set of classes that define various types of reading material: books, novels, magazines, technical journals, textbooks, and so on. Include data values that describe various attributes of the material, such as the number of pages and the names of the primary characters. Include methods that are named appropriately for each class and that print an appropriate message. Create a driver class to instantiate and exercise several of the classes.

PP 8.4 Design and implement a set of classes that keep track of various sports statistics. Have each low-level class represent a specific sport. Tailor the services of the classes to the sport in question, and move common attributes to the higher-level classes as appropriate. Create a driver class to instantiate and exercise several of the classes.

PP 8.5 Design and implement a set of classes that keep track of demographic information about a set of people, such as age, nationality, occupation, income, and so on. Design each class to focus on a particular aspect of data collection. Create a driver class to instantiate and exercise several of the classes.

PP 8.6 Design and implement a set of classes that define a series of three-dimensional geometric shapes. For each shape, store fundamental data about its size, and provide methods to access and modify the data. In addition, provide appropriate methods to compute each shape's circumference, area, and volume. In your design, consider how shapes are related and thus where inheritance can be implemented. Create a driver class to instantiate several shapes of differing types and exercise the behavior you provided.

PP 8.7 Design and implement a set of classes that define various types of electronics equipment (computers, cell phones, pagers, digital cameras, and so on). Include data values that describe various attributes of the electronics, such as the weight, cost, power usage, and name of the manufacturer. Include methods that are named appropriately for each class and that print an appropriate message. Create a driver class to instantiate and exercise several of the classes.

PP 8.8 Design and implement a set of classes that define various courses in your curriculum. Include information about each course, such as its title, number, and description and the department that teaches the course. Consider the categories of classes that make up your curriculum when designing your inheritance structure. Create a driver class to instantiate and exercise several of the classes.

Answers to Self-Review Questions

SRA 8.1 A child class is derived from a parent class using inheritance. The methods and variables of the parent class automatically become a part of the child class, subject to the rules of the visibility modifiers used to declare them.

SRA 8.2 Because a new class can be derived from an existing class, the characteristics of the parent class can be reused without the error-prone process of copying and modifying code.

SRA 8.3 Each inheritance derivation should represent an is-a relationship: the child *is-a* more specific version of the parent. If this relationship does not hold, then inheritance is being used improperly.

SRA 8.4 The `protected` modifier establishes a visibility level (such as `public` and `private`) that takes inheritance into account. A variable or method declared with protected visibility can be referenced by name in the derived class, while retaining some level of encapsulation. Protected visibility allows access from any class in the same package.

SRA 8.5 The `super` reference can be used to call the parent's constructor, which cannot be invoked directly by name. It can also be used to invoke the parent's version of an overridden method.

SRA 8.6 With single inheritance, a class is derived from only one parent, whereas with multiple inheritance, a class can be derived from multiple parents, inheriting the properties of each. The problem with multiple inheritance is that collisions must be resolved in the cases when two or more parents contribute an attribute or method with the same name. Java supports only single inheritance.

SRA 8.7 A child class may prefer its own definition of a method in favor of the definition provided for it by its parent. In this case, the child overrides (redefines) the parent's definition with its own.

SRA 8.8 All classes in Java are derived, directly or indirectly, from the `Object` class. Therefore, all public methods of the `Object` class, such as `equals` and `toString`, are available to every object.

SRA 8.9 An abstract class is a representation of a general concept. Common characteristics and method signatures can be defined in an abstract class so that they are inherited by child classes derived from it.

SRA 8.10 A class member is not inherited if it has private visibility, meaning that it cannot be referenced by name in the child class. However, such members do exist for the child and can be referenced indirectly.

SRA 8.11 The `final` modifier can be applied to a particular method, which keeps that method from being overridden in a child class. It can also be applied to an entire class, which keeps that class from being extended at all.

Polymorphism

9

CHAPTER OBJECTIVES

- Define polymorphism and explore its benefits.
- Discuss the concept of dynamic binding.
- Use inheritance to create polymorphic references.
- Explore the purpose and syntax of Java interfaces.
- Use interfaces to create polymorphic references.
- Discuss object-oriented design in the context of polymorphism.

This chapter discusses polymorphism, another fundamental principle of object-oriented software. We first explore the concept of binding and discuss how it is related to polymorphism. Then we look at two distinct ways to implement a polymorphic reference in Java: inheritance and interfaces. Next we explore Java interfaces in general, establishing the similarities between them and abstract classes, and bringing the polymorphism discussion full circle. The chapter concludes with a discussion of the design issues related to polymorphism.

9.1 Dynamic Binding

Often, the type of a reference variable exactly matches the class of the object to which it refers. For example, consider the following reference:

```
ChessPiece bishop;
```

The `bishop` variable may be used to point to an object that is created by instantiating the `ChessPiece` class. However, it doesn't have to. The variable type and the object it refers to must be compatible, but their types need not be exactly the same. The relationship between a reference variable and the object it refers to is more flexible than that.

KEY CONCEPT

A polymorphic reference can refer to different types of objects over time.

The term *polymorphism* can be defined as "having many forms." A *polymorphic reference* is a reference variable that can refer to different types of objects at different points in time. The specific method invoked through a polymorphic reference (the actual code executed) can change from one invocation to the next.

Consider the following line of code:

```
obj.doIt();
```

If the reference `obj` is polymorphic, it can refer to different types of objects at different times. Thus, if that line of code is in a loop, or if it's in a method that is called more than once, that line of code could call a different version of the `doIt` method each time it is invoked.

At some point, the commitment is made to execute certain code to carry out a method invocation. This commitment is referred to as *binding* a method invocation to a method definition. In many situations, the binding of a method invocation to a method definition can occur at compile-time. For polymorphic references, however, the decision cannot be made until run-time. The method definition that is used is determined by the type of the object being referenced at the moment of invocation. This deferred commitment is called *dynamic binding* or *late binding*. It is slightly less efficient than binding at compile-time, because the decision is made during the execution of the program. This overhead is generally acceptable in light of the flexibility that a polymorphic reference provides.

KEY CONCEPT

The binding of a method invocation to its definition is performed at run-time for a polymorphic reference.

We can create a polymorphic reference in Java in two ways: using inheritance and using interfaces. Let's look at each in turn.

9.2 Polymorphism via Inheritance

When we declare a reference variable using a particular class name, it can be used to refer to any object of that class. In addition, it can refer to any object of any class that is related to its declared type by inheritance. For example, if the class `Mammal` is the parent of the class `Horse`, then a `Mammal` reference can be used to refer to an object of class `Horse`. This ability is shown in the following code segment:

```
Mammal pet;
Horse secretariat = new Horse();
pet = secretariat;  // a valid assignment
```

The ability to assign an object of one class to a reference of another class may seem like a deviation from the concept of strong typing discussed in Chapter 2, but it's not. Strong typing asserts that a variable can be assigned only a value consistent with its declared type. Well, that's what's happening here. Remember, inheritance establishes an is-a relationship. A horse *is-a* mammal. Therefore, assigning a `Horse` object to a `Mammal` reference is perfectly reasonable.

The reverse operation, assigning the `Mammal` object to a `Horse` reference, can also be done, but it requires an explicit cast. Assigning a reference in this direction is generally less useful and more likely to cause problems, because although a horse has all the functionality of a mammal, the reverse is not necessarily true.

KEY CONCEPT
A reference variable can refer to any object created from any class related to it by inheritance.

This relationship works throughout a class hierarchy. If the `Mammal` class were derived from a class called `Animal`, the following assignment would also be valid:

```
Animal creature = new Horse();
```

Carrying this idea to the limit, an `Object` reference can be used to refer to any object, because ultimately all classes are descendants of the `Object` class.

The reference variable `creature` can be used polymorphically, because at any point in time it can refer to an `Animal` object, a `Mammal` object, or a `Horse` object. Suppose that all three of these classes have a method called `move` that is implemented in different ways (because the child class overrode the definition it inherited). The following invocation calls the `move` method, but the particular version of the method it calls is determined at run-time:

```
creature.move();
```

When this line is executed, if `creature` currently refers to an `Animal` object, the `move` method of the `Animal` class is invoked. Likewise, if `creature` currently refers to a `Mammal` object, the `Mammal` version of `move` is invoked. Similarly, if it currently refers to a `Horse` object, the `Horse` version of `move` is invoked.

Of course, since Animal and Mammal represent general concepts, they may be defined as abstract classes. This situation does not eliminate the ability to have polymorphic references. Suppose the move method in the Mammal class is abstract and is given unique definitions in the Horse, Dog, and Whale classes (all derived from Mammal). A Mammal reference variable can be used to refer to any objects created from any of the Horse, Dog, and Whale classes, and it can be used to execute the move method on any of them, even though Mammal itself is abstract.

KEY CONCEPT

The type of the object, not the type of the reference, determines which version of a method is invoked.

Let's look at another situation. Consider the class hierarchy shown in Figure 9.1. The classes in it represent various types of employees that might be employed at a particular company. Let's explore an example that uses this hierarchy to pay a set of employees of various types.

The Firm class shown in Listing 9.1 on page 416 contains a main driver that creates a Staff of employees and invokes the payday method to pay them all. The program output includes information about each employee and how much each is paid (if anything).

The Staff class shown in Listing 9.2 on page 417 maintains an array of objects that represent individual employees of various kinds. Note that the array is declared to hold StaffMember references, but it is actually filled with objects created from several other classes, such as Executive and Employee. These classes are all descendants of the StaffMember class, so the assignments are valid. The staffList array is filled with polymorphic references.

The payday method of the Staff class scans through the list of employees, printing their information and invoking their pay methods to determine how much each employee should be paid. The invocation of the pay method is polymorphic because each class has its own version of the pay method.

The StaffMember class shown in Listing 9.3 on page 419 is abstract. It does not represent a particular type of employee and is not intended to be instantiated. Rather, it serves as the ancestor of all employee classes and contains information that applies to all employees. Each employee has a name, address, and phone number, so variables to store these values are declared in the StaffMember class and are inherited by all descendants.

The StaffMember class contains a toString method to return the information managed by the StaffMember class. It also contains an abstract method called pay, which takes no parameters and returns a value of type double. At the generic StaffMember level, it would be inappropriate to give a definition for this method. However, each descendant of StaffMember provides its own specific definition for pay.

This example shows the essence of polymorphism. Each class knows best how it should handle a specific behavior, in this case paying an employee. Yet in one sense it's all the same behavior—the employee is getting paid. Polymorphism lets us treat similar objects in consistent but unique ways.

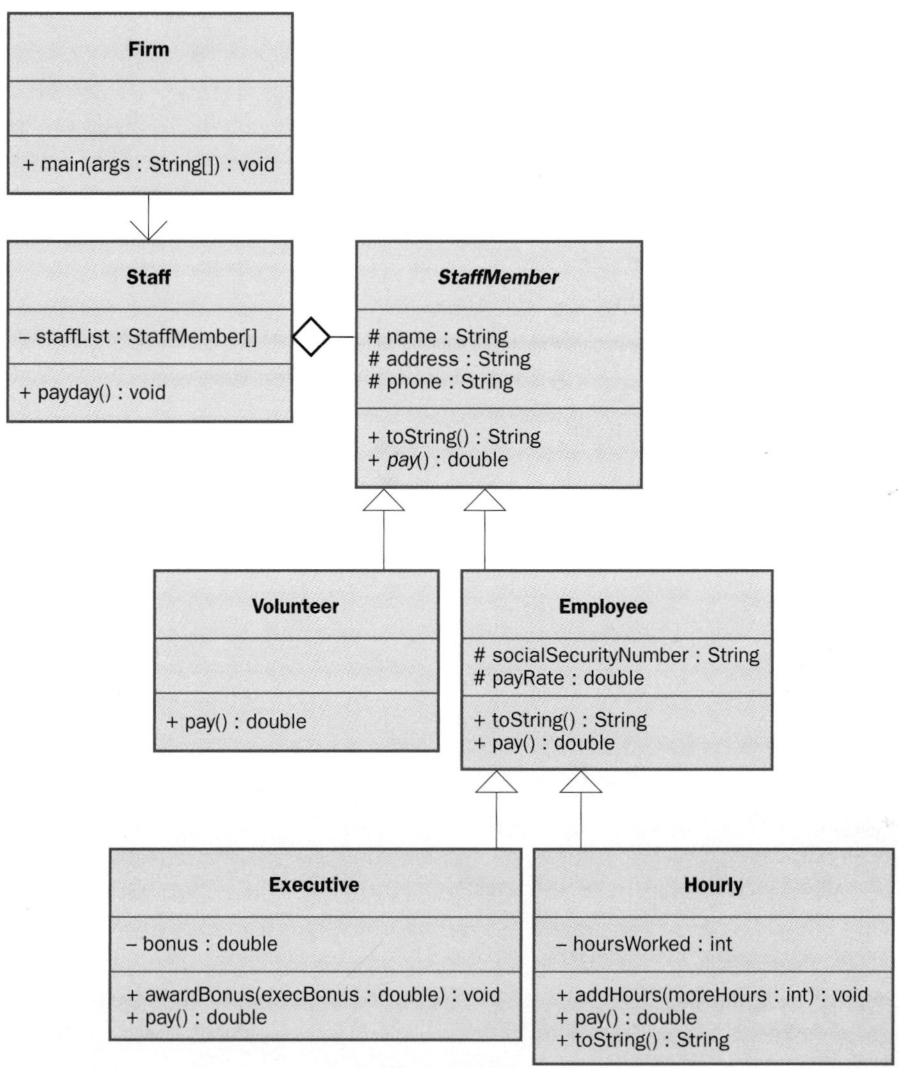

FIGURE 9.1 A class hierarchy of employees

Because `pay` is defined abstractly in `StaffMember`, the `payday` method of `Staff` can pay each employee polymorphically. If the `pay` method were not established in `StaffMember`, the compiler would complain when `pay` was invoked through an element of the `staffList` array. The abstract method guarantees the compiler that any object referenced through the `staffList` array has a `pay` method defined for it.

LISTING 9.1

```
//********************************************************************
//  Firm.java       Java Foundations
//
//  Demonstrates polymorphism via inheritance.
//********************************************************************

public class Firm
{
   //-----------------------------------------------------------------
   //  Creates a staff of employees for a firm and pays them.
   //-----------------------------------------------------------------
   public static void main(String[] args)
   {
      Staff personnel = new Staff();

      personnel.payday();
   }
}
```

OUTPUT

```
Name: Tony
Address: 123 Main Line
Phone: 555-0469
Social Security Number: 123-45-6789
Paid: 2923.07
-----------------------------------
Name: Paulie
Address: 456 Off Line
Phone: 555-0101
Social Security Number: 987-65-4321
Paid: 1246.15
-----------------------------------
Name: Vito
Address: 789 Off Rocker
Phone: 555-0000
Social Security Number: 010-20-3040
Paid: 1169.23
-----------------------------------
```

LISTING 9.1 *continued*

```
Name: Michael
Address: 678 Fifth Ave.
Phone: 555-0690
Social Security Number: 958-47-3625
Current hours: 40
Paid: 422.0
-----------------------------------
Name: Adrianna
Address: 987 Babe Blvd.
Phone: 555-8374
Thanks!
-----------------------------------
Name: Benny
Address: 321 Dud Lane
Phone: 555-7282
Thanks!
-----------------------------------
```

LISTING 9.2

```
//********************************************************************
//  Staff.java       Java Foundations
//
//  Represents the personnel staff of a particular business.
//********************************************************************

public class Staff
{
   private StaffMember[] staffList;

   //-----------------------------------------------------------------
   //  Constructor: Sets up the list of staff members.
   //-----------------------------------------------------------------
   public Staff()
   {
      staffList = new StaffMember[6];
```

LISTING 9.2 *continued*

```
      staffList[0] = new Executive("Tony", "123 Main Line",
         "555-0469", "123-45-6789", 2423.07);
      staffList[1] = new Employee("Paulie", "456 Off Line",
         "555-0101", "987-65-4321", 1246.15);
      staffList[2] = new Employee("Vito", "789 Off Rocker",
         "555-0000", "010-20-3040", 1169.23);

      staffList[3] = new Hourly("Michael", "678 Fifth Ave.",
         "555-0690", "958-47-3625", 10.55);

      staffList[4] = new Volunteer("Adrianna", "987 Babe Blvd.",
         "555-8374");
      staffList[5] = new Volunteer("Benny", "321 Dud Lane",
         "555-7282");

      ((Executive)staffList[0]).awardBonus(500.00);

      ((Hourly)staffList[3]).addHours(40);
   }

   //-----------------------------------------------------------------
   //  Pays all staff members.
   //-----------------------------------------------------------------
   public void payday()
   {
      double amount;

      for (int count=0; count < staffList.length; count++)
      {
         System.out.println(staffList[count]);

         amount = staffList[count].pay();   // polymorphic

         if (amount == 0.0)
            System.out.println("Thanks!");
         else
            System.out.println("Paid: " + amount);

         System.out.println("-----------------------------------");
      }
   }
}
```

LISTING 9.3

```
//********************************************************************
//  StaffMember.java      Java Foundations
//
//  Represents a generic staff member.
//********************************************************************

abstract public class StaffMember
{
   protected String name;
   protected String address;
   protected String phone;

   //-----------------------------------------------------------------
   //  Constructor: Sets up this staff member using the specified
   //  information.
   //-----------------------------------------------------------------
   public StaffMember(String eName, String eAddress, String ePhone)
   {
      name = eName;
      address = eAddress;
      phone = ePhone;
   }

   //-----------------------------------------------------------------
   //  Returns a string including the basic employee information.
   //-----------------------------------------------------------------
   public String toString()
   {
      String result = "Name: " + name + "\n";

      result += "Address: " + address + "\n";
      result += "Phone: " + phone;

     return result;
   }

   //-----------------------------------------------------------------
   //  Derived classes must define the pay method for each type of
   //  employee.
   //-----------------------------------------------------------------
   public abstract double pay();
}
```

LISTING 9.4

```
//********************************************************************
//  Volunteer.java      Java Foundations
//
//  Represents a staff member that works as a volunteer.
//********************************************************************

public class Volunteer extends StaffMember
{
   //-----------------------------------------------------------------
   //  Constructor: Sets up this volunteer using the specified
   //  information.
   //-----------------------------------------------------------------
   public Volunteer(String eName, String eAddress, String ePhone)
   {
      super(eName, eAddress, ePhone);
   }

   //-----------------------------------------------------------------
   //  Returns a zero pay value for this volunteer.
   /------------------------------------------------------------------
   public double pay()
   {
      return 0.0;
   }
}
```

The `Volunteer` class shown in Listing 9.4 represents a person who is not compensated monetarily for his or her work. We keep track only of a volunteer's basic information, which is passed into the constructor of `Volunteer`, which in turn passes it to the `StaffMember` constructor using the `super` reference. The `pay` method of `Volunteer` simply returns a zero pay value. If `pay` had not been overridden, the `Volunteer` class would have been considered abstract and could not have been instantiated.

VideoNote
Exploring the `Firm` program

Note that when a volunteer gets "paid" in the `payday` method of `Staff`, a simple expression of thanks is printed. In all other situations, where the pay value is greater than zero, the payment itself is printed.

The `Employee` class shown in Listing 9.5 represents an employee who gets paid at a particular rate each pay period. The pay rate and the employee's Social Security number are passed, along with the other basic information, to the `Employee` constructor. The basic information is passed to the constructor of `StaffMember` using the `super` reference.

The `toString` method of `Employee` is overridden to concatenate the additional information that `Employee` manages to the information returned by the parent's version of `toString`, which is called using the `super` reference. The `pay` method of an `Employee` simply returns the pay rate for that employee.

LISTING 9.5

```
//********************************************************************
//  Employee.java       Java Foundations
//
//  Represents a general paid employee.
//********************************************************************

public class Employee extends StaffMember
{
   protected String socialSecurityNumber;
   protected double payRate;

   //-----------------------------------------------------------------
   //  Constructor: Sets up this employee with the specified
   //  information.
   //-----------------------------------------------------------------
   public Employee(String eName, String eAddress, String ePhone,
                   String socSecNumber, double rate)
   {
      super(eName, eAddress, ePhone);

      socialSecurityNumber = socSecNumber;
      payRate = rate;
   }

   //-----------------------------------------------------------------
   //  Returns information about an employee as a string.
   //-----------------------------------------------------------------
   public String toString()
   {
      String result = super.toString();
```

LISTING 9.5 *continued*

```
      result += "\nSocial Security Number: " + socialSecurityNumber;

      return result;
   }

   //-----------------------------------------------------------------
   //  Returns the pay rate for this employee.
   //-----------------------------------------------------------------
   public double pay()
   {
      return payRate;
   }
}
```

The `Executive` class shown in Listing 9.6 represents an employee who may earn a bonus in addition to his or her normal pay rate. The `Executive` class is derived from `Employee` and therefore inherits from both `StaffMember` and `Employee`. The constructor of `Executive` passes along its information to the `Employee` constructor and sets the executive bonus to zero.

A bonus is awarded to an executive using the `awardBonus` method. This method is called in the `payday` method in `Staff` for the only executive that is part of the `staffList` array. Note that the generic `StaffMember` reference must be cast into an `Executive` reference to invoke the `awardBonus` method (because it doesn't exist for a `StaffMember`).

The `Executive` class overrides the `pay` method so that it first determines the payment as it would for any employee; then it adds the bonus. The `pay` method of the `Employee` class is invoked using `super` to obtain the normal payment amount. This technique is better than using just the `payRate` variable, because if we choose to change how `Employee` objects get paid, the change will automatically be reflected in `Executive`. After the bonus is awarded, it is reset to zero.

The `Hourly` class shown in Listing 9.7 on page 424 represents an employee whose pay rate is applied on an hourly basis. It keeps track of the number of hours worked in the current pay period, which can be modified by calls to the `addHours` method. This method is called from the `payday` method of `Staff`. The `pay` method of `Hourly` determines the payment on the basis of the number of hours worked and then resets the hours to zero.

LISTING 9.6

```
//********************************************************************
//  Executive.java       Java Foundations
//
//  Represents an executive staff member, who can earn a bonus.
//********************************************************************

public class Executive extends Employee
{
   private double bonus;

   //-----------------------------------------------------------------
   //  Constructor: Sets up this executive with the specified
   //  information.
   //-----------------------------------------------------------------
   public Executive(String eName, String eAddress, String ePhone,
                    String socSecNumber, double rate)
   {
      super(eName, eAddress, ePhone, socSecNumber, rate);

      bonus = 0; // bonus has yet to be awarded
   }

   //-----------------------------------------------------------------
   //  Awards the specified bonus to this executive.
   //-----------------------------------------------------------------
   public void awardBonus(double execBonus)
   {
      bonus = execBonus;
   }

   //-----------------------------------------------------------------
   //  Computes and returns the pay for an executive, which is the
   //  regular employee payment plus a one-time bonus.
   //-----------------------------------------------------------------
   public double pay()
   {
      double payment = super.pay() + bonus;

      bonus = 0;

      return payment;
   }
}
```

LISTING 9.7

```
//********************************************************************
//  Hourly.java      Java Foundations
//
//  Represents an employee that gets paid by the hour.
//********************************************************************

public class Hourly extends Employee
{
   private int hoursWorked;

   //-----------------------------------------------------------------
   //  Constructor: Sets up this hourly employee using the specified
   //  information.
   //-----------------------------------------------------------------
   public Hourly(String eName, String eAddress, String ePhone,
                 String socSecNumber, double rate)
   {
      super(eName, eAddress, ePhone, socSecNumber, rate);

      hoursWorked = 0;
   }

   //-----------------------------------------------------------------
   //  Adds the specified number of hours to this employee's
   //  accumulated hours.
   //-----------------------------------------------------------------
   public void addHours(int moreHours)
   {
      hoursWorked += moreHours;
   }

   //-----------------------------------------------------------------
   //  Computes and returns the pay for this hourly employee.
   //-----------------------------------------------------------------
   public double pay()
   {
      double payment = payRate * hoursWorked;

      hoursWorked = 0;

      return payment;
   }
```

LISTING 9.7 *continued*

```
   //-----------------------------------------------------------------
   //  Returns information about this hourly employee as a string.
   //-----------------------------------------------------------------
   public String toString()
   {
      String result = super.toString();

      result += "\nCurrent hours: " + hoursWorked;
      count--;

      return result;
   }
}
```

9.3 Interfaces

In Chapter 5 we used the term *interface* to refer to the set of public methods through which we can interact with an object. That definition is consistent with our use of it in this section, but now we are going to formalize this concept using a Java language construct. Interfaces provide another way to create polymorphic references.

A Java *interface* is a collection of constants and abstract methods. As discussed in Chapter 8, an abstract method is a method that does not have an implementation. That is, there is no body of code defined for an abstract method. The header of the method, including its parameter list, is simply followed by a semicolon. An interface cannot be instantiated.

KEY CONCEPT
An interface is a collection of abstract methods and therefore cannot be instantiated.

Listing 9.8 on page 426 shows an interface called `Encryptable`. It contains two abstract methods: `encrypt` and `decrypt`.

An abstract method can be preceded by the reserved word `abstract`, although in interfaces it usually is not. Methods in interfaces have public visibility by default.

A class *implements* an interface by providing method implementations for each of the abstract methods defined in the interface. The `Secret` class, shown in Listing 9.9 on page 426, implements the `Encryptable` interface.

LISTING 9.8

```
//********************************************************************
//  Encryptable.java       Java Foundations
//
//  Represents the interface for an object that can be encrypted
//  and decrypted.
//********************************************************************

public interface Encryptable
{
   public void encrypt();
   public String decrypt();
}
```

LISTING 9.9

```
//********************************************************************
//  Secret.java       Java Foundations
//
//  Represents a secret message that can be encrypted and decrypted.
//********************************************************************

import java.util.Random;

public class Secret implements Encryptable
{
   private String message;
   private boolean encrypted;
   private int shift;
   private Random generator;

   //-----------------------------------------------------------------
   //  Constructor: Stores the original message and establishes
   //  a value for the encryption shift.
   //-----------------------------------------------------------------
   public Secret(String msg)
   {
      message = msg;
      encrypted = false;
```

LISTING 9.9 *continued*

```
      generator = new Random();
      shift = generator.nextInt(10) + 5;
   }

   //-----------------------------------------------------------------
   //  Encrypts this secret using a Caesar cipher. Has no effect if
   //  this secret is already encrypted.
   //-----------------------------------------------------------------
   public void encrypt()
   {
      if (!encrypted)
      {
         String masked = "";
         for (int index=0; index < message.length(); index++)
            masked = masked + (char)(message.charAt(index)+shift);
         message = masked;
         encrypted = true;
      }
   }

   //-----------------------------------------------------------------
   //  Decrypts and returns this secret. Has no effect if this
   //  secret is not currently encrypted.
   //-----------------------------------------------------------------
   public String decrypt()
   {
      if (encrypted)
      {
         String unmasked = "";
         for (int index=0; index < message.length(); index++)
            unmasked = unmasked + (char)(message.charAt(index)-shift);
         message = unmasked;
         encrypted = false;
      }

      return message;
   }

   //-----------------------------------------------------------------
   //  Returns true if this secret is currently encrypted.
   //-----------------------------------------------------------------
   public boolean isEncrypted()
```

LISTING 9.9 *continued*

```
   {
      return encrypted;
   }

   //-----------------------------------------------------------------
   //  Returns this secret (may be encrypted).
   //-----------------------------------------------------------------
   public String toString()
   {
      return message;
   }
}
```

A class that implements an interface uses the reserved word `implements` followed by the interface name in the class header. If a class asserts that it implements a particular interface, it must provide a definition for all methods in the interface. The compiler will produce errors if any of the methods in the interface is not given a definition in the class.

In the class `Secret`, both the `encrypt` method and the `decrypt` method are implemented, which satisfies the contract established by the interface. These methods must be declared with the same signatures as their abstract counterparts in the interface. In the `Secret` class, the encryption is implemented using a simple Caesar cipher, which shifts the characters of the message a certain number of places. Another class that implements the `Encryptable` interface may use a completely different technique for encryption.

Note that the `Secret` class also implements additional methods that are not part of the `Encryptable` interface. Specifically, it defines the methods `isEncrypted` and `toString`, which have nothing to do with the interface. The interface guarantees that the class implements certain methods, but it does not restrict it from having others. In fact, it is common for a class that implements an interface to have other methods.

Listing 9.10 shows a program called `SecretTest`, which creates some `Secret` objects.

An interface and its relationship to a class can be shown in a UML class diagram. An interface is represented similarly to a class node except that the designation

LISTING 9.10

```
//********************************************************************
//  SecretTest.java       Java Foundations
//
//  Demonstrates the use of a formal interface.
//********************************************************************

public class SecretTest
{
   //-----------------------------------------------------------------
   //  Creates a Secret object and exercises its encryption.
   //-----------------------------------------------------------------
   public static void main(String[] args)
   {
      Secret hush = new Secret("Wil Wheaton is my hero!");
      System.out.println(hush);

      hush.encrypt();
      System.out.println(hush);

      hush.decrypt();
      System.out.println(hush);
   }
}
```

OUTPUT

```
Wil Wheaton is my hero!
asv*arok~yx*s}*w?*ro|y+
Wil Wheaton is my hero!
```

`<<interface>>` is inserted above the interface name. A dotted arrow with a triangular arrowhead is drawn from the class to the interface that it implements. Figure 9.2 on page 430 shows a UML class diagram for the `SecretTest` program.

Multiple classes can implement the same interface, providing their own definitions for the methods. For example, we could implement a class called `Password` that also implements the `Encryptable` interface. And, as mentioned earlier, each class that implements an interface may do so in different ways. The interface specifies which methods are implemented, not how they are implemented.

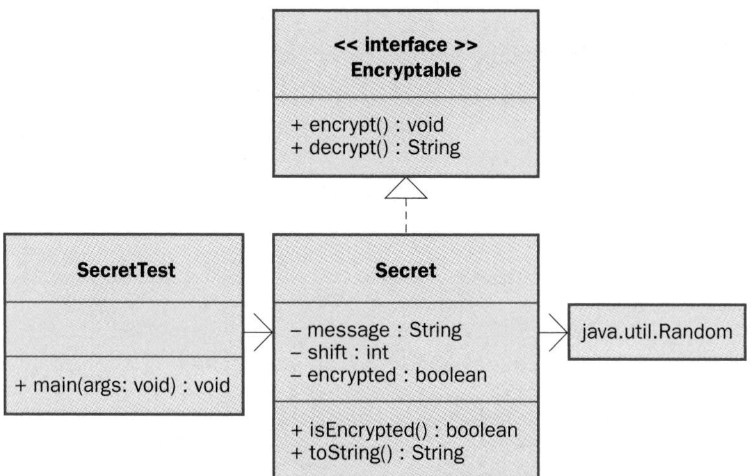

FIGURE 9.2 A UML class diagram for the `SecretTest` program

A class can implement more than one interface. In these cases, the class must provide an implementation for all methods in all interfaces listed. To show that a class implements multiple interfaces, they are listed in the `implements` clause, separated by commas. Here is an example:

```
class ManyThings implements Interface1, Interface2, Interface3
{
   // implements all methods of all interfaces
}
```

In addition to, or instead of, abstract methods, an interface can contain constants defined using the `final` modifier. When a class implements an interface, it gains access to all the constants defined in it.

Interface Hierarchies

The concept of inheritance can be applied to interfaces as well as to classes. That is, one interface can be derived from another interface. These relationships can form an *interface hierarchy*, which is similar to a class hierarchy. Inheritance relationships between interfaces are shown in UML diagrams using the same connection (an arrow with an open arrowhead) that is used to show inheritance relationships between classes.

> **KEY CONCEPT**
> Inheritance can be applied to interfaces so that one interface can be derived from another.

When a parent interface is used to derive a child interface, the child inherits all abstract methods and constants of the parent. Any class that implements the child interface must implement all of the methods. There are no visibility issues when dealing with inheritance between interfaces (as there are with protected and private members of a class), because all members of an interface are public.

Class hierarchies and interface hierarchies do not overlap. That is, an interface cannot be used to derive a class, and a class cannot be used to derive an interface. A class and an interface interact only when a class is designed to implement a particular interface.

Before we see how interfaces support polymorphism, let's take a look at a couple of useful interfaces that are defined in the Java standard class library: `Comparable` and `Iterator`.

The `Comparable` Interface

The Java standard class library contains interfaces as well as classes. The `Comparable` interface, for example, is defined in the `java.lang` package. The `Comparable` interface contains only one method, `compareTo`, which takes an object as a parameter and returns an integer.

The purpose of this interface is to provide a common mechanism for comparing one object to another. One object calls the method and passes another as a parameter as follows:

```
if (obj1.compareTo(obj2) < 0)
    System.out.println("obj1 is less than obj2");
```

As specified by the documentation for the interface, the integer that is returned from the `compareTo` method should be negative if `obj1` is less than `obj2`, 0 if they are equal, and positive if `obj1` is greater than `obj2`. It is up to the designer of each class to decide what it means for one object of that class to be less than, equal to, or greater than another.

In Chapter 4, we mentioned that the `String` class contains a `compareTo` method that operates in this manner. Now we can clarify that the `String` class has this method because it implements the `Comparable` interface. The `String` class implementation of this method bases the comparison of strings on the lexicographic ordering defined by the Unicode character set.

The `Iterator` Interface

The `Iterator` interface is another interface defined in the Java standard class library. It is used by a class that represents a collection of objects, providing a means to move through the collection one object at a time.

In Chapter 4, we defined the concept of an iterator, using a loop to process all elements in the collection. Most iterators, including objects of the `Scanner` class, are defined using the `Iterator` interface.

The two primary methods in the `Iterator` interface are `hasNext`, which returns a boolean result, and `next`, which returns an object. Neither of these methods takes any parameters. The `hasNext` method returns true if there are items left to process, and `next` returns the next object. It is up to the designer of the class that implements the `Iterator` interface to decide in what order objects will be delivered by the `next` method.

We should note that, in accordance with the spirit of the interface, the `next` method does not remove the object from the underlying collection; it simply returns a reference to it. The `Iterator` interface also has a method called `remove`, which takes no parameters and has a `void` return type. A call to the `remove` method removes the object that was most recently returned by the `next` method from the underlying collection.

We've seen how we can use iterators to process information from the `Scanner` class (in Chapter 4) and from arrays (in Chapter 7). Recall that the foreach version of the `for` loop simplifies this processing in many cases. We will continue to use `iterators` as appropriate. They are an important part of the development of collection classes, which we discuss in detail in the later chapters of this text (Chapters 14 and beyond).

9.4 Polymorphism via Interfaces

Now let's examine how we can create polymorphic references using interfaces. As we've seen many times, a class name can be used to declare the type of an object reference variable. Similarly, an interface name can be used as the type of a reference variable as well. An interface reference variable can be used to refer to any object of any class that implements that interface.

KEY CONCEPT
An interface name can be used to declare an object reference variable.

Suppose we declare an interface called `Speaker` as follows:

```
public interface Speaker
{
   public void speak();
   public void announce(String str);
}
```

The interface name, `Speaker`, can now be used to declare an object reference variable:

```
Speaker current;
```

The reference variable `current` can be used to refer to any object of any class that implements the `Speaker` interface. For example, if we define a class called `Philosopher` such that it implements the `Speaker` interface, we can then assign a `Philosopher` object to a `Speaker` reference as follows:

```
current = new Philosopher();
```

This assignment is valid because a `Philosopher` is a `Speaker`. In this sense, the relationship between a class and its interface is the same as the relationship between a child class and its parent. It is an is-a relationship, similar to the relationship created via inheritance. And that relationship forms the basis of the polymorphism.

KEY CONCEPT

An interface reference can refer to any object of any class that implements that interface.

The flexibility of an interface reference allows us to create polymorphic references. As we saw earlier in this chapter, using inheritance, we can create a polymorphic reference that can refer to any one of a set of objects as long as they are related by inheritance. Using interfaces, we can create similar polymorphic references among objects that implement the same interface.

For example, if we create a class called `Dog` that also implements the `Speaker` interface, it can be assigned to a `Speaker` reference variable as well. The same reference variable, in fact, can at one point refer to a `Philosopher` object and then later refer to a `Dog` object. The following lines of code illustrate this:

```
Speaker guest;
guest = new Philosopher();
guest.speak();
guest = new Dog();
guest.speak();
```

In this code, the first time the `speak` method is called, it invokes the `speak` method defined in the `Philosopher` class. The second time it is called, it invokes the `speak` method of the `Dog` class. As with polymorphic references via inheritance, it is not the type of the reference that determines which method gets invoked; this is based on the type of the object that the reference points to at the moment of invocation.

Note that when we are using an interface reference variable, we can invoke only the methods defined in the interface, even if the object it refers to has other methods to which it can respond. For example, suppose the `Philosopher` class also defined a public method called `pontificate`. The second line of the following code segment would generate a compiler error, even though the object can in fact contain the `pontificate` method:

```
Speaker special = new Philosopher();
special.pontificate();     // generates a compiler error
```

The problem is that the compiler can determine only that the object is a `Speaker`, and therefore can guarantee only that the object can respond to the `speak` and `announce` methods. Because the reference variable `special` could refer to a `Dog` object (which cannot pontificate), it does not allow the invocation. If we know in a particular situation that such an invocation is valid, we can cast the object into the appropriate reference so that the compiler will accept it, as follows:

```
((Philosopher)special).pontificate();
```

KEY CONCEPT
A parameter to a method can be polymorphic, which gives the method flexible control of its arguments.

Just as with polymorphic references based in inheritance, we can use an interface name as the type of a method parameter. In such situations, any object of any class that implements the interface can be passed into the method. For example, the following method takes a `Speaker` object as a parameter. Therefore, both a `Dog` object and a `Philosopher` object can be passed into it in separate invocations:

```
public void sayIt(Speaker current)
{
   current.speak();
}
```

Using a polymorphic reference as the formal parameter to a method is a powerful technique. It allows the method to control the types of parameters passed into it, yet gives it the flexibility to accept arguments of various types.

Let's now examine a particular use of polymorphism via interfaces.

Event Processing

In Chapter 6 we examined the processing of events in a Java GUI. Recall that, in order to respond to an event, we must establish a relationship between an event listener object and a particular component that may fire the event. We establish the relationship between the listener and the component it listens to by making a method call that adds the listener to the component. This situation is actually an example of polymorphism.

Suppose a class called `MyButtonListener` represents an action listener. To set up a listener to respond to a `JButton` object, we might do the following:

```
JButton button = new JButton();
button.addActionListener(new MyButtonListener());
```

Once this relationship is established, the listener will respond whenever the button fires an action event (because the user pressed it). Now think about the `addActionListener` method carefully. It is a method of the `JButton` class, which was written by someone at Sun Microsystems years ago. On the other hand, we might have written the `MyButtonListener` class today. How can a method written years ago take a parameter whose class was just written?

The answer is polymorphism. If you examine the source code for the `addActionListener` method, you'll discover that it accepts a parameter of type `ActionListener`, the interface. Therefore, instead of accepting a parameter of only one object type, the `addActionListener` method can accept any object of any class that implements the `ActionListener` interface. All other methods that add listeners work in similar ways.

KEY CONCEPT

The relationship between a listener and the component it listens to is established using polymorphism.

The `JButton` object doesn't know anything in particular about the object that is passed to the `addActionListener` method, except for the fact that it implements the `ActionListener` interface (otherwise, the code wouldn't compile). The `JButton` object simply stores the listener object and invokes its `performAction` method when the event occurs.

In Chapter 6 we mentioned that we can also create a listener by extending an adaptor class. This is another example of polymorphism via interfaces, even though the listener class is created via inheritance. Each adaptor class is written to implement the appropriate listener interface, providing empty methods for all event handlers. By extending an adaptor class, the new listener class automatically implements the corresponding listener interface. And that is what really makes it a listener such that it can be passed to an appropriate add listener method.

Thus, no matter how a listener object is created, we are using polymorphism via interfaces to set up the relationship between a listener and the component it listens to. GUI events are a wonderful example of the power and versatility provided by polymorphism.

Polymorphism, whether implemented via inheritance or interfaces, is a fundamental object-oriented technique that we will use as appropriate throughout the remainder of this text.

Summary of Key Concepts

- A polymorphic reference can refer to different types of objects over time.
- The binding of a method invocation to its definition is performed at run-time for a polymorphic reference.
- A reference variable can refer to any object created from any class related to it by inheritance.
- The type of the object, not the type of the reference, determines which version of a method is invoked.
- An interface is a collection of abstract methods and therefore cannot be instantiated.
- Inheritance can be applied to interfaces so that one interface can be derived from another.
- An interface name can be used to declare an object reference variable.
- An interface reference can refer to any object of any class that implements that interface.
- A parameter to a method can be polymorphic, which gives the method flexible control of its arguments.
- The relationship between a listener and the component it listens to is established using polymorphism.

Summary of Terms

binding The process of determining which method definition is used to fulfill a given method invocation.

dynamic binding The binding of a method invocation to its definition at run-time. Also called late binding.

interface A collection of abstract methods, used to define a set of operations that can be used to interact with an object.

interface hierarchy The hierarchy formed when interfaces are derived from other interfaces. Interface hierarchies are distinct from class hierarchies.

polymorphism The ability to define an operation that has more than one meaning by having the operation dynamically bound to methods of various objects.

polymorphic reference A reference variable that can refer to different types of objects at different points in time.

Self-Review Questions

SR 9.1 What is polymorphism?

SR 9.2 How does inheritance support polymorphism?

SR 9.3 How is overriding related to polymorphism?

SR 9.4 Why is the `StaffMember` class in the `Firm` example declared as abstract?

SR 9.5 Why is the `pay` method declared in the `StaffMember` class, given that it is abstract and has no body at that level?

SR 9.6 What is the difference between a class and an interface?

SR 9.7 How do class hierarchies and interface hierarchies intersect?

SR 9.8 Describe the `Comparable` interface.

SR 9.9 How can polymorphism be accomplished using interfaces?

Exercises

EX 9.1 Draw and annotate a class hierarchy that represents various types of faculty at a university. Show what characteristics would be represented in the various classes of the hierarchy. Explain how polymorphism could play a role in the process of assigning courses to each faculty member.

EX 9.2 Draw and annotate a class hierarchy that represents various types of animals in a zoo. Show what characteristics would be represented in the various classes of the hierarchy. Explain how polymorphism could play a role in guiding the feeding of the animals.

EX 9.3 Draw and annotate a class hierarchy that represents various types of sales transactions in a store (cash, credit, and so on). Show what characteristics would be represented in the various classes of the hierarchy. Explain how polymorphism could play a role in the payment process.

EX 9.4 What would happen if the `pay` method were not defined as an abstract method in the `StaffMember` class of the `Firm` program?

EX 9.5 Create an interface called `Visible` that includes two methods: `makeVisible` and `makeInvisible`. Both methods should take no parameters and should return a boolean result. Describe how a class might implement this interface.

EX 9.6 Draw a UML class diagram that shows the relationships among the elements of Exercise 9.5.

EX 9.7 Create an interface called `VCR` that has methods that represent the standard operations on a video cassette recorder (play, stop, and so on). Define the method signatures any way you desire. Describe how a class might implement this interface.

EX 9.8 Draw a UML class diagram that shows the relationships among the elements of Exercise 9.7.

EX 9.9 Explain how a call to the `addMouseListener` method in a GUI-based program represents a polymorphic situation.

Programming Projects

PP 9.1 Modify the `Firm` example from this chapter such that it accomplishes its polymorphism using an interface called `Payable`.

PP 9.2 Modify the `Firm` example from this chapter such that all employees can be given different vacation options depending on their classification. Modify the driver program to demonstrate this new functionality.

PP 9.3 Modify the `RationalNumber` class from Chapter 5 so that it implements the `Comparable` interface. To perform the comparison, compute an equivalent floating point value from the numerator and denominator for both `RationalNumber` objects, and then compare them using a tolerance value of 0.0001. Write a `main` driver to test your modifications.

PP 9.4 Create a class called `Password` that implements the `Encryptable` interface from this chapter. Then create a `main` driver that instantiates a `Secret` object and a `Password` object, using the same reference variable, and exercises their methods. Use any type of encryption desired for `Password`, other than the Caesar cipher used by `Secret`.

PP 9.5 Implement the `Speaker` interface defined in this chapter. Create three classes that implement `Speaker` in various ways. Create a driver class whose `main` method instantiates some of these objects and tests their abilities.

PP 9.6 Design a Java interface called `Priority` that includes two methods: `setPriority` and `getPriority`. The interface should define a way to establish numeric priority among a set of objects. Design and implement a class called `Task` that represents a task (such as on a to-do list) that implements the `Priority` interface. Create a driver class to exercise some `Task` objects.

PP 9.7 Modify the `Task` class from Programming Project 9.6 so that it also implements the `Comparable` interface from the Java standard class library. Implement the interface such that the tasks are ranked by priority. Create a driver class whose `main` method shows these new features of `Task` objects.

PP 9.8 Design a Java interface called `Lockable` that includes the following methods: `setKey`, `lock`, `unlock`, and `locked`. The `setKey`, `lock`, and `unlock` methods take an integer parameter that represents the key. The `setKey` method establishes the key. The `lock` and `unlock` methods lock and unlock the object, but only if the key passed in is correct. The `locked` method returns a boolean that indicates whether or not the object is locked. A `Lockable` object represents an object whose regular methods are protected: If the object is locked, the methods cannot be invoked; if it is unlocked, they can be invoked. Redesign and implement a version of the `Coin` class from Chapter 5 so that it is `Lockable`.

PP 9.9 Redesign and implement a version of the `Account` class from Chapter 5 so that it is `Lockable` as defined by Programming Project 9.8.

Answers to Self-Review Questions

SRA 9.1 Polymorphism is the ability of a reference variable to refer to objects of various types at different times. A method invoked through such a reference is bound to different method definitions at different times, depending on the type of the object referenced.

SRA 9.2 In Java, a reference variable declared using a parent class can be used to refer to an object of the child class. If both classes contain a method with the same signature, the parent reference can be polymorphic.

SRA 9.3 When a child class overrides the definition of a parent's method, two versions of that method exist. If a polymorphic reference is used to invoke the method, the version of the method that is invoked is determined by the type of the object being referred to, not by the type of the reference variable.

SRA 9.4 The `StaffMember` class is abstract because it is not intended to be instantiated. It serves as a placeholder in the inheritance hierarchy to help organize and manage the objects polymorphically.

SRA 9.5 The `pay` method has no meaning at the `StaffMember` level, so it is declared as abstract. But by declaring it there, we guarantee that every object of its children will have a `pay` method. This allows us to create an array of `StaffMember` objects, which is actually filled with various types of staff members, and to pay each one. The details of being paid are determined by each class, as appropriate.

SRA 9.6 A class can be instantiated; an interface cannot. An interface can contain only abstract methods and constants. A class provides the implementation for an interface.

SRA 9.7 Class hierarchies and interface hierarchies do not intersect. A class can be used to derive a new class, and an interface can be used to derive a new interface, but these two types of hierarchies do not overlap.

SRA 9.8 The `Comparable` interface contains a single method called `compareTo`, which should return an integer that is less than zero, equal to zero, or greater than zero if the executing object is less than, equal to, or greater than the object to which it is being compared, respectively.

SRA 9.9 An interface name can be used as the type of a reference. Such a reference variable can refer to any object of any class that implements that interface. Because all classes implement the same interface, they have methods with common signatures, which can be dynamically bound.

Exceptions

10

CHAPTER OBJECTIVES

- Discuss the purpose of exceptions.
- Examine exception messages and the call stack trace.
- Examine the `try-catch` statement for handling exceptions.
- Explore the concept of exception propagation.
- Describe the exception class hierarchy in the Java standard class library.
- Explore I/O exceptions and the ability to write text files.

Exception handling is an important part of an object-oriented software system. Exceptions represent problems or unusual situations that may occur in a program. Java provides various ways to handle exceptions when they occur. We explore the class hierarchy from the Java standard library used to define exceptions, as well as the ability to define our own exception objects. This chapter also discusses the use of exceptions when dealing with input and output, and it presents an example that writes a text file.

10.1 Exception Handling

KEY CONCEPT
Errors and exceptions are objects that represent unusual or invalid processing.

As we've discussed briefly in other parts of the text, problems that arise in a Java program may generate exceptions or errors. An *exception* is an object that defines an unusual or erroneous situation. An exception is thrown by a program or the run-time environment and can be caught and handled appropriately if desired. An *error* is similar to an exception, except that an error generally represents an unrecoverable situation and should not be caught.

Java has a predefined set of exceptions and errors that may occur during the execution of a program. If the predefined exceptions don't suffice, a programmer may choose to design a new class that represents an exception that is specific to a particular situation.

Problem situations represented by exceptions and errors can have various kinds of root causes. Here are some examples of situations that cause exceptions to be thrown:

- Attempting to divide by zero
- An array index that is out of bounds
- A specified file that could not be found
- A requested I/O operation that could not be completed normally
- Attempting to follow a null reference
- Attempting to execute an operation that violates some kind of security measure

These are just a few examples. There are dozens of others that address very specific situations.

As many of these examples show, an exception can represent a truly erroneous situation. But, as the name implies, an exception may simply represent an exceptional situation. That is, an exception may represent a situation that won't occur under usual conditions. Exception handling is set up to be an efficient way to deal with such situations, especially given that they don't happen too often.

We have several options when it comes to dealing with exceptions. A program can be designed to process an exception in one of three ways. It can

- not handle the exception at all,
- handle the exception where it occurs, or
- handle the exception at another point in the program.

We explore each of these approaches in the following sections.

10.2 Uncaught Exceptions

If a program does not handle the exception at all, it will terminate abnormally and produce a message that describes what exception occurred and where in the code it was produced. The information in an exception message is often helpful in tracking down the cause of a problem.

Let's look at the output of an exception. The program shown in Listing 10.1 below throws an `ArithmeticException` when an invalid arithmetic operation is attempted. In this case, the program attempts to divide by zero.

LISTING 10.1

```
//********************************************************************
//  Zero.java       Java Foundations
//
//  Demonstrates an uncaught exception.
//********************************************************************

public class Zero
{
   //-----------------------------------------------------------------
   //  Deliberately divides by zero to produce an exception.
   //-----------------------------------------------------------------
   public static void main(String[] args)
   {
      int numerator = 10;
      int denominator = 0;

      System.out.println("Before the attempt to divide by zero.");

      System.out.println(numerator / denominator);

      System.out.println("This text will not be printed.");
   }
}
```

OUTPUT

```
Before the attempt to divide by zero.
Exception in thread "main" java.lang.ArithmeticException: / by zero
        at Zero.main(Zero.java:19)
```

Because there is no code in this program to handle the exception explicitly, it terminates when the exception occurs, printing specific information about the exception. Note that the last `println` statement in the program never executes, because the exception occurs first.

The first line of the exception output indicates which exception was thrown and provides some information about why it was thrown. The remaining lines are the *call stack trace*; they indicate where the exception occurred. In this case, there is only one line in the call stack trace, but there may be several, depending on where the exception originated. The first trace line indicates the method, file, and line number where the exception occurred. The other trace lines, if present, indicate the methods that were called to get to the method that produced the exception. In this program, there is only one method, and it produced the exception; therefore, there is only one line in the trace.

KEY CONCEPT
The messages printed when an exception is thrown provide a method call stack trace.

The call stack trace information is also available by calling methods of the exception class that is being thrown. The method `getMessage` returns a string explaining the reason the exception was thrown. The method `printStackTrace` prints the call stack trace.

10.3 The `try-catch` Statement

Let's now examine how we catch and handle an exception when it is thrown. The *try-catch* statement identifies a block of statements that may throw an exception. A *catch clause*, which follows a `try` block, defines how a particular kind of exception is handled. A `try` block can have several `catch` clauses associated with it. Each `catch` clause is called an *exception handler*.

When a `try` statement is executed, the statements in the `try` block are executed. If no exception is thrown during the execution of the `try` block, processing continues with the statement following the `try` statement (after all of the `catch` clauses). This situation is the normal execution flow and should occur most of the time.

If an exception is thrown at any point during the execution of the `try` block, control is immediately transferred to the appropriate catch handler if it is present. That is, control transfers to the first `catch` clause whose exception class corresponds to the class of the exception that was thrown. After execution of the statements in the `catch` clause, control transfers to the statement after the entire `try-catch` statement.

KEY CONCEPT
Each `catch` clause handles a particular kind of exception that may be thrown within the `try` block.

Let's look at an example. Suppose a hypothetical company uses codes to represent its various products. A product code includes, among other information, a character in the tenth position that

The `try` Statement

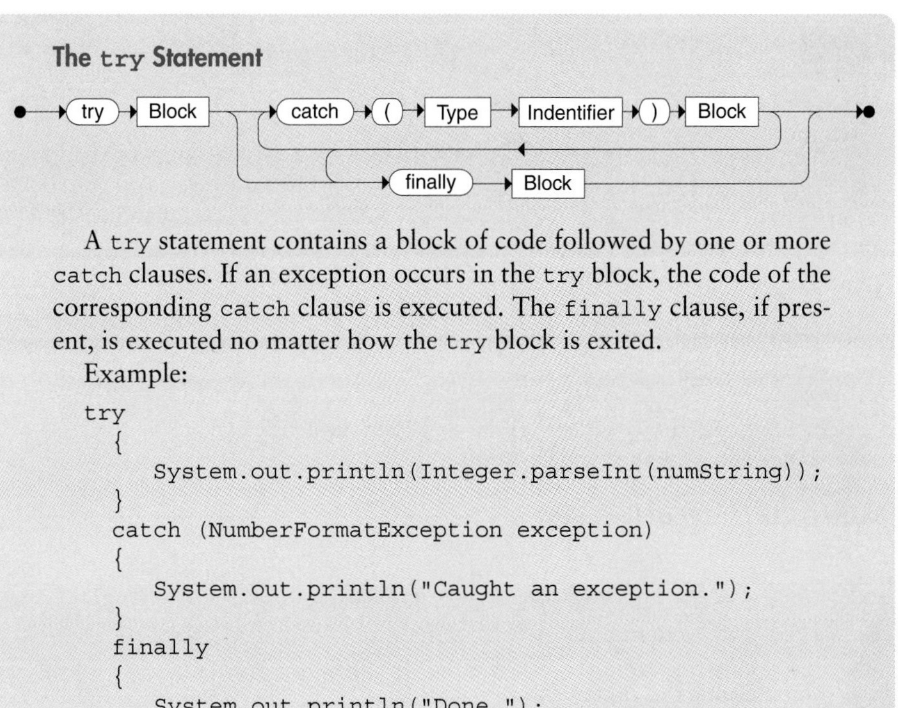

A `try` statement contains a block of code followed by one or more `catch` clauses. If an exception occurs in the `try` block, the code of the corresponding `catch` clause is executed. The `finally` clause, if present, is executed no matter how the `try` block is exited.

Example:

```
try
   {
      System.out.println(Integer.parseInt(numString));
   }
   catch (NumberFormatException exception)
   {
      System.out.println("Caught an exception.");
   }
   finally
   {
      System.out.println("Done.");
   }
```

represents the zone from which that product was made, and a four-digit integer in positions 4 through 7 that represents the district in which it will be sold. As a consequence of some reorganization, the sale of products from zone R is banned in districts with a designation of 2000 or higher. The program shown in Listing 10.2 on the next page reads product codes from the user and counts the number of banned codes entered.

The programming statements in the `try` block attempt to pull out the zone and district information, and then determine whether it represents a banned product code. If there is any problem extracting the zone and district information, the product code is considered to be invalid and is not processed further. For example, a `StringIndexOutOfBoundsException` could be thrown by either the `charAt` method or the `substring` method. Furthermore, a `NumberFormatException` will be thrown by the `parseInt` method if the `substring` method does not contain a valid integer. A particular message is printed, depending on which exception is thrown. In either case, because the exception is caught and handled, processing continues normally.

LISTING 10.2

```
//********************************************************************
//  ProductCodes.java       Java Foundations
//
//  Demonstrates the use of a try-catch block.
//********************************************************************

import java.util.Scanner;

public class ProductCodes
{
   //-----------------------------------------------------------------
   //  Counts the number of product codes that are entered with a
   //  zone of R and district greater than 2000.
   //-----------------------------------------------------------------
   public static void main(String[] args)
   {
      String code;
      char zone;
      int district, valid = 0, banned = 0;

      Scanner scan = new Scanner(System.in);

      System.out.print("Enter product code (STOP to quit): ");
      code = scan.nextLine();

      while (!code.equals("STOP"))
      {
         try
         {
            zone = code.charAt(9);
            district = Integer.parseInt(code.substring(3, 7));
            valid++;
            if (zone == 'R' && district > 2000)
               banned++;
         }
         catch (StringIndexOutOfBoundsException exception)
         {
            System.out.println("Improper code length: " + code);
         }
         catch (NumberFormatException exception)
         {
            System.out.println("District is not numeric: " + code);
         }
```

LISTING 10.2 *continued*

```
            System.out.print("Enter product code (STOP to quit): ");
            code = scan.nextLine();
        }

        System.out.println("# of valid codes entered: " + valid);
        System.out.println("# of banned codes entered: " + banned);
    }
}
```

OUTPUT

```
Enter product code (STOP to quit): TRV2475A5R-14
Enter product code (STOP to quit): TRD1704A7R-12
Enter product code (STOP to quit): TRL2k74A5R-11
District is not numeric: TRL2k74A5R-11
Enter product code (STOP to quit): TRQ2949A6M-04
Enter product code (STOP to quit): TRV2105A2
Improper code length: TRV2105A2
Enter product code (STOP to quit): TRQ2778A7R-19
Enter product code (STOP to quit): STOP
# of valid codes entered: 4
# of banned codes entered: 2
```

Note that for each code examined, the integer variable `valid` is incremented only if no exception is thrown. If an exception is thrown, control transfers immediately to the appropriate `catch` clause. Likewise, the zone and district are tested by the `if` statement only `if` no exception is thrown.

The `finally` Clause

A `try-catch` statement can have an optional *finally clause*. The `finally` clause defines a section of code that is executed no matter how the `try` block is exited. Most often, a `finally` clause is used to manage resources or to guarantee that particular parts of an algorithm are executed.

> **KEY CONCEPT**
> The `finally` clause is executed whether the `try` block is exited normally or because of a thrown exception.

If no exception is generated, the statements in the `finally` clause are executed after the `try` block is complete. If an exception is generated in the `try` block, control first transfers to the appropriate `catch` clause. After execution of the exception-handling code, control transfers to the finally clause and its statements are executed. A finally clause, if present, must be listed after the catch clauses.

Note that a try block does not need to have a catch clause at all. If there are no catch clauses, a finally clause may be used by itself if that is appropriate for the situation.

10.4 Exception Propagation

We can design our software so that an exception is caught and handled at an outer level in the method-calling hierarchy. If an exception is not caught and handled in the method where it occurs, control is immediately returned to the method that invoked the method that produced the exception. If it isn't caught there, control returns to the method that called it, and so on. This process is called *exception propagation*.

KEY CONCEPT
If an exception is not caught and handled where it occurs, it is propagated to the calling method.

An exception will be propagated until it is caught and handled or until it is passed out of the main method, which causes the program to terminate and produces an exception message. To catch an exception at any level, the method that produces the exception must be invoked inside a try block that has catch clauses to handle it.

The Propagation program shown in Listing 10.3 succinctly demonstrates the process of exception propagation. The main method invokes method level1 in the ExceptionScope class (see Listing 10.4 on page 450), which invokes level2, which invokes level3, which produces an exception. Method level3 does not catch and handle the exception, so control is transferred back to level2. The level2 method does not catch and handle the exception either, so control is transferred back to level1. Because the invocation of level2 is made inside a try block (in method level1), the exception is caught and handled at that point.

VideoNote
Proper exception handling

Note that the program output does not include the messages indicating that the methods level3 and level2 are ending. These println statements are never executed, because an exception occurred and had not yet been caught. However, after method level1 handles the exception, processing continues normally from that point, printing the messages indicating that method level1 and the program are ending.

KEY CONCEPT
A programmer must carefully consider how and where exceptions should be handled, if at all.

Note also that the catch clause that handles the exception uses the getMessage and printStackTrace methods to output that information. The stack trace shows the methods that were called when the exception occurred.

DESIGN FOCUS

A programmer must pick the most appropriate level at which to catch and handle an exception. There is no single best way to do this. It depends on the situation and the design of the system. Sometimes the right approach will be not to catch an exception at all and let the program terminate.

LISTING 10.3

```
//********************************************************************
//  Propagation.java       Java Foundations
//
//  Demonstrates exception propagation.
//********************************************************************

public class Propagation
{
   //-----------------------------------------------------------------
   //  Invokes the level1 method to begin the exception demonstration.
   //-----------------------------------------------------------------
   public static void main(String[] args)
   {
      ExceptionScope demo = new ExceptionScope();

      System.out.println("Program beginning.");
      demo.level1();
      System.out.println("Program ending.");
   }
}
```

OUTPUT

```
Program beginning.
Level 1 beginning.
Level 2 beginning.
Level 3 beginning.

The exception message is: / by zero
The call stack trace:
```

LISTING 10.3 *continued*

```
java.lang.ArithmeticException: / by zero
        at ExceptionScope.level3(ExceptionScope.java:54)
        at ExceptionScope.level2(ExceptionScope.java:41)
        at ExceptionScope.level1(ExceptionScope.java:18)
        at Propagation.main(Propagation.java:17)

Level 1 ending.
Program ending.
```

LISTING 10.4

```
//********************************************************************
//  ExceptionScope.java       Java Foundations
//
//  Demonstrates exception propagation.
//********************************************************************

public class ExceptionScope
{
   //-----------------------------------------------------------------
   //  Catches and handles the exception that is thrown in level3.
   //-----------------------------------------------------------------
   public void level1()
   {
      System.out.println("Level 1 beginning.");

      try
      {
         level2();
      }
      catch (ArithmeticException problem)
      {
         System.out.println();
         System.out.println("The exception message is: " +
                            problem.getMessage());
         System.out.println();
```

LISTING 10.4 *continued*

```
         System.out.println("The call stack trace:");
         problem.printStackTrace();
         System.out.println();
      }

      System.out.println("Level 1 ending.");
   }

   //-----------------------------------------------------------------
   //  Serves as an intermediate level. The exception propagates
   //  through this method back to level1.
   //-----------------------------------------------------------------
   public void level2()
   {
      System.out.println("Level 2 beginning.");
      level3 ();
      System.out.println("Level 2 ending.");
   }

   //-----------------------------------------------------------------
   //  Performs a calculation to produce an exception. It is not
   //  caught and handled at this level.
   //-----------------------------------------------------------------
   public void level3()
   {
      int numerator = 10, denominator = 0;

      System.out.println("Level 3 beginning.");
      int result = numerator / denominator;
      System.out.println("Level 3 ending.");
   }
}
```

10.5 The Exception Class Hierarchy

The classes that define various exceptions are related by inheritance, creating a class hierarchy that is shown in part in Figure 10.1 on the next page.

The `Throwable` class is the parent of both the `Error` class and the `Exception` class. Many types of exceptions are derived from the `Exception` class, and these

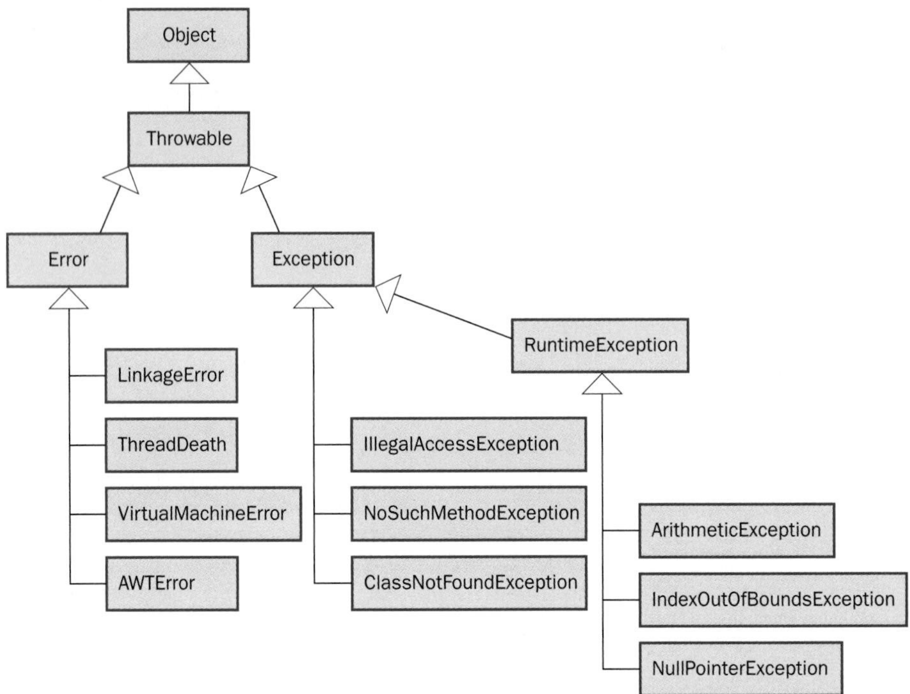

FIGURE 10.1 Part of the `Error` and `Exception` class hierarchy

classes also have many children. Although these high-level classes are defined in the `java.lang` package, many child classes that define specific exceptions are part of other packages. Inheritance relationships can span package boundaries.

We can define our own exceptions by deriving a new class from `Exception` or one of its descendants. The class we choose as the parent depends on what situation or condition the new exception represents.

The program in Listing 10.5 on page 453 instantiates an exception object and throws it. The exception is created from the `OutOfRangeException` class, which is shown in Listing 10.6 on page 454. This exception is not part of the Java standard class library. It was created to represent the situation in which a value is outside a particular valid range.

KEY CONCEPT
A new exception is defined by deriving a new class from the `Exception` class or one of its descendants.

After reading in an input value, the `main` method evaluates it to see whether it is in the valid range. If not, the *throw statement* is executed. A `throw` statement is used to begin exception propagation. Because the `main` method does not catch and handle the exception, the program will terminate if the exception is thrown, printing the message associated with the exception.

LISTING 10.5

```
//********************************************************************
//  CreatingExceptions.java       Java Foundations
//
//  Demonstrates the ability to define an exception via inheritance.
//********************************************************************

import java.util.Scanner;

public class CreatingExceptions
{
   //-----------------------------------------------------------------
   //  Creates an exception object and possibly throws it.
   //-----------------------------------------------------------------
   public static void main(String[] args) throws OutOfRangeException
   {
      final int MIN = 25, MAX = 40;

      Scanner scan = new Scanner(System.in);

      OutOfRangeException problem =
         new OutOfRangeException("Input value is out of range.");

      System.out.print("Enter an integer value between " + MIN +
                       " and " + MAX + ", inclusive: ");
      int value = scan.nextInt();

      // Determine if the exception should be thrown
      if (value < MIN || value > MAX)
         throw problem;

      System.out.println("End of main method."); // may never reach
   }
}
```

OUTPUT

```
Enter an integer value between 25 and 40, inclusive: 69
Exception in thread "main" OutOfRangeException:
        Input value is out of range.
        at CreatingExceptions.main(CreatingExceptions.java:20)
```

LISTING 10.6

```
//********************************************************************
//  OutOfRangeException.java       Java Foundations
//
//  Represents an exceptional condition in which a value is out of
//  some particular range.
//********************************************************************

public class OutOfRangeException extends Exception
{
   //-----------------------------------------------------------------
   // Sets up the exception object with a particular message.
   //-----------------------------------------------------------------
   OutOfRangeException(String message)
   {
      super(message);
   }
}
```

We created the `OutOfRangeException` class by extending the `Exception` class. Often, a new exception is nothing more than what you see in this example: an extension of some existing exception class that stores a particular message describing the situation it represents. The important point is that the class is ultimately a descendant of the `Exception` class and the `Throwable` class, which gives it the ability to be thrown using a `throw` statement.

The type of situation handled by this program, in which a value is out of range, does not need to be represented as an exception. We've previously handled such situations using conditionals or loops alone. Whether you handle a situation by using an exception or take care of it in the normal flow of your program is an important design decision.

Throwing an Exception

```
if (count > MAX)
   throw new MaxException("Count exceeds maximum.");
```

throw — Java keyword

new MaxException("Count exceeds maximum.") — create exception object

Checked and Unchecked Exceptions

Some exceptions are checked, whereas others are unchecked. A *checked exception* must either be caught by a method or be listed in the *throws clause* of any method that may throw or propagate it. A `throws` clause is appended to the header of a method definition to formally acknowledge that the method will throw or propagate a particular exception if it occurs. An *unchecked* exception requires no `throws` clause.

> **KEY CONCEPT**
> The `throws` clause on a method header must be included for checked exceptions that are not caught and handled in the method.

The only unchecked exceptions in Java are objects of type `RuntimeException` or any of its descendants. All other exceptions are considered checked exceptions. The `main` method of the `CreatingExceptions` program has a `throws` clause, indicating that it may throw an `OutOfRangeException`. This `throws` clause is required because the `OutOfRangeException` was derived from the `Exception` class, making it a checked exception.

10.6 I/O Exceptions

Processing input and output is a task that often produces tenuous situations, given that it relies on external resources such as user data and files. These resources can have various problems that lead to exceptions being thrown. Let's explore some I/O issues and the problems that may arise.

A *stream* is an ordered sequence of bytes. The term *stream* comes from the analogy that as we read and write information, the data flow from a source to a destination (or *sink*) as water flows down a stream. The source of the information is like a spring filling the stream, and the destination is like a cave into which the stream flows.

> **KEY CONCEPT**
> A stream is a sequential sequence of bytes; it can be used as a source of input or as a destination for output.

In a program, we treat a stream either as an *input stream*, from which we read information, or as an *output stream*, to which we write information. A program can deal with multiple input and output streams at one time. A particular store of data, such as a file, can serve either as an input stream or as an output stream to a program, but it generally cannot be both at the same time.

There are three streams that are referred to as the standard I/O streams. They are listed in Figure 10.2. The `System` class contains three object reference variables (`in`, `out`, and `err`) that represent the three standard I/O streams. These references are declared as both `public` and `static`, which allows them to be accessed directly through the `System` class.

> **KEY CONCEPT**
> Three public reference variables in the `System` class represent the standard I/O streams.

We've been using the standard output stream, with calls to `System.out.prinln` for instance, in examples throughout this text. We've also used the standard input stream to create a `Scanner` object when we want to process input

Standard I/O Stream	Description
`System.in`	Standard input stream.
`System.out`	Standard output stream.
`System.err`	Standard error stream (output for error messages).

FIGURE 10.2 Standard I/O streams

read interactively from the user. The `Scanner` class manages the input read from the standard input stream in various ways that make our programming tasks easier. It also processes various I/O exceptions internally, producing an `InputMismatchException` when needed.

The standard I/O streams, by default, represent particular I/O devices. `System.in` typically represents keyboard input, whereas `System.out` and `System.err` typically represent a particular window on the monitor screen. The `System.out` and `System.err` streams write output to the same window by default (usually the one in which the program was executed), although they could be set up to write to different places. The `System.err` stream is usually where error messages are sent.

KEY CONCEPT
The Java class library contains many classes for defining I/O streams with various characteristics.

In addition to the standard input streams, the `java.io` package of the Java standard class library provides many classes that enable us to define streams with particular characteristics. Some of the classes deal with files, others with memory, and others with strings. Some classes assume that the data they handle consist of characters, whereas others assume the data consist of raw bytes of binary information. Some classes provide the means to manipulate the data in the stream in some way, such as buffering the information or numbering it. By combining classes in appropriate ways, we can create objects that represent a stream of information that has exactly the characteristics we want for a particular situation.

The broad topic of Java I/O and the sheer number of classes in the `java.io` package prohibit us from covering it in detail in this text. Our focus for the moment is on I/O exceptions.

Many operations performed by I/O classes can potentially throw an `IOException`. The `IOException` class is the parent of several exception classes that represent problems when trying to perform I/O.

An `IOException` is a checked exception. As described earlier in this chapter, that means that either the exception must be caught or all methods that propagate it must list it in a `throws` clause of the method header.

Because I/O often deals with external resources, many problems can arise in programs that attempt to perform I/O operations. For example, a file from which we want to read might not exist; when we attempt to open the file, an exception will be thrown because that file can't be found. In general, we should try to design programs to be as robust as possible when dealing with potential problems.

We've seen in previous examples how we can use the `Scanner` class to read and process input read from a text file. Now let's explore an example that writes data to a text output file. Writing output to a text file requires simply that we use the appropriate classes to create the output stream and then call the appropriate methods to write the data.

Suppose we want to test a program we are writing, but we don't have the real data available. We could write a program that generates a test data file that contains random values. The program shown in Listing 10.7 generates a file that contains random integer values within a particular range. It also writes one line of standard output, confirming that the data file has been written.

LISTING 10.7

```
//********************************************************************
//  TestData.java Java   Foundations
//
//  Demonstrates I/O exceptions and the use of a character file
//  output stream.
//********************************************************************

import java.util.Random;
import java.io.*;

public class TestData
{
   //-----------------------------------------------------------------
   //  Creates a file of test data that consists of ten lines each
   //  containing ten integer values in the range 10 to 99.
   //-----------------------------------------------------------------
   public static void main(String[] args) throws IOException
   {
      final int MAX = 10;
      int value;
      String file = "test.dat";

      Random rand = new Random();

      FileWriter fw = new FileWriter(file);
      BufferedWriter bw = new BufferedWriter(fw);
      PrintWriter outFile = new PrintWriter(bw);
```

LISTING 10.7 *continued*

```
      for (int line=1; line <= MAX; line++)
      {
         for (int num=1; num <= MAX; num++)
         {
            value = rand.nextInt(90) + 10;
            outFile.print(value + " ");
         }
         outFile.println();
      }

      outFile.close();
      System.out.println("Output file has been created: " + file);
   }
}
```

OUTPUT

```
Output file has been created: test.dat
```

The `FileWriter` class represents a text output file but has minimal method support for manipulating data. The `PrintWriter` class provides `print` and `println` methods similar to the standard I/O `PrintStream` class.

Although we do not need to do so for the program to work, we have added a layer in the file stream configuration to include a `BufferedWriter`. This addition simply gives the output stream buffering capabilities, which makes the processing more efficient. Although buffering is not crucial in this situation, it is usually a good idea when writing text files.

Note that in the `TestData` program, we have eliminated explicit exception handling. That is, if something goes wrong, we simply allow the program to terminate instead of specifically catching and handling the problem. Because all `IOExceptions` are checked exceptions, we must include the `throws` clause on the method header to indicate that they may be thrown. For each program, we must carefully consider how best to handle the exceptions that may be thrown. This requirement is especially important when dealing with I/O, which is fraught with potential problems that cannot always be foreseen.

KEY CONCEPT

Output file streams should be explicitly closed, or they may not correctly retain the data written to them.

The `TestData` program uses nested `for` loops to compute random values and write them to the output file. After all values are printed, the file is closed. Output files must be closed explicitly to ensure that the data are retained. In general, it is good practice to close all file streams explicitly when they are no longer needed.

The data contained in the file `test.dat` after the `TestData` program is run might look like this:

```
85 90 93 15 82 79 52 71 70 98
74 57 41 66 22 16 67 65 24 84
86 61 91 79 18 81 64 41 68 81
98 47 28 40 69 10 85 82 64 41
23 61 27 10 59 89 88 26 24 76
33 89 73 36 54 91 42 73 95 58
19 41 18 14 63 80 96 30 17 28
24 37 40 64 94 23 98 10 78 50
89 28 64 54 59 23 61 15 80 88
51 28 44 48 73 21 41 52 35 38
```

Summary of Key Concepts

- Errors and exceptions are objects that represent unusual or invalid processing.
- The messages printed when an exception is thrown provide a method call stack trace.
- Each `catch` clause handles a particular kind of exception that may be thrown within the `try` block.
- The `finally` clause is executed whether the `try` block is exited normally or because of a thrown exception.
- If an exception is not caught and handled where it occurs, it is propagated to the calling method.
- A programmer must carefully consider how and where exceptions should be handled, if at all.
- A new exception is defined by deriving a new class from the `Exception` class or one of its descendants.
- The `throws` clause on a method header must be included for checked exceptions that are not caught and handled in the method.
- A stream is a sequential sequence of bytes; it can be used as a source of input or as a destination for output.
- Three public reference variables in the `System` class represent the standard I/O streams.
- The Java class library contains many classes for defining I/O streams with various characteristics.
- Output file streams should be explicitly closed, or they may not correctly retain the data written to them.

Summary of Terms

call stack trace A list of the method calls that resulted in an exception being thrown.

`catch` clause The portion of a `try-catch` statement that handles a particular category of exception.

checked exception An exception that must be caught by a method or listed in the `throws` clause of the method header.

error An object that represents a problem from which the program cannot recover.

exception An object that represents an unusual or erroneous situation.

exception handler Code that responds to a particular type of exception when it is thrown. It is usually implemented using a `catch` clause in a `try-catch` statement.

exception propagation The process of an exception, when thrown, cascading up the call stack until it is caught or causes the program to abnormally terminate.

`finally` clause A clause in a `try-catch` statement that is executed no matter how the `try` block is exited (with a thrown exception or not).

input stream Any source of data.

output stream Any place to which data are written.

`try-catch` statement A statement used to intercept a thrown exception and respond in an appropriate way.

unchecked exception An exception that is not required to be caught or explicitly declared.

Self-Review Questions

SR 10.1 In what ways might a thrown exception be handled?

SR 10.2 What is a `catch` phrase?

SR 10.3 What happens if an exception is not caught?

SR 10.4 What is a `finally` clause?

SR 10.5 What is a checked exception?

SR 10.6 What is a stream?

SR 10.7 What are the standard I/O streams?

Exercises

EX 10.1 Create a UML class diagram for the `ProductCodes` program.

EX 10.2 Describe the output for the `ProductCodes` program if a `finally` clause were added to the `try` statement that printed the string `"Got here!"`.

EX 10.3 What would happen if the `try` statement were removed from the `level1` method of the `ExceptionScope` class in the `Propagation` program?

EX 10.4 What would happen if the `try` statement described in the previous exercise were moved to the `level2` method?

EX 10.5 What happens when the `Exception` class is used in a `catch` clause to catch an exception?

EX 10.6 Look up the following exception classes in the online Java API documentation, and describe their purpose:

a. `ArithmeticException`

b. `NullPointerException`

c. `NumberFormatException`

d. `PatternSyntaxException`

EX 10.7 Describe the output file used in the `TestData` program in terms of the classes that were used to create it.

Programming Projects

PP 10.1 Design and implement a program that reads a series of 10 integers from the user and prints their average. Read each input value as a string, and then attempt to convert it to an integer using the `Integer.parseInt` method. If this process throws a `NumberFormatException` (meaning that the input is not a valid number), print an appropriate error message and prompt for the number again. Continue reading values until 10 valid integers have been entered.

PP 10.2 Design and implement a program that creates an exception class called `StringTooLongException`, designed to be thrown when a string is discovered that has too many characters in it. In the `main` driver of the program, read strings from the user until the user enters `"DONE"`. If a string that has too many characters (say 20) is entered, throw the exception. Allow the thrown exception to terminate the program.

PP 10.3 Modify the solution to Programming Project 10.2 such that it catches and handles the exception if it is thrown. Handle the exception by printing an appropriate message, and then continue processing more strings.

PP 10.4 Design and implement a program that creates an exception class called `InvalidDocumentCodeException`, designed to be thrown when an improper designation for a document is encountered during processing. Suppose that in a particular business, all documents are given a two-character designation starting with U, C, or P, which stand for unclassified, confidential, or proprietary. If a document designation is encountered that doesn't fit that description, the exception is thrown. Create a driver program to test the exception, allowing it to terminate the program.

PP 10.5 Modify the solution to Programming Project 10.4 such that it catches and handles the exception if it is thrown. Handle the exception by printing an appropriate message, and then continue processing.

PP 10.6 Write a program that reads strings from the user and writes them to an output file called `userStrings.dat`. Terminate processing when the user enters the string `"DONE"`. Do not write the sentinel string to the output file.

PP 10.7 Suppose a library is processing an input file containing the titles of books in order to remove duplicates. Write a program that reads all of the titles from an input file called `bookTitles.inp` and writes them to an output file called `noDuplicates.out`. When complete, the output file should contain all unique titles found in the input file.

Answers to Self-Review Questions

SRA 10.1 A thrown exception can be handled in one of three ways. It can be ignored, which will cause a program to terminate; it can be handled where it occurs using a `try` statement; or it can be caught and handled higher in the method-calling hierarchy.

SRA 10.2 A `catch` phrase of a `try` statement defines the code that will handle a particular type of exception.

SRA 10.3 If an exception is not caught immediately when thrown, it begins to propagate up through the methods that were called to get to the point where it was generated. The exception can be caught and handled at any point during that propagation. If it propagates out of the `main` method, the program terminates.

SRA 10.4 The `finally` clause of a `try-catch` statement is executed no matter how the `try` block is exited. If no exception is thrown, the `finally` clause is executed after the `try` block is complete. If an exception is thrown, the appropriate `catch` clause is executed, and then the `finally` clause is executed.

SRA 10.5 A checked exception is an exception that must be either (1) caught and handled or (2) listed in the `throws` clause of any method that may throw or propagate it. This establishes a set of exceptions that must be formally acknowledged in the program one way or another. Unchecked exceptions can be ignored completely in the code, if desired.

SRA 10.6 A stream is a sequential series of bytes that serves as a source of input or a destination for output.

SRA 10.7 The standard I/O streams in Java are `System.in`, the standard input stream; `System.out`, the standard output stream; and `System.err`, the standard error stream. Usually, standard input comes from the keyboard, and standard output and errors go to a default window on the monitor screen.

Analysis of Algorithms

11

CHAPTER OBJECTIVES

- Discuss the goals of software development with respect to efficiency.
- Introduce the concept of algorithm analysis.
- Explore the concept of asymptotic complexity.
- Compare various growth functions.

It is important that we understand the concepts surrounding the efficiency of algorithms before we begin building data structures. A data structure built correctly and with an eye toward efficient use of both the CPU and memory is one that can be reused effectively in many different applications. However, using a data structure that is not built efficiently is similar to using a damaged original as the master from which to make copies.

11.1 Algorithm Efficiency

One of the most important computer resources is CPU time. The efficiency of an algorithm we use to accomplish a particular task is a major factor that determines how fast a program executes. Although the techniques that we will discuss here may also be used to analyze an algorithm in terms of the amount of memory it uses, we will focus our discussion on the efficient use of processing time.

KEY CONCEPT
Algorithm analysis is a fundamental computer science topic.

The *analysis of algorithms* is a fundamental computer science topic and involves a variety of techniques and concepts. It is a primary theme that we return to throughout this text. This chapter introduces the issues related to algorithm analysis and lays the groundwork for using analysis techniques.

Let's start with an everyday example: washing dishes by hand. If we assume that washing a dish takes 30 seconds and drying a dish takes an additional 30 seconds, then we can see quite easily that it would take n minutes to wash and dry n dishes. This computation could be expressed as follows:

$$\begin{aligned}\text{Time } (n \text{ dishes}) &= n * (30 \text{ seconds wash time } + 30 \text{ seconds dry time}) \\ &= 60n \text{ seconds}\end{aligned}$$

or, written more formally,

$$f(x) = 30x + 30x$$
$$f(x) = 60x$$

On the other hand, suppose we were careless while washing the dishes and splashed too much water around. Suppose each time we washed a dish, we had to dry not only that dish but also all of the dishes we had washed before that one. It would still take 30 seconds to wash each dish, but now it would take 30 seconds to dry the last dish (once), 2 * 30 or 60 seconds to dry the second-to-last dish (twice), 3 * 30 or 90 seconds to dry the third-to-last dish (three times), and so on. This computation could be expressed as follows:

$$\text{Time } (n \text{ dishes}) = n * (30 \text{ seconds wash time } + \sum_{i=1}^{n}(i * 30)$$

When we use the formula for an arithmetic series, $\sum_{1}^{n} i = n(n + 1)/2$, the function becomes

$$\begin{aligned}\text{Time } (n \text{ dishes}) &= 30n + 30n(n + 1)/2 \\ &= 15n^2 + 45n \text{ seconds}\end{aligned}$$

If there were 30 dishes to wash, the first approach would take 30 minutes, whereas the second (careless) approach would take 247.5 minutes. The more dishes we wash, the worse that discrepancy becomes. For example, if there were 300 dishes to wash, the first approach would take 300 minutes, or 5 hours, whereas the second approach would take 908,315 minutes, or roughly 15,000 hours!

11.2 Growth Functions and Big-Oh Notation

For every algorithm we want to analyze, we need to define the size of the problem. For our dishwashing example, the size of the problem is the number of dishes to be washed and dried. We also must determine the value that represents efficient use of time or space. For time considerations, we often pick an appropriate processing step that we'd like to minimize, such as our goal to minimize the number of times a dish has to be washed and dried. The overall amount of time spent on the task is directly related to how many times we have to perform that task. The algorithm's efficiency can be defined in terms of the problem size and the processing step.

Consider an algorithm that sorts a list of numbers into increasing order. One natural way to express the size of the problem would be the number of values to be sorted. The processing step we are trying to optimize could be expressed as the number of comparisons we have to make for the algorithm to put the values in order. The more comparisons we make, the more CPU time is used.

KEY CONCEPT

A growth function shows time or space utilization relative to the problem size.

A *growth function* shows the relationship between the size of the problem (n) and the value we hope to optimize. This function represents the *time complexity* or *space complexity* of the algorithm.

The growth function for our second dishwashing algorithm is

$$t(n) = 15n^2 + 45n$$

However, it is not typically necessary to know the exact growth function for an algorithm. Instead, we are mainly interested in the *asymptotic complexity* of an algorithm. That is, we want to focus on the general nature of the function as n increases. This characteristic is based on the *dominant term* of the expression—the term that increases most quickly as n increases. As n gets very large, the value of the dishwashing growth function is dominated by the n^2 term because the n^2 term grows much faster than the n term. The constants, in this case 15 and 45, and the secondary term, in this case $45n$, quickly become irrelevant as n increases. That is to say, the value of n^2 dominates the growth in the value of the expression.

The table in Figure 11.1 shows how the two terms and the value of the expression grow. As you can see from the table, as n gets larger, the $15n^2$ term dominates the value of the expression. It is important to note that the $45n$ term is larger for

Number of dishes (n)	15n²	45n	15n² + 45n
1	15	45	60
2	60	90	150
5	375	225	600
10	1,500	450	1,950
100	150,000	4,500	154,500
1,000	15,000,000	45,000	15,045,000
10,000	1,500,000,000	450,000	1,500,450,000
100,000	150,000,000,000	4,500,000	150,004,500,000
1,000,000	15,000,000,000,000	45,000,000	15,000,045,000,000
10,000,000	1,500,000,000,000,000	450,000,000	1,500,000,450,000,000

FIGURE 11.1 Comparison of terms in growth function

very small values of n. Saying that a term is the dominant term as n gets large does not mean that it is larger than the other terms for all values of n.

The asymptotic complexity is called the *order* of the algorithm. Thus, our second dishwashing algorithm is said to have order n^2 time complexity, which is written $O(n^2)$. Our first, more efficient dishwashing example, with growth function $t(n) = 60(n)$, would have order n time complexity, which is written $O(n)$. Thus the reason for the difference between our $O(n)$ original algorithm and our $O(n^2)$ sloppy algorithm is the fact each dish will have to be dried multiple times.

KEY CONCEPT
The order of an algorithm is found by eliminating constants and all but the dominant term in the algorithm's growth function.

This notation is referred to as O(), or Big-Oh, notation. A growth function that executes in constant time regardless of the size of the problem is said to have O(1). In general, we are concerned only with executable statements in a program or algorithm in determining its growth function and efficiency. Keep in mind, however, that some declarations may include initializations, and some of these may be complex enough to factor into the efficiency of an algorithm.

As an example, assignment statements and if statements that are executed only once, regardless of the size of the problem, are O(1). Therefore, it does not matter how many of those you string together; it is still O(1). Loops and method calls may result in higher-order growth functions because they may result in a statement or series of statements being executed more than once based on the size of the problem. We will discuss these separately in later sections of this chapter. Figure 11.2 shows several growth functions and their asymptotic complexity.

KEY CONCEPT
The order of an algorithm provides an upper bound to the algorithm's growth function.

More formally, saying that the growth function $t(n) = 15n^2 + 45n$ is $O(n^2)$ means that there exist a constant m and some value of n (n_0), such that $t(n) \leq m * n^2$ for all $n > n_0$. Another way of stating this is to say that the order of an algorithm provides an upper bound to its growth function. It is also important to note that there are other related notations such as

Growth Function	Order	Label
$t(n) = 17$	$O(1)$	constant
$t(n) = 3\log n$	$O(\log n)$	logarithmic
$t(n) = 20n - 4$	$O(n)$	linear
$t(n) = 12n \log n + 100n$	$O(n \log n)$	n log n
$t(n) = 3n^2 + 5n - 2$	$O(n^2)$	quadratic
$t(n) = 8n^3 + 3n^2$	$O(n^3)$	cubic
$t(n) = 2^n + 18n^2 + 3n$	$O(2^n)$	exponential

FIGURE 11.2 Some growth functions and their asymptotic complexities

omega (Ω), which refers to a function that provides a lower bound, and theta (Θ), which refers to a function that provides both an upper and a lower bound. Our discussion will focus on order.

Because the order of the function is the key factor, the other terms and constants are often not even mentioned. All algorithms within a given order are considered to be generally equivalent in terms of efficiency. For example, even though two algorithms to accomplish the same task may have different growth functions, if they are both $O(n^2)$, then they are considered to be roughly equivalent with respect to efficiency.

11.3 Comparing Growth Functions

One might assume that, with the advances in the speed of processors and the availability of large amounts of inexpensive memory, algorithm analysis would no longer be necessary. However, nothing could be further from the truth. Processor speed and memory cannot make up for the differences in efficiency of algorithms. Keep in mind that constants are often eliminated as irrelevant when one is discussing the order of an algorithm. Increasing processor speed simply adds a constant to the growth function. When possible, finding a more efficient algorithm is a better solution than finding a faster processor.

Another way of looking at the effect of algorithm complexity was proposed by Aho, Hopcroft, and Ullman (1974). If a system can currently handle a problem of size n in a given time period, what happens to the allowable size of the problem if we increase the speed of the processor tenfold? As shown in Figure 11.3, the linear case is relatively simple. Algorithm A, with a linear time complexity of n, is indeed improved by a factor of 10, which means that this algorithm can process 10 times as much data in the same amount of time, given a tenfold speedup of the processor. However, algorithm B, with a time complexity of n^2, is improved by a factor of only 3.16. Why do we not get the full tenfold increase in problem size? Because the complexity of algorithm B is n^2, our effective speedup is only the square root of 10, or 3.16.

Algorithm	Time Complexity	Max Problem Size Before Speedup	Max Problem Size After Speedup
A	n	s_1	$10s_1$
B	n^2	s_2	$3.16s_2$
C	n^3	s_3	$2.15s_3$
D	2^n	s_4	$s_4 + 3.3$

FIGURE 11.3 Increase in problem size with a tenfold increase in processor speed

Similarly, algorithm C, with complexity n^3, is improved by a factor of only 2.15, or the cube root of 10. For algorithms with *exponential complexity* like algorithm D, in which the size variable is in the exponent of the complexity term, the situation is far worse. The speedup is $\log_2 n$, or in this case, 3.3. Note that this is not a factor of 3, but the original problem size plus 3. In the grand scheme of things, if an algorithm is inefficient, speeding up the processor will not help.

KEY CONCEPT
When the algorithm is inefficient, a faster processor will not help in the long run.

Figure 11.4 illustrates various growth functions graphically for relatively small values of n. Note that when n is small, there is little difference between the algorithms. That is, if you can guarantee a very small problem size (5 or less), it doesn't really matter which algorithm is used.

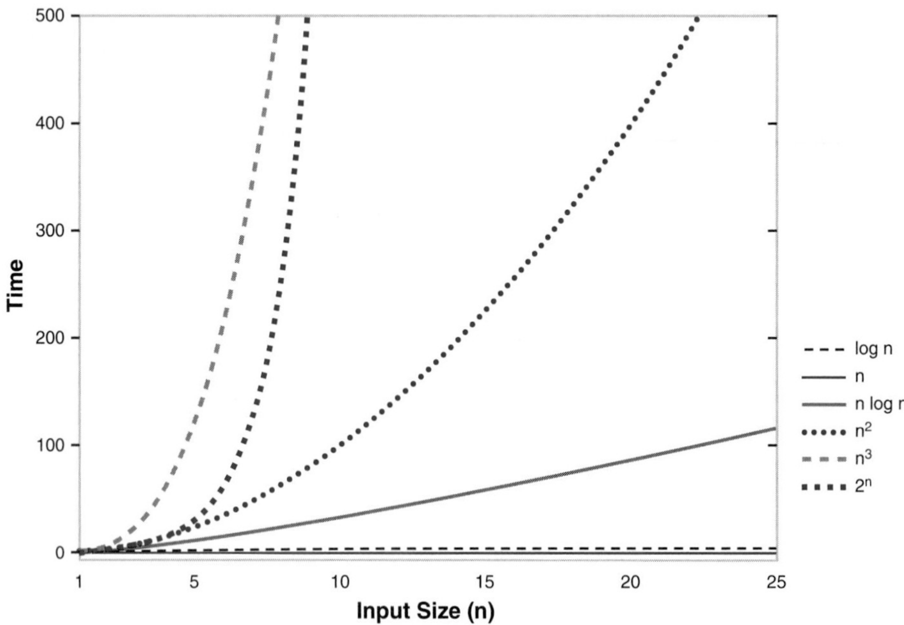

FIGURE 11.4 Comparison of typical growth functions for small values of n

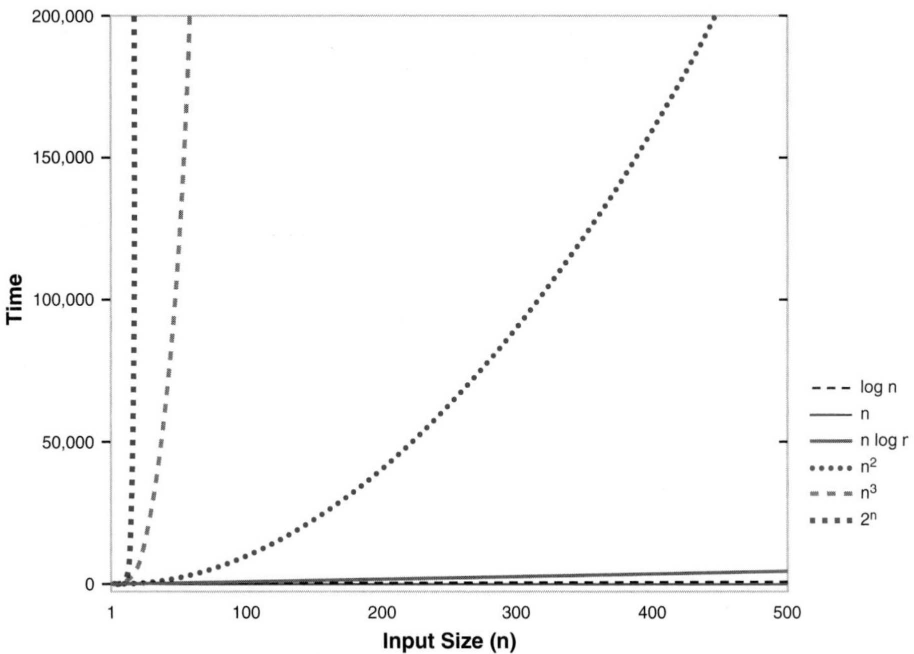

FIGURE 11.5 Comparison of typical growth functions for large values of n

However, notice that in Figure 11.5, as n gets very large, the differences between the growth functions become obvious.

11.4 Determining Time Complexity

Analyzing Loop Execution

To determine the order of an algorithm, we have to determine how often a particular statement or set of statements gets executed. Therefore, we often have to determine how many times the body of a loop is executed. To analyze loop execution, first determine the order of the body of the loop, and then multiply that by the number of times the loop will execute relative to n. Keep in mind that n represents the problem size.

KEY CONCEPT
Analyzing algorithm complexity often requires analyzing the execution of loops.

Assuming that the body of a loop is O(1), then a loop such as

```
for (int count = 0; count < n; count++)
{
   /* some sequence of O(1) steps */
}
```

will have $O(n)$ time complexity. This is due to the fact that the body of the loop has $O(1)$ complexity but is executed n times by the loop structure. In general, if a loop structure steps through n items in a linear fashion and the body of the loop is $O(1)$, then the loop is $O(n)$. Even in a case where the loop is designed to skip some number of elements, as long as the progression of elements to skip is linear, the loop is still $O(n)$. For example, if the preceding loop skipped every other number (e.g., count += 2), the growth function of the loop would be $n/2$, but since constants don't affect the asymptotic complexity, the order is still $O(n)$.

Let's look at another example. If the progression of the loop is logarithmic, as it is in the loop

```
count = 1
while (count < n)
{
   count *= 2;
   /* some sequence of O(1) steps */
}
```

KEY CONCEPT
The time complexity of a loop is found by multiplying the complexity of the body of the loop by how many times the loop will execute.

then the loop is said to be $O(\log n)$. Note that when we use a logarithm in an algorithm complexity, we almost always mean log base 2. This can be explicitly written as $O(\log^2 n)$. Since each time through the loop the value of `count` is multiplied by 2, the number of times the loop is executed is $\log^2 n$.

Nested Loops

A slightly more interesting scenario arises when loops are nested. In this case, we must multiply the complexity of the outer loop by the complexity of the inner loop to find the resulting complexity. For example, the nested loops

```
for (int count = 0; count < n; count++)
{
   for (int count2 = 0; count2 < n; count2++)
   {
      /* some sequence of O(1) steps */
   }
}
```

have complexity $O(n^2)$. The body of the inner loop is $O(1)$ and the inner loop will execute n times. This means the inner loop is $O(n)$. Multiplying this result by the number of times the outer loop will execute (n) results in $O(n^2)$.

What is the complexity of the following nested loop?

```
for (int count = 0; count < n; count++)
{
   for (int count2 = count; count2 < n; count2++)
   {
      /* some sequence of O(1) steps */
   }
}
```

KEY CONCEPT
The analysis of nested loops must take into account both the inner loop and the outer loop.

In this case, the inner loop index is initialized to the current value of the index for the outer loop. The outer loop executes n times. The inner loop executes n times the first time, $n - 1$ times the second time, and so on. However, remember that we are interested only in the dominant term, not in constants or any lesser terms. If the progression is linear, then regardless of whether some elements are skipped, the order is still $O(n)$. Thus the complexity for this code is $O(n^2)$.

Method Calls

Let's suppose that we have the following segment of code:

```
for (int count = 0; count < n; count++)
{
   printsum(count);
}
```

We know from our previous discussion that we find the order of the loop by multiplying the order of the body of the loop by the number of times the loop will execute. In this case, however, the body of the loop is a method call. Therefore, we must determine the order of the method before we can determine the order of the code segment. Let's suppose that the purpose of the method is to print the sum of the integers from 1 to n each time it is called. We might be tempted to create a brute force method such as the following:

```
public void printsum(int count)
{
   int sum = 0;
   for (int i = 1; i < count; i++)
      sum += i;
   System.out.println(sum);
}
```

What is the time complexity of this `printsum` method? Keep in mind that only executable statements contribute to the time complexity, so in this case, all of the executable statements are O(1) except for the loop. The loop, on the other hand, is O(n), and thus the method itself is O(n). Now, to compute the time complexity of the original loop that called the method, we simply multiply the complexity of the method, which is the body of the loop, by the number of times the loop will execute. Our result, then, is O(n^2) using this implementation of the printsum method.

However, we know from our earlier discussion that we do not have to use a loop to calculate the sum of the numbers from 1 to n. In fact, we know that $\sum_1^n i = n(n + 1)/2$. Now let's rewrite our printsum method and see what happens to our time complexity:

```
public void printsum(int count)
{
   sum = count*(count+1)/2;
   System.out.println (sum);
}
```

Now the time complexity of the printsum method is made up of an assignment statement, which is O(1), and a print statement, which is also O(1). The result of this change is that the time complexity of the printsum method is now O(1), which means that the loop that calls this method goes from O(n^2) to O(n). We know from our earlier discussion and from Figure 11.5 that this is a very significant improvement. Once again, we see that there is a difference between delivering correct results and doing so efficiently.

What if the body of a method is made up of multiple method calls and loops? Consider the following code using our printsum method above:

```
public void sample(int n)
{
  printsum(n);                          /* this method call is O(1) */
  for (int count = 0; count < n; count++) /* this loop is O(n) */
    printsum (count);
  for (int count = 0; count < n; count++)    /* this loop is O(n²) */
      for (int count2 = 0; count2 < n; count2++)
        System.out.println (count, count2);
}
```

The initial call to the printsum method with the parameter temp is O(1), because the method is O(1). The for loop containing the call to the printsum method with the parameter count is O(n), because the method is O(1) and the loop executes n times. The nested loops are O(n^2), because the inner loop will execute n times each time the outer loop executes, and the outer loop will also execute n times. The entire method is then O(n^2) since only the dominant term matters.

More formally, the growth function for the method sample is given by

$$f(x) = 1 + n + n^2$$

Then, given that we eliminate constants and all but the dominant term, the time complexity is $O(n^2)$.

There is one additional issue we must deal with when analyzing the time complexity of method calls, and that is recursion, the situation wherein a method calls itself. We will save that discussion for Chapter 17.

Summary of Key Concepts

- Software must make efficient use of resources such as CPU time and memory.
- Algorithm analysis is a fundamental computer science topic.
- A growth function shows time or space utilization relative to the problem size.
- The order of an algorithm is found by eliminating constants and all but the dominant term in the algorithm's growth function.
- The order of an algorithm provides an upper bound to the algorithm's growth function.
- When the algorithm is inefficient, a faster processor will not help in the long run.
- Analyzing algorithm complexity often requires analyzing the execution of loops.
- The time complexity of a loop is found by multiplying the complexity of the body of the loop by the number of times the loop will execute.
- The analysis of nested loops must take into account both the inner loop and the outer loop.

Summary of Terms

analysis of algorithms The computer science topic area that focuses on the efficiency of software algorithms.

Big-Oh notation The notation used to represent the order, or asymptotic complexity, of a function.

growth function A function that describes time or space utilization relative to the problem size.

asymptotic complexity A limit on a growth function, defined by the growth function's dominant term and characterizing similar functions into a general category.

Self-Review Questions

SR 11.1 What is the difference between the growth function of an algorithm and the order of that algorithm?

SR 11.2 Why does speeding up the CPU not necessarily speed up the process by the same amount?

SR 11.3 How do we use the growth function of an algorithm to determine its order?

SR 11.4 How do we determine the time complexity of a loop?

SR 11.5 How do we determine the time complexity of a method call?

Exercises

EX 11.1 What is the order of each of the following growth functions?

a. $10n^2 + 100n + 1000$
b. $10n^3 - 7$
c. $2^n + 100n^3$
d. $n^2 \log n$

EX 11.2 Arrange the growth functions of the previous exercise in ascending order of efficiency for $n = 10$ and again for $n = 1{,}000{,}000$.

EX 11.3 Write the code necessary to find the largest element in an unsorted array of integers. What is the time complexity of this algorithm?

EX 11.4 Determine the growth function and order of the following code fragment:

```
for (int count=0; count < n; count++)
{
   for (int count2=0; count2 < n; count2=count2+2)
   {
      System.out.println(count + ", " + count2);
   }
}
```

EX 11.5 Determine the growth function and order of the following code fragment:

```
for (int count=0; count < n; count++)
{
   for (int count2=1; count2 < n; count2=count2*2)
   {
      System.out.println(count + ", " + count2);
   }
}
```

EX 11.6 The table in Figure 11.1 shows how the terms of the growth function for our dishwashing example are related to one another as n grows. Write a program that will create such a table for any given growth function.

Answers to Self-Review Questions

SRA 11.1 The growth function of an algorithm represents the exact relationship between the problem size and the time complexity of the solution. The order of the algorithm is the asymptotic time complexity. As the size of the problem grows, the complexity of the algorithm approaches the asymptotic complexity.

SRA 11.2 Linear speedup occurs only if the algorithm has constant order, O(1), or linear order, O(n). As the complexity of the algorithm grows, faster processors have significantly less impact.

SRA 11.3 The order of an algorithm is found by eliminating constants and all but the dominant term from the algorithm's growth function.

SRA 11.4 The time complexity of a loop is found by multiplying the time complexity of the body of the loop by the number of times the loop will execute.

SRA 11.5 The time complexity of a method call is found by determining the time complexity of the method and then substituting that for the method call.

References

Aho, A. V., J. E. Hopcroft, and J. D. Ullman. *The Design and Analysis of Computer Algorithms*. Reading, Mass.: Addison-Wesley, 1974.

Introduction to Collections—Stacks

12

CHAPTER OBJECTIVES

- Define the concepts and terminology related to collections.
- Explore the basic structure of the Java Collections API.
- Discuss the abstract design of collections.
- Define a stack collection.
- Use a stack collection to solve a problem.
- Examine an array implementation of a stack.

This chapter begins our exploration of collections and the underlying data structures used to implement them. It lays the groundwork for the study of collections by carefully defining the issues and goals related to their design. This chapter also introduces a collection called a stack and uses it to exemplify the issues related to the design, implementation, and use of collections.

12.1 Collections

A *collection* is an object that gathers and organizes other objects. It defines the specific ways in which those objects, which are called *elements* of the collection, can be accessed and managed. The user of a collection, which is usually another class or object in the software system, must interact with the collection only in the prescribed ways.

KEY CONCEPT
A collection is an object that gathers and organizes other objects.

Over time, several specific types of collections have been defined by software developers and researchers. Each type of collection lends itself to solving particular kinds of problems. A large portion of this text is devoted to exploring these classic collections.

Collections can be separated into two broad categories: linear and nonlinear. As the name implies, a *linear collection* is one in which the elements of the collection are organized in a straight line. A *nonlinear collection* is one in which the elements are organized in something other than a straight line, such as a hierarchy or a network. For that matter, a nonlinear collection may not have any organization at all.

KEY CONCEPT
Elements in a collection are typically organized in terms of the order of their addition to the collection or in terms of some inherent relationship among the elements.

Figure 12.1 shows a linear collection and a nonlinear collection. It usually doesn't matter whether the elements in a linear collection are depicted horizontally or vertically.

The organization of the elements in a collection, relative to each other, is usually determined by one of two things:

- The order in which they were added to the collection
- Some inherent relationship among the elements themselves

FIGURE 12.1 A linear collection and a nonlinear collection

For example, one linear collection may always add new elements to one end of the line, so the order of the elements is determined by the order in which they are added. Another linear collection may be kept in sorted order based on some characteristic of the elements. For example, a list of people may be kept in alphabetic order based on the characters that make up their name. The specific organization of the elements in a nonlinear collection can be determined in either of these two ways as well.

Abstract Data Types

An *abstraction* hides certain details at certain times. Dealing with an abstraction is easier than dealing with too many details at one time. In fact, we couldn't get through a day without relying on abstractions. For example, we couldn't possibly drive a car if we had to worry about all the details that make the car work: the spark plugs, the pistons, the transmission, and so on. Instead, we can focus on the *interface* to the car: the steering wheel, the pedals, and a few other controls. These controls are an abstraction, hiding the underlying details and allowing us to control an otherwise very complicated machine.

A collection, like any well-designed object, is an abstraction. A collection defines the interface operations through which the user can manage the objects in the collection, such as adding and removing elements. The user interacts with the collection through this interface, as depicted in Figure 12.2. However, the details of how a collection is implemented to fulfill that definition are another issue altogether. A class that implements the collection's interface must fulfill the conceptual definition of the collection, but it can do so in many ways.

> **KEY CONCEPT**
> A collection is an abstraction where the details of the implementation are hidden.

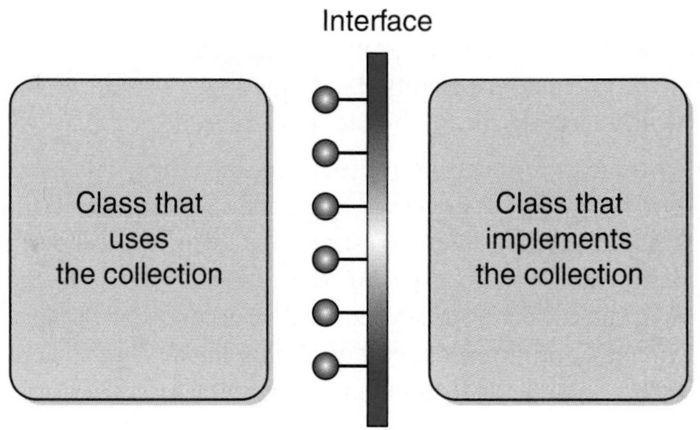

FIGURE 12.2 A well-defined interface masks the implementation of the collection

Abstraction is another important software engineering concept. In large software systems, it is virtually impossible for any one person to grasp all of the details of the system at once. Instead, the system is divided into abstract subsystems such that the purpose of those subsystems and the interactions among them can be specified. Subsystems may then be assigned to different developers or groups of developers who will develop the subsystem to meet its specification.

An object is the perfect mechanism for creating a collection, because if it is designed correctly, the internal workings of an object are *encapsulated* from the rest of the system. In most cases, the instance variables defined in a class should be declared with private visibility. Therefore, only the methods of that class can access and modify them. The only interaction a user has with an object should be through its public methods, which represent the services that the object provides.

As we progress through our exploration of collections, we will always stress the idea of separating the interface from the implementation. Therefore, for every collection that we examine, we should consider the following:

- How does the collection operate, conceptually?
- How do we formally define the interface to the collection?
- What kinds of problems does the collection help us solve?
- What support is already available to us for this type of collection?
- In which various ways might we implement the collection?
- What are the benefits and costs of each implementation?

Before we continue, let's carefully define some other terms related to the exploration of collections. A *data type* is a group of values and the operations defined on those values. The primitive data types defined in Java are the primary examples. For example, the integer data type defines a set of numeric values and the operations (addition, subtraction, etc.) that can be used on them.

An *abstract data type* (ADT) is a data type whose values and operations are not inherently defined within a programming language. It is abstract only in that the details of its implementation must be defined and should be hidden from the user. A collection, therefore, is an abstract data type.

A *data structure* is the collection of programming constructs used to implement a collection. For example, a collection might be implemented using a fixed-size structure such as an array. One interesting artifact of these definitions and our design decision to separate the interface from the implementation (i.e., the collection from the data structure that implements it) is that we may, and often do, end up with a linear data structure, such as an array, being used to implement a nonlinear collection, such as a tree.

KEY CONCEPT

A data structure is the underlying programming construct used to implement a collection.

Historically, the terms *ADT* and *data structure* have been used in various ways. We carefully define them here to avoid any confusion, and we will use them consistently. Throughout this text, we will examine various data structures and how they can be used to implement various collections.

The Java Collections API

The Java programming language is accompanied by a very large library of classes that can be used to support the development of software. Parts of the library are organized into *application programming interfaces* (APIs). The *Java Collections API* is a set of classes that represent a few specific types of collections, implemented in various ways.

You might ask why we should learn how to design and implement collections if a set of collections has already been provided for us. There are several reasons. First, the Java Collections API provides only a subset of the collections you may want to use. Second, the classes that are provided may not implement the collections in the ways you desire. Third, and perhaps most important, the study of software development requires a deep understanding of the issues involved in the design of collections and the data structures used to implement them.

As we explore various types of collections, we will also examine the appropriate classes of the Java Collections API. In each case, we will analyze the various implementations that we develop and compare them to the approach used by the classes in the standard library.

12.2 A Stack Collection

Let's look at an example of a collection. A *stack* is a linear collection whose elements are added to, and removed from, the same end. We say that a stack is processed in a *last in, first out* (LIFO) manner. That is, the last element to be put on a stack will be the first one that gets removed. Said another way, the elements of a stack are removed in the reverse order of their placement on it. In fact, one of the principal uses of a stack in computing is to reverse the order of something (such as an undo operation).

KEY CONCEPT

Stack elements are processed in a LIFO manner—the last element in is the first element out.

The processing of a stack is shown in Figure 12.3. Usually a stack is depicted vertically, and we refer to the end to which elements are added and from which they are removed as the *top* of the stack.

Recall from our earlier discussions that we define an abstract data type (ADT) by identifying a specific set of operations that establishes the valid ways in which we can manage the elements stored in the data structure. We always want to use this concept to formally define the operations for a collection and work within

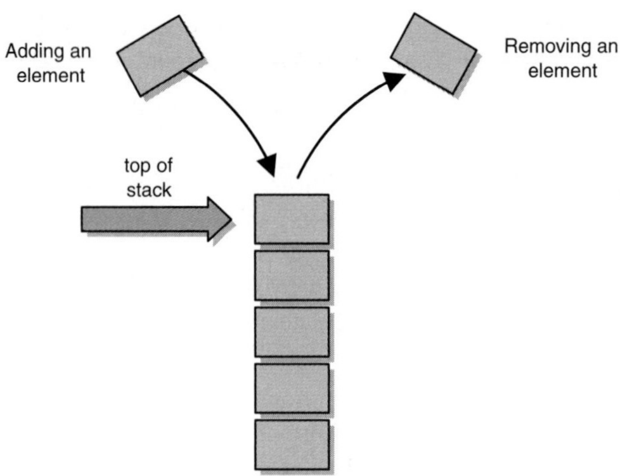

FIGURE 12.3 A conceptual view of a stack

the functionality it provides. That way, we can cleanly separate the interface to the collection from any particular implementation technique used to create it.

The operations for a stack ADT are listed in Figure 12.4. In stack terminology, we *push* an element onto a stack, and we *pop* an element off a stack. We can also *peek* at the top element of a stack, examining it or using it as needed, without actually removing it from the collection. And there are general operations that enable us to determine whether the stack is empty and, if it is not empty, how many elements it contains.

KEY CONCEPT
A programmer should choose the structure that is appropriate for the type of data management needed.

Sometimes there are variations on the naming conventions for the operations on a collection. For a stack, the use of the terms *push* and *pop* is relatively standard. The `peek` operation is sometimes referred to as *top*.

Operation	Description
`push`	Adds an element to the top of the stack.
`pop`	Removes an element from the top of the stack.
`peek`	Examines the element at the top of the stack.
`isEmpty`	Determines if the stack is empty.
`size`	Determines the number of elements on the stack.

FIGURE 12.4 The operations on a stack

DESIGN FOCUS

In the design of the stack ADT, we see the separation between the role of the stack and the role of the application that is using the stack. Notice that any implementation of this stack ADT is expected to throw an exception if a `pop` or `peek` operation is requested on an empty stack. The role of the collection is not to determine how such an exception is handled but merely to report it back to the application using the stack. Similarly, the concept of a full stack does not exist in the stack ADT. Thus, it is the role of the stack collection to manage its own storage to eliminate the possibility of being full.

Keep in mind that the definition of a collection is not universal. You will find variations in the operations defined for specific data structures from one text to another. We've been very careful in this text to define the operations on each collection so that they are consistent with its purpose.

For example, note that none of the stack operations in Figure 12.4 enables us to reach down into the stack to modify, remove, or reorganize the elements in the stack. That is the very nature of a stack—all activity occurs at one end. If we discover that, to solve a particular problem, we need to access the elements in the middle or at the bottom of the collection, then a stack is not the appropriate collection to use.

We do provide a `toString` operation for the collection. This is not a classic operation defined for a stack, and it could be argued that this operation violates the prescribed behavior of a stack. However, it provides a convenient means to traverse and display the stack's contents without allowing modification of the stack and this is quite useful for debugging purposes.

12.3 Crucial OO Concepts

Now let's consider what we will store in our stack. One possibility would be to simply recreate our stack data structure each time we need it and create it to store the specific object type for that application. For example, if we needed a stack of strings, we would simply copy and paste our stack code and change the object type to `String`. Even though copy, paste, and modify is technically a form of reuse, this brute force type of reuse is not our goal. Reuse, in its purest form, should mean that we create a collection that is written once, is compiled into byte code once, and will then handle any objects we choose to store in it safely, efficiently, and effectively. To accomplish these goals, we must take *type compatibility* and *type checking* into account. Type compatibility indicates whether a particular assignment of an object to a reference is legal. For example, the following assignment is not legal because you cannot assign a reference declared to be of type `String` to point to an object of type `Integer`.

```
String x = new Integer(10);
```

Java provides compile-time type checking that will flag this invalid assignment. A second possibility of what to store in our collection is to take advantage of the concepts of *inheritance* and *polymorphism* to create a collection that can store objects of any class.

Inheritance and Polymorphism

A complete discussion of the concepts of inheritance and polymorphism is provided in Appendix B. To review, a *polymorphic reference* is a reference variable that can refer to different types of objects at different points in time. Inheritance can be used to create a class hierarchy where a reference variable can be used to point to any object related to it by inheritance.

Carrying this to the extreme, an `Object` reference can be used to refer to any object, because ultimately all classes are descendants of the `Object` class. An `ArrayList`, for example, uses polymorphism in that it is designed to hold `Object` references. That's why an `ArrayList` can be used to store any kind of object. A particular `ArrayList` can hold several different types of objects at one time, because they are all objects compatible with type `Object`.

The result of this discussion would seem to be that we could simply store `Object` references in our stack and take advantage of polymorphism via inheritance to create a collection that can store any type of objects. However, this possible solution creates some unexpected consequences. Because in this chapter we focus on implementing a stack with an array, let's examine what can happen when dealing with polymorphic references and arrays. Consider our classes represented in Figure 12.5. Since `Animal` is a superclass of all of the other classes in this diagram, an assignment such as the following is allowable:

```
Animal creature = new Bird();
```

However, this also means that the following assignments will compile as well:

```
Animal[] creatures = new Mammal[];
creatures[1] = new Reptile();
```

Note that by definition, `creatures[1]` should be both a `Mammal` and an `Animal`, but not a `Reptile`. This code will compile but will generate a

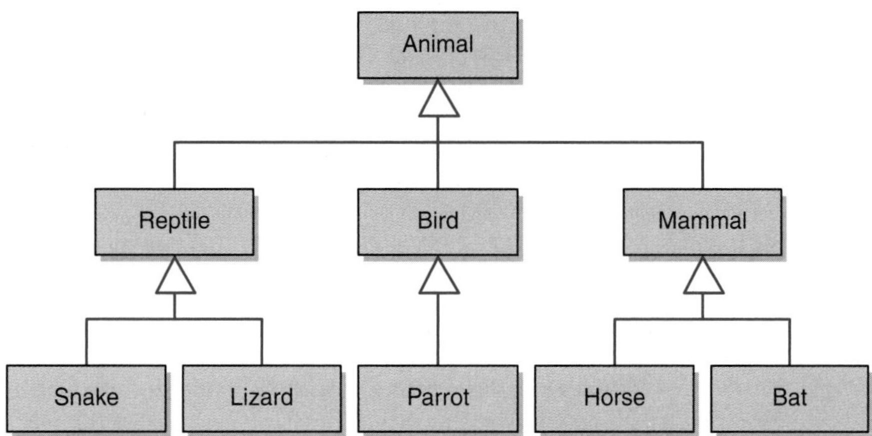

FIGURE 12.5 A UML class diagram showing a class hierarchy

`java.lang.ArrayStoreException` at run-time. Thus, because using the `Object` class will not provide us with compile-time type checking, we should look for a better solution.

Generics

Beginning with Java 5.0, Java enables us to define a class based on a *generic type*. That is, we can define a class so that it stores, operates on, and manages objects whose type is not specified until the class is instantiated. Generics are an integral part of our discussions of collections and their underlying implementations throughout the rest of this text.

Let's assume we need to define a class called `Box` that stores and manages other objects. As we discussed, using polymorphism, we could simply define `Box` so that internally it stores references to the `Object` class. Then, any type of object could be stored inside a box. In fact, multiple types of unrelated objects could be stored in `Box`. We lose a lot of control with that level of flexibility in our code.

A better approach is to define the `Box` class to store a generic type `T`. (We can use any identifier we want for the generic type, but using `T` has become a convention.) The header of the class contains a reference to the type in angle brackets. For example:

```
class Box<T>
{
   // declarations and code that manage objects of type T
}
```

Then, when a Box is needed, it is instantiated with a specific class used in place of T. For example, if we wanted a Box of Widget objects, we could use the following declaration:

```
Box<Widget> box1 = new Box<Widget>();
```

The type of the box1 variable is Box<Widget>. In essence, for the box1 object, the Box class replaces T with Widget. Now suppose we wanted a Box in which to store Gadget objects; we could make the following declaration:

```
Box<Gadget> box2 = new Box<Gadget>();
```

For box2, the Box class essentially replaces T with Gadget. So, although the box1 and box2 objects are both boxes, they have different types because the generic type is taken into account. This is a safer implementation, because at this point we cannot use box1 to store gadgets (or anything else for that matter), nor could we use box2 to store widgets. A generic type such as T cannot be instantiated. It is merely a placeholder to allow us to define the class that will manage a specific type of object that is established when the class is instantiated.

Given that we now have a mechanism using generic types for creating a collection that can be used to store any type of object safely and effectively, let's continue on with our discussion of the stack collection.

The following section explores in detail an example of using a stack to solve a problem.

12.4 Using Stacks: Evaluating Postfix Expressions

Traditionally, arithmetic expressions are written in *infix* notation, meaning that the operator is placed between its operands in the form

<operand> <operator> <operand>

such as in the expression

```
4 + 5
```

When evaluating an infix expression, we rely on precedence rules to determine the order of operator evaluation. For example, the expression

```
4 + 5 * 2
```

evaluates to 14 rather than 18 because of the precedence rule that in the absence of parentheses, multiplication evaluates before addition.

In a *postfix* expression, the operator comes after its two operands. Therefore, a postfix expression takes the form

<operand> <operator> <operand>

For example, the postfix expression

```
6 9 -
```

is equivalent to the infix expression

```
6 - 9
```

A postfix expression is generally easier to evaluate than an infix expression because precedence rules and parentheses do not have to be taken into account. The order of the values and operators in the expression is sufficient to determine the result. For this reason, programming language compilers and run-time environments often use postfix expressions in their internal calculations.

The process of evaluating a postfix expression can be stated in one simple rule: *Scanning from left to right, apply each operation to the two operands immediately preceding it and replace the operator with the result.* At the end we are left with the final value of the expression.

Consider the infix expression we looked at earlier:

```
4 + 5 * 2
```

In postfix notation, this expression would be written

```
4 5 2 * +
```

Let's use our evaluation rule to determine the final value of this expression. We scan from the left until we encounter the multiplication (`*`) operator. We apply this operator to the two operands immediately preceding it (`5` and `2`) and replace it with the result (`10`), which leaves us with

```
4 10 +
```

Continuing our scan from left to right, we immediately encounter the plus (`+`) operator. Applying this operator to the two operands immediately preceding it (`4` and `10`) yields `14`, which is the final value of the expression.

Let's look at a slightly more complicated example. Consider the following infix expression:

```
(3 * 4 - (2 + 5)) * 4 / 2
```

The equivalent postfix expression is

```
3 4 * 2 5 + - 4 * 2 /
```

Applying our evaluation rule results in

```
        12 2 5 + - 4 * 2 /
then    12 7 - 4 * 2 /
then    5 4 * 2 /
then    20 2 /
then    10
```

Now let's consider the design of a program that will evaluate a postfix expression. The evaluation rule relies on being able to retrieve the previous two operands whenever we encounter an operator. Furthermore, a large postfix expression will have many operators and operands to manage. It turns out that a stack is the perfect collection to use in this case. The operations provided by a stack coincide nicely with the process of evaluating a postfix expression.

KEY CONCEPT

A stack is the ideal data structure to use when evaluating a postfix expression.

The algorithm for evaluating a postfix expression using a stack can be expressed as follows: Scan the expression from left to right, identifying each token (operator or operand) in turn. If it is an operand, push it onto the stack. If it is an operator, pop the top two elements off the stack, apply the operation to them, and push the result onto the stack. When we reach the end of the expression, the element remaining on the stack is the result of the expression. If at any point we attempt to pop two elements off the stack but there are not two elements on the stack, then our postfix expression was not properly formed. Similarly, if we reach the end of the expression and more than one element remains on the stack, then our expression was not well formed. Figure 12.6 depicts the use of a stack to evaluate a postfix expression.

The `PostfixTester` program in Listing 12.1 evaluates multiple postfix expressions entered by the user. It uses the `PostfixEvaluator` class shown in Listing 12.2.

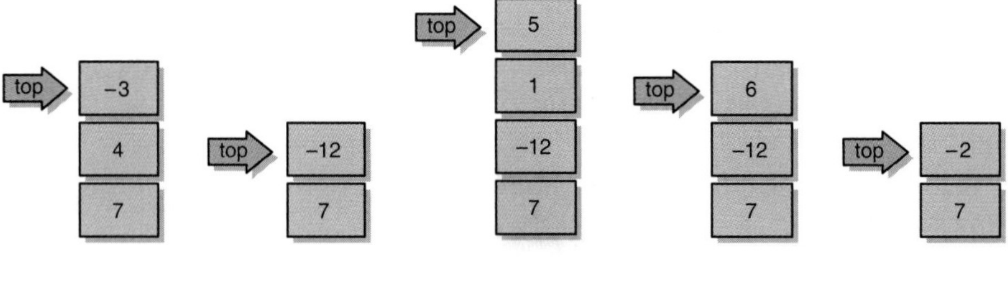

FIGURE 12.6 Using a stack to evaluate a postfix expression

LISTING 12.1

```
import java.util.Scanner;

/**
 * Demonstrates the use of a stack to evaluate postfix expressions.
 *
 * @author Java Foundations
 * @version 4.0
 */
public class PostfixTester
{

   /**
    * Reads and evaluates multiple postfix expressions.
    */
   public static void main(String[] args)
   {
      String expression, again;
      int result;

      Scanner in = new Scanner(System.in);

      do
      {
         PostfixEvaluator evaluator = new PostfixEvaluator();
         System.out.println("Enter a valid post-fix expression one token " +
            "at a time with a space between each token (e.g. 5 4 + 3 2 1 - + *)");

         System.out.println("Each token must be an integer or an operator (+,-,*,/)");
         expression = in.nextLine();

         result = evaluator.evaluate(expression);
         System.out.println();
         System.out.println("That expression equals " + result);

         System.out.print("Evaluate another expression [Y/N]? ");
         again = in.nextLine();
         System.out.println();
      }
      while (again.equalsIgnoreCase("y"));
   }
}
```

LISTING 12.2

```
import java.util.Stack;
import java.util.Scanner;

/**
 * Represents an integer evaluator of postfix expressions. Assumes
 * the operands are constants.
 *
 * @author Java Foundations
 * @version 4.0
 */
public class PostfixEvaluator
{
  private final static char ADD = '+';
  private final static char SUBTRACT = '-';
  private final static char MULTIPLY = '*';
  private final static char DIVIDE = '/';

  private Stack<Integer> stack;

  /**
   * Sets up this evalutor by creating a new stack.
   */
  public PostfixEvaluator()
  {
      stack = new Stack<Integer>();
  }

  /**
   * Evaluates the specified postfix expression. If an operand is
   * encountered, it is pushed onto the stack. If an operator is
   * encountered, two operands are popped, the operation is
   * evaluated, and the result is pushed onto the stack.
   * @param expr string representation of a postfix expression
   * @return value of the given expression
   */
  public int evaluate(String expr)
  {
     int op1, op2, result = 0;
     String token;
     Scanner parser = new Scanner(expr);

     while (parser.hasNext())
     {
        token = parser.next();
```

LISTING 12.2 *continued*

```
        if (isOperator(token))
          {
             op2 = (stack.pop()).intValue();
             op1 = (stack.pop()).intValue();
             result = evaluateSingleOperator(token.charAt(0), op1, op2);
             stack.push(new Integer(result));
         }
         else
           stack.push(new Integer(Integer.parseInt(token)));
      }
      return result;
    }

    /**
     * Determines if the specified token is an operator.
     * @param token the token to be evaluated
     * @return true if token is operator
     */
    private boolean isOperator(String token)
    {
      return ( token.equals("+") || token.equals("-") ||
               token.equals("*") || token.equals("/") );
    }

    /**
     * Peforms integer evaluation on a single expression consisting of
     * the specified operator and operands.
     * @param operation operation to be performed
     * @param op1 the first operand
     * @param op2 the second operand
     * @return value of the expression
     */
    private int evaluateSingleOperator(char operation, int op1, int op2)
    {
      int result = 0;

      switch (operation)
      {
         case ADD:
             result = op1 + op2;
             break;
         case SUBTRACT:
```

LISTING 12.2 *continued*

```
                result = op1 - op2;
                break;
            case MULTIPLY:
                result = op1 * op2;
                break;
            case DIVIDE:
                result = op1 / op2;
        }

        return result;
    }
}
```

To keep things simple, this program assumes that the operands to the expression are integers and are literal values (not variables). When executed, the program repeatedly accepts and evaluates postfix expressions until the user chooses not to.

The `PostfixEvaluator` class uses the `java.util.Stack` class to create the stack attribute. The `java.util.Stack` class is one of two stack implementations provided by the Java Collections API. We revisit the other implementation, the `Deque` interface in Chapter 13.

The `evaluate` method performs the evaluation algorithm described earlier, supported by the `isOperator` and `evalSingleOp` methods. Note that in the `evaluate` method, only operands are pushed onto the stack. Operators are used as they are encountered and are never put on the stack. This is consistent with the evaluation algorithm we discussed. An operand is put on the stack as an `Integer` object, instead of as an `int` primitive value, because the stack data structure is designed to store objects.

When an operator is encountered, the two most recent operands are popped off the stack. Note that the first operand popped is actually the second operand in the expression and that the second operand popped is the first operand in the expression. This order doesn't matter in the cases of addition and multiplication, but it certainly matters for subtraction and division.

Note also that the postfix expression program assumes that the postfix expression entered is valid, meaning that it contains a properly organized set of operators and operands. A postfix expression is invalid if either (1) two operands are not available on the stack when an operator is encountered or (2) there is more than one value on the stack when the tokens in the expression are exhausted. Either situation indicates that there was something wrong with the format of the expression, and both can be caught by examining the state of the stack at the appropriate point in the program. We will discuss how we might deal with these situations and other exceptional cases in the next section.

Perhaps the most important aspect of this program is the use of the class that defined the stack collection. At this point, we don't know how the stack was implemented. We simply trusted the class to do its job. In this example, we used the class `java.util.Stack`, but we could have used any class that implemented a stack as long as it performed the stack operations as expected. From the point of view of evaluating postfix expressions, the manner in which the stack is implemented is largely irrelevant. Figure 12.7 shows a UML class diagram for the postfix expression evaluation program. The diagram illustrates that the `PostfixEvaluator` class uses an `Integer` instance of the `java.util.Stack` class and represents the binding of the `Integer` to the generic type `T`. We will not always include this level of detail in our UML diagrams.

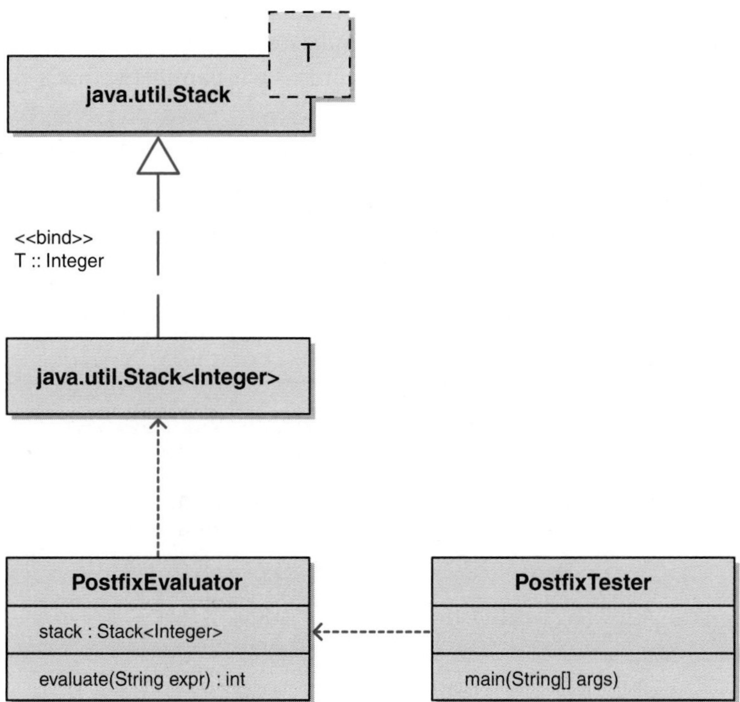

FIGURE 12.7 UML class diagram for the postfix expression evaluation program

Javadoc

Before moving on, let's mention the documentation style used for comments in Listing 12.1 and 12.2. These are *Javadoc comments*, which are written in a format that allows the javadoc tool to parse the comments and extract information about the classes and methods. Javadoc comments begin with a `/**` and end with a `*/`.

Javadoc is used to create online documentation in HTML about a set of classes. You've already seen the results; the online Java API documentation is created using this technique. When changes are made to the API classes (and their comments), the javadoc tool is run again to generate the documentation. It's a clever way to ensure that the documentation does not lag behind the evolution of the code.

There's nothing special about the Java API classes in this regard. Documentation for any program or set of classes can be generated using Javadoc. And even if it's not used to generate online documentation, the Javadoc commenting style is the official standard for adding comments to Java code.

Javadoc tags are used to identify particular types of information. For example, the `@author` tag is used to identify the programmer who wrote the code. The `@version` tag is used to specify the version number of the code. In the header of a method, the `@return` tag is used to indicate what value is returned by the method and the `@param` tag is used to identify each parameter that's passed to the method.

We won't discuss Javadoc further at this point, but we will use the Javadoc commenting style throughout the remainder of this text.

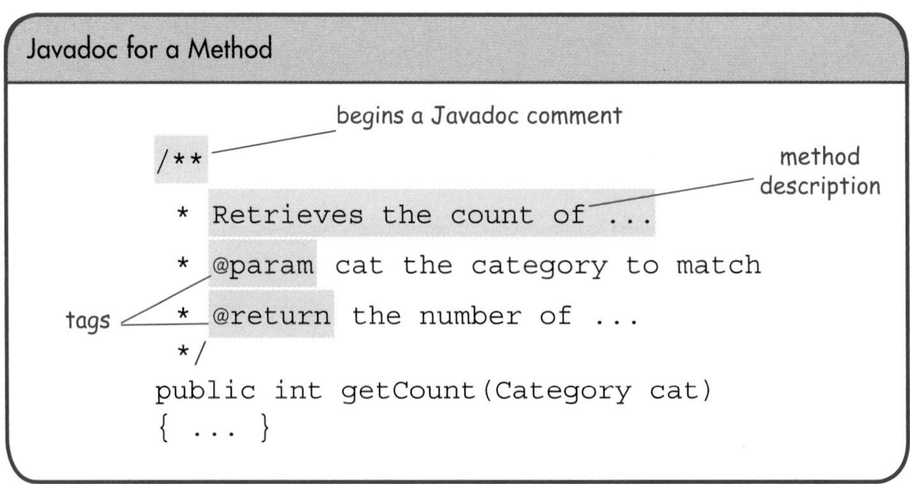

12.5 Exceptions

One concept that we will explore with each of the collections we discuss is that of exceptional behavior. What action should the collection take in the exceptional case? There are some such cases that are inherent in the collection itself. For example, in the case of a stack, what should happen if an attempt is made to pop an element from an empty stack? In this case, it does not matter what data structure is being used to implement the collection; the exception will still apply. Some such cases are artifacts of the data structure being used to implement the collection. For example, if we are using an array to implement a stack, what should happen if an attempt is made to push an element onto the stack but the array is full? Let's take a moment to explore this concept further.

As discussed in Chapter 10, problems that arise in a Java program may generate exceptions or errors. An *exception* is an object that defines an unusual or erroneous situation. An exception is thrown by a program or the run-time environment, and it can be caught and handled appropriately if desired. An *error* is similar to an exception, except that an error generally represents an unrecoverable situation, and it should not be caught. Java has a predefined set of exceptions and errors that may occur during the execution of a program.

In our postfix evaluation example, there were several potential exceptional situations. For example:

- If the stack were full on a push
- If the stack were empty on a pop
- If the stack held more than one value at the completion of the evaluation

Let's consider each of these separately. The possibility that the stack might be full on a push is an issue for the underlying data structure, not the collection. Conceptually speaking, there is no such thing as a full stack. Now we know that this is not reality and that all data structures will eventually reach a limit. However, even when this physical limit is reached, the stack is not full; only the data structure that implements the stack is full. We will discuss strategies for handling this situation as we implement our stack in the next section.

What if the stack is empty on a pop? This is an exceptional case that has to do with the problem, not the underlying data structure. In our postfix evaluation example, if we attempt to pop two operands and there are not two operands available on the stack, our postfix expression was not properly formed. This is a case where the collection needs to report the exception and the application then must interpret that exception in context.

The third case is equally interesting. What if the stack holds more than one value at the completion of the evaluation? From the perspective of the stack

KEY CONCEPT
Errors and exceptions represent unusual or invalid processing.

collection, this is not an exception. However, from the perspective of the application, this is a problem that means once again that the postfix expression was not well formed. Because it will not generate an exception from the collection, this is a condition for which the application must test.

Appendix B includes a complete discussion of exceptions and exception handling, including exception propagation and the try/catch statement. As we explore particular implementation techniques for a collection, we will also discuss the appropriate use of exceptions.

12.6 A Stack ADT

To facilitate separation of the interface operations from the methods that implement them, we can define a Java interface structure for a collection. A Java interface provides a formal mechanism for defining the set of operations for any collection.

KEY CONCEPT
A Java interface defines a set of abstract methods and is useful in separating the concept of an abstract data type from its implementation.

Recall that a Java interface defines a set of abstract methods, specifying each method's signature but not its body. A class that implements an interface provides definitions for the methods defined in the interface. The interface name can be used as the type of a reference, which can be assigned any object of any class that implements the interface.

Listing 12.3 defines a Java interface for a stack collection. We name a collection interface using the collection name followed by the abbreviation ADT (for abstract data type). Thus, `StackADT.java` contains the interface for a stack collection. It is defined as part of the `jsjf` package, which contains all of the collection classes and interfaces presented in this book.

KEY CONCEPT
By using the interface name as a return type, we ensure that the interface doesn't commit the method to the use of any particular class that implements a stack.

Note that the stack interface is defined as `StackADT<T>`, operating on a generic type `T`. In the methods of the interface, the type of various parameters and return values is often expressed using the generic type `T`. When this interface is implemented, it will be based on a type that is substituted for `T`.

Each time we introduce an interface, a class, or a system in this text, we will accompany that description with the UML description of that interface, class, or system. This should help you become accustomed to reading UML descriptions and to creating them for other classes and systems. Figure 12.8 illustrates the UML description of the `StackADT` interface.

Stacks are used quite frequently in the computing world. For example, the undo operation in a word processor is usually implemented using a stack. As we

LISTING 12.3

```
package jsjf;

/**
 * Defines the interface to a stack collection.
 *
 * @author Java Foundations
 * @version 4.0
 */
public interface StackADT<T>
{
  /**
   * Adds the specified element to the top of this stack.
   * @param element element to be pushed onto the stack
   */
  public void push(T element);

  /**
   * Removes and returns the top element from this stack.
   * @return the element removed from the stack
   */
  public T pop();

  /**
   * Returns without removing the top element of this stack.
   * @return the element on top of the stack
   */
  public T peek();

  /**
   * Returns true if this stack contains no elements.
   * @return true if the stack is empty
   */
  public boolean isEmpty();

  /**
   * Returns the number of elements in this stack.
   * @return the number of elements in the stack
   */
  public int size();

  /**
   * Returns a string representation of this stack.
   * @return a string representation of the stack
   */
  public String toString();
}
```

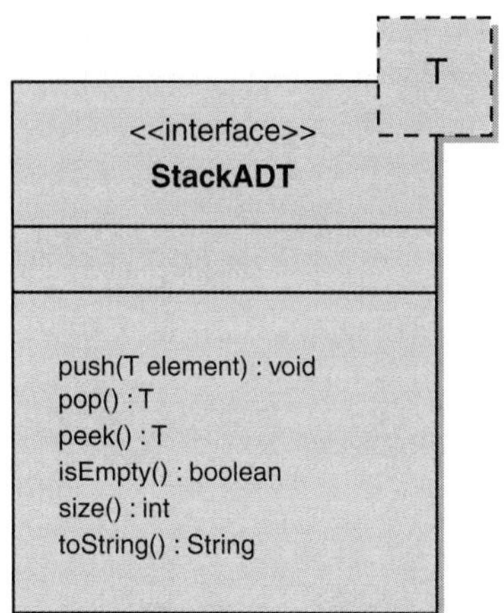

FIGURE 12.8 The `StackADT` interface in UML

Stack Interface

reserved word — interface name — generic type parameter

```
public interface StackADT <T>
{
   . . .
}
```

(`interface`: reserved word; `StackADT`: interface name; `<T>`: generic type parameter; `. . .`: list of method signatures)

make changes to a document (add data, delete data, make format changes, etc.), the word processor keeps track of each operation by pushing some representation of it onto a stack. If we choose to undo an operation, the word processing software pops the most recently performed operation off the stack and reverses it.

DESIGN FOCUS

Undo operations are often implemented using a special type of stack called a drop-out stack. The basic operations on a drop-out stack are the same as those for a stack (`push`, `pop`, and `peek`). The only difference is that a drop-out stack has a limit to the number of elements it will hold, and once that limit is reached, the element on the bottom of the stack drops off the stack when a new element is pushed on. The development of a drop-out stack is left as an exercise.

If we choose to undo again (undoing the second-to-last operation we performed), another element is popped from the stack. In most word processors, many operations can be reversed in this manner.

12.7 Implementing a Stack: With Arrays

So far in our discussion of a stack collection we have described its basic conceptual nature and the operations that allow the user to interact with it. In software engineering terms, we would say that we have done the analysis for a stack collection. We have also used a stack, without knowing the details of how it was implemented, to solve a particular problem. Now let's turn our attention to the implementation details. There are various ways to implement a class that represents a stack. As mentioned earlier, the Java Collections API provides multiple implementations including the `Stack` class and the `Deque` interface. In this section, we examine an implementation strategy that uses an array to store the objects contained in the stack. In the next chapter, we examine a second technique for implementing a stack.

KEY CONCEPT
The implementation of the collection operations should not affect the way users interact with the collection.

To explore this implementation, we must recall several key characteristics of Java arrays. The elements stored in an array are indexed from 0 to $n - 1$, where n is the total number of cells in the array. An array is an object, which is instantiated separately from the objects it holds. And when we talk about an array of objects, we are actually talking about an array of references to objects, as illustrated in Figure 12.9.

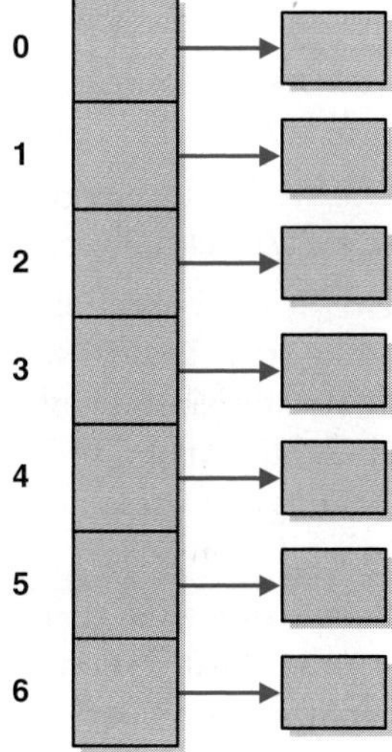

FIGURE 12.9 An array of object references

Keep in mind the separation between the collection and the underlying data structure used to implement it. Our goal is to design an efficient implementation that provides the functionality of every operation defined in the stack abstract data type. The array is just a convenient data structure in which to store the objects.

Managing Capacity

When an array object is created, it is allocated a specific number of cells into which elements can be stored. For example, the following instantiation creates an array that can store 500 elements, indexed from 0 to 499:

```
Object[] collection = Object[500];
```

The number of cells in an array is called its *capacity*. This value is stored in the `length` constant of the array. The capacity of an array cannot be changed once the array has been created.

When using an array to implement a collection, we have to deal with the situation in which all cells of the array are being used to store elements. That is, because we are using a fixed-size data structure, at some point the data structure may become "full." However, just because the data structure is full, should that mean that the collection is full?

A crucial question in the design of a collection is what to do in the case in which a new element is added to a full data structure. Three basic options exist:

- We could implement operations that add an element to the collection such that they throw an exception if the data structure is full.
- We could implement the `add` operations to return a status indicator that can be checked by the user to see whether the `add` operation was successful.
- We could automatically expand the capacity of the underlying data structure whenever necessary so that, essentially, it would never become full.

In the first two cases, the user of the collection must be aware that the collection could get full and must take steps to deal with it when needed. For these solutions we would also provide extra operations that allow the user to check to see whether the collection is full and to expand the capacity of the data structure as desired. The advantage of these approaches is that they give the user more control over the capacity.

KEY CONCEPT

How we handle exceptional conditions determines whether the collection or the user of the collection controls the particular behavior.

However, given that our goal is to separate the interface from the implementation, the third option is attractive. The capacity of the underlying data structure is an implementation detail that, in general, should be hidden from the user. Furthermore, the capacity issue is particular to this implementation. Other techniques used to implement the collection, such as the one we explore in the next chapter, are not restricted by a fixed capacity and therefore never have to deal with this issue.

In the solutions presented in this text, we opt to implement fixed data structure solutions by automatically expanding the capacity of the underlying data structure. Occasionally, other options are explored as programming projects.

12.8 The `ArrayStack` Class

In the Java Collections API framework, class names indicate both the underlying data structure and the collection. We follow that naming convention in this text. Thus, we define a class called `ArrayStack` to represent a stack with an underlying array-based implementation.

To be more precise, we define a class called `ArrayStack<T>` that represents an array-based implementation of a stack collection that stores objects of generic type `T`. When we instantiate an `ArrayStack` object, we specify what the generic type `T` represents.

An array implementation of a stack can be designed by making the following four assumptions: The array is an array of object references (type determined when the stack is instantiated), the bottom of the stack is always at index 0 of the array, the elements of the stack are stored in order and contiguously in the array, and there is an integer variable `top` that stores the index of the array immediately following the top element in the stack.

KEY CONCEPT
For efficiency, an array-based stack implementation keeps the bottom of the stack at index 0.

Figure 12.10 illustrates this configuration for a stack that currently contains the elements A, B, C, and D, assuming that they have been pushed on in that order. To simplify the figure, the elements are shown in the array itself rather than as objects referenced from the array. Note that the variable `top` represents both the next cell into which a pushed element should be stored and the count of the number of elements currently in the stack.

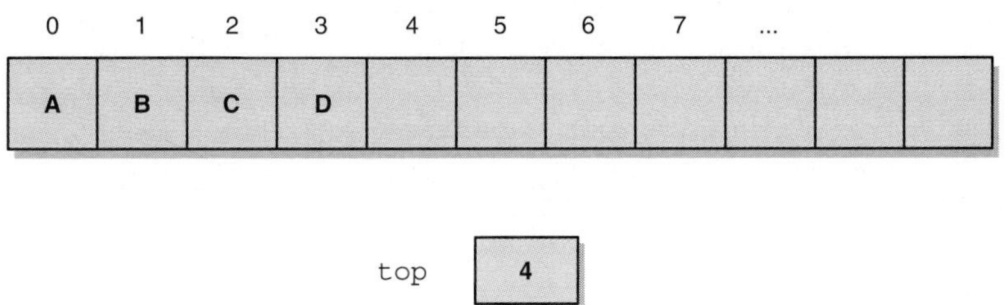

FIGURE 12.10 An array implementation of a stack

VideoNote
An overview of the ArrayStack implementation.

In this implementation, the bottom of the stack is always held at index 0 of the array, and the stack grows and shrinks at the higher indexes. This is considerably more efficient than if the stack were reversed within the array. Consider the processing that would be necessary if the top of the stack were kept at index 0.

From these assumptions, we can determine that our class will need a constant to store the default capacity, a variable to keep track of the top of the stack, and a variable for the array to store the stack. This results in the following class header. Note that our `ArrayStack` class will be part of the `jsjf` package and will make use of a package called `jsjf.exceptions`.

```
package jsjf;

import jsjf.exceptions.*;
import java.util.Arrays;

/**
 * An array implementation of a stack in which the bottom of the
 * stack is fixed at index 0.
 *
 * @author Java Foundations
 * @version 4.0
 */
public class ArrayStack<T> implements StackADT<T>
{
  private final static int DEFAULT_CAPACITY = 100;

  private int top;
  private T[] stack;
```

The Constructors

Our class will have two constructors, one to use the default capacity and the other to use a specified capacity.

```
/**
 * Creates an empty stack using the default capacity.
 */
public ArrayStack()
{
   this(DEFAULT_CAPACITY);
}
```

```
   /**
    * Creates an empty stack using the specified capacity.
    * @param initialCapacity the initial size of the array
    */
   public ArrayStack(int initialCapacity)
   {
      top = 0;
      stack = (T[])(new Object[initialCapacity]);
   }
```

Just to refresh our memory, this is an excellent example of method overloading (that is, two methods with the same name that differ only in the parameter list). It is also interesting to note that the constructor for the default capacity makes use of the other constructor by passing it the `DEFAULT_CAPACITY` constant.

From our previous discussion of generics we recall that you cannot instantiate a generic type. This also means that you cannot instantiate an array of a generic type. This results in an interesting line of code in our constructor:

```
stack = (T[])(new Object[initialCapacity]);
```

Note that in this line, we are instantiating an array of Objects and then casting it as an array of our generic type. This will create a compile-time warning for an unchecked type conversion because the Java compiler cannot guarantee the type safety of this cast. As we have seen, it is worth dealing with this warning to gain the flexibility and type safety of generics. This warning can be suppressed using the following Java annotation placed before the offending statement:

```
@SuppressWarnings("unchecked")
```

COMMON ERROR

A common error made by programmers new to generics is to attempt to create an array of a generic type:

```
stack = new T[initialCapacity];
```

Generic types cannot be instantiated, and that includes arrays of a generic type. That's why we have to create an array that holds `Object` references, and then cast it into an array of the generic type.

Creating an Array of Generic Elements

create an array of `object`

```
stack = (T[]) (new Object[initialCapacity]);
```

cast as an array of generic type `T`

The `push` Operation

To push an element onto the stack, we simply insert it in the next available position in the array as specified by the variable `top`. Before doing so, however, we must determine whether the array has reached its capacity and expand it if necessary. After storing the value, we must update the value of `top` so that it continues to represent the number of elements in the stack.

Implementing these steps results in the following code:

```
/**
 * Adds the specified element to the top of this stack, expanding
 * the capacity of the array if necessary.
 * @param element generic element to be pushed onto stack
 */
public void push(T element)
{
   if (size() == stack.length)
      expandCapacity();

   stack[top] = element;
   top++;
}
```

The `expandCapacity` method is implemented to double the size of the array as needed. Of course, since an array cannot be resized once it is instantiated, this method simply creates a new, larger array and copies the contents of the old array

```
/**
 * Creates a new array to store the contents of this stack with
 * twice the capacity of the old one.
 */
private void expandCapacity()
{
  stack = Arrays.copyOf(stack, stack.length * 2);
}
```

into the new one. It serves as a support method of the class and can therefore be implemented with private visibility.

Figure 12.11 illustrates the result of pushing an element E onto the stack that was depicted in Figure 12.10.

The `push` operation for the array implementation of a stack consists of the following steps:

- Make sure that the array is not full.
- Set the reference in position `top` of the array to the object being added to the stack.
- Increment the values of `top` and `count`.

Each of these steps is O(1). Thus the operation is O(1). We might wonder about the time complexity of the `expandCapacity` method and the impact it might have on the analysis of the `push` method. This method does contain a linear `for` loop and, intuitively, we would call that O(n). However, given how seldom the `expandCapacity` method is called relative to the number of times `push` may be called, we can amortize that complexity across all instances of `push`.

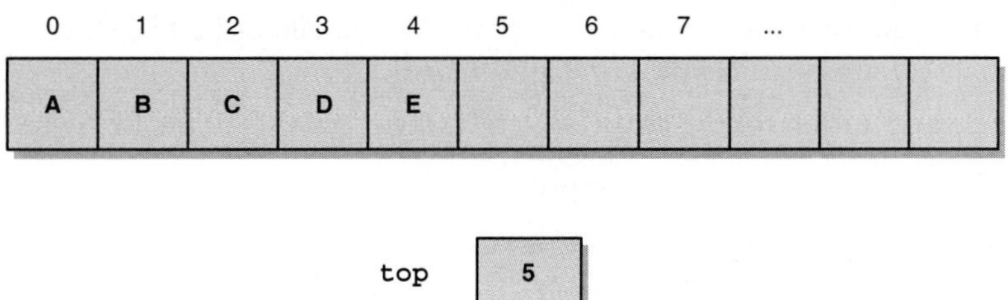

FIGURE 12.11 The stack after pushing element E

The pop Operation

The pop operation removes and returns the element at the top of the stack. For an array implementation, that means returning the element at index top-1. Before attempting to return an element, however, we must ensure that there is at least one element in the stack to return.

The array-based version of the pop operation can be implemented as follows:

```
/**
 * Removes the element at the top of this stack and returns a
 * reference to it.
 * @return element removed from top of stack
 * @throws EmptyCollectionException if stack is empty
 */
public T pop() throws EmptyCollectionException
{
   if (isEmpty())
      throw new EmptyCollectionException("stack");

   top--;
   T result = stack[top];
   stack[top] = null;

   return result;
}
```

If the stack is empty when the pop method is called, an EmptyCollectionException is thrown. Otherwise, the value of top is decremented and the element stored at that location is stored into a temporary variable so that it can be returned. That cell in the array is then set to null. Note that the value of top ends up with the appropriate value relative to the now smaller stack. Figure 12.12 illustrates the results of a pop operation on the stack from Figure 12.11, which brings it back to its earlier state (identical to Figure 12.10).

The pop operation for the array implementation consists of the following steps:

- Make sure the stack is not empty.
- Decrement the top counter.
- Set a temporary reference equal to the element in stack[top].
- Set stack[top] equal to null.
- Return the temporary reference.

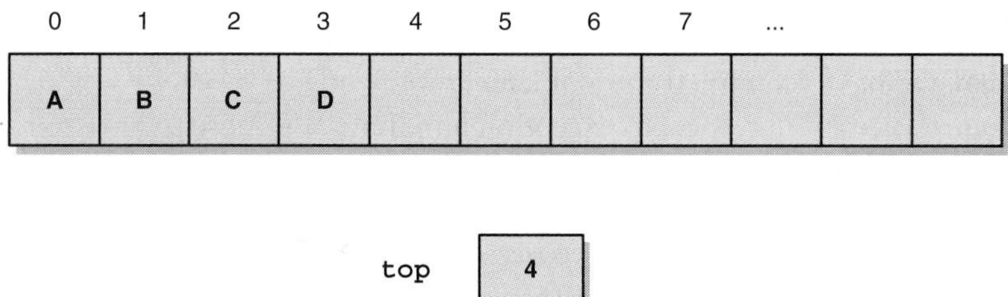

FIGURE 12.12 The stack after popping the top element

All of these steps are also O(1). Thus, the pop operation for the array implementation has time complexity O(1).

The peek Operation

The peek operation returns a reference to the element at the top of the stack without removing it from the array. For an array implementation, that means returning a reference to the element at position top-1. This one step is O(1) and thus the peek operation is O(1) as well.

```
/**
 * Returns a reference to the element at the top of this stack.
 * The element is not removed from the stack.
 * @return element on top of stack
 * @throws EmptyCollectionException if stack is empty
 */
public T peek() throws EmptyCollectionException
{
   if (isEmpty())
      throw new EmptyCollectionException("stack");

   return stack[top-1];
}
```

Other Operations

The isEmpty, size, and toString operations and their analysis are left as programming projects and exercises.

The `EmptyCollectionException` Class

Now that we have examined the implementation of our `ArrayStack` class, lets revisit our choices with respect to exception handling. We chose to have our collection handle the case where the underlying data structure becomes full, because that is an issue that is internal to the collection. On the other hand, we chose to throw an exception if an attempt is made to access an element in the collection through either a `pop` or `peek` operation when the collection is empty. This situation reveals a problem with the use of the collection, not with the collection itself.

Exceptions are classes in Java, so we have the choice of using existing exceptions provided in the Java API or creating our own. In this case, we could have chosen to create a specific empty stack exception. However, creating a parameterized exception enables us to reuse this exception with any of our collections classes. Listing 12.4 shows the `EmptyCollectionException` class. Notice that our exception class extends the `RuntimeException` class and then makes use of the parent's constructor by using a `super` reference.

LISTING 12.4

```
package jsjf.exceptions;

/**
 * Represents the situation in which a collection is empty.
 *
 * @author Java Foundations
 * @version 4.0
 */
public class EmptyCollectionException extends RuntimeException
{
   /**
    * Sets up this exception with an appropriate message.
    * @param collection the name of the collection
    */
   public EmptyCollectionException(String collection)
   {
      super("The " + collection + " is empty.");
   }
}
```

Other Implementations

In this chapter we examined the concept of a stack, used the Stack class available in Java API to solve a postfix evaluation problem, and then implemented our own `ArrayStack` class that used an array to store the underlying elements on a stack.

We're not finished with stacks yet, though. In Chapter 13, we'll examine another technique for implementing collections using linked structures instead of arrays, and implement a `LinkedStack` class.

Armed with these two broad implementation techniques—array-based and linked-based—we'll be set to explore many other collections.

Summary of Key Concepts

- A collection is an object that gathers and organizes other objects.
- Elements in a collection are typically organized in terms of the order of their addition to the collection or in terms of some inherent relationship among the elements.
- A collection is an abstraction wherein the details of the implementation are hidden.
- A data structure is the underlying programming construct used to implement a collection.
- Stack elements are processed in a LIFO manner—the last element in is the first element out.
- A programmer should choose the structure that is appropriate for the type of data management needed.
- A stack is the ideal data structure to use when evaluating a postfix expression.
- Errors and exceptions represent unusual or invalid processing.
- A Java interface defines a set of abstract methods and is useful in separating the concept of an abstract data type from its implementation.
- By using the interface name as a return type, we ensure that the interface doesn't commit the method to the use of any particular class that implements a stack.
- A programmer must carefully consider how exceptions should be handled, if at all, and at what level.
- The implementation of the collection operations should not affect the way users interact with the collection.
- How we handle exceptional conditions determines whether the collection or the user of the collection controls the particular behavior.
- For efficiency, an array-based stack implementation keeps the bottom of the stack at index 0.

Summary of Terms

abstraction A point of view that hides or ignores certain details, usually to make concepts easier to manage.

abstract data type A data type whose values and operations are not inherently defined within a programming language.

class hierarchy The relationship among classes created by inheritance in which the child of one parent can itself be the parent of other classes.

collection An object that gathers and organizes other objects.

data structure (1) An organization of objects that allows certain operations to be performed efficiently; (2) The programming constructs used to implement a collection.

exception An object that defines an unusual or erroneous situation.

generic type A placeholder for an object type that is not made concrete until the class that refers to it is instantiated.

inheritance The object-oriented principle of deriving one class from an existing class.

interface (1) The manner in which one thing interacts with another; (2) A set of public methods that enables one object to interact with another.

Java Collections API The subset of the Java application programming interfaces API that represent or deal with collections.

LIFO (1) Last-in, first-out; (2) A description of a collection in which the last element added will be the first element removed.

polymorphism The object-oriented principle that enables a reference variable to point to related but distinct types of objects over time, and in which method invocations are bound to code at run-time.

pop A stack operation in which an element is removed from the top of a stack.

push A stack operation in which an element is added to the top of a stack.

stack A linear collection whose elements are added and removed from the same end in a LIFO manner.

Self-Review Questions

SR 12.1 What is a collection?

SR 12.2 What is a data type?

SR 12.3 What is an abstract data type?

SR 12.4 What is a data structure?

SR 12.5 What is abstraction and what advantage does it provide?

SR 12.6 Why is a class an excellent representation of an abstract data type?

SR 12.7 What is the characteristic behavior of a stack?

SR 12.8 What are the five basic operations on a stack?

SR 12.9 What are some of the other operations that might be implemented for a stack?

SR 12.10 Define the term *inheritance*.

SR 12.11 Define the term *polymorphism*.

SR 12.12 Given the example in Figure 12.5, list the subclasses of `Mammal`.

SR 12.13 Given the example in Figure 12.5, will the following code compile?

```
Animal creature = new Parrot();
```

SR 12.14 Given the example in Figure 12.5, will the following code compile?

```
Horse creature = new Mammal();
```

SR 12.15 What is the purpose of generics in the Java language?

SR 12.16 What is the advantage of postfix notation?

Exercises

EX 12.1 Compare and contrast data types, abstract data types, and data structures.

EX 12.2 List the collections in the Java Collections API and mark the ones that are covered in this text.

EX 12.3 Define the concept of abstraction and explain why it is important in software development.

EX 12.4 Hand trace an initially empty stack X through the following operations:

```
X.push(new Integer(4));
X.push(new Integer(3));
Integer Y = X.pop();
X.push(new Integer(7));
X.push(new Integer(2));
X.push(new Integer(5));
X.push(new Integer(9));
Integer Y = X.pop();
X.push(new Integer(3));
X.push(new Integer(9));
```

EX 12.5 Given the resulting stack X from the previous exercise, what would be the result of each of the following?

```
a. Y = X.peek();
b. Y = X.pop();
   Z = X.peek();
c. Y = X.pop();
   Z = X.peek();
```

EX 12.6 What should be the time complexity of the `isEmpty()`, `size()`, and `toString()` methods?

EX 12.7 Show how the undo operation in a word processor can be supported by the use of a stack. Give specific examples and draw the contents of the stack after various actions are taken.

EX 12.8 In the postfix expression evaluation example, the two most recent operands are popped when an operator is encountered so that the subexpression can be evaluated. The first operand popped is treated as the second operand in the subexpression, and the second operand popped is the first. Give and explain an example that demonstrates the importance of this aspect of the solution.

EX 12.9 Draw an example using the five integers (12, 23, 1, 45, 9) of how a stack could be used to reverse the order (9, 45, 1, 23, 12) of these elements.

EX 12.10 Explain what would happen to the algorithms and the time complexity of an array implementation of the stack if the top of the stack were at position 0.

Programming Projects

PP 12.1 Complete the implementation of the `ArrayStack` class presented in this chapter. Specifically, complete the implementations of the `isEmpty`, `size`, and `toString` methods.

PP 12.2 Design and implement an application that reads a sentence from the user and prints the sentence with the characters of each word backwards. Use a stack to reverse the characters of each word.

PP 12.3 Modify the solution to the postfix expression evaluation problem so that it checks for the validity of the expression that is entered by the user. Issue an appropriate error message when an erroneous situation is encountered.

PP 12.4 The array implementation in this chapter keeps the top variable pointing to the next array position above the actual top of the stack. Rewrite the array implementation such that `stack[top]` is the actual top of the stack.

PP 12.5 There is a data structure called a drop-out stack that behaves like a stack in every respect except that if the stack size is n, when the $n + 1$ element is pushed, the first element is lost. Implement a drop-out stack using an array. (*Hint:* A circular array implementation would make sense.)

PP 12.6 Implement an integer adder using three stacks.

PP 12.7 Implement an infix-to-postfix translator using stacks.

PP 12.8 Implement a class called reverse that uses a stack to output a set of elements input by the user in reverse order.

PP 12.9 Create a graphical application that provides a button for push and pop from a stack, a text field to accept a string as input for push, and a text area to display the contents of the stack after each operation.

Answers to Self-Review Questions

SRA 12.1 A collection is an object that gathers and organizes other objects.

SRA 12.2 A data type is a set of values and operations on those values defined within a programming language.

SRA 12.3 An abstract data type is a data type that is not defined within the programming language and must be defined by the programmer.

SRA 12.4 A data structure is the set of objects necessary to implement an abstract data type.

SRA 12.5 Abstraction is the concept of hiding the underlying implementation of operations and data storage in order to simplify the use of a collection.

SRA 12.6 Classes naturally provide abstraction since only those methods that provide services to other classes have public visibility.

SRA 12.7 A stack is a last in, first out (LIFO) structure.

SRA 12.8 The operations are

push—adds an element to the end of the stack
pop—removes an element from the front of the stack
peek—returns a reference to the element at the front of the stack
isEmpty—returns true if the stack is empty, returns false otherwise
size—returns the number of elements in the stack

SRA 12.9 `makeEmpty(), destroy(), full()`

SRA 12.10 Inheritance is the process in which a new class is derived from an existing one. The new class automatically contains some or all of the variables and methods in the original class. Then, to tailor the class as needed, the programmer can add new variables and methods to the derived class, or modify the inherited ones.

SRA 12.11 The term *polymorphism* can be defined as "having many forms." A *polymorphic reference* is a reference variable that can refer to different types of objects at different points in time. The specific method invoked through a polymorphic reference can change from one invocation to the next.

SRA 12.12 The subclasses of `Mammal` are `Horse` and `Bat`.

SRA 12.13 Yes, a reference variable of a parent class or any superclass may hold a reference to one of its descendants.

SRA 12.14 No, a reference variable for a child or subclass may not hold a reference to a parent or superclass. To make this assignment, you would have to explicitly cast the parent class into the child class `(Horse creature = (Horse)(new Mammal());`

SRA 12.15 Beginning with Java 5.0, Java enables us to define a class based on a *generic type*. That is, we can define a class so that it stores, operates on, and manages objects whose type is not specified until the class is instantiated. This allows for the creation of structures that can manipulate "generic" elements and still provide type checking.

SRA 12.16 Postfix notation avoids the need for precedence rules that are required to evaluate infix expressions.

Linked Structures—Stacks

13

CHAPTER OBJECTIVES

- Describe the use of references to create linked structures.
- Compare linked structures to array-based structures.
- Explore the techniques for managing a linked list.
- Discuss the need for a separate node object to form linked structures.
- Implement a stack collection using a linked list.

This chapter explores a technique for creating data structures using references to create links between objects. Linked structures are fundamental to the development of software, especially the design and implementation of collections. This approach has both advantages and disadvantages when compared to a solution using arrays.

13.1 References as Links

In Chapter 12, we discussed the concept of collections and explored one collection in particular: a stack. We defined the operations on a stack collection and designed an implementation using an underlying array-based data structure. In this chapter, we explore an entirely different approach to designing a data structure.

A *linked structure* is a data structure that uses object reference variables to create links between objects. Linked structures are the primary alternative to an array-based implementation of a collection. After discussing various issues involved in linked structures, we will define a new implementation of a stack collection that uses an underlying linked data structure.

KEY CONCEPT
Object reference variables can be used to create linked structures.

Recall that an object reference variable holds the address of an object, indicating where the object is stored in memory. The following declaration creates a variable called `obj` that is only large enough to hold the numeric address of an object:

```
Object obj;
```

Usually the specific address that an object reference variable holds is irrelevant. That is, even though it is important to be able to use the reference variable to access an object, the specific location in memory where it is stored is unimportant. Therefore, instead of showing addresses, we usually depict a reference variable as a name that "points to" an object, as shown in Figure 13.1. A reference variable, used in this context, is sometimes called a *pointer*.

Consider the situation in which a class defines as instance data a reference to another object of the same class. For example, suppose we have a class named `Person` that contains a person's name, address, and other relevant information. Now suppose that in addition to these data, the `Person` class also contains a reference variable to another `Person` object:

```
public class Person
{
   private String name;
   private String address;

   private Person next; // a link to another Person object

   // whatever else
}
```

Using only this one class, we can create a linked structure. One `Person` object contains a link to a second `Person` object. This second object also contains a

FIGURE 13.1 An object reference variable pointing to an object

reference to a `Person`, which contains another, and so on. This type of object is sometimes called *self-referential.*

This kind of relationship forms the basis of a *linked list*, which is a linked structure in which one object refers to the next, creating a linear ordering of the objects in the list. A linked list is depicted in Figure 13.2. Often the objects stored in a linked list are referred to generically as the *nodes* of the list.

KEY CONCEPT
A linked list is composed of objects that each point to the next object in the list.

Note that a separate reference variable is needed to indicate the first node in the list. The list is terminated in a node whose `next` reference is `null`.

A linked list is only one kind of linked structure. If a class is set up to have multiple references to objects, a more complex structure can be created, such as the one depicted in Figure 13.3. The way in which the links are managed dictates the specific organization of the structure.

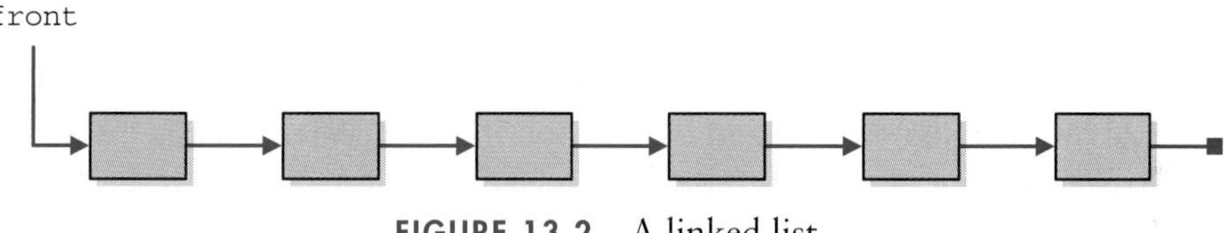

FIGURE 13.2 A linked list

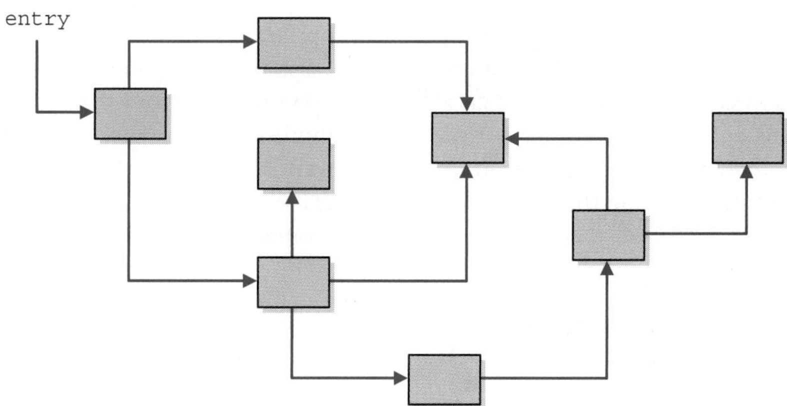

FIGURE 13.3 A complex linked structure

KEY CONCEPT
A linked list dynamically grows as needed and essentially has no capacity limitations.

For now, we will focus on the details of a linked list. Many of these techniques apply to more complicated linked structures as well.

Unlike an array, which has a fixed size, a linked list has no upper bound on its capacity other than the limitations of memory in the computer. A linked list is considered to be a *dynamic* structure because its size grows and shrinks as needed to accommodate the number of elements stored. In Java, all objects are created dynamically from an area of memory called the *system heap* or *free store*.

The next section explores some of the primary ways in which a linked list is managed.

13.2 Managing Linked Lists

Keep in mind that our goal is to use linked lists and other linked structures to create collections—specifically, in this chapter, to create a stack. Because the principal purpose of a collection is to be able to add, remove, and access elements, we must first examine how to accomplish these fundamental operations using links. We will focus our discussion in this chapter on adding and removing from the end of a linked list as we will need to do for our stack. We will revisit this discussion in later chapters as the situation warrants.

No matter what a linked list is used to store, there are a few basic techniques involved in managing the nodes in the list. Specifically, elements in the list are accessed, elements are inserted into the list, and elements are removed from the list.

Accessing Elements

Special care must be taken when dealing with the first node in the list so that the reference to the entire list is maintained appropriately. When using linked lists, we maintain a pointer to the first element in the list. To access other elements, we must access the first one and then follow the next pointer from that one to the next one and so on. Consider our previous example of a `person` class containing the attributes `name`, `address`, and `next`. If we wanted to find the fourth person in the list, and assuming that we had a variable `first` of type `Person` that pointed to the first person in the list and that the list contained at least four nodes, we might use the following code:

```
Person current = first;
for (int i = 0; i < 3; i++)
    current = current.next;
```

After executing this code, `current` will point to the fourth person in the list. Notice that it is very important to create a new reference variable, in this case current, and then start by setting that reference variable to point to the first element in the list. Consider what would happen if we used the first pointer in the loop instead of current. Once we moved the first pointer to point to the second element in the list, we would no longer have a pointer to the first element and would not be able to access it. Keep in mind that with a linked list, the only way to access the elements in the list is to start with the first element and progress through the list.

Of course, a more likely scenario is that we would need to search our list for a particular person. Assuming that the Person class overrides the equals method such that it returns true if the given String matches the name stored for that person, then the following code will search the list for Tom Jones:

```
String searchstring = "Tom Jones";
Person current = first;
while ((not(current.equals(searchstring)) && (current.next != null))
    current = current.next;
```

Note that this loop will terminate when the string is found or when the end of the list is encountered. Now that we have seen how to access elements in a linked list, let's consider how to insert elements into a list.

Inserting Nodes

A node may be inserted into a linked list at any location: at the front of the list, among the interior nodes in the middle of the list, or at the end of the list. Adding a node to the front of the list requires resetting the reference to the entire list, as shown in Figure 13.4. First, the next reference of the added node is set to point to the current first node in the list. Second, the reference to the front of the list is reset to point to the newly added node.

KEY CONCEPT
The order in which references are changed is crucial to maintaining a linked list.

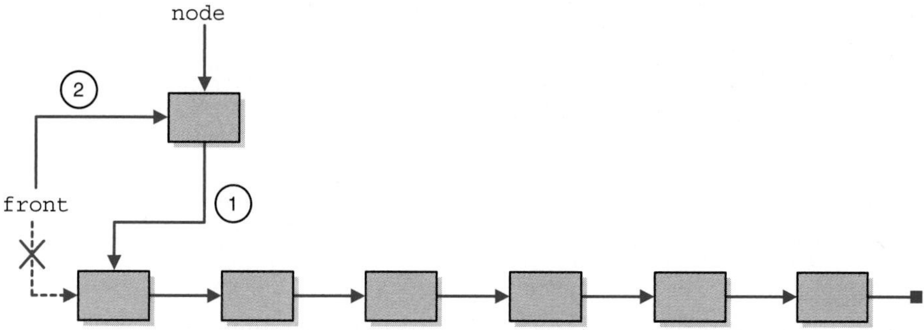

FIGURE 13.4 Inserting a node at the front of a linked list

Note that difficulties would arise if these steps were reversed. If we were to reset the `front` reference first, we would lose the only reference to the existing list and it could not be retrieved.

Inserting a node into the middle of a list requires some additional processing but is not needed for our stack collection. We will come back to this topic in Chapter 15.

Deleting Nodes

Any node in the list can be deleted. We must maintain the integrity of the list no matter which node is deleted. As with the process of inserting a node, dealing with the first node in the list represents a special case.

KEY CONCEPT
Dealing with the first node in a linked list often requires special handling.

To delete the first node in a linked list, we reset the reference to the front of the list so that it points to the current second node in the list. This process is shown in Figure 13.5. If the deleted node is needed elsewhere, we must set up a separate reference to it before resetting the `front` reference. The general case of deleting a node from the interior of the list is left for Chapter 15.

DESIGN FOCUS

We've described insertion into and deletion from a list as having two cases: the case when dealing with the first node and the case when dealing with any other node. It is possible to eliminate the special case involving the first node by introducing a *sentinel node* or *dummy node* at the front of the list. A sentinel node serves as a false first node and doesn't actually represent an element in the list. When a sentinel node is used, all insertions and deletions will fall under the second case and the implementations will not have as many special situations to consider.

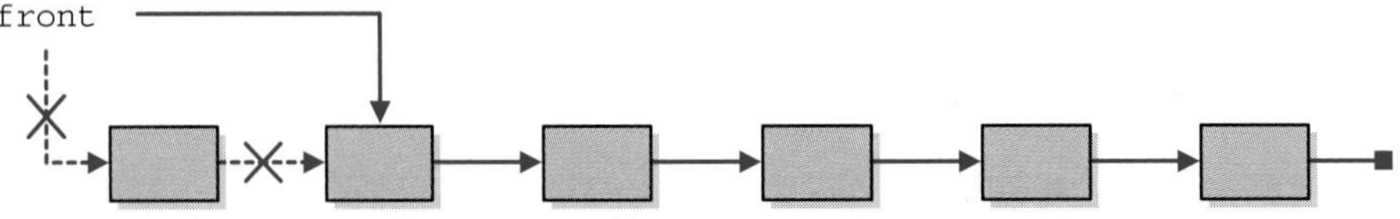

FIGURE 13.5 Deleting the first node in a linked list

13.3 Elements without Links

Now that we have explored some of the techniques needed to manage the nodes of a linked list, we can turn our attention to using a linked list as an alternative implementation approach for a collection. To do so, however, we need to carefully examine one other key aspect of linked lists. We must separate the details of the linked list structure from the elements that the list stores.

Earlier in this chapter we discussed the idea of a `Person` class that contains, among its other data, a link to another `Person` object. The flaw in this approach is that the self-referential `Person` class must be designed so that it "knows" it may become a node in a linked list of `Person` objects. This assumption is impractical, and it violates our goal of separating the implementation details from the parts of the system that use the collection.

> **KEY CONCEPT**
> Objects that are stored in a collection should not contain any implementation details of the underlying data structure.

The solution to this problem is to define a separate node class that serves to link the elements together. A node class is fairly simple, containing only two important references: one to the next node in the linked list and another to the element that is being stored in the list. This approach is depicted in Figure 13.6.

The linked list of nodes can still be managed using the techniques discussed in the previous section. The only additional aspect is that the actual elements stored in the list are accessed using separate references in the node objects.

Doubly Linked Lists

An alternative implementation for linked structures is the concept of a doubly linked list, as illustrated in Figure 13.7. In a doubly linked list, two references are maintained: one to point to the first node in the list and another to point to the last node in the list. Each node in the list stores both a reference to the next element

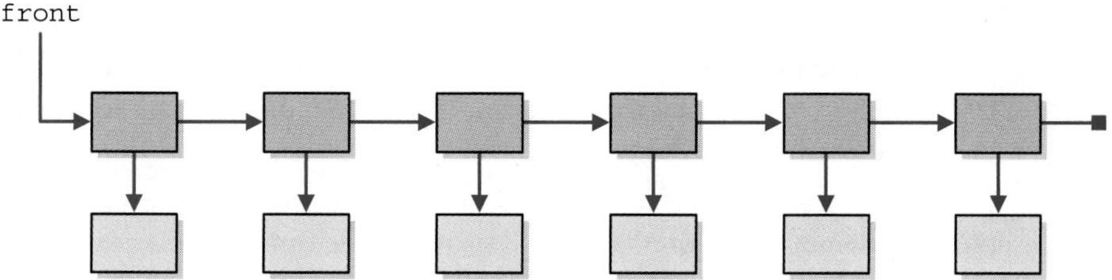

FIGURE 13.6 Using separate node objects to store and link elements

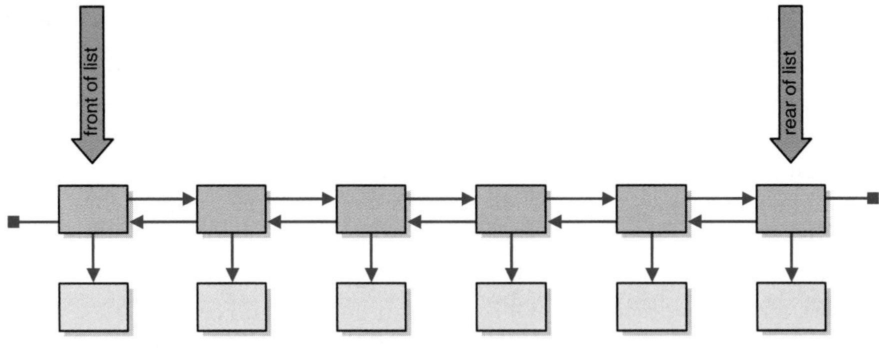

FIGURE 13.7 A doubly linked list

and a reference to the previous one. If we were to use sentinel nodes with a doubly linked list, we would place sentinel nodes on both ends of the list. We discuss doubly linked lists further in Chapter 15.

13.4 Stacks in the Java API

In Chapter 12, we used the `java.util.Stack` class from the Java Collections API to solve the postfix expression problem. The `Stack` class is an array-based implementation of a stack provided in the Java Collections API framework. This implementation provides the same basic operations we have been discussing:

- The `push` operation accepts a parameter item that is a reference to an object to be placed on the stack.
- The `pop` operation removes the object on top of the stack and returns a reference to it.
- The `peek` operation returns a reference to the object on top of the stack.

KEY CONCEPT
The `java.util.Stack` class is derived from `Vector`, which gives a stack inappropriate operations.

The `Stack` class is derived from the `Vector` class and uses its inherited capabilities to store the elements in the stack. Because this implementation is built on a vector, it exhibits the characteristics of both a vector and a stack and thus allows operations that violate the basic premise of a stack.

The `Deque` interface implemented by the `LinkedList` class provides a linked implementation of a stack and provides the same basic stack operations. A deque (pronounced like "deck") is a double-ended queue, and we discuss that concept further in Chapter 14. Unfortunately, since a `Deque` operates on both ends of the collection, there are a variety of operations available that violate the premise of a stack. It is up to developers to limit themselves to the use of stack operations. Let's see how we use a `Deque` as a stack.

13.5 Using Stacks: Traversing a Maze

Another classic use of a stack data structure is to keep track of alternatives in maze traversal or other similar algorithms that involve trial and error. Suppose that we build a grid as a two-dimensional array of integer values where each number represents either a path (1) or a wall (0) in a maze. We store our grid in a file where the first line of the file describes the number of rows and columns in the grid.

```
9 13
1 1 1 0 1 1 0 0 0 1 1 1 1
1 0 0 1 1 0 1 1 1 1 0 0 1
1 1 1 1 1 0 1 0 1 0 1 0 0
0 0 0 0 1 1 1 0 1 0 1 1 1
1 1 1 0 1 1 1 0 1 0 1 1 1
1 0 1 0 0 0 0 1 1 1 0 0 1
1 0 1 1 1 1 1 1 0 1 1 1 1
1 0 0 0 0 0 0 0 0 0 0 0 0
1 1 1 1 1 1 1 1 1 1 1 1 1
```

The goal is to start in the top-left corner of this grid and traverse to the bottom-right corner of this grid, traversing only positions that are marked as a path. Valid moves will be those that are within the bounds of the grid and are to cells in the grid marked with a 1. We will mark our path as we go by changing the 1's to 2's, and we will push only valid moves onto the stack.

Starting in the top-left corner, we have two valid moves: down and right. We push these moves onto the stack, pop the top move off of the stack (right), and then move to that location. This means that we moved right one position:

```
2 2 1 0 1 1 0 0 0 1 1 1 1
1 0 0 1 1 0 1 1 1 1 0 0 1
1 1 1 1 1 0 1 0 1 0 1 0 0
0 0 0 0 1 1 1 0 1 0 1 1 1
1 1 1 0 1 1 1 0 1 0 1 1 1
1 0 1 0 0 0 0 1 1 1 0 0 1
1 0 1 1 1 1 1 1 0 1 1 1 1
1 0 0 0 0 0 0 0 0 0 0 0 0
1 1 1 1 1 1 1 1 1 1 1 1 1
```

We now have only one valid move. We push that move onto the stack, pop the top element off of the stack (right), and then move to that location. Again we moved right one position:

```
2 2 2 0 1 1 0 0 0 1 1 1 1
1 0 0 1 1 0 1 1 1 1 0 0 1
1 1 1 1 1 0 1 0 1 0 1 0 0
0 0 0 0 1 1 1 0 1 0 1 1 1
1 1 1 0 1 1 1 0 1 0 1 1 1
1 0 1 0 0 0 0 1 1 1 0 0 1
1 0 1 1 1 1 1 0 1 1 1 1 1
1 0 0 0 0 0 0 0 0 0 0 0 0
1 1 1 1 1 1 1 1 1 1 1 1 1
```

From this position, we do not have any valid moves. At this point, however, our stack is not empty. Keep in mind that we still have a valid move on the stack left from the first position. We pop the next (and currently last) element off of the stack (down from the first position). We move to that position, push the valid move(s) from that position onto the stack, and continue processing.

```
2 2 2 0 1 1 0 0 0 1 1 1 1
2 0 0 1 1 0 1 1 1 1 0 0 1
1 1 1 1 1 0 1 0 1 0 1 0 0
0 0 0 0 1 1 1 0 1 0 1 1 1
1 1 1 0 1 1 1 0 1 0 1 1 1
1 0 1 0 0 0 0 1 1 1 0 0 1
1 0 1 1 1 1 1 0 1 1 1 1 1
1 0 0 0 0 0 0 0 0 0 0 0 0
1 1 1 1 1 1 1 1 1 1 1 1 1
```

Using a stack in this way is actually simulating *recursion*, a process whereby a method calls itself either directly or indirectly. Recursion, which we discuss in detail in Chapter 17, uses the concept of a program stack. A *program stack* (or *run-time stack*) is used to keep track of methods that are invoked. Every time a method is called, an *activation record* that represents the invocation is created and pushed onto the program stack. Therefore, the elements on the stack represent the series of method invocations that occurred to reach a particular point in an executing program.

For example, when the `main` method of a program is called, an activation record for it is created and pushed onto the program stack. When `main` calls another method (say `m2`), an activation record for `m2` is created and pushed onto the stack. If `m2` calls method `m3`, then an activation record for `m3` is created and pushed onto the stack. When method `m3` terminates, its activation record is popped off the stack and control returns to the calling method (`m2`), which is now on the top of the stack.

If an exception occurs during the execution of a Java program, the programmer can examine the *call stack trace* to see what method the problem occurred within and what method calls were made to arrive at that point.

KEY CONCEPT
Recursive processing can be simulated using a stack to keep track of the appropriate data.

An activation record contains various administrative data to help manage the execution of the program. It also contains a copy of the method's data (local variables and parameters) for that invocation of the method.

Because of the relationship between stacks and recursion, we can always rewrite a recursive program into a nonrecursive program that uses a stack. Instead of using recursion to keep track of the data, we can create our own stack to do so.

VideoNote
Using a stack to solve a maze

Listings 13.1, 13.2 and 13.3 illustrate the `Maze`, `MazeSolver` and `MazeTester` classes that implement our stack-based solution to traversing a maze. We will revisit this same example in our discussion of recursion in Chapter 17.

Note that the constructor of the `Maze` class reads the initial maze data from a file specified by the user. This solution assumes that all issues regarding the file I/O will proceed without a problem, which, of course, is not a safe assumption. The file might not be present; the data might not be in the correct format, and so forth. Several different exceptions could occur during the execution of the constructor, which doesn't catch or handle them. If any occur, the program will terminate. In a more robust program, these exceptions would be handled more elegantly.

This solution uses a class called `Position` to encapsulate the coordinates of a position within the maze. The `traverse` method loops, popping the top position off the stack, marking it as tried, and then testing to see whether we are done. If we are not done, then all of the valid moves from this position are pushed onto the stack, and the loop continues. A private method called `pushNewPos` has been created to handle the task of putting the valid moves from the current position onto the stack:

```
private StackADT<Position> push_new_pos(int x, int y,
StackADT<Position> stack)
{
   Position npos = new Position();
   npos.setx(x);
   npos.sety(y);
   if (valid(npos.getx(),npos.gety()))
     stack.push(npos);
   return stack;
}
```

LISTING 13.1

```
import java.util.*;
import java.io.*;

/**
 * Maze represents a maze of characters. The goal is to get from the
 * top left corner to the bottom right, following a path of 1's. Arbitrary
 * constants are used to represent locations in the maze that have been TRIED
 * and that are part of the solution PATH.
 *
 * @author Java Foundations
 * @version 4.0
 */
public class Maze
{
  private static final int TRIED = 2;
  private static final int PATH = 3;

  private int numberRows, numberColumns;
  private int[][] grid;

  /**
   * Constructor for the Maze class. Loads a maze from the given file.
   * Throws a FileNotFoundException if the given file is not found.
   *
   * @param filename the name of the file to load
   * @throws FileNotFoundException if the given file is not found
   */
  public Maze(String filename) throws FileNotFoundException
  {
     Scanner scan = new Scanner(new File(filename));
     numberRows = scan.nextInt();
     numberColumns = scan.nextInt();

     grid = new int[numberRows][numberColumns];
     for (int i = 0; i < numberRows; i++)
         for (int j = 0; j < numberColumns; j++)
             grid[i][j] = scan.nextInt();
  }

  /**
   * Marks the specified position in the maze as TRIED
   *
   * @param row the index of the row to try
   * @param col the index of the column to try
   */
```

LISTING 13.1 *continued*

```
   public void tryPosition(int row, int col)
   {
      grid[row][col] = TRIED;
   }

   /**
    * Return the number of rows in this maze
    *
    * @return the number of rows in this maze
    */
   public int getRows()
   {
      return grid.length;
   }

   /**
    * Return the number of columns in this maze
    *
    * @return the number of columns in this maze
    */
   public int getColumns()
   {
      return grid[0].length;
   }

  /**
    * Marks a given position in the maze as part of the PATH
    *
    * @param row the index of the row to mark as part of the PATH
    * @param col the index of the column to mark as part of the PATH
    */
   public void markPath(int row, int col)
   {
      grid[row][col] = PATH;
   }

   /**
    * Determines if a specific location is valid. A valid location
    * is one that is on the grid, is not blocked, and has not been TRIED.
    *
    * @param row the row to be checked
    * @param column the column to be checked
    * @return true if the location is valid
    */
```

LISTING 13.1 *continued*

```
  public boolean validPosition(int row, int column)
  {
     boolean result = false;

     // check if cell is in the bounds of the matrix

     if (row >= 0 && row < grid.length &&
         column >= 0 && column < grid[row].length)

     //  check if cell is not blocked and not previously tried

         if (grid[row][column] == 1)
            result = true;
      return result;
  }

  /**
   * Returns the maze as a string.
   *
   * @return a string representation of the maze
   */
  public String toString()
  {
     String result = "\n";

     for (int row=0; row < grid.length; row++)
     {
        for (int column=0; column < grid[row].length; column++)
            result += grid[row][column] + "";
        result += "\n";
     }
      return result;
  }
}
```

LISTING 13.2

```
import java.util.*;

/**
 * MazeSolver attempts to recursively traverse a Maze. The goal is to get from the
 * given starting position to the bottom right, following a path of 1's. Arbitrary
 * constants are used to represent locations in the maze that have been TRIED
 * and that are part of the solution PATH.
 *
 * @author Java Foundations
 * @version 4.0
 */
public class MazeSolver
{
  private Maze maze;

  /**
   * Constructor for the MazeSolver class.
   */
  public MazeSolver(Maze maze)
  {
     this.maze = maze;
  }

  /**
   * Attempts to recursively traverse the maze. Inserts special
   * characters indicating locations that have been TRIED and that
   * eventually become part of the solution PATH.
   *
   * @param row row index of current location
   * @param column column index of current location
   * @return true if the maze has been solved
   */
  public boolean traverse()
  {
     boolean done = false;
     int row, column;
     Position pos = new Position();
     Deque<Position> stack = new LinkedList<Position>();
     stack.push(pos);
```

LISTING 13.2 *continued*

```
      while (!(done) && !stack.isEmpty())
      {
         pos = stack.pop();
         maze.tryPosition(pos.getx(),pos.gety());  // this cell has been tried
         if (pos.getx() == maze.getRows()-1 && pos.gety() == maze.getColumns()-1)
              done = true;  // the maze is solved
         else
         {
            push_new_pos(pos.getx() - 1,pos.gety(), stack);
            push_new_pos(pos.getx() + 1,pos.gety(), stack);
            push_new_pos(pos.getx(),pos.gety() - 1, stack);
            push_new_pos(pos.getx(),pos.gety() + 1, stack);
         }
      }

      return done;
   }

   /**
    * Push a new attempted move onto the stack
    * @param x represents x coordinate
    * @param y represents y coordinate
    * @param stack the working stack of moves within the grid
    * @return stack of moves within the grid
    */
   private void push_new_pos(int x, int y,
                                        Deque<Position> stack)
   {
      Position npos = new Position();
      npos.setx(x);
      npos.sety(y);
      if (maze.validPosition(x,y))
          stack.push(npos);
   }

}
```

LISTING 13.3

```
import java.util.*;
import java.io.*;

/**
 * MazeTester uses recursion to determine if a maze can be traversed.
 *
 * @author Java Foundations
 * @version 4.0
 */
public class MazeTester
{
  /**
   * Creates a new maze, prints its original form, attempts to
   * solve it, and prints out its final form.
   */
  public static void main(String[] args) throws FileNotFoundException
  {
     Scanner scan = new Scanner(System.in);
     System.out.print("Enter the name of the file containing the maze: ");
     String filename = scan.nextLine();

     Maze labyrinth = new Maze(filename);

     System.out.println(labyrinth);

     MazeSolver solver = new MazeSolver(labyrinth);

     if (solver.traverse())
         System.out.println("The maze was successfully traversed!");
     else
         System.out.println("There is no possible path.");

     System.out.println(labyrinth);
  }
}
```

The UML description for the maze problem is left as an exercise.

13.6 Implementing a Stack: With Links

Let's use a linked list to implement a stack collection, which was defined in Chapter 12. Note that we are not changing the way in which a stack works. Its conceptual nature remains the same, as does the set of operations defined for it. We are merely changing the underlying data structure used to implement it.

KEY CONCEPT
Any implementation of a collection can be used to solve a problem as long as it validly implements the appropriate operations.

The purpose of the stack, and the solutions it helps us to create, also remains the same. The postfix expression evaluation example from Chapter 12 used the `java.util.Stack<T>` class, but any valid implementation of a stack could be used instead. Once we create the `LinkedStack<T>` class to define an alternative implementation, we could substitute it into the postfix expression solution without having to change anything but the class name. That is the beauty of abstraction.

In the following discussion, we show and discuss the methods that are important to understanding the linked-list implementation of a stack. Some of the stack operations are left as programming projects.

The `LinkedStack` Class

The `LinkedStack<T>` class implements the `StackADT<T>` interface, just as the `ArrayStack<T>` class from Chapter 12 does. Both provide the operations defined for a stack collection.

Because we are using a linked-list approach, there is no array in which we store the elements of the collection. Instead, we need only a single reference to the first node in the list. We will also maintain a count of the number of elements in the list. The header and class-level data of the `LinkedStack<T>` class are therefore:

```
package jsjf;

import jsjf.exceptions.*;
import java.util.Iterator;

/**
 * Represents a linked implementation of a stack.
 *
 * @author Java Foundations
 * @version 4.0
 */
public class LinkedStack<T> implements StackADT<T>
{
    private int count;
    private LinearNode<T> top;
```

The `LinearNode<T>` class serves as the node class, containing a reference to the next `LinearNode<T>` in the list and a reference to the element stored in that node. Each node stores a generic type that is determined when the node is instantiated. In our `LinkedStack<T>` implementation, we simply use the same type for the node as used to define the stack. The `LinearNode<T>` class also contains methods to set and get the element values. The `LinearNode<T>` class is shown in Listing 13.4.

LISTING 13.4

```
package jsjf;

/**
 * Represents a node in a linked list.
 *
 * @author Java Foundations
 * @version 4.0
 */
public class LinearNode<T>
{
  private LinearNode<T> next;
  private T element;

  /**
   * Creates an empty node.
   */
  public LinearNode()
  {
     next = null;
     element = null;
  }

  /**
   * Creates a node storing the specified element.
   * @param elem element to be stored
   */
  public LinearNode(T elem)
  {
     next = null;
     element = elem;
  }

  /**
   * Returns the node that follows this one.
   * @return reference to next node
   */
```

LISTING 13.4 *continued*

```
   public LinearNode<T> getNext()
   {
      return next;
   }

   /**
    * Sets the node that follows this one.
    * @param node node to follow this one
    */
   public void setNext(LinearNode<T> node)
   {
      next = node;
   }

   /**
    * Returns the element stored in this node.
    * @return element stored at the node
    */
   public T getElement()
   {
      return element;
   }

   /**
    * Sets the element stored in this node.
    * @param elem element to be stored at this node
    */
   public void setElement(T elem)
   {
      element = elem;
   }
}
```

KEY CONCEPT

A linked implementation of a stack adds and removes elements from one end of the linked list.

Note that the `LinearNode<T>` class is not tied to the implementation of a stack collection. It can be used in any linear linked-list implementation of a collection. We will use it for other collections as needed.

Using the `LinearNode<T>` class and maintaining a count of elements in the collection creates the implementation strategy depicted in Figure 13.8.

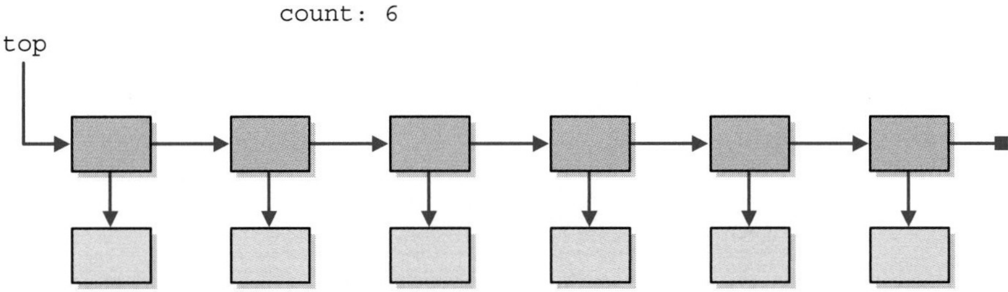

FIGURE 13.8 A linked implementation of a stack collection

The constructor of the `LinkedStack<T>` class sets the count of elements to zero and sets the front of the list, represented by the variable `top`, to `null`. Note that because a linked-list implementation does not have to worry about capacity limitations, there is no need to create a second constructor as we did in the `ArrayStack<T>` class of Chapter 12.

```
/**
 * Creates an empty stack.
 */
public LinkedStack()
{
   count = 0;
   top = null;
}
```

Because the nature of a stack is to only allow elements to be added to, or removed from, only one end, we will only need to operate on one end of our linked list. We could choose to push the first element into the first position in the linked list, the second element into the second position, and so on. This would mean that the top of the stack would always be at the tail end of the list. However, if we consider the efficiency of this strategy, we realize that it would mean we would have to traverse the entire list on every `push` and every `pop` operation. Instead, we can choose to operate on the front of the list, making the front of the list the top of the stack. In this way, we do not have to traverse the list for either the `push` or the `pop` operation. Figure 13.9 illustrates this configuration for a stack containing four elements, A, B, C, and D, that have been pushed onto the stack in that order.

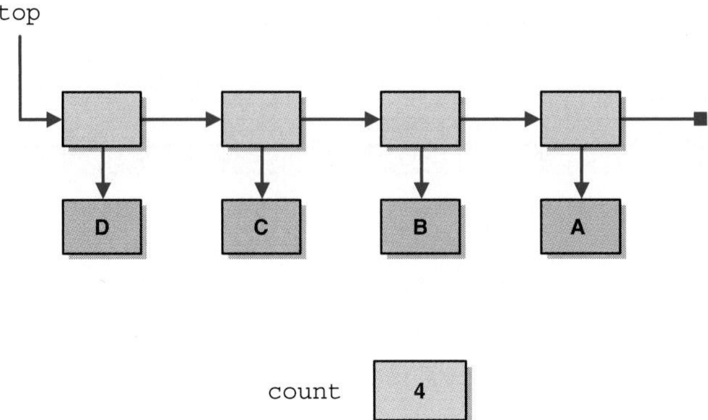

FIGURE 13.9 A linked implementation of a stack

Let's explore the implementation of the stack operations for the `LinkedStack` class.

The `push` Operation

Every time a new element is pushed onto the stack, a new `LinearNode` object must be created to store it in the linked list. To position the newly created node at the top of the stack, we must set its `next` reference to the current top of the stack and reset the `top` reference to point to the new node. We must also increment the `count` variable.

Implementing these steps results in the following code:

```
/**
 * Adds the specified element to the top of this stack.
 * @param element element to be pushed on stack
 */
public void push(T element)
{
   LinearNode<T> temp = new LinearNode<T>(element);

   temp.setNext(top);
   top = temp;
   count++;
}
```

Figure 13.10 shows the result of pushing the element E onto the stack depicted in Figure 13.9.

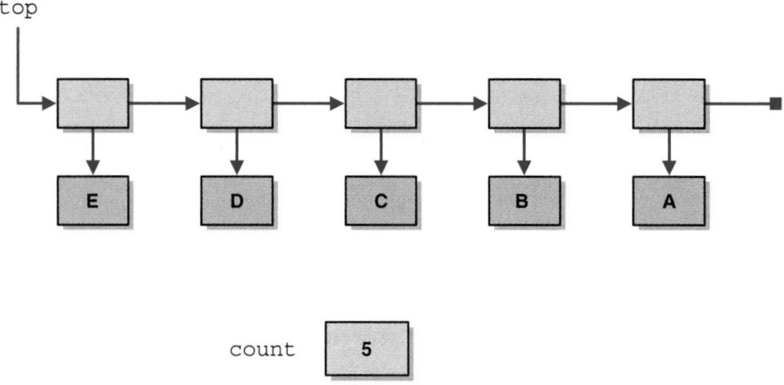

FIGURE 13.10 The stack after pushing element E

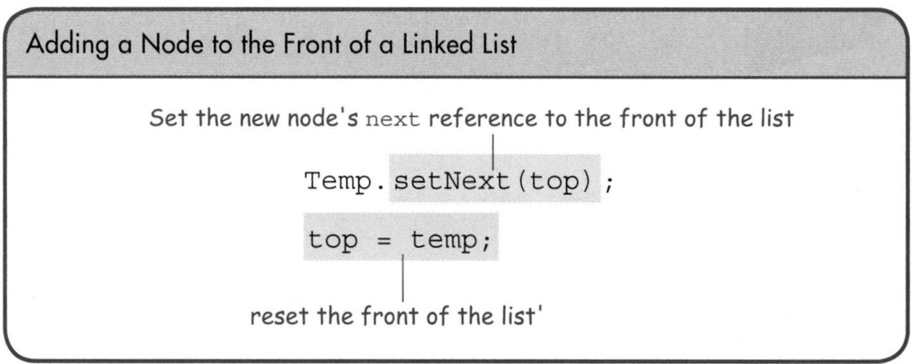

The push operation for the linked implementation of a stack consists of the following steps:

- Create a new node containing a reference to the object to be placed on the stack.
- Set the next reference of the new node to point to the current top of the stack (which will be null if the stack is empty).
- Set the top reference to point to the new node.
- Increment the count of elements in the stack.

All of these steps have time complexity O(1) because they require only one processing step regardless of the number of elements already in the stack. Each of these steps would have to be accomplished once for each of the elements to be pushed. Thus, using this method, the push operation would be O(1).

The pop Operation

The pop operation is implemented by returning a reference to the element currently stored at the top of the stack and adjusting the top reference to the new top of the stack. Before attempting to return any element, however, we must first ensure that there is at least one element to return. This operation can be implemented as follows:

```
/**
 * Removes the element at the top of this stack and returns a
 * reference to it.
 * @return element from top of stack
 * @throws EmptyCollectionException if the stack is empty
 */
public T pop() throws EmptyCollectionException
{
   if (isEmpty())
       throw new EmptyCollectionException("stack");

   T result = top.getElement();
   top = top.getNext();
   count--;

   return result;
}
```

If the stack is empty, as determined by the isEmpty method, an EmptyCollectionException is thrown. If there is at least one element to pop, it is stored in a temporary variable so that it can be returned. Then the reference to the top of the stack is set to the next element in the list, which is now the new top of the stack. The count of elements is decremented as well.

Figure 13.11 illustrates the result of a pop operation on the stack from Figure 13.8. Notice that this figure is identical to our original configuration in Figure 13.7. This illustrates the fact that the pop operation is the inverse of the push operation.

The pop operation for the linked implementation consists of the following steps:

- Make sure the stack is not empty.
- Set a temporary reference equal to the element on top of the stack.
- Set the top reference equal to the next reference of the node at the top of the stack.

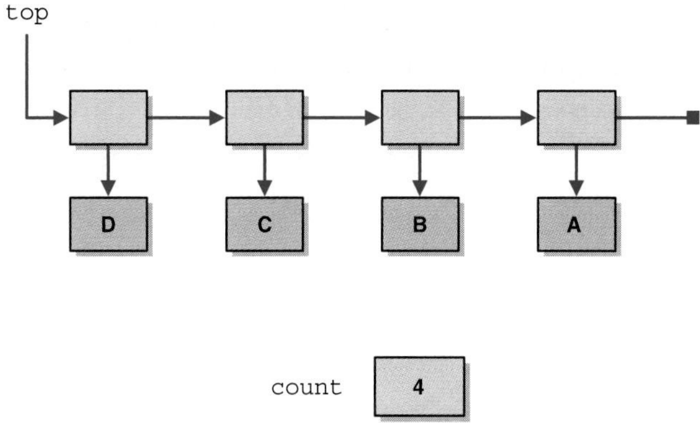

FIGURE 13.11 The stack after a pop operation

- Decrement the count of elements in the stack.
- Return the element pointed to by the temporary reference.

As with our previous examples, each of these operations consists of a single comparison or a simple assignment and is therefore O(1). Thus, the pop operation for the linked implementation is O(1).

Other Operations

Using a linked implementation, the `peek` operation is implemented by returning a reference to the element pointed to by the node pointed to by the top pointer. The `isEmpty` operation returns true if the count of elements is 0, and false otherwise. The `size` operation simply returns the count of elements in the stack. The `toString` operation can be implemented by traversing the linked list. These operations are left as programming projects.

Summary of Key Concepts

- Object reference variables can be used to create linked structures.
- A linked list is composed of objects that each point to the next object in the list.
- A linked list dynamically grows as needed and essentially has no capacity limitations.
- The order in which references are changed is crucial to maintaining a linked list.
- Dealing with the first node in a linked list often requires special handling.
- Objects that are stored in a collection should not contain any implementation details of the underlying data structure.
- The `java.util.Stack` class is derived from `Vector`, which gives a stack inappropriate operations.
- Any implementation of a collection can be used to solve a problem as long as it validly implements the appropriate operations.
- A linked implementation of a stack adds elements to, and removes elements from, one end of the linked list.
- Recursive processing can be simulated using a stack to keep track of the appropriate data.

Summary of Terms

activation record An object that represents a method invocation.

doubly linked list A linked list in which each node has references to both the next node and the previous node in the list.

linked list A linked structure in which one object refers to the next, creating a linear ordering.

linked structure A data structure that uses object reference variables to create links between objects.

node A class that represents a single element in a linked structure.

program stack A stack of activation records used to keep track of method invocations during program execution.

sentinel node A node at the front or end of a linked list that serves as a marker and does not represent an element in the list.

Self-Review Questions

SR 13.1 How do object references help us define data structures?

SR 13.2 Compare and contrast a linked list and an array.

SR 13.3 What special case exists when managing linked lists?

SR 13.4 Why should a linked list node be separate from the element stored on the list?

SR 13.5 What do the `LinkedStack<T>` and `ArrayStack<T>` classes have in common?

SR 13.6 What would be the time complexity of the `push` operation if we chose to push at the end of the list instead of at the front?

SR 13.7 What is the difference between a doubly linked list and a singly linked list?

SR 13.8 What impact would the use of sentinel nodes or dummy nodes have on a doubly linked list implementation?

SR 13.9 What are the advantages of using a linked implementation as opposed to an array implementation?

SR 13.10 What are the advantages of using an array implementation as opposed to a linked implementation?

SR 13.11 What are the advantages of the `java.util.Stack` implementation of a stack?

SR 13.12 What is the potential problem with the `java.util.Stack` implementation?

Exercises

EX 13.1 Explain what will happen if the steps depicted in Figure 13.4 are reversed.

EX 13.2 Explain what will happen if the steps depicted in Figure 13.5 are reversed.

EX 13.3 Draw a UML diagram showing the relationships among the classes involved in the linked-list implementation of a stack.

EX 13.4 Write an algorithm for the `add` method that will add at the end of the list instead of at the beginning. What is the time complexity of this algorithm?

EX 13.5 Modify the algorithm from the previous exercise so that it makes use of a rear reference. How does this affect the time complexity of this and the other operations?

EX 13.6 Discuss the effect on all the operations if there were not a count variable in the implementation.

EX 13.7 Discuss the impact (and draw an example) of using a sentinel node or dummy node at the head of a list.

EX 13.8 Draw the UML class diagram for the iterative maze solver example from this chapter.

Programming Projects

PP 13.1 Complete the implementation of the `LinkedStack<T>` class by providing the definitions for the `peek`, `size`, `isEmpty`, and `toString` methods.

PP 13.2 Modify the `postfix` program from Chapter 3 so that it uses the `LinkedStack<T>` class instead of the `ArrayStack<T>` class.

PP 13.3 Create a new version of the `LinkedStack<T>` class that makes use of a dummy record at the head of the list.

PP 13.4 Create a simple graphical application that will allow a user to perform `push`, `pop`, and `peek` operations on a stack, and display the resulting stack (using `toString`) in a text area.

PP 13.5 Design and implement an application that reads a sentence from the user and prints the sentence with the characters of each word backwards. Use a stack to reverse the characters of each word.

PP 13.6 Complete the solution to the iterative maze solver so that your solution marks the successful path.

PP 13.7 The linked implementation in this chapter uses a `count` variable to keep track of the number of elements in the stack. Rewrite the linked implementation without a `count` variable.

PP 13.8 There is a data structure called a drop-out stack that behaves like a stack in every respect except that if the stack size is n, then when the n+1 element is pushed, the first element is lost. Implement a drop-out stack using links.

PP 13.9 Modify the maze problem in this chapter so that it can start from a user-defined starting position (other than 0, 0) and search for a user-defined ending point (other than row-1, column-1).

Answers to Self-Review Questions

SRA 13.1 An object reference can be used as a link from one object to another. A group of linked objects can form a data structure, such as a linked list, on which a collection can be based.

SRA 13.2 A linked list has no capacity limitations, whereas an array does. However, arrays provide direct access to elements using indexes, whereas a linked list must be traversed one element at a time to reach a particular point in the list.

SRA 13.3 The primary special case in linked-list processing occurs when dealing with the first element in the list. A special reference variable is maintained that specifies the first element in the list. If that element is deleted, or if a new element is added in front of it, the front reference must be carefully maintained.

SRA 13.4 It is unreasonable to assume that every object that we may want to put in a collection can be designed to cooperate with the collection implementation. Furthermore, the implementation details are supposed to be kept distinct from the user of the collection, including the elements that the user chooses to add to the collection.

SRA 13.5 Both the LinkedStack<T> and ArrayStack<T> classes implement the StackADT<T> interface. This means that they both represent a stack collection, providing the necessary operations needed to use a stack. Although they both have distinct approaches to managing the collection, they are functionally interchangeable from the user's point of view.

SRA 13.6 To push at the end of the list, we would have to traverse the list to reach the last element. This traversal would cause the time complexity to be $O(n)$. An alternative would be to modify the solution to add a rear reference that always pointed to the last element in the list. This would help the time complexity for add but would have consequences if we try to remove the last element.

SRA 13.7 A singly linked list maintains a reference to the first element in the list and then a next reference from each node to the following node in the list. A doubly linked list maintains two references: front and rear. Each node in the doubly linked list stores both a next and a previous reference.

SRA 13.8 It would take two dummy records in a doubly linked list, one at the front and one at the rear, to eliminate the special cases when dealing with the first and last nodes.

SRA 13.9 A linked implementation allocates space only as it is needed and has a theoretical limit on the size of the hardware.

SRA 13.10 An array implementation uses less space per object since it only has to store the object and not an extra pointer. However, the array implementation will allocate much more space than it needs initially.

SRA 13.11 Because the `java.util.Stack` implementation is an extension of the `Vector` class, it can keep track of the positions of elements in the stack using an index and thus does not require each node to store an additional pointer. This implementation also allocates space only as it is needed, like the linked implementation.

SRA 13.12 The `java.util.Stack` implementation is an extension of the `Vector` class and thus inherits a large number of operations that violate the basic assumptions of a stack.

14 Queues

CHAPTER OBJECTIVES

- Examine queue processing.
- Demonstrate how a queue can be used to solve problems.
- Define a queue abstract data type.
- Examine various queue implementations.
- Compare queue implementations.

A queue is another collection with which we are inherently familiar. A queue is a waiting line, such as a line of customers waiting in a bank for their opportunity to talk to a teller. In fact, in many countries the word *queue* is used habitually in this way. In such countries, a person might say "join the queue" rather than "get in line." Other examples of queues include a checkout line at the grocery store and cars waiting at a stoplight. In any queue, an item enters on one end and leaves from the other. Queues have a variety of uses in computer algorithms.

14.1 A Conceptual Queue

A *queue* is a linear collection whose elements are added on one end and removed from the other. Therefore, we say that queue elements are processed in a *first in, first out* (FIFO) manner. Elements are removed from a queue in the same order in which they are placed on the queue.

This is consistent with the general concept of a waiting line. When a customer arrives at a bank, he or she begins waiting at the end of the line. When a teller becomes available, the customer at the beginning of the line leaves the line to receive service. Eventually every customer who started out at the end of the line moves to the front of the line and exits. For any given set of people, the first person to get in line is the first person to leave it.

KEY CONCEPT
Queue elements are processed in a FIFO manner—the first element in is the first element out.

The processing of a queue is pictured in Figure 14.1. Usually a queue is depicted horizontally. One end is established as the *front* of the queue and the other as the *rear* of the queue. Elements go onto the rear of the queue and come off of the front. Sometimes the front of the queue is called the *head* and the rear of the queue the *tail*.

Compare and contrast the processing of a queue to the LIFO (last in, first out) processing of a stack, which was discussed in Chapters 12 and 13. In a stack, the processing occurs at only one end of the collection. In a queue, processing occurs at both ends.

The operations defined for a queue ADT are listed in Figure 14.2. The term *enqueue* is used to refer to the process of adding a new element to the end of a queue. Likewise, *dequeue* is the process of removing the element at the front of a queue. The *first* operation enables the user to examine the element at the front of the queue without removing it from the collection.

Remember that naming conventions are not universal for collection operations. Sometimes `enqueue` is simply called `add`, `insert`, or `offer`. The `dequeue` operation is sometimes called `remove`, `poll`, or `serve`. The `first` operation is sometimes called `front` or `peek`.

FIGURE 14.1 A conceptual view of a queue

Operation	Description
`enqueue`	Adds an element to the rear of the queue.
`dequeue`	Removes an element from the front of the queue.
`first`	Examines the element at the front of the queue.
`isEmpty`	Determines if the queue is empty.
`size`	Determines the number of elements on the queue.
`toString`	Returns a string representation of the queue.

FIGURE 14.2 The operations on a queue

Note that there is a general similarity between the operations on a queue and those on a stack. The `enqueue`, `dequeue`, and `first` operations correspond to the stack operations `push`, `pop`, and `peek`. As is true of a stack, there are no operations that allow the user to "reach into" the middle of a queue and reorganize or remove elements. If that type of processing is required, perhaps the appropriate collection to use is a list of some kind, such as those discussed in the next chapter.

14.2 Queues in the Java API

Unfortunately, the Java Collections API is not consistent in its implementations of collections. There are a couple of important differences between the way the stack and queue collections are implemented:

- The Java Collections API provides the `java.util.Stack` class that implements a stack collection. Instead of a queue class, a `Queue` interface is provided and is implemented by several classes including the `LinkedList` class.
- The `java.util.Stack` class provides the traditional `push`, `pop`, and `peek` operations. The `Queue` interface does not implement the traditional `enqueue`, `dequeue`, and `first` operations. Instead, the `Queue` interface defines two alternatives for adding elements to, and removing elements from, a queue. These alternatives behave differently in terms of how the exceptional cases are handled. One set provides a boolean return value, whereas the other throws an exception.

The `Queue` interface defines an `element` method that is the equivalent of our conceptual `first`, `front`, or `peek`. This method retrieves the element at the head of the queue but does not remove it.

The `Queue` interface provides two methods for adding an element to the queue: `add` and `offer`. The `add` operation ensures that the queue contains the given element. This operation will throw an exception if the given element cannot be added to the queue. The `offer` operation inserts the given element into this queue, returning `true` if the insertion is successful and `false` otherwise.

The `Queue` interface also provides two methods for removing an element from the queue: `poll` and `remove`. Just like the difference between the `add` and `offer` methods, the difference between `poll` and `remove` is in how the exceptional case is handled. In this instance, the exceptional case `occurs` when an attempt is made to remove an element from an empty queue. The `poll` method will return `null` if the queue is empty, whereas the `remove` method will throw an exception.

Queues have a wide variety of applications within computing. Whereas the principal purpose of a stack is to reverse order, the principal purpose of a queue is to preserve order. Before exploring various ways to implement a queue, let's examine some ways in which a queue can be used to solve problems.

14.3 Using Queues: Code Keys

A *Caesar cipher* is a simple approach to encoding messages by shifting each letter in a message along the alphabet by a constant amount k. For example, if k equals 3, then in an encoded message, each letter is shifted three characters forward: a is replaced with d, b with e, c with f, and so on. The end of the alphabet wraps back around to the beginning. Thus w is replaced with z, x with a, y with b, and z with c.

To decode the message, each letter is shifted the same number of characters backwards. Therefore, if k equals 3, then the encoded message

```
vlpsolflwb iroorzv frpsohalwb
```

would be decoded into

```
simplicity follows complexity
```

Julius Caesar actually used this type of cipher in some of his secret government correspondence (hence the name). Unfortunately, the Caesar cipher is fairly easy to break. There are only 26 possibilities for shifting the characters, and the code can be broken by trying various key values until one works.

This encoding technique can be improved by using a *repeating key*. Instead of shifting each character by a constant amount, we can shift each character by a different amount using a list of key values. If the message is longer than the list of key values, we just start using the key over again from the beginning. For example, if the key values are

```
3 1 7 4 2 5
```

then the first character is shifted by three, the second character by one, the third character by seven, and so on. After shifting the sixth character by five, we start

Encoded Message:	n	o	v	a	n	j	g	h	l		m	u		u	r	x	l	v
Key:	3	1	7	4	2	5	3	1	7		4	2		5	3	1	7	4
Decoded Message:	k	n	o	w	l	e	d	g	e		i	s		p	o	w	e	r

FIGURE 14.3 An encoded message using a repeating key

using the key over again. The seventh character is shifted by three, the eighth by one, and so on.

Figure 14.3 shows the message "knowledge is power" encoded using this repeating key. Note that this encryption approach encodes the same letter into different characters, depending on where it occurs in the message (and thus on which key value is used to encode it). Conversely, the same character in the encoded message is decoded into different characters.

The program in Listing 14.1 uses a repeating key to encode and decode a message. The key of integer values is stored in a queue. After a key value is used, it is put back on the end of the queue so that the key continually repeats as needed for long messages. The key in this

KEY CONCEPT
A queue is a convenient collection for storing a repeating code key.

LISTING 14.1

```
import java.util.*;

/**
 * Codes demonstrates the use of queues to encrypt and decrypt messages.
 *
 * @author Java Foundations
 * @version 4.0
 */
public class Codes
{
   /**
    * Encode and decode a message using a key of values stored in
    * a queue.
    */
public static void main(String[] args)
{
   int[] key = {5, 12, -3, 8, -9, 4, 10};
   Integer keyValue;
   String encoded = "", decoded = "";
```

LISTING 14.1 *continued*

```
      String message = "All programmers are playwrights and all " +
                       "computers are lousy actors.";
      Queue<Integer> encodingQueue = new LinkedList<Integer>();
      Queue<Integer> decodingQueue = new LinkedList<Integer>();

      // load key queues

      for (int scan = 0; scan < key.length; scan++)
      {
         encodingQueue.add(key[scan]);
         decodingQueue.add(key[scan]);
      }

      // encode message

      for (int scan = 0; scan < message.length(); scan++)
      {
         keyValue = encodingQueue.remove();
         encoded += (char) (message.charAt(scan) + keyValue);
         encodingQueue.add(keyValue);
      }

      System.out.println ("Encoded Message:\n" + encoded + "\n");

      // decode message

      for (int scan = 0; scan < encoded.length(); scan++)
      {
         keyValue = decodingQueue.remove();
         decoded += (char) (encoded.charAt(scan) - keyValue);
         decodingQueue.add(keyValue);
      }
      System.out.println ("Decoded Message:\n" + decoded);
   }
}
```

example uses both positive and negative values. Figure 14.4 illustrates the UML description of the `Codes` class. As we saw in Chapter 12, the UML diagram illustrates the binding of the generic type `T` to an `Integer`. Unlike the earlier example, in this case we have two different bindings illustrated: one for the `LinkedList` class and one for the `Queue` interface.

This program actually uses two copies of the key stored in two separate queues. The idea is that the person encoding the message has one copy of the key, and the person decoding the message has another. Two copies of the key are helpful in

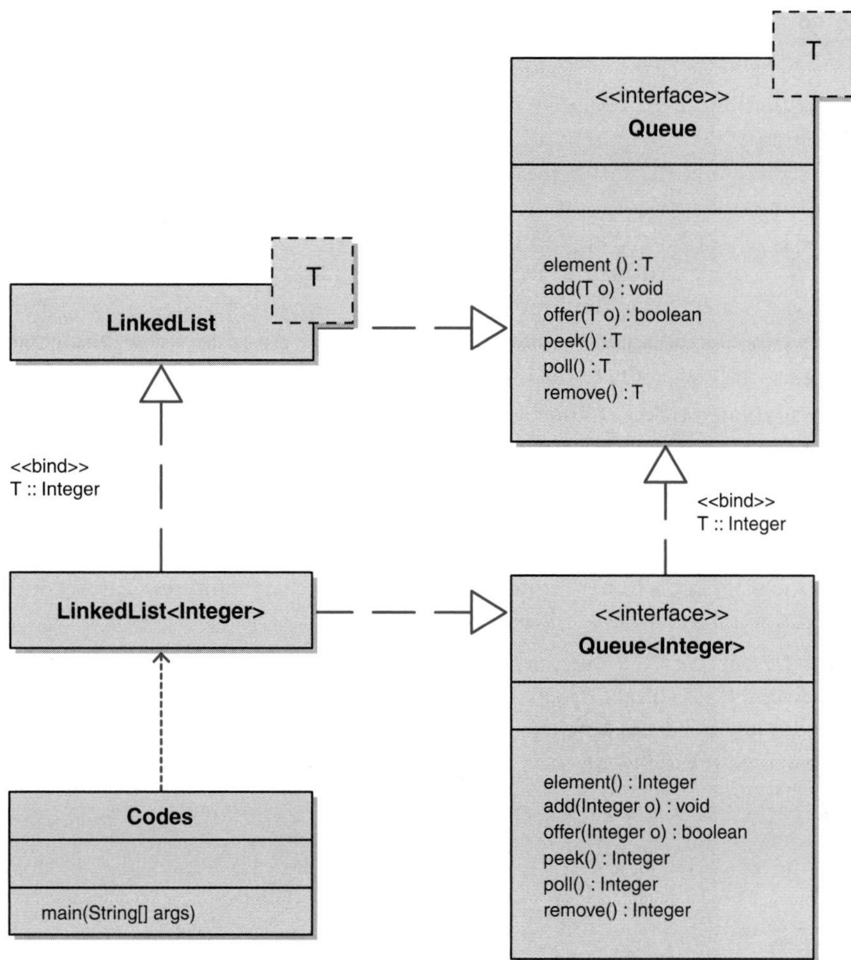

FIGURE 14.4 UML description of the `Codes` program

this program because the decoding process needs to match up the first character of the message with the first value in the key.

Also, note that this program doesn't bother to wrap around the end of the alphabet. It encodes any character in the Unicode character set by shifting it to some other position in the character set. Therefore, we can encode any character, including uppercase letters, lowercase letters, and punctuation. Even spaces get encoded.

Using a queue to store the key makes it easy to repeat the key by putting each key value back onto the queue as soon as it is used. The nature of a queue keeps the key values in the proper order, and we don't have to worry about reaching the end of the key and starting over.

14.4 Using Queues: Ticket Counter Simulation

Let's look at another example using queues. Consider the situation in which you are waiting in line to purchase tickets at a movie theater. In general, the more cashiers there are, the faster the line moves. The theater manager wants to keep his customers happy, but he doesn't want to employ any more cashiers than necessary. Suppose the manager wants to keep the total time needed by a customer to less than seven minutes. Being able to simulate the effect of adding more cashiers during peak business hours enables the manager to plan more effectively. And, as we've discussed, a queue is the perfect collection for representing a waiting line.

KEY CONCEPT
Simulations are often implemented using queues to represent waiting lines.

Our simulated ticket counter will use the following assumptions:

- There is only one line, and it is first come first served (a queue).
- Customers arrive on average every 15 seconds.
- If there is a cashier available, processing begins immediately upon arrival.
- Processing a customer request takes on average two minutes (120 seconds) from the time the customer reaches a cashier.

First we can create a `Customer` class, as shown in Listing 14.2. A `Customer` object keeps track of the time the customer arrives and the time the customer departs after purchasing a ticket. The total time spent by the customer is therefore the departure time minus the arrival time. To keep things simple, our simulation will

LISTING 14.2

```
/**
 * Customer represents a waiting customer.
 *
 * @author Java Foundations
 * @version 4.0
 */
public class Customer
{
  private int arrivalTime, departureTime;

   /**
    * Creates a new customer with the specified arrival time.
    * @param arrives the arrival time
    */
```

LISTING 14.2 *continued*

```
   public Customer(int arrives)
   {
      arrivalTime = arrives;
      departureTime = 0;
   }

   /**
    * Returns the arrival time of this customer.
    * @return the arrival time
    */
   public int getArrivalTime()
   {
      return arrivalTime;
   }

   /**
    * Sets the departure time for this customer.
    * @param departs the departure time
    **/
   public void setDepartureTime(int departs)
   {
      departureTime = departs;
   }

   /**
    * Returns the departure time of this customer.
    * @return the departure time
    */
   public int getDepartureTime()
   {
      return departureTime;
   }

   /**
    * Computes and returns the total time spent by this customer.
    * @return the total customer time
    */
   public int totalTime()
   {
      return departureTime - arrivalTime;
   }
}
```

measure time in elapsed seconds, so a time value can be stored as a single integer. Our simulation will begin at time 0.

Our simulation will create a queue of customers and then see how long it takes to process those customers if there is only one cashier. Then we will process the same queue of customers with two cashiers. Then we will do it again with three cashiers. We continue this process for up to ten cashiers. At the end we compare the average times that it takes to process a customer.

Because of our assumption that customers arrive every 15 seconds (on average), we can preload a queue with customers. We will process 100 customers in this simulation.

The program shown in Listing 14.3 conducts our simulation. The outer loop determines how many cashiers are used in each pass of the simulation. For each pass, the customers are taken from the queue in turn and processed by a cashier. The total elapsed time is tracked, and at the end of each pass the average time is computed. Figure 14.5 shows the UML description of the `TicketCounter` and `Customer` classes.

LISTING 14.3

```
import java.util.*;

/**
 * TicketCounter demonstrates the use of a queue for simulating a line of
 * customers
 *
 * @author Java Foundations
 * @version 4.0
 */
public class TicketCounter
{
  private final static int PROCESS = 120;
  private final static int MAX_CASHIERS = 10;
  private final static int NUM_CUSTOMERS = 100;

  public static void main(String[] args)
  {
     Customer customer;
     Queue<Customer> customerQueue = new LinkedList<Customer>();
     int[] cashierTime = new int[MAX_CASHIERS];
     int totalTime, averageTime, departs, start;

     // run the simulation for various number of cashiers
```

LISTING 14.3 *continued*

```
      for (int cashiers = 0; cashiers < MAX_CASHIERS; cashiers++)
      {
         // set each cashiers time to zero initially

         for (int count = 0; count < cashiers; count++)
            cashierTime[count] = 0;

         // load customer queue

         for (int count = 1; count <= NUM_CUSTOMERS; count++)
            customerQueue.add(new Customer(count * 15));

         totalTime = 0;

         // process all customers in the queue

         while (!(customerQueue.isEmpty()))
         {
            for (int count = 0; count <= cashiers; count++)
            {
               if (!(customerQueue.isEmpty()))
               {
                  customer = customerQueue.remove();
                  if (customer.getArrivalTime() > cashierTime[count])
                     start = customer.getArrivalTime();
                  else
                     start = cashierTime[count];
                  departs = start + PROCESS;
                  customer.setDepartureTime(departs);
                  cashierTime[count] = departs;
                  totalTime += customer.totalTime();
               }
            }
         }

         // output results for this simulation

         averageTime = totalTime / NUM_CUSTOMERS;
         System.out.println("Number of cashiers: " + (cashiers + 1));
         System.out.println("Average time: " + averageTime + "\n");
      }
   }
}
```

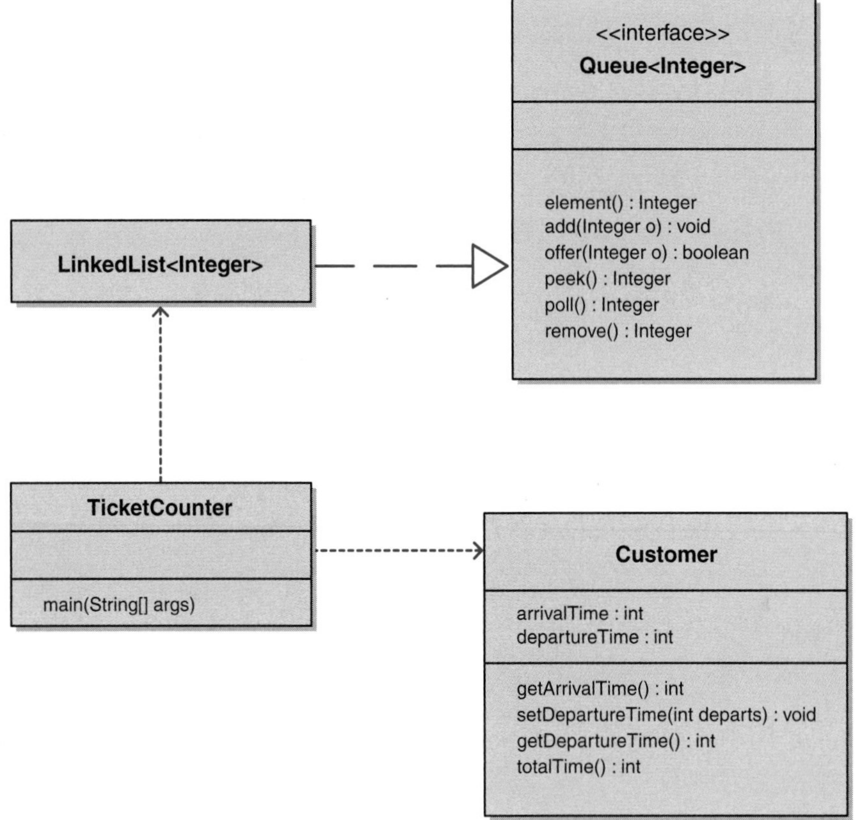

FIGURE 14.5 UML description of the `TicketCounter` program

The results of the simulation are shown in Figure 14.6. Note that with eight cashiers, the customers do not wait at all. The time of 120 seconds reflects only the time it takes to walk up and purchase the ticket. Increasing the number of cashiers to nine or ten or more will not improve the situation. Since the manager has decided he wants to keep the total average time to less than seven minutes (420 seconds), the simulation tells him that he should have six cashiers.

Number of Cashiers:	1	2	3	4	5	6	7	8	9	10
Average Time (sec):	5317	2325	1332	840	547	355	219	120	120	120

FIGURE 14.6 The results of the ticket counter simulation

14.5 A Queue ADT

As we did with stacks, we define a generic `QueueADT` interface that represents the queue operations, separating the general purpose of the operations from the variety of ways in which they could be implemented. A Java version of the `QueueADT` interface is shown in Listing 14.4, and its UML description is shown in Figure 14.7.

Note that in addition to the standard queue operations, we have included a `toString` method, just as we did with our stack collection. It is included for convenience and is not generally considered a classic operation on a queue.

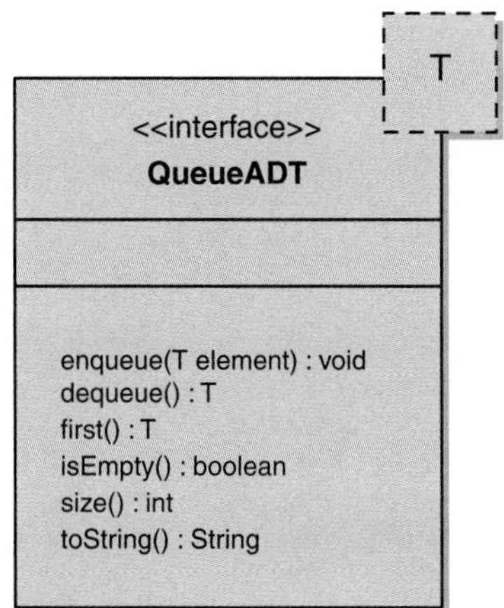

FIGURE 14.7 The `QueueADT` interface in UML

LISTING 14.4

```
package jsjf;

/**
 * QueueADT defines the interface to a queue collection.
 *
 * @author Java Foundations
 * @version 4.0
 */
public interface QueueADT<T>
{
   /**
    * Adds one element to the rear of this queue.
    * @param element  the element to be added to the rear of the queue
    */
```

LISTING 14.4 *continued*

```
    public void enqueue(T element);

    /**
     * Removes and returns the element at the front of this queue.
     * @return the element at the front of the queue
     */
    public T dequeue();

    /**
     * Returns without removing the element at the front of this queue.
     * @return the first element in the queue
     */
    public T first();

    /**
     * Returns true if this queue contains no elements.
     * @return true if this queue is empty
     */
    public boolean isEmpty();

    /**
     * Returns the number of elements in this queue.
     * @return the integer representation of the size of the queue
     */
    public int size();

    /**
     * Returns a string representation of this queue.
     * @return the string representation of the queue
     */
    public String toString();
}
```

14.6 A Linked Implementation of a Queue

Because a queue is a linear collection, we can implement a queue as a linked list of `LinearNode` objects, as we did with stacks. The primary difference is that we will have to operate on both ends of the list. Therefore, in addition to a reference (called `head`) pointing to the first element in the list, we will also keep track of a second reference (called `tail`) that points to the last element in the list. We will also use an integer variable called `count` to keep track of the number of elements in the queue.

Does it make a difference to which end of the list we add or enqueue elements and from which end of the list we remove or dequeue elements? If our linked list is singly linked, meaning that each node has only a pointer to the node behind it in the list, then yes, it does make a difference. In the case of the `enqueue` operation, it will not matter whether we add new elements to the head or the tail of the list. The processing steps will be very similar. If we add to the head of the list then we will set the `next` pointer of the new node to point to the `head` of the list and will set the `head` variable to point to the new node. If we add to the `tail` of the list, then we will set the `next` pointer of the node at the `tail` of the list to point to the new node and will set the `tail` of the list to point to the new node. In both cases, all of these processing steps are O(1), so the time complexity of the `enqueue` operation will be O(1).

KEY CONCEPT

A linked implementation of a queue is facilitated by references to the first and last elements of the linked list.

The difference between our two choices, adding to the `head` or the `tail` of the list, occurs with the `dequeue` operation. If we `enqueue` at the `tail` of the list and `dequeue` from the `head` of the list, then to `dequeue` we simply set a temporary variable to point to the element at the `head` of the list and then set the `head` variable to the value of the next pointer of the first node. Both processing steps are O(1), so the operation will be O(1). However, if we `enqueue` at the `head` of the list and `dequeue` at the `tail` of the list, our processing steps become more interesting. In order to `dequeue` from the `tail` of the list, we must set a temporary variable to point to the element at the `tail` of the list and then set the `tail` pointer to point to the node before the current `tail`. Unfortunately, in a singly linked list, we cannot get to this node without traversing the list. Therefore, if we chose to `enqueue` at the `head` and `dequeue` at the `tail`, the `dequeue` operation will be $O(n)$ instead of O(1) as it is with our other choice. Thus, we choose to `enqueue` at the `tail` and `dequeue` at the `head` of our singly linked list. Keep in mind that a doubly linked list would solve the problem of having to traverse the list and thus it would not matter which end was which in a doubly linked implementation.

Figure 14.8 depicts this strategy for implementing a queue. It shows a queue that has had the elements A, B, C, and D added to the queue, or enqueued, in that order.

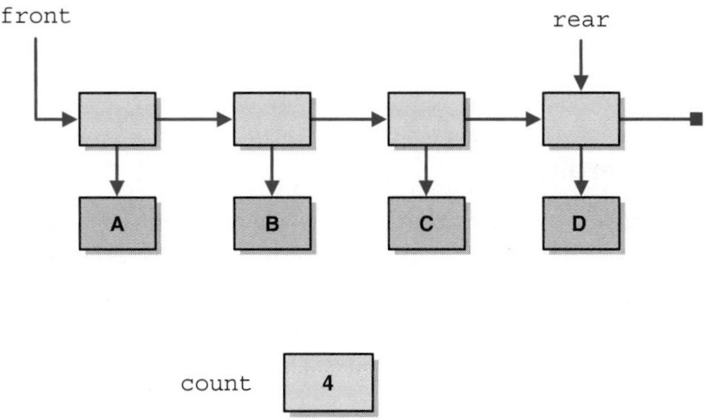

FIGURE 14.8 A linked implementation of a queue

Remember that Figure 14.8 depicts the general case. We always have to be careful to maintain our references accurately in special cases. For an empty queue, the head and tail references are both null and the count is zero. If there is exactly one element in the queue, both the head and tail references point to the same object.

Let's explore the implementation of the queue operations using this linked list approach. The header, class-level data, and constructors for our linked implementation of a queue are provided for context.

```
package jsjf;

import jsjf.exceptions.*;

/**
 * LinkedQueue represents a linked implementation of a queue.
 *
 * @author Java Foundations
 * @version 4.0
 */
public class LinkedQueue<T> implements QueueADT<T>
{
   private int count;
   private LinearNode<T> head, tail;

   /**
    * Creates an empty queue.
    */
   public LinkedQueue()
   {
      count = 0;
      head = tail = null;
   }
```

The enqueue Operation

The enqueue operation requires that we put the new element on the tail of the queue. In the general case, that means setting the next reference of the current last element to the new one, and resetting the tail reference to the new last element. However, if the queue is currently empty, the head reference must also be set to the new (and only) element. This operation can be implemented as follows:

```
/**
 * Adds the specified element to the tail of this queue.
 * @param element the element to be added to the tail of the queue
 */
public void enqueue(T element)
{
   LinearNode<T> node = new LinearNode<T>(element);

   if (isEmpty())
      head = node;
   else
      tail.setNext(node);

   tail = node;
   count++;
}
```

Note that the next reference of the new node need not be explicitly set in this method because it has already been set to null in the constructor for the `LinearNode` class. The `tail` reference is set to the new node in either case and the `count` is incremented. Implementing the queue operations with sentinel nodes is left as an exercise. As we discussed earlier, this operation is O(1).

Figure 14.9 shows the queue from Figure 14.8 after element E has been added.

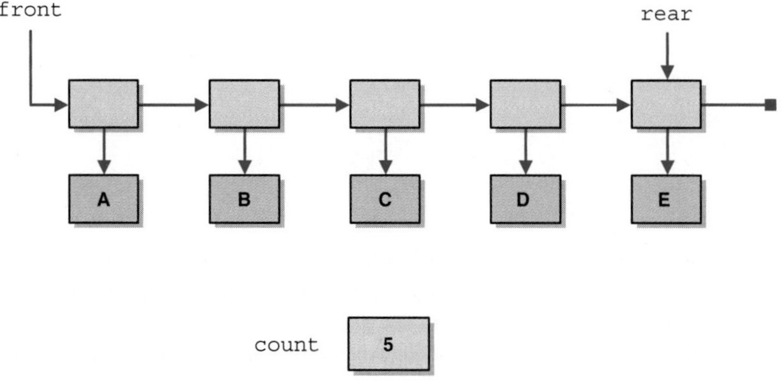

FIGURE 14.9 The queue after adding element E

The `dequeue` Operation

The first thing to do when implementing the dequeue operation is to ensure that there is at least one element to return. If not, an EmptyCollectionException is thrown. As we did with our stack collection in Chapters 12 and 13, it makes sense to employ a generic EmptyCollectionException to which we can pass a parameter specifying which collection we are dealing with. If there is at least one element in the queue, the first one in the list is returned, and the head reference is updated:

```
/**
 * Removes the element at the head of this queue and returns a
 * reference to it.
 * @return the element at the head of this queue
 * @throws EmptyCollectionException if the queue is empty
 */
public T dequeue() throws EmptyCollectionException
{
   if (isEmpty())
       throw new EmptyCollectionException("queue");

   T result = head.getElement();
   head = head.getNext();
   count--;

   if (isEmpty())
       tail = null;

   return result;
}
```

For the dequeue operation, we must consider the situation in which we are returning the only element in the queue. If, after removal of the head element, the queue is now empty, then the tail reference is set to null. Note that in this case, the head will be null because it was set equal to the next reference of the last element in the list. Again, as we discussed earlier, the dequeue operation for our implementation is O(1).

KEY CONCEPT

The enqueue and dequeue operations work on opposite ends of the collection.

DESIGN FOCUS

The same goals of reuse that apply to other classes apply to exceptions as well. The `EmptyCollectionException` class is a good example of this. It is an example of an exceptional case that will be the same for any collection that we create (such as attempting to perform an operation on the collection that cannot be performed if the collection is empty). Thus, creating a single exception with a parameter that allows us to designate which collection has thrown the exception is an excellent example of designing for reuse.

Figure 14.10 shows the result of a `dequeue` operation on the queue from Figure 14.9. The element A at the head of the queue is removed and returned to the user.

Note that, unlike the `push` and `pop` operations on a stack, the `dequeue` operation is not the inverse of `enqueue`. That is, Figure 14.10 is not identical to our original configuration shown in Figure 14.8, because the `enqueue` and `dequeue` operations are working on opposite ends of the collection.

Other Operations

The remaining operations in the linked queue implementation are fairly straightforward and are similar to those in the stack collection. The `first` operation is implemented by returning a reference to the element at the head of the queue. The `isEmpty` operation returns true if the count of elements is 0, and false otherwise. The `size` operation simply returns the count of elements in the queue. Finally, the `toString` operation returns a string made up of the `toString` results of each individual element. These operations are left as programming projects.

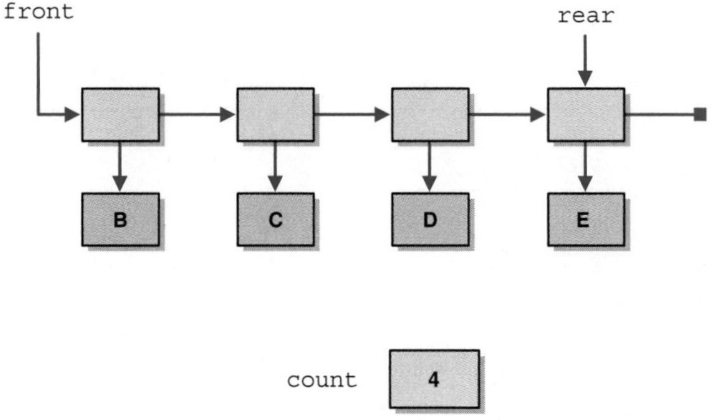

FIGURE 14.10 The queue after a `dequeue` operation

14.7 Implementing Queues: With Arrays

VideoNote
An array-based queue implementation.

One array-based strategy for implementing a queue is to fix one end of the queue (say, the front) at index 0 of the array. The elements are stored contiguously in the array. Figure 14.11 depicts a queue stored in this manner, assuming elements A, B, C, and D have been added to the queue in that order.

KEY CONCEPT
Because queue operations modify both ends of the collection, fixing one end at index 0 requires that elements be shifted.

In a manner similar to the `top` variable in the `ArrayStack` implementation, the integer variable `rear` is used to indicate the next open cell in the array. Note that it also represents the number of elements in the queue.

This strategy assumes that the first element in the queue is always stored at index 0 of the array. Because queue processing affects both ends of the collection, this strategy will require that we shift the elements whenever an element is removed from the queue. This required shifting of elements would make the `dequeue` operation O(n). Just as in our discussion of the complexity of our singly linked list implementation above, making a poor choice in our array implementation could lead to less than optimal efficiency.

KEY CONCEPT
The shifting of elements in a noncircular array implementation creates an O(*n*) complexity.

Would it make a difference if we fixed the rear of the queue, instead of the front, at index 0 of the array? Keep in mind that when we enqueue an element onto the queue, we do so at the rear of the queue. This would mean that each `enqueue` operation would result in shifting all of the elements in the queue up one position in the array, making the `enqueue` operation O(*n*).

The key is to not fix either end. As elements are dequeued, the front of the queue will move further into the array. As elements are enqueued, the rear of the queue will also move further into the array. The challenge comes when the rear of the queue reaches the end of the array. Enlarging the array at this point is not a

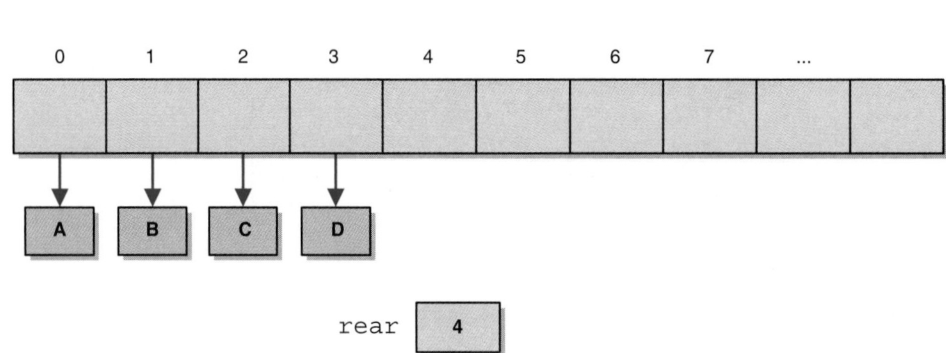

FIGURE 14.11 An array implementation of a queue

DESIGN FOCUS

It is important to note that this fixed array implementation strategy, which was very effective in our implementation of a stack, is not nearly as efficient for a queue. This is an important example of matching the data structure used to implement a collection with the collection itself. The fixed array strategy was efficient for a stack because all of the activity (adding and removing elements) was on one end of the collection and thus on one end of the array. With a queue, now that we are operating on both ends of the collection and order does matter, the fixed array implementation is much less efficient.

practical solution, and it does not make use of the now-empty space in the lower indexes of the array.

KEY CONCEPT
Treating arrays as circular eliminates the need to shift elements in an array queue implementation.

To make this solution work, we will use a *circular array* to implement the queue, defined in a class called `CircularArrayQueue`. A circular array is not a new construct—it is just a way to think about the array used to store the collection. Conceptually, the array is used as a circle, whose last index is followed by the first index. A circular array storing a queue is shown in Figure 14.12.

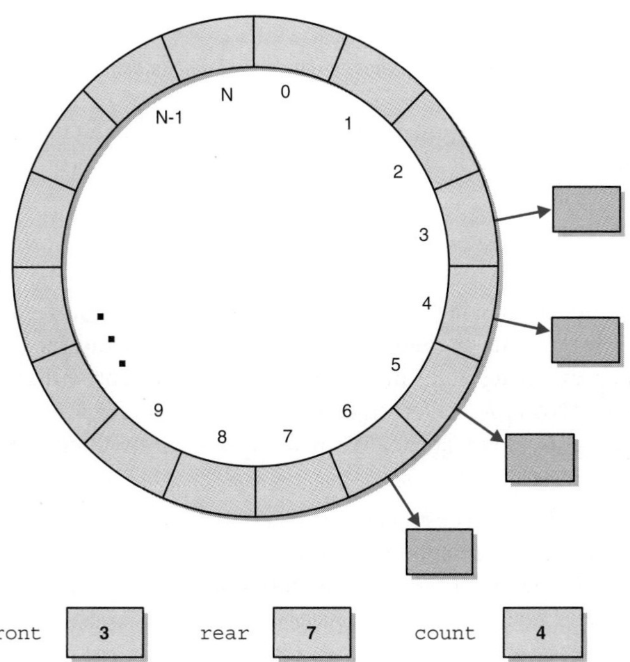

FIGURE 14.12 A circular array implementation of a queue

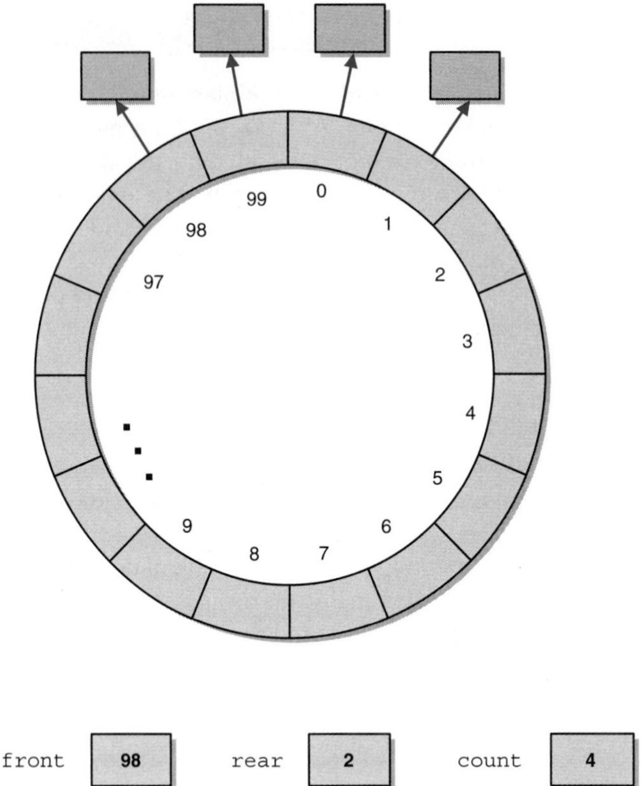

FIGURE 14.13 A queue straddling the end of a circular array

Two integer values are used to represent the front and rear of the queue. These values change as elements are added and removed. Note that the value of `front` represents the location where the first element in the queue is stored, and the value of `rear` represents the next available slot in the array (not where the last element is stored). Using `rear` in this manner is consistent with our other array implementation. Note, however, that the value of `rear` no longer represents the number of elements in the queue. We will use a separate integer value to keep a count of the elements.

When the rear of the queue reaches the end of the array, it "wraps around" to the front of the array. The elements of the queue can therefore straddle the end of the array, as shown in Figure 14.13, which assumes the array can store 100 elements.

Using this strategy, once an element has been added to the queue, it stays in one location in the array until it is removed with a `dequeue` operation. No elements need to be shifted as elements are added or removed. This approach requires, however, that we carefully manage the values of `front` and `rear`.

Let's look at another example. Figure 14.14 shows a circular array (drawn linearly) with a capacity of ten elements. Initially it is shown after elements A through H have been enqueued. It is then shown after the first four elements (A through D) have been dequeued. Finally, it is shown after elements I, J, K, and L have been enqueued, which causes the queue to wrap around the end of the array.

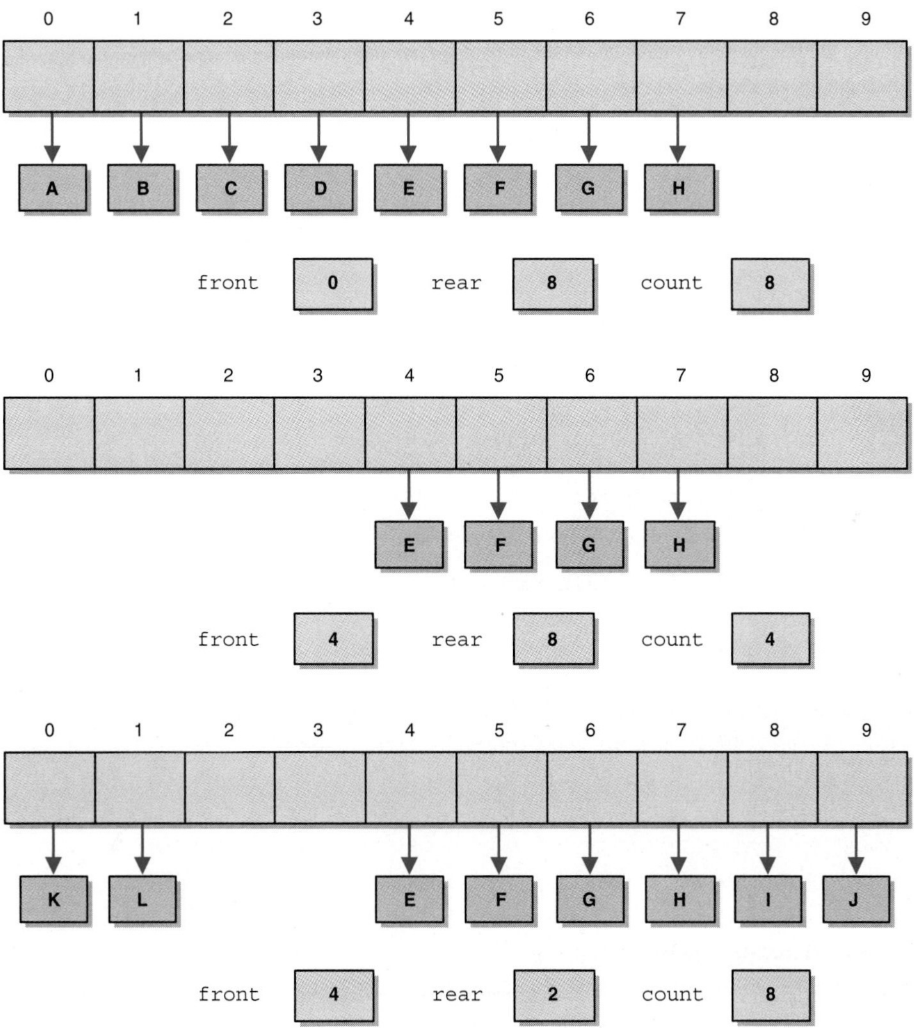

FIGURE 14.14 Changes in a circular array implementation of a queue

The header, class-level data, and constructors for our circular array implementation of a queue are provided for context:

```
package jsjf;

import jsjf.exceptions.*;

/**
 * CircularArrayQueue represents an array implementation of a queue in
 * which the indexes for the front and rear of the queue circle back to 0
 * when they reach the end of the array.
 *
 * @author Java Foundations
 * @version 4.0
 */
public class CircularArrayQueue<T> implements QueueADT<T>
{
   private final static int DEFAULT_CAPACITY = 100;
   private int front, rear, count;
   private T[] queue;

   /**
    * Creates an empty queue using the specified capacity.
    * @param initialCapacity the initial size of the circular array queue
    */
   public CircularArrayQueue (int initialCapacity)
   {
      front = rear = count = 0;
      queue = (T[]) (new Object[initialCapacity]);
   }

   /**
    * Creates an empty queue using the default capacity.
    */
   public CircularArrayQueue()
   {
      this(DEFAULT_CAPACITY);
   }
```

The `enqueue` Operation

In general, after an element is enqueued, the value of `rear` is incremented. But when an `enqueue` operation fills the last cell of the array (at the largest index), the value of `rear` must be set to 0, indicating that the next element should be stored at index 0. The appropriate update to the value of `rear` can be accomplished in one calculation by using the remainder operator (%). Recall that the remainder operator returns the remainder after dividing the first operand by the second. Therefore, if queue is the name of the array storing the queue, the following line of code will update the value of rear appropriately:

```
rear = (rear+1) % queue.length;
```

Let's try this calculation, assuming we have an array of size 10. If rear is currently 5, it will be set to 6%10, or 6. If rear is currently 9, it will be set to 10%10 or 0. Try this calculation using various situations to see that it works no matter how big the array is.

Given this strategy, the enqueue operation can be implemented as follows:

```
/**
 * Adds the specified element to the rear of this queue, expanding
 * the capacity of the queue array if necessary.
 * @param element the element to add to the rear of the queue
 */
public void enqueue(T element)
{
   if (size() == queue.length)
       expandCapacity();

   queue[rear] = element;
   rear = (rear+1) % queue.length;

   count++;
}
```

Circular Increment

increment regularly

```
rear = (rear + 1) % queue.length;
```

wrap back to 0 if appropriate

Note that this implementation strategy will still allow the array to reach capacity. As with any array-based implementation, all cells in the array may become filled. This implies that the rear of the queue has "caught up" to the front of the queue. To add another element, the array would have to be enlarged. Keep in mind, however, that the elements of the existing array must be copied into the new array in their proper order in the queue, which is not necessarily the order in which they appear in the current array. This makes the private `expandCapacity` method slightly more complex than the one we used for stacks:

```
/**
 * Creates a new array to store the contents of this queue with
 * twice the capacity of the old one.
 */
private void expandCapacity()
{
   T[] larger = (T[]) (new Object[queue.length *2]);

   for (int scan = 0; scan < count; scan++)
   {
      larger[scan] = queue[front];
      front = (front + 1) % queue.length;
   }
   front = 0;
   rear = count;
   queue = larger;
}
```

The `dequeue` Operation

Likewise, after an element is dequeued, the value of `front` is incremented. After enough `dequeue` operations, the value of `front` will reach the last index of the array. After removal of the element at the largest index, the value of `front` must be set to 0 instead of being incremented. The same calculation we used to set the value of `rear` in the `enqueue` operation can be used to set the value of `front` in the `dequeue` operation:

```
/**
 * Removes the element at the front of this queue and returns a
 * reference to it.
 * @return the element removed from the front of the queue
 * @throws EmptyCollectionException  if the queue is empty
 */
```

```
public T dequeue() throws EmptyCollectionException
{
   if (isEmpty())
       throw new EmptyCollectionException("queue");

   T result = queue[front];
   queue[front] = null;
   front = (front+1) % queue.length;

   count--;

   return result;
}
```

Other Operations

Operations such as `toString` become a bit more complicated using this approach, because the elements are not stored starting at index 0 and may wrap around the end of the array. These methods have to take the current situation into account. All of the other operations for a circular array queue are left as programming projects.

14.8 Double-Ended Queues (Dequeue)

A deque, or double-ended queue, is an extension of the concept of a queue that allows adding, removing, and viewing elements from both ends of the queue. As mentioned in Chapter 12, the Java API provides the `Deque` interface, which like the `Queue` interface, is implemented by the `LinkedList` class. Just like the `Queue` interface, the `Deque` interface provides two versions of each operation: one that will throw an exception and one that will return a `boolean`.

Interestingly, the `Deque` interface also provides implementations of the basic stack operations `push`, `pop`, and `peek`. In fact, Oracle now recommends that the `Deque` interface be used in place of the `java.util.stack` class.

Summary of Key Concepts

- Queue elements are processed in a FIFO manner—the first element in is the first element out.
- A queue is a convenient collection for storing a repeating code key.
- Simulations are often implemented using queues to represent waiting lines.
- A linked implementation of a queue is facilitated by references to the first and last elements of the linked list.
- The `enqueue` and `dequeue` operations work on opposite ends of the collection.
- Because queue operations modify both ends of the collection, fixing one end at index 0 requires that elements be shifted.
- The shifting of elements in a noncircular array implementation creates an $O(n)$ complexity.
- Treating arrays as circular eliminates the need to shift elements in an array queue implementation.

Summary of Terms

Caesar cipher A simple message encoding technique in which letters are shifted along the alphabet by a constant amount.

circular array An array that is treated as circular, meaning that incrementing the last index value in the array wraps around back to the first element.

dequeue A queue operation in which an element is removed from the front of the queue.

enqueue A queue operation in which an element is added to the rear of the queue.

FIFO (1) First in, first out; (2) A description of a collection in which the first element added will be the first element removed.

queue A linear collection whose elements are added on one end and removed from the other.

repeating key A list of integer values used to shift letters by varying amounts in an improved version of a Caesar cipher.

Self-Review Questions

SR 14.1 What is the difference between a queue and a stack?

SR 14.2 What are the five basic operations on a queue?

SR 14.3 What are some of the other operations that might be implemented for a queue?

SR 14.4 Is it possible for the `head` and `tail` references in a linked implementation to be equal?

SR 14.5 Is it possible for the `front` and `rear` references in a circular array implementation to be equal?

SR 14.6 Which implementation has the worst time complexity?

SR 14.7 Which implementation has the worst space complexity?

Exercises

EX 14.1 Hand trace a queue X through the following operations:

```
X.enqueue(new Integer(4));
X.enqueue(new Integer(1));
Object Y = X.dequeue();
X.enqueue(new Integer(8));
X.enqueue(new Integer(2));
X.enqueue(new Integer(5));
X.enqueue(new Integer(3));
Object Y = X.dequeue();
X.enqueue(new Integer(4));
X.enqueue(new Integer(9));
```

EX 14.2 Given the queue X that results from Exercise 14.1, what would be the result of each of the following?

```
a.X.first();
b.Y = X.dequeue();
  X.first();
c.Y = X.dequeue();
d.X.first();
```

EX 14.3 What would be the time complexity of the `size` operation for each of the implementations if there were not a `count` variable?

EX 14.4 Under what circumstances could the `head` and `tail` references for the linked implementation of the `front` and `rear` references of the array implementation be equal?

EX 14.5 Hand trace the ticket counter problem for 22 customers and 4 cashiers. Graph the total process time for each person. What can you surmise from these results?

EX 14.6 Compare and contrast the `enqueue` method of the `LinkedQueue` class to the `push` method of the `LinkedStack` class from Chapter 13.

EX 14.7 Describe two different ways in which the `isEmpty` method of the `LinkedQueue` class could be implemented.

EX 14.8 Name five everyday examples of a queue other than those discussed in this chapter.

EX 14.9 Explain why the array implementation of a stack does not require elements to be shifted but the noncircular array implementation of a queue does.

EX 14.10 Suppose the `count` variable was not used in the `CircularArrayQueue` class. Explain how you could use the values of `front` and `rear` to compute the number of elements in the list.

Programming Projects

PP 14.1 Complete the implementation of the `LinkedQueue` class presented in this chapter. Specifically, complete the implementations of the `first`, `isEmpty`, `size`, and `toString` methods.

PP 14.2 Complete the implementation of the `CircularArrayQueue` class described in this chapter, including all methods.

PP 14.3 Write a version of the `CircularArrayQueue` class that grows the list in the direction opposite to the direction in which the version described in this chapter grows the list.

PP 14.4 All of the implementations in this chapter use a `count` variable to keep track of the number of elements in the queue. Rewrite the linked implementation without a `count` variable.

PP 14.5 All of the implementations in this chapter use a `count` variable to keep track of the number of elements in the queue. Rewrite the circular array implementation without a `count` variable.

PP 14.6 A data structure called a deque is closely related to a queue. The name *deque* stands for "double-ended queue. " The difference between the two is that with a deque, you can insert, remove, or view from either end of the queue. Implement a deque using arrays.

PP 14.7 Implement the deque from Programming Project 14.6 using links. (*Hint*: Each node will need a `next` and a `previous` reference.)

PP 14.8 Create a graphical application that provides buttons for enqueue and dequeue from a queue, a text field to accept a string as input for enqueue, and a text area to display the contents of the queue after each operation.

PP 14.9 Create a system using a stack and a queue to test whether a given string is a palindrome (that is, whether the characters read the same both forwards and backwards).

PP 14.10 Create a system to simulate vehicles at an intersection. Assume that there is one lane going in each of four directions, with stoplights facing each direction. Vary the arrival average of vehicles in each direction and the frequency of the light changes to view the "behavior" of the intersection.

Answers to Self-Review Questions

SRA 14.1 A queue is a first in, first out (FIFO) collection, whereas a stack is a last in, first out (LIFO) collection.

SRA 14.2 The basic queue operations are

`enqueue`–adds an element to the end of the queue
`dequeue`–removes an element from the front of the queue
`first`–returns a reference to the element at the front of the queue
`isEmpty`–returns true if the queue is empty, returns false otherwise

SRA 14.3 `makeEmpty()`, `destroy()`, `full()`

SRA 14.4 Yes, it happens when the queue is empty (both `head` and `tail` are null) and when there is only one element on the queue.

SRA 14.5 Yes, it can happen under two circumstances: when the queue is empty and when the queue is full.

SRA 14.6 The noncircular array implementation with an O(n) `dequeue` or `enqueue` operation has the worst time complexity.

SRA 14.7 Both of the array implementations waste space for unfilled elements in the array. The linked implementation uses more space per element stored.

15 Lists

CHAPTER OBJECTIVES

- Examine various types of list collections.
- Demonstrate how lists can be used to solve problems.
- Define a list abstract data type.
- Examine and compare list implementations.

The concept of a list is familiar to all of us. You may make to-do lists, lists of items to buy at the grocery store, and lists of friends to invite to a party. You might number the items in a list or keep them in alphabetical order. In other situations you may simply keep the items in a particular order that simply makes the most sense to you. This chapter explores the concept of a list collection and some ways in which such collections can be managed.

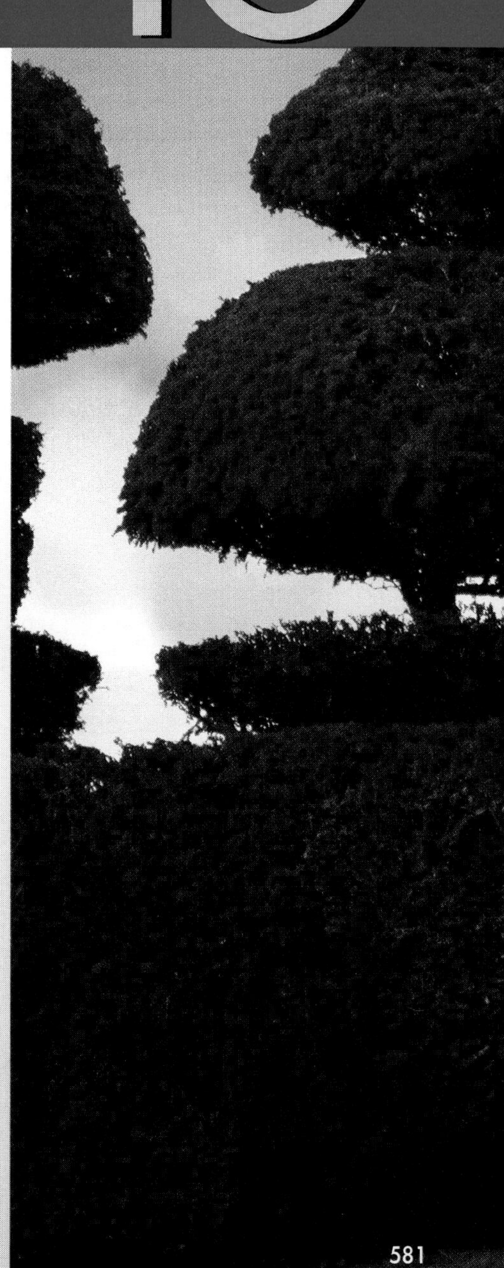

15.1 A List Collection

Let's begin by differentiating between a linked list and the concept of a list collection. As we've seen in previous chapters, a linked list is an implementation strategy that uses references to create links between objects. We used linked lists in Chapters 13 and 14 to help us implement stack and queue collections, respectively.

VideoNote
List categories.

A list collection, on the other hand, is a conceptual notion—the idea of keeping things organized in a linear list. Just like stacks and queues, a list can be implemented using linked lists or arrays. A list collection has no inherent capacity; it can grow as large as needed.

Both stacks and queues are linear structures and might be thought of as lists, but elements can be added and removed only on the ends. List collections are more general; elements can be added and removed in the middle of the list as well as on the ends.

Furthermore, there are three types of list collections:

- *Ordered lists*, whose elements are ordered by some inherent characteristic of the elements
- *Unordered lists*, whose elements have no inherent order but are ordered by their placement in the list
- *Indexed lists*, whose elements can be referenced using a numeric index

KEY CONCEPT
List collections can be categorized as ordered, unordered, or indexed.

KEY CONCEPT
The elements of an ordered list have an inherent relationship defining their order.

An ordered list is based on some particular characteristic of the elements in the list. For example, you may keep a list of people ordered alphabetically by name, or you may keep an inventory list ordered by part number. The list is sorted on the basis of some key value. Any element added to an ordered list has a proper location in the list, given its key value and the key values of the elements already in the list. Figure 15.1 shows a conceptual view of an ordered list, in which the elements are ordered by an integer key value. Adding a value to the list involves finding the new element's proper, sorted position among the existing elements.

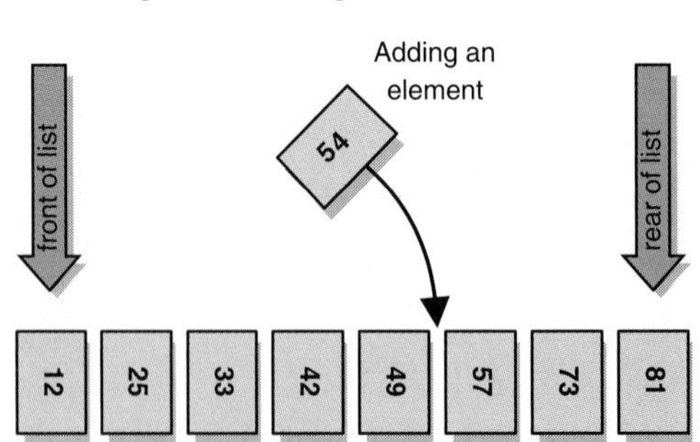

FIGURE 15.1 A conceptual view of an ordered list

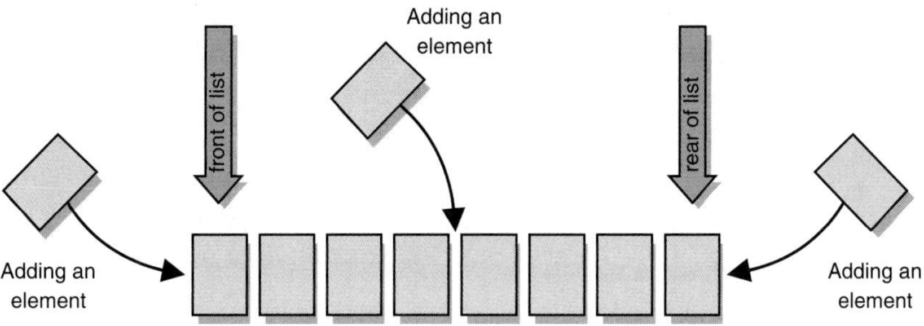

FIGURE 15.2 A conceptual view of an unordered list

The placement of elements in an unordered list is not based on any inherent characteristic of the elements. Don't let the name mislead you. The elements in an unordered list are kept in a particular order, but that order is not based on the elements themselves. The client using the list determines the order of the elements. Figure 15.2 shows a conceptual view of an unordered list. A new element can be put at the front or rear of the list, or it can be inserted after a particular element already in the list.

> **KEY CONCEPT**
> The elements of an unordered list are kept in whatever order the client chooses.

An indexed list is similar to an unordered list in that there is no inherent relationship among the elements that determines their order in the list. The client using the list determines the order of the elements. However, in addition, each element can be referenced by a numeric index that begins at 0 at the front of the list and continues contiguously until the end of the list. Figure 15.3 shows a conceptual view of an indexed list. A new element can be inserted into the list at any position, including at the front or rear of the list. Every time a change occurs in the list, the indexes are adjusted to stay in order and contiguous.

> **KEY CONCEPT**
> An indexed list maintains a contiguous numeric index range for its elements.

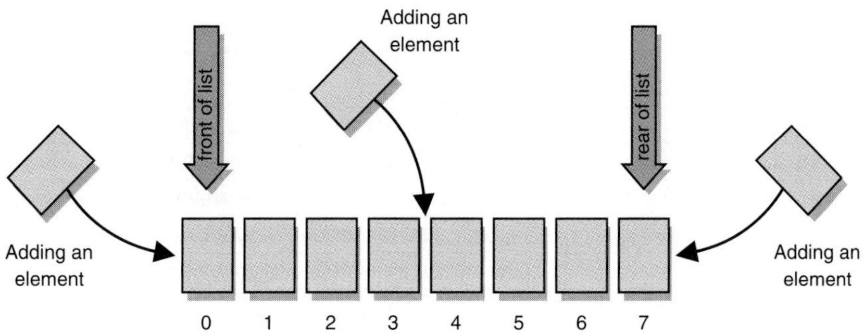

FIGURE 15.3 A conceptual view of an indexed list

DESIGN FOCUS

Is it possible that a list could be both an ordered list and an indexed list? Possible perhaps but not very meaningful. If a list were both ordered and indexed, what would happen if a client application attempted to add an element at a particular index or to change an element at a particular index such that it is not in the proper order? Which rule would have precedence, index position or order?

Note the primary difference between an indexed list and an array: An indexed list keeps its indexes contiguous. If an element is removed, the positions of other elements "collapse" to eliminate the gap. When an element is inserted, the indexes of other elements are shifted to make room.

15.2 Lists in the Java Collections API

The list classes provided in the Java API primarily support the concept of an indexed list. To some extent, they overlap with the concept of an unordered list. Note, though, that the Java API does not have any classes that directly implement an ordered list as described above.

KEY CONCEPT

The Java API does not provide a class that implements an ordered list.

You're probably already familiar with the `ArrayList` class from the Java API. It is a favorite among Java programmers, because it provides a quick way to manage a set of objects. Its counterpart, the `LinkedList` class, provides the same basic functionality with, as the name implies, an underlying linked implementation. Both store elements defined by a generic parameter `E`.

Both `ArrayList` and `LinkedList` implement the `java.util.List` interface. Some of the methods in the `List` interface are shown in Figure 15.4.

Before looking at our own implementation of lists, let's look at a couple of examples that use lists provided by the Java API.

Method	Description
`add(E element)`	Adds an element to the end of the list.
`add(int index, E element)`	Inserts an element at the specified index.
`get(int index)`	Returns the element at the specified index.
`remove(int index)`	Removes the element at the specified index.
`remove(E object)`	Removes the first occurrence of the specified object.
`set(int index, E element)`	Replaces the element at the specified index.
`size()`	Returns the number ofelements in the list.

FIGURE 15.4 Some methods in the `java.util.List` interface

15.3 Using Unordered Lists: Program of Study

The list of courses a student takes in order to fulfill degree requirements is sometimes called a program of study. Let's look at an example that manages a simplified program of study. We'll use the `LinkedList` class from the Java API, adding some unordered list operations, to manage the list of courses.

Listing 15.1 contains a `main` method that creates a `ProgramOfStudy` object and uses it to manage a few specific courses. It first adds a few initial courses, one after the other to the end of the list. Then a second CS course is inserted into the list after the existing CS course. Then a specific THE course is found, and its grade is updated. Finally, a GER course is replaced by a FRE course.

LISTING 15.1

```
import java.io.IOException;

/**
 * Demonstrates the use of a list to manage a set of objects.
 *
 * @author Java Foundations
 * @version 4.0
 */
public class POSTester
{
   /**
    * Creates and populates a Program of Study. Then saves it using serialization.
    */
   public static void main(String[] args) throws IOException
   {
      ProgramOfStudy pos = new ProgramOfStudy();

      pos.addCourse(new Course("CS", 101, "Introduction to Programming", "A-"));
      pos.addCourse(new Course("ARCH", 305, "Building Analysis", "A"));
      pos.addCourse(new Course("GER", 210, "Intermediate German"));
      pos.addCourse(new Course("CS", 320, "Computer Architecture"));
      pos.addCourse(new Course("THE", 201, "The Theatre Experience"));

      Course arch = pos.find("CS", 320);
      pos.addCourseAfter(arch, new Course("CS", 321, "Operating Systems"));
      Course theatre = pos.find("THE", 201);
      theatre.setGrade("A-");
```

LISTING 15.1 *continued*

```
        Course german = pos.find("GER", 210);
        pos.replace(german, new Course("FRE", 110, "Beginning French", "B+"));

        System.out.println(pos);

        pos.save("ProgramOfStudy");
    }
}
```

After manipulating the list of courses in these specific ways, the `main` method prints the entire `ProgramOfStudy` object and then saves it to disk so that it can be retrieved and modified further at a later time.

The `ProgramOfStudy` class is shown in Listing 15.2 and the `Course` class is shown in Listing 15.3. First note that the instance variable called `list` is declared to be of type `List<Course>`, which refers to the interface. In the constructor, a new `LinkedList<Course>` object is instantiated. If desired, this could be changed to an `ArrayList<Course>` object without any other changes to the class.

LISTING 15.2

```
import java.io.FileInputStream;
import java.io.FileNotFoundException;
import java.io.FileOutputStream;
import java.io.IOException;
import java.io.ObjectInputStream;
import java.io.ObjectOutputStream;
import java.io.Serializable;
import java.util.Iterator;
import java.util.LinkedList;
import java.util.List;

/**
 * Represents a Program of Study, a list of courses taken and planned, for an
 * individual student.
 *
 * @author Java Foundations
 * @version 4.0
 */
```

LISTING 15.2 *continued*

```
public class ProgramOfStudy implements Iterable<Course>, Serializable
{
  private List<Course> list;

  /**
   * Constructs an initially empty Program of Study.
   */
  public ProgramOfStudy()
  {
     list = new LinkedList<Course>();
  }

  /**
   * Adds the specified course to the end of the course list.
   *
   * @param course the course to add
   */
  public void addCourse(Course course)
  {
     if (course != null)
         list.add(course);
  }

  /**
   * Finds and returns the course matching the specified prefix and number.
   *
   * @param prefix the prefix of the target course
   * @param number the number of the target course
   * @return the course, or null if not found
   */
  public Course find(String prefix, int number)
  {
     for (Course course : list)
         if (prefix.equals(course.getPrefix()) &&
                 number == course.getNumber())
             return course;

     return null;
  }

  /**
   * Adds the specified course after the target course. Does nothing if
   * either course is null or if the target is not found.
   *
```

LISTING 15.2 *continued*

```
     * @param target the course after which the new course will be added
     * @param newCourse the course to add
     */
    public void addCourseAfter(Course target, Course newCourse)
    {
       if (target == null || newCourse == null)
          return;

       int targetIndex = list.indexOf(target);
       if (targetIndex != -1)
          list.add(targetIndex + 1, newCourse);
    }

    /**
     * Replaces the specified target course with the new course. Does nothing if
     * either course is null or if the target is not found.
     *
     * @param target the course to be replaced
     * @param newCourse the new course to add
     */
    public void replace(Course target, Course newCourse)
    {
       if (target == null || newCourse == null)
          return;

       int targetIndex = list.indexOf(target);
       if (targetIndex != -1)
          list.set(targetIndex, newCourse);
    }

    /**
     * Creates and returns a string representation of this Program of Study.
     *
     * @return a string representation of the Program of Study
     */
    public String toString()
    {
       String result = "";
       for (Course course : list)
          result += course + "\n";
       return result;
    }
```

LISTING 15.2 *continued*

```
   /**
    * Returns an iterator for this Program of Study.
    *
    * @return an iterator for the Program of Study
    */
   public Iterator<Course> iterator()
   {
      return list.iterator();
   }

   /**
    * Saves a serialized version of this Program of Study to the specified
    * file name.
    *
    * @param fileName the file name under which the POS will be stored
    * @throws IOException
    */
   public void save(String fileName) throws IOException
   {
      FileOutputStream fos = new FileOutputStream(fileName);
      ObjectOutputStream oos = new ObjectOutputStream(fos);
      oos.writeObject(this);
      oos.flush();
      oos.close();
   }

   /**
    * Loads a serialized Program of Study from the specified file.
    *
    * @param fileName the file from which the POS is read
    * @return the loaded Program of Study
    * @throws IOException
    * @throws ClassNotFoundException
    */
   public static ProgramOfStudy load(String fileName) throws IOException,
   ClassNotFoundException
   {
      FileInputStream fis = new FileInputStream(fileName);
      ObjectInputStream ois = new ObjectInputStream(fis);
      ProgramOfStudy pos = (ProgramOfStudy) ois.readObject();
      ois.close();

      return pos;
   }
}
```

LISTING 15.3

```
import java.io.Serializable;

/**
 * Represents a course that might be taken by a student.
 *
 * @author Java Foundations
 * @version 4.0
 */
public class Course implements Serializable
{
  private String prefix;
  private int number;
  private String title;
  private String grade;

  /**
   * Constructs the course with the specified information.
   *
   * @param prefix the prefix of the course designation
   * @param number the number of the course designation
   * @param title the title of the course
   * @param grade the grade received for the course
   */
  public Course(String prefix, int number, String title, String grade)
  {
     this.prefix = prefix;
     this.number = number;
     this.title = title;
     if (grade == null)
         this.grade = "";
     else
         this.grade = grade;
  }

  /**
   * Constructs the course with the specified information, with no grade
   * established.
   *
   * @param prefix the prefix of the course designation
   * @param number the number of the course designation
   * @param title the title of the course
   */
  public Course(String prefix, int number, String title)
```

LISTING 15.3 *continued*

```
   {
      this(prefix, number, title, "");
   }

   /**
    * Returns the prefix of the course designation.
    *
    * @return the prefix of the course designation
    */
   public String getPrefix()
   {
      return prefix;
   }

   /**
    * Returns the number of the course designation.
    *
    * @return the number of the course designation
    */
   public int getNumber()
   {
      return number;
   }

   /**
    * Returns the title of this course.
    *
    * @return the prefix of the course
    */
   public String getTitle()
   {
      return title;
   }

   /**
    * Returns the grade for this course.
    *
    * @return the grade for this course
    */
   public String getGrade()
   {
      return grade;
   }
```

LISTING 15.3 *continued*

```
   /**
    * Sets the grade for this course to the one specified.
    *
    * @param grade the new grade for the course
    */
   public void setGrade(String grade)
   {
      this.grade = grade;
   }

   /**
    * Returns true if this course has been taken (if a grade has been received).
    *
    * @return true if this course has been taken and false otherwise
    */
   public boolean taken()
   {
      return !grade.equals("");
   }

   /**
    * Determines if this course is equal to the one specified, based on the
    * course designation (prefix and number).
    *
    * @return true if this course is equal to the parameter
    */
   public boolean equals(Object other)
   {
      boolean result = false;
      if (other instanceof Course)
      {
         Course otherCourse = (Course) other;
         if (prefix.equals(otherCourse.getPrefix()) &&
               number == otherCourse.getNumber())
            result = true;
      }
      return result;
   }

   /**
    * Creates and returns a string representation of this course.
    *
    * @return a string representation of the course
    */
```

LISTING 15.3 *continued*

```
   public String toString()
   {
      String result = prefix + " " + number + ": " + title;
      if (!grade.equals(""))
          result += "  [" + grade + "]";
      return result;
   }
}
```

The methods `addCourse`, `find`, `addCourseAfter`, and `replace` perform the various core operations needed to update the program of study. They essentially add unordered list operations to the basic list operations provided by the `LinkedList` class.

The `iterator` method returns an `Iterator` object. This method was not used in the `ProgramOfStudyTester` program, but it is a key operation. Iterators are discussed in detail in Chapter 16.

Finally, the `save` and `load` methods are used to write the `ProgramOfStudy` object to a file and read it back in, respectively. Unlike text-based I/O operations we've seen in previous examples, this one uses a process called serialization to read and write the object as a binary stream. So with just a few lines of code, an object can be stored with its current state completely intact. In this case, that means all courses currently stored in the Program of Study list are stored as part of the object.

Note that the `ProgramOfStudy` and `Course` classes implement the `Serializable` interface. In order for an object to be saved using *serialization*, its class must implement `Serializable`. There are no methods in the `Serializable` inteface—it is used simply to indicate that the object may be converted to a

Serializable

```
public class Course implements Serializable
```

indicates that this class can be serialized

The Serializable interface contains no methods.

serialized representation. The `ArrayList` and `LinkedList` classes implement `Serializable`.

A UML class diagram that describes the relationships among the classes in the Program of Study example is shown in Figure 15.5.

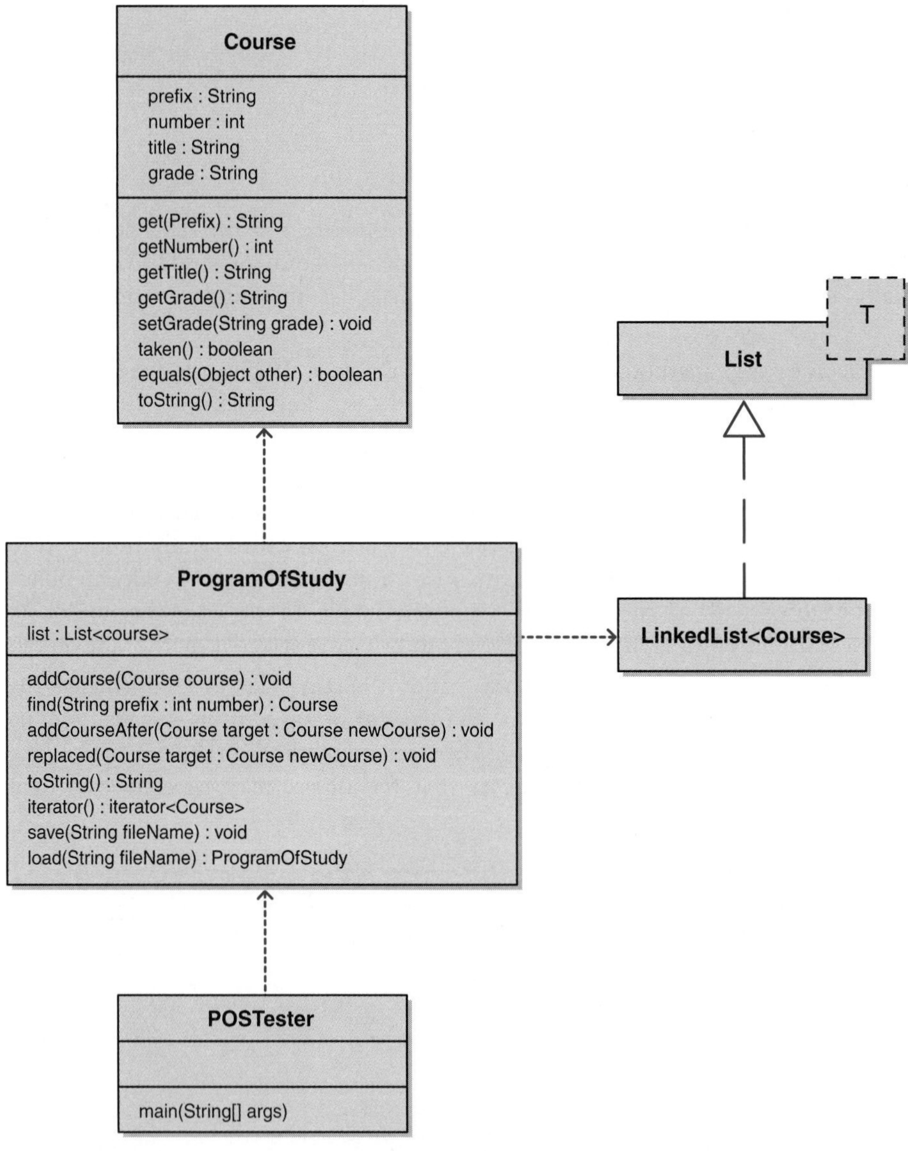

FIGURE 15.5 UML description of the Program of Study program

15.4 Using Indexed Lists: Josephus

Flavius Josephus was a Jewish historian of the first century. Legend has it that he was one of a group of 41 Jewish rebels who decided to kill themselves rather than surrender to the Romans, who had them trapped. They decided to form a circle and to kill every third person until no one was left. Josephus, not wanting to die, calculated where he needed to stand so that he would be the last one alive and thus would not have to die. Thus was born a class of problems referred to as the Josephus problem. These problems involve finding the order of events when events in a list are not taken in order but, rather, they are taken every ith element in a cycle until none remains.

KEY CONCEPT

The Josephus problem is a classic computing problem that is appropriately solved with indexed lists.

For example, suppose that we have a list of seven elements numbered from 1 to 7:

```
1 2 3 4 5 6 7
```

If we were to remove every third element from the list, the first element to be removed would be number 3, leaving the list

```
1 2 4 5 6 7
```

The next element to be removed would be number 6, leaving the list

```
1 2 4 5 7
```

The elements are thought of as being in a continuous cycle, so when we reach the end of the list, we continue counting at the beginning. Therefore, the next element to be removed would be number 2, leaving the list

```
1 4 5 7
```

The next element to be removed would be number 7, leaving the list

```
1 4 5
```

The next element to be removed would be number 5, leaving the list

```
1 4
```

The next-to-last element to be removed would be number 1, leaving the number 4 as the last element on the list.

Listing 15.4 illustrates a generic implementation of the Josephus problem, allowing the user to input the number of items in the list and the gap between elements. Initially, a list is filled with integers representing the soldiers. Each element is then removed from the list one at a time by computing the next index position in the list to be removed.

The one complication in this process is computation of the next index position to be removed. This is particularly interesting because the list collapses on itself as elements are removed. For example, the element number 6 from our previous example should be the second element removed from the list. However, once element 3 has been removed from the list, element 6 is no longer in its original position. Instead of being at index position 5 in the list, it is now at index position 4.

LISTING 15.4

```
import java.util.*;

/**
 * Demonstrates the use of an indexed list to solve the Josephus problem.
 *
 * @author Java Foundations
 * @version 4.0
 */
public class Josephus
{
  /**
   * Continue around the circle eliminating every nth soldier
   * until all of the soldiers have been eliminated.
   */
  public static void main(String[] args)
  {
     int numPeople, skip, targetIndex;
     List<String> list = new ArrayList<String>();
     Scanner in = new Scanner(System.in);

     // get the initial number of soldiers

     System.out.print("Enter the number of soldiers: ");
     numPeople = in.nextInt();
     in.nextLine();

     // get the number of soldiers to skip

     System.out.print("Enter the number of soldiers to skip: ");
     skip = in.nextInt();

     // load the initial list of soldiers

     for (int count = 1; count <= numPeople; count++)
     {
        list.add("Soldier " + count);
     }
```

LISTING 15.4 *continued*

```
      targetIndex = skip;
      System.out.println("The order is: ");

      // Treating the list as circular, remove every nth element
      // until the list is empty

      while (!list.isEmpty())
      {
         System.out.println(list.remove(targetIndex));
         if (list.size() > 0)
            targetIndex = (targetIndex + skip) % list.size();
      }
   }
}
```

15.5 A List ADT

Now let's explore our own implementation of a list collection. We'll go beyond what the Java API provides and include full implementations of unordered and ordered.

There is a set of operations that is common to both ordered and unordered lists. These common operations are shown in Figure 15.6. They include operations to remove and examine elements, as well as classic operations such as `isEmpty` and `size`. The `contains` operation is also supported by both list types, which allows the user to determine if a list contains a particular element.

KEY CONCEPT
Many common operations can be defined for all list types. The differences between them stem from how elements are added.

Operation	Description
`removeFirst`	Removes the first element from the list.
`removeLast`	Removes the last element from the list.
`remove`	Removes a particular element from the list.
`first`	Examines the element at the front of the list.
`last`	Examines the element at the rear of the list.
`contains`	Determines if the list contains a particular element.
`isEmpty`	Determines if the list is empty.
`size`	Determines the number of elements on the list.

FIGURE 15.6 The common operations on a list

Adding Elements to a List

The differences between ordered and unordered lists generally center on how elements are added to the list. In an ordered list, we need only specify the new element to add. Its position in the list is based on its key value. This operation is shown in Figure 15.7.

An unordered list supports three variations of the `add` operation. Elements can be added to the front of the list, to the rear of the list, or after a particular element that is already in the list. These operations are shown in Figure 15.8.

Conceptually, the operations particular to an indexed list make use of its ability to reference elements by their index. A new element can be inserted into the list at a particular index, or it can be added to the rear of the list without specifying an index at all. Note that if an element is inserted or removed, the elements at higher indexes are either shifted up to make room or shifted down to close the gap. Alternatively, the element at a particular index can be set, which overwrites the element currently at that index and therefore does not cause other elements to shift.

We can capitalize on the fact that both ordered lists and unordered lists share a common set of operations. These operations need to be defined only once. Therefore, we will define three list interfaces: one with the common operations and two with the operations particular to each list type. Inheritance can be used with interfaces just as it can with classes. The interfaces of the particular list types extend the common list definition. This relationship among the interfaces is shown in Figure 15.9.

Listings 15.5 through 15.7 show the Java interfaces corresponding to the UML diagram in Figure 15.9.

Operation	Description
`add`	Adds an element to the list.

FIGURE 15.7 The operation particular to an ordered list

Operation	Description
`addToFront`	Adds an element to the front of the list.
`addToRear`	Adds an element to the rear of the list.
`addAfter`	Adds an element after a particular element already in the list.

FIGURE 15.8 The operations particular to an unordered list

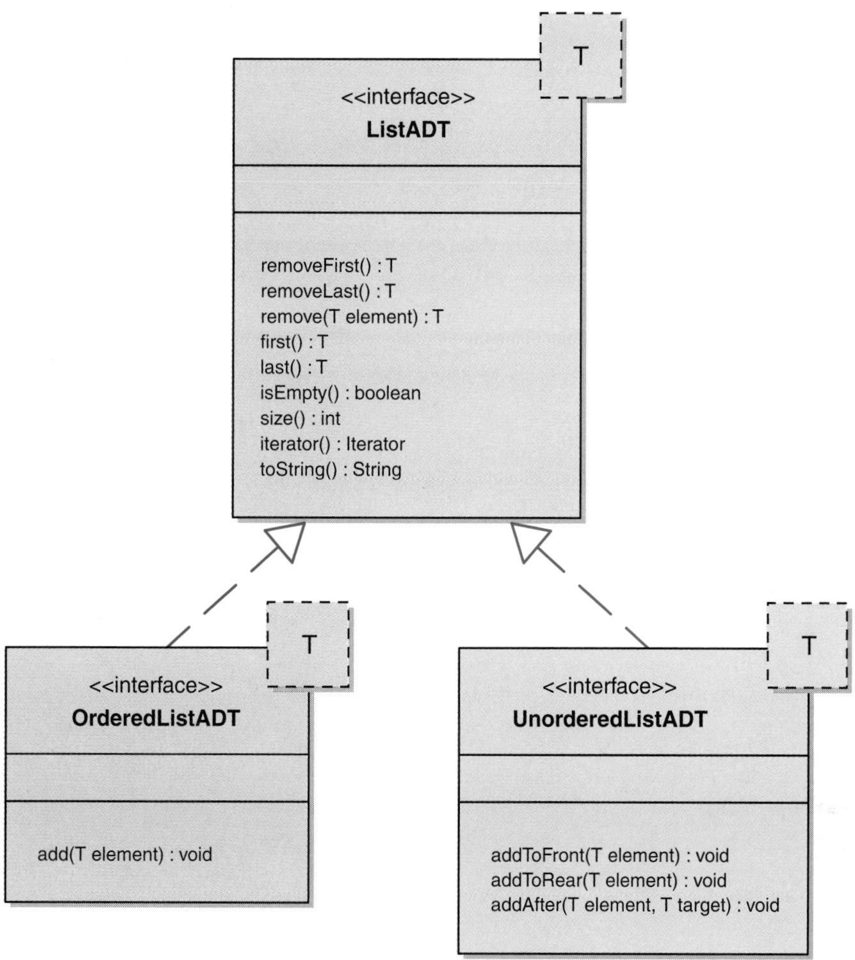

FIGURE 15.9 Using inheritance to define list interfaces

LISTING 15.5

```
package jsjf;
import java.util.Iterator;

/**
 * ListADT defines the interface to a general list collection. Specific
 * types of lists will extend this interface to complete the
 * set of necessary operations.
 *
```

LISTING 15.5 *continued*

```
 * @author Java Foundations
 * @version 4.0
 */
public interface ListADT<T> extends Iterable<T>
{
  /**
   * Removes and returns the first element from this list.
   *
   * @return the first element from this list
   */
  public T removeFirst();

  /**
   * Removes and returns the last element from this list.
   *
   * @return the last element from this list
   */
  public T removeLast();

  /**
   * Removes and returns the specified element from this list.
   *
   * @param element the element to be removed from the list
   */
  public T remove(T element);

  /**
   * Returns a reference to the first element in this list.
   *
   * @return a reference to the first element in this list
   */
  public T first();

  /**
   * Returns a reference to the last element in this list.
   *
   * @return a reference to the last element in this list
   */
  public T last();

  /**
   * Returns true if this list contains the specified target element.
   *
   * @param target the target that is being sought in the list
   * @return true if the list contains this element
   */
```

LISTING 15.5 *continued*

```
  public boolean contains(T target);

  /**
   * Returns true if this list contains no elements.
   *
   * @return true if this list contains no elements
   */
  public boolean isEmpty();

  /**
   * Returns the number of elements in this list.
   *
   * @return the integer representation of number of elements in this list
   */
  public int size();

  /**
   * Returns an iterator for the elements in this list.
   *
   * @return an iterator over the elements in this list
   */
  public Iterator<T> iterator();

  /**
   * Returns a string representation of this list.
   *
   * @return a string representation of this list
   */
  public String toString();
}
```

LISTING 15.6

```
package jsjf;

/**
 * OrderedListADT defines the interface to an ordered list collection. Only
 * Comparable elements are stored, kept in the order determined by
 * the inherent relationship among the elements.
 *
 * @author Java Foundations
 * @version 4.0
 */
```

LISTING 15.6 *continued*

```
public interface OrderedListADT<T> extends ListADT<T>
{
   /**
    * Adds the specified element to this list at the proper location
    *
    * @param element the element to be added to this list
    */
   public void add(T element);
}
```

LISTING 15.7

```
package jsjf;

/**
 * UnorderedListADT defines the interface to an unordered list collection.
 * Elements are stored in any order the user desires.
 *
 * @author Java Foundations
 * @version 4.0
 */
public interface UnorderedListADT<T> extends ListADT<T>
{
   /**
    * Adds the specified element to the front of this list.
    *
    * @param element the element to be added to the front of this list
    */
   public void addToFront(T element);

   /**
    * Adds the specified element to the rear of this list.
    *
    * @param element the element to be added to the rear of this list
    */
   public void addToRear(T element);
```

LISTING 15.7 *continued*

```
    /**
     * Adds the specified element after the specified target.
     *
     * @param element the element to be added after the target
     * @param target  the target is the item that the element will be added
     *                after
     */
    public void addAfter(T element, T target);
}
```

15.6 Implementing Lists with Arrays

As we've seen in previous chapters, an array-based implementation of a collection can fix one end of the list at index 0 and shift elements as needed. This is similar to our array-based implementation of a stack from Chapter 12. We dismissed that approach for queue in Chapter 14 because its operations add and remove elements from both ends. General lists also add and remove from either end, but they insert and remove in the middle of the list as well. So shifting of elements cannot be avoided. A circular array approach could be used, but that will not eliminate the need to shift elements when adding or removing elements from the middle of the list.

Figure 15.10 depicts an array implementation of a list with the front of the list fixed at index 0. The integer variable `rear` represents the number of elements in the list and the next available slot for adding an element to the rear of the list.

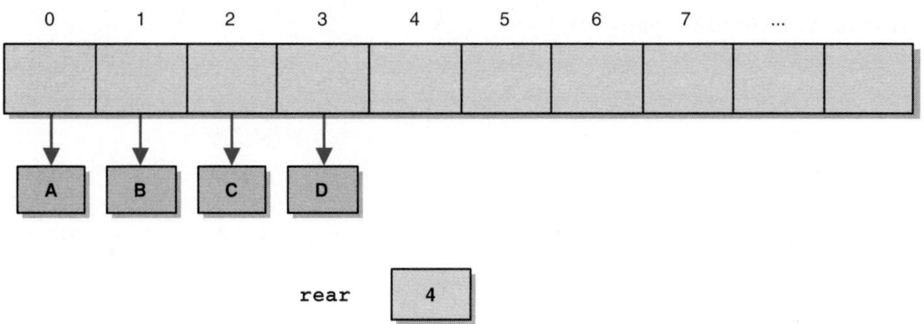

FIGURE 15.10 An array implementation of a list

Note that Figure 15.10 applies to both ordered and unordered lists. First we will explore the common operations. Here are the header and class-level data of the `ArrayList` class:

```
/**
 * ArrayList represents an array implementation of a list. The front of
 * the list is kept at array index 0. This class will be extended
 * to create a specific kind of list.
 *
 * @author Java Foundations
 * @version 4.0
 */
public abstract class ArrayList<T> implements ListADT<T>, Iterable<T>
{
   private final static int DEFAULT_CAPACITY = 100;
   private final static int NOT_FOUND = -1;

   protected int rear;
   protected T[] list;
   protected int modCount;

   /**
    * Creates an empty list using the default capacity.
    */
   public ArrayList()
   {
      this(DEFAULT_CAPACITY);
   }

   /**
    * Creates an empty list using the specified capacity.
    *
    * @param initialCapacity the size of the array list
    */
   public ArrayList(int initialCapacity)
   {
      rear = 0;
      list = (T[])(new Object[initialCapacity]);
      modCount = 0;
   }
```

The `ArrayList` class implements the `ListADT` interface defined earlier. It also implements the `Iterable` interface. That interface, and the `modCount` variable, are discussed in Chapter 16.

The `remove` Operation

This variation of the `remove` operation requires that we search for the element passed in as a parameter and remove it from the list if it is found. Then, elements at higher indexes in the array are shifted down in the list to fill in the gap. Consider what happens if the element to be removed is the first element in the list. In this case, there is a single comparison to find the element followed by n–1 shifts to shift the elements down to fill the gap. On the opposite extreme, what happens if the element to be removed is the last element in the list? In this case, we would require n comparisons to find the element and none of the remaining elements would need to be shifted. As it turns out, this implementation of the `remove` operation will always require exactly n comparisons and shifts and thus the operation is O(n). Note that if we were to use a circular array implementation, it would only improve the performance of the special case when the element to be removed is the first element. This operation can be implemented as follows:

```
/**
 * Removes and returns the specified element.
 *
 * @param  element the element to be removed and returned from the list
 * @return the removed elememt
 * @throws ElementNotFoundException if the element is not in the list
 */
public T remove(T element)
{
  T result;
  int index = find(element);

  if (index == NOT_FOUND)
      throw new ElementNotFoundException("ArrayList");

  result = list[index];
  rear--;

  // shift the appropriate elements

  for (int scan=index; scan < rear; scan++)
      list[scan] = list[scan+1];

  list[rear] = null;
  modCount++;

  return result;
}
```

The remove method makes use of a method called find, which finds the element in question, if it exists in the list, and returns its index. The find method returns a constant called NOT_FOUND if the element is not in the list. The NOT_FOUND constant is equal to –1 and is defined in the ArrayList class. If the element is not found, a NoSuchElementException is generated. If it is found, the elements at higher indexes are shifted down, the rear value is updated, and the element is returned.

The find method supports the implementation of a public operation on the list, rather than defining a new operation. Therefore, the find method is declared with private visibility. The find method can be implemented as follows:

```
/**
 * Returns the array index of the specified element, or the
 * constant NOT_FOUND if it is not found.
 *
 * @param target the target element
 * @return the index of the target element, or the
 *         NOT_FOUND constant
 */
private int find(T target)
{
  int scan = 0;
  int result = NOT_FOUND;

  if (!isEmpty())
      while (result == NOT_FOUND && scan < rear)
          if (target.equals(list[scan]))
              result = scan;
          else
              scan++;

  return result;
}
```

Note that the find method relies on the equals method to determine whether the target has been found. It's possible that the object passed into the method is an exact copy of the element being sought. In fact, it may be an alias of the element in the list. However, if the parameter is a separate object, it may not contain all aspects of the element being sought. Only the key characteristics on which the equals method is based are important.

The logic of the find method could have been incorporated into the remove method, though it would have made the remove method somewhat complicated.

When appropriate, such support methods should be defined to keep each method readable. Furthermore, in this case, the `find` support method is useful in implementing the `contains` operation, as we will now explore.

DESIGN FOCUS

The overriding of the `equals` method and the implementation of the `Comparable` interface are excellent examples of the power of object-oriented design. We can create implementations of collections that can handle classes of objects that have not yet been designed as long as those objects provide a definition of equality and/or a method of comparison between objects of the class.

DESIGN FOCUS

Separating out private methods such as the `find` method in the `ArrayList` class provides multiple benefits. First, it simplifies the definition of the already complex `remove` method. Second, it allows us to use the `find` method to implement the `contains` operation as well as the `addAfter` method for an `ArrayUnorderedList`. Notice that the `find` method does not throw an `ElementNotFound` exception. It simply returns a value (–1), signifying that the element was not found. In this way, the calling routine can decide how to handle the fact that the element was not found. In the `remove` method, that means throwing an exception. In the `contains` method, that means returning false.

The `contains` Operation

The purpose of the `contains` operation is to determine whether a particular element is currently contained in the list. As we discussed, we can use the `find` support method to create a fairly straightforward implementation:

```
/**
 * Returns true if this list contains the specified element.
 *
 * @param target the target element
 * @return true if the target is in the list, false otherwise
 */
public boolean contains(T target)
{
   return (find(target) != NOT_FOUND);
}
```

If the target element is not found, the contains method returns false. If it is found, it returns true. A carefully constructed return statement ensures the proper return value. Because this method is performing a linear search of our list, our worst case will be that the element we are searching for is not in the list. This case would require n comparisons. We would expect this method to require, on average, n/2 comparisons, which results in the operation being O(n).

The add Operation for an Ordered List

The add operation is the only way an element can be added to an ordered list. No location is specified in the call because the elements themselves determine their order. Very much like the remove operation, the add operation requires a combination of comparisons and shifts: comparisons to find the correct location in the list and then shifts to open a position for the new element. Looking at the two extremes, if the element to be added to the list belongs at the front of the list, that will require one comparison and then the other n – 1 elements in the list will need to be shifted. If the element to be added belongs at the rear of the list, this will require n comparisons, and none of the other elements in the list will need to be shifted. Like the remove operation, the add operation requires n comparisons and shifts each time it is executed, and thus the operation is O(n). The add operation can be implemented as follows:

```
/**
 * Adds the specified Comparable element to this list, keeping
 * the elements in sorted order.
 *
 * @param element the element to be added to the list
 */
public void add(T element)
{
   if (!(element instanceof Comparable))
       throw new NonComparableElementException("OrderedList");

   Comparable<T> comparableElement = (Comparable<T>)element;

   if (size() == list.length)
       expandCapacity();

   int scan = 0;

   // find the insertion location

   while (scan < rear && comparableElement.compareTo(list[scan]) > 0)
       scan++;
```

```
    // shift existing elements up one

    for (int shift=rear; shift > scan; shift--)
        list[shift] = list[shift-1];

    // insert element

    list[scan] = element;
    rear++;
    modCount++;
}
```

Note that only `Comparable` objects can be stored in an ordered list. If the element isn't `Comparable`, an exception is thrown. If it is `Comparable`, but cannot be validly compared to the elements in the list, a `ClassCastException` will result, when the `compareTo` method is invoked.

KEY CONCEPT
Only `Comparable` objects can be stored in an ordered list.

Recall that the `Comparable` interface defines the `compareTo` method that returns a negative integer, zero, or positive integer value if the executing object is less than, equal to, or greater than the parameter, respectively.

The unordered and indexed versions of a list do not require that the elements they store be `Comparable`. It is a testament to the utility of object-oriented programming that the various classes that implement these list variations can exist in harmony despite these differences.

Operations Particular to Unordered Lists

The `addToFront` and `addToRear` operations are similar to operations from other collections and are therefore left as programming projects. Keep in mind that the `addToFront` operation must shift the current elements in the list first to make room at index 0 for the new element. Thus we know that the `addToFront` operation will be O(n) because it requires n–1 elements to be shifted. Like the push operation on a stack, the `addToRear` operation will be O(1).

The `addAfter` Operation for an Unordered List

The `addAfter` operation accepts two parameters: one that represents the element to be added and one that represents the target element that determines the placement of the new element. The `addAfter` method must first find the target element, shift the elements at higher indexes to make room, and then insert the new element after it. Very much like the `remove` operation and the `add` operation for ordered lists, the `addAfter` method will require a combination of n comparisons and shifts and will be O(n).

```
/**
 * Adds the specified element after the specified target element.
 * Throws an ElementNotFoundException if the target is not found.
 *
 * @param element the element to be added after the target element
 * @param target  the target that the element is to be added after
 */
public void addAfter(T element, T target)
{
   if (size() == list.length)
         expandCapacity();

   int scan = 0;

   // find the insertion point

   while (scan < rear && !target.equals(list[scan]))
         scan++;

   if (scan == rear)
         throw new ElementNotFoundException("UnorderedList");

   scan++;

   // shift elements up one

   for (int shift=rear; shift > scan; shift--)
         list[shift] = list[shift-1];

   // insert element

   list[scan] = element;
   rear++;
   modCount++;
}
```

15.7 Implementing Lists with Links

As we have seen with other collections, the use of a linked list is often another convenient way to implement a linear collection. The common operations that apply for ordered and unordered lists, as well as the particular operations for each type, can be implemented with techniques similar to the ones we have used before. We will examine a couple of the more interesting operations but will leave most of them as programming projects.

First, the class header, class-level data, and constructor for our `LinkedList` class are provided for context:

```
/**
 * LinkedList represents a linked implementation of a list.
 *
 * @author Java Foundations
 * @version 4.0
 */
public abstract class LinkedList<T> implements ListADT<T>, Iterable<T>
{
   protected int count;
   protected LinearNode<T> head, tail;
   protected int modCount;

  /**
   * Creates an empty list.
   */
   public LinkedList()
   {
      count = 0;
      head = tail = null;
      modCount = 0;
   }
```

The `remove` Operation

The `remove` operation is part of the `LinkedList` class shared by both implementations: unordered and ordered lists. The `remove` operation consists of making sure that the list is not empty, finding the element to be removed, and then handling one of four cases: the element to be removed is the only element in the list, the element to be removed is the first element in the list, the element to be removed is the last element in the list, or the element to be removed is in the middle of the list. In all cases, the `count` is decremented by one. Unlike the `remove` operation for the array version, the linked version does not require elements to be shifted to close the gap. However, given that the worst case still requires n comparisons to determine that the target element is not in the list, the `remove` operation is still O(n). An implementation of the `remove` operation follows.

```
/**
 * Removes the first instance of the specified element from this
 * list and returns it. Throws an EmptyCollectionException
 * if the list is empty. Throws a ElementNotFoundException if the
 * specified element is not found in the list.
 *
 * @param  targetElement the element to be removed from the list
 * @return a reference to the removed element
 * @throws EmptyCollectionException if the list is empty
 * @throws ElementNotFoundException if the target element is not found
 */
public T remove(T targetElement) throws EmptyCollectionException,
  ElementNotFoundException
{
   if (isEmpty())
      throw new EmptyCollectionException("LinkedList");

  boolean found = false;
  LinearNode<T> previous = null;
  LinearNode<T> current = head;

  while (current != null && !found)
      if (targetElement.equals(current.getElement()))
         found = true;
      else
      {
         previous = current;
         current = current.getNext();
      }

  if (!found)

      throw new ElementNotFoundException("LinkedList");
  if (size() == 1)  // only one element in the list
      head = tail = null;

  else if (current.equals(head))  // target is at the head
      head = current.getNext();

  else if (current.equals(tail))  // target is at the tail
  {
     tail = previous;
     tail.setNext(null);
  }
  else  // target is in the middle

      previous.setNext(current.getNext());

  count--;

  modCount++;
  return current.getElement();
}
```

Summary of Key Concepts

- List collections can be categorized as ordered, unordered, or indexed.
- The elements of an ordered list have an inherent relationship defining their order.
- The elements of an unordered list are kept in whatever order the client chooses.
- An indexed list maintains a contiguous numeric index range for its elements.
- The Jave API does not provide a class that implements an ordered list.
- Many common operations can be defined for all list types. The differences between them stem from how elements are added.
- Interfaces can be used to derive other interfaces. The child interface contains all abstract methods of the parent.
- An interface name can be used to declare an object reference variable. An interface reference can refer to any object of any class that implements the interface.
- Interfaces enable us to make polymorphic references in which the method that is invoked is based on the particular object being referenced at the time.
- The Josephus problem is a classic computing problem that is appropriately solved with indexed lists.
- Only `Comparable` objects can be stored in an ordered list.

Summary of Terms

indexed list A list whose elements can be referenced using a numeric index.

Josephus problem A classic computing problem whose goal is to find the order in which elements are selected from a list by taking every ith element cyclically until none remains.

natural ordering An expression of the ordering criteria used to determine whether one object comes before another, often implemented using the `compareTo` method.

ordered list A list whose elements are ordered in terms of some inherent characteristic of the elements.

serialization A technique for representing an object as a stream of binary digits, which allows objects to be read and written from files with their state maintained.

unordered list A list whose elements have no inherent order but are ordered by their placement in the list.

Self-Review Questions

SR 15.1 What is the difference between an indexed list, an ordered list, and an unordered list?

SR 15.2 What are the basic methods for accessing an indexed list?

SR 15.3 What are the additional operations required of implementations that are part of the Java Collections API framework?

SR 15.4 What are the trade-offs in space complexity between an `ArrayList` and a `LinkedList`?

SR 15.5 What are the trade-offs in time complexity between an `ArrayList` and a `LinkedList`?

SR 15.6 What is the time complexity of the `contains` operation and the `find` operation for both implementations?

SR 15.7 Why is the time to increase the capacity of the array on an `add` operation considered negligible for the `ArrayList` implementation?

SR 15.8 Why is a circular array implementation not as attractive as an implementation for a list as it was for a queue?

Exercises

EX 15.1 Hand trace an ordered list X through the following operations:

```
X.add(new Integer(4));
X.add(new Integer(7));
Object Y = X.first();
X.add(new Integer(3));
X.add(new Integer(2));
X.add(new Integer(5));
Object Y = X.removeLast();
Object Y = X.remove(new Integer(7));
X.add(new Integer(9));
```

EX 15.2 Given the resulting list X from Exercise 15.1, what would be the result of each of the following?

a. `X.last();`

b. `z = X.contains(new Integer(3));`
   `X.first();`

c. `Y = X.remove(new Integer(2));`
   `X.first();`

EX 15.3 What would be the time complexity of the `size` operation for the linked implementation if there were not a `count` variable?

EX 15.4 In the linked implementation, under what circumstances could the `head` and `tail` references be equal?

EX 15.5 In the array implementation, under what circumstances could the `rear` reference equal 0?

EX 15.6 Hand trace an unordered list through the following operations.

```
X.addToFront(new Integer(4));
X.addToRear(new Integer(7));
Object Y = X.first();
X.addAfter(new Integer(3), new Integer(4));
X.addToFront(new Integer(2));
X.addToRear(new Integer(5));
Object Y = X.removeLast();
Object Y = X.remove(new Integer(7));
X.addAfter(new Integer(9), new Integer(3));
```

EX 15.7 If there were not a `rear` variable in the array implementation, how could you determine whether or not the list was full?

Programming Projects

PP 15.1 Implement a stack using a `LinkedList`.

PP 15.2 Implement a stack using an `ArrayList`.

PP 15.3 Implement a queue using a `LinkedList`.

PP 15.4 Implement a queue using an `ArrayList`.

PP 15.5 Implement the Josephus problem using a queue, and compare the performance of that algorithm to the `ArrayList` implementation from this chapter.

PP 15.6 Implement an `OrderedList` using a `LinkedList`.

PP 15.7 Implement an `OrderedList` using an `ArrayList`.

PP 15.8 Complete the implementation of the `ArrayList` class.

PP 15.9 Complete the implementation of the `ArrayOrderedList` class.

PP 15.10 Complete the implementation of the `ArrayUnorderedList` class.

PP 15.11 Write an implementation of the `LinkedList` class.

PP 15.12 Write an implementation of the `LinkedOrderedList` class.

PP 15.13 Write an implementation of the `LinkedUnorderedList` class.

PP 15.14 Create an implementation of a doubly linked `DoubleOrderedList` class. You will need to create a `DoubleNode` class, a `DoubleList` class, and a `DoubleIterator` class.

PP 15.15 Create a graphical application that provides a button for `add` and `remove` from an ordered list, a text field to accept a string as input for `add`, and a text area to display the contents of the list after each operation.

PP 15.16 Create a graphical application that provides a button for `addToFront`, `addToRear`, `addAfter`, and `remove` from an unordered list. Your application must provide a text field to accept a string as input for any of the `add` operations. The user should be able to select the element to be added after, and select the element to be removed.

PP 15.17 Modify the `Course` class from this chapter so that it implements the `Comparable` interface. Order the courses first by department and then by course number. Then write a program that uses an ordered list to maintain a list of courses.

Answers to Self-Review Questions

SRA 15.1 An indexed list is a collection of objects with no inherent order that are ordered by index value. An ordered list is a collection of objects ordered by value. An unordered list is a collection of objects with no inherent order.

SRA 15.2 Access to the list is accomplished in one of three ways: by accessing a particular index position in the list, by accessing the ends of the list, or by accessing an object in the list by value.

SRA 15.3 All Java Collections API framework classes implement the `Collections` interface, the `Serializable` interface, and the `Cloneable` interface.

SRA 15.4 The linked implementation requires more space per object to be inserted in the list simply because of the space allocated for the references. Keep in mind that the `LinkedList` class is actually a doubly linked list and thus requires twice as much space for references. The `ArrayList` class is more efficient at managing space than the array-based implementations we have discussed previously. This is because `ArrayList` collections are resizable and thus can dynamically allocate space as needed. Therefore, there need not be a large amount of wasted space allocated all at once. Rather, the list can grow as needed.

SRA 15.5 The major difference between the two is access to a particular index position of the list. The `ArrayList` implementation can access any element of the list in the same amount of time if the index value is known. The LinkedList implementation requires the list to be traversed from one end or the other to reach a particular index position.

SRA 15.6 The contains and find operations for both implementations are O(n) because they are simply linear searches.

SRA 15.7 Averaged over the total number of insertions into the list, the time to enlarge the array has little effect on the total time.

SRA 15.8 The circular array implementation of a queue improved the efficiency of the dequeue operation from O(n) to O(1) because it eliminated the need to shift elements in the array. That is not the case for a list because we can add or remove elements anywhere in the list, not just at the front or the rear.

Iterators

CHAPTER OBJECTIVES

- Define an iterator and explore its use.
- Discuss the `Iterator` and `Iterable` interfaces.
- Explore the concept of fail-fast collections.
- Use iterators in various situations.
- Explore implementation options related to iterators.

We mentioned iterators in Chapter 15 in our discussion of lists, but didn't explore them in any detail. They are important enough to deserve their own chapter. Conceptually, they provide a standard way to access each element of a collection in turn, which is a common operation. And their implementation in the Java API has some interesting nuances that are worth exploring carefully.

16.1 What's an Iterator?

An *iterator* is an object that allows the user to acquire and use each element in a collection one at a time. It works in conjunction with a collection but is a separate object. An iterator is a mechanism for helping implement a collection.

KEY CONCEPT
An iterator is an object that provides a way to access each element in a collection in turn.

Embracing the concept of an iterator consistently over the implementation of multiple collections makes it much easier to process and manage those collections and the elements they contain. The Java API has a consistent approach to iterators that are implemented by nearly all collections in the class library. We will follow this approach in our own implementations.

Iterators are implemented in the Java API using two primary interfaces:

- `Iterator` – used to define an object that can be used as an iterator.
- `Iterable` – used to define a collection from which an iterator can be extracted.

A collection is `Iterable`, which commits it to providing an `Iterator` when requested. For example, a `LinkedList` is `Iterable`, which means it provides a method called `iterator` that can be called to get an iterator over of the elements in the list. The names of the interfaces make it fairly easy to keep them straight.

KEY CONCEPT
A collection is often defined as `Iterable`, which means it provides an `Iterator` when needed.

The abstract methods defined in these two interfaces are shown in Figures 16.1 and 16.2. Both interfaces operate on a generic type, which is denoted by `E` in these figures.

The `Iterable` interface has only one method, called `iterator`, that returns an `Iterator` object. When you create the collection, you commit to the element type, which is used to define the elements in the iterator.

Method	Description
`boolean hasNext()`	Returns true if the iteration has more elements.
`E next()`	Returns the next element in the iteration.
`void remove()`	Removes the last element returned by the iteration from the underlying collection.

FIGURE 16.1 The methods in the `Iterator` interface

Method	Description
`Iterator<E> iterator()`	Returns an iterator over a set of elements of type E.

FIGURE 16.2 The methods in the `Iterable` interface

The `Iterator` interface contains three methods. The first two, `hasNext` and `next`, can be used in concert to access the elements in turn. For example, if `myList` is an `ArrayList` of `Book` objects, you could use the following code to print all books in the list:

```
Iterator<Book> itr = myList.iterator();
while (itr.hasNext())
    System.out.println(itr.next());
```

In this example, the first line calls the `iterator` method of the collection to obtain the `Iterator<Book>` object. Then a call to the `hasNext` method of the iterator is used as the condition of the while loop. Inside the loop, the `next` method of the iterator is called to get the next book. When the iteration is exhausted, the loop terminates.

The `remove` operation of the `Iterator` interface is provided as a convenience to allow you to remove an element from a collection while iterating over it. The `remove` method is considered an optional operation, and not all iterators will implement it.

Now, you've probably realized that you could access the elements of a collection using a for-each loop as we've done in the past. The following code does the same thing that the previous while loop accomplishes:

```
for (Book book : myList)
    System.out.println(book);
```

The for-each code is cleaner and shorter than the while loop code, and it will often be the technique you'll want to use. But you should be aware that both of these examples are using iterators. Java provides the for-each construct specifically to simplify the processing of iterators. Behind the scenes, the for-each code is translated into code that explicitly calls the iterator methods.

In fact, you can use a for-each loop only on an `Iterable` collection. Most of the collections in the Java API are `Iterable`, and you can define your own collection objects to be `Iterable` as well.

So why would you ever use an explicit iterator with a while loop instead of the cleaner for-each loop? Well, there are two basic reasons. First, you may not want to process all elements in the iteration. If you're looking for a particular element, for example, and do not wish to process them all, you may choose to use an explicit iterator. (You could break out of the loop, but that may not be as clean.)

You may also choose to use an explicit iterator if you want to call the iterator's `remove` method. The for-each loop does not provide explicit access to the iterator, so the only way you could do it would be to call the `remove` method of the collection, and that would cause a completely separate traversal of the collection data structure in order to reach the element (again) to remove it.

KEY CONCEPT

The optional `remove` method of an iterator makes it possible to remove an element without having to traverse the collection again.

Other Iterator Issues

We should note a couple of other issues to point out related to iterators before we continue. First, there is no assumption about the order in which an `Iterator` object delivers the elements from the collection. In the case of a list, there is a linear order to the elements, so the iterator would probably follow that order. In other cases, an iterator may follow a different order that makes sense for that collection and its underlying data structures. Read the API documentation carefully before making any assumptions about how an iterator delivers its elements.

KEY CONCEPT
You should make no assumptions about the order in which an iterator delivers elements unless it is explicitly stated.

Second, you should be aware that there is an intimate relationship between an iterator and its collection. An iterator references elements that are still stored in the collection. Therefore, while an iterator is in use there are at least two objects with references to the element objects. Because of this relationship, the structure of the underlying collection should not be modified while an iterator on that collection is actively being used.

KEY CONCEPT
Most iterators are fail-fast, and will throw an exception if the collection is modified while an iterator is active.

Embracing this assumption, most of the iterators provided by collections in the Java API are implemented to be *fail-fast*, which means that they will throw a `ConcurrentModificationException` if the collection is modified while an iterator is active. The idea is that the iterator will fail quickly and cleanly, rather than permitting a problem to be introduced that won't be discovered until some unknown point in the future.

16.2 Using Iterators: Program of Study Revisited

In Chapter 15 we examined a program that created a program of study for a student, consisting of a list of the courses the student has taken and is planning to take. Recall that a `Course` object stores course information such as the number and title, as well as the grade the student received if she or he has already taken the course.

The `ProgramOfStudy` class maintains an unordered list of `Course` objects. In Chapter 15 we examined various aspects of this class. Now we will focus on aspects of it that pertain to iterators. The `ProgramOfStudy` class is reprinted in Listing 16.1 for convenience.

Note first that the `ProgramOfStudy` class implements the `Iterable` interface using the `Course` class as the generic type. As discussed in the previous section, that commits this class to implementing the `iterator` method, which returns an `Iterator` object for the program of study. In this implementation, the `iterator` method simply returns the `Iterator` object obtained from the `LinkedList` object that stores the courses.

Thus a `ProgramOfStudy` object is `Iterable`, and the `LinkedList` it uses to store the `Course` objects is `Iterable` as well. We'll see both in use.

LISTING 16.1

```
import java.io.FileInputStream;
import java.io.FileNotFoundException;
import java.io.FileOutputStream;
import java.io.IOException;
import java.io.ObjectInputStream;
import java.io.ObjectOutputStream;
import java.io.Serializable;
import java.util.Iterator;
import java.util.LinkedList;
import java.util.List;

/**
 * Represents a Program of Study, a list of courses taken and planned, for an
 * individual student.
 *
 * @author Java Foundations
 * @version 4.0
 */
public class ProgramOfStudy implements Iterable<Course>, Serializable
{
   private List<Course> list;

  /**
   * Constructs an initially empty Program of Study.
   */
  public ProgramOfStudy()
  {
     list = new LinkedList<Course>();
  }

  /**
   * Adds the specified course to the end of the course list.
   *
   * @param course the course to add
   */
  public void addCourse(Course course)
  {
     if (course != null)
         list.add(course);
  }

  /**
   * Finds and returns the course matching the specified prefix and number.
   *
   * @param prefix the prefix of the target course
```

LISTING 16.1 *continued*

```
     * @param number the number of the target course
     * @return the course, or null if not found
     */
    public Course find(String prefix, int number)
    {
       for (Course course : list)
          if (prefix.equals(course.getPrefix()) &&
                number == course.getNumber())
             return course;
       return null;
    }

    /**
     * Adds the specified course after the target course. Does nothing if
     * either course is null or if the target is not found.
     *
     * @param target the course after which the new course will be added
     * @param newCourse the course to add
     */
    public void addCourseAfter(Course target, Course newCourse)
    {
       if (target == null || newCourse == null)
          return;

       int targetIndex = list.indexOf(target);
       if (targetIndex != -1)
          list.add(targetIndex + 1, newCourse);
    }

    /**
     * Replaces the specified target course with the new course. Does nothing if
     * either course is null or if the target is not found.
     *
     * @param target the course to be replaced
     * @param newCourse the new course to add
     */
    public void replace(Course target, Course newCourse)
    {
       if (target == null || newCourse == null)
          return;

       int targetIndex = list.indexOf(target);
       if (targetIndex != -1)
          list.set(targetIndex, newCourse);
    }
```

LISTING 16.1 *continued*

```
/**
 * Creates and returns a string representation of this Program of Study.
 *
 * @return a string representation of the Program of Study
 */
public String toString()
{
   String result = "";
   for (Course course : list)
       result += course + "\n";
   return result;
}

/**
 * Returns an iterator for this Program of Study.
 *
 * @return an iterator for the Program of Study
 */
public Iterator<Course> iterator()
{
   return list.iterator();
}

/**
 * Saves a serialized version of this Program of Study to the specified
 * file name.
 *
 * @param fileName the file name under which the POS will be stored
 * @throws IOException
 */
public void save(String fileName) throws IOException
{
   FileOutputStream fos = new FileOutputStream(fileName);
   ObjectOutputStream oos = new ObjectOutputStream(fos);
   oos.writeObject(this);
   oos.flush();
   oos.close();
}

/**
 * Loads a serialized Program of Study from the specified file.
 *
 * @param fileName the file from which the POS is read
 * @return the loaded Program of Study
```

LISTING 16.1 *continued*

```
    * @throws IOException
    * @throws ClassNotFoundException
    */
   public static ProgramOfStudy load(String fileName) throws IOException,
       ClassNotFoundException
   {
      FileInputStream fis = new FileInputStream(fileName);
      ObjectInputStream ois = new ObjectInputStream(fis);
      ProgramOfStudy pos = (ProgramOfStudy) ois.readObject();
      ois.close();

      return pos;
   }
}
```

Consider the `toString` method in the `ProgramOfStudy` class. It uses a for-each loop on the linked list to scan through the list and append the description of each course to the overall description. It can do this only because the `LinkedList` class is `Iterable`.

The `find` method of `ProgramOfStudy` is similar in that it uses a for-each loop to scan through the list of `Course` objects. In this case, however, the `return` statement jumps out of the loop (and the method) as soon as the target course is found.

Printing Certain Courses

Now let's examine a driver program that exercises our program of study in a new way. Listing 16.2 contains a `main` method that first reads a previously created `ProgramOfStudy` object stored in a file. (Recall that the `ProgramOfStudy` class uses serialization to store the list of courses.) Then, after printing the entire list, it prints only those courses that have been taken and in which the student received a grade of A or A–.

Note that a for-each loop is used to examine each course and print only those with high grades. That loop iterates over the `ProgramOfStudy` object called `pos`. This is possible only because the `ProgramOfStudy` class is `Iterable`.

LISTING 16.2

```
import java.io.FileInputStream;
import java.io.IOException;
import java.io.ObjectInputStream;

/**
 * Demonstrates the use of an Iterable object (and the technique for reading
 * a serialzed object from a file).
 *
 * @author Lewis and Chase
 */
public class POSGrades
{
     /**
     * Reads a serialized Program of Study, then prints all courses in which
     * a grade of A or A- was earned.
     */
  public static void main(String[] args) throws Exception
  {
     ProgramOfStudy pos = ProgramOfStudy.load("ProgramOfStudy");

     System.out.println(pos);

     System.out.println("Classes with Grades of A or A-\n");

     for (Course course : pos)
     {
        if (course.getGrade().equals("A") || course.getGrade().equals("A-"))
            System.out.println(course);
     }
  }
}
```

Removing Courses

Listing 16.3 contains yet another driver program. This example removes, from a program of study, any course that doesn't already have a grade. After an existing `ProgramOfStudy` object is read from a file and printed, each course is examined in turn, and if it has no grade, it is removed from the list.

This time, however, a for-each loop is not used to iterate over the `Course` objects. Instead, the `iterator` method of the `ProgramOfStudy` object is called explicitly, which returns an `Iterator` object. Then, using the `hasNext` and `next` methods of the iterator, a while loop is used to iterate over the courses. An explicit iterator is used in this case because of the `remove` operation. To remove a `Course` object, we call the `remove` method of the `iterator`. If we had done this in a for-each loop, we would have triggered a `ConcurrentModificationException`, as discussed in the first section of this chapter.

LISTING 16.3

```
import java.io.FileInputStream;
import java.io.ObjectInputStream;
import java.util.Iterator;

/**
 * Demonstrates the use of an explicit iterator.
 *
 * @author Java Foundations
 */
public class POSClear
{
   /**
    * Reads a serialized Program of Study, then removes all courses that
    * don't have a grade.
    */
   public static void main(String[] args) throws Exception
   {
      ProgramOfStudy pos = ProgramOfStudy.load("ProgramOfStudy");

      System.out.println(pos);

      System.out.println("Removing courses with no grades.\n");

      Iterator<Course> itr = pos.iterator();
      while (itr.hasNext())
      {
         Course course = itr.next();
         if (!course.taken())
            itr.remove();
      }

      System.out.println(pos);

      pos.save("ProgramOfStudy");
   }
}
```

16.3 Implementing Iterators: With Arrays

In Chapter 15 we explored the implementation of an array-based list. One thing we didn't show then was the implementation of the iterator for our own `ArrayList` class. Let's explore it now.

Listing 16.4 contains the `ArrayListIterator` class. It's defined as a private class, and therefore would actually be an inner class, part of the `ArrayList` class from Chapter 15. This is an appropriate use for an inner class, which has an intimate relationship with its outer class.

> **KEY CONCEPT**
> An iterator class is often implemented as an inner class of the collection to which it belongs.

The `ArrayListIterator` class maintains two integers: one for the index of the current element in the iteration, and one to keep track of the number of modifications made through the iterator. The constructor sets `current` to 0 (the first element in the array) and the `iteratorModCount` to be equal to the `modCount` of the collection itself.

The `modCount` variable is an integer defined in the outer `ArrayList` class. If you go back to Chapter 15, you'll see that anytime the collection was modified (such as something being added to the collection), the `modCount` was incremented. So when a new iterator is created, its modification count is set equal to the count of the collection itself. If those two values get out of synch (because the collection was updated), then the iterator will throw a `ConcurrentModificationException`.

The `hasNext` method checks the modification count and then returns true if there are still elements to process, which in this case is true if the `current` iterator index is less than the `rear` counter. Recall that the `rear` counter is maintained by the outer collection class.

> **KEY CONCEPT**
> An iterator checks the modification count to ensure that it stays consistent with the mod count from the collection when it was created.

LISTING 16.4

```
/**
 * ArrayListIterator iterator over the elements of an ArrayList.
 */
private class ArrayListIterator implements Iterator<T>
{
   int iteratorModCount;
   int current;

   /**
    * Sets up this iterator using the specified modCount.
    *
    * @param modCount the current modification count for the ArrayList
    */
```

LISTING 16.4 *continued*

```
public ArrayListIterator()
{
   iteratorModCount = modCount;
   current = 0;
}

/**
 * Returns true if this iterator has at least one more element
 * to deliver in the iteration.
 *
 * @return  true if this iterator has at least one more element to deliver
 *          in the iteration
 * @throws  ConcurrentModificationException if the collection has changed
 *          while the iterator is in use
 */
public boolean hasNext() throws ConcurrentModificationException
{
   if (iteratorModCount != modCount)
       throw new ConcurrentModificationException();

   return (current < rear);
}

/**
 * Returns the next element in the iteration. If there are no
 * more elements in this iteration, a NoSuchElementException is
 * thrown.
 *
 * @return  the next element in the iteration
 * @throws  NoSuchElementException if an element not found exception occurs
 * @throws  ConcurrentModificationException if the collection has changed
 */
public T next() throws ConcurrentModificationException
{
   if (!hasNext())
       throw new NoSuchElementException();

   current++;

   return list[current - 1];
}

/**
 * The remove operation is not supported in this collection.
 *
 * @throws UnsupportedOperationException if the remove method is called
 */
```

LISTING 16.4 *continued*

```
    public void remove() throws UnsupportedOperationException
    {
       throw new UnsupportedOperationException();
    }
}
```

The next method returns the next element in the iteration and increments the current index value. If the next method is invoked and there are no elements left to process, then a NoSuchElementException is thrown.

In this implementation of the iterator, the remove operation is not supported (remember, it's considered optional). If this method is called, then an UnsupportedOperationException is thrown.

16.4 Implementing Iterators: With Links

Similarly, an iterator for a collection using links can also be defined. Like the ArrayListIterator class, the LinkedListIterator class is implemented as a private inner class. The LinkedList outer class maintains its own modCount that must stay in synch with the iterator's stored value.

In this iterator, though, the value of current is a pointer to a LinearNode instead of an integer index value. The hasNext method, therefore, simply confirms that current is pointing to a valid node. The next method returns the element at the current node and moves the current reference to the next node. As with our ArrayListIterator, the remove method is not supported.

LISTING 16.5

```
/**
 * LinkedListIterator represents an iterator for a linked list of linear nodes.
 */
private class LinkedListIterator implements Iterator<T>
{
   private int iteratorModCount;  // the number of elements in the collection
   private LinearNode<T> current;  // the current position
```

LISTING 16.5 *continued*

```
   /**
    * Sets up this iterator using the specified items.
    *
    * @param collection  the collection the iterator will move over
    * @param size        the integer size of the collection
    */
   public LinkedListIterator()
   {
      current = head;
      iteratorModCount = modCount;
   }

   /**
    * Returns true if this iterator has at least one more element
    * to deliver in the iteration.
    *
    * @return  true if this iterator has at least one more element to deliver
    *          in the iteration
    * @throws  ConcurrentModificationException if the collection has changed
    *          while the iterator is in use
    */
   public boolean hasNext() throws ConcurrentModificationException
   {
      if (iteratorModCount != modCount)
          throw new ConcurrentModificationException();

      return (current != null);
   }

   /**
    * Returns the next element in the iteration. If there are no
    * more elements in this iteration, a NoSuchElementException is
    * thrown.
    *
    * @return the next element in the iteration
    * @throws NoSuchElementException if the iterator is empty
    */
   public T next() throws ConcurrentModificationException
   {
      if (!hasNext())
          throw new NoSuchElementException();
      T result = current.getElement();
      current = current.getNext();
       return result;
   }
```

LISTING 16.5 *continued*

```
   /**
    * The remove operation is not supported.
    *
    * @throws UnsupportedOperationException if the remove operation is called
    */
   public void remove() throws UnsupportedOperationException
   {
      throw new UnsupportedOperationException();
   }
}
```

Summary of Key Concepts

- An iterator is an object that provides a way to access each element in a collection in turn.
- A collection is often defined as `Iterable`, which means it provides an `Iterator` when needed.
- The optional `remove` method of an iteratormakes it possible to remove an element without having to traverse the collection again.
- Most iterators are fail-fast and will throw an exception if the collection is modified while an iterator is active.
- You should make no assumptions about the order in which an iterator delivers elements unless it is explicitly stated.
- An iterator class is often implemented as an inner class of the collection to which it belongs.
- An iterator checks the modification count to ensure that it stays consistent with the mod count from the collection when it was created.

Summary of Terms

iterator An object that allows the user to acquire and use each element in the collection one at a time.

fail-fast An iterator that throws an exception if its collection is modified in any way except through the iterator itself.

Self-Review Questions

SR 16.1 What is an iterator?

SR 16.2 What does the `Iterable` interface represent?

SR 16.3 What does the `Iterator` interface represent?

SR 16.4 What is the relationship between a for-each loop and iterators?

SR 16.5 Why might you need to use an explicit iterator instead of a for-each loop?

SR 16.6 What does it mean for an iterator to be fail-fast?

SR 16.7 How is the fail-fast characteristic implemented?

Exercises

EX 16.1 Write a for-each loop that prints all elements in a collection of `Student` objects called `role`. What is required for that loop to work?

EX 16.2 Write a while loop that uses an explicit iterator to accomplish the same thing as Exercise 16.1.

EX 16.3 Write a for-each loop that calls the `addInterest` method on each `BankAccount` object in a collection called `accounts`. What is required for that loop to work?

EX 16.4 Write a while loop that uses an explicit iterator to accomplish the same thing as Exercise 16.3.

Answers to Self-Review Questions

SRA 16.1 An iterator is an object that is used to process each element in a collection one at a time.

SRA 16.2 The `Iterable` interface is implemented by a collection to formally commit to providing an iterator when it is needed.

SRA 16.3 The `Iterator` interface is implemented by an interface and provides methods for checking for, accessing, and removing elements.

SRA 16.4 A for-each loop can be used only with collections that implement the `Iterable` interface. It is a syntactic simplification that can also be accomplished using an iterator explicitly.

SRA 16.5 You may need to use an explicit iterator rather than a for-each loop if you don't plan on processing all elements in a collection or if you may use the iterator's `remove` method.

SRA 16.6 A fail-fast iterator will fail quickly and cleanly if the underlying collection has been modified by something other than the iterator itself.

SRA 16.7 An iterator notes the modification count of the collection when it is created and on subsequent operations makes sure that that value hasn't changed. If it has, the iterator throws a `ConcurrentModificationException`.

Recursion

17

CHAPTER OBJECTIVES

- Explain the underlying concepts of recursion.
- Examine recursive methods and unravel their processing steps.
- Define infinite recursion and discuss ways to avoid it.
- Explain when recursion should and should not be used.
- Demonstrate the use of recursion to solve problems.

Recursion is a powerful programming technique that provides elegant solutions to certain problems. It is particularly helpful in the implementation of various data structures and in the process of searching and sorting data. This chapter provides an introduction to recursive processing. It contains an explanation of the basic concepts underlying recursion and then explores the use of recursion in programming.

17.1 Recursive Thinking

We know that one method can call another method to help it accomplish its goal. Similarly, a method can also call itself to help accomplish its goal. *Recursion* is a programming technique in which a method calls itself to fulfill its overall purpose.

KEY CONCEPT

Recursion is a programming technique in which a method calls itself. A key to being able to program recursively is to be able to think recursively.

Before we get into the details of how we use recursion in a program, we need to explore the general concept of recursion. The ability to think recursively is essential to being able to use recursion as a programming technique.

In general, recursion is the process of defining something in terms of itself. For example, consider the following definition of the word *decoration*:

decoration: n. any ornament or adornment used to decorate something

The word *decorate* is used to define the word *decoration*. You may recall your grade-school teacher telling you to avoid such recursive definitions when explaining the meaning of a word. However, in many situations, recursion is an appropriate way to express an idea or definition. For example, suppose we want to formally define a list of one or more numbers, separated by commas. Such a list can be defined recursively either as a number or as a number followed by a comma followed by a list. This definition can be expressed as follows:

A list is a:	`number`
or a:	`number comma list`

This recursive definition of a list defines each of the following lists of numbers:

```
24, 88, 40, 37
96, 43
14, 64, 21, 69, 32, 93, 47, 81, 28, 45, 81, 52, 69
70
```

No matter how long a list is, the recursive definition describes it. A list of one element, such as in the last example, is defined completely by the first (nonrecursive) part of the definition. For any list longer than one element, the recursive part of the definition (the part that refers to itself) is used as many times as necessary, until the last element is reached. The last element in the list is always defined by the nonrecursive part of this definition. Figure 17.1 shows how one particular list of numbers corresponds to the recursive definition of *list*.

Infinite Recursion

Note that this definition of a list contains one option that is recursive, and one option that is not. The part of the definition that is not recursive is called the *base case*.

Method	Description
boolean hasNext()	Returns true if the iteration has more elements.
E next()	Returns the next element in the iteration.
void remove()	Removes the last element returned by the iteration from the underlying collection.

FIGURE 17.1 Tracing the recursive definition of a list

If all options had a recursive component, then the recursion would never end. For example, if the definition of a list were simply "a number followed by a comma followed by a list," then no list could ever end. This problem is called *infinite recursion*. It is similar to an infinite loop, except that the "loop" occurs in the definition itself.

KEY CONCEPT
Any recursive definition must have a nonrecursive part, called the base case, that permits the recursion to eventually end.

As in the infinite loop problem, a programmer must be careful to design algorithms so that they avoid infinite recursion. Any recursive definition must have a base case that does not result in a recursive option. The *base case* of the list definition is a single number that is not followed by anything. In other words, when the last number in the list is reached, the base case option terminates the recursive path.

Recursion in Math

Let's look at an example of recursion in mathematics. The value referred to as N! (which is pronounced *N factorial*) is defined for any positive integer N as the product of all integers between 1 and N inclusive. Therefore,

```
3! = 3*2*1 = 6
```

and

```
5! = 5*4*3*2*1 = 120
```

Mathematical formulas are often expressed recursively. The definition of N! can be expressed recursively as

```
1! = 1
N! = N * (N-1)! for N > 1
```

The base case of this definition is 1!, which is defined to be 1. All other values of N! (for N > 1) are defined recursively as N times the value (N–1)!. The recursion is that the factorial function is defined in terms of the factorial function.

KEY CONCEPT
Mathematical problems and formulas are often expressed recursively.

COMMON ERROR

A common error made by programmers new to recursion is to provide an incomplete base case. The reason why the base case for the factorial problem (N = 1) works is that factorial is defined only for positive integers. A common error would be to set a base case of N = 1 when there is some possibility that N could be less than 1. It is important to account for all of the possibilities: N > 1, N = 1, and N < 1.

Using this definition, 50! is equal to 50 * 49!. And 49! is equal to 49 * 48!. And 48! is equal to 48 * 47!. This process continues until we get to the base case of 1. Because N! is defined only for positive integers, this definition is complete and will always conclude with the base case.

The next section describes how recursion is accomplished in programs.

17.2 Recursive Programming

Let's use a simple mathematical operation to demonstrate the concepts of recursive programming. Consider the process of summing the values between 1 and N inclusive, where N is any positive integer. The sum of the values from 1 to N can be expressed as N plus the sum of the values from 1 to N–1. That sum can be expressed similarly, as shown in Figure 17.2.

KEY CONCEPT
Each recursive call to a method creates new local variables and parameters.

For example, the sum of the values between 1 and 20 is equal to 20 plus the sum of the values between 1 and 19. Continuing this approach, the sum of the values between 1 and 19 is equal to 19 plus the sum of the values between 1 and 18. This may sound like a strange way to think about this problem, but it is a straightforward example that can be used to demonstrate how recursion is programmed.

In Java, as in many other programming languages, a method can call itself. Each call to the method creates a new environment in which to work. That is, all local variables and parameters are newly defined with their own unique data space

$$
\begin{aligned}
\sum_{i=1}^{N} i &= N + \sum_{i=1}^{N-1} i = N + N-1 + \sum_{i=1}^{N-2} i \\
&= N + N-1 + N-2 + \sum_{i=1}^{N-3} i \\
&\;\;\vdots \\
&= N + N-1 + N-2 + \cdots + 2 + 1
\end{aligned}
$$

FIGURE 17.2 The sum of the numbers 1 through N, defined recursively

every time the method is called. Each parameter is given an initial value based on the new call. Each time a method terminates, processing returns to the method that called it (which may be an earlier invocation of the same method). These rules are no different from those governing any "regular" method invocation.

A recursive solution to the summation problem is defined by the following recursive method called sum:

```
// This method returns the sum of 1 to num

public int sum(int num)
{
   int result;
   if (num == 1)
      result = 1;
   else
      result = num + sum(num-1);
   return result;
}
```

Note that this method essentially embodies our recursive definition that the sum of the numbers between 1 and N is equal to N plus the sum of the numbers between 1 and N–1. The sum method is recursive because sum calls itself. The parameter passed to sum is decremented each time sum is called, until it reaches the base case of 1. Recursive methods usually contain an if-else statement, with one of the branches representing the base case.

Recursive Call

```
public int sum (int num)
{
    ...
    result = num + sum(num-1);
    ...
}
```

calling a method within itself with a different parameter value

Suppose the main method calls sum, passing it an initial value of 1, which is stored in the parameter num. Because num is equal to 1, the result of 1 is returned to main, and no recursion occurs.

KEY CONCEPT
A careful trace of recursive processing can provide insight into the way it is used to solve a problem.

Now let's trace the execution of the sum method when it is passed an initial value of 2. Because num does not equal 1, sum is called again with an argument of num-1, or 1. This is a new call to the method sum, with a new parameter num and a new local variable result. Because this num is equal to 1 in this invocation, the result of 1 is returned without further recursive calls. Control returns to the first version of sum that was invoked. The return value of 1 is added to the initial value of num in that call to sum, which is 2. Therefore, result is assigned the value 3, which is returned to the main method. The method called from main correctly calculates the sum of the integers from 1 to 2 and returns the result of 3.

The base case in the summation example is when num equals 1, at which point no further recursive calls are made. The recursion begins to fold back into the earlier versions of the sum method, returning the appropriate value each time. Each return value contributes to the computation of the sum at the higher level. Without the base case, infinite recursion would result. Because of each call to a method requires additional memory space, infinite recursion often results in a run-time error indicating that memory has been exhausted.

Trace the sum function with different initial values of num until this processing becomes familiar. Figure 17.3 illustrates the recursive calls when main invokes sum to determine the sum of the integers from 1 to 4. Each box represents a copy of the method as it is invoked, indicating the allocation of space to store the formal parameters and any local variables. Invocations are shown as solid lines, and returns are shown as dotted lines. The return value result is shown at each step. The recursive path is followed completely until the base case is reached; then the calls begin to return their result up through the chain.

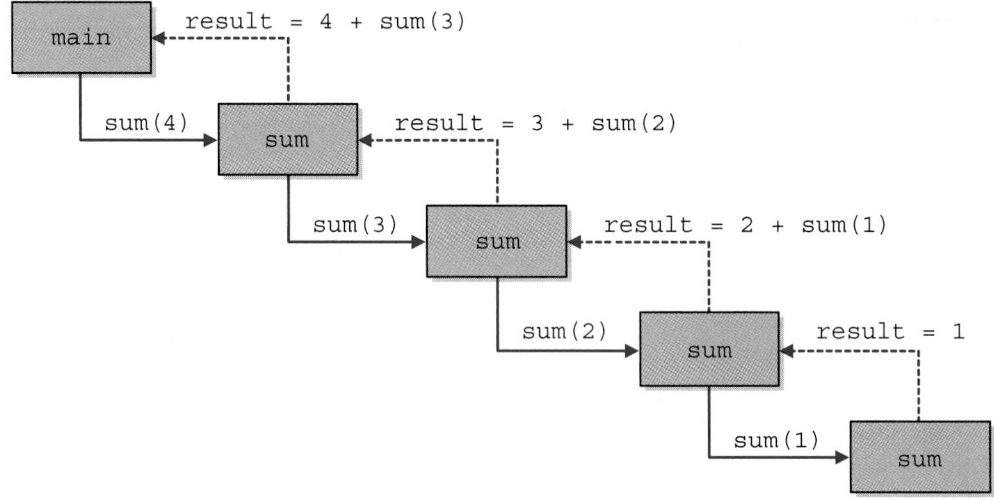

FIGURE 17.3 Recursive calls to the sum method

Recursion versus Iteration

Of course, there is an iterative solution to the summation problem we just explored:

```
sum = 0;
for (int number = 1; number <= num; number++)
    sum += number;
```

This solution is certainly more straightforward than the recursive version. If you recall our discussion from Chapter 11, we also learned that the sum of the numbers from 1 to N can be computed in a single step:

```
sum = num(num+1)/2;
```

It is important to know when recursion provides an appropriate solution to a problem. We used the summation problem to demonstrate recursion because it is a simple problem to understand, not because one would use recursion to solve it under normal conditions. Recursion has the overhead of multiple method invocations and, in this case, presents a more complicated solution than either its iterative or its computational counterparts.

KEY CONCEPT
Recursion is the most elegant and appropriate way to solve some problems, but for others it is less intuitive than an iterative solution.

A programmer must learn when to use recursion and when not to use it. Determining which approach is best is another important software engineering decision that depends on the problem being solved. All problems can be solved in an iterative manner, but in some cases the iterative version is much more complicated. For some problems, recursion enables us to create relatively short, elegant programs.

Direct versus Indirect Recursion

Direct recursion occurs when a method invokes itself, such as when `sum` calls `sum`. *Indirect recursion* occurs when a method invokes another method, eventually resulting in the original method being invoked again. For example, if method `m1` invokes method `m2`, and `m2` invokes method `m1`, we can say that `m1` is indirectly recursive. The amount of indirection could be several levels deep, as when `m1` invokes `m2`, which invokes `m3`, which invokes `m4`, which invokes `m1`. Figure 17.4 depicts a situation that involves indirect recursion. Method invocations are shown with solid lines, and returns are shown with dotted lines. The entire invocation path is followed, and then the recursion unravels following the return path.

Indirect recursion requires paying just as much same attention to base cases as direct recursion does. Furthermore, indirect recursion can be more difficult to trace because of the intervening method calls. Therefore, extra care is warranted when designing or evaluating indirectly recursive methods. Ensure that the indirection is truly necessary and that it is clearly explained in documentation.

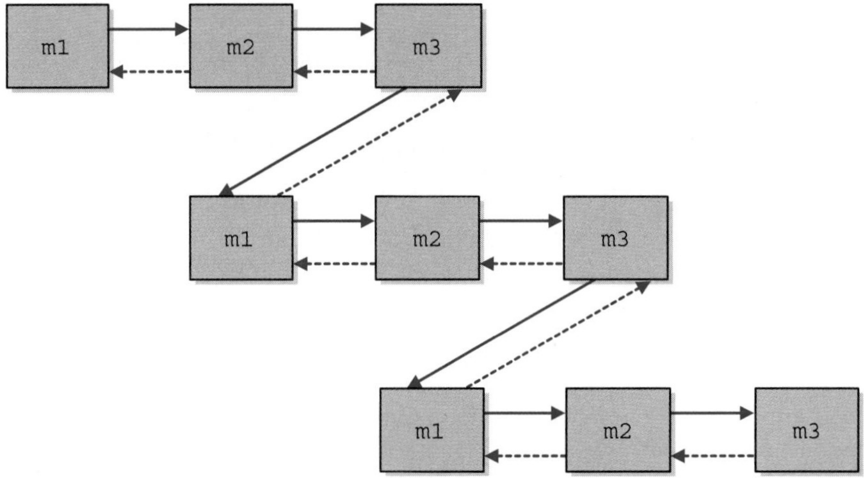

FIGURE 17.4 Indirect recursion

17.3 Using Recursion

The following sections describe problems that we solve using a recursive technique. For each one, we examine exactly how recursion plays a role in the solution and how a base case is used to terminate the recursion. As you explore these examples, consider how complicated a nonrecursive solution for each problem would be.

Traversing a Maze

As we discussed in Chapter 13, solving a maze involves a great deal of trial and error: following a path, backtracking when you cannot go farther, and trying other, untried options. Such activities often are handled nicely using recursion. In Chapter 13, we solved this problem iteratively using a stack to keep track of our potential moves. However, we can also solve this problem recursively by using the run-time stack to keep track of our progress. The `MazeTester` program shown in Listing 17.1 creates a `Maze` object and attempts to traverse it.

The `Maze` class, shown in Listing 17.2, uses a two-dimensional array of integers to represent the maze. The maze is loaded from a file. The goal is to move from the top-left corner (the entry point) to the bottom-right corner (the exit point). Initially, a 1 indicates a clear path, and a 0 indicates a blocked path. As the maze is solved, these array elements are changed to other values to indicate attempted paths and, ultimately, a successful path through the maze if one exists. Figure 17.5 shows the UML illustration of this solution.

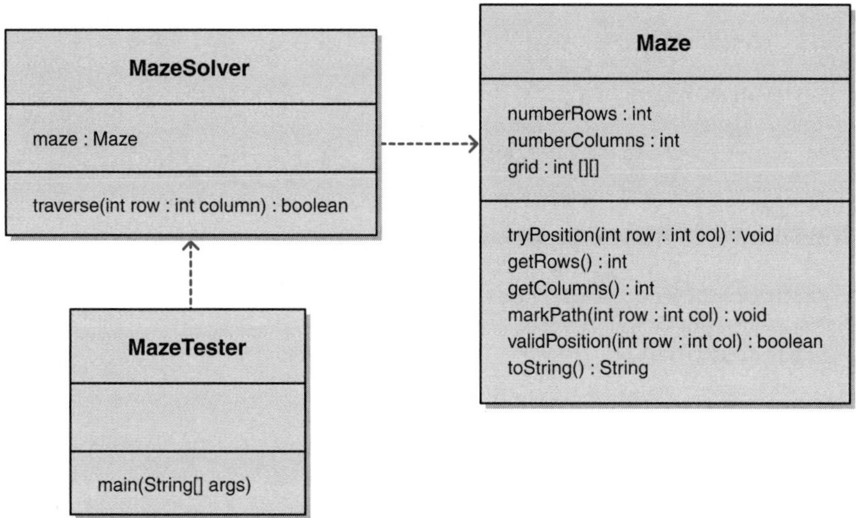

FIGURE 17.5 UML description of the maze-solving program

LISTING 17.1

```
import java.util.*;
import java.io.*;

/**
 * MazeTester uses recursion to determine if a maze can be traversed.
 *
 * @author Java Foundations
 * @version 4.0
 */
public class MazeTester
{
   /**
    * Creates a new maze, prints its original form, attempts to
    * solve it, and prints out its final form.
    */
   public static void main(String[] args) throws FileNotFoundException
   {
      Scanner scan = new Scanner(System.in);
      System.out.print("Enter the name of the file containing the maze: ");
      String filename = scan.nextLine();

      Maze labyrinth = new Maze(filename);
```

LISTING 17.1 *continued*

```
      System.out.println(labyrinth);

      MazeSolver solver = new MazeSolver(labyrinth);

      if (solver.traverse(0, 0))
          System.out.println("The maze was successfully traversed!");
      else
          System.out.println("There is no possible path.");

      System.out.println(labyrinth);
   }
}
```

LISTING 17.2

```
import java.util.*;
import java.io.*;

/**
 * Maze represents a maze of characters. The goal is to get from the
 * top left corner to the bottom right, following a path of 1's. Arbitrary
 * constants are used to represent locations in the maze that have been TRIED
 * and that are part of the solution PATH.
 *
 * @author Java Foundations
 * @version 4.0
 */
public class Maze
{
   private static final int TRIED = 2;
   private static final int PATH = 3;

   private int numberRows, numberColumns;
   private int[][] grid;

  /**
   * Constructor for the Maze class. Loads a maze from the given file.
   * Throws a FileNotFoundException if the given file is not found.
   *
```

LISTING 17.2 *continued*

```
   * @param filename the name of the file to load
   * @throws FileNotFoundException if the given file is not found
   */
  public Maze(String filename) throws FileNotFoundException
  {
     Scanner scan = new Scanner(new File(filename));
     numberRows = scan.nextInt();
     numberColumns = scan.nextInt();

     grid = new int[numberRows][numberColumns];
     for (int i = 0; i < numberRows; i++)
         for (int j = 0; j < numberColumns; j++)
             grid[i][j] = scan.nextInt();
  }

  /**
   * Marks the specified position in the maze as TRIED
   *
   * @param row the index of the row to try
   * @param col the index of the column to try
   */
   public void tryPosition(int row, int col)
   {
      grid[row][col] = TRIED;
 }

  /**
   * Return the number of rows in this maze
   *
   * @return the number of rows in this maze
   */
  public int getRows()
  {
     return grid.length;
  }

  /**
   * Return the number of columns in this maze
   *
   * @return the number of columns in this maze
   */
  public int getColumns()
```

LISTING 17.2 *continued*

```
{
   return grid[0].length;
}

/**
 * Marks a given position in the maze as part of the PATH
 *
 * @param row the index of the row to mark as part of the PATH
 * @param col the index of the column to mark as part of the PATH
 */
public void markPath(int row, int col)
{
   grid[row][col] = PATH;
}

/**
 * Determines if a specific location is valid. A valid location
 * is one that is on the grid, is not blocked, and has not been TRIED.
 *
 * @param row the row to be checked
 * @param column the column to be checked
 * @return true if the location is valid
 */
public boolean validPosition(int row, int column)
{
   boolean result = false;

   // check if cell is in the bounds of the matrix

   if (row >= 0 && row < grid.length &&
       column >= 0 && column < grid[row].length)

       //  check if cell is not blocked and not previously tried

       if (grid[row][column] == 1)
           result = true;

   return result;
}

/**
 * Returns the maze as a string.
 *
 * @return a string representation of the maze
 */
```

LISTING 17.2 *continued*

```
   public String toString()
   {
      String result = "\n";

      for (int row=0; row < grid.length; row++)
      {
         for (int column=0; column < grid[row].length; column++)
            result += grid[row][column] + "";
         result += "\n";
      }

      return result;
   }
}
```

The only valid moves through the maze are in the four primary directions: down, right, up, and left. No diagonal moves are allowed. Listing 17.3 shows the `MazeSolver` class.

Let's think this through recursively. The maze can be traversed successfully if it can be traversed successfully from position (0, 0). Therefore, the maze can be traversed successfully if it can be traversed successfully from any position adjacent to (0, 0)—namely, position (1, 0), position (0, 1), position (–1, 0), or position (0, –1). Picking a potential next step, say (1, 0), we find ourselves in the same type of situation as before. To traverse the maze successfully from the new current position, we must successfully traverse it from an adjacent position. At any point, some of the adjacent positions may be invalid, may be blocked, or may represent a possible successful path. We continue this process recursively. If the base case position is reached, the maze has been traversed successfully.

The recursive method in the `MazeSolver` class is called `traverse`. It returns a `boolean` value that indicates whether a solution was found. First the method determines whether a move to the specified row and column is valid. A move is considered valid if it stays within the grid boundaries and if the grid contains a 1 in that location, indicating that a move in that direction is not blocked. The initial call to `traverse` passes in the upper-left location (0, 0).

If the move is valid, the grid entry is changed from a 1 to a 2, marking this location as visited so that we don't later retrace our steps. Then the `traverse` method determines whether the maze has been completed by having reached

LISTING 17.3

```
/**
 * MazeSolver attempts to recursively traverse a Maze. The goal is to get from the
 * given starting position to the bottom right, following a path of 1's. Arbitrary
 * constants are used to represent locations in the maze that have been TRIED
 * and that are part of the solution PATH.
 *
 * @author Java Foundations
 * @version 4.0
 */
public class MazeSolver
{
   private Maze maze;

   /**
    * Constructor for the MazeSolver class.
    */
   public MazeSolver(Maze maze)
   {
      this.maze = maze;
   }

   /**
    * Attempts to recursively traverse the maze. Inserts special
    * characters indicating locations that have been TRIED and that
    * eventually become part of the solution PATH.
    *
    * @param row row index of current location
    * @param column column index of current location
    * @return true if the maze has been solved
    */
   public boolean traverse(int row, int column)
   {
      boolean done = false;

      if (maze.validPosition(row, column))
      {
         maze.tryPosition(row, column);   // mark this cell as tried

         if (row == maze.getRows()-1 && column == maze.getColumns()-1)
              done = true;  // the maze is solved
         else
         {
            done = traverse(row+1, column);      // down
            if (!done)
                done = traverse(row, column+1);  // right
```

LISTING 17.3 *continued*

```
                if (!done)
                    done = traverse(row-1, column);  // up
                if (!done)
                    done = traverse(row, column-1);  // left
            }

            if (done)  // this location is part of the final path
                maze.markPath(row, column);
        }

        return done;
    }
}
```

the bottom-right location. Therefore, there are actually three possibilities of the base case for this problem that will terminate any particular recursive path:

- An invalid move because the move is out of bounds or blocked
- An invalid move because the move has been tried before
- A move that arrives at the final location

If the current location is not the bottom-right corner, we search for a solution in each of the primary directions, if necessary. First, we look down by recursively calling the `traverse` method and passing in the new location. The logic of the `traverse` method starts all over again using this new position. Either a solution is ultimately found by first attempting to move down from the current location, or it is not found. If it's not found, we try moving right. If that fails, we try moving up. Finally, if no other direction has yielded a correct path, we try moving left. If no direction from the current location yields a correct solution, then there is no path from this location, and `traverse` returns false. If the very first invocation of the `traverse` method returns false, then there is no possible path through this maze.

If a solution is found from the current location, then the grid entry is changed to a 3. The first 3 is placed in the bottom-right corner. The next 3 is placed in the location that led to the bottom-right corner, and so on until the final 3 is placed in the upper-left corner. Therefore, when the final maze is printed, 0 still indicates a blocked path, 1 indicates an open path that was never tried, 2 indicates a path that was tried but failed to yield a correct solution, and 3 indicates a part of the final solution of the maze.

Here are a sample maze input file and its corresponding output:

```
5 5
1 0 0 0 0
1 1 1 1 0
0 1 0 0 0
1 1 1 1 0
0 1 0 1 1

3 0 0 0 0
3 3 1 1 0
0 3 0 0 0
1 3 3 3 0
0 2 0 3 3
```

Note that there are several opportunities for recursion in each call to the `traverse` method. Any or all of them might be followed, depending on the maze configuration. Although there may be many paths through the maze, the recursion terminates when a path is found. Carefully trace the execution of this code while following the maze array to see how the recursion solves the problem. Then consider the difficulty of producing a nonrecursive solution.

The Towers of Hanoi

The *Towers of Hanoi* puzzle was invented in the 1880s by Edouard Lucas, a French mathematician. It has become a favorite among computer scientists because its solution is an excellent demonstration of recursive elegance.

The puzzle consists of three upright pegs (towers) and a set of disks with holes in the middle so that they slide onto the pegs. Each disk has a different diameter. Initially, all of the disks are stacked on one peg in order of size such that the largest disk is on the bottom, as shown in Figure 17.6.

The goal of the puzzle is to move all of the disks from their original (first) peg to the destination (third) peg. We can use the "extra" peg as a temporary place to put disks, but we must obey the following three rules:

- We can move only one disk at a time.
- We cannot place a larger disk on top of a smaller disk.
- All disks must be on some peg except for the disk that is in transit between pegs.

FIGURE 17.6 The Towers of Hanoi puzzle

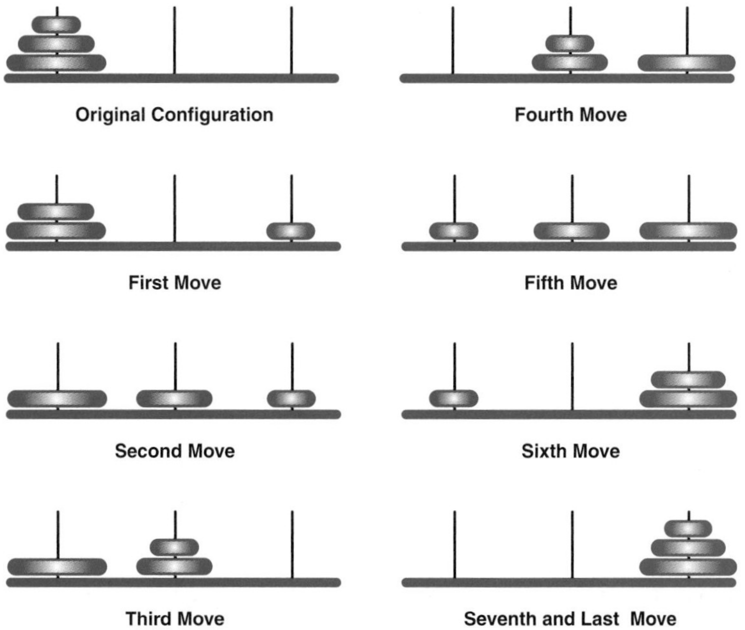

FIGURE 17.7 A solution to the three-disk Towers of Hanoi puzzle

These rules imply that we must move smaller disks "out of the way" in order to move a larger disk from one peg to another. Figure 17.7 shows the step-by-step solution for the Towers of Hanoi puzzle using three disks. To move all three disks from the first peg to the third peg, we first have to get to the point where the smaller two disks are out of the way on the second peg so that the largest disk can be moved from the first peg to the third peg.

The first three moves shown in Figure 17.7 can be thought of as "moving the smaller disks out of the way." The fourth move puts the largest disk in its final place. The last three moves put the smaller disks in their final place on top of the largest one.

Let's use this idea to form a general strategy. To move a stack of N disks from the original peg to the destination peg:

- Move the topmost N–1 disks from the original peg to the extra peg.
- Move the largest disk from the original peg to the destination peg.
- Move the N–1 disks from the extra peg to the destination peg.

This strategy lends itself nicely to a recursive solution. The step to move the N–1 disks out of the way is the same problem all over again: moving a stack of disks. For this subtask, though, there is one less disk, and our destination peg is what we were originally calling the extra peg. An analogous situation occurs after we have moved the largest disk, and we have to move the original N–1 disks again.

LISTING 17.4

```
/**
 * SolveTowers uses recursion to solve the Towers of Hanoi puzzle.
 *
 * @author Java Foundations
 * @version 4.0
 */
public class SolveTowers
{
   /**
    * Creates a TowersOfHanoi puzzle and solves it.
    */
   public static void main(String[] args)
   {
      TowersOfHanoi towers = new TowersOfHanoi(4);
      towers.solve();
   }
}
```

The base case for this problem occurs when we want to move a "stack" that consists of only one disk. That step can be accomplished directly and without recursion.

The program in Listing 17.4 creates a `TowersOfHanoi` object and invokes its `solve` method. The output is a step-by-step list of instructions that describes how the disks should be moved to solve the puzzle. This example uses four disks, which is specified by a parameter to the `TowersOfHanoi` constructor.

The `TowersOfHanoi` class, shown in Listing 17.5, uses the `solve` method to make an initial call to `moveTower`, the recursive method. The initial call indicates that all of the disks should be moved from peg 1 to peg 3, using peg 2 as the extra position.

LISTING 17.5

```
/**
 * TowersOfHanoi represents the classic Towers of Hanoi puzzle.
 *
 * @author Java Foundations
 * @version 4.0
 */
```

LISTING 17.5 *continued*

```
public class TowersOfHanoi
{
   private int totalDisks;

  /**
   * Sets up the puzzle with the specified number of disks.
   *
   * @param disks the number of disks
   */
  public TowersOfHanoi(int disks)
  {
     totalDisks = disks;
  }

  /**
   * Performs the initial call to moveTower to solve the puzzle.
   * Moves the disks from tower 1 to tower 3 using tower 2.
   */
  public void solve()
  {
     moveTower(totalDisks, 1, 3, 2);
  }

  /**
   * Moves the specified number of disks from one tower to another
   * by moving a subtower of n-1 disks out of the way, moving one
   * disk, then moving the subtower back. Base case of 1 disk.
   *
   * @param numDisks  the number of disks to move
   * @param start     the starting tower
   * @param end       the ending tower
   * @param temp      the temporary tower
   */
  private void moveTower(int numDisks, int start, int end, int temp)
  {
     if (numDisks == 1)
         moveOneDisk(start, end);
     else
     {
        moveTower(numDisks-1, start, temp, end);
        moveOneDisk(start, end);
        moveTower(numDisks-1, temp, end, start);
     }
  }
```

LISTING 17.5 *continued*

```
   /**
    * Prints instructions to move one disk from the specified start
    * tower to the specified end tower.
    *
    * @param start  the starting tower
    * @param end    the ending tower
    */
   private void moveOneDisk(int start, int end)
   {
      System.out.println("Move one disk from " + start + " to " + end);
   }
}
```

The `moveTower` method first considers the base case (a "stack" of one disk). When that occurs, it calls the `moveOneDisk` method, which prints a single line describing that particular move. If the stack contains more than one disk, we call `moveTower` again to get the N–1 disks out of the way, then move the largest disk, then move the N–1 disks to their final destination with yet another call to `moveTower`.

Note that the parameters to `moveTower` describing the pegs are switched around as needed to move the partial stacks. This code follows our general strategy and uses the `moveTower` method to move all partial stacks. Trace the code carefully for a stack of three disks to understand the processing. Figure 17.8 shows the UML diagram for this problem.

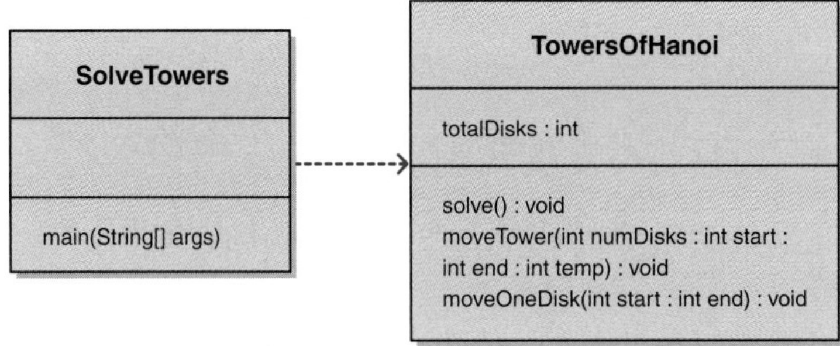

FIGURE 17.8 UML description of Towers of Hanoi puzzle solution

17.4 Analyzing Recursive Algorithms

In Chapter 11, we explored the concept of analyzing an algorithm to determine its complexity (usually its time complexity) and expressed it in terms of a growth function. The growth function gave us the order of the algorithm, which can be used to compare it to other algorithms that accomplish the same task.

KEY CONCEPT
The order of a recursive algorithm can be determined using techniques similar to those used in analyzing iterative processing.

When analyzing a loop, we determined the order of the body of the loop and multiplied it by the number of times the loop was executed. Analyzing a recursive algorithm uses similar thinking. Determining the order of a recursive algorithm is a matter of determining the order of the recursion (the number of times the recursive definition is followed) and multiplying that by the order of the body of the recursive method.

Consider the recursive method presented in Section 17.2 that computes the sum of the integers from 1 to some positive value. We reprint it here for convenience:

```
// This method returns the sum of 1 to num

public int sum (int num)
{
   int result;
   if (num == 1)
      result = 1;
   else
      result = num + sum (num-1);
   return result;
}
```

The size of this problem is naturally expressed as the number of values to be summed. Because we are summing the integers from 1 to `num`, the number of values to be summed is `num`. The operation of interest is the act of adding two values together. The body of the recursive method performs one addition operation, and therefore is O(1). Each time the recursive method is invoked, the value of `num` is decreased by 1. Therefore, the recursive method is called `num` times, so the order of the recursion is O(n). Thus, because the body is O(1) and the recursion is O(n), the order of the entire algorithm is O(n).

We will see that in some algorithms the recursive step operates on half as much data as the previous call, thus creating an order of recursion of O(log n). If the body of the method is O(1), then the whole algorithm is O(log n). If the body of the method is O(n), then the whole algorithm is O(n log n).

Now consider the Towers of Hanoi puzzle. The size of the puzzle is naturally the number of disks, and the processing operation of interest is the step of moving one disk from one peg to another. Each call to the recursive method `moveTower` results in one disk being moved. Unfortunately, except for the base case, each recursive call results in calling itself *twice more*, and each call operates on a stack of disks that is only one less than the stack that is passed in as the parameter. Thus, calling `moveTower` with 1 disk results in 1 disk being moved, calling `moveTower` with 2 disks results in 3 disks being moved, calling `moveTower` with 3 disks results in 7 disks being moved, calling `moveTower` with 4 disks results in 15 disks being moved, and so on. Looking at it another way, if `f(n)` is the growth function for this problem, then:

VideoNote
Analyzing recursive algorithms

$$f(n) + 1 \text{ when n is equal to } 1$$

for $n > 1$,

$$\begin{aligned} f(n) &= 2^*(f(n - 1) + 1) \\ &= 2^n - 1 \end{aligned}$$

Contrary to its short and elegant implementation, the solution to the Towers of Hanoi puzzle is terribly inefficient. To solve the puzzle with a stack of n disks, we have to make $2^n - 1$ individual disk moves. Therefore, the Towers of Hanoi algorithm is $O(2^n)$. This order is an example of exponential complexity. As the number of disks increases, the number of required moves increases exponentially.

KEY CONCEPT
The Towers of Hanoi solution has exponential complexity, which is very inefficient, yet the code is remarkably short and elegant.

Legend has it that priests of Brahma are working on this puzzle in a temple at the center of the world. They are using 64 gold disks, moving them between pegs of pure diamond. The downside is that when the priests finish the puzzle, the world will end. The upside is that even if they move one disk every second of every day, it will take them over 584 billion years to complete it. That's with a puzzle of only 64 disks! It is certainly an indication of just how intractable exponential algorithm complexity is.

Summary of Key Concepts

- Recursion is a programming technique in which a method calls itself. A key to being able to program recursively is to be able to think recursively.
- Any recursive definition must have a nonrecursive part, called the base case, that permits the recursion to eventually end.
- Mathematical problems and formulas are often expressed recursively.
- Each recursive call to a method creates new local variables and parameters.
- A careful trace of recursive processing can provide insight into the way it is used to solve a problem.
- Recursion is the most elegant and appropriate way to solve some problems, but for others it is less intuitive than an iterative solution.
- The order of a recursive algorithm can be determined using techniques similar to those used in analyzing iterative processing.
- The Towers of Hanoi solution has exponential complexity, which is very inefficient, yet the code is incredibly short and elegant.

Summary of Terms

base case The part of an operation's definition that is not recursive.

direct recursion The type of recursion in which a method invokes itself firectly (as opposed to indirect recursion).

indirect recursion The type of recursion in which a method calls another method, which may call yet another, and so on until the original method is called (as opposed to direction recursion).

infinite recursion The problem that occurs when a base case is never reached or not defined for an operation.

recursion A programming technique in which a method calls itself to fulfill its overall purpose.

Towers of Hanoi A classic computing puzzle in which the goal is to move disks from one tower to another under specific rules.

Self-Review Questions

SR 17.1 What is recursion?

SR 17.2 What is infinite recursion?

SR 17.3 When is a base case needed for recursive processing?

SR 17.4 Is recursion necessary?

SR 17.5 When should recursion be avoided?

SR 17.6 What is indirect recursion?

SR 17.7 Explain the general approach to solving the Towers of Hanoi puzzle. How is it related to recursion?

Exercises

EX 17.1 Write a recursive definition of a valid Java identifier.

EX 17.2 Write a recursive definition of x^y (x raised to the power y), where x and y are integers and $y > 0$.

EX 17.3 Write a recursive definition of i * j (integer multiplication), where $i > 0$. Define the multiplication process in terms of integer addition. For example, 4 * 7 is equal to 7 added to itself 4 times.

EX 17.4 Write a recursive definition of the Fibonacci numbers, a sequence of integers, each of which is the sum of the previous two numbers. The first two numbers in the sequence are 0 and 1. Explain why you would not normally use recursion to solve this problem.

EX 17.5 Modify the method that calculates the sum of the integers between 1 and N shown in this chapter. Have the new version match the following recursive definition: The sum of 1 to N is the sum of 1 to (N/2) plus the sum of (N/2 + 1) to N. Trace your solution using an N of 8.

EX 17.6 Write a recursive method that returns the value of N! (N factorial) using the definition given in this chapter. Explain why you would not normally use recursion to solve this problem.

EX 17.7 Write a recursive method to reverse a string. Explain why you would not normally use recursion to solve this problem.

EX 17.8 Design a new maze for the `MazeSearch` program in this chapter, and rerun the program. Explain the processing in terms of your new maze, giving examples of a path that was tried but failed, a path that was never tried, and the ultimate result.

EX 17.9 Annotate the lines of output of the `SolveTowers` program in this chapter to show the recursive steps.

EX 17.10 Produce a chart showing the number of moves required to solve the Towers of Hanoi puzzle using the following numbers of disks: 2, 3, 4, 5, 6, 7, 8, 9, 10, 15, 20, and 25.

EX 17.11 Determine and explain the order of your solution to Exercise 17.4.

EX 17.12 Determine and explain the order of your solution to Exercise 17.5.

EX 17.13 Determine and explain the order of your solution to Exercise 17.6.

EX 17.14 Determine the order of the recursive maze solution presented in this chapter.

Programming Projects

PP 17.1 Design and implement a program that implements Euclid's algorithm for finding the greatest common divisor of two positive integers. The greatest common divisor is the largest integer that divides both values without producing a remainder. In a class called `DivisorCalc`, define a static method called `gcd` that accepts two integers, `num1` and `num2`. Create a driver to test your implementation. The recursive algorithm is defined as follows:

```
gcd (num1, num2) is num2 if num2 <= num1 and num2
divides num1
gcd (num1, num2) is gcd (num2, num1) if num1 < num2
gcd (num1, num2) is gcd (num2, num1%num2) otherwise
```

PP 17.2 Modify the `Maze` class so that it prints out the path of the final solution as it is discovered, without storing it.

PP 17.3 Design and implement a program that traverses a 3D maze.

PP 17.4 Design and implement a recursive program that solves the Nonattacking Queens problem. That is, write a program to determine how eight queens can be positioned on an eight-by-eight chessboard so that none of them is in the same row, column, or diagonal as any other queen. There are no other chess pieces on the board.

PP 17.5 In the language of an alien race, all words take the form of Blurbs. A Blurb is a Whoozit followed by one or more Whatzits. A Whoozit is the character `'x'` followed by zero or more `'y'`s. A Whatzit is a `'q'` followed by either a `'z'` or a `'d'`, followed by a Whoozit. Design and implement a recursive program that generates random Blurbs in this alien language.

PP 17.6 Design and implement a recursive program to determine whether a string is a valid Blurb as defined in the previous project description.

PP 17.7 Design and implement a recursive program to determine and print the Nth line of Pascal's Triangle, as shown below. Each interior value is the sum of the two values above it. (*Hint*: Use an array to store the values on each line.)

```
                1
              1   1
            1   2   1
          1   3   3   1
        1   4   6   4   1
      1   5  10  10   5   1
    1   6  15  20  15   6   1
  1   7  21  35  35  21   7   1
1   8  28  56  70  56  28   8   1
```

PP 17.8 Design and implement a graphical version of the Towers of Hanoi puzzle. Allow the user to set the number of disks used in the puzzle. The user should be able to interact with the puzzle in two main ways. The user can move the disks from one peg to another using the mouse, in which case the program should ensure that each move is legal. The user can also watch a solution take place as an animation, with pause/resume buttons. Permit the user to control the speed of the animation.

Answers to Self-Review Questions

SR 17.1 Recursion is a programming technique in which a method calls itself, solving a smaller version of the problem each time, until the terminating condition is reached.

SR 17.2 Infinite recursion occurs when there is no base case that serves as a terminating condition, or when the base case is improperly specified. The recursive path is followed forever. In a recursive program, infinite recursion often results in an error that indicates that available memory has been exhausted.

SR 17.3 A base case is always needed to terminate recursion and begin the process of returning through the calling hierarchy. Without the base case, infinite recursion results.

SR 17.4 Recursion is not necessary. Every recursive algorithm can be written in an iterative manner. However, some problem solutions are much more elegant and straightforward when they are written recursively.

SR 17.5 Avoid recursion when the iterative solution is simpler and more easily understood and programmed. Recursion has the overhead of multiple method calls and is not always intuitive.

SR 17.6 Indirect recursion occurs when a method calls another method, which calls another method, and so on until one of the called methods invokes the original method. Indirect recursion is usually more difficult to trace than direct recursion, in which a method calls itself.

SR 17.7 The Towers of Hanoi puzzle of N disks is solved by moving N–1 disks out of the way onto an extra peg, moving the largest disk to its destination, then moving the N–1 disks from the extra peg to the destination. This solution is inherently recursive because we can use the same process to move the whole substack of N–1 disks.

Searching and Sorting

CHAPTER OBJECTIVES

- Examine the linear search and binary search algorithms.
- Examine several sort algorithms.
- Discuss the complexity of these algorithms.

Two common tasks in the world of software development are searching for a particular element within a group and sorting a group of elements into a particular order. There are a variety of algorithms that can be used to accomplish these tasks, and the differences among them are worth exploring carefully. These topics go hand in hand with the study of collections and data structures.

18.1 Searching

Searching is the process of finding a designated *target element* within a group of items, or determining that the target does not exist within the group. The group of items to be searched is sometimes called the *search pool*.

> **KEY CONCEPT**
> Searching is the process of finding a designated target within a group of items or determining that it doesn't exist.

This section examines two common approaches to searching: a linear search and a binary search. Later in this book, other search techniques are presented that use the characteristics of particular data structures to facilitate the search process.

Our goal is to perform the search as efficiently as possible. In terms of algorithm analysis, we want to minimize the number of comparisons we have to make to find the target. In general, the more items there are in the search pool, the more comparisons it will take to find the target. Thus, the size of the problem is defined by the number of items in the search pool.

> **KEY CONCEPT**
> An efficient search minimizes the number of comparisons made.

To be able to search for an object, we must be able to compare one object to another. Our implementations of these algorithms search an array of `Comparable` objects. Therefore, the elements involved must implement the `Comparable` interface and be comparable to each other. We might attempt to accomplish this restriction in the header for the `Searching` class in which all of our searching methods are located by doing something like:

```
public class Searching<T extends Comparable<T>>
```

The net effect of this generic declaration is that we can instantiate the `Searching` class with any class that implements the `Comparable` interface. Recall that the `Comparable` interface contains one method, `compareTo`, which is designed to return an integer that is less than zero, equal to zero, or greater than zero (respectively) if the object is less than, equal to, or greater than the object to which it is being compared. Therefore, any class that implements the `Comparable` interface defines the relative order of any two objects of that class.

Declaring the `Searching` class in this manner, however, will cause us to have to instantiate the class any time we want to use one of the search methods. This is awkward at best for a class that contains nothing but service methods. A better solution would be to declare all of the methods as static and generic. Let's first remind ourselves about the concept of static methods, and then we will explore generic static methods.

Static Methods

As discussed in Chapter 5, a *static method* (also called a *class method*) can be invoked through the class name (all the methods of the `Math` class are static methods, for example). You don't have to instantiate an object of the class to invoke a static method. For example, the `sqrt` method is called through the `Math` class as follows:

```
System.out.println ("Square root of 27: " + Math.sqrt(27));
```

A method is made static by using the `static` modifier in the method declaration. As we have seen, the `main` method of a Java program must be declared with the `static` modifier; this is so that `main` can be executed by the interpreter without instantiating an object from the class that contains `main`.

Because static methods do not operate in the context of a particular object, they cannot reference instance variables, which exist only in an instance of a class. The compiler will issue an error if a static method attempts to use a nonstatic variable. A static method can, however, reference static variables, because static variables exist independent of specific objects. Therefore, the `main` method can access only static and local variables.

KEY CONCEPT
A method is made static by using the `static` modifier in the method declaration.

The methods in the `Math` class perform basic computations based on values passed as parameters. There is no object state to maintain in these situations; therefore, there is no good reason to force us to create an object in order to request these services.

Generic Methods

In a manner similar to what we have done in creating generic classes, we can also create generic methods. That is, instead of creating a class that refers to a generic type parameter, we can create an individual method that does so. A generic parameter applies only to that method.

To create a generic method, we insert a generic declaration in the header of the method immediately preceding the return type.

```
public static <T extends Comparable<T>> boolean
     linearSearch(T[] data, int min, int max, T target)
```

Now that method, including the return type and the types of the parameters, can make use of the generic type parameter. It makes sense that the generic declaration has to come before the return type so that, although this example doesn't do so, the generic type can be used in the return type.

Generic Method

generic type parameter applies to this method

```
public static <T extends Comparable<T>> boolean
  linearSearch(T[] data, int min, int max, T target)
```

generic type can be used in method parameters and return type

Now that we can create a generic static method, we do not need to instantiate the `Searching` class each time we need one of the methods. Instead, we can simply invoke the static method using the class name and including our type to replace the generic type. For example, an invocation of the `linearSearch` method to search an array of Strings might look like this:

```
Searching.linearSearch(targetarray, min, max, target);
```

Note that it is not necessary to specify the type to replace the generic type. The compiler will infer the type from the arguments provided. Thus for this line of code, the compiler will replace the generic type T with whatever the element type is for `targetarray` and the type of `target`.

Linear Search

If the search pool is organized into a list of some kind, one straightforward way to perform the search is to start at the beginning of the list and compare each value in turn to the target element. Eventually, we will either find the target or come to the end of the list and conclude that the target doesn't exist in the group. This approach is called a *linear search* because it begins at one end and scans the search pool in a linear manner. This process is depicted in Figure 18.1.

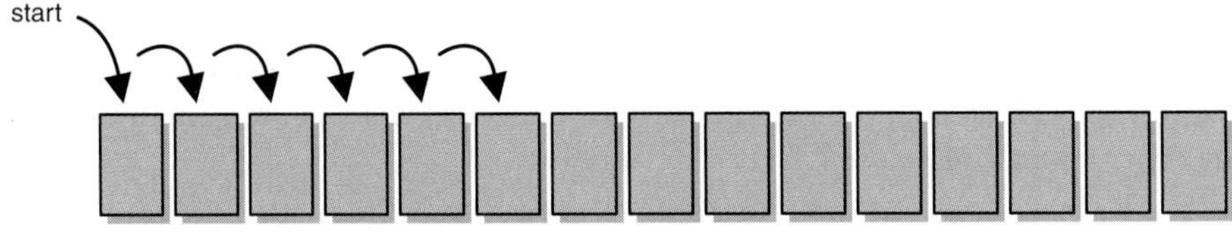

FIGURE 18.1 A linear search

The following method implements a linear search. It accepts the array of elements to be searched, the beginning and ending index for the search, and the target value sought. The method returns a `boolean` value that indicates whether or not the target element was found.

```
/**
 * Searches the specified array of objects using a linear search
 * algorithm.
 *
 * @param data   the array to be searched
 * @param min    the integer representation of the minimum value
 * @param max    the integer representation of the maximum value
 * @param target the element being searched for
 * @return       true if the desired element is found
 */
public static <T>
   boolean linearSearch(T[] data, int min, int max, T target)
{
   int index = min;
   boolean found = false;

   while (!found && index <= max)
   {
      found = data[index].equals(target);
      index++;
   }

   return found;
}
```

The `while` loop steps through the elements of the array, terminating when either the element is found or when the end of the array is reached. The `boolean` variable `found` is initialized to `false` and is changed to `true` only if the target element is located.

Variations on this implementation could return the element found in the array if it is found and return a null reference if it is not found. Alternatively, an exception could be thrown if the target element is not found.

The `linearSearch` method could be incorporated into any class. Our version of this method is defined as part of a class containing methods that provide various searching capabilities.

The linear search algorithm is fairly easy to understand, although it is not particularly efficient. Note that a linear search does not require the elements in the search pool to be in any particular order within the array. The only criterion is that we must be able to examine them one at a time in turn. The binary search algorithm, described next, improves on the efficiency of the search process, but it works only if the search pool is ordered.

Binary Search

If the group of items in the search pool is sorted, then our approach to searching can be much more efficient than that of a linear search. A *binary search* algorithm eliminates large parts of the search pool with each comparison by capitalizing on the fact that the search pool is in sorted order.

KEY CONCEPT
A binary search capitalizes on the fact that the search pool is sorted.

Instead of starting the search at one end or the other, a binary search begins in the middle of the sorted list. If the target element is not found at that middle element, then the search continues. And because the list is sorted, we know that if the target is in the list, it will be on one side of the array or the other, depending on whether the target is less than or greater than the middle element. Thus, because the list is sorted, we eliminate half of the search pool with one carefully chosen comparison. The remaining half of the search pool represents the *viable candidates* in which the target element may yet be found.

The search continues in this same manner, examining the middle element of the viable candidates, eliminating half of them. Each comparison reduces the viable candidates by half until eventually the target element is found or there are no more viable candidates, which means the target element is not in the search pool. The process of a binary search is depicted in Figure 18.2.

Let's look at an example. Consider the following sorted list of integers:

10 12 18 22 31 34 40 46 59 67 69 72 80 84 98

Suppose we were trying to determine whether the number 67 is in the list. Initially, the target could be anywhere in the list (all items in the search pool are viable candidates).

The binary search approach begins by examining the middle element, in this case 46. That element is not our target, so we must continue searching. But since we know that the list is sorted, we know that if 67 is in the list, it must be in the

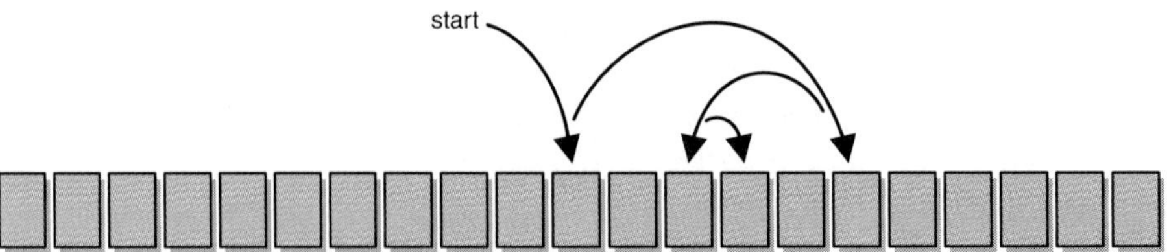

FIGURE 18.2 A binary search

second half of the data, because all data items to the left of the middle have values of 46 or less. This leaves the following viable candidates to search (shown in bold):

10 12 18 22 31 34 40 46 **59 67 69 72 80 84 98**

Continuing the same approach, we examine the middle value of the viable candidates (72). Again, this is not our target value, so we must continue the search. This time we can eliminate all values higher than 72, which leaves (again in bold)

10 12 18 22 31 34 40 46 **59 67 69** 72 80 84 98

Note that in only two comparisons, we have reduced the viable candidates from 15 items down to 3 items. Employing the same approach again, we select the middle element, 67, and find the element we are seeking. If 67 had not been our target, we would have continued with this process until we had either found the target value or eliminated all possible data.

KEY CONCEPT
A binary search eliminates half of the viable candidates with each comparison.

With each comparison, a binary search eliminates approximately half of the data remaining (it also eliminates the middle element). That is, a binary search eliminates half of the data with the first comparison, another quarter of the data with the second comparison, another eighth of the data with the third comparison, and so on.

VideoNote
Demonstration of a binary search

The following method implements a binary search. Like the `linearSearch` method, it accepts an array of `Comparable` objects to be searched as well as the target value. It also takes integer values representing the minimum index and maximum index that define the portion of the array to search (the viable candidates).

```
/**
 * Searches the specified array of objects using a binary search
 * algorithm.
 *
 * @param data   the array to be searched
 * @param min    the integer representation of the minimum value
 * @param max    the integer representation of the maximum value
 * @param target the element being searched for
 * @return       true if the desired element is found
 */
public static <T extends Comparable<T>>
   boolean binarySearch(T[] data, int min, int max, T target)
{
   boolean found = false;
   int midpoint = (min + max) / 2;  // determine the midpoint
```

```
    if (data[midpoint].compareTo(target) == 0)
        found = true;

    else if (data[midpoint].compareTo(target) > 0)
    {
       if (min <= midpoint - 1)
           found = binarySearch(data, min, midpoint - 1, target);
    }
    else if (midpoint + 1 <= max)
       found = binarySearch(data, midpoint + 1, max, target);

    return found;
 }
```

Note that the `binarySearch` method is implemented recursively. If the target element is not found, and there are more data to search, the method calls itself, passing parameters that shrink the size of viable candidates within the array. The `min` and `max` indexes are used to determine whether there are still more data to search. That is, if the reduced search area does not contain at least one element, the method does not call itself, and a value of false is returned.

At any point in this process, we may have an even number of values to search—and therefore two "middle" values. As far as the algorithm is concerned, the midpoint used can be either of the two middle values as long as the same choice is made consistently. In this implementation of the binary search, the calculation that determines the midpoint index discards any fractional part and therefore picks the first of the two middle values.

Comparing Search Algorithms

For a linear search, the best case occurs when the target element happens to be the first item we examine in the group. The worst case occurs when the target is not in the group, and we have to examine every element before we determine that it isn't present. The expected case is that we will have to search half of the list before we find the element. That is, if there are n elements in the search pool, then on average we will have to examine n/2 elements before finding the one for which we were searching.

Therefore, the linear search algorithm has a linear time complexity of O(n). Because the elements are searched one at a time in turn, the complexity is linear—in direct proportion to the number of elements to be searched.

A binary search, on the other hand, is generally much faster. Because we can eliminate half of the remaining data with each comparison, we can find the element much more quickly. The best case is that we find the target in one comparison—that is, the target element happens to be at the midpoint of the array. The worst case occurs when the element is not present in the list, in which case we have to make approximately $\log_2 n$ comparisons before we eliminate all of the data. Thus, the expected case for finding an element that is in the search pool is approximately $(\log_2 n)/2$ comparisons.

Therefore, binary search is a *logarithmic algorithm* and has a time complexity of $O(\log_2 n)$. Compared to a linear search, a binary search is much faster for large values of n.

KEY CONCEPT
A binary search has logarithmic complexity, which makes it a very efficient way to examine a large search pool.

A question might be asked here: If a binary search is more efficient than a linear search, why would we ever use a linear search? First, a linear search is generally simpler than a binary search, and it is therefore easier to program and debug. Second, a linear search does not require the additional overhead of sorting the search list. Thus, conducting a binary search involves a trade-off: Achieving maximum efficiency requires investing the effort to keep the search pool sorted.

For small problems, there is little practical difference between the two types of algorithms. However, as n gets larger, the binary search becomes increasingly attractive. Suppose a given set of data contains a million elements. In a linear search, we would have to examine each of the one million elements to determine that a particular target element is not in the group. In a binary search, we could make that conclusion in roughly 20 comparisons.

18.2 Sorting

Sorting is the process of arranging a group of items into a defined order, either ascending or descending, based on some criterion. For example, you may want to alphabetize a list of names or put a list of survey results into descending numeric order.

KEY CONCEPT
Sorting is the process of arranging a list of items into a defined order based on some criterion.

Many sort algorithms have been developed and critiqued over the years. In fact, sorting is considered a classic area of study in computer science. Like search algorithms, sort algorithms generally are divided into two categories based on efficiency: *Sequential sorts* typically use a pair of nested loops and require roughly n^2 comparisons to sort n elements, and *logarithmic sorts* typically require roughly $n\log_2 n$ comparisons to sort n elements. As with the search algorithms, when n is small, there is little practical difference between the two categories of algorithms.

In this chapter, we examine three sequential sorts—selection sort, insertion sort, and bubble sort—and two logarithmic sorts—quick sort and merge sort. We also take a look at one additional sort algorithm—radix sort—that sorts without comparing elements.

Before we dive into particular sort algorithms, let's look at a general sorting problem to solve. The `SortPhoneList` program, shown in Listing 18.1, creates an array of `Contact` objects, sorts those objects, and then prints the sorted list. In this implementation, the `Contact` objects are sorted using a call to the `selectionSort` method, which we examine later in this chapter. However, any other sorting method described in this chapter could be used to achieve the same results.

LISTING 18.1

```
/**
 * SortPhoneList driver for testing an object selection sort.
 *
 * @author Java Foundations
 * @version 4.0
 */
public class SortPhoneList
{
   /**
    * Creates an array of Contact objects, sorts them, then prints
    * them.
    */
   public static void main(String[] args)
   {
      Contact[] friends = new Contact[7];

      friends[0] = new Contact("John", "Smith", "610-555-7384");
      friends[1] = new Contact("Sarah", "Barnes", "215-555-3827");
      friends[2] = new Contact("Mark", "Riley", "733-555-2969");
      friends[3] = new Contact("Laura", "Getz", "663-555-3984");
      friends[4] = new Contact("Larry", "Smith", "464-555-3489");
      friends[5] = new Contact("Frank", "Phelps", "322-555-2284");
      friends[6] = new Contact("Marsha", "Grant", "243-555-2837");

      Sorting.insertionSort(friends);

      for (Contact friend : friends)
         System.out.println(friend);
   }
}
```

Each `Contact` object represents a person with a last name, a first name, and a phone number. The `Contact` class is shown in Listing 18.2. The UML description of these classes is left as an exercise.

The `Contact` class implements the `Comparable` interface and therefore provides a definition of the `compareTo` method. In this case, the contacts are sorted by last name; if two contacts have the same last name, their first names are used.

LISTING 18.2

```
/**
 * Contact represents a phone contact.
 *
 * @author Java Foundations
 * @version 4.0
 */
public class Contact implements Comparable<Contact>
{
   private String firstName, lastName, phone;

  /**
   * Sets up this contact with the specified information.
   *
   * @param first     a string representation of a first name
   * @param last      a string representation of a last name
   * @param telephone a string representation of a phone number
   */
  public Contact(String first, String last, String telephone)
  {
     firstName = first;
     lastName = last;
     phone = telephone;
  }

  /**
   * Returns a description of this contact as a string.
   *
   * @return a string representation of this contact
   */
  public String toString()
  {
     return lastName + ", " + firstName + "\t" + phone;
  }
```

LISTING 18.2 *continued*

```
   /**
    * Uses both last and first names to determine lexical ordering.
    *
    * @param other the contact to be compared to this contact
    * @return the integer result of the comparison
    */
   public int compareTo(Contact other)
   {
      int result;

      if (lastName.equals(other.lastName))
          result = firstName.compareTo(other.firstName);
      else
          result = lastName.compareTo(other.lastName);

      return result;
   }
}
```

Now let's examine several sort algorithms and their implementations. Any of these could be used to put the `Contact` objects into sorted order.

Selection Sort

The *selection sort* algorithm sorts a list of values by repetitively putting a particular value into its final, sorted position. In other words, for each position in the list, the algorithm selects the value that should go in that position and puts it there.

The general strategy of the selection sort algorithm is as follows: Scan the entire list to find the smallest value. Exchange that value with the value in the first position of the list. Scan the rest of the list (all but the first value) to find the smallest value, and then exchange it with the value in the second position of the list. Scan the rest of the list (all but the first two values) to find the smallest value, and then exchange it with the value in the third position of the list. Continue this process for each position in the list. When complete, the list is sorted. The selection sort process is illustrated in Figure 18.3.

KEY CONCEPT
The selection sort algorithm sorts a list of values by repetitively putting a particular value into its final, sorted position.

The following method defines an implementation of the selection sort algorithm. It accepts an array of objects as a parameter. When it returns to the calling method, the elements within the array are sorted.

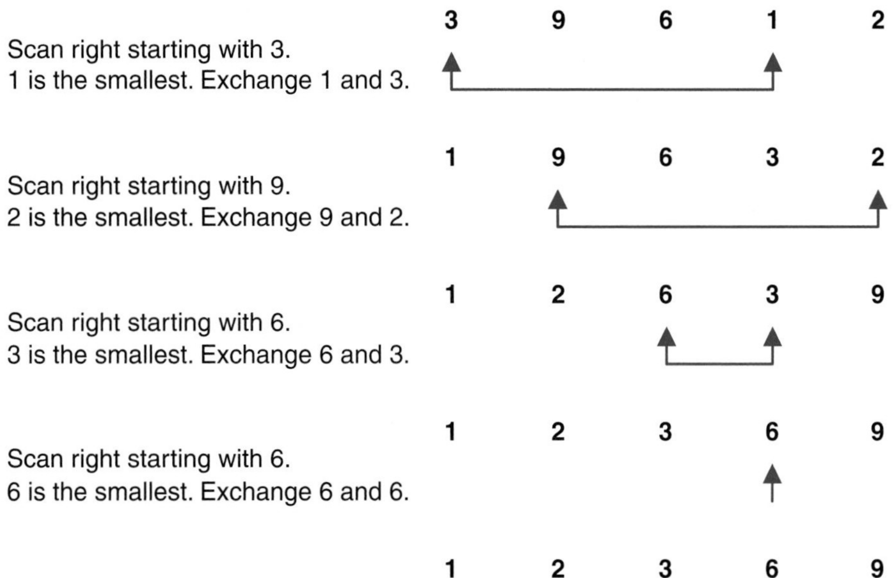

FIGURE 18.3 Example of selection sort processing

```
/**
 * Sorts the specified array of integers using the selection
 * sort algorithm.
 *
 * @param data the array to be sorted
 */
public static <T extends Comparable<T>>
        void selectionSort(T[] data)
{
    int min;
    T temp;

    for (int index = 0; index < data.length-1; index++)
    {
        min = index;
        for (int scan = index+1; scan < data.length; scan++)
            if (data[scan].compareTo(data[min])<0)
                min = scan;

        swap(data, min, index);
    }
}
```

The implementation of the `selectionSort` method uses two loops to sort an array. The outer loop controls the position in the array where the next smallest value will be stored. The inner loop finds the smallest value in the rest of the list by scanning all positions greater than or equal to the index specified by the outer loop. When the smallest value is determined, it is exchanged with the value stored at `index`. This exchange is accomplished by three assignment statements using an extra variable called `temp`. This type of exchange is called *swapping* and makes use of a private `swap` method. This method is also used by several of our other sorting algorithms.

```
/**
 * Swaps to elements in an array. Used by various sorting algorithms.
 *
 * @param data   the array in which the elements are swapped
 * @param index1 the index of the first element to be swapped
 * @param index2 the index of the second element to be swapped
 */
private static <T extends Comparable<T>>
   void swap(T[] data, int index1, int index2)
{
   T temp = data[index1];
   data[index1] = data[index2];
   data[index2] = temp;
}
```

Note that because this algorithm finds the smallest value during each iteration, the result is an array sorted in ascending order (that is, from smallest to largest). The algorithm can easily be changed to put values in descending order by finding the largest value each time.

Insertion Sort

The *insertion sort* algorithm sorts a list of values by repetitively inserting a particular value into a subset of the list that has already been sorted. One at a time, each unsorted element is inserted at the appropriate position in that sorted subset until the entire list is in order.

KEY CONCEPT

The insertion sort algorithm sorts a list of values by repetitively inserting a particular value into a subset of the list that has already been sorted.

The general strategy of the insertion sort algorithm is as follows: Sort the first two values in the list relative to each other by exchanging them if necessary. Insert the list's third value into the appropriate position relative to the first two (sorted) values. Then insert the

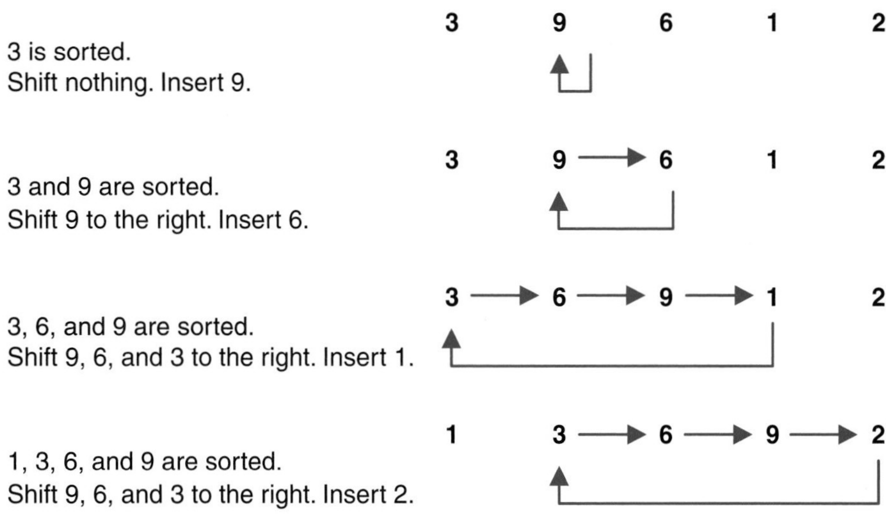

FIGURE 18.4 Example of insertion sort processing

fourth value into its proper position relative to the first three values in the list. Each time an insertion is made, the number of values in the sorted subset increases by one. Continue this process until all values in the list are completely sorted. The insertion process requires that the other values in the array shift to make room for the inserted element. Figure 18.4 illustrates the insertion sort process.

The following method implements an insertion sort:

```
/**
 * Sorts the specified array of objects using an insertion
 * sort algorithm.
 *
 * @param data the array to be sorted
 */
public static <T extends Comparable<T>>
    void insertionSort(T[] data)
{
   for (int index = 1; index < data.length; index++)
   {
      T key = data[index];
      int position = index;

   // shift larger values to the right
```

```
        while (position > 0 && data[position-1].compareTo(key) > 0)
        {
           data[position] = data[position-1];
           position--;
        }

        data[position] = key;
     }
  }
```

Like the selection sort implementation, the `insertionSort` method uses two loops to sort an array of objects. In the insertion sort, however, the outer loop controls the index in the array of the next value to be inserted. The inner loop compares the current insert value with values stored at lower indexes (which make up a sorted subset of the entire list). If the current insert value is less than the value at `position`, then that value is shifted to the right. Shifting continues until the proper position is opened to accept the insert value. Each iteration of the outer loop adds one more value to the sorted subset of the list, until the entire list is sorted.

Bubble Sort

A *bubble sort* is another sequential sort algorithm that uses two nested loops. It sorts values by repeatedly comparing neighboring elements in the list and swapping their position if they are not in order relative to each other.

KEY CONCEPT

The bubble sort algorithm sorts a list by repeatedly comparing neighboring elements and swapping them if necessary.

The general strategy of the bubble sort algorithm is as follows: Scan through the list comparing adjacent elements, and exchange them if they are not in relative order. This has the effect of "bubbling" the largest value to the last position in the list, which is its appropriate position in the final, sorted list. Then scan through the list again, bubbling up the second-to-last value. This process continues until all elements have been bubbled into their correct positions.

Each pass through the bubble sort algorithm moves the largest value to its final position. A pass may also reposition other elements as well. For example, if we started with the list

9 6 8 12 3 1 7

we would first compare 9 and 6 and, finding them not in the correct order, swap them, which yields

6 9 8 12 3 1 7

Then we would compare 9 to 8 and, again, finding them not in the correct order, swap them, which yields

6 8 9 12 3 1 7

Then we would compare 9 to 12. Since they are in the correct order, we don't swap them. Instead, we move to the next pair of values to compare. That is, we then compare 12 to 3. Because they are not in order, we swap them, which yields

6 8 9 3 12 1 7

We then compare 12 to 1 and swap them, which yields

6 8 9 3 1 12 7

We then compare 12 to 7 and swap them, which yields

6 8 9 3 1 7 12

This completes one pass through the data to be sorted. After this first pass, the largest value in the list (12) is in its correct position, but we cannot be sure about any of the other numbers. Each subsequent pass through the data guarantees that one more element is put into the correct position. Thus we make n–1 passes through the data, because if n–1 elements are in the correct, sorted positions, then the nth item must also be in the correct location.

An implementation of the bubble sort algorithm is shown in the following method:

```
/**
 * Sorts the specified array of objects using a bubble sort
 * algorithm.
 *
 * @param data the array to be sorted
 */
public static <T extends Comparable<T>>
      void bubbleSort(T[] data)
{
   int position, scan;
   T temp;
```

```
    for (position =  data.length - 1; position >= 0; position--)
    {
       for (scan = 0; scan <= position - 1; scan++)
       {
          if (data[scan].compareTo(data[scan+1]) > 0)
               swap(data, scan, scan + 1);
       }
    }
}
```

The outer `for` loop in the `bubbleSort` method represents the n–1 passes through the data. The inner `for` loop scans through the data, performs the pairwise comparisons of the neighboring data, and swaps them if necessary.

Note that the outer loop also has the effect of decreasing the position that represents the maximum index to examine in the inner loop. That is, after the first pass, which puts the last value in its correct position, there is no need to consider that value in future passes through the data. After the second pass, we can forget about the last two, and so on. Thus the inner loop examines one less value on each pass.

Quick Sort

The sort algorithms we have discussed thus far in this chapter (selection sort, insertion sort, and bubble sort) are relatively simple, but they are inefficient sequential sorts that use a pair of nested loops and require roughly n^2 comparisons to sort a list of n elements. Now we can turn our attention to more efficient sorts that lend themselves to a recursive implementation.

KEY CONCEPT
The quick sort algorithm sorts a list by partitioning the list and then recursively sorting the two partitions.

The *quick sort* algorithm sorts a list by partitioning the list using an arbitrarily chosen *partition element* and then recursively sorting the sublists on either side of the partition element. The general strategy of the quick sort algorithm is as follows: First, choose one element of the list to act as a partition element. Next, partition the list so that all elements less than the partition element are to the left of that element and all elements greater than the partition element are to the right. Finally, apply this quick sort strategy (recursively) to both partitions.

If the order of the data is truly random, the choice of the partition element is arbitrary. We will use the element in the middle of the section we want to partition. For efficiency reasons, it is nice if the partition element happens to divide the list roughly in half, but the algorithm works no matter what element is chosen as the partition.

Let's look at an example of creating a partition. If we started with the list

305 65 7 90 120 110 8

we would choose 90 as our partition element. We would then rearrange the list, swapping the elements that are less than 90 to the left side and those that are greater than 90 to the right side, which would yield

8 65 7 90 120 110 305

We would then apply the quick sort algorithm separately to both partitions. This process continues until a *partition* contains only one element, which is inherently sorted. Thus, after the algorithm is applied recursively to either side, the entire list is sorted. Once the initial partition element is determined and placed, it is never considered or moved again.

The following method implements the quick sort algorithm. It accepts an array of objects to sort and the minimum and maximum index values used for a particular call to the method. Notice that the public method takes the array to be sorted and then calls the private method providing the array, the min, and the max.

```
/**
 * Sorts the specified array of objects using the quick sort algorithm.
 *
 * @param data the array to be sorted
 */
public static <T extends Comparable<T>>
   void quickSort(T[] data)
{
   quickSort(data, 0, data.length - 1);
}

/**
 * Recursively sorts a range of objects in the specified array using the
 * quick sort algorithm.
 *
 * @param data the array to be sorted
 * @param min  the minimum index in the range to be sorted
 * @param max  the maximum index in the range to be sorted
 */
```

```
private static <T extends Comparable<T>>
   void quickSort(T[] data, int min, int max)
{
   if (min < max)
   {
      // create partitions

      int indexofpartition = partition(data, min, max);

      // sort the left partition (lower values)

      quickSort(data, min, indexofpartition - 1);

      // sort the right partition (higher values)

      quickSort(data, indexofpartition + 1, max);
   }
}
```

The `quickSort` method relies heavily on the `partition` method, which it calls initially to divide the sort area into two partitions. The `partition` method returns the index of the partition value. Then the `quickSort` method is called twice (recursively) to sort the two partitions. The base case of the recursion, represented by the `if` statement in the `quickSort` method, is a list of one element or less, which is already inherently sorted. An example of the `partition` method follows.

```
/**
 * Used by the quick sort algorithm to find the partition.
 *
 * @param data the array to be sorted
 * @param min  the minimum index in the range to be sorted
 * @param max  the maximum index in the range to be sorted
 */
private static <T extends Comparable<T>>
   int partition(T[] data, int min, int max)
{
   T partitionelement;
   int left, right;
   int middle = (min + max) / 2;
```

```
        // use the middle data value as the partition element

        partitionelement = data[middle];

        // move it out of the way for now

        swap(data, middle, min);
        left = min;
        right = max;
        while (left < right)
        {
            // search for an element that is > the partition element

            while (left < right && data[left].compareTo(partitionelement) <= 0)
                left++;

            // search for an element that is < the partition element

            while (data[right].compareTo(partitionelement) > 0)
                right--;

            // swap the elements

            if (left < right)
                swap(data, left, right);
        }

        // move the partition element into place

        swap(data, min, right);
        return right;
    }
```

The two inner `while` loops of the `partition` method are used to find elements to swap that are in the wrong partitions. The first loop scans from left to right looking for an element that is greater than the partition element. The second loop scans from right to left looking for an element that is less than the partition element. When these two elements are found, they are swapped. This process continues until the right and left indexes meet in the "middle" of the list. The location where they meet also indicates where the partition element (which isn't moved from its initial location until the end) will ultimately reside.

What happens if we get a poor partition element? If the partition element is near the smallest or the largest element in the list, then we effectively waste a pass through the data. One way to ensure a better partition element is to choose the middle of three elements. For example, the algorithm could check the first, middle, and last elements in the list and choose the middle value as the partition element. This middle-of-three approach is left as a programming project.

Merge Sort

The *merge sort* algorithm, another recursive sort algorithm, sorts a list by recursively dividing the list in half until each sublist has one element and then recombining these sublists in order.

KEY CONCEPT

The merge sort algorithm sorts a list by recursively dividing the list in half until each sublist has one element and then merging these sublists into the sorted order.

The general strategy of the merge sort algorithm is as follows: Begin by dividing the list into two roughly equal parts and then recursively calling itself with each of those lists. Continue the recursive decomposition of the list until the base case of the recursion is reached, where the list is divided into lists of length one, which are by definition sorted. Then, as control passes back up the recursive calling structure, the algorithm merges the two sorted sublists resulting from the two recursive calls into one sorted list.

For example, if we started with the initial list from our example in the previous section, the recursive decomposition portion of the algorithm would yield the results shown in Figure 18.5.

The merge portion of the algorithm would then recombine the list as shown in Figure 18.6.

An implementation of the merge sort algorithm is shown below. Note that, just as for the quick sort algorithm, we make use of a public method that accepts the array to be sorted and then a private method accepts the array as well as the min and max indexes of the section of the array to be sorted. This algorithm also makes use of a private `merge` method to recombine the sorted sections of the array.

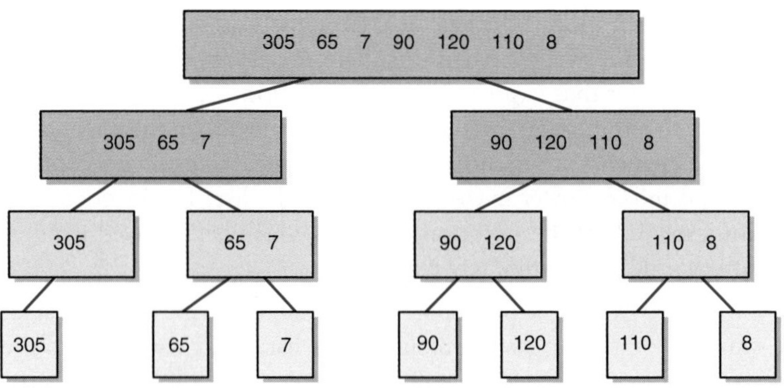

FIGURE 18.5 The decomposition of merge sort

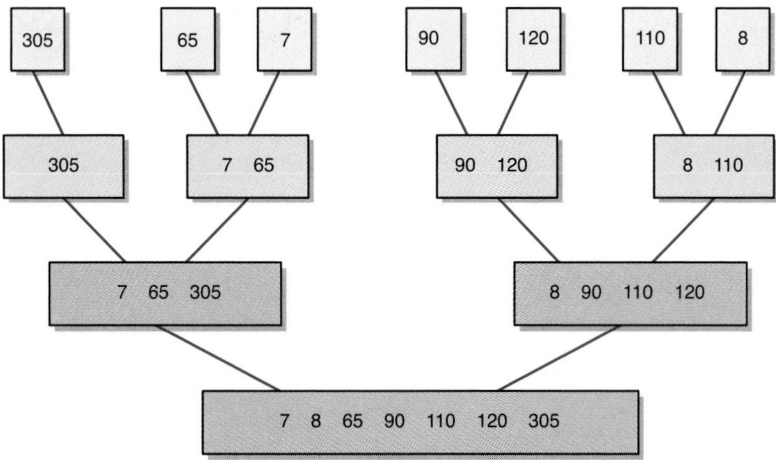

FIGURE 18.6 The merge portion of the merge sort algorithm

```
/**
 * Sorts the specified array of objects using the merge sort
 * algorithm.
 *
 * @param data the array to be sorted
 */
public static <T extends Comparable<T>>
   void mergeSort(T[] data)
{
   mergeSort(data, 0, data.length - 1);
}

/**
 * Recursively sorts a range of objects in the specified array using the
 * merge sort algorithm.
 *
 * @param data the array to be sorted
 * @param min  the index of the first element
 * @param max  the index of the last element
 */
private static <T extends Comparable<T>>
   void mergeSort(T[] data, int min, int max)
{
   if (min < max)
```

```
   {
      int mid = (min + max) / 2;
      mergeSort(data, min, mid);
      mergeSort(data, mid+1, max);
      merge(data, min, mid, max);
   }
}
```

```
/**
 * Merges two sorted subarrays of the specified array.
 *
 * @param data the array to be sorted
 * @param first the beginning index of the first subarray
 * @param mid the ending index of the first subarray
 * @param last the ending index of the second subarray
 */
@SuppressWarnings("unchecked")
private static <T extends Comparable<T>>
   void merge(T[] data, int first, int mid, int last)
{
   T[] temp = (T[])(new Comparable[data.length]);

   int first1 = first, last1 = mid;  // endpoints of first subarray
   int first2 = mid+1, last2 = last;  // endpoints of second subarray
   int index = first1;  // next index open in temp array

   //  Copy smaller item from each subarray into temp until one
   //  of the subarrays is exhausted

   while (first1 <= last1 && first2 <= last2)
   {
      if (data[first1].compareTo(data[first2]) < 0)
      {
         temp[index] = data[first1];
         first1++;
      }
      else
      {
         temp[index] = data[first2];
         first2++;
      }
         index++;
   }
    //  Copy remaining elements from first subarray, if any

    while (first1 <= last1)
```

```
    {
       temp[index] = data[first1];
       first1++;
       index++;
    }

    //  Copy remaining elements from second subarray, if any

    while (first2 <= last2)
    {
       temp[index] = data[first2];
       first2++;
       index++;
    }

    //  Copy merged data into original array

    for (index = first; index <= last; index++)
       data[index] = temp[index];
 }
```

18.3 Radix Sort

To this point, all of the sorting techniques we have discussed have involved comparing elements within the list to each other. As we have seen, the best of these comparison-based sorts is O(nlogn). What if there were a way to sort elements without comparing them directly to each other? It might then be possible to build a more efficient sorting algorithm. We can find such a technique by revisiting our discussion of queues from Chapter 5.

KEY CONCEPT
A radix sort is inherently based on queue processing.

A sort is based on some particular value, called the *sort key*. For example, a set of people might be sorted by their last name. A *radix sort*, rather than comparing items by sort key, is based on the structure of the sort key. Separate queues are created for each possible value of each digit or character of the sort key. The number of queues, or the number of possible values, is called the *radix*. For example, if we were sorting strings made up of lowercase alphabetic characters, the radix would be 26. We would use 26 separate queues, one for each possible character. If we were sorting decimal numbers, then the radix would be 10, one for each digit 0 through 9.

Let's look at an example that uses a radix sort to put ten three-digit numbers in order. To keep things manageable, we will restrict the digits of these numbers to 0 through 5, which means we will need only six queues.

Each three-digit number to be sorted has a 1s position (right digit), a 10s position (middle digit), and a 100s position (left digit). The radix sort will make three passes through the values, one for each digit position. On the first pass, each number is put on the queue corresponding to its 1s digit. On the second pass, each number is put on the queue corresponding to its 10s digit. And finally, on the third pass, each number is put on the queue corresponding to its 100s digit.

Originally, the numbers are loaded into the queues from the original list. On the second pass, the numbers are taken from the queues in a particular order. They are retrieved from the digit 0 queue first, and then from the digit 1 queue, and so on. For each queue, the numbers are processed in the order in which they come off the queue. This processing order is crucial to the operation of a radix sort. Likewise, on the third pass, the numbers are again taken from the queues in the same way. When the numbers are pulled off of the queues after the third pass, they will be completely sorted.

Figure 18.7 shows the processing of a radix sort for ten three-digit numbers. The number 442 is taken from the original list and put onto the queue corresponding to digit 2. Then 503 is put onto the queue corresponding to digit 3. Then 312 is put onto the queue corresponding to digit 2 (following 442). This continues for all values, resulting in the set of queues for the 1s position.

Assume, as we begin the second pass, that we have a fresh set of six empty digit queues. In actuality, the queues can be used over again if processed carefully. To begin the second pass, the numbers are taken from the 0 digit queue first. The number 250 is put onto the queue for digit 5, and then 420 is put onto the queue for digit 2. Then we can move to the next queue, taking 341 and putting it onto the queue for digit 4. This continues until all numbers have been taken off of the 1s position queues, resulting in the set of queues for the 10s position.

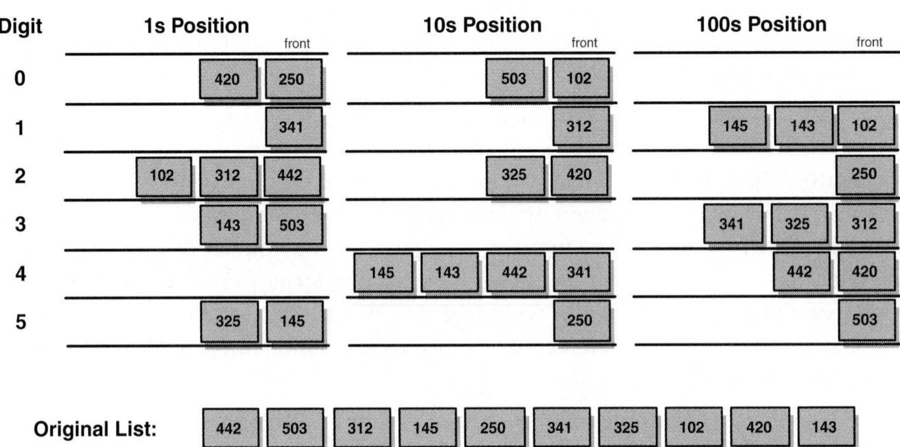

FIGURE 18.7 A radix sort of ten three-digit numbers

For the third pass, the process is repeated. First, 102 is put onto the queue for digit 1, then 503 is put onto the queue for digit 5, and then 312 is put onto the queue for digit 3. This continues until we have the final set of digit queues for the 100s position. These numbers are now in sorted order if taken off of each queue in turn.

Let's now look at a program that implements the radix sort. For this example, we will sort four-digit numbers, and we won't restrict the digits used in those numbers. Listing 18.3 shows the `RadixSort` class, which contains a single `main` method. Using an array of ten queue objects (one for each digit 0 through 9), this

LISTING 18.3

```
import java.util.*;

/**
 * RadixSort driver demonstrates the use of queues in the execution of a radix sort.
 *
 * @author Java Foundations
 * @version 4.0
 */
public class RadixSort
{
   /**
    * Performs a radix sort on a set of numeric values.
    */
   public static void main(String[] args)
   {
      int[] list = {7843, 4568, 8765, 6543, 7865, 4532, 9987, 3241,
                    6589, 6622, 1211};

      String temp;
      Integer numObj;
      int digit, num;

      Queue<Integer>[] digitQueues = (LinkedList<Integer>[])(new LinkedList[10]);
      for (int digitVal = 0; digitVal <= 9; digitVal++)
         digitQueues[digitVal] = (Queue<Integer>)(new LinkedList<Integer>());

      // sort the list

      for (int position=0; position <= 3; position++)
      {
         for (int scan=0; scan < list.length; scan++)
```

LISTING 18.3 *continued*

```
         {
            temp = String.valueOf(list[scan]);
            digit = Character.digit(temp.charAt(3-position), 10);
            digitQueues[digit].add(new Integer(list[scan]));
         }

            // gather numbers back into list

            num = 0;
            for (int digitVal = 0; digitVal <= 9; digitVal++)
            {
               while (!(digitQueues[digitVal].isEmpty()))
               {
                  numObj = digitQueues[digitVal].remove();
                  list[num] = numObj.intValue();
                  num++;
               }
            }
      }

      // output the sorted list

      for (int scan=0; scan < list.length; scan++)
         System.out.println(list[scan]);
   }
}
```

method carries out the processing steps of a radix sort. Figure 18.8 shows the UML description of the `RadixSort` class.

In the `RadixSort` program, the numbers are originally stored in an array called `list`. After each pass, the numbers are pulled off the queues and stored back into the `list` array in the proper order. This allows the program to reuse the original array of ten queues for each pass of the sort.

The concept of a radix sort can be applied to any type of data as long as the sort key can be dissected into well-defined positions. Note that unlike the sorts we discussed earlier in this chapter, it's not reasonable to create a generic radix sort for any object, because dissecting the key values is an integral part of the process.

So what is the time complexity of a radix sort? In this case, there is not any comparison or swapping of elements. Elements are simply removed from a queue

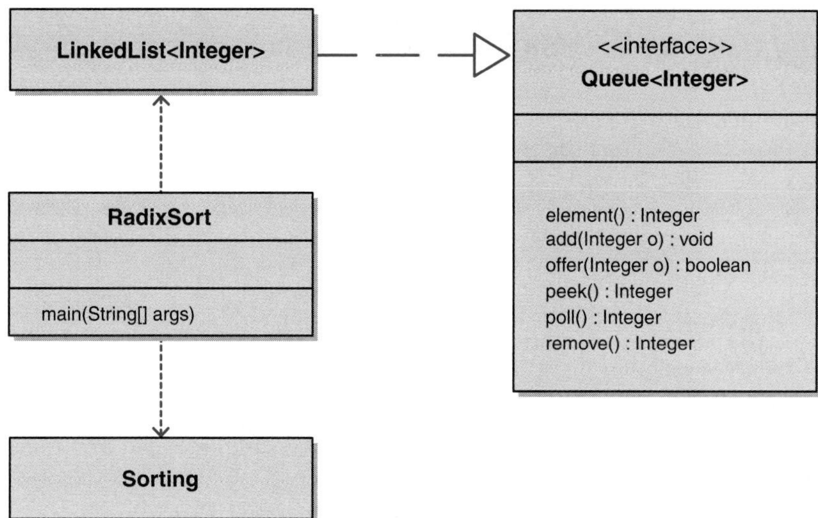

FIGURE 18.8 UML description of the `RadixSort` program

and placed in another one on each pass. For any given radix, the number of passes through the data is a constant based on the number of characters in the key; let's call it c. Then the time complexity of the algorithm is simply c*n. Keep in mind, from our discussion in Chapter 11, that we ignore constants when computing the time complexity of an algorithm. Thus the radix sort algorithm is O(n). So why not use radix sort for all of our sorting? First, each radix sort algorithm has to be designed specifically for the key of a given problem. Second, for keys where the number of digits in the key (c) and the number of elements in the list (n) are very close together, the actual time complexity of the radix sort algorithm mimics n^2 instead of n. In addition, we also need to keep in mind that there is another constant that affects space complexity; it is the radix, or the number of possible values for each position or character in the key. Imagine, for example, trying to implement a radix sort for a key that allows any character from the Unicode character set. Because this set has more than 100,000 characters, we would need that many queues!

Summary of Key Concepts

- Searching is the process of finding a designated target within a group of items or determining that the target doesn't exist.
- An efficient search minimizes the number of comparisons made.
- A method is made static by using the static modifier in the method declaration.
- A binary search capitalizes on the fact that the search pool is sorted.
- A binary search eliminates half of the viable candidates with each comparison.
- A binary search has logarithmic complexity, making it very efficient for a large search pool.
- Sorting is the process of arranging a list of items into a defined order based on some criterion.
- The selection sort algorithm sorts a list of values by repetitively putting a particular value into its final, sorted position.
- The insertion sort algorithm sorts a list of values by repetitively inserting a particular value into a subset of the list that has already been sorted.
- The bubble sort algorithm sorts a list by repeatedly comparing neighboring elements and swapping them if necessary.
- The quick sort algorithm sorts a list by partitioning the list and then recursively sorting the two partitions.
- The merge sort algorithm sorts a list by recursively dividing the list in half until each sublist has one element and then merging these sublists into the sorted order.
- A radix sort is inherently based on queue processing.

Summary of Terms

binary search A search that occurs on a sorted list and in which each comparison eliminates approximately half of the remaining viable candidates.

bubble sort A sorting algorithm that sorts elements by repeatedly comparing adjacent values and swapping them.

class method See *static method*.

generic method A method that includes the definition of a type parameter in the header of the method.

insertion sort A sorting algorithm that sorts elements by repetitively inserting a particular element into a previously sorted sublist.

linear search A search that begins at one end of a list of items and continues linearly until the element is found or the end of the list is reached.

logarithmic algorithm An algorithm that has a time complexity of $O(\log_2 n)$, such as a binary search.

logarithmic sort A sorting algorithm that requires approximately $n\log_2 n$ comparisons to sort n elements.

merge sort A sorting algorithm that sorts elements by recursively dividing the list in half until each sublist has one element and then merging the sublists.

partition A set of unsorted elements used by the quick sort algorithm that are all either less than or greater than a chosen partition element.

partition element An element used by the quick sort algorithm to separate unsorted elements into two distinct partitions.

quick sort A sorting algorithm that sorts elements by partitioning the unsorted elements into two partitions and then recursively sorting each partition.

radix sort A sorting algorithm that sorts elements using a sort key instead of directly comparing elements.

searching The process of finding a designated target element within a group of elements, or determining that the target is not in the group.

search pool A group of items to be searched.

selection sort A sorting algorithm that sorts elements by repetitively finding a particular element and putting it in its final position.

sequential sort A sorting algorithm that typically uses nested loops and requires approximately n^2 comparisons to sort n elements.

sorting The process of arranging a group of items into a particular order based on some criterion.

static method A method that is invoked through the class name and that cannot refer to instance data. Also called a class method.

target element The element that is being sought during a search operation.

viable candidates The elements in a search pool among which the target element may still be found.

Self-Review Questions

SR 18.1 When would a linear search be preferable to a logarithmic search?

SR 18.2 Which searching method requires that the list be sorted?

SR 18.3 When would a sequential sort be preferable to a recursive sort?

SR 18.4 The insertion sort algorithm sorts using what technique?

SR 18.5 The bubble sort algorithm sorts using what technique?

SR 18.6 The selection sort algorithm sorts using what technique?

SR 18.7 The quick sort algorithm sorts using what technique?

SR 18.8 The merge sort algorithm sorts using what technique?

SR 18.9 How many queues would it take to use a radix sort to sort names stored as all lowercase?

Exercises

EX 18.1 Compare and contrast the `linearSearch` and `binarySearch` algorithms by searching for the numbers 45 and 54 in the list 3, 8, 12, 34, 54, 84, 91, 110.

EX 18.2 Using the list from Exercise 18.1, construct a table showing the number of comparisons required to sort that list for each of the sort algorithms (selection sort, insertion sort, bubble sort, quick sort, and merge sort).

EX 18.3 Consider the same list from Exercise 18.1. What happens to the number of comparisons for each of the sort algorithms if the list is already sorted?

EX 18.4 Consider the following list:

90 8 7 56 123 235 9 1 653

Show a trace of execution for:

a. selection sort
b. insertion sort
c. bubble sort
d. quick sort
e. merge sort

EX 18.5 Given the resulting sorted list from Exercise 18.4, show a trace of execution for a binary search, searching for the number 235.

EX 18.6 Draw the UML description of the `SortPhoneList` example.

EX 18.7 Hand trace a radix sort for the following list of five-digit student ID numbers:

13224

32131

54355

12123

22331

21212

33333

54312

EX 18.8 What is the time complexity of a radix sort?

Programming Projects

PP 18.1 The bubble sort algorithm shown in this chapter is less efficient than it could be. If a pass is made through the list without exchanging any elements, this means that the list is sorted and there is no reason to continue. Modify this algorithm so that it will stop as soon as it recognizes that the list is sorted. *Do not* use a `break` statement!

PP 18.2 There is a variation of the bubble sort algorithm called a *gap sort* that, rather than comparing neighboring elements each time through the list, compares elements that are some number i positions apart, where i is an integer less than n. For example, the first element would be compared to the (i + 1) element, the second element would be compared to the (i + 2) element, the nth element would be compared to the (n − i) element, and so on. A single iteration is completed when all of the elements that can be compared, have been compared. On the next iteration, i is reduced by some number greater than 1 and the process continues until i is less than 1. Implement a gap sort.

PP 18.3 Modify the sorts listed in the chapter (selection sort, insertion sort, bubble sort, quick sort, and merge sort) by adding code to each to tally the total number of comparisons and total execution time of each algorithm. Execute the sort algorithms against the same list, recording information for the total number of comparisons and total execution time for each algorithm. Try several different lists, including at least one that is already in sorted order.

PP 18.4 Modify the quick sort method to choose the partition element using the middle-of-three technique described in the chapter. Run this new version against the old version for several sets of data, and compare the total execution time.

Answers to Self-Review Questions

SR 18.1 A linear search would be preferable for relatively small, unsorted lists and in languages where recursion is not supported.

SR 18.2 Binary search.

SR 18.3 A sequential sort would be preferable for relatively small data sets and in languages where recursion is not supported.

SR 18.4 The insertion sort algorithm sorts a list of values by repetitively inserting a particular value into a subset of the list that has already been sorted.

SR 18.5 The bubble sort algorithm sorts a list by repeatedly comparing neighboring elements in the list and swapping their positions if they are not already in order.

SR 18.6 The selection sort algorithm, which is an $O(n^2)$ sort algorithm, sorts a list of values by repetitively putting a particular value into its final, sorted position.

SR 18.7 The quick sort algorithm sorts a list by partitioning the list using an arbitrarily chosen partition element and then recursively sorting the sublists on either side of the partition element.

SR 18.8 The merge sort algorithm sorts a list by recursively dividing the list in half until each sublist has one element and then recombining these sublists in order.

SR 18.9 It would require 27 queues, one for each of the 26 letters in the alphabet and one to store the whole list before, during, and after sorting.

19 Trees

CHAPTER OBJECTIVES

- Define trees as data structures.
- Define the terms associated with trees.
- Discuss the possible implementations of trees.
- Analyze tree implementations of collections.
- Discuss methods for traversing trees.
- Examine a binary tree example.

This chapter begins our exploration of nonlinear collections and data structures. We discuss the use and implementation of trees, define the terms associated with trees, analyze possible tree implementations, and look at examples of implementing and using trees.

19.1 Trees

> **KEY CONCEPT**
> A tree is a nonlinear structure whose elements are organized into a hierarchy.

The collections we have examined up to this point in the book (stacks, queues, and lists) are all linear data structures, which means that their elements are arranged in order one after another. A *tree* is a nonlinear structure in which elements are organized into a hierarchy. This section describes trees in general and establishes some important terminology.

Conceptually, a tree is composed of a set of *nodes* in which elements are stored and *edges* that connect one node to another. Each node is at a particular *level* in the tree hierarchy. The *root* of the tree is the only node at the top level of the tree. There is only one root node in a tree. Figure 19.1 shows a tree that helps to illustrate these terms.

The nodes at lower levels of the tree are the *children* of nodes at the previous level. In Figure 19.1, the nodes labeled B, C, D, and E are the children of A. Nodes F and G are the children of B. A node can have only one parent, but a node may have multiple children. Nodes that have the same parent are called *siblings*. Thus, nodes H, I, and J are siblings because they are all children of node D.

> **KEY CONCEPT**
> Trees are described by a large set of related terms.

The root node is the only node in a tree that does not have a parent. A node that does not have any children is called a *leaf*. A node that is not the root and has at least one child is called an *internal node*. Note that the tree analogy is upside-down. Our trees "grow" from the root at the top of the tree to the leaves toward the bottom of the tree.

The root is the entry point into a tree structure. We can follow a *path* through the tree from parent to child. For example, the path from node A to node N in Figure 19.1 is A, D, I, N. A node is the *ancestor* of another node if it is above it

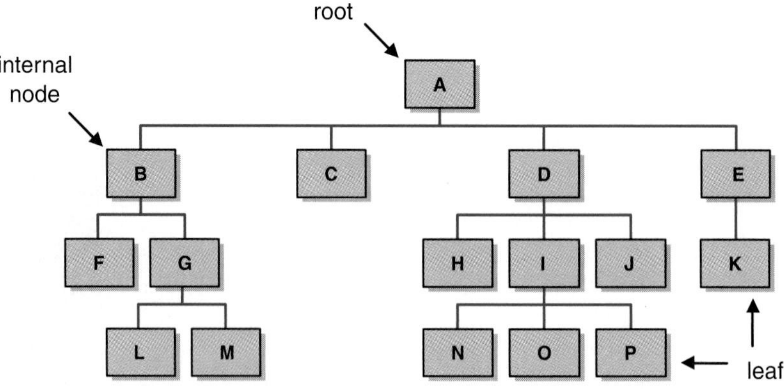

FIGURE 19.1 Tree terminology

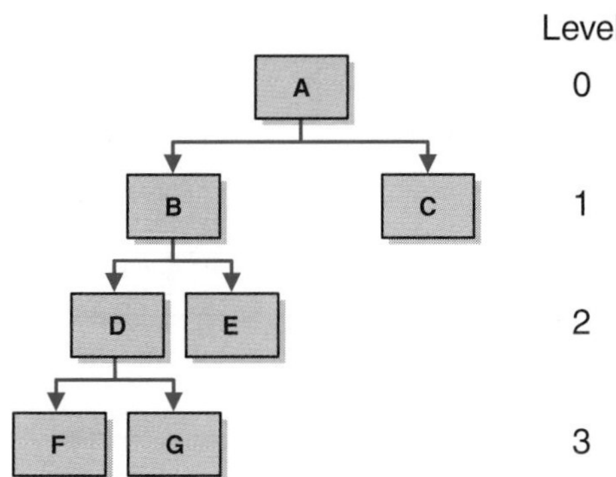

FIGURE 19.2 Path length and level

on the path from the root. Thus the root is the ultimate ancestor of all nodes in a tree. Nodes that can be reached by following a path from a particular node are the *descendants* of that node.

The level of a node is also the length of the path from the root to the node. This *path length* is determined by counting the number of edges that must be followed to get from the root to the node. The root is considered to be level 0, the children of the root are at level 1, the grandchildren of the root are at level 2, and so on. Path length and level are depicted in Figure 19.2.

The *height* of a tree is the length of the longest path from the root to a leaf. Thus the height of the tree in Figure 19.2 is 3, because the path length from the root to leaves F and G is 3. The path length from the root to leaf C is 1.

Tree Classifications

Trees can be classified in many ways. The most important criterion is the maximum number of children any node in the tree may have. This value is sometimes referred to as the *order* of the tree. A tree that has no limit to the number of children a node may have is called a *general tree*. A tree that limits each node to no more than n children is referred to as an *n-ary tree*.

One n-ary tree is of particular importance. A tree in which nodes may have at most two children is called a *binary tree*. This type of tree is helpful in many situations. Much of our exploration of trees will focus on binary trees.

Another way to classify a tree is in terms of whether it is balanced or not. There are many definitions of balance depending on the algorithms being used. We will explore some of these algorithms in the next chapter. Roughly speaking, a tree is considered to be *balanced* if all of the leaves of the tree are on the same level or at least within one level of each other. Thus, the tree shown on the left in Figure 19.3 is balanced, and the one on the right is not. A balanced n-ary tree

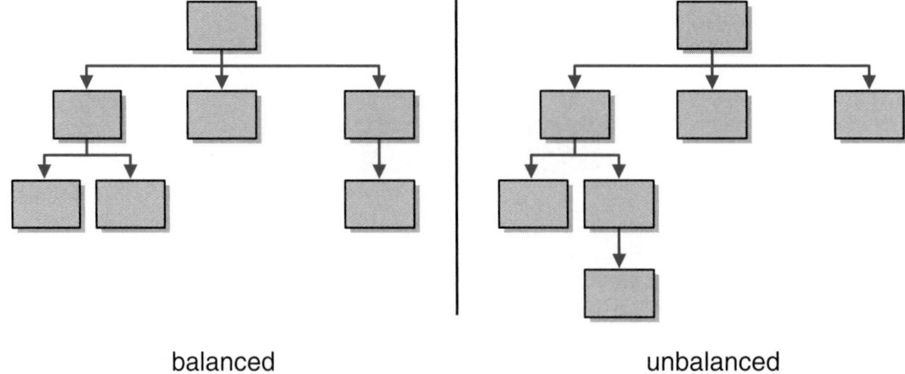

FIGURE 19.3 Balanced and unbalanced trees

with m elements has a height of $\log_n m$. Thus a balanced binary tree with n nodes has a height of $\log_2 n$.

The concept of a complete tree is related to the balance of a tree. A tree is considered *complete* if it is balanced and all of the leaves at the bottom level are on the left side of the tree. Although it seems arbitrary, this definition has implications for how the tree is stored in certain implementations. Another way to express this concept is to say that a complete binary tree has 2^k nodes at every level k except the last, where the nodes must be leftmost.

A related concept is the notion of a full tree. An n-ary tree is considered *full* if all the leaves of the tree are at the same level and every node is either is a leaf or has exactly n children. The balanced tree in Figure 19.3 is not considered complete. Among the 3-ary (or tertiary) trees shown in Figure 19.4, the trees in parts (a) and (c) are complete, but only the tree in part (c) is full.

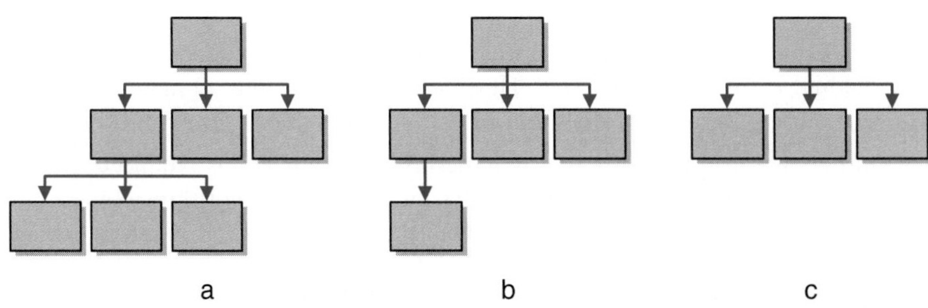

FIGURE 19.4 Some complete trees

19.2 Strategies for Implementing Trees

Let's examine some general strategies for implementing trees. The most obvious implementation of a tree is a linked structure. Each node could be defined as a `TreeNode` class, similar to what we did with the `LinearNode` class for linked lists. Each node would contain a pointer to the element to be stored in that node as well as pointers for each of the possible children of the node. Depending on the implementation, it may also be useful for each node to store a pointer to its parent. This use of pointers is similar to the concept of a doubly linked list, where each node points not only to the next node in the list, but to the previous node as well.

Another possibility would be to implement a tree recursively using links. This strategy would involve defining each node as a tree with attributes for each of its children. Thus each node, and all of its descendants, represents a tree unto itself. The implementation of this strategy is left as a programming project.

Because a tree is a nonlinear structure, it may not seem reasonable to try to implement it using an underlying linear structure such as an array. However, sometimes that approach is useful. The strategies for array implementations of a tree may be less obvious. There are two principal approaches: a computational strategy and a simulated link strategy.

Computational Strategy for Array Implementation of Trees

For certain types of trees, specifically binary trees, a computational strategy can be used for storing a tree using an array. One possible strategy is as follows: For any element stored in position n of the array, that element's left child will be stored in position (2 * n + 1) and that element's right child will be stored in position (2 * (n + 1)). This strategy is very effective and can be managed in terms of capacity in much the same way as managing capacity for the array implementations of lists, queues, and stacks. However, despite the conceptual elegance of this solution, it is not without drawbacks. For example, if the tree that we are storing is not complete or is only relatively complete, we may be wasting large amounts of memory allocated in the array for positions of the tree that do not contain data. The computational strategy is illustrated in Figure 19.5.

KEY CONCEPT
One possible computational strategy places the left child of element n at position (2 * n + 1) and the right child at position (2 * (n + 1)).

Simulated Link Strategy for Array Implementation of Trees

A second possible array implementation of trees is modeled after the way operating systems manage memory. Instead of assigning elements of the tree to array

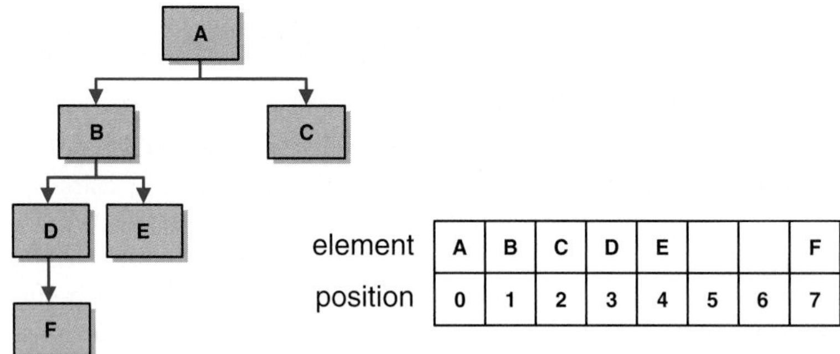

element	A	B	C	D	E			F
position	0	1	2	3	4	5	6	7

FIGURE 19.5 Computational strategy for array implementation of trees

positions by location in the tree, array positions are allocated contiguously on a first-come, first-served basis. Each element of the array will be a node class similar to the `TreeNode` class that we discussed earlier. However, instead of storing object reference variables as pointers to its children (and perhaps its parent), each node would store the array index of each child (and perhaps its parent). This approach allows elements to be stored contiguously in the array so that space is not wasted. However, this approach increases the overhead for deleting elements in the tree, because it requires either that remaining elements be shifted to maintain contiguity or that a *freelist* be maintained. This strategy is illustrated in Figure 19.6. The order of the elements in the array is determined simply by their entry order into the tree. In this case, the entry order is assumed to have been A, C, B, E, D, F.

> **KEY CONCEPT**
> The simulated link strategy allows array positions to be allocated contiguously, regardless of the completeness of the tree.

This same strategy may also be used when tree structures need to be stored directly on disk using a direct I/O approach. In this case, rather than using an array index as a pointer, each node will store the relative position in the file of its children so that an offset can be calculated given the base address of the file.

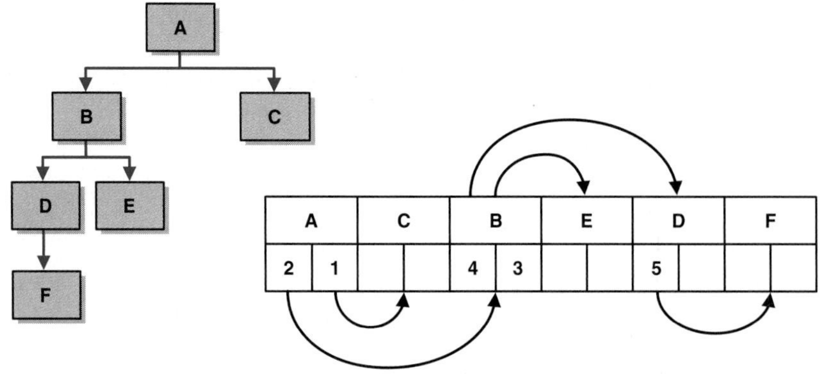

FIGURE 19.6 Simulated link strategy for array implementation of trees

DESIGN FOCUS 

When does it begin to make sense to define an ADT for a collection? At this point, we have defined many of the terms for a tree and we have a general understanding of how a tree might be used, but are we ready to define an ADT? Not really. Trees, in the general sense, are more of an abstract data structure than a collection, so trying to define an ADT for a general tree is not likely to be very useful. Instead, we will wait until we have specified more details about the type of the tree and its use before we attempt to define an interface.

Analysis of Trees

As we noted earlier, trees are a useful and efficient way to implement other collections. Let's consider an ordered list as an example. In our analysis of list implementations in Chapter 15, we described the `find` operation as having efficiency n/2 or O(n). However, if we were to implement an ordered list using a balanced *binary search tree*—a binary tree with the added property that the left child is always less than the parent, which is always less than or equal to the right child—then we could improve the efficiency of the `find` operation to O(log n). We will discuss binary search trees in much greater detail in Chapter 20.

This increased efficiency is due to the fact that the height of such a tree will always be $\log_2 n$, where n is the number of elements in the tree. This is very similar to our discussion of the binary search in Chapter 18. In fact, for any balanced n-ary tree with m elements, the tree's height will be $\log_n m$. With the added ordering property of a binary search tree, you are guaranteed to search, at worst, one path from the root to a leaf, and that path can be no longer than $\log_n m$.

KEY CONCEPT

In general, a balanced n-ary tree with m elements will have height $\log_n m$.

DESIGN FOCUS 

If trees provide more efficient implementations than linear structures, why would we ever use linear structures? There is an overhead associated with trees in terms of maintaining the structure and order of the tree that may not be present in other structures; thus there is a trade-off between this overhead and the size of the problem. With a relatively small n, the difference between the analysis of tree implementations and that of linear structures is not particularly significant relative to the overhead involved in the tree. However, as n increases, the efficiency of a tree becomes more attractive.

19.3 Tree Traversals

Because a tree is a nonlinear structure, the concept of traversing a tree is generally more interesting than the concept of traversing a linear structure. There are four basic methods for traversing a tree:

- *Preorder traversal*, which is accomplished by visiting each node, followed by its children, starting with the root
- *Inorder traversal*, which is accomplished by visiting the left child of the node, then the node, and then any remaining nodes, starting with the root
- *Postorder traversal*, which is accomplished by visiting the children, and then the node, starting with the root
- *Level-order traversal*, which is accomplished by visiting all of the nodes at each level, one level at a time, starting with the root

KEY CONCEPT
There are four basic methods for traversing a tree: preorder, inorder, postorder, and level-order traversals.

Each of these definitions applies to all trees. However, as an example, let us examine how each of these definitions would apply to a binary tree (that is, a tree in which each node has at most two children).

Preorder Traversal

Given the tree shown in Figure 19.7, a preorder traversal would produce the sequence A, B, D, E, C. The definition stated previously says that preorder traversal is accomplished by visiting each node, followed by its children, starting with the root. So, starting with the root, we visit the root, giving us A. Next we traverse to the first child of the root, which is the node containing B. We then use the same algorithm by first visiting the current node, which yields B, and then visiting its children. Next we traverse to the first child of B, which is the node containing D. We then use the same algorithm again by first visiting the current node, which yields D, and then visiting its children. Only this time, there are no children. We then traverse to any other children of B. This yields E, and because E has no children, we then traverse to any other children of A. This brings us to the node containing C, where we again use the same algorithm, first visiting the node, which yields C, and then visiting any children. Because there are no children of C and no more children of A, the traversal is complete.

KEY CONCEPT
Preorder traversal means visit the node, then the left child, and then the right child.

Stated in pseudocode for a binary tree, the algorithm for a preorder traversal is

```
Visit node
Traverse(left child)
Traverse(right child)
```

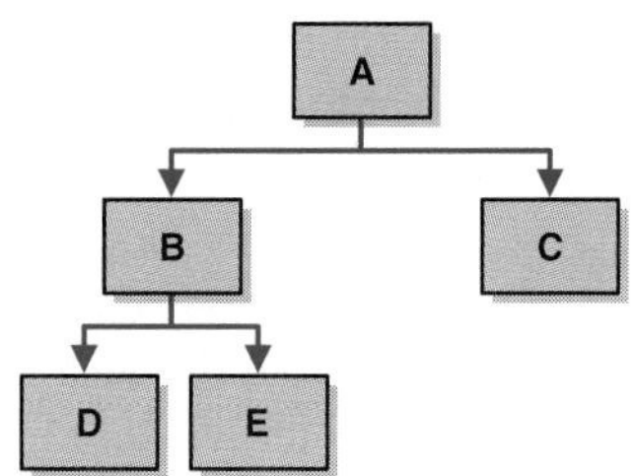

FIGURE 19.7 A complete tree

Inorder Traversal

Given the tree shown in Figure 19.7, an inorder traversal would produce the sequence D, B, E, A, C. As defined earlier, inorder traversal is accomplished by visiting the left child of the node, then the node, and then any remaining nodes, starting with the root. So, starting with the root, we traverse to the left child of the root, the node containing B. We then use the same algorithm again and traverse to the left child of B, the node containing D. Note that we have not yet visited any nodes. Using the same algorithm again, we attempt to traverse to the left child of D. Because there is no such left child, we then visit the current node, which yields D. Continuing the same algorithm, we attempt to traverse to any remaining children of D. Because there are no children, we then visit the previous node, which yields B. We then attempt to traverse to any remaining children of B. This brings us to the node containing E. Because E does not have a left child, we visit the node, which yields E. Because E has no right child, we then visit the previous node, which yields A. We then traverse to any remaining children of A, which takes us to the node containing C. Using the same algorithm, we then attempt to traverse to the left child of C. Because there is no such left child, we then visit the current node, which yields C. We then attempt to traverse to any remaining children of C. Because there are no such, we return to the previous node, which happens to be the root. Because there are no more children of the root, the traversal is complete.

KEY CONCEPT
Inorder traversal means visit the left child, then the node, and then the right child.

Stated in pseudocode for a binary tree, the algorithm for an inorder traversal is

```
Traverse(left child)
Visit node
Traverse(right child)
```

Postorder Traversal

Given the tree shown in Figure 19.7, a postorder traversal would produce the sequence D, E, B, C, A. As previously defined, postorder traversal is accomplished

KEY CONCEPT

Postorder traversal means visit the left child, then the right child, and then the node.

by visiting the children and then the node, starting with the root. So, starting from the root, we traverse to the left child, the node containing B. Repeating that process, we traverse to the left child again, the node containing D. Because that node does not have any children, we then visit that node, which yields D. Returning to the previous node, we visit the right child, the node containing E. Because this node does not have any children, we visit the node, which yields E, and then return to the previous node and visit it, which yields B. Returning to the previous node, in this case the root, we find that it has a right child, so we traverse to the right child, the node containing C. Because this node does not have any children, we visit it, which yields C. Returning to the previous node (the root), we find that it has no remaining children, so we visit it, which yields A, and the traversal is complete.

Stated in pseudocode for a binary tree, the algorithm for a postorder traversal is

```
Traverse(left child)
Traverse(right child)
Visit node
```

Level-Order Traversal

Given the tree shown in Figure 19.7, a level-order traversal would produce the sequence A, B, C, D, E. As defined earlier, a level-order traversal is accomplished by visiting all of the nodes at each level, one level at a time, starting with the root. Using this definition, we first visit the root, which yields A. Next we visit the left child of the root, which yields B, then the right child of the root, which yields C, and then the children of B, which yields D and E.

Stated in pseudocode for a binary tree, an algorithm for a level-order traversal is

```
Create a queue called nodes
Create an unordered list called results
Enqueue the root onto the nodes queue
While the nodes queue is not empty
{
   Dequeue the first element from the queue
   If that element is not null
     Add that element to the rear of the results list
     Enqueue the children of the element on the nodes queue
   Else
      Add null on the result list
}
Return an iterator for the result list
```

This algorithm for a level-order traversal is only one of many possible solutions. However, it does have some interesting properties. First, note that we are using collections—namely a queue and a list—to solve a problem within another collection—namely a binary tree. Second, recall that in our earlier discussions of iterators, we talked about their behavior with respect to the collection if the collection is modified while the iterator is in use. In this case, using a list to store the elements in the proper order and then returning an iterator over the list, this iterator behaves like a snapshot of the binary tree and is not affected by any concurrent modifications. This can be either a positive or a negative attribute, depending on how the iterator is used.

KEY CONCEPT
Level-order traversal means visit the nodes at each level, one level at a time, starting with the root.

VideoNote
Demonstration of the four basic tree traversals

19.4 A Binary Tree ADT

Let's take a look at a simple binary tree implementation using links. In Section 19.5 and 19.6, we will consider examples using this implementation. As we discussed earlier in this chapter, it is difficult to abstract an interface for all trees. However, once we have narrowed our focus to binary trees, the task becomes more reasonable. One possible set of operations for a binary tree ADT is listed in Figure 19.8. Keep in mind that the definition of a collection is not universal. You will find variations in the operations defined for specific collections from one text to another. We have been very careful in this text to define the operations on each collection so that they are consistent with its purpose.

Notice that in all of the operations listed, there are no operations to add elements to the tree or remove elements from it. This is because until we specify the purpose and organization of the binary tree, there is no way to know how

Operation	Description
`getRoot`	Returns a reference to the root of the binary tree
`isEmpty`	Determines whether the tree is empty
`size`	Returns the number of elements in the tree
`contains`	Determines whether the specified target is in the tree
`find`	Returns a reference to the specified target element if it is found
`toString`	Returns a string representation of the tree
`iteratorInOrder`	Returns an iterator for an inorder traversal of the tree
`iteratorPreOrder`	Returns an iterator for a preorder traversal of the tree
`iteratorPostOrder`	Returns an iterator for a postorder traversal of the tree
`iteratorLevelOrder`	Returns an iterator for a level-order traversal of the tree

FIGURE 19.8 The operations on a binary tree

or—more specifically—where to add an element to the tree. Similarly, any operation to remove one or more elements from the tree may violate the purpose or structure of the tree as well. As with adding an element, we do not yet have enough information to know how to remove an element. When we were dealing with stacks in Chapters 12 and 13, we could think about the concept of removing an element from a stack, and it was easy to conceptualize the state of the stack after removal of the element. The same can be said of queues, because we could remove an element from only one end of the linear structures. Even with lists, where we could remove an element from the middle of the linear structure, it was easy to conceptualize the state of the resulting list.

With a tree, however, upon removing an element, we have many issues to handle that will affect the state of the tree. What happens to the children and other descendants of the element that is removed? Where does the child pointer of the element's parent now point? What if the element we are removing is the root? As we will see in our example using expression trees later in this chapter, there will be applications of trees where there is no concept of the removal of an element from the tree. Once we have specified more detail about the use of the tree, we may then decide that a `removeElement` method is appropriate. An excellent example of this is binary search trees, as we will see in Chapter 20.

Listing 19.1 shows the `BinaryTreeADT` interface. Figure 19.9 shows the UML description for the `BinaryTreeADT` interface.

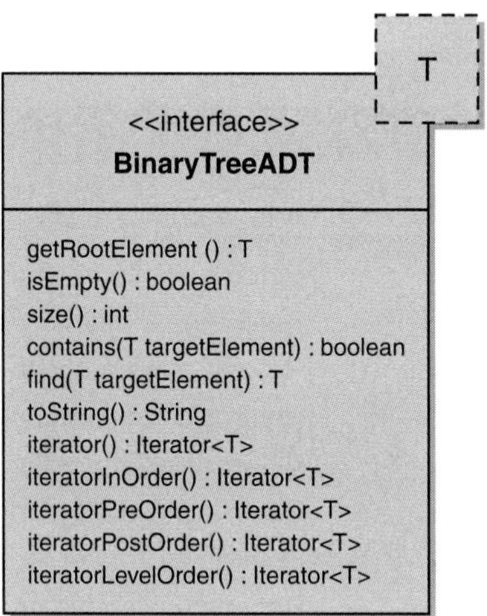

FIGURE 19.9 UML description of the `BinaryTreeADT` interface

LISTING 19.1

```
package jsjf;

import java.util.Iterator;

/**
 * BinaryTreeADT defines the interface to a binary tree data structure.
 *
 * @author Java Foundations
 * @version 4.0
 */
public interface BinaryTreeADT<T>
{
  /**
   * Returns a reference to the root element
   *
   * @return a reference to the root
   */
  public T getRootElement();

  /**
   * Returns true if this binary tree is empty and false otherwise.
   *
   * @return true if this binary tree is empty, false otherwise
   */
  public boolean isEmpty();

  /**
   * Returns the number of elements in this binary tree.
   *
   * @return the number of elements in the tree
   */
  public int size();

  /**
   * Returns true if the binary tree contains an element that matches
   * the specified element and false otherwise.
   *
   * @param targetElement the element being sought in the tree
   * @return true if the tree contains the target element
   */
  public boolean contains(T targetElement);

  /**
   * Returns a reference to the specified element if it is found in
```

LISTING 19.1 *continued*

```
     * this binary tree.  Throws an exception if the specified element
     * is not found.
     *
     * @param targetElement the element being sought in the tree
     * @return a reference to the specified element
     */
    public T find(T targetElement);

    /**
     * Returns the string representation of this binary tree.
     *
     * @return a string representation of the binary tree
     */
    public String toString();

    /**
     * Returns an iterator over the elements of this tree.
     *
     * @return an iterator over the elements of this binary tree
     */
    public Iterator<T> iterator();

    /**
     * Returns an iterator that represents an inorder traversal on this binary tree.
     *
     * @return an iterator over the elements of this binary tree
     */
    public Iterator<T> iteratorInOrder();

    /**
     * Returns an iterator that represents a preorder traversal on this binary tree.
     *
     * @return an iterator over the elements of this binary tree
     */
    public Iterator<T> iteratorPreOrder();

    /**
     * Returns an iterator that represents a postorder traversal on this binary tree.
     *
     * @return an iterator over the elements of this binary tree
     */
    public Iterator<T> iteratorPostOrder();
```

LISTING 19.1 *continued*

```
    /**
     * Returns an iterator that represents a levelorder traversal on the binary tree.
     *
     * @return an iterator over the elements of this binary tree
     */
    public Iterator<T> iteratorLevelOrder();
}
```

19.5 Using Binary Trees: Expression Trees

In Chapter 12, we used a stack algorithm to evaluate postfix expressions. In this section, we modify that algorithm to construct an expression tree using an `ExpressionTree` class that extends our definition of a binary tree. Figure 19.10 illustrates the concept of an expression tree. Notice that the root and all of the internal nodes of an expression tree contain operations and that all of the leaves contain operands. An expression tree is evaluated from the bottom up. In this case, the (5 − 3) term is evaluated first, which yields 2. That result is then multiplied by 4, which yields 8. Finally, the result of that term is added to 9, which yields 17.

Listing 19.2 illustrates our `ExpressionTree` class. The Java Collections API does not provide an implementation of a tree collection. Instead, the use of

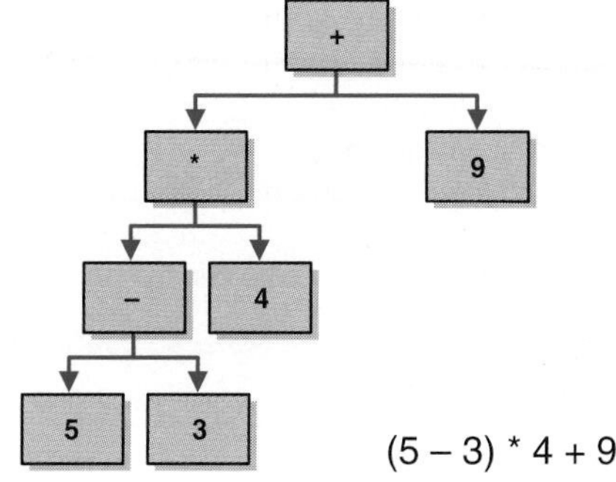

FIGURE 19.10 An example of an expression tree

trees in the API is limited to their use as an implementation strategy for sets and maps. Thus we will use our own implementation of a linked binary tree for this example. The `LinkedBinaryTree` class is presented in Section 19.7.

The `ExpressionTree` class extends the `LinkedBinaryTree` class, providing a new constructor that will combine expression trees to make a new tree and providing an `evaluate` method to recursively evaluate an expression tree once it has been constructed.

LISTING 19.2

```
import jsjf.*;

/**
 * ExpressionTree represents an expression tree of operators and operands.
 *
 * @author Java Foundations
 * @version 4.0
 */
public class ExpressionTree extends LinkedBinaryTree<ExpressionTreeOp>
{
   /**
    * Creates an empty expression tree.
    */
   public ExpressionTree()
   {
      super();
   }

   /**
    * Constructs a expression tree from the two specified expression
    * trees.
    *
    * @param element      the expression tree for the center
    * @param leftSubtree  the expression tree for the left subtree
    * @param rightSubtree the expression tree for the right subtree
    */
   public ExpressionTree(ExpressionTreeOp element,
          ExpressionTree leftSubtree, ExpressionTree rightSubtree)
   {
      root = new BinaryTreeNode<ExpressionTreeOp>(element, leftSubtree, right
      Subtree);
   }

   /**
    * Evaluates the expression tree by calling the recursive
    * evaluateNode method.
```

LISTING 19.2 *continued*

```
    *
    * @return the integer evaluation of the tree
    */
   public int evaluateTree()
   {
      return evaluateNode(root);
   }

   /**
    * Recursively evaluates each node of the tree.
    *
    * @param root the root of the tree to be evaluated
    * @return the integer evaluation of the tree
    */
   public int evaluateNode(BinaryTreeNode root)
   {
      int result, operand1, operand2;
      ExpressionTreeOp temp;

       if (root==null)
           result = 0;
       else
       {
          temp = (ExpressionTreeOp)root.getElement();

          if (temp.isOperator())
          {
             operand1 = evaluateNode(root.getLeft());
             operand2 = evaluateNode(root.getRight());
             result = computeTerm(temp.getOperator(), operand1, operand2);
          }
          else
             result = temp.getValue();
      }

      return result;
   }

   /**
    * Evaluates a term consisting of an operator and two operands.
    *
    * @param operator  the operator for the expression
    * @param operand1  the first operand for the expression
    * @param operand2  the second operand for the expression
    */
```

LISTING 19.2 *continued*

```
private int computeTerm(char operator, int operand1, int operand2)
{
   int result=0;
   if (operator == '+')
        result = operand1 + operand2;
   else if (operator == '-')
       result = operand1 - operand2;
   else if (operator == '*')
       result = operand1 * operand2;
   else
       result = operand1 / operand2;

   return result;
}

/**
 * Generates a structured string version of the tree by performing
 * a levelorder traversal.
 *
 * @return a string representation of this binary tree
 */
public String printTree()
{
   UnorderedListADT<BinaryTreeNode<ExpressionTreeOp>> nodes =
     new ArrayUnorderedList<BinaryTreeNode<ExpressionTreeOp>>();
   UnorderedListADT<Integer> levelList =
     new ArrayUnorderedList<Integer>();
   BinaryTreeNode<ExpressionTreeOp> current;
   String result = "";
   int printDepth = this.getHeight();
   int possibleNodes = (int)Math.pow(2, printDepth + 1);
   int countNodes = 0;

   nodes.addToRear(root);
   Integer currentLevel = 0;
   Integer previousLevel = -1;
   levelList.addToRear(currentLevel);

   while (countNodes < possibleNodes)
   {
      countNodes = countNodes + 1;
      current = nodes.removeFirst();
```

LISTING 19.2 *continued*

```
        currentLevel = levelList.removeFirst();
        if (currentLevel > previousLevel)
        {
           result = result + "\n\n";
           previousLevel = currentLevel;
           for (int j = 0; j < ((Math.pow(2, (printDepth - currentLevel))) - 1); j++)
             result = result + " ";
        }
        else
        {
           for (int i = 0; i < ((Math.pow(2, (printDepth - currentLevel + 1)) -
             1)) ; i++)
           {
               result = result + " ";
           }
        }
        if (current != null)
        {
           result = result + (current.getElement()).toString();
           nodes.addToRear(current.getLeft());
           levelList.addToRear(currentLevel + 1);
           nodes.addToRear(current.getRight());
           levelList.addToRear(currentLevel + 1);
        }
        else {
           nodes.addToRear(null);
           levelList.addToRear(currentLevel + 1);
           nodes.addToRear(null);
           levelList.addToRear(currentLevel + 1);
           result = result + " ";
        }

     }

     return result;
  }
}
```

The `evaluateTree` method calls the recursive `evaluateNode` method. The `evaluateNode` method returns the value if the node contains a number, or, if the node contains an operation, it returns the result of the operation using the value of the left and right `subtrees`. The `ExpressionTree` class uses the `ExpressionTreeOp` class as the element to store at each node of the tree. The `ExpressionTreeOp` class enables us to keep track of whether the element is a number or an operator and of which operator or what value is stored there. The `ExpressionTreeOp` class is illustrated in Listing 19.3.

LISTING 19.3

```
import jsjf.*;

/**
 * ExpressionTreeOp represents an element in an expression tree.
 *
 * @author Java Foundations
 * @version 4.0
 */
public class ExpressionTreeOp
{
   private int termType;
   private char operator;
   private int value;

   /**
    * Creates a new expression tree object with the specified data.
    *
    * @param type the integer type of the expression
    * @param op   the operand for the expression
    * @param val  the value for the expression
    */
   public ExpressionTreeOp(int type, char op, int val)
   {
      termType = type;
      operator = op;
      value = val;
   }

   /**
    * Returns true if this object is an operator and false otherwise.
    *
    * @return true if this object is an operator, false otherwise
    */
```

LISTING 19.3 *continued*

```
   public boolean isOperator()
   {
      return (termType == 1);
   }

   /**
    *Returns the operator of this expression tree object.
    *
    * @return the character representation of the operator
    */
   public char getOperator()
   {
      return operator;
   }

   /**
    * Returns the value of this expression tree object.
    *
    * @return the value of this expression tree object
    */
   public int getValue()
   {
      return value;
   }

   public String toString()
   {
      if (termType == 1)
          return operator + "";
      else
          return value + "";
   }
}
```

The `PostfixTester` and `PostfixEvaluator` classes are a modification of our solution from Chapter 12. This solution employs the `ExpressionTree` class to build, print and evaluate an expression tree. Figure 19.11 illustrates this process for the expression tree from Figure 19.10. Note that the top of the expression tree stack is on the right.

The `PostfixTester` class is shown in Listing 19.4, and the `PostfixEvaluator` class is shown in Listing 19.5. The UML description of the `Postfix` class is shown in Figure 19.12.

Input in Postfix: 5 3 – 4 * 9 +

Token	Processing Steps	Expression Tree Stack (top at right)
5	push(new ExpressionTree(5, null, null)	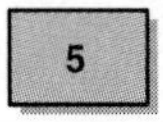
3	push(new ExpressionTree(3, null, null)	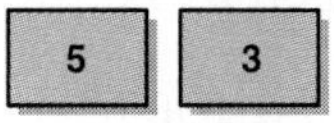
–	op2 = pop op1 = pop push(new ExpressionTree(–, op1, op2)	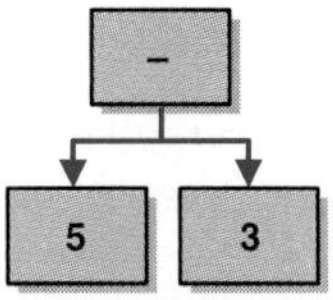
4	push(new ExpressionTree(4, null, null)	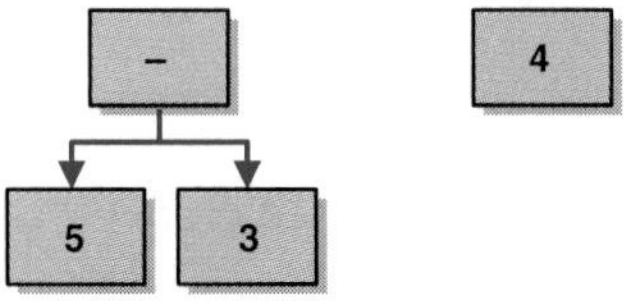
*	op2 = pop op1 = pop push(new ExpressionTree(*, op1, op2)	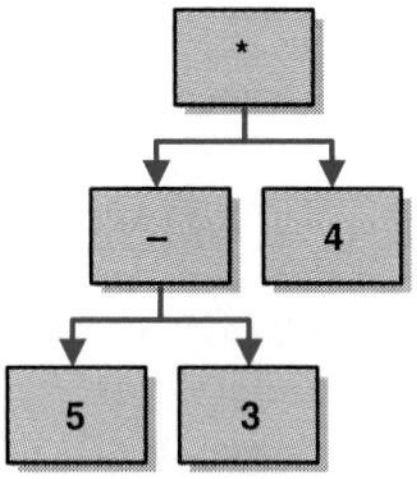
9	push(new ExpressionTree(9, null, null)	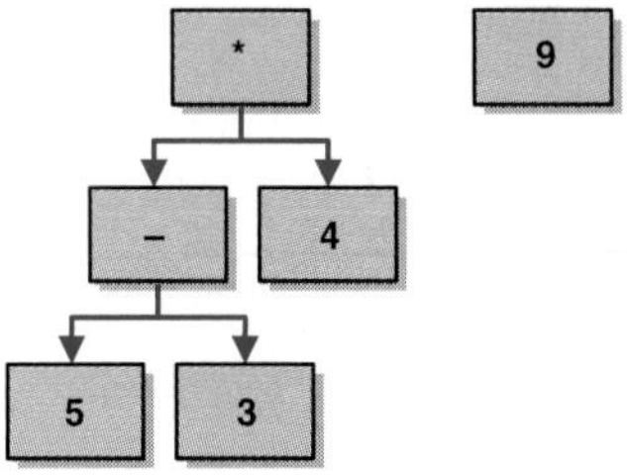
+	op2 = pop op1 = pop push(new ExpressionTree(+, op1, op2)	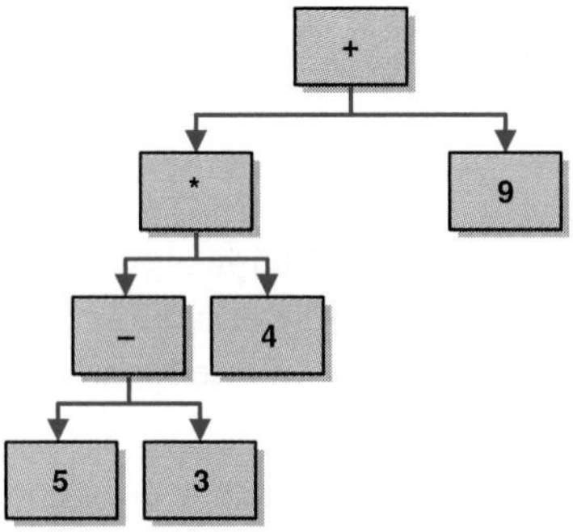

FIGURE 19.11 Building an expression tree from a postfix expression

LISTING 19.4

```
import java.util.Scanner;

/**
 * Demonstrates the use of a stack to evaluate postfix expressions.
 *
 * @author Java Foundations
 * @version 4.0
 */
public class PostfixTester
{
   /**
    * Reads and evaluates multiple postfix expressions.
    */
   public static void main(String[] args)
   {
      String expression, again;
      int result;

      Scanner in = new Scanner(System.in);

      do
      {
         PostfixEvaluator evaluator = new PostfixEvaluator();
         System.out.println("Enter a valid post-fix expression one token " +
                  "at a time with a space between each token (e.g. 5 4 + 3 2
                  1 - + *)");
         System.out.println("Each token must be an integer or an operator
         (+,-,*,/)");
         expression = in.nextLine();

         result = evaluator.evaluate(expression);
         System.out.println();
         System.out.println("That expression equals " + result);

         System.out.println("The Expression Tree for that expression is: ");
         System.out.println(evaluator.getTree());

         System.out.print("Evaluate another expression [Y/N]? ");
         again = in.nextLine();
         System.out.println();
      }
      while (again.equalsIgnoreCase("y"));
   }
}
```

LISTING 19.5

```
import jsjf.*;
import jsjf.exceptions.*;
import java.util.*;
import java.io.*;

/**
 * PostfixEvaluator this modification of our stack example uses a
 * stack to create an expression tree from a VALID integer postfix expression
 * and then uses a recursive method from the ExpressionTree class to
 * evaluate the tree.
 *
 * @author Java Foundations
 * @version 4.0
 */
public class PostfixEvaluator
{
   private String expression;
   private Stack<ExpressionTree> treeStack;

   /**
    * Sets up this evalutor by creating a new stack.
    */
   public PostfixEvaluator()
   {
      treeStack = new Stack<ExpressionTree>();
   }

   /**
    * Retrieves and returns the next operand off of this tree stack.
    *
    * @param treeStack  the tree stack from which the operand will be returned
    * @return the next operand off of this tree stack
    */
   private ExpressionTree getOperand(Stack<ExpressionTree> treeStack)
   {
      ExpressionTree temp;
      temp = treeStack.pop();

      return temp;
   }

   /**
    * Evaluates the specified postfix expression by building and evaluating
    * an expression tree.
    *
```

LISTING 19.5 *continued*

```
    * @param expression string representation of a postfix expression
    * @return value of the given expression
    */
   public int evaluate(String expression)
   {
      ExpressionTree operand1, operand2;
      char operator;
      String tempToken;

      Scanner parser = new Scanner(expression);

      while (parser.hasNext())
      {
         tempToken = parser.next();
         operator = tempToken.charAt(0);

         if ((operator == '+') || (operator == '-') || (operator == '*') ||
              (operator == '/'))
         {
            operand1 = getOperand(treeStack);
            operand2 = getOperand(treeStack);
            treeStack.push(new ExpressionTree
                     (new ExpressionTreeOp(1,operator,0), operand2, operand1));
         }
         else
         {
             treeStack.push(new ExpressionTree(new ExpressionTreeOp
                     (2,' ',Integer.parseInt(tempToken)), null, null));
         }

      }
       return (treeStack.peek()).evaluateTree();
   }

   /**
    * Returns the expression tree associated with this postfix evaluator.
    *
    * @return string representing the expression tree
    */
   public String getTree()
   {
      return (treeStack.peek()).printTree();
   }
}
```

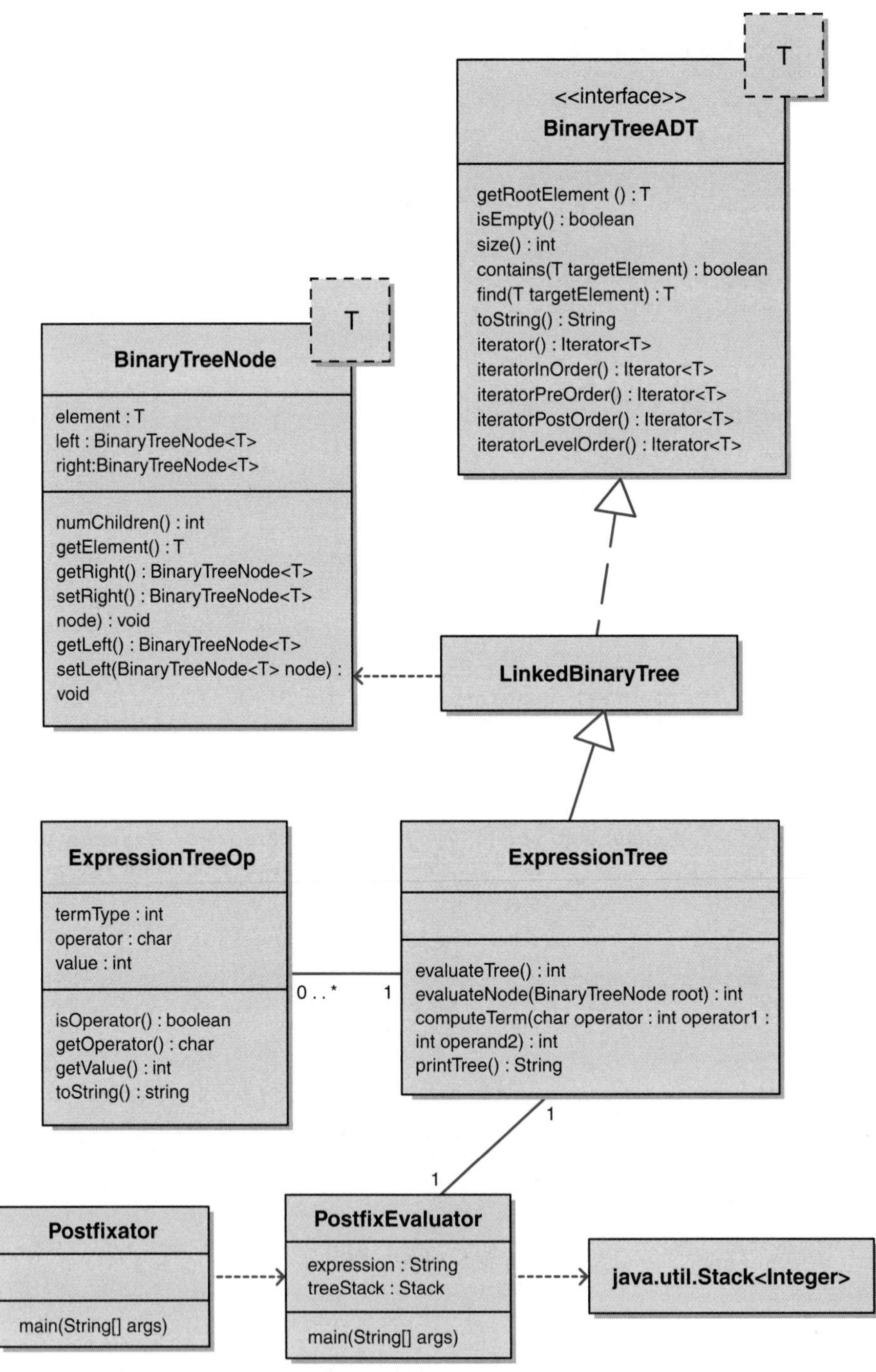

FIGURE 19.12 UML description of the Postfix example

19.6 A Backpain Analyzer

Notice that the `ExpressionTree` class extended the `LinkedBinaryTree` class. Keep in mind that when one class is derived from another it creates an is-a relationship. This extension to create the `ExpressionTree` class is natural given that an expression tree is a binary tree.

Let's look at another example where our solution uses the `LinkedBinaryTree` class but does not extend it. A *decision tree* is a tree whose nodes represent decision points and whose children represent the options available at that point. The leaves of a decision tree represent the possible conclusions that might be drawn based on the answers.

A simple decision tree, with yes/no questions, can be modeled by a binary tree. Figure 19.13 shows a decision tree that helps to diagnose the cause of back pain. For each question, the left child represents the answer No, and the right child represents the answer Yes. To perform a diagnosis, begin with the question at the root and follow the appropriate path, based on the answers, until a leaf is reached.

Decision trees are sometimes used as a basis for an *expert system*, which is software that attempts to represent the knowledge of an expert in a particular field. For instance, a particular expert system might be used to model the expertise of a doctor, a car mechanic, or an accountant. Obviously, the greatly simplified decision tree in Figure 19.13 is not fleshed out enough to do a good job diagnosing the real cause of back pain, but it should give you a feel for how such systems might work.

KEY CONCEPT
A decision tree can be used as the basis for an expert system.

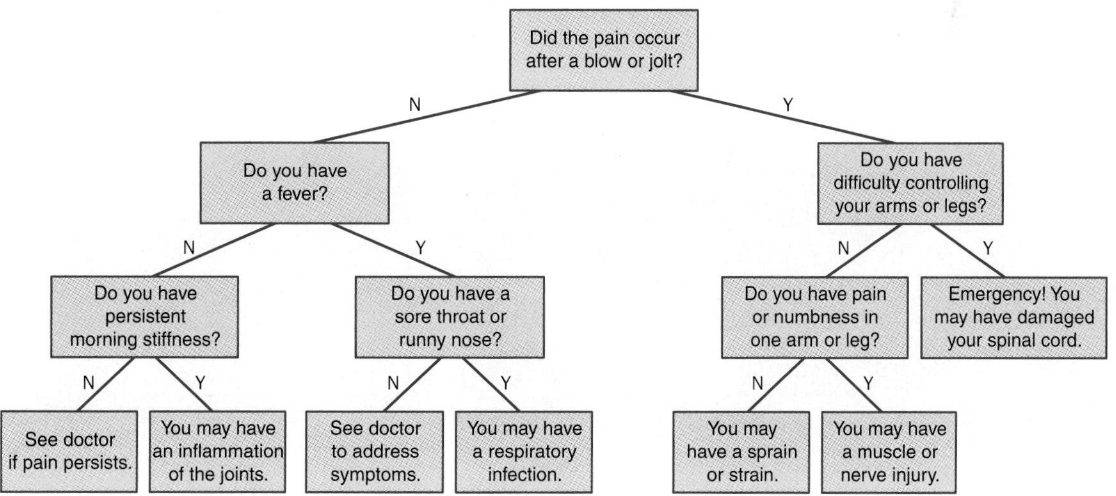

FIGURE 19.13 A decision tree for diagnosing back pain

Let's look at an example that uses the `LinkedBinaryTree` implementation discussed in the previous section to represent a decision tree. The program in Listing 19.6 uses the tree pictured in Figure 19.13 to hold a dialog with the user and draw a conclusion. The UML description of our solution to the back pain analyzer problem is presented in Figure 19.14.

The tree is constructed and used in the `DecisionTree` class, shown in Listing 19.7. The only instance data is the variable `tree` that represents the entire decision tree, which is defined to store `String` objects as elements. Note that this

LISTING 19.6

```
import java.io.*;

/**
 * BackPainAnaylyzer demonstrates the use of a binary decision tree to
 * diagnose back pain.
 */
public class BackPainAnalyzer
{
   /**
    *  Asks questions of the user to diagnose a medical problem.
    */
   public static void main (String[] args) throws FileNotFoundException
   {
      System.out.println ("So, you're having back pain.");

      DecisionTree expert = new DecisionTree("input.txt");
      expert.evaluate();
   }
}
```

OUTPUT

```
So, you're having back pain
Did the pain occur after a blow or jolt?
Y
Do you have difficulty controlling your arms or legs?
N
Do you have pain or numbness in one arm or leg?
Y
You may have a muscle or nerve injury.
```

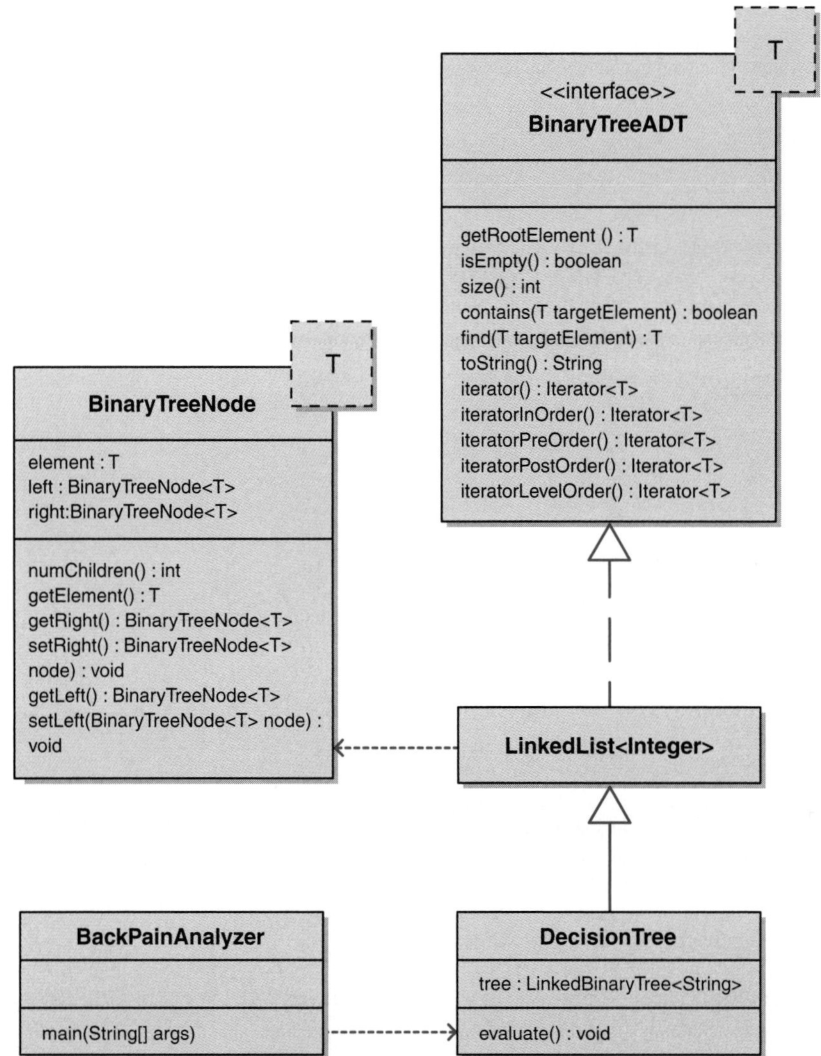

FIGURE 19.14 UML description of the back pain analyzer

version of the `DecisionTree` class is not specific to the back pain analyzer. It could be used for any binary decision tree.

The constructor of `DecisionTree` reads the various string elements to be stored in the tree nodes from the given file. Then the nodes themselves are created, with no children for the leaves and with previously defined nodes (or subtrees) as children for internal nodes. The tree is basically created from the bottom up.

LISTING 19.7

```
import jsjf.*;
import java.util.*;
import java.io.*;

/**
 * The DecisionTree class uses the LinkedBinaryTree class to implement
 * a binary decision tree. Tree elements are read from a given file and
 * then the decision tree can be evaluated based on user input using the
 * evaluate method.
 *
 * @author Java Foundations
 * @version 4.0
 */
public class DecisionTree
{
  private LinkedBinaryTree<String> tree;

  /**
   * Builds the decision tree based on the contents of the given file
   *
   * @param filename the name of the input file
   * @throws FileNotFoundException if the input file is not found
   */
  public DecisionTree(String filename) throws FileNotFoundException
  {
     File inputFile = new File(filename);
     Scanner scan = new Scanner(inputFile);
     int numberNodes = scan.nextInt();
     scan.nextLine();
     int root = 0, left, right;

     List<LinkedBinaryTree<String>> nodes = new java.util.ArrayList<LinkedBinaryTree
     <String>>();
     for (int i = 0; i < numberNodes; i++)
          nodes.add(i,new LinkedBinaryTree<String>(scan.nextLine()));

      while (scan.hasNext())
      {
         root = scan.nextInt();
         left = scan.nextInt();
         right = scan.nextInt();
         scan.nextLine();

         nodes.set(root,
             new LinkedBinaryTree<String>((nodes.get(root)).getRootElement(),
             nodes.get(left), nodes.get(right)));
```

LISTING 19.7 *continued*

```
      }
      tree = nodes.get(root);
   }

   /**
    *  Follows the decision tree based on user responses.
    */
   public void evaluate()
   {
      LinkedBinaryTree<String> current = tree;
      Scanner scan = new Scanner(System.in);

      while (current.size() > 1)
      {
         System.out.println (current.getRootElement());
         if (scan.nextLine().equalsIgnoreCase("N"))
            current = current.getLeft();
         else
            current = current.getRight();
      }

      System.out.println (current.getRootElement());
   }
}
```

The `evaluate` method uses the variable `current` to indicate the current node in the tree being processed, beginning at the root. The `while` loop continues until a leaf is found. The current question is printed, and the answer is read from the user. If the answer is No, then `current` is updated to point to the left child. Otherwise, it is updated to point to the right child. After falling out of the loop, the element stored in the leaf (the conclusion) is printed.

19.7 Implementing Binary Trees with Links

We will examine how some of these methods might be implemented using a linked implementation; others will be left as exercises. The `LinkedBinaryTree` class implementing the `BinaryTreeADT` interface will need to keep track of the node that is at the root of the tree and the number of elements on the tree. The `LinkedBinaryTree` header and instance data could be declared as

```
package jsjf;

import java.util.*;
import jsjf.exceptions.*;

/**
 * LinkedBinaryTree implements the BinaryTreeADT interface
 *
 * @author Java Foundations
 * @version 4.0
 */
public class LinkedBinaryTree<T> implements BinaryTreeADT<T>, Iterable<T>
{
  protected BinaryTreeNode<T> root;
  protected int modCount;
```

The constructors for the `LinkedBinaryTree` class should handle three cases: We want to create a binary tree with nothing in it, we want to create a binary tree with a single element but no children, and we want to create a binary tree with a particular element at the root and two given trees as children. With these goals in mind, the `LinkedBinaryTree` class might have the following constructors. Note that each of the constructors must account for both the `root` and `count` attributes.

```
/**
 * Creates an empty binary tree.
 */
public LinkedBinaryTree()
{
   root = null;
}

/**
 * Creates a binary tree with the specified element as its root.
 *
 * @param element the element that will become the root of the binary tree
 */
public LinkedBinaryTree(T element)
{
   root = new BinaryTreeNode<T>(element);
}

/**
 * Creates a binary tree with the specified element as its root and the
```

```
     * given trees as its left child and right child
     *
     * @param element the element that will become the root of the binary tree
     * @param left the left subtree of this tree
     * @param right the right subtree of this tree
     */
    public LinkedBinaryTree(T element, LinkedBinaryTree<T> left,
                 LinkedBinaryTree<T> right)
    {
       root = new BinaryTreeNode<T>(element);
       root.setLeft(left.root);
       root.setRight(right.root);
    }
```

Note that both the instance data and the constructors use an additional class called `BinaryTreeNode`. As discussed earlier, this class keeps track of the element stored at each location as well as pointers to the left and right subtree or children of each node. In this particular implementation, we chose not to include a pointer back to the parent of each node. Listing 19.8 shows the `BinaryTreeNode` class. The `BinaryTreeNode` class also includes a recursive method to return the number of children of the given node.

LISTING 19.8

```
package jsjf;

/**
 * BinaryTreeNode represents a node in a binary tree with a left and
 * right child.
 *
 * @author Java Foundations
 * @version 4.0
 */
public class BinaryTreeNode<T>
{
  protected T element;
  protected BinaryTreeNode<T> left, right;

  /**
   * Creates a new tree node with the specified data.
   *
   * @param obj the element that will become a part of the new tree node
  */
```

LISTING 19.8 *continued*

```
public BinaryTreeNode(T obj)
{
   element = obj;
   left = null;
   right = null;
}

/**
 * Creates a new tree node with the specified data.
 *
 * @param obj the element that will become a part of the new tree node
 * @param left the tree that will be the left subtree of this node
 * @param right the tree that will be the right subtree of this node
 */
public BinaryTreeNode(T obj, LinkedBinaryTree<T> left, LinkedBinaryTree<T> right)
{
   element = obj;
   if (left == null)
       this.left = null;
   else
       this.left = left.getRootNode();

   if (right == null)
       this.right = null;
   else
       this.right = right.getRootNode();
}

/**
 * Returns the number of non-null children of this node.
 *
 * @return the integer number of non-null children of this node
 */
public int numChildren()
{
   int children = 0;

   if (left != null)
       children = 1 + left.numChildren();

   if (right != null)
        children = children + 1 + right.numChildren();
```

LISTING 19.8 *continued*

```
      return children;
   }

   /**
    * Return the element at this node.
    *
    * @return the element stored at this node
    */
   public T getElement()
   {
      return element;
   }

   /**
    * Return the right child of this node.
    *
    * @return the right child of this node
    */
   public BinaryTreeNode<T> getRight()
   {
      return right;
   }

   /**
    * Sets the right child of this node.
    *
    * @param node the right child of this node
    */
   public void setRight(BinaryTreeNode<T> node)
   {
      right = node;
   }

  /**
    * Return the left child of this node.
    *
    * @return the left child of the node
    */
   public BinaryTreeNode<T> getLeft()
   {
      return left;
   }

  /**
    * Sets the left child of this node.
```

LISTING 19.8 *continued*

```
     *
     * @param node the left child of this node
     */
    public void setLeft(BinaryTreeNode<T> node)
    {
       left = node;
    }
}
```

There are a variety of other possibilities for implementation of a tree node or binary tree node class. For example, methods could be included to test whether the node is a leaf (does not have any children), to test whether the node is an internal node (has at least one child), to test the depth of the node from the root, or to calculate the height of the left and right subtrees.

Another alternative would be to use polymorphism such that, rather than testing a node to see if it has data or has children, we would create various implementations, such as an `emptyTreeNode`, an `innerTreeNode`, and a `leafTreeNode`, that would distinguish the various possibilities.

The `find` Method

As with our earlier collections, our `find` method traverses the tree using the `equals` method of the class stored in the tree to determine equality. This puts the definition of equality under the control of the class being stored in the tree. The `find` method throws an exception if the target element is not found.

Many methods associated with trees may be written either recursively or iteratively. Often, when written recursively, these methods require the use of a private support method because the signature and/or the behavior of the first call and each successive call may not be the same. The `find` method in our simple implementation is an excellent example of this strategy.

We have chosen to use a recursive `findAgain` method. We know that the first call to `find` will start at the root of the tree, and if that instance of the `find` method completes without finding the target, we need to throw an exception. The private `findAgain` method enables us to distinguish between this first instance of the `find` method and each successive call.

```
/**
 * Returns a reference to the specified target element if it is
 * found in this binary tree. Throws a ElementNotFoundException if
 * the specified target element is not found in the binary tree.
 *
 * @param targetElement the element being sought in this tree
 * @return a reference to the specified target
 * @throws ElementNotFoundException if the element is not in the tree
 */
public T find(T targetElement) throws ElementNotFoundException
{
   BinaryTreeNode<T> current = findNode(targetElement, root);

   if (current == null)
      throw new ElementNotFoundException("LinkedBinaryTree");

   return (current.getElement());
}

/**
 * Returns a reference to the specified target element if it is
 * found in this binary tree.
 *
 * @param targetElement the element being sought in this tree
 * @param next the element to begin searching from
 */
private BinaryTreeNode<T> findNode(T targetElement,
                    BinaryTreeNode<T> next)
{
   if (next == null)
      return null;

   if (next.getElement().equals(targetElement))
      return next;

   BinaryTreeNode<T> temp = findNode(targetElement, next.getLeft());

   if (temp == null)
      temp = findNode(targetElement, next.getRight());

   return temp;
}
```

As seen in earlier examples, the contains method can make use of the find method. Our implementation of this is left as a programming project.

The iteratorInOrder Method

Another interesting operation is the iteratorInOrder method. The task is to create an Iterator object that will allow a user class to step through the elements of the tree in an inorder traversal. The solution to this problem provides another example of using one collection to build another. We simply traverse the tree using a definition of "visit" from earlier pseudocode that adds the contents of the node onto an unordered list. We then use the list iterator to create an new TreeIterator. This approach is possible because of the linear nature of an unordered list and the way that we implemented the iterator method for a list. The iterator method for a list returns an Iterator that starts with the element at the front of the list and steps through the list in a linear fashion. It is important to understand that this behavior is not a requirement for an iterator associated with a list. It is simply an artifact of the way that we chose to implement the iterator method for a list. What would happen if we simply returned the Iterator for our list without creating a TreeIterator? The problem with that solution would be that our Iterator would no longer be fail-fast (that is, it would no longer throw a concurrent modification exception if the underlying tree were modified while the iterator was in use).

Like the find operation, we use a private helper method in our recursion.

```
/**
 * Performs an inorder traversal on this binary tree by calling an
 * overloaded, recursive inorder method that starts with
 * the root.
 *
 * @return an in order iterator over this binary tree
 */
public Iterator<T> iteratorInOrder()
{
   ArrayUnorderedList<T> tempList = new ArrayUnorderedList<T>();
   inOrder(root, tempList);

   return new TreeIterator(tempList.iterator());
}

/**
 * Performs a recursive inorder traversal.
```

```
     *
     * @param node the node to be used as the root for this traversal
     * @param tempList the temporary list for use in this traversal
     */
    protected void inOrder(BinaryTreeNode<T> node,
                           ArrayUnorderedList<T> tempList)
    {
       if (node != null)
       {
          inOrder(node.getLeft(), tempList);
          tempList.addToRear(node.getElement());
          inOrder(node.getRight(), tempList);
       }
    }
```

The other iterator operations are similar and are left as exercises. Likewise, the array implementation of a binary tree is left as an exercise and will be revisited in Chapter 21.

Summary of Key Concepts

- A tree is a nonlinear structure whose elements are organized into a hierarchy.
- Trees are described by a large set of related terms.
- The simulated link strategy allows array positions to be allocated contiguously regardless of the completeness of the tree.
- In general, a balanced n-ary tree with m elements will have height $\log_n m$.
- There are four basic methods for traversing a tree: preorder, inorder, postorder, and level-order traversals.
- Preorder traversal means visit the node, then the left child, then the right child.
- Inorder traversal means visit the left child, then the node, then the right child.
- Postorder traversal means visit the left child, then the right child, then the node.
- Level-order traversal means visit the nodes at each level, one level at a time, starting with the root.
- A decision tree can be used as the basis for an expert system.

Summary of Terms

tree A tree is a nonlinear structure whose elements are organized into a hierarchy.

node A location within a tree.

edge A connection between two nodes of a tree.

root The node at the top level of a tree and the one node in the tree that does not have a parent.

level The position of a node relative to the root of the tree.

child A node that is below the current node in tree and directly connected to it by an edge.

siblings Nodes that are children of the same node.

leaf A node in a tree that does not have any children.

internal node A node in a tree that is not the root and has at least one child.

path The collection of edges that directly connects a node to another node of the tree.

ancestor A node that is above the current node on the path from the root.

descendant A node that is below the current node in the tree and is on a path from the current node to a leaf (including the leaf).

path length The number of edges that must be followed to connect one node to another.

tree height The length of the longest path from the root to a leaf.

tree order The maximum number of children that any node in the tree may have.

general tree A tree that has no limit on the number of children a node may have.

nary tree A tree that limits each node to no more than n children.

binary tree A tree in which nodes may have at most two children.

balanced Roughly speaking, a tree is considered to be balanced if all of the leaves of the tree are on the same level or at least within one level of each other.

complete A tree is considered complete if it is balanced and all of the leaves at the bottom level are on the left side of the tree.

full An n-ary tree is considered full if all the leaves of the tree are at the same level and every node either is a leaf or has exactly n children.

freelist A list of available positions in an array implementation of a tree.

binary search tree A binary tree with the added property that the left child is always less than the parent, which is always less than or equal to the right child.

preorder traversal A tree traversal accomplished by visiting each node, followed by its children, starting with the root.

inorder traversal A tree traversal accomplished by visiting the left child of the node, then the node, and then any remaining nodes, starting with the root.

postorder traversal A tree traversal accomplished by visiting the children and then the node, starting with the root.

level-order traversal A tree traversal accomplished by visiting all of the nodes at each level, one level at a time, starting with the root.

Self-Review Questions

SR 19.1 What is a tree?

SR 19.2 What is a node?

SR 19.3 What is the root of a tree?

SR 19.4 What is a leaf?

SR 19.5 What is an internal node?

SR 19.6 Define the height of a tree.

SR 19.7 Define the level of a node.

SR 19.8 What are the advantages and disadvantages of the computational strategy?

SR 19.9 What are the advantages and disadvantages of the simulated link strategy?

SR 19.10 What attributes should be stored in the `TreeNode` class?

SR 19.11 Which method of traversing a tree would result in a sorted list for a binary search tree?

SR 19.12 We used a list to implement the iterator methods for a binary tree. What must be true for this strategy to be successful?

Exercises

EX 19.1 Develop a pseudocode algorithm for a level-order traversal of a binary tree.

EX 19.2 Draw either a matrilineage (following your mother's lineage) or a patrilineage (following your father's lineage) diagram for a couple of generations. Develop a pseudocode algorithm for inserting a person into the proper place in the tree.

EX 19.3 Develop a pseudocode algorithm to build an expression tree from a prefix expression.

EX 19.4 Develop a pseudocode algorithm to build an expression tree from an infix expression.

EX 19.5 Calculate the time complexity of the `find` method.

EX 19.6 Calculate the time complexity of the `iteratorInOrder` method.

EX 19.7 Develop a pseudocode algorithm for the `size` method assuming that there is not a `count` variable.

EX 19.8 Develop a pseudocode algorithm for the `isEmpty` operation assuming that there is not a `count` variable.

EX 19.9 Draw an expression tree for the expression (9 + 4) * 5 + (4 − (6 − 3)).

Programming Projects

PP 19.1 Complete the implementation of the `getRoot` and `toString` operations of a binary tree.

PP 19.2 Complete the implementation of the `size` and `isEmpty` operations of a binary tree, assuming that there is not a `count` variable.

PP 19.3 Create boolean methods for our `BinaryTreeNode` class to determine whether the node is a leaf or an internal node.

PP 19.4 Create a method called `depth` that will return an `int` representing the level or depth of the given node from the root.

PP 19.5 Complete the implementation of the `contains` method for a binary tree.

PP 19.6 Implement the `contains` method for a binary tree without using the `find` operation.

PP 19.7 Complete the implementation of the iterator methods for a binary tree.

PP 19.8 Implement the iterator methods for a binary tree without using a list.

PP 19.9 Modify the `ExpressionTree` class to create a method called `draw` that will graphically depict the expression tree.

PP 19.10 We use postfix notation in the example in this chapter because it eliminates the need to parse an infix expression by precedence rules and parentheses. Some infix expressions do not need parentheses to modify precedence. Implement a method for the `ExpressionTree` class that will determine if an integer expression would require parentheses if it were written in infix notation.

PP 19.11 Create an array-based implementation of a binary tree using the computational strategy.

PP 19.12 Create an array-based implementation of a binary tree using the simulated link strategy.

PP 19.13 Create an implementation of a binary tree using the recursive approach introduced in the chapter. In this approach, each node is a binary tree. Thus a binary tree contains a reference to the element stored at its root as well as references to its left and right subtrees. You may also want to include a reference to its parent.

Answers to Self-Review Questions

SRA 19.1. A tree is a nonlinear structure defined by the concept that each node in the tree, other than the first node or root node, has exactly one parent.

SRA 19.2. A node is a location in the tree where an element is stored.

SRA 19.3. The root of a tree is the node at the base of the tree or the one node in the tree that does not have a parent.

SRA 19.4 A leaf is a node that does not have any children.

SRA 19.5 An internal node is any non-root node that has at least one child.

SRA 19.6 The height of the tree is the length of the longest path from the root to a leaf.

SRA 19.7 The level of a node is measured by the number of links that must be followed to reach that node from the root.

SRA 19.8 The computational strategy does not have to store links from parent to child because that relationship is fixed by position. However, this strategy may lead to substantial wasted space for trees that are not balanced and/or not complete.

SRA 19.9 The simulated link strategy stores array index values as pointers between parent and child and allows the data to be stored contiguously no matter how balanced and/or complete the tree. However, this strategy increases the overhead in terms of maintaining a freelist or shifting elements in the array.

SRA 19.10 The `TreeNode` class must store a pointer to the element stored in that position as well as pointers to each of the children of that node. The class may also contain a pointer to the parent of the node.

SRA 19.11 Inorder traversal of a binary search tree would result in a sorted list in ascending order.

SRA 19.12 For this strategy to be successful, the iterator for a list must return the elements in the order in which they were added. For this particular implementation of a list, we know this is indeed the case.

Binary Search Trees

20

CHAPTER OBJECTIVES

- Define a binary search tree abstract data structure
- Demonstrate how a binary search tree can be used to solve problems
- Examine a binary search tree implementation
- Discuss strategies for balancing a binary search tree

In this chapter, we will explore the concept of binary search trees and options for their implementation. We will examine algorithms for adding and removing elements from binary search trees and for maintaining balanced binary search trees. We will discuss the analysis of these implementations and also explore various uses of binary search trees.

20.1 A Binary Search Tree

A *binary search tree* is a binary tree with the added property that for each node, the left child is less than the parent, which is less than or equal to the right child. As we discussed in Chapter 19, it is very difficult to abstract a set of operations for a tree without knowing what type of tree it is and its intended purpose. With the added ordering property that must be maintained, we can now extend our definition to include the operations on a binary search tree listed in Figure 20.1.

KEY CONCEPT
A binary search tree is a binary tree with the added property that the left child is less than the parent, which is less than or equal to the right child.

KEY CONCEPT
The definition of a binary search tree is an extension of the definition of a binary tree.

As we discussed in Chapter 19, the Java Collections API does not provide an implementation of a general tree. Instead, trees are used as an implementation strategy for Sets and Maps. We will discuss the API treatment of trees in Chapter 22. In the meantime, we will build upon our own linked implementation of trees from Chapter 19.

We must keep in mind that the definition of a binary search tree is an extension of the definition of a binary tree discussed in the last chapter. Thus, these operations are in addition to the ones defined for a binary tree. At this point we are simply discussing binary search trees, but as we will see shortly, the interface for a balanced binary search tree will be the same. Listing 20.1 and Figure 20.2 describe a `BinarySearchTreeADT`.

Operation	Description
`addElement`	Add an element to the tree.
`removeElement`	Remove an element from the tree.
`removeAllOccurrences`	Remove all occurrences of element from the tree.
`removeMin`	Remove the minimum element in the tree.
`removeMax`	Remove the maximum element in the tree.
`findMin`	Returns a reference to the minimum element in the tree.
`findMax`	Returns a reference to the maximum element in the tree.

FIGURE 20.1 The operations on a binary search tree

LISTING 20.1

```
package jsjf;

/**
 * BinarySearchTreeADT defines the interface to a binary search tree.
 *
 * @author Java Foundations
 * @version 4.0
 */
```

LISTING 20.1 *continued*

```
public interface BinarySearchTreeADT<T> extends BinaryTreeADT<T>
{
   /**
    * Adds the specified element to the proper location in this tree.
    *
    * @param element the element to be added to this tree
    */
   public void addElement(T element);

   /**
    * Removes and returns the specified element from this tree.
    *
    * @param targetElement the element to be removed from the tree
    * @return the element to be removed from the tree
    */
   public T removeElement(T targetElement);

   /**
    * Removes all occurences of the specified element from this tree.
    *
    * @param targetElement the element to be removed from the tree
    */
   public void removeAllOccurrences(T targetElement);

   /**
    * Removes and returns the smallest element from this tree.
    *
    * @return the smallest element from the tree.
    */
   public T removeMin();

   /**
    * Removes and returns the largest element from this tree.
    *
    * @return the largest element from the tree
    */
   public T removeMax();

   /**
    * Returns the smallest element in this tree without removing it.
    *
```

LISTING 20.1 *continued*

```
    * @return the smallest element in the tree
    */
   public T findMin();

   /**
    * Returns the largest element in this tree without removing it.
    *
    * @return the largest element in the tree
    */
   public T findMax();
}
```

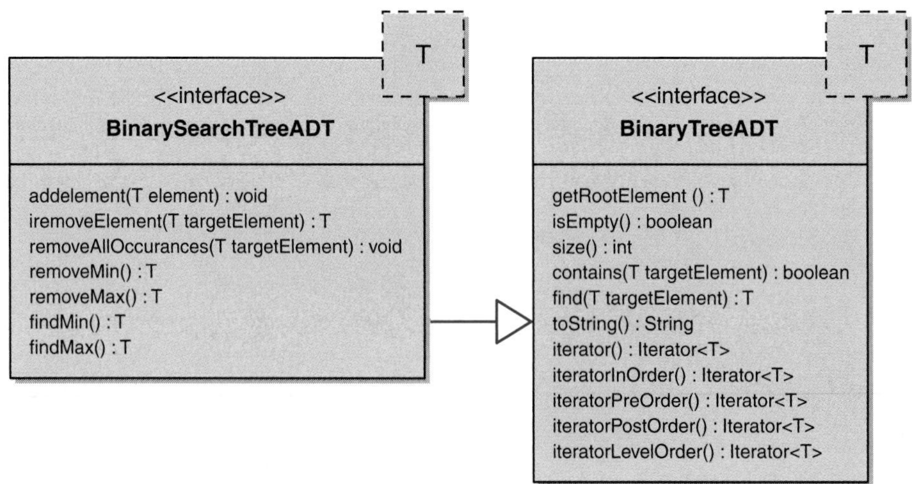

FIGURE 20.2 UML description of the `BinarySearchTreeADT`

20.2 Implementing Binary Search Trees: With Links

> **KEY CONCEPT**
> Each `BinaryTreeNode` object maintains a reference to the element stored at that node, as well as references to each of the node's children.

In Chapter 19, we introduced a simple implementation of a `LinkedBinaryTree` class using a `BinaryTreeNode` class to represent each node of the tree. Each `BinaryTreeNode` object maintains a reference to the element stored at that node, as well as references to each of the node's children. We can simply extend that definition with a `LinkedBinarySearchTree` class implementing the BinarySearchTreeADT interface. Because we are extending the LinkedBinaryTree class from Chapter 19, all of the methods we discussed are still supported, including the various traversals.

Our LinkedBinarySearchTree class offers two constructors: one to create an empty LinkedBinarySearchTree and the other to create a LinkedBinarySearchTree with a particular element at the root. Both of these constructors simply refer to the equivalent constructors of the super class (that is, the LinkedBinaryTree class).

```
/**
* Creates an empty binary search tree.
*/
public LinkedBinarySearchTree()
{
   super();
}

/**
 * Creates a binary search with the specified element as its root.
 *
 * @param element the element that will be the root of the new binary
 *      search tree
 */
public LinkedBinarySearchTree(T element)
{
   super(element);

   if (!(element instanceof Comparable))
       throw new
           NonComparableElementException("LinkedBinarySearchTree");
}
```

The addElement Operation

The addElement(element) method adds a given element to the appropriate location in the tree using the private, recursive addElement(element, tree) method. If the element is not Comparable, the method throws a NonComparableElementException. If the tree is empty, the new element becomes the root. If the tree is not empty, the new element is compared to the element at the root. If it is less than the element stored at the root and the left child of the root is null, then the new element becomes the left child of the root. If the new element is less than the element stored at the root and the left child of the root is not null, then we recursively add the element to the left subtree of the root. If the new element is greater than or equal to the element stored at the root and the right child of the root is null, then the new element becomes the right child of the root. If the new element

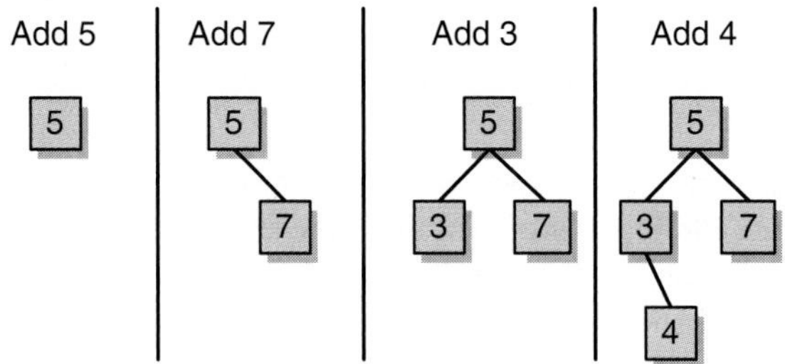

FIGURE 20.3 Adding elements to a binary search tree

is greater than or equal to the element stored at the root and the right child of the root is not null, then we recursively add the element to the right subtree of the root. Figure 20.3 illustrates this process of adding elements to a binary search tree. As in any recursive algorithm, we could have chosen to implement the add operation iteratively. The iterative version of the add operation is left as a programming project.

DESIGN FOCUS

Once we have a definition of the type of tree that we wish to construct and how it is to be used, we have the ability to define an interface and implementations. In Chapter 19, we defined a binary tree that enabled us to define a very basic set of operations. Now that we have limited our scope to a binary search tree, we can fill in more details of the interface and the implementation. Determining the level at which to build interface descriptions and determining the boundaries between parent and child classes are design choices . . . and they are not always easy design choices.

```
/**
 * Adds the specified object to the binary search tree in the
 * appropriate position according to its natural order.  Note that
 * equal elements are added to the right.
 *
 * @param element the element to be added to the binary search tree
 */
public void addElement(T element)
{
   if (!(element instanceof Comparable))
       throw new NonComparableElementException("LinkedBinarySearchTree");

   Comparable<T> comparableElement = (Comparable<T>)element;
```

```
      if (isEmpty())
         root = new BinaryTreeNode<T>(element);
      else
      {
         if (comparableElement.compareTo(root.getElement()) < 0)
         {
            if (root.getLeft() == null)
                 this.getRootNode().setLeft(new BinaryTreeNode<T>(element));
            else
                 addElement(element, root.getLeft());
         }
         else
         {
            if (root.getRight() == null)
                this.getRootNode().setRight(new BinaryTreeNode<T>(element));
            else
                addElement(element, root.getRight());
         }
      }
      modCount++;
   }

   /**
    * Adds the specified object to the binary search tree in the
    * appropriate position according to its natural order.  Note that
    * equal elements are added to the right.
    *
    * @param element the element to be added to the binary search tree
    */
   private void addElement(T element, BinaryTreeNode<T> node)
   {
      Comparable<T> comparableElement = (Comparable<T>)element;

      if (comparableElement.compareTo(node.getElement()) < 0)
      {
         if (node.getLeft() == null)
             node.setLeft(new BinaryTreeNode<T>(element));
         else
             addElement(element, node.getLeft());
      }
      else
      {
         if (node.getRight() == null)
             node.setRight(new BinaryTreeNode<T>(element));
         else
             addElement(element, node.getRight());
      }
   }
```

The `removeElement` Operation

The `removeElement` method removes a given `Comparable` element from a binary search tree or throws an `ElementNotFoundException` if the given target is not found in the tree. Unlike our earlier study of linear structures, we cannot simply remove the node by making the reference point around the node to be removed. Instead, another node will have to be *promoted* to replace the one being removed. The protected method `replacement` returns a reference to a node that will replace the one specified for removal. There are three cases for selecting the replacement node:

KEY CONCEPT
In removing an element from a binary search tree, another node must be promoted to replace the node being removed.

- If the node has no children, `replacement` returns null.
- If the node has only one child, `replacement` returns that child.
- If the node to be removed has two children, `replacement` returns the inorder successor of the node to be removed (because equal elements are placed to the right).

Like our recursive `addElement` method, the `removeElement(targetElement)` method is recursive and makes use of the private `removeElement(targetElement,`

```
/**
 * Removes the first element that matches the specified target
 * element from the binary search tree and returns a reference to
 * it.  Throws a ElementNotFoundException if the specified target
 * element is not found in the binary search tree.
 *
 * @param targetElement the element being sought in the binary search tree
 * @throws ElementNotFoundException if the target element is not found
 */
public T removeElement(T targetElement)
                throws ElementNotFoundException
{
   T result = null;

   if (isEmpty())
       throw new ElementNotFoundException("LinkedBinarySearchTree");
   else
   {
       BinaryTreeNode<T> parent = null;
       if (((Comparable<T>)targetElement).equals(root.element))
       {
          result =  root.element;
          BinaryTreeNode<T> temp = replacement(root);
          if (temp == null)
              root = null;
          else
```

```
            {
               root.element = temp.element;
               root.setRight(temp.right);
               root.setLeft(temp.left);
            }

            modCount--;
         }
         else
         {
            parent = root;
            if (((Comparable)targetElement).compareTo(root.element) < 0)
               result = removeElement(targetElement, root.getLeft(), parent);
            else
               result = removeElement(targetElement, root.getRight(), parent);
         }
      }

      return result;
   }

   /**
    * Removes the first element that matches the specified target
    * element from the binary search tree and returns a reference to
    * it.  Throws a ElementNotFoundException if the specified target
    * element is not found in the binary search tree.
    *
    * @param targetElement the element being sought in the binary search tree
    * @param node the node from which to search
    * @param parent the parent of the node from which to search
    * @throws ElementNotFoundException if the target element is not found
    */
   private T removeElement(T targetElement, BinaryTreeNode<T> node,
   BinaryTreeNode<T> parent) throws ElementNotFoundException
   {
      T result = null;

      if (node == null)
          throw new ElementNotFoundException("LinkedBinarySearchTree");
      else
      {
         if (((Comparable<T>)targetElement).equals(node.element))
         {
            result =  node.element;
            BinaryTreeNode<T> temp = replacement(node);
            if (parent.right == node)
               parent.right = temp;
```

```
            else
                parent.left = temp;

            modCount--;
        }
        else
        {
            parent = node;
            if (((Comparable)targetElement).compareTo(node.element) < 0)
                result = removeElement(targetElement, node.getLeft(), parent);
            else
                result = removeElement(targetElement, node.getRight(), parent);
        }
    }

    return result;
}
```

node, parent) method. In this way the special case of removing the root element can be handled separately.

The following code illustrates the replacement method. Figure 20.4 further illustrates the process of removing elements from a binary search tree.

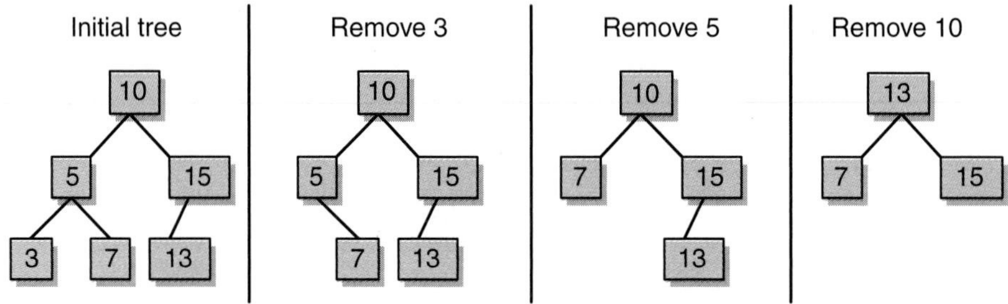

FIGURE 20.4 Removing elements from a binary tree

```
/**
 * Returns a reference to a node that will replace the one
 * specified for removal.  In the case where the removed node has
 * two children, the inorder successor is used as its replacement.
 *
 * @param node the node to be removed
```

```
 * @return a reference to the replacing node
 */
private BinaryTreeNode<T> replacement(BinaryTreeNode<T> node)
{
   BinaryTreeNode<T> result = null;

   if ((node.left == null) && (node.right == null))
       result = null;

   else if ((node.left != null) && (node.right == null))
       result = node.left;

   else if ((node.left == null) && (node.right != null))
       result = node.right;

   else
   {
      BinaryTreeNode<T> current = node.right;
      BinaryTreeNode<T> parent = node;

      while (current.left != null)
      {
         parent = current;
         current = current.left;
      }

      current.left = node.left;
      if (node.right != current)
      {
         parent.left = current.right;
         current.right = node.right;
      }

      result = current;
   }

   return result;
}
```

The `removeAllOccurrences` Operation

The `removeAllOccurrences` method removes all occurrences of a given element from a binary search tree and throws an `ElementNotFoundException` if the given element is not found in the tree. This method also throws a `ClassCastException` if the element given is not `Comparable`. This method makes use of the `removeElement` method by calling it once, which guarantees that the exception will be thrown if there is not at least one occurrence of the element in the tree. The `removeElement` method is then called again as long as the tree contains the target element. Note that the `removeAllOccurrences` method makes use of the `contains` method of the `LinkedBinaryTree` class. Note that the `find` method has been overridden in the `LinkedBinarySearchTree` class to take advantage of the ordering property of a binary search tree.

```
/**
 * Removes elements that match the specified target element from
 * the binary search tree. Throws a ElementNotFoundException if
 * the sepcified target element is not found in this tree.
 *
 * @param targetElement the element being sought in the binary search tree
 * @throws ElementNotFoundException if the target element is not found
 */
public void removeAllOccurrences(T targetElement)
         throws ElementNotFoundException
{
   removeElement(targetElement);

   try
   {
      while (contains((T)targetElement))
          removeElement(targetElement);
   }
   catch (Exception ElementNotFoundException)
   {
   }
}
```

The `removeMin` Operation

KEY CONCEPT
The leftmost node in a binary search tree will contain the minimum element whereas the rightmost node will contain the maximum element.

There are three possible cases for the location of the minimum element in a binary search tree:

- If the root has no left child, then the root is the minimum element and the right child of the root becomes the new root.
- If the leftmost node of the tree is a leaf, then it is the minimum element and we simply set its parent's left child reference to null.

- If the leftmost node of the tree is an internal node, then we set its parent's left child reference to point to the right child of the node to be removed.

Figure 20.5 illustrates these possibilities. Given these possibilities, the code for the `removeMin` operation is relatively straightforward.

```
/**
 * Removes the node with the least value from the binary search
 * tree and returns a reference to its element.  Throws an
 * EmptyCollectionException if this tree is empty.
 *
 * @return a reference to the node with the least value
 * @throws EmptyCollectionException if the tree is empty
 */
public T removeMin() throws EmptyCollectionException
{
   T result = null;

   if (isEmpty())
       throw new EmptyCollectionException("LinkedBinarySearchTree");
   else
   {
      if (root.left == null)
      {
         result = root.element;
         root = root.right;
      }
      else
      {
         BinaryTreeNode<T> parent = root;
         BinaryTreeNode<T> current = root.left;
         while (current.left != null)
         {
            parent = current;
            current = current.left;
         }
         result =  current.element;
         parent.left = current.right;
      }

      modCount--;
   }

   return result;
}
```

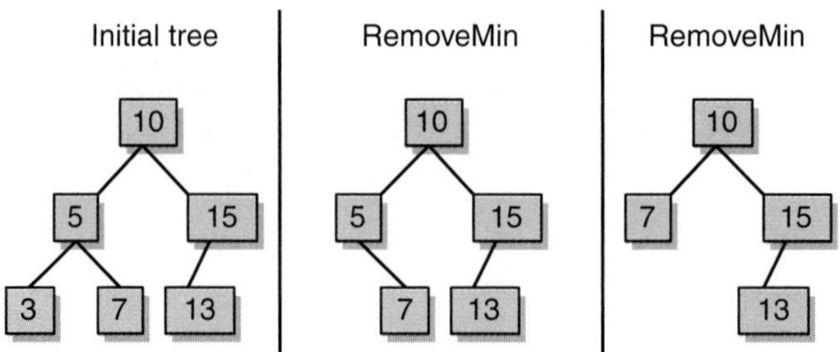

FIGURE 20.5 Removing the minimum element from a binary search tree

The `removeMax`, `findMin`, and `findMax` operations are left as exercises.

Implementing Binary Search Trees: With Arrays

In Chapter 19, we discussed two array implementation strategies for trees: the computational strategy and the simulated link strategy. For now, both implementations are left as programming projects. We will revisit these array-based tree implementations in Chapter 21.

20.3 Using Binary Search Trees: Implementing Ordered Lists

As we discussed in Chapter 19, one of the uses of trees is to provide efficient implementations of other collections. The `OrderedList` collection from Chapter 15 provides an excellent example. Figure 20.6 reminds us of the common operations for lists, and Figure 20.7 reminds us of the operations particular to an ordered list.

Operation	Description
`removeFirst`	Removes the first element from the list.
`removeLast`	Removes the last element from the list.
`remove`	Removes a particular element from the list.
`first`	Examines the element at the front of the list.
`last`	Examines the element at the rear of the list.
`contains`	Determines if the list contains a particular element.
`isEmpty`	Determines if the list is empty.
`size`	Determines the number of elements on the list.

FIGURE 20.6 The common operations on a list

Operation	Description
add	Adds an element to the list.

FIGURE 20.7 The operation particular to an ordered list

Using a binary search tree, we can create an implementation called BinarySearchTreeList that is a more efficient implementation than those we discussed in Chapter 6.

KEY CONCEPT
One of the uses of trees is to provide efficient implementations of other collections.

For simplicity, we have implemented both the ListADT and the OrderedListADT interfaces with the BinarySearchTreeList class, as shown in Listing 20.2. For some of the methods, the same method from either the LinkedBinaryTree or LinkedBinarySearchTree class will suffice. This is the case for the contains, isEmpty, and size operations. For the rest of the operations, there is a one-to-one correspondence between methods of the LinkedBinaryTree or the LinkedBinarySearchTree classes and the required methods for an ordered list. Thus, each of these methods is implemented by simply calling the associated method for a LinkedBinarySearchTree. This is the case for the add, removeFirst, removeLast, remove, first, last, and iterator methods.

LISTING 20.2

```
package jsjf;

import jsjf.exceptions.*;
import java.util.Iterator;

/**
 * BinarySearchTreeList represents an ordered list implemented using a binary
 * search tree.
 *
 * @author Java Foundations
 * @version 4.0
 */
public class BinarySearchTreeList<T> extends LinkedBinarySearchTree<T>
              implements ListADT<T>, OrderedListADT<T>, Iterable<T>
{
   /**
    * Creates an empty BinarySearchTreeList.
    */
   public BinarySearchTreeList()
```

LISTING 20.2 *continued*

```
{
   super();
}

/**
 * Adds the given element to this list.
 *
 * @param element the element to be added to the list
 */
public void add(T element)
{
   addElement(element);
}

/**
 * Removes and returns the first element from this list.
 *
 * @return the first element in the list
 */
public T removeFirst()
{
   return removeMin();
}

/**
 * Removes and returns the last element from this list.
 *
 * @return the last element from the list
 */
public T removeLast()
{
   return removeMax();
}

/**
 * Removes and returns the specified element from this list.
 *
 * @param element the element being sought in the list
 * @return the element from the list that matches the target
 */
public T remove(T element)
{
```

LISTING 20.2 *continued*

```
        return removeElement(element);
    }

    /**
     * Returns a reference to the first element on this list.
     *
     * @return a reference to the first element in the list
     */
    public T first()
    {
        return findMin();
    }

    /**
     * Returns a reference to the last element on this list.
     *
     * @return a reference to the last element in the list
     */
    public T last()
    {
        return findMax();
    }

    /**
     * Returns an iterator for the list.
     *
     * @return an iterator over the elements in the list
     */
    public Iterator<T> iterator()
    {
        return iteratorInOrder();
    }
}
```

Analysis of the `BinarySearchTreeList` Implementation

For the sake of our analysis, we will assume that the `LinkedBinarySearchTree` implementation used in the `BinarySearchTreeList` implementation is a balanced binary search tree with the added property that the maximum depth of any node is $\log_2(n)$, where n is the number of elements stored in the tree.

Operation	LinkedList	BinarySearchTreeList
`removeFirst`	O(1)	O(log n)
`removeLast`	O(n)	O(log n)
`remove`	O(n)	O(log n)*
`first`	O(1)	O(log n)
`last`	O(n)	O(log n)
`contains`	O(n)	O(log n)
`isEmpty`	O(1)	O(1)
`size`	O(1)	O(1)
`add`	O(n)	O(log n)*
*both the `add` and `remove` operations may cause the tree to become unbalanced		

FIGURE 20.8 Analysis of linked list and binary search tree implementations of an ordered list

This is a tremendously important assumption, as we will see over the next several sections. With that assumption, Figure 20.8 shows a comparison of the order of each operation for a singly linked implementation of an ordered list and our `BinarySearchTreeList` implementation.

Note that given our assumption of a balanced binary search tree, both the `add` and `remove` operations could cause the tree to need to be rebalanced, which, depending on the algorithm used, could affect the analysis. It is also important to note that although some operations are more efficient in the tree implementation, such as `removeLast`, `last`, and `contains`, are more efficient in the tree implementation, others, such as `removeFirst` and `first`, are less efficient when implemented using a tree.

20.4 Balanced Binary Search Trees

Why is our balance assumption important? What would happen to our analysis if the tree were not balanced? As an example, let's assume that we read the following list of integers from a file and added them to a binary search tree:

> **KEY CONCEPT**
> If a binary search tree is not balanced, it may be less efficient than a linear structure.

3 5 9 12 18 20

Figure 20.9 shows the resulting binary search tree. This resulting binary tree, which is referred to as a *degenerate tree*, looks more like a linked list, and in fact it is less efficient than a linked list because of the additional overhead associated with each node.

If this is the tree we are manipulating, then our analysis from the previous section will look far worse. For example, without our balance assumption, the `addElement`

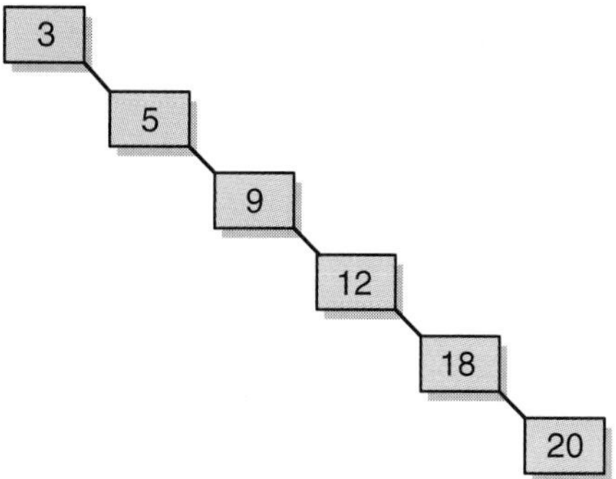

FIGURE 20.9 A degenerate binary tree

operation would have worst-case time complexity of O(n) instead of O(log n) because of the possibility that the root is the smallest element in the tree and the element we are inserting might be the largest element.

Our goal instead is to keep the maximum path length in the tree at or near $\log_2 n$. There are a variety of algorithms available for balancing or maintaining balance in a tree. There are brute force methods, which are not elegant or efficient, but get the job done. For example, we could write an inorder traversal of the tree to an array and then use a recursive method (much like binary search) to insert the middle element of the array as the root, and then build balanced left and right subtrees. Although such an approach would work, there are more elegant solutions, such as AVL trees and red/black trees, which we examine later in this chapter.

However, before we move on to these techniques, we need to understand some additional terminology that is common to many balancing techniques. The methods described here will work for any subtree of a binary search tree as well. For those subtrees, we simply replace the reference to root with the reference to the root of the subtree.

Right Rotation

Figure 20.10 shows a binary search tree that is not balanced and the processing steps necessary to rebalance it. The maximum path length in this tree is 3 and the minimum path length is 1. With only 6 elements in the tree, the maximum path length should be $\log_2 6$, or 2. To get this tree into balance, we need to

- Make the left child element of the root the new root element.
- Make the former root element the right child element of the new root.
- Make the right child of what was the left child of the former root the new left child of the former root.

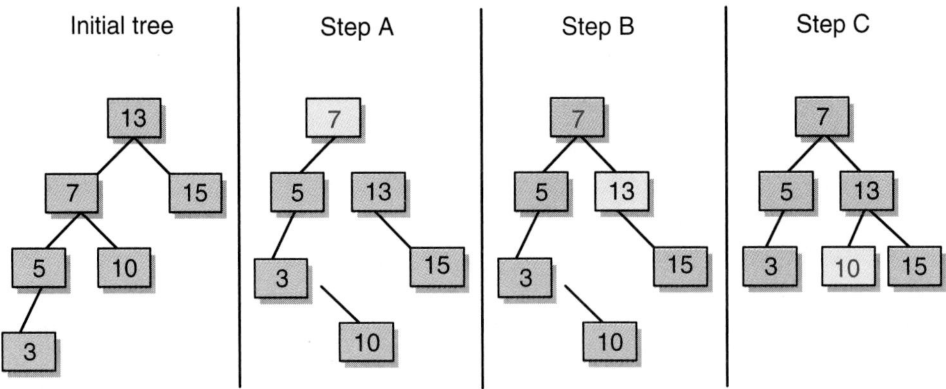

FIGURE 20.10 An unbalanced tree and the balanced tree that results from a right rotation

This *right rotation* is often referred to as a right rotation of the left child around the parent. The last image in Figure 20.10 shows the same tree after a right rotation. The same kind of rotation can be done at any level of the tree. This single rotation to the right will solve the imbalance if the imbalance is caused by a long path length in the left subtree of the left child of the root.

Left Rotation

Figure 20.11 shows another binary search tree that is not balanced. Again, the maximum path length in this tree is 3 and the minimum path length is 1.

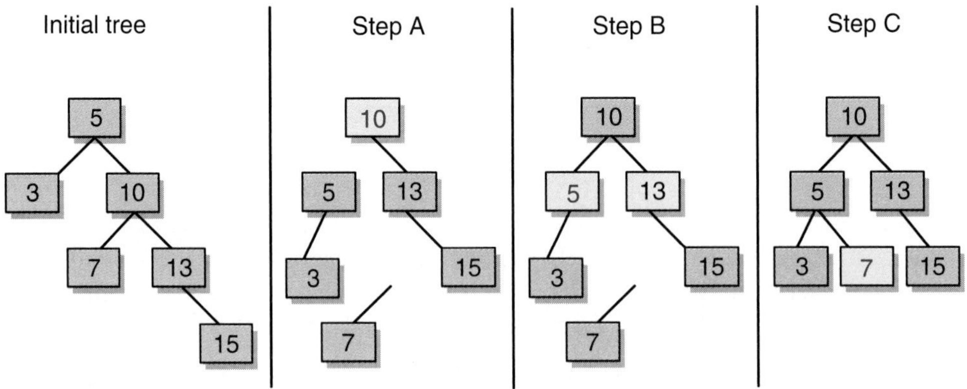

FIGURE 20.11 An unbalanced tree and the balanced tree that results from a left rotation

However, this time the larger path length is in the right subtree of the right child of the root. To get this tree into balance, we need to

- Make the right child element of the root the new root element.
- Make the former root element the left child element of the new root.
- Make the left child of what was the right child of the former root the new right child of the former root.

This *left rotation* is often referred to as a left rotation of the right child around the parent. Figure 20.11 shows the same tree through the processing steps of a left rotation. The same kind of rotation can be done at any level of the tree. This single rotation to the left will solve the imbalance if the imbalance is caused by a long path length in the right subtree of the right child of the root.

Rightleft Rotation

Unfortunately, not all imbalances can be solved by single rotations. If the imbalance is caused by a long path length in the left subtree of the right child of the root, we must first perform a right rotation of the left child of the right child of the root around the right child of the root, and then perform a left rotation of the resulting right child of the root around the root. Figure 20.12 illustrates this process.

Leftright Rotation

Similarly, if the imbalance is caused by a long path length in the right subtree of the left child of the root, we must first perform a left rotation of the right child of the left child of the root around the left child of the root, and then perform a right rotation of the resulting left child of the root around the root. Figure 20.13 illustrates this process.

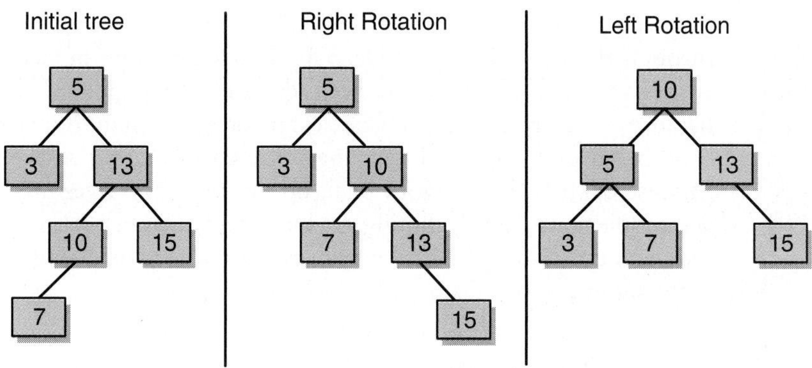

FIGURE 20.12 A rightleft rotation

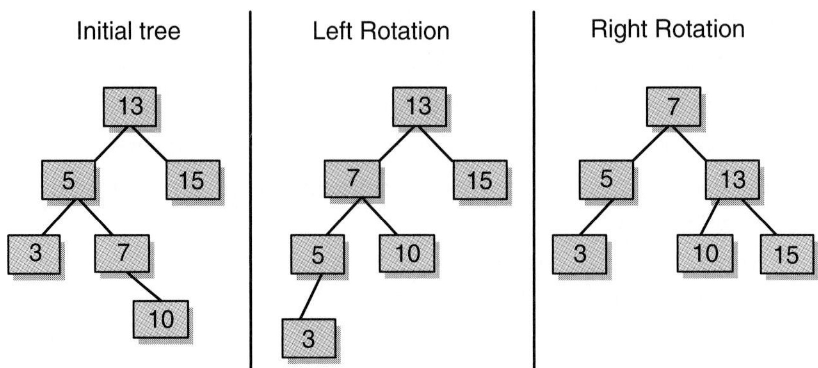

FIGURE 20.13 A leftright rotation

VideoNote
Demonstration of the four basic tree rotations.

20.5 Implementing Binary Search Trees: AVL Trees

We have been discussing a generic method for balancing a tree where the maximum path length from the root must be no more than $\log_2 n$ and the minimum path length from the root must be no less than $\log_2 n-1$. Adel'son-Vel'skii and Landis developed a method called *AVL trees* that is a variation on this theme. For each node in the tree, we will keep track of the height of the left and right subtrees. For any node in the tree, if the *balance factor*, or the difference in the heights of its subtrees (height of the right subtree minus height of the left subtree), is greater than 1 or less than –1, then the subtree with that node as the root needs to be rebalanced.

KEY CONCEPT
The height of the right subtree minus the height of the left subtree is called the balance factor of a node.

KEY CONCEPT
There are only two ways in which a tree, or any subtree of a tree, can become unbalanced: through the insertion of a node or through the deletion of a node.

There are only two ways in which a tree, or any subtree of a tree, can become unbalanced: through the insertion of a node or through the deletion of a node. Thus, each time one of these operations is performed, the balance factors must be updated and the balance of the tree must be checked starting at the point of insertion or removal of a node and working up toward the root of the tree. Because of this need to work back up the tree, AVL trees are often best implemented by including a parent reference in each node. In the diagrams that follow, all edges are represented as a single bidirectional line.

The cases for rotation that we discussed in the last section apply here as well, and by using this method, we can easily identify when to use each.

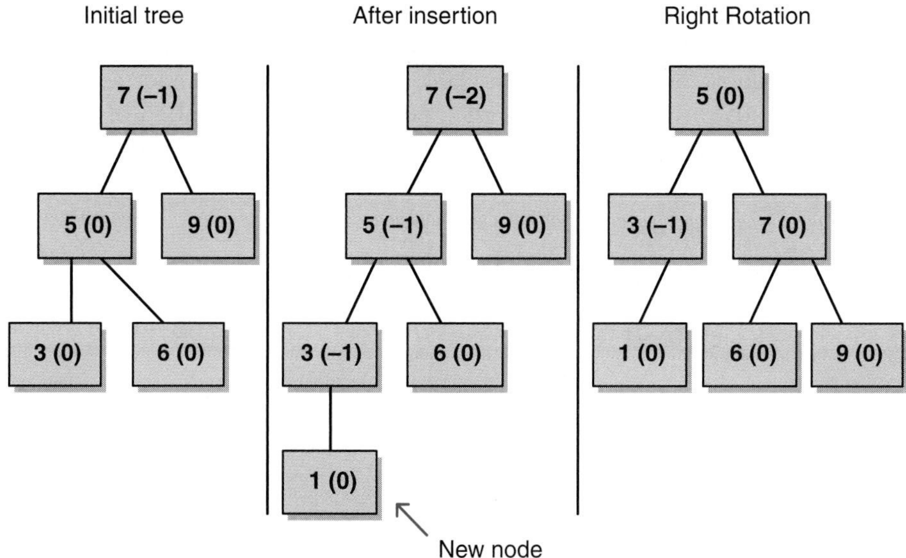

FIGURE 20.14 A right rotation in an AVL tree

Right Rotation in an AVL Tree

If the balance factor of a node is −2, this means that the node's left subtree has a path that is too long. We then check the balance factor of the left child of the original node. If the balance factor of the left child is −1, this means that the long path is in the left subtree of the left child, and therefore a simple right rotation of the left child around the original node will rebalance the tree. Figure 20.14 shows how an insertion of a node could cause an imbalance and how a right rotation would resolve it. Note that we are representing both the values stored at each node and the balance factors, with the balance factors shown in parentheses.

Left Rotation in an AVL Tree

If the balance factor of a node is +2, this means that the node's right subtree has a path that is too long. We then check the balance factor of the right child of the original node. If the balance factor of the right child is +1, this means that the long path is in the right subtree of the right child and therefore a simple left rotation of the right child around the original node will rebalance the tree.

Rightleft Rotation in an AVL Tree

If the balance factor of a node is +2, this means that the node's right subtree has a path that is too long. We then check the balance factor of the right child of the original node. If the balance factor of the right child is −1, this means that the long path is in the left subtree of the right child and therefore a rightleft double rotation will rebalance the tree. This is accomplished by first performing a right rotation of the left child of the right child of the original node around the right child of the original node, and then performing a left rotation of the right child of the original node around the original node. Figure 20.15 shows how the

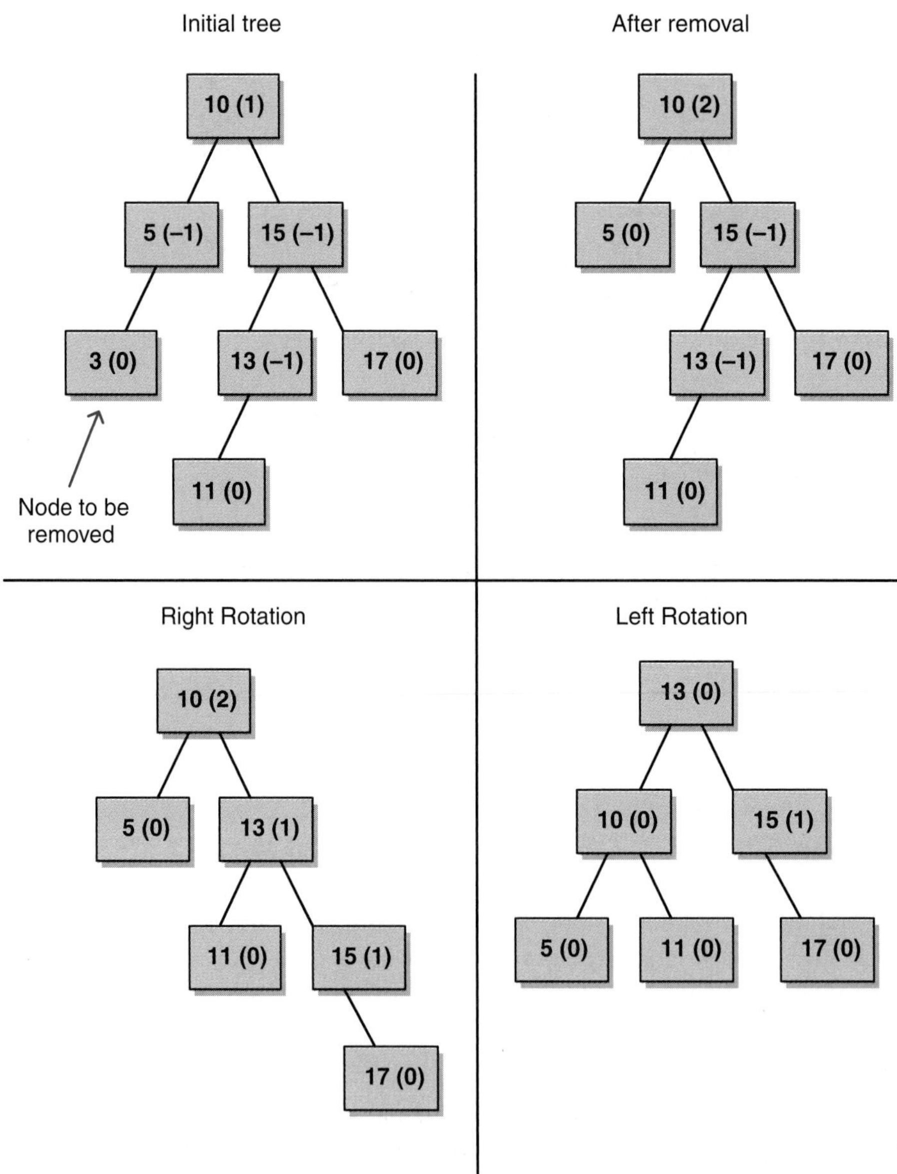

FIGURE 20.15 A rightleft rotation in an AVL tree

removal of an element from the tree could cause an imbalance and how a rightleft rotation would resolve it. Again, note that we are representing both the values stored at each node and the balance factors, with the balance factors shown in parentheses.

Leftright Rotation in an AVL Tree

If the balance factor of a node is –2, this means that the node's left subtree has a path that is too long. We then check the balance factor of the left child of the original node. If the balance factor of the left child is +1, this means that the long path is in the right subtree of the left child and therefore a leftright double rotation will rebalance the tree. This is accomplished by first performing a left rotation of the right child of the left child of the original node around the left child of the original node, and then performing a right rotation of the left child of the original node around the original node.

20.6 Implementing Binary Search Trees: Red/Black Trees

Another alternative to the implementation of binary search trees is the concept of a *red/black tree*, which was developed by Bayer and extended by Guibas and Sedgewick. A red/black tree is a balanced binary search tree in which we will store a color with each node (either red or black, usually implemented as a `boolean` value with false being equivalent to red). The following rules govern the color of a node:

- The root is black.
- All children of a red node are black.
- Every path from the root to a leaf contains the same number of black nodes.

Figure 20.16 shows three valid red/black trees (the lighter-shade nodes are "red"). Notice that the balance restriction on a red/black tree is somewhat less strict than that for AVL trees or for our earlier theoretical discussion. However, finding an element in both implementations is still an O(log n) operation. Because no red node can have a red child, at most half of the nodes in a path could be red nodes and at least half of the nodes in a path are black. From this we can argue that the maximum height of a red/black tree is roughly 2*log n and thus the traversal of the longest path is still order log n.

KEY CONCEPT
The balance restriction on a red/black tree is somewhat less strict than that for AVL trees.

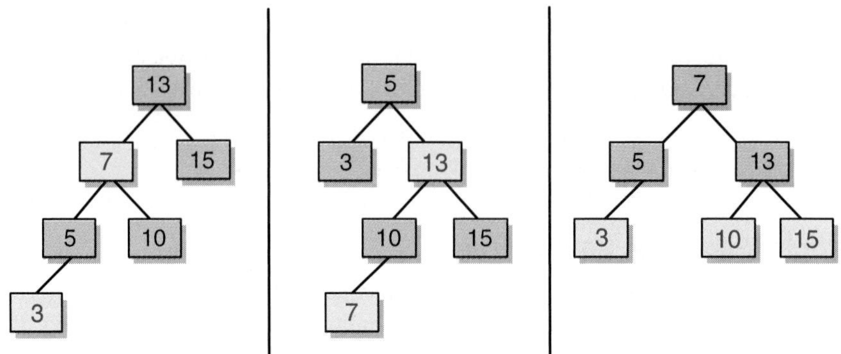

FIGURE 20.16 Valid red/black trees

As with AVL trees, the only time we need to be concerned about balance is after an insertion or removal of an element in the tree. But unlike the case with AVL trees, insertion and removal are handled quite separately.

Insertion into a Red/Black Tree

Insertion into a red/black tree progresses much as it did in our earlier `addElement` method. However, we always begin by setting the color of the new element to red. Once the new element has been inserted, we rebalance the tree as needed and change the color of elements as needed to maintain the properties of a red/black tree. As a last step, we always set the color of the root of the tree to black. For purposes of our discussion, we will simply refer to the color of a node as `node.color`. However, it may be more elegant in an actual implementation to create a method to return the color of a node.

The rebalancing (and recoloring) process after insertion is an iterative (or recursive) one starting at the point of insertion and working up the tree toward the root. Therefore, like AVL trees, red/black trees are best implemented by including a parent reference in each node. The termination conditions for this process are (`current == root`), where `current` is the node we are currently processing, or (`current.parent.color == black`) (that is, the color of the parent of the current node is black). The first condition terminates the process because we will always set the root color to black, and the root is included in all paths and therefore cannot violate the rule that each path have the same number of black elements. The second condition terminates the process because the node pointed to by `current` will always be a red node. This means that if the parent of the current node is black, then all of the rules are met as well since a red node does not affect the number of black nodes in a path and because we are working from the point of insertion up, we will have already balanced the subtree under the current node.

In each iteration of the rebalancing process, we will focus on the color of the sibling of the parent of the current node. Keep in mind that there are two possibilities for the parent of the current node: `current.parent` could be a left child or a right child. Assuming that the parent of `current` is a right child, we can get the color information by using `current.parent.parent.left.color`, but for purposes of our discussion, we will use the terms `parentsleftsibling.color` and `parentsrightsibling.color`. It is also important to keep in mind that the color of a null element is considered to be black.

In the case where the parent of `current` is a right child, there are two cases: `(parentsleftsibling.color == red)` or `(parentsleftsibling.color == black)`. Keep in mind that in either case, we are describing processing steps that are occurring inside of a loop with the termination conditions described earlier. Figure 20.17 shows a red/black tree after insertion with this first case (`parentsleftsibling.color==red`). The processing steps in this case are

- Set the color of `current`'s parent to black.
- Set the color of `parentsleftsibling` to black.
- Set the color of `current`'s grandparent to red.
- Set `current` to point to the grandparent of `current`.

In Figure 20.17, we inserted 8 into our tree. Keep in mind that `current` points to our new node and that `current.color` is set to red. Following the processing steps, we set the parent of `current` to black, we set the left sibling of the parent of `current` to black, and we set the grandparent of `current` to red. We then set `current` to point to the grandparent. Because the grandparent is the root, the loop terminates. Finally, we set the root of the tree to black.

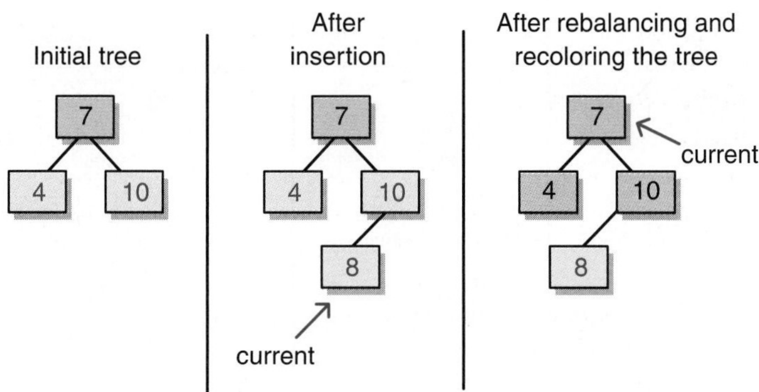

FIGURE 20.17 Red/black tree after insertion

However, if (`parentsleftsibling.color == black`), then we first need to check to see whether `current` is a left or a right child. If `current` is a left child, then we must set `current` equal to its parent and then rotate `current.left` to the right (around `current`) before continuing. Once this is accomplished, the processing steps are the same as they would be if `current` had been a right child to begin with:

- Set the color of `current`'s parent to black.
- Set the color of `current`'s grandparent to red.
- If `current`'s grandparent does not equal null, then rotate `current`'s parent to the left around `current`'s grandparent.

In the case where the parent of `current` is a left child, there are two cases: `parentsrightsibling.color == red`) or (`parentsrightsibling.color == black`). Keep in mind that in either case, we are describing processing steps that are occurring inside of a loop with the termination conditions described earlier. Figure 20.18 shows a red/black tree after insertion in this case (`parentsrightsibling.color==red`). The processing steps in this case are

- Set the color of `current`'s parent to black.
- Set the color of `parentsrightsibling` to black.
- Set the color of `current`'s grandparent to red.
- Set `current` to point to the grandparent of `current`.

In Figure 20.18. we inserted 5 into our tree, setting `current` to point to the new node and setting `current.color` to red. Again, following our processing steps,

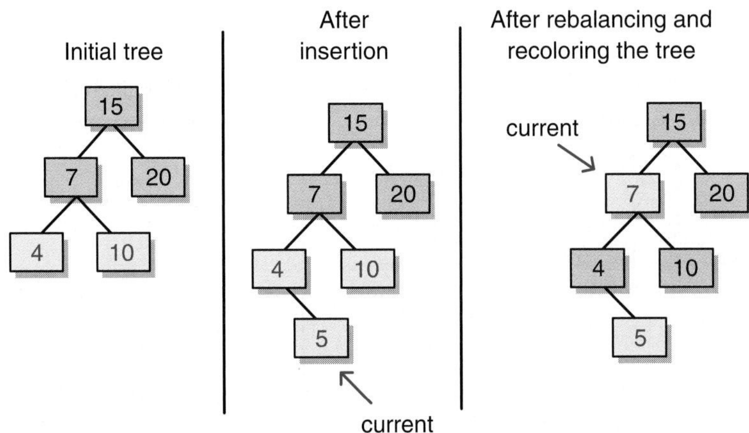

FIGURE 20.18 Red/black tree after insertion

we set the parent of `current` to black, we set the right sibling of the parent of `current` to black, and we set the grandparent of `current` to red. We then set `current` to point to its grandparent. Because the parent of the new `current` is black, our loop terminates. Last, we set the color of the root to black.

If (`parentsrightsibling.color == black`), then we first need to check to see whether `current` is a left or a right child. If `current` is a right child, then we must set `current` equal to `current.parent` and then rotate `current.right` to the left (around `current`) before continuing. Once this is accomplished, the processing steps are the same as they would be if `current` had been a left child to begin with:

- Set the color of `current`'s parent to black.
- Set the color of `current`'s grandparent to red.
- If `current`'s grandparent does not equal null, then rotate `current`'s parent to the right around `current`'s grandparent.

As you can see, the cases, depending on whether `current`'s parent is a left or a right child, are symmetrical.

Element Removal from a Red/Black Tree

As with insertion, the `removeElement` operation behaves much as it did before, only with the additional step of rebalancing (and recoloring) the tree. This rebalancing (and recoloring) process after removal of an element is an iterative one starting at the point of removal and working up the tree toward the root. Therefore, as stated earlier, red/black trees are often best implemented by including a parent reference in each node. The termination conditions for this process are (`current == root`), where `current` is the node we are currently processing, or (`current.color == red`).

As with the cases for insertion, the cases for removal are symmetrical depending upon whether `current` is a left or a right child. We will examine only the case where `current` is a right child. The other cases are easily derived by simply substituting left for right and right for left in the following cases.

In insertion, we were most concerned with the color of the sibling of the parent of the current node. For removal, we will focus on the color of the sibling of `current`. We could reference this color using `current.parent.left.color`, but we will simply refer to it as `sibling.color`. We will also look at the color of the children of the sibling. It is important to note that the default for color is black. Therefore, if at any time we are attempting to get the color of a null object, the result will be black. Figure 20.19 shows a red/black tree after the removal of an element.

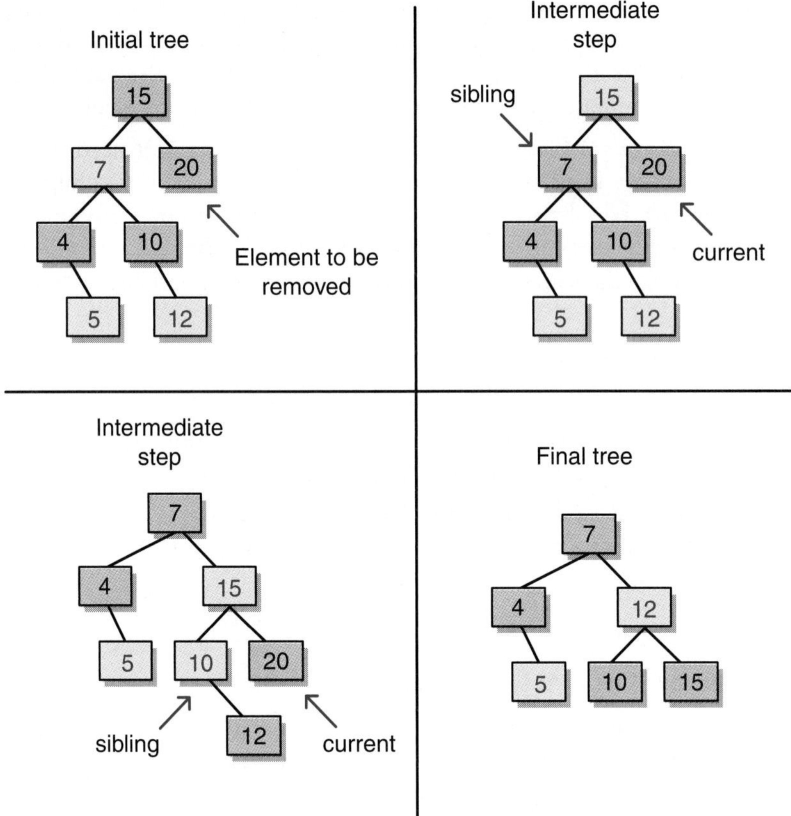

FIGURE 20.19 Red/black tree after removal

If the sibling's color is red, then before we do anything else, we must complete the following processing steps:

- Set the color of the sibling to black.
- Set the color of `current`'s parent to red.
- Rotate the sibling right around `current`'s parent.
- Set the sibling equal to the left child of `current`'s parent.

Next, our processing continues regardless of whether the original sibling was red or black. Now our processing is divided into one of two cases based upon the color of the children of the sibling. If both children of the sibling are black (or null), then we do the following:

- Set the color of the sibling to red.
- Set `current` equal to `current`'s parent.

If the children of the sibling are not both black, then we check to see whether the left child of the sibling is black. If it is, we must complete the following steps before continuing:

- Set the color of the sibling's right child to black.
- Set the color of the sibling to red.
- Rotate the sibling's right child left around the sibling.
- Set the sibling equal to the left child of `current`'s parent.

Then to complete the process when both of the sibling's children are not black, we must

- Set the color of the sibling to the color of `current`'s parent.
- Set the color of `current`'s parent to black.
- Set the color of the sibling's left child to black.
- Rotate the sibling right around `current`'s parent.
- Set `current` equal to the root.

Once the loop terminates, we must always then remove the node and set its parent's child reference to null.

Summary of Key Concepts

- A binary search tree is a binary tree with the added property that the left child is less than the parent, which is less than or equal to the right child.
- The definition of a binary search tree is an extension of the definition of a binary tree.
- Each `BinaryTreeNode` object maintains a reference to the element stored at that node as well as references to each of the node's children.
- In removing an element from a binary search tree, another node must be promoted to replace the node being removed.
- The leftmost node in a binary search tree will contain the minimum element, whereas the rightmost node will contain the maximum element.
- One of the uses of trees is to provide efficient implementations of other collections.
- If a binary search tree is not balanced, it may be less efficient than a linear structure.
- The height of the right subtree minus the height of the left subtree is called the balance factor of a node.
- There are only two ways in which a tree, or any subtree of a tree, can become unbalanced: through the insertion of a node and through the deletion of a node.
- The balance restriction on a red/black tree is somewhat less strict than that for AVL trees. However, in both cases, the `find` operation is order log n.

Summary of Terms

binary search tree A *binary search tree* is a binary tree with the added property that, for each node, the left child is less than the parent, which is less than or equal to the right child.

promoted A term used to describe the concept of a node in a tree being moved up to replace a parent node or other ancestor node that is being removed from the tree.

degenerate tree A tree that does not branch.

right rotation A single rotation strategy for rebalancing a tree when the long path is in the left subtree of the left child of the root.

left rotation A single rotation strategy for rebalancing a tree when the long path is in the right subtree of the right child of the root.

rightleft rotation A double rotation strategy for rebalancing a tree when the long path is in the left subtree of the right child of the root.

leftright rotation A double rotation strategy for rebalancing a tree when the long path is in the right subtree of the left child of the root.

AVL trees A strategy for keeping a binary search tree balanced that makes use of the balance factor of each node.

balance factor A property of a node that is computed by subtracting the height of the left subtree from the height of the right subtree. If the result is either greater than 1 or less than –1, then the tree is unbalanced.

red/black trees A strategy for keeping a binary search tree balanced making use of a color (either red or black) associated with each node.

Self-Review Questions

SR 20.1 What is the difference between a binary tree and a binary search tree?

SR 20.2 Why are we able to specify `addElement` and `removeElement` operations for a binary search tree but unable to do so for a binary tree?

SR 20.3 Assuming that the tree is balanced, what is the time complexity (order) of the `addElement` operation?

SR 20.4 Without the balance assumption, what is the time complexity (order) of the `addElement` operation?

SR 20.5 As stated in this chapter, a degenerate tree might actually be less efficient than a linked list. Why?

SR 20.6 Our `removeElement` operation uses the inorder successor as the replacement for a node with two children. What would be another reasonable choice for the replacement?

SR 20.7 The `removeAllOccurrences` operation uses both the `contains` and `removeElement` operations. What is the resulting time complexity (order) for this operation?

SR 20.8 `RemoveFirst` and `first` were O(1) operations for our earlier implementation of an ordered list. Why are they less efficient for our `BinarySearchTreeOrderedList`?

SR 20.9 Why does the `BinarySearchTreeOrderedList` class have to define the `iterator` method? Why can't it just rely on the `iterator` method of its parent class, as it does for `size` and `isEmpty`?

SR 20.10 What is the time complexity of the `addElement` operation after modifying to implement an AVL tree?

SR 20.11 What imbalance is fixed by a single right rotation?

SR 20.12 What imbalance is fixed by a leftright rotation?

SR 20.13 What is the balance factor of an AVL tree node?

SR 20.14 In our discussion of the process for rebalancing an AVL tree, we never discussed the possibility of the balance factor of a node being either +2 or −2 and the balance factor of one of its children being either +2 or −2. Why not?

SR 20.15 We noted that the balance restriction for a red/black tree is less strict than that of an AVL tree and yet we still claim that traversing the longest path in a red/black tree is still O(log n). Why?

Exercises

EX 20.1 Draw the binary search tree that results from adding the following integers (34 45 3 87 65 32 1 12 17). Assume our simple implementation with no balancing mechanism.

EX 20.2 Starting with the tree resulting from 20.1, draw the tree that results from removing (45 12 1), again using our simple implementation with no balancing mechanism.

EX 20.3 Repeat Exercise 20.1, this time assuming an AVL tree. Include the balance factors in your drawing.

EX 20.4 Repeat Exercise 20.2, this time assuming an AVL tree and using the result of Exercise 20.3 as a starting point. Include the balance factors in your drawing.

EX 20.5 Repeat Exercise 20.1, this time assuming a red/black tree. Label each node with its color.

EX 20.6 Repeat Exercise 20.2, this time assuming a red/black tree and using the result of Exercise 20.5 as a starting point. Label each node with its color.

EX 20.7 Starting with an empty red/black tree, draw the tree after insertion and before rebalancing, and after rebalancing (if necessary) for the following series of inserts and removals:

```
AddElement(40);
AddElement(25):
AddElement(10);
AddElement(5);
```

```
AddElement(1);
AddElement(45);
AddElement(50);
RemoveElement(40);
RemoveElement(25);
```

EX 20.8 Repeat Exercise 20.7, this time with an AVL tree.

Programming Projects

PP 20.1 Develop an array implementation of a binary search tree using the computational strategy described in Chapter 19.

PP 20.2 The `LinkedBinarySearchTree` class is currently using the `find` and `contains` methods of the `LinkedBinaryTree` class. Implement these methods for the `LinkedBinarySearchTree` class so that they will be more efficient by making use of the ordering property of a binary search tree.

PP 20.3 Implement the `removeMax`, `findMin`, and `findMax` operations for our linked binary search tree implementation.

PP 20.4 Modify the linked implementation of a binary tree so that it will no longer allow duplicates.

PP 20.5 Implement a balance tree method for the linked implementation using the brute force method described in Section 20.4.

PP 20.6 Implement a balance tree method for the array implementation from Project 20.1 using the brute force method described in Section 20.4.

PP 20.7 Develop an array implementation of a binary search tree built upon an array implementation of a binary tree by using the simulated link strategy. Each element of the array will need to maintain both a reference to the data element stored there and the array positions of the left child and the right child. You also need to maintain a list of available array positions where elements have been removed, in order to reuse those positions.

PP 20.8 Modify the linked binary search tree implementation to make it an AVL tree.

PP 20.9 Modify the linked binary search tree implementation to make it a red/black tree.

PP 20.10 Modify the add operation for the linked implementation of a binary search tree to use an iterative algorithm.

Answers to Self-Review Questions

SRA 20.1 A binary search tree has the added ordering property that the left child of any node is less than the node, and the node is less than or equal to its right child.

SRA 20.2 With the added ordering property of a binary search tree, we are now able to define what the state of the tree should be after an `add` or `remove`. We were unable to define that state for a binary tree.

SRA 20.3 If the tree is balanced, finding the insertion point for the new element will take at worst log n steps, and since inserting the element is simply a matter of setting the value of one reference, the operation is O(log n).

SRA 20.4 Without the balance assumption, the worst case would be a degenerate tree, which is effectively a linked list. Therefore, the `addElement` operation would be O(n).

SRA 20.5 A degenerate tree will waste space with unused references, and many of the algorithms will check for null references before following the degenerate path, thus adding steps that the linked list implementation does not have.

SRA 20.6 The best choice is the inorder successor because we are placing equal values to the right.

SRA 20.7 With our balance assumption, the `contains` operation uses the `find` operation, which will be rewritten in the `BinarySearchTree` class to take advantage of the ordering property and will be O(log n). The `removeElement` operation is O(log n). The `while` loop will iterate some constant (k) number of times depending on how many times the given element occurs within the tree. The worst case would be that all n elements of the tree were the element to be removed, which would make the tree degenerate, and in which case the complexity would be n*2*n or $O(n^2)$. However, the expected case would be some small constant (0<=k<n) occurrences of the element in a balanced tree, which would result in a complexity of k*2*log n or O(log n).

SRA 20.8 In our earlier linked implementation of an ordered list, we had a reference that kept track of the first element in the list, which made it quite simple to remove it or return it. With a binary search tree, we have to traverse to get to the leftmost element before knowing that we have the first element in the ordered list.

SRA 20.9 Remember that the iterators for a binary tree are all followed by which traversal order to use. That is why the `iterator` method for the `BinarySearchTreeOrderedList` class calls the `iteratorInOrder` method of the `BinaryTree` class.

SRA 20.10 Keep in mind that an `addElement` method affects only one path of the tree, which in a balanced AVL tree has a maximum length of log n. As we have discussed previously, finding the position to insert and setting the reference is O(log n). We then have to progress back up the same path, updating the balance factors of each node (if necessary) and rotating if necessary. Updating the balance factors is an O(1) step and rotation is also an O(1) step. Each of these will have to be done at most log n times. Therefore, `addElement` has time complexity 2*log n or O(log n).

SRA 20.11 A single right rotation will fix the imbalance if the long path is in the left subtree of the left child of the root.

SRA 20.12 A leftright rotation will fix the imbalance if the long path is in the right subtree of the left child of the root.

SRA 20.13 The balance factor of an AVL tree node is the height of the right subtree minus the height of the left subtree.

SRA 20.14 Rebalancing an AVL tree is done after either an insertion or a deletion and it is done starting at the affected node and working up along a single path to the root. As we progress upward, we update the balance factors and rotate if necessary. We will never encounter a situation where both a child and a parent have balance factors of +/−2 because we would have already fixed the child before we ever reached the parent.

SRA 20.15 Because no red node can have a red child, then at most half of the nodes in a path could be red nodes and at least half of the nodes in a path are black. From this we can argue that the maximum height of a red/black tree is roughly 2*log n and thus the traversal of the longest path is O(log n).

References

Adel'son-Vel'skii, G. M., and E. M. Landis. "An Algorithm for the Organization of Information." *Soviet Mathematics* 3 (1962): 1259–1263.

Bayer, R. "Symmetric Binary B-trees: Data Structure and Maintenance Algorithms." *Acta Informatica* (1972): 290–306.

Collins, W. J. *Data Structures and the Java Collections Framework*. New York: McGraw-Hill, 2002.

Cormen, T., C. Leierson, and R. Rivest. *Introduction to Algorithms*. New York: McGraw-Hill, 1992.

Guibas, L., and R. Sedgewick. "A Diochromatic Framework for Balanced Trees." *Proceedings of the 19th Annual IEEE Symposium on Foundations of Computer Science* (1978): 8–21.

Heaps and Priority Queues

21

CHAPTER OBJECTIVES

- Define a heap abstract data structure.
- Demonstrate how a heap can be used to solve problems.
- Examine various heap implementations.
- Compare heap implementations.

In this chapter, we will look at another ordered extension of binary trees. We will examine heaps, including both linked and array implementations, and the algorithms for adding and removing elements from a heap. We will also examine some uses for heaps including the implementation of priority queues.

21.1 A Heap

A *heap* is a binary tree with two added properties:

- It is a complete tree, as described in Chapter 19.
- For each node, the node is less than or equal to both the left child and the right child.

KEY CONCEPT
A minheap is a complete binary tree in which each node is less than or equal to both of its children.

KEY CONCEPT
A minheap stores its smallest element at the root of the binary tree, and both children of the root of a minheap are also minheaps.

This definition describes a *minheap*. A heap can also be a *maxheap*, in which the node is greater than or equal to its children. We will focus our discussion in this chapter on minheaps. All of the same processes work for maxheaps by reversing the comparisons.

Figure 21.1 describes the operations on a heap. The heap is defined as an extension of a binary tree and thus inherits all of those operations as well. Note that because the implementation of a binary tree does not have any operations to add or remove elements from the tree, there are not any operations that would violate the properties of a heap. Listing 21.1 shows the interface definition for a heap. Figure 21.2 shows the UML description of the `HeapADT`.

Operation	Description
`addElement`	Adds the given element to the heap.
`removeMin`	Removes the minimum element in the heap.
`findMin`	Returns a reference to the minimum element in the heap.

FIGURE 21.1 The operations on a heap

LISTING 21.1

```
package jsjf;

/**
 * HeapADT defines the interface to a Heap.
 *
 * @author Java Foundations
 * @version 4.0
 */
public interface HeapADT<T> extends BinaryTreeADT<T>
{
    /**
     * Adds the specified object to this heap.
     *
```

LISTING 21.1 *continued*

```
     * @param obj the element to be added to the heap
     */
    public void addElement(T obj);

    /**
     * Removes element with the lowest value from this heap.
     *
     * @return the element with the lowest value from the heap
     */
    public T removeMin();

      /**
       * Returns a reference to the element with the lowest value in
       * this heap.
       *
       * @return a reference to the element with the lowest value in the heap
       */
    public T findMin();
}
```

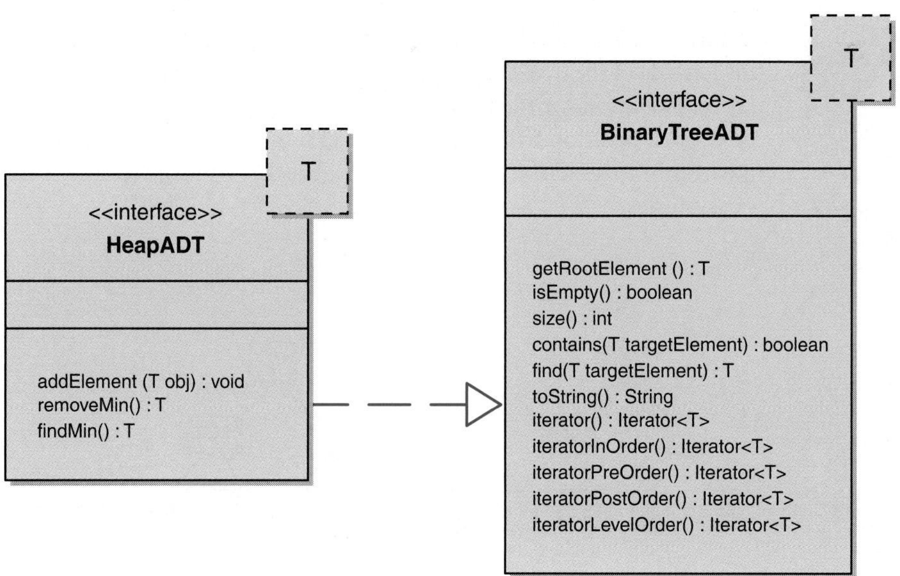

FIGURE 21.2 UML description of the `HeapADT`

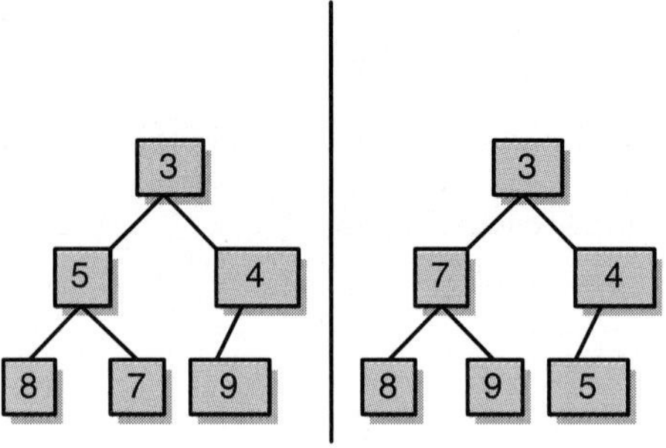

FIGURE 21.3 Two minheaps containing the same data

Simply put, a minheap will always store its smallest element at the root of the binary tree, and both children of the root of a minheap are also minheaps. Figure 21.3 illustrates two valid minheaps with the same data. Let's look at the basic operations on a heap and examine generic algorithms for each.

The `addElement` Operation

The `addElement` method adds a given element to the appropriate location in the heap, maintaining both the completeness property and the ordering property of the heap. This method throws a `ClassCastException` if the given element is not `Comparable`. A binary tree is considered *complete* if it is balanced, meaning that all of the leaves are at level h or h – 1, where h is $\log_2 n$ and n is the number of elements in the tree, and all of the leaves at level h are on the left side of the tree. Because a heap is a complete tree, there is only one correct location for the insertion of a new node, and that is either the next open position from the left at level h or, if level h is full, the first position on the left at level h + 1. Figure 21.4 illustrates these two possibilities.

> **KEY CONCEPT**
> The `addElement` method adds a given `Comparable` element to the appropriate location in the heap, maintaining both the completeness property and the ordering property of the heap.

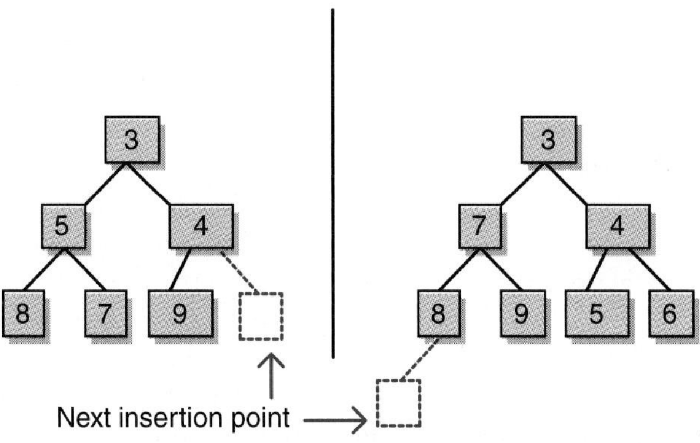

FIGURE 21.4 Insertion points for a heap

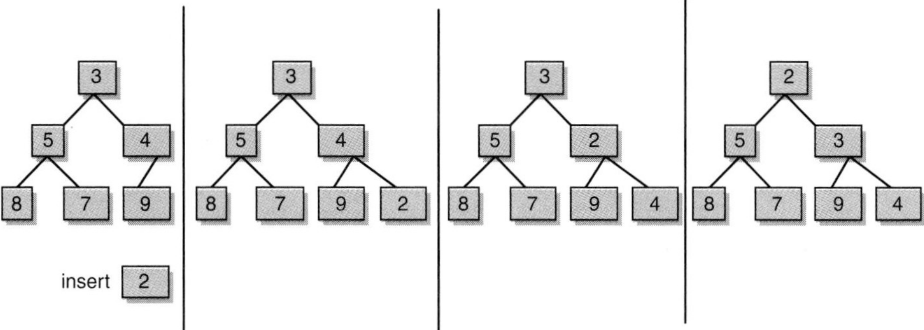

FIGURE 21.5 Insertion and reordering in a heap

Once we have located the new node in the proper position, we must account for the ordering property. To do this, we simply compare the new value to its parent value and swap the values if the new node is less than its parent. We continue this process up the tree until the new value either is greater than its parent or is in the root of the heap. Figure 21.5 illustrates this process for inserting a new element into a heap. Typically, in heap implementations, we keep track of the position of the last node or, more precisely, the last leaf in the tree. After an `addElement` operation, the last node is set to the node that was inserted.

> **KEY CONCEPT**
> Because a heap is a complete tree, there is only one correct location for the insertion of a new node, and that is either the next open position from the left at level h or, if level h is full, the first position on the left at level h + 1.

The `removeMin` Operation

The `removeMin` method removes the minimum element from the minheap and returns it. Because the minimum element is stored in the root of a minheap, we need to return the element stored at the root and replace it with another element in the heap. As with the `addElement` operation, to maintain the completeness of the tree, there is only one valid element to replace the root, and that is the element stored in the last leaf in the tree. This last leaf will be the rightmost leaf at level h of the tree. Figure 21.6 illustrates this concept of the last leaf under a variety of circumstances.

> **KEY CONCEPT**
> Typically, in heap implementations, we keep track of the position of the last node or, more precisely, the last leaf in the tree.

Once the element stored in the last leaf has been moved to the root, the heap will then have to be reordered to maintain the heap's ordering property. This is accomplished by comparing the new root element to the smaller of its children and then swapping them if the child is smaller. This process is repeated on down the tree until the element either is in a leaf or is less than both of its children. Figure 21.7 illustrates the process of removing the minimum element and then reordering the tree.

> **KEY CONCEPT**
> To maintain the completeness of the tree, there is only one valid element to replace the root, and that is the element stored in the last leaf in the tree.

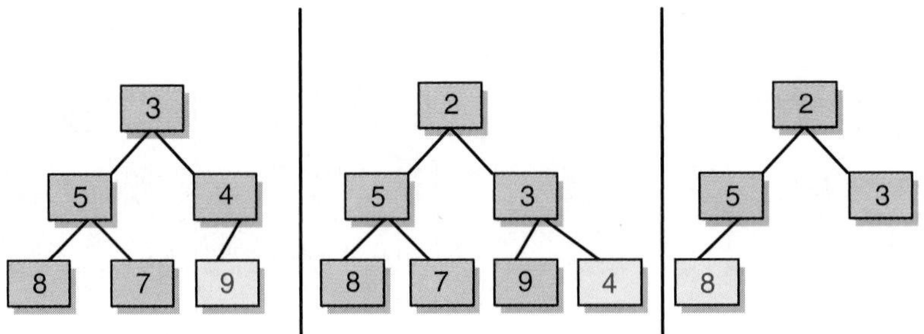

FIGURE 21.6 Examples of the last leaf in a heap

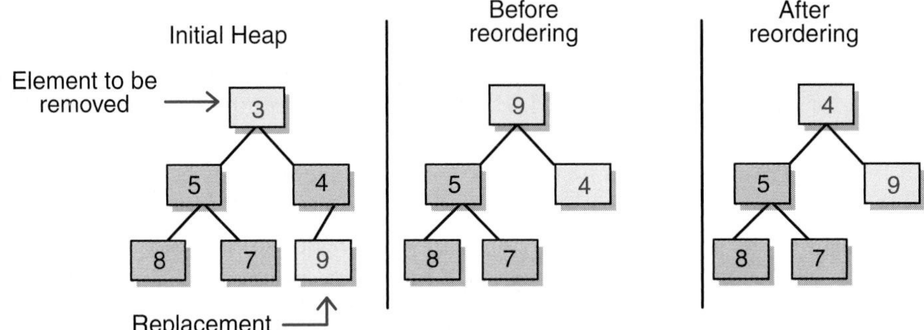

FIGURE 21.7 Removal and reordering in a heap

The `findMin` Operation

The `findMin` method returns a reference to the smallest element in the minheap. Because that element is always stored in the root of the tree, this method is simply implemented by returning the element stored in the root.

21.2 Using Heaps: Priority Queues

A *priority queue* is a collection that follows two ordering rules. First, items with higher priority go first. Second, items with the same priority are ordered in accordance with the first in, first out principle. Priority queues have a variety of applications (such as task scheduling in an operating system, traffic scheduling on a network, and even job scheduling at your local auto mechanic).

A priority queue could be implemented using a list of queues where each queue represents items of a given priority. Another solution to this problem is to use a minheap. Sorting the heap by priority accomplishes the first ordering (higher-priority items go first). However, the first in, first out ordering of items with the same priority is something we will have to manipulate. The solution is to create a `PrioritizedObject` object that stores the element to be placed on the queue, the priority of the element, and the order in which elements are placed on the queue. Then, we simply define the `compareTo` method for the `PrioritizedObject` class to compare priorities first and then compare order if there is a tie. Listing 21.2 shows the `PrioritizedObject` class, and Listing 21.3 shows the `PriorityQueue` class. The UML description of the `PriorityQueue` class is left as an exercise.

KEY CONCEPT
Even though it is not a queue at all, a minheap provides an efficient implementation of a priority queue.

LISTING 21.2

```
/**
 * PrioritizedObject represents a node in a priority queue containing a
 * comparable object, arrival order, and a priority value.
 *
 * @author Java Foundations
 * @version 4.0
 */
public class PrioritizedObject<T> implements Comparable<PrioritizedObject>
{
   private static int nextOrder = 0;
   private int priority;
   private int arrivalOrder;
   private T element;

  /**
   * Creates a new PrioritizedObject with the specified data.
   *
   * @param element the element of the new priority queue node
   * @param priority the priority of the new queue node
   */
  public PrioritizedObject(T element, int priority)
  {
     this.element = element;
     this.priority = priority;
     arrivalOrder = nextOrder;
     nextOrder++;
  }

  /**
   * Returns the element in this node.
   *
   * @return the element contained within the node
   */
  public T getElement()
```

LISTING 21.2 *continued*

```
{
   return element;
}

/**
 * Returns the priority value for this node.
 *
 * @return the integer priority for this node
 */
public int getPriority()
{
   return priority;
}

/**
 * Returns the arrival order for this node.
 *
 * @return the integer arrival order for this node
 */
public int getArrivalOrder()
{
   return arrivalOrder;
}

/**
 * Returns a string representation for this node.
 *
 */
public String toString()
{
   return (element + "  " + priority + "  " + arrivalOrder);
}

/**
 * Returns 1 if the this object has higher priority than
 * the given object and -1 otherwise.
 *
 * @param obj the object to compare to this node
 * @return the result of the comparison of the given object and
 *     this one
 */
public int compareTo(PrioritizedObject obj)
```

LISTING 21.2 *continued*

```
   {
      int result;
      if (priority > obj.getPriority())
         result = 1;
      else if (priority < obj.getPriority())
         result = -1;
      else if (arrivalOrder > obj.getArrivalOrder())
         result = 1;
      else
         result = -1;
      return result;
   }
}
```

LISTING 21.3

```
import jsjf.*;

/**
 * PriorityQueue implements a priority queue using a heap.
 *
 * @author Java Foundations
 * @version 4.0
 */
public class PriorityQueue<T> extends ArrayHeap<PrioritizedObject<T>>
{
   /**
    * Creates an empty priority queue.
    */
   public PriorityQueue()
   {
      super();
   }

   /**
    * Adds the given element to this PriorityQueue.
    *
    * @param object the element to be added to the priority queue
    * @param priority the integer priority of the element to be added
    */
   public void addElement(T object, int priority)
```

LISTING 21.3 *continued*

```
   {
      PrioritizedObject<T> obj = new PrioritizedObject<T>(object, priority);
      super.addElement(obj);
   }

   /**
    * Removes the next highest priority element from this priority
    * queue and returns a reference to it.
    *
    * @return a reference to the next highest priority element in this queue
    */
   public T removeNext()
   {
      PrioritizedObject<T> obj = (PrioritizedObject<T>)super.removeMin();
      return obj.getElement();
   }
}
```

21.3 Implementing Heaps: With Links

All of our implementations of trees thus far have been illustrated using links. Thus it is natural to extend that discussion to a linked implementation of a heap. Because of the requirement that we be able to traverse up the tree after an insertion, it is necessary for the nodes in a heap to store a pointer to their parent. Because our `BinaryTreeNode` class did not have a parent pointer, we start our linked implementation by creating a `HeapNode` class that extends our `BinaryTreeNode` class and adds a parent pointer. Listing 21.4 shows the `HeapNode` class.

KEY CONCEPT
Because of the requirement that we be able to traverse up the tree after an insertion, it is necessary for the nodes in a heap to store a pointer to their parent.

The additional instance data for a linked implementation will consist of a single reference to a `HeapNode` called `lastNode` so that we can keep track of the last leaf in the heap:

```
public HeapNode lastNode;
```

The `addElement` Operation

The `addElement` method must accomplish three tasks: add the new node at the appropriate location, reorder the heap to maintain the ordering property, and then reset the `lastNode` pointer to point to the new last node.

LISTING 21.4

```
package jsjf;

/**
 * HeapNode represents a binary tree node with a parent pointer for use
 * in heaps.
 *
 * @author Java Foundations
 * @version 4.0
 */
public class HeapNode<T> extends BinaryTreeNode<T>
{
   protected HeapNode<T> parent;

  /**
   * Creates a new heap node with the specified data.
   *
   * @param obj the data to be contained within the new heap node
   */
  public HeapNode(T obj)
  {
     super(obj);
     parent = null;
  }

  /**
   * Return the parent of this node.
   *
   * @return the parent of the node
   */
  public HeapNode<T> getParent()
  {
     return parent;
  }

  /**
   * Sets the element stored at this node.
   *
   * @param the element to be stored
   */
  public void setElement(T obj)
  {
     element = obj;
  }
```

LISTING 21.4 *continued*

```
  /**
   * Sets the parent of this node.
   *
   * @param node the parent of the node
   */
  public void setParent(HeapNode<T> node)
  {
    parent = node;
  }
}
```

```
  /**
   * Adds the specified element to this heap in the appropriate
   * position according to its key value.
   *
   * @param obj the element to be added to the heap
   */
  public void addElement(T obj)
  {
    HeapNode<T> node = new HeapNode<T>(obj);

    if (root == null)
        root=node;
      else
      {
        HeapNode<T> nextParent = getNextParentAdd();
        if (nextParent.getLeft() == null)
            nextParent.setLeft(node);
        else
            nextParent.setRight(node);

        node.setParent(nextParent);
      }
      lastNode = node;
      modCount++;
      if (size() > 1)
        heapifyAdd();
   }
```

This method also uses two private methods: `getNextParentAdd`, which returns a reference to the node that will be the parent of the node to be inserted, and `heapifyAdd`, which accomplishes any necessary reordering of the heap starting with the new leaf and working up toward the root. Both of those methods are shown below.

```
/**
 * Returns the node that will be the parent of the new node
 *
 * @return the node that will be the parent of the new node
 */
private HeapNode<T> getNextParentAdd()
{
   HeapNode<T> result = lastNode;

   while ((result != root) && (result.getParent().getLeft() != result))
        result = result.getParent();

   if (result != root)
        if (result.getParent().getRight() == null)
            result = result.getParent();
        else
        {
           result = (HeapNode<T>)result.getParent().getRight();
           while (result.getLeft() != null)
               result = (HeapNode<T>)result.getLeft();
        }
   else
        while (result.getLeft() != null)
            result = (HeapNode<T>)result.getLeft();

   return result;
}
```

```
/**
 * Reorders this heap after adding a node.
 */
private void heapifyAdd()
{
   T temp;
   HeapNode<T> next = lastNode;
   temp = next.getElement();
   while ((next != root) &&
        (((Comparable)temp).compareTo(next.getParent().getElement()) < 0))
```

```
    {
       next.setElement(next.getParent().getElement());
       next = next.parent;
    }
    next.setElement(temp);
}
```

In this linked implementation, the first step in the process of adding an element is to determine the parent of the node to be inserted. Because, in the worst case, this involves traversing from the bottom-right node of the heap up to the root and then down to the bottom-left node of the heap, this step has time complexity 2 × log n. The next step is to insert the new node. Because it involves only simple assignment statements, this step has constant time complexity (O(1)). The last step is to reorder the path from the inserted leaf to the root if necessary. This process involves at most log n comparisons because that is the length of the path. Thus the `addElement` operation for the linked implementation has time complexity 2 × log n + 1 + log n or O(log n).

Note that the `heapifyAdd` method does not perform a full swap of parent and child as it moves up the heap. Instead, it simply shifts parent elements down until a proper insertion point is found and then assigns the new value into that location. This does not actually improve the O() of the algorithm, because it would be O(log n) even if we were performing full swaps. However, it does improve the efficiency, because it reduces the number of assignments performed at each level of the heap.

The `removeMin` Operation

The `removeMin` method must accomplish three tasks: replace the element stored in the root with the element stored in the last node, reorder the heap if necessary, and return the original root element. Like the `addElement` method, the `removeMin` method uses two additional methods: `getNewLastNode`, which returns a reference to the node that will be the new last node, and `heapifyRemove`, which accomplishes any necessary reordering of the tree starting from the root down. All three of these methods are shown below.

```
/**
 * Remove the element with the lowest value in this heap and
 * returns a reference to it. Throws an EmptyCollectionException
 * if the heap is empty.
 *
 * @return the element with the lowest value in this heap
 * @throws EmptyCollectionException if the heap is empty
 */
```

```
public T removeMin() throws EmptyCollectionException
 {
   if (isEmpty())
       throw new EmptyCollectionException("LinkedHeap");
   T minElement = root.getElement();
   if (size() == 1)
   {
      root = null;
      lastNode = null;
   }
   else
   {
      HeapNode<T> nextLast = getNewLastNode();
      if (lastNode.getParent().getLeft() == lastNode)
          lastNode.getParent().setLeft(null);
      else
          lastNode.getParent().setRight(null);

      ((HeapNode<T>)root).setElement(lastNode.getElement());
      lastNode = nextLast;
      heapifyRemove();
   }
   modCount++;

   return minElement;
 }
```

```
/**
 * Returns the node that will be the new last node after a remove.
 *
 * @return the node that willbe the new last node after a remove
 */
private HeapNode<T> getNewLastNode()
{
   HeapNode<T> result = lastNode;

   while ((result != root) && (result.getParent().getLeft() == result))
       result = result.getParent();

   if (result != root)
       result = (HeapNode<T>)result.getParent().getLeft();

   while (result.getRight() != null)
       result = (HeapNode<T>)result.getRight();

   return result;
}
```

```
/**
 * Reorders this heap after removing the root element.
 */
private void heapifyRemove()
{
   T temp;
   HeapNode<T> node = (HeapNode<T>)root;
   HeapNode<T> left = (HeapNode<T>)node.getLeft();
   HeapNode<T> right = (HeapNode<T>)node.getRight();
   HeapNode<T> next;

   if ((left == null) && (right == null))
         next = null;
   else if (right == null)
         next = left;
   else if (((Comparable)left.getElement()).compareTo(right.getElement()) < 0)
         next = left;
   else
         next = right;

   temp = node.getElement();
   while ((next != null) &&
                     (((Comparable)next.getElement()).compareTo(temp) < 0))
   {
      node.setElement(next.getElement());
      node = next;
      left = (HeapNode<T>)node.getLeft();
      right = (HeapNode<T>)node.getRight();

      if ((left == null) && (right == null))
          next = null;
      else if (right == null)
          next = left;
      else if (((Comparable)left.getElement()).compareTo(right.getElement()) < 0)
          next = left;
      else
          next = right;
   }
      node.setElement(temp);
 }
```

The `removeMin` method for the linked implementation must remove the root element and replace it with the element from the last node. Because this is simply assignment statements, this step has time complexity 1. Next, this method must reorder the heap, if necessary, from the root down to a leaf. Because the maximum path length from the root to a leaf is log n, this step has time complexity log n. Finally, we must determine the new last node. Like the process for determining the next parent node for the `addElement` method, the worst case is that we must traverse from a leaf through the root and down to another leaf. Thus the time complexity of this step is 2*log n. The resulting time complexity of the `removeMin` operation is 2*log n + log n + 1 or O(log n).

The `findMin` Operation

The `findMin` method simply returns a reference to the element stored at the root of the heap and therefore is O(1).

21.4 Implementing Heaps: With Arrays

To this point, we have focused our discussion of the implementation of trees around linked structures. If you recall, however, in Chapter 19 we discussed a couple of different array implementation strategies for trees: the computational strategy and the simulated link strategy. An array implementation of a heap may provide a simpler alternative than our linked implementation. Many of the intricacies of the linked implementation are related to the need to traverse up and down the tree to determine the last leaf of the tree or to determine the parent of the next node to insert. Many of those difficulties do not exist in the array implementation because we are able to determine the last node in the tree by looking at the last element stored in the array.

KEY CONCEPT

In an array implementation of a binary tree, the root of the tree is in position 0, and for each node n, n's left child is in position 2n + 1, and n's right child is in position 2(n + 1).

As we discussed in Chapter 10, a simple array implementation of a binary tree can be created using the notion that the root of the tree is in position 0, and that for each node n, n's left child will be in position 2n+1 of the array and n's right child will be in position 2(n + 1) of the array. Of course, the inverse is also true. For any node n other than the root, n's parent is in position (n – 1)/2. Because of our ability to calculate the location of both parent and child, the array implementation (unlike the linked implementation) does not require the creation of a `HeapNode` class. The UML description of the array implementation of a heap is left as an exercise.

Just as the `LinkedHeap` class extends the `LinkedBinaryTree` class, the `ArrayHeap` class will extend the `ArrayBinaryTree` class. The class header, attributes and constructors for both classes are provided for context.

```
package jsjf;

import java.util.*;
import jsjf.exceptions.*;

/**
 * ArrayBinaryTree implements the BinaryTreeADT interface using an array
 *
 * @author Java Foundations
 * @version 4.0
 */
public class ArrayBinaryTree<T> implements BinaryTreeADT<T>, Iterable<T>
{
    private static final int DEFAULT_CAPACITY = 50;

    protected int count;
    protected T[] tree;
    protected int modCount;

   /**
     * Creates an empty binary tree.
     */
   public ArrayBinaryTree()
   {
      count = 0;
      tree = (T[]) new Object[DEFAULT_CAPACITY];
   }

   /**
     * Creates a binary tree with the specified element as its root.
     *
     * @param element the element which will become the root of the new tree
     */
   public ArrayBinaryTree(T element)
   {
      count = 1;
      tree = (T[]) new Object[DEFAULT_CAPACITY];
      tree[0] = element;
   }
```

```
package jsjf;
import jsjf.exceptions.*;

/**
 * ArrayHeap provides an array implementation of a minheap.
 *
 * @author Java Foundations
 * @version 4.0
 */
public class ArrayHeap<T> extends ArrayBinaryTree<T> implements HeapADT<T>
{
   /**
    * Creates an empty heap.
    */
    public ArrayHeap()
    {
       super();
    }
```

The `addElement` Operation

The `addElement` method for the array implementation must accomplish three tasks: add the new node at the appropriate location, reorder the heap to maintain the ordering property, and increment the count by one. Of course, as with all of our array implementations, the method must first check for available space and expand the capacity of the array if necessary. Like the linked implementation, the `addElement` operation of the array implementation uses a private method called heapifyAdd to reorder the heap if necessary.

```
   /**
    * Adds the specified element to this heap in the appropriate
    * position according to its key value.
    *
    * @param obj the element to be added to the heap
    */
   public void addElement(T obj)
   {
      if (count == tree.length)
         expandCapacity();

      tree[count] = obj;
```

```
        count++;
        modCount++;

        if (count > 1)
            heapifyAdd();
    }
```

```
    /**
     * Reorders this heap to maintain the ordering property after
     * adding a node.
     */
    private void heapifyAdd()
    {
        T temp;
        int next = count - 1;

        temp = tree[next];

        while ((next != 0) &&
            (((Comparable)temp).compareTo(tree[(next-1)/2]) < 0))
        {
            tree[next] = tree[(next-1)/2];
            next = (next-1)/2;
        }
        tree[next] = temp;
    }
```

KEY CONCEPT
The `addElement` operation for both the linked implementation and the array implementation is O(log n).

Unlike the linked implementation, the array implementation does not require the first step of determining the parent of the new node. However, both of the other steps are the same as those for the linked implementation. Thus the time complexity for the `addElement` operation for the array implementation is 1 + log n or O(log n). Granted, the two implementations have the same Order( ), but the array implementation is more efficient and more elegant.

The `removeMin` Operation

The `removeMin` method must accomplish three tasks: replace the element stored in the root with the element stored in the last element, reorder the heap if necessary, and return the original root element. In the case of the array implementation, we know the last element of the heap is stored in position `count1` of the array. We then use a private method heapifyRemove to reorder the heap as necessary.

```
/**
 * Remove the element with the lowest value in this heap and
 * returns a reference to it. Throws an EmptyCollectionException if
 * the heap is empty.
 *
 * @return a reference to the element with the lowest value in this heap
 * @throws EmptyCollectionException if the heap is empty
 */
public T removeMin() throws EmptyCollectionException
{
   if (isEmpty())
       throw new EmptyCollectionException("ArrayHeap");

   T minElement = tree[0];
   tree[0] = tree[count-1];
   heapifyRemove();
   count--;
   modCount--;

   return minElement;
}
```

```
/**
 * Reorders this heap to maintain the ordering property
 * after the minimum element has been removed.
 */
private void heapifyRemove()
{
   T temp;
   int node = 0;
   int left = 1;
   int right = 2;
   int next;

   if ((tree[left] == null) && (tree[right] == null))
       next = count;
   else if (tree[right] == null)
       next = left;
   else if (((Comparable)tree[left]).compareTo(tree[right]) < 0)
       next = left;
   else
```

```
            next = right;
        temp = tree[node];

        while ((next < count) &&
            (((Comparable)tree[next]).compareTo(temp) < 0))
        {
            tree[node] = tree[next];
            node = next;
            left = 2 * node + 1;
            right = 2 * (node + 1);
            if ((tree[left] == null) && (tree[right] == null))
                next = count;
            else if (tree[right] == null)
                next = left;
            else if (((Comparable)tree[left]).compareTo(tree[right]) < 0)
                next = left;
            else
                next = right;
        }
        tree[node] = temp;
    }
```

KEY CONCEPT
The `removeMin` operation for both the linked implementation and the array implementation is O(log n).

Like the `addElement` method, the array implementation of the `removeMin` operation looks just like the linked implementation except that it does not have to determine the new last node. Thus the resulting time complexity is log n + 1 or O(log n).

The `findMin` Operation

Like the linked implementation, the `findMin` method simply returns a reference to the element stored at the root of the heap or position 0 of the array and therefore is O(1).

21.5 Using Heaps: Heap Sort

Now that we have examined an array implementation of a heap, lets consider another way we might use it. In Chapter 18, we introduced a variety of sorting techniques, some of which were sequential sorts (bubble sort, selection sort, and insertion sort) and some of which were logarithmic sorts (merge sort and quick sort). In that chapter, we also introduced a queue-based sort called a radix sort. Given the ordering property of a heap, it is natural to think of using a heap to sort a list of numbers. A brute force approach to a heap sort would be to add each of the elements of the list to a heap and then remove them one at a time from the root. In the case of a minheap, the result will be the list in ascending order. In the case of a maxheap, the result will be the list in descending order. Because both the `add` operation and the `remove` operation are O(log n), it might be tempting to conclude that a heap sort is also O(log n). However, keep in mind that those operations are O(log n) to add or remove a single element in a list of n elements. Insertion into a heap is O(log n) for any given node and thus would be O(n log n) for n nodes. Removal is also O(log n) for a single node and thus O(n log n) for n nodes. With the heap sort algorithm, we are performing both operations, `addElement` and `removeMin`, n times, once for each of the elements in the list. Therefore, the resulting time complexity is 2 × n log n × or O(n log n).

KEY CONCEPT
The heapSort method consists of adding each of the elements of the list to a heap and then removing them one at a time.

It is also possible to "build" a heap in place using the array to be sorted. Because we know the relative position of each parent and child in the heap, we can simply start with the first non-leaf node in the array, compare it to its children, and swap if necessary. We then work backward in the array until we reach the root. Because, at most, this will require us to make two comparisons for each non-leaf node, this approach is O(n) to build the heap. However, with this approach, removing each element from the heap and maintaining the properties of the heap would still be O(n log n). Thus, even though this approach is slightly more efficient, roughly 2 × n + n log n, it is still O(n log n). The implementation of this approach is left as an exercise. The `heapSort` method could be added to our class of sort methods described in Chapter 18. Listing 21.5 illustrates how it might be created as a standalone class.

VideoNote
Demonstration of a heap sort on an array

KEY CONCEPT
Heap sort is O(n log n).

LISTING 21.5

```
package jsjf;

/**
 * HeapSort sorts a given array of Comparable objects using a heap.
 *
 * @author Java Foundations
 * @version 4.0
 */
public class HeapSort<T>
```

LISTING 21.5 *continued*

```
{
  /**
   * Sorts the specified array using a Heap
   *
   * @param data the data to be added to the heapsort
   */
  public void HeapSort(T[]data)
  {
     ArrayHeap<T> temp = new ArrayHeap<T>();

     // copy the array into a heap

     for (int i = 0; i < data.length; i++)
         temp.addElement(data[i]);

     // place the sorted elements back into the array

     int count = 0;
     while (!(temp.isEmpty()))
     {
        data[count] = temp.removeMin();
        count++;
     }
  }
}
```

Summary of Key Concepts

- A minheap is a complete binary tree in which each node is less than or equal to both the left child and the right child.
- A minheap stores its smallest element at the root of the binary tree, and both children of the root of a minheap are also minheaps.
- The `addElement` method adds a given `Comparable` element to the appropriate location in the heap, maintaining both the completeness property and the ordering property of the heap.
- Because a heap is a complete tree, there is only one correct location for the insertion of a new node, and that is either the next open position from the left at level h or, if level h is full, the first position on the left at level h + 1.
- Typically, in heap implementations, we keep track of the position of the last node or, more precisely, the last leaf in the tree.
- To maintain the completeness of the tree, there is only one valid element to replace the root, and that is the element stored in the last leaf in the tree.
- Even though it is not a queue at all, a minheap provides an efficient implementation of a priority queue.
- Because of the requirement that we be able to traverse up the tree after an insertion, it is necessary for the nodes in a heap to store a pointer to their parent.
- In an array implementation of a binary tree, the root of the tree is in position 0, and for each node n, n's left child is in position 2n + 1 and n's right child is in position 2(n + 1).
- The `addElement` operation for both the linked implementation and the array implementation is O(log n).
- The `removeMin` operation for both the linked implementation and the array implementation is O(log n).
- The `heapSort` method consists of adding each of the elements of the list to a heap and then removing them one at a time.
- Heap sort is O(n log n).

Summary of Terms

heap A binary tree that is complete and is either a minheap or a maxheap.

minheap A binary tree with two added properties: It is a complete tree and for each node, the node is less than or equal to both the left child and the right child.

maxheap A binary tree with two added properties: It is a complete tree and for each node, the node is greater than or equal to both the left child and the right child.

complete A balanced tree in which all of the leaves at level h (the lowest level of the tree) on the left side of the tree.

priority queue A collection that follows two ordering rules: Items with higher priority go first, and items with the same priority are ordered in accordance with the first in, first out principle.

Self-Review Questions

SR 21.1 What is the difference between a heap (a minheap) and a binary search tree?

SR 21.2 What is the difference between a minheap and a maxheap?

SR 21.3 What does it mean for a binary tree to be complete?

SR 21.4 Does a heap ever have to be rebalanced?

SR 21.5 The `addElement` operation for the linked implementation must determine the parent of the next node to be inserted. Why?

SR 21.6 Why does the `addElement` operation for the array implementation not have to determine the parent of the next node to be inserted?

SR 21.7 The `removeMin` operation for both implementations replaces the element at the root with the element in the last leaf of the heap. Why is this the proper replacement?

SR 21.8 What is the time complexity of the `addElement` operation?

SR 21.9 What is the time complexity of the `removeMin` operation?

SR 21.10 What is the time complexity of heap sort?

Exercises

EX 21.1 Draw the heap that results from adding the following integers (34 45 3 87 65 32 1 12 17).

EX 21.2 Starting with the tree resulting from Exercise 21.1, draw the heap that results from performing a `removeMin` operation.

EX 21.3 Starting with an empty minheap, draw the heap after each of the following operations.

```
addElement(40);
addElement(25):
```

```
removeMin();
addElement(10);
removeMin();
addElement(5);
addElement(1);
removeMin();
addElement(45);
addElement(50);
```

EX 21.4 Repeat Exercise 21.3, this time with a maxheap.

EX 21.5 Draw the UML description for the `PriorityQueue` class described in this chapter.

EX 21.6 Draw the UML description for the array implementation of heap described in this chapter.

Programming Projects

PP 21.1 Implement a queue using a heap. Keep in mind that a queue is a first in, first out structure. Thus the comparison in the heap will have to be according to order entry into the queue.

PP 21.2 Implement a stack using a heap. Keep in mind that a stack is a last in, first out structure. Thus the comparison in the heap will have to be according to order entry into the queue.

PP 21.3 Implement a maxheap using an array implementation.

PP 21.4 Implement a maxheap using a linked implementation.

PP 21.5 As described in Section 21.5, it is possible to make the heap sort algorithm more efficient by writing a method that will build a heap in place using the array to be sorted. Implement such a method, and rewrite the heap sort algorithm to make use of it.

PP 21.6 Use a heap to implement a simulator for a process scheduling system. In this system, jobs will be read from a file consisting of the job id (a six-character string), the length of the job (an `int` representing seconds), and the priority of the job (an `int` where the higher the number the higher the priority). Each job will also be assigned an arrival number (an `int` representing the order of its arrival). The simulation should output the job id, the priority, the length of the job, and the completion time (relative to a simulation start time of 0).

PP 21.7 Create a birthday reminder system using a minheap such that the ordering on the heap is done each day according to days remaining until the individual's birthday. Keep in mind that when a birthday passes, the heap must be reordered.

PP 21.8 Complete the implementation of an `ArrayHeap` including the `ArrayBinaryTree` class that the `ArrayHeap` extends.

PP 21.9 Complete the implementation of the `LinkedHeap` class.

Answers to Self-Review Questions

SRA 21.1 A binary search tree has the ordering property that the left child of any node is less than the node, and the node is less than or equal to its right child. A minheap is complete and has the ordering property that the node is less than both of its children.

SRA 21.2 A minheap has the ordering property that the node is less than both of its children. A maxheap has the ordering property that the node is greater than both of its children.

SRA 21.3 A binary tree is considered complete if it is balanced, which means that all of the leaves are at level h or h – 1, where h is $\log_2 n$ and n is the number of elements in the tree, and all of the leaves at level h are on the left side of the tree.

SRA 21.4 No. By definition, a complete heap is balanced and the algorithms for `add` and `remove` maintain that balance.

SRA 21.5 The `addElement` operation must determine the parent of the node to be inserted so that a child pointer of that node can be set to the new node.

SRA 21.6 The `addElement` operation for the array implementation does not have to determine the parent of the new node because the new element is inserted in position `count` of the array and its parent is determined by position in the array.

SRA 21.7 To maintain the completeness of the tree, the only valid replacement for the element at the root is the element at the last leaf. Then the heap must be reordered as necessary to maintain the ordering property.

SRA 21.8 For both implementations, the `addElement` operation is O(log n). However, despite having the same order, the array implementation is somewhat more efficient because it does not have to determine the parent of the node to be inserted.

SRA 21.9 For both implementations, the `removeMin` operation is O(log n). However, despite having the same order, the array implementation is somewhat more efficient because it does not have to determine the new last leaf.

SRA 21.10 The heap sort algorithm is O(n log n).

Sets and Maps

22

CHAPTER OBJECTIVES

- Introduce the Java set and map collections.
- Explore the use of sets and maps to solve problems.
- Introduce the concept of hashing.
- Discuss how the Java API implements sets and maps.

This chapter introduces the Java concepts of sets and maps. We will explore these collections and compare and contrast them with our previous implementations. We will also introduce the concept of hashing.

22.1 Set and Map Collections

A *set* can be defined as a collection of elements with no duplicates. You should not assume that there is any particular positional relationship among the elements of a set.

For the most part, set collections in Java can be thought of in the mathematical sense of a set. They represent a collection of unique elements that can be used to determine the relationship of an element to the set. That is, the primary purpose of a set is to determine whether a particular element is a member of the set or not.

KEY CONCEPT
A set is a unique collection of objects generally used to determine whether a particular element is a member of the set.

Of course, other collections (such as a list) have the ability to test for containment. However, if such tests are an important part of a program, you should consider using sets. The implementation of a set is explicitly designed to be efficient when searching for an element.

A *map* is a collection that establishes a relationship between keys and values, providing an efficient way to retrieve a value given its key. The keys of a map must be unique, and each key can map to only one value. For example, you could use a unique membership id (a `String`) to retrieve the information about that member of a club (a `Member` object).

It doesn't have to be a one-to-one mapping, however. Multiple keys could map to the same object. For example, in a situation where information about a topic is being looked up, multiple keywords can map to the same topic entry. The key "gardening" and the key "mulch beds" and the key "flowers" could all map to the `Topic` object describing gardening, for instance.

KEY CONCEPT
A map is a collection of objects that can be retrieved using a unique key.

The keys of a map don't have to be character strings, although they often are. Both the keys and the values of a map can be any type of object.

VideoNote
A comparison of sets and maps

Like that of a set, a map's implementation is specifically designed to provide efficient lookup. In fact, as we'll see in more detail later in this chapter, the set and map classes defined in the Java API are implemented using similar underlying techniques.

22.2 Sets and Maps in the Java API

The Java API defines interfaces called `Set` and `Map` to define the public interaction available for these types of collections. In the remainder of this chapter, we'll explore the interfaces for these classes, use them to solve some problems, and then discuss the underlying implementation strategies.

The operations of the `Set` interface are listed in Figure 22.1. Like other collections, a set has operations that allow the user to add elements, remove elements, and to check whether a particular element is in the collection. Some operations such as `isEmpty` and `size` are common to nearly all collections as well. The `contains` and `containsAll` methods perform the key operations of determining whether the set contains particular elements.

Method Summary	
`boolean`	`add(E e)` Adds the specified element to this set if it is not already present (optional operation).
`boolean`	`addAll(Collection<? extends E> c)` Adds all of the elements in the specified collection to this set if they are not already present (optional operation).
`void`	`clear()` Removes all of the elements from this set (optional operation).
`boolean`	`contains(Object o)` Returns `true` if this set contains the specified element.
`boolean`	`containsAll(Collection<?> c)` Returns `true` if this set contains all of the elements of the specified collection.
`boolean`	`equals(Object o)` Compares the specified object with this set for equality.
`int`	`hashCode()` Returns the hash code value for this set.
`boolean`	`isEmpty()` Returns `true` if this set contains no elements.
`Iterator`	`iterator()` Returns an iterator over the elements in this set.
`boolean`	`remove(Object o)` Removes the specified element from this set if it is present (optional operation).
`boolean`	`removeAll(Collection<?> c)` Removes from this set all of its elements that are contained in the specified collection (optional operation).
`boolean`	`retainAll(Collection<?> c)` Retains only the elements in this set that are contained in the specified collection (optional operation).
`int`	`size()` Returns the number of elements in this set (its cardinality).

Method Summary *(continued)*	
`Object[]`	`toArray()` Returns an array containing all of the elements in this set.
`<T> T[]`	`toArray(T[] a)` Returns an array containing all of the elements in this set; the run-time type of the returned array is that of the specified array.

FIGURE 22.1 The operations in the `Set` interface

Like most collections, the elements of a `set` are defined using a generic type parameter (E in this case). The only objects that can be added to a set are those that are type compatible with the generic type established when a set object is instantiated.

Figure 22.2 illustrates the operations in the `Map` interface. Elements are added to a map using the `put` operation, which accepts both the key object and its corresponding value as parameters. A particular element is retrieved from the map using the `get` operation, which accepts the key object as a parameter.

Method Summary	
`void`	`clear()` Removes all of the mappings from this map (optional operation).
`boolean`	`containsKey(Object key)` Returns `true` if this map contains a mapping for the specified key.
`boolean`	`containsValue(Object value)` Returns `true` if this map maps one or more keys to the specified value.
`Set<Map.Entry<K,V>>`	`entrySet()` Returns a `Set` view of the mappings contained in this map.
`boolean`	`equals(Object o)` Compares the specified object with this map for equality.
`V`	`get(Object key)` Returns the value to which the specified key is mapped, or `null` if this map contains no mapping for the key.
`int`	`hashCode()` Returns the hash code value for this map.
`boolean`	`isEmpty()` Returns `true` if this map contains no key-value mappings.
`Set<K>`	`keySet()` Returns a `Set` view of the keys contained in this map.

Method Summary (continued)	
V	`put(K key, V value)` Associates the specified value with the specified key in this map (optional operation).
void	`putAll(Map<? extends K,? extends V> m)` Copies all of the mappings from the specified map to this map (optional operation).
V	`remove(Object key)` Removes the mapping for a key from this map if it is present (optional operation).
int	`size()` Returns the number of key-value mappings in this map.
Collection<V>	`values()` Returns a Collection view of the values contained in this map.

FIGURE 22.2 The operations in the `Map` interface

The Map interface has two generic type parameters, one for the key (K) and one for the value (V). When a class implementing a Map is instantiated, both types are established for that particular map, and all subsequent operations work in terms of those types.

The Java API provides two implementation classes for each interface: `TreeSet` and `HashSet` are two implementations of the `Set` interface; `TreeMap` and `HashMap` are two implementations of the `Map` interface. As the names imply, the classes use two different underlying implementation techniques: trees and hashing.

Next we'll explore some examples that use these classes to solve some problems, and then we will discuss each implementation strategy in more detail.

22.3 Using Sets: Domain Blocker

One of the primary purposes of a set is to test for membership in the set. Let's consider an example that tests web site domains against a list of blocked domains. We could use a simple list of blocked domains, but when we use a `TreeSet` instead, each check for a particular domain is accomplished in log n steps instead of in n steps.

Suppose that the following list of blocked domains is held in a text input file called `blockedDomains.txt`:

```
dontgothere.com
ohno.org
badstuff.com
badstuff.org
```

```
badstuff.net
whatintheworld.com
notinthislifetime.org
letsnot.com
eeewwwwww.com
```

Listing 22.1 illustrates the `DomainBlocker` class, which keeps track of the blocked domains and checks candidates against them as needed. The constructor for this class reads the file and sets up a `TreeSet` containing all of the blocked domains. The `isBlocked` method that determines whether a given domain is in the set.

In this example, the set of blocked domains is represented by a `TreeSet` object. The domains themselves are simply character strings.

In Listing 22.2 we see the `DomainChecker` class. As the driver for this example, this class creates an instance of the `DomainBlocker` class and then allows the user to enter domains interactively to check to see whether they are blocked.

LISTING 22.1

```java
import java.io.File;
import java.io.FileNotFoundException;
import java.util.Scanner;
import java.util.TreeSet;

/**
 * A URL domain blocker.
 *
 * @author Java Foundations
 * @version 4.0
 */
public class DomainBlocker
{
   private TreeSet<String> blockedSet;

   /**
    * Sets up the domain blocker by reading in the blocked domain names from
    * a file and storing them in a TreeSet.
    * @throws FileNotFoundException
    */
   public DomainBlocker() throws FileNotFoundException
   {
      blockedSet = new TreeSet<String>();

      File inputFile = new File("blockedDomains.txt");
      Scanner scan = new Scanner(inputFile);

      while (scan.hasNextLine())
      {
```

LISTING 22.1 *continued*

```
         blockedSet.add(scan.nextLine());
      }
   }

   /**
    * Checks to see if the specified domain has been blocked.
    *
    * @param domain the domain to be checked
    * @return true if the domain is blocked and false otherwise
    */
   public boolean domainIsBlocked(String domain)
   {
      return blockedSet.contains(domain);
   }
}
```

LISTING 22.2

```
import java.io.FileNotFoundException;
import java.util.Scanner;

/**
 * Domain checking driver.
 *
 * @author Java Foundations
 * @version 4.0
 */
public class DomainChecker
{
   /**
    * Repeatedly reads a domain interactively from the user and checks to
    * see if that domain has been blocked.
    */
   public static void main(String[] args) throws FileNotFoundException
   {
      DomainBlocker blocker = new DomainBlocker();
      Scanner scan = new Scanner(System.in);
      String domain;
```

LISTING 22.2 *continued*

```
      do
      {
         System.out.print("Enter a domain (DONE to quit): ");
         domain = scan.nextLine();

         if (!domain.equalsIgnoreCase("DONE"))
         {
            if (blocker.domainIsBlocked(domain))
               System.out.println("That domain is blocked.");
            else
               System.out.println("That domain is fine.");
         }
      }  while (!domain.equalsIgnoreCase("DONE"));
   }
}
```

22.4 Using Maps: Product Sales

Let's look at an example using the `TreeMap` class. What if we were trying to keep track of product sales? Suppose that each time a product is sold, its product code is entered into a sales file. Here's a sample of how that information might appear in a file. Note that there are duplicates in the list.

```
OB311
HR588
DX555
EW231
TT232
TJ991
HR588
TT232
GB637
BV693
CB329
NP466
CB329
EW231
BV693
DX555
GB637
VA838
```

Our system would need to read the sales file and update the product information for each entry. We could organize our collection by product code but then keep that separate from the actual product information. Listing 22.3 shows the `Product` class and Listing 22.4 shows the `ProductSales` class.

LISTING 22.3

```
/**
 * Represents a product for sale.
 *
 * @author Java Foundations
 * @version 4.0
 */
public class Product implements Comparable<Product>
{
   private String productCode;
   private int sales;

   /**
    * Creates the product with the specified code.
    *
    * @param productCode a unique code for this product
    */
   public Product(String productCode)
   {
      this.productCode = productCode;
      this.sales = 0;
   }

   /**
    * Returns the product code for this product.
    *
    * @return the product code
    */
   public String getProductCode()
   {
      return productCode;
   }

   /**
    * Increments the sales of this product.
    */
   public void incrementSales()
   {
      sales++;
   }
```

LISTING 22.3 *continued*

```
   /**
    * Compares this product to the specified product based on the product
    * code.
    *
    * @param other the other product
    * @return an integer code result
    */
   public int compareTo(Product obj)
   {
      return productCode.compareTo(obj.getProductCode());
   }

   /**
    * Returns a string representation of this product.
    *
    * @return a string representation of the product
    */
   public String toString()
   {
      return productCode + "\t(" + sales + ")";
   }
}
```

LISTING 22.4

```
import java.io.File;
import java.io.IOException;
import java.util.Scanner;
import java.util.TreeMap;

/**
 * Demonstrates the use of a TreeMap to store a sorted group of Product
 * objects.
 *
 * @author Java Foundations
 * @version 4.0
 */
```

LISTING 22.4 *continued*

```
public class ProductSales
{
   /**
    * Processes product sales data and prints a summary sorted by
    * product code.
    */
  public static void main(String[] args) throws IOException
  {
     TreeMap<String, Product> sales = new TreeMap<String, Product>();

     Scanner scan = new Scanner(new File("salesData.txt"));

     String code;
     Product product;
     while (scan.hasNext())
     {
       code = scan.nextLine();
       product = sales.get(code);
       if (product == null)
        sales.put(code, new Product(code));
       else
        product.incrementSales();
     }

     System.out.println("Products sold this period:");
     for (Product prod : sales.values())
      System.out.println(prod);
  }
}
```

OUTPUT

```
Products sold this period:
BR742  (67)
BV693  (69)
CB329  (67)
DX555  (67)
DX699  (72)
EW231  (66)
GB637  (56)
HR588  (66)
LF845  (69)
LH933  (59)
```

LISTING 22.4 *continued*

```
NP466  (67)
OB311  (50)
TJ991  (79)
TT232  (74)
UI294  (75)
VA838  (60)
WL023  (76)
WL310  (81)
WL812  (65)
YG904  (78)
```

In our previous collections, when we wanted to retrieve or find an object in the collection, we would have had to instantiate an object of the same type and with the same critical information in order to look for it. One of the advantages of using a `Map` is that we no longer have to do that. In this example, our key is a `String`. Therefore, we were able to search the `Map` using a `String` rather than having to create a dummy `Product` object.

In the `main` method, a `while` loop is used to read all values from the input file. For each product code, we attempt to get the corresponding `Product` object from the map using the product code as the key. If the result is null, then no sales of that product have been recorded yet, and a new `Product` object is created and added to the map. If it was successfully retrieved from the map, the `incrementSales` method is called.

The output of the program lists only unique product codes found in the input file, followed by the number of sales in parentheses. Note that the coutput shown in Listing 22.4 is based on a much larger input file than the sample given earlier in the chapter.

The output is accomplished by a for-each loop in the `main` method, which retrieves a list of all `Product` objects stored in the map using a call to the `values` method. The values are returned in order by product code, because that's how `Product` objects rank themselves using the `compareTo` method of `Product`.

22.5 Using Maps: User Management

Suppose we wanted to create a system to manage users. Our system could maintain a map of users and allow searches for particular users based on a user id. Listing 22.5 illustrates our `User` class, representing an individual user, and Listing 22.6 represents the `Users` class, representing the collection of users.

LISTING 22.5

```
/**
 * Represents a user with a userid.
 *
 * @author Java Foundations
 * @version 4.0
 */
public class User
{
   private String userId;
   private String firstName;
   private String lastName;

   /**
    * Sets up this user with the specified information.
    *
    * @param userId a user identification string
    * @param firstName the user's first name
    * @param lastName the user's last name
    */
   public User(String userId, String firstName, String lastName)
   {
      this.userId = userId;
      this.firstName = firstName;
      this.lastName = lastName;
   }

   /**
    * Returns the user id of this user.
    *
    * @return the user id of the user
    */
   public String getUserId()
   {
      return userId;
   }

   /**
    * Returns a string representation of this user.
    *
    * @return a string representation of the user
    */
   public String toString()
   {
      return userId + ":\t" + lastName + ", " + firstName;
   }
}
```

LISTING 22.6

```
import java.util.HashMap;
import java.util.Set;

/**
 * Stores and manages a map of users.
 *
 * @author Java Foundations
 * @version 4.0
 */
public class Users
{
   private HashMap<String, User> userMap;

   /**
    * Creates a user map to track users.
    */
   public Users()
   {
      userMap = new HashMap<String, User>();
   }

   /**
    * Adds a new user to the user map.
    *
    * @param user the user to add
    */
   public void addUser(User user)
   {
      userMap.put(user.getUserId(), user);
   }

   /**
    * Retrieves and returns the specified user.
    *
    * @param userId the user id of the target user
    * @return the target user, or null if not found
    */
   public User getUser(String userId)
   {
      return userMap.get(userId);
   }
```

LISTING 22.6 *continued*

```
   /**
    * Returns a set of all user ids.
    *
    * @return a set of all user ids in the map
    */
   public Set<String> getUserIds()
   {
      return userMap.keySet();
   }
}
```

In the `Users` class, individual `User` objects are stored in a `HashMap` object, using a user id (string) as a key. The `addUser` and `getUser` methods simply store and retrieve the `User` objects as needed. The `getUserIds` method returns a `Set` of user ids using a call to the `keySet` method of the map.

Listing 22.7 shows the `UserManagement` class that contains the `main` method of our program. It creates and adds several users, allows the user to search for them interactively, and then prints all of the users in the collection.

LISTING 22.7

```
import java.io.IOException;
import java.util.Scanner;

/**
 * Demonstrates the use of a map to manage a set of objects.
 *
 * @author Java Foundations
 * @version 4.0
 */
public class UserManagement
{
   /**
    * Creates and populates a group of users. Then prompts for interactive
    * searches, and finally prints all users.
    */
```

LISTING 22.7 *continued*

```
   public static void main(String[] args) throws IOException
   {
      Users users = new Users();

      users.addUser(new User("fziffle", "Fred", "Ziffle"));
      users.addUser(new User("geoman57", "Marco", "Kane"));
      users.addUser(new User("rover322", "Kathy", "Shear"));
      users.addUser(new User("appleseed", "Sam", "Geary"));
      users.addUser(new User("mon2016", "Monica", "Blankenship"));

      Scanner scan = new Scanner(System.in);
      String uid;
      User user;

      do
      {
         System.out.print("Enter User Id (DONE to quit): ");
         uid = scan.nextLine();
         if (!uid.equalsIgnoreCase("DONE"))
         {
            user = users.getUser(uid);
            if (user == null)
               System.out.println("User not found.");
            else
               System.out.println(user);
         }
      } while (!uid.equalsIgnoreCase("DONE"));

      // print all users

      System.out.println("\nAll Users:\n");
      for (String userId : users.getUserIds())
         System.out.println(users.getUser(userId));
   }
}
```

OUTPUT

```
Enter User Id (DONE to quit): DONE

All Users:

geoman57:  Kane, Marco
appleseed: Geary, Sam
rover322:  Shear, Kathy
fziffle:   Ziffle, Fred
mon2016:   Blankenship, Monica
```

22.6 Implementing Sets and Maps Using Trees

As the names imply, the `TreeSet` and `TreeMap` classes use an underlying tree structure to hold the elements in the set or map. In previous chapters, we explored trees as collections in their own right, first as general trees in Chapter 19, then as binary search trees in Chapter 20. As we discussed in those chapters, the Java API does not treat trees as collections, but only as a means to implement other collections.

KEY CONCEPT

The Java API treats trees as implementing data structures rather than as collections.

The tree used to implement `TreeSet` and `TreeMap` is a red-black implementation of a balanced binary search tree. Recall the discussion of red-black trees in Chapter 20. They guarantee that the search tree remains balanced as elements are added and removed, which in turn results in nearly all of the basic operations being executed with O(log n) efficiency. These trees use the so-called natural ordering of elements, based on the `Comparable` interface, unless an explicit `Comparator` object is provided.

KEY CONCEPT

Both `TreeSet` and `TreeMap` use a red-black balanced binary search tree.

Furthermore, it turns out that the `TreeSet` and `TreeMap` classes in the API don't have their own unique implementations of the underlying tree. The `TreeSet` class is built upon a backing instance of a `TreeMap`.

KEY CONCEPT

In the Java API, `TreeSet` is built using an underlying `TreeMap`.

22.7 Implementing Sets and Maps Using Hashing

The `HashSet` and `HashMap` classes are implemented using an underlying technique called *hashing* as the means by which elements are stored and retrieved. First we will discuss hashing in general; then we will consider how it is used to implement sets and maps.

In all of our discussions of the implementations of collections, we have proceeded with one of two assumptions about the order of elements in a collection:

- Order is determined by the order in which elements are added to and/or removed from our collection, as in the case of stacks, queues, unordered lists, and indexed lists.
- Order is determined by comparing the values of the elements (or some key component of the elements) to be stored in the collection, as in the case of ordered lists and binary search trees.

With hashing, however, the order—and, more specifically, the location of an item within the collection—is determined by some function of the value of the element to be stored, or some function of a key value of the element to be stored.

KEY CONCEPT
In hashing, elements are stored in a hash table, and their location in the table is determined by a hashing function.

In hashing, elements are stored in a *hash table*, with their location in the table determined by a *hashing function*. Each location in the table may be referred to as a *cell* or a *bucket*.

A complete discussion of hashing functions is included in Appendix I, but we'll discuss just the basics here.

Consider a simple example where we create an array that will hold 26 elements. Wishing to store names in our array, we create a hashing function that equates each name to the position in the array associated with the first letter of the name (for example, a first letter of A would be mapped to position 0 of the array, a first letter of D would be mapped to position 3 of the array, and so on). Figure 22.3 illustrates this scenario after several names have been added.

Notice that, unlike our earlier implementations of collections, using a hashing approach results in the access time to a particular element being independent of the number of elements in the table. This means that all of the operations on an element of a hash table should be O(1). This is the result of no longer having to do comparisons to find a particular element or to locate the appropriate position for a given element. Using hashing, we simply calculate where a particular element should be.

KEY CONCEPT
The situation in which two elements or keys map to the same location in a hash table is called a collision.

However, this efficiency is fully realized only if each element maps to a unique position in the table. Consider our example from Figure 22.3. What will happen if we attempt to store the name "Ann" and the name "Andrew"? This situation, where two elements or keys map to the same location in a hash table, is called a *collision*.

KEY CONCEPT
A hashing function that maps each element to a unique position in the hash table is said to be a perfect hashing function.

A hashing function that maps each element to a unique position in the hash table is said to be a *perfect hashing function*. Although it is possible in some situations to develop a perfect hashing function, a hashing function that does a good job of distributing the elements among the table positions will still result in constant time (O(1)) access to elements in the table and an improvement over our earlier algorithms that were either O(n) in the case of our linear approaches or O(log n) in the case of search trees.

A complete discussion of hashing is included in Appendix I. Now, let's consider how the Java API uses hashing to create a set implementation.

Just as the `TreeSet` class was built upon a backing `TreeMap` instance, the `HashSet` class is built upon a backing instance of the `HashMap` class. The `HashSet` class provides constant time (O(1)) access for the basic operations as long as the hash function does a reasonable job of distributing elements in the hash table. The two parameters to the constructor that affect the efficiency of the hash function are the *initial capacity* and *load factor*.

The initial capacity determines the initial size of the hash table. The load factor determines how full the table is allowed to be before its size is increased. The default for the initial capacity is 16 and the default for the load factor is 0.75. With these defaults the table size would be doubled once 12 elements had been added.

When an element is added to a `HashSet`, the object's `hashCode` method is called to produce an integer hashcode for the object. If the `hashCode` method has not been overridden, then the `hashCode` method of the `java.lang.Object` class is used. Whether it uses this method or an overridden version, the requirements of the `hashCode` method as stated in the Java API are the same:

- Whenever it is invoked on the same object more than once during an execution of a Java application, the `hashCode` method must consistently return the same integer, provided that no information used in equals comparisons on the object is modified. This integer need not remain consistent from one execution of an application to another execution of the same application.
- If two objects are equal according to the `equals(Object)` method, then calling the `hashCode` method on each of the two objects must produce the same integer result.
- It is not required that if two objects are unequal according to the `equals(Object)` method, then calling the `hashCode` method on each of the two objects must produce distinct integer results. However, the programmer should be aware that producing distinct integer results for unequal objects may improve the performance of hashtables.

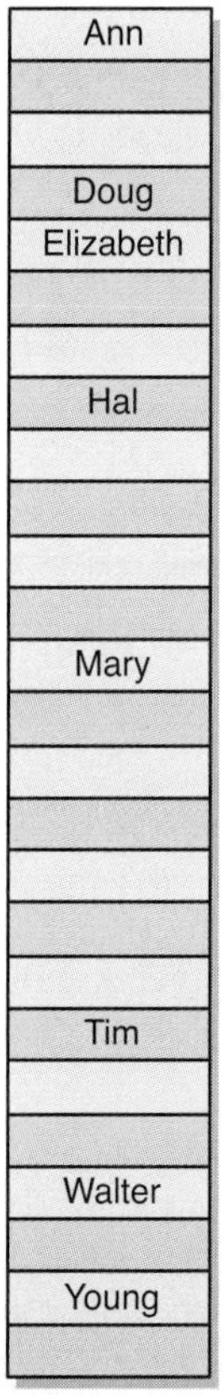

FIGURE 22.3
A simple hashing example

Summary of Key Concepts

- A set is a unique collection of objects generally used to determine whether a particular element is a member of the set.
- A map is a collection of objects that can be retrieved using a unique key.
- The Java API treats trees as implementing data structures rather than as collections.
- In the Java API, `TreeSet` is built using a backing `TreeMap`.
- Both `TreeSet` and `TreeMap` use a red-black balanced binary search tree.
- In hashing, elements are stored in a hash table, and their location in the table is determined by a hashing function.
- The situation in which two elements or keys map to the same location in the table is called a collision.
- A hashing function that maps each element to a unique position in the table is said to be a perfect hashing function.

Summary of Terms

set A unique set of objects generally used to determine whether a particular element is a member of the set.

map A collection of objects that can be retrieved using a unique key.

collision The situation in which two elements or keys map to the same location in a hash table.

hashing A technique by which elements are stored in, and retrieved from, a hash table, and their location in the table is determined by a hashing function.

hash table A table where elements are stored in the hashing technique.

hashing function In the hashing technique, the function that determines where elements are stored in a hash table.

cell A location in a hash table.

bucket A location in a hash table.

perfect hashing function A hashing function that maps each element to a unique position in a hash table.

initial capacity The parameter that determines the initial size of a hash table.

load factor The parameter that determines how full a hash table is allowed to be before its size is increased.

Self-Review Questions

SR 22.1 What is a set?

SR 22.2 What is a map?

SR 22.3 How are sets and maps implemented in the Java API?

SR 22.4 What is the relationship between a `TreeSet` and a `TreeMap`?

SR 22.5 What is the relationship between a `HashSet` and a `HashMap`?

SR 22.6 How does a hash table differ from the other implementation strategies we have discussed?

SR 22.7 What is the potential advantage of a hash table over other implementation strategies?

SR 22.8 Define the terms *collision* and *perfect hashing function*.

Exercises

EX 22.1 Define the concept of a set. List additional operations that might be considered for a set.

EX 22.2 The `TreeSet` class is built upon a backing instance of the `TreeMap` class. Discuss the advantages and disadvantages of this strategy for reuse.

EX 22.3 Given the nature of a set, one could implement the Set interface using any one of a variety of other collections or data structures. Describe how you might implement the Set interface using a `LinkedList`. Discuss the advantages and disadvantages of this approach.

EX 22.4 A bag is a very similar construct to a set except that duplicates are allowed in a bag. What changes would have to be made to extend a `TreeSet` to create an implementation of a bag?

EX 22.5 Draw a UML diagram showing the relationships among the classes involved in the Product Sales example from this chapter.

EX 22.6 Draw a UML diagram showing the relationships among the classes in the User Management example from this chapter.

EX 22.7 Describe two hashing functions that might be appropriate for a data set organized by name (e.g. last name, first name, middle initial).

EX 22.8 Explain when it might be preferable to use a map instead of a set.

Programming Projects

PP 22.1 Create an array based implementation of a set called `ArraySet<T>` that implements the `Set` interface.

PP 22.2 Create a linked implementation of a set call `LinkedSet<T>` that implements the `Set` interface.

PP 22.3 Create a tree-based implementation of a `TreeBag<T>` class. Remember, the difference is that a bag allows duplicates.

PP 22.4 Create a hash table based implementation of a `HashBag<T>` class. Remember, the difference is that a bag allows duplicates.

PP 22.5 Extend the `TreeSet` class to create a class called `AlgebraicTreeSet`. In addition to the methods of the `Set` interface, this class will provide the basic algebraic set operations of union, intersection, and difference.

PP 22.6 Create the `AlgebraicTreeSet` class of PP22.5 by extending the `HashSet` class.

PP 22.7 Building upon PP 22.1, create an array implementation of a map.

PP 22.8 Building upon PP 22.2, create a linked implementation of a map.

PP 22.9 Using a `TreeMap` develop a rolodex application to keep track of Contact objects as described in Chapter 9.

PP 22.10 Using a `HashMap` develop a new implementation of the `ProgramofStudy` application from Chapter 6.

Answers to Self-Review Questions

SRA 22.1 A set is a unique set of objects generally used to determine whether a particular element is a member of the set.

SRA 22.2 A map is a collection of objects that can be retrieved using a unique key.

SRA 22.3 Sets and maps are implemented in the Java API both with Red/Black Binary Trees (`TreeSet` and `TreeMap`) and with hash-tables (`HashSet` and `HashMap`).

SRA 22.4 A `TreeSet` is implemented using a backing instance of a `TreeMap`.

SRA 22.5 A `HashSet` is implemented using a backing instance of a `HashMap`.

SRA 22.6 Using a hash table, the location of an element in the table is determined using a hashing function. In this way, each element in the hash table can be accessed in equal, O(1), time.

SRA 22.7 Given the O(1) access time to each element in a hash table, assuming a good hashing function, then a hash table has the potential to be more efficient than some of our other strategies. For example, a binary search tree might require O(log n) time to access a given element as opposed to the O(1) access time of a hash table.

SRA 22.8 A *collision* occurs in a hash-table when two or more different elements are hashed to the same location in the table. A *perfect hashing function* is one that does not produce any collisions.

Multi-way Search Trees

23

CHAPTER OBJECTIVES

- Examine 2-3 and 2-4 trees.
- Introduce the generic concept of a B-tree.
- Examine some specialized implementations of B-trees.

When we first introduced the concept of efficiency of algorithms, we said that we were interested in issues such as processing time and memory. In this chapter, we explore multi-way trees that were specifically designed with a concern for the use of space and the effect that a particular use of space could have on the total processing time for an algorithm.

23.1 Combining Tree Concepts

In Chapter 19, we established the difference between a general tree, which has a varying number of children per node, and a binary tree, which has at most two children per node. Then in Chapter 20, we discussed the concept of a search tree, which has a specific ordering relationship among the elements in the nodes to allow efficient searching for a target value. In particular, we focused on binary search trees. Now we can combine these concepts and extend them further.

KEY CONCEPT
A multi-way search tree can have more than two children per node and can store more than one element in each node.

In a *multi-way search tree*, each node might have more than two child nodes, and, because it is a search tree, there is a specific ordering relationship among the elements. Furthermore, a single node in a multi-way search tree may store more than one element.

This chapter examines three specific forms of a multi-way search tree:

- 2-3 trees
- 2-4 trees
- B-trees

23.2 2-3 Trees

A *2-3 tree* is a multi-way search tree in which each node has two children (referred to as a *2-node*) or three children (referred to as a *3-node*). A 2-node contains one element and, as in a binary search tree, the left subtree contains elements that are less than that element and the right subtree contains elements that are greater than or equal to that element. However, unlike the case in a binary search tree, a 2-node can have either no children or two children—it cannot have just one child.

A 3-node contains two elements, one designated as the smaller element and one designated as the larger element. A 3-node has either no children or three children. If a 3-node has children, then the left subtree contains elements that are less than the smaller element, and the right subtree contains elements that are greater than or equal to the larger element. The middle subtree contains elements that are greater than or equal to the smaller element and less than the larger element.

KEY CONCEPT
A 2-3 tree contains nodes that contain either one or two elements and have either zero, two, or three children.

All of the leaves of a 2-3 tree are on the same level. Figure 23.1 illustrates a valid 2-3 tree.

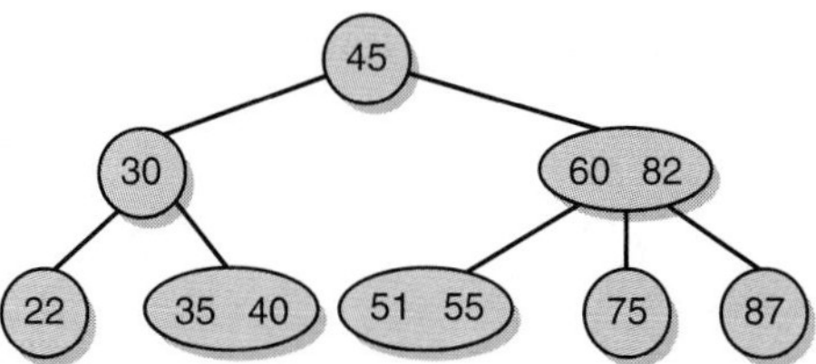

FIGURE 23.1 A 2-3 tree

Inserting Elements into a 2-3 Tree

Similar to a binary search tree, all insertions into a 2-3 tree occur at the leaves of the tree. That is, the tree is searched to determine where the new element will go; then it is inserted. Unlike a binary tree, however, the process of inserting an element into a 2-3 tree can have a ripple effect on the structure of the rest of the tree.

Inserting an element into a 2-3 tree has three cases. The first, and simplest, case is that the tree is empty. In this case, a new node is created containing the new element, and this node is designated as the root of the tree.

The second case occurs when we want to insert a new element at a leaf that is a 2-node. That is, we traverse the tree to the appropriate leaf (which may also be the root) and find that the leaf is a 2-node (containing only one element). In this case, the new element is added to the 2-node, making it a 3-node. Note that the new element may be less than or greater than the existing element. Figure 23.2 illustrates this case by inserting the value 27 into the tree shown in Figure 23.1. The leaf node containing 22 is a 2-node, so 27 is inserted into that node, making it a 3-node. Note that neither the number of nodes in the tree nor the height of the tree changed because of this insertion.

The third insertion situation occurs when we want to insert a new element at a leaf that is a 3-node (containing two elements). In this case, because the 3-node cannot hold any more elements, it is split, and the middle element is moved up a

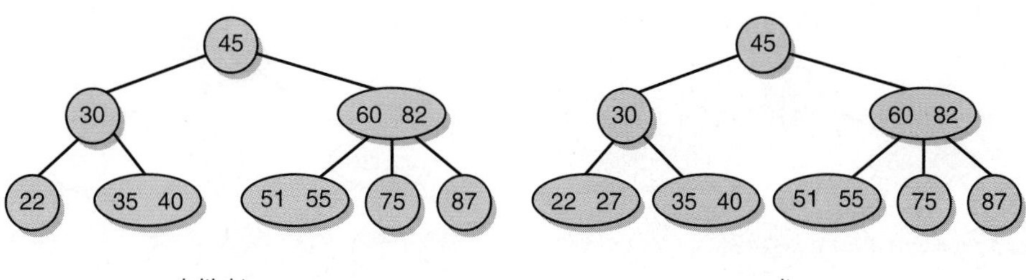

FIGURE 23.2 Inserting 27

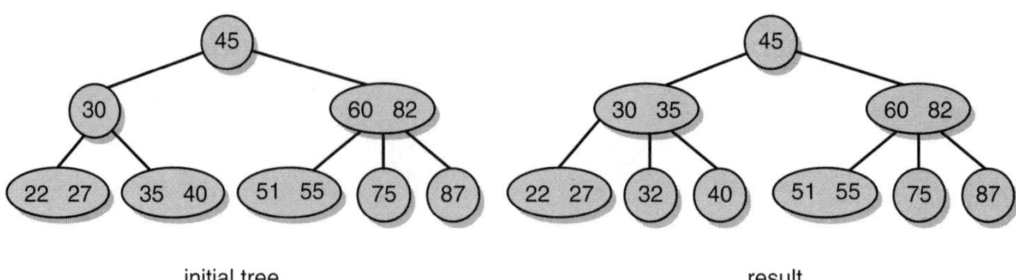

FIGURE 23.3 Inserting 32

level in the tree. The middle element that moves up a level can be either of the two elements that already existed in the 3-node, or it can be the new element being inserted. It depends on the relationship among those three elements.

Figure 23.3 shows the result of inserting the element 32 into the tree shown in Figure 23.2. Searching the tree, we reach the 3-node that contains the elements 35 and 40. That node is split, and the middle element (35) is moved up to join its parent node. Thus the internal node that contains 30 becomes a 3-node that contains both 30 and 35. Note that the act of splitting a 3-node results in two 2-nodes at the leaf level. In this example, we are left with one 2-node that contains 32 and another 2-node that contains 40.

Now consider the situation in which we must split a 3-node whose parent is already a 3-node. The middle element that is promoted causes the parent to split, moving an element up yet another level in the tree. Figure 23.4 shows the effect of inserting the element 57 into the tree shown in Figure 23.3. Searching the tree, we reach the 3-node leaf that contains 51 and 55. This node is split, causing the middle element 55 to move up a level. But that node is already a 3-node, containing the values 60 and 82, so we split that node as well, promoting the element 60, which joins the 2-node containing 45 at the root. Therefore, inserting an element into a 2-3 tree can cause a ripple effect that changes several nodes in the tree.

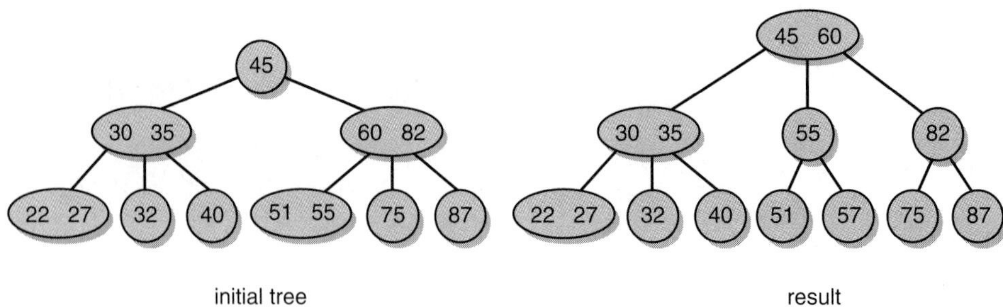

FIGURE 23.4 Inserting 57

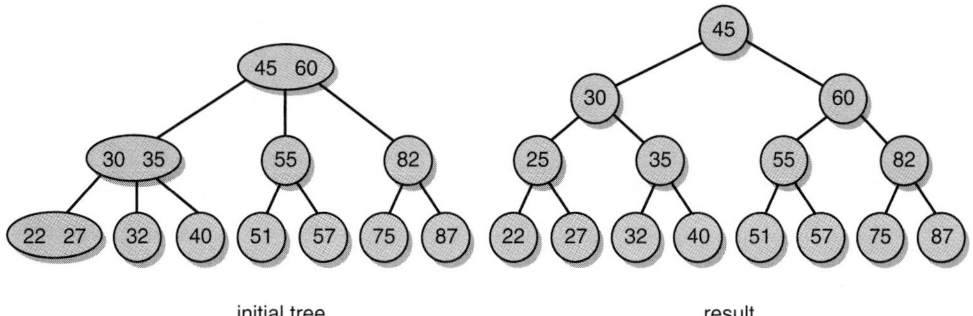

FIGURE 23.5 Inserting 25

If this effect propagates all the way to the root of the entire tree, a new 2-node root is created. For example, inserting the element 25 into the tree shown in Figure 23.4 results in the tree depicted in Figure 23.5. The 3-node containing 22 and 27 is split, promoting 25. This causes the 3-node containing 30 and 35 to split, promoting 30. This causes the 3-node containing 45 and 60 (which happens to be the root of the entire tree) to split, creating a new 2-node root that contains 45.

KEY CONCEPT
If the propagation effect of a 2-3 tree insertion causes the root to split, the tree increases in height.

Note that when the root of the tree splits, the height of the tree increases by one. The insertion strategy for a 2-3 tree keeps all of the leaves at the same level.

Removing Elements from a 2-3 Tree

Removal of elements from a 2-3 tree also has three cases. The first case is that the element to be removed is in a leaf that is a 3-node. In this case, removal is simply a matter of removing the element from the node. Figure 23.6 illustrates this process by removing the element 51 from the tree we began with in Figure 23.1. Note that the properties of a 2-3 tree are maintained.

VideoNote
Inserting elements into, and removing elements from, a 2-3 tree

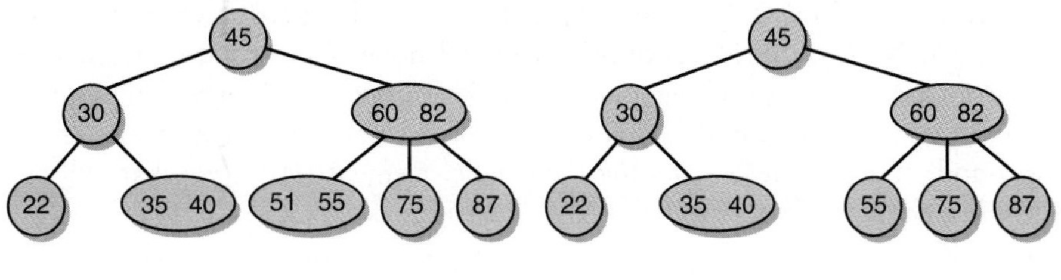

FIGURE 23.6 Removal from a 2-3 tree (case 1)

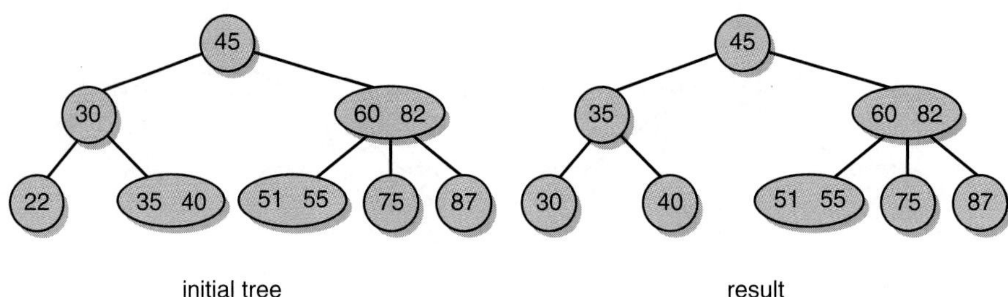

FIGURE 23.7 Removal from a 2-3 tree (case 2.1)

The second case is that the element to be removed is in a leaf that is a 2-node. This condition is called *underflow* and creates a situation in which we must rotate the tree and/or reduce the tree's height in order to maintain the properties of the 2-3 tree. This situation can be broken down into four subordinate cases that we will refer to as cases 2.1, 2.2, 2.3, and 2.4. Figure 23.7 illustrates case 2.1 and shows what happens if we remove the element 22 from our initial tree shown in Figure 23.1. In this case, because the parent node has a right child that is a 3-node, we can maintain the properties of a 2-3 tree by rotating the smaller element of the 3-node around the parent. The same process will work if the element being removed from a 2-node leaf is the right child and the left child is a 3-node.

What happens if we now remove the element 30 from the resulting tree in Figure 23.7? We can no longer maintain the properties of a 2-3 tree through a local rotation. Keep in mind that a node in a 2-3 tree cannot have just one child. Because the leftmost child of the right child of the root is a 3-node, we can rotate the smaller element of that node around the root to maintain the properties of a 2-3 tree. This process is illustrated in Figure 23.8 and represents case 2.2. Notice that the element 51 moves to the root, the element 45 becomes the larger element in a 3-node leaf, and then the smaller element of that leaf is rotated around its parent. Once element 51 was moved to the root and element 45 was moved to a 3-node leaf, we were back in the same situation as case 2.1.

Given the resulting 2-3 tree in Figure 23.8, what happens if we now remove element 55? None of the leaves of this tree is a 3-node. Thus, rotation from a leaf, even from a distance, is no longer an option. However, because the parent node is a 3-node, all that is required to maintain the properties of a 2-3 node is to change this 3-node to a 2-node by rotating the smaller element (60) into what will now be the left child of the node. Figure 23.9 illustrates case 2.3.

If we then remove element 60 (using case 1), the resulting tree contains nothing but 2-nodes. Now, if we remove another element, perhaps element 45, rotation is no longer an option. We must instead reduce the height of the tree in order to

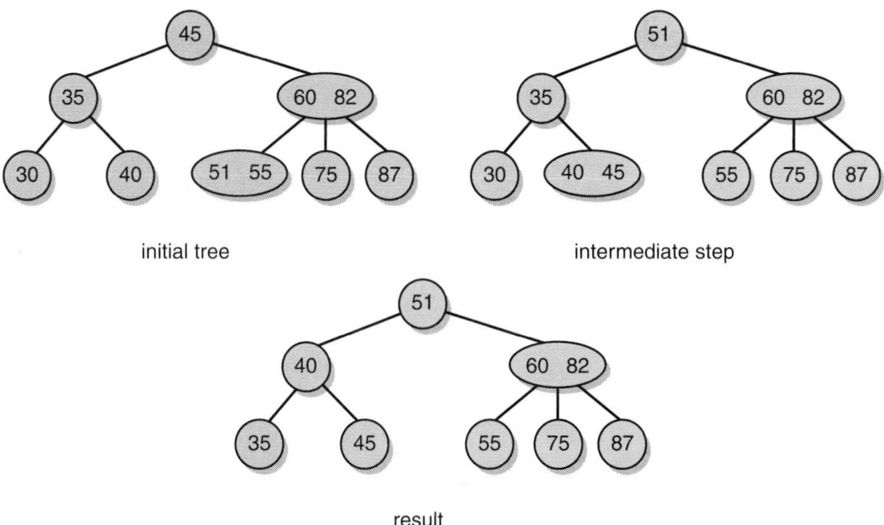

FIGURE 23.8 Removal from a 2-3 tree (case 2.2)

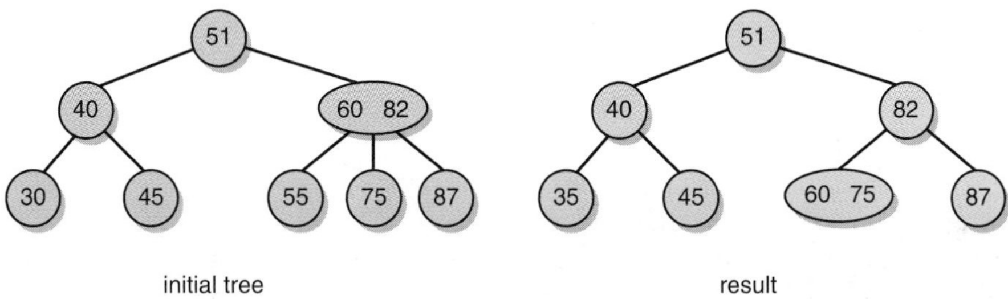

FIGURE 23.9 Removal from a 2-3 tree (case 2.3)

maintain the properties of a 2-3 tree. This is case 2.4. To accomplish this, we simply combine each of the leaves with its parent and siblings in order. If any of these combinations contains more than two elements, we split it into two 2-nodes and promote or propagate the middle element. Figure 23.10 illustrates this process for reducing the height of the tree.

The third case is that the element to be removed is in an internal node. Just as we did with binary search trees, we can simply replace the element to be removed with its inorder successor. In a 2-3 tree, the inorder successor of an internal element will always be a leaf, which, if it is a 2-node, will bring us back to our first case, and if it is a 3-node, requires no further action. Figure 23.11 illustrates these possibilities by removing the element 30 from our original tree from Figure 23.1 and then by removing the element 60 from the resulting tree.

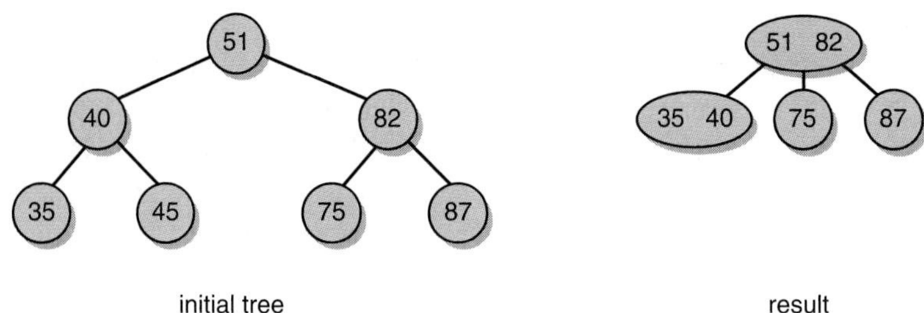

FIGURE 23.10 Removal from a 2-3 tree (case 2.4)

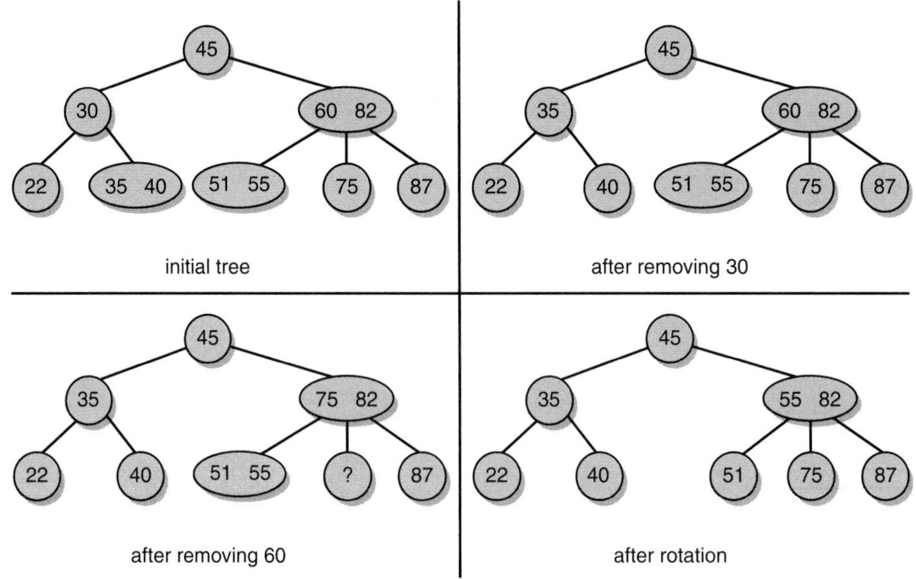

FIGURE 23.11 Removal from a 2-3 tree (case 3)

23.3 2-4 Trees

A *2-4 tree* is similar to a 2-3 tree, adding the characteristic that a node can contain three elements. Expanding on the same principles as a 2-3 tree, a *4-node* contains three elements and has either no children or four children. The same ordering property applies: The left child will be less than the leftmost element of a node, which will be less than or equal to the second child of the node, which will be less than the second element of the node, which will be less than or equal to the third child

KEY CONCEPT
A 2-4 tree expands on the concept of a 2-3 tree to include the use of 4-nodes.

of the node, which will be less than the third element of the node, which will be less than or equal to the fourth child of the node.

The same cases for insertion and removal of elements apply, with 2-nodes and 3-nodes behaving similarly on insertion and 3-nodes and 4-nodes behaving similarly on removal. Figure 23.12 illustrates a series of insertions into a 2-4 tree. Figure 23.13 illustrates a series of removals from a 2-4 tree.

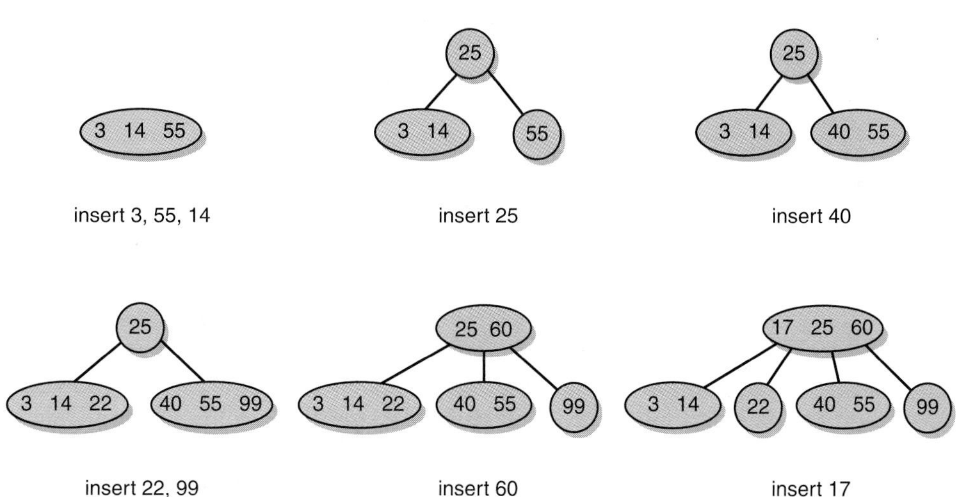

FIGURE 23.12 Insertions into a 2-4 tree

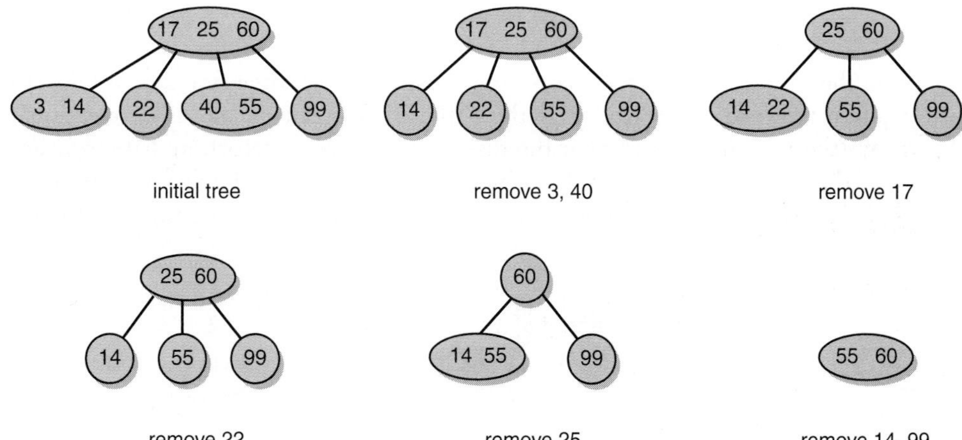

FIGURE 23.13 Removals from a 2-4 tree

23.4 B-Trees

Both 2-3 and 2-4 trees are examples of a larger class of multi-way search trees called *B-trees*. We refer to the maximum number of children of each node as the *order* of the B-tree. Thus 2-3 trees are B-trees of order 3, and 2-4 trees are B-trees of order 4.

KEY CONCEPT
A B-tree extends the concept of 2-3 and 2-4 trees so that nodes can have an arbitrary maximum number of elements.

B-trees of order m have the following properties:

- The root has at least two subtrees unless it is a leaf.
- Each non-root internal node n holds k–1 elements and k children where $\lceil m/2 \rceil \leq k \leq m$.
- Each leaf n holds k-1 elements where $\lceil m/2 \rceil \leq k \leq m$.
- All leaves are on the same level.

Figure 23.14 illustrates a B-tree of order 6.

The reasoning behind the creation and use of B-trees is an interesting study of the effects of algorithm and data structure design. To understand this reasoning, we must understand the context of most all of the collections we have discussed thus far. Our assumption has always been that we were dealing with a collection in primary memory. However, what if the data set that we are manipulating is too large for primary memory? In that case, our data structure would be paged in and out of memory from a disk or some other secondary storage device. An interesting thing happens to time complexity once a secondary storage device is involved. No longer is the time to access an element of the collection simply a function of how many comparisons are needed to find the element. Now we must also consider the access time of the secondary storage device and how many separate accesses we will make to that device.

KEY CONCEPT
Access to secondary storage is very slow relative to access to primary storage, which is motivation to use structures such as B-trees.

In the case of a disk, this access time consists of seek time (the time it takes to position the read-write head over the appropriate track on the disk), rotational delay (the time it takes to spin the disk to the correct sector), and the transfer time (the time it takes to transfer a block of memory from the disk into primary memory). Adding this "physical" complexity to the access time for a collection

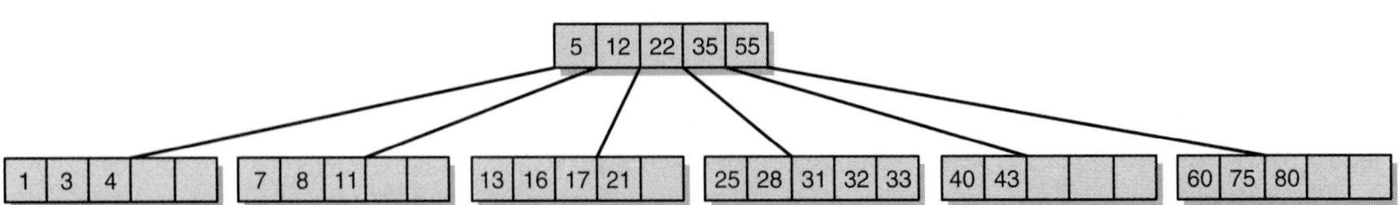

FIGURE 23.14 A B-tree of order 6

can be very costly. Access to secondary storage devices is very slow relative to access to primary storage.

Given this added time complexity, it makes sense to develop a structure that minimizes the number of times the secondary storage device must be accessed. A B-tree can be just such a structure. B-trees are typically tuned so that the size of a node is the same as the size of a block on secondary storage. In this way, we get the maximum amount of data for each disk access. Because B-trees can have many more elements per node than a binary tree, they are much flatter structures than binary trees. This reduces the number of nodes and/or blocks that must be accessed, thus improving performance.

We have already demonstrated the processes of insertion and removal of elements for 2-3 and 2-4 trees, both of which are B-trees. The process for any B-tree of order m is similar. Let's now briefly examine some interesting variations of B-trees that were designed to solve specific problems.

B*-Trees

One of the potential problems with a B-tree is that even though we are attempting to minimize access to secondary storage, we have actually created a data structure that may be half empty. To minimize this problem, B*-trees were developed. *B*-trees* have all of the same properties as B-trees except that, instead of each node having k children where $\lceil m/2 \rceil \leq k \leq m$, in a B*-tree each node has k children where $\lceil (2m - 1)/3 \rceil \leq k \leq m$. This means that each non-root node is at least two-thirds full.

This is accomplished by delaying splitting of nodes by rebalancing across siblings. Once siblings are full, instead of splitting one node into two, creating two half-full nodes, we split two nodes into three, creating three nodes that are two-thirds full.

B⁺-Trees

Another potential problem with B-trees is sequential access. As with any tree, we can use an inorder traversal to look at the elements of the tree sequentially. However, this means that we are no longer taking advantage of the blocking structure of secondary storage. In fact, we have made it much worse, because now we will access each block containing an internal node many separate times as we pass through it during the traversal.

B^+-trees provide a solution to this problem. In a B-tree, each element appears only once in the tree, regardless of whether it appears in an internal node or in a leaf. In a B^+-tree, each element appears in a leaf, regardless of whether or not it appears

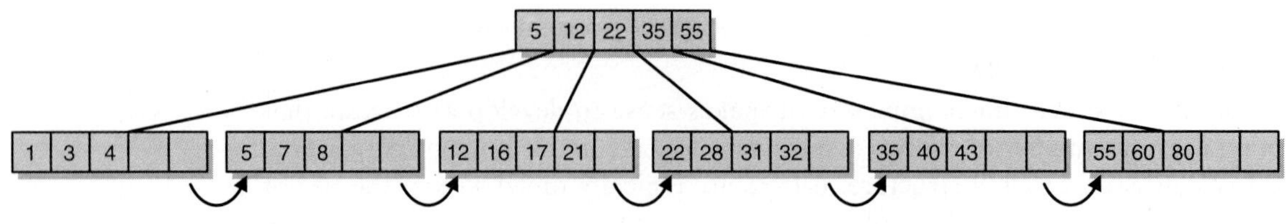

FIGURE 23.15 A B^+-tree of order 6

in an internal node. Elements appearing in an internal node will be listed again as the inorder successor (which is a leaf) of their position in the internal node. Additionally, each leaf node will maintain a pointer to the following leaf node. In this way, a B^+-tree provides indexed access through the B-tree structure and sequential access through a linked list of leaves. Figure 23.15 illustrates this strategy.

Analysis of B-Trees

With balanced binary search trees, we were able to say that searching for an element in the tree was $O(\log_2 n)$. This is because, at worst, we had to search a single path from the root to a leaf in the tree and, at worst, the length of that path would be $\log_2 n$. Analysis of B-trees is similar. At worst, searching a B-tree, we will have to search a single path from the root to a leaf and, at worst, that path length will be $\log_m n$, where m is the order of the B-tree and n is the number of elements in the tree. However, finding the appropriate node is only part of the search. The other part of the search is finding the appropriate path from each node and then finding the target element in a given node. Because there are up to m–1 elements per node, it may take up to m–1 comparisons per node to find the appropriate path and/or to find the appropriate element. Thus, the analysis of a search of a B-tree yields $O((m-1)\log_m n)$. Because m is a constant for any given implementation, we can say that searching a B-tree is O(log n).

The analysis of insertion into and deletion from a B-tree is similar and is left as an exercise.

23.5 Implementation Strategies for B-Trees

We have already discussed insertion of elements into B-trees, removal of elements from B-trees, and the balancing mechanisms necessary to maintain the properties of a B-tree. What remains is to discuss strategies for storing B-trees. Keep in mind that the B-tree structure was developed specifically to address the issue of a collection that must move in and out of primary memory from secondary storage. If we attempt to use object reference variables to create a linked implementation, we are actually storing a primary memory address for an object. Once that object is moved back to secondary storage, that address is no longer valid. Therefore, if interaction with secondary memory is part of your motivation to use a B-tree, then an array implementation may be a better solution.

KEY CONCEPT
Arrays may provide a better solution both within a B-tree node and for collecting B-tree nodes, because they are effective in both primary memory and secondary storage.

A solution is to think of each node as a pair of arrays. The first array would be an array of m–1 elements and the second array would be an array of m children. Next, if we think of the tree itself as one large array of nodes, then the elements stored in the array of children in each node would simply be integer indexes into this array of nodes.

In primary memory, this strategy works because when we use an array, as long as we know the index position of the element within the array, it does not matter to us where the array is loaded in primary memory. For secondary memory, this same strategy works because, given that each node is of fixed length, the address in memory of any given node is given by

The base address of the file + (index of the node − 1) × length of a node.

The array implementations of 2-3, 2-4, and larger B-trees are left as a programming project.

Summary of Key Concepts

- A multi-way search tree can have more than two children per node and can store more than one element in each node.
- A 2-3 tree contains nodes that contain either one or two elements and have zero, two, or three children.
- Inserting an element into a 2-3 tree can have a ripple effect up the tree.
- If the propagation effect of a 2-3 tree insertion causes the root to split, the tree increases in height.
- A 2-4 tree expands on the concept of a 2-3 tree to include the use of 4-nodes.
- A B-tree extends the concept of 2-3 and 2-4 trees so that nodes can have an arbitrary maximum number of elements.
- Access to secondary storage is very slow relative to access to primary storage, which is motivation to use structures such as B-trees.
- Arrays may provide a better solution both within a B-tree node and for collecting B-tree nodes because they are effective in both primary memory and secondary storage.

Summary of Terms

multi-way search tree A search tree where each node might have more than two child nodes and there is a specific ordering relationship among the elements.

2-3 tree A multi-way search tree in which each node has two children (referred to as a 2-node) or three children (referred to as a 3-node).

2-node A 2-node contains one element and, as in a binary search tree, the left subtree contains elements that are less than that element, and the right subtree contains elements that are greater than or equal to that element.

3-node A 3-node contains two elements, one designated as the smaller element and one designated as the larger element. A 3-node has either no children or three children. If a 3-node has children, the left subtree contains elements that are less than the smaller element, and the right subtree contains elements that are greater than or equal to the larger element. The middle subtree contains elements that are greater than or equal to the smaller element and less than the larger element.

underflow A situation in which we must rotate the tree and/or reduce the tree's height in order to maintain the properties of the 2-3 tree.

2-4 tree A 2-4 tree is similar to a 2-3 tree, adding the characteristic that a node can contain three elements.

4-node A 4-node contains three elements and has either no children or four children.

B-tree A B-tree extends the concept of 2-3 and 2-4 trees so that nodes can have an arbitrary maximum number of elements.

B*-trees B*-trees have all of the same properties as B-trees except that, instead of each node having k children where in a B*-tree, each node has k children where $\lceil m/2 \rceil \leq k \leq m$, in a B*-tree each node has k children where $\lceil (2m - 1)/3 \rceil \leq k \leq m$.

B+-trees In a B+-tree, each element appears in a leaf, regardless of whether or not it appears in an internal node. Elements appearing in an internal node will be listed again as the inorder successor (which is a leaf) of their position in the internal node. Additionally, each leaf node will maintain a pointer to the following leaf node. In this way, a B+-tree provides indexed access through the B-tree structure and sequential access through a linked list of leaves.

Self-Review Questions

SR 23.1 Describe the nodes in a 2-3 tree.

SR 23.2 When does a node in a 2-3 tree split?

SR 23.3 How can splitting a node in a 2-3 tree affect the rest of the tree?

SR 23.4 Describe the process of deleting an element from a 2-3 tree.

SR 23.5 Describe the nodes in a 2-4 tree.

SR 23.6 How do insertions and deletions in a 2-4 tree compare to insertions and deletions in a 2-3 tree?

SR 23.7 When is rotation no longer an option for rebalancing a 2-3 tree after a deletion?

Exercises

EX 23.1 Draw the 2-3 tree that results from adding the following elements into an initially empty tree:

34 45 3 87 65 32 1 12 17

EX 23.2 Using the resulting tree from Exercise 23.1, draw the resulting tree after removing each of the following elements:

3 87 12 17 45

EX 23.3 Repeat Exercise 23.1 using a 2-4 tree.

EX 23.4 Repeat Exercise 23.2 using the resulting 2-4 tree from Exercise 23.3.

EX 23.5 Draw the B-tree of order 8 that results from adding the following elements into an initially empty tree:

34 45 3 87 65 32 1 12 17 33 55 23 67 15 39 11 19 47

EX 23.6 Draw the B-tree that results from removing the following from the resulting tree from Exercise 23.5:

1 12 17 33 55 23 19 47

EX 23.7 Describe the complexity (order) of insertion into a B-tree.

EX 23.8 Describe the complexity (order) of deletion from a B-tree.

Programming Projects

PP 23.1 Create an implementation of a 2-3 tree using the array strategy discussed in Section 23.5.

PP 23.2 Create an implementation of a 2-3 tree using a linked strategy.

PP 23.3 Create an implementation of a 2-4 tree using the array strategy discussed in Section 23.5.

PP 23.4 Create an implementation of a 2-4 tree using a linked strategy.

PP 23.5 Create an implementation of a B-tree of order 7 using the array strategy discussed in Section 23.5.

PP 23.6 Create an implementation of a B^+-tree of order 9 using the array strategy discussed in Section 23.5.

PP 23.7 Create an implementation of a B^*-tree of order 11 using the array strategy discussed in Section 23.5.

PP 23.8 Implement a graphical system to manage employees using an employee id, employee name, and years of service. The system should use a B-tree of order 7 to store employees, and it must provide the ability to add and remove employees. After each operation, your system must update a sorted list of employees sorted by name on the screen.

Answers to Self-Review Questions

SRA 23.1 A 2-3 tree node can have either one element or two and can have no children, two children, or three children. If it has one element, then it is a 2-node and has either no children or two children. If it has two elements, then it is a 3-node and has either no children or three children.

SRA 23.2 A 2-3 tree node splits when it has three elements. The smallest element becomes a 2-node, the largest element becomes a 2-node, and the middle element is promoted or propagated to the parent node.

SRA 23.3 If the split and resulting propagation force the root node to split, then splitting the node will increase the height of the tree.

SRA 23.4 Deletion from a 2-3 tree falls into one of three cases. Case 1, deletion of an element from a 3-node leaf, means simply removing the element and has no impact on the rest of the tree. Case 2, deletion of an element from a 2-node leaf, results in one of four cases. Case 2.1, deletion of an element from a 2-node that has a 3-node sibling, is resolved by rotating either the inorder predecessor or the inorder successor of the parent, depending upon whether the 3-node is a left child or a right child, around the parent. Case 2.2, deletion of an element from a 2-node when there is a 3-node leaf elsewhere in the tree, is resolved by rotating an element out of that 3-node and propagating that rotation until a sibling of the node being deleted becomes a 3-node; then this case becomes case 2.1. Case 2.3, deletion of a 2-node where there is a 3-node internal node, can be resolved through rotation as well. Case 2.4, deletion of a 2-node when there are no 3-nodes in the tree, is resolved by reducing the height of the tree.

SRA 23.5 Nodes in a 2-4 tree are exactly like those in a 2-3 tree, except that 2-4 trees also allow 4-nodes, or nodes containing three elements and having four children.

SRA 23.6 Insertions and deletions in a 2-4 tree are exactly like those in a 2-3 tree, except that splits occur when there are four elements instead of three as in a 2-3 tree.

SRA 23.7 If all of the nodes in a 2-3 tree are 2-nodes, then rotation is not an option for rebalancing.

References

Bayer, R. "Symmetric Binary B-trees: Data Structure and Maintenance Algorithms." *Acta Informatica* (1972): 290–306.

Comer, D. "The Ubiquitous B-Tree." *Computing Surveys 11*(1979): 121–137.

Wedeking, H. "On the Selection of Access Paths in a Data Base System." In *Data Base Management*, edited by J. W. Klimbie and K. L. Koffeman, pp. 385–397. Amsterdam: North-Holland, 1974.

Graphs

24

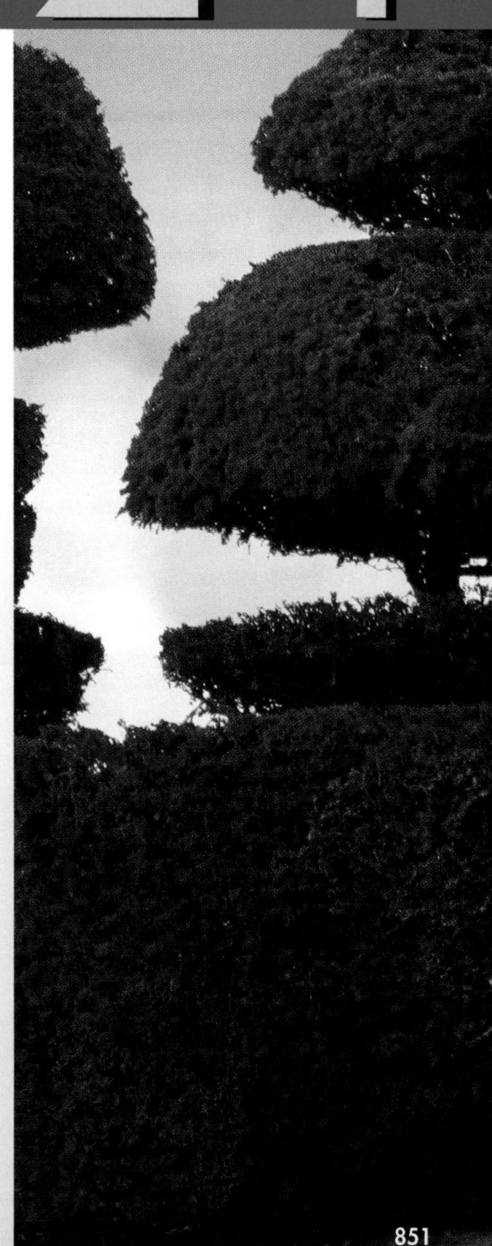

CHAPTER OBJECTIVES

- Define undirected graphs.
- Define directed graphs.
- Define weighted graphs or networks.
- Explore common graph algorithms.

In Chapter 19, we introduced the concept of a tree, a nonlinear structure defined by the concept that each node in the tree, other than the root node, has exactly one parent. If we were to violate that premise and allow each node in the tree to be connected to a variety of other nodes with no notion of parent or child, the result would be the concept of a graph, which we explore in this chapter. Graphs and graph theory make up entire subdisciplines of both mathematics and computer science. In this chapter, we introduce the basic concepts of graphs and their implementation.

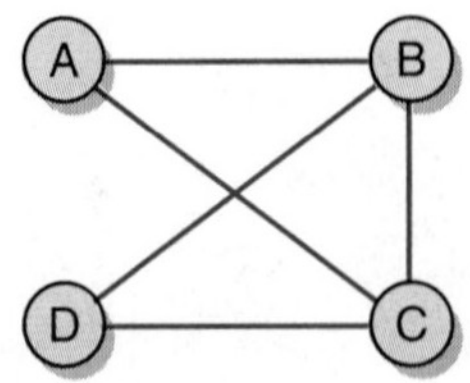

FIGURE 24.1 An example of an undirected graph

24.1 Undirected Graphs

Like trees, a graph is made up of nodes and the connections between those nodes. In graph terminology, we refer to the nodes as *vertices* and refer to the connections among them as *edges*. Vertices are typically identified by a name or a label. For example, we might label vertices A, B, C, and D. Edges are referred to by pairing the vertices that they connect. For example, we might have an edge (A, B), which means there is an edge from vertex A to vertex B.

An *undirected graph* is a graph where the pairings that represent the edges are unordered. Thus, listing an edge as (A, B) means that there is a connection between A and B that can be traversed in either direction. In an undirected graph, listing an edge as (A, B) means exactly the same thing as listing the edge as (B, A). Figure 24.1 illustrates the following undirected graph:

> **KEY CONCEPT**
> An undirected graph is a graph where the pairings that represent the edges are unordered.

Vertices: A, B, C, D

Edges: (A, B), (A, C), (B, C), (B, D), (C, D)

Two vertices in a graph are *adjacent* if there is an edge connecting them. For example, in the graph of Figure 24.1, vertices A and B are adjacent, and vertices A and D are not. Adjacent vertices are sometimes referred to as *neighbors*. An edge of a graph that connects a vertex to itself is called a *self-loop* or a *sling* and is represented by listing the vertex twice. For example, listing an edge (A, A) would mean that there is a sling connecting A to itself.

> **KEY CONCEPT**
> Two vertices in a graph are adjacent if there is an edge connecting them.

> **KEY CONCEPT**
> An undirected graph is considered complete if it has the maximum number of edges connecting vertices.

An undirected graph is considered *complete* if it has the maximum number of edges connecting vertices. For the first vertex, it requires (n – 1) edges to connect it to the other vertices. For the second vertex, it requires only (n – 2) edges because it is already connected to the first vertex. For the third vertex, it requires (n – 3) edges. This sequence continues until the final vertex requires no additional edges because all the other vertices have already been connected to it. Remember from Chapter 11 that the summation from 1 to n is

$$\sum_{1}^{n} i = n(n + 1)/2$$

Thus, in this case, because we are summing only from 1 to (n – 1), the resulting summation is

$$\sum_{1}^{n-1} i = n(n - 1)/2$$

This means that for any undirected graph with n vertices, it would require n(n – 1)/2 edges to make the graph complete. This, of course, assumes that none of those edges is a sling.

A *path* is a sequence of edges that connect two vertices in a graph. For example, in our graph from Figure 24.1, A, B, D is a path from A to D. Notice that each sequential pair, (A, B) and then (B, D), is an edge. A path in an undirected graph is bi-directional. For example, A, B, D is the path from A to D, but because the edges are undirected, the inverse, D, B, A, is also the path from D to A. The *length* of a path is the number of edges in the path (or the number of vertices – 1). So for our previous example, the path length is 2. Notice that this definition of path length is identical to the definition that we used in discussing trees. In fact, trees are a special case of graphs.

KEY CONCEPT
A path is a sequence of edges that connects two vertices in a graph.

KEY CONCEPT
A cycle is a path in which the first and last vertices are the same, and none of the edges is repeated.

An undirected graph is considered *connected* if for any two vertices in the graph, there is a path between them. Our graph from Figure 24.1 is connected. The same graph with a minor modification is not connected, as illustrated in Figure 24.2.

Vertices: A, B, C, D

Edges: (A, B), (A, C), (B, C)

KEY CONCEPT
An undirected tree is a connected, acyclic, undirected graph with one element designated as the root.

A *cycle* is a path in which the first and last vertices are the same, and none of the edges is repeated. In Figure 24.2, we would say that the path A, B, C, A is a cycle. A graph that has no cycles is called *acyclic*. Earlier we mentioned the relationship between graphs and trees. Now that we have introduced these definitions, we can formalize that relationship. An undirected tree is a connected, acyclic, undirected graph with one element designated as the root.

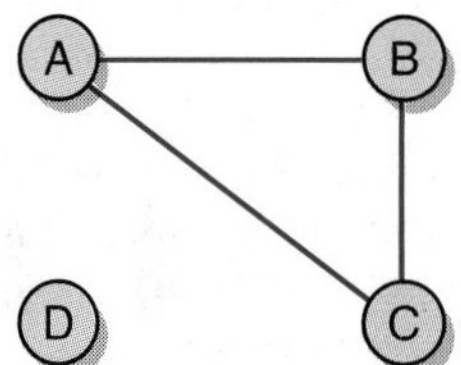

FIGURE 24.2 An example of an undirected graph that is not connected

24.2 Directed Graphs

A *directed graph*, sometimes referred to as a *digraph*, is a graph where the edges are ordered pairs of vertices. This means that the edges (A, B) and (B, A) are separate, directional edges in a directed graph. In our previous example, we had the following description for an undirected graph:

Vertices: A, B, C, D

Edges: (A, B), (A, C), (B, C), (B, D), (C, D)

KEY CONCEPT
A directed graph, sometimes referred as a digraph, is a graph where the edges are ordered pairs of vertices.

Figure 24.3 shows what happens if we interpret this earlier description as a directed graph. We represent each of the edges now

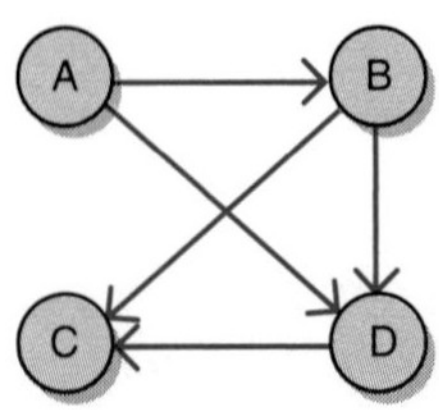

FIGURE 24.3 An example of a directed graph

with the direction of traversal specified by the ordering of the vertices. For example, the edge (A, B) allows traversal from A to B but not traversal in the other direction.

Our previous definitions change slightly for directed graphs. For example, a path in a directed graph is a sequence of directed edges that connects two vertices in a graph. In our undirected graph, we listed the path A, B, D as the path from A to D, and that is still true in our directed interpretation of the graph description. However, paths in a directed graph are not bi-directional, so the inverse is no longer true: D, B, A is not a valid path from D to A, unless we add directional edges (D, B) and (B, A).

KEY CONCEPT
A path in a directed graph is a sequence of directed edges that connects two vertices in the graph.

Our definition for a connected directed graph sounds the same as it did for undirected graphs. A directed graph is connected if for any two vertices in the graph, there is a path between them. However, keep in mind that our definition of a path is different. Look at the two graphs shown in Figure 24.4. The first one is connected. The second one is not connected, because there is no path from any other vertex to vertex 1.

If a directed graph has no cycles, it is possible to arrange the vertices such that vertex A precedes vertex B if an edge exists from A to B. The order of vertices resulting from this arrangement is called *topological order* and is very useful for examples such as course prerequisites.

As we discussed earlier, trees are graphs. In fact, most of our previous much work with trees actually focused on directed trees. A directed tree is a directed graph that has an element designated as the root and has the following properties:

- There are no connections from other vertices to the root.
- Every non-root element has exactly one connection to it.
- There is a path from the root to every other vertex.

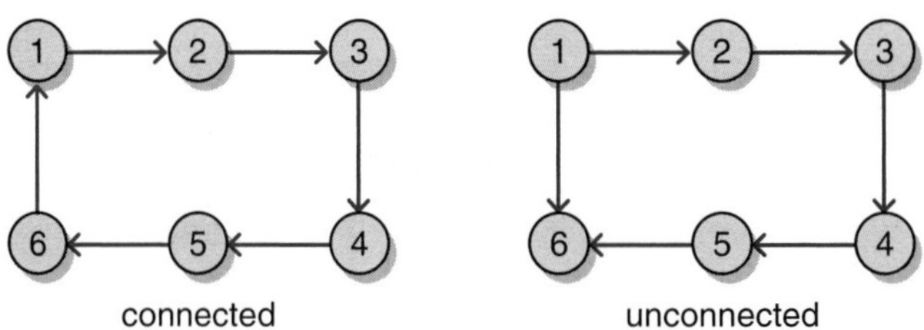

FIGURE 24.4 Examples of a connected directed graph and an unconnected directed graph

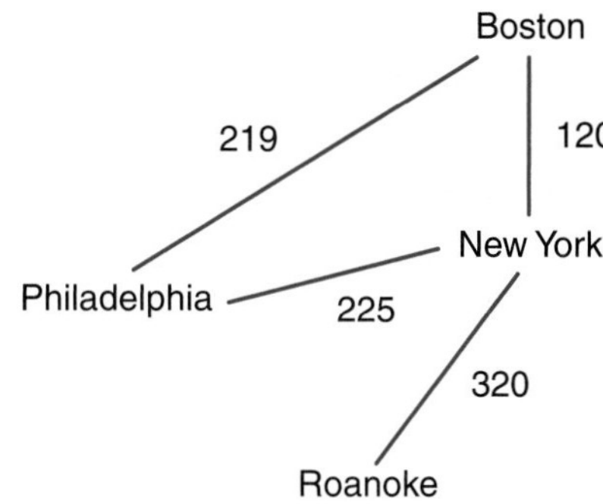

FIGURE 24.5 An undirected network

24.3 Networks

A *network*, or a *weighted graph*, is a graph with weights or costs associated with each edge. Figure 24.5 shows an undirected network of the connections and the airfares between cities. This weighted graph, or network, could then be used to determine the cheapest path from one city to another. The weight of a path in a weighted graph is the sum of the weights of the edges in the path.

KEY CONCEPT
A network, or a weighted graph, is a graph with weights or costs associated with each edge.

Networks may be either undirected or directed, depending on the need. Take our airfare example from Figure 24.5. What if the airfare to fly from New York to Boston is one price but the airfare to fly from Boston to New York is a different price? This would be an excellent application of a directed network, as illustrated in Figure 24.6.

For networks, we represent each edge with a triple that includes the starting vertex, the ending vertex, and the weight. Keep in mind that for undirected net-

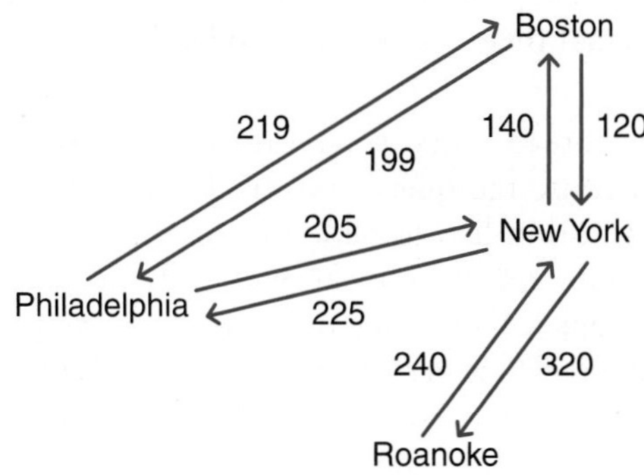

FIGURE 24.6 A directed network

works, the starting and ending vertices could be swapped with no impact. However, for directed networks, a triple must be included for every directional connection. For example, the network of Figure 24.6 would be represented as follows:

Vertices: Boston, New York, Philadelphia, Roanoke

Edges: (Boston, New York, 120), (Boston, Philadelphia, 199), (New York, Boston, 140), (New York, Philadelphia, 225), (New York, Roanoke, 320), (Philadelphia, Boston, 219), (Philadelphia, New York, 205), (Roanoke, New York, 240)

24.4 Common Graph Algorithms

There are a number of common graph algorithms that may apply to undirected graphs, directed graphs, and/or networks. These include various traversal algorithms similar to what we explored with trees, as well as algorithms for finding the shortest path, algorithms for finding the least costly path in a network, and algorithms to answer simple questions about the graph such as whether the graph is connected and what the shortest path is between two vertices.

Traversals

In our discussion of trees in Chapter 19, we defined four types of traversals and then implemented them as iterators: preorder traversal, inorder traversal, postorder traversal, and level-order traversal. Because we know that a tree is a graph, we know that for certain types of graphs these traversals would still apply. Generally, however, we divide graph traversal into two categories: a *breadth-first* traversal, which behaves very much like the level-order traversal of a tree, and a *depth-first* traversal, which behaves very much like the preorder traversal of a tree. One difference here is that there is not a root node. Thus our traversal may start at any vertex in the graph.

We can construct a breadth-first traversal for a graph using a queue and an unordered list. We will use the queue (traversal-queue) to manage the traversal and the unordered list (result-list) to build our result. The first step is to enqueue the starting vertex into the traversal-queue and mark the starting vertex as visited. We then begin a loop that will continue until the traversal-queue is empty. Within this loop, we will take the first vertex off the traversal-queue and add that vertex to the rear of the result-list. Next, we will enqueue each of the vertices that are adjacent to the current one, and have not already been marked as visited, into the traversal-queue, mark each of them as visited, and then repeat the loop.

We simply repeat this process for each of the visited vertices until the traversal-queue is empty, meaning we can no longer reach any new vertices. The result-list now contains the vertices in breadth-first order from the given starting point. Very similar logic can be used to construct a breadth-first iterator. The `iteratorBFS` shows an iterative algorithm for this traversal for an array implementation of a graph. The determination of vertices that are adjacent to the current one depends on the implementation we choose to represent edges in a graph. This particular method assumes an implementation using an adjacency matrix. We will discuss this further in Section 24.5.

VideoNote
Illustration of depth-first and breadth-first traversals of a graph

A depth-first traversal for a graph can be constructed using virtually the same logic by simply replacing the traversal-queue with a traversal-stack. One other difference in the algorithm, however, is that we do not want to mark a vertex as visited until it has been added to the result-list. The `iteratorDFS` method illustrates this algorithm for an array implementation of a graph.

KEY CONCEPT
The only difference between a depth-first traversal of a graph and a breadth-first traversal is that the depth-first traversal uses a stack instead of a queue to manage the traversal.

```
/**
 * Returns an iterator that performs a breadth first
 * traversal starting at the given index.
 *
 * @param startIndex the index from which to begin the traversal
 * @return an iterator that performs a breadth first traversal
 */
public Iterator<T> iteratorBFS(int startIndex)
{
   Integer x;
   QueueADT<Integer> traversalQueue = new LinkedQueue<Integer>();
   UnorderedListADT<T> resultList = new ArrayUnorderedList<T>();

   if (!indexIsValid(startIndex))
        return resultList.iterator();

   boolean[] visited = new boolean[numVertices];
   for (int i = 0; i < numVertices; i++)
        visited[i] = false;

   traversalQueue.enqueue(new Integer(startIndex));
   visited[startIndex] = true;

   while (!traversalQueue.isEmpty())
   {
      x = traversalQueue.dequeue();
      resultList.addToRear(vertices[x.intValue()]);
```

```
         //Find all vertices adjacent to x that have not been visited
         //      and queue them up

         for (int i = 0; i < numVertices; i++)
         {
            if (adjMatrix[x.intValue()][i] && !visited[i])
            {
               traversalQueue.enqueue(new Integer(i));
               visited[i] = true;
            }
         }
      }
      return new GraphIterator(resultList.iterator());
   }

   /**
    * Returns an iterator that performs a depth first traversal
    * starting at the given index.
    *
    * @param startIndex the index from which to begin the traversal
    * @return an iterator that performs a depth first traversal
    */
   public Iterator<T> iteratorDFS(int startIndex)
   {
      Integer x;
      boolean found;
      StackADT<Integer> traversalStack = new LinkedStack<Integer>();
      UnorderedListADT<T> resultList = new ArrayUnorderedList<T>();
      boolean[] visited = new boolean[numVertices];

      if (!indexIsValid(startIndex))
          return resultList.iterator();

      for (int i = 0; i < numVertices; i++)
          visited[i] = false;

      traversalStack.push(new Integer(startIndex));
      resultList.addToRear(vertices[startIndex]);
      visited[startIndex] = true;

      while (!traversalStack.isEmpty())
      {
         x = traversalStack.peek();
         found = false;

         //Find a vertex adjacent to x that has not been visited
         //      and push it on the stack
```

```
        for (int i = 0; (i < numVertices) && !found; i++)
        {
            if (adjMatrix[x.intValue()][i] && !visited[i])
            {
                traversalStack.push(new Integer(i));
                resultList.addToRear(vertices[i]);
                visited[i] = true;
                found = true;
            }
        }
        if (!found && !traversalStack.isEmpty())
            traversalStack.pop();
    }
    return new GraphIterator(resultList.iterator());
}
```

Let's look at an example. Figure 24.7 shows a sample undirected graph where each vertex is labeled with an integer. For a breadth-first traversal starting from vertex 9, we do the following:

1. Add 9 to the traversal-queue and mark it as visited.
2. Dequeue 9 from the traversal-queue.
3. Add 9 to the result-list.
4. Add 6, 7, and 8 to the traversal-queue, marking each of them as visited.
5. Dequeue 6 from the traversal-queue.
6. Add 6 to the result-list.

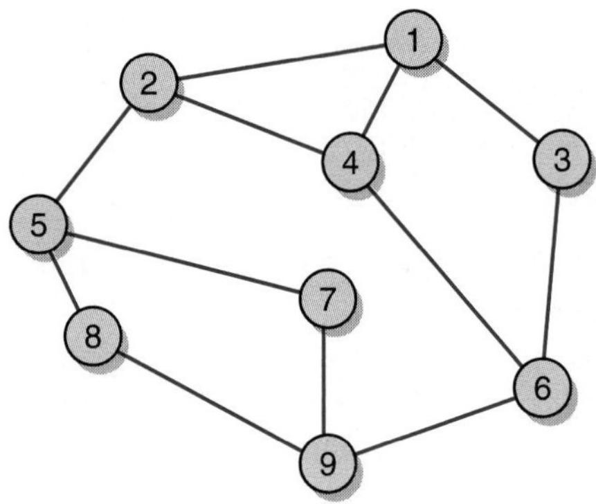

FIGURE 24.7 A traversal example

7. Add 3 and 4 to the traversal-queue, marking them both as visited.
8. Dequeue 7 from the traversal-queue and add it to the result-list.
9. Add 5 to the traversal-queue, marking it as visited.
10. Dequeue 8 from the traversal-queue and add it to the result-list. (We do not add any new vertices to the traversal-queue because there are no neighbors of 8 that have not already been visited.)
11. Dequeue 3 from the traversal-queue and add it to the result-list.
12. Add 1 to the traversal-queue, marking it as visited.
13. Dequeue 4 from the traversal-queue and add it to the result-list.
14. Add 2 to the traversal-queue, marking it as visited.
15. Dequeue 5 from the traversal-queue and add it to the result-list. (Because there are no unvisited neighbors, we continue without adding anything to the traversal-queue.)
16. Dequeue 1 from the traversal-queue and add it to the result-list. (Because there are no unvisited neighbors, we continue without adding anything to the traversal-queue.)
17. Dequeue 2 from the traversal-queue and add it to the result-list.

The result-list now contains the breadth-first order starting at vertex 9: 9, 6, 7, 8, 3, 4, 5, 1, and 2. Try tracing a depth-first search on the same graph from Figure 24.7.

Of course, both of these algorithms could be expressed recursively. For example, the following algorithm recursively defines a depth-first search:

```
DepthFirstSearch(node x)
{
  visit(x)
  result-list.addToRear(x)
  for each node y adjacent to x
      if y not visited
          DepthFirstSearch(y)
}
```

Testing for Connectivity

KEY CONCEPT

A graph is connected if and only if the number of vertices in the breadth-first traversal is the same as the number of vertices in the graph regardless of the starting vertex.

In our earlier discussion, we defined a graph as *connected* if for any two vertices in the graph, there is a path between them. This definition holds true for both undirected and directed graphs. Given the algorithm we just discussed, there is a simple solution to the question of whether a graph is connected: The graph is connected if and only if for each vertex v in a graph containing n vertices, the size of the result of a breadth-first traversal starting at v is n.

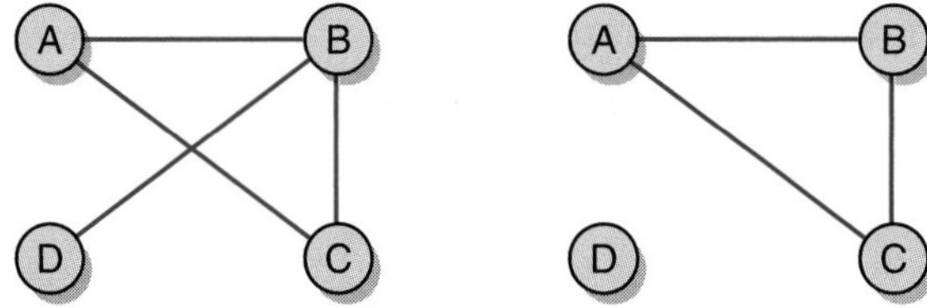

FIGURE 24.8 Connectivity in an undirected graph

Starting Vertex	Breadth-First Traversal
A	A, B, C, D
B	B, A, D, C
C	C, B, A, D
D	D, B, A, C

FIGURE 24.9 Breadth-first traversal for a connected undirected graph

Let's look at the examples of undirected graphs in Figure 24.8. We stated earlier that the graph on the left is connected and that the graph on the right is not. Let's confirm that by following our algorithm. Figure 24.9 shows the breadth-first traversals for the graph on the left using each of the vertices as a starting point. As you can see, all of the traversals yield n = 4 vertices, so the graph is connected. Figure 24.10 shows the breadth-first traversals for the graph on the right using each of the vertices as a starting point. Not only does none of the traversals contain n = 4 vertices, but the one starting at vertex D has only the one vertex. Thus the graph is not connected.

Starting Vertex	Breadth-First Traversal
A	A, B, C
B	B, A, C
C	C, B, A
D	D

FIGURE 24.10 Breadth-first traversal for an unconnected undirected graph

KEY CONCEPT
A spanning tree is a tree that includes all of the vertices of a graph and some, but possibly not all, of the edges.

KEY CONCEPT
A minimum spanning tree is a spanning tree where the sum of the weights of the edges is less than or equal to the sum of the weights for any other spanning tree for the same graph.

Minimum Spanning Trees

A *spanning tree* is a tree that includes all of the vertices of a graph and some, but possibly not all, of the edges. Because trees are also graphs, for some graphs the graph itself will be a spanning tree, and thus the only spanning tree for that graph will include all of the edges. Figure 24.11 shows a spanning tree for our graph from Figure 24.7.

One interesting application of spanning trees is to find a minimum spanning tree for a weighted graph. A *minimum spanning tree* is a spanning tree where the sum of the weights of the edges is less than or equal to the sum of the weights for any other spanning tree for the same graph.

The algorithm for developing a minimum spanning tree was developed by Prim (1957) and is quite elegant. As we discussed earlier, each edge is represented by a triple that includes the starting vertex, the ending vertex, and the weight. We then pick an arbitrary starting vertex (it does not matter which one) and add it to our minimum spanning tree (MST). Next we add all of the edges that include our starting vertex to a minheap ordered by weight. Keep in mind that if we are dealing with a directed network, we will add only edges that start at the given vertex.

Next we remove the minimum edge from the minheap and add the edge and the new vertex to our MST. Next we add to our minheap all of the edges that include this new vertex and whose other vertex is not already in our MST. We continue this process until either our MST includes all of the vertices in our original graph or the minheap is empty. Figure 24.12 shows a weighted network and its associated minimum spanning tree. The `getMST` method illustrates this algorithm.

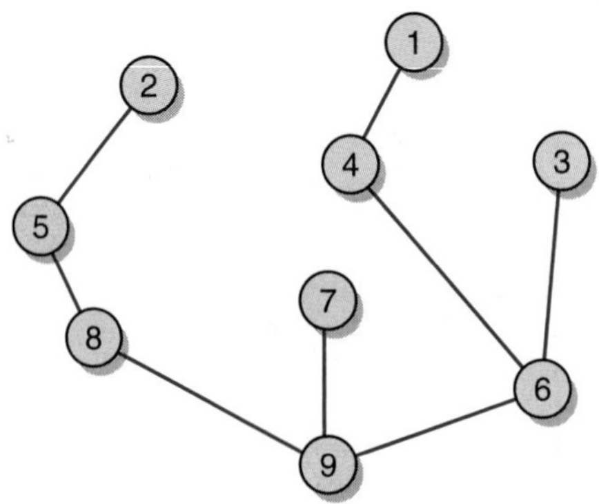

FIGURE 24.11 A spanning tree

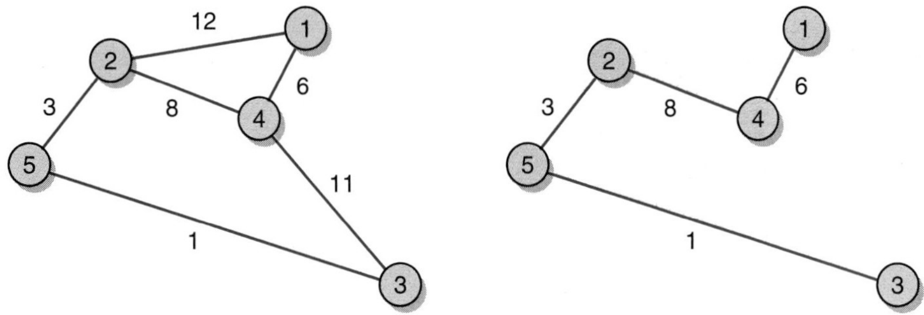

FIGURE 24.12 A network and its minimum spanning tree

```
/**
 * Returns a minimum spanning tree of the network.
 *
 * @return a minimum spanning tree of the network
 */
public Network mstNetwork()
{
    int x, y;
    int index;
    double weight;
    int[] edge = new int[2];
    HeapADT<Double> minHeap = new LinkedHeap<Double>();
    Network<T> resultGraph = new Network<T>();

    if (isEmpty() || !isConnected())
        return resultGraph;

    resultGraph.adjMatrix = new double[numVertices][numVertices];
    for (int i = 0; i < numVertices; i++)
        for (int j = 0; j < numVertices; j++)
            resultGraph.adjMatrix[i][j] = Double.POSITIVE_INFINITY;
    resultGraph.vertices = (T[])(new Object[numVertices]);

    boolean[] visited = new boolean[numVertices];
    for (int i = 0; i < numVertices; i++)
        visited[i] = false;

    edge[0] = 0;
    resultGraph.vertices[0] = this.vertices[0];
     resultGraph.numVertices++;
     visited[0] = true;
```

```
    // Add all edges, which are adjacent to the starting vertex,
    // to the heap

    for (int i = 0; i < numVertices; i++)
        minHeap.addElement(new Double(adjMatrix[0][i]));

    while ((resultGraph.size() < this.size()) && !minHeap.isEmpty())
    {

       // Get the edge with the smallest weight that has exactly
       // one vertex already in the resultGraph

       do
       {
          weight = (minHeap.removeMin()).doubleValue();
          edge = getEdgeWithWeightOf(weight, visited);
       } while (!indexIsValid(edge[0]) || !indexIsValid(edge[1]));

       x = edge[0];
       y = edge[1];
       if (!visited[x])
           index = x;
       else
           index = y;

       // Add the new edge and vertex to the resultGraph

       resultGraph.vertices[index] = this.vertices[index];
       visited[index] = true;
       resultGraph.numVertices++;

       resultGraph.adjMatrix[x][y] = this.adjMatrix[x][y];
       resultGraph.adjMatrix[y][x] = this.adjMatrix[y][x];

       // Add all edges, that are adjacent to the newly added vertex,
       // to the heap

       for (int i = 0; i < numVertices; i++)
       {
          if (!visited[i] && (this.adjMatrix[i][index] <
                           Double.POSITIVE_INFINITY))
          {
             edge[0] = index;
             edge[1] = i;
             minHeap.addElement(new Double(adjMatrix[index][i]));
          }
       }
    }
     return resultGraph;
}
```

Determining the Shortest Path

There are two possibilities for determining the "shortest" path in a graph. The first, and perhaps simplest, possibility is to determine the literal shortest path between a starting vertex and a target vertex—that is, the least number of edges between the two vertices. This turns out to be a simple variation of our earlier breadth-first traversal algorithm.

To convert this algorithm to find the shortest path, we simply store two additional pieces of information for each vertex during our traversal: the path length from the starting vertex to this vertex, and the vertex that is the predecessor of this vertex in that path. Then we modify our loop to terminate when we reach our target vertex. The path length for the shortest path is simply the path length to the predecessor of the target + 1, and if we wish to output the vertices along the shortest path, we can simply backtrack along the chain of predecessors.

The second possibility for determining the shortest path is to look for the cheapest path in a weighted graph. Dijkstra (1959) developed an algorithm for this possibility that is similar to our previous algorithm. However, instead of using a queue of vertices that causes us to progress through the graph in the order in which we encounter vertices, we use a minheap or a priority queue storing vertex and weight pairs based on total weight (the sum of the weights from the starting vertex to this vertex) so that we always traverse through the graph following the cheapest path first. For each vertex, we must store the label of the vertex, the weight of the cheapest path (thus far) to that vertex from our starting point, and the predecessor of that vertex along that path. On the minheap, we will store vertex and weight pairs for each possible path that we have encountered but not yet traversed. As we remove a (vertex, weight) pair from the minheap, if we encounter a vertex with a weight less than the one already stored with the vertex, we update the cost.

24.5 Strategies for Implementing Graphs

Let us begin our discussion of implementation strategies by examining what operations will need to be available for a graph. Of course, we will need to be able to add vertices and edges to the graph and to remove them from it. There will need to be traversals (perhaps breadth-first and depth-first) beginning with a particular vertex, and these might be implemented as iterators, as we did for binary trees. Other operations like `size`, `isEmpty`, `toString`, and `find` will be useful as well. In addition to these, operations to determine the shortest path from a particular vertex to a particular target vertex, to determine the adjacency of two vertices, to construct a minimum spanning tree, and to test for connectivity will all probably need to be implemented.

Whatever storage mechanism we use for vertices must allow us to mark vertices as visited during traversals and other algorithms. This can be accomplished by simply adding a Boolean variable to the class representing the vertices.

Adjacency Lists

Because trees are graphs, perhaps the best introduction to how we might implement graphs is to consider the discussions and examples that we have already seen concerning the implementation of trees. One might immediately think of using a set of nodes where each node contains an element and n–1 links to other nodes. When we use this strategy with trees, the number of connections from any given node is limited by the order of the tree (e.g., a maximum of two directed edges starting at any particular node in a binary tree). Because of this limitation, we can specify, for example, that a binary node has a left and a right child pointer. Even if the binary node is a leaf, the pointer still exists. It is simply set to null.

In the case of a *graph node*, because each node could have up to n – 1 edges connecting it to other nodes, it would be better to use a dynamic structure such as a linked list to store the edges within each node. This list is called an *adjacency list*. In the case of a network or a weighted graph, each edge would be stored as a triple including the weight. In the case of an undirected graph, an edge (A, B) would appear in the adjacency list of both vertex A and vertex B.

Adjacency Matrices

Keep in mind that we must somehow efficiently (in terms of both space and access time) store both vertices and edges. Because vertices are just elements, we can use any of our collections to store the vertices. In fact, we often talk about a "set of vertices," the term *set* implying an implementation strategy. However, another solution for storing edges is motivated by our use of array implementations of trees, but instead of using a one-dimensional array, we will use a two-dimensional array that we call an *adjacency matrix*. In an adjacency matrix, each position of the two-dimensional array represents an intersection between two vertices in the graph. Each of these intersections is represented by a Boolean value indicating whether or not the two vertices are connected. Figure 24.13 shows the undirected graph that we began with at the beginning of this chapter. Figure 24.14 shows the adjacency matrix for this graph.

For any position (row, column) in the matrix, that position is true if and only if the edge (v_{row}, v_{column}) is in the graph. Because edges in an undirected graph are bi-directional, if (A, B) is an edge in the graph, then (B, A) is also in the graph.

Notice that this matrix is symmetrical—that is, each side of the diagonal is a mirror image of the other. This is because we are representing an undirected graph. For undirected graphs, it may not be necessary to represent the entire matrix; one side or the other of the diagonal may be enough.

	A	B	C	D
A	F	T	T	F
B	T	F	T	T
C	T	T	F	F
D	F	T	F	F

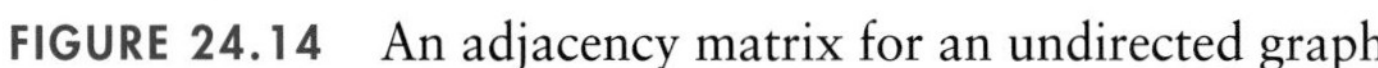

FIGURE 24.14 An adjacency matrix for an undirected graph

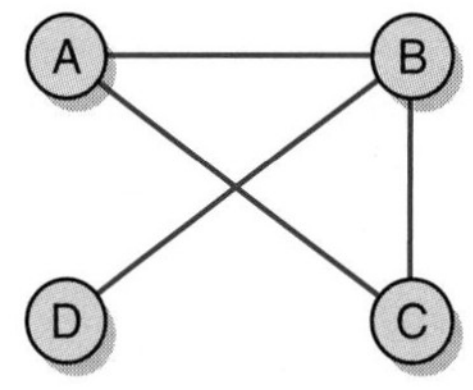

FIGURE 24.13 An undirected graph

However, for directed graphs, because all of the edges are directional, the result can be quite different. Figure 24.15 shows a directed graph, and Figure 24.16 shows the adjacency matrix for this graph.

Adjacency matrices may also be used with networks or weighted graphs by simply storing an object at each position of the matrix to represent the weight of the edge. Positions in the matrix where edges do not exist would simply be set to null.

24.6 Implementing Undirected Graphs with an Adjacency Matrix

Like the other collections we have discussed, the first step in implementing a graph is to determine its interface. Listing 24.1 illustrates the `GraphADT` interface. Listing 24.2 illustrates the `NetworkADT` interface that extends the `GraphADT` interface. Note that our interfaces include methods to add and remove vertices, methods to add and remove edges, iterators for both breadth-first and depth-first traversals, methods to determine the shortest path between two vertices and to determine whether the graph is connected, and our usual collection of methods to determine the size of the collection, to determine whether it is empty, and to return a string representation of it.

	A	B	C	D
A	F	T	T	F
B	F	F	T	T
C	F	F	F	F
D	F	F	F	F

FIGURE 24.16 The adjacency matrix for the directed graph shown in Figure 24.15

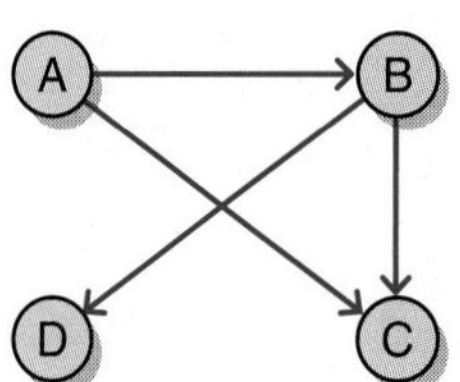

FIGURE 24.15 A directed graph

LISTING 24.1

```
package jsjf;
import java.util.Iterator;

/**
 * GraphADT defines the interface to a graph data structure.
 *
 * @author Java Foundations
 * @version 4.0
 */
public interface GraphADT<T>
{
  /**
   * Adds a vertex to this graph, associating object with vertex.
   *
   * @param vertex the vertex to be added to this graph
   */
  public void addVertex(T vertex);

  /**
   * Removes a single vertex with the given value from this graph.
   *
   * @param vertex the vertex to be removed from this graph
   */
  public void removeVertex(T vertex);

  /**
   * Inserts an edge between two vertices of this graph.
   *
   * @param vertex1 the first vertex
   * @param vertex2 the second vertex
   */
  public void addEdge(T vertex1, T vertex2);

  /**
   * Removes an edge between two vertices of this graph.
   *
   * @param vertex1 the first vertex
   * @param vertex2 the second vertex
   */
  public void removeEdge(T vertex1, T vertex2);

  /**
   * Returns a breadth first iterator starting with the given vertex.
   *
```

LISTING 24.1 *continued*

```
     * @param startVertex the starting vertex
     * @return a breadth first iterator beginning at the given vertex
     */
    public Iterator iteratorBFS(T startVertex);

    /**
     * Returns a depth first iterator starting with the given vertex.
     *
     * @param startVertex the starting vertex
     * @return a depth first iterator starting at the given vertex
     */
    public Iterator iteratorDFS(T startVertex);

    /**
     * Returns an iterator that contains the shortest path between
     * the two vertices.
     *
     * @param startVertex the starting vertex
     * @param targetVertex the ending vertex
     * @return an iterator that contains the shortest path
     *    between the two vertices
     */
    public Iterator iteratorShortestPath(T startVertex, T targetVertex);

    /**
     * Returns true if this graph is empty, false otherwise.
     *
     * @return true if this graph is empty
     */
    public boolean isEmpty();

    /**
     * Returns true if this graph is connected, false otherwise.
     *
     * @return true if this graph is connected
     */
    public boolean isConnected();

    /**
     * Returns the number of vertices in this graph.
     *
     * @return the integer number of vertices in this graph
     */
    public int size();
```

LISTING 24.1 *continued*

```
    /**
     * Returns a string representation of the adjacency matrix.
     *
     * @return a string representation of the adjacency matrix
     */
    public String toString();
}
```

LISTING 24.2

```
package jsjf;

import java.util.Iterator;

/**
 * NetworkADT defines the interface to a network.
 *
 * @author Java Foundations
 * @version 4.0
 */
public interface NetworkADT<T> extends GraphADT<T>
{
    /**
     * Inserts an edge between two vertices of this graph.
     *
     * @param vertex1 the first vertex
     * @param vertex2 the second vertex
     * @param weight the weight
     */
    public void addEdge(T vertex1, T vertex2, double weight);

    /**
     * Returns the weight of the shortest path in this network.
     *
     * @param vertex1 the first vertex
     * @param vertex2 the second vertex
     * @return the weight of the shortest path in this network
     */
    public double shortestPathWeight(T vertex1, T vertex2);
}
```

Of course, this interface could be implemented a variety of ways, but we will focus our discussion on an adjacency matrix implementation. The other implementations of undirected graphs and networks, as well as the implementations of directed graphs and networks, are left as programming projects. The header and instance data for our implementation are presented to provide context. Note that the adjacency matrix is represented by a two-dimensional Boolean array.

```
package jsjf;

import jsjf.exceptions.*;
import java.util.*;

/**
 * Graph represents an adjacency matrix implementation of a graph.
 *
 * @author Java Foundations
 * @version 4.0
 */
public class Graph<T> implements GraphADT<T>
{
   protected final int DEFAULT_CAPACITY = 5;
   protected int numVertices;    // number of vertices in the graph
   protected boolean[][] adjMatrix;    // adjacency matrix
   protected T[] vertices;    // values of vertices
   protected int modCount;
```

Our constructor simply initializes the number of vertices to zero, constructs the adjacency matrix, and sets up an array of generic objects (`T[]`) to represent the vertices.

```
/**
 * Creates an empty graph.
 */
public Graph()
{
   numVertices = 0;
   this.adjMatrix = new boolean[DEFAULT_CAPACITY][DEFAULT_CAPACITY];
   this.vertices = (T[])(new Object[DEFAULT_CAPACITY]);
}
```

The `addEdge` Method

Once we have established our list of vertices and our adjacency matrix, adding an edge is simply a matter of setting the appropriate locations in the adjacency matrix to true. Our `addEdge` method uses the `getIndex` method to locate the proper indices and calls a different version of the `addEdge` method to make the assignments if the indices are valid.

```
/**
 * Inserts an edge between two vertices of the graph.
 *
 * @param vertex1  the first vertex
 * @param vertex2  the second vertex
 */
public void addEdge(T vertex1, T vertex2)
{
   addEdge(getIndex(vertex1), getIndex(vertex2));
}
```

```
/**
 * Inserts an edge between two vertices of the graph.
 *
 * @param index1  the first index
 * @param index2  the second index
 */
public void addEdge(int index1, int index2)
{
   if (indexIsValid(index1) && indexIsValid(index2))
   {
      adjMatrix[index1][index2] = true;
      adjMatrix[index2][index1] = true;
      modCount++;
   }
}
```

The `addVertex` Method

Adding a vertex to the graph involves adding the vertex in the next available position in the array and setting all of the appropriate locations in the adjacency matrix to false.

```
/**
 * Adds a vertex to the graph, expanding the capacity of the graph
 * if necessary.  It also associates an object with the vertex.
 *
 * @param vertex  the vertex to add to the graph
 */
public void addVertex(T vertex)
{
    if ((numVertices + 1) == adjMatrix.length)
        expandCapacity();

    vertices[numVertices] = vertex;
    for (int i = 0; i < numVertices; i++)
    {
        adjMatrix[numVertices][i] = false;
        adjMatrix[i][numVertices] = false;
    }
    numVertices++;
    modCount++;
}
```

The `expandCapacity` Method

The `expandCapacity` method for our adjacency matrix implementation of a graph is more interesting than the similar method in other array implementations. It is no longer just a case of expanding one array and copying the contents. Keep in mind that for our graph, we must not only expand the array of vertices and copy the existing vertices into the new array; we must also expand the capacity of the adjacency list and copy the old contents into the new list.

```
/**
 * Creates new arrays to store the contents of the graph with
 * twice the capacity.
 */
protected void expandCapacity()
{
    T[] largerVertices = (T[])(new Object[vertices.length*2]);
    boolean[][] largerAdjMatrix =
         new boolean[vertices.length*2][vertices.length*2];

    for (int i = 0; i < numVertices; i++)
    {
        for (int j = 0; j < numVertices; j++)
          {
```

```
            largerAdjMatrix[i][j] = adjMatrix[i][j];
        }
        largerVertices[i] = vertices[i];
    }
    vertices = largerVertices;
    adjMatrix = largerAdjMatrix;
}
```

Other Methods

The remaining methods for our graph implementation are left as programming projects, as is the implementation of a network.

Summary of Key Concepts

- An undirected graph is a graph where the pairings that represent the edges are unordered.
- Two vertices in a graph are adjacent if there is an edge connecting them.
- An undirected graph is considered complete if it has the maximum number of edges connecting vertices.
- A path is a sequence of edges that connects two vertices in a graph.
- A cycle is a path in which the first and last vertices are the same and none of the edges is repeated.
- An undirected tree is a connected, acyclic, undirected graph with one element designated as the root.
- A directed graph, sometimes referred as a digraph, is a graph where the edges are ordered pairs of vertices.
- A path in a directed graph is a sequence of directed edges that connects two vertices in the graph.
- A network, or a weighted graph, is a graph with weights or costs associated with each edge.
- The only difference between a depth-first traversal of a graph and a breadth-first traversal is that the depth-first traversal uses a stack instead of a queue to manage the traversal.
- A graph is connected if and only if the number of vertices in the breadth-first traversal is the same as the number of vertices in the graph, regardless of the starting vertex.
- A spanning tree is a tree that includes all of the vertices of a graph and some, but possibly not all, of the edges.
- A minimum spanning tree is a spanning tree where the sum of the weights of the edges is less than or equal to the sum of the weights for any other spanning tree for the same graph.

Summary of Terms

graph A graph is made up of nodes and the connections between those nodes.

vertices Nodes within a graph.

edges Connections between nodes in a graph.

undirected graph A graph where the pairings that represent the edges are unordered.

adjacent Two vertices are adjacent if there is an edge connecting them.

self-loop An edge of a graph that connects a vertex to itself.

complete An undirected graph is considered complete if it has the maximum number of edges connecting vertices.

path A path is a sequence of edges that connects two vertices in a graph.

path length The number of edges in the path (or the number of vertices – 1).

connected An undirected graph is considered connected if for any two vertices in the graph, there is a path between them.

cycle A path in which the first and last vertices are the same and none of the edges is repeated.

acyclic A graph that has no cycles.

directed graph (digraph) A graph where the edges are ordered pairs of vertices.

topological order The order of vertices for an acyclic directed graph where A precedes B if an edge exists from A to B.

network (weighted graph) A graph with weights or costs associated with each edge.

breadth-first traversal A traversal of a graph that behaves like a level-order traversal of a tree.

depth-first traversal A traversal of a graph that behaves like a preorder traversal of a tree.

spanning tree A tree that includes all of the vertices of a graph and some, but possibly not all, of the edges.

minimum spanning tree A spanning tree for a network where the sum of the weights of the edges is less than or equal to the sum of the weights for any other spanning tree.

adjacency list For any given node in a graph, the list of edges connecting it to other nodes. In the case of a network, each entry in the list also includes the weight or cost of the edge.

adjacency matrix A two-dimensional array where each location in the array represents the intersection between two vertices in the graph. In the case of an undirected graph, each position in the array is simply a Boolean. In the case of a weighted graph, the weight of the edge is stored in the array.

Self-Review Questions

SR 24.1 What is the difference between a graph and a tree?

SR 24.2 What is an undirected graph?

SR 24.3 What is a directed graph?

SR 24.4 What does it mean to say that a graph is complete?

SR 24.5 What is the maximum number of edges for an undirected graph? What is the maximum number of edges for a directed graph?

SR 24.6 Give the definition of path and the definition of a cycle.

SR 24.7 What is the difference between a network and a graph?

SR 24.8 What is a spanning tree? What is a minimum spanning tree?

Exercises

EX 24.1 Draw the undirected graph that is represented as follows:

```
Vertices: 1, 2, 3, 4, 5, 6, 7

Edges: (1, 2), (1, 4), (2, 3), (2, 4), (3, 7), (4, 7),
(4, 6), (5, 6), (5, 7), (6, 7)
```

EX 24.2 Is the graph from Exercise 24.1 connected? Is it complete?

EX 24.3 List all of the cycles in the graph from Exercise 24.1.

EX 24.4 Draw a spanning tree for the graph from Exercise 24.1.

EX 24.5 Using the data in Exercise 24.1, draw the resulting directed graph.

EX 24.6 Is the directed graph of Exercise 24.5 connected? Is it complete?

EX 24.7 List all of the cycles in the graph of Exercise 24.5.

EX 24.8 Draw a spanning tree for the graph of Exercise 24.5.

EX 24.9 Consider the weighted graph shown in Figure 24.10. List all of the possible paths from vertex 2 to vertex 3 along with the total weight of each path.

Programming Projects

PP 24.1 Implement an undirected graph using an adjacency list. Keep in mind that you must store both vertices and edges. Your implementation must implement the `GraphADT` interface.

PP 24.2 Repeat Programming Project 24.1 for a directed graph.

PP 24.3 Complete the implementation of a graph using an adjacency matrix that was presented in this chapter.

PP 24.4 Extend the adjacency matrix implementation presented in this chapter to create an implementation of a weighted graph or network.

PP 24.5 Extend the adjacency matrix implementation presented in this chapter to create a directed graph.

PP 24.6 Extend your implementation from Programming Project 24.1 to create a weighted, undirected graph.

PP 24.7 Create a limited airline scheduling system that will allow a user to enter city-to-city connections and their prices. Your system should then allow a user to enter two cities and should return the shortest path and the cheapest path between the two cities. Your system should report if there is no connection between two cities. Assume an undirected network.

PP 24.8 Repeat Programming Project 24.7 assuming a directed network.

PP 24.9 Create a simple graphical application that will produce a textual representation of the shortest path and the cheapest path between two vertices in a network.

PP 24.10 Create a network routing system that, given the point-to-point connections in the network and the costs of utilizing each, will produce cheapest-path connections from each point to each point in the network and will report any disconnected locations.

Answers to Self-Review Questions

SRA 24.1 A graph is the more general concept without the restriction that each node have one and only one parent except for the root, which does not have a parent. In the case of a graph, there is no root, and each vertex can be connected to up to n – 1 other vertices.

SRA 24.2 An undirected graph is a graph where the pairings that represent the edges are unordered.

SRA 24.3 A directed graph, sometimes referred as a digraph, is a graph where the edges are ordered pairs of vertices.

SRA 24.4 A graph is considered complete if it has the maximum number of edges connecting vertices.

SRA 24.5 The maximum number of edges for an undirected graph is n (n – 1)/2. For a directed graph, it is n(n – 1).

SRA 24.6 A path is a sequence of edges that connects two vertices in a graph. A cycle is a path in which the first and last vertices are the same and none of the edges is repeated.

SRA 24.7 A network is a graph, either directed or undirected, with weights or costs associated with each edge.

SRA 24.8 A spanning tree is a tree that includes all of the vertices of a graph and some, but possibly not all, of the edges. A minimum spanning tree is a spanning tree where the sum of the weights of the edges is less than or equal to the sum of the weights for any other spanning tree for the same graph.

References

Collins, W. J. *Data Structures: An Object-Oriented Approach*. Reading, Mass.: Addison-Wesley, 1992.

Dijkstra, E. W. "A Note on Two Problems in Connection with Graphs." *Numerische Mathematik 1* (1959): 269–271.

Drosdek, A. *Data Structures and Algorithms in Java*. Pacific Grove, Cal.: Brooks/Cole, 2001.

Prim, R. C. "Shortest Connection Networks and Some Generalizations." *Bell System Technical Journal 36* (1957): 1389–1401.

Databases

25

CHAPTER OBJECTIVES

- Understand the basic concept of a database as it relates to data storage.
- Explain the concepts behind relational databases.
- Examine how Java programs can connect to databases for the purposes of creating, reading, updating, and deleting data.
- Briefly introduce the syntax of several different types of SQL statements.

This chapter provides an introduction to databases and interacting with databases using Java. A database is a large repository of data organized for efficient storage and searching. Discussing databases and the way we interact with them through a Java program is a natural extension of the concept of collections that has been a major theme throughout this book.

25.1 Introduction to Databases

A *database* is a potentially large repository of data, organized so that the data can be quickly stored, searched, and organized in various ways. A *database management system* is software that provides the ability to quickly search or query the data contained within the database and generally perform four primary operations on the data: create, read, update, and delete (also known as CRUD). Applications such as a university's class scheduling system and an airline reservation system use a database to organize and manage large amounts of data.

KEY CONCEPT
Databases are software applications used to provide data to other programs.

There are many different types of databases, each with its own strengths and weaknesses. For example, there are object-oriented databases, flat-file databases, and relational databases. A comprehensive discussion of the various types of databases is beyond the scope of this text, but we will focus on the most commonly used type of database in existence today—a relational database. A relational database organizes its basic information into one or more *tables*. And, perhaps more important, the relationships among various data elements are also stored in tables.

A simple example of a relational database (or a database that uses the relational model) appears in the following two tables, which we shall call Person and Location. Let's look at each more closely. The Person table contains a series of rows, which are called records. Each record in the table contains the information about one person in our database. Each person's record provides a number of fields, including that person's first name, her or his last name, and two integer values: `personID` and `locationID`. The `personID` is a unique integer value (that is, unique within the Person table) used to identify a particular record. For example, Peter's `personalID` is 1. John's `personalID` is 2. Each record also contains a `locationID`. This value is used to find (or "look up") a particular matching record in the `Location` table; hence the name `locationID` that contains the table name as part of the field name.

Person			
personID	firstName	LastName	locationID
0	Matthew	Williamson	0
1	Peter	DePasquale	0
2	John	Lewis	1
3	Jason	Smithson	2

Location		
locationID	city	state
0	Portsmouth	RI
1	Blacksburg	VA
2	Maple Glen	PA
3	San Jose	CA

Thus, by using the `locationID` value in Peter's record in the Person table, and finding that value in the Location table, we can determine that Peter lives in Portsmouth, RI. Matthew Williamson lives there as well. But what do these tables really get us? There are several answers to that question. First of all, we pointed out that both Matt and Peter live in the same town in the same state. If we didn't have a `Location` table in use, the city and state strings would probably be a part of the `Person` table, so we would be using more space in our database to replicate the same values over and over. By using the Location table, we can conserve space by avoiding data replication.

There's another advantage to the use of tables in this manner. We can easily query our database (ask it a question) to determine which people live in Portsmouth, RI. Each record of each person that we have stored in the `Person` table will contain the value 0 in the `locationID` field. There's actually a more complex way of *joining* the tables to determine the answer to our query, but that's really outside the scope of this text.

KEY CONCEPT

A relational database creates relationships between records in different tables by using unique identifiers.

Our query can be quickly executed because we are using the strength of the relational database model. If we were replicating our data ("Portsmouth", "RI") over and over in several records of the Person table, searching for all residents of Portsmouth would be rather inefficient and time-consuming, because we'd be searching each record looking for two string values.

Tables in our database are related by the use of the `locationID`. A `locationID` value helps to relate a specific person record in the `Person` table to a specific record in the Location table. Additionally, as you may have noted, each record in the Location table has its own unique identifier (`locationID`). The use of these identifiers and the way we utilize them between tables enable us to establish the relationships between the records in our tables.

KEY CONCEPT

The JDBC API is used to establish a connection to a database.

For the purposes of this discussion, we will be using the open source database MySQL (see http://www.mysql.com to obtain a copy). There are other databases that we could have chosen, including Oracle, SQLServer, Access, and PostgreSQL. Some of these databases are open source and freely available; others can be purchased for a fee.

Before we can interact with a database in a Java program, we must first establish a connection to it. To do that, we'll use the Java Database Connectivity (JDBC) API. The JDBC API provides us the classes and methods required to manage our data from within the Java program. Fortunately, the JDBC API has been a component of the Java Development Environment (JDK) since JDK 1.1, so we won't have to download any additional software to obtain the API functionality. However, to connect to our database, we will need a database-specific driver, discussed in the next section.

25.2 Establishing a Connection to a Database

In order to establish communications to our database, we'll need a specialized piece of software that communicates our database requests to the database application (known as the server, which generally resides on another machine). This software is known as a *driver*. The response from the database is communicated back to our program via the driver, as well.

Obtaining a Database Driver

There are over two hundred JDBC drivers available for various databases. To find one for your system, check Java's JDBC Data Access API web page at developers.sun.com/product/jdbc/drivers. We'll be using the MySQL connector driver (www.mysql.com/products/connector/) to provide our connection to a database hosted on another computer. We downloaded our connector in jar file form from the MySQL website and placed in it a directed named "connector."

Once installed, we need only refer to its location via the CLASSPATH environment variable (during compilation and execution). Depending on your configuration, you can save these values in a shell configuration or just provide them on the command line. As we demonstrate the coding steps necessary to create and issue queries, and obtain and process responses from the server, we'll also show you how to include the driver into the CLASSPATH.

In Listing 25.1, we have a simple program that includes the use of several JDBC-specific classes. The code demonstrates the loading of our JDBC driver, attempting to establish a connection to our database server, and closing the connection once we have confirmed that the connection was opened.

The program starts by attempting to load our JDBC driver (`com.mysql.jdbc.Driver`) from our downloaded jar file. When our driver is loaded, it will create an instance of itself and register itself with the `DriverManager` (`java.sql.DriverManager`) class.

Next, we attempt to establish a connection to our database through the `DriverManager` class. The `DriverManager` will attempt to select an appropriate driver from among the set of drivers registered with the `DriverManager`. In our case, this will be easy; we're using only one driver for this program, and it is the only possible driver that can be selected. The call to the `getConnection` method of the `DriverManager` accepts a URL that defines our database instance. It comprises several components that we must provide, including the hostname (the name of the machine where our database server is residing), the name of the database, and the username and password that will provide us access to the selected database.

LISTING 25.1

```
import java.sql.*;

/**
 * Demonstrates the establishment of a JDBC connector.
 *
 * @author Java Foundations
 * @version 4.0
 */
public class DatabaseConnector
{
   /**
   * Establishes the connection to the database and prints an
   * appropriate confirmation message.
   */
    public static void main (String args[])
    {
       try
       {
          Connection conn = null;

          // Loads the class object for the mysql driver into the DriverManager.

          Class.forName("com.mysql.jdbc.Driver");

          // Attempt to establish a connection to the specified database via the
          // DriverManager

          conn = DriverManager.getConnection("jdbc:mysql://comtor.org/"+
             "javafoundations?user=jf2e&password=hirsch");

          if (conn != null)
          {
             System.out.println("We have connected to our database!");
             conn.close();
          }

       } catch (SQLException ex) {
          System.out.println("SQLException: " + ex.getMessage());
          ex.printStackTrace();
    }     catch (Exception ex) {
```

LISTING 25.1 *continued*

```
        System.out.println("Exception: " + ex.getMessage());
        ex.printStackTrace();
      }
    }
  }
```

If all goes well, and there are no problems (such as the database server not running, or a communications issue between our machine where our Java program is executing and the host on which the database server is executing), we will be returned a `Connection` (`java.sql.Connection`) object. This object represents a single connection to our database and will be the conduit for our queries to, and responses from, the database. Finally, our program checks to determine whether we did in fact receive a non-null `Connection` object, and if so, it prints a success message to the user and then closes the connection to the database.

In order to execute a program called `Example1`, the CLASSPATH will need to reflect the location of the driver. It is not necessary for it to do so when we compile the `Example1` program, because we need only the `Driver` class from the JDBC jar file at run-time when the program attempts to load and register the `Driver` object. Working on the UNIX command line, after successful compilation, we can execute the program with the following command:

```
$ java -cp .:../connector/mysql-connector-java-5.1.7-bin.jar
Example1
```

Under Windows, the command will be

```
java -cp .;..\connector\mysql-connector-java-5.1.7-bin.jar
Example1
```

The resulting output is

```
We have connected to our database!
```

This assumes that the download location of our JDBC jar file is the adjacent connector directory from the current directory. We could have placed our jar file in the same directory where the source code is located, but we prefer not to mix our source code and jar files, so they are placed in the connector directory.

We'll do more with our database in the next section, including creating and altering tables in our database.

25.3 Creating and Altering Database Tables

In the previous section, we showed how to establish a connection to our database, check that the connection was successful, and disconnect. Let's expand on those abilities and create a new database table.

Create Table

The start of the SQL statement to create a database table is `CREATE TABLE <tablename>`. We will also need to specify the name of the table and any fields that will be present at creation. For example, let's create a new table of students. For now, this table will contain an ID value (known as a key) and the students' first and last names. To do so, our creation command will be the following string:

> **KEY CONCEPT**
> The `CREATE TABLE` SQL statement is used to create new database tables.

```
CREATE TABLE Student (student_ID INT UNSIGNED NOT NULL
AUTO_INCREMENT, PRIMARY KEY (student_ID), firstName
varchar(255), lastName varchar(255))
```

Each field of the table is specified in the comma-separated list in the parentheses that follow the table name (`Student`). Our table will initially include the following fields:

- `student_ID`—an unsigned integer value, which cannot be null and will automatically increment each time we add a new student to the table.
- `firstName`—a variable-length character string up to 255 characters in length.
- `lastName`—a variable-length character string up to 255 characters in length.

You may be asking yourself about the `PRIMARY KEY` field that we skipped mentioning. It isn't really a field but a setting on the table itself that specifies which field or fields make the record unique among the other records. Because each student will have a unique identifier, the `student_ID` field will be sufficient to be our table's key. Again, this is a database topic that you really need to study in the database course, so we will leave it at that for now.

To create the table in our existing code from Listing 1, we'll add the following lines immediately after the successful connection message.

```
Statement stmt = conn.createStatement();
boolean result = stmt.execute("CREATE TABLE Student " +
  " (student_ID INT UNSIGNED NOT NULL AUTO_INCREMENT, " +
  " PRIMARY KEY (student_ID), firstName varchar(255), " +
  " lastName varchar(255))");
System.out.print("\tTable creation result: " + result + "\t");
System.out.println("(false is the expected result)");
```

The Statement class (java.sql.Statement) is an interface class, which we will use to prepare and execute our SQL statement(s). We can ask our Connection object to create our Statement object for us. Once we have our Statement object, we can call its execute method and pass it the SQL query string (our CREATE TABLE string) for execution by the database. The execute method returns a TRUE value if there is a ResultSet object (we'll talk about this shortly) returned after the call, or returns a false otherwise.

When we execute our code, we anticipate that we will be returned a FALSE value and the table will be created. In fact, that is what happens (see the output below). However, note that if an attempt to execute the same program is again made, the program will throw an exception stating that the table already exists. That's fine for now. We'll discuss removal of tables later in this chapter.

```
We have connected to our database!
  Table creation result: false (false is the expected result)
```

Alter Table

So far, so good! Our new database has a new table called Student. Now let's add a few fields in our new table. Often the structure of a table will be established when it is created and will not be changed subsequently, but from time to time the need to alter an existing table arises. We could drop (delete) the existing table and create a new one from scratch. But if we do, we'll lose the data currently stored in the table. It's usually preferable to add new fields or remove existing fields (and their data) from an existing table.

KEY CONCEPT
The ALTER TABLE SQL statement can be used to modify an existing database table.

Let's add age and gpa fields for our students. For the age field, we can use the smallest unsigned integer field possible (conserving the most amount of space). This is an unsigned tinyint for MySQL (be sure to check the datatype listing for your database); it will range from 0 to 255, sufficient for an age field. We'll also need an additional column for our gpa field. Here we will use an unsigned float that uses three digits total, and two digits for the fractional part.

In order to modify our table and add the missing fields, we need to create a new Statement object and use the ALTER TABLE <tablename> ADD COLUMN SQL statement. Following the ADD COLUMN portion of the string, we specify our new fields in a parenthetical list, separated by commas. Once the string is constructed, we call the execute method of the Statement object to execute the query. Again here, we expect a FALSE value to be returned, indicating that no result set is returned to us.

```
Statement stmt2 = conn.createStatement();
result = stmt2.execute("ALTER TABLE Student ADD COLUMN " +
  " (age tinyint UNSIGNED, gpa FLOAT (3,2) unsigned)");

System.out.print("\tTable modification result: " + result + "\t");
System.out.println("(false is the expected result)");
```

Our output is not surprising:

```
We have connected to our database!
  Table creation result: false (false is the expected result)
  Table modification result: false (false is the expected result)
```

Drop Column

Of course, we may also wish to alter a table by dropping a column, rather than adding one or more. To do so, we can use the `ALTER TABLE` Sql statement and follow the table name with the `DROP COLUMN` command. `DROP COLUMN` is followed by one or more column names, separated by commas. For example, if we wanted to drop the `firstName` column of our `Student` table, we could use the following statements:

```
Statement stmt3 = conn.createStatement();
result = stmt3.execute("ALTER TABLE Student DROP COLUMN first-
Name");

System.out.print("\tTable modification result: " + result + "\t");
System.out.println("(false is the expected result)");
```

Again, our output is fairly straightforward:

```
We have connected to our database!
  Table creation result: false (false is the expected result)
  Table modification result: false (false is the expected result)
  Table modification result: false (false is the expected result)
```

But how do we know this is really modifying the table? What we really want to be able to do is ask the database to tell us what the structure of our table is at any point in time. We'll discuss that in the next section.

25.4 Querying the Database

At this point, we have a single table in our database with no data. One of the activities we would like to do at this point is query the database regarding the structure of our table. To do this, we will build another `Statement` and send it to the database server for processing. However, the difference here, compared to our earlier examples, is that we expect to be returned a `ResultSet` object—an object that manages a set of records that contains our result.

How to obtain and use a `ResultSet` is an important piece of the knowledge we will need to master in order to obtain information from our database. A `ResultSet` functions in much the same way a `Scanner` object does; it provides a method of accessing and traversing through a set of data (in this case, data obtained from our database). A default `ResultSet` object permits moving through the data from the first object to the last object in the set, and it cannot be updated. Other variations of the `ResultSet` object can permit bidirectional movement and the ability to be updated.

Show Columns

The simplest example we can provide of using a `ResultSet` is querying the database about the structure of our table. In the following sections of this chapter, we will use the `ResultSet` in more complex ways. In the code below, we form our query and submit it to the server. Apart from the syntax of the `SHOW COLUMNS <tablename>` statement, the remainder of the code is very straightforward and similar to our previous examples. Note that we are expecting a `ResultSet` object to be returned from our execution of the query.

KEY CONCEPT

The `SHOW COLUMNS` SQL statement can be used to obtain a list of a table's columns and configuration settings.

```
Statement stmt5 = conn.createStatement();
ResultSet rSet = stmt5.executeQuery("SHOW COLUMNS FROM Student");
```

Once we have our results returned from the query, we can obtain some information from the `ResultSet`'s `ResultSetMetaData` object (which contains "meta" information about the results returned). For instance, in the next two lines of code, we use information from the `ResultSetMetaData` object to produce output for the user (including the table name and the number of columns in the result).

```
ResultSetMetaData rsmd = rSet.getMetaData();
int numColumns = rsmd.getColumnCount();
```

Our `ResultSet` is essentially a two-dimensional table that contains columns (our fields) and rows of data (records in the result). By utilizing the metadata regarding the number of columns in the `ResultSet`, we can print out some basic information about the structure of our `Student` table.

```
String resultString = null;
if (numColumns > 0)
```

```
{
  resultString = "Table: Student\n" +
    "========================================================" +
    "========================================================\n\t";
  for (int colNum = 1; colNum <= numColumns; colNum++)
    resultString += rsmd.getColumnLabel(colNum) + '\t';
}
System.out.println(resultString);
System.out.println(
  "========================================================" +
  "========================================================\n\t");
```

The program will now print out a table of our column headers in the `ResultSet`, which is really a list of property names for each field in our table.

```
We have connected to our database!
  Table creation result: false (false is the expected result)
  Table modification result: false (false is the expected result)
  Table modification result: false (false is the expected result)
Table: Student
========================================================
  Field Type Null Key Default Extra
========================================================
```

Let's get the rows of data as well from the `ResultSet` so that we can see the full structure of our table. We need to add additional statements to our program that will iterate through the `ResultSet` rows and obtain the value of each column as a string.

```
We have connected to our database!
  Table creation result: false (false is the expected result)
  Table modification result: false (false is the expected result)
  Table modification result: false (false is the expected result)
Table: Student
========================================================
Field   Type   Null   Key   Default   Extra
========================================================
student_ID   int(10) unsigned   NO   PRI   auto_increment
--------------------------------------------------------
lastName   varchar(255)   YES
--------------------------------------------------------
age   tinyint(3) unsigned   YES
--------------------------------------------------------
gpa   float(3,2) unsigned   YES
--------------------------------------------------------
```

It's not very pretty, but we can now see the basic configuration information for each field in our table. Each record from the `ResultSet` contains the field name, the field (data) type, whether the field can hold a null value, whether the field is part of a key, the default value for the field (if not provided), and any extra information.

Let's turn this printed table into something easier to read. With a little more work, we could have attempted to output the table structure in a format like the one shown in the following table. This is left up to you as a string formatting exercise.

Field	Type	Null	Key	Default	Extra
student_ID	int(10) unsigned	NO	PRI	auto_increment	
lastName	varchar(255)	YES			
age	tinyint(3) unsigned	YES			
gpa	float(3, 2) unsigned	YES			

We used our `Statement` object as the vehicle to obtain information from our database. In this case, the information we sought was the structure of the `Student` table. However, we can change our `Statement` string and query the database quite easily.

In terms of outputting the results, we'll do the same iteration through the `ResultSet`. However, there's one problem. Our `Student` table does not yet have any data in it. We'll address that problem in the next section and then show how to query the table.

25.5 Inserting, Viewing, and Updating Data

A table without data is like a day without sunshine. It's time to put some real data into our `Student` table. Since the `studentID` field is an `auto_increment` field (it will automatically increment by 1 each time data are placed into the table), we really only needed to insert data for student `lastnames`, `age`, and `gpa`. Let's add the following values into our database.

lastName	age	gpa
Campbell	19	3.79
Garcia	28	2.37
Fuller	19	3.18
Cooper	26	2.13
Walker	27	2.14
Griego	31	2.10

Insert

To insert the data, we need to create a new `Statement` and use the `INSERT <tablename>` SQL statement. The `INSERT` statement takes the form

```
INSERT <tablename> (column name, ...) VALUES (expression, ...)
```

Following the `tablename`, one or more columns are specified by name. Then the values to be placed in the specified fields, respectively, are listed in the same order in which the columns are specified. For example, to insert the Campbell row into the database, we will create a SQL statement that looks like this:

KEY CONCEPT

The `INSERT SQL` statement is used to add new data to a database table.

```
INSERT Student (lastName, age, gpa) VALUES ("Campbell", 19, 3.79)
```

We can use the following two lines of source code to perform the insertion on the table.

```
Statement stmt2 = conn.createStatement(ResultSet.TYPE_FORWARD_ONLY,
  ResultSet.CONCUR_UPDATABLE);
int rowCount = stmt2.executeUpdate("INSERT Student " +
  "(lastName, age, gpa) VALUES (\"Campbell\", 19, 3.79)");
```

In order for the update of the table's data values to take place, we need to make two method calls different from those we have done previously. First, when we construct the `Statement` object (via the `createStatement` method), we specify that the resulting `ResultSet`'s pointer may move only forward and that changes to the `ResultSet` are passed on to the database.

Second, we called the `executeUpdate` method, rather than the `execute` or `executeQuery` methods used earlier. The `executeUpdate` method returns the number of rows affected by the update query; in this case, only 1 row was modified. Similar `executeQuery` statements can follow, enabling us to insert each row of students shown in Table 1. Alternatively, we could read our data from an input file and use a loop to process the data from the input file into the database.

It's been a while since we have seen the full body of code of our program. Along the way we have made a number of additions and changes. Listing 25.2 on the next page updates us on the source code we're using in discussing our database connections.

SELECT . . . FROM

One of the actions we perform most frequently on a database is issuing queries to view to retrieve the data. The `SELECT . . . FROM` SQL statement permits users to construct a request for data based on a number of criteria. The basic syntax of the `SELECT . . . FROM` statement is as follows:

KEY CONCEPT

The `SELECT` SQL statement is used to retrieve data from a database table.

LISTING 25.2

```
import java.sql.*;

/**
 * Demonstrates interaction between a Java program and a database.
 *
 * @author Java Foundations
 * @version 4.0
 */
public class DatabaseModification
{
   /**
   * Carries out various CRUD operations after establishing the
   * database connection.
   */
   public static void main (String args[])
   {
      Connection conn = null;
      try
      {

         // Loads the class object for the mysql driver into the DriverManager.
         Class.forName("com.mysql.jdbc.Driver");

         // Attempt to establish a connection to the specified database via the
         // DriverManager

         conn = DriverManager.getConnection("jdbc:mysql://comtor.org/" +
           "javafoundations?user=jf2e&password=hirsch");

         // Check the connection

         if (conn != null)
         {
            System.out.println("We have connected to our database!");

             // Create the table and show the table structure

             Statement stmt = conn.createStatement();
             boolean result = stmt.execute("CREATE TABLE Student " +
               " (student_ID INT UNSIGNED NOT NULL AUTO_INCREMENT, " +
               " PRIMARY KEY (student_ID), lastName varchar(255), " +
               " age tinyint UNSIGNED, gpa FLOAT (3,2) unsigned)");
```

LISTING 25.2 *continued*

```
         System.out.println("\tTable creation result: " + result);
         DatabaseModification.showColumns(conn);

         //  Insert the data into the database and show the values in the table

         Statement stmt2 = conn.createStatement(ResultSet.TYPE_FORWARD_ONLY,
           ResultSet.CONCUR_UPDATABLE);
         int rowCount = stmt2.executeUpdate("INSERT Student " +
           "(lastName, age, gpa) VALUES (\"Campbell\", 19, 3.79)");
         DatabaseModification.showValues(conn);

         //  Close the database

         conn.close();
      }

    } catch (SQLException ex) {
       System.out.println("SQLException: " + ex.getMessage());
       ex.printStackTrace();

    } catch (Exception ex) {
       System.out.println("Exception: " + ex.getMessage());
       ex.printStackTrace();
    }
  }

/**
 * Obtains and displays a ResultSet from the Student table.
 */
public static void showValues(Connection conn)
{
   try
   {
      Statement stmt = conn.createStatement();
      ResultSet rset = stmt.executeQuery("SELECT * FROM Student");
      DatabaseModification.showResults("Student", rset);
   } catch (SQLException ex) {
      System.out.println("SQLException: " + ex.getMessage());
      ex.printStackTrace();
   }
}

  /**
   * Displays the structure of the Student table.
   */
```

LISTING 25.2 *continued*

```
public static void showColumns(Connection conn)
{
   try
   {
      Statement stmt = conn.createStatement();
      ResultSet rset = stmt.executeQuery("SHOW COLUMNS FROM Student");
      DatabaseModification.showResults("Student", rset);
   } catch (SQLException ex) {
      System.out.println("SQLException: " + ex.getMessage());
      ex.printStackTrace();
   }
}

/**
* Displays the contents of the specified ResultSet.
*/
public static void showResults(String tableName, ResultSet rSet)
{
   try
   {
      ResultSetMetaData rsmd = rSet.getMetaData();
      int numColumns = rsmd.getColumnCount();
      String resultString = null;
      if (numColumns > 0)
      {
         resultString = "\nTable: " + tableName + "\n" +
           "=======================================================\n";
         for (int colNum = 1; colNum <= numColumns; colNum++)
           resultString += rsmd.getColumnLabel(colNum) + " ";
      }
      System.out.println(resultString);
      System.out.println(
        "=======================================================");

      while (rSet.next())
      {
        resultString = "";
        for (int colNum = 1; colNum <= numColumns; colNum++)
        {
           String column = rSet.getString(colNum);
           if (column != null)
             resultString += column + " ";
        }
        System.out.println(resultString + '\n' +
        "------------------------------------------------------------");
    }
```

LISTING 25.2 *continued*

```
        } catch (SQLException ex) {
            System.out.println("SQLException: " + ex.getMessage());
            ex.printStackTrace();
        }
    }
}
```

```
SELECT <columns, ...> FROM <tablename> WHERE <condition, ...>
```

The `SELECT` statement has many parts (most of which are beyond the scope of this text). We will talk about just a few to get you started using the statement.

The `SELECT` statement allows you to ask for only certain columns to be returned following the query. For example, if we wanted only a list of student `lastNames` and `gpas` from our `Student` table, we would construct our query as follows:

```
SELECT lastName, gpa FROM Student
```

If we wanted to make our query even more specific, and get the `lastNames` and `gpas` only of students whose `age` is 21 and over, our statement would look like this:

```
SELECT lastName, gpa FROM Student WHERE age >= 21
```

The `WHERE condition` clause is optional, and if it is not provided, all rows from the specified table will be selected. A condition is an expression that must evaluate to `TRUE` and can contain functions and operators such as `&&` (and), `||` (or), and many others. For example, we can further refine our query to limit results to those students who are 21 years old or older and who have a grade point average of 3.0 or less:

```
SELECT lastName, gpa FROM Student WHERE age >= 21 && gpa <= 3.0
```

The selected items to return (`lastName` and `gpa` in our examples above) are specified by listing them with a comma between them. However, if you wish to have all of the columns from a table returned, you can substitute an asterisk (`*`) for the column listings:

```
SELECT * FROM Student WHERE age >= 21 && gpa <= 3.0
```

As like our INSERT statement, the SELECT statement will be a parameter to an executeQuery method call. The output from the execution of this statement would look something like

```
Table: Student
=========================================================
student_ID   lastName   age   gpa
=========================================================
2   Jones   22   2.40
---------------------------------------------------------
```

There are a number of other capabilities that the SELECT SQL statement provides, including the ability to join two or more tables, to limit our output to a set number of rows, and to group our results by one or more columns. Often, the most useful additional clause is ORDER BY <columnname> <direction>.

The ORDER BY clause, appended to the statement following the where clause, will direct the statement to sort our results in an ascending or descending fashion. To specify ascending, place the string ASC in the direction portion; to specify descending, use DESC. For example, the query

```
SELECT * FROM Student ORDER BY gpa DESC
```

produces the following results:

```
Table: Student
=========================================================
lastName   age   gpa
=========================================================
Hampton   31   3.88
---------------------------------------------------------
Campbell   19   3.79
---------------------------------------------------------
Smith   21   3.69
---------------------------------------------------------
Jones   22   2.40
---------------------------------------------------------
```

Update

Updating data in a database is another frequently used skill. Fortunately, it is a rather simple process. We can break the process down into three steps. First, we obtain a ResultSet and navigate to the row we wish to update. Second, we update the ResultSet's value that we wish to change. Finally, we update the database with the record from the ResultSet.

Let's look at these steps in more detail. We first want to obtain a ResultSet on which we will operate. The type of change you wish to make to the database (updating one row vs. updating multiple rows) will likely direct the ResultSet you obtain to operate on the data. Generally speaking, it's a good idea to limit your ResultSet to the database rows you wish to modify. Thus, if you are going to change only one row's values, your ResultSet should really comprise only that row.

KEY CONCEPT
Updates to a database can be performed through changes to a ResultSet.

Once we have our ResultSet, we need to navigate the ResultSet cursor (a pointer into the set). You may have noted from Listing 25.2 that we iterated through the ResultSet by repeatedly calling the next method on the ResultSet object. We can actually navigate via a number of methods (first, last, next, previous, and so on). Because the cursor is placed prior to the first row in a ResultSet, we simply used the next method to move forward each time we attempted to read a row of data.

If we are modifying only one row of data and our ResultSet contains only one row, we can just jump to the first row by executing a call to our set's first method. Then, we can modify our data by using the updateXXX methods (updateString, updateFloat, and so on) on our set. We make our changes permanent in the database by calling the updateRow method. Here is an example:

```
ResultSet rst = stmt2.executeQuery("SELECT * FROM Student
WHERE " +
  "lastName=\"Jones\"");
rst.first();
rst.updateFloat("gpa", 3.41f);
rst.updateRow();
```

Obviously, if we are attempting to update multiple rows of records from a ResultSet, the navigation and updating statements will be more involved, possibly utilizing a loop. Additionally, prior to inserting, we can update any number of values in the row or rows in the ResultSet. The updateRow call simply communicates the changes back to the database once the ResultSet contains all of the necessary changes.

25.6 Deleting Data and Database Tables

The last piece of our JDBC knowledge is the ability to delete data and tables from the database. We'll first look at the deleting of data.

Deleting Data

The SQL statement that deletes data from a table is the DELETE FROM statement. This statement has the syntax

```
DELETE FROM <tablename> WHERE condition
```

KEY CONCEPT
The DELETE FROM SQL statement is used to delete data from a database table.

The WHERE condition clause is optional, and if it is not provided, all rows from the specified table will be deleted. A condition is an expression that must evaluate to TRUE and can contain functions and operators such as && (and), || (or), and many others. For example, if we wished to delete all of the students whose age is greater than or equal to 30, we would use the following SQL statement.

```
DELETE FROM Student WHERE age >= 30
```

If we wished to delete all students whose age is greater than or equal to 30 and whose gpa is less than 3.5, we would use

```
DELETE FROM Student WHERE age >=30 && gpa < 3.5
```

As with the INSERT statement in the previous section, we will need to use a Statement that produces RecordSet objects that are forward-scrolling only (ResultSet.TYPE_FORWARD_ONLY), and that update the database (ResultSet.CONCUR_UPDATABLE).

Deleting Database Tables

Deleting tables from our database is rather simple to accomplish. We use the executeUpdate method of a Statement object and pass it the DROP TABLE <tablename> SQL statement.

KEY CONCEPT
The DROP TABLE SQL statement is used to delete data from a database table.

For example, if we wanted to drop the Student table, we could do so using the following Java statement in our program.

```
int rowCount = stmt.executeUpdate("DROP TABLE
Student");
```

Keep in mind that when the table is dropped, any data stored within the table are dropped as well.

Summary of Key Concepts

- Databases are software applications used to provide data to other programs.
- A relational database creates relationships between records in different tables by using unique identifiers.
- The JDBC API is used to establish a connection to a database.
- The `CREATE TABLE` SQL statement is used to create new database tables.
- The `ALTER TABLE` SQL statement can be used to modify an existing database table.
- The `SHOW COLUMNS` SQL statement can be used to obtain a list of a table's columns and configuration settings.
- The `INSERT` SQL statement is used to add new data to a database table.
- The `SELECT` SQL statement is used to retrieve data from a database table.
- The `DELETE FROM` SQL statement is used to delete data from a database table.
- The `DROP TABLE` SQL statement is used to delete an entire database table.
- Updates to a database can be performed through changes to a `ResultSet`.

Self-Review Questions

SR 25.1 What are the four primary operations on database data?

SR 25.2 In relational databases, where are the relationships stored, and how are they stored?

SR 25.3 Name two popular database products on the market today.

SR 25.4 Where can one obtain the JDBC?

SR 25.5 What role does a database driver play?

SR 25.6 What does the `java.sql.DriverManager` class assist with?

SR 25.7 Which class do we use to prepare and execute SQL statements?

SR 25.8 Which JDBC class is used to manage a set of records that is usually the result of a database query?

SR 25.9 Which SQL statement is used to add new data to a database table?

SR 25.10 Which SQL statement is used to remove a database table from the database?

Exercises

EX 25.1 Design a table for storing the names and contact information (addresses, phone numbers, email addresses) of your closest friends and family members. What fields would you use?

EX 25.2 Design one or more tables for managing a list of courses run by your university. How many tables do you need? What fields are in each table? Be sure to include such data as the instructor's names, the number of credits awarded for successful completion of the course, the department that offers the course, and the current enrollment in the course.

EX 25.3 Research the SQL statements needed to perform the CRUD operations on an Oracle database, on an Access database, and on a PostgreSQL database. How do they differ from those presented in this chapter?

EX 25.4 Using the MySQL documentation (http://dev.mysql.com/doc), determine how to create a temporary table and what the implications of using a temporary table are.

EX 25.5 How would you go about modifying a table and adding a new column in front of an existing one?

EX 25.6 What is the SQL statement needed to add a new column named `employeeNumber` to a table named `Employees`? Assume that the `employeeNumber` is a 7-digit integer value.

EX 25.7 What is the SQL statement needed to delete a column named `ProductCode` from a table named `Products`?

EX 25.8 Given the `Person` and `Location` tables provided at the beginning of this chapter, indicate what SQL statement is needed to return a query that lists all of the states that any person resides in.

EX 25.9 What SQL statement is needed to insert, in the `Student` table discussed earlier in this chapter, a new field that will store the total number of credits each student has accumulated? What data type should be used, and why?

EX 25.10 What SQL statement is needed to delete the age column from the `Student` table discussed earlier in this chapter?

Programming Projects

Use the MySQL world database (http://dev.mysql.com/doc/world-setup/en/world-setup.html) to populate a database and complete Programming Projects 25.1 through 25.5.

PP 25.1 Write a program to query the world database to obtain a list of all the cities of the world that contain a population that exceeds 5 million residents.

PP 25.2 Write a Java program that queries the world database to determine the total population of all cities in New Jersey.

PP 25.3 Write a program that queries the world database to determine in which country the residents have the greatest life expectancy.

PP 25.4 Research how to accomplish a `JOIN` on two tables (see http://en.wikipedia.org/wiki/Join_(SQL)). Then write a program that queries the world database to list the population of the capitol city for any country in Asia.

PP 25.5 Write a program with a graphical user interface that connects to a database, creates a CDs table (if it does not already exist), and provides the user the ability to manage a music album database. The database should include fields for the album title, artist name, number of tracks, and price. The user should be able to enter new album information, delete existing albums, and obtain a list of albums in the database.

PP 25.6 Using the free tool at http://www.fakenamegenerator.com, create 1,000 fake identifications to a text file. Then write a Java program that will populate a database table with the fake names from the text file. Finally, print a list of individuals in the database whose first (given) name is John and who live in Tennessee.

PP 25.7 Write a program that connects to a database, creates a Movies table (if it does not already exist), and provides the user the ability to manage a movie listing database. The database should include fields for a movie's name, run-time, rating code, date of release, and two primary stars. The user should be able to enter new movie information, delete existing movies, and obtain a list of movies in the database.

PP 25.8 Write a program with a graphical user interface that prompts the user to enter a database hostname, username, password, and database name. Once connected, the program should allow the user to browse the database by selecting a table and then choose to display either the structure of the table (`SHOW COLUMNS`) or the data contained within the selected table.

PP 25.9 Write a program that connects to a database, creates two tables (`Teams` and `Games`, if they don't already exist), and allows the user to manage a series of games between different opponents.

`Games` includes a score value for each team, a unique identifier for each game. `Teams` includes identifiers for each team, as well as their names and overall win/loss records. This problem can be solved with or without the knowledge of table joins in SQL statements. The user should be able enter new game results, add new teams, and navigate through each table or read the data.

PP 25.10 Write program that connects to a database, creates and populates the `Student` table, prints a display of the data contained in the `Student` table, and then deletes the `Student` table along with its data.

Answers to Self-Review Questions

SRA 25.1 The four primary database operations are create, read, update, and delete.

SRA 25.2 Relational databases store their relationships in the database tables themselves in the form of unique identifiers that are used to join the database tables.

SRA 25.3 Some popular database products are MySQL, PostgreSQL, SQLServer, Oracle, and Access.

SRA 25.4 As of JDK 1.1, the JDBC API is part of the JDK.

SRA 25.5 A database driver helps to establish communications from our JDBC statements to the specific database we are attempting to communicate with.

SRA 25.6 The `java.sql.DriverManager` class registers and manages each of the database drivers loaded at run-time.

SRA 25.7 The `java.sql.Statement` is used to prepare and execute SQL statements.

SRA 25.8 The `ResultSet` object is a JDBC class that is used to manage a set of database query result records.

SRA 25.9 The `INSERT` SQL statement is used to add new data to a database table.

SRA 25.10 The `DROP TABLE` SQL statement is used to delete a database table and its data.

Appendix A

Glossary

abstract—A Java reserved word that serves as a modifier for classes, interfaces, and methods. An `abstract` class cannot be instantiated and is used to specify bodiless abstract methods that are given definitions by derived classes. Interfaces are inherently abstract.

abstract class—*See* abstract.

abstract data type (ADT)—A collection of data and the operations that are defined on those data. An abstract data type might be implemented in a variety of ways, but the interface operations are consistent.

abstract method—*See* abstract.

Abstract Windowing Toolkit (AWT)—The package in the Java API (`java.awt`) that contains classes related to graphics and GUIs. *See also* Swing.

abstraction—The concept of hiding details. If the right details are hidden at the right times, abstraction can significantly help control complexity and focus attention on appropriate issues.

access—The ability to reference a variable or invoke a method from outside the class in which it is declared. Controlled by the visibility modifier used to declare the variable or method. Also called the level of encapsulation. *See also* visibility modifier.

access modifier—*See* visibility modifier.

actual parameter—The value passed to a method as a parameter. *See also* formal parameter.

adaptor class—*See* listener adaptor class.

address—(1) A numeric value that uniquely identifies a particular memory location in a computer's main memory. (2) A designation that uniquely identifies a computer among all others on a network.

adjacency list—A list of all the edges in a graph grouped by the vertices that each edge touches. *See also* edge, graph, vertex.

adjacency matrix—A matrix (two-dimensional array) that stores the list of edges in a graph. Each position in the array represents an intersection between two vertices in the graph. *See also* array, edge, graph, vertex.

ADT—*See* abstract data type (ADT).

aggregate object—An object that contains variables that are references to other objects. *See also* has-a relationship.

aggregation—Something that is composed, at least in part, of other things. *See also* aggregate object.

algorithm—A step-by-step process for solving a problem. A program is based on one or more algorithms.

alias—A reference to an object that is currently also referred to by another reference. Each reference is an alias of the other.

analog—A representation that is in direct proportion to the source of the information. *See also* digital.

animation—A series of images or drawings that gives the appearance of movement when displayed in order at a particular speed.

ANT—A build tool generally used with Java program development. *See also* build tool.

API—*See* application programming interface (API).

applet—A Java program that is linked into an HTML document and is then retrieved and executed using a Web browser, as opposed to a stand-alone Java application.

appletviewer—A software tool that interprets and displays Java applets through links in HTML documents. Part of the Java Development Kit.

application—(1) A generic term for any program. (2) A Java program that can be run without the use of a Web browser, as opposed to a Java applet.

application programming interface (API)—A set of classes that defines services for a programmer. Not part of the language itself, but often relied on to perform even basic tasks. *See also* class library.

arc angle—In the definition of an arc, the radial distance that defines the arc's length. *See also* start angle.

architectural design—A high-level design that identifies the large portions of a software system and key data structures. *See also* detailed design.

architecture—*See* computer architecture.

architecture neutral—Not specific to any particular hardware platform. Java code is considered architecture neutral because it is compiled into bytecode and then interpreted on any machine with a Java interpreter. *See also* bytecode.

arithmetic operator—An operator that performs a basic arithmetic computation, such as addition or multiplication.

arithmetic promotion—The act of promoting the type of a numeric operand to be consistent with the other operand.

array—A programming language construct used to store an ordered list of primitive values or objects. Each element in the array is referenced using a numeric index from 0 to *N*–1, where *N* is the size of the array.

array element—A value or object that is stored in an array.

array element type—The type of the values or objects that are stored in an array.

ASCII—A popular character set used by many programming languages. ASCII stands for American Standard Code for Information Interchange. It is a subset of the Unicode character set, which is used by Java.

assembly language—A low-level language that uses mnemonics to represent program commands.

assert—A Java reserved word that is used to make an assertion that a condition is fulfilled. *See also* assertion.

assertion—A programming language construct that is used to declare a programmatic assumption (that is usually true). Assertions are used by JUnit for the purposes of unit testing. *See also* JUnit, unit testing.

assignment conversion—Some data types can be converted to another data type in an assignment statement. *See* widening conversion.

assignment operator—An operator that results in an assignment to a variable. The `=` operator performs basic assignment. Many other assignment operators, such as the `*=` operator, perform additional operations prior to the assignment.

association—A relationship between two classes in which one uses the other or is related to it in some way. *See also* operator association, use relationship.

asymptotic complexity—The order, or dominant term, of a growth function. *See also* dominant term, growth function.

AWT—*See* Abstract Windowing Toolkit.

background color—(1) The color of the background of a GUI component. (2) The color of the background of an HTML page. *See also* foreground color.

bag—A collection that facilitates the selection of random elements from a group. *See also* collection.

balanced tree—A tree whose leaves are all on the same level or within one level of each other. *See also* leaf, tree.

base—The numeric value on which a particular number system is based. It determines the number of digits available in that number system and the place value of each digit in a number. *See also* binary, decimal, hexadecimal, octal, place value.

base 2—*See* binary.

base 8—*See* octal.

base 10—*See* decimal.

base 16—*See* hexadecimal.

base case—The situation that terminates recursive processing, allowing the active recursive methods to begin returning to their point of invocation.

base class—*See* superclass.

behavior—The functional characteristics of an object, defined by its methods. *See also* identity, state.

binary—The base-2 number system. Modern computer systems store information as strings of binary digits (bits).

binary operator—An operator that uses two operands.

binary search—A searching algorithm that requires that the list be sorted. It repetitively compares the "middle" element of the list to the target value, narrowing the scope of the search each time. *See also* linear search.

binary search tree—A binary tree with the added property that for each node, the left child is less than the parent, and the right child is greater than or equal to the parent. *See also* node, tree.

binary string—A series of binary digits (bits).

binary tree—A tree data structure in which each node can have no more than two child nodes.

binding—The process of associating an identifier with the construct that it represents. For example, the process of binding a method name to the specific definition that it invokes.

bit—A binary digit, either 0 or 1.

bit shifting—The act of shifting the bits of a data value to the left or right, losing bits on one end and inserting bits on the other.

bits per second (bps)—A measurement rate for data transfer devices.

bitwise operator—An operator that manipulates individual bits of a value, either by calculation or by shifting.

black-box testing—Producing and evaluating test cases on the basis of the input and expected output of a software component. The test cases focus on covering the equivalence categories and boundary values of the input. *See also* white-box testing.

block—A group of programming statements and declarations delimited by braces ({}).

boolean—A Java reserved word representing a logical primitive data type that can take only the value `true` or the value `false`.

boolean expression—An expression that evaluates to a true or false result; such expressions are used primarily as conditions in selection and repetition statements.

boolean operator—Any of the bitwise operators AND (`&`), OR (`|`), and XOR (`^`) when applied to `boolean` operands. The results are equivalent to their logical counterparts, except that boolean operators are not short-circuited.

border—A graphical edge around a GUI component to enhance its appearance or to group components visually. An empty border creates a buffer of space around a component.

boundary values—The input values corresponding to the edges of equivalence categories. Used in black-box testing.

bounding rectangle—A rectangle that delineates a region in which an oval or arc is defined.

bounds checking—The process of determining whether an array index is in bounds, given the size of the array. Java performs automatic bounds checking.

bps—*See* bits per second.

breadth-first traversal—A graph traversal that starts at a given vertex, then visits all neighboring vertices one edge from the starting vertex, then visits all vertices two edges from the starting vertex, and so on. *See also* depth-first traversal, graph, vertex.

break—A Java reserved word used to interrupt the flow of control by breaking out of the current loop or `switch` statement.

breakpoints—A special flag or tag in a debugger that pauses execution of the program being debugged when the execution reaches the breakpoint.

browser—Software that retrieves HTML documents across network connections and formats them for viewing. A browser is the primary vehicle for accessing the World Wide Web.

bubble sort—A sorting algorithm in which values are repeatedly compared to neighboring elements in the list and their positions are swapped if they are not in order relative to each other. *See also* heap sort, insertion sort, merge sort, quick sort, radix sort, selection sort.

bug—A slang term for a defect or error in a computer program.

build-and-fix approach—An approach to software development in which a program is created without any significant planning or design and then is modified until it reaches some level of acceptance. It is a prevalent, but unwise, approach.

build tool—A software application used to automate, define, and execute a consistent process for building software applications.

bus—A group of wires in the computer that carries data between components such as the CPU and main memory.

button—A GUI component that allows the user to initiate an action, set a condition, or choose an option with a mouse click. There are several kinds of GUI buttons. *See also* check box, push button, radio button.

byte—(1) A unit of binary storage equal to 8 bits. (2) A Java reserved word that represents a primitive integer type, stored using 8 bits in two's complement format.

byte stream—An I/O stream that manages 8-bit bytes of raw binary data. *See also* character stream.

bytecode—The low-level format into which the Java compiler translates Java source code. The bytecode is interpreted and executed by the Java interpreter, perhaps after transportation over the Internet.

capacity—*See* storage capacity.

case—(1) A Java reserved word that is used to identify each unique option in a `switch` statement. (2) The orientation of an alphabetic character (uppercase or lowercase).

case sensitive—Differentiating between the uppercase and lowercase versions of an alphabetic letter. Java is case sensitive; therefore, the identifier `total` and the identifier `Total` are considered to be different identifiers.

cast—A Java operation expressed using a type or class name in parentheses to explicitly convert and return a value of one data type into another.

catch—A Java reserved word that is used to specify an exception handler, defined after a `try` block.

CD-Recordable (CD-R)—A compact disc on which information can be stored once using a home computer with an appropriate drive. *See also* CD-Rewritable, CD-ROM.

CD-Rewritable (CD-RW)—A compact disc on which information can be stored and rewritten multiple times using a home computer with an appropriate drive. *See also* CD-Recordable, CD-ROM.

CD-ROM—An optical secondary memory medium that stores binary information in a manner similar to a musical compact disc.

central processing unit (CPU)—The hardware component that controls the main activity of a computer, including the flow of information and the execution of commands.

char—A Java reserved word that represents the primitive character type. All Java characters are members of the Unicode character set and are stored using 16 bits.

character font—A specification that defines the distinct look of a character when it is printed or drawn.

character set—An ordered list of characters, such as the ASCII and the Unicode character sets. Each character corresponds to a specific, unique numeric value within a given character set. A programming language adopts a particular character set to use for character representation and management.

character stream—An I/O stream that manages 16-bit Unicode characters. *See also* byte stream.

character string—A series of ordered characters. Represented in Java using the `String` class and string literals such as `"hello"`.

check box—A GUI component that allows the user to set a boolean condition with a mouse click. A check box can be used alone or independently among other check boxes. *See also* radio button.

checked exception—A Java exception that must be either caught or explicitly thrown to the calling method. *See also* unchecked exception.

child class—*See* subclass.

circular array—Conceptually, an array whose last index is followed by the first index.

class—(1) A Java reserved word used to define a class. (2) The blueprint of an object—the model that defines the variables and methods an object will contain when instantiated.

class diagram—A diagram that shows the relationships between classes, including inheritance and use relationships. *See also* Unified Modeling Language.

class hierarchy—A tree-like structure created when classes are derived from other classes through inheritance. *See also* interface hierarchy.

class library—A set of classes that defines useful services for a programmer. *See also* application programming interface (API).

class method—A method that can be invoked using only the class name. An instantiated object is not required, as it is with instance methods. Defined in a Java program by using the `static` reserved word.

class variable—A variable that is shared among all objects of a class. It can also be referenced through the class name, without instantiating any object of that class. Defined in a Java program by using the `static` reserved word.

CLASSPATH—An operating system setting that determines where the Java interpreter searches for class files.

client-server model—A manner in which to construct a software design based on objects (clients) making use of the services provided by other objects (servers).

coding guidelines—A series of conventions that describe how programs should be constructed. They make programs easier to read, exchange, and integrate. Sometimes referred to as coding standards, especially when they are enforced.

coding standard—*See* coding guidelines.

cohesion—The strength of the relationship among the parts within a software component. *See also* coupling.

collection—An object that serves as a repository for other objects.

collision—The process of two hash values producing the same hash code. *See also* hash code, hashing.

color chooser—A GUI component, often displayed as a dialog box, that allows the user to select or specify a color.

combo box—A GUI component that allows the user to select one of several options. A combo box displays the most recent selection. *See also* list.

command-line arguments—The values that follow the program name on the command line. Accessed within a Java program through the `String` array parameter to the `main` method.

command shell—A text-based user interface for issuing commands to a computer operating system.

comment—A programming language construct that allows a programmer to embed human-readable annotations into the source code. *See also* documentation.

compile-time error—Any error that occurs during the compilation process, often indicating that a program does not conform to the language syntax or that an operation was attempted on an inappropriate data type. *See also* logical error, run-time error, syntax error.

compiler—A program that translates code from one language to equivalent code in another language. The Java compiler translates Java source code into Java bytecode. *See also* interpreter.

complete tree—A tree that is balanced and all of whose leaves at the bottom level are on the left side of the tree. *See also* balanced tree, leaf.

component—Any portion of a software system that performs a specific task, transforming input to output. *See also* GUI component.

computer architecture—The structure and interaction of the hardware components of a computer.

concatenation—*See* string concatenation.

condition—A boolean expression used to determine whether the body of a selection or repetition statement should be executed.

conditional coverage—A strategy used in white-box testing in which all conditions in a program are executed, producing both `true` and `false` results. *See also* statement coverage.

conditional operator—A Java ternary operator that evaluates one of two expressions on the basis of a condition.

conditional statement—*See* selection statement.

connected graph—A graph in which a path exists between any two vertices. *See also* graph, path, vertex.

const—A Java reserved word that is not currently used.

constant—An identifier that contains a value that cannot be modified. Used to make code more readable and to facilitate changes. Defined in Java using the `final` modifier.

constant complexity—A growth function of an algorithm that executes in a set amount of time regardless of the size of the problem. *See also* growth function.

constructor—A special method in a class that is invoked when an object is instantiated from the class. Used to initialize the object.

container—A Java GUI component that can hold other components. *See also* containment hierarchy.

containment hierarchy—The relationships among graphical components of a user interface. *See also* container.

content pane—The part of a top-level container to which components are added.

control characters—*See* nonprintable characters.

controllers—Hardware devices that control the interaction between a computer system and a particular kind of peripheral.

coupling—The strength of the relationship between two software components. *See also* cohesion.

CPU—*See* central processing unit.

cycle—A path in a graph in which the first and last vertices are the same and none of the edges are repeated. *See also* graph.

data stream—An I/O stream that represents a particular source or destination for data, such as a file. *See also* processing stream.

data structure—Any programming construct, defined either in the language or by a programmer, used to organize data into a format to facilitate access and processing. Arrays, linked lists, and stacks can all be considered data structures.

data transfer device—A hardware component, such as a modem, that makes it possible to send information between computers.

data type—A designation that specifies a set of values (which may be infinite). For example, each variable has a data type that specifies the kinds of values that can be stored in it.

debugger—A software tool that allows a programmer to step through an executing program and examine the value of variables at any point. *See also* jdb.

debugging—The act of locating and correcting run-time and logical errors in a program.

decimal—The base-10 number system, which humans use in everyday life. *See also* binary.

default—A Java reserved word that is used to indicate the default case of a `switch` statement. Used if no other cases match.

default visibility—The level of access designated when no explicit visibility modifier is used to declare a class, interface, method, or variable. Sometimes referred to as package visibility. Classes and interfaces declared with default visibility can be used within their package. A method or variable declared with default visibility is inherited and accessible by all subclasses in the same package.

defect testing—Testing designed to uncover errors in a program.

defined—Existing for use in a derived class, even if it can be accessed only indirectly. *See also* inheritance.

degenerate tree—A tree whose nodes are located primarily on one side. *See also* tree.

delimiter—Any symbol or word used to set the boundaries of a programming language construct, such as the braces ({}) used to define a Java block.

deprecated—Something, such as a particular method, that is considered old-fashioned and should not be used.

depth-first traversal—A graph traversal that starts at a given vertex and traverses as far as possible along a sequence of edges before backtracking and traversing alternative, skipped edges. *See also* breadth-first traversal, graph, vertex.

derived class—*See* subclass.

design—(1) The plan for implementing a program, which includes a specification of the classes and objects used and an expression of the important program algorithms. (2) The process of creating a program design.

desk check—A type of review in which a developer carefully examines a design or program to find errors.

detailed design—(1) The low-level algorithmic steps of a method. (2) The development stage at which low-level algorithmic steps are determined.

development stage—The software life-cycle stage in which a software system is first created; this stage precedes use, maintenance, and eventual retirement.

dialog box—A graphical window that pops up to allow brief, specific user interaction.

digital—A representation that breaks information down into pieces, which are in turn represented as numbers. All modern computer systems are digital.

digitize—The act of converting an analog representation into a digital one by breaking it down into pieces.

digraph—*See* directed graph.

dimension—The number of index levels of a particular array.

direct recursion—The process of a method invoking itself. *See also* indirect recursion.

directed graph—A graph data structure in which each edge has a specific direction. *See also* edge.

disable—Make a GUI component inactive so that it cannot be used. A disabled component is grayed to indicate its disabled status. *See also* enable.

DNS—*See* Domain Name System.

do—A Java reserved word that represents a repetition construct. A `do` statement is executed one or more times. *See also* for, while.

documentation—Supplemental information about a program, including comments in a program's source code and printed reports such as a user's guide.

domain name—The portion of an Internet address that specifies the organization to which the computer belongs.

Domain Name System (DNS)—Software that translates an Internet address into an IP address using a domain server.

domain server—A file server that maintains a list of Internet addresses and their corresponding IP addresses.

dominant term—The term in a growth function that increases the most as the problem size (n) increases. The dominant term is the basis of determining the order of an algorithm. *See also* growth function, order.

double—A Java reserved word that represents a primitive floating point numeric type, stored using 64 bits in IEEE 754 format.

doubly linked list—A linked list with two references in each node: one that refers to the next node in the list and one that refers to the previous node in the list.

dynamic binding—The process of associating an identifier with its definition during run-time. *See also* binding.

dynamic structure—A set of objects that are linked using references, which can be modified as needed during program execution.

edge—A connector (in a linked structure, a reference) between two nodes in a tree or graph. *See also* graph, node, tree.

editor—A software tool that allows the user to enter and store a file of characters on a computer. Often used by programmers to enter the source code of a program.

efficiency—The characteristic of an algorithm that specifies the required number of a particular operation in order to complete its task. For example, the efficiency of a sort can be measured by the number of comparisons required to sort a list. *See also* order.

element—A value or object stored in another object such as an array.

element type—*See* array element type.

else—A Java reserved word that designates the portion of code in an `if` statement that will be executed if the condition is false.

enable—Make a GUI component active so that it can be used. *See also* disable.

encapsulation—The characteristic of an object that limits access to the variables and methods contained in it.

All interaction with an object occurs through a well-defined interface that supports a modular design.

environment variable—A variable located in the system's settings or command shell that can store a value (typically the path to a file or directory). Environment variables can be used within a command shell or program for configuration purposes. *See also* command shell.

equality operator—One of two Java operators that returns a boolean result based on whether two values are equal (`==`) or not equal (`!=`).

equivalence category—A range of functionally equivalent input values as specified by the requirements of the software component. Used when developing black-box test cases.

error—(1) Any defect in a design or program. (2) An object that can be thrown and processed by special `catch` blocks, although errors should not usually be caught. *See also* compile-time error, exception, logical error, run-time error, syntax error.

escape sequence—In Java, a sequence of characters that begins with the backslash character (\) and is used to indicate a special situation when printing values. For example, the escape sequence `\t` specifies that a horizontal tab should be printed.

exception—(1) A situation that arises during program execution that is erroneous or out of the ordinary. (2) An object that can be thrown and processed by special `catch` blocks. *See also* error.

exception handler—The code in a `catch` clause of a `try` statement, executed when a particular type of exception is thrown.

exception propagation—The process that occurs when an exception is thrown: control returns to each calling method in the stack trace until the exception is caught and handled or until the exception is thrown from the `main` method, terminating the program.

exponent—The portion of a floating point value's internal representation that specifies how far the decimal point is shifted. *See also* mantissa.

exponential complexity—An equation that specifies the efficiency of an algorithm and whose dominant term contains the problem size as an exponent (for example, 2^n). *See also* growth function.

expression—A combination of operators and operands that produces a result.

extends—A Java reserved word used to specify the parent class in the definition of a child class.

event—(1) A user action, such as a mouse click or key press. (2) An object that represents a user action, to which the program can respond. *See also* event-driven programming.

event-driven programming—An approach to software development in which the program is designed to acknowledge that an event has occurred and to act accordingly. *See also* event.

factorial—The product of all integers between 1 and any positive integer N (written $N!$).

false—A Java reserved word that serves as one of the two boolean literals (`true` and `false`).

fetch-decode-execute—The cycle through which the CPU continually obtains instructions from main memory and executes them.

FIFO—*See* first-in, first-out (FIFO).

file—A named collection of data stored on a secondary storage device such as a disk. *See also* text file.

file chooser—A GUI component, usually displayed as a dialog box, that allows the user to select a file from a storage device.

file server—A computer in a network, usually with a large secondary storage capacity, that is dedicated to storing software needed by many network users.

filtering stream—*See* processing stream.

final—A Java reserved word that serves as a modifier for classes, methods, and variables. A final class cannot be used to derive a new class. A final method cannot be overridden. A final variable is a constant.

finalize—A Java method defined in the `Object` class that can be overridden in any other class. It is called after the object becomes a candidate for garbage collection and before it is destroyed. It can be used to perform "clean-up" activity that is not performed automatically by the garbage collector.

finalizer method—A Java method, known as `finalize`, that is called before an object is destroyed. *See also* finalize.

finally—A Java reserved word that designates a block of code to be executed when an exception is thrown, after any appropriate catch handler is processed.

first-in, first-out (FIFO)—A data management technique in which the first value that is stored in a data structure is the first value that comes out. *See also* last-in, first-out (LIFO); queue.

float—A Java reserved word that represents a primitive floating point numeric type, stored using 32 bits in IEEE 754 format.

flushing—The process of forcing the contents of the output buffer to be displayed on the output device.

font—*See* character font.

for—A Java reserved word that represents a repetition construct. A `for` statement is executed zero or more times and is generally used when a precise number of iterations is known.

foreground color—The color in which any current drawing will be rendered. *See also* background color.

formal parameter—An identifier that serves as a parameter name in a method. It receives its initial value from the actual parameter passed to it. *See also* actual parameter.

fourth-generation language—A high-level language that provides built-in functionality, such as automatic report generation or database management, beyond that of traditional high-level languages.

full tree—An n-ary tree whose leaves are all on the same level and in which every node is a leaf or has exactly *n* children. *See also* leaf, level, node, tree.

function—A named group of declarations and programming statements that can be invoked (executed) when needed. A function that is part of a class is called a method. Java has no functions because all code is part of a class.

garbage—(1) An unspecified or uninitialized value in a memory location. (2) An object that cannot be accessed anymore because all references to it have been lost.

garbage collection—The process of reclaiming unneeded, dynamically allocated memory. Java performs automatic garbage collection of objects that no longer have any valid references to them.

general tree—A tree with no limit to the number of children a node may contain or reference. *See also* node, tree.

generic type—A class designed so that it stores, operates on, and manages objects whose type is not specified until the class is instantiated.

gigabyte (GB)—A unit of binary storage, equal to 2^{30} (approximately 1 billion) bytes.

glass-box testing—*See* white-box testing.

goto—(1) A Java reserved word that is not currently used. (2) An unconditional branch.

grammar—A representation of language syntax that specifies how reserved words, symbols, and identifiers can be combined into valid programs.

graph—A nonlinear data structure made up of vertices and edges that connect the vertices. *See also* directed graph, undirected graph, vertex, edge.

graphical user interface (GUI)—Software that provides the means to interact with a program or operating system by making use of graphical images and point-and-click mechanisms such as buttons and text fields.

graphics context—The drawing surface and related coordinate system on which a drawing is rendered or GUI components are placed.

growth function—A function that shows the complexity of an algorithm relative to the size of the problem (n). A growth function can represent the time complexity or space complexity of the algorithm. *See also* order.

GUI—*See* graphical user interface (GUI).

GUI component—A visual element, such as a button or text field, that is used to make up a GUI.

hardware—The tangible components of a computer system, such as the keyboard, monitor, and circuit boards.

has-a relationship—The relationship between two objects in which one is composed, at least in part, of one or more of the other. *See also* aggregate object, is-a relationship.

hash code—An integer value calculated from any given data value or object, used to determine where a value should be stored in a hash table. Also called a hash value. *See also* hashing.

hash method—A method that calculates a hash code from a data value or object. The same data value or object will always produce the same hash code. Also called a hash function. *See also* hashing.

hash table—A data structure in which values are stored for efficient retrieval. *See also* hashing.

hashing—A technique for storing items so that they can be found efficiently. Items are stored in a hash table at a position specified by a calculated hash code. *See also* hash method.

heap—A complete binary tree in which each element is greater than or equal to both of its children. *See also* binary tree, minheap.

heap sort—A sorting algorithm in which a set of elements is sorted by adding each one to a heap and then removing them one at a time. *See also* bubble sort, merge sort, quick sort, radix sort, selection sort.

hexadecimal—The base-16 number system, often used as an abbreviated representation of binary strings.

hierarchy—An organizational technique in which items are layered or grouped to reduce complexity.

high-level language—A programming language in which each statement represents many machine-level instructions.

HTML—*See* HyperText Markup Language.

hybrid object-oriented language—A programming language that can be used to implement a program in a procedural manner or an object-oriented manner, at the programmer's discretion. *See also* pure object-oriented language.

hypermedia—The concept of hypertext extended to include other media types such as graphics, audio, video, and programs.

hypertext—A document representation that allows a user to navigate through it easily in other than a linear fashion. Links to other parts of the document are embedded at the appropriate places to allow the user to jump from one part of the document to another. *See also* hypermedia.

HyperText Markup Language (HTML)—The notation used to define Web pages. *See also* browser, World Wide Web.

icon—A small, fixed-sized picture, often used to decorate a GUI. *See also* image.

IDE—*See* integrated development environment.

identifier—Any name that a programmer makes up to use in a program, such as a class name or variable name.

identity—The designation of an object, which, in Java, is an object's reference name. See also *state, behavior*.

IEEE 754—A standard for representing floating point values. Used by Java to represent `float` and `double` data types.

if—A Java reserved word that specifies a simple conditional construct. *See also* else.

image—A picture, often specified using a GIF or JPEG format. *See also* icon.

IMAP—*See* Internet Message Access Protocol.

immutable—Unchanging. For example, the contents of a Java character string are immutable once the string has been defined.

implementation—(1) The process of translating a design into source code. (2) The source code that defines a method, class, abstract data type, or other programming entity.

implements—A Java reserved word that is used in a class declaration to specify that the class implements the methods specified in a particular interface.

import—A Java reserved word that is used to specify the packages and classes that are used in a particular Java source code file.

index—The integer value used to specify a particular element in an array.

index operator—The brackets (`[]`) in which an array index is specified.

indirect recursion—The process of a method invoking another method, which eventually results in the original method being invoked again. *See also* direct recursion.

infinite loop—A loop that does not terminate because the condition controlling the loop never becomes false.

infinite recursion—A recursive series of invocations that does not terminate because the base case is never reached. *See also* base case.

infix expression—An expression in which the operators are positioned between the operands on which they work. *See also* postfix expression.

inheritance—The ability to derive a new class from an existing one. Inherited variables and methods of the original (parent) class are available in the new (child) class just as if they were declared locally.

initialize—To give an initial value to a variable.

initializer list—A comma-separated list of values, delimited by braces (`{}`), used to initialize and specify the size of an array.

inline documentation—Comments that are included in the source code of a program.

inner class—A nonstatic, nested class.

inorder traversal—A tree traversal that is accomplished by visiting the left child of the node, then the node, and then any remaining nodes. *See also* level-order traversal, postorder traversal, preorder traversal.

input/output buffer—A storage location for data on their way from the user to the computer (input buffer) or from the computer to the user (output buffer).

input/output devices—Hardware components that allow the human user to interact with the computer, such as a keyboard, mouse, and monitor.

input/output stream—A sequence of bytes that represents a source of data (input stream) or a destination for data (output stream).

insertion sort—A sorting algorithm in which each value, one at a time, is inserted into a sorted subset of the entire list. *See also* bubble sort, heap sort, merge sort, quick sort, radix sort, selection sort.

inspection—*See* walkthrough.

instance—An object created from a class. Multiple objects can be instantiated from a single class.

instance method—A method that must be invoked through a particular instance of a class, as opposed to a class method.

instance variable—A variable that must be referenced through a particular instance of a class, as opposed to a class variable.

instanceof—A Java reserved word that is also an operator, used to determine the class or type of a variable.

instantiation—The act of creating an object from a class.

int—A Java reserved word that represents a primitive integer type, stored using 32 bits in two's complement format.

integrated development environment (IDE)—A software application used by software developers to create and debug programs.

integration test—The process of testing software components that are made up of other interacting components. Stresses the communication between components rather than the functionality of individual components.

interface—(1) A Java reserved word that is used to define a set of abstract methods that will be implemented by particular classes. (2) The set of messages to which an object responds, defined by the methods that can be invoked from outside of the object. (3) The techniques through which a human user interacts with a program, often graphically. *See also* graphical user interface.

interface hierarchy—A tree-like structure created when interfaces are derived from other interfaces through inheritance. *See also* class hierarchy.

internal node—A tree node that is not the root node and that has at least one child. *See also* node, root, tree.

Internet—The most pervasive wide-area network in the world; it has become the primary vehicle for computer-to-computer communication. *See also* wide-area network.

Internet address—A designation that uniquely identifies a particular computer or device on the Internet.

Internet Message Access Protocol (IMAP)—Protocol that defines the communications commands required to communicate with another machine for the purposes of reading email.

Internet Naming Authority—The governing body that approves all Internet addresses.

interpreter—A program that translates and executes code on a particular machine. The Java interpreter translates and executes Java bytecode. *See also* compiler.

invisible component—A GUI component that can be added to a container to provide buffering space between other components.

invocation—*See* method invocation.

I/O devices—*See* input/output devices.

IP address—A series of several integer values, separated by periods (.), that uniquely identifies a particular computer or device on the Internet. Each Internet address has a corresponding IP address.

is-a relationship—The relationship created through properly derived classes via inheritance. The subclass *is-a* more specific version of the superclass. *See also* has-a relationship.

ISO-Latin-1—A 128-character extension to the ASCII character set defined by the International Organization for Standardization (ISO). The characters correspond to the numeric values 128 through 255 in both ASCII and Unicode.

iteration—(1) One execution of the body of a repetition statement. (2) One pass through a cyclic process, such as an iterative development process.

iteration statement—*See* repetition statement.

iterative development process—A step-by-step approach for creating software, which contains a series of stages that are performed repetitively.

jar—A file format used by Java to package and compress a group of files and directories, suitable for exchanging with another computer. The jar file format is based on the zip file format. *See also* zip.

java—The Java command-line interpreter, which translates and executes Java bytecode. Part of the Java Development Kit (JDK).

Java—The programming language used throughout this text to demonstrate software development concepts. Described by its developers as object-oriented, robust, secure, architecture neutral, portable, high-performance, interpreted, threaded, and dynamic.

Java API—*See* application programming interface (API).

Java Development Kit (JDK)—A collection of software tools available free from Sun Microsystems, the creators of the Java programming language. *See also* Software Development Kit.

Java Virtual Machine (JVM)—The conceptual device, implemented in software, on which Java bytecode is executed. Bytecode, which is architecture neutral, does not run on a particular hardware platform; instead, it runs on the JVM.

javac—The Java command-line compiler, which translates Java source code into Java bytecode. Part of the Java Development Kit.

javadoc—A software tool that creates external documentation in HTML format about the contents and structure of a Java software system. Part of the Java Development Kit.

javah—A software tool that generates C header and source files, used for implementing `native` methods. Part of the Java Development Kit.

javap—A software tool that disassembles a Java class file, containing unreadable bytecode, into a human-readable version. Part of the Java Development Kit.

jdb—The Java command-line debugger. Part of the Java Development Kit.

JDK—*See* Java Development Kit.

JUnit—A unit testing framework for Java applications. *See also* unit testing.

JVM—*See* Java Virtual Machine.

kilobit (Kb)—A unit of binary storage, equal to 2^{10}, or 1024, bits.

kilobyte (K or KB)—A unit of binary storage, equal to 2^{10}, or 1024, bytes.

label—(1) A GUI component that displays text, an image, or both. (2) An identifier in Java used to specify a particular line of code. The `break` and `continue` statements can jump to a specific, labeled line in the program.

LAN—*See* local-area network.

last-in, first-out (LIFO)—A data management technique in which the last value that is stored in a data structure is the first value that comes out. *See also* first-in, first-out (FIFO); stack.

layout manager—An object that specifies the presentation of GUI components. Each container is governed by a particular layout manager.

leaf—A tree node that has no children. *See also* node, tree.

level—A conceptual horizontal line in a tree on which all elements that are the same distance from the root node are located.

level-order traversal—A tree traversal that is accomplished by visiting all of the nodes at each level, one level at a time. *See also* inorder traversal, level, postorder traversal, preorder traversal.

lexicographic ordering—The ordering of characters and strings based on a particular character set such as Unicode.

life cycle—The stages through which a software product is developed and used.

LIFO—*See* last-in, first-out (LIFO).

linear search—A search algorithm in which each item in the list is compared to the target value until the target is found or the list is exhausted. *See also* binary search.

link—(1) A designation in a hypertext document that "jumps" to a new document (or to a new part of the same document) when clicked. (2) An object reference used to connect two items in a dynamically linked structure.

linked list—A structure in which one object refers to the next, creating a linear ordering of the objects in the list. *See also* linked structure.

linked structure—A dynamic data structure in which objects are connected using references.

Linux—A computer operating system, similar to Unix, developed by hobbyists and generally available free. *See also* operating system, Unix.

list—(1) A GUI component that presents a list of items from which the user can choose. The current selection is highlighted in the list. *See also* combo box. (2) A collection of objects arranged in a linear manner. *See also* linked list.

listener—An object that is set up to respond to an event when it occurs.

listener adaptor class—A class defined with empty methods corresponding to the methods invoked when particular events occur. A listener object can be derived from an adaptor class. *See also* listener interface.

listener interface—A Java interface that defines the methods invoked when particular events occur. A listener object can be created by implementing a listener interface. *See also* listener adaptor class.

literal—A primitive value used explicitly in a program, such as the numeric literal `147` or the string literal `"hello"`.

local-area network (LAN)—A computer network designed to span short distances and connect a relatively small number of computers. *See also* wide-area network.

local variable—A variable, defined within a method, that does not exist except during the execution of the method.

logarithmic complexity—An equation that specifies the efficiency of an algorithm and whose dominant term contains the problem size as the base of a logarithm (for example, $\log_2 n$). *See also* growth function.

logical error—A problem stemming from inappropriate processing in the code. It does not cause an abnormal termination of the program, but it produces incorrect results. *See also* compile-time error, run-time error, syntax error.

logical line of code—A logical programming statement in a source code program, which may extend over multiple physical lines. *See also* physical line of code.

logical operator—One of the operators that perform a logical NOT (`!`), AND (`&&`), or OR (`||`), returning a boolean result. The logical operators are short-circuited, meaning that if their left operand is sufficient to determine the result, the right operand is not evaluated.

long—A Java reserved word that represents a primitive integer type, stored using 64 bits in two's complement format.

loop—*See* repetition statement.

loop control variable—A variable whose value specifically determines how many times a loop body is executed.

low-level language—Either machine language or assembly language, which are considered "low-level" because they are conceptually closer to the basic processing of a computer than high-level languages are.

machine language—The native language of a particular CPU. Any software that runs on a particular CPU must be translated into its machine language.

main memory—The volatile hardware storage device where programs and data are held when they are actively needed by the CPU. *See also* secondary memory.

maintenance—(1) The process of fixing errors in, or making enhancements to, a released software product. (2) The software life-cycle phase in which the software is in use and changes are made to it as needed.

make—A build tool generally used with C and C++ program development. *See also* build tool.

mantissa—The portion of a floating point value's internal representation that specifies the magnitude of the number. *See also* exponent.

max heap—A complete binary tree in which each element is greater than or equal to both of its children. *See also* binary tree, min heap.

megabyte (MB)—A unit of binary storage, equal to 2^{20} (approximately 1 million) bytes.

member—A variable or method in an object or class.

memory—Hardware devices that store programs and data. *See also* main memory, secondary memory.

memory location—An individual, addressable cell inside main memory in which data can be stored.

memory management—The process of controlling dynamically allocated portions of main memory, especially the act of returning allocated memory when it is no longer required. *See also* garbage collection.

merge sort—A sorting algorithm in which a list is recursively divided in half until each sublist has one element. Then the sublists are recombined in order. *See also* bubble sort, heap sort, insertion sort, quick sort, radix sort, selection sort.

method—A named group of declarations and programming statements that can be invoked (executed) when needed. A method is part of a class.

method call conversion—The automatic widening conversion that can occur when a value of one type is passed to a formal parameter of another type.

method definition—The specification of the code that gets executed when the method is invoked. The definition includes declarations of local variables and formal parameters.

method invocation—A line of code that causes a method to be executed. It specifies any values that are passed to the method as parameters.

method overloading—*See* overloading.

min heap—A complete binary tree in which each element is less than or equal to both of its children. *See also* binary tree, max heap.

minimum spanning tree—A spanning tree where the sum of the weights of the edges is less than or equal to the sum of the weights of the edges for any other spanning tree for the same graph. *See also* edge, spanning tree.

mnemonic—(1) A word or identifier that specifies a command or data value in an assembly language. (2) A keyboard character used as a alternative means to activate a GUI component such as a button.

modal—Having multiple modes (such as a dialog box).

modem—A data transfer device that allows information to be sent along a telephone line.

modifier—A designation used in a Java declaration that specifies particular characteristics to the construct being declared.

monitor—The screen in the computer system that serves as an output device.

multidimensional array—An array that uses more than one index to specify a value stored in it.

multiple inheritance—Deriving a class from more than one parent, inheriting methods and variables from each. Multiple inheritance is not supported in Java.

multiplicity—The numeric relationship between two objects, often shown in class diagrams.

n-ary tree—A tree that limits to the value of n the number of children a node can contain or reference.

NaN—An abbreviation that stands for "not a number," which is the designation for an inappropriate or undefined numeric value.

narrowing conversion—A conversion between two values of different but compatible data types. Narrowing conversions could lose information because the converted type usually has an internal representation smaller than the original storage space. *See also* widening conversion.

native—A Java reserved word that serves as a modifier for methods. A native method is implemented in another programming language.

natural language—A language that humans use to communicate, such as English or French.

negative infinity—A special floating point value that represents the "lowest possible" value. *See also* positive infinity.

nested class—A class declared within another class in order to facilitate implementation and restrict access.

nested if statement—An `if` statement that has another `if` statement as its body.

network—(1) Two or more computers connected together so that they can exchange data and share resources. (2) *See* weighted graph.

network address—*See* address.

new—A Java reserved word that is also an operator, used to instantiate an object from a class.

newline character—A nonprintable character that indicates the end of a line.

nodes—Objects in a collection that generally manage the structure of the collection. Nodes can be found in linked implementations of graphs, linked structures, and trees. *See also* graph, linked structure, trees.

nonprintable character—Any character, such as an escape or newline character, that does not have a symbolic representation that can be displayed on a monitor or printed by a printer. *See also* printable character.

nonvolatile—The characteristic of a memory device that retains its stored information even after the power supply is turned off. Secondary memory devices are nonvolatile. *See also* volatile.

null—A Java reserved word that is a reference literal, used to indicate that a reference does not currently refer to any object.

number system—A set of values and operations defined by a particular base value that determines the number of digits available and the place value of each digit.

object—(1) The primary software construct in the object-oriented paradigm. (2) An encapsulated collection of data variables and methods. (3) An instance of a class.

object diagram—A visual representation of the objects in a program at a given point in time, often showing the status of instance data.

object-oriented programming—An approach to software design and implementation that revolves around objects and classes. *See also* procedural programming.

octal—The base-8 number system, sometimes used to abbreviate binary strings. *See also* binary, hexadecimal.

off-by-one error—An error caused by a calculation or condition being off by one, such as when a loop is set up to access one too many array elements.

operand—A value on which an operator performs its function. For example, in the expression 5 + 2, the values 5 and 2 are operands.

operating system—The collection of programs that provides the primary user interface to a computer and manages its resources, such as memory and the CPU.

operator—A symbol that represents a particular operation in a programming language, such as the addition operator (+).

operator association—The order in which operators within the same precedence level are evaluated, either right to left or left to right. *See also* operator precedence.

operator overloading—Assigning additional meaning to an operator. Operator overloading is not supported in Java, although method overloading is.

operator precedence—The order in which operators are evaluated in an expression as specified by a well-defined hierarchy.

order—The dominant term in an equation that specifies the efficiency of an algorithm. For example, selection sort is of order n^2.

order of tree—The maximum number of children a tree node may contain or reference. *See also* node, tree.

overflow—A problem that occurs when a data value grows too large for its storage size, which can cause inaccurate arithmetic processing. *See also* underflow.

overloading—Assigning additional meaning to a programming language construct, such as a method or operator. Method overloading is supported by Java, but operator overloading is not.

overriding—The process of modifying the definition of an inherited method to suit the purposes of the subclass. *See also* shadowing variables.

package—A Java reserved word that is used to specify a group of related classes.

package visibility—*See* default visibility.

panel—A GUI container that holds and organizes other GUI components.

parameter—(1) A value passed from a method invocation to its definition. (2) The identifier in a method definition that accepts the value passed to it when the method is invoked. *See also* actual parameter, formal parameter.

parameter list—The list of actual or formal parameters to a method.

parameterized type—*See* generic type.

parent class—*See* superclass.

partition element—An arbitrarily chosen element in a list of values that is used by the quick sort algorithm to partition the list for recursive processing. *See also* quick sort.

pass by reference—The process of passing a reference to a value into a method as the parameter. In Java, all objects are managed using references, so an object's formal parameter is an alias to the original. *See also* pass by value.

pass by value—The process of making a copy of a value and passing the copy into a method. Therefore, any change made to the value inside the method is not reflected in the original value. All Java primitive types are passed by value.

path—A sequence of edges in a tree or graph that connects two nodes. *See* also edge, graph, node, tree.

PDL—*See* Program Design Language.

peripheral—Any hardware device other than the CPU or main memory.

persistence—The ability of an object to stay in existence after the executing program that creates it terminates. *See also* serialize.

physical line of code—A line in a source code file, terminated by a newline or similar character. *See also* logical line of code.

pixel—A picture element. A digitized picture is made up of many pixels.

place value—The value of each digit position in a number, which determines the overall contribution of that digit to the value. *See also* number system.

point-to-point connection—The link between two networked devices that are connected directly by a wire.

pointer—A variable that can hold a memory address. Instead of pointers, Java uses references, which provide essentially the same functionality as pointers but without the complications.

polyline—A shape made up of a series of connected line segments. A polyline is similar to a polygon, but the shape is not closed.

polymorphism—An object-oriented technique by which a reference that is used to invoke a method can result in different methods being invoked at different times. All Java method invocations are potentially polymorphic in that they invoke the method of the object type, not that of the reference type.

polynomial complexity—An equation that specifies the efficiency of an algorithm and whose dominant term contains the problem size raised to a power (for example, n^2). *See also* growth function.

POP—*See* Post Office Protocol.

portability—The ability of a program to be moved from one hardware platform to another without having to be changed. Because Java bytecode is not related to any particular hardware environment, Java programs are considered portable. *See also* architecture neutral.

positive infinity—A special floating point value that represents the "highest possible" value. *See also* negative infinity.

Post Office Protocol—Protocol that defines the communications commands required to communicate with another machine for the purposes of reading email.

postfix expression—An expression in which an operator is positioned after the operands on which it works. *See also* infix expression.

postfix operator—In Java, an operator that is positioned behind its single operand and whose evaluation yields the value prior to the operation being performed. Both the increment operator (++) and the decrement operator (--) can be applied postfix. *See also* prefix operator.

postorder traversal—A tree traversal that is accomplished by visiting the children and then the node. *See also* inorder traversal, level-order traversal, preorder traversal.

precedence—*See* operator precedence.

prefix operator—In Java, an operator that is positioned in front of its single operand and whose evaluation yields the value after the operation has been performed. Both the increment operator (++) and the decrement operator (--) can be applied prefix. *See also* postfix operator.

preorder traversal—A tree traversal that is accomplished by visiting each node and then its children. *See also* inorder traversal, level-order traversal, postorder traversal.

primitive data type—A data type that is predefined in a programming language.

printable character—Any character that has a symbolic representation that can be displayed on a monitor or printed by a printer. *See also* nonprintable character.

private—A Java reserved word that serves as a visibility modifier for methods and variables. Private methods and variables are not inherited by subclasses, and they can be accessed only in the class in which they are declared.

procedural programming—An approach to software design and implementation that revolves around procedures (or functions) and their interaction. *See also* object-oriented programming.

processing stream—An I/O stream that performs some type of manipulation on the data in the stream. Sometimes called a filtering stream. *See also* data stream.

program—A series of instructions executed by hardware, one after another.

Program Design Language (PDL)—A language in which a program's design and algorithms are expressed. *See also* pseudocode.

programming language—A specification of the syntax and semantics of the statements used to create a program.

programming language statement—An individual instruction in a given programming language.

prompt—A message or symbol used to request information from the user.

propagation—*See* exception propagation.

protected—A Java reserved word that serves as a visibility modifier for methods and variables. Protected methods and variables are inherited by all subclasses and are accessible from all classes in the same package.

prototype—A program used to explore an idea or prove the feasibility of a particular approach.

pseudocode—Structured and abbreviated natural language used to express the algorithmic steps of a program. *See also* Program Design Language.

pseudo-random number—A value generated by software that performs extensive calculations based on an initial seed value. The result is not truly random because it is based on a calculation, but it is usually random enough for most purposes.

public—A Java reserved word that serves as a visibility modifier for classes, interfaces, methods, and variables. A public class or interface can be used anywhere. A public method or variable is inherited by all subclasses and is accessible anywhere.

pure object-oriented language—A programming language that enforces, to some degree, software development using an object-oriented approach. *See also* hybrid object-oriented language.

push button—A GUI component that allows the user to initiate an action with a mouse click. *See also* check box, radio button.

queue—An abstract data type that manages information in a first-in, first-out manner.

quick sort—A sorting algorithm in which the list to sort is partitioned on the basis of an arbitrarily chosen element. Then the sublists on either side of the partition element are recursively sorted. *See also* bubble sort, heap sort, insertion sort, merge sort, radix sort, selection sort.

radio button—A GUI component that allows the user to choose one of a set of options with a mouse click. A radio button is useful only as part of a group of other radio buttons. *See also* check box.

radix—The base, or number of possible unique digits, of a number system.

radix sort—A sorting algorithm that utilizes a series of queues. *See also* bubble sort, heap sort, insertion sort, merge sort, selection sort, quick sort.

RAM—*See* random access memory (RAM).

random access device—A memory device whose information can be directly accessed. *See also* random access memory, sequential access device.

random access memory (RAM)—A term basically interchangeable with main memory. Should probably be called read-write memory, to distinguish it from read-only memory.

random-number generator—Software that produces a pseudo-random number, generated by calculations based on a seed value.

read-only memory (ROM)—Any memory device whose stored information is stored permanently when the device is created. It can be read from but not written to.

recursion—The process of a method invoking itself, either directly or indirectly. Recursive algorithms sometimes provide elegant, though perhaps inefficient, solutions to a problem.

refactoring—The process of modifying existing source code to clean up redundant portions introduced during the development of additional source code.

reference—A variable that holds the address of an object. In Java, a reference can be used to interact with an object, but its address cannot be accessed, set, or operated on directly.

refinement—One iteration of an evolutionary development cycle in which a particular aspect of the system, such as the user interface or a particular algorithm, is addressed.

refinement scope—The specific issues that are addressed in a particular refinement during evolutionary software development.

register—A small area of storage in the CPU of the computer.

regression testing—The process of re-executing test cases after the addition of a new feature or the correction of an existing bug to ensure that code modifications did not introduce any new problems.

relational operator—One of several operators that determine the ordering relationship between two values: less than (<), less than or equal to (<=), greater than (>), and greater than or equal to (>=). *See also* equality operator.

release—A version of a software product that is made available to the customer.

repetition statement—A programming construct that allows a set of statements to be executed repetitively as long as a particular condition is true. The body of the repetition statement should eventually make the condition false. Also called an iteration statement or loop. *See also* do, for, while.

requirements—(1) The specification of what a program must do and what it must not do. (2) An early phase of the software development process in which the program requirements are established.

reserved word—A word that has special meaning in a programming language and cannot be used for any other purpose.

retirement—The phase of a program's life cycle in which the program is taken out of active use.

return—A Java reserved word that causes the flow of program execution to return from a method to the point of invocation.

return type—The type of value returned from a method, specified before the method name in the method declaration. Could be `void`, which indicates that no value is returned.

reuse—Using existing software components to create new ones.

review—The process of critically examining a design or program to discover errors. There are many types of reviews. *See also* desk check, walkthrough.

RGB value—A collection of three values that defines a color. Each value represents the contribution of the primary colors red, green, and blue.

ROM—*See* read-only memory (ROM).

rotation—An operation on a tree that seeks to relocate nodes in an attempt to assist in the balance of the tree. *See also* balanced tree, node.

run-time error—A problem that occurs during program execution and causes the program to terminate abnormally. *See also* compile-time error, logical error, syntax error.

scope—The areas within a program in which an identifier, such as a variable, can be referenced. *See also* access.

scroll pane—A GUI container that offers a limited view of a component and provides horizontal and/or vertical scroll bars to change that view.

SDK—*See* Software Development Kit (SDK).

search pool—A group of items over which a search is performed.

search tree—A tree whose elements are structured to facilitate finding a particular element when needed. *See also* tree.

searching—The process of determining the existence or location of a target value within a list of values. *See also* binary search, linear search.

secondary memory—Hardware storage devices, such as magnetic disks or tapes, that store information in a relatively permanent manner. *See also* main memory.

seed value—A value used by a random-number generator as a base for the calculations that produce a pseudo-random number.

selection sort—A sorting algorithm in which each value, one at a time, is placed in its final, sorted position. *See also* bubble sort, heap sort, insertion sort, merge sort, quick sort, radix sort.

selection statement—A programming construct that allows a set of statements to be executed if a particular condition is true. *See also* if, switch.

self-loop—An edge of a graph that connects a vertex to itself.

self-referential object—An object that contains a reference to a second object of the same type.

semantics—The interpretation of a program or programming construct.

sentinel value—A specific value used to indicate a special condition, such as the end of input.

serialize—The process of converting an object into a linear series of bytes so that it can be saved to a file or sent across a network. *See also* persistence.

service methods—Methods in an object that are declared with public visibility and define a service that the object's client can invoke.

shadowing variables—The process of defining a variable in a subclass that supersedes an inherited version.

shell—*See* command shell.

short—A Java reserved word that represents a primitive integer type, stored using 16 bits in two's complement format.

siblings—Two items in a tree or hierarchy, such as a class inheritance hierarchy, that have the same parent.

sign bit—A bit in a numeric value that represents the sign (positive or negative) of that value.

signed numeric value—A value that stores a sign (positive or negative). All Java numeric values are signed. A Java character is stored as an unsigned value.

signature—The number, types, and order of the parameters of a method. Overloaded methods must each have a unique signature.

Simple Mail Transfer Protocol—A protocol that defines the communications commands required to send email.

slider—A GUI component that allows the user to specify a numeric value within a bounded range by moving a knob to the appropriate place in the range.

sling—*See* self-loop.

SMTP—*See* Simple Mail Transfer Protocol.

software—(1) Programs and data. (2) The intangible components of a computer system.

software component—*See* component.

Software Development Kit (SDK)—A collection of software tools that assists in the development of software. The Java Software Development Kit is another name for the Java Development Kit.

software engineering—The discipline within computer science that addresses the process of developing high-quality software within practical constraints.

sort key—A particular value that is present in each member of a collection of objects and on which a sort is based.

sorting—The process of putting a list of values into a well-defined order. *See also* bubble sort, heap sort, insertion sort, merge sort, radix sort, selection sort, quick sort.

spanning tree—A tree that includes all of the vertices of a graph and some, but possibly not all, of the edges. *See also* edge, vertex.

split pane—A GUI container that displays two components, either side by side or one on top of the other, separated by a moveable divider bar.

stack—An abstract data type that manages data in a last-in, first-out manner.

stack trace—The series of methods called to reach a certain point in a program. When an exception is thrown, the stack trace can be analyzed to assist the programmer in tracking down the problem.

standard I/O stream—One of three common I/O streams representing standard input (usually the keyboard), standard output (usually the monitor screen), and standard error (also usually the monitor). *See also* stream.

start angle—In the definition of an arc, the angle at which the arc begins. *See also* arc angle.

state—The state of being of an object, defined by the values of its data. *See also* behavior, identity.

statement—*See* programming language statement.

statement coverage—A strategy used in white-box testing in which all statements in a program are executed. *See also* condition coverage.

static—A Java reserved word that serves as a modifier for methods and variables. A static method is also called a class method and can be referenced without an instance of the class. A static variable is also called a class variable and is common to all instances of the class.

static data structure—A data structure that has a fixed size and cannot grow and shrink as needed. *See also* dynamic data structure.

step—The execution of a single program statement in a debugger. *See also* debugger.

storage capacity—The total number of bytes that can be stored in a particular memory device.

stream—A source of input or a destination for output.

strictfp—A Java reserved word that is used to control certain aspects of floating point arithmetic.

string—*See* character string.

string concatenation—The process of attaching the beginning of one character string to the end of another, resulting in one longer string.

strongly typed language—A programming language in which each variable is associated with a particular data type for the duration of its existence. Variables are not allowed to take on values or be used in operations that are inconsistent with their type.

structured programming—An approach to program development in which each software component has one entry and exit point and in which the flow of control does not cross unnecessarily.

stub—A method that simulates the functionality of a particular software component. Often used during unit testing. *See also* unit testing.

subclass—A class derived from another class via inheritance. Also called a derived class or child class. *See also* superclass.

subscript—*See* index.

super—A Java reserved word that is a reference to the parent class of the object making the reference. Often used to invoke a parent's constructor.

super reference—*See* super.

superclass—The class from which another class is derived via inheritance. Also called a base class or parent class. *See also* subclass.

support methods—Methods in an object that are not intended for use outside the class. They provide support functionality for service methods. Thus they are usually not declared with public visibility.

swapping—The process of exchanging the values of two variables.

Swing—The package in the Java API (`javax.swing`) that contains classes related to GUIs. Swing provides alternatives to components in the Abstract Windowing Toolkit package but does not replace it.

switch—A Java reserved word that specifies a compound conditional construct.

synchronization—The process of ensuring that data shared among multiple threads cannot be accessed by more than one thread at a time. *See also* synchronized.

synchronized—A Java reserved word that serves as a modifier for methods. Separate threads of a process can execute concurrently in a method, unless the method is synchronized, making it a mutually exclusive resource. Methods that access shared data should be synchronized.

syntax error—An error produced by the compiler because a program did not conform to the syntax of the programming language. Syntax errors are a subset of compile-time errors. *See also* compile-time error, logical error, run-time error, syntax rules.

syntax rules—The set of specifications that govern how the elements of a programming language can be put together to form valid statements.

system test—The process of testing an entire software system. Alpha and beta tests (also known as alpha and beta releases of software applications) are system tests.

tabbed pane—A GUI container that presents a set of cards from which the user can choose. Each card contains its own GUI components.

target element—*See* target value.

target value—The value that is sought when performing a search on a collection of data.

targets—User-defined groups of actions present in an ANT build file.

TCP/IP—Software that controls the movement of messages across the Internet. The abbreviation stands for Transmission Control Protocol/Internet Protocol.

terabyte (TB)—A unit of binary storage, equal to 2^{40} (approximately 1 trillion) bytes.

termination—The point at which a program stops executing.

ternary operator—An operator that uses three operands.

test case—A set of input values and user actions, along with a specification of the expected output, used to find errors in a system.

test-driven development—A software development style that encourages the developer to write test cases first and then develop just enough source code to see the test cases pass.

test fixture—A method used to instantiate objects used during a test.

test suite—A set of tests that covers various aspects of the system.

testing—(1) The process of running a program with various test cases in order to discover problems. (2) The process of critically evaluating a design or program.

text area—A GUI component that displays, or allows the user to enter, multiple lines of data.

text field—A GUI component that displays, or allows the user to enter, a single line of data.

text file—A file that contains data formatted as ASCII or Unicode characters.

this—A Java reserved word that is a reference to the object executing the code making the reference.

thread—An independent process executing within a program. A Java program can have multiple threads running in a program at one time.

throw—A Java reserved word that is used to start an exception propagation.

throws—A Java reserved word that specifies that a method may throw a particular type of exception.

timer—An object that generates an event at regular intervals.

token—A portion of a string defined by a set of delimiters.

tool tip—A short line of text that appears when the mouse pointer is allowed to rest on top of a particular component. Usually, tool tips are employed to inform the user of the component's purpose.

top-level domain—The last part of a network domain name, such as edu or com.

transient—A Java reserved word that serves as a modifier for variables. A transient variable does not contribute to the object's persistent state and therefore does not need to be saved. *See also* serialize.

tree—A nonlinear data structure that forms a hierarchy stemming from a single root node.

true—A Java reserved word that serves as one of the two boolean literals (`true` and `false`).

truth table—A complete enumeration of all permutations of values involved in a boolean expression, as well as the computed result.

try—A Java reserved word that is used to define the context in which certain exceptions will be handled if they are thrown.

two-dimensional array—An array that uses two indices to specify the location of an element. The two dimensions are often thought of as the rows and columns of a table. *See also* multidimensional array.

two's complement—A technique for representing numeric binary data. Used by all Java integer primitive types (`byte`, `short`, `int`, `long`).

type—*See* data type.

UML—*See* Unified Modeling Language (UML).

unary operator—An operator that uses only one operand.

unchecked exception—A Java exception that does not need to be caught or dealt with if the programmer so chooses.

underflow—A problem that occurs when a floating point value becomes too small for its storage size, which can cause inaccurate arithmetic processing. *See also* overflow.

undirected graph—A graph data structure in which each edge can be traversed in either direction. *See also* edge.

Unicode—The international character set used to define valid Java characters. Each character is represented using a 16-bit unsigned numeric value.

Unified Modeling Language (UML)—A graphical notation for visualizing relationships among classes and objects. There are many types of UML diagrams. *See also* class diagrams.

uniform resource locator (URL)—A designation for a resource that can be located through a Web browser.

unit testing—The process of testing an individual software component. May require the creation of stub modules to simulate other system components.

Unix—A computer operating system developed by AT&T Bell Labs. *See also* Linux, operating system.

unsigned numeric value—A value that does not store a sign (positive or negative). The bit usually reserved to represent the sign is included in the value, doubling the magnitude of the number that can be stored. Java characters are stored as unsigned numeric values, but there are no primitive numeric types that are unsigned.

URL—*See* uniform resource locator (URL).

use relationship—A relationship between two classes, often shown in a class diagram, that establishes that one class uses another in some way, such as relying on its services. *See also* association.

user interface—The manner in which the user interacts with a software system, which is often graphical. *See also* graphical user interface (GUI).

variable—An identifier in a program that represents a memory location in which a data value is stored.

vertex—A node in a graph. *See also* graph.

visibility modifier—A Java modifier that defines the scope in which a construct can be accessed. The Java visibility modifiers are `public`, `protected`, `private`, and default (no modifier used).

void—A Java reserved word that can be used as a return value for a method, indicating that no value is returned.

volatile—(1) A Java reserved word that serves as a modifier for variables. A volatile variable might be changed asynchronously and therefore indicates that the compiler should not attempt optimizations on it. (2) The characteristic of a memory device that loses stored information when the power supply is interrupted. Main memory is a volatile storage device. *See also* nonvolatile.

von Neumann architecture—The computer architecture, named after John von Neumann, in which programs and data are stored together in the same memory devices.

walkthrough—A form of review in which a group of developers, managers, and quality assurance personnel examine a design or program in order to find errors. Sometimes referred to as an inspection. *See also* desk check.

WAN—*See* wide-area network.

waterfall model—One of the earliest software development process models. It defines a basically linear interaction among the requirements, design, implementation, and testing stages.

Web—*See* World Wide Web.

weighted graph—A graph with weights or costs associated with each edge. Weighted graphs are also sometimes known as networks.

while—A Java reserved word that represents a repetition construct. A `while` statement is executed zero or more times. *See also* do, for.

white-box testing—Producing and evaluating test cases on the basis of the interior logic of a software component. The test cases focus on stressing decision points and ensuring coverage. *See also* black-box testing, condition coverage, statement coverage.

white space—Spaces, tabs, and blank lines that are used to set off sections of source code to make programs more readable.

wide-area network (WAN)—A computer network that connects two or more local-area networks, usually across long geographic distances. *See also* local-area network.

widening conversion—A conversion between two values of different but compatible data types. Widening conversions usually leave the data value intact because the converted type has an internal representation equal to or larger than the original storage space. *See also* narrowing conversion.

word—A unit of binary storage. The size of a word varies by computer but is usually 2, 4, or 8 bytes. The word size indicates the amount of information that can be moved through the machine at one time.

World Wide Web (WWW or Web)—Software that makes the exchange of information across a network easier by providing a common GUI for multiple types of information. Web browsers are used to retrieve and format HTML documents.

wrapper class—A class designed to store a primitive type in an object. Generally used when an object reference is needed and a primitive type will not suffice.

WWW—*See* World Wide Web.

zip—A file format used to compress and store one or more files and directories into a single file suitable for exchanging to another computer.

Appendix B
Number Systems

This appendix contains a detailed introduction to number systems and their underlying characteristics. The particular focus is on the binary number system, its use with computers, and its similarities to other number systems. This introduction also covers conversions between bases.

In our everyday lives, we use the *decimal number system* to represent values, to count, and to perform arithmetic. The decimal system is also referred to as the *base-10 number system*. We use ten digits (0 through 9) to represent values in the decimal system.

Computers use the *binary number system* to store and manage information. The binary system, also called the *base-2 number system*, has only two digits (0 and 1). Each 0 and 1 is called a *bit*, which is short for "binary digit." A series of bits is called a *binary string*.

There is nothing particularly special about either the binary or the decimal system. Long ago, humans adopted the decimal number system, probably because we have ten fingers on our hands. If humans had twelve fingers, we would probably be using a base-12 number system regularly and finding it just as easy to deal with as we do the decimal system now. As you explore and use the binary system, it will become more familiar and natural.

Binary is used for computer processing because the devices used to manage and store information are less expensive and more reliable if they have to represent only two possible values. Computers have been made that use the decimal system, but they are not as convenient.

There are an infinite number of number systems, and they all follow the same basic rules. You already know how the binary number system works, but you just might not be aware that you do. It all goes back to the basic rules of arithmetic.

Place Value

In the decimal number system, we represent the values of 0 through 9 using only one digit. To represent any value higher than 9, we must use more than one digit. The position of each digit has a *place value* that indicates the amount it contributes to the overall value. In the decimal system, we refer to the one's column, the ten's column, the hundred's column, and so on forever.

Each place value is determined by the *base* of the number system, raised to increasing powers as we move from right to left. In the decimal number system, the place value of the digit farthest to the right is 10^0, or 1. The place value of the next digit is 10^1, or 10. The place value of the third digit from the right is 10^2, or 100, and so on. Figure B.1 shows how each digit in a decimal number contributes to the value.

The binary number system works the same way, except that we exhaust the available digits much sooner. We can represent 0 and 1 with a single bit, but to represent any value higher than 1, we must use multiple bits.

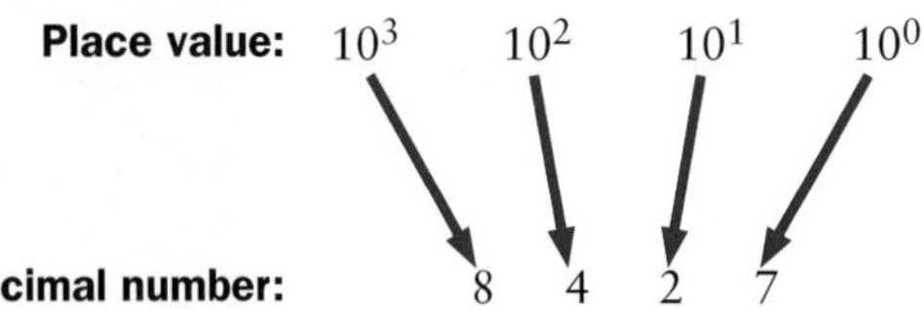

Decimal number: $8 * 10^3 + 4 * 10^2 + 2 * 10^1 + 7 * 10^0 =$

$8 * 1000 + 4 * 100 + 2 * 10 + 7 * 1 = 8427$

FIGURE B.1 Place values in the decimal number system

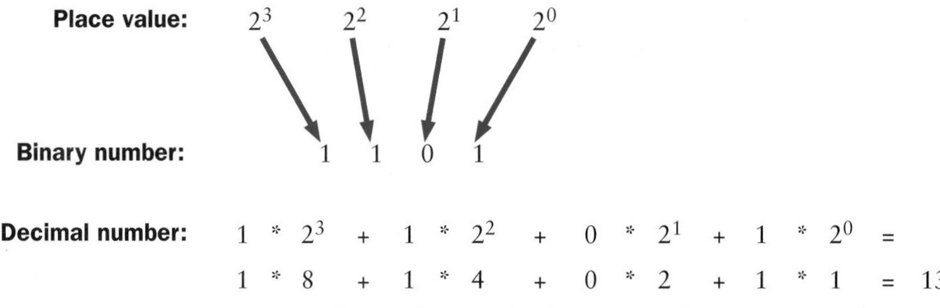

FIGURE B.2 Place values in the binary number system

The place values in binary are determined by increasing powers of the base as we move right to left, just as they are in the decimal system. However, in binary, the base value is 2. Therefore, the place value of the bit farthest to the right is 2^0, or 1. The place value of the next bit is 2^1, or 2. The place value of the third bit from the right is 2^2, or 4, and so on. Figure B.2 shows a binary number and its place values.

The number 1101 is a valid binary number, but it is a valid decimal number as well. Sometimes, to make it clear which number system is being used, the base value is appended as a subscript to the end of a number. Therefore, you can distinguish between 1101_2, which is equivalent to 13 in decimal, and 1101_{10} (one thousand one hundred and one), which in binary is represented as 10001001101_2.

A number system with base N has N digits (0 through N – 1). As we have seen, the decimal system has ten digits (0 through 9), and the binary system has two digits (0 and 1). They all work the same way. For instance, the base-5 number system has five digits (0 through 4).

Note that in any number system, the place value of the digit farthest to the right is 1, because any base raised to the zero power is 1. Also note that the value 10, which we refer to as "ten" in the decimal system, always represents the base value in any number system. In base 10, 10 is one 10 and zero 1's. In base 2, 10 is one 2 and zero 1's. In base 5, 10 is one 5 and zero 1's.

You may have seen the following geeky joke on a t-shirt: There are 10 types of people in the world, those who understand binary, and those who don't.

Bases Higher Than 10

Because all number systems with base N have N digits, base 16 has 16 digits. But what are they? We are used to the digits 0 through 9, but in bases higher than 10, we need a single digit, a single symbol, that represents the decimal value 10. In *base 16*, which is also called *hexadecimal*, we need digits that represent the decimal values 10 through 15.

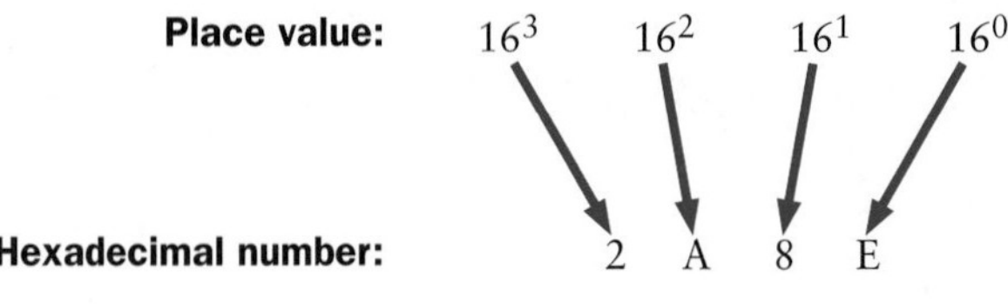

Decimal number: $2 * 16^3 + 10 * 16^2 + 8 * 16^1 + 14 * 16^0 =$

$2 * 4096 + 10 * 256 + 8 * 16 + 14 * 1 = 10893$

FIGURE B.3 Place values in the hexadecimal number system

For number systems higher than 10, we use alphabetic characters as single digits for values greater than 9. The hexadecimal digits are 0 through F, where 0 through 9 represent the first 10 digits, and A represents the decimal value 10, B represents 11, C represents 12, D represents 13, E represents 14, and F represents 15.

Therefore, the number 2A8E is a valid hexadecimal number. The place values are determined as they are for decimal and binary, using increasing powers of the base. So in hexadecimal, the place values are powers of 16. Figure B.3 shows how the place values of the hexadecimal number 2A8E contribute to the overall value.

All number systems with bases greater than 10 use letters as digits. For example, base 12 has the digits 0 through B, and base 19 has the digits 0 through I. However, apart from each system having a different set of digits and a different base, the rules governing all number systems are the same.

Keep in mind that when we change number systems, we are simply changing the way we represent values, not the values themselves. If you have 18_{10} pencils, it may be written as 10010 in binary or as 12 in hexadecimal, but it is still the same number of pencils.

Figure B.4 shows the representations of the decimal values 0 through 20 in several bases, including *base 8*, which is also called *octal*. Note that the larger the base, the higher the value that can be represented in a single digit.

Conversions

We've already seen how a number in another base is converted to decimal by determining the place value of each digit and computing the result. This process can be used to convert any number in any base to its equivalent value in base 10.

Now let's reverse the process, converting a base-10 value to another base. First, find the highest place value in the new number system that is less than or equal to the original value. Then divide the original number by that place value to

Binary (base 2)	Octal (base 8)	Decimal (base 10)	Hexadecimal (base 16)
0	0	0	0
1	1	1	1
10	2	2	2
11	3	3	3
100	4	4	4
101	5	5	5
110	6	6	6
111	7	7	7
1000	10	8	8
1001	11	9	9
1010	12	10	A
1011	13	11	B
1100	14	12	C
1101	15	13	D
1110	16	14	E
1111	17	15	F
10000	20	16	10
10001	21	17	11
10010	22	18	12
10011	23	19	13
10100	24	20	14

FIGURE B.4 Counting in various number systems

determine the digit that belongs in that position. The remainder is the value that must be represented in the remaining digit positions. Continue this process, position by position, until the entire value is represented.

For example, Figure B.5 shows the process of converting the decimal value 180 to binary. The highest place value in binary that is less than or equal to 180 is 128 (or 2^7), which is the eighth bit position from the right. Dividing 180 by 128 yields 1 with 52 remaining. Therefore, the first bit is 1, and the decimal value 52 must be represented in the remaining seven bits. Dividing 52 by 64, which is the next place value (2^6), yields 0 with 52 remaining. So the second bit is 0. Dividing 52 by 32 yields 1 with 20 remaining. So the third bit is 1, and the remaining five bits must represent the value 20. Dividing 20 by 16 yields 1 with 4 remaining. Dividing 4 by 8 yields 0 with 4 remaining. Dividing 4 by 4 yields 0 with 0 remaining.

Place value	Number	Digit
128	180	1
64	52	0
32	52	1
16	20	1
8	4	0
4	4	1
2	0	0
1	0	0

$180_{10} = 10110100_2$

FIGURE B.5 Converting a decimal value to binary

Because the number has been completely represented, the rest of the bits are zero. Therefore, 180_{10} is equivalent to 10110100 in binary. This can be confirmed by converting the new binary number back to decimal to make sure we get the original value.

This process works to convert any decimal value to any target base. For each target base, the place values and possible digits change. If you start with the correct place value, each division operation will yield a valid digit in the new base.

In the example in Figure B.5, the only digits that could have resulted from each division operation were 1 and 0, since we were converting to binary. However, when we are converting to other bases, any digit valid in the new base can result. For example, Figure B.6 shows the process of converting the decimal value 1967 to hexadecimal.

The place value 256, which is 16^2, is the highest place value less than or equal to the original number, because the next highest place value is 16^3, or 4096. Dividing 1967 by 256 yields 7 with 175 remaining. Dividing 175 by 16 yields

Place value	Number	Digit
256	1967	7
16	175	A
1	15	F

$1967_{10} = 7AF_{16}$

FIGURE B.6 Converting a decimal value to hexadecimal

10 with 15 remaining. Remember that 10 in decimal can be represented as the single digit A in hexadecimal. The 15 remaining can be represented as the digit F. Therefore, 1967_{10} is equivalent to 7AF in hexadecimal.

Shortcut Conversions

We have established techniques for converting any value in any base to its equivalent representation in base 10, and from base 10 to any other base. Therefore, you can now convert a number in any base to any other base by going through base 10. However, an interesting relationship between the bases that are powers of 2, such as binary, octal, and hexadecimal, makes possible very quick conversions between them.

To convert from binary to hexadecimal, for instance, you can simply group the bits of the original value into groups of four, starting from the right, and then convert each group of four into a single hexadecimal digit. The example in Figure B.7 demonstrates this process.

To go from hexadecimal to binary, we reverse this process, expanding each hexadecimal digit into four binary digits. Note that you may have to add leading zeros to the binary version of each expanded hexadecimal digit to make four binary digits. Figure B.8 shows the conversion of the hexadecimal value 40C6 to binary.

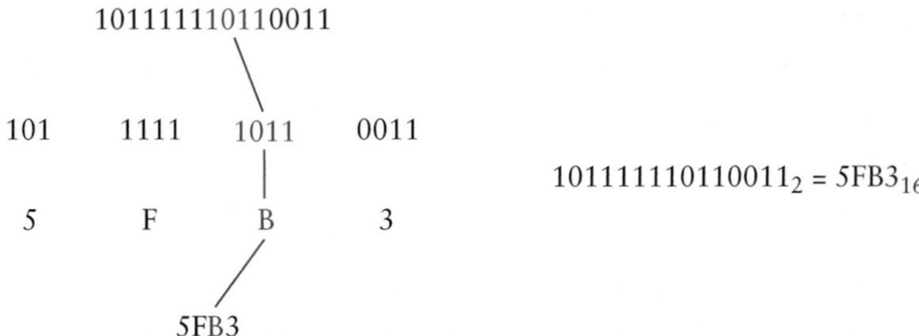

FIGURE B.7 A shortcut conversion from binary to hexadecimal

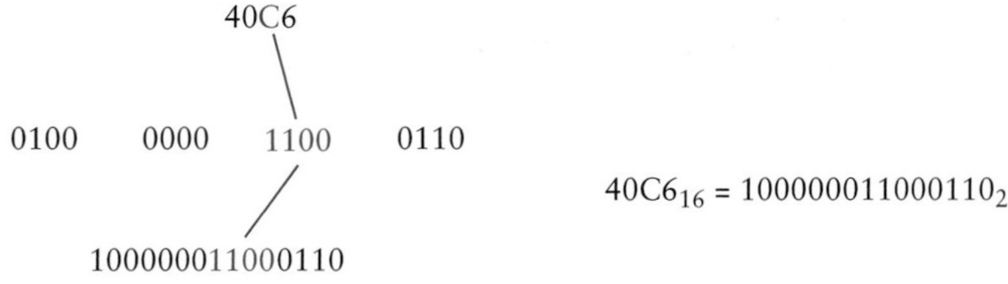

FIGURE B.8 A shortcut conversion from hexadecimal to binary

Why do we use groups of four bits when converting between binary and hexadecimal? The answer comes from the relationship between the bases 2 and 16. We use groups of four bits because $2^4 = 16$. The shortcut conversions work between binary and any base that is a power of 2. We section the bits into groups of that power.

Therefore, converting from binary to octal is the same process, except that the bits are sectioned into groups of three, because $2^3 = 8$. Likewise, when converting from octal to binary, we expand each octal digit into three bits.

To convert between, say, hexadecimal and octal is now a process of doing two shortcut conversions. First convert from hexadecimal to binary; then take that result and perform a shortcut conversion from binary to octal.

By the way, these types of shortcut conversions can be performed between any base B and any base that is a power of B. For example, conversions between base 3 and base 9 can be accomplished using the shortcut grouping technique, sectioning or expanding digits into groups of two, because $3^2 = 9$.

Exercises

EX B.1 What is the difference between the binary and decimal number systems?

EX B.2 Why do modern computers use a binary number system to represent information?

EX B.3 How many digits are used in the base-6 number system? What are they?

EX B.4 How many digits are used in the base-12 number system? What are they?

EX B.5 Convert the following binary numbers to decimal.

a. 10

b. 10110

c. 11100

d. 10101010

e. 11001011

f. 10000000001

EX B.6 Convert the following octal numbers to decimal.

a. 10

b. 125

c. 5401

d. 7777

e. 46034

f. 65520

EX B.7 Convert the following hexadecimal numbers to decimal.

a. 10

b. 904

c. 6C3

d. ABC

e. 5D0BF

f. FFF

EX B.8 Convert the following decimal numbers to binary.

a. 2
b. 10
c. 64
d. 80
e. 145
f. 256

EX B.9 Convert the following decimal numbers to octal.

a. 8
b. 10
c. 512
d. 406
e. 349
f. 888

EX B.10 Convert the following decimal numbers to hexadecimal.

a. 16
b. 10
c. 175
d. 256
e. 422
f. 4199

EX B.11 Convert the following binary numbers to hexadecimal.

a. 101000110110
b. 1110101111
c. 1100110000010111
d. 1000000000011011
e. 1010111100010
f. 11000111000010001111000

EX B.12 Convert the following binary numbers to octal.

a. 101011111011
b. 1001101011
c. 111111000101110

d. 11010000110111110001

e. 1111101011000110100001

f. 11000100011101011110111001111

EX B.13 Convert the following hexadecimal numbers to binary.

a. 555

b. B74

c. 47A9

d. FDCB

e. 10101010

f. 5B60F9D

EX B.14 Convert the following octal numbers to binary.

a. 555

b. 760

c. 152

d. 3032

e. 76543

f. 6351732

The Unicode Character Set

Appendix C

The Java programming language uses the Unicode character set for managing text. A *character set* is simply an ordered list of characters, each corresponding to a particular numeric value. Unicode is an international character set that contains letters, symbols, and ideograms for languages all over the world. Each character is represented as a 16-bit unsigned numeric value. Unicode, therefore, can support over 65,000 unique characters. In fact, with a technique that uses more than two bytes in some cases, it can represent more than that.

Many programming languages still use the ASCII character set. ASCII stands for the American Standard Code for Information Interchange. The 8-bit extended ASCII set is quite small, so the developers of Java opted to use Unicode in order to support international users. However, ASCII is essentially a subset of Unicode, including the corresponding numeric values, so programmers who are accustomed to using ASCII should have no problems with Unicode.

Figure C.1 shows a list of commonly used characters and their Unicode numeric values. These characters also happen to be ASCII characters. All of the characters in Figure C.1 are called *printable characters*, because they have a symbolic representation that can be displayed on a monitor or printed by a printer. Characters that have no such symbolic representation are called *nonprintable characters*. Note that the space character (numeric value 32) is considered a printable character, even though no symbol is printed when it is displayed. Nonprintable characters are sometimes called *control characters*, because many of them can be generated by holding down the control key on a keyboard and pressing another key.

The Unicode characters with numeric values 0 through 31 are nonprintable characters. Also, the delete character, with numeric value 127, is a nonprintable character. All of these characters are ASCII characters as well. Many of them have

Value	Char	Value	Char	Value	Char	Value	Char	Value	Char
32	*space*	51	3	70	F	89	Y	108	l
33	!	52	4	71	G	90	Z	109	m
34	"	53	5	72	H	91	[	110	n
35	#	54	6	73	I	92	\	111	o
36	$	55	7	74	J	93	]	112	p
37	%	56	8	75	K	94	^	113	q
38	&	57	9	76	L	95	_	114	r
39	'	58	:	77	M	96	`	115	s
40	(	59	;	78	N	97	a	116	t
41	)	60	<	79	O	98	b	117	u
42	*	61	=	80	P	99	c	118	v
43	+	62	>	81	Q	100	d	119	w
44	,	63	?	82	R	101	e	120	x
45	–	64	@	83	S	102	f	121	y
46	.	65	A	84	T	103	g	122	z
47	/	66	B	85	U	104	h	123	{
48	0	67	C	86	V	105	i	124	|
49	1	68	D	87	W	106	j	125	}
50	2	69	E	88	X	107	k	126	~

FIGURE C.1 The printable ASCII subset of the Unicode character set

Value	Character
0	*null*
7	*bell*
8	*backspace*
9	*tab*
10	*line feed*
12	*form feed*
13	*carriage return*
27	*escape*
127	*delete*

FIGURE C.2 Some nonprintable characters in the Unicode character set

fairly common and well-defined uses, whereas others are more general. The table in Figure C.2 lists a small sample of the nonprintable characters.

Nonprintable characters are used in many situations to represent special conditions. For example, certain nonprintable characters can be stored in a text document to indicate, among other things, the beginning of a new line. An editor will process these characters by starting the text that follows it on a new line, instead of printing a symbol to the screen. Various types of computer systems use different nonprintable characters to represent particular conditions.

Except for having no visible representation, nonprintable characters are essentially equivalent to printable characters. They can be stored in a Java character variable and can be part of a character string. They are stored using 16 bits, can be converted to their numeric value, and can be compared using relational operators.

The first 128 characters of the Unicode character set correspond to the common ASCII character set. The first 256 characters correspond to the ISO-Latin-1 extended ASCII character set. Many operating systems and Web browsers will handle these characters, but they may not be able to print the other Unicode characters.

The Unicode character set contains most alphabets in use today, including Greek, Hebrew, Cyrillic, and various Asian ideographs. It also includes Braille and several sets of symbols used in mathematics and music. Figure C.3 shows a few characters from non-Western alphabets.

Value	Character	Source
1071	Я	Russian (Cyrillic)
3593	ฉ	Thai
5098	Ꮺ	Cherokee
8478	℞	Letterlike Symbols
8652	⇌	Arrows
10287	⠯	Braille
13407	㑟	Chinese/Japanese/Korean (Common)

FIGURE C.3 Some non-Western characters in the Unicode character set

Appendix D
Java Operators

Java operators are evaluated according to the precedence hierarchy shown in Figure D.1. Operators at low precedence levels are evaluated before operators at higher levels. Operators within the same precedence level are evaluated according to the specified association, either right to left (R to L) or left to right (L to R). Operators in the same precedence level are not listed in any particular order.

The order of operator evaluation can always be forced by the use of parentheses. It is sometimes a good idea to use parentheses even when they are not required, to make it explicitly clear to a human reader how an expression is evaluated.

Precedence Level	Operator	Operation	Associates
1	[ ] . (*parameters*) ++ --	array indexing object member reference parameter evaluation and method invocation postfix increment postfix decrement	L to R
2	++ -- + - ~ !	prefix increment prefix decrement unary plus unary minus bitwise NOT logical NOT	R to L
3	new (*type*)	object instantiation cast	R to L
4	* / %	multiplication division remainder	L to R
5	+ + -	addition string concatenation subtraction	L to R
6	<< >> >>>	left shift right shift with sign right shift with zero	L to R
7	< <= > >= instanceof	less than less than or equal greater than greater than or equal type comparison	L to R
8	== !=	equal not equal	L to R

FIGURE D.1 Java operator precedence

For some operators, the operand types determine which operation is carried out. For instance, if the + operator is used on two strings, string concatenation is performed, but if it is applied to two numeric types, they are added in the arithmetic sense. If only one of the operands is a string, the other is converted to a string, and string concatenation is performed. Similarly, the operators &, ^, and | perform bitwise operations on numeric operands but perform boolean operations on boolean operands.

The boolean operators & and | differ from the logical operators && and || in a subtle way. The logical operators are "short-circuited" in that if the result of an expression can be determined by evaluating only the left operand, the right operand

<table>
<tr><th>Precedence Level</th><th>Operator</th><th>Operation</th><th>Associates</th></tr>
<tr><td>9</td><td>&
&</td><td>bitwise AND
boolean AND</td><td>L to R</td></tr>
<tr><td>10</td><td>^
^</td><td>bitwise XOR
boolean XOR</td><td>L to R</td></tr>
<tr><td>11</td><td>|
|</td><td>bitwise OR
boolean OR</td><td>L to R</td></tr>
<tr><td>12</td><td>&&</td><td>logical AND</td><td>L to R</td></tr>
<tr><td>13</td><td>||</td><td>logical OR</td><td>L to R</td></tr>
<tr><td>14</td><td>?:</td><td>conditional operator</td><td>R to L</td></tr>
<tr><td>15</td><td>=
+=
+=
-=
*=
/=
%=
<<=
>>=
>>>=
&=
&=
^=
^=
|=
|=</td><td>assignment
addition, then assignment
string concatenation, then assignment
subtraction, then assignment
multiplication, then assignment
division, then assignment
remainder, then assignment
left shift, then assignment
right shift (sign), then assignment
right shift (zero), then assignment
bitwise AND, then assignment
boolean AND, then assignment
bitwise XOR, then assignment
boolean XOR, then assignment
bitwise OR, then assignment
boolean OR, then assignment</td><td>R to L</td></tr>
</table>

FIGURE D.1 Java operator precedence (continued)

is not evaluated. The boolean versions always evaluate both sides of the expression. There is no logical operator that performs an exclusive OR (XOR) operation.

Java Bitwise Operators

The Java *bitwise operators* operate on individual bits within a primitive value. Because they are not discussed in the chapters of this book, we explore them further here. The bitwise operators are defined only for integers and characters. They are unique among all Java operators, because they let us work at the lowest level of binary storage. Figure D.2 on the next page lists the Java bitwise operators.

Three of the bitwise operators are similar to the logical operators `!`, `&&`, and `||`. The bitwise NOT, AND, and OR operations work in basically the same way

Operator	Description
~	bitwise NOT
&	bitwise AND
|	bitwise OR
^	bitwise XOR
<<	left shift
>>	right shift with sign
>>>	right shift with zero fill

FIGURE D.2 The Java bitwise operators

as their logical counterparts, except they work on individual bits of a value. The rules are essentially the same. Figure D.3 shows the results of bitwise operators on all combinations of two bits. Compare this chart to the truth tables for the logical operators in Chapter 4 to see the similarities.

The bitwise operators include the XOR operator, which stands for *exclusive OR*. The logical || operator is an *inclusive OR* operation, which means that it returns true if both operands are true. The | bitwise operator is also inclusive and yields a 1 if both corresponding bits are 1. However, the exclusive OR operator (^) yields a 0 if both operands are 1. There is no logical exclusive OR operator in Java.

When the bitwise operators are applied to integer values, the operation is performed individually on each bit in the value. For example, suppose the integer variable `number` is declared to be of type byte and currently holds the value 45. Stored as an 8-bit byte, it is represented in binary as `00101101`. When the bitwise complement operator (~) is applied to `number`, each bit in the value is inverted, yielding `11010010`. Because integers are stored using two's complement representation, the value represented is now negative, specifically −46.

a	b	~ a	a & b	a | b	a ^ b
0	0	1	0	0	0
0	1	1	0	1	1
1	0	0	0	1	1
1	1	0	1	1	0

FIGURE D.3 Bitwise operations on individual bits

num1 & num2	num1 | num2	num1 ^ num2
00101101	00101101	00101101
& 00001110	| 00001110	^ 00001110
= 00001100	= 00101111	= 00100011

FIGURE D.4 Bitwise operations on bytes

Similarly, for all bitwise operators, the operations are applied bit by bit, which is where the term *bitwise* comes from. For binary operators (with two operands), the operations are applied to corresponding bits in each operand. For example, assume that `num1` and `num2` are byte integers, `num1` holds the value 45, and `num2` holds the value 14. Figure D.4 shows the results of several bitwise operations.

The operators `&`, `|`, and `^` can also be applied to boolean values, and they have basically the same meaning as their logical counterparts. When used with boolean values, they are called *boolean operators*. However, unlike the operators `&&` and `||`, which are "short-circuited," the boolean operators are not short-circuited. Both sides of the expression are evaluated every time.

Like the other bitwise operators, the three bitwise shift operators manipulate the individual bits of an integer value. They all take two operands. The left operand is the value whose bits are shifted; the right operand specifies how many positions they should move. Before a shift is performed, byte and short values are promoted to int for all shift operators. Furthermore, if either of the operands is long, the other operand is promoted to long. For readability, we use only 16 bits in the examples in this section, but the concepts are the same when carried out to 32- or 64-bit strings.

When bits are shifted, some bits are lost off one end, and others need to be filled in on the other. The *left-shift* operator (`<<`) shifts bits to the left, filling the right bits with zeros. For example, if the integer variable `number` currently has the value 13, then the statement

```
number = number << 2;
```

stores the value 52 into `number`. Initially, `number` contains the bit string `0000000000001101`. When shifted to the left, the value becomes `0000000000110100`, or 52. Notice that for each position shifted to the left, the original value is multiplied by 2.

The sign bit of a number is shifted along with all of the others. Therefore, the sign of the value can change if enough bits are shifted to change the sign bit. For example, the value –8 is stored in binary two's complement form as `1111111111111000`.

When shifted left two positions, it becomes `1111111111100000`, which is –32. However, if enough positions are shifted, a negative number can become positive, and vice versa.

There are two forms of the right-shift operator: one that preserves the sign of the original value (`>>`) and one that fills the leftmost bits with zeros (`>>>`).

Let's examine two examples of the *right-shift-with-sign-fill* operator. If the int variable `number` currently has the value 39, the expression `(number >> 2)` results in the value 9. The original bit string stored in `number` is `0000000000100111`, and the result of a right shift two positions is `0000000000001001`. The leftmost sign bit, which in this case is a zero, is used to fill from the left.

If `number` has an original value of –16, or `1111111111110000`, the right-shift (with sign fill) expression `(number >>> 3)` results in the binary string `1111111111111110`, or –2. The leftmost sign bit is a 1 in this case and is used to fill in the new left bits, maintaining the sign.

If maintaining the sign is not desirable, the *right-shift-with-zero-fill* operator (`>>>`) can be used. It operates similarly to the `>>` operator but fills with zero no matter what the sign of the original value is.

Appendix E

Java Modifiers

This appendix summarizes the modifiers that give particular characteristics to Java classes, interfaces, methods, and variables. For discussion purposes, the set of all Java modifiers is divided into two groups: visibility modifiers and all others.

Java Visibility Modifiers

The table in Figure E.1 describes the effect of Java visibility modifiers on various constructs. Some relationships are not applicable (N/A). For instance, a class cannot be declared with protected visibility. Note that each visibility modifier operates in the same way on classes and interfaces and in the same way on methods and variables.

Default visibility means that no visibility modifier was explicitly used. Default visibility is sometimes called *package visibility,* but you cannot use the reserved word `package` as a modifier. Classes and interfaces can have default or public visibility; this visibility determines whether a class or interface can be referenced outside of its package. Only an inner class can have private visibility, in which case only the enclosing class may access it.

A Visibility Example

Consider the situation depicted in Figure E.2. Class `P` is the parent class that is used to derive child classes `C1` and `C2`. Class `C1` is in the same package as class `P`, but class `C2` is not. Class `P` contains four methods, each with different visibility modifiers. One object has been instantiated from each of these classes.

The public method `a()` has been inherited by `C1` and `C2`, and any code with access to object `x` can invoke `x.a()`. The private method `d()` is not visible to `C1` or `C2`, so objects `y` and `z` have no such method available to them. Furthermore, `d()` is fully encapsulated and can be invoked only from within object `x`.

Modifier	Classes and interfaces	Methods and variables
default (no modifier)	Visible in its package.	Visible to any class in the same package as its class.
public	Visible anywhere.	Visible anywhere.
protected	N/A	Visible by any class in the same package as its class.
private	Visible to the enclosing class only	Not visible by any other class.

FIGURE E.1 Java visibility modifiers

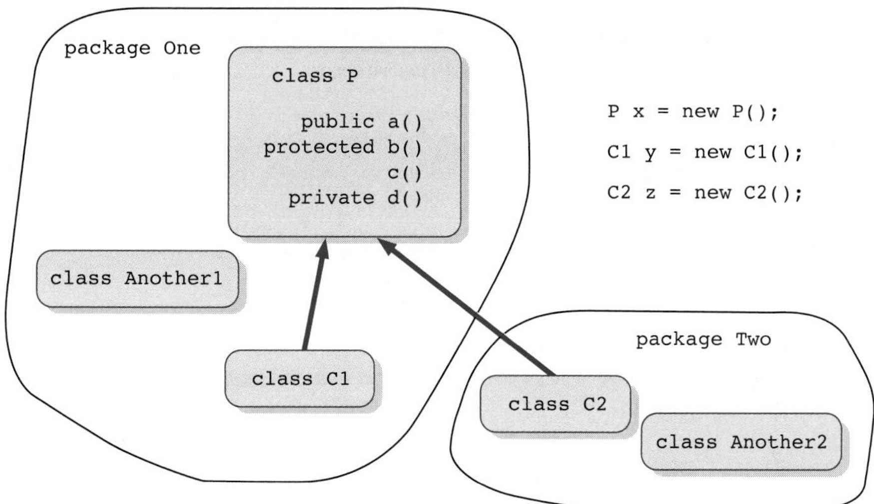

FIGURE E.2 A situation demonstrating Java visibility modifiers

The protected method `b()` is visible in both `C1` and `C2`. A method in `y` could invoke `x.b()`, but a method in `z` could not. Furthermore, an object of any class in package `One` could invoke `x.b()`, even those that are not related to class `P` by inheritance, such as an object created from class `Another1`.

Method `c()` has `default` visibility, because no visibility modifier was used to declare it. Therefore, object `y` can refer to the method `c()` as if it were declared locally, but object `z` cannot. Object `y` can invoke `x.c()`, as can an object instantiated from any class in package `One`, such as `Another1`. Object `z` cannot invoke `x.c()`.

These rules generalize in the same way for variables. The visibility rules may appear complicated initially, but they can be mastered with a little effort.

Other Java Modifiers

Figure E.3 summarizes the rest of the Java modifiers, which address a variety of issues. These modifiers have different effects on classes, interfaces, methods, and variables. Some modifiers cannot be used with certain constructs and therefore are listed as not applicable (N/A).

Modifier	Class	Interface	Method	Variable
`abstract`	The class may contain abstract methods. It cannot be instantiated.	All interfaces are inherently abstract. The modifier is optional.	No method body is defined. The method requires implementation when inherited.	N/A
`final`	The class cannot be used to derive new classes.	N/A	The method cannot be overridden.	The variable is a constant, whose value cannot be changed once initially set.
`native`	N/A	N/A	No method body is necessary since implementation is in another language.	N/A
`static`	N/A	N/A	Defines a class method. It does not require an instantiated object to be invoked. It cannot reference non-static methods or variables. It is implicitly final.	Defines a class variable. It does not require an instantiated object to be referenced. It is shared (common memory space) among all instances of the class.
`synchronized`	N/A	N/A	The execution of the method is mutually exclusive among all threads.	N/A
`transient`	N/A	N/A	N/A	The variable will not be serialized.
`volatile`	N/A	N/A	N/A	The variable is changed asynchronously. The compiler should not perform optimizations on it.

FIGURE E.3 The rest of the Java modifiers

The `transient` modifier is used to indicate data that need not be stored in a persistent (serialized) object. That is, when an object is written to a serialized stream, the object representation will include all data that are not specified as transient.

Appendix F

Java Graphics

Chapter 6 covers the issues related to developing a graphical user interface (GUI) for a Java program, but it does not discuss the mechanisms for drawing shapes and managing color. This appendix is provided to introduce the concepts and techniques used to manage Java graphics.

A picture is represented on a computer by breaking it down into *pixels*, a term that is short for "picture elements." A complete picture is stored by storing the color of each individual pixel. The more pixels used to represent a picture, the more realistic it looks when it is reproduced. The number of pixels used to represent a picture is called the *picture resolution*. The number of pixels that can be displayed by a monitor is called the *monitor resolution*.

Coordinate Systems

When drawn, each pixel is mapped to a pixel on the monitor screen. Each computer system and programming language defines a coordinate system so that we can refer to particular pixels.

A traditional two-dimensional Cartesian coordinate system has two axes that meet at the origin. Values on either axis can be negative or positive. The Java programming language has a relatively simple coordinate system in which all of the visible coordinates are positive. Figure F.1 compares a traditional coordinate system to the Java coordinate system.

Each point in the Java coordinate system is represented using an (x, y) pair of values. Each graphical component in a Java program, such as a panel, has its own coordinate system, with the origin in the top-left corner at coordinates (0, 0). The x-axis coordinates get larger as you move to the right, and the y-axis coordinates get larger as you move down.

Representing Color

There are various ways to represent the color of a pixel. In the Java programming language, every color is represented as a mix of what the Java language refers to as the three *primary colors*: red, green, and blue. A color is specified using three numbers that are collectively referred to as an *RGB value*. RGB stands for Red-Green-Blue. Each number represents the relative contribution of a primary color.

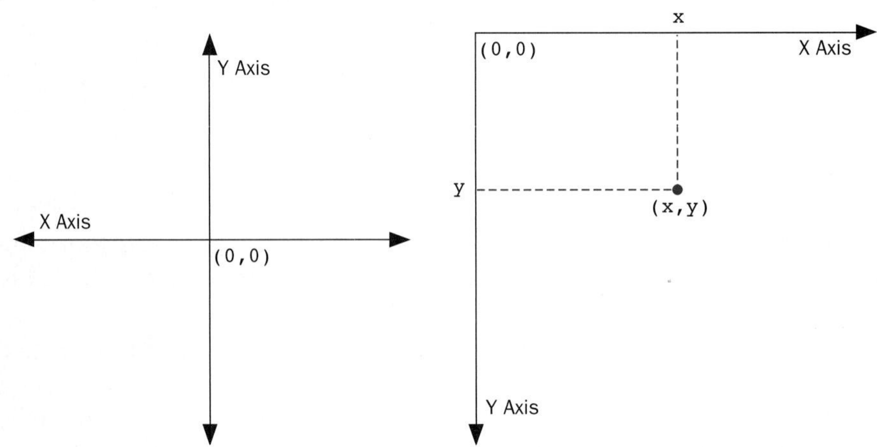

FIGURE F.1 A traditional coordinate system and the Java coordinate system

Color	Object	RGB Value
black	`Color.black`	0, 0, 0
blue	`Color.blue`	0, 0, 255
cyan	`Color.cyan`	0, 255, 255
gray	`Color.gray`	128, 128, 128
dark gray	`Color.darkGray`	64, 64, 64
light gray	`Color.lightGray`	192, 192, 192
green	`Color.green`	0, 255, 0
magenta	`Color.magenta`	255, 0, 255
orange	`Color.orange`	255, 200, 0
pink	`Color.pink`	255, 175, 175
red	`Color.red`	255, 0, 0
white	`Color.white`	255, 255, 255
yellow	`Color.yellow`	255, 255, 0

FIGURE F.2 Predefined colors in the `Color` class

Using 1 byte (8 bits) to store each of the three components of an RGB value, the numbers can range from 0 to 255. The level of each primary color determines the overall color. For example, high values of red and green combined with a low level of blue results in a shade of yellow.

In Java, a programmer uses the `Color` class, which is part of the `java.awt` package, to define and manage colors. Each object of the `Color` class represents a single color. The class contains several instances of itself to provide a basic set of predefined colors. Figure F.2 lists the predefined colors of the `Color` class. It also contains methods to define and manage many other colors.

Drawing Shapes

The Java standard class library provides many classes that enable us to present and manipulate graphical information. The `Graphics` class, which is defined in the `java.awt` package, is fundamental to all such processing.

The `Graphics` class contains various methods that enable us to draw shapes, including lines, rectangles, and ovals. Figure F.3 on the next page lists some of the fundamental drawing methods of the `Graphics` class. These methods also let us draw circles and squares, which are just specific types of ovals and rectangles, respectively.

```
void drawLine (int x1, int y1, int x2, int y2)
```
Paints a line from point (x1, y1) to point (x2, y2).

```
void drawRect (int x, int y, int width, int height)
```
Paints a rectangle with upper left corner (x, y) and dimensions width and height.

```
void drawOval (int x, int y, int width, int height)
```
Paints an oval bounded by the rectangle with an upper left corner of (x, y) and dimensions width and height.

```
void drawString (String str, int x, int y)
```
Paints the character string str at point (x, y), extending to the right.

```
void drawArc (int x, int y, int width, int height, int
startAngle, int arcAngle)
```
Paints an arc along the oval bounded by the rectangle defined by x, y, width, and height. The arc starts at startAngle and extends for a distance defined by arcAngle.

```
void fillRect (int x, int  y, int width, int height)
```
Same as their draw counterparts, but filled with the current foreground color.

```
void fillOval (int x, int y, int width, int height)
```

```
void fillArc (int x, int y, int width, int height,
int startAngle, int arcAngle)
```

```
Color getColor ()
```
Returns this graphics context's foreground color.

```
void setColor (Color color)
```
Sets this graphics context's foreground color to the specified color.

FIGURE F.3 Some methods of the `Graphics` class

The methods of the `Graphics` class allow us to specify whether we want a shape filled or unfilled. An unfilled shape shows only the outline of the shape and is otherwise transparent (you can see any underlying graphics). A filled shape is solid between its boundaries and covers any underlying graphics.

Many of these methods accept parameters that specify the coordinates at which the shape should be drawn. Shapes drawn at coordinates that are outside the visible area will not be seen.

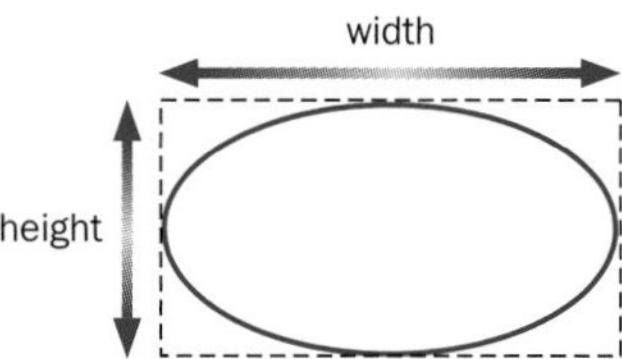

FIGURE F.4 An oval and its bounding rectangle

Many of the `Graphics` drawing methods are self-explanatory, but some require a little more discussion. Note, for instance, that an oval drawn by the `drawOval` method is defined by the coordinate of the upper-left corner and dimensions that specify the width and height of a *bounding rectangle*. Shapes with curves, such as ovals, are often defined by a rectangle that encompasses their perimeters. Figure F.4 depicts a bounding rectangle for an oval.

An arc can be thought of as a segment of an oval. To draw an arc, we specify the oval of which the arc is a part and the portion of the oval in which we're interested. The starting point of the arc is defined by the *start angle* and the ending point of the arc is defined by the *arc angle*. The arc angle does not indicate where the arc ends, but rather its range. The start angle and the arc angle are measured in degrees. The origin for the start angle is an imaginary horizontal line passing through the center of the oval and can be referred to as 0°, as shown in Figure F.5.

Every graphics context has a current *foreground color* that is used whenever shapes or strings are drawn. Every surface that can be drawn on has a

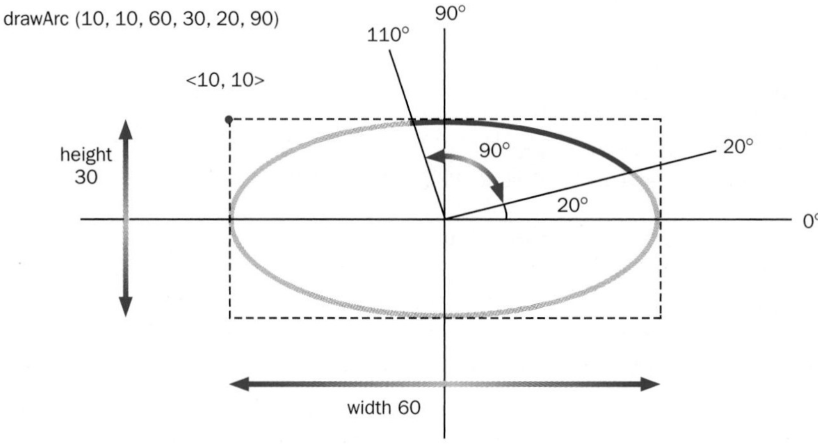

FIGURE F.5 An arc defined by an oval, a start angle, and an arc angle

background color. The foreground color is set using the `setColor` method of the `Graphics` class, and the background color is set using the `setBackground` method of the component on which we are drawing, such as the panel.

Listing F.1 shows a program that uses various drawing and color methods to draw a winter scene featuring a snowman. The drawing is done on a `JPanel`, defined by the `SnowmanPanel` class, which is shown in Listing F.2.

The `paintComponent` method of a graphical component is called automatically when the component is rendered on the screen. Note that the `paintComponent` method accepts a `Graphics` object as a parameter. A `Graphics` object defines a particular *graphics context* with which we can interact. The graphics context passed into a panel's `paintComponent` method represents the graphics context in which the panel is drawn.

LISTING F.1

```
//********************************************************************
//  Snowman.java       Java Foundations
//
//  Demonstrates the use of basic drawing methods.
//********************************************************************

import javax.swing.JFrame;
public class Snowman
{
   //-----------------------------------------------------------------
   //  Displays a winter scene featuring a snowman.
   //-----------------------------------------------------------------
   public static void main (String[] args)
   {
      JFrame frame = new JFrame ("Snowman");
      frame.setDefaultCloseOperation (JFrame.EXIT_ON_CLOSE);

      frame.getContentPane().add(new SnowmanPanel());

      frame.pack();
      frame.setVisible(true);
   }
}
```

LISTING F.1 *continued*

DISPLAY

LISTING F.2

```
//********************************************************************
//  SnowmanPanel.java       Java Foundations
//
//  Represents the primary drawing panel for the Snowman application.
//********************************************************************

import java.awt.*;
import javax.swing.*;

public class SnowmanPanel extends JPanel
{
   private final int MID = 150;
   private final int TOP = 50;
```

LISTING F.2 *continued*

```
   //-----------------------------------------------------------------
   //  Sets up the snowman panel.
   //-----------------------------------------------------------------
   public SnowmanPanel ()
   {
      setPreferredSize (new Dimension(300, 225));
      setBackground (Color.cyan);
   }

   //-----------------------------------------------------------------
   //  Draws a snowman.
   //-----------------------------------------------------------------
   public void paintComponent (Graphics page)
   {
      super.paintComponent (page);
      page.setColor (Color.blue);
      page.fillRect (0, 175, 300, 50); // ground

      page.setColor (Color.yellow);
      page.fillOval (-40, -40, 80, 80); // sun

      page.setColor (Color.white);
      page.fillOval (MID-20, TOP, 40, 40);      // head
      page.fillOval (MID-35, TOP+35, 70, 50);   // upper torso
      page.fillOval (MID-50, TOP+80, 100, 60); // lower torso

      page.setColor (Color.black);
      page.fillOval (MID-10, TOP+10, 5, 5); // left eye
      page.fillOval (MID+5, TOP+10, 5, 5);  // right eye

      page.drawArc (MID-10, TOP+20, 20, 10, 190, 160); // smile

      page.drawLine (MID-25, TOP+60, MID-50, TOP+40); // left arm
      page.drawLine (MID+25, TOP+60, MID+55, TOP+60); // right arm

      page.drawLine (MID-20, TOP+5, MID+20, TOP+5);  // brim of hat
      page.fillRect (MID-15, TOP-20, 30, 25);        // top of hat
   }
}
```

The drawing of the snowman figure is based on two constant values called `MID` and `TOP`, which define the midpoint of the snowman (left to right) and the top of the snowman's head. The entire snowman figure is drawn relative to these values. Using constants like these makes it easier to create the snowman and to make modifications later. For example, to shift the snowman to the right or left in our picture, we need change only one constant declaration.

The call to the `super.paintComponent` method as the first line in the `paintComponent` method ensures that the background color will be painted. The version of `paintComponent` defined in the `JPanel` class handles the display of the panel's background. The examples in Chapter 6, which add graphical components such as buttons to a panel, do not need this call. If a panel contains graphical components, the parent's `paintComponent` method is automatically called. This is a key distinction between drawing on a component and adding a component to a container.

Let's look at another example. The `Splat` class shown in Listing F.3 simply draws a few filled circles. The interesting thing about this program is not what it does but how it does it—each circle drawn in this program is represented by its own object.

LISTING F.3

```
//********************************************************************
//  Splat.java       Java Foundations
//
//  Demonstrates the use of graphical objects.
//********************************************************************

import javax.swing.JFrame;

public class Splat
{
   //-----------------------------------------------------------------
   //  Presents a set of circles.
   //-----------------------------------------------------------------
   public static void main (String[] args)
   {
      JFrame frame = new JFrame ("Splat");
      frame.setDefaultCloseOperation (JFrame.EXIT_ON_CLOSE);
      frame.getContentPane().add(new SplatPanel());
```

LISTING F.3 *continued*

```
        frame.pack();
        frame.setVisible(true);
    }
}
```

DISPLAY

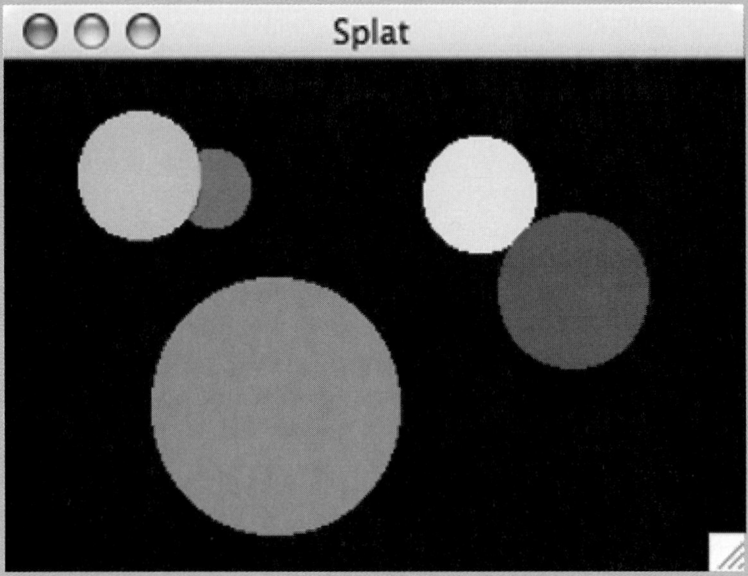

Splat

The `main` method instantiates a `SplatPanel` object and adds it to the frame. The `SplatPanel` class is shown in Listing F.4. It is derived from `JPanel`, and it holds as instance data five `Circle` objects, which are instantiated in the panel's constructor. The `paintComponent` method in the `SplatPanel` class draws the panel by calling the `draw` method of each circle.

The `Circle` class is shown in Listing F.5 on page 974. It defines instance data to store the size of the circle, its (x, y) location, and its color. The `draw` method of the `Circle` class simply draws the circle based on the values of its instance data.

The design of the `Splat` program embodies fundamental object-oriented thinking. Each circle manages itself and will draw itself in whatever graphics context you pass it. The `Circle` class is defined in a way that can be used in other situations and programs. There is a clean separation between the object being drawn and the component on which it is drawn.

LISTING F.4

```
//********************************************************************
//  SplatPanel.java       Java Foundations
//
//  Demonstrates the use of graphical objects.
//********************************************************************

import javax.swing.*;
import java.awt.*;

public class SplatPanel extends JPanel
{
   private Circle circle1, circle2, circle3, circle4, circle5;

   //-----------------------------------------------------------------
   //  Creates five Circle objects.
   //-----------------------------------------------------------------
   public SplatPanel()
   {
      circle1 = new Circle (30, Color.red, 70, 35);
      circle2 = new Circle (50, Color.green, 30, 20);
      circle3 = new Circle (100, Color.cyan, 60, 85);
      circle4 = new Circle (45, Color.yellow, 170, 30);
      circle5 = new Circle (60, Color.blue, 200, 60);
      setPreferredSize (new Dimension(300, 200));
      setBackground (Color.black);
   }

   //-----------------------------------------------------------------
   //  Draws this panel by requesting that each circle draw itself.
   //-----------------------------------------------------------------
   public void paintComponent (Graphics page)
   {
      super.paintComponent(page);
      circle1.draw(page);
      circle2.draw(page);
      circle3.draw(page);
      circle4.draw(page);
      circle5.draw(page);
   }
}
```

LISTING F.5

```
//********************************************************************
//  Circle.java        Java Foundations
//
//  Represents a circle with a particular position, size, and color.
//********************************************************************

import java.awt.*;

public class Circle
{
   private int diameter, x, y;
   private Color color;

   //-----------------------------------------------------------------
   //  Sets up this circle with the specified values.
   //-----------------------------------------------------------------
   public Circle (int size, Color shade, int upperX, int upperY)
   {
      diameter = size;
      color = shade;
      x = upperX;
      y = upperY;
   }

   //-----------------------------------------------------------------
   //  Draws this circle in the specified graphics context.
   //-----------------------------------------------------------------
   public void draw (Graphics page)
   {
      page.setColor (color);
      page.fillOval (x, y, diameter, diameter);
   }
}
```

Polygons and Polylines

A polygon is a multisided shape that is defined in Java using a series of (x, y) points that indicate the vertices of the polygon. Arrays are often used to store the list of coordinates.

Polygons are drawn using methods of the `Graphics` class, in a manner similar to how we draw rectangles and ovals. Like these other shapes, a polygon can be drawn filled or unfilled. The methods used to draw a polygon are called `drawPolygon` and `fillPolygon`. Both of these methods are overloaded. One version uses arrays of integers to define the polygon, and the other uses an object of the `Polygon` class to define the polygon. We discuss the `Polygon` class later in this appendix.

In the version that uses arrays, the `drawPolygon` and `fillPolygon` methods take three parameters. The first is an array of integers representing the *x* coordinates of the points in the polygon, the second is an array of integers representing the corresponding y coordinates of those points, and the third is an integer that indicates how many points are used from each of the two arrays. Taken together, the first two parameters represent the (*x*, *y*) coordinates of the vertices of the polygons.

A polygon is always closed. A line segment is always drawn from the last point in the list to the first point in the list.

Much like a polygon, a *polyline* contains a series of points connected by line segments. Polylines differ from polygons in that the first and last coordinates are not automatically connected when they are drawn. Since a polyline is not closed, it cannot be filled. Therefore there is only one method, called `drawPolyline`, used to draw a polyline. The parameters of the `drawPolyline` method are similar to those of the `drawPolygon` method.

The program shown in Listing F.6 below uses polygons to draw a rocket. In the `RocketPanel` class, shown in Listing F.7 on page 815, the arrays called `xRocket` and `yRocket` define the points of the polygon that make up the main body of the rocket. The first point in the arrays is the upper tip of the rocket, and the points progress clockwise from there. The `xWindow` and `yWindow` arrays specify the points for the polygon that form the window in the rocket. Both the rocket and the window are drawn as filled polygons.

LISTING F.6

```
//********************************************************************
//  Rocket.java       Java Foundations
//
//  Demonstrates the use of polygons and polylines.
//********************************************************************

import javax.swing.JFrame;

public class Rocket
{
   //-----------------------------------------------------------------
   //  Displays a rocket in flight.
```

LISTING F.6 *continued*

```
   //-----------------------------------------------------------------
   public static void main (String[] args)
   {
      JFrame frame = new JFrame ("Rocket");
      frame.setDefaultCloseOperation (JFrame.EXIT_ON_CLOSE);

      frame.getContentPane().add(new RocketPanel());

      frame.pack();
      frame.setVisible(true);
   }
}
```

DISPLAY

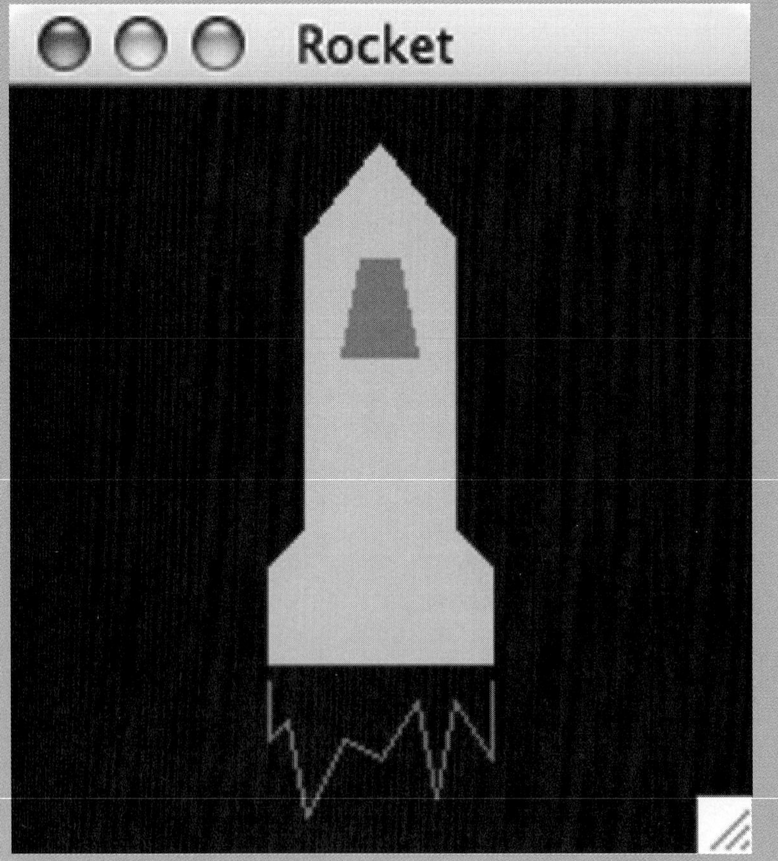

LISTING F.7

```
//********************************************************************
//  RocketPanel.java       Java Foundations
//
//  Demonstrates the use of polygons and polylines.
//********************************************************************

import javax.swing.JPanel;
import java.awt.*;

public class RocketPanel extends JPanel
{
   private int[] xRocket = {100, 120, 120, 130, 130, 70, 70, 80, 80};
   private int[] yRocket = {15, 40, 115, 125, 150, 150, 125, 115, 40};

   private int[] xWindow = {95, 105, 110, 90};
   private int[] yWindow = {45, 45, 70, 70};

   private int[] xFlame = {70, 70, 75, 80, 90, 100, 110, 115, 120,
                           130, 130};
   private int[] yFlame = {155, 170, 165, 190, 170, 175, 160, 185,
                           160, 175, 155};

   //-----------------------------------------------------------------
   //  Sets up the basic characteristics of this panel.
   //-----------------------------------------------------------------
   public RocketPanel()
   {
      setBackground (Color.black);
      setPreferredSize (new Dimension(200, 200));
   }

   //-----------------------------------------------------------------
   //  Draws a rocket using polygons and polylines.
   //-----------------------------------------------------------------
   public void paintComponent (Graphics page)
   {
      super.paintComponent (page);
```

LISTING F.7 *continued*

```
      page.setColor (Color.cyan);
      page.fillPolygon (xRocket, yRocket, xRocket.length);

      page.setColor (Color.gray);
      page.fillPolygon (xWindow, yWindow, xWindow.length);
      page.setColor (Color.red);
      page.drawPolyline (xFlame, yFlame, xFlame.length);
   }
}
```

The `xFlame` and `yFlame` arrays define the points of a polyline that are used to create the image of flame shooting out of the tail of the rocket. Because it is drawn as a polyline, not as a polygon, the flame is not closed or filled.

The `Polygon` Class

A polygon can also be defined explicitly using an object of the `Polygon` class, which is defined in the `java.awt` package of the Java standard class library. Two versions of the overloaded `drawPolygon` and `fillPolygon` methods take a single `Polygon` object as a parameter.

A `Polygon` object encapsulates the coordinates of the polygon sides. The constructors of the `Polygon` class allow the creation of an initially empty polygon, or one defined by arrays of integers representing the point coordinates. The `Polygon` class contains methods to add points to the polygon and to determine whether a given point is contained within the polygon shape. It also contains methods to get a representation of a bounding rectangle for the polygon, as well as a method to translate all of the points in the polygon to another position. Figure F.6 lists these methods.

`Polygon ()`
Constructor: Creates an empty polygon.

`Polygon (int[] xpoints, int[] ypoints, int npoints)`
Constructor: Creates a polygon using the (*x*, *y*) coordinate pairs in corresponding entries of `xpoints` and `ypoints`.

`void addPoint (int x, int y)`
Appends the specified point to this polygon.

`boolean contains (int x, int y)`
Returns true if the specified point is contained in this polygon.

`boolean contains (Point p)`
Returns true if the specified point is contained in this polygon.

`Rectangle getBounds ()`
Gets the bounding rectangle for this polygon.

`void translate (int deltaX, int deltaY)`
Translates the vertices of this polygon by `deltaX` along the *x* axis and `deltaY` along the *y* axis.

FIGURE F.6 Some methods of the `Polygon` class

Exercises

EX F.1 Compare and contrast a traditional coordinate system and the coordinate system used by Java graphical components.

EX F.2 How many bits are needed to store a color picture that is 400 pixels wide and 250 pixels high? Assume that color is represented using the RGB technique described in this appendix and that no special compression is done.

EX F.3 Assuming you have a `Graphics` object called `page`, write a statement that will draw a line from point (20, 30) to point (50, 60).

EX F.4 Assuming you have a `Graphics` object called `page`, write a statement that will draw a rectangle with height 70 and width 35, such that its upper-left corner is at point (10, 15).

EX F.5 Assuming you have a `Graphics` object called `page`, write a statement that will draw a circle centered on point (50, 50) with a radius of 20 pixels.

EX F.6 The following lines of code draw the eyes of the snowman in the `Snowman` program. The eyes seem centered on the face when drawn, but the first parameters of each call are not equally offset from the midpoint. Explain.

```
page.fillOval (MID-10, TOP+10, 5, 5);
page.fillOval (MID+5, TOP+10, 5, 5);
```

EX F.7 Write a method called `randomColor` that creates and returns a `Color` object that represents a random color.

EX F.8 Write a method called `drawCircle` that draws a circle based on the method's parameters: a `Graphics` object through which to draw the circle, two integer values representing the (x, y) coordinates of the center of the circle, another integer that represents the circle's radius, and a `Color` object that defines the circle's color. The method does not return anything.

Programming Projects

PP F.1 Create a revised version of the `Snowman` program with the following modifications:

- Add two red buttons to the upper torso.
- Make the snowman frown instead of smile.
- Move the sun to the upper-right corner of the picture.
- Display your name in the upper-left corner of the picture.
- Shift the entire snowman 20 pixels to the right.

PP F.2 Write a program that writes your name using the `drawString` method.

PP F.3 Write a program that draws the Big Dipper. Add some extra stars in the night sky.

PP F.4 Write a program that draws some balloons tied to strings. Make the balloons various colors.

PP F.5 Write a program that draws the Olympic logo. The circles in the logo should be colored (from left to right) blue, yellow, black, green, and red.

PP F.6 Write a program that displays a business card of your own design. Include both graphics and text.

PP F.7 Write a program that shows a pie chart with eight equal slices, all colored differently.

PP F.8 Write a program that draws a house with a door (and doorknob), windows, and a chimney. Add some smoke coming out of the chimney and some clouds in the sky.

PP F.9 Modify the program from Programming Project F.8 to include a simple fence with vertical, equally spaced slats backed by two horizontal support boards. Make sure the house is visible between the slats in the fence.

PP F.10 Write a program that draws 20 horizontal, evenly spaced parallel lines of random length.

PP F.11 Write a program that draws the side view of stair steps from the lower left to the upper right.

PP F.12 Write a program that draws 100 circles of random color and random diameter in random locations. Ensure that, in each case, the entire circle appears in the visible area of the applet.

PP F.13 Write a program that draws 10 concentric circles of random radius.

PP F.14 Write a program that draws a brick wall pattern in which each row of bricks is offset from the row above and the row below it.

PP F.15 Design and implement a program that draws a rainbow. Use tightly spaced concentric arcs to draw each part of the rainbow in a particular color.

PP F.16 Design and implement a program that draws 20,000 points in random locations within the visible area. Make the points on the left half of the panel appear in red and the points on the right half of the panel appear in green. Draw each point by drawing a line with a length of only one pixel.

PP F.17 Design and implement a program that draws 10 circles of random radius in random locations. Fill in the largest circle in red.

PP F.18 Write a program that draws a quilt in which a simple pattern is repeated in a grid of squares.

PP F.19 Modify the program from Programming Project F.18 such that it draws a quilt using a separate class called `Pattern` that represents a particular pattern. Allow the constructor of the `Pattern` class to vary some characteristics of the pattern, such as its color scheme. Instantiate two separate `Pattern` objects and incorporate them in a checkerboard layout in the quilt.

PP F.20 Design and implement a class called `Building` that represents a graphical depiction of a building. Allow the parameters to the constructor to specify the building's width and height. Each building should be colored black and should contain a few random windows of yellow. Create a program that draws a random skyline of buildings.

PP F.21 Write a program that displays a graphical seating chart for a dinner party. Create a class called `Diner` (as in one who dines) that stores the person's name, gender, and location at the dinner table. A diner is graphically represented as a circle, color-coded by gender, with the person's name printed in the circle.

PP F.22 Create a class called `Crayon` that represents one crayon of a particular color and length (height). Design and implement a program that draws a box of crayons.

PP F.23 Create a class called `Star` that represents a graphical depiction of a star. Let the constructor of the star accept the number of points in the star (4, 5, or 6), the radius of the star, and the center point location. Write a program that draws a sky containing various types of stars.

PP F.24 Design and implement an application that displays an animation of a horizontal line segment moving across the screen, eventually passing across a vertical line. As the vertical line is passed, the horizontal line should change color. The change of color should occur while the horizontal line crosses the vertical line; therefore, while it is crossing, the horizontal line will be two different colors.

PP F.25 Create a class that represents a spaceship, which can be drawn (side view) in any particular location. Use it to create a program that displays the spaceship so that it follows the movement of the mouse. When the mouse button in pressed down, have a laser beam shoot out of the front of the spaceship (one continuous beam, not a moving projectile) until the mouse button is released.

Appendix G
Java Applets

There are two kinds of Java programs: Java applications and Java applets. A Java *application* is a stand-alone program that can be executed using a Java interpreter. The programs presented in the main chapters of this text are Java applications. A Java *applet* is a Java program that is intended to be embedded into an HTML document, transported across a network, and executed using a Web browser. This appendix explores Java applets.

The Web enables users to send and receive various types of media, such as text, graphics, and sound, using a point-and-click interface that is extremely convenient and easy to use. Java applets are considered just another type of medium that can be exchanged across the Web.

When we surf the Web, we tend to think in terms of visiting a site. Of course, the reality is that we are downloading a page to our local computer to view it. Therefore, security is an issue with applets. As you browse Web pages, you may download a page containing an applet, and suddenly an unknown program is executing on your machine. Because of the dangers inherent in that process, applets are restricted in the kinds of operations they can perform. For instance, an applet cannot write data to a local drive.

Even though Java applets are generally intended to be transported across a network, they don't have to be. They can be viewed locally using a Web browser. For that matter, they don't even have to be executed through a Web browser. A tool in Sun's Java Software Development Kit called *appletviewer* can be used to interpret and execute an applet. We use appletviewer to display applets in this appendix. However, the point of making a Java applet is usually to provide a link to it on a Web page and allow it to be retrieved and executed by Web users anywhere in the world.

Java bytecode (not Java source code) is linked to an HTML document and sent across the Web. A version of the Java interpreter embedded in a Web browser is used to execute the applet once it reaches its destination. A Java applet must be compiled into bytecode format before it can be used with the Web.

There are some important differences between the structure of a Java applet and the structure of a Java application. Because the Web browser that executes an applet is already running, applets can be thought of as a part of a larger program. As such, they do not have a `main` method where execution starts. The `paint` method in an applet is automatically invoked when the applet program executes. Consider the program in Listing G.1, in which the `paint` method is used to draw a few shapes and write a quotation by Albert Einstein to the screen.

A class that defines an applet extends the `JApplet` class, as indicated in the header line of the `Einstein` class declaration. Applet classes must be declared as `public`.

LISTING G.1

```
//********************************************************************
//  Einstein.java       Java Foundations
//
//  Demonstrates a basic applet.
//********************************************************************

import javax.swing.JApplet;
import java.awt.*;

public class Einstein extends JApplet
{
   //-----------------------------------------------------------------
   //  Draws a quotation by Albert Einstein among some shapes.
   //-----------------------------------------------------------------
   public void paint (Graphics page)
```

LISTING G.1 *continued*

```
   {
      page.drawRect (50, 50, 40, 40);    // square
      page.drawRect (60, 80, 225, 30);   // rectangle
      page.drawOval (75, 65, 20, 20);    // circle
      page.drawLine (35, 60, 100, 120);  // line

      page.drawString ("Out of clutter, find simplicity.", 110, 70);
      page.drawString ("-- Albert Einstein", 130, 100);
   }
}
```

DISPLAY

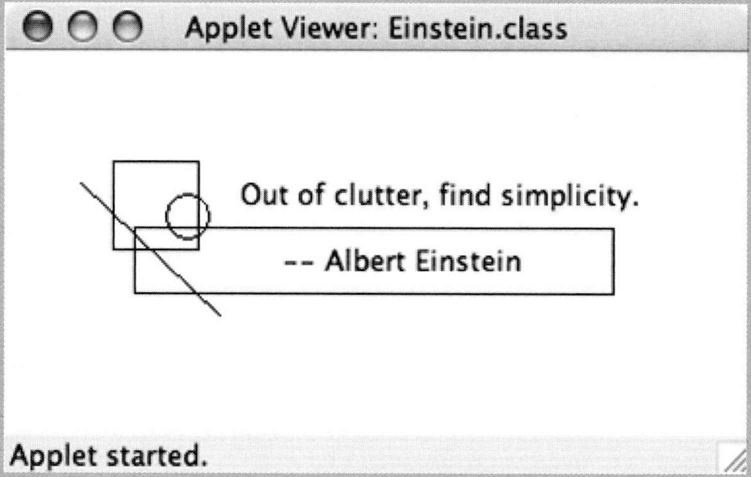

Applet Viewer: Einstein.class

Out of clutter, find simplicity.

-- Albert Einstein

Applet started.

The `paint` method is one of several applet methods that have particular significance. It is invoked automatically whenever the graphical elements of the applet need to be painted to the screen, such as when the applet is first run or when another window that was covering it is moved.

Note that the `paint` method accepts a `Graphics` object as a parameter. As discussed in Appendix F, a `Graphics` object defines the *graphics context* of a component and provides a variety of methods for drawing shapes on a component. The graphics context passed into an applet's `paint` method represents the applet window.

Embedding Applets in HTML

In order for the applet to be executed, either by the appletviewer or by being transmitted over the Web and executed by a browser, it must be referenced in a HyperText Markup Language (HTML) document. An HTML document contains *tags* that specify formatting instructions and identify the special types of media that are to be included in a document.

An HTML tag is enclosed in angle brackets. The following is an example of an applet tag:

```
<applet code="Einstein.class" width="350" height="175">
</applet>
```

This tag dictates that the bytecode stored in the file `Einstein.class` should be transported over the network and executed on the machine that wants to view this particular HTML document. The applet tag also indicates the width and height of the applet.

There are other tags that can be used to reference an applet in an HTML file, including the `<object>` tag and the `<embed>` tag. The `<object>` tag is actually the tag that should be used, according to the World Wide Web Consortium (W3C). However, browser support for the `<object>` tag is not consistent. For now, the most reliable solution is to use the `<applet>` tag.

Note that the applet tag refers to the bytecode file of the `Einstein` applet, not to the source code file. Before an applet can be transported using the Web, it must be compiled into its bytecode format. Then, as shown in Figure G.1, the document can be loaded using a Web browser, which will automatically interpret and execute the applet.

More Applet Methods

An applet has several other methods that perform specific duties. Because an applet is designed to work with Web pages, some applet methods are specifically designed with that concept in mind. Figure G.2 lists several applet methods.

The `init` method is executed once when the applet is first loaded, such as when the browser or appletviewer initially views the applet. Therefore, the `init` method is the place to initialize the applet's environment and permanent data.

The `start` and `stop` methods of an applet are called when the applet becomes active or inactive, respectively. For example, after we use a browser to initially load an applet, the applet's `start` method is called. We may then leave that page to visit another one, at which point the applet becomes inactive and the `stop`

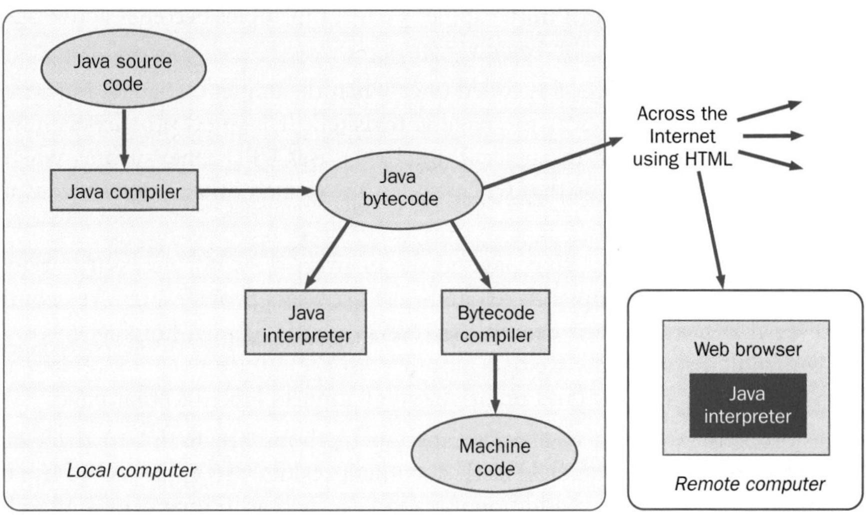

FIGURE G.1 The Java translation and execution process, including applets

```
public void init ()
```
Initializes the applet. Called just after the applet is loaded.

```
public void start ()
```
Starts the applet. Called just after the applet is made active.

```
public void stop ()
```
Stops the applet. Called just after the applet is made inactive.

```
public void destroy ()
```
Destroys the applet. Called when the browser is exited.

```
public URL getCodeBase ()
```
Returns the URL at which this applet's bytecode is located.

```
public URL getDocumentBase ()
```
Returns the URL at which the HTML document containing this applet is located.

```
public AudioClip getAudioClip (URL url, String name)
```
Retrieves an audio clip from the specified URL.

```
public Image getImage (URL url, String name)
```
Retrieves an image from the specified URL.

FIGURE G.2 Some methods of the `JApplet` class

method is called. If we return to the applet's page, the applet becomes active again and the `start` method is called again.

Note that the `init` method is called once when the applet is loaded, but `start` may be called several times as the page is revisited. It is good practice to implement `start` and `stop` for an applet if it actively uses CPU time, such as when it is showing an animation, so that CPU time is not wasted on an applet that is not visible.

Note that reloading the Web page in the browser does not necessarily reload the applet. To force the applet to reload, most browsers provide some key combination for that purpose. For example, in Netscape Navigator, holding down the Shift key while pressing the Reload button with the mouse not only reloads the Web page but also reloads (and reinitializes) all applets linked to that page.

The `getCodeBase` and `getDocumentBase` methods are useful to determine where the applet's bytecode or HTML document resides. An applet could use the appropriate URL to retrieve additional resources, such as an image or audio clip, using the method `getImage` or the method `getAudioClip`.

Let's look at another example of an applet. Carefully examine the display for the `TiledPictures` applet shown in Listing G.2. There are actually three unique images among the menagerie. The entire area is divided into four equal quadrants. A picture of the world (with a circle indicating the Himalayan mountain region) is shown in the bottom-right quadrant. The bottom-left quadrant contains a picture of Mt. Everest. In the top-right quadrant is a picture of a mountain goat.

The interesting part of the picture is the top-left quadrant. It contains a copy of the entire collage, including itself. In this smaller version you can see the three simple pictures in their three quadrants. And again, in the top-left corner, the picture is repeated (including itself). This repetition continues for several levels. It is similar to the effect you can create when looking at a mirror in the reflection of another mirror.

This visual effect is created using recursion. The applet's `init` method initially loads the three images. The `paint` method then invokes the `drawPictures` method, which accepts a parameter that defines the size of the area in which pictures are displayed. It draws the three images using the `drawImage` method, with parameters that scale the picture to the correct size and location. The `drawPictures` method is then called recursively to draw the upper-left quadrant.

On each invocation, if the drawing area is large enough, the `drawPictures` method is invoked again, using a smaller drawing area. Eventually, the drawing area becomes so small that the recursive call is not performed. Note that `drawPictures` assumes the origin (0, 0) coordinate as the relative location of the new images, no matter what their size is.

LISTING G.2

```
//********************************************************************
//  TiledPictures.java       Java Foundations
//
//  Demonstrates an applet.
//********************************************************************

import java.awt.*;
import javax.swing.JApplet;

public class TiledPictures extends JApplet
{
   private final int APPLET_WIDTH = 320;
   private final int APPLET_HEIGHT = 320;
   private final int MIN = 20;  // smallest picture size

   private Image world, everest, goat;

   //-----------------------------------------------------------------
   //  Loads the images.
   //-----------------------------------------------------------------
   public void init()
   {
      world = getImage (getDocumentBase(), "world.gif");
      everest = getImage (getDocumentBase(), "everest.gif");
      goat = getImage (getDocumentBase(), "goat.gif");
      setSize (APPLET_WIDTH, APPLET_HEIGHT);
   }

   //-----------------------------------------------------------------
   //  Draws the three images, then calls itself recursively.
   //-----------------------------------------------------------------
   public void drawPictures (int size, Graphics page)
   {
      page.drawImage (everest, 0, size/2, size/2, size/2, this);
      page.drawImage (goat, size/2, 0, size/2, size/2, this);
      page.drawImage (world, size/2, size/2, size/2, size/2, this);
      if (size > MIN)
         drawPictures (size/2, page);
   }
```

LISTING G.2 *continued*

```
   //-----------------------------------------------------------------
   //  Performs the initial call to the drawPictures method.
   //-----------------------------------------------------------------
   public void paint (Graphics page)
   {
      drawPictures (APPLET_WIDTH, page);
   }
}
```

DISPLAY

The base case of the recursion in this problem specifies a minimum size for the drawing area. Because the size is decreased each time, the base case eventually is reached and the recursion stops. This is why the upper-left corner is empty in the smallest version of the collage.

GUIs in Applets

In Chapter 6, we explored issues related to the development of programs that use graphical user interfaces (GUIs). The examples in those sections are presented as Java applications, using `JFrame` components as the primary heavyweight container. An applet can also be used to present GUI-based programs. Like a `JFrame`, a `JApplet` is a heavyweight container.

Let's look at an applet that contains interactive components. Our example will contain buttons that determine the level of a displayed fractal. A *fractal* is a geometric shape that can be made up of the same pattern repeated at different scales and orientations. The nature of a fractal lends itself to a recursive definition. Interest in fractals has grown immensely in recent years, largely thanks to Benoit Mandelbrot, a Polish mathematician born in 1924. He demonstrated that fractals occur in many places in mathematics and nature. Computers have made fractals much easier to generate and investigate. Over the past quarter-century, the bright, interesting images that can be created with fractals have come to be considered as much an art form as a mathematical phenomenon.

One particular example of a fractal is called the Koch snowflake, named after Helge von Koch, a Swedish mathematician. It begins with an equilateral triangle, which is considered to be the Koch fractal of order 1. Koch fractals of higher orders are constructed by repeatedly modifying all of the line segments in the shape.

To create the Koch fractal of the next higher order, each line segment in the shape is modified by replacing its middle third with a sharp protrusion made of two line segments, each having the same length as the replaced part. Relative to the entire shape, the protrusion on any line segment always points outward. Figure G.3

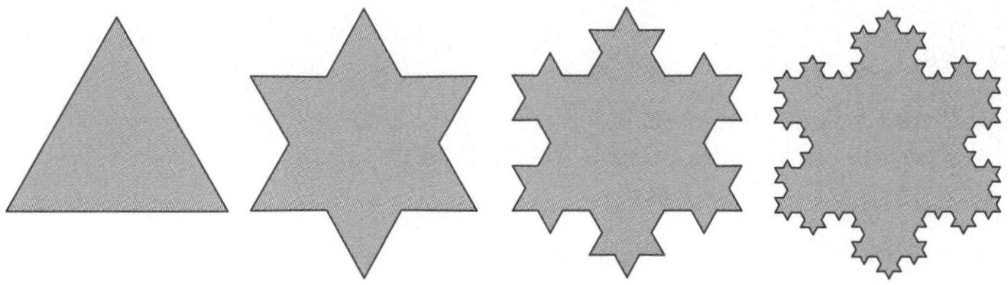

FIGURE G.3 Several orders of the Koch snowflake

shows several orders of Koch fractals. As the order increases, the shape begins to look like a snowflake.

The applet shown in Listing G.3 draws a Koch snowflake of several different orders. The buttons at the top of the applet enable the user to increase and decrease the order of the fractal. Each time a button is pressed, the fractal image is redrawn. The applet serves as the listener for the buttons.

LISTING G.3

```
//********************************************************************
//  KochSnowflake.java       Java Foundations
//
//  Demonstrates the use of recursion in graphics.
//********************************************************************

import java.awt.*;
import java.awt.event.*;
import javax.swing.*;

public class KochSnowflake extends JApplet implements ActionListener
{
   private final int APPLET_WIDTH = 400;
   private final int APPLET_HEIGHT = 440;

   private final int MIN = 1, MAX = 9;

   private JButton increase, decrease;
   private JLabel titleLabel, orderLabel;
   private KochPanel drawing;
   private JPanel appletPanel, tools;

   //-----------------------------------------------------------------
   //  Sets up the components for the applet.
   //-----------------------------------------------------------------
   public void init()
   {
      tools = new JPanel ();
      tools.setLayout (new BoxLayout(tools, BoxLayout.X_AXIS));
      tools.setPreferredSize (new Dimension (APPLET_WIDTH, 40));
      tools.setBackground (Color.yellow);
      tools.setOpaque (true);
      titleLabel = new JLabel ("The Koch Snowflake");
      titleLabel.setForeground (Color.black);
```

LISTING G.3 *continued*

```
      increase = new JButton (new ImageIcon ("increase.gif"));
      increase.setPressedIcon (new ImageIcon ("increasePressed.gif"));
      increase.setMargin (new Insets (0, 0, 0, 0));
      increase.addActionListener (this);

      decrease = new JButton (new ImageIcon ("decrease.gif"));
      decrease.setPressedIcon (new ImageIcon ("decreasePressed.gif"));
      decrease.setMargin (new Insets (0, 0, 0, 0));
      decrease.addActionListener (this);

      orderLabel = new JLabel ("Order: 1");
      orderLabel.setForeground (Color.black);

      tools.add (titleLabel);
      tools.add (Box.createHorizontalStrut (40));
      tools.add (decrease);
      tools.add (increase);
      tools.add (Box.createHorizontalStrut (20));
      tools.add (orderLabel);

      drawing = new KochPanel (1);

      appletPanel = new JPanel();
      appletPanel.add (tools);
      appletPanel.add (drawing);

      getContentPane().add (appletPanel);

      setSize (APPLET_WIDTH, APPLET_HEIGHT);
   }

   //-----------------------------------------------------------------
   //  Determines which button was pushed, and sets the new order
   //  if it is in range.
   //-----------------------------------------------------------------
   public void actionPerformed (ActionEvent event)
   {
      int order = drawing.getOrder();
      if (event.getSource() == increase)
         order++;
      else
         order--;
```

LISTING G.3 *continued*

```
         if (order >= MIN && order <= MAX)
         {
            orderLabel.setText ("Order: " + order);
            drawing.setOrder (order);
            repaint();
         }
      }
   }
```

DISPLAY

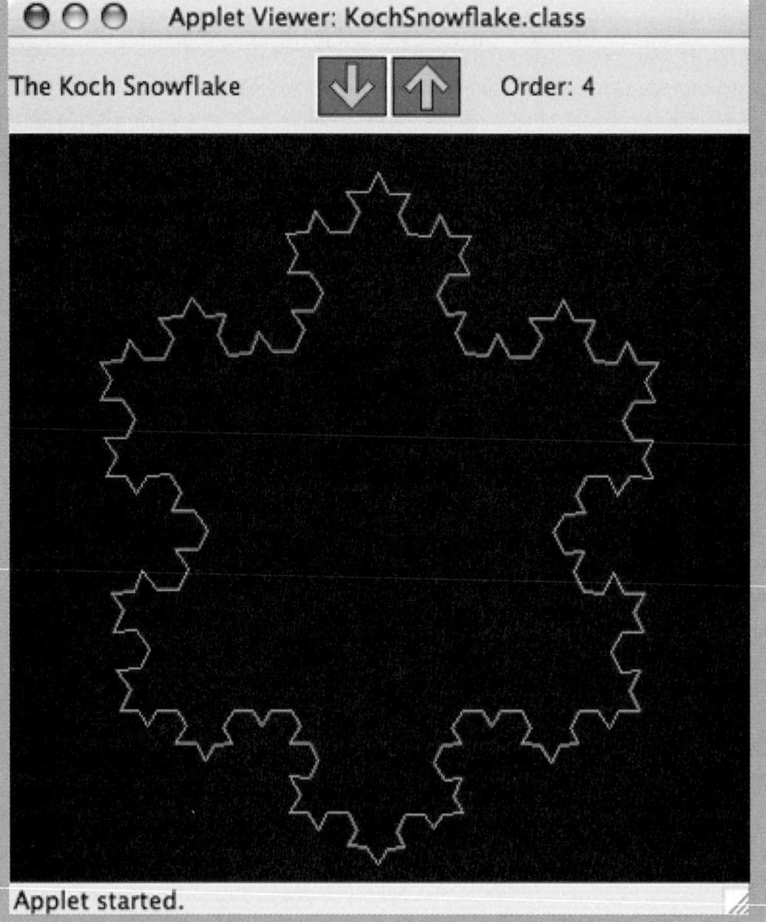

The fractal image is drawn on a panel defined by the `KochPanel` class shown in Listing G.4. The `paint` method makes the initial calls to the recursive method `drawFractal`. The three calls to `drawFractal` in the paint method represent the original three sides of the equilateral triangle that make up a Koch fractal of order 1.

LISTING G.4

```
//********************************************************************
//  KochPanel.java       Java Foundations
//
//  Represents a drawing surface on which to paint a Koch Snowflake.
//********************************************************************

import java.awt.*;
import javax.swing.JPanel;

public class KochPanel extends JPanel
{
   private final int PANEL_WIDTH = 400;
   private final int PANEL_HEIGHT = 400;

   private final double SQ = Math.sqrt(3.0) / 6;

   private final int TOPX = 200, TOPY = 20;
   private final int LEFTX = 60, LEFTY = 300;
   private final int RIGHTX = 340, RIGHTY = 300;

   private int current; // current order

   //-----------------------------------------------------------------
   //  Sets the initial fractal order to the value specified.
   //-----------------------------------------------------------------
   public KochPanel (int currentOrder)
   {
      current = currentOrder;
      setBackground (Color.black);
      setPreferredSize (new Dimension(PANEL_WIDTH, PANEL_HEIGHT));
   }
```

LISTING G.4 *continued*

```
   //-----------------------------------------------------------------
   //  Draws the fractal recursively. The base case is order 1 for
   //  which a simple straight line is drawn. Otherwise three
   //  intermediate points are computed, and each line segment is
   //  drawn as a fractal.
   //-----------------------------------------------------------------
   public void drawFractal (int order, int x1, int y1, int x5, int y5,
                            Graphics page)
   {
      int deltaX, deltaY, x2, y2, x3, y3, x4, y4;

      if (order == 1)
         page.drawLine (x1, y1, x5, y5);
      else
      {
         deltaX = x5 - x1; // distance between end points
         deltaY = y5 - y1;

         x2 = x1 + deltaX / 3; // one third
         y2 = y1 + deltaY / 3;

         x3 = (int) ((x1+x5)/2 + SQ * (y1-y5)); // tip of projection
         y3 = (int) ((y1+y5)/2 + SQ * (x5-x1));

         x4 = x1 + deltaX * 2/3; // two thirds
         y4 = y1 + deltaY * 2/3;

         drawFractal (order-1, x1, y1, x2, y2, page);
         drawFractal (order-1, x2, y2, x3, y3, page);
         drawFractal (order-1, x3, y3, x4, y4, page);
         drawFractal (order-1, x4, y4, x5, y5, page);
      }
   }

   //-----------------------------------------------------------------
   //  Performs the initial calls to the drawFractal method.
   //-----------------------------------------------------------------
   public void paintComponent (Graphics page)
   {
      super.paintComponent (page);

      page.setColor (Color.green);
```

LISTING G.4 *continued*

```
      drawFractal (current, TOPX, TOPY, LEFTX, LEFTY, page);
      drawFractal (current, LEFTX, LEFTY, RIGHTX, RIGHTY, page);
      drawFractal (current, RIGHTX, RIGHTY, TOPX, TOPY, page);
   }

   //-----------------------------------------------------------------
   //  Sets the fractal order to the value specified.
   //-----------------------------------------------------------------
   public void setOrder (int order)
   {
      current = order;
   }

   //-----------------------------------------------------------------
   //  Returns the current order.
   //-----------------------------------------------------------------
   public int getOrder ()
   {
      return current;
   }
}
```

The variable `current` represents the order of the fractal to be drawn. Each recursive call to `drawFractal` decrements the order by 1. The base case of the recursion occurs when the order of the fractal is 1, which results in a simple line segment between the coordinates specified by the parameters.

If the order of the fractal is higher than 1, three additional points are computed. In conjunction with the parameters, these points form the four line segments of the modified fractal. Figure G.4 on the next page shows the transformation.

Based on the position of the two end points of the original line segment, a point one-third of the way between them and a point two-thirds of the way between them are computed. The calculation of $<x_3, y_3>$, the point at the tip of the protrusion, is more convoluted and uses a simplifying constant that incorporates multiple geometric relationships. The calculations to determine the three new points actually have nothing to do with the recursive technique employed to draw the fractal, and so we won't discuss the details of these computations here.

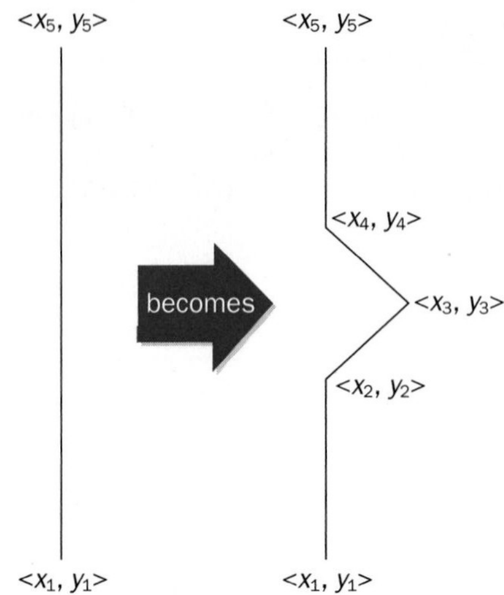

FIGURE G.4 The transformation of each line segment of a Koch snowflake

An interesting mathematical feature of a Koch snowflake is that it has an infinite perimeter but a finite area. As the order of the fractal increases, the perimeter grows exponentially larger, with a mathematical limit of infinity. However, a rectangle large enough to surround the second-order fractal for the Koch snowflake is large enough to contain all higher-order fractals. The shape is restricted forever in area, but its perimeter gets infinitely greater.

Programming Projects

PP G.1 Convert any of the applications described by the programming projects in Appendix F (on Java graphics) into applets.

PP G.2 Convert any of the applications described by the programming projects in Chapter 7 (on GUIs) into applets, excluding those that require data written to a file.

Appendix H

Regular Expressions

Throughout this text, we've used the `Scanner` class to read interactive input from the user and parse strings into individual tokens such as words. In Chapter 4 we also used it to read input from a data file. Usually we used the default whitespace delimiters for tokens in the scanner input.

The `Scanner` class can also be used to parse its input according to a *regular expression*, which is a character string that represents a pattern. A regular expression can be used to set the delimiters used when extracting tokens, or it can be used in methods such as `findInLine` to match a particular string.

Some of the general rules for constructing regular expressions follow.

- The dot (`.`) character matches any single character.
- The asterisk (`*`) character, which is called the Kleene star, matches zero or more characters.
- A string of characters in brackets (`[]`) matches any single character in the string.
- The \ character followed by a special character (such as the ones in this list) matches the character itself.
- The \ character followed by a character matches the pattern specified by that character (see Figure H.1) on the next page.

Regular Expression	Matches
`x`	The character x
`.`	Any character
`[ abc]`	a, b, or c
`[^abc]`	Any character except a, b, or c (negation)
`[a-z][A-Z]`	a through z or A through Z, inclusive (range)
`[a-o[m-p]]`	a through d or m through p (union)
`[a-z&&[ def]]`	d, e, or f (intersection)
`[a-z&&[ ^bc]]`	a through z, except for b and c (subtraction)
`[a-z&&[ ^m-p]]`	a through z but not m through p (subtraction)
`\d`	A digit: [0–9]
`\D`	A non-digit: [^0–9]
`\s`	A whitespace character
`\S`	A non-whitespace character
`^`	The beginning of a line
`$`	The end of a line

FIGURE H.1 Some patterns that can be specified in a Java regular expression

For example, the regular expression `B.b*` matches `Bob`, `Bubba`, and `Baby`. The regular expression `T[aei]*ing` matches `Taking`, `Tickling`, and `Telling`.

Figure H.1 shows some of the patterns that can be matched in a Java regular expression. This list is not complete—see the online documentation for the `Pattern` class for a complete list.

Appendix

Hashing

In Chapter 11, we discussed the idea that a binary search tree is, in effect, an efficient implementation of a set or a map. In this appendix, we examine hashing, an approach to implementing a set or map collection that can be even more efficient than binary search trees.

I.1 A Hashing

In all of our discussions of the implementations of collections, we have proceeded with one of two assumptions about the order of elements in a collection:

- Order is determined by the order in which elements are added to and/or removed from our collection, as in the case of stacks, queues, unordered lists, and indexed lists.
- Order is determined by comparing the values of the elements (or some key component of the elements) to be stored in the collection, as in the case of ordered lists and binary search trees.

In this appendix, we will explore the concept of *hashing*, which means that the order—and, more specifically, the location of an item within the collection—is determined by some function of the value of the element to be stored, or some function of a key value of the element to be stored. In hashing, elements are stored in a *hash table*, and the location of each element in the table is determined by a *hashing function*. Each location in the table may be referred to as a *cell* or a *bucket*. We will discuss hashing functions further in Section I.2. We will discuss implementation strategies and algorithms, and we will leave the implementations as programming projects.

KEY CONCEPT
In hashing, elements are stored in a hash table, and the location of each element in the table is determined by a hashing function.

Consider a simple example where we create an array that will hold 26 elements. Wishing to store names in our array, we create a hashing function that equates each name to the position in the array associated with the first letter of the name. (For example, a first letter of A would be mapped to position 0 of the array, a first letter of D would be mapped to position 3 of the array, and so on.) Figure I.1 illustrates this scenario after several names have been added.

Notice that, unlike our earlier implementations of collections, using a hashing approach results in the access time to a particular element being independent of the number of elements in the table. This means that all of the operations on an element of a hash table should be O(1). This is the result of no longer having to do comparisons to find a particular element or to locate the appropriate position for a given element. Using hashing, we simply calculate where a particular element should be.

KEY CONCEPT
The situation where two elements or keys map to the same location in the table is called a collision.

However, this efficiency is fully realized only if each element maps to a unique position in the table. Consider our example from Figure I.1. What will happen if we attempt to store the name "Ann" and the name "Andrew"? This situation, where two elements or keys map to the same location in the table, is called a *collision*. We will discuss how to resolve collisions in Section I.3.

KEY CONCEPT
A hashing function that maps each element to a unique position in the table is said to be a perfect hashing function.

A hashing function that maps each element to a unique position in the table is said to be a *perfect hashing function*. Although it is possible in some situations to develop a perfect hashing function, a hashing function that does a good job of distributing the elements among the table positions will still result in constant time (O(1)) access to elements in the table and an improvement over our earlier algorithms that were either O(n) in the case of our linear approaches or O(log n) in the case of search trees.

Another issue surrounding hashing is the question of how large the table should be. If the data set is of known size and a perfect hashing function can be used, then we simply make the table the same size as the data set. If a perfect hashing function is not available or practical but the size of the data set is known, a good rule of thumb is to make the table 150 percent of the size of the data set.

The third case is very common and far more interesting. What if we do not know the size of the data set? In this case, we depend on *dynamic resizing*. Dynamic resizing of a hash table involves creating a new hash table that is larger than—perhaps even twice as large as—the original, inserting all of the elements of the original table into the new table, and then discarding the original table. When to resize is also an interesting question. One possibility is to use the same method we used with our earlier array implementations and simply expand the table when it is full. However, it is the nature of hash tables that their performance seriously degrades as they become full. A better approach is to use a *load factor*. The load factor of a hash table is the percentage occupancy of the table at which the table will be resized. For example, if the load factor were set to 0.50, then the table would be resized each time it reached 50 percent capacity.

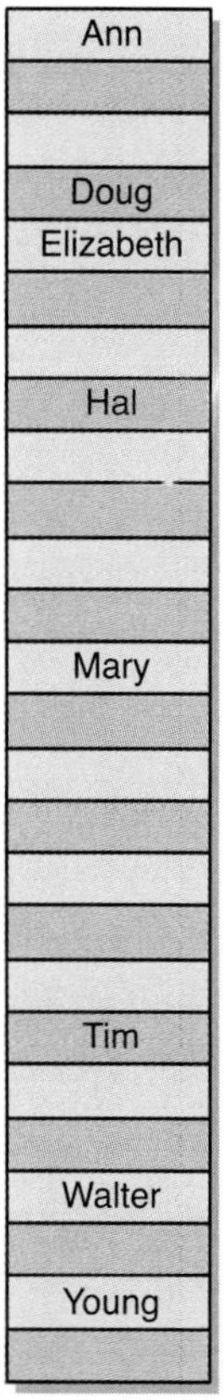

FIGURE I.1 A simple hashing example

I.2 Hashing Functions

Although perfect hashing functions are possible if the data set is known, we do not need the hashing function to be perfect to get good performance from the hash table. Our goal is simply to develop a function that does a reasonably good job of distributing our elements in the table such that we avoid collisions. A reasonably good hashing function will still result in constant time access (O(1)) to our data set.

> **KEY CONCEPT**
> Extraction involves using only a part of the element's value or key to compute the location at which to store the element.

There are a variety of approaches to developing a hashing function for a particular data set. The method that we used in our example in the previous section is called *extraction*. Extraction involves using only a part of the element's value or key to compute the location at which to store the element. In our previous example, we simply extracted the first letter of a string and computed its value relative to the letter A.

Other examples of extraction include storing phone numbers according to the last four digits and storing information about cars according to the first three characters of the license plate.

The Division Method

Creating a hashing function by *division* simply means using the remainder of the key divided by some positive integer p as the index for the given element. This function could be defined as follows:

```
Hashcode(key) = Math.abs(key)%p
```

This function will yield a result in the range of 0 to p–1. If we use our table size as p, we then have an index that maps directly to a location in the table.

Using a prime number p as the table size and the divisor helps provide a better distribution of keys to locations in the table.

For example, if our key value is 79 and our table size is 43, then the division method will result in an index value of 36. The division method is very effective when one is dealing with an unknown set of key values.

The Folding Method

In the *folding method*, the key is divided into parts that are then combined or folded together to create an index into the table. This is done by first dividing the key into parts where each of the parts of the key will be the same length as the desired index, except possibly the last one. In the *shift folding method*, these parts are then added together to create the index. For example, if our key were the Social Security number 987-65-4321, we might divide this into three parts: 987, 654, and 321. Adding these together would yield 1962. Assuming that we are looking for a three-digit key, at this point we could use either division or extraction to get our index.

KEY CONCEPT
In the shift folding method, the parts of the key are added together to create the index.

A second possibility is *boundary folding*. There are a number of variations on this approach. However, generally, they involve reversing some of the parts of the key before adding. One variation on this approach is to imagine that the parts of the key are written side by side on a piece of paper and that the piece of paper is folded along the boundaries of the parts of the key. In this way, if we begin with the same key (987-65-4321), we first divide it into parts: 987, 654, and 321. We then reverse every other part of the key, which yields 987, 456, and 321. Adding these together yields 1764, and once again we can proceed with either extraction or division to get our index. Other variations on folding use different algorithms to determine which parts of the key to reverse.

Folding may also be a useful method for building a hashing function for a key that is a string. One approach to this is to divide the string into substrings the same length (in bytes) as the desired index and then combine these strings using an *exclusive-or* function. This is also a useful way to convert a string into a number so that other methods, such as division, may be applied to strings.

The Mid-Square Method

In the *mid-square method*, the key is multiplied by itself, and then the extraction method is used to extract the appropriate number of digits from the middle of the squared result to serve as an index. The same "middle" digits must be chosen each time, to provide consistency. For example, if our key were 4321, we would multiply the key by itself, which would yield 18671041. Assuming that we need a three-digit key, we might extract 671 or 710, depending on how we construct our algorithm. It is also possible to extract bits instead of digits and then construct the index from the extracted bits.

The mid-square method may also be effectively used with strings by manipulating the binary representations of the characters in the string.

The Radix Transformation Method

In the *radix transformation method*, the key is transformed into another numeric base. For example, if our key were 23 in base 10, we might convert it into 32 in base 7. We would then use the division method and divide the converted key by the table size and use the remainder as our index. Continuing our previous example, if our table size were 17, we would compute the function

```
Hashcode(23) = Math.abs(32)%17
             =  15
```

The Digit Analysis Method

In the *digit analysis method*, the index is formed by extracting, and then manipulating, specific digits from the key. For example, if our key were 1234567, we might select the digits in positions 2 through 4, obtaining 234, and then manipulate them to form our index. This manipulation can take many forms, including simply reversing the digits (which yields 432), performing a circular shift to the right (which yields 423), performing a circular shift to the left (which yields 342), swapping each pair of digits (which yields 324), or any number of other possibilities, including the methods we have already discussed. The goal is simply to provide a function that does a reasonable job of distributing keys to locations in the table.

The Length-Dependent Method

In the *length-dependent method*, the key and the length of the key are combined in some way to form either the index itself or an intermediate value that is then used with one of our other methods to form the index. For example, if our key were 8765, we might multiply the first two digits by the length and then divide by the last digit, which would yield 69. If our table size were 43, we would then use the division method, which would result in an index of 26.

KEY CONCEPT
The length-dependent method and the mid-square method may also be effectively used with strings by manipulating the binary representations of the characters in the string.

The length-dependent method may also be effectively used with strings by manipulating the binary representations of the characters in the string.

Hashing Functions in the Java Language

The `java.lang.Object` class defines a method called `hashcode` that returns an integer based on the memory location of the object. This is generally not very useful. Classes that are derived from `Object` often override the inherited definition of `hashcode` to provide their own version. For example, the `String` and `Integer` classes define their own `hashcode` methods. These more specific `hashcode` functions can be very effective for hashing. Having the `hashcode` method defined in the `Object` class means that all Java objects can be hashed. However, it is also possible—and often preferable—to define your own `hashcode` method for any class that you intend to store in a hash table.

KEY CONCEPT
Although Java provides a `hashcode` method for all objects, it is often preferable to define a specific hashing function for any particular class.

I.3 Resolving Collisions

If we are able to develop a perfect hashing function for a particular data set, then we do not need to concern ourselves with collisions, the situation where more than one element or key map to the same location in the table. However, when a perfect hashing function is not possible or practical, there are a number of ways to handle collisions. Similarly, if we are able to develop a perfect hashing function for a particular data set, then we do not need to concern ourselves with the size of the table. In this case, we will simply make the table the exact size of the data set.

Otherwise, if the size of the data set is known, it is generally a good idea to set the initial size of the table to about 150 percent of the expected element count. If the size of the data set is not known, then dynamic resizing of the table becomes an issue.

Chaining

The *chaining method* for handling collisions simply treats the hash table conceptually as a table of collections rather than as a table of individual cells. Thus each cell is a pointer to the collection associated with that location in the table. Usually this internal collection is either an unordered list or an ordered list. Figure I.2 illustrates this conceptual approach.

KEY CONCEPT
The chaining method for handling collisions simply treats the hash table conceptually as a table of collections rather than as a table of individual cells.

Chaining can be implemented in a variety of ways. One approach is to make the array holding the table larger than the number of cells in the table and use the extra space as an overflow area to store the linked lists associated with each table location. In this method, each position in the array can store both an element (or a key) and the array index of the next element in its list. The first element mapped to a particular location in the table would actually be stored in that location. The next element mapped to that location would be stored in a free location in this overflow area, and the array index of this second element would be stored with the first element in the table. If a third element were mapped to the same location, the third element would also be stored in this overflow area, and the index of the third element would be stored with the second element. Figure I.3 illustrates this strategy.

Note that when this method is used, the table itself can never be full. However, if the table is implemented as an array, the array can become full, requiring a decision on whether to throw an exception or simply expand capacity. In our earlier collections, we chose to expand the capacity of the array. In this case, expanding the capacity of the array but leaving the embedded table the original size would have disastrous effects on efficiency. A more satisfactory solution is to expand the array and expand the embedded table within the array. This will, however, require that all of the elements in the table be rehashed using the new table size. We will discuss the dynamic resizing of hash tables further in Section I.5.

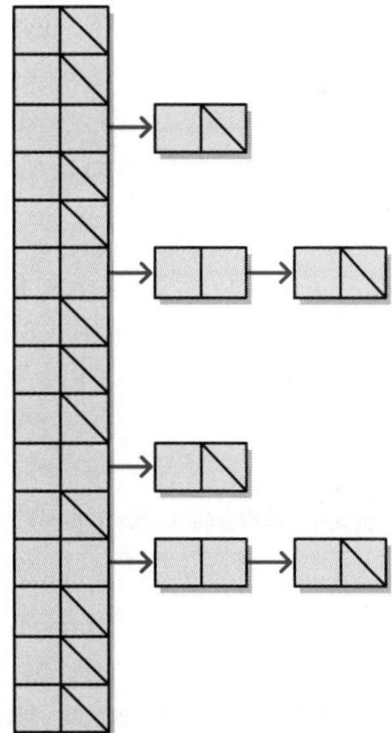

FIGURE I.2 The chaining method of collision handling

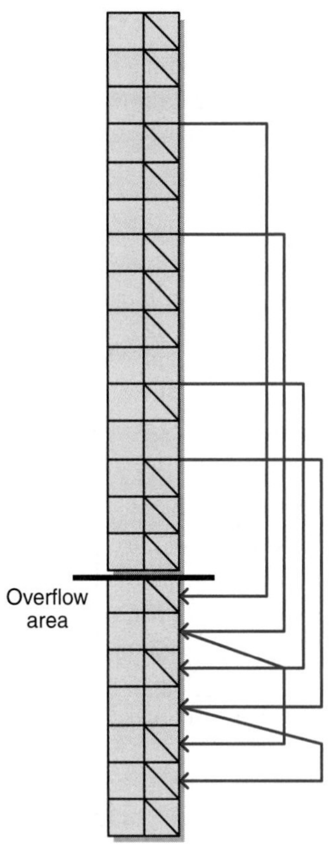

FIGURE I.3 Chaining using an overflow area

With this method, the worst case is that our hashing function will not do a good job of distributing elements to locations in the table, and consequently we end up with one linked list of n elements, or a small number of linked lists with roughly n/k elements each, where k is some relatively small constant. In this case, hash tables become O(n) for both insertions and searches. Thus you can see how important it is to develop a good hashing function.

A second method for implementing chaining is using links. In this method, each cell or bucket in the hash table would be something like the `LinearNode` class used earlier in this text to construct linked lists. In this way, as a second element is mapped to a particular bucket, we simply create a new `LinearNode`, set the `next` reference of the existing node to point to the new node, set the `element` reference of the new node to the element being inserted, and set the `next` reference of the new node to null. The result is an implementation model that looks exactly like the conceptual model shown in Figure I.2.

A third method for implementing chaining is to literally make each position in the table a pointer to a collection. In this way, we could represent each position in the table with a list or perhaps even a more efficient collection (such as a balanced binary search tree), and this would improve our worst case. Keep in mind, however, that if our hashing function is doing a good job of distributing elements to locations in the table, this approach may incur a great deal of overhead while achieving very little improvement.

Open Addressing

The *open addressing method* for handling collisions looks for an open position in the table other than the one to which the element is originally hashed. There are a variety of methods for finding another available location in the table. We will examine three of these methods: linear probing, quadratic probing, and double hashing.

The simplest of these methods is *linear probing*. In linear probing, if an element hashes to position p, and position p is already occupied, we simply try position (p + 1)%s, where s is the size of the table. If position (p + 1)%s is already occupied, we try position (p + 2)%s, and so on until either we find an open position or we find ourselves back at the original position. If we find an open position, we insert the new element. What to do if we do not find an open position is a design decision made when creating a hash table. As we have discussed before, one possibility is to throw an exception if the table is full. Another possibility is to expand the capacity of the table and rehash the existing entries.

KEY CONCEPT

The open addressing method for handling collisions looks for an open position in the table other than the one to which the element is originally hashed.

The problem with linear probing is that it tends to create clusters of filled positions within the table, and these clusters then affect the performance of insertions and searches. Figure I.4 illustrates the linear probing method and the creation of a cluster using our earlier hashing function of extracting the first character of the string.

In this example, Ann was entered, followed by Andrew. Because Ann already occupied position 0 of the array, Andrew was placed in position 1. Later, Bob was entered. Because Andrew already occupied position 1, Bob was placed in the next open position, which was position 2. Doug and Elizabeth were already in the table by the time Betty arrived, so Betty could not be placed in position 1, 2, 3, or 4 and was placed in the next open position, position 5. After Barbara, Hal, and Bill were added, we find that there is now a nine-location cluster at the front of the table, which will continue to grow as more names are added. Thus we see that linear probing may not be the best approach.

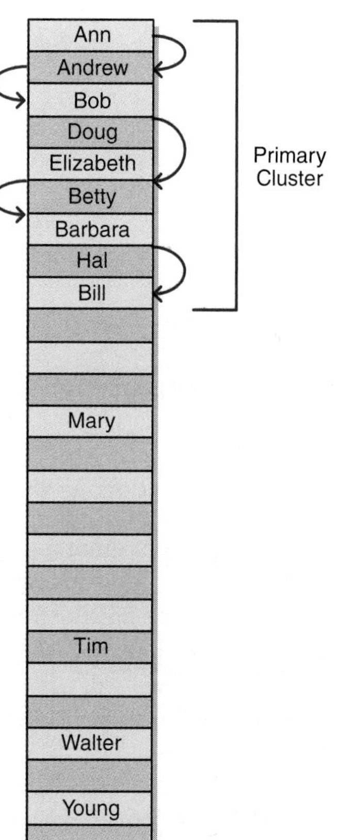

FIGURE I.4 Open addressing using linear probing

A second form of the open addressing method is *quadratic probing*. If we use quadratic probing, instead of a linear approach, then once we have a collision, we follow a formula such as

$$newhashcode(x) = hashcode(x) + (-1)^{i-1}((i + 1)/2)^2$$

for i in the range of 1 to s–1, where s is the table size.

The result of this formula is the search sequence p, p+1, p−1, p+4, p−4, p+9, p−9, ... Of course, this new hash code is then put through the division method to keep it within the table range. As with linear probing, the same possibility exists that we will eventually get back

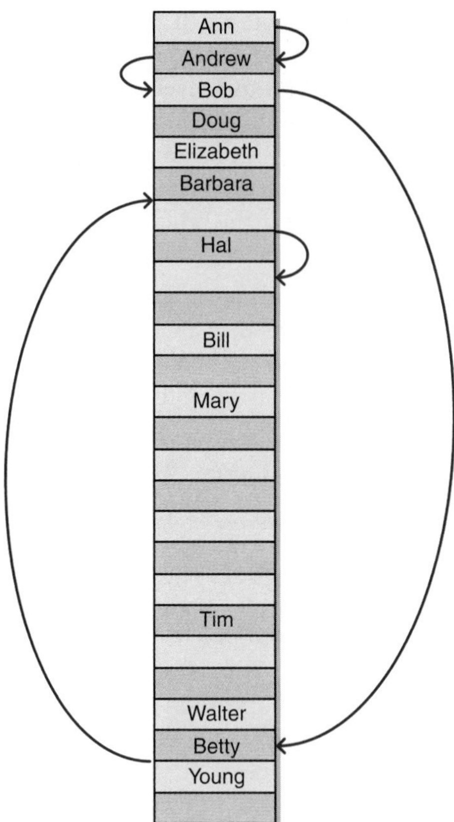

FIGURE I.5 Open addressing using quadratic probing

to the original hash code without having found an open position in which to insert. This "full" condition can be handled in all of the same ways that we described for chaining and linear probing. The benefit of the quadratic probing method is that it does not have as strong a tendency toward clustering as linear probing. Figure I.5 illustrates quadratic probing for the same key set and hashing function that we used in Figure I.4. Notice that after the same data have been entered, we still have a cluster at the front of the table. However, this cluster occupies only six buckets instead of the nine-bucket cluster created by linear probing.

A third form of the open addressing method is *double hashing*. Using the double hashing method, we resolve collisions by providing a secondary hashing function to be used when the primary hashing function results in a collision. For example, if a key x hashes to a position p that is already occupied, then the next position p´ that we try is

```
p" = p + secondaryhashcode(x)
```

If this new position is also occupied, then we look to position

```
p" = p + 2 * secondaryhashcode(x)
```

We continue searching in this way, of course using the division method to maintain our index within the bounds of the table, until an open position is found. This method, although it is somewhat more costly because of the introduction of an additional function, tends to further reduce clustering beyond the improvement gained by quadratic probing. Figure I.6 illustrates this approach, again using the same key set and hashing function as our previous examples. For this example, the secondary hashing function is the length of the string. Notice that with the same data, we no longer have a cluster at the front of the table. However, we have developed a six-bucket cluster from Doug through Barbara. The advantage of double hashing is that even after a cluster has been created, it will tend to grow more slowly than it would if we were using linear probing or even quadratic probing.

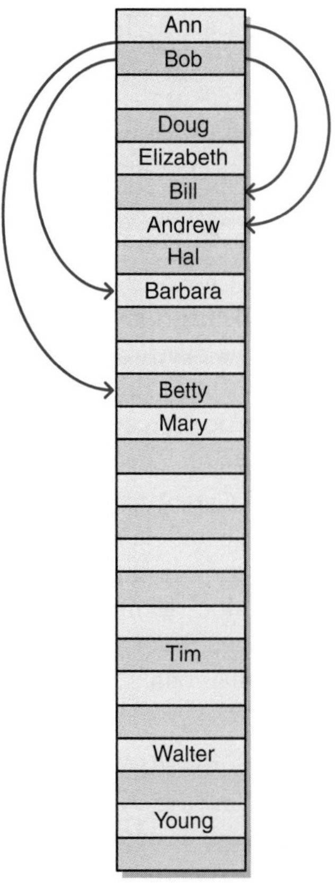

FIGURE I.6 Open addressing using double hashing

I.4 Deleting Elements from a Hash Table

Thus far, our discussion has centered on the efficiency of insertion of and searching for elements in a hash table. What happens if we remove an element from a hash table? The answer to this question depends on which implementation we have chosen.

Deleting from a Chained Implementation

If we have chosen to implement our hash table using a chained implementation and an array with an overflow area, then removing an element falls into one of five cases:

Case 1 The element we are attempting to remove is the only one mapped to the particular location in the table. In this case, we simply remove the element by setting the table position to null.

Case 2 The element we are attempting to remove is stored in the table (not in the overflow area) but has an index into the overflow area for the next element at the same position. In this case, we replace the element and the next index value in the table with the element and next index value of the array position pointed to by the element to be removed. We then also must set the position in the overflow area to null and add it back to whatever mechanism we are using to maintain a list of free positions.

Case 3 The element we are attempting to remove is at the end of the list of elements stored at that location in the table. In this case, we set its position in the overflow area to null, and we set the next index value of the previous element in the list to null as well. We then also must set the position in the overflow area to null and add it back to whatever mechanism we are using to maintain a list of free positions.

Case 4 The element we are attempting to remove is in the middle of the list of elements stored at that location in the table. In this case, we set its position in the overflow area to null, and we set the next index value of the previous element in the list to the next index value of the element being removed. We then also must add it back to whatever mechanism we are using to maintain a list of free positions.

Case 5 The element we are attempting to remove is not in the list. In this case, we throw an `ElementNotFoundException`.

If we have chosen to implement our hash table using a chained implementation where each element in the table is a collection, then we simply remove the target element from the collection.

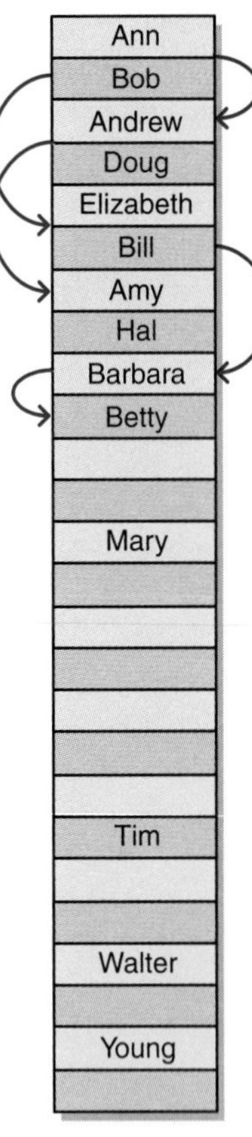

FIGURE I.7 Open addressing and deletion

Deleting from an Open Addressing Implementation

If we have chosen to implement our hash table using an open addressing implementation, then deletion creates more of a challenge. Consider the example in Figure I.7. Note that the elements "Ann," "Andrew," and "Amy" all mapped to the same location in the table and the collision was resolved using linear probing. What happens if we now remove "Andrew"? If we then search for "Amy" we will not find that element because the search will find "Ann" and then follow the linear probing rule to look in the next position, find it null, and return an exception.

The solution to this problem is to mark items as deleted but not actually remove them from the table until some future point when the deleted element is overwritten by a new inserted element or the entire table is rehashed, either because it is being expanded or because we have reached some predetermined threshold for the percentage of deleted records in the table. This means that we will need to add a `boolean` flag to each node in the table and modify all of our algorithms to test and/or manipulate that flag.

I.5 Hash Tables in the Java Collections API

The Java Collections API provides seven implementations of hashing: `Hashtable`, `HashMap`, `HashSet`, `IdentityHashMap`, `LinkedHashSet`, `LinkedHashMap`, and `WeakHashMap`. To understand these different solutions we must first remind ourselves of the distinction between a *set* and a *map* in the Java Collections API as well as some of our other pertinent definitions.

A *set* is a collection of objects where in order to find an object, we must have an exact copy of the object we are looking for. A *map*, on the other hand, is a collection that stores key-value pairs so that, given the key, we can find the associated value.

KEY CONCEPT
The load factor is the maximum percentage occupancy allowed in the hash table before it is resized.

Another definition that will be useful to us as we explore the Java Collections API implementations of hashing is that of a *load factor*. The load factor, as stated earlier, is the maximum percentage occupancy allowed in the hash table before it is resized. For the implementations that we are going to discuss here, the default is 0.75. Thus, using this default, when one of these implementations becomes 75 percent full, a new hash table is created that is twice the size of the current one, and then all of the elements from the current table are inserted into the new table. The load factor of these implementations can be altered when the table is created.

All of these implementations rely on the `hashcode` method of the object being stored to return an integer. This integer is then processed using the division method (using the table size) to produce an index within the bounds of the table. As stated earlier, the best practice is to define your own `hashcode` method for any class that you intend to store in a hash table.

Let's look at each of these implementations.

The `Hashtable` Class

The `Hashtable` implementation of hashing is the oldest of the implementations in the Java Collections API. In fact, it predates the Collections API and was modified in version 1.2 to implement the `Map` interface so that it would become a part of the Collections API. Unlike the newer Java Collections implementations, `Hashtable` is synchronized. Figure I.8 shows the operations for the `Hashtable` class.

Creation of a `Hashtable` requires two parameters: initial capacity (with a default of 11) and load factor (with a default of 0.75). The capacity is the number of cells or locations in the initial table. As we noted earlier, the load factor is the maximum percentage occupancy allowed in the hash table before it is resized. `Hashtable` uses the chaining method for resolving collisions.

The `Hashtable` class is a legacy class that will be most useful if you are connecting to legacy code or require synchronization. Otherwise, it is preferable to use the `HashMap` class.

Return Value	Method	Description
	`Hashtable()`	Constructs a new, empty hash table with a default initial capacity (11) and load factor, which is 0.75.
	`Hashtable(int initialCapacity)`	Constructs a new, empty hash table with the specified initial capacity and default load factor, which is 0.75.
	`Hashtable(int initialCapacity, float loadFactor)`	Constructs a new, empty hash table with the specified initial capacity and the specified load factor.
	`Hashtable (Map t)`	Constructs a new hash table with the same mappings as the given `Map`.
`void`	`clear()`	Clears this hash table so that it contains no keys.
`Object`	`clone()`	Creates a shallow copy of this hash table.
`boolean`	`contains(Object value)`	Tests if some key maps into the specified value in this hash table.
`boolean`	`containsKey(Object key)`	Tests if the specified object is a key in this hash table.
`boolean`	`containsValue (Object value)`	Returns true if this hash table maps one or more keys to this value.
`Enumeration`	`elements()`	Returns an enumeration of the values in this hash table.
`Set`	`entrySet()`	Returns a `Set` view of the entries contained in this hash table.
`boolean`	`equals(Object o)`	Compares the specified `Object` with this `Map` for equality, as per the definition in the `Map` interface.
`Object`	`get(Object key)`	Returns the value to which the specified key is mapped in this hash table.
`int`	`hashCode()`	Returns the hash code value for this `Map` as per the definition in the `Map` interface.
`boolean`	`isEmpty()`	Tests if this hash table maps no keys to values.
`Enumeration`	`keys()`	Returns an enumeration of the keys in this hash table.
`Set`	`keysSet()`	Returns a `Set` view of the keys contained in this hash table.
`Object`	`put(Object key Object value)`	Maps the specified key to the specified value in this hash table.
`void`	`putAll(Map t)`	Copies all of the mappings from the specified `Map` to this hash table. These mappings will replace any mappings that this hash table had for any of the keys currently in the specified `Map`.
`protected void`	`rehash()`	Increases the capacity of and internally reorganizes this hash table, in order to accommodate and access its entries more efficiently.
`Object`	`remove(Object key)`	Removes the key (and its corresponding value) from this hash table.
`int`	`size()`	Returns the number of keys in this hash table.
`String`	`toString()`	Returns a string representation of this hash table object in the form of a set of entries, enclosed in braces and separated by the ASCII characters comma and space.
`Collection`	`values()`	Returns a `Collection` view of the values contained in this hash table.

FIGURE I.8 Operations on the `Hashtable` class

The `HashSet` Class

The `HashSet` class implements the `Set` interface using a hash table. The `HashSet` class, like most of the Java Collections API implementations of hashing, uses chaining to resolve collisions (each table position effectively being a linked list). The `HashSet` implementation does not guarantee the order of the set on iteration and does not guarantee that the order will remain constant over time. This is because the iterator simply steps through the table in order. Because the hashing function will somewhat randomly distribute the elements to table positions, order cannot be guaranteed. Further, if the table is expanded, all of the elements are rehashed relative to the new table size, and the order may change.

Like the `Hashtable` class, the `HashSet` class requires two parameters: initial capacity and load factor. The default for the load factor is the same as it is for `Hashtable` (0.75). The default for initial capacity is currently unspecified (originally it was 101). Figure I.9 shows the operations for the `HashSet` class. The `HashSet` class is not synchronized and permits null values.

The `HashMap` Class

The `HashMap` class implements the `Map` interface using a hash table. The `HashMap` class also uses a chaining method to resolve collisions. Like the `HashSet` class, the `HashMap` class is not synchronized and allows null values. Also like the previous

Return Value	Method	Description
	`HashSet()`	Constructs a new, empty set; the backing `HashMap` instance has the default capacity and load factor, which is 0.75.
	`HashSet(Collection c)`	Constructs a new set containing the elements in the specified collection.
	`HashSet(int initialCapacity)`	Constructs a new, empty set; the backing `HashMap` instance has the specified initial capacity and default load factor, which is 0.75.
	`HashSet(int initial Capacity, float loadFactor)`	Constructs a new, empty set; the backing `HashMap` instance has the specified initial capacity and the specified load factor.
`boolean`	`add(Object o)`	Adds the specified element to this set if it is not already present.
`void`	`clear()`	Removes all of the elements from this set.
`Object`	`clone()`	Returns a shallow copy of this `HashSet` instance: the elements themselves are not cloned.
`boolean`	`contains(Object o)`	Returns true if this set contains the specified element.
`boolean`	`isEmpty()`	Returns true if this set contains no elements.
`iterator()`	`iterator()`	Returns an iterator over the elements in this set.
`boolean`	`remove(Object o)`	Removes the given element from this set if it is present.
`int`	`size()`	Returns the number of elements in this set (its cardinality).

FIGURE I.9 Operations on the `HashSet` class

implementations, the default load factor is 0.75. Like the `HashSet` class, the current default initial capacity is unspecified, although it was also originally 101.

Figure I.10 shows the operations on the `HashMap` class.

The `IdentityHashMap` Class

The `IdentityHashMap` class implements the `Map` interface using a hash table. The difference between this and the `HashMap` class is that the `IdentityHashMap` class uses reference-equality instead of object-equality when comparing both keys and values. This is the difference between using `key1==key2` and using `key1.equals(key2)`.

This class has one parameter: expected maximum size. This is the maximum number of key-value pairs that the table is expected to hold. If the table exceeds this maximum, then the table size will be increased and the table entries rehashed.

Return Value	Method	Description
	`HashMap()`	Constructs a new, empty map with a default capacity and load factor, which is 0.75.
	`HashMap(int initialCapacity)`	Constructs a new, empty map with the specified initial capacity and default load factor, which is 0.75.
	`HashMap(int initialCapacity, float loadFactor)`	Constructs a new, empty map with the specified initial capacity and the specified load factor.
	`HashMap(Map t)`	Constructs a new map with the same mappings as the given map.
`void`	`clear()`	Removes all mappings from this map.
`Object`	`clone()`	Returns a shallow copy of this `HashMap` instance: the keys and values themselves are not cloned.
`boolean`	`containsKey(Object key)`	Returns true if this map contains a mapping for the specified key.
`boolean`	`containsValue (Object value)`	Returns true if this map maps one or more keys to the specified value.
`set`	`entrySet()`	Returns a collection view of the mappings contained in this map.
`Object`	`get(Object key)`	Returns the value to which this map maps the specified key.
`boolean`	`isEmpty()`	Returns true if this map contains no key-value mappings.
`Set`	`keySet()`	Returns a set view of the keys contained in this map.
`Object`	`put(Object key, Object value)`	Associates the specified value with the specified key in this map.
`void`	`putAll(Map t)`	Copies all of the mappings from the specified map to this one.
`Object`	`remove(Object key)`	Removes the mapping for this key from this map if present.
`int`	`size()`	Returns the number of key-value mappings in this map.
`Collection`	`values()`	Returns a collection view of the values contained in this map.

FIGURE I.10 Operations on the `HashMap` class

Return Value	Method	Description
	`IdentityHashMap()`	Constructs a new, empty identity hash map with a default expected maximum size (21).
	`IdentityHashMap(int expectedMaxSize)`	Constructs a new, empty map with the specified expected maximum size.
	`IdentityHashMap(Map m)`	Constructs a new identity hash map containing the key-value mappings in the specified map.
`void`	`clear()`	Removes all mappings from this map.
`Object`	`clone()`	Returns a shallow copy of this identity hash map: the keys and values themselves are not cloned.
`boolean`	`containsKey(Object key)`	Tests whether the specified object reference is a key in this identity hash map.
`boolean`	`containsValue (Object value)`	Tests whether the specified object reference is a value in this identity hash map.
`Set`	`entrySet()`	Returns a set view of the mappings contained in this map.
`boolean`	`equals(Object o)`	Compares the specified object with this map for equality.
`Object`	`get(Object key)`	Returns the value to which the specified key is mapped in this identity hash map, or null if the map contains no mapping for this key.
`int`	`hashCode()`	Returns the hash code value for this map.
`boolean`	`isEmpty()`	Returns true if this identity hash map contains no key-value mappings.
`Set`	`keySet()`	Returns an identity-based set view of the keys contained in this map.
`Object`	`put(Object key, Object value)`	Associates the specified value with the specified key in this identity hash map.
`void`	`putAll(Map t)`	Copies all of the mappings from the specified map to this map. These mappings will replace any mappings that this map had for any of the keys currently in the specified map.
`Object`	`remove(Object key)`	Removes the mapping for this key from this map if present.
`int`	`size()`	Returns the number of key-value mappings in this identity hash map.
`Collection`	`values()`	Returns a collection view of the values contained in this map.

FIGURE I.11 Operations on the `IdentityHashMap` class

Figure I.11 shows the operations on the `IdentityHashMap` class.

The `WeakHashMap` Class

The `WeakHashMap` class implements the `Map` interface using a hash table. This class is specifically designed with weak keys so that an entry in a `WeakHashMap` will automatically be removed when its key is no longer in use. In other words, if the use of the key in a mapping in the `WeakHashMap` is the only remaining use of the key, the garbage collector will collect it anyway.

Return Value	Method	Description
	WeakHashMap()	Constructs a new, empty WeakHashMap with the default initial capacity and the default load factor, which is 0.75.
	WeakHashMap(int initialCapacity)	Constructs a new, empty WeakHashMap with the given initial capacity and the default load factor, which is 0.75.
	WeakHashMap(int initial Capacity, float loadFactor)	Constructs a new, empty WeakHashMap with the given initial capacity and the given load factor.
	WeakHashMap(Map t)	Constructs a new WeakHashMap with the same mappings as the specified map.
void	clear()	Removes all mappings from this map.
boolean	containsKey(Object key)	Returns true if this map contains a mapping for the specified key.
Set	entrySet()	Returns a set view of the mappings in this map.
Object	get(Object key)	Returns the value to which this map maps the specified key.
boolean	isEmpty()	Returns true if this map contains no key-value mappings.
Set	keySet()	Returns a set view of the keys contained in this map.
Object	put(Object key, Object value)	Associates the specified value with the specified key in this map.
void	putAll(Map t)	Copies all of the mappings from the specified map to this map. These mappings will replace any mappings that this map had for any of the keys currently in the specified map.
Object	remove(Object key)	Removes the mapping for the given key from this map, if present.
int	size()	Returns the number of key-value mappings in this map.
Collection	values()	Returns a collection view of the values contained in this map.

FIGURE I.12 Operations on the `WeakHashMap` class

The `WeakHashMap` class allows both null values and null keys, and it has the same tuning parameters as the `HashMap` class: initial capacity and load factor.

Figure I.12 shows the operations on the `WeakHashMap` class.

`LinkedHashSet` and `LinkedHashMap`

The two remaining hashing implementations are extensions of previous classes. The `LinkedHashSet` class extends the `HashSet` class, and the `LinkedHashMap` class extends the `HashMap` class. Both of them are designed to solve the problem of iterator order. These implementations maintain a doubly linked list running through the entries to maintain the insertion order of the elements. Thus the iterator order for these implementations is the order in which the elements were inserted.

Figure I.13 shows the additional operations on the `LinkedHashSet` class. Figure I.14 shows the additional operations on the `LinkedHashMap` class.

Return Value	Method	Description
	LinkedHashSet()	Constructs a new, empty linked hash set with the default initial capacity (16) and load factor (0.75).
	LinkedHashSet (Collection c)	Constructs a new linked hash set with the same elements as the specified collection.
	LinkedHashSet (int initialCapacity)	Constructs a new, empty linked hash set with the specified initial capacity and the default load factor (0.75).
	LinkedHashSet(int initialCapacity, float loadFactor)	Constructs a new, empty linked hash set with the specified initial capacity and load factor.

FIGURE I.13 Additional operations on the `LinkedHashSet` class

Return Value	Method	Description
	LinkedHashMap()	Constructs an empty insertion-ordered `LinkedHashMap` instance with a default capacity (16) and load factor (0.75).
	LinkedHashMap (int initialCapacity)	Constructs an empty insertion-ordered `LinkedHashMap` instance with the specified initial capacity and a default load factor (0.75).
	LinkedHashMap (int initialCapacity, float loadFactor)	Constructs an empty insertion-ordered `LinkedHashMap` instance with the specified initial capacity and load factor.
	LinkedHashMap (int initialCapacity, float loadFactor, boolean accessOrder)	Constructs an empty `LinkedHashMap` instance with the specified initial capacity, load factor, and ordering mode.
	LinkedHashMap(Map m)	Constructs an insertion-ordered `LinkedHashMap` instance with the same mappings as the specified map.
void	clear()	Removes all mappings from this map.
boolean	containsValue (Object value)	Returns true if this map maps one or more keys to the specified value.
Object	get(Object key)	Returns the value to which this map maps the specified key.
protected boolean	removeEldestEntry (Map.Entry eldest)	Returns true if this map should remove its eldest entry.

FIGURE I.14 Additional operations on the `LinkedHashMap` class

Summary of Key Concepts

- In hashing, elements are stored in a hash table, and their location in the table is determined by a hashing function.
- The situation where two elements or keys map to the same location in the table is called a collision.
- A hashing function that maps each element to a unique position in the table is said to be a perfect hashing function.
- Extraction involves using only a part of the element's value or key to compute the location at which to store the element.
- The division method is very effective when one is dealing with an unknown set of key values.
- In the shift folding method, the parts of the key are added together to create the index.
- The length-dependent method and the mid-square method may also be effectively used with strings by manipulating the binary representations of the characters in the string.
- Although Java provides a `hashcode` method for all objects, it is often preferable to define a specific hashing function for any particular class.
- The chaining method for handling collisions simply treats the hash table conceptually as a table of collections rather than as a table of individual cells.
- The open addressing method for handling collisions looks for an open position in the table other than the one to which the element is originally hashed.
- The load factor is the maximum percentage occupancy allowed in the hash table before it is resized.

Self-Review Questions

SR I.1 What is the difference between a hash table and the other collections we have discussed?

SR I.2 What is a collision in a hash table?

SR I.3 What is a perfect hashing function?

SR I.4 What is our goal for a hashing function?

SR I.5 What is the consequence of not having a good hashing function?

SR I.6 What is the extraction method?

SR I.7 What is the division method?

SR I.8 What is the shift folding method?

SR I.9 What is the boundary folding method?

SR I.10 What is the mid-square method?

SR I.11 What is the radix transformation method?

SR I.12 What is the digit analysis method?

SR I.13 What is the length-dependent method?

SR I.14 What is chaining?

SR I.15 What is open addressing?

SR I.16 What are linear probing, quadratic probing, and double hashing?

SR I.17 Why is deletion from an open addressing implementation a problem?

SR I.18 What is the load factor, and how does it affect table size?

Exercises

EX I.1 Draw the hash table that results from adding the following integers (34 45 3 87 65 32 1 12 17) to a hash table of size 11 using the division method and linked chaining.

EX I.2 Draw the hash table from Exercise I.1 using a hash table of size 11 and array chaining with a total array size of 20.

EX I.3 Draw the hash table from Exercise I.1 using a table size of 17 and open addressing with linear probing.

EX I.4 Draw the hash table from Exercise I.1 using a table size of 17 and open addressing with quadratic probing.

EX I.5 Draw the hash table from Exercise I.1 using a table size of 17 and double hashing using extraction of the first digit as the secondary hashing function.

EX I.6 Draw the hash table that results from adding the following integers (1983, 2312, 6543, 2134, 3498, 7654, 1234, 5678, 6789) to a hash table using shift folding of the first two digits with the last two digits. Use a table size of 13.

EX I.7 Draw the hash table from Exercise I.6 using boundary folding.

EX I.8 Draw a UML diagram that shows how all of the various implementations of hashing within the Java Collections API are constructed.

Programming Projects

PP I.1 Implement the hash table illustrated in Figure I.1 using the array version of chaining.

PP I.2 Implement the hash table illustrated in Figure I.1 using the linked version of chaining.

PP I.3 Implement the hash table illustrated in Figure I.1 using open addressing with linear probing.

PP I.4 Implement a dynamically resizable hash table to store people's names and Social Security numbers. Use the extraction method with division using the last four digits of the Social Security number. Use an initial table size of 31 and a load factor of 0.80. Use open addressing with double hashing using an extraction method on the first three digits of the Social Security number.

PP I.5 Implement the problem from Programming Project I.4 using linked chaining.

PP I.6 Implement the problem from Programming Project I.4 using the `HashMap` class of the Java Collections API.

PP I.7 Create a new implementation of the bag collection called `HashtableBag` using a hash table.

PP I.8 Implement the problem from Programming Project I.4 using shift folding with the Social Security number divided into three equal three-digit parts.

PP I.9 Create a graphical system that will allow a user to add and remove employees where each employee has an employee id (a six-digit number), an employee name, and years of service. Use the `hashcode` method of the `Integer` class as your hashing function, and use one of the Java Collections API implementations of hashing.

PP I.10 Complete Programming Project I.9 using your own `hashcode` function. Use extraction of the first three digits of the employee id as the hashing function and use one of the Java Collections API implementations of hashing.

PP I.11 Complete Programming Project I.9 using your own `hashcode` function and your own implementation of a hash table.

PP I.12 Create a system that will allow a user to add and remove vehicles from an inventory system. Vehicles will be represented by license number (an eight-character string), make, model, and color. Use your own array-based implementation of a hash table using chaining.

PP I.13 Complete Programming Project I.12 using a linked implementation with open addressing and double hashing.

Answers to Self-Review Questions

SRA I.1 Elements are placed into a hash table at an index produced by a function of the value of the element or a key of the element. This is different from other collections, where the position/location of an element in the collection is determined either by comparison with the other values in the collection or by the order in which the elements were added or removed from the collection.

SRA I.2 The situation where two elements or keys map to the same location in the table is called a collision.

SRA I.3 A hashing function that maps each element to a unique position in the table is said to be a perfect hashing function.

SRA I.4 We need a hashing function that will do a good job of distributing elements into positions in the table.

SRA I.5 If we do not have a good hashing function, the result will be too many elements mapped to the same location in the table. This will result in poor performance.

SRA I.6 Extraction involves using only a part of the element's value or key to compute the location at which to store the element.

SRA I.7 The division method involves dividing the key by some positive integer p (usually the table size and usually prime) and then using the remainder as the index.

SRA I.8 Shift folding involves dividing the key into parts (usually the same length as the desired index) and then adding the parts. Extraction or division is then used to get an index within the bounds of the table.

SRA I.9 Like shift folding, boundary folding involves dividing the key into parts (usually the same length as the desired index). However, some of the parts are then reversed before adding. One example is to imagine that the parts are written side by side on a piece of paper, which is then folded on the boundaries between parts. In this way, every other part is reversed.

SRA I.10 The mid-square method involves multiplying the key by itself and then extracting some number of digits or bytes from the middle of the result. Division can then be used to guarantee an index within the bounds of the table.

SRA I.11 The radix transformation method is a variation on the division method where the key is first converted to another numeric base and then divided by the table size with the remainder used as the index.

SRA I.12 In the digit analysis method, the index is formed by extracting, and then manipulating, specific digits from the key.

SRA I.13 In the length-dependent method, the key and the length of the key are combined in some way to form either the index itself or an intermediate value that is then used with one of our other methods to form the index.

SRA I.14 The chaining method for handling collisions simply treats the hash table conceptually as a table of collections, rather than as a table of individual cells. Thus each cell is a pointer to the collection associated with that location in the table. This internal collection usually is either an unordered list or an ordered list.

SRA I.15 The open addressing method for handling collisions looks for an open position in the table other than the one to which the element is originally hashed.

SRA I.16 Linear probing, quadratic probing, and double hashing are methods for determining the next table position to try if the original hash causes a collision.

SRA I.17 Because of the way a path is formed in open addressing, deleting an element from the middle of that path can cause elements beyond that point on the path to be unreachable.

SRA I.18 The load factor is the maximum percentage occupancy allowed in the hash table before it is resized. Once the load factor has been reached, a new table is created that is twice the size of the current table, and then all of the elements in the current table are inserted into the new table.

Appendix J

Java Syntax

This appendix contains syntax diagrams that collectively describe the way in which Java language elements can be constructed. Rectangles indicate something that is further defined in another syntax diagram, and ovals indicate a literal word or character. Though largely complete, not all Java constructs are represented in this collection of syntax diagrams.

Compilation Unit

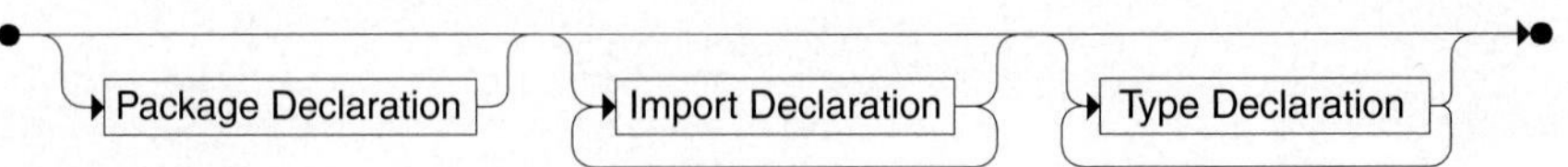

Package Declaration

Import Declaration

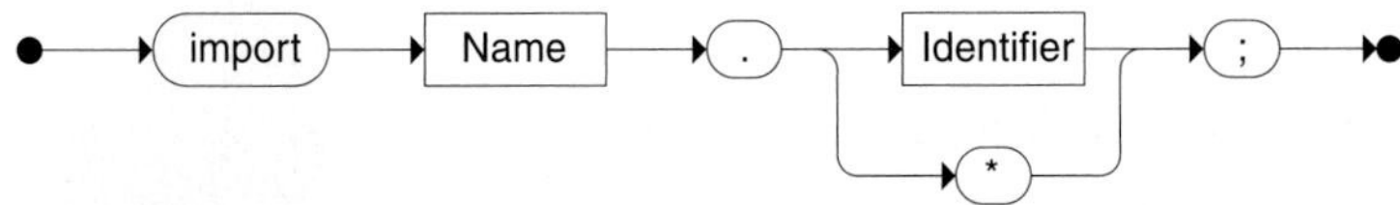

Type Declaration

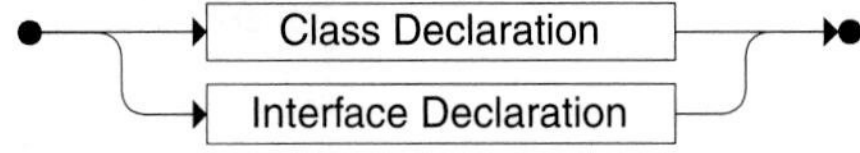

Class Declaration

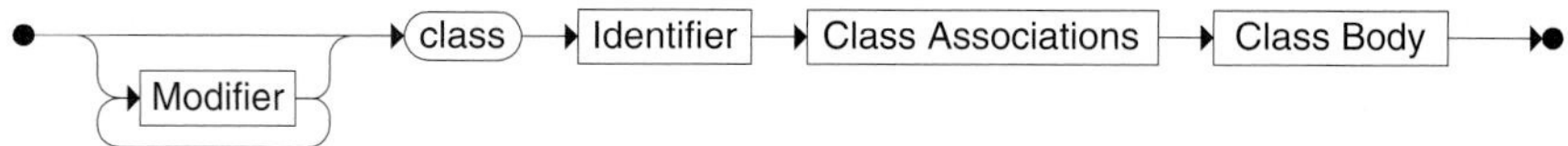

Class Associations

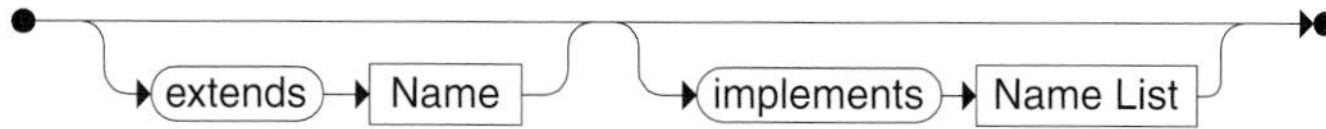

Class Body

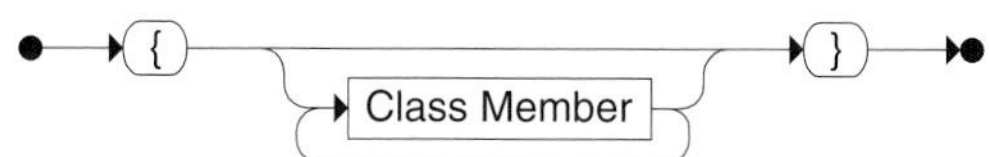

Class Member

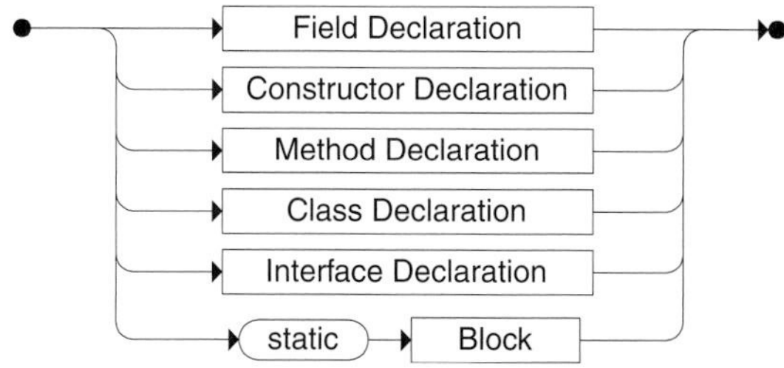

Interface Declaration

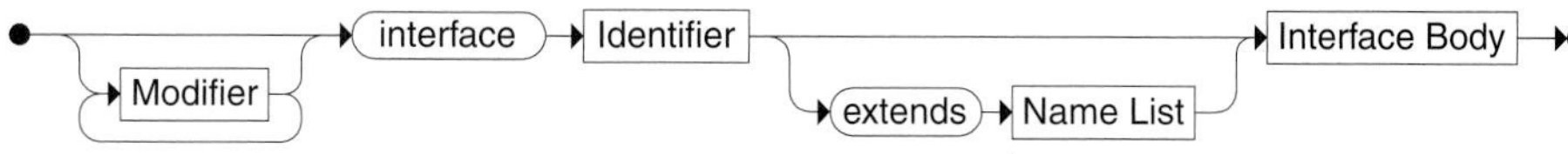

Interface Body

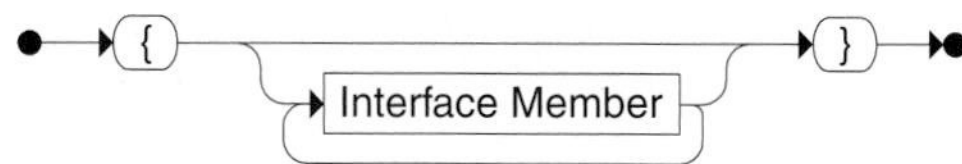

Interface Member

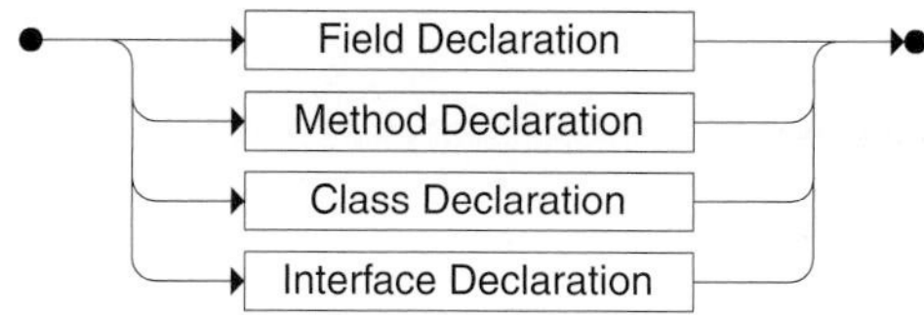

Field Declaration

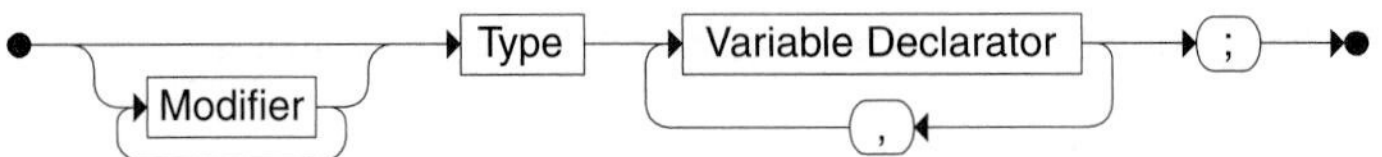

Variable Declarator

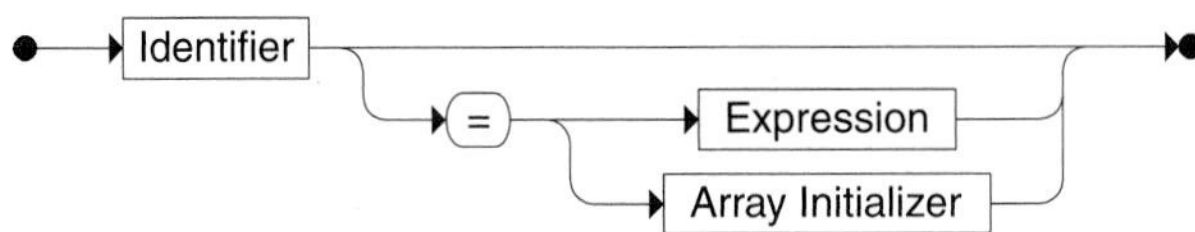

Type

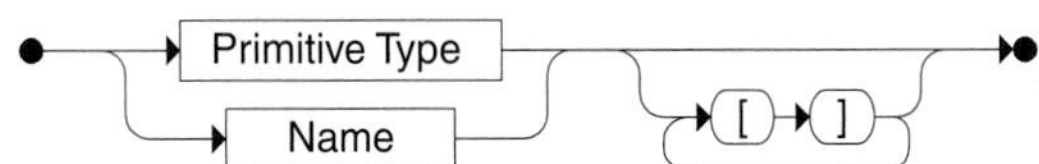

Modifier

Primitive Type

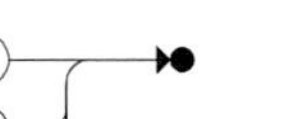
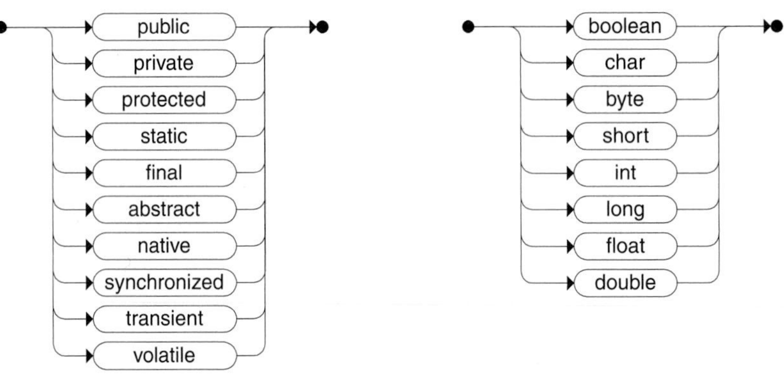

Array Initializer

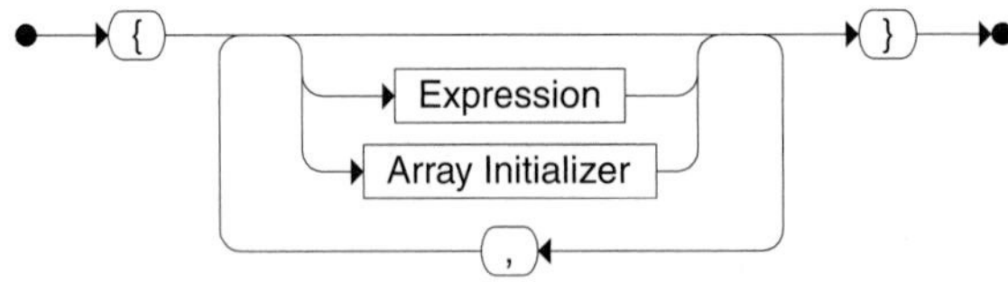

Name

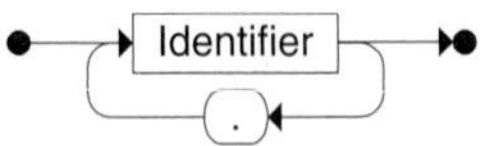

Name List

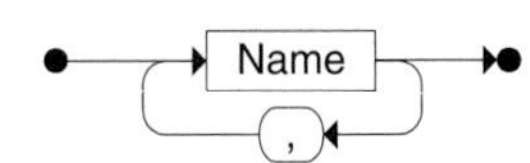

Method Declaration

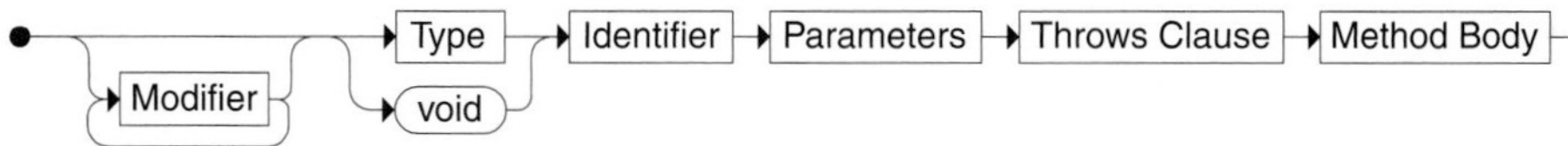

Parameters

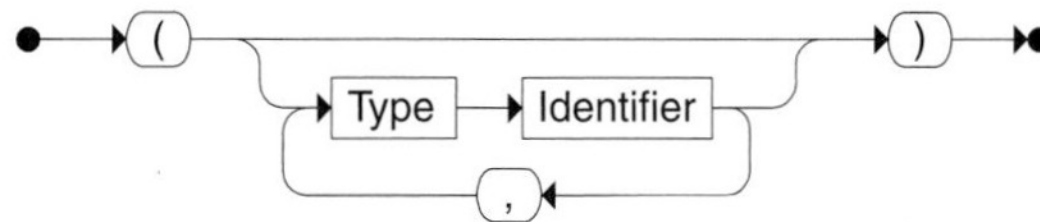

Throws Clause

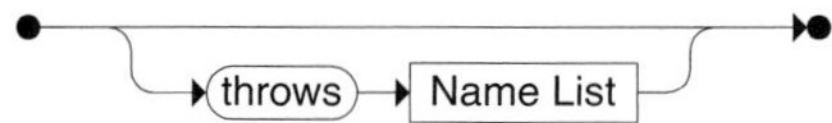

Method Body

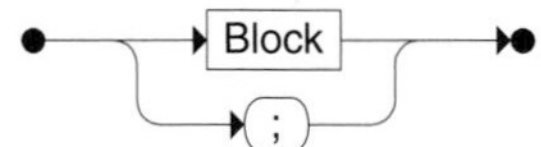

Constructor Declaration

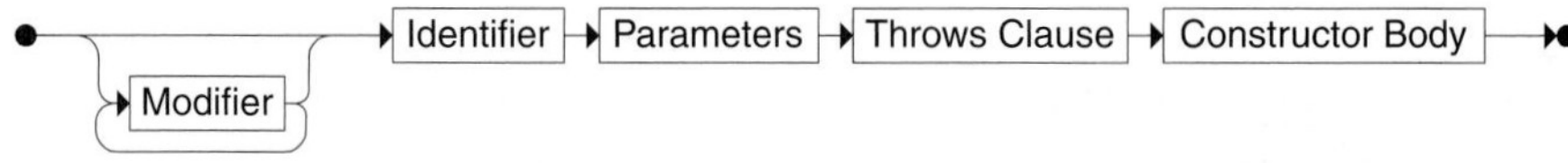

Constructor Body

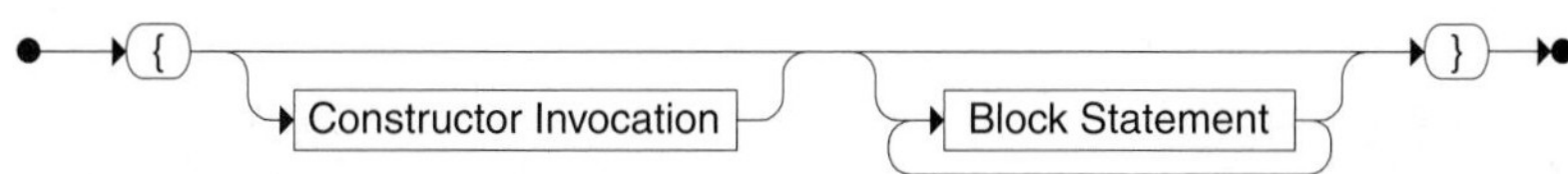

Constructor Invocation

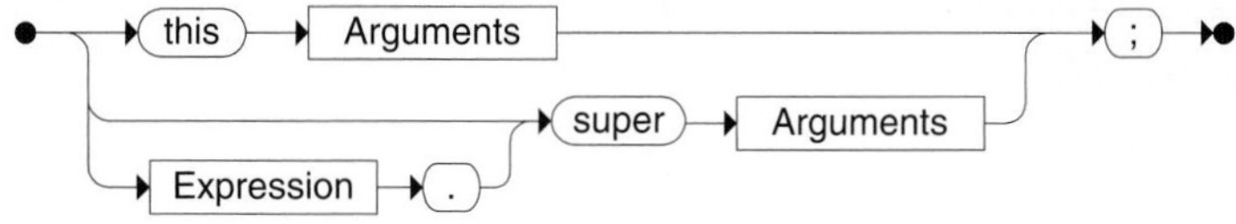

Block

Block Statement

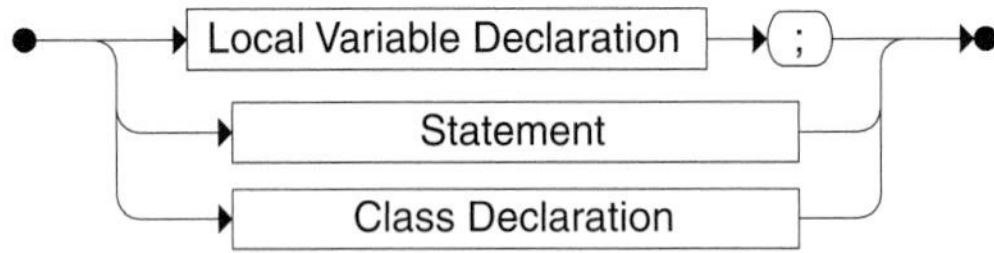

Local Variable Declaration

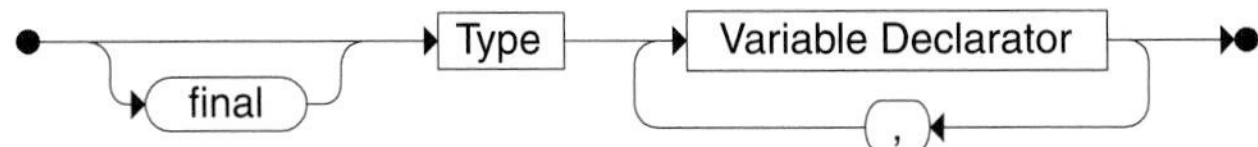

Statement

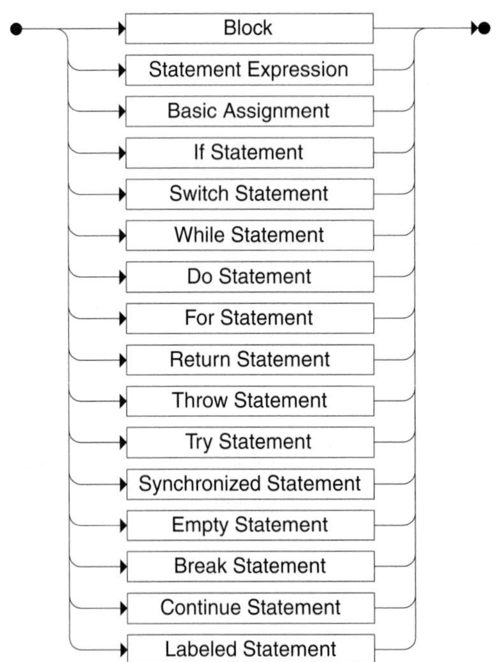

If Statement

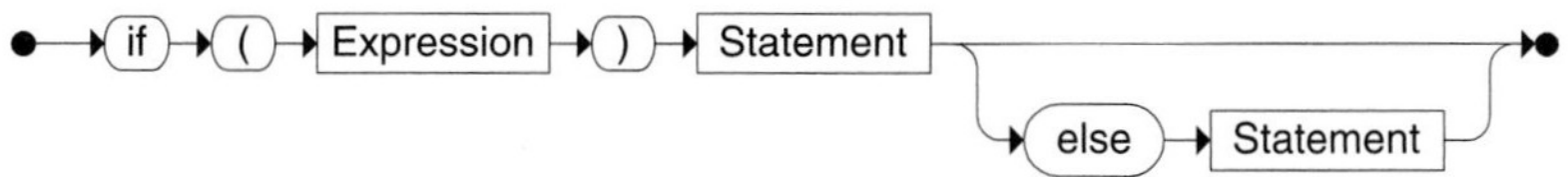

Switch Statement

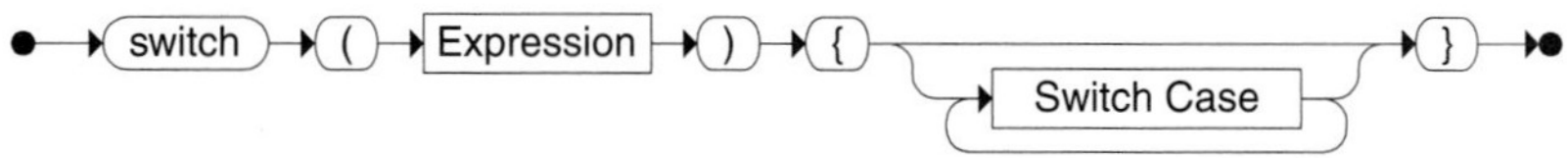

Switch Case

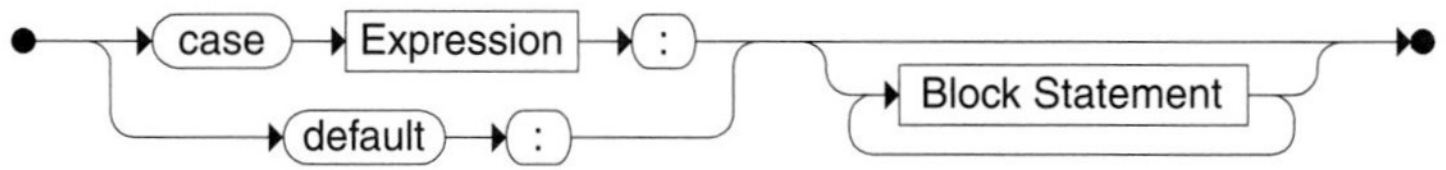

While Statement

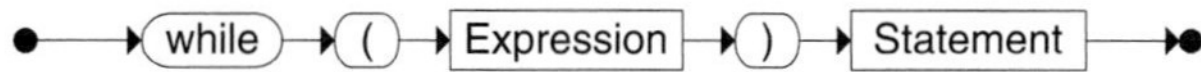

Do Statement

For Statement

For Init

For Update

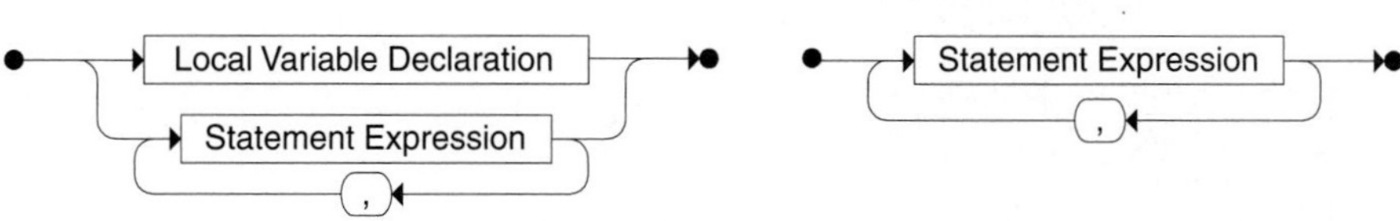

Basic Assignment

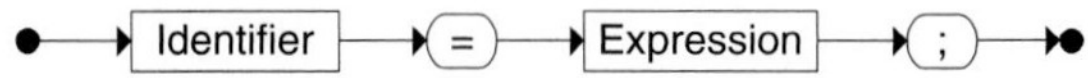

Return Statement

Throw Statement

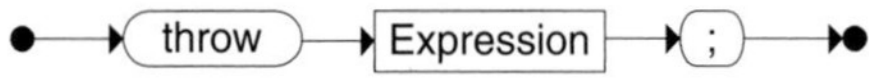

Try Statement

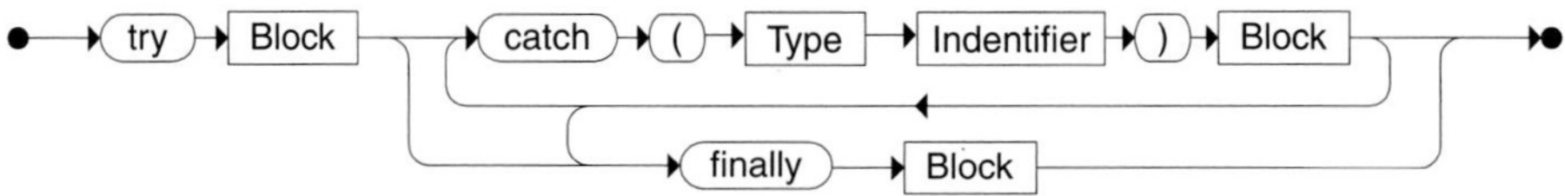

Synchronized Statement

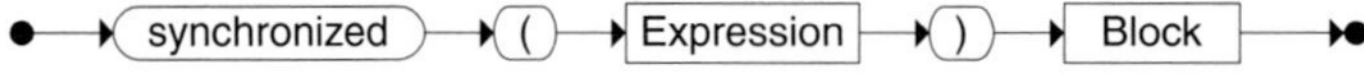

Empty Statement

Break Statement

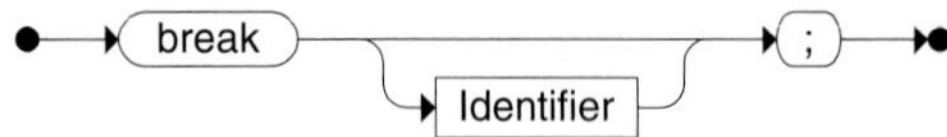

Continue Statement

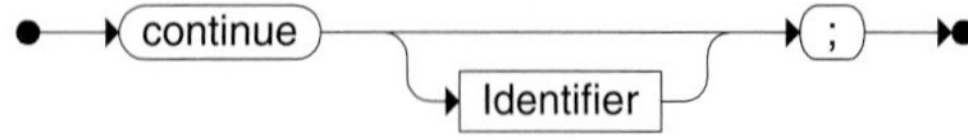

Labeled Statement

Expression

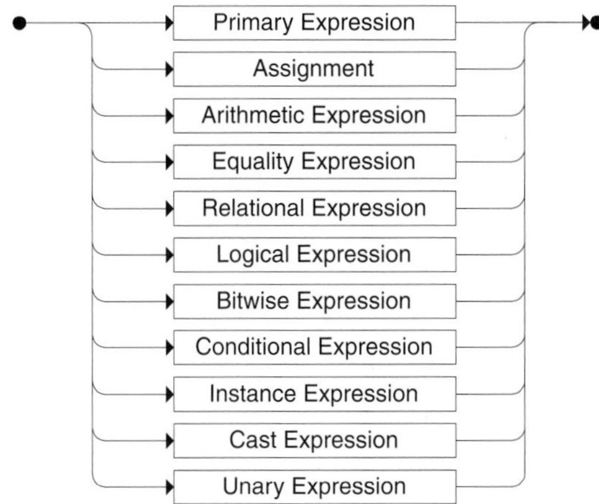

Primary Expression

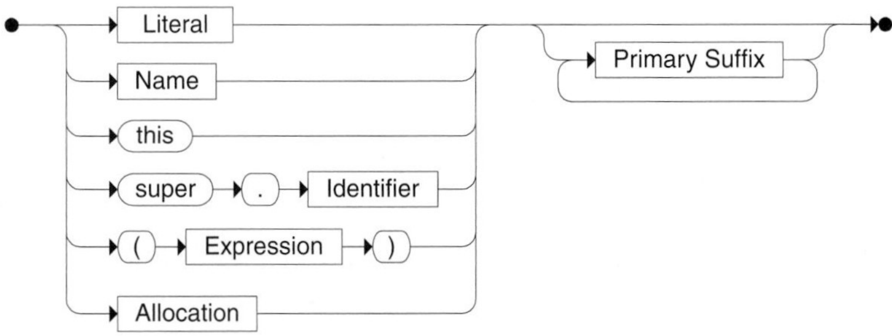

Primary Suffix

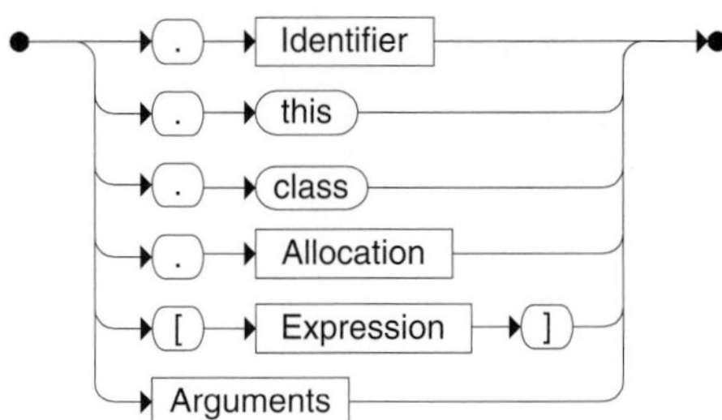

Arguments

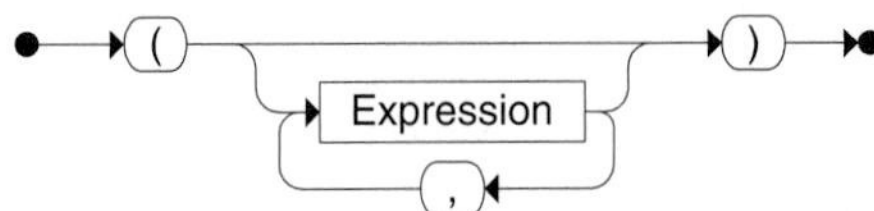

Allocation

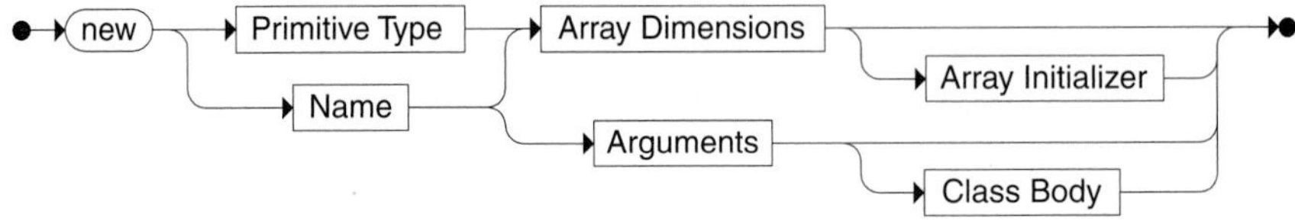

Array Dimensions

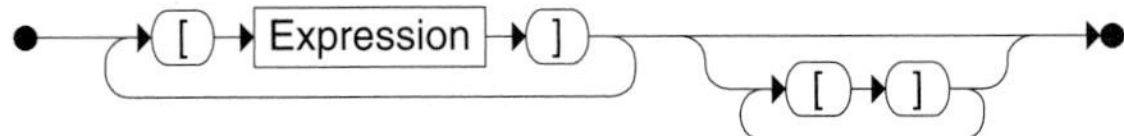

Statement Expression

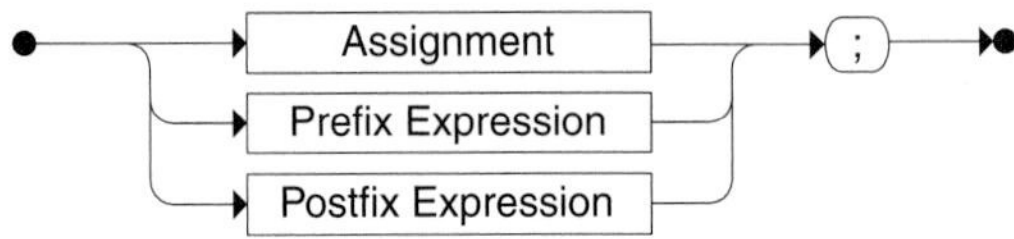

Assignment

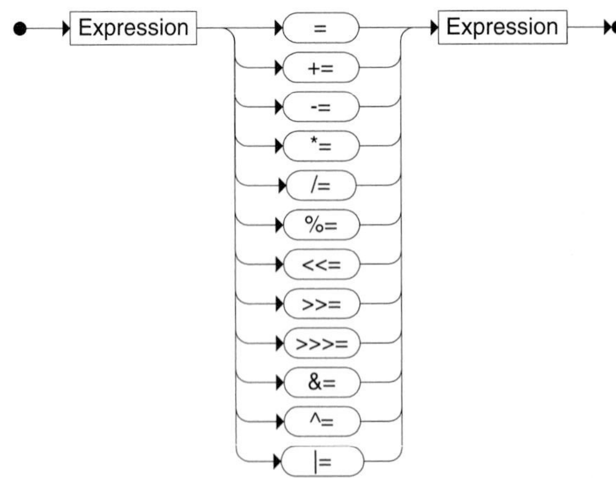

Arithmetic Expression

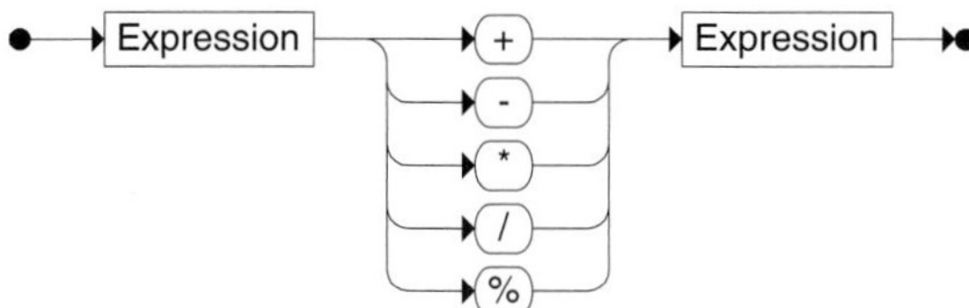

Equality Expression

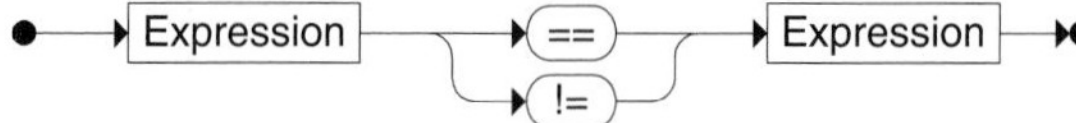

Relational Expression

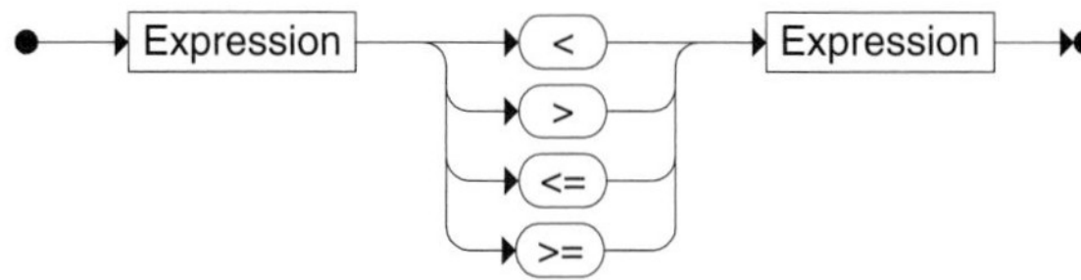

Logical Expression

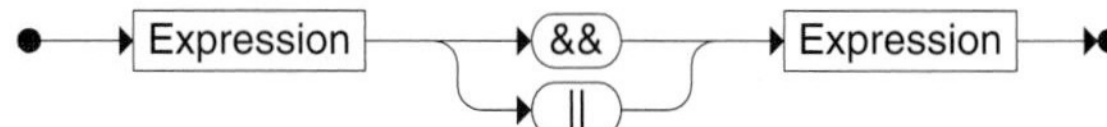

Bitwise Expression

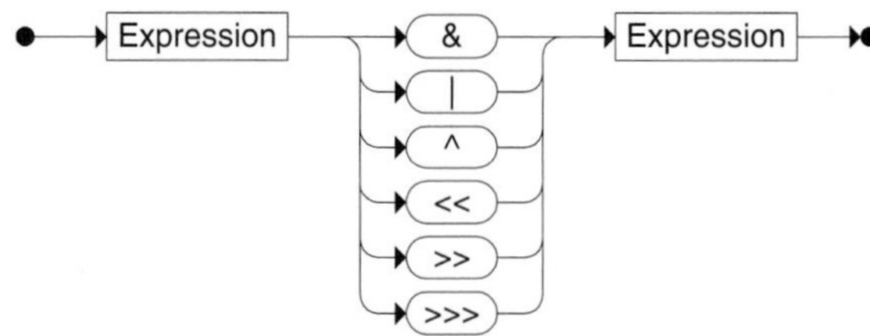

Conditional Expression

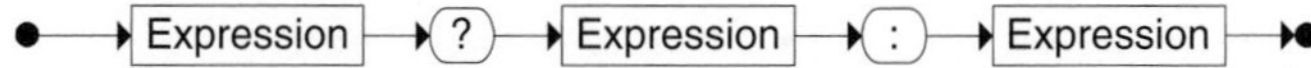

Instance Expression

Cast Expression

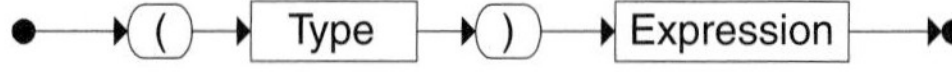

Unary Expression

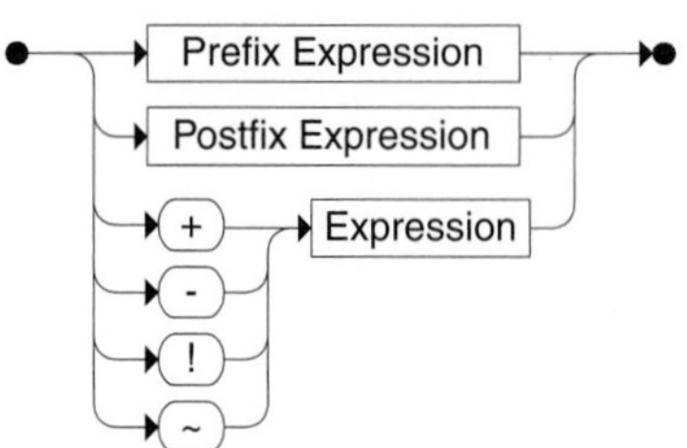

Prefix Expression

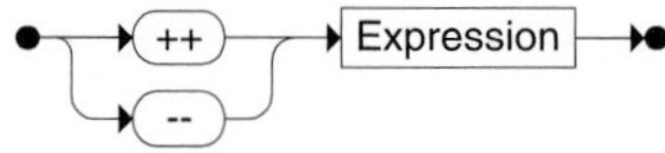

Postfix Expression

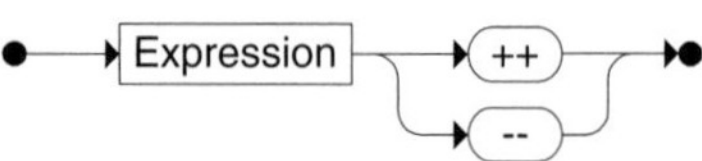

Literal

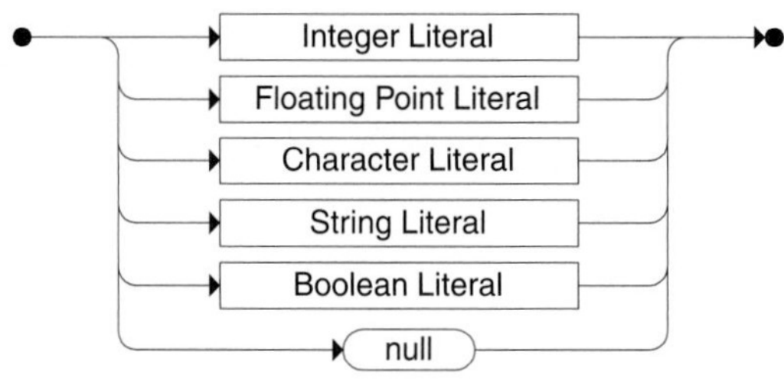

Integer Literal

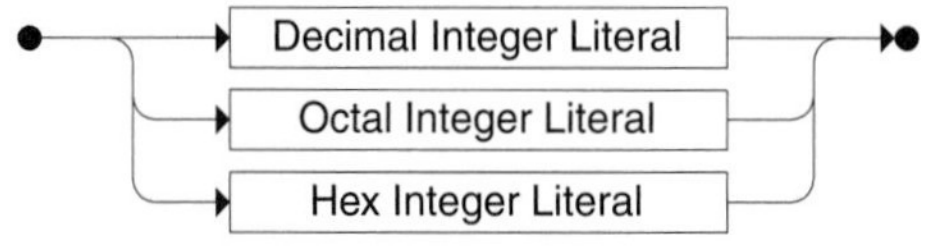

Decimal Integer Literal

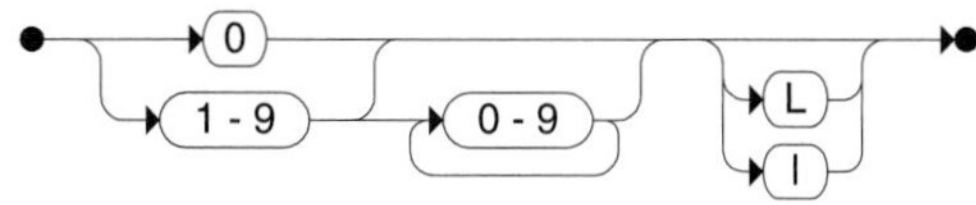

Octal Integer Literal

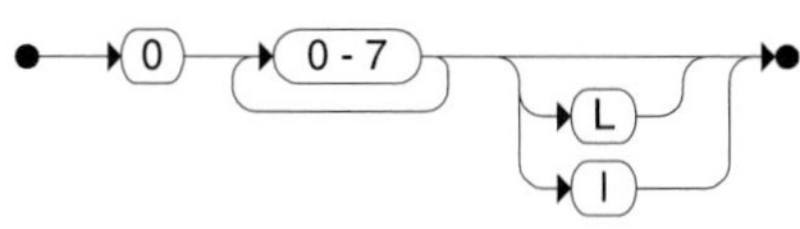

Hex Digit

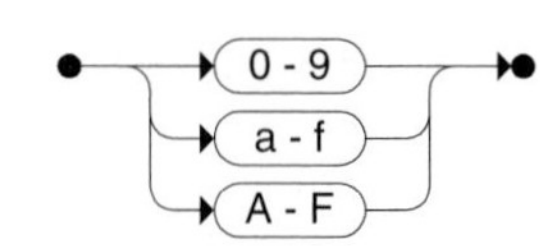

Hex Integer Literal

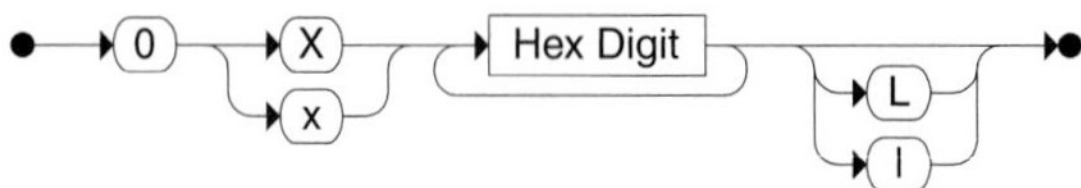

Floating Point Literal

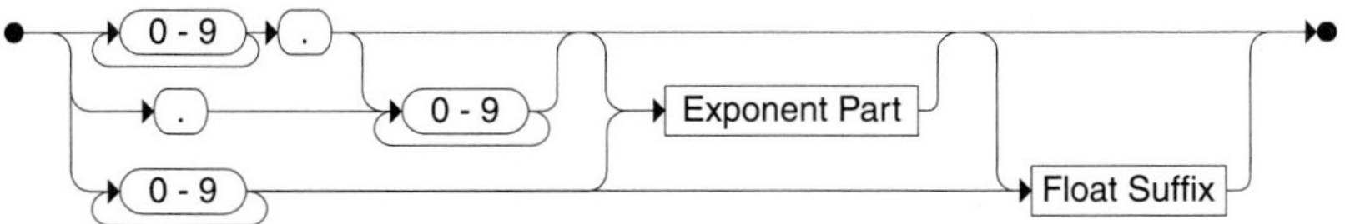

Exponent Part

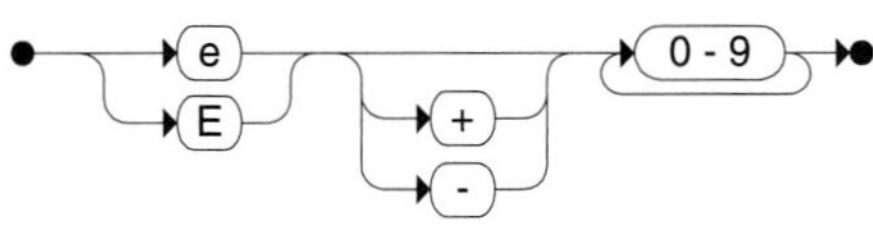

Float Suffix

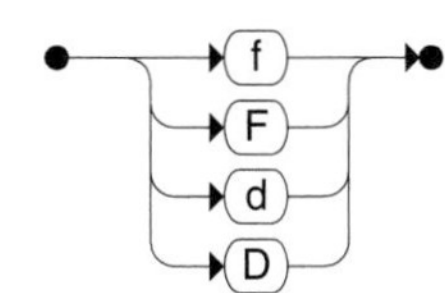

Character Literal

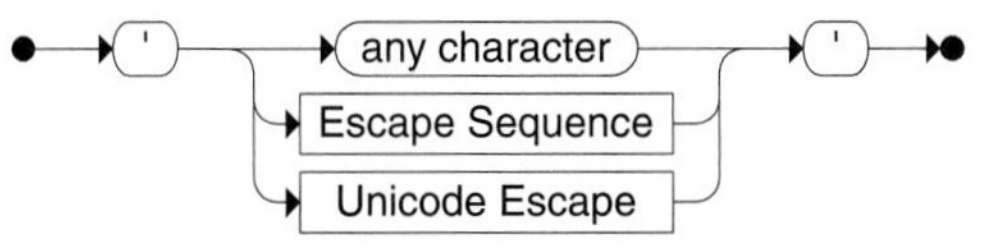

Boolean Literal

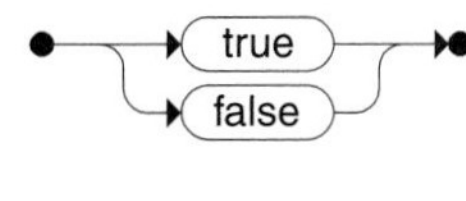

String Literal

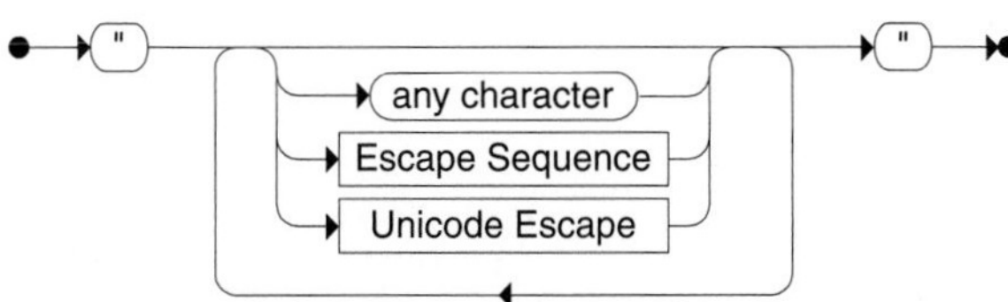

Escape Sequence

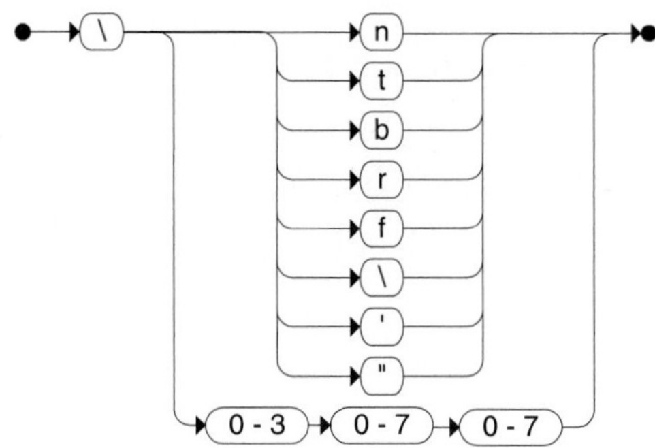

Identifier

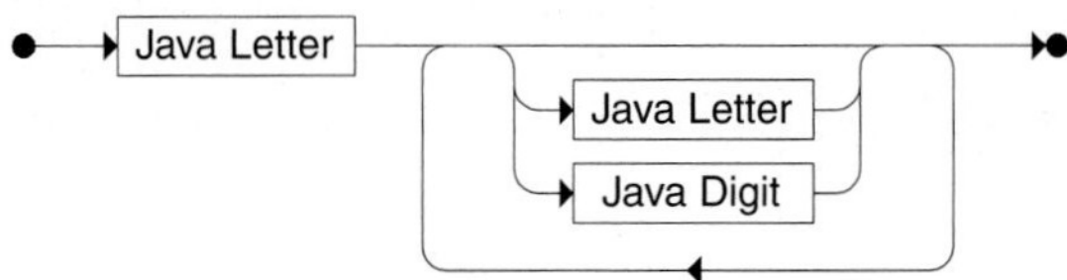

Java Letter

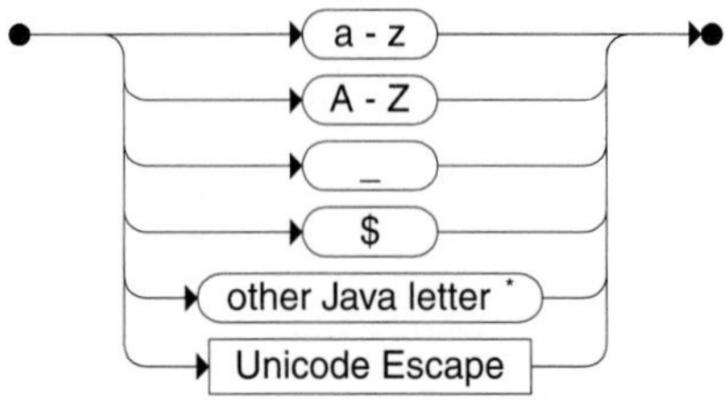

* The "other Java letter" category includes letters from many languages other than English.

Java Digit

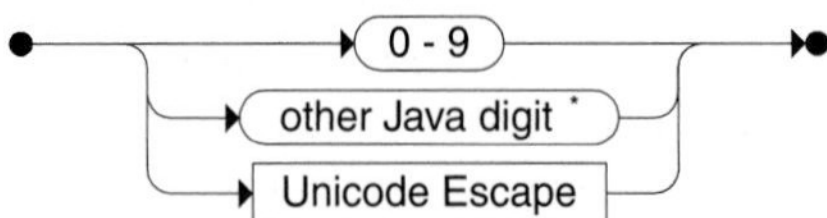

* The "other Java digit" category includes additional digits defined in Unicode.

Unicode Escape*

* In some contexts, the character represented by a Unicode Escape is restricted.

Symbols

A

B

E

M

P

S

U

V

LISTING 6.1: DISPLAY

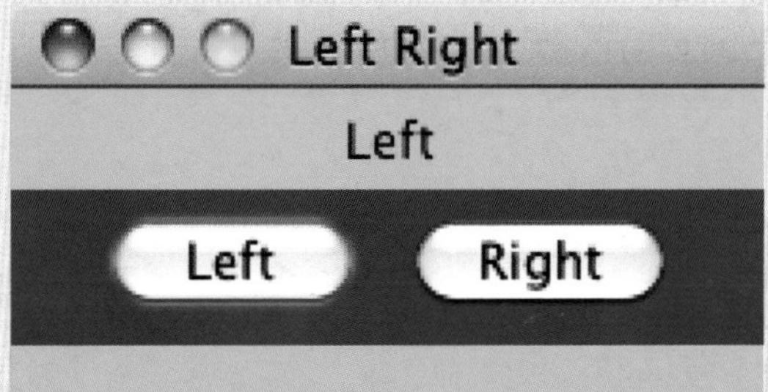

LISTING 6.3: DISPLAY

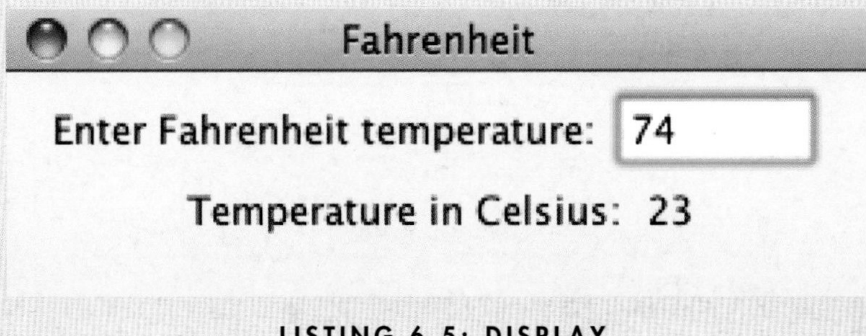

LISTING 6.5: DISPLAY

LISTING 6.7: DISPLAY

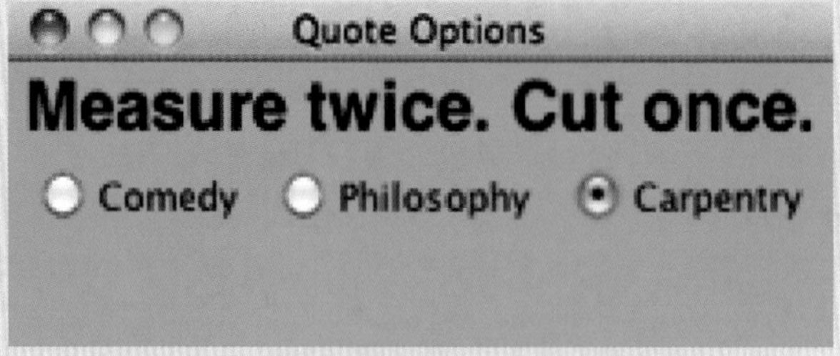

LISTING 6.9: DISPLAY

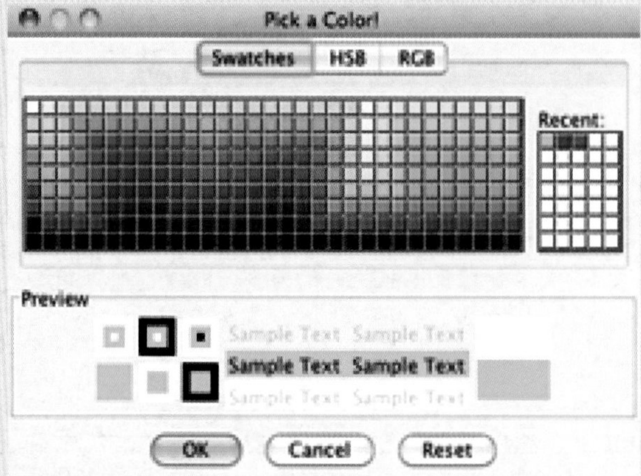

FIGURE 6.10: A color chooser dialog box

LISTING 6.10: DISPLAY

LISTING 6.11: DISPLAY

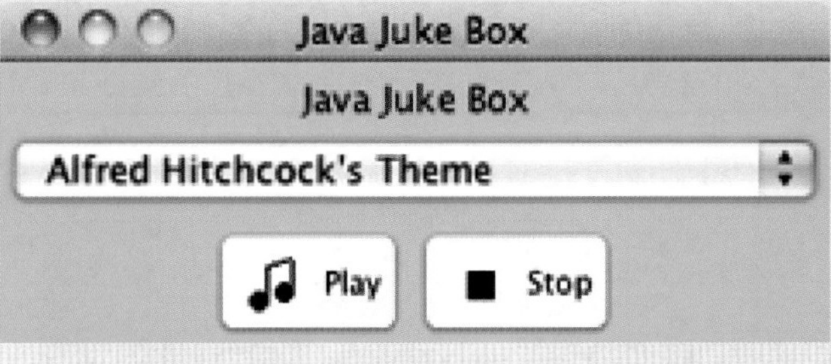

LISTING 6.13: DISPLAY

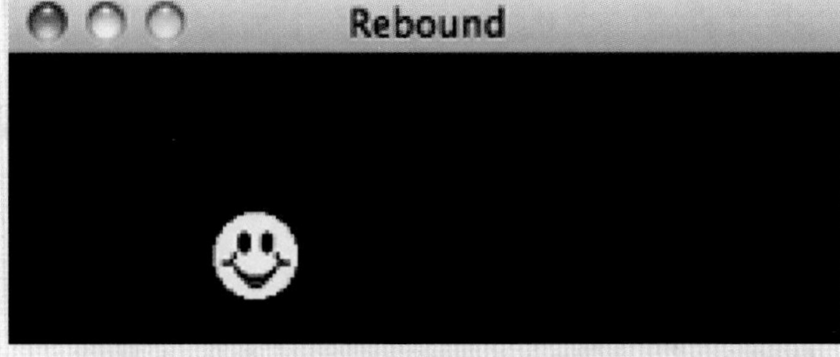

LISTING 6.15: DISPLAY

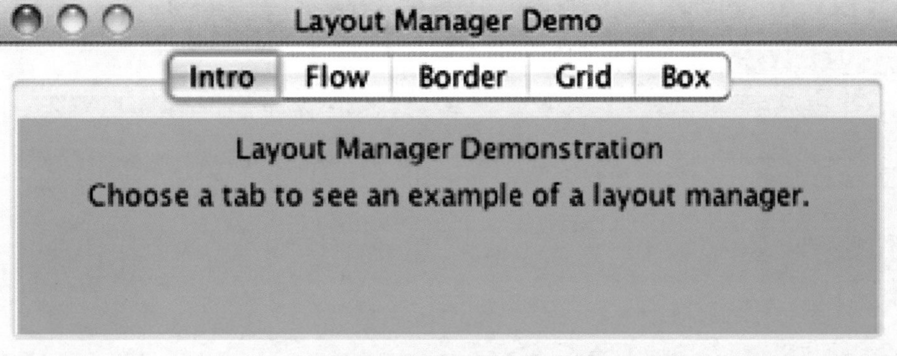

LISTING 6.18: DISPLAY

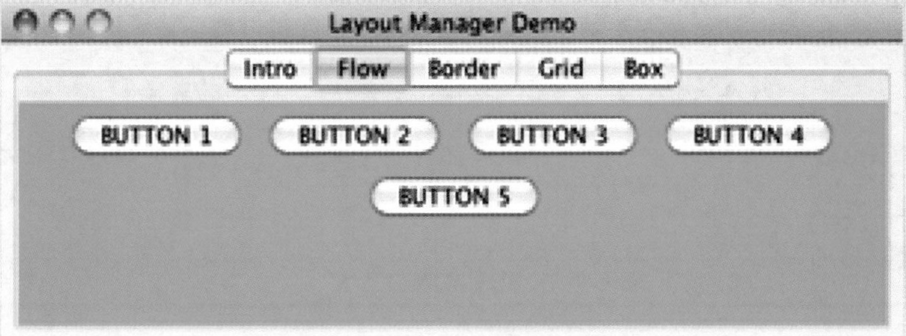

LISTING 6.19: DISPLAY

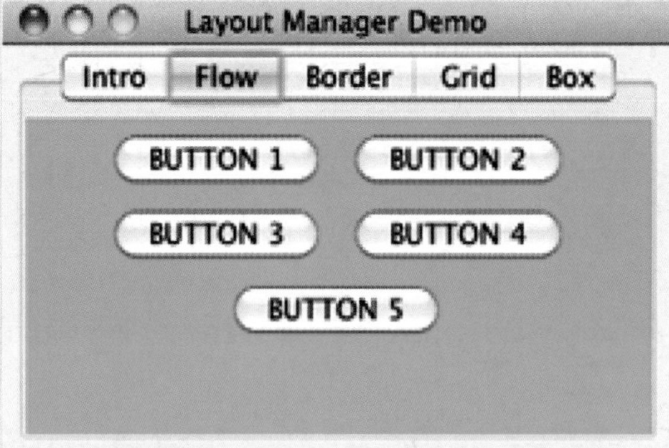

LISTING 6.19: DISPLAY (continued)

Layout Manager Demo
Intro Flow Border Grid Box
BUTTON 2
BUTTON 5
BUTTON 1
BUTTON 4
BUTTON 3

LISTING 6.20: DISPLAY

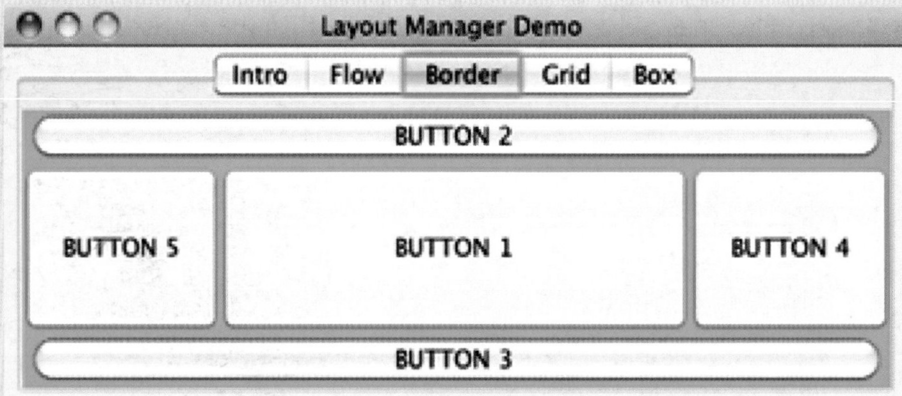

LISTING 6.20: DISPLAY (continued)

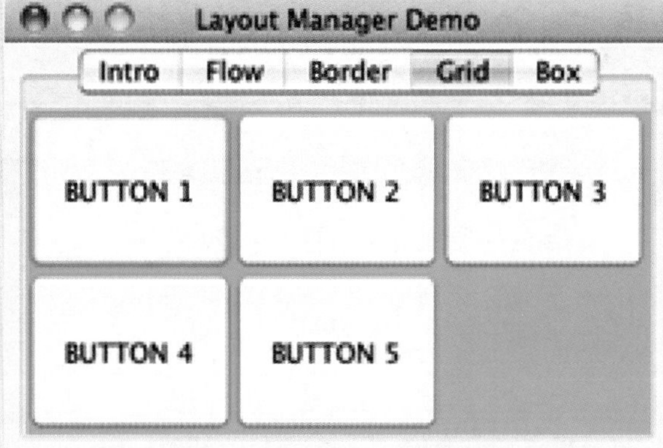

LISTING 6.21: DISPLAY

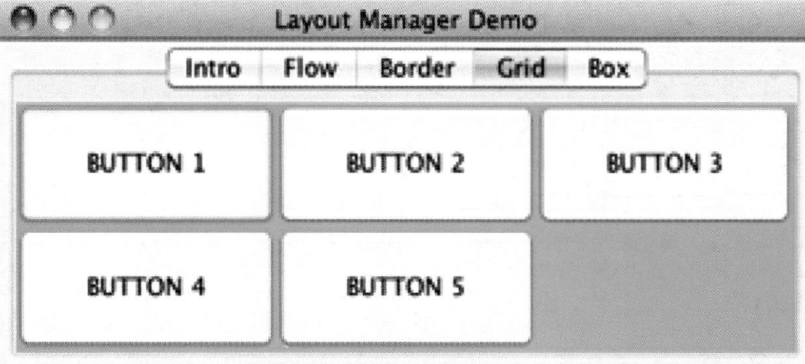

LISTING 6.21: DISPLAY (continued)

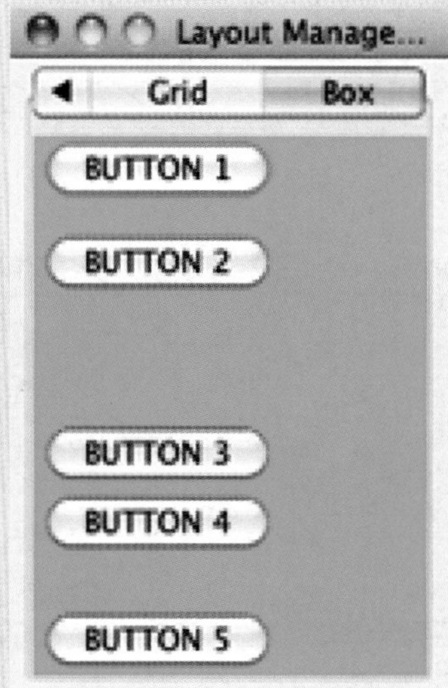

LISTING 6.22: DISPLAY

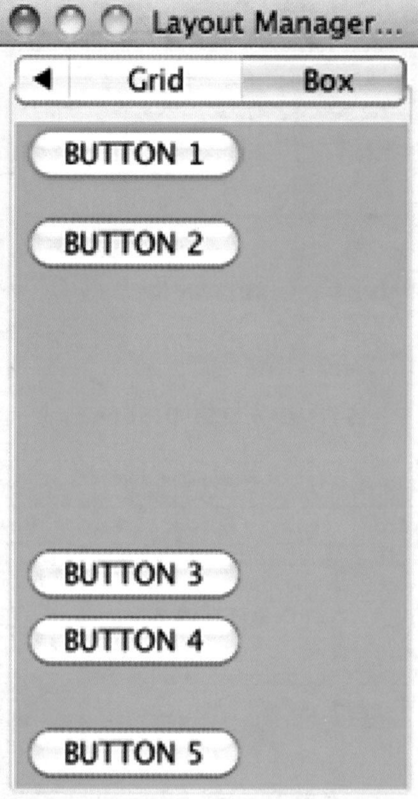

LISTING 6.22: DISPLAY (continued)

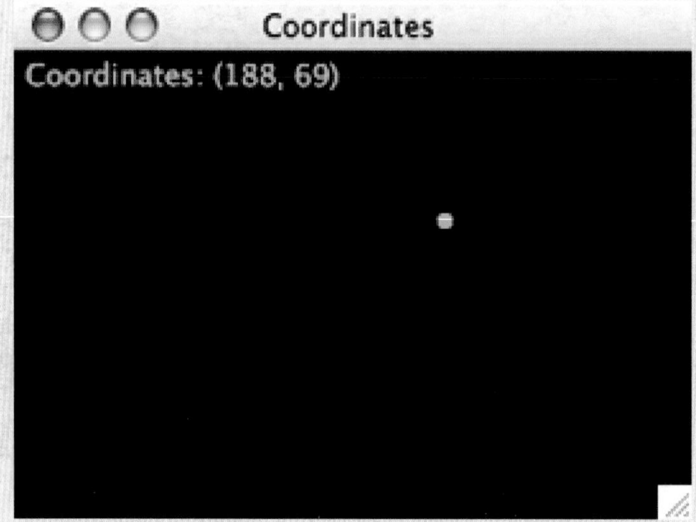

LISTING 6.23: DISPLAY

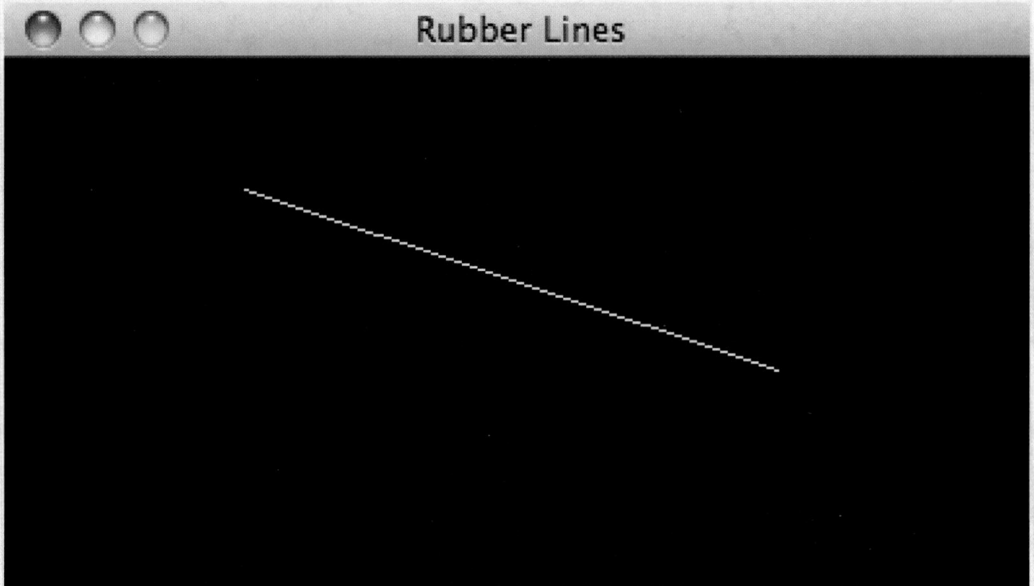

LISTING 6.25: DISPLAY

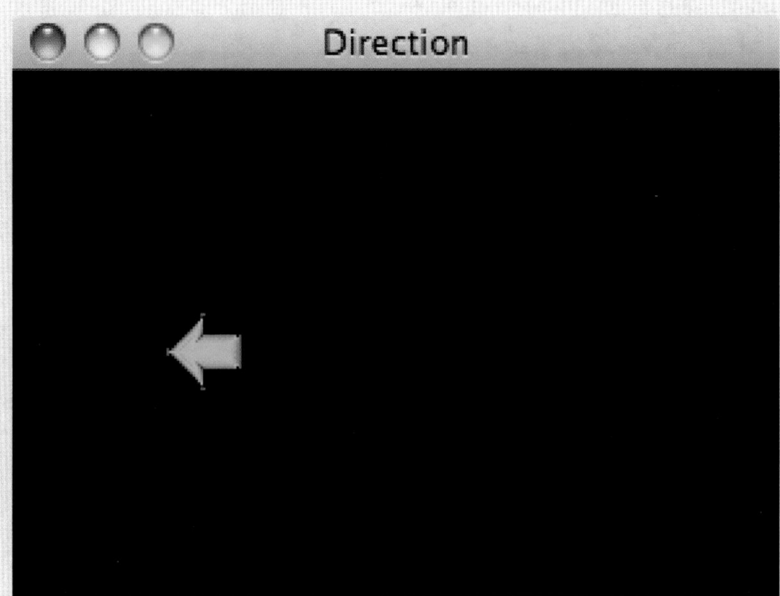

LISTING 6.27: DISPLAY

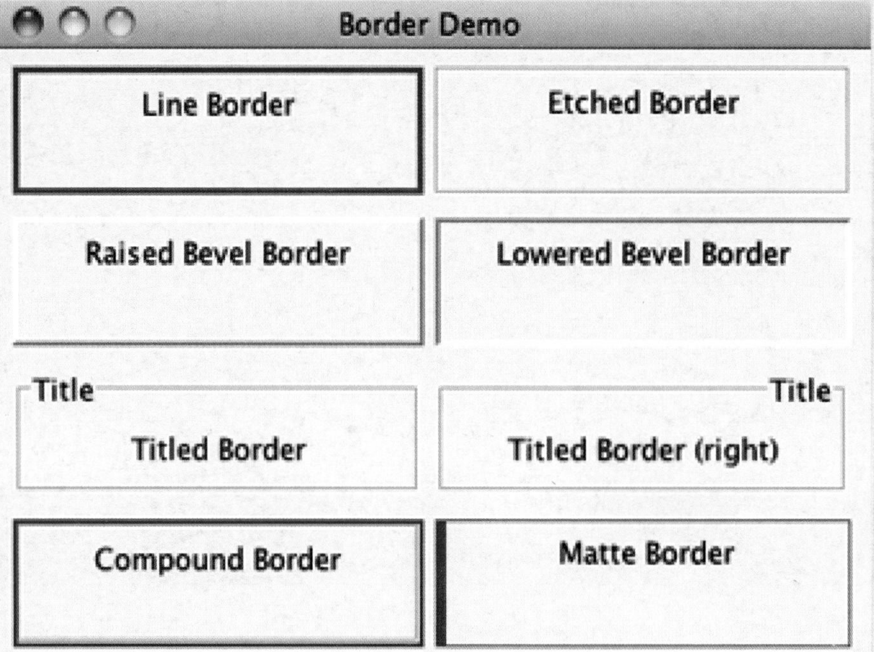

LISTING 6.31: DISPLAY

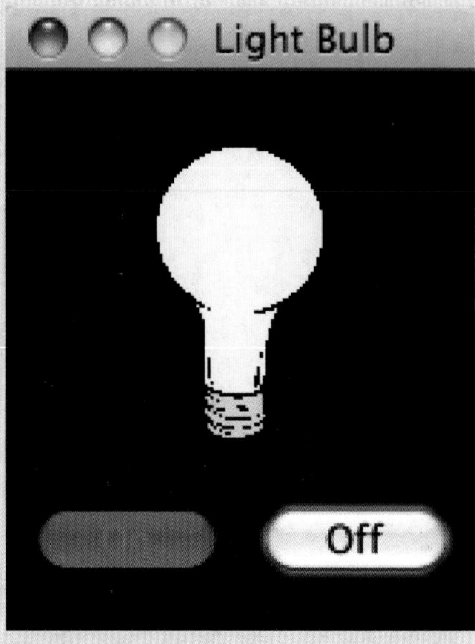

LISTING 6.32: DISPLAY